MANAGEMENT

RICHARD L. DAFT AND ALAN BENSON

CENGAGE
Learning™

Australia • Brazil • Japan • Korea • Mexico • Singapore • Spain • United Kingdom • United States

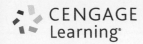

Management, 1st Edition
Richard L. Daft & Alan Benson

Publisher: Annabel Ainscow

Commissioning Editor: Abbie Jones

Content Project Manager: Melissa Beavis

Manufacturing Buyer: Elaine Bevan

Marketing Manager: Vicky Pavlicic

Typesetter: Cenveo Publisher Services

Cover design: Adam Renvoize Creative

Text design: Design Deluxe Ltd

Front cover image: rayjunk/Shutterstock Inc

Printed in China by RR Donnelley
Print Number 01 Print Year 2015

For product information and technology assistance, contact **emea.info@cengage.com.**

For permission to use material from this text or product, and for permission queries, email **emea.permissions@cengage.com.**

This work is adapted from Management 11th edition by Richard L. Daft published by South-Western, Cengage Learning © 2014.

British Library Cataloguing-in-Publication Data
A catalogue record for this book is available from the British Library.

ISBN: 978-1-4080-6385-9

Cengage Learning EMEA
Cheriton House, North Way, Andover, Hampshire, SP10 5BE
United Kingdom

Cengage Learning products are represented in Canada by Nelson Education Ltd.

For your lifelong learning solutions, visit **www.cengage.co.uk**

Purchase your next print book, e-book or e-chapter at **www. cengagebrain.com**

BRIEF CONTENTS

CONTENTS

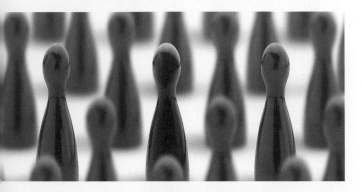

PART 5 LEADING 407

13 Leadership 409

14 Managing human resources 445

15 Managing communication 497

PREFACE

The ethos of this textbook is to provide as up-to-date content as we can, up to the point of the textbook's 2016 publication. It is recognized that many of our readers are in education, mostly in a full-time capacity. However, with the expansion of internships many students of management will increasingly be able to engage more strongly in class discussions; as they will bring some experiential learning to their formative and summative college learning in classrooms or chat rooms. We recognize that education is moving towards greater deployment of technology and that some modules will be delivered and further assessed by technology. The main objective of management education is to develop synthesizers that provide links to the challenges that managers are likely to encounter. These challenges, in an increasingly interconnected business environment, doubtless will contain economic shocks – many, but not all, will be unforeseeable. During the first 15 years of this century we have observed two major economic shocks: the 2000 dot.com bubble bursting and more recently the 2008 financial crisis and its ramifications, including distrust of bankers and more intense government agency supervision of their actions. There will be more shocks in the future and it is important to learn from these major interruptions to national and international trading that rely on stable institutions such as banks.

What has emerged in the field of management is that softer qualities are being recognized and the role of management requires empathy to subordinates and the peer groups within which they are team players. So what are the qualities required of managers in the future? There is no standard answer as it depends on the context of the firm and the industry dynamics that the firm operates in.

Another major set of variables is that of government; they exercise varying levels of control, regulation and of course determine the legal framework that governments create and revise to ensure a balance between stakeholder interests. The level of fairness in different regimes is of course variable, and we can only aspire to hope that best practice is adopted to harmonize a world of stark differences between those who have and those sectors of societies marginalized by unethical business practices. In China and India, two of the world's biggest economies, we are seeing a concerted drive to reduce the levels of systemic and often endemic corruption that induce unethical business practices. An emerging and highly significant theme of management research is to investigate leadership behaviours in top executive teams and in particular determine what desirable qualities senior executives and their chief executive officers (CEOs) should have. There is a consensus in the literature that high levels of self-efficacy are required, but there is recognition that board cohesion is at risk from CEOs who are inadequately influenced by controls and behave in a dysfunctional manner. More research is required in this area as executive overconfidence, if unconstrained, can have adverse impacts if there are no checks and balances provided from robust management control systems.

The issue of ethical behaviour has been embraced by the academic community and has found itself within a blossoming discipline of corporate governance, which includes corporate social responsibility.

Sustainability of the earth's resources is a major area that the corporate world is addressing with a greater sense of urgency. We must be grateful for government intervention and the ongoing influence of non-governmental organizations (NGOs) that have been effective pressure groups in the past. There is a recognition that self-control is a virtue and that corporate core values that are well drafted and enforced are influential in guiding employees to carry out their duties in line with corporate objectives. Indeed, some firms use core values to facilitate hiring the right people and in the event of non-compliance they can support dismissal.

A modern-day manager cannot rely on just his/her status and power to influence direct reports and those affected by his/her decisions. The management style of command and control is no longer the appropriate way to motivate employees and get their commitment. There might be exceptions to this rule, such as an organization that is failing and teetering on the brink of bankruptcy or liquidation. The new workplace still values stability and efficiency, but over-commitment to the status quo has seen the demise of many organizations that were seen as exemplar 20 years or less ago. The world managers will find themselves in, during the coming decade, is unpredictable – future disruptions of both a natural and social order will have to be dealt with. Two major drivers of change have particularly influenced business since the beginning of this century: the Internet and Globalization. However, we as authors hold the view that the world is contoured (not flat) and despite considerable convergence there remain areas of the world where homogeneous business practices and standardized products do not prevail. Cultural sensitivity is still an essential quality for managers to develop, as ethnocentric market strategies have demonstrably shown to have caused market exits for a number of very well-known multinational corporations (MNCs).

It is not possible to provide a checklist of requirements for an ideal manager, as the portfolio of skills required are contextual at the micro as well as the macro level. Several themes are emerging from academic research of desirable management traits including being critical, innovative and reactive to critical incidents. The quality of humility is being more recognized as a valuable characteristic but new ventures entering yet-to-exist markets have, as a requirement, aspects of managerial over-confidence and the courage to act. There is a need for high performance in today's marketplaces but this must be subject to checks and balances within the executive board, facilitated by sound internal and external management control systems. There has to be synchronization of systems with the corporate culture and the organization structure, otherwise the implementation of corporate strategies will be compromised. Organizational change is the 'new normal' and using Darwinian thinking, only the fittest firms will survive and grow. Thus, change should be on the agenda as a continuous process and optimistically as interventions involving incremental change, rather than disruptive radical change initiatives.

Our approach to management education is to provide, within this textbook, content that students of management will find stimulating and thus provide knowledge of best practice. Our blend of content has been influenced by including material from real life and data from research with consultancies, learned contributors and academic research papers. We have included a considerable amount of topical material and data from experiential learning. History may not always repeat itself but we contend that themes do, so we have continued to include solid coverage of the historical development of management as in previous textbooks authored by Professor Daft.

This textbook contains chapter-based self-assessment exercises that students can complete. These in-chapter exercises provide useful formative individual feedback, such as on their attitudes and where personal development may be required to bring out their greatest potential as managers. The text has been compiled with strong visual content to illustrate the topics discussed in the narrative, and opinions and contributions have been italicized to encourage critical analysis of the data.

The end-of-chapter discussion questions and those relating to the case studies are designed to be ones that are challenging for students of management. The questions encourage students to provide answers that present a critical debate of the topic and are typical of university level questions that are often faced in closed-book situations.

In conclusion, we contend that we have produced a textbook for the facilitation of managerial development by incorporating pedagogical features that stimulate deeper learning. Such learning can be achieved through seeking evidence-based solutions that have been rigorously diagnosed and debated.

ABOUT THE AUTHORS

RICHARD L. DAFT is the Brownlee O. Currey, Jr. Professor of Management in the Owen Graduate School of Management at Vanderbilt University. Professor Daft specializes in the study of organization theory and leadership and is a fellow of the Academy of Management. He has served on the editorial boards of the *Academy of Management Journal, Administrative Science Quarterly* and *Journal of Management Education*. He was the associate editor-in-chief of *Organization Science* and served for 3 years as associate editor of *Administrative Science Quarterly*.

Professor Daft has authored or co-authored 14 books, including *Building Management Skills: An Action-First Approach* (with Dorothy Marcic, South-Western, 2014); *The Executive and the Elephant: A Leader's Guide for Building Inner Excellence* (Jossey-Bass, 2010); *Organization Theory and Design* (South-Western, 2013); *The Leadership Experience* (South-Western, 2011); and *Fusion Leadership: Unlocking the Subtle Forces That Change People and Organizations* (with Robert Lengel, Berrett-Koehler, 2000). He has also written dozens of scholarly articles, papers and chapters in other books. His work has been published in *Administrative Science Quarterly, Academy of Management Journal, Academy of Management Review, Strategic Management Journal, Journal of Management, Accounting Organizations and Society, Management Science, MIS Quarterly, California Management Review,* and *Organizational Behavior Teaching Review*. Professor Daft is also an active teacher and consultant. He has taught management, leadership, organizational change, organizational theory and organizational behaviour.

In addition, Professor Daft has served as associate dean, produced for-profit theatrical productions and helped manage a start-up enterprise. He has been involved in management development and consulting for many companies and government organizations, including the American Banking Association, Bridgestone, Bell Canada, the National Transportation Research Board, Nortel, the Tennessee Valley Authority (TVA), Pratt & Whitney, State Farm Insurance, Tenneco, the US Air Force, the US Army, J.C. Bradford & Co., Central Parking System, Entergy Sales and Service, Bristol-Myers Squibb, First American National Bank and the Vanderbilt University Medical Centre.

ALAN BENSON is a Senior Lecturer in the Management Discipline of the University of Exeter Business School. He is the module leader for the MSc module 'Managing in a Multinational Context' and 'Business Projects' in the undergraduate degree programmes. He is a supervisor of Master's dissertations and supervises students in internships.

Before he became a full-time academic he gained practical management experience in several industrial sectors, mostly in engineering and manufacturing companies. He became a Fellow of the Chartered Association of Certified Accountants in 1982.

In 1986 he gained an MBA from Cranfield University School of Management, where his interest in entrepreneurship was stimulated. His particular interests (both in teaching and research) include the use and value of network relationships, entrepreneurial learning and business failure studies (primarily qualitative research).

Recently, his interests have extended into research into the impacts (positive and negative) arising from behaviours of over-confident hubristic executives. Alan gained his DBA from the University of Hull in 2005 and has published three articles between 2010 and 2012, regarding SME support in the UK and entrepreneurial learning.

Dr Benson's teaching interests coincide well with his research areas, and he is very keen to apply innovative teaching and assessment methods. Between 2000–2010 he taught and assessed intensive MBA programmes in Bahrain, Oman, Saudi Arabia, Dubai, Singapore, Hong Kong and Indonesia.

He is a reviewer for two UK academic journals that cover a range of topics in management education and ethical business management (analysis and control).

ACKNOWLEDGEMENTS

The authors would like to thank Dr Anne Cox at the University of Wollongong, Australia for her work on Chapter 14, *Managing Human Resources*, and Dr Bobby Mackie at the University of the West of Scotland for his case study contributions. The authors would also like to thank Abbie Jones for her consistent helpfulness and encouragement.

The publisher would like to thank the following academics for their helpful and insightful comments at various stages of the development of this book:

David Biggs, University of Gloucestershire, UK

Alistair Norman, University of Leeds, UK

Hans Schlappa, University of Hertfordshire, UK

Angela Sutherland, Glasgow Caledonian University, UK

Peter van Hooijdonk, TIO Utrecht, Netherlands

PART 1

INTRODUCTION TO MANAGEMENT

CHAPTER 1

INTRODUCTION TO MANAGEMENT

LEARNING OBJECTIVES

After studying this chapter, you should be able to:

1 Describe the four major management functions and the type of management activities associated with each.

2 Explain the difference between efficiency and effectiveness and their importance for optimal organizational performance.

3 Describe conceptual, human and technical skills and their relevance for C20 managers.

4 Describe management types and the differences between them.

5 Define ten roles that managers typically perform in organizations.

6 Appreciate the managerial role in small businesses and not-for-profit organizations.

7 Understand the personal challenges involved when taking a management appointment.

8 Discuss the innovative competencies needed to be an effective manager in tomorrow's business environments.

When Steve Jobs died in October 2011, Apple, the company he cofounded in 1976, was the most valuable company in the world in terms of market capitalization. Millions of people are devoted to Apple's innovative products, such as the iPhone and iPad. After Jobs's death, multimedia publications abounded concerning the legendary Apple CEO's rich legacy and his quirky management style. In his 600-plus-page biography of Jobs, Walter Isaacson calls him *'the greatest business executive of our era,'* and *managers around the world began reading the book to tap into the power of Jobs's management ideas.*[1] It seems hard to believe that 26 years earlier, after founding Apple, Jobs had been fired by its CEO John Sully at the age of 30. During his first 10 years with Apple, Jobs was clearly a visionary and highly innovative, possessing unique characteristics that he continued to display throughout his lifetime. Lack of attention to the 'traditional management issues' led to a humiliating and humbling dismissal by Apple's CEO. However, Jobs made a very successful equity founding investment in PIXAR, which once liquidated, took him back to controlling the Apple Corporation, producing one of the greatest 'Lazarus' comebacks this century. The concept of experiential learning from failure exemplified by Jobs will be further developed in this and other chapters. The fear of failure (arising from making poor management decisions) needs to be balanced against potential 'value-added' activities, some of which might be exploratory in nature.

For most people, being a manager doesn't come naturally. Steve Jobs had both positive and negative qualities as a manager, but over the course of his career, he learned how to motivate people effectively to accomplish amazing end results. The nature of management is very much to motivate and coordinate others to cope with diverse and far-reaching foreseen and unforeseen challenges. Many new managers expect to have power, to be in control, and to be personally responsible for departmental outcomes. However, managers depend on subordinates much more than the reverse, and they are evaluated on the outputs of other people, rather than on their own achievements. Managers have a responsibility to set up and maintain appropriate systems and cultural values that facilitate others to perform optimally.

TAKE A MOMENT

What makes a good manager? Refer to the Small Group Breakout Exercise online that pertains to the qualities and characteristics of effective and ineffective managers.

In the past, many managers exercised tight control over employees. But the field of lean management requires managers to do more with less, to engage employees' hearts and minds, as well as their physical energy. The adaptive manager needs to see change, rather than a continuity of stability, as the new norm, inspiring visionary interpretation of the future business environment, establishing hire and fire cultural values that allow teams to create a truly collaborative and productive workplace. This textbook introduces and explains the process of management and the changing ways of sense-making in the search for the best way forward. There will be various phenomena to deal with in your career and past experience may not be useful in dealing with unexpected future events. It is essential for managers to develop both criticality and creativity. By observing the actions of successful and less than successful managers, you will learn the fundamentals of best practice management. By the end of this chapter, you will already recognize some of the characteristics and skills that managers use to keep organizations on track, and to understand how managers can achieve astonishing results with and through people. By the end of this textbook, we believe that you will have a deeper understanding of the four fundamental management skills: planning, organizing, leading and controlling a department, or even an entire organization. Arguably, these skills are still the right ones to develop and maintain in tomorrow's world. However, there are specific competencies to be developed. These include *inter alia*: obtaining and allocating scarce resources, time management, crisis management and ensuring that corporate strategies are synchronized with the right corporate culture and right organization structure. There is a need to gain and maintain respect within and without the organization, as increasingly senior managers are subject to public scrutiny to an unprecedented level of intensity. Failures of good commercial judgement can be value-destroying. The primary role of company management is *not* to maximize financial returns – it is much richer than that! The UK Companies Act of 2006 provides the following requirements of directors of limited liability companies.

The Companies Act 2006 outlines the statutory duties of company directors as seven fiduciary duties:

1   to act within your powers as a company director

2   to promote the success of your company

3   to exercise independent judgement

4   to exercise reasonable care, skill and diligence

5   to avoid conflicts of interest

6   not to accept benefits from third parties

7   to declare interest in proposed transaction or arrangement with the company.

CONCEPT CONNECTION

In Kenya, an emerging economy, Safaricom is one of several new companies providing affordable mobile telephone service to the region. The company's innovative managers continuously search for better ways to serve customers and expand the business. In 2012, Safaricom was awarded a Global Mobile Award for developing a mobile application that allows its customers to use their mobile phones to purchase clean drinking water: critical in such countries where purified H_2O is not freely available through piped systems.

Why innovative management matters

'*By inventing Twitter, Jack may have well brought down dictators in North Africa and the Middle East,*' said Virgin Group CEO, Richard Branson.[2] He was talking about Jack Dorsey, one of the cofounders of the microblogging service Twitter. As Branson's comment reflects, tweeting should not be about gossiping or boasting. It's used for all sorts of activities, from organizing protests and spreading the word about political turbulence or natural disasters, to marketing products and gathering customer feedback. However, a number of politicians and executives have misused the medium in recent years and have been reprimanded and/or dismissed for bringing their organizations into disrepute. Your university or organization could well have a policy on appropriate use of social media and its potential impacts on the organization from mis-tweeting – even out of office hours!

Innovative management really does matter. Innovations in products, product services, management control systems, production processes, corporate values and other aspects of the organization are what keep companies growing, changing and thriving. Without innovation, no company can survive over the long run. Industries, technologies, economies, governments and societies are in constant flux, and managers are responsible for helping their organizations navigate through the unpredictable with flexibility and innovation.[3] Events in tumultuous global economies, especially the meltdown of the housing and finance industries in the USA, involving the bankruptcy of Lehman Brothers, seriously impacted on the UK clearing banks, necessitating large scale government bailouts and nationalization of several major banks. Energy remains an area of great concern in the world, from both supplier and consumer perspectives. We have observed volatile oil prices and the demise of the once all-powerful OPEC cartel's influence on market prices; sweeping geo-government changes; disasters (such as an earthquake and tsunami in Japan and the resulting accidents at the Fukushima Daiichi nuclear power plant); continuing threats of planned and random terrorism; wars and the displacement of millions from their home countries; and last but not least global health scares, including ebola and avian flu. All of these 'shocks' have confirmed for managers and policy makers the naivety of managing for economic stability. The exponential growth and expertise of companies in fast developing countries, particularly China and India, is becoming evident. Chinese companies such as Haier and Huwai are now on the world stage with innovative products. The Chinese government has acquired considerable tracts of agricultural land in Africa and is now investing heavily in European assets (especially intellectual property). Many US and European CEOs have learned expensive lessons too, when their foreign direct investments (FDI) in China resulted in huge balance sheet write-downs. eBay with Alibaba and Beiersdorf (Nivea) with C-Bons are case studies of two very expensive FDI misinvestments made by their respective executive boards. In such a turbulent and intensely competitive global business environment, innovation and interpretation and timely reaction to global trends requires ongoing surveillance and awareness. Lethargic corporations that were exemplar in prior years can and do fail, despite strong balance sheets. Two well-publicized case study examples of corporate failure, mostly due to lack of timely technical product innovation that our readers might explore, are those of RIM (BlackBerry) and NOKIA.

💡 INNOVATIVE WAY

Band leaders

Leadership: Learning from Jazz Bands (Ucbasaran et al.)

The Grateful Dead (Barnes)

The novel approach taken by the three authors of the above paper was to record how Jazz Band leaders, such as Duke Ellington, managed the very talented musicians in their bands that were at the forefront of developing new forms of expression of Jazz.

Barry Barnes, a US business professor lectures to business leaders about the Grateful Dead, saying that the band's ability to think and behave innovatively at all times, is a lesson for today's managers. The band thrived for decades, through bad times as well as good. *'If you're going to survive this economic downturn,'* Barnes says, *'...you better be able to turn on a dime. The Dead were exemplars.'*[4]

Uchbasaran *et al.* hold the view that leaders should facilitate innovation by allowing degrees of improvisation within their teams, thus facilitating an entrepreneurial culture to continuously develop with individual differences (a source of conflict) being facilitated.

Innovation has become the new imperative, despite the need for companies to control costs in today's economy. In a recent survey of corporate executives in Asia, North America, Europe and Latin America, 80 per cent agreed that *'innovation is more important than cost-reduction for long-term success.'*[5] Throughout this text, we will spotlight various companies that reflect managers' ability to think and act innovatively, such as the Grateful Dead band did. In addition, Chapter 11 discusses innovation and change in much more detail. First, let's begin our journey into the world of management by learning some basics about what it means to be a manager.

The definition of management

Every day, managers solve difficult problems, turn organizations around, and achieve astonishing performances. To be successful, every organization needs good managers.

What do managers actually do? The late US management guru, Professor Peter Drucker, often credited with creating the modern study of management, summarized the job of the manager by specifying five tasks, outlined in Exhibit 1.1.[6] In essence, managers set goals, organize activities, motivate and communicate, measure performance and develop people. These five manager activities apply not only to present and past senior executives such as Mark Zuckerberg at Facebook and Alan Mulally at the Ford Motor Company. They apply also to the manager of a restaurant in your home town, the leader of an airport security team, a supervisor at a Web hosting service or the director of sales and marketing for a regional business.

The activities outlined in Exhibit 1.1 fall into four core management functions: planning (setting goals and deciding activities); organizing (organizing activities and people); leading (motivating, communicating with and developing people); and controlling (establishing targets and measuring performance). Depending on their job situation, managers perform numerous and varied tasks, but they all can be categorized under these four primary functions. Thus, our summarized definition of management is as follows:

Management is the attainment of organizational goals in an effective and efficient manner through planning, organizing, leading and controlling organizational resources. This definition includes two important ideas: (1) the four functions of planning, organizing, leading and controlling and (2) the attainment of organizational goals in an effective and efficient manner. Let's first look at the four primary management functions. Later in this chapter we'll discuss organizational effectiveness and efficiency, as well as the multitude of skills that managers use to perform their jobs successfully. There is considerable fertile topical debate concerning corporate responsibility in the media and academic publications. This includes developing models and diagnostics to

EXHIBIT 1.1 What do managers do?

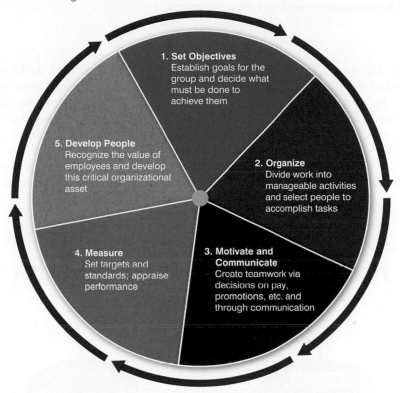

1. **Set Objectives**
Establish goals for the group and decide what must be done to achieve them

2. **Organize**
Divide work into manageable activities and select people to accomplish tasks

3. **Motivate and Communicate**
Create teamwork via decisions on pay, promotions, etc. and through communication

4. **Measure**
Set targets and standards; appraise performance

5. **Develop People**
Recognize the value of employees and develop this critical organizational asset

SOURCE: 'What Do Managers Do?' *The Wall Street Journal Online,* www.guides.wsj.com/management/developinga-leadership-style/what-do-managers-do/ (accessed August 11, 2010), article adapted from Alan Murray, *The Wall Street Journal Essential Guide to Management* (New York: Harper Business, 2010).

facilitate the recognition of dysfunctional value-destroying executive behaviours. The material for this section is to be found online in Chapter 17, as it is a developing area that requires real-time updating.

Management means, in the last analysis, the substitution of thought for brawn and muscle, of knowledge for folklore and superstition, and of cooperation for force. …'

— PETER DRUCKER, MANAGEMENT GURU

REFLECTION

- Managers get things done by coordinating and motivating other people.
- Management often is a different experience from what people expect.
- Innovative management is critical in today's turbulent world.

- The success of Twitter and Facebook can be attributed to the effectiveness of their innovative managers.
- **Management** is defined as the attainment of organizational goals in an effective and efficient manner through planning, organizing, leading and controlling organizational resources.

The four management functions

Exhibit 1.2 illustrates the process of how managers use resources to attain organizational goals through the functions of planning, organizing, leading and controlling. Chapters of this book are devoted to the multiple activities and skills associated with each function, as well as to the environment, global competitiveness and ethics that influence how managers perform these functions.

Planning

Planning means identifying goals for future organizational performance and deciding on the tasks and use of resources needed to attain them. In other words, managerial planning defines where the organization wants to be in the future and how to get there. A good example of planning comes from General Electric (GE), where managers have sold divisions such as plastics, insurance and media to focus company resources on four key business areas: energy, aircraft engines, health care and financial services. GE used to relocate senior executives every few years to different divisions so that they developed broad, general expertise. In line with the strategic refocusing, the company now will keep people in their business units longer so they gain a deeper understanding of products and customers within each of the four core businesses.[7]

EXHIBIT 1.2 The process of management

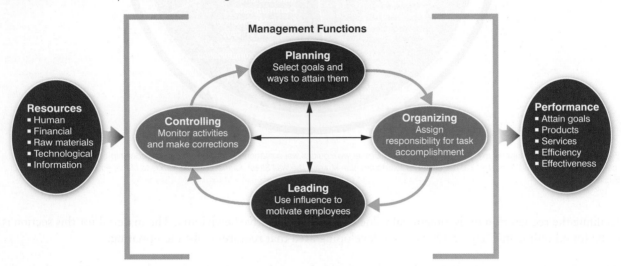

Organizing

Organizing typically follows planning and reflects how the organization tries to accomplish the plan. Organizing involves assigning tasks, grouping tasks into departments, delegating authority and allocating resources across the organization. In recent years, organizations as diverse as IBM, the Catholic Church, Estée Lauder and the Federal Bureau of Investigation (FBI) have undergone structural reorganization to accommodate their changing plans. Organizing is a key task for Oprah Winfrey as she strives to turn around her struggling start-up cable network, OWN. She took over as CEO of the company, repositioned some executives and hired new ones, and cut jobs to reduce costs and streamline the company. She is hoping the structural changes will bring a lean, entrepreneurial approach that will get OWN on solid ground. Winfrey said '*I prided myself on leanness*,' referring to the early days of her TV talk show. '*The opposite was done here.*'[8]

Leading

Leading is the use of influence to motivate employees to achieve organizational goals. Leading means creating a shared culture and values, communicating goals to people throughout the organization and infusing employees with the desire to perform at a high level. As CEO of Chrysler Group, Sergio Marchionne spends about 2 weeks a month in Michigan meeting with executive teams from sales, marketing and industrial operations to talk about his plans and motivate people to accomplish ambitious goals. Marchionne, who spends half his time in Italy running Fiat, rejected the 15th-floor executive suite at Chrysler headquarters so he could provide more hands-on leadership from an office close to the engineering centre.[9] One doesn't have to be a top manager of a big corporation to be an exceptional leader. Many managers working quietly in both large and small organizations around the world provide strong leadership within departments, teams, non-profits and small businesses.

Controlling

Controlling is the fourth function in the management process. Controlling means monitoring employees' activities, determining whether the organization is moving towards its goals, and making corrections as necessary. One trend in recent years is for companies to place less emphasis on top-down control and more emphasis on training employees to monitor and correct themselves. However, the ultimate responsibility for control still rests with managers.

In 2012, the US Secret Service agency became embroiled in a public relations nightmare, partly due to a breakdown of managerial control. When news broke that members of the security team sent to prepare for President Barack Obama's visit to Cartagena, Colombia, engaged in a night of heavy drinking, visited strip clubs and brought prostitutes to their hotel rooms, there was a public and legislative uproar. Several agents were fired, and director Mark Sullivan and other managers were called before a Senate subcommittee to explain the breakdown in control. The widespread investigation has brought other allegations of agent misconduct and 'morally repugnant behaviour' to light. One response from managers has been to create stricter rules of conduct, rules that apply even when agents are off duty.[10]

REFLECTION

- Managers perform a wide variety of activities that fall within four primary management functions.
- Planning is the management function concerned with defining goals for future performance and how to attain them.
- Organizing involves assigning tasks, grouping tasks into departments and allocating resources.
- Leading means using influence to motivate employees to achieve the organization's goals.
- Controlling is concerned with monitoring employees' activities, keeping the organization on track towards meeting its goals and making corrections as necessary.
- The US Secret Service agency prostitution scandal can be traced partly to a breakdown of management control.

Organizational performance

The second part of our definition of management is the attainment of organizational goals in an efficient and effective manner. Management is so important because organizations are so important. In an industrialized society where complex technologies dominate, organizations bring together knowledge, people and raw materials to perform tasks that no individual could do alone. Without organizations, how could technology be provided that enables us to share information around the world in an instant; electricity be produced from huge dams and nuclear power plants; and millions of songs, videos and games be available for our entertainment at any time and place? Organizations pervade our society, and managers are responsible for seeing that resources are used wisely to attain organizational goals.

Our formal definition of an organization is a social entity that is goal directed and deliberately structured. *Social entity* means being made up of two or more people. *Goal directed* means designed to achieve some outcome, such as make a profit (Waitrose), win pay increases for members (Unison), meet spiritual needs (Methodist Church) or provide social satisfaction (a university club or association). *Deliberately structured* means that tasks are divided, and responsibility for their performance is assigned to

 GREEN **POWER**

Local Impact

Logistics giant **Deutsche Post DHL Group** planned for corporate social responsibility with sustainability at the *local* level. Deutsche Post DHL Group's commitment to social responsibility is reflected in its three pillars: *Go Green* (climate protection), *Go Help* (disaster relief) and *Go Teach* (education). Each pillar in this corporate plan is indicative of broad goals – such as a 30 per cent reduction in CO_2 emissions by 2020 – that are customized to fit local needs and cultures.

For example, DHL has 38 locations in Thailand, where Buddhist teachings about caring for one another lend themselves to helping and teaching the local population. By pinpointing local needs and issues, DHL planned site-specific strategies, such as efficient lighting and the reduction of air conditioner demand in Thailand's hot climate, and the installation of global positioning satellite (GPS) systems to minimize fuel consumption. In addition, DHL Thailand asks potential business partners to buy into the company's Go Green philosophy, reflecting a giant leap in sustainability at the local level.

SOURCE: David Ferguson, 'CSR in Asian Logistics: Operationalization within DHL (Thailand)', *Journal of Management Development* 30, no. 10 (2011): 985–999.

 INNOVATIVE **WAY**

Illumination Entertainment

You can't quite make a blockbuster movie on a dime, but Christopher Meledandri is out to prove that strict cost controls and big hit animated films aren't mutually exclusive. Most computer-generated animated films cost at least $100 million, with some budgets pushing $150 million. In contrast, Illumination Entertainment made the hit film *Despicable Me* for only $69 million. The budget for *Hop* came in at a mere $63 million. And the company produced its third blockbuster, *Dr. Seuss' The Lorax,* for $70 million – less than the movie brought in at the box office on its opening weekend.

Managers at the company use many approaches to increase efficiency. For example, when making *Despicable Me*, they decided to eliminate details such as animal fur, which the audience couldn't see on the screen. Other details that were extremely costly to render in computer graphics but that weren't central to the story were also cut, saving the detail work for sets that were used repeatedly. The company paid big bucks for the voice of Steve Carell, but it hired other vocal talent with less star power, a practice that managers follow for all their films. They also seek out first-time directors and young, enthusiastic, less-experienced animators, who often cost less than half what a more experienced artist commands. Organizational details also contribute to efficiency – Meledandri keeps layers of the hierarchy to a minimum so that decisions can be made fast and movies don't languish for years in development, eating up money. Offices are in a low-rent area behind a cement plant rather than being housed in sumptuous surroundings.

Illumination Entertainment is quickly becoming the envy of Hollywood. Movie-going in general is down, but animated family films are hot. And Illumination has had some of the hottest ones going. Peter Chernin, former president of News Corporation, said of Meledandri: *'It is rare to find people whose business sense is as strong as their creative sense.'* Meledandri and his management team are using their business sense to run an efficient operation, and their creative instincts to put money in the right places to produce popular, often critically acclaimed animated films.[11]

organization members. This definition applies to all organizations, including both profit and non-profit. Small, offbeat and non-profits are more numerous than large, visible corporations – and just as important to society.

Based on our definition of management, the manager's responsibility is to coordinate resources in an effective and efficient manner to accomplish the organization's goals. Organizational effectiveness is the degree to which the organization achieves a *stated goal*, or succeeds in accomplishing what it tries to do. Organizational effectiveness means providing a product or service that customers value. Organizational efficiency refers to the amount of resources used to achieve an organizational goal. It is based on how much raw material, money and people are necessary for producing a given volume of output. Efficiency can be calculated as the amount of resources used to produce a product or service. Efficiency and effectiveness can both be high in the same organization. Managers at Illumination Entertainment, the film production company behind *Dr Seuss' The Lorax*, continually look for ways to increase efficiency while also meeting the company's goal of producing creative and successful animated films.

So far, Illumination Entertainment has managed to adhere to its efficient, low-cost model as well as be highly effective in meeting its goals. Meledandri is committed to keeping things 'lean and mean' so that costs don't creep up over time and require harsh cost slashing measures later on. All managers have to pay attention to costs, but severe cost-cutting to improve efficiency can sometimes hurt organizational effectiveness. The ultimate responsibility of managers is to achieve high performance, which is the attainment of organizational goals by using resources in an efficient *and* effective manner. Consider what happened at music company EMI. Weak sales led managers to focus on financial efficiency, which successfully trimmed waste and boosted operating income. However, the efficiencies damaged the company's ability to recruit new artists, which are vital to record companies, and also led to internal turmoil that caused some long-time acts like the Rolling Stones to leave the label. Thus, the company's overall performance suffered. *Managers are struggling to find the right balance between efficiency and effectiveness to get EMI back on the right track.*[12]

REFLECTION

- **An organization** is a social entity that is goal-directed and deliberately structured.
- Good management is important because organizations contribute so much to society.
- **Efficiency** pertains to the amount of resources – raw materials, money and people – used to produce a desired volume of output.
- **Effectiveness** refers to the degree to which the organization achieves a stated goal.

- **Performance** is defined as the organization's ability to attain its goals by using resources in an efficient and effective manner.
- Managers at Illumination Entertainment are concerned both with keeping costs low (efficiency) and producing animated films such as *The Lorax* that are critically and financially successful (effectiveness).

Management skills

A manager's job requires a range of skills. Although some management theorists propose a long list of skills, the necessary skills for managing a department or an organization can be placed in three categories: conceptual, human and technical.[13] As illustrated in Exhibit 1.3, the application of these skills changes dramatically when a person is promoted to management. Although the degree of each skill that is required at different levels of an organization may vary, all managers must possess some skill in each of these important areas to perform effectively.

EXHIBIT 1.3 Relationship of conceptual, human and technical skills to management

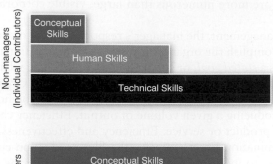

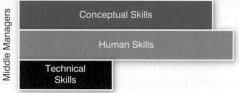

Holding degrees in both physics and economics, entrepreneur Elon Musk certainly possesses his share of **technical skills**. He designed and created the first viable electric car – the Tesla Roadster – as well as the Web-based payment service PayPal and a spacecraft that will enable private citizens to travel to outer space. But it is his stellar **conceptual skills** that allow him to lead the innovative companies that are making these products and services available to people worldwide.

Conceptual skills

Conceptual skill is the cognitive ability to see the organization as a whole system and the relationships among its parts. Conceptual skill involves knowing where one's team fits into the total organization and how the organization fits into the industry, the community, and the broader business and social environment. It means the ability to *think strategically* – to take the broad, long-term view – and to identify, evaluate and solve complex problems.[14]

Conceptual skills are needed by all managers, but especially for managers at the top. Many of the responsibilities of top managers, such as decision-making, resource allocation and innovation, require a broad view. For example, Ursula Burns, who in 2009 became the first African-American woman to lead a major US corporation, needs superb conceptual skills to steer Xerox through the tough economy and the rapidly changing technology industry. Sales of copiers and printers have remained flat, prices have declined and Xerox is battling stronger competitors in a consolidating industry. To keep the company thriving, Burns needs a strong understanding not only of the company, but also of shifts in the industry and the larger environment.[15]

Human skills

Human skill is the manager's ability to work with and through other people and to work effectively as a group member. Human skill is demonstrated in the way a manager relates to other people, including the ability to motivate, facilitate, coordinate, lead, communicate and resolve conflicts. Human skills are essential for frontline managers who work with employees directly on a daily basis.[16] However, human skills are increasingly important for managers at all levels and in all types of organizations.[17]

Even at a company such as Google that depends on technical expertise, human skills are considered essential for managers. Google analyzed performance reviews and feedback surveys to find out what makes a good manager of technical people and found that technical expertise ranked last among a list of eight desired manager qualities, as shown in Exhibit 1.4. The exhibit lists eight effective behaviours of good managers. Notice that almost all of them relate to human skills, such as communication, coaching and teamwork. *People want managers who listen to them, build positive relationships and show an interest in their lives and careers.*[18] A recent survey comparing the importance of managerial skills today with those from the late 1980s found a decided increase in the role of skills for building relationships with others.[19]

Technical skills

Technical skill is the understanding of and proficiency in the performance of specific tasks. Technical skill includes mastery of the methods, techniques and equipment involved in specific functions such as engineering, manufacturing or finance. Technical skill also includes specialized knowledge, analytical ability and the competent use of tools and techniques to solve problems in that specific discipline. Technical skills are particularly important at lower organizational levels. Many managers get promoted to their first management jobs by having excellent technical skills. However, technical skills become less important than human and conceptual skills as managers move up the hierarchy. Top managers with strong technical skills sometimes have to learn to step back so others can do their jobs effectively. David Sacks, founder and CEO of Yammer, designed the first version of the product himself, but now the company has 200 employees and a dozen or so product managers and design teams. Sacks used to '*walk around and look over the designers' shoulders to see what they were doing,*' *but says that habit prevented some people from doing their best work.*[20]

When skills fail

Everyone has flaws and weaknesses, and these shortcomings become most apparent under conditions of rapid change, uncertainty or crisis.[21] Consider how Tony Hayward, a geologist by training, handled the BP Deepwater Horizon crisis in the Gulf of Mexico that ended his career as CEO and further damaged BP's reputation. Until the spring of 2010, Hayward had been praised for leading a successful turnaround at the oil giant. However, after an oil rig drilling a well for BP exploded in April 2010, killing 11 workers and sending hundreds of millions of gallons of oil spewing into the Gulf of Mexico, Hayward faltered in his role as a crisis leader. His ill-advised comment that he wanted the crisis over as much as anyone because he 'wanted his life back' showed an insensitivity and lack of diplomacy that roiled the public. Hayward's poor handling of the crisis eventually led to calls for his dismissal, and he resigned in July 2010.[22]

During turbulent times, managers really have to stay on their toes and apply all their skills and competencies in a way that benefits the organization and its stakeholders – employees, customers, investors, the community and so forth. In recent years, numerous highly publicized examples have shown what happens when managers fail to apply their skills effectively to meet the demands of an uncertain, rapidly changing world. Ethical and financial scandals have left people cynical about business managers and even less willing to overlook mistakes.

Crises and examples of corporate deceit and greed grab the headlines, but many more companies falter or fail less spectacularly. Managers fail to listen to customers, are unable to motivate employees or can't build a cohesive team. For example, the reputation of Netflix went from 'beloved icon of innovation to just another big, bad company ripping off customers' because managers didn't listen. Reed Hastings and other top executives couldn't help but hear the angry complaints from customers when they decided to increase prices and split the company's mail-order and streaming businesses at the same time, causing users to have to manage their accounts in two places. However, managers clearly weren't listening, as the company pushed forward with its plans despite growing customer frustration and resentment.[23]

Exhibit 1.5 shows the top ten factors that cause managers to fail to achieve desired results, based on a survey of managers in US organizations operating in rapidly changing business environments.[24] Notice that

TAKE A MOMENT

Complete the Experiential Exercise online that pertains to management skills. Reflect on the strength of your preferences among the three types of skills and the implications for you as a manager.

EXHIBIT 1.4 Google's rules: eight good behaviours for managers

To know how to build better managers, Google executives studied performance reviews, feedback surveys and award nominations to see what qualities made a good manager. Here are the 'Eight Good Behaviours' they found, in order of importance:

1 Be a good coach.
2 Empower your team and don't micromanage.
3 Express interest in team members' success and personal well-being.
4 Don't be a sissy: be productive and results-oriented.
5 Be a good communicator and listen to your team.
6 Help your employees with career development.
7 Have a clear vision and strategy for the team.
8 Have key technical skills so you can help to advise the team.

SOURCE: Google's Quest to Build a Better Boss, by Adam Bryant, published March 12, 2011 in the *New York Times*. Courtesy of Google, Inc.

EXHIBIT 1.5 Top causes of manager failure

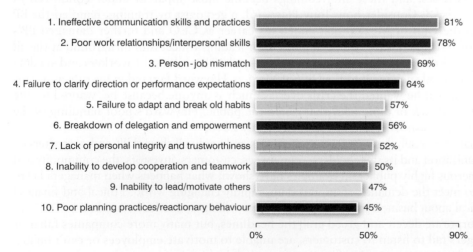

1. Ineffective communication skills and practices	81%
2. Poor work relationships/interpersonal skills	78%
3. Person-job mismatch	69%
4. Failure to clarify direction or performance expectations	64%
5. Failure to adapt and break old habits	57%
6. Breakdown of delegation and empowerment	56%
7. Lack of personal integrity and trustworthiness	52%
8. Inability to develop cooperation and teamwork	50%
9. Inability to lead/motivate others	47%
10. Poor planning practices/reactionary behaviour	45%

SOURCE: Clinton O. Longenecker, Mitchell J. Neubert and Laurence S. Fink, 'Causes and Consequences of Managerial Failure in Rapidly Changing Organizations', *Business Horizons* 50 (2007): 145–155, Table 1, with permission from Elsevier.

many of these factors are due to poor human skills, such as the inability to develop good work relationships, a failure to clarify direction and performance expectations or an inability to create cooperation and teamwork. The number one reason for manager failure is ineffective communication skills and practices, cited by 81 per cent of managers surveyed. Especially in times of uncertainty or crisis, if managers do not communicate effectively, including listening to employees and customers and showing genuine care and concern, organizational performance and reputation suffer.

REFLECTION

- Managers have complex jobs that require a range of abilities and skills.
- Conceptual skill is the cognitive ability to see the organization as a whole and the relationship among its parts.
- Human skill refers to a manager's ability to work with and through other people and to work effectively as part of a group.

- Technical skill is the understanding of and proficiency in the performance of specific tasks.
- The two major reasons that managers fail are poor communication and poor interpersonal skills.
- A manager's weaknesses become more apparent during stressful times of uncertainty, change or crisis.

Management types

Managers use conceptual, human and technical skills to perform the four management functions of planning, organizing, leading and controlling in all organizations – large and small, manufacturing and service, profit and non-profit, traditional and Internet-based. But not all managers' jobs are the same. Managers are responsible for different departments, work at different levels in the hierarchy, and meet different requirements for achieving high performance. Twenty-five-year-old Daniel Wheeler is a first-line supervisor in his first management job at Del Monte Foods, directly involved in promoting products, approving packaging sleeves and organizing people to host sampling events.[25] Kevin Kurtz is a middle manager at Lucasfilm, where he works with employees to develop marketing campaigns for some of the entertainment company's hottest films.[26] And Domenic Antonellis is CEO of the New England Confectionary Co. (Necco), the company that makes those tiny pastel candy hearts stamped with phrases such as 'Be Mine' and 'Kiss Me'.[27] All three are managers and must contribute to planning, organizing, leading and controlling their organizations – but in different amounts and ways.

Vertical differences

An important determinant of the manager's job is the hierarchical level. Exhibit 1.6 illustrates the three levels in the hierarchy. A study of more than 1400 managers examined how the manager's job differs across these three hierarchical levels and found that the primary focus changes at different levels.[28] For first-level managers, the main concern is facilitating individual employee performance. Middle managers, though, are concerned less with individual performance and more with linking groups of people, such as allocating resources, coordinating teams or putting top management plans into action across the organization. For top-level managers, the primary focus is monitoring the external environment and determining the best strategy to be competitive.

Let's look in more detail at differences across hierarchical levels. Top managers are at the top of the hierarchy and are responsible for the entire organization. They have titles such as president, chairperson, executive director, CEO and executive vice president. Top managers are responsible for setting organizational goals, defining strategies for achieving them, monitoring and interpreting the external environment, and making decisions that affect the entire organization. They look to the long-term future and concern themselves with general environmental trends and the organization's overall success. Top managers are also responsible for communicating a shared vision for the organization, shaping corporate culture and nurturing an entrepreneurial spirit that can help the company innovate and keep pace with rapid change.[29]

Middle managers work at middle levels of the organization and are responsible for business units and major departments. Examples of middle managers are department head, division head, manager of quality control and director of the research lab. Middle managers typically have two or more management levels beneath them. They are responsible for implementing the overall strategies and policies defined by top managers. Middle managers generally are concerned with the near future, rather than with long-range planning.

The middle manager's job has changed dramatically over the past two decades. Many organizations improved efficiency by laying off middle managers and slashing middle management levels. Traditional pyramidal organization charts were flattened to allow information to flow quickly from top to bottom and decisions to be made with greater speed. In addition, technology has taken over many tasks once performed by middle managers, such as monitoring performance and creating reports.[30] Exhibit 1.6 illustrates the shrinking middle management.

EXHIBIT 1.6 Management levels in the organizational hierarchy

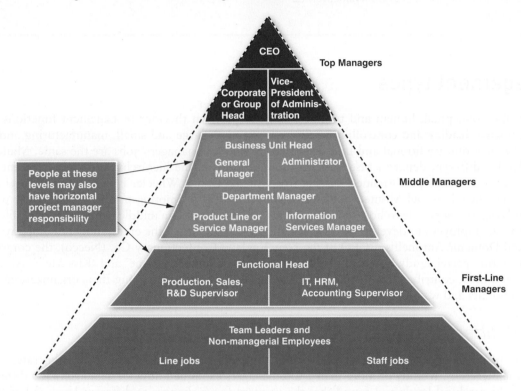

SOURCE: Thomas V. Bonoma and Joseph C. Lawler, 'Chutes and Ladders: Growing the General Manager', *Sloan Management Review* (Spring 1989): 27–37.

Yet even as middle management levels have been reduced, the middle manager's job has taken on a new vitality. Research shows that middle managers play a crucial role in driving innovation and enabling organizations to respond to rapid shifts in the environment.[31] As Ralph Stayer, a US CEO said, *'Leaders can design wonderful strategies, but the success of the organization resides in the execution of those strategies. The people in the middle are the ones who make it work.'*[32] A study by Nicholas Bloom and John Van Reenen seems to support Stayer's observation. In an experiment with textile factories in India, improved middle management practices were introduced into 20 factories in India, and the results were compared to factories that did not improve management procedures. After just 4 months of training in better management methods, the 20 factories cut defects by 50 per cent, boosted productivity and output, and improved profits by $200 000 a year.[33]

Middle managers' status also has escalated because of the growing use of teams and projects. A project manager is responsible for a temporary work project that involves the participation of people from various functions and levels of the organization, and perhaps from outside the company as well. Many of today's middle managers work with a variety of projects and teams at the same time, some of which cross geographical and cultural boundaries as well as functional ones.

First-line managers are directly responsible for the production of goods and services. They are the first or second level of management and have such titles as supervisor, line manager, section chief and office manager.

They are responsible for teams and non-management employees. Their primary concern is the application of rules and procedures to achieve efficient production, provide technical assistance and motivate subordinates. The time horizon at this level is short, with the emphasis on accomplishing day-to-day goals. For example, Alistair Boot manages the menswear department for a John Lewis department store in Cheadle, England.[34] Boot's duties include monitoring and supervising shop floor employees to make sure that sales procedures, safety rules and customer service policies are followed. This type of managerial job might also involve motivating and guiding young, often inexperienced workers, providing assistance as needed and ensuring adherence to company policies.

Horizontal differences

The other major difference in management jobs occurs horizontally across the organization. Functional managers are responsible for departments that perform a single functional task and have employees with similar training and skills. Functional departments include advertising, sales, finance, human resources, manufacturing and accounting. *Line managers* are responsible for the manufacturing and marketing departments that make or sell the product or service. *Staff managers* are in charge of departments, such as finance and human resources, supporting line departments.

General managers are responsible for several departments that perform different functions. A general manager is responsible for a self-contained division, such as a Nordstrom department store or a Honda assembly plant, and for all the functional departments within it. Project managers also have general management responsibility because they coordinate people across several departments to accomplish a specific project.

REFLECTION

- There are many types of managers, based on their purpose and location in an organization.
- A **top manager** is one who is at the apex of the organizational hierarchy and is responsible for the entire organization.
- **Middle managers** work at the middle level of the organization and are responsible for major divisions or departments.
- A **project manager** is a manager who is responsible for a temporary work project that involves people from various functions and levels of the organization.

- Most new managers are **first-line managers** – managers who are at the first or second level of the hierarchy and are directly responsible for overseeing groups of production employees.
- A **functional manager** is responsible for a department that performs a single functional task, such as finance or marketing.
- **General managers** are responsible for several departments that perform different functions, such as the manager of a Macy's department store or a Ford automobile factory.

What is it like to be a manager?

'*Despite a proliferation of management gurus, management consultants and management schools, it remains murky to many of us what managers actually do and why we need them in the first place,*' wrote Ray Fisman, a Columbia Business School professor.[35] Unless someone has actually performed managerial work, it is hard to understand exactly what managers do on an hour-by-hour, day-to-day basis. One preliminary answer to the question of what managers actually do to plan, organize, lead and control was provided by Henry Mintzberg, who followed managers around and recorded all their activities.[36] He developed a description of managerial work that included three general characteristics and ten roles. These characteristics and roles, discussed in detail later in this section, have been supported by other research.[37]

Researchers also have looked at what managers *like* to do. Both male and female managers across five different countries report that they most enjoy activities such as leading others, networking and leading innovation. *Activities managers like least include controlling subordinates, handling paperwork and managing time pressures.*[38] Many new managers in particular find the intense time pressures of management, the load of administrative paperwork, and the challenge of directing others, to be quite stressful as they adjust to their new roles and responsibilities. Indeed, the initial leap into management can be one of the scariest moments in a person's career.

Making the leap: becoming a new manager

Many people who are promoted into a manager position have little idea what the job actually entails and receive little training about how to handle their new role. It's no wonder that, among managers, first-line supervisors tend to experience the most job burnout and attrition.[39]

Making the shift from individual contributor to manager is often tricky. Mark Zuckerberg, whose company, Facebook, went public a week before he turned 28-years-old, provides an example. In a sense, the public has been able to watch as Zuckerberg 'grows up' as a manager. He was a strong individual performer in creating the social media platform and forming the company, but he fumbled with day-to-day management, such as interactions with employees and communicating with people both inside and outside Facebook. Zuckerberg was smart enough to hire seasoned managers, including former Google executive Sheryl Sandberg, and cultivate advisors and mentors who have coached him in areas where he is weak. He also shadowed David Graham at the offices of The Post Company (publisher of *The Washington Post*) for 4 days to try to learn what it is like to manage a large organization. Now that Facebook is a public company, Zuckerberg will be watched more closely than ever to see if he has what it takes to be a manager of a big public corporation.[40]

EXHIBIT 1.7 Making the leap from individual performer to manager

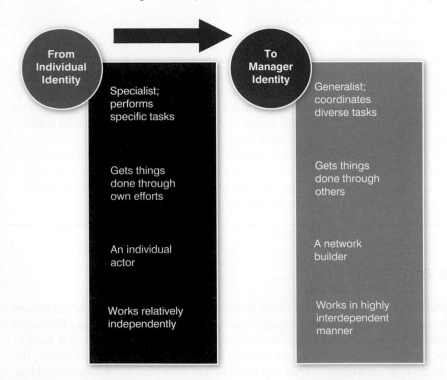

SOURCE: Exhibit 1.1, 'Transformation of Identity', in Linda A. Hill, *Becoming a Manager: Mastery of a New Identity*, 2nd ed. (Boston, MA: Harvard Business School Press, 2003), p. 6.

Harvard professor Linda Hill followed a group of 19 managers over the first year of their managerial careers and found that one key to success is to recognize that becoming a manager involves more than learning a new set of skills. Rather, becoming a manager means a profound transformation in the way people think of themselves, called *personal identity*, which includes letting go of deeply held attitudes and habits and learning new ways of thinking.[41] Exhibit 1.7 outlines the transformation from individual performer to manager. Recall our earlier discussion of the role of manager as the person who builds systems rather than doing specific tasks. The individual performer is a specialist and a 'doer'. His or her mind is conditioned to think in terms of performing specific tasks and activities as expertly as possible. The manager, on the other hand, has to be a generalist and learn to coordinate a broad range of activities. Whereas the individual performer strongly identifies with his or her specific tasks, the manager has to identify with the broader organization and industry.

TAKE A MOMENT

Can you make a personal transformation from individual performer to manager, accomplishing work by engaging and coordinating other people? Complete the questionnaire on page 29 of this chapter to see how your priorities align with the demands placed on a manager.

In addition, the individual performer gets things done mostly through his or her own efforts and develops the habit of relying on self rather than others. The manager, though, gets things done through other people. Indeed, one of the most common mistakes that new managers make is wanting to do all the work themselves, rather than delegating to others and developing others' abilities.[42] Hill offers a reminder that, as a manager, you must *be an instrument to get things done in the organization by working with and through others, rather than being the one doing the work.*[43]

Another problem for many new managers is that they expect to have greater freedom to do what they think is best for the organization. In reality, though, managers find themselves hemmed in by interdependencies. Being a successful manager means thinking in terms of building teams and networks and becoming a motivator and organizer within a highly interdependent system of people and work. Although the distinctions may sound simple in the abstract, they are anything but. In essence, becoming a manager means becoming a new person and viewing oneself in a completely new way.

Many new managers have to make the transformation in a 'trial by fire', learning on the job as they go, but organizations are beginning to be more responsive to the need for new manager training. The cost to organizations of losing good employees who can't make the transition is greater than the cost of providing training to help new managers cope, learn and grow. In addition, some organizations use great care in selecting people for managerial positions, including ensuring that each candidate understands what management involves and really wants to be a manager.

TAKE A MOMENT

How will you make the transition to a new manager's position and effectively manage your time to keep up with the hectic pace? Complete the New Manager Self-Test on page 20 to see how good you are at time management.

Manager activities

Most new managers are unprepared for the variety of activities that managers routinely perform. One of the most interesting findings about managerial activities is how busy managers are and how hectic the average workday can be.

Adventures in multitasking

Managerial activity is characterized by variety, fragmentation and brevity.[44] The widespread and voluminous nature of a manager's tasks leaves little time for quiet reflection. A study by a team from the London School of Economics and Harvard Business School found that the time CEOs spend working alone averages a mere 6 hours a week. The rest of their time is spent in meetings, on the telephone, travelling and talking with others inside and outside the organization.[45]

NEW MANAGER SELF-TEST

Managing your time

INSTRUCTIONS Think about how you normally handle tasks during a typical day at work or school. Read each item and check whether it is 'Mostly true' or 'Mostly false' for you.

	Mostly true	Mostly false
1 I frequently take on too many tasks.	☐	☐
2 I spend too much time on enjoyable but unimportant activities.	☐	☐
3 I feel that I am in excellent control of my time.	☐	☐
4 Frequently during the day, I am not sure what to do next.	☐	☐
5 There is little room for improvement in the way I manage my time.	☐	☐
6 I keep a schedule for events, meetings and deadlines.	☐	☐
7 My workspace and paperwork are well organized.	☐	☐
8 I am good at record keeping.	☐	☐
9 I make good use of waiting time.	☐	☐
10 I am always looking for ways to increase task efficiency.	☐	☐

SCORING & INTERPRETATION For questions 3 and 5–10, give yourself one point for each 'Mostly true' answer. For questions 1, 2 and 4, give yourself one point for each 'Mostly false' answer. Your total score pertains to the overall way you use time. Items 1–5 relate to taking mental control over how you spend your time. Items 6–10 pertain to some mechanics of good time management. Good mental and physical habits make effective time management much easier. Busy managers have to learn to control their time. If you scored 8 or higher, your time-management ability is good. If your score is 4 or lower, you may want to re-evaluate your time-management practices if you aspire to be a manager. How important is good time management to you? Read the Manager's Shoptalk box on page 21 for ideas to improve your time management skills.

Managers shift gears quickly. In his study, Mintzberg found that the average time a top executive spends on any one activity is less than 9 minutes, and another survey indicates that some first-line supervisors average one activity every 48 seconds![46] Significant crises are interspersed with trivial events in no predictable sequence.

Life on speed dial

The manager performs a great deal of work at an unrelenting pace.[47] Managers' work is fast paced and requires great energy. Most top executives routinely work at least 12 hours a day and spend 50 per cent or more of their time travelling.[48] Calendars are often booked months in advance, but unexpected disturbances erupt every day. Mintzberg found that the majority of executives' meetings and other contacts are ad hoc, and even scheduled meetings are typically surrounded by other events such as quick telephone calls, scanning of email or spontaneous encounters. During time away from the office, executives catch up on work-related reading, paperwork, telephone calls and email. Technology, such as email, text messaging, smartphones and laptops intensifies the pace.

🌐 MANAGER'S SHOPTALK

Time management (TM) tips for new managers

Becoming a manager is considered by most people to be a positive, forward-looking career move and, indeed, life as a manager offers many appealing aspects. However, it also holds many challenges, not the least of which is the increased workload and the difficulty of finding the time to accomplish everything on one's expanded list of duties and responsibilities. The following classic time management techniques can help you eliminate major time-wasters in your daily routines.

- **Keep a to-do list.** If you don't use any other system for keeping track of your responsibilities and commitments, at the very least you should maintain a 'To-Do' list that identifies all the things you need to do during the day/week. Although the nature of management means that new responsibilities and shifting priorities occur frequently, it's a fact that people accomplish more with a list than without one.

- **Remember your ABCs.** This is a highly effective system for prioritizing tasks or activities on your To-Do list:

  - An 'A' item is something highly important. It *must* be done, or you'll face serious consequences.

  - A 'B' item is a *should do*, but consequences will tend to be minor if you don't get it done.

  - 'C' items are things that would be nice to get done, but there are no consequences at all if you don't urgently accomplish them.

  - 'D' items are often tasks that you can delegate to someone else.

- **Do a daily review and look ahead.** Spend 10–15 minutes each evening (before leaving the office) reviewing the day and thinking ahead to the next day. Reviewing what has worked well and what didn't will increase your awareness of your

behaviour and subsequently could reduce your bad habits. Then, look ahead and plan what you want to accomplish the next day/week. Some TM experts propose that every minute spent in planning saves around 10 minutes in task execution.

- **Do one thing at a time.** Multitasking has become the motto of the early twenty first century, but too much multitasking is a time waster. Research has shown that multitasking *reduces* rather than enhances productivity. The authors of one study suggest that an inability to focus on one thing at a time could reduce efficiency by 20 to 40 per cent. Even for those whose job requires numerous brief activities, the ability to concentrate fully on each one (sometimes called *spotlighting*) saves time. Give each task your full attention, and you'll get more done and get it done better, too.

SOURCES: Pamela Dodd and Doug Sundheim, *The 25 Best Time Management Tools & Techniques* (Ann Arbor, MI: Peak Performance Press, Inc., 2005); Brian Tracy, *Eat That Frog: 21 Great Ways to Stop Procrastinating and Get More Done in Less Time* (San Francisco: Berrett-Koehler, 2002); Joshua S. Rubinstein, David E. Meyer, and Jeffrey E. Evans, 'Executive Control of Cognitive Processes in Task Switching', *Journal of Experimental Psychology: Human Perception and Performance* 27, no. 4 (August 2001): 763–797; and Sue Shellenbarger, 'Multitasking Makes You Stupid: Studies Show Pitfalls of Doing Too Much at Once', *The Wall Street Journal* (February 27, 2003): D1.

Where does a manager find the time to manage the business?

With so many responsibilities and so many competing demands on their time, how do managers cope? *The Wall Street Journal*'s 'Lessons in Leadership' video series asked CEOs of large companies how they managed their time and found that many of them carve out time just to think about how to manage their time.[49] *Time is a manager's most valuable resource, and one characteristic that identifies successful managers is that they know how to use time effectively to accomplish the important things first and the less important things later.*[50] Time management refers to using techniques that enable you to get more done in less time and with better results, be more relaxed, and have more time to enjoy your work and your social and family life. New managers, in particular, often struggle with the increased workload, the endless paperwork, the incessant meetings and the constant interruptions that come with a management position. Learning to manage their time effectively is one of the greatest challenges that new managers face. There is a much publicized case study of the CEO of Lloyds Bank, António Horta-Osório, who honestly informed his executive board and the bank's primary stakeholders in 2013 that he would have to take time off to deal with the fatigue he was experiencing from the demanding job that he had inherited. The board agreed with their CEO and he was granted a period of time off to recharge his energy levels. This chapter's Manager's Shoptalk box offers some tips for optimal time management. Some of these useful tips may well apply to your studies and preparation for assessments.

Manager roles

Mintzberg's observations and subsequent research indicate that diverse manager activities can be organized into ten roles.[51] A role is a set of expectations for a manager's behaviour. Exhibit 1.8 describes activities

EXHIBIT 1.8 Ten manager roles

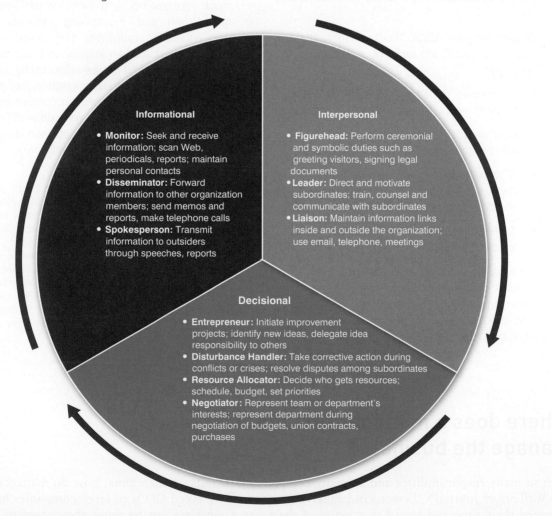

Informational
- **Monitor:** Seek and receive information; scan Web, periodicals, reports; maintain personal contacts
- **Disseminator:** Forward information to other organization members; send memos and reports, make telephone calls
- **Spokesperson:** Transmit information to outsiders through speeches, reports

Interpersonal
- **Figurehead:** Perform ceremonial and symbolic duties such as greeting visitors, signing legal documents
- **Leader:** Direct and motivate subordinates; train, counsel and communicate with subordinates
- **Liaison:** Maintain information links inside and outside the organization; use email, telephone, meetings

Decisional
- **Entrepreneur:** Initiate improvement projects; identify new ideas, delegate idea responsibility to others
- **Disturbance Handler:** Take corrective action during conflicts or crises; resolve disputes among subordinates
- **Resource Allocator:** Decide who gets resources; schedule, budget, set priorities
- **Negotiator:** Represent team or department's interests; represent department during negotiation of budgets, union contracts, purchases

SOURCE: Henry Mintzberg, *The Nature of Managerial Work* (New York: Harper & Row, 1973), pp. 92–93; and Henry Mintzberg, 'Managerial Work: Analysis from Observation', *Management Science* 18 (1971), B97–B110.

associated with each of the roles. These roles are divided into three conceptual categories: **informational** (managing by information), **interpersonal** (managing through people) and **decisional** (managing through action). Each role represents activities that managers undertake to ultimately accomplish the functions of planning, organizing, leading and controlling. Although it is necessary to separate the components of the manager's job to understand the different roles and activities of a manager, it is important to remember that the real job of management isn't practised as a set of independent parts; all the roles can and do interact simultaneously in the real world of management.

Informational roles

Informational roles describe the activities used to maintain and develop an information network. General managers spend about 75 per cent of their time communicating with other people. The *monitor* role involves seeking current information from many sources. The manager acquires information from others and scans written materials to stay well informed. The *disseminator* and *spokesperson* roles are just the opposite: The manager transmits current information to others, both inside and outside the organization, who can use it. Steve Jobs of Apple was a master of the spokesperson role when introducing new Apple products to the public, and employees and the media have assessed Apple's CEO Tim Cook to see if he can match his predecessor's proficiency. Cook seemingly has a distinctly different style from Jobs, being less passionate and more controlled, but the comments about his first appearance as spokesperson for Apple, at the 2012 'D: All Things Digital' conference were generally positive.[52]

Interpersonal roles

Interpersonal roles pertain to relationships with others and are related to the human skills described earlier. The *figurehead* role involves handling ceremonial and symbolic activities for the department or organization. The manager represents the organization in his or her formal managerial capacity, as the head of the unit. The presentation of employee awards by a branch manager for a Commercial Bank is an example of the figurehead role. The *leader* role encompasses relationships with subordinates, including motivation, communication and influence. The *liaison* role pertains to the development of information sources both inside and outside the organization.

Consider the challenge of the leader and liaison roles for managers at National Foods, Pakistan's largest maker of spices and pickles. Managers in companies throughout Pakistan struggle with ever growing political instability, frequent power outages, a high level of government corruption and inefficiency, and increasing threats of terrorism, all of which makes the leader role even more challenging. '*In the morning, I assess my workers,*' says Sajjad Farooqi, a supervisor at National Foods. If Mr Farooqi finds people who are too stressed out or haven't slept the night before, he changes their shift, or gives them easier work. Mr Farooqi also pays a lot of attention to incentives because people are under so much pressure. *As for the liaison role, managers have to develop information sources not only related to the business, but related to safety and security concerns.*[53]

Decisional roles

Decisional roles pertain to those events about which the manager must make a choice and take action. These roles often require conceptual as well as human skills. The *entrepreneur* role involves the initiation of often radical change. *Managers are constantly thinking about the future and how to get there.*[54] The *disturbance handler* role involves resolving conflicts among subordinates, or between the manager's department and other departments. The *resource allocator* role pertains to decisions of how to assign people, time, equipment, money and other resources to attain desired outcomes. The manager must decide which projects receive budget allocations, which of several customer complaints receive priority, and even how to spend his or her own time. The founders and co-CEOs of Research in Motion (RIM), Mike Lazaridis and Jim Balsillie, were ineffective in fulfilling their decisional roles in the several years before the two resigned, under pressure from angry shareholders and frustrated board members in early 2012. Rather than pushing for innovative new products and change at RIM, they kept pouring more resources into the [non-smartphone] keyboard BlackBerry, even as the iPhone and Android models devastated market share.[55]

CONCEPT CONNECTION

Small business owners often assume multiple management roles. Here, Susan Solovic (right), founder and CEO of sbtv.com, an Internet news and information site for small business, functions as a **spokesperson** in an interview with Phoenix anchor Tess Rafols of KTVK. When Solovic develops new ideas for sbtv.com, she functions as an **entrepreneur**, while she fills the **monitor** role when she keeps an eye on current trends that might benefit her evolving company and the small businesses her channel serves.

The relative emphasis that a manager puts on these ten roles depends on a number of factors, for example: the manager's position and influence in the hierarchy; his/her natural skills and abilities; the type of organization; or specific departmental goals to be achieved. For example, Exhibit 1.9 illustrates the varying importance of the leader and his/her liaison roles, as reported in a survey of top, middle and lower-level managers. NB: the importance of the leader role typically declines, while the importance of the liaison role increases, as a manager moves up the organizational hierarchy.

Other factors, such as changing environmental conditions, also may determine which roles are more important for a manager at any given time. Robert Dudley, who took over as CEO of troubled oil giant BP after Tony Hayward was forced out due to mishandling the Deepwater Horizon crisis, has found informational roles and decisional roles at the top of his list as he has personally worked to repair relationships with US government officials, mend fences with local communities, carve a path towards restoring the company's reputation, and take steps to prevent such a disastrous event from ever happening again.[56] Managers stay alert to needs both within and outside the organization to determine which roles are most critical at various times. A top manager may regularly put more emphasis on the roles of spokesperson, figurehead and negotiator, but the emergence of new competitors may require more attention to the monitor role, or a severe decline in employee morale and direction may mean that the CEO has to put more emphasis on the leader role. A marketing manager may focus on interpersonal roles because of the importance of personal contacts in the marketing process, whereas a financial manager may be more likely to emphasize decisional roles, such as resource allocator and negotiator. Despite these differences, all managers carry out informational, interpersonal and decisional roles to meet the needs of their organizations.

Managing in small businesses and not-for-profit organizations

Small businesses are growing in importance. Hundreds of small businesses open every month, but the environment for small business today is highly complicated. Chapter 10 provides more detailed information about managing in small businesses and entrepreneurial startups.

One interesting finding is that managers in small businesses tend to emphasize roles that are different from those of managers in large corporations. Managers in small companies often see their most important role as that of spokesperson, because they must promote the small, growing company to the outside world. The entrepreneur role is also critical in small businesses, because managers have to be innovative and help their organizations develop new ideas to remain competitive. At LivingSocial, for example, founder and CEO Tim O'Shaughnessy spends much of his time promoting the rapidly growing daily-deal site and talking with department heads about potential new products and services.[57] Small business managers tend to rate lower on the leader role and on information-processing roles, compared with their counterparts in large corporations.

EXHIBIT 1.9 Hierarchical levels and importance of leader and liaison roles

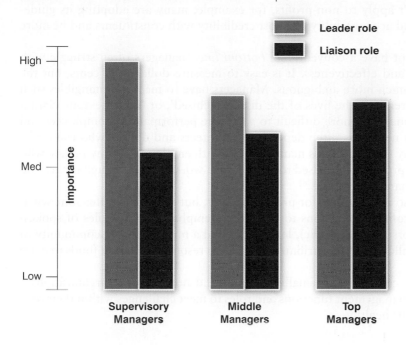

SOURCE: A. I. Kraut, P. R. Pedigo, D. D. McKenna and M. D. Dunnette, 'The Role of the Manager: What's Really Important in Different Management Jobs', *Academy of Management Executive* 3 (1989), 286–293.

REFLECTION

- Becoming a new manager requires a shift in thinking from being an individual performer to playing an interdependent role of coordinating and developing others.
- Because of the interdependent nature of management, new managers often have less freedom and control than they expect to have.
- The job of a manager is highly diverse and fast-paced, so managers need good time management skills.

- A **role** is a set of expectations for one's behaviour.
- Managers at every level perform ten roles, which are grouped into informational roles, interpersonal roles and decisional roles.
- Since the death of Steve Jobs, Tim Cook has taken over the role of *spokesperson* for introducing new products at Apple.

Not-for-profit organizations also represent a major application of management talent.[58] Organizations such as the Salvation Army, The National Trust, Boy Scouts and Girl Guides, all require excellent management. The functions of planning, organizing, leading and controlling apply to not-for-profits, just as they do to business organizations, and managers in non-profits use similar skills and perform similar activities. The primary difference is that managers in businesses direct their activities towards earning money for the company, whereas managers in non-profits direct their efforts towards generating social impacts. The characteristics and needs of non-profits, created by this distinction, present unique challenges for managers.[59]

Financial resources for non-profits typically come from government appropriations, grants and public and private donations, rather than from the sale of products or services to customers. In businesses, managers focus on improving the organization's products and services to increase sales revenues. In non-profits, however, services are typically provided to non-paying clients, and a major problem for many organizations is securing a steady stream of funds to continue operating. Non-profit managers, committed to serving clients with limited resources, must focus on keeping organizational costs as low as possible.[60] Donors generally want their money to go directly to helping clients rather than for overhead costs. If non-profit managers can't demonstrate a highly efficient use of resources, they might have a hard time securing additional donations or government appropriations. Although the Sarbanes-Oxley Act (the 2002 corporate governance reform law for US-domiciled companies) doesn't apply to non-profits, for example, many are adopting its guidelines, striving for greater transparency and accountability to boost credibility with constituents and be more competitive when seeking funding.[61]

In addition, because non-profits do not have a conventional *bottom line*, managers often struggle with the question of what constitutes results and effectiveness. It is easy to measure dollars and cents, but the metrics of success in not-for-profits are much more ambiguous. Managers have to measure intangibles such as 'improve public health', 'make a difference in the lives of the disenfranchised', or 'increase appreciation for the arts'. This intangible nature also makes it more difficult to gauge the performance of employees and managers. An added complication is that managers often depend on volunteers and donors who cannot be supervised and controlled in the same way that a business manager deals with employees. Many people who move from the corporate world to a non-profit are surprised to find that the work hours are often longer and the stress greater than in their previous management jobs.[62]

The ten roles defined by Mintzberg also apply to not-for-profit managers, but these may differ somewhat. We might expect managers in not-for-profit organizations to place more emphasis on the roles of spokesperson (to 'sell' the organization to donors and the public), leader (to build a mission-driven community of employees and volunteers) and resource allocator (to distribute government resources or grant funds that are often assigned top-down).

Managers in all organizations – large corporations, small businesses and not-for-profit organizations – should carefully integrate and adjust the management functions and roles to meet challenges within their own circumstances and keep their organizations healthy.

REFLECTION

- Good management practices are just as important for small businesses and not-for-profit organizations as they are for large corporations.
- Managers in dynamic organizations adjust and integrate the various management functions, activities and roles to meet the unique challenges they face.
- Managers in small businesses often see their most important roles as being the agent of the major

stakeholder for the business and acting as an *entrepreneur* for the firm's benefit.
- Managers in not-for-profit organizations direct their main efforts towards generating social impact, rather than making money for the organization.
- Not-for-profit organizations don't have a conventional accounting, so managers often struggle with what constitutes effectiveness.

State-of-the-art management competencies

In recent years, rapid environmental shifts have caused a fundamental transformation in what is required of truly effective managers. Technological advances and the rise of virtual work, global market forces, and shifting employee and customer expectations, have led to a decline in organizational hierarchies and more empowered workers, which calls for a new approach to management that may be quite different from managing in the past.[63] Exhibit 1.10 shows the shift from the traditional management approach to the new management competencies that are effective in today's environment.

'I was once a command-and-control guy, but the environment's different today. I think now it's a question of making people feel they're making a contribution.'
— JOSEPH J. PLUMERI, CHAIRMAN AND CEO OF WILLIS GROUP HOLDINGS

Instead of being a *controller*, today's effective manager is an *enabler* who helps people do and be their best. Managers have the obligation to get the resources subordinates need, negating obstacles, providing learning and growth opportunities, and offering constructive feedback, coaching and career guidance. Instead of 'management by keeping tabs', they employ an empowering leadership style. Much work these days is done in teams rather than by individuals, so team leadership skills are crucial. People in many organizations work in dispersed locations, so managers can't monitor their behaviour continually. In addition, managers sometimes are coordinating the work of people who aren't under their direct control, such as those in partner organizations, sometimes (for example Apple and Samsung) even working with their competitors. Managing relationships based on authentic conversation and collaboration is essential for successful net outcomes. In addition, today's best managers are 'future-facing'. That is, they redesign the organization and corporate culture for creativity, adaptation and innovation rather than maintaining the status quo. The world is constantly changing, and future success depends much on innovation and continuous improvement. Luck should not be overlooked!

EXHIBIT 1.10 State-of-the-art management competencies for today's world

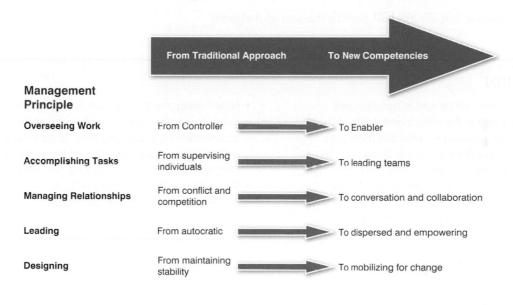

TAKE A MOMENT

Read the Ethical Dilemma at the end of this chapter that pertains to managing in the new workplace. Evaluate what you could do and thus begin to gain a fuller understanding of how to resolve 'thorny' management problems.

One manager who exemplifies the new management competencies is Vineet Nayar, CEO of India's Hindustan Computers Ltd (HCL), with 80 000 employees and operations in more than 25 countries. When he took over as CEO, HCL was a traditional, hierarchical, command-and-control workplace, but Nayar shifted the mindset to treat employees like customers. Nayar is constantly on the lookout to upgrade management competencies, to serve employees and help them do their jobs better. When HCL needed to cut expenses by $100 million due to the [last] global recession, managers asked the employees to come up with ideas for cutting costs without issuing massive layoffs.[64] The shift to a new way of managing isn't easy for traditional managers who are accustomed to being 'in full charge', making all the decisions, and knowing where their subordinates are and what they're doing at every moment.

Even more changes and challenges are on the horizon for organizations and managers. The world is not flat as some systems thinkers postulate. This is an exciting and challenging time to be entering the field of management. Throughout this book, you will learn much more about the new workplace, about the new and dynamic roles managers will be playing in the twenty-first century, and about how you can be a more effective manager in a complex, ever-changing world. Our approach is to provide a stimulating framework for students of Management to gain a sound grasp of the connections between the dynamic forces that are shaping world events. Synthesizers and heuristics, coupled with reality checks and balances, facilitate better interpretation of trends and events. But there is not just one future, there are several possible futures, so planning does not always provide for dealing with economic shocks as some occur by stealth. The modern manager must be prepared to deal with chaos and uncertainty as well as dealing with fair-weather sailing. A major task of management is not to accept bold statements about the nature and impacts of *globalization;* but to argue and debate with counter-hypotheses to challenge prevailing myths. Peter Dicken (2011, p. 8) provides some poignant challenges to inevitable end state scenarios by 'management gurus':

1 The world is not flat (contra Friedman)

2 The world is nor borderless (contra Ohmae)

3 Global companies do not rule the world (contra Korten)

4 Globalization is not always good (contra the neo-liberal hyper-globalizers)

5 Globalization is not always bad (contra the anti-globalizers)

REFLECTION

- Turbulent environmental forces have caused a significant shift in the nature and depth of competencies required for effective managers.
- Traditional management competencies typically included a command-and-control leadership style, a focus on individual tasks and standardizing procedures to maintain stability. In tomorrow's world stability will be the exception not the norm.

- New management competencies include the ability to be an enabler, rather than a controller, using an empowering leadership style, encouraging collaboration, leading teams and mobilizing the corporate culture for change and innovation.
- Vineet Nayar, CEO of India's HCL, illustrates many of the new management competencies.

DISCUSSION QUESTIONS

1 Management responsibilities in today's world are said to be characterized by uncertainty, ambiguity and sudden changes or threats from the environment. Describe some managerial skills and qualities that are of the most importance to managers working in these challenging conditions.

2 Many organizations seem to have a new CEO every 5 years, whereas others have senior executives who stay with the company for many years (e.g., Jack Welch's 20 years as CEO at GE). Determine the likely factors regarding the manager, or his/her company, which might account for this significant longitudinal difference.

3 As a bright, hard-working, entry-level manager you fully intend to rapidly rise up through the hierarchy. Your performance evaluation gives

you high recognition for your technical skills, but low marks when it comes to empathy with people. Arguing that people skills can be developed, identify and discuss the various means of gaining these skills.

4 Organizations and jobs have changed significantly over the past 10 years. Discuss the major changes you anticipate will occur over the next 10 years. a) To what extent could these changes affect the manager's job? and b) What additional skills will be needed to be successful?

5 Is Management more of an art, science or practice? Explain your view.

6 What problems and opportunities do you think globalization, climate change and workplace diversity present for managers? Discuss.

Are you ready to be a practising manager?[65]

Welcome to the world of management. To what extent are you ready for it? This end-of-chapter questionnaire will help you see whether your priorities align with the demands placed on tomorrow's managers.

INSTRUCTIONS Rate each of the following items, based on what you think is the appropriate emphasis for that task, to your success as a new manager of a department. Your task is to rate the top four priority items as 'High priority' and the other four as 'Low priority'.

	High priority	Low priority
1 Spend 50 per cent or more of your time in the care and feeding of people.	☐	☐
2 Make sure that people understand you are in control of the department.	☐	☐
3 Use lunches to meet and network with peers in other departments.	☐	☐
4 Implement the changes that you believe will improve department performance.	☐	☐
5 Spend as much time as possible talking with and listening to subordinates.	☐	☐
6 Make sure that jobs get out on time.	☐	☐
7 Reach out to your boss to discuss his or her expectations for you and your department.	☐	☐
8 Make sure that you set clear expectations and policies for your department.	☐	☐

SCORING & INTERPRETATION All eight items in the list may be important, but the odd-numbered items are considered more important than the even-numbered items for long-term success as a manager. If you checked three or four of the odd-numbered items, consider yourself ready for a management position. A successful new manager discovers that a lot of time has to be spent in the care and feeding of people, including subordinates and colleagues. People who fail in new management jobs often do so because they have poor working relationships or they misjudge management philosophy or cultural values. Developing good relationships in all directions is typically more important than holding on to old work skills or emphasizing control and task outcomes. Successful outcomes typically will occur when relationships are solid. After a year or so in a managerial role, successful people learn that more than half their time is spent networking and building relationships.

APPLY YOUR SKILLS: ETHICAL DILEMMA

Can management afford to look the other way?[66]

Harry Rull had been with Shellington Pharmaceuticals (SP) for 30 years. After a tour of duty in the various plants and 7 years overseas, Harry was back at US headquarters, looking forward to his new role as vice president of US marketing.

Two weeks into his new job, Harry received some unsettling news about one of the managers that he supervises. During a casual lunch conversation, Sally Barton, the director of human resources, mentioned that Harry should expect a telephone call about Roger Jacobs, manager of new product development. Jacobs had a history of being 'pretty horrible' to his subordinates, she said, and one disgruntled employee asked to speak to someone in senior management. After lunch, Harry did some follow-up work. Jacobs's performance reviews have been stellar, but his personnel file also contains a large number of notes documenting charges of Jacobs's mistreatment of subordinates. The complaints ranged from 'inappropriate and derogatory remarks' to charges of sexual harassment (which were subsequently dropped). What was more disturbing was the fact that the number and the severity of the complaints have increased with each of Jacobs's 10 years with the company.

When Harry questioned the company president about the issue, he was told, 'Yeah, he's had some problems, but you can't just replace someone with an eye for new products. You're a bottom-line guy; you understand why we let these things slide.' Not sure how to handle the situation, Harry met briefly with Jacobs and reminded him to 'keep the team's morale up'. Just after the meeting, Barton called to let him know that the problem that she'd mentioned over lunch had been worked out. However, she warned, another employee has now come forward, demanding that her complaints be addressed by senior management.

What would you do?

1 Ignore the problem. Jacobs's contributions to new product development are too valuable to risk losing him, and the problems over the past 10 years have always worked themselves out anyway. There's no sense starting something that could make you look bad.

2 Launch a full-scale investigation of employee complaints about Jacobs and make Jacobs aware that his documented history over the past 10 years has put him on thin ice.

3 Meet with Jacobs and the employee to try to resolve the current issue, and then start working with Barton and other senior managers to develop stronger policies regarding sexual harassment and treatment of employees, including clear-cut procedures for handling complaints.

APPLY YOUR SKILLS: CASE FOR CRITICAL ANALYSIS

The management standards
Background

The Management Standards Centre (MSC) is the UK Government recognized standards setting body for management and leadership. The functional areas covered by the management and leadership standards were identified by consulting widely with employers, individual managers and other key stakeholders during the course of the standards review project.

Employers globally are seeking to access practical and well-designed guidelines on how to achieve high quality management and leadership for their businesses and industries.

Too often, supply has not been meeting employers' expectations. Many businesses need:

■ Better access to high quality managers and leaders.

■ Guidance on educating or developing potential managers and leaders from their existing workforce.

■ Individuals who are prepared to take up the challenge for on going self-development that can benefit themselves and business objectives.

Management and leadership standards have been developed in the UK with employers and individuals to provide a useful and practical framework for management and leadership development. The MSC's aim is to influence employers by developing case studies to demonstrate how the new standards can help them equip managers and leaders to realize their business potential. By working alongside employers, funding decision-makers and awarding bodies, the MSC encourages them to incorporate some of the best practice units, thus ensuring they are fit for purpose for their business and/or industry and will help current and future managers and leaders to be skilled at:

1 Managing self and personal development

2 Providing direction

3 Facilitating change

4   Working with people

5   Using resources

6   Achieving results

Managers and leaders continuously develop their knowledge, skills and performance as part of their professional and contractual professional codes of practice, employment conditions and supply-chain agreements should encourage and require owners and managers in all organizations, regardless of size or sector, to update their knowledge and develop their skills continuously to improve their performance. Organizations and their managers accurately pinpoint their learning and development priorities. Guidance and easy-to-use tools should be provided to enable organizations to identify knowledge and skills gaps and prioritize learning needs for their managers.

Learning and qualifications deliver real benefits for managers and their organizations. Employers and managers should take the lead in designing relevant learning and qualifications that deliver measurable improvements in performance in line with the organization's strategy and the manager's career aspirations. Experienced managers should be able to find programmes to help them reflect on their experience and take their management knowledge and skills to a new level. Learning and qualifications should support the transfer of knowledge, skills and competence from one situation to another, helping managers to progress both vertically (promotion) and horizontally (change of job or redeployment).

Stimulating active take-up by all the identified key players to improve management and leadership within the UK is an important step forward. Providing employers with greater access to competent individuals that possess relevant and up-to-date management and leadership skills can improve business productivity and performance. Improving the core skills of existing managers and leaders can create a positive culture of continuous improvement to achieve better business performance. Management standards can provide a critical management and leadership benchmark for all UK employers, whatever the size of their business, to be sustainable and competitive on the global stage.

A functional mapping exercise was undertaken which asked individual managers and employers at all levels to identify the functions that managers undertake in the workplace. This led to the development of a purpose statement and functional map. The standards now include behaviours that underpin effective performance. This is in recognition of feedback from employers that the soft skills which managers bring to their role are as important as the hard technical skills they possess.

The standards are proven benchmarks of best practice and have been developed based on extensive consultation with genuine managers doing real management jobs. They offer a practical resource to aid decisions in everything from day-to-day matters like recruitment and selection to long-term issues such as the recognition and development of future leaders.

This revised set of standards builds on the 2004 suite with the addition of new units covering fresh areas such as knowledge management, environmental management and quality assurance. The standards are both clear and accessible while still providing enough detail to be robust and measureable.

Questions

1   Defining management has been a challenge for theorists for many years, analyze the advantages of the management standards approach.

2   'How contemporary managers think and work are the basis for arguing that a new form of managerial style has arrived (Drucker, P. F. (2015, p.11)). Discuss the extent to which management has changed since Henry Mintzberg's *The Nature of Managerial Work* (1973).

3   Predict the ways in which management will change in the future.

END NOTES

1. This example is based on Jon Katzenbach, 'The Steve Jobs Way', *Strategy + Business* (Summer 2012), www.strategy-business.com/article/00109?gko=d331b (accessed June 11, 2012); Leslie Kwoh and Emma Silverman, 'Bio as Bible: Managers Imitate Steve Jobs', *The Wall Street Journal* (March 31, 2012), B1; and Joel Siegel, 'When Steve Jobs Got Fired by Apple', *ABC News* (October 6, 2011), www.abcnews.go.com/Technology/steve-jobs-fire-company/story?id =14683754 (accessed June 11, 2012).

2. Quoted in Ellen McGirt. '05: Square, For Making Magic Out of the Mercantile', *Fast Company* (March 2012), 82–85, 146–147 (part of the section, 'The World's 50 Most Innovative Companies').

3. See Joshua Cooper Ramo, *The Age of the Unthinkable: Why the New World Disorder Constantly Surprises Us and What We Can Do About It* (New York: Little Brown, 2009); and Richard Florida, *The Great Reset: How New Ways of Living and Working Drive Post-Crash Prosperity* (New York: Harper Collins, 2010).

4. Joshua Green, 'Management Secrets of the Grateful Dead', *The Atlantic* (March 2010): 64–67; Jordan Timm, 'Jerry Bears, Doobage and the Invention of Social Networking', *Canadian Business* (September 2010): 74–75; David Meerman Scott and Brian Halligan, *Marketing Lessons from the Grateful Dead: What Every Business Can Learn from the Most Iconic Band in History* (New York: John Wiley & Sons, 2010); and Barry Barnes, *Everything I Know About Business I Learned from the Grateful Dead* (New York: Business Plus, 2011).

5. Darrell Rigby and Barbara Bilodeau, 'Management Tools and Trends 2011', Bain and Company, Inc., www .bain. com/publications/articles/Management-tools-trends-2011. aspx (accessed June 22, 2012).

6. 'What Do Managers Do?' *The Wall Street Journal Online*, www.guides.wsj.com/management/developing-a-leadership-style/what-do-managers-do/ (accessed August 11, 2010); article adapted from Alan Murray, *The Wall Street Journal Essential Guide to Management* (New York: Harper Business, 2010).

7. Kate Linebaugh, 'The New GE Way: Go Deep, Not Wide', *The Wall Street Journal* (March 7, 2012), B1.

8. Christopher S. Stewart, 'Oprah Struggles to Build Her Network', *The Wall Street Journal* (May 7, 2012), A1.

9. Jeff Bennett and Neal E. Boudette, 'Boss Sweats Details of Chrysler Revival', *The Wall Street Journal* (January 31, 2011), A1.

10. Ed O'Keefe, 'Lieberman Calls for Wider Inquiry into Secret Service Scandal', *The Washington Post* (April 23, 2012), A3; Laurie Kellman and Alicia A. Caldwell, 'Inquiry Hears of Wider Secret Service Misbehavior', *The Salt Lake Tribune* (May 25, 2012); and 'Secret Service Toughens Agent Conduct Rules after Prostitution Scandal: Political Notebook', *The Boston Globe* (April 28, 2012), A8.

11. Based on Lauren A. E. Schuker, 'Movie Budget Lesson #1: Skip the Fur', *The Wall Street Journal* (July 15, 2010), B1; Brooks Barnes, 'Animation Meets Economic Reality', *The New York Times* (April 4, 2011), B1; and Allison Corneau, '*The Lorax* Tops Weekend Box Office', *US Weekly* (March 4, 2012), www.usmagazine .com/entertainment/news/the-lorax-tops-weekend-box-office-201243 (accessed June 12, 2012).

12. Aaron O. Patrick, 'EMI Deal Hits a Sour Note', *The Wall Street Journal,* August 15, 2009.

13. Robert L. Katz, 'Skills of an Effective Administrator', *Harvard Business Review* 52 (September–October 1974): 90–102.

14. Troy V. Mumford, Michael A. Campion and Frederick P. Morgeson, 'The Leadership Skills Strataplex: Leadership Skills Requirements Across Organizational Levels', *The Leadership Quarterly* 18 (2007): 154–166.

15. Nanette Byrnes and Roger O. Crockett, 'An Historic Succession at Xerox', *BusinessWeek* (June 8, 2009): 18–22.

16. Sue Shellenbarger, 'From Our Readers: The Bosses That Drove Me to Quit My Job', *The Wall Street Journal,* February 7, 2000.

17. Boris Groysberg, L. Kevin Kelly and Bryan MacDonald, 'The New Path to the C-Suite', *Harvard Business Review* (March 2011): 60–68; Jeanne C. Meister and Karie Willyerd, 'Leadership 2020: Start Preparing People Now', *Leadership Excellence* (July 2010): 5; Neena Sinha, N. K. Kakkar and Vikas Gupta, 'Uncovering the Secrets of the Twenty-First-Century Organization', *Global Business and Organizational Excellence* (January–February 2012): 49–63; and Rowena Crosbie, 'Learning the Soft Skills of Leadership', *Industrial and Commercial Training*, 37, no. 1 (2005).

18. Adam Bryant, 'The Quest to Build a Better Boss', *The New York Times* (March 13, 2011), BU1.

19. William A. Gentry, Lauren S. Harris, Becca A. Baker and Jean Brittain Leslie, 'Managerial Skills: What Has Changed Since the Late 1980s?' *Leadership and Organization Development Journal* 29, no. 2 (2008): 167–181.

20. David Sacks, 'The Way I Work: Yammer', *Inc.* (November 2011): 122–124.

21. Clinton O. Longenecker, Mitchell J. Neubert and Laurence S. Fink, 'Causes and Consequences of Managerial Failure in Rapidly Changing Organizations', *Business Horizons* 50 (2007): 145–155.

22. Paul Sonne, 'The Gulf Oil Spill: Hayward Fell Short of Modern CEO Demands', *The Wall Street Journal*, July 26, 2010.

23. Sydney Finkelstein, 'The Worst CEOs of 2011', *The New York Times*, December 27, 2011; and Ethan Smith, 'Netflix CEO Unbowed: Ignoring Customers' Anger, Company Says Separating DVD Business Is Essential', *The Wall Street Journal*, September 20, 2011.

24. Longenecker, Neubert and Fink, 'Causes and Consequences of Managerial Failure in Rapidly Changing Organizations'.

25. Eileen Sheridan, 'Rise: Best Day, Worst Day', *The Guardian*, September 14, 2002.

26. Heath Row, 'Force Play' (Company of Friends column), *Fast Company* (March 2001): 46.

27. Charles Fishman, 'Sweet Company', *Fast Company* (February 2001): 136–145.

28. A. I. Kraut, P. R. Pedigo, D. D. McKenna and M. D. Dunnette, 'The Role of the Manager: What's Really Important in Different Management Jobs', *Academy of Management Executive* 19, no. 4 (2005): 122–129.

29. Christopher A. Bartlett and Sumantra Ghoshal, 'Changing the Role of Top Management: Beyond Systems to People', *Harvard Business Review* (May–June 1995): 132–142; and Sumantra Ghoshal and Christopher A. Bartlett, 'Changing the Role of Top Management: Beyond Structure to Processes', *Harvard Business Review* (January–February 1995): 86–96.

30. Lynda Gratton, 'The End of the Middle Manager', *Harvard Business Review* (January–February 2011): 36.

31. Paul Osterman, 'Recognizing the Value of Middle Management', *Ivey Business Journal* (November–December 2009), www.iveybusinessjournal.com/article.asp?intArticle_id=866; Quy Nguyen Huy, 'In Praise of Middle Managers', *Harvard Business Review* (September 2003): 72–79;

Rosabeth Moss Kanter, *On the Frontiers of Management* (Boston: Harvard Business School Press, 2003).

32. Quoted in Lisa Haneberg, 'Reinventing Middle Management', *Leader to Leader* (Fall 2005): 13–18.

33. Reported in Ray Fisman, 'In Defense of Middle Management', *The Washington Post*, October 16, 2010, www.washingtonpost.com/wp-dyn/content/article/2010/10/16/AR2010101604266_pf.html (accessed June 13, 2012).

34. Miles Brignall, 'Rise; Launch Pad: The Retailer; Alistair Boot, an Assistant Manager at the John Lewis Store in Cheadle, Talks to Miles Brignall', *The Guardian*, October 4, 2003.

35. Fisman, 'In Defense of Middle Management'.

36. Henry Mintzberg, *Managing* (San Francisco: Berrett-Kohler Publishers, 2009); Mintzberg, *The Nature of Managerial Work* (New York: Harper & Row, 1973); and Mintzberg, 'Rounding Out the Manager's Job', *Sloan Management Review* (Fall 1994): 11–26.

37. Robert E. Kaplan, 'Trade Routes: The Manager's Network of Relationships', *Organizational Dynamics* (Spring 1984): 37–52; Rosemary Stewart, 'The Nature of Management: A Problem for Management Education', *Journal of Management Studies* 21 (1984): 323–330; John P. Kotter, 'What Effective General Managers Really Do', *Harvard Business Review* (November–December 1982): 156–167; and Morgan W. McCall, Jr., Ann M. Morrison and Robert L. Hannan, 'Studies of Managerial Work: Results and Methods', Technical Report No. 9, Center for Creative Leadership, Greensboro, NC, 1978.

38. Alison M. Konrad, Roger Kashlak, Izumi Yoshioka, Robert Waryszak and Nina Toren, 'What Do Managers *Like* to Do? A Five-Country Study', *Group and Organizational Management* 26, no. 4 (December 2001): 401–433.

39. For a review of the problems faced by first-time managers, see Linda A. Hill, 'Becoming the Boss', *Harvard Business Review* (January 2007): 49–56; Loren B. Belker and Gary S. Topchik, *The First-Time Manager: A Practical Guide to the Management of People*, 5th ed. (New York: AMACOM, 2005); J. W. Lorsch and P. F. Mathias, 'When Professionals Have to Manage', *Harvard Business Review* (July–August 1987): 78–83; R. A. Webber, *Becoming a Courageous Manager: Overcoming Career Problems of New Managers* (Englewood Cliffs, NJ: Prentice Hall, 1991); D. E. Dougherty, *From Technical Professional to Corporate Manager: A Guide to Career Transition* (New York: Wiley, 1984); J. Falvey, 'The Making of a Manager', *Sales and Marketing Management* (March 1989): 42–83; M. K. Badawy, *Developing Managerial Skills in Engineers and Scientists: Succeeding as a Technical Manager* (New York: Van Nostrand Reinhold, 1982); and M. London, *Developing Managers: A Guide to Motivating and Preparing People for Successful Managerial Careers* (San Francisco, CA: Jossey-Bass, 1985).

40. Based on Evelyn Rusli, Nicole Perlroth and Nick Bilton, 'The Hoodie amid the Pinstripes: As Facebook IPO Nears, Is Its Chief up to Running a Public Company?' *International Herald Tribune*, May 14, 2012, 17.

41. This discussion is based on Linda A. Hill, *Becoming a Manager: How New Managers Master the Challenges of Leadership*, 2d ed. (Boston, MA: Harvard Business School Press, 2003), 6–8; and Hill, 'Becoming the Boss'.

42. See also the 'Boss's First Steps' sidebar in White, 'Learning to Be the Boss'; and Belker and Topchik, *The First-Time Manager*.

43. Quoted in Eileen Zimmerman, 'Are You Cut Out for Management?' (Career Couch column), *The New York Times*, January 15 2011, www.nytimes.com/2011/01/16/jobs/16career.html (accessed June 14, 2012).

44. Henry Mintzberg, *Managing*, 17–41.

45. Study reported in Rachel Emma Silverman, 'Where's The Boss? Trapped in a Meeting', *The Wall Street Journal*, February 14, 2012, www.online.wsj.com/article/SB10001424052970204642604577215013504567548.html (accessed June 14, 2012).

46. *Ibid*.

47. Mintzberg, *Managing*, 17–41.

48. Carol Hymowitz, 'Packed Calendars Rule', *The Asian Wall Street Journal*, June 16, 2009; and 'The 18-Hour Day', *The Conference Board Review* (March–April 2008): 20.

49. 'Four CEOs' Tips on Managing Your Time', *The Wall Street Journal*, February 14, 2012, www.online.wsj.com/article/SB10001424052970204883304577221551714492724.html (accessed June 14, 2012).

50. A. Garrett, 'Buying Time to Do the Things That Really Matter', *Management Today* (July 2000): 75; and Robert S. Kaplan, 'What to Ask the Person in the Mirror', *Harvard Business Review* (January 2007): 86–95.

51. Mintzberg, *Managing*; Lance B. Kurke and Howard E. Aldrich, 'Mintzberg Was Right! A Replication and Extension of *The Nature of Managerial Work*', *Management Science* 29 (1983): 975–984; Cynthia M. Pavett and Alan W. Lau, 'Managerial Work: The Influence of Hierarchical Level and Functional Specialty', *Academy of Management Journal* 26 (1983): 170–177; and Colin P. Hales, 'What Do Managers Do? A Critical Review of the Evidence', *Journal of Management Studies* 23 (1986): 88–115.

52. Jessica E. Vascellaro, 'Apple Chief Executive Cook to Climb on a New Stage', *The Wall Street Journal*, May 29, 2012, B2; Walt Mossberg and Kara Swisher, 'All Things Digital (A Special Report) – Apple After Jobs', *The Wall Street Journal*, June 4, 2012, R3; and Troy Wolverton, 'Apple CEO Tim Cook Isn't Trying to Be the Next Steve Jobs', *Oakland Tribune*, May 29, 2012.

53. Naween Mangi, 'Convoys and Patdowns: A Day at the Office in Pakistan', *Bloomberg Businessweek* (July 25–July 31, 2011): 11–13.

54. Harry S. Jonas III, Ronald E. Fry and Suresh Srivastva, 'The Office of the CEO: Understanding the Executive Experience', *Academy of Management Executive* 4 (August 1990): 36–48.

55. Will Connors and Chip Cummins, 'RIM CEOs Give up Top Posts in Shuffle', *The Wall Street Journal Online*, January 23, 2012, www.online.wsj.com/article/SB10001424052970204624204577177184275959856.html (accessed July 9, 2012); and Finkelstein, 'The Worst CEOs of 2011'.

56. Guy Chazan and Monica Langley, 'Dudley Faces Daunting To-Do List', *The Wall Street Journal Europe*, July 27, 2010.

57. Tim O'Shaughnessy, 'The Way I Work: LivingSocial', *Inc.* (March 2012): 104–108.

58. Jean Crawford, 'Profiling the Non-Profit Leader of Tomorrow', *Ivey Business Journal* (May–June 2010),

www.iveybusinessjournal.com/topics/leadership/profiling-the-non-profit-leader-of-tomorrow (accessed June 14, 2012).

59. The following discussion is based on Peter F. Drucker, *Managing the Non-Profit Organization: Principles and Practices* (New York: Harper Business, 1992); and Thomas Wolf, *Managing a Nonprofit Organization* (New York: Fireside/Simon & Schuster, 1990).

60. Christine W. Letts, William P. Ryan and Allen Grossman, *High Performance Nonprofit Organizations* (New York: Wiley & Sons, 1999), pp. 30–35.

61. Carol Hymowitz, 'In Sarbanes-Oxley Era, Running a Non-profit Is Only Getting Harder', *The Wall Street Journal*, June 21, 2005; and Bill Birchard, 'Nonprofits by the Numbers', *CFO* (June 2005): 50–55.

62. Eilene Zimmerman, 'Your True Calling Could Suit a Non-profit' (interview, Career Couch column), *The New York Times,* April 6, 2008.

63. This discussion is based on ideas in Stephen Denning, 'Masterclass: The Reinvention of Management', *Strategy & Leadership* 39, no. 2 (2011): 9–17; Julian Birkinshaw and Jules Goddard, 'What Is Your Management Model?' *MIT Sloan Management Review* (Winter 2009): 81–90; Paul McDonald, 'It's Time for Management Version 2.0: Six Forces Redefining the Future of Modern Management', *Futures* (October 2011): 797ff; Jeanne C. Meister and Karie Willyerrd, 'Leadership 2020: Start Preparing People Now', *Leadership Excellence* (July 2010): 5.

64. Described in Birkinshaw and Goddard, 'What Is Your Management Model?'; Denning, 'The Reinvention of Management'; and Traci L. Fenton, 'Inspiring Democracy in the Workplace: From Fear-Based to Freedom-Centered Organizations', *Leader to Leader* (Spring 2012): 57–63.

65. This questionnaire is adapted from research findings reported in Linda A. Hill, *Becoming a Manager: How New Managers Master the Challenges of Leadership*, 2nd ed. (Boston, MA: Harvard Business School Press, 2003); and John J. Gabarro, *The Dynamics of Taking Charge* (Boston, MA: Harvard Business School Press, 1987).

66. Based on Doug Wallace, 'A Talent for Mismanagement: What Would You Do?' *Business Ethics* 2 (November–December 1992): 3–4.

CHAPTER 2
THE EVOLUTION OF MANAGEMENT THINKING

LEARNING OBJECTIVES

After studying this chapter, you should be able to:

1 Understand how historical forces influence the practice of management.

2 Identify and explain major developments in the history of management thought.

3 Describe the major components of the classical and humanistic management perspectives.

4 Discuss the management science approach and its current use in organizations.

5 Explain the major concepts of systems thinking, the contingency view and total quality management.

6 Name contemporary management tools and some reasons that management trends change over time.

7 Describe the management changes brought about by a technology-driven workplace, including the role of social media programs, customer relationship management and supply chain management.

What do managers at India's Tata Group, US-based General Electric (GE) and Africa's M-Pesa mobile money transfer service have in common with eighteenth-century inventor and statesman Benjamin Franklin? The authors of a recent book on innovation say they have all applied a concept called *jugaad* (pronounced joo-gaardh). *Jugaad* is a Hindi word that basically refers to creating something of benefit from limited resources. Benjamin Franklin, the authors say, is a great historical example because he faced scarcity first-hand, but he improvised to create inventions that were for the benefit of the masses.[1]

Management – like most disciplines – loves buzzwords, and *jugaad* is one of the most recent to appear on the radar. *Jugaad* basically refers to an innovation mindset, used widely by Indian companies, that strives to meet customers' immediate needs quickly and inexpensively. With research and development budgets strained in today's economy, Western managers have quickly picked up on the approach, sometimes calling it *frugal engineering*.[2] Will this be a buzzword that quickly fades from managers' vocabularies, or will it become as ubiquitous in management circles as terms such as total quality or *kaizen*?

Managers are always on the lookout for fresh ideas, innovative management approaches and new tools and techniques. Management philosophies and organizational forms change over time to meet new needs. The questionnaire at the end of this chapter describes two differing philosophies about how people should be managed, and you will learn more about these ideas in this chapter.

If management is always changing, why does history matter to managers? The workplace of today is different from what it was 50 years ago – indeed, from what it was even 10 years ago – yet historical concepts form the backbone of management education.[3] One reason is that a historical perspective provides managers with a broader way of thinking, a way of searching for patterns and determining whether they recur across time periods. It is a way of learning from others' mistakes so as not to repeat them; learning from others' successes so as to repeat them in the appropriate situation; and most of all, learning to understand why things happen to improve organizations in the future. Certain management practices that seem modern, such as open-book management or employee stock ownership, have actually been around for a long time. These techniques have repeatedly gained and lost popularity since the early twentieth century because of shifting historical forces.[4]

This chapter provides a historical overview of the ideas, theories and management philosophies that have contributed to making the workplace what it is today. The final section of the chapter looks at some recent trends and current approaches that build on the basis of management understanding. This foundation illustrates that the value of studying management lies not in learning current facts and research, but in developing a perspective that will facilitate the broad, long-term view needed for management success.

TAKE A MOMENT

Go to the Small Group Breakout Exercise online that pertains to how historical events and forces shape the lives of individuals.

 ## GREEN **POWER**

Drop back and punt

Glenn Rink's great product – popcorn-like sponges for absorbing oil spills – received a cool reception in the 1990s. Corporate sceptics said that traditional skimming of oil off water remained the preferred choice for disaster cleanup. Blocked by resistance to his product, Rink, founder of **Abtech Industries**, followed the historic and time-honoured tradition of American football teams, which sometimes need to drop back and punt before they can go on the offensive again.

Rink decided to focus on smaller-scale disasters instead. For more than a decade, Abtech Industries built a reputation for offering low-cost alternatives to address the cleanup needs of cities struggling with a variety of water pollution problems. The strategy paid off. In 2011, a revitalized Abtech, maker of the Smart Sponge Plus, partnered with the huge company Waste Management Inc. as the exclusive North American distributor to cities, and oil cleanup orders began pouring in. To date, Smart Sponge Plus has been used in more than 15 000 spill locations worldwide.

SOURCE: 'Innovation #71: Glenn Rink, Founder of Abtech Industries', *Fast Company* (June 2012): 136 (part of 'The 100 Most Creative People in Business 2012', pp. 78–156).

Management and organization

Studying history doesn't mean merely arranging events in chronological order; it means developing an understanding of the impact of societal forces on organizations. Studying history is a way to achieve strategic thinking, see the big picture and improve conceptual skills. Let's begin by examining how social, political and economic forces have influenced organizations and the practice of management.[5]

Social forces refer to those aspects of a culture that guide and influence relationships among people. What do people value? What do people need? What are the standards of behaviour among people? These forces shape what is known as the *social contract*, which refers to the unwritten, common rules and perceptions about relationships among people and between employees and management.

One social force is the changing attitudes, ideas and values of Generation Y employees (sometimes called Millennials).[6] These young workers, arguably the most educated generation in history USA, grew up technologically adept and globally conscious. Unlike many workers of the past, they typically are not hesitant to question their superiors and challenge the status quo. They want a flexible, collaborative work environment that is challenging and supportive, with access to cutting-edge technology, opportunities to learn and further their careers and personal goals, and the power to make substantive decisions and changes in the workplace.

Political forces refer to the influence of political and legal institutions on people and organizations. One significant political force is the increased role of government in business after the collapse of companies in the financial services sector and major problems in the auto industry. Some managers expect increasing government regulation in the coming years.[7] Political forces also include basic assumptions underlying the political system, such as the desirability of self-government, property rights, contract rights, the definition of justice and the determination of innocence or guilt of a crime.

Economic forces pertain to the availability, production and distribution of resources in a society. Governments, military agencies, churches, schools and business organizations in every society need resources to achieve their goals, and economic forces influence the allocation of scarce resources. Companies in every industry have been affected by the recent financial crisis, which is the worst since the Great Depression of the 1930s. Reduced consumer spending and tighter access to credit have curtailed growth and left companies scrambling to meet goals with limited resources. Although liquidity for large corporations has increased, smaller companies continued to struggle to find funding.[8] Another economic trend that affects managers worldwide is the growing economic power of countries such as China, India and Brazil.[9]

Management practices and perspectives vary in response to these social, political and economic forces in the larger society. Exhibit 2.1 illustrates the evolution of significant management perspectives over time. The timeline reflects the dominant time period for each approach, but elements of each are still used in today's organizations.[10]

EXHIBIT 2.1 Management perspectives over time

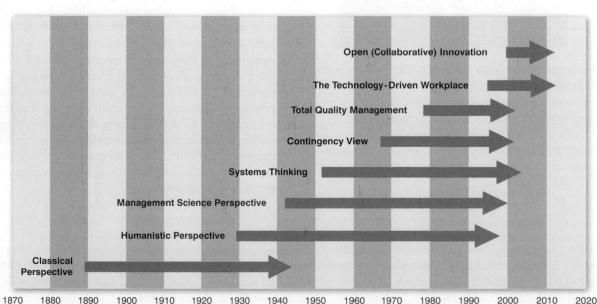

REFLECTION

- Managers are always on the lookout for new techniques and approaches to meet shifting organizational needs.
- Looking at history gives managers a broader perspective for interpreting and responding to current opportunities and problems.
- Management and organizations are shaped by forces in the larger society.
- **Social forces** are aspects of a society that guide and influence relationships among people, such as their values, needs and standards of behaviour.

- **Political forces** relate to the influence of political and legal institutions on people and organizations.
- The increased role of government in business is one example of a political force.
- **Economic forces** affect the availability, production and distribution of a society's resources.

 CONCEPT CONNECTION

Frederick Winslow Taylor (1856–1915). Taylor's theory that labour productivity could be improved by scientifically determined management practices earned him the title of 'father of scientific management'.

This perspective contains three subfields, each with a slightly different emphasis: scientific management, bureaucratic organizations and administrative principles.[14]

Classical perspective

The practice of management can be traced to 3000 BC, to the first government organizations developed by the Sumerians and Egyptians, but the formal study of management is relatively recent.[11] The early study of management as we know it today began with what is now called the classical perspective.

The classical perspective on management emerged during the nineteenth and early twentieth centuries. The factory system that began to appear in the 1800s posed challenges that earlier organizations had not encountered. Problems arose in tooling the plants, organizing managerial structure, training employees (many of them non-English-speaking immigrants), scheduling complex manufacturing operations, and dealing with increased labour dissatisfaction and resulting strikes.

These myriad new problems and the development of large, complex organizations demanded a new approach to coordination and control, and a 'new sub-species of economic man – the salaried manager'[12] – was born. Between 1880 and 1920, the number of professional managers in the USA grew from 161 000 to more than 1 million.[13] These professional managers began developing and testing solutions to the mounting challenges of organizing, coordinating and controlling large numbers of people and increasing worker productivity. Thus began the evolution of modern management with the classical perspective.

Scientific management

Scientific management emphasizes scientifically determined jobs and management practices as the way to improve efficiency and labour productivity. In the late 1800s, a young engineer, Frederick Winslow Taylor (1856–1915), proposed that workers 'could be retooled like machines, their physical and mental gears recalibrated for better productivity'.[15] Taylor insisted that improving productivity meant that management itself would have to change and, further, that the manner of change could be determined only by scientific study; hence, the label *scientific management* emerged. Taylor suggested that decisions based on rules of thumb and tradition be replaced with precise procedures developed after careful study of individual situations.[16]

The scientific management approach is illustrated by the unloading of iron from rail cars and reloading finished steel for the Bethlehem Steel plant in 1898. Taylor calculated that with the correct movements, tools and sequencing, each man was capable of loading 47.5 tons per day instead of the typical 12.5 tons. He also worked out an incentive system that paid each man $1.85 a day for meeting the new standard, an increase from the previous rate of $1.15. Productivity at Bethlehem Steel shot up overnight.

Although known as the *father of scientific management*, Taylor was not alone in this area. Henry Gantt, an associate of Taylor's, developed the *Gantt chart*, a bar graph that measures planned and completed work along each stage of production by time elapsed. Two other important pioneers in this area were the husband-and-wife team of Frank B. and Lillian M. Gilbreth. Frank B. Gilbreth (1868–1924) pioneered *time and motion study* and arrived

CONCEPT CONNECTION

Automaker Henry Ford made extensive use of Frederick Taylor's **scientific management** techniques, as illustrated by this assembly of an automobile at a Ford plant, circa 1930. Ford replaced workers with machines for heavy lifting and moving autos from one worker to the next. This reduced worker hours and improved efficiency and productivity. Under this system, a Ford car rolled off the assembly line every 10 seconds.

at many of his management techniques independent of Taylor. He stressed efficiency and was known for his quest for the one best way to do work. Although Gilbreth is known for his early work with bricklayers, his work had great impact on medical surgery by drastically reducing the time that patients spent on the operating table. Surgeons were able to save countless lives through the application of time and motion study. Lillian M. Gilbreth (1878–1972) was more interested in the human aspect of work. When her husband died at the age of 56, she had 12 children aged 2 to 19. The undaunted 'first lady of management' went right on with her work. She presented a paper in place of her late husband, continued their seminars and consulting, lectured and eventually became a professor at Purdue University.[17] She pioneered in the field of industrial psychology and made substantial contributions to human resource management.

There were other advantages accruing to Ford's production lines, as the multitude of steps required to make a Model T Ford could be defined. Immigrant labour, with low literacy in English, were thus able to follow a simplified set of instructions from a worksheet. Worker activity (efficiency) measurement against standard times and practices is still practised in many call centres and physical goods dispatching warehouses (e.g. Amazon).

Exhibit 2.2 shows the basic ideas of scientific management. To use this approach, managers should develop standard methods for doing each job, select workers with the appropriate abilities, train workers in the standard methods, support workers and eliminate interruptions, and provide wage incentives.

The ideas of scientific management that began with Taylor dramatically increased productivity across all industries, and they are still important today. Indeed, the idea of engineering work for greater productivity has enjoyed a renaissance in the retail industry. Supermarket chains such as Meijer Inc. and Hannaford, for example, use computerized labour waste elimination systems based on scientific management principles. The system breaks down tasks such as greeting a customer, working the register, scanning items and so forth, into quantifiable units and devises standard times to complete each task. Executives say the computerized system has allowed them to staff stores more efficiently because people are routinely monitored by computer and

EXHIBIT 2.2 Characteristics of scientific management

General approach

- Developed standard method for performing each job.
- Selected workers with appropriate abilities for each job.
- Trained workers in standard methods.
- Supported workers by planning their work and eliminating interruptions.
- Provided wage incentives to workers for increased output.

Contributions

- Demonstrated the importance of compensation for performance.
- Initiated the careful study of tasks and jobs.
- Demonstrated the importance of personnel selection and training.

Criticisms

- Did not appreciate the social context of work and higher needs of workers.
- Did not acknowledge variance among individuals.
- Tended to regard workers as uninformed and ignored their ideas and suggestions.

are expected to meet strict standards.[18] Interestingly, F.W. Taylor characterized managerial responsibility in four ways:

First, each element of a man's work should be measured not assessed on a rule of thumb approach.

Second, managers should be responsible for selecting and training workers and developing them.

Third, managers should wholeheartedly cooperate with the workers to ensure that work is being done according to the scientific principles applied.

Fourth, there should be almost equal division of the work and responsibility between the managers and the workers.

A *Harvard Business Review* article discussing innovations that shaped modern management puts scientific management at the top of its list of 12 influential innovations. Indeed, the ideas of creating a system for maximum efficiency and organizing work for maximum productivity are deeply embedded in our organizations.[19] However, because scientific management ignores the social context and workers' needs, it can lead to increased conflict and clashes between managers and employees. The United Food and Commercial Workers Union, for instance, filed a grievance against Meijer in connection with its cashier-performance system. Under such performance management systems, workers often feel exploited – a sharp contrast from the harmony and cooperation that Taylor and his followers had envisioned.

Bureaucratic organizations

A systematic approach developed in Europe that looked at the organization as a whole is the bureaucratic organizations approach, a subfield within the classical perspective. Max Weber (1864–1920), a German theorist, introduced most of the concepts on bureaucratic organizations.[20]

During the late 1800s, many European organizations were managed on a personal, family-like basis. Employees were loyal to a single individual rather than to the organization or its mission. The dysfunctional consequence of this management practice was that resources were used to realize individual desires rather than organizational goals. Employees in effect owned the organization and used resources for their own gain rather than to serve customers. Weber envisioned organizations that would be managed on an impersonal, rational basis. This form of organization was called a *bureaucracy*. Exhibit 2.3 summarizes the six characteristics of bureaucracy as specified by Weber.

'Students would be more likely to have a positive impact on the future of management if they were more engaged with the history and traditions of management – particularly that of a German sociologist [Weber] who died nearly 100 years ago.'
— STEPHEN CUMMINGS AND TODD BRIDGMAN, VICTORIA UNIVERSITY OF WELLINGTON, NEW ZEALAND

Weber believed that an organization based on rational authority would be more efficient and adaptable to change because continuity is related to formal structure and positions rather than to a particular person, who may leave or die. To Weber, rationality in organizations meant employee selection and advancement based not on whom you know, but rather on competence and technical qualifications, which are assessed by examination or according to specific training and experience. The organization relies on rules and written records for continuity. In addition, rules and procedures are impersonal and applied uniformly to all employees. A clear division of labour arises from distinct definitions of authority and responsibility, legitimized as official duties. Positions are organized in a hierarchy, with each position under the authority of a higher one. The manager gives orders successfully not on the basis of his or her personality, but on the legal power invested in the managerial position.

The term *bureaucracy* has taken on a negative meaning in today's organizations and is associated with endless rules and red tape. We have all been frustrated by waiting in long lines or following seemingly silly procedures. However, the value of bureaucratic principles is still evident in many organizations, such as United Parcel Service (UPS), sometimes nicknamed *Big Brown*.

EXHIBIT 2.3 Characteristics of Weberian bureaucracy

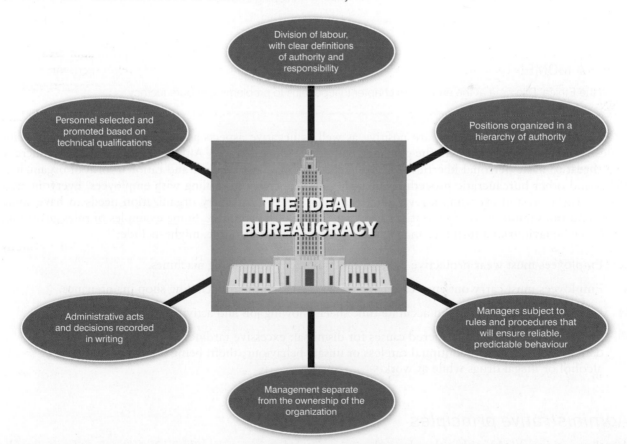

SOURCE: Max Weber, *The Theory of Social and Economic Organizations*, ed. and trans. A. M. Henderson and Talcott Parsons (New York: Free Press, 1947), pp. 328–337.

INNOVATIVE WAY

UPS

UPS is the largest package delivery company in the world and a leading global provider of specialized transportation and logistics services. The company operates in more than 200 countries and territories worldwide.

Why has UPS been so successful? One important factor is the concept of bureaucracy. UPS operates according to strict rules and regulations. It teaches drivers an astounding 340 steps for how to deliver a package correctly, such as how to load the truck, how to fasten their seat belts, how to walk and how to carry their keys. Specific safety rules apply to drivers, loaders, clerks and managers. Strict dress codes are enforced – clean uniforms (called *browns*), every day, black or brown polished shoes with non-slip soles, no beards, no hair below the collar, no tattoos visible during deliveries and so on. Before each shift, drivers conduct a 'Z-scan', a Z-shaped inspection of the sides

and front of their vehicles. Employees are asked to clean off their desks at the end of each day so they can start fresh the next morning. Managers are given copies of policy books with the expectation that they will use them regularly, and memos on various policies and rules circulate by the hundreds every day.

UPS has a well-defined division of labour. Each plant consists of specialized drivers, loaders, clerks, washers, sorters and maintenance personnel. UPS thrives on written records, and it has been a leader in using new technology to enhance reliability and efficiency. All drivers have daily worksheets that specify performance goals and work output. Technical qualification is the criterion for hiring and promotion. The UPS policy book says the leader is expected to have the knowledge and capacity to justify the position of leadership. Favouritism is forbidden. The bureaucratic model works just fine at UPS, 'the tightest ship in the shipping business'.[21]

TAKE A MOMENT

Read the Ethical Dilemma at the end of this chapter that pertains to problems with bureaucracy.

As this example shows, there are positive as well as negative aspects associated with bureaucratic principles. Weber also struggled with the good and bad sides of bureaucracy.[22] Although he perceived bureaucracy as a threat to basic personal liberties, he recognized it as the most efficient and rational form of organizing. Rules and other bureaucratic procedures provide a standard way of dealing with employees. Everyone gets equal treatment, and everyone knows what the rules are. Almost every organization needs to have some rules, and rules multiply as organizations grow larger and more complex. Some examples of rules governing employee behaviour in a furniture manufacturing company, for example, might include:[23]

■ Employees must wear protective eye and ear equipment when using machines.

■ Employees must carry out any reasonable duty assigned to them, including shop maintenance.

■ Employees must maintain an accurate time sheet, showing job and activity.

■ The following will be considered causes for dismissal: excessive tardiness or absenteeism; willful damage to equipment; continual careless or unsafe behaviour; theft; being under the influence of alcohol or illegal drugs while at work.

Administrative principles

Another major subfield within the classical perspective is known as the *administrative principles* approach. Whereas scientific management focused on the productivity of the individual worker, the administrative principles approach focused on the total organization. The major contributor to this approach was Henri

Fayol (1841–1925), a French mining engineer who worked his way up to become head of a large mining group known as Comambault. Pieces of Comambault survive today as part of ArcelorMittal, the world's largest steel and mining company. In his later years, Fayol wrote down his concepts on administration, based largely on his own management experiences.[24]

TAKE A MOMENT

What would it be like for you to be a manager in a bureaucratic organization? Complete the Experiential Exercise online to find out if you would thrive in that type of environment.

In his most significant work, *General and Industrial Management*, Fayol discussed 14 general principles of management, several of which are part of management philosophy today. For example:

- ◼ *Unity of command.* Each subordinate receives orders from one – and only one – superior.

- ◼ *Division of work.* Managerial work and technical work are amenable to specialization to produce more and better work with the same amount of effort.

- ◼ *Unity of direction.* Similar activities in an organization should be grouped together under one manager.

- ◼ *Scalar chain.* A chain of authority extends from the top to the bottom of the organization and should include every employee.

Fayol felt that these principles could be applied in any organizational setting. He also identified five basic functions or elements of management: *planning, organizing, commanding, coordinating* and *controlling*. These functions underlie much of the general approach to today's management theory.

The overall classical perspective as an approach to management was very powerful and gave companies fundamental new skills for establishing high productivity and effective treatment of employees. Indeed, the USA surged ahead of the world in management techniques, and other countries, especially Japan, borrowed heavily from American ideas.

REFLECTION

- The study of modern management began in the late nineteenth century with the **classical perspective**, which took a rational, scientific approach to management and sought to turn organizations into efficient operating machines.
- **Scientific management** is a subfield of the classical perspective that emphasizes scientifically determined changes in management practices as the solution to improving labour productivity.
- Frederick Winslow Taylor is known as 'the father of scientific management'.
- Scientific management is considered one of the most significant innovations influencing modern management.
- Some supermarket chains are using computerized systems based on scientific management principles to schedule employees for maximum efficiency.

- Another subfield of the classical perspective is the **bureaucratic organizations approach**, which emphasizes management on an impersonal, rational basis through elements such as clearly defined authority and responsibility, formal recordkeeping, and separation of management and ownership.
- Max Weber introduced most of the concepts about bureaucratic organizations.
- The **administrative principles approach** is a subfield of the classical perspective that focuses on the total organization rather than the individual worker and delineates the management functions of planning, organizing, commanding, coordinating and controlling.
- Henri Fayol, a major contributor to the administrative principles approach, outlined 14 general principles of management, several of which are a part of management philosophy today.

CONCEPT CONNECTION

Mary Parker Follett. Follett was an early advocate of the **humanistic perspective** on management. Her emphasis on worker participation and shared goals among managers was embraced by many business-people of the day and has been recently 'rediscovered' by corporate America.

Humanistic perspective

The humanistic perspective on management emphasized the importance of understanding human behaviours, needs and attitudes in the workplace, as well as social interactions and group processes.[25] There are three primary subfields based on the humanistic perspective: the human relations movement, the human resources perspective and the behavioural sciences approach.

Early advocates

Two early advocates of a more humanistic approach were Mary Parker Follett and Chester Barnard. Mary Parker Follett (1868–1933) was trained in philosophy and political science, but she applied herself in many fields, including social psychology and management. She wrote of the importance of common superordinate goals for reducing conflict in organizations.[26] Her work was popular with businesspeople of her day but was often overlooked by management scholars.[27] Follett's ideas served as a contrast to scientific management and are re-emerging as applicable for modern managers dealing with rapid changes in today's global environment. Her approach to leadership stressed the importance of people rather than engineering techniques. She offered the pithy admonition, 'Don't hug your blueprints', and analyzed the dynamics of management-organization interactions. Follett addressed issues that are timely today, such as ethics, power and leading, in a way that encourages employees to give their best. The concepts of *empowerment*, facilitating rather than controlling employees, and allowing employees to act depending on the authority of the situation opened new areas for theoretical study by Chester Barnard and others.[28]

Chester I. Barnard (1886–1961) studied economics at Harvard but failed to receive a degree because he did not take a course in laboratory science. He went to work in the statistical department of AT&T, and in 1927, he became president of New Jersey Bell. One of Barnard's significant contributions was the concept of the *informal organization*. The *informal organization* occurs in all formal organizations and includes cliques, informal networks and naturally occurring social groupings. Barnard argued that organizations are not machines and stressed that informal relationships are powerful forces that can help the organization if properly managed. Another significant contribution was the *acceptance theory of authority*, which states that people have free will and can choose whether to follow management orders. People typically follow orders because they perceive positive benefit to themselves, but they do have a choice. Managers should treat employees properly because their acceptance of authority may be critical to organization success in important situations.[29]

Human relations management

The human relations movement was based on the idea that truly effective control comes from within the individual worker rather than from strict, authoritarian control.[30] This school of thought recognized and directly responded to social pressures for enlightened treatment of employees. The early work on industrial psychology and personnel selection received little attention because of the prominence of scientific management. Then a series of studies at a Chicago electric company, which came to be known as the Hawthorne studies, changed all that.

Beginning about 1895, a struggle developed between manufacturers of gas and electric lighting fixtures for control of the residential and industrial market.[31] By 1909, electric lighting was beginning to win, but the increasingly efficient electric fixtures used less total power, which was less profitable for the electric companies. The electric companies began a campaign to convince industrial users that they needed more light to get more productivity. When advertising did not work, the industry began using experimental tests to demonstrate their argument. Managers were sceptical about the results, so the Committee on Industrial Lighting (CIL) was set up to run the tests. To further add to the tests' credibility, Thomas Edison was made honorary chairman of the CIL. In one test location – the Hawthorne plant of the Western Electric Company – some interesting events occurred.

The major part of this work involved four experimental and three control groups. In all, five different tests were conducted. These pointed to the importance of factors *other* than illumination in affecting productivity. To examine these factors more carefully, numerous other experiments were conducted.[32] The results of the most famous study,

CONCEPT CONNECTION

This 1914 photograph shows the initiation of a new arrival at a Nebraska planting camp. This initiation was not part of the formal rules and illustrates the significance of the **informal organization** described by Barnard. Social values and behaviours were powerful forces that could help or hurt the planting organization, depending on how they were managed.

the first Relay Assembly Test Room (RATR) experiment, were extremely controversial. Under the guidance of two Harvard professors, Elton Mayo and Fritz Roethlisberger, the RATR studies lasted nearly 6 years (10 May 1927 to 4 May 1933) and involved 24 separate experimental periods. So many factors were changed and so many unforeseen factors uncontrolled that scholars disagree on the factors that truly contributed to the general increase in performance over that time period. Most early interpretations, however, agreed on one point: Money was not the cause of the increased output.[33] It was believed that the factor that best explained increased output was *human relations*. Employees performed better when managers treated them in a positive manner. Recent re-analyses of the experiments have revealed that a number of factors were different for the workers involved, and some suggest that money may well have been the single most important factor.[34] An interview with one of the original participants revealed that just getting into the experimental group meant a huge increase in income.[35]

TAKE A MOMENT

Before reading on, take the New Manager Self-Test on page 47. This test will give you feedback about your personal approach to getting things done through others.

These new data clearly show that money mattered a great deal at Hawthorne. In addition, worker productivity increased, partly as a result of the increased feelings of importance and group pride that employees

CONCEPT CONNECTION

This is the Relay Room of the Western Electric Hawthorne, Illinois, plant in 1927. Six women worked in this relay assembly test room during the controversial experiments on employee productivity. Professors Mayo and Roethlisberger evaluated conditions such as rest breaks and workday length, physical health, amount of sleep and diet. Experimental changes were fully discussed with the women and were abandoned if they disapproved. Gradually the researchers began to realize they had created a change in supervisory style and **human relations**, which they believed was the true cause of the increased productivity.

felt by virtue of being selected for this important project.[36] One unintended contribution of the experiments was a rethinking of field research practices. Researchers and scholars realized that the researcher can influence the outcome of an experiment by being too closely involved with research subjects. This phenomenon has come to be known as the *Hawthorne effect* in research methodology. Subjects behaved differently because of the active participation of researchers in the Hawthorne experiments.[37]

From a historical perspective, whether the studies were academically sound is less important than the fact that they stimulated an increased interest in looking at employees as more than extensions of production machinery. The interpretation that employees' output increased when managers treated them in a positive manner started a revolution in worker treatment for improving organizational productivity. Despite flawed methodology or inaccurate conclusions, the findings provided the impetus for the human relations movement. This approach shaped management theory and practice for well over a quarter-century, and the belief that human relations is the best area of focus for increasing productivity persists today.

Human resources perspective

The human relations movement initially espoused a *dairy farm* view of management – just as contented cows give more milk, satisfied workers will produce more work. Gradually, views with deeper content began to emerge. The human resources perspective maintained an interest in worker participation and considerate leadership but shifted the emphasis to consider the daily tasks that people perform. The human resources perspective combines prescriptions for design of job tasks with theories of motivation.[38] In the human resources view, jobs should be designed so that tasks are not perceived as dehumanizing or demeaning but instead allow workers to use their full potential. Two of the best-known contributors to the human resources perspective were Abraham Maslow and Douglas McGregor.

Abraham Maslow (1908–1970), a practicing psychologist, observed that his patients' problems usually stemmed from an inability to satisfy their needs. Thus, he generalized his work and suggested a hierarchy of needs. Maslow's hierarchy started with physiological needs and progressed to safety, belongingness, esteem, and, finally, self-actualization needs. Chapter 16 discusses his ideas in more detail.

Douglas McGregor (1906–1964) had become frustrated with the early simplistic human relations notions while president of Antioch College in Ohio. He challenged both the classical perspective and the early human relations assumptions about human behaviour. Based on his experiences as a manager and consultant, his training as a psychologist, and the work of Maslow, McGregor formulated Theory X and Theory Y, which are explained in Exhibit 2.4.[39] McGregor believed that the classical perspective was based on Theory X assumptions about workers. He also felt that a slightly modified version of Theory X fit early human relations ideas. In other words, human relations ideas did not go far enough. McGregor proposed Theory Y as a more realistic view of workers for guiding management thinking.

NEW MANAGER SELF-TEST

What's your Mach?

INSTRUCTIONS Managers differ in how they view human nature and the tactics that they use to get things done through others. Answer the questions below based on how you view others. Think carefully about each question and be honest about what you feel inside. Please answer whether each item below is 'Mostly false' or 'Mostly true' for you.

		Mostly true	Mostly false
1	Overall, it is better to be humble and honest than to be successful and dishonest?	☐	☐
2	If you trust someone completely, you are asking for trouble.	☐	☐
3	A leader should take action only when it is morally right.	☐	☐
4	A good way to handle people is to tell them what they like to hear.	☐	☐
5	There is no excuse for telling a white lie to someone.	☐	☐
6	It makes sense to flatter important people.	☐	☐
7	Most people who get ahead as leaders have led very moral lives.	☐	☐
8	It is better not to tell people the real reason you did something unless it benefits you to do so.	☐	☐
9	The vast majority of people are brave, good and kind.	☐	☐
10	It is hard to get to the top without sometimes cutting corners.	☐	☐

SCORING & INTERPRETATION To compute your Mach score, give yourself one point for each 'Mostly false' answer to items 1, 3, 5, 7 and 9, and one point for each 'Mostly true' answer to items 2, 4, 6, 8 and 10. These items were drawn from the works of Niccoló Machiavelli, an Italian political philosopher who wrote *The Prince* in 1513 to describe how a prince can retain control of his kingdom. Successful management intrigue at the time of Machiavelli was believed to require behaviours that today would be considered ego-centred and manipulative, which is almost the opposite of more enlightened management that arose from the human relations movement. A score of 8–10 points suggests that you have a high Mach score. From 4–7 points indicates a moderate score, and 0–3 points would indicate a low Mach score. Having a high Mach score does not mean that the individual is a sinister or vicious person, but it probably means that he or she has a cool detachment, sees life as a game, and is not personally engaged with other people. Discuss your results with other students, and talk about whether you think politicians and top executives would have a high or a low Mach score.

SOURCE: R. Christie and F. L. Geis, *Studies in Machiavellianism* (New York: Academic Press, 1970).

The point of Theory Y is that organizations can take advantage of the imagination and intellect of all their employees. Employees will exercise self-control and will contribute to organizational goals when given the opportunity. A few companies today still use Theory X management, but many are using Theory Y techniques. Consider how Semco applies Theory Y assumptions to tap into employee creativity and mind power.

EXHIBIT 2.4 Theory X and Theory Y

Assumptions of Theory X

- The average human being has an inherent dislike of work and will avoid it if possible.
- Because of the human characteristic of dislike for work, most people must be coerced, controlled, directed or threatened with punishment to get them to put forth adequate effort towards the achievement of organizational objectives.
- The average human being prefers to be directed, wishes to avoid responsibility, has relatively little ambition and wants security above all.

Assumptions of Theory Y

- The expenditure of physical and mental effort in work is as natural as play or rest. The average human being does not inherently dislike work.
- External control and the threat of punishment are not the only means for bringing about effort towards organizational objectives. A person will exercise self-direction and self-control in the service of objectives to which he or she is committed.
- The average human being learns, under proper conditions, not only to accept but to seek responsibility.
- The capacity to exercise a relatively high degree of imagination, ingenuity and creativity in the solution of organizational problems is widely, not narrowly, distributed in the population.
- Under the conditions of modern industrial life, the intellectual potentialities of the average human being are only partially utilized.

SOURCE: Douglas McGregor, *The Human Side of Enterprise* (New York: McGraw-Hill, 1960), pp. 33–48. ©McGraw-Hill Companies, Inc. Reprinted by permission.

 INNOVATIVE WAY

Semco

The Brazil-based company Semco's fundamental operating principle is to harness the wisdom of all its employees. It does so by letting people control their work hours, location and even pay plans. Employees also participate in all organizational decisions, including what businesses Semco should pursue.

Semco leaders believe that economic success requires creating an atmosphere that puts power and control directly in the hands of employees. People can veto any new product idea or business venture. They choose their own leaders and manage themselves to accomplish goals. Information is openly and broadly shared so that everyone knows where they and the company stand.

Instead of dictating Semco's identity and strategy, leaders allow it to be shaped by individual interests and efforts. People are encouraged to seek challenges, explore new ideas and business opportunities, and question the ideas of anyone in the company.

This high level of trust in employees has helped Semco achieve decades of high profitability and growth despite fluctuations in the economy and shifting markets. 'At Semco, we don't play by the rules,' says Ricardo Semler. Semler, whose father started the company in the 1950s, says it doesn't unnerve him to 'step back and see nothing on the company's horizon.' He is happy to watch the company and its employees 'ramble through their days, running on instinct and opportunity. . . .'[40]

For managers like Ricardo Semler, command and control is a thing of the past, with the future belonging to those companies that build leadership throughout the organization. The Theory Y approach has helped Semco succeed in a tough environment. Although few go as far as Semco, other companies are also using Theory Y principles that are more in line with today's emphasis on employee empowerment and involvement.

TAKE A MOMENT

When you have completed the questionnaire related to Theory X and Theory Y at the end of this chapter, consider how your management assumptions about people fit into an organization today.

Behavioural sciences approach

The behavioural sciences approach uses scientific methods and draws from sociology, psychology, anthropology, economics and other disciplines to develop theories about human behaviour and interaction in an organizational setting. This approach can be seen in practically every organization. When a company such as Zappos.com conducts research to determine the best set of tests, interviews and employee profiles to use when selecting new employees, it is using behavioural science techniques. When Best Buy electronics stores train new managers in the techniques of employee motivation, most of the theories and findings are rooted in behavioural science research.

One specific set of management techniques based in the behavioural sciences approach is *organization development* (OD). In the 1970s, OD evolved as a separate field that applied the behavioural sciences to improve the organization's health and effectiveness through its ability to cope with change, improve internal relationships and increase problem-solving capabilities.[41] The techniques and concepts of OD have since been broadened and expanded to address the increasing complexity of organizations and the environment, and OD is still a vital approach for managers. OD will be discussed in detail in Chapter 11. Other concepts that grew out of the behavioural sciences approach include matrix organizations, self-managed teams, ideas about corporate culture and management by wandering around. Indeed, the behavioural sciences approach has influenced the majority of tools, techniques and approaches that managers have applied to organizations since the 1970s.

All the remaining chapters of this book contain research findings and management applications that can be attributed to the behavioural sciences approach.

REFLECTION

- The humanistic perspective emphasized understanding human behaviour, needs and attitudes in the workplace.
- Mary Parker Follett and Chester Barnard were early advocates of a more humanistic approach to management.
- Follett emphasized worker participation and empowerment, shared goals and facilitating rather than controlling employees. Barnard's contributions include the acceptance theory of authority.
- The human relations movement stresses the satisfaction of employees' basic needs as the key to increased productivity.

- The Hawthorne studies were important in shaping ideas concerning how managers should treat workers.
- The human resources perspective suggests that jobs should be designed to meet people's higher-level needs by allowing employees to use their full potential.
- The behavioural sciences approach draws from psychology, sociology and other social sciences to develop theories about human behaviour and interaction in an organizational setting.
- Many current management ideas and practices can be traced to the behavioural sciences approach.

Management science

World War II caused many management changes. The massive and complicated problems associated with modern global warfare presented managerial decision-makers with the need for more sophisticated tools than ever before. Management science, also referred to as the *quantitative perspective*, provided a way to address those problems. This view is distinguished for its application of mathematics, statistics and other quantitative techniques to management decision-making and problem-solving. During World War II, groups of mathematicians, physicists and other scientists were formed to solve military problems that frequently involved moving massive amounts of materials and large numbers of people quickly and efficiently. Managers soon saw how quantitative techniques could be applied to large-scale business firms.[42]

Management scholar Peter Drucker's 1946 book *Concept of the Corporation* sparked a dramatic increase in the academic study of business and management. Picking up on techniques developed for the military, scholars began cranking out numerous mathematical tools for corporate managers, such as the application of linear programming for optimizing operations, statistical process control for quality management and the capital asset pricing model.[43]

These efforts were enhanced with the development and perfection of the computer. Coupled with the growing body of statistical techniques, computers made it possible for managers to collect, store and process large volumes of data for quantitative decision-making, and the quantitative approach is widely used today by managers in a variety of industries. The Walt Disney Company used quantitative techniques to develop FASTPASS, a sophisticated computerized system that spares parents the ordeal of standing in long lines for the most popular rides. Disney theme parks have machines that issue coupons with a return time that's been calculated based on the number of people standing in the actual line, the number who have already obtained passes, and each ride's capacity. The next generation of technology, xPass, will let visitors book times for rides before they even leave home.[44] Let's look at three subsets of management science.

Operations research grew directly out of the World War II military groups (called *operational research teams* in Great Britain and *operations research teams* in the USA).[45] It consists of mathematical model building and other applications of quantitative techniques to managerial problems.

Operations management refers to the field of management that specializes in the physical production of goods or services. Operations management specialists use management science to solve manufacturing problems. Some commonly used methods are forecasting, inventory modelling, linear and non-linear programming, queuing theory, scheduling, simulation and break-even analysis.

Information technology (IT) is the most recent subfield of management science, which is often reflected in management information systems designed to provide relevant information to managers in a timely and cost-efficient manner. IT has evolved to include intranets and extranets, as well as various software programs that help managers estimate costs, plan and track production, manage projects, allocate resources or schedule employees. Most of today's organizations have IT specialists who use quantitative techniques to solve complex organizational problems.

However, as events in the mortgage and finance industries show, relying too heavily on quantitative techniques can cause problems for managers. Mortgage companies used quantitative models that showed their investments in subprime mortgages would be okay even if default rates hit historically high proportions. However, the models didn't take into account that no one before in history had thought it made sense to give $500 000 loans to people earning the minimum wage![46] 'Quants' also came to dominate organizational decisions in other financial firms. The term quants refers to financial managers and others who base their decisions on complex quantitative analysis, under the assumption that using advanced mathematics and sophisticated computer technology can accurately predict how the market works and help them reap huge profits. The virtually exclusive use of these quantitative models led aggressive traders and managers to take enormous risks. When the market began to go haywire as doubts about subprime mortgages grew, the models went haywire as well. Stocks predicted to go up went down and vice versa. Events that were predicted to happen only once every 10 000 years happened 3 days in a row in the market madness. Scott Patterson, a *Wall Street Journal* reporter and author of *The Quants: How a New Breed of Math Whizzes Conquered Wall Street and Nearly Destroyed It*, suggests that the financial crisis that began in 2008 is partly due to the quants' failure to observe market fundamentals, pay attention to human factors and heed their own intuition.[47]

REFLECTION

- Management science became popular based on its successful application in solving military problems during World War II.
- **Management science**, also called the *quantitative perspective,* uses mathematics, statistical techniques and computer technology to facilitate management decision-making, particularly for complex problems.
- The Walt Disney Company uses management science to solve the problem of long lines for popular rides and attractions at its theme parks.

- Three subsets of management science are operations research, operations management and information technology.
- Quants have come to dominate decision-making in financial firms, and the Wall Street meltdown in 2007–2008 shows the danger of relying too heavily on a quantitative approach.

- Management scholar Peter Drucker's classic 1946 book *Concept of the Corporation* sparked a dramatic increase in the academic study of business and management.

Recent historical trends

Despite recent heavy use of management science techniques by some managers, among the approaches that we've discussed so far the humanistic perspective has remained most prevalent from the 1950s until today. The post-World War II period saw the rise of new concepts, along with a continued strong interest in the human aspect of managing, such as team and group dynamics and other ideas that relate to the humanistic perspective. Three new concepts that appeared were systems thinking, the contingency view and total quality management.

Systems thinking

Systems thinking is the ability to see both the distinct elements of a system or situation and the complex and changing interaction among those elements. A system is a set of interrelated parts that function as a whole to achieve a common purpose.[48] Subsystems are parts of a system, such as an organization, that depend on one another. Changes in one part of the system (the organization) affect other parts. Managers need to understand the synergy of the whole organization, rather than just the separate elements, and to learn to reinforce or change whole system patterns.[49] Synergy means that the whole is greater than the sum of its parts. The organization must be managed as a coordinated whole. Managers who understand subsystem interdependence and synergy are reluctant to make changes that do not recognize subsystem impact on the organization as a whole.

Many people have been trained to solve problems by breaking a complex system, such as an organization, into discrete parts and working to make each part perform as well as possible. However, the success of each piece does not add up to the success of the whole. In fact, sometimes changing one part to make it better actually makes the whole system function less effectively. For example, a small city embarked on a road-building programme to solve traffic congestion without whole systems thinking. With new roads available, more people began moving to the suburbs. Rather than reduce congestion, the solution actually increased traffic congestion, delays and pollution by enabling suburban sprawl.[50]

It is the *relationship* among the parts that form a whole system – whether a community, an automobile, a non-profit agency, a human being or a business organization – that matters. Systems thinking enables managers to look for patterns of movement over time and focus on the qualities of rhythm, flow, direction, shape and networks of relationships that accomplish the performance of the whole. When managers can see the structures that underlie complex situations, they can facilitate improvement. But doing that requires a focus on the big picture.

An important element of systems thinking is to discern circles of causality. Peter Senge, author of *The Fifth Discipline*, argues that reality is made up of circles rather than straight lines. For example, Exhibit 2.5 shows circles of influence for increasing a retail firm's profits. The events in the circle on the left are caused by the decision to increase advertising; hence the retail firm adds to the advertising budget to aggressively promote its products. The advertising promotions increase sales, which increase profits, which provide money to further increase the advertising budget.

But another circle of causality is being influenced as well. The decision by marketing managers will have consequences for the operations department. As sales and profits increase, operations will be forced to stock up with greater inventory. Additional inventory will create a need for additional warehouse space. Building a new warehouse will cause a delay in stocking up. After the warehouse is built, new people will be hired, all of which adds to company costs, which will have a negative impact on profits. Thus, understanding all the

EXHIBIT 2.5 Systems thinking and circles of causality

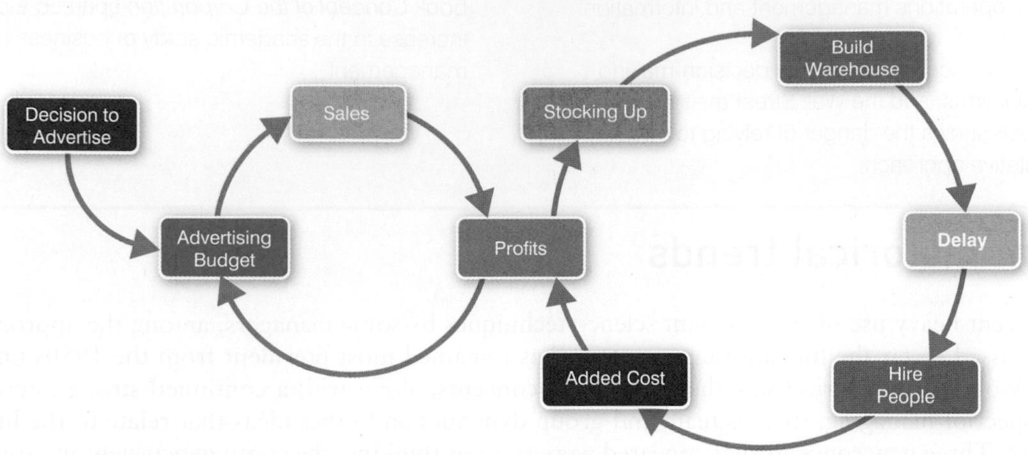

Decision to Advertise → Advertising Budget → Sales → Profits → Stocking Up → Build Warehouse → Delay → Hire People → Added Cost → Profits

SOURCE: Peter M. Senge, *The Fifth Discipline: The Art and Practice of the Learning Organization* (New York: Doubleday/Currency, 1990).

consequences of their decisions via circles of causality enables company leaders to plan and allocate resources to warehousing as well as to advertising to ensure stable increases in sales and profits. Without understanding system causality, top managers would fail to understand why increasing advertising budgets could cause inventory delays and temporarily reduce profits.

Contingency view

A second recent extension to management thinking is the contingency view. The classical perspective assumed a *universalist* view. Management concepts were thought to be universal; that is, whatever worked in terms of management style, bureaucratic structure and so on in one organization, would work in any other one. In business education, however, an alternative view exists. In this *case* view, each situation is believed to be unique. Principles are not universal, and one learns about management by experiencing a large number of case problem situations. Managers face the task of determining what methods will work in every new situation.

To integrate these views, the contingency view emerged, as illustrated in Exhibit 2.6.[51] Here, neither of the other views is seen as entirely correct. Instead, certain contingencies, or variables, exist for helping managers identify and understand situations. The contingency view tells us that what works in one setting might not work in another. Contingency means that one thing depends on other things and a manager's response to a situation depends on identifying key contingencies in an organizational situation.

One important contingency, for example, is the industry in which the organization operates. The organizational structure that is effective for an Internet company, such as Google, would not be successful for a large auto manufacturer, such as Ford. A management-by-objectives (MBO) system that works well in a

EXHIBIT 2.6 Contingency view of management

Case View — 'Every situation is unique.'

Universalist View — 'There is one best way.'

Contingency View

Organizational phenomena exist in logical patterns. Managers devise and apply similar responses to common types of problems.

manufacturing firm, in turn, might not be right for a school system. When managers learn to identify important patterns and characteristics of their organizations, they can fit solutions to those characteristics.

Total quality management

The theme of quality is another concept that permeates current management thinking. The quality movement is strongly associated with Japanese companies, but these ideas emerged partly as a result of American influence after World War II. The ideas of W. Edwards Deming, known as the 'father of the quality movement', were initially scoffed at in the USA, but the Japanese embraced his theories and modified them to help rebuild their industries into world powers.[52] Japanese companies achieved a significant departure from the American model by gradually shifting from an inspection-oriented approach to quality control towards an approach that emphasized employee involvement in the prevention of quality problems.[53]

During the 1980s and into the 1990s, total quality management (TQM), which focuses on managing the total organization to deliver better quality to customers, moved to the forefront in helping managers deal with global competition. The approach infuses high-quality values throughout every activity within a company, with frontline workers intimately involved in the process. Four significant elements of quality management are employee involvement, focus on the customer, benchmarking and continuous improvement, often referred to as *kaizen*.

Employee involvement means that achieving better quality requires company-wide participation in quality control. All employees are *focused on the customer*; companies find out

CONCEPT CONNECTION

Hyundai Motor Company's rise from 1 per cent of the US market in 1999 to about 9 per cent of the US market in 2011 shows how commitment to **total quality management** can improve a company's products and market position. First, managers increased the quality team from 100 to 865 people and held quality seminars to train employees. Then they **benchmarked** products, using vehicle lifts and high-intensity spotlights to compare against competing brands. Today, Hyundai earns quality ratings comparable to its main competitors, Honda and Toyota.

what customers want and try to meet their needs and expectations. *Benchmarking* refers to a process whereby companies find out how others do something better than they do and then try to imitate or improve on it. *Continuous improvement* is the implementation of small, incremental improvements in all areas of the organization on an ongoing basis. TQM is not a quick fix, but companies such as GE, Texas Instruments, Procter & Gamble and DuPont achieved astonishing results in efficiency, quality and customer satisfaction through total quality management.[54] TQM is still an important part of today's organizations, and managers consider benchmarking in particular a highly effective and satisfying management technique.[55]

Some of today's companies pursue highly ambitious quality goals to demonstrate their commitment to improving quality. For example, *Six Sigma*, popularized by Motorola and GE, specifies a goal of no more than 3.4 defects per million parts. However, the term also refers to a broad quality control approach that emphasizes a disciplined and relentless pursuit of higher quality and lower costs. TQM will be discussed in detail in Chapter 17 online.

REFLECTION

- A **system** is a set of interrelated parts that function as a whole to achieve a common purpose. An organization is a system.
- **Systems thinking** means looking not just at discrete parts of an organizational situation, but also at the continually changing interactions among the parts.
- When managers think systemically and understand subsystem interdependence and synergy, they can get a better handle on managing in a complex environment.
- **Subsystems** are parts of a system that depend on one another for their functioning.
- The concept of **synergy** says that the whole is greater than the sum of its parts. The organization must be managed as a whole.

- The **contingency view** tells managers that what works in one organizational situation might not work in others. Managers can identify important *contingencies* that help guide their decisions regarding the organization.
- The quality movement is associated with Japanese companies, but it emerged partly as a result of American influence after World War II.
- W. Edwards Deming is known as the 'father of the quality movement'.
- **Total quality management** focuses on managing the total organization to deliver quality to customers.
- Four significant elements of TQM are employee involvement, focus on the customer, benchmarking and continuous improvement.

Innovative management thinking for a changing world

All of the ideas and approaches discussed so far in this chapter go into the mix that makes up modern management. Dozens of ideas and techniques in current use can trace their roots to these historical perspectives.[56] In addition, innovative concepts continue to emerge to address new management challenges. Smart managers heed the past but know that they and their organizations have to change with the times. General Motors (GM) was the 'ideal' organizational model in a post-World War II environment, but by 2009, it had collapsed into bankruptcy and sought billions of dollars in government aid because managers failed to pay attention as the world changed around them. GM managers assumed that the pre-eminence of their company would shelter it from change, and they stuck far too long with a strategy, culture and management approach that was out of tune with the shifting environment.

Contemporary management tools

Recall from the beginning of this chapter our discussion of *jugaad*, an approach to innovation management used in India that many Western managers are trying. Management fads and fashions come and go, but managers are always looking for new techniques and approaches that more adequately respond to customer needs and the demands of the environment. A recent survey of European managers reflects that managers pay attention to currently fashionable management concepts. The following table lists the percentage of managers reporting that they were aware of these selected management trends that have been popular over the past decade.[57]

Concept	Awareness percentage
e-Business	99.41
Decentralization	99.12
Customer relationship management	97.50
Virtual organization	91.19
Empowerment	83.41
Re-engineering	76.65

Managers especially tend to look for fresh ideas to help them cope during difficult times. For instance, recent challenges such as the tough economy and volatile stock market, environmental and organizational crises, lingering anxieties over war and terrorism, and public suspicion and scepticism resulting from the crisis on Wall Street, have left today's executives searching for any management tool – new or old – that can help them get the most out of limited resources. The Manager's Shoptalk lists a wide variety of ideas and techniques used by today's managers. Management idea life cycles have been growing shorter as the pace of change has increased. A study by professors at the University of Louisiana at Lafayette found that, from the 1950s to the 1970s, it typically took more than a decade for interest in a popular management idea to peak. Now, the interval has shrunk to fewer than 3 years, and some trends come and go even faster.[58]

Managing the technology-driven workplace

Two popular contemporary tools that have shown some staying power (as reflected in the Shoptalk box) are customer relationship management and supply chain management. These techniques are related to the shift to a technology-driven workplace. A more recent tool in the technology-driven workplace, social media, is also growing in use and importance.

Social media programs

Companies use social media programs to interact electronically with employees, customers, partners and other stakeholders. Although only 29 per cent of managers surveyed by Bain & Company said their companies used social media programs in 2010, more than half said they planned to use them.[59] Social media programs include company online community pages, social media sites such as Faccbook or LinkedIn, microblogging platforms such as Twitter and China's Weibo, and company online forums. One frequent, and controversial, use of social media has been to look into the backgrounds and activities of job candidates. A survey by CareerBuilder found that 37 per cent of hiring managers said they had used social media sites to see if job applicants present themselves professionally, to learn more about an applicant's qualifications, or to see if the candidate would be a good fit with the organizational culture.[60] Other uses of social media programs include generating awareness about the company's products and services, sharing ideas and seeking feedback from customers and partners, strengthening relationships among employees and selling products. One concern for many managers is how to measure the effectiveness of the use of social media programs.

 CONCEPT CONNECTION

The success and popularity of **social media** tools continues to drive innovation on the Web. In 2012, after an initial launch in France, Muxi went international. Muxi's creators describe it as a combination of the professional networking power of LinkedIn and the truly social aspects of Facebook.

MANAGER'S SHOPTALK

Management tools and trends

Over the history of management, many fashions and fads have appeared. Critics argue that new techniques may not represent permanent solutions. Others feel that managers must adopt new techniques for continuous improvement in a fast-changing world.

In 1993, Bain & Company started a large research project to interview and survey thousands of corporate executives about the 25 most popular management tools and techniques. The list and usage rates for 2010–2011 are shown below. How many of the tools do you know? For more information on specific tools, see Bain's *Management Tools 2011: An Executive's Guide* at www.bain.com/publications/articles/management-tools-2011-executives-guide.aspx.

Popularity. In the 2010–2011 survey, benchmarking held onto the top spot as the most popular tool, reflecting managers' concern with efficiency and cost-cutting in a difficult economy. Mergers and acquisitions have decreased in popularity, with only 35 per cent of managers using this technique. Three tools that

ranked high in both use and satisfaction were *strategic planning, mission and vision statements* and *customer segmentation*, tools that can guide managers' thinking on strategic issues during times of rapid change.

Global trends. For the first time, firms in emerging markets reported using more tools than those in developed markets. More than half of emerging market executives reported using the *balanced scorecard*. North American managers decreased their use of *outsourcing* and were the largest users of *social media programs*. Managers in Latin American companies used more tools than any other region, but they were the lightest users of *downsizing* and *customer relationship management (CRM)*. Asian companies were the greatest users of *knowledge management*. *Benchmarking* and *change management programs* were top tools for managers in Europe, where acute economic uncertainty continues.

SOURCE: Darrell Rigby and Barbara Bilodeau, 'Management Tools and Trends 2011', Copyright © 2011, Bain and Company, Inc., www.bain.com/publications/articles/Management-tools-trends-2011.aspx. Reprinted by permission.

EXHIBIT 2.7 Supply chain for a retail organization

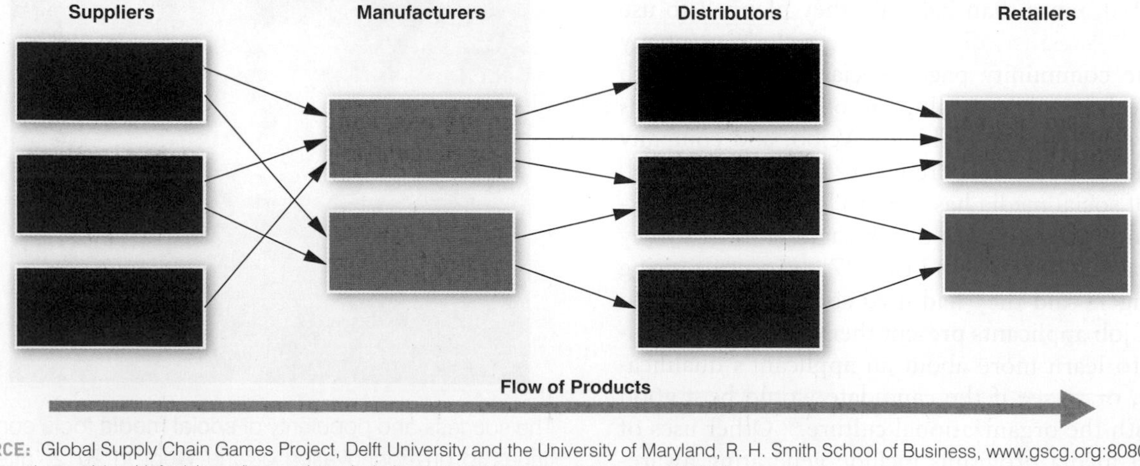

SOURCE: Global Supply Chain Games Project, Delft University and the University of Maryland, R. H. Smith School of Business, www.gscg.org:8080/opencms/export/sites/default/gscg/images/supplychain_simple.gif (accessed February 6, 2008).

Customer relationship management

Unlike social media, many managers have become quite comfortable and adept at using technology for customer relationship management (CRM). CRM systems use the latest information technology to keep in close touch with customers and to collect and manage large amounts of customer data. These systems can help managers be more accurate in their sales forecasts, coordinate sales and service staff more easily, improve product design and marketing, and act quickly to respond to shifting customer needs and desires. There has been an explosion of interest in CRM. In the Manager's Shoptalk, 58 per cent of surveyed managers reported their companies used CRM in 2010, whereas only 35 per cent of companies reported using this technique in 2000.

'The first rule of any technology used in a business is that automation applied to an efficient operation will magnify the efficiency. The second is that automation applied to an inefficient operation will magnify the inefficiency.'

— BILL GATES, FOUNDER AND CHAIRMAN OF MICROSOFT

Supply chain management

Supply chain management refers to managing the sequence of suppliers and purchasers, covering all stages of processing from obtaining raw materials to distributing finished goods to consumers.[61] Exhibit 2.7 illustrates a basic supply chain model. A *supply chain* is a network of multiple businesses and individuals that are connected through the flow of products or services.[62] Many organizations manage the supply chain with sophisticated electronic technology. In India, for example, Walmart managers have invested in an efficient supply chain that electronically links farmers and small manufacturers directly to the stores, maximizing value for both ends.[63] Supply chain management will be discussed in detail in the Appendix online.

REFLECTION

- Modern management is a lively mix of ideas and techniques from varied historical perspectives, but new concepts continue to emerge.
- Managers tend to look for innovative ideas and approaches, particularly during turbulent times.
- Many of today's popular techniques are related to the transition to a technology-driven workplace.
- Social media programs include online community pages, social media sites such as Facebook and LinkedIn, microblogging platforms such as Twitter and company online forums that enable managers to interact electronically with employees, customers, partners and other stakeholders.

- Customer relationship management (CRM) systems use information technology to keep in close touch with customers, collect and manage large amounts of customer data, and provide superior customer value.
- Supply chain management refers to managing the sequence of suppliers and purchasers, covering all stages of processing from obtaining raw materials to distributing finished goods to consumers.
- These new approaches require managers to think in fresh ways about managing their relationships with employees, customers and business partners.

DISCUSSION QUESTIONS

1 An understanding of the different perspectives and approaches to management theory, which have evolved throughout the history of organizations, is of considerable benefit to 2016–2018 management entry trainees. Discuss this statement.

2 Societal forces influence the practice and theory of management and new management techniques are often implemented in response to these forces. Compare and contrast how the application of management theory differs across the world's major trading regions.

3 As organizations become more technology-driven, which will become more important? a) Management of the human element of the organization or b) The management of technology? Discuss.

4 Describe the difference between the universalist view and the classical view. Why could approaches to management differ between an internet company and a food production company?

5 Based on your experience at work or school, describe some of the ways in which the principles of scientific management and bureaucracy are still used in organizations. Do you believe these characteristics will ever cease to be a part of organizational life? Discuss.

6 A management professor once said that for successful management, studying the present was most important, studying the past was next, and studying the future was least important. What is your perspective of this view?

Are you a new-style or an old-style manager?[64]

INSTRUCTIONS The following are various behaviours in which a manager may engage when relating to subordinates. Read each statement carefully and rate each one 'Mostly true' or 'Mostly false', to reflect the extent to which you would use that behaviour.

		Mostly true	Mostly false
1	Supervise my subordinates closely to get better work from them.	☐	☐
2	Set the goals and objectives for my subordinates and sell them on the merits of my plans.	☐	☐
3	Set up controls to ensure that my subordinates are getting the job done.	☐	☐
4	Make sure that my subordinates' work is planned out for them.	☐	☐
5	Check with my subordinates daily to see if they need any help.	☐	☐
6	Step in as soon as reports indicate that progress on a job is slipping.	☐	☐
7	Push my people if necessary in order to meet schedules.	☐	☐
8	Have frequent meetings to learn from others what is going on.	☐	☐

SCORING AND INTERPRETATION Add the total number of 'Mostly true' answers and mark your score on the scale below. Theory X tends to be 'old-style' management, and Theory Y 'new-style', because the styles are based on different assumptions about people. To learn more about these assumptions, you can refer to Exhibit 2.4 and review the assumptions related to Theory X and Theory Y. Strong Theory X assumptions are typically considered inappropriate for today's workplace. Where do you fit on the X-Y scale? Does your score reflect your perception of yourself as a current or future manager?

X-Y Scale

Theory X ← 10_____ 5 _____0 → Theory Y

APPLY YOUR SKILLS: ETHICAL DILEMMA

The new test[65]

The civil service board in a midsize city in Indiana decided that a written exam should be given to all candidates being considered for promotion to supervisor. A written test would assess mental skills and would open access to all personnel who wanted to apply for the position. The board believed a written exam for promotion would be completely fair and objective because it eliminated subjective judgements and personal favouritism regarding a candidate's qualifications.

Maxine Othman, manager of a social service agency, loved to see her employees learn and grow to their full potential. When a rare opening for a supervising clerk occurred, Maxine quickly decided to give Sheryl Hines a shot at the job. Sheryl had been with the agency for 17 years and had shown herself to be a true leader. Sheryl worked hard at becoming a good supervisor, just as she had always worked hard at being a top-notch clerk. She paid attention to the human aspects of employee problems and introduced modern management techniques that strengthened the entire agency. Because of the board's new ruling, Sheryl would have to complete the exam in an open competition – anyone could sign up and take it, even a new employee. The board wanted the candidate with the highest score to get the job but allowed Maxine, as manager of the agency, to have the final say.

Because Sheryl had accepted the provisional opening and proved herself on the job, Maxine was upset that the entire clerical force was deemed qualified to take the test. When the results came back, she was devastated. Sheryl was placed twelfth in the field of candidates, while one of her newly hired clerks was placed first. The civil service board, impressed by the high score, urged Maxine to give the new clerk the permanent supervisory job; however, it was still Maxine's choice. Maxine wonders whether it is fair to base her decision only on the results of a written test. The board is pushing her to honour the objective written test, but could the test really assess fairly who was the right person for the job?

What would you do?

1 Ignore the test. Sheryl has proved herself via work experience and deserves the job.

2 Give the job to the candidate with the highest score. You don't need to make enemies on the civil service board, and, although it is a bureaucratic procedure, the test is an objective way to select a permanent placement.

3 Press the board to devise a more comprehensive set of selection criteria – including test results as well as supervisory experience, ability to motivate employees and knowledge of agency procedures – that can be explained and justified to the board and to employees.

APPLY YOUR SKILLS: CASE FOR CRITICAL ANALYSIS

Social media and employee engagement

The Diamond Bar Group is a global relocation service provider and has developed an enterprise social media learning environment (SMLE) to build a common corporate culture across the group. The SMLE is also used to provide employees with bite-sized learning opportunities to enable them to access personal development opportunities, any time any place, providing personal development as well as exchanging knowledge and understanding of work-related problems and their solutions.

John Adam, the Director of People and Development, asserted that 'social media's use as a personal development tool has grown exponentially in the Diamond Bar Group'. However, not all employees access the SMLE but those who do, according to Adam, experience a personal benefit as well as being able to support colleagues and to exert direct influence over issues in the wider organization. 'People scan the SMLE on a regular basis and it has become a company Facebook surrogate' according to Jane Bowe, Head of Corporate Communications at the Diamond Bar Group.

Visibility and recognition for contributing to the SMLE gives employees a sense of achievement and this is supported by regular communications from senior management highlighting particular contributions which have had an impact on people and organizational performance. This can help distribute leadership and enhance individual careers according to Jack Carr, a recently promoted first-line supervisor.

The Diamond Bar Group also promotes an annual employee conference using social media contributions to identify employees to take on important roles and responsibilities in the planning and running of the conference. Employees, through the annual 'Employee Engagement Survey', have expressed a clear view that social media enhances employee voice and influence across a dispersed organization making it easier to communicate with people within your own location and work group.

The views expressed by the employees of the Diamond Bar Group do not contradict the argument expressed in the Chartered Institute of Personnel and Development (UK) Survey Report (2013) 'Social technology, social business?' in which it is stated that the use of social media is 'less narcissistic and more collaborative' than it is given credit for.

Organizational social media such as the Diamond Bar Group's SMLE can be utilized by the organization to identify leadership talent and supporting succession planning. There is a strong link in such approaches to challenge existing leadership practices and to facilitate opportunities for distributed leadership throughout the organization. In distributed leadership, knowledge and expertise are valued according to the situation and therefore leadership activity is context specific (contingency-dependent).

Distributed leadership varies from organization to organization but there is no doubt that its progress within an organization can be greatly accelerated through the use of social media, particularly organization bespoke social media. Employees find social media platforms such as Diamond Bar's SMLE engaging because they are interactive and democratic and as such provide an excellent channel to promote employee voice and are preferred to more traditional channels such as employee surveys. In particular, enterprise specific social networks provide in-house channels of communication where employees can discuss personal and organization-specific issues more openly and more quickly. Employees can voice support and dissent, can contribute to discussions and can add knowledge and understanding to a range of issues resulting in enhanced morale and potentially improving management processes, products and services and the quality of working life.

References Chartered Institute of Personnel and Development (CIPD) (UK) *Survey Report (2013) 'Social technology, social business?'* London, CIPD.

Questions

1 Evaluate the statement that 'social media (company specific) always leads to a more participative and open culture'.

2 Discuss who is best placed to manage the Diamond Bar Group's social media learning environment.

3 The case study clearly identifies a range of potential benefits in establishing a social media learning environment. Appraise the dangers of the approach adopted by the Diamond Bar Group?

END NOTES

1. 'Q&A: Why the West Needs "Jugaad" Creativity' (an interview with Navi Radjou, Jaideep Prabhu and Simone Ahuja), *The Wall Street Journal India Online*, June 6, 2012, www.blogs.wsj.com/indiarealtime/2012/06/06/qa-why-the-west-needs-jugaad-creativity/ (accessed June 19, 2012); and Navi Radjou, Jaideep Prabhu and Simone Ahuja, *Jugaad Innovation: Think Frugal, Be Flexible, Generate Breakthrough Growth* (San Francisco: Jossey-Bass, 2012).

2. Devita Saraf, 'India's Indigenous Genius: Jugaad', *The Wall Street Journal Online*, July 13, 2009, www.online.wsj.com/article/SB124745880685131765.html (accessed June 19, 2012); Nirmalya Kumar and Phanish Puranam','Frugal Engineering: An Emerging Innovation Paradigm', *Ivey Business Journal* (March–April 2012) www.iveybusinessjournal.com/topics/innovation/frugal-engineering-an-emerging-innovation-paradigm (accessed June 19, 2012).

3. M. S. S. el Namaki, 'Does the Thinking of Yesterday's Management Gurus Imperil Today's Companies?' *Ivey Business Journal* (March–April 2012), www.iveybusinessjournal.com/topics/strategy/does-the-thinking-of-yesterdays-management-gurus-imperil-todays-companies (accessed June 19, 2012).

4. Eric Abrahamson, 'Management Fashion', *Academy of Management Review* 21, no. 1 (January 1996): 254–285. Also see '75 Years of Management Ideas and Practice', a supplement to the *Harvard Business Review* (September–October 1997), for a broad overview of historical trends in management thinking.

5. The following discussion is based on Daniel A. Wren, *The Evolution of Management Thought*, 4th ed. (New York: Wiley, 1994).

6. Based on Todd Henneman, 'Talkin' About Their Generations: The Workforce of the '50s and Today', *Workforce* (April 2, 2012), www.workforce.com/article/20120402/WORKFORCE90/120319965/talkin-about-their- generations-the-workforce-of-the-50s-and-today (accessed June 19, 2012); and Stephanie Armour, 'Generation Y: They've Arrived at Work with a New Attitude', *USA Today*, November 6, 2005, www.usatoday.com/money/workplace/2005-11-06-gen-y_x.htm (accessed November 10, 2005).

7. Jena McGregor, "There Is No More Normal," *Business-Week* (March 23 and 30, 2009): 30–34.

8. Michael Aneiro, 'Credit Market Springs to Life', *The Wall Street Journal*, March 11, 2010.

9. Aziz Hannifa, 'India, China Growth Dominates World Bank Meet', *India Abroad* (New York edition), November 2, 2007.

10. Robert Tell and Brian Kleiner, 'Organizational Change Can Rescue Industry', *Industrial Management* (March–April 2009): 20–24.

11. Daniel A. Wren, 'Management History: Issues and Ideas for Teaching and Research', *Journal of Management* 13 (1987): 339–350.

12. Business historian Alfred D. Chandler, Jr., quoted in Jerry Useem, 'Entrepreneur of the Century', *Inc.* (20th Anniversary Issue, 1999): 159–174.

13. Useem, 'Entrepreneur of the Century'.

14. The following is based on Wren, *Evolution of Management Thought*, Chapters 4 and 5; and Claude S. George, Jr., *The History of Management Thought* (Englewood Cliffs, NJ: Prentice-Hall, 1968), Chapter 4.

15. Cynthia Crossen, 'Early Industry Expert Soon Realized a Staff Has Its Own Efficiency', *The Wall Street Journal*, November 6, 2006.

16. Alan Farnham, 'The Man Who Changed Work Forever', *Fortune* (July 21, 1997): 114; Charles D. Wrege and Ann Marie Stoka, 'Cooke Creates a Classic: The Story Behind F. W. Taylor's Principles of Scientific Management', *Academy of Management Review* (October 1978): 736–749; Robert Kanigel, *The One Best Way: Frederick Winslow Taylor and the Enigma of Efficiency* (New York: Viking, 1997); and 'The X and Y Factors: What Goes Around Comes Around', special section in 'The New Organisation: A Survey of the Company', *The Economist* (January 21–27, 2006): 17–18.

17. Wren, *Evolution of Management Thought*, 171; and George, *History of Management Thought*, 103–104.

18. Vanessa O'Connell, 'Stores Count Seconds to Trim Labor Costs', *The Wall Street Journal*, November 17, 2008; and Vanessa O'Connell, 'Retailers Reprogram Workers in Efficiency Push', *The Wall Street Journal*, September 10, 2008.

19. Gary Hamel, 'The Why, What and How of Management Innovation', *Harvard Business Review* (February 2006): 72–84; Peter Coy, 'Cog or CoWorker?' *BusinessWeek* (August 20 and 27, 2007): 58–60.

20. Max Weber, *General Economic History*, trans. Frank H. Knight (London: Allen & Unwin, 1927); Max Weber, *The Protestant Ethic and the Spirit of Capitalism*, trans. Talcott Parsons (New York: Scribner, 1930); and Max Weber, *The Theory of Social and Economic Organizations*, ed. and trans. A. M. Henderson and Talcott Parsons (New York: Free Press, 1947).

21. Nadira A. Hira, 'The Making of a UPS Driver', *Fortune* (November 12, 2007), 118–129; David J. Lynch, 'Thanks to Its CEO, UPS Doesn't Just Deliver', *USA Today*, July 24, 2006, www.usatoday.com/money/companies/management/2006-07-23-ups_x.htm?tab1=t2 (accessed July 24, 2006); Kelly Barron, 'Logistics in Brown', *Forbes* (January 10, 2000): 78–83; Scott Kirsner, 'Venture Vérité: United Parcel Service', *Wired* (September 1999): 83–96; 'UPS', *The Atlanta Journal and Constitution*, April 26, 1992; Kathy Goode, Betty Hahn and Cindy Seibert, 'United Parcel Service: The Brown Giant' (unpublished manuscript, Texas A&M University, 1981); and 'About UPS', UPS corporate website, www.ups.com/content/us/en/about/index.html (accessed June 19, 2012).

22. Stephen Cummings and Todd Bridgman, 'The Relevant Past: Why the History of Management Should Be Critical to Our Future', *Academy of Management Learning & Education* 10, no. 1 (2011): 77–93.

23. These are based on Paul Downs, 'How I Fire People', You're the Boss blog, *The New York Times*, June 4, 2012, www.boss.blogs.nytimes.com/2012/06/04/how-i-fire-people/ (accessed June 20, 2012).

24. Henri Fayol, *Industrial and General Administration*, trans. J. A. Coubrough (Geneva: International Management Institute, 1930); Henri Fayol, *General and Industrial Management*, trans. Constance Storrs (London: Pitman and Sons, 1949); and W. J. Arnold et al., *Business-Week, Milestones in Management* (New York: McGraw-Hill, vol. I, 1965; vol. II, 1966).

25. Gregory M. Bounds, Gregory H. Dobbins and Oscar S. Fowler, *Management: A Total Quality Perspective* (Cincinnati, OH: South-Western Publishing, 1995), pp. 52–53.

26. Mary Parker Follett, *The New State: Group Organization: The Solution of Popular Government* (London: Longmans, Green, 1918); and Mary Parker Follett, *Creative Experience* (London: Longmans, Green, 1924).

27. Henry C. Metcalf and Lyndall Urwick, eds., *Dynamic Administration: The Collected Papers of Mary Parker Follett* (New York: Harper & Row, 1940); Arnold, *Business-Week, Milestones in Management*.

28. Follett, *The New State*; Metcalf and Urwick, *Dynamic Administration* (London: Sir Isaac Pitman, 1941).

29. William B. Wolf, *How to Understand Management: An Introduction to Chester I. Barnard* (Los Angeles: Lucas Brothers, 1968); and David D. Van Fleet, 'The Need-Hierarchy and Theories of Authority', *Human Relations* 9 (Spring 1982): 111–118.

30. Curt Tausky, *Work Organizations: Major Theoretical Perspectives* (Itasca, IL: F. E. Peacock, 1978), p. 42.

31. Charles D. Wrege, 'Solving Mayo's Mystery: The First Complete Account of the Origin of the Hawthorne Studies – The Forgotten Contributions of Charles E. Snow and Homer Hibarger', paper presented to the Management History Division of the Academy of Management (August 1976).

32. Ronald G. Greenwood, Alfred A. Bolton and Regina A. Greenwood, 'Hawthorne a Half Century Later: Relay Assembly Participants Remember', *Journal of Management* 9 (Fall/Winter 1983): 217–231.

33. F. J. Roethlisberger, W. J. Dickson and H. A. Wright, *Management and the Worker* (Cambridge, MA: Harvard University Press, 1939).

34. H. M. Parson, 'What Happened at Hawthorne?' *Science* 183 (1974): 922–932; John G. Adair, 'The Hawthorne Effect: A Reconsideration of the Methodological Artifact', *Journal of*

Applied Psychology 69, no. 2 (1984): 334–345; and Gordon Diaper, 'The Hawthorne Effect: A Fresh Examination', *Educational Studies* 16, no. 3 (1990): 261–268.

35. R. G. Greenwood, A. A. Bolton and R. A. Greenwood, 'Hawthorne a Half Century Later', 219–221.

36. F. J. Roethlisberger and W. J. Dickson, *Management and the Worker*.

37. Ramon J. Aldag and Timothy M. Stearns, *Management*, 2d ed. (Cincinnati, OH: South-Western Publishing, 1991), pp. 47–48.

38. Tausky, *Work Organizations: Major Theoretical Perspectives*, p. 55.

39. Douglas McGregor, *The Human Side of Enterprise* (New York: McGraw-Hill, 1960), pp. 16–18; Robert A. Cunningham, 'Douglas McGregor: A Lasting Impression', *Ivey Business Journal* (October 2011): 5–7.

40. Ricardo Semler, 'Out of This World: Doing Things the Semco Way', *Global Business and Organizational Excellence* (July–August 2007): 13–21.

41. Wendell L. French and Cecil H. Bell Jr., 'A History of Organizational Development', in Wendell L. French, Cecil H. Bell Jr. and Robert A. Zawacki, *Organization Development and Transformation: Managing Effective Change* (Burr Ridge, IL: Irwin McGraw-Hill, 2000), pp. 20–42.

42. Mansel G. Blackford and K. Austin Kerr, *Business Enterprise in American History* (Boston: Houghton Mifflin, 1986), Chapters 10 and 11; and Alex Groner and the editors of *American Heritage* and *BusinessWeek, The American Heritage History of American Business and Industry* (New York: American Heritage Publishing, 1972), Chapter 9.

43. Geoffrey Colvin, 'How Alfred P. Sloan, Michael Porter and Peter Drucker Taught Us All the Art of Management', *Fortune* (March 21, 2005): 83–86.

44. Brooks Barnes, 'Disney Technology Tackles a Theme-Park Headache: Lines', *The New York Times*, December 28, 2010, B1; and 'Disney Cracks Down on FastPass Enforcement', *Tampa Bay Times*, March 9, 2012, B2.

45. Larry M. Austin and James R. Burns, *Management Science* (New York: Macmillan, 1985).

46. Dan Heath and Chip Heath, 'In Defense of Feelings: Why Your Gut Is More Ethical Than Your Brain', *Fast Company* (July–August 2009): 58–59.

47. Scott Patterson, *The Quants: How a New Breed of Math Whizzes Conquered Wall Street and Nearly Destroyed It* (New York: Crown Business, 2010); and Harry Hurt III, 'In Practice, Stock Formulas Weren't Perfect', *The New York Times*, February 21, 2010.

48. Ludwig von Bertalanffy et al., 'General Systems Theory: A New Approach to Unity of Science', *Human Biology* 23 (December 1951): 302–361; and Kenneth E. Boulding, 'General Systems Theory – The Skeleton of Science', *Management Science* 2 (April 1956): 197–208.

49. This section is based on Peter M. Senge, *The Fifth Discipline: The Art and Practice of the Learning Organization* (New York: Doubleday, 1990); John D. Sterman, 'Systems Dynamics Modeling: Tools for Learning in a Complex World', *California Management Review* 43, no. 4 (Summer 2001): 8–25; Andrea Gabor, 'Seeing Your Company as a System', *Strategy + Business* (Summer 2010), www.strategy-business.

com/article/10210?gko=20cca (accessed June 20, 2012); and Ron Zemke, 'Systems Thinking', *Training* (February 2001): 40–46.

50. This example is cited in Sterman, 'Systems Dynamics Modeling'.

51. Fred Luthans, 'The Contingency Theory of Management: A Path Out of the Jungle', *Business Horizons* 16 (June 1973): 62–72; and Fremont E. Kast and James E. Rosenzweig, *Contingency Views of Organization and Management* (Chicago: Science Research Associates, 1973).

52. Samuel Greengard, '25 Visionaries Who Shaped Today's Workplace', *Workforce* (January 1997): 50–59; and Ann Harrington, 'The Big Ideas', *Fortune* (November 22, 1999): 152–154.

53. Mauro F. Guillen, 'The Age of Eclecticism: Current Organizational Trends and the Evolution of Managerial Models', *Sloan Management Review* (Fall 1994): 75–86.

54. Jeremy Main, 'How to Steal the Best Ideas Around', *Fortune* (October 19, 1992): 102–106.

55. Darrell Rigby and Barbara Bilodeau, 'Management Tools and Trends 2009', Bain & Company Inc., 2009, www.bain. com/management_tools/home.asp (accessed March 10, 2010).

56. David Hurst, 'The New Ecology of Leadership: Revisiting the Foundations of Management', *Ivey Business Journal* (May–June 2012): 1–5; Michael Murphy, 'The Race to Failure' (a review of *Crash Course* by Paul Ingrassia, Random House 2010), *The Wall Street Journal*, January 29, 2010, A13.

57. Annick Van Rossem and Kees Van Veen, 'Managers' Awareness of Fashionable Management Concepts: An Empirical Study', *European Management Journal* 29 (2011): 206–216.

58. Study reported in Phred Dvorak, 'Why Management Trends Quickly Fade Away' (Theory and Practice column), *The Wall Street Journal*, June 26, 2006.

59. Darrell Rigby and Barbara Bilodeau, 'Management Tools and Trends 2011', Bain and Company, Inc., www.bain.com/ publications/articles/Management-tools-trends-2011.aspx (accessed June 22, 2012).

60. 'Survey: 37% Use Social Media to Check Candidates', *Workforce* (April 18, 2012), www.workforce.com/article/20120418/NEWS01/120419964 (accessed June 22, 2012).

61. Definition based on Steven A. Melnyk and David R. Denzler, *Operations Management: A Value-Driven Approach* (Burr Ridge, IL: Richard D. Irwin, 1996): p. 613.

62. The Global Supply Chain Games project, www.gscg.org (accessed July 16, 2008).

63. Eric Bellman and Cecilie Rohwedder, 'Western Grocer Modernizes Passage to India's Markets', *The Wall Street Journal*, November 28, 2007.

64. This questionnaire is from William Pfeiffer and John E. Jones, eds., 'Supervisory Attitudes: The X-Y Scale', in *The 1972 Annual Handbook for Group Facilitators* (New York: John Wiley & Sons, 1972), pp. 65–68. This material is used by permission of John Wiley & Sons, Inc. The X-Y scale was adapted from an instrument developed by Robert N. Ford of AT&T for in-house manager training.

65. Based on Betty Harrigan, 'Career Advice', *Working Woman* (July 1986): 22–24.

THE CLEAN-ENERGY FUTURE IS NOW

As *Green Car Journal* prepared to publish its much-anticipated 'Green Car of the Year' edition for 2012, audiences might have expected a tribute to the Toyota Prius, Nissan Leaf or another innovation in electric motoring. Instead, the panel of environmental and automotive experts assembled by the magazine made a surprising choice – one that signalled a sea change in green energy. The judges selected the 2012 Honda Civic Natural Gas, an alternative-fuel, partial-zero emissions vehicle that operates solely on compressed natural gas. As the journal noted, not only is the Civic's sticker price of $26 155 more affordable than electric vehicles, and not only does the model possess a driving range and horsepower on par with conventional compacts, but the Civic's alternative fuel costs approximately half the price of gasoline and is sourced almost entirely from abundant reserves in the USA.

Against a backdrop of ubiquitous marketing for electric cars and hybrids, the choice of a natural gas vehicle for Green Car of the Year was an unmistakable nod to a development in green energy that is so immense that it promises to transform the US energy grid and end North American dependence on foreign oil. That development is the discovery of the Marcellus Shale. Located throughout the Appalachian Basin of the eastern USA, the Marcellus Shale is a massive sedimentary rock formation deep beneath the Earth's surface that contains one of the largest methane deposits anywhere in the world. Once thought to possess a modest 1.9 trillion cubic feet of natural gas, this 600-mile-wide black shale formation below Pennsylvania, Ohio, New York and West Virginia was explored by geologists in 2004 and was found to contain between 168 trillion and 516 trillion cubic feet of natural gas. Combined with other US shale plays, including the Barnett Shale in Texas, the discovery of the Marcellus led the International Energy Agency (IEA) to rank the USA the new number one natural gas producer in the world, edging out resource-rich Russia. In addition, the Marcellus has triggered a green-energy boom known as the Great Shale Gas Rush, which is creating thousands of green jobs, revitalizing the nation's economy and pointing the way to a clean-energy future.

The breakthrough couldn't have come at a better time. In a highly turbulent business environment shaken by a global recession and new government restrictions on traditional energy, today's business managers struggle to know which energy alternatives are viable, or even affordable. The unexpected bankruptcy of well-funded green-energy darlings Solyndra and Beacon Power further underscore the uncertainty of the alternative energy marketplace. To gain stability for their organizations, managers need solutions that are reliable now, not decades into the future.

Thanks to an abundant supply of affordable natural gas, the green energy future has arrived. According to the US Environmental Protection Agency (EPA) profile on clean energy, natural gas is a clean-burning fuel that generates roughly half the carbon emissions of coal and oil while releasing zero sulfur dioxide or mercury emissions. Given its low price relative to other energy sources, natural gas has game-changing implications for trucking fleets, consumer autos, electric power generation and commercial heating – not to mention natural gas ovens, clothes dryers, water heaters and other appliances.

While shale gas is a win–win for business and the environment, its impact on green jobs and the economy is equally important. According to a 2011 IHS Global Insight study, shale gas production – currently 34 per cent of all natural gas production in the USA – supported more than 600 000 green jobs in 2010, a number that will increase to 870 000 jobs by 2015. As for the national economy, shale gas contributed $76.9 billion to the US gross domestic product (GDP) in 2010 and is projected to contribute

$118.2 billion by 2015. Over the next 25 years, shale gas will raise more than $933 billion in tax revenue for local, state and federal governments. The news about natural gas is good for average consumers as well. In 2011, property owners in the Marcellus region received $400 million in natural gas royalties – a number that will climb even higher in the next decade. Additionally, individual US consumers can expect $926 in new disposable income per year from cost savings related to natural gas. Combined, this economic activity equates to much-needed relief in hard times.

What does the switch to natural gas mean for industry-leading companies? For automakers like Honda and Volvo, natural gas vehicles have begun making their way into regular assembly-line production. Transport businesses such as UPS are converting fleets from diesel to natural gas as part of the White House's National Clean Fleets Partnership. Transit leaders like Navistar and Clean Energy Fuels have launched strategic partnerships to build America's Natural Gas Highway. Manufacturers such as Westport Innovations have made organizational changes to become leading producers of liquefied and compressed natural gas engines. Utility companies like Dominion are replacing coal-based electricity with gas-fired electric generation. And drillers like Range Resources are finding new ways to improve the quality and safety of natural gas exploration while controlling costs.

There are no limits to the possibilities of the Great Shale Gas Rush. However, it will take visionary leadership and skilful management to deliver on the promise of a truly sustainable clean-energy future.

Integrative case questions

1   What turbulent forces are causing business leaders to rethink their use of energy?

2   Which managers – top managers, middle managers or first-line managers – would make companywide decisions about energy use? How might *the new workplace* enable all managers to capitalize on the Great Shale Gas Rush?

3   Which historical management perspectives have particular relevance to the exploration and extraction of natural gas? Explain.

SOURCES: 'Honda Civic Natural Gas Is 2012 Green Car of the Year', *Green Car Journal*, November 17, 2011, www.greencar.com/articles/honda-civic-natural-gas-2012-green-car-year.php (accessed June 7, 2012); Elwin Green, 'Natural Gas Locked in the Marcellus Shale Has Companies Rushing to Cash in on Possibilities', *Pittsburgh Post-Gazette*, March 16, 2012, www.post-gazette.com/stories/business/news/natural-gas-locked-in-the-marcellus-shale-has-companies-rushing-to-cash-in-on-possibilities-370058/ (accessed June 7, 2012); Kevin Begos, 'Gas Drillers Generate About $3.5 Billion in Revenues From Marcellus Shale', Associated Press, May 5, 2012, www.timesunion.com/business/article/AP-Pa-gas-drilling-brought-3-5-billion-in-2011-3536873.php (accessed June 8, 2012); Timothy J. Considine, Robert Watson and Seth Blumsack, *The Pennsylvania Marcellus Natural Gas Industry: Status, Economic Impacts and Future Potential*, John and Willie Leone Family Department of Energy and Mineral Engineering, Penn State University, July 20, 2011, www.marcelluscoalition.org/wp-content/uploads/2011/07/Final-2011-PA-Marcellus-Economic-Impacts.pdf (accessed June 8, 2012); IHS, 'Shale Gas Supports More than 600 000 American Jobs Today; by 2015, Shale Gas Predicted to Support Nearly 870 000 Jobs and Contribute $118.2 Billion to GDP', press release, December 6, 2011, www.press.ihs.com/press-release/energy-power/shale-gas-supports-more-600000-american-jobs-today-2015-shale-gas-predict (accessed June 8, 2012); 'IEA: US to Overtake Russia as Top Gas Producer, Reuters, Jun 5, 2012, www.af.reuters.com/article/energyOilNews/idAFL3E-8H45WZ20120605 (accessed June 8, 2012); Environmental Protection Agency, 'Clean Energy: Air Emissions', www.epa.gov/cleanenergy/energy-and-you/affect/air-emissions.html (accessed June 8, 2012); Clifford Krauss, 'There's Gas in Those Hills, *The New York Times*, April 8, 2008, www.nytimes.com/2008/04/08/business/08gas.html (accessed June 8, 2012).

PART 2

MANAGING EXTERNAL AND INTERNAL ENVIRONMENTS

PART 2

MANAGING EXTERNAL AND INTERNAL ENVIRONMENTS

CHAPTER 3

THE ORGANIZATION AND CORPORATE CULTURE

LEARNING OBJECTIVES

After studying this chapter, you should be able to:

1 Define an organizational ecosystem and understand how general and task environments affect an organization's ability to survive and thrive.

2 Explain the strategies that managers use to help organizations adapt to an uncertain and/or turbulent future environment.

3 Define corporate culture providing organizational examples.

4 Interpret organizational symbols, stories, heroes, villains, slogans and ceremonies and their interrelationships within a corporate culture.

5 Describe four main types of corporate culture and how corporate culture relates to the environment.

6 Define cultural leadership and explain the tools that a cultural leader uses to create a high performance culture.

Most managers don't pop on a crash helmet and fire-resistant suit to guide an organization through a period of tumultuous change. But when Toyota Motor Corporation's president, Akio Toyoda, faced a series of calamities during his first few years as president, he tapped into his personal skills as a certified test car driver – high endurance, precise steering and strong mental focus – leading Toyota to a surprising rebound. In 2011, Toyota was toppled from its number one position as the world's largest automaker to third, behind General Motors and Volkswagen, after suffering the multiple effects of a global recession, the recall of 8 million vehicles, and a deadly tsunami in Japan. Within the organization, storms were also brewing as there was an awareness that Toyota's tortuous bureaucracy had slowed down decision-making and response times. Furthermore, Toyota had lost touch with its customers. Toyota's growth had been underpinned by 'quality, dependability and reliability', but customers also wanted style and design, and they were flocking to Hyundai, which had seized design leadership.[1]

These environmental factors, both external and internal, served as abrupt wake-up calls for a company that had grown complacent. Akio Toyoda's response was to revise the corporate culture and create a more responsive organization – one that could navigate with greater ease, through even subtle environmental shifts. This chapter explores in full detail the components of the external environment and how they affect an organization. It also examines a major part of the organization's internal environment: the corporate culture. Corporate culture is shaped by the external environment and also strongly influences how managers respond to changes in the external environment. A useful approach for analyzing a corporate culture is to visualize it as an iceberg. The aspects above the surface are ones that can be detected by radar; the aspects below the waterline can only be seen by sonar.

The external environment

The environmental changes that shook Toyota's leadership position in the auto industry – a global recession, natural disasters and changing customer needs – were part of its external organizational environment. The external organizational environment includes all elements existing outside the boundary of the organization that have the potential to affect the organization.[2] The environment includes competitors, resources, technology and economic conditions that will influence the organization.

The organization's external environment can be conceptualized further as having two main components: general and task environments, as illustrated in Exhibit 3.1.[3]

The general environment mostly affects organizations indirectly, including social, economic, legal-political, international, natural and technological factors that can influence all organizations with differing impacts. Changes in national and regional regulations, or economic shocks, are events within the organization's general environment. Such events may not directly change day-to-day operations, but they do affect organizations, eventually. The task environment is closer to the organization itself and includes the sectors that conduct day-to-day transactions with the organization and directly influence its basic operations and performance. The task environment is generally considered to include competitors, suppliers, customers and the labour market.

A new view of the environment argues that organizations are now evolving into business ecosystems. An organizational ecosystem is a system formed by the interaction amongst a community of organizations, within the environment. *An ecosystem includes organizations in all the sectors of the task and general environments that provide the resource and information transactions, flows and linkages necessary for an organization to thrive.*[4]

For example, Apple's ecosystem includes hundreds of suppliers and millions of customers for the products that it produces across several industries, including consumer electronics, Internet services, mobile phones,

EXHIBIT 3.1 Dimensions of the organization's general, task and internal environments

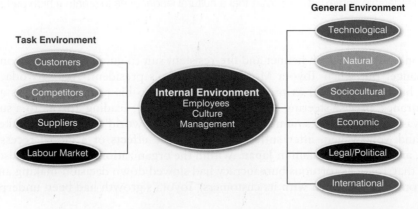

personal computers and entertainment.[5] An organization also has an internal environment, which includes all the elements within the organization's boundaries. The internal environment is composed of current employees, management and particularly its corporate culture, which defines required employee behaviour in the internal environment and is highly indicative of how well the organization will adapt to the external environment.

'It is not the strongest of the species that survives, nor the most intelligent that survives. It is the one that is the most adaptable to change.'

— CHARLES DARWIN (1809–1882), NATURALIST

Exhibit 3.1 illustrates the relationship amongst the general, task and internal environments. As an open system, the organization draws resources from the external environment and releases goods and services back to it. We will now discuss the two components of the external environment in more detail. Then we will discuss corporate culture, the key element in the internal environment. Other aspects of the internal environment, such as structure and technology, will be covered in later chapters of this book.

General environment

The dimensions of the general environment include international, technological, sociocultural, economic, legal-political and natural.

International

In his 2007 book 'The World Is Flat', Thomas Friedman challenges managers to view global markets as a level playing field where geographical divisions are irrelevant.[6] A flat world, Friedman argues, creates opportunities

EXHIBIT 3.2 China PRC 2015 – Onwards and upwards

Motto: *Listen, watch, learn, practice, innovate, lead*

The PRC decadal movements: Moved from 'cheap China' to 'consuming China' to 'demanding China' to 'ownership China' to the ultimate stage of becoming the **world leader**.

Who's who: PRC fast forwarding to becoming the MNC world leader – major challenges to US and EU MNCs

Profitability issues: Watch the PRC's rising MNCs – such as Haier & Huawei

Type of investments vehicle: Joint ventures enable leverage, franchising, spreads branding and gains know-how

Industry types: Service manufacturing for Chinese markets

Market: Mega domestic as well as global – but there are many markets (not homogeneous)

Consumer habits: Mega increased online buying – highly tech-savvy PRC consumers; is the middle-class expansion a myth or reality?

Taxes: VIP changes will amplify future opportunities

Where: PRC has four main regions – coastal, inland, 3/4 tier cities, north – therefore demand cultural and economic variations

Government role: Central political system, Five Year Plan visualizing the nation, shared services and outsourcing, payments, world-class cloud computing initiatives

SOURCE: Patricia Walker, Associate Professor Hon Researcher Institute of Cultural Industries, Peking University, China

for companies to expand into global markets and build a global supply chain. Other authors, such as Peter Dicken, present counter arguments as not all the world is flat! The world is indeed contoured with some regions being quite 'mountainous'. China and Africa should not be viewed as singular and very large markets, as they both contain many different markets. The Chinese nation has changed dramatically as illustrated by Exhibit 3.2 provided by Patricia Walker, a visiting Professor at the Peking University and editorial author of China's Creative Industries.

As managers plan for expansion into global markets, they have to consider the international dimension of the external environment, which includes events originating in foreign countries, as facilitating new opportunities for EU and US companies in other countries. The international environment provides new competitors, customers and suppliers, and shapes social, technological and economic trends as well. However, the relative levels of corruption, business regulation and maturity of legal systems represent considerable complexity, that requires due diligence by executives. Descriptions and tolerance of corruption/unethical business practices vary throughout the world and some notable examples include Blat (Russia), Graft (USA), Sleaze (UK) and Guan Xi (China). A detailed discussion of Guan Xi follows later in this chapter and one could take a view that it is a form of relationship marketing. The nature of Guan Xi is very wide indeed, from being benevolent to grossly unethical! Starbucks experienced mixed results as it expanded into European markets. Starbucks devotees have packed stores in Germany and the UK, but sales and profits in the company's French stores were disappointing. In fact, after its first 8 years of operating 63 stores, Starbucks did not report a profit in France. What international factors hindered the company's success in France? A sluggish economy and Europe's debt crisis arguably hurt sales. Also, Starbucks faced high rent and labour costs in France that eroded profits. The company was also very slow to tailor the Starbucks experience to the French café culture. Whereas a New Yorker might collect a disposable cup of coffee 'to go', the French much prefer to linger over a large, ceramic mug of coffee with friends and colleagues in a café-style environment. To respond to these challenges, Starbucks launched a multimillion-dollar campaign in France that included an upscale makeover of stores, with more seating and customized beverages and blends that appeal to local tastes.[7]

 CONCEPT CONNECTION

Changes in the **technological dimension** of the environment have enabled many firms to expand their services, as well as their marketing practices, on the Web. In the UK this has facilitated 'crowdsourcing' to develop. The most well-known UK ones are Kickstart and Crowdcube. The ease of raising finance through this medium has enabled a good number of new start entrepreneurial firms to raise capital from small sum investors.

As geographic boundaries become permeable and more transaction opportunities arise, especially in fast developing economies such as China, more companies are finding considerable advantages in the global marketplace. For example, Coca-Cola's CEO Muhtar Kent predicted that its China division will double its sales of Coke products, helping to meet Kent's goal of doubling Coke's overall business, by 2020. '*China will be Coke's largest market,*' Kent promised. '*I can't give you a time, but it will happen.*'[8] With more companies establishing a competitive presence in China, managers working in that country recognize that their competitive success begins with their ability to build personal relationships and emotional bonds with their Chinese contacts. The Manager's Shoptalk, in this chapter, offer tips for creating successful and enduring business relationships in China.

Technological

The technological dimension of the general environment includes scientific and technological advancements in a specific industry, as well as in

⊕ MANAGER'S SHOPTALK

Creating and benefiting from Guanxi in China

With its lower labour costs against mature economies and huge potential regional markets, China is luring thousands of EU and US companies in search of growth opportunities. Yet many multinationals (MNCs) doing business in China have been very disappointed with the poor financial returns from their foreign direct investment (FDI). A major reason for many Western businesses falling short of expectations, experts agree, is that they have failed to grasp the centuries-old concept of *guanxi,* at the very heart of Chinese culture. Another reason for failure in China has been the ethnocentric attitude of US corporations, typified by ebay who were driven out of the Chinese market by Jack Ma's Alibaba, in 2006. Alibaba's subsequent initial public offering (IPO) in 2014 was the biggest in US corporate history at $250 billion! At its very simplest level, *guanxi* is a supportive, mutually beneficial connection between two people. Eventually, those personal relationships are linked together into a network, and it is through networks like this that real business gets done. Anyone considering doing business in China should keep in mind the following basic rules:

- **Business is always personal.** It is impossible to translate 'Don't take it so personally – it's only business' into Chinese. Western managers tend to believe that if they conclude a successful transaction, a good business relationship will follow. The development of a personal relationship is an added bonus, but it is not really necessary when it comes to getting things done. In the Chinese business world, however, a personal relationship must be in place before managers even consider entering a business transaction. Western managers doing business in China should cultivate personal relationships – both during and outside business hours. Accept any and all social invitations – for drinks, a meal, or even a potentially embarrassing visit to a karaoke bar, which some Chinese businessmen consider an important part of solidifying good business relationships.

- **Don't minimize the small talk.** Getting right down to business and bypassing the small talk during a meeting, might feel like an efficient use of time to an American manager. To the Chinese, however, this approach neglects the all-important work of forging an emotional bond. Be aware that the real purpose of your initial meetings with potential business partners is to begin building a relationship, so keep your patience if the deal that you are planning to discuss never even comes up – there's always another opportunity tomorrow.

- **Remember that relationships are not short-term.** The work of establishing and nurturing *guanxi* relationships in China is never done. Western managers must put aside their usual focus on short-term results and recognize that it takes a long time for foreigners to be accepted into a *guanxi* network. Often, foreign companies must prove their trustworthiness and reliability over time.

- **Make contact frequently.** Some experts recommend hiring ethnic Chinese staff members and then letting them do the heavy work of relationship building. Others emphasize that Westerners themselves should put plenty of time and energy into forging links with Chinese contacts; those efforts will pay off because the contacts can smooth the way by tapping into their own *guanxi* networks. Whatever the strategy, contact should be frequent and personal. In addition, be sure to keep careful track of the contacts that you make. In China, any and all relationships are bound to be important at some point in time.

SOURCES: Michelle Dammon Loyalka, 'Before You Set Up Shop in China', part of the 'Doing Business in China' special report, *BusinessWeek Online,* January 4, 2006, www.businessweek.com/smallbiz/content/jan2006/sb20060104_466114.htm (accessed January 6, 2006); Los Angeles Chinese Learning Center, 'Chinese Business Culture', www.chinese-school.netfirms.com/guanxi.html; Beijing British Embassy, 'Golden Hints for Doing Business in China', www.chinese-school.netfirms.com/goldenhints.html; and Emily Flitter, 'Faux Pas: With Karaoke, a Deal in China for a Song', *The Wall Street Journal Online*, June 9, 2008, www.online.wsj.com/article/SB121268021240548769.html (accessed 24 September 2012).

society at large. In recent years, the economic recovery in the USA sputtered forward, with managers buying equipment and software that has enabled them to accomplish more work with fewer employees. Motivated by temporary tax breaks and historically low interest rates, US-based companies increased spending on machines and software but were very slow to put more employees on the payroll, leading to a 'jobless recovery'. Instead of hiring more workers, for example, companies such as Cincinnati-based Sunny Delight Beverages Company invested in technology to make operations faster and more productive. In fact, since the US economy began growing again in 2009, spending on equipment and software has surged 31 per cent. On the other hand, [US] private-sector jobs have grown just 1.4 per cent over the same span.[9]

Advances in technology drive competition and help innovative companies gain market share. They also have the potential to transform consumer expectations of an entire industry. Driven by the popularity of e-readers, Barnes & Noble reinvented its traditional bookstore image with a new digital strategy that they hope will help it compete with rivals Amazon, Apple and Google on the digital book front. With its renewed focus as a seller of downloads, reading devices, and apps, and a market share of 27 per cent of the e-book market, Barnes & Noble is using its brick-and-mortar bookstores to introduce customers to its Nook e-readers and build e-book audiences.[10]

Sociocultural

The sociocultural dimension of the general environment represents demographic characteristics as well as the norms, customs and values of the general population. Important sociocultural characteristics are geographical distribution and population density, age and education levels. Today's demographic profiles are the foundation of tomorrow's workforce and consumers. By understanding these profiles and addressing them in the organization's business plans, managers prepare their organizations for long-term success. Smart managers may want to consider how the following sociocultural trends are changing the consumer and business landscape:

1 A new generation of technologically savvy consumers, often called the *Connected Generation* or *Generation C*, has intimately woven technology into every aspect of their lives. Their primary digital devices (PDDs) shape the way they communicate, shop, travel and earn college credits. Generation C (typically defined as people born after 1990) will make up 40 per cent of the population in the USA and Europe by 2020 and will constitute the largest cohort of consumers worldwide.[11]

2 As the US population, together with many EU countries and Japan, continues to age, organizations are rushing to create senior-friendly products and services. Currently, the US population includes 78 million 'baby boomers', and roughly one-third were 62 years old or older in 2013.[12] Organizations realize that it makes good business sense to create products and services for this ageing demographic.

3 US census data show that more than half of all babies born in 2011 were members of minority groups, the first time that has happened in US history. Hispanics, African-Americans, Asians and other minorities in 2011 represented 50.4 per cent of births. The nation's growing diversity has huge implications for business. 'Children are in the vanguard of this transition,' says Kenneth Johnson, a demographer at the University of New Hampshire's Carsey Institute.[13]

Economic

The economic dimension represents the general economic health of the country or region in which the organization operates. Consumer purchasing power, the unemployment rate and interest rates are part of an organization's economic environment. Because many organizations today are operating in a globalized environment, the economic dimension has become exceedingly complex and creates enormous uncertainty for managers. The global economic environment will be discussed in much more detail in the next chapter.

In the USA and the EU, many industries such as banking, are finding it difficult to make a strong comeback, despite the slowly rebounding economies. Regulators are now applying stress testing to the banking industry which we believe will signal even closer future control of the banking institutions so important to interlinked free market economies.

Legal-political

The legal-political dimension includes government regulations at the local, state and federal levels, as well as political activities designed to influence company behaviour. The US political system encourages capitalism, and the government tries not to overregulate business. However, government laws do specify rules of the game. The federal government influences organizations through the Occupational Safety and Health Administration (OSHA), Environmental Protection Agency (EPA), fair trade practices, libel statutes allowing lawsuits against business, consumer protection and privacy legislation, product safety requirements, import and export restrictions, and information and labeling requirements. The US has a very high number of lawyers in the business world as well as in its government agencies. This accounts for a 'rules-based' society with due deference to their Bill of Rights. On the other hand, China has educated a great number of engineers and as a consequence they have been able to allocate them against large-scale infrastructure projects. Interestingly, the flow of Chinese FDI into Europe has accelerated in recent years. Up to 2013 Chinese FDI was concentrated into agricultural land, especially in Africa.

Many companies work closely with national lawmakers, educating them about products and services and legislation's impact on their business strategies. Long before its NASDAQ debut in May 2012, Facebook had been befriending the nation's top lawmakers. Facebook hired former political aides with access to top leaders in both parties and had them lead training sessions on using Facebook to communicate with voters. In addition, Facebook stepped up its lobbying efforts and set up a political action committee. *'It's smart advocacy,'* said Rey Ramsey, CEO of TechNet, an industry grouping that includes Facebook. *'It starts with giving people an education. Then you start explaining more of your business model. What you ultimately want is for a legislator to understand the consequences of their actions.'*[14]

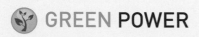 **GREEN POWER**

Reaching Mythical Proportions

In Greek mythology, Nike was the winged goddess of victory. With headquarters in Portland, Oregon – considered one of the world's 'greenest' cities – **Nike Inc.** has a corporate culture definitely centred on a commitment to victory, both on the athletic field and as one of the top 100 most sustainable corporations. Some companies give insufficient commitment to sustainability in the context of reducing toxins, but Nike goes much further. The company's predictive tool, the Considered Design Index, monitors the total environmental impact of the running shoe production cycle, scoring everything from fabric to reducing waste. Victory in sustainability also means influencing other companies. Nike's corporate social responsibility (CSR) staff spearheaded the 'GreenXchange', which brought together companies to explore opportunities, share information and keep abreast of trends and issues. As Nike's sustainability influence grows, its cultural mantra reflects the winged deity: 'There is no finish line for environmental efforts – we can always go further'.

SOURCES: Marc J. Epstein, Adriana Rejc Buhovac and Kristi Yuthas (2010) 'Why Nike Kicks Butt in Sustainability', *Organizational Dynamics* 39: 353–356; and 'Sustainable Business at Nike, Inc.', Nike corporate website, www.nikeinc.com/pages/responsibility (accessed 24 July 2012).

Natural

In response to pressure from environmental advocates, organizations have become increasingly sensitive to the Earth's diminishing natural resources and the environmental impact of their products and business practices. As a result, the natural dimension of the external environment is growing in importance. The natural dimension includes all elements that occur naturally on Earth, including plants, animals, rocks and resources such as air, water and climate. Protection of the natural environment is emerging as a critical policy focus around the world. Governments are increasingly under pressure to explain their performance on pollution control and natural resource management. Nations with the best environmental performance, along with some comparison countries, are listed in Exhibit 3.3. Note: one of the top national performers is Switzerland, which gets most of its power from renewable sources – hydropower and geothermal energy. Solomon and Solomon have notably recognized animals as primary stakeholders of the Earth and other authors have developed the concept of 'ecocide' expressing the view that permanent damage to the Earth is a criminal offence. CSEAR, the research centre at St Andrews University in Wales, is a very useful source of data on topical sustainability issues.

The natural dimension is very different from other sectors of the general environment because it has no voice of its own. Influence on managers to meet needs in the natural environment may come from other sectors, such as government regulation, consumer concerns, the media, competitors' actions or even employees.[15] For example, environmental groups described as non-governmental organizations (NGOs) advocate various action and policy goals that include reduction and clean ups of pollution, development of renewable energy resources, reduction of greenhouse gases such as carbon dioxide, and sustainable use of scarce resources such as water, land and air. The oil spill in the Gulf of Mexico in 2010 brought environmental issues to the forefront. Many months after the BP-Transocean rig at the Deepwater Horizon oil well exploded, hundreds of thousands of gallons of oil were still flowing into open water each day, adding to the millions of gallons already contaminating the water and beaches along the coasts of Louisiana, Mississippi, Alabama and Florida, and threatening the region's fish, birds, turtles and vegetation. '*One of the last pristine, most biologically diverse coastal habitats in the country is about to get wiped out*,' said Felicia Coleman, who directs the Florida State University Coastal and Marine Laboratory. '*And there's not much we can do about it*'. The effects of the devastating spill are likely to continue for many years.[16] Even in 2015 the compensation issues for BP have not been fully resolved with class actions prevailing.

EXHIBIT 3.3 2012 environmental performance index

Rank	Country	Score
1	Switzerland	76.69
2	Latvia	70.37
3	Norway	69.92
4	Luxembourg	69.20
5	Costa Rica	69.03
6	France	69.00
7	Austria	68.92
8	Italy	68.90
9	Sweden	68.82
10	UK	68.82
11	Germany	66.91
12	Slovakia	66.62
13	Iceland	66.28
14	New Zealand	66.05
15	Albania	65.85
37	Canada	58.41
49	USA	56.59
116	China	42.24
125	India	36.23
132	Iraq	25.32

SOURCE: 2012 Environmental Performance Index, Yale Center for Environmental Law and Policy, Yale University, www.epi.yale.edu/epi2012/rankings; and Center for International Earth Science Information Network, Columbia University.
Note: The scores for each country are based on 25 performance indicators covering both environmental public health and ecosystem vitality, such as air pollution and greenhouse gas emissions.

CONCEPT CONNECTION

Whether they are motivated by a desire to preserve natural resources, to impress their customers with their social responsibility or to comply with new legislation, many companies are looking for ways to treat the **natural environment** better. Some are doing it by switching to renewable energy sources, while others are trying to reduce pollution. Promoting the use of cloth carrying bags, such as these, is just one example of how retailers can help minimize the amount of rubbish going into the world's landfills.

Task environment

As described earlier, the task environment includes those sectors that have a direct working relationship with the organization, among them customers, competitors, suppliers and the labour market.

Customers

Those people and organizations in the environment that acquire goods or services from the organization are customers. As recipients of the organization's output, customers are important because they determine the organization's success. Organizations have to be responsive to marketplace changes. The Hershey Company, which practically invented modern chocolate bars; with its popular Hershey's bars and Hershey's Kisses, experienced serious losses in profits, market share and stakeholder confidence after failing to understand customers' tastes. Hershey assumed that customers would embrace its dizzying array of Hershey's Kisses featuring different types of chocolate (milk, dark and white), different fillings (caramel, peanut butter and truffle), different flavours (orange, mint and cherry) and with or without nuts. Instead, people saw a confusing tangle of flavours, and retailers were unhappy trying to find shelf space for all these varieties. With sales and profits sagging, Hershey refocused its efforts to understand its customers' desires, needs and tastes better. Hershey then aligned its management teams in a strategic focus to meet those needs. The resulting turnabout and focus on customer needs rescued the company and restored its lustre.[17]

Competitors

Organizations in the same industry or type of business that provide goods or services to the same set of customers are referred to as competitors. Competitors are constantly battling for loyalty from the same group of customers. For example, managers at the US retailer Target realized customers were price matching merchandise in Target stores and later buying it at lower prices via Amazon. This procedure, known in the USA as 'showrooming', means that customers check out products in stores and then buy them cheaper online, which really hurts the bottom lines of traditional retailers, such as Target. In response to this new trend, Target managers immediately began pushing suppliers to offer products that were exclusively available at Target, as well as expanding the number of items available at Target.com. Walmart also felt the pinch of showrooming and started promoting the convenience of in-store pickups for online orders – many available the same day they are purchased.[18]

REFLECTION

- The **organizational environment** consists of both general and task environments and includes all elements, existing outside the boundaries of the organization, which have the potential to affect the organization.
- An **organizational ecosystem** includes organizations in all the sectors of the task and general environments that provide resource and information transactions, being flows and linkages necessary for an organization to thrive.
- The **general environment** indirectly influences all organizations within an industry and includes six dimensions.
- The **task environment** includes the sectors that conduct day-to-day transactions with the organization and directly influence its basic operations and performance.
- The **international dimension** of the external environment represents events originating in foreign countries, as well as opportunities for national companies in other countries.

- The **technological dimension** of the general environment includes scientific and technological advances in society.
- The **sociocultural dimension** includes demographic characteristics, norms, customs and values of a population, within which the organization operates.
- The **economic dimension** represents the general economic health of the country or region in which the organization operates.
- The **legal-political dimension** includes government regulations at the local, state and federal levels, as well as political activities designed to influence company behaviour.
- The **internal environment** includes elements within the organization's boundaries, such as employees, management and corporate culture.
- The **natural dimension** includes all elements that occur naturally on Earth, including plants, animals, rocks and natural resources such as air, water and climate.

Suppliers

Suppliers provide the raw materials that the organization uses to produce its output. A confectionary manufacturer, for example, may use suppliers from around the globe for ingredients such as cocoa beans, sugar and cream. A *supply chain* is a network of multiple businesses and individuals that are connected through the flow of products or services. For Toyota, the supply chain includes over 500 global parts suppliers organized by a production strategy called just-in-time (JIT).[19]

JIT improves an organization's return on investment, quality and efficiency because much less money is invested in idle inventory. In the 1970s, the Japanese taught US companies how to boost profit by keeping inventories lean through JIT. '*Instead of months' worth of inventory, there are now days and even hours of inventory*,' says Jim Lawton, head of supply management solutions at consultant Dun & Bradstreet. Lawton points out that there is a downside, however – one that became dramatically clear after a March 2011 earthquake in Japan: '*If supply is disrupted, as in this situation, there's nowhere to get the product*'.[20]

The recent crisis in Japan revealed the fragility of today's JIT supply chains. A powerful earthquake along the Pacific coastline triggered massive tsunami waves and caused the second-worst nuclear disaster in history at the Fukushima power plant. Japanese parts suppliers for the global auto industry were shut down, disrupting production at auto factories around the world. '*Even a missing $5 part can stop an assembly line*,' said a Morgan Stanley representative.[21]

Because of this natural disaster, Toyota's production was down 800 000 vehicles – 10 per cent of its annual output. Most organizations aren't willing to boost inventory to minimize risks of supply-chain disruptions. Boosting inventory even slightly to provide a cushion against disruptions can cost big companies millions of dollars. '*I don't see any of us moving away from a very disciplined supply chain management*,' said Ford Motor Company's finance chief, Lewis Booth.[22]

Labour market

The labour market represents people in the environment who can be hired to work for the organization. Every organization needs a supply of trained, qualified personnel. Unions, employee associations and the availability of certain classes of employees, can influence the organization's labour market. Labour market forces typically affecting organizations include: (1) the growing need for computer-literate knowledge workers, (2) the necessity for continuous investment in human resources through recruitment, education and training to meet the competitive demands of the borderless world and (3) the effects of international trading blocs, automation, outsourcing and shifting facility locations on labour dislocations, creating unused labour pools in some areas and labour shortages in others.

Changes in these various sectors of the general and task environments can create tremendous challenges, especially for organizations operating in complex, rapidly changing industries. Costco Wholesale Corporation, with warehouses throughout the world, is an example of an organization operating in a highly complex environment.

 INNOVATIVE WAY

Costco Wholesale Corporation

Costco Wholesale Corporation, a no-frills, self-service warehouse club, operates an international chain of membership warehouses offering a limited selection of products at reduced prices. Costco's business model focuses on maintaining its image as a pricing authority, consistently providing the most competitive prices. *'Everything we do is to provide goods and services to the customer at a lower price,'* said Jim Sinegal, its CEO and founder. Costco warehouses are designed to operate efficiently and to communicate value to members. The warehouse decor – high ceilings, metal roofs, exposed trusses – keeps costs low and contributes to the perception that Costco is for serious shoppers seeking serious bargains. Other strategies for keeping prices low include offering only 3600 unique products at a time (Walmart offers over 100 000) and negotiating low prices with suppliers.

Only about a quarter of sales come from outside the USA, but same store sales in overseas markets have been growing about four times faster than those in the USA. Costco plans to expand its customer base by delving further into the Asian markets, where consumer spending and growth is higher than mature US and European markets. Costco's complex environment is illustrated in Exhibit 3.4.

Costco's biggest competitive advantage is its workforce. *'Costco compensates employees very well, well above the industry in terms of wages and benefits*,' says R.J. Hottovey, a retail analyst at Morningstar. *'When retailers are cutting health benefits, Costco employees don't have to worry about that*,' he says. The happiness and morale of employees is often overlooked in the retail industry, but not at Costco. Thanks to its good treatment of workers, Costco has one of the lowest turnovers in the retail industry (only 6 per cent), and it earns $530 000 of revenue per employee.[23]

REFLECTION

- **Customers** are part of the task environment and include people and organizations that acquire goods or services from the organization.
- **Competitors** are organizations within the same industry or type of business that vie for the same set of customers.
- Traditional stores such as Target and Walmart are competing with online retailers such as Amazon and Zappos. In response they have set up their own clicks and bricks operations. Other retailers have installed PCs so that in-store shoppers can order goods online.
- **Suppliers** provide the raw materials the organization uses to produce its output.
- The **labour market** represents the people available for hire by the organization.

EXHIBIT 3.4 The external environment of Costco Wholesale Corporation

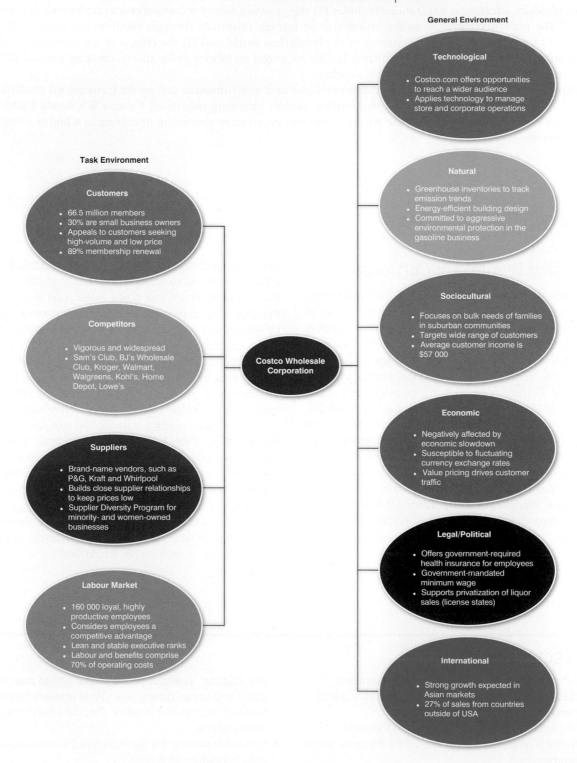

SOURCES: Costco Wholesale Corporation website,www.costco.com (accessed July 10, 2012); 'Costco Wholesale Corporation', *Marketline* (April 30, 2012): 3–9; Alaric DeArment, 'Costco's Lobbying Changes WA's Liquor Laws: Who Is Next?' DrugstoreNews.com, December 12, 2011, p. 12 (www.drugstorenews.com/article/costco%E2%80%99s-lobbying-changes-%E2%80%A9wa%E2%80%99s-liquor-laws-who-next); and Sharon Edelson, 'Costco Keeps Formula As It Expands', *Women's Wear Daily* (30 January 2012): 1.

Organization–environment relationship

Why do organizations care so much about factors in the external environment? The reason is that the environment often creates great uncertainty for organization managers, and they must be willing and able to respond by designing the organization to be adaptable to the environment. The consequences of non-response could be one of demise. Nokia and BlackBerry are prime examples of business failure with Microsoft and Google acquiring valuable intellectual property from the assets they respectively acquired.

Environmental uncertainty

Uncertainty means that managers do not have sufficient information about environmental factors to understand and predict environmental needs and changes.[24]

As indicated in Exhibit 3.5, environmental characteristics that influence uncertainty are the number of factors that affect the organization and the extent to which those factors change. Managers at a large multinational, such as Costco, must deal with thousands of factors in the external environment that create uncertainty. When external factors change rapidly, the organization experiences high uncertainty; examples are telecommunications and aerospace firms, computer and electronics companies, and Internet organizations. When MySpace's audience plummeted 27 per cent in 2010, managers struggled to identify the factors that were upending this fledgling social media service. One factor included the changing tastes of fickle social media customers, which are difficult to predict. When Facebook provided a better customer experience and a simple Google-like interface, customers left MySpace in droves. In fact, MySpace lost 9 million customers between 2009 and 2010.

When an organization deals with only a few external factors and these factors are relatively stable, such as those affecting soft-drink bottlers or food processors, managers experience low uncertainty and can devote less attention to external issues.

Adapting to the environment

Environmental changes may evolve unexpectedly, such as shifting customer tastes for social media sites, or they may occur violently, such as the devastating Japanese earthquake and tsunami. The level of turbulence

EXHIBIT 3.5 The external environment and uncertainty

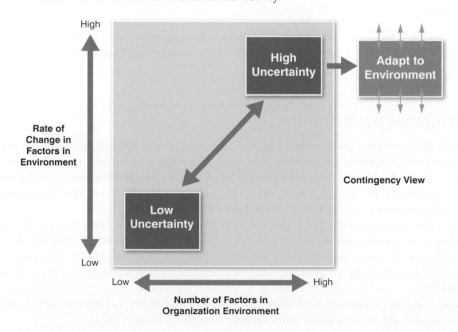

created by an environmental shift will determine the type of response that managers must make in order for the organization to survive. Managers should continuously scan the business horizon for both subtle and dramatic environmental changes, also called *strategic issues*, and identify those that require strategic responses. Strategic issues are events or forces either inside or outside an organization that are likely to alter its ability to achieve its objectives. As environmental turbulence increases, strategic issues emerge more frequently.[25]

Managers use several strategies to adapt to these strategic issues, including boundary-spanning roles, interorganizational partnerships and mergers or joint ventures.

Boundary-spanning roles

Boundary-spanning roles link to and coordinate the organization with key elements in the external environment. Boundary spanners serve two purposes for the organization: They detect and process information about changes in the environment, and they represent the organization's interests to the environment.[26]

As an example of boundary spanning, General Electric has recorded expenditure of $39.3 million on political lobbying to influence government officials to take actions that positively affect the company's business performance. GE's political lobbyists serve to span the boundary between the organization and the government, a critical aspect of the external environment.[27]

Another approach to boundary spanning is the use of *business intelligence*, which results from using sophisticated software to search through large amounts of internal and external data to spot patterns, trends and relationships that might be significant. For example, Verizon uses business intelligence software to monitor customer interactions and fix problems almost immediately.[28]

Business intelligence is related to the growing area of boundary spanning known as *competitive intelligence (CI)*, which refers to activities to get as much information as possible about one's rivals.[29]

Visa has an employee who searches the Web for 2 hours each day for insights on MasterCard and other competitors. Harley-Davidson hires an outside research firm to search through massive amounts of data and reveal patterns that help decipher and predict competitors' actions.[30]

Boundary spanning is an increasingly important task in organizations because environmental shifts can happen quickly in today's world. Managers need good information about their competitors, customers and other elements of the environment to make good decisions. Thus, the most successful companies involve everyone in boundary-spanning activities. The approach outlined above is nowadays often referred to as BIG DATA.

TAKE A MOMENT

Read the Ethical Dilemma at the end of this chapter that pertains to competitive intelligence (CI). Do you have the courage to risk your job by challenging the boss's inappropriate use of confidential information?

Interorganizational partnerships

With tough global competition, constantly changing technology and shifting government regulations, few companies can compete effectively unless they join with other firms in various partnerships. Organizations around the world are embedded in complex networks of confusing relationships – collaborating in some markets, competing fiercely in others. The number of corporate alliances has been increasing at a rate of 25 per cent annually, and many of those have been between competitors.[31]

For example, in the auto industry, Ford and General Motors (GM) compete fiercely, but the two joined together to develop a six-speed transmission. Hyundai, Chrysler and Mitsubishi jointly run the Global Engine Manufacturing Alliance to build four-cylinder engines. Volvo is now owned by Zhejiang Geely Holding Group of China, but it maintains an alliance with its previous owner, Ford, to supply engines and certain other components.[32]

In a partnership, each organization both supports and depends on the others for success, and perhaps for survival, but that doesn't mean they don't still compete fiercely in certain areas.[33]

Managers in partnering organizations shift from an adversarial orientation to a partnership orientation. The new paradigm, shown in Exhibit 3.6, is based on trust and the ability of partners to work out equitable solutions to conflicts, so that everyone profits from the relationship. Managers work to reduce costs and add value to both sides, rather than trying to get all the benefits for their own company. The new model is also characterized by a high level of information sharing, including e-business links for automatic ordering, payments and other transactions. In addition, person-to-person interaction provides corrective feedback and solves problems. People from other companies may be on-site, or they may participate in virtual teams to enable close coordination. Partners are frequently involved in one another's product design and production, and they are committed for the long term. It is not unusual for business partners to help one another, even outside of what is specified in the contract.[34]

EXHIBIT 3.6 The shift to a partnership paradigm

From adversarial orientation ⟶	To partnership orientation
Suspicion, competition, arm's length	Trust, value added to both sides
Price, efficiency, own profits	Equity, fair dealing, everyone profits
Information and feedback limited	e-Business links to share information and conduct digital transactions
Lawsuits to resolve conflict	Close coordination; virtual teams and people on-site
Minimal involvement and up front investment	Involvement in partner's product design and production
Short-term contracts	Long-term contracts
Contracts limit the relationship	Business assistance goes beyond the contract

CONCEPT CONNECTION

Already the largest drugstore chain in the USA, Walgreens decided to expand its business through a major acquisition in 2011. The company paid nearly $400 million to purchase the online health and beauty care product retailer, Drugstore.com. Mergers and acquisitions are one way organizations **adapt to an uncertain environment**.

Mergers and joint ventures

A step beyond strategic partnerships is for companies to become involved in mergers or joint ventures to reduce environmental uncertainty. A frenzy of merger and acquisition activity both in the USA and internationally in recent years is an attempt by organizations to cope with the tremendous volatility of the environment.[35]

A merger occurs when two or more organizations combine to become one. When managers saw sales of Corn Flakes and Rice Krispies fall flat as price-conscious consumers chose generic, private-label cereals instead, Kellogg bought Pringles from Procter & Gamble (P&G) in May 2012 to bolster its foreign snacks divisions. Growth for Kellogg, as well as for rivals PepsiCo and Frito-Lay, is in snack foods in foreign markets. 'We're not happy with our performance the last couple of years,' says Kellogg CEO, John A. Bryant. 'We have to keep bringing new foods to consumers and delighting them, because if we stand still, people catch up'. With the merger, Kellogg gains not only a snack that is already hugely popular internationally, but also a group of P&G merchandisers that understand global markets.[36]

A joint venture involves a strategic alliance or programme by two or more organizations. A joint venture typically occurs when a project is too complex, expensive or uncertain for one firm to handle alone. Sikorsky Aircraft and Lockheed Martin, for example, teamed up to bid on a new contract for a fleet of Marine One helicopters. The joint venture would have Sikorsky building the helicopters and Lockheed Martin providing the vast array of specialized systems that each one uses. Although the two companies have previously competed to build presidential helicopters, they joined together to be more competitive against rivals such as Boeing, Bell Helicopters, and Finmeccanica SpA's Agusta Westland.[37]

Joint ventures are on the rise as companies strive to keep pace with rapid technological change and compete in the global economy.

REFLECTION

- When external factors change rapidly, the organization experiences high uncertainty.
- Strategic issues are events and forces that alter an organization's ability to achieve its goals. As environmental turbulence increases, strategic issues emerge more frequently.
- Boundary-spanning roles link to and coordinate the organization with key elements in the external environment.

- Interorganizational partnerships reduce boundaries and increase collaboration with other organizations.
- A merger occurs when two or more organizations combine to become one.
- A joint venture is a strategic alliance or program by two or more organizations.

The international environment: corporate culture

The internal environment within which managers work includes corporate culture, production technology, organization structure and physical facilities. Of these, corporate culture surfaces as extremely important to competitive advantage. The internal culture must fit the needs of the external environment and company strategy. When this fit occurs, highly committed employees create a high-performance organization that is tough to beat.[38]

Most people don't think about culture; it's just 'how we do things around here' or 'the way things are here'. However, managers have to think about culture because it typically plays a significant role in organizational success.[39]

Organizational culture has been defined and studied in many and varied ways. For the purposes of this chapter, we define culture as the set of key values, beliefs, understandings and norms shared by members of an organization. The concept of culture helps managers understand the hidden, complex aspects of organizational life. Culture is a pattern of shared values and assumptions about how things are done within the organization. This pattern is learned by members as they cope with external and internal problems and taught to new members as the correct way to perceive, think and feel. Corruption of core values has been seen by many commentators as being a major contributing factor to the 2008 crisis that affected the global financial industry. At its peak the markets froze and major banks would not lend to each other.

The excessive self-efficacy of Lehman Bros CEO was aptly described by Partnoy, in the *Financial Times*, as hubris, Richard Fuld of Lehman Bros being nominated as an exemplar of negative hubristic behaviour. The headline of 14 September 2008 read *Fulds – thou art Hubris*.

Although strong corporate cultures are important, they can also sometimes promote negative values and behaviours. When the actions of top leaders are unethical, for instance, the entire culture can become contaminated. Consider what happened at News Corporation, a corporate giant with a lucrative string of media properties all over the world. Rupert Murdoch, chairman and CEO, has been accused of frequently applying unethical, sometimes seedy tactics in his business dealings. In addition, Murdoch has allegedly used 'blunt force' spending to cover up unscrupulous tactics and silence critics with multimillion dollar payoffs. '*Bury your mistakes*,' Murdoch was fond of saying.[40]

But he couldn't bury the scandal that rocked the organization after journalists working for News Corporation newspapers allegedly hacked private voicemail messages and offered bribes to police in the pursuit of hot scoops. Journalists went so far as to hack the voicemail of a murdered 13-year-old girl, Milly Dowler, while she was still listed as missing.[41]

As this example illustrates, the values and behaviours of top leaders have the potential to shape significantly the decisions made by employees throughout the organization.[42]

Mark Lewis, the lawyer for the family of the murdered girl, pointed out: '*This is not just about one individual, but about the culture of an organization*'.

Culture can be analyzed at two levels, as illustrated in Exhibit 3.7.[43]

EXHIBIT 3.7 Levels of corporate culture

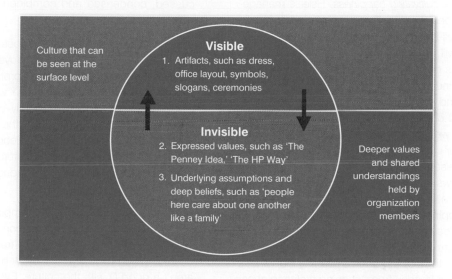

At the surface level are visible artefacts, which include aspects such as manner of dress, patterns of behaviour, physical symbols, organizational ceremonies and office layout. Visible artefacts are all the things one can see, hear and observe by watching members of the organization. At a deeper, less obvious level are values and beliefs, which are not observable but can be discerned from how people explain and justify what they do. Members of the organization hold some values at a conscious level. These values can be interpreted from the stories, language and symbols that organization members use to represent them.

Some values become so deeply embedded in a culture that members are no longer consciously aware of them. These basic, underlying assumptions and beliefs are the essence of culture and subconsciously guide behaviour and decisions. In some organizations, a basic assumption might be that people are essentially lazy and will shirk their duties whenever possible; thus, employees are closely supervised and given little freedom, and colleagues are frequently suspicious of one another. More enlightened organizations operate on the basic assumption that people want to do a good job; in these organizations, employees are given more freedom and responsibility and colleagues trust one another and work cooperatively. At the Zappos Family of companies, a culture of well-being and happiness has been instrumental in the growth of this successful online retailer.

The Zappos Family of companies has created a unique culture that is reflected in its core values. Fundamental values are demonstrated in organizations through symbols, stories, heroes, slogans and ceremonies. Zappos also uses the core values to facilitate dismissal of employees. Thus they are 'hire and fire' corporate values.

Symbols

A symbol is an object, act, or event that conveys meaning to others. Symbols can be considered a rich non-verbal language, which vibrantly conveys the organization's important core values concerning how people relate to one another and interact with the environment. Mindy Grossman, CEO of HSN Inc., found that

💡 INNOVATIVE WAY

Zappos Family

Zappos.com, an online retail site best known for its wide selection of shoes and its free shipping, boldly proclaims its unique culture in an offbeat set of ten core values. CEO Tony Hsieh believes that these values illustrate the company's innovative culture and demonstrate its ultimate business goal – *cultivating happiness*. Hsieh's management theory goes like this: If you create a work culture that fosters well-being and good practices, (eventually) good profits will naturally flow out of the operation. So far, his theory is producing outstanding business results. Zappos.com, Inc. is achieving $1 billion plus of annual gross sales, and employees widely report that their work is exciting and challenging. '*We really buy into the idea that the better we treat each other, the better we'll all be able to treat our customers,*' says Rebecca Ratner, director of human resources.

Hsieh knows first-hand how important a strong, positive culture is when it comes to employee and customer happiness. Before Zappos, he had experienced the joyless grind of working in a job that had no meaning, where technical skill was all that mattered. Hsieh decided to write the book *Delivering Happiness* to document his journey from 'chasing profits to chasing passion', the life lessons he has learned, and how those lessons have been applied at Zappos. Here are some key points for business leaders:

- *Get the right values.* Zappos has a set of ten core values that include 'Create fun and a little

weirdness'; 'Deliver WOW through service'; 'Embrace and drive change'; 'Be adventurous, creative and open-minded'; 'Pursue growth and learning'; and 'Be humble'. But Hsieh didn't dictate the values from on high. He sent an email to all employees asking them what values should guide the company. The responses were discussed, condensed and combined to come up with the final list.

- *Get the right people.* Zappos does two sets of interviews when hiring new employees. The first focuses on relevant experience, professional and technical skills, and the ability to work with the team. The second focuses purely on culture fit. There are questions for each of the core values, such as 'How weird are you?' People are carefully selected to fit the Zappos culture, even if that means rejecting people with stronger technical skills.

- *Make culture a top priority.* All employees attend a 4-week training session and commit the core values to memory. At the end of training, they're offered $2000 to resign if they believe that they aren't a good fit with the culture. Every year, Zappos puts out a *Culture Book*, in which employees share their own stories about what the Zappos culture means to them.

SOURCE: Copyright © 2010 Zappos.com, Inc. or its affiliates. Used by permission.

something as simple as an office chair can be symbolic. When Grossman became HSN's eighth CEO in 10 years, she inherited a downtrodden workforce. During her first few months, Grossman learned as much about the business as possible. '*As I grew to understand the business, it became clear that it was fundamentally broken. To fix it, I needed to dramatically alter the company's culture,*' she said. Part of the cultural transformation included improving the work environment, which had dirty offices full of broken-down office furniture and clutter. '*I looked around and realized we had 40 different kinds of office chairs. So I bought several thousand Herman Miller Aeron chairs,*' said Grossman. She received over 100 emails expressing appreciation on the day they were delivered.[44] For Grossman, the new office chairs were an important symbol of a new company value of caring for employees.

Stories

A story is a narrative based on true events and is repeated frequently and shared among organizational employees. Stories paint pictures that help symbolize the firm's vision and values and help employees personalize and absorb them.[45]

CONCEPT CONNECTION

Toyota's handling of its 2010 recall crisis drove some observers to characterize Toyota's **corporate culture** as parochial. Critics attributed the company's reticence to go public with its quality problems to its deep roots in Japanese culture, in which airing dirty linen in public is impolite. However, the Toyota culture has also been historically linked with a powerful commitment to quality, which enabled the company, under the leadership of president and CEO Akio Toyoda (pictured here at an award ceremony after the FIFA World Cup in Japan), to return to its previous strong market position within a couple of years.

A frequently told story at UPS (a highly regulated organization) concerns an employee who, without authorization, ordered an extra Boeing 737 to ensure timely delivery of a load of Christmas packages that had been left behind in the holiday rush. As the story goes, rather than punishing the worker, UPS rewarded his initiative. By telling this story, UPS workers communicate that the company stands behind its commitment to worker autonomy and customer service.[46]

Heroes

A hero is a figure who exemplifies the deeds, character and attributes of a strong culture. Heroes are role models for employees to follow. Heroes with strong legacies may continue to influence a culture even after they are gone. Many people have wondered if the culture that Steve Jobs created at Apple would be sustained after his death in 2011. Jobs exemplified the creativity, innovation, risk-taking and boundary-breaking thinking that made the company famous.[47]

When Jobs's health began to fail, Apple's board began considering replacements who could sustain the fertile culture that Jobs created. They chose Tim Cook, who long had served as second-in-command. Cook now cultivates a culture that reflects the values and behaviours of Apple's hero, Steve Jobs. '*Apple has a culture of excellence that is, I think, so unique and so special. I'm not going to witness or permit the change of it,*' he said.[48]

Slogans

A slogan is a phrase or sentence that succinctly expresses a key corporate value. Many companies use a slogan or saying to convey special meaning to employees. For example, Disney uses the slogan 'The happiest place on earth'. The Ritz-Carlton Hotel adopted the slogan, 'Ladies and gentlemen taking care of ladies and gentlemen' to demonstrate its cultural commitment to take care of both employees and customers. '*We're in the service business, and service comes only from people. Our promise is to take care of them, and provide a happy place for them to work,*' said general manager, Mark DeCocinis, who managed the Portman Hotel in Shanghai, recipient of the 'Best Employer in Asia' award for 3 consecutive years.[49]

Cultural values can also be discerned in written public statements, such as corporate mission statements or other formal statements that express the core values of the organization. The mission statement for Hallmark Cards, for example, emphasizes values of excellence, ethical and moral conduct in all relationships, business innovation and corporate social responsibility.[50]

Ceremonies

A ceremony is a planned activity at a special event that is conducted for the benefit of an audience. Managers hold ceremonies to provide dramatic examples of company values. Ceremonies are special occasions that reinforce valued accomplishments, create a bond among people by allowing them to share an important event and anoint and celebrate heroes.[51]

In a ceremony to mark its 20th anniversary, Southwest Airlines rolled out a speciality plane called the 'Lone Star One', which had the Texas state flag painted on it to signify the company's start in Texas. Later, when the National Basketball Association (NBA) chose Southwest Airlines as the league's official airline, Southwest launched another speciality plane, the 'Slam Dunk One', coloured blue and orange with a large basketball painted on the nose of the plane. Today, ten speciality planes celebrate significant milestones in Southwest's history and demonstrate key cultural values.[52]

REFLECTION

- Organizational culture is the set of key values, beliefs, understandings and norms shared by members of an organization.
- A symbol is an object, act or event that conveys meaning to others.
- A story is a narrative based on true events and is repeated frequently and shared among organizational employees.
- A hero is a figure who exemplifies the deeds, character and attributes of a strong culture.
- Steve Jobs was a hero at Apple, representing the creativity, risk-taking and striving for excellence values that define the company's culture.

- A slogan, such as Disney's 'The happiest place on earth', succinctly expresses a key corporate value.
- Managers hold ceremonies, planned activities at special events, to reinforce company values.
- Dysfunctional executives can cause havoc and chaos and the consequences are value destruction and poor corporate morale – checks and balances need to be in place (See Chapter 17 online).
- Legislation to encourage and protect 'whistle-blowers' has been enacted in the UK and the USA in recent years and scholars are attempting to develop detection frameworks and models (termed legitimate dissent).

Types of culture

A big influence on internal corporate culture is the external environment. Cultures can vary widely across organizations; however, organizations within the same industry often reveal similar cultural characteristics because they are operating in similar environments.[53]

The internal culture should embody what it takes to succeed in the environment. If the external environment requires extraordinary customer service, the culture should encourage good service; if it calls for careful technical decision-making, cultural values should reinforce managerial decision-making.

In considering what cultural values are important for the organization, managers consider the external environment as well as the company's strategy and goals. Studies suggest that the right fit between culture, strategy and the environment is associated with four categories or types of culture, as illustrated in Exhibit 3.8. These categories are based on two dimensions. First, the extent to which the external environment requires flexibility or stability. Second, the extent to which a company's strategic focus is internal or external. The four categories associated with these differences are adaptability, achievement, involvement and consistency.[54]

Adaptability culture

The adaptability culture emerges in an environment that requires fast response and high-risk decision-making. Managers encourage values that support the company's ability to rapidly detect, interpret and translate signals from the environment into new behaviours. Employees have the autonomy to make decisions and act freely to meet new needs, and responsiveness to customers is highly valued. Managers also actively create change by encouraging and rewarding creativity, experimentation and risk taking. Lush Cosmetics, a fast-growing maker of shampoos, lotions and bath products,[55] provides a good example of an adaptability culture. A guiding motto at the company is '*We reserve the right to make mistakes*'. Founder and CEO, Mark Constantine, is passionately devoted to change and encourages employees to break boundaries, experiment and take risks. The company kills off one-third of its product line every year to offer new and offbeat products. Other companies in the cosmetics industry, as well as those involved in electronics, e-commerce and fashion, often use an adaptability culture because they must move quickly to respond to rapid changes in the environment. There is, however, an inherent danger that a risk-taking culture can become dysfunctional and be value-destroying.

EXHIBIT 3.8 Four types of corporate culture

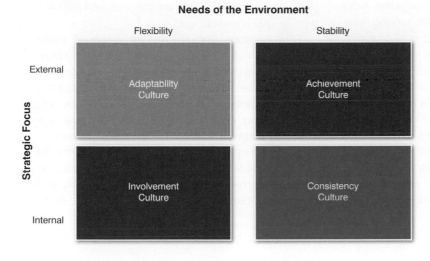

SOURCES: D. R. Denison and A. K. Mishra, 'Toward a Theory of Organizational Culture and Effectiveness', *Organization Science* 6, no. 2 (March–April 1995): 204–223; R. Hooijberg and F. Petrock, 'On Cultural Change: Using the Competing Values Framework to Help Leaders Execute a Transformational Strategy', *Human Resource Management* 32, no.1 (1993): 29–50; and R. E. Quinn, *Beyond Rational Management: Mastering the Paradoxes and Competing Demands of High Performance* (San Francisco: Jossey-Bass, 1988).

Achievement culture

The achievement culture is suited to organizations concerned with serving specific customers in the external environment, but without the intense need for flexibility and rapid change. This results-oriented culture values competitiveness, aggressiveness, personal initiative, cost cutting and willingness to work long and hard to achieve results. An emphasis on winning and achieving specific ambitious goals is the glue that holds the organization together.[56]

Brewing giant InBev provides an example. When InBev bought Anheuser-Busch, it replaced lavish perks and generous spending with a no-frills culture, focused intently on cost cutting and meeting strict profit goals. Managers also created an incentive-based compensation system to reflect 'an increased focus on meritocracy'. The system handsomely rewards high performers rather than spreading dollars more evenly among employees. '*We always say, the leaner the business, the more money we'll have at the end of the year to share,*' Carlos Brito, InBev's CEO.[57]

Involvement culture

The involvement culture emphasizes an internal focus on the involvement and participation of employees to adapt rapidly to changing needs from the environment. This culture places high value on meeting the needs of employees, and the organization may be characterized by a caring, family-like atmosphere. Managers emphasize values such as cooperation, consideration of both employees and customers, and avoiding status differences. Consider the Four Seasons hotel chain, where the culture embodies a commitment to the company's greatest asset – its employees. Such a culture values empathy towards frontline staff – not just the customers.

INNOVATIVE WAY

Four Seasons

Four Seasons is considered by many people to be the world's premier hospitality company, offering a worldwide chain of luxury hotels and resorts. One reason is that it consistently inspires employees to provide exceptional, customized 24-hour service and strive for the goal of creating *the world's best hospitality experience'*. The company has been named one of the '100 Best Companies to Work For' by *Fortune* magazine every year since the survey's inception in 1998, ranking number 85 in 2012. With 86 luxury properties in 35 countries, Four Seasons has nurtured a corporate culture that values employees above all other assets. This relentless commitment to employees has sustained Four Seasons during an economic recession that battered many companies in the hospitality industry. With most of the industry in shambles as holidaymakers and business travellers cancelled travel plans, how did Four Seasons stay on track and position itself for future success?

Managers created a unified culture where employees rallied behind an inspiring purpose. The purpose of Four Seasons – to create the world's best hospitality experience – is a deeply instilled belief that each employee takes personally. *'We have 34 000 employees who get up every morning thinking about how to serve our guests even better than the day before,'* said CEO, Katie Taylor. *'So while all of this trouble is swirling around us, our brand's promise of providing the most exceptional guest experience, wherever and whenever you visit us, is instilled in the hearts and minds of our dedicated employees. They are the ones who fulfill that promise day in and day out'.*

Four Seasons also clarified its corporate vision by ensuring that it could be personalized by employees and provide stability through an unpredictable recession. The 2012 vision included: (1) achieving a first-choice ranking among guests, (2) being the best employer and (3) being the industry's number one builder of sustainable value. These clear and meaningful statements provided a compelling and aspirational vision that motivates employees to do their best. The results were that bookings went up dramatically, and employee engagement scores were higher than ever.

Consistency culture

The final category of culture, the consistency culture, uses an internal focus and a consistency orientation for a stable environment. Following the rules and being thrifty are valued, and the culture supports and rewards a methodical, rational, orderly way of doing things. In today's fast-changing world, few companies operate in a stable environment, and most managers are shifting towards cultures that are more flexible and in tune with changes in the environment. eBay founder Pierre Omidyar's attitude was to work a standard day and recruit senior managers to run the business (such as Meg Whitman who joined from Playskool). A detailed profile of his modus operandus is provided in Chapter 16.

Each of these four categories of culture can be successful. In addition, organizations usually have values that fall into more than one category. The relative emphasis on various cultural values depends on the needs of the environment and the organization's focus. Managers are responsible for instilling the cultural values the organization needs to be successful in its environment.

Shaping corporate culture for innovative response

Research conducted by a Stanford University professor indicates that the one factor that increases a company's value the most is people and how they are treated.[58]

In addition, surveys show that CEOs often cite organizational culture as their most important mechanism for attracting, motivating and retaining talented employees, a capability considered the single best predictor of overall organizational excellence.[59]

In a survey of Canadian senior executives, fully 82 per cent believe a direct correlation exists between culture and financial performance.[60] Consider how an 'employees first' corporate culture drives stellar financial performance at Southwest Airlines. Profitable for 38 consecutive years and touting the lowest ratio

NEW MANAGER SELF-TEST

Culture Preference

INSTRUCTIONS The fit between a new manager and organizational culture can determine success and satisfaction. To understand your culture preference, rank the items below from 1 to 8 based on the strength of your preference (1 = strongest preference).

1 The organization is very personal, much like an extended family.

2 The organization is dynamic and changing, where people take risks.

3 The organization is achievement oriented, with the focus on competition and getting jobs done.

4 The organization is stable and structured, with clarity and established procedures.

5 Management style is characterized by teamwork and participation.

6 Management style is characterized by innovation and risk taking.

7 Management style is characterized by high performance demands and achievement

8 Management style is characterized by security and predictability.

SCORING & INTERPRETATION Each question pertains to one of the four types of culture in Exhibit 3.8. To compute your preference for each type of culture, add together the scores for each set of two questions as follows:

Involvement culture – total for questions 1, 5: _____

Adaptability culture – total for questions 2, 6: _____

Achievement culture – total for questions 3, 7: _____

Consistency culture – total for questions 4, 8: _____

A lower score means a stronger culture preference. You will probably be more comfortable and more effective as a new manager in a corporate culture that is compatible with your personal preferences. A higher score means the culture would not fit your expectations, and you would have to change your style and preference to be comfortable. Review the text discussion of the four culture types. Do your cultural preference scores seem correct to you? Can you think of companies that fit your culture preference?

SOURCE: Kim S. Cameron and Robert D. Quinn, *Diagnosing and Changing Organizational Culture* (Reading, MA: Addison-Wesley, 1999).

REFLECTION

- For an organization to be effective, corporate culture should be aligned with organizational strategy and the needs of the external environment.
- Organizations within the same industry often reveal similar cultural characteristics because they are operating in similar environments.
- The adaptability culture is characterized by values that support the company's ability to interpret and translate signals from the environment into new behaviour responses.

- An achievement culture is a results-oriented culture that values competitiveness, personal initiative and achievement.
- A culture that places high value on meeting the needs of employees and values cooperation and equality is an involvement culture.
- A consistency culture values and rewards a methodical, rational, orderly way of doing things.

of complaints per passengers in the industry, Southwest offers industry-leading salaries and benefits, intense career development programmes, and a commitment to diversity among its workforce. In addition, Southwest promotes a strong collaborative culture and fosters good relationships with organized labour.[61]

At Southwest, a positive culture that reflects an intense commitment to employees results in a competitive advantage.

Corporate culture plays a key role in creating an organizational climate that enables learning and innovative responses to threats from the external environment, challenging new opportunities or organizational crises. However, managers realize they can't focus all their effort on values; they also need a commitment to solid business performance.

Managing the high-performance culture

Companies that succeed in a turbulent world are those that pay careful attention to both cultural values *and* business performance. Cultural values can energize and motivate employees by appealing to higher ideals and unifying people around shared goals. In addition, values boost performance by shaping and guiding employee behaviour, so that everyone's actions are aligned with strategic priorities.[62]

Exhibit 3.9 illustrates four organizational outcomes based on the relative attention managers pay to cultural values and business performance.[63] For example, a company in Quadrant C pays little attention to either values or business results and is unlikely to survive for long. Managers in Quadrant D organizations are highly focused on creating a strong cohesive culture, but they don't tie organizational values directly to goals and desired business results.

When cultural values aren't connected to business performance, they aren't likely to benefit the organization during hard times. The corporate culture at the LEGO Group, with headquarters in Billund, Denmark, nearly doomed the toymaker in the 1990s when sales plummeted as children turned from traditional toys to video games. At that time, LEGO reflected the characteristics found in Quadrant D of Exhibit 3.9. Imagination and creativity, not business performance, were what guided the company. The attitude among employees was, 'We're doing great stuff for kids – don't bother us with financial goals'. A new CEO, Jørgen Vig Knudstorp, upended the corporate culture with a new employee motto: 'I am here to make money for the company'.

EXHIBIT 3.9 Combining culture and performance

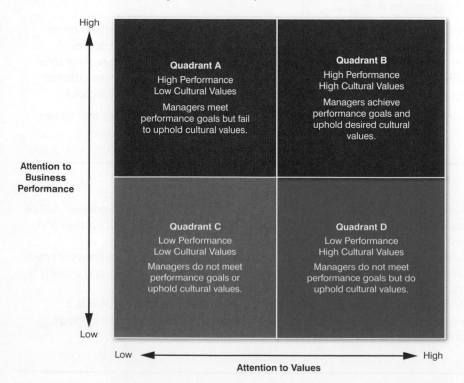

SOURCES: Jeff Rosenthal and Mary Ann Masarech, 'High-performance cultures: How values can drive business results', *Journal of Organizational Excellence* (Spring 2003): 3–18; and Dave Ulrich, Steve Kerr and Ron Ashkenas, Figure 11-2, GE leadership decision matrix, the GE work-out: How to implement GE's revolutionary method for busting bureaucracy and attacking organizational problems – fast! (New York: McGraw-Hill, 2002), p. 230.

CONCEPT CONNECTION

Furthering Target's partnerships with unique designer brands, the idea to create the new Shops at Target in-store boutiques was born in Target's **high-performance culture**. Target has quarterly Big Idea internal contests, in which departments compete for additional budget allocations awarded for innovative ideas. The fun, creative competition encourages a sense of employee ownership and reinforces shared values. Tapping into employee talent helps Target meet its mission of providing customers with more for less.

The shift to bottom-line results had a profound impact, and LEGO has become one of the most successful companies in the toy industry.[64]

'If you see your job not as chief strategy officer and the guy who has all the ideas, but rather as the guy who is obsessed with enabling employees to create value, I think you will succeed.'
— VINEET NAYAR, CEO OF HCL
TECHNOLOGIES

Quadrant A represents organizations that are focused primarily on bottom-line results and pay little attention to organizational values. This approach may be profitable in the short run, but the success is difficult to sustain over the long term because the 'glue' that holds the organization together – that is, shared cultural values – is missing. Consider how a bottom-line focus at Zynga, the Web's largest social games company, damaged the organization. Zynga, founded in July 2007 and led by CEO Mark Pincus, recorded a phenomenal $828 million in revenue in the first 9 months of 2011, more than double the amount earned a year earlier. Zynga also met ambitious profitability goals, rare among Internet start-ups. With this type of financial performance, one might assume working for Zynga would be all fun and games. Instead, autonomous teams for each game, like FarmVille and CityVille, worked under aggressive deadlines and were continuously challenged to meet lofty performance goals. Managers emphasized performance reports, relentlessly aggregating data, and using the data to demote or fire weak employees. Little attention was paid to cultural values that bind people into a unified whole, during these formative years.

The relentless focus on financial performance began to take a toll when employees started voicing their frustration, complaining about long hours and aggressive deadlines. Former employees describe emotionally charged encounters, including loud outbursts from Pincus, threats from top managers, and moments when colleagues broke down in tears. The company's success probably cannot be sustained without an increased focus on building a more positive culture. Already, valued employees are being lured away by competitors in an industry where talent is scarce.[65]

Finally, companies in Quadrant B put high emphasis on both culture and solid business performance as drivers of organizational success. Managers in these organizations align values with the company's day-to-day operations – hiring practices, performance management, budgeting, criteria for promotions and rewards and so forth. Consider the approach that General Electric (GE) took to accountability and performance management. When he was CEO, Jack Welch helped GE become one of the world's most successful and admired companies. He achieved this by creating a culture in which risk was rewarded and accountability and measurable goals were keys to individual success and company profitability.[66]

The company's traditional approach had achieved stellar financial results, but managers motivated people to perform primarily through control, intimidation and reliance on a small circle of staff. Welch was interested in more than just financial results – he wanted managers to exhibit the following cultural values in addition to 'making their numbers':[67]

■ Have a passion for excellence and hate bureaucracy.

■ Be open to ideas from anywhere.

■ 'Live' quality, and drive cost and speed for competitive advantage.

Welch knew that for the company to succeed in a rapidly changing world, managers needed to pay careful attention to both cultural values and business performance. Quadrant D organizations represent the high-performance culture, a culture that (1) is based on a solid organizational mission or purpose, (2) embodies shared adaptive values that guide decisions and business practices and (3) encourages individual employee ownership of both bottom-line results and the organization's cultural backbone.[68]

One of the most important things managers do is create and influence organizational culture to meet strategic goals because culture has a significant impact on performance.[69]

In *Corporate Culture and Performance*, John Kotter and James Heskett provided evidence that companies that intentionally managed cultural values outperformed similar companies that did not. Recent research validates that elements of corporate culture are positively correlated with higher financial performance. But there is evidence that a culture that is weak on corporate ethics without 'checks and balances' can go off the rails.

Following the departure of Bob Diamond of Barclays Bank Plc, a UK government agency under Anthony Salz conducted an enquiry costing almost £15 million into the bank's mis-governance and provided 34 recommendations to change the corporate culture and eschew a level of corporate governance appropriate to an international bank.

Cultural leadership

A primary way in which managers shape cultural norms and values to build a high-performance culture is through *cultural leadership*. Managers must *overcommunicate* to ensure that employees understand the new culture values, and they signal these values in actions as well as words.

A cultural leader defines and uses signals and symbols to influence corporate culture. Cultural leaders influence culture in two key areas:

1   *The cultural leader articulates a vision for the organizational culture that employees can believe in.* The leader defines and communicates central values that employees believe in and will rally around. Values are tied to a clear and compelling mission, or core purpose.

2   *The cultural leader heeds the day-to-day activities that reinforce the cultural vision.* The leader makes sure that work procedures and reward systems match and reinforce the values. Actions speak louder than words, so cultural leaders 'walk their talk'.[70]

Managers widely communicate the cultural values through words and actions. Values statements that aren't reinforced by management behaviour are meaningless, or even harmful, for employees and the organization. Whole Foods founder and CEO John Mackey wants his managers to place more value on creating 'a better person, company, and world' than on pursuing personal financial gain. To demonstrate his personal commitment to this belief, he asked the board of directors to donate all his future stock options to the company's two foundations:[71] the Animal Compassion Foundation and the Whole Planet Foundation.

Leaders should also uphold their commitment to values during difficult times or crises. Upholding the cultural values helps organizations weather a crisis and come out stronger on the other side. Creating and maintaining a high-performance culture is not easy in today's turbulent environment and changing workplace, but through their words – and particularly their actions – cultural leaders let everyone in the organization know what really counts.

REFLECTION

- Managers emphasize both values and business results to create a **high-performance culture**.
- Culture enables solid business performance through the alignment of motivated employees with the mission and goals of the company.
- Managers create and sustain adaptive high-performance cultures through cultural leadership.
- **Cultural leaders** define and articulate important values that are tied to a clear and compelling mission, which they communicate widely and uphold through their actions.

DISCUSSION QUESTIONS

1   a) Evaluate the characteristics of a flat world (a term used by Thomas Friedman to describe a homogenized business environment), discussing the challenges that a hyper-globalist world view of globalization poses and b) Suggest how managers can prepare to manage effectively should this become the new natural order.

2   Compare and contrast the task environment for a mobile phone provider to that of a government agency.

3   Determine the specific resource issues that have the potential to create geopolitical uncertainty in two of the following industries: a) Agriculture b) Clothing, c) Automobiles and d) Logistics and Distribution.

4   Many companies are 'going green' or adopting more environmentally friendly business strategies. What do they hope to gain and what is the likelihood that they will be successful?

5   Cultural symbols are usually noticed through sight, sound, touch and smell. Compare and contrast a discount retailer, such as Aldi, to that of a major long-established bank. What do these elements communicate as symbols between Aldi's and your choice of bank's respective corporate cultures?

6   As public sector organizations seek to become more 'business-like' to what extent do they need to gain a better understanding of their 'customers' and external environment? How might this impact on the internal culture of their organization?

Are you fit for managerial uncertainty?[72]

In an organization in a highly uncertain environment, everything seems to be in a state of flux. In this context an important quality for a new manager is '*mindfulness*'. This includes the qualities of being open-minded, critical, analytical and deploying creative approaches to decision-making. In a stable environment, a manager with a closed mindset may perform adequately because much work can still be done in the same tried and tested ways. In an uncertain environment, even a new manager needs to facilitate new thinking, new ideas and new ways of working. A high score on the test items suggests a higher level of mindfulness and thus a better fit with an uncertain environment. The authors share the view that criticality is an essential management attribute and the need to seek and use factual evidence, as well as feelings, is of paramount importance.

INSTRUCTIONS Do you approach uncertainty with an open mind? Think back to how you thought or behaved during a time of uncertainty when you were in a formal or informal leadership position. Please answer whether each of the following items was 'Mostly true' or 'Mostly false' in that circumstance.

	High priority	Low priority
1 Enjoyed hearing about new ideas even when trying to meet a deadline.	☐	☐
2 Welcomed unusual viewpoints of others, even if we were working under pressure.	☐	☐
3 Made it a point to attend industry trade shows and company events.	☐	☐
4 Specifically encouraged others to express opposing ideas and arguments.	☐	☐
5 Asked 'dumb' questions.	☐	☐
6 Always offered comments on the meaning of data or issues.	☐	☐
7 Expressed a controversial opinion to bosses and peers.	☐	☐
8 Suggested ways of improving my and others' ways of doing things.	☐	☐

SCORING & INTERPRETATION Give yourself one point for each item that you marked as Mostly True. If you scored less than 5, you might want to start your career as a manager in a stable rather than an unstable environment. A score of 5 or above suggests a higher level of mindfulness and a better fit for a new manager in an organization with an uncertain environment.

In an organization in a highly uncertain environment, everything seems to be in a state of flux. In this context an important quality for a new manager is 'mindfulness', which includes the qualities of being open-minded and an independent thinker. In a stable environment a manager with a closed mind may perform adequately because much work can still be done in the same old way. In an uncertain environment, even a new manager needs to facilitate new thinking, new ideas and new ways of working. A high score on the preceding items suggests higher mindfulness and a better fit with an uncertain environment.

APPLY YOUR SKILLS: ETHICAL DILEMMA

Competitive intelligence predicament[73]

Miquel Vasquez was proud of his job as a new product manager for a biotechnology start-up, and he loved the high stakes and tough decisions that went along with the job. But as he sat in his den after a long day, he was troubled, struggling over what had happened earlier that day and the information that he now possessed.

Just before lunch, Miquel's boss had handed him a stack of private strategic documents from their closest competitor. It was a competitive intelligence gold mine – product plans, pricing strategies, partnership agreements and other documents, most of them clearly marked 'proprietary and confidential'. When Miquel asked where the documents came from, his boss told him with a touch of pride that he had taken them right off the competing firm's server. 'I got into a private section of their intranet and downloaded everything that looked interesting,' he said. Later, realizing Miquel was suspicious, the boss would say only that he had obtained 'electronic access' via a colleague and had not personally broken any passwords. Maybe not, Miquel thought to himself, but this situation wouldn't pass the *60 Minutes* test. If word of this acquisition of a competitor's confidential data ever got out to the press, the company's reputation would be ruined.

Miquel didn't feel good about using these materials. He spent the afternoon searching for answers to his dilemma, but found no clear company policies or regulations that offered any guidance. His sense of fair play told him that using the information was unethical, if not downright illegal. What bothered him even more was the knowledge that this kind of thing might happen again. Using this confidential information would certainly give him and his company a competitive advantage, but Miquel wasn't sure that he wanted to work for a firm that would stoop to such tactics.

What would you do?

1   Go ahead and use the documents to the company's benefit, but make clear to your boss that you don't want him passing confidential information to you in the future. If he threatens to fire you, threaten to leak the news to the press.

2   Confront your boss privately and let him know you're uncomfortable with how the documents were obtained and what possession of them says about the company's culture. In addition to the question of the legality of using the information, point out that it is a public relations nightmare waiting to happen.

3   Talk to the company's legal counsel and contact the Society of Competitive Intelligence Professionals for guidance. Then, with their opinions and facts to back you up, go to your boss.

APPLY YOUR SKILLS: CASE FOR CRITICAL ANALYSIS

Corporate culture: The Asian Steel Corporation's Code of Conduct

The Asian Steel Corporation's (ASC) core purpose is to improve the quality of life of the communities it serves globally, through long-term stakeholder value creation based on leadership with trust.

Good corporate citizenship is part of ASC's corporate philosophy and a substantial percentage of the equity of ASC is held by philanthropic trusts. As a result of this unique ownership structure and ethos of serving the community, the ASC name has gained global respect and is trusted for its adherence to strong values and business ethics.

Anchored in Asia and wedded to traditional values and strong ethics, ASC is building multinational businesses that achieve growth through excellence and innovation, while balancing the interests of shareholders, employees and civil society. With a work culture that embraces ethics, value systems, comfortable and safe environments and learning opportunities, ASC encourages holistic growth amongst its most valuable asset, its people.

Like many other companies ASC has developed a Code of Conduct which serves as the ethical road map for employees and subsidiary companies, and provides the guidelines by which ASC conducts its businesses. The ASC Code of Conduct is a set of principles that guide and govern the conduct of management and employees in all matters relating to business. The Code lays down the ethical standards that management and employees have to observe in their professional lives, and it defines the value system at the heart of ASC and its many business entities. The Code is a dynamic document that reinforces honourable behaviour in business. While it has remained unaltered at its core, the Code has been modified down the years to keep it in step with changing regulatory norms in the different parts of the world where ASC now does business. These modifications have reinforced the Code, and have enabled it to reflect the diverse business, cultural and other factors that have a bearing on the health of the ASC brand.

Every employee of ASC, including full-time directors and the chief executive, is required to exhibit culturally appropriate behaviour There must be no tolerance of ethnocentric beliefs and behaviours in the countries they operate in, and all organisational activity on behalf of the company must re-enforce the high standard of professionalism, honesty and integrity expected of ASC organizational members, while conforming to high moral and ethical standards. The conduct of all ASC employees must be fair and transparent and be perceived to be so by all who interact with ASC. Every employee of ASC is required to preserve the human rights of every individual and the community, and must strive to honour organizational commitments to people, communities and governments. Every employee is responsible for the implementation of and compliance with the Code in his/her environment. Failure to adhere to the Code can attract severe consequences, including termination of employment.

Although perceived by some organizational members as being too prescriptive and lacking the involvement of ordinary employees in its development, nevertheless senior management constantly promote adherence to the Code as a key performance indicator (KPI) for the Asian Steel Corporation.

Reference Prakash, S.P. (2011) *Globalization and the Good Corporation*, Springer.

Questions

1　Discuss the extent to which the ASC Code of Conduct is an exercise in creating an ethical adaptive culture.

2　According to Sethi (2009) 'The large corporation, and especially the multinational corporation, must become an active agent for social change if it is to make the world safe for democracy and indeed, for capitalism'. Evaluate the assertion that when organizations globalize, their corporate cultures cannot remain the same.

3　Propose an approach which can help organizations develop environmental and cultural sensitivity.

END NOTES

1. Geoff Colvin, 'How It Works', *Fortune* (February 27, 2012): 72–79.

2. This section is based on Richard L. Daft, *Organization Theory and Design*, 10th ed. (Cincinnati, OH: South-Western, 2010), pp. 140–143.

3. L. J. Bourgeois, 'Strategy and Environment: A Conceptual Integration', *Academy of Management Review 5* (1980): 25–39.

4. James Moore, *The Death of Competition: Leadership and Strategy in the Age of Business Ecosystems* (New York: HarperCollins, 1996).

5. David J. Teece, 'Dynamic Capabilities: A Guide for Managers', *Ivey Business Journal* (March/April, 2011), www.iveybusinessjournal.com/topics/strategy/dynamic-capabilities-a-guide-for-managers (accessed June 12, 2012).

6. Thomas L. Friedman, *The World Is Flat: A Brief History of the Twenty-First Century* (New York: Farrar, Straus and Giroux, 2005), pp. 3–23.

7. Liz Alderman, 'In Europe, Starbucks Adjusts to a Café Culture', *The New York Times*, March 30, 2012.

8. Patricia Sellers, 'The New Coke', *Fortune* (May 21, 2012): 140.

9. Timothy Aeppel, 'Man vs. Machine, A Jobless Recovery', *The Wall Street Journal Online* (January 17, 2012), www.online.wsj.com/article/SB10001424052970204468004577164710231081398.html (accessed June 12, 2012).

10. Jeffrey A. Trachtenberg, 'Barnes & Noble Focuses on E-Books', *The Wall Street Journal Online* (July 20, 2011), www.allthingsd.com/20110720/barnes-noble-focuses-on-e-books/ (accessed June 12, 2012).

11. Roman Friedrich, Michael Peterson, and Alex Koster, 'The Rise of Generation C', *Strategy + Business*, Issue 62 (Spring 2011), www.strategy-business.com/article/11110?gko=64e54 (accessed June 25, 2012).

12. Sara Lin, 'Designing for the Senior Surge', *The Wall Street Journal*, April 25, 2008.

13. Dennis Cauchon and Paul Overberg, 'Census Data Shows Minorities Now a Majority of US Births', *USA TODAY* (May 17, 2012), www.usatoday.com/news/nation/story/2012-05-17/minority-births-census/55029100/1 (accessed June 12, 2012).

14. Somini Sengupta, 'Facebook Builds Network of Friends in Washington', *The New York Times Online* (May 18, 2012), www.nytimes.com/2012/05/19/technology/facebook-builds-network-of-friends-in-washington.html?_r=1&emc=eta1 (accessed June 12, 2012).

15. Dror Etzion, 'Research on Organizations and the Natural Environment', *Journal of Management* 33 (August 2007): 637–654.

16. Elizabeth Weise and Doyle Rice, 'Even the 'Best' Outcome Won't Be Good; The Oil Spill's Potential Toll Is Becoming Clear', *USA Today*, June 9, 2010.

17. Rick Kash, 'The Hershey Company: Aligning Inside to Win on the Outside', *Ivey Business Journal* (March–April 2012), www.iveybusinessjournal.com/topics/strategy/the-hershey-company-aligning-inside-to-win-on-the-outside-2 (accessed June 12, 2012).

18. Ann Zimmerman, 'Can Retailers Halt Showrooming?' *The Wall Street Journal Online* (April 11, 2012), www.online.wsj.com/article/SB10001424052702304587704577334370670243032.html (accessed June 13, 2012).

19. Geoff Colvin, 'Toyota's Comeback Kid', *Fortune* (February 2, 2012): 73.

20. 'Downsides of Just-in-Time Inventory', *Bloomberg Businessweek* (March 28–April 3, 2011): 17–18.

21. Peter Valdes-Dapena, 'Japan Earthquake Impact Hits US Auto Plants', *CNNMoney* (March 30, 2011), www.money.cnn.com/2011/03/28/autos/japan_earthquake_autos_outlook/index.htm# (accessed June 13, 2012).

22. Maxwell Murphy, 'Reinforcing the Supply Chain', *The Wall Street Journal*, January 11, 2012, B6.

23. Sharon Edelson, 'Costco Keeps Formula as It Expands', *Women's Wear Daily*, Issue 19 (January 30, 2012): 1; Andria Cheng, 'Costco Cracks Taiwan Market', *The Wall Street Journal*, April 2, 2010, B5; and 'Form 10-K for Costco Wholesale Corporation', Item 7 – Management's Discussion and Analysis of Financial Conditions and Results of Operations, *Costco Annual Report*, www.sec.gov/Archives/edgar/data/909832/000119312511271844/d203874d10k.htm#toc203874_9 (accessed July 10, 2012).

24. Robert B. Duncan, 'Characteristics of Organizational Environment and Perceived Environmental Uncertainty', *Administrative Science Quarterly* 17 (1972): 313–327; and Daft, *Organization Theory and Design*, pp. 144–148.

25. Bruce E. Perrott, 'Strategic Issue Management as Change Catalyst', *Strategy & Leadership* 39, no. 5 (2011): 20–29.

26. David B. Jemison, 'The Importance of Boundary Spanning Roles in Strategic Decision-Making', *Journal of Management Studies* 21 (1984): 131–152; and Marc J. Dollinger, 'Environmental Boundary Spanning and Information Processing Effects on Organizational Performance', *Academy of Management Journal* 27 (1984): 351–368.

27. Sean Lux, T. Russell Crook and Terry Leap, 'Corporate Political Activity: The Good, the Bad, and the Ugly', *Business Horizons* 55, no. 3 (May–June 2012): 307–312.

28. Tom Duffy, 'Spying the Holy Grail', *Microsoft Executive Circle* (Winter 2004): 38–39.

29. Alexander Garrett, 'Crash Course in Competitive Intelligence', *Management Today* (May 1, 2011): 18.

30. Kim Girard, 'Snooping on a Shoestring', *Business 2.0* (May 2003): 64–66.

31. Jonathan Hughes and Jeff Weiss, 'Simple Rules for Making Alliances Work', *Harvard Business Review* (November 2007): 122–131; Howard Muson, 'Friend? Foe? Both? The Confusing World of Corporate Alliances', *Across the Board* (March–April 2002): 19–25; and Devi R. Gnyawali and Ravindranath Madhavan, 'Cooperative Networks and Competitive Dynamics: A Structural Embeddedness Perspective', *Academy of Management Review* 26, no. 3 (2001): 431–445.

32. Katie Merx, 'Automakers Interconnected Around World', *Edmonton Journal* April 6, 2007, H14; and Keith Bradsher, 'Ford Agrees to Sell Volvo to a Fast-Rising Chinese Company', *The New York Times Online* (March 28, 2010), www.nytimes.com/2010/03/29/business/global/29auto.html (accessed August 1, 2011).

33. Thomas Petzinger, Jr., *The New Pioneers: The Men and Women Who Are Transforming the Workplace and Marketplace* (New York: Simon & Schuster, 1999), pp. 53–54.

34. Stephan M. Wagner and Roman Boutellier, 'Capabilities for Managing a Portfolio of Supplier Relationships', *Business Horizons* (November–December 2002): 79–88; Peter Smith Ring and Andrew H. Van de Ven, 'Developmental Processes of Corporate Interorganizational Relationships', *Academy of Management Review* 19 (1994): 90–118; Myron Magnet, 'The New Golden Rule of Business', *Fortune* (February 21, 1994): 60–64; and Peter Grittner, 'Four Elements of Successful Sourcing Strategies', *Management Review* (October 1996): 41–45.

35. Richard L. Daft, 'After the Deal: The Art of Fusing Diverse Corporate Cultures into One', paper presented at the Conference on International Corporate Restructuring, Institute of Business Research and Education, Korea University, Seoul, Korea (June 16, 1998).

36. David Segal, 'When a Sugar High Isn't Enough', *The New York Times Online* (April 21, 2012), www.nytimes.com/2012/04/22/business/kellogg-takes-aim-at-snack-foods.html?pagewanted=all (accessed June 15, 2012).

37. Peter Sanders, 'Sikorsky's Business Heads Up', *The Wall Street Journal Online* (April 19, 2010), www.online.wsj.com/article/SB10001424052702304180804575188821353177134.html (accessed April 19, 2010).

38. Yoash Wiener, 'Forms of Value Systems: A Focus on Organizational Effectiveness and Culture Change and Maintenance', *Academy of Management Review* 13 (1988): 534–545; V. Lynne Meek, 'Organizational Culture: Origins and Weaknesses', *Organization Studies* 9 (1988): 453–473; John J. Sherwood, 'Creating Work Cultures with Competitive Advantage', *Organizational Dynamics* (Winter 1988): 5–27; and Andrew D. Brown and Ken Starkey, 'The Effect of Organizational Culture on Communication and Information', *Journal of Management Studies* 31, no. 6 (November 1994): 807–828.

39. Joanne Martin, *Organizational Culture: Mapping the Terrain* (Thousand Oaks, CA: Sage Publications, 2002); Ralph H. Kilmann, Mary J. Saxton and Roy Serpa, 'Issues in Understanding and Changing Culture', *California Management Review* 28 (Winter 1986): 87–94; and Linda Smircich, 'Concepts of Culture and Organizational Analysis', *Administrative Science Quarterly* 28 (1983): 339–358.

40. David Carr, 'Troubles That Money Can't Dispel', *The New York Times Online* (July 17, 2011), www.nytimes.com/2011/07/18/business/media/for-news-corporation-troubles-that-money-cant-dispel.html?pagewanted=all (accessed June 13, 2012).

41. John F. Burns and Jeremy W. Peters, 'Two Top Deputies Resign as Crisis Isolates Murdoch', *The New York Times Online* (July 16, 2011), www.hongkong-mart.com/forum/viewtopic.php?f=2&t=367 (accessed June 13, 2012).

42. Carr, 'Troubles That Money Can't Dispel'.

43. Based on Edgar H. Schein, *Organizational Culture and Leadership*, 2d ed. (San Francisco: Jossey-Bass, 1992): 3–27.

44. Mindy Grossman, 'HSN's CEO on Fixing the Shopping Network's Culture', *Harvard Business Review* (December 2011): 43–46.

45. Chip Jarnagin and John W. Slocum, Jr., 'Creating Corporate Cultures through Mythopoetic Leadership', *Organizational Dynamics* 36, no. 3 (2007): 288–302.

46. Robert E. Quinn and Gretchen M. Spreitzer, 'The Road to Empowerment: Seven Questions Every Leader Should Consider', *Organizational Dynamics* (Autumn 1997): 37–49.

47. Yukari Iwatani Kane and Jessica E. Vascellaro, 'Successor Faces Tough Job at Apple', *The Wall Street Journal Online* (August 26, 2011), www.allthingsd.com/20110826/successor-faces-tough-job-at-apple/ (accessed June 13, 2012).

48. Based on an interview with Tim Cook conducted by *Wall Street Journal's* Walt Mossberg and Kara Swisher (June 4, 2012), www.online.wsj.com/article/SB10001424052702303552104577436952829794614.html?KEYWORDS=steve+jobs+apple+culture (accessed June 16, 2012).

49. Arthur Yeung, 'Setting People up for Success: How the Portman Ritz-Carlton Hotel Gets the Best from Its People', *Human Resource Management* 45, no. 2 (Summer 2006): 267–275.

50. Patricia Jones and Larry Kahaner, *Say It and Live It: 50 Corporate Mission Statements That Hit the Mark* (New York: Currency Doubleday, 1995).

51. Harrison M. Trice and Janice M. Beyer, 'Studying Organizational Cultures Through Rites and Ceremonials', *Academy of Management Review* 9 (1984): 653–669.

52. PRWeb, 'Southwest Airlines Launches New NBA-Themed Specialty Airplane; Slam Dunk One Marks First Southwest Specialty Plane with a Partner in 17 Years', November 3, 2005, www.prweb.com/releases/2005/11/prweb306461.php (accessed February 7, 2008).

53. Jennifer A. Chatman and Karen A. Jehn, 'Assessing the Relationship Between Industry Characteristics and Organizational Culture: How Different Can You Be?' *Academy of Management Journal* 37, no. 3 (1994): 522–553.

54. This discussion is based on Paul McDonald and Jeffrey Gandz, 'Getting Value from Shared Values', *Organizational Dynamics* 21, no. 3 (Winter 1992): 64–76; Daniel R. Denison and Aneil K. Mishra, 'Toward a Theory of Organizational Culture and Effectiveness', *Organization Science* 6,

no. 2 (March–April 1995): 204–223; and Richard L. Daft, *The Leadership Experience*, 3d ed. (Cincinnati, OH: South-Western, 2005), pp. 570–573.

55. Lucas Conley, 'Rinse and Repeat', *Fast Company* (July 2005): 76–77.

56. Robert Hooijberg and Frank Petrock, 'On Cultural Change: Using the Competing Values Framework to Help Leaders Execute a Transformational Strategy', *Human Resource Management* 32, no. 1 (1993): 29–50.

57. David Kesmodel and Suzanne Vranica, 'Unease Brewing at Anheuser as New Owners Slash Costs', *The Wall Street Journal Online*, April 23, 2009, www.online.wsj.com/article/SB124096182942565947.html (accessed June 22, 2012).

58. Jeffrey Pfeffer, *The Human Equation: Building Profits by Putting People First* (Boston, MA: Harvard Business School Press, 1998).

59. Jeremy Kahn, 'What Makes a Company Great?' *Fortune* (October 26, 1998): 218; James C. Collins and Jerry I. Porras, *Built to Last: Successful Habits of Visionary Companies* (New York: HarperCollins, 1994); and James C. Collins, 'Change Is Good – But First Know What Should Never Change', *Fortune* (May 29, 1995): 141.

60. Andrew Wahl, 'Culture Shock', *Canadian Business* (October 10–23, 2005): 115–116.

61. Based on information in Alison Beard and Richard Hornik, 'It's Hard to Be Good', *Harvard Business Review* (November, 2011): 88–96.

62. Jennifer A. Chatman and Sandra Eunyoung Cha, 'Leading by Leveraging Culture', *California Management Review* 45, no. 4 (Summer 2003): 20–34.

63. This section is based on Jeff Rosenthal and Mary Ann Masarech, 'High-Performance Cultures: How Values Can Drive Business Results', *Journal of Organizational Excellence* (Spring 2003): 3–18.

64. Nelson D. Schwartz, 'One Brick at a Time', *Fortune* (June 12, 2006): 45–46; and Nelson D. Schwartz, 'Lego Rebuilds

Legacy', *International Herald Tribune* (September 5, 2009).

65. Evelyn M. Ruslie, 'Zynga's Tough Culture Risks a Talent Drain', *The New York Times Online* (November 27, 2011), www.dealbook.nytimes.com/2011/11/27/zyngas-tough-culture-risks-a-talent-drain/ (accessed June 18, 2012).

66. This example is based on Dave Ulrich, Steve Kerr and Ron Ashkenas, *The GE Work-Out* (New York: McGraw-Hill, 2002), pp. 238–230.

67. From Ulrich et al., 'GE Values', in *The GE Work-Out*, Figure 11–2.

68. Rosenthal and Masarech, "High-Performance Cultures."

69. John P. Kotter and James L. Heskett, *Corporate Culture and Performance* (New York: The Free Press, 1992); Eric Flamholtz and Rangapriya Kannan-Narasimhan, 'Differential Impact of Cultural Elements on Financial Performance', *European Management Journal* 23, no. 1 (2005): 50–64. Also see J. M. Kouzes and B. Z. Posner, *The Leadership Challenge: How to Keep Getting Extraordinary Things Done in Organizations*, 3d ed. (San Francisco: Jossey-Bass, 2002).

70. Rosenthal and Masarech, 'High-Performance Cultures'; Patrick Lencioni, 'Make Your Values Mean Something', *Harvard Business Review* (July 2002): 113–117; and Thomas J. Peters and Robert H. Waterman, Jr., *In Search of Excellence* (New York: Warner, 1988).

71. Jarnagin and Slocum, 'Creating Corporate Cultures through Mythopoetic Leadership'.

72. These questions are based on ideas from R. L. Daft and R. M. Lengel, *Fusion Leadership* (San Francisco: Berrett Koehler, 2000): Chapter 4; B. Bass and B. Avolio, *Multifactor Leadership Questionnaire*, 2d ed. (Menlo Park, CA: Mind Garden, Inc., 2004); and Karl E. Weick and Kathleen M. Sutcliffe, *Managing the Unexpected: Assuring High Performance in an Age of Complexity* (San Francisco: Jossey-Bass, 2001).

73. Adapted from Kent Weber, 'Gold Mine or Fool's Gold?' *Business Ethics* (January–February 2001): 18.

CHAPTER 4

THE DYNAMICS OF ALTERNATIVE ORGANIZATIONAL FORMS

LEARNING OBJECTIVES

After studying this chapter, you should be able to:

1   Discuss the fundamental characteristics of organizing, including concepts such as work specialization, chain of command, span of management and centralization versus decentralization.

2   Describe functional and divisional approaches to structure.

3   Explain the matrix approach to structure and its application to both domestic and international organizations.

4   Describe the contemporary team and virtual network structures and why they are being adopted by organizations.

5   Explain why organizations need coordination across departments and hierarchical levels, and describe mechanisms for achieving coordination.

6   Identify how structure can be used to achieve an organization's strategic goals.

7   Define production technology and explain how it influences organization structure.

Valve Software Corporation, which makes some of the most popular video and digital games in the world, has more than 300 employees, provides free food and massage rooms, and offers on-site laundry service. But it is what the company *doesn't* have that's really interesting, as it has no bosses. Valve's unique organization structure caused a minor media blitz after someone posted the employee handbook online in the spring of 2012, but Valve has been functioning smoothly without bosses since it was founded in 1996. Founders Gabe Newell and Mike Harrington, former Microsoft employees, wanted to create a flat, fast organization that allowed employees maximum flexibility to be creative. The company prizes 'fast and flexible' so much that desks are on wheels. Employees recruit colleagues to work on a project they think is worthwhile, and people wheel their desks around to form teamwork areas as they choose. It sounds like a dream for employees, but many people don't adapt to the 'no structure structure' and leave for more traditional jobs.[1]

Could you work in a company with no bosses, no permanent offices, and no clearly defined structure? Valve is unusual, but many companies are flattening their hierarchies and cutting out layers of management to improve efficiency and be more flexible. Some people thrive in less hierarchical organizations, whereas others have difficulty without a clearly defined vertical structure. New managers in particular are typically more comfortable and more effective working in an organization system that is compatible with their leadership beliefs and core values.

In your career as a manager, you will have to understand and learn to work within a variety of structural configurations. All organizations wrestle with the question of optimum structural design, and reorganization often is necessary to reflect a new strategy, changing market conditions, and/or innovative and often disruptive technology. In recent years, many companies have realigned departmental groupings, chains of command, and horizontal coordination mechanisms to attain new strategic goals or to cope with a turbulent environment. Managers at Hachette Filipacchi Media US, which owns magazines such as *Elle* and *Woman's Day*, created brand officer positions to increase horizontal coordination across departments and make sure everyone from editorial to event marketing is in the information loop. Michael Dell created a separate division at his company that will focus specifically on products such as mobile phones and other portable devices, the fastest-growing part of the computer industry. At Sony, executives added a new position of chief information security officer (CISO) to the hierarchy, after hackers accessed millions of customer files on the supposedly secure Sony network. The company had to shut down the PlayStation Network temporarily to figure out what went wrong, leading to lost revenue, investigation expenses and the loss of customer loyalty and goodwill. The newly created position of CISO, said a Sony spokesman, *'will keep a dynamic focus on the latest security threats and advanced defences . . . to uphold our unwavering commitment to protect our customers' data'.*[2] Each of these organizations is using fundamental concepts of organizing. Sony was hacked again in 2014 by GOP, a North Korean sponsored hacking agency, inter alia compromising the secrecy of the development of the latest Bond movie (Spectre) and emails from Sony Pictures Entertainment's chairwomen, including making inappropriate remarks concerning the likely films that President Obama might enjoy (such as 12 Years a Slave), resulted in her giving a public apology. Ms Pascal resigned her position as co-chairwoman in 2014, but it was later reported in 2015 that she was fired from her head position at Sony Pictures.

Organizing is the deployment of organizational resources to achieve strategic goals. The deployment of resources is reflected in the organization's division of labour into specific departments and jobs, formal lines of authority and mechanisms for coordinating diverse organization tasks.

Organizing is important because it facilitates the implementation of strategy – the topic included in Part Four of this book. Strategy defines *what* to do; organizing defines *how* to do it. Structure (with lines of power and influence) is a powerful tool for reaching strategic goals, and a strategy's success often is determined by its fit with organizational structure. Part Five of this book explains the variety of organizing principles and HRM concepts used by managers. This chapter covers fundamental concepts that apply to all organizations and departments, including organizing the traditional vertical structure and using mechanisms for optimum horizontal coordination. Chapter 12 discusses how organizations can be structured to facilitate innovation and change. Senior management must consider how to use human resources to the best advantage within an organization's structure.

Organizing the vertical structure

The organizing process leads to the creation of organization structure, which defines how tasks are divided and resources deployed. Organization structure is defined as: First, the set of formal tasks assigned to individuals and departments; second, formal reporting relationships, including lines of authority, decision responsibility, number of hierarchical levels and span of managers' control; and third, the design of systems to ensure effective coordination of employees across departments.[3] Ensuring the fullest coordination across departments is just as critical as defining the departments within the structure. Without effective coordination and auditing systems, no organization structure is complete. Changes to systems should be systemically desirable and culturally feasible. Powerful coalitions can and do exercise considerable power in organizations, especially if they are information gatekeepers, as well as having legitimate position power in an organization. Critical systems heuristics should be influenced by valid concerns including social systems, organizational cybernetics and soft systems thinking.

The set of formal tasks and formal reporting relationships provides a framework for vertical control of the organization. The characteristics of vertical structure are portrayed in the organization chart, which is the visual representation of an organization's structure.

A sample organization chart for a water bottling plant is illustrated in Exhibit 4.1. The plant has four major departments – accounting, human resources, production and marketing. The organization chart delineates the chain of command, indicates departmental tasks and how they fit together, and provides order and logic for the organization. Every employee has an appointed task, line of authority and decision responsibility. The following sections discuss several important features of vertical structure in more detail.

EXHIBIT 4.1 Organization chart for a water bottling plant

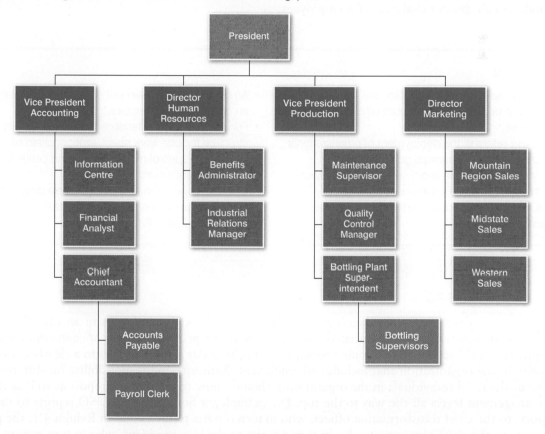

Work specialization

Organizations perform a wide variety of tasks. A fundamental principle (per the structuralist school) is that work can be performed more efficiently if employees task-specialize.[4] Indeed, Max Weber postulated that the ideal type of organization was that of a bureaucracy – but one with several defined characteristics. One aspect of his thinking was that there was a need for work specialization, sometimes called *division of labour*: the degree to which organizational tasks are subdivided into separate jobs. Work specialization in Exhibit 4.1 is illustrated by the separation of production tasks into bottling, quality control and maintenance. Employees within each department perform only the tasks relevant to their specialized function. When organizations face new strategic issues, managers often create new positions or departments to deal with them, just as Sony created a new position of chief information security officer, described earlier in the chapter. Many corporations have created a new position for chief diversity officer because of the importance today of creating an environment where minorities and women can flourish. Even the position of chief information officer (CIO) was practically unheard of even a decade ago, but almost every government agency, non-profit organization and business firm has a CIO today. In 2009, President Barack Obama appointed Vivek Kundra as the first CIO for the US government.[5]

When work specialization is extensive, employees specialize in a single task. Jobs tend to be small, but they can be performed efficiently. Work specialization is readily visible on an automobile assembly line, where each employee performs the same task over and over again. It would not be efficient to have a single employee build the entire automobile, or even perform a large number of unrelated jobs.

Despite the apparent advantages of specialization, many organizations are moving away from this principle. With too much specialization, employees are isolated and do only a single, boring job. In addition, too much specialization creates separation and hinders the coordination that is essential for organizations to be effective. Many enlightened companies are implementing teams and other mechanisms that enhance coordination and provide greater challenges for employees.

REFLECTION

- Managers in every organization face the question about how to organize for maximum efficiency and effectiveness.
- **Organizing** refers to the deployment of organizational resources to achieve strategic goals.
- **Organization structure** is defined as the framework in which the organization defines how tasks are divided, resources are deployed and departments are coordinated.
- An **organization chart** is the visual representation of an organization's structure.
- Fundamental characteristics of vertical organization structure include work specialization, chain of command, span of management, and centralization and decentralization.
- **Work specialization**, sometimes called *division of labour*, is the degree to which organizational tasks are subdivided into individual jobs.

Chain of command

The chain of command is an unbroken line of authority that links all employees in an organization and shows who reports to whom. It is associated with two underlying principles. *Unity of command* means that each employee is held accountable to only one supervisor. The *scalar principle* refers to a clearly defined line of authority in the organization that includes all employees. Authority and responsibility for different tasks should be distinct. All individuals in the organization should know to whom they report as well as the successive management levels all the way to the top. For example, at Sony, the new CISO reports to the CIO, who reports to the chief transformation officer, who in turn reports to the CEO.[6] In Exhibit 4.1, the payroll clerk reports to the chief accountant, who in turn reports to the vice president, who in turn reports to the company president.

Authority, responsibility and delegation

The chain of command illustrates the authority structure of the organization. Authority is the formal and legitimate right of a manager to make decisions, issue orders and allocate resources to achieve organizationally desired outcomes. Authority is distinguished by three characteristics:[7]

1 *Authority is vested in organizational positions, not people.* Managers have authority because of the positions they hold, and other people in the same positions would have the same authority.

CONCEPT CONNECTION

Cognizant Technology Solutions Corporation, a US-based outsourcing firm, has an unusual **chain of command** referred to as 'two in a box'. Originally, project managers supervised company staff in India while living in the USA, where most customers were located. Because spanning that many time zones was difficult, former chief operating officer Francisco D'Souza (now CEO, pictured second from right) implemented a solution: assign two managers to each project – one in India and one at the client's site. Each is equally responsible for the project's success. The model works because it enhances the company's customer responsiveness, even though it violates the principle of **unity of command**.

2 ***Authority flows down the vertical hierarchy.*** Positions at the top of the hierarchy are vested with more formal authority than are positions at the bottom.

3 ***Authority is accepted by subordinates.*** Although authority flows from the top down, subordinates comply because they believe that managers have a legitimate right to issue orders. The *acceptance theory of authority* argues that a manager has authority only if subordinates choose to accept his or her commands. If subordinates refuse to obey because the order is outside their zone of acceptance, a manager's authority disappears.[8]

Responsibility is the flip side of the authority coin. Responsibility is the duty to perform the task or activity as assigned. Typically, managers are assigned authority commensurate with responsibility. When managers have responsibility for task outcomes but little authority, the job is possible but difficult. They rely on persuasion and luck. When managers have authority exceeding responsibility, they may become tyrants, using authority to achieve frivolous outcomes.[9]

Accountability is the mechanism through which authority and responsibility are brought into alignment. Accountability means that the people with authority and responsibility are subject to reporting and justifying task outcomes to those above them in the chain of command.[10] For organizations to function well, everyone needs to know what they are accountable for and accept the responsibility and authority for performing it. At Apple, the late Steve Jobs instituted an accountability mindset throughout the organization. The term *DRI*, meaning 'directly responsible individual', typically appears on meeting agendas and so forth, so that everyone knows who is responsible for what.[11]

Another important concept related to authority is delegation.[12] Delegation is the process managers use to transfer authority and responsibility to positions below them in the hierarchy. Most organizations today encourage managers to delegate authority to the lowest possible level to provide maximum flexibility to meet customer needs and adapt to shifts in the environment. Consider how top managers at Meetup.com revived the company by pushing authority and responsibility down to the front lines.

'I think the most difficult transition for anybody from being a worker bee to a manager is this issue of delegation. What do you give up? How can you have the team do what you would do yourself without you doing it?'
— TACHI YAMADA, PRESIDENT OF THE BILL AND MELINDA GATES FOUNDATION'S GLOBAL HEALTH PROGRAMME

As illustrated by this example, delegating decision-making to lower-level managers and employees can be highly motivating and improve speed, flexibility and creativity. However, many managers find delegation difficult. When managers can't delegate, they undermine the role of their subordinates and prevent people from doing their jobs effectively.

INNOVATIVE WAY

Meetup.com

Meetup.com is the company known for organizing Howard Dean's US presidential campaign in 2004. As an organization that helps other people create organizations, Meetup has been instrumental in setting up local groups for everything from protests to gardening clubs. When Meetup.com went through a period of rapid expansion, top executives implemented a command-and-control structure as a way to regulate and monitor performance. The company even had a 'review board' that worked with managers to oversee what employees could and could not do. The trouble was, '*productivity went through the floor,*' says chief technology officer

Greg Whalin. One day, a senior manager pulled CEO Scott Heiferman into a conference room and showed him a list of complaints, including *We aren't a creative company* and *I hate the organization chart.*

Heiferman decided to go in the opposite direction and push authority and responsibility down to his employees. Now, Meetup's employees have almost total freedom to select the projects they work on and how and when they accomplish them. With the authority and responsibility for setting priorities and making decisions, employee creativity soared. In addition, many people began working harder than ever before. '*We got more done in 6 weeks than in 6 months last year,*' said Heiferman.[13]

🌐 NEW MANAGER SELF-TEST

Delegation

INSTRUCTIONS How do you share tasks with others at school or work, such as when performing group assignments or club activities? Answer whether each of the following statements is 'Mostly true' or 'Mostly false' for you.

	Mostly true	Mostly false
1 I completely trust other people to do good work.	☐	☐
2 I give assignments by patiently explaining the rationale and desired outcomes.	☐	☐
3 I genuinely believe that others can do a job as well as I can.	☐	☐
4 I leave people alone after I delegate a task to them.	☐	☐
5 I am better at managing the work of others than actually doing it.	☐	☐
6 I often end up doing tasks myself.	☐	☐
7 I get upset when someone doesn't do the task correctly.	☐	☐
8 I really enjoy doing task details to get them just right.	☐	☐
9 I try to do the work better than anyone else.	☐	☐
10 I set very high standards for myself.	☐	☐

SCORING & INTERPRETATION The questions above represent two related aspects of delegating work – delegation and perfectionism. Give yourself one point for each 'Mostly true' answer:

   Delegation, sum questions 1–5: ___
   Perfectionism, sum questions 6–10: ___

Delegation and perfectionism are opposite sides of the same coin. Your score for delegation reflects your attitude towards entrusting others with work for which you are responsible. Your score for perfectionism indicates your desire to be in personal control, which prevents delegation. Perfectionists want to do everything themselves so it is just exactly the way they want it. A lower score for delegation (0–2) and a higher score for perfectionism (4–5) probably means that delegation of authority will not come easily for you. When managers cannot delegate tasks to individuals and teams, an organization will struggle to decentralize authority and engage people in coordination. How does your delegation score compare to your perfectionism score? What would you need to change about yourself to be a better delegator?

TAKE A MOMENT

As a manager, how effective will you be at delegating? Get an idea by completing the New Manager Self-Test above.

Line and staff authority

An important distinction in many organizations is between line authority and staff authority, reflecting whether managers work in line or staff departments in the organization's structure. *Line departments* perform tasks that reflect the organization's primary goal and mission. In a software company, line departments make and sell the product. In an Internet-based company, line departments would be those that develop and manage online offerings and sales. *Staff departments* include all those that provide specialized skills in support of line departments. Staff departments have an advisory relationship with line departments and typically include marketing, labour relations, research, accounting and human resources.

 GREEN **POWER**

A New Department

Systems, Applications and Products in Data Processing (SAP) created its first-ever chief sustainability officer position in 2009, and Peter Graf, formerly a computer scientist, leads a global team that oversees sustainability initiatives. To change SAP, Graf and his team focused on the top of the hierarchy, educating SAP's board of directors as their first target. Regular emails and newsletters to board members defined terminology and answered questions (such as, 'What does "offset" mean in regard to sustainability?'). In addition, Graf and his team reminded board members of incidents within SAP's own corporate history, such as the decision by a major German customer to stop ordering SAP software because SAP had no sustainability code of conduct.

By the time SAP's board held its next official meeting, members were fully engaged in adopting sustainability policies, speaking with an informed, unified voice as they assisted the new department's efforts to change the sustainability thinking of employees, suppliers and customers.

SOURCE: Michael S. Hopkins, 'How SAP Made the Business Case for Sustainability', *MIT Sloan Management Review* 52, no. 1 (Fall 2010): 69–72.

Line authority means that people in management positions have formal authority to direct and control immediate subordinates. Staff authority is narrower and includes the right to advise, recommend and counsel in the staff specialists' area of expertise. Staff authority is a communication relationship; staff specialists advise managers in technical areas. For example, the finance department of a manufacturing firm would have staff authority to coordinate with line departments about which accounting forms to use to facilitate equipment purchases and standardize payroll services. BP's new safety department, created in the wake of the 2010 BP-Transocean Deepwater Horizon oil rig explosion in the Gulf of Mexico that killed 11 crew members and set off an environmental disaster, advises managers in line departments regarding risk management, agreements with contractors and other safety-related issues. Safety staff specialists are embedded throughout the company, including on exploration projects and in refineries. Unlike many staff specialists, BP's safety unit has broad power to challenge line managers' decisions if it considers them too risky.[14]

To understand the importance of the chain of command and clear lines of authority, responsibility and delegation, consider the Deepwater Horizon oil rig explosion. Activities were so loosely organized that no one seemed to know who was in charge or what their level of authority and responsibility was. When the explosion occurred, confusion reigned. Twenty-three-year-old Andrea Fleytas issued a mayday (distress signal) over the radio when she realized no one else had done so, but she was chastised for overstepping her authority. One manager says he didn't call for help because he wasn't sure he had authorization to do so. Still another said he tried to call to shore but was told that the order needed to come from someone else. Crew members knew the emergency shutdown needed to be triggered, but there was confusion over who had the authority to give the OK. As fire spread, several minutes passed before people were given directions to evacuate. Again, an alarmed Fleytas turned on the public address system and announced that the crew was abandoning the rig. 'The scene was very chaotic,' said worker Carlos Ramos. 'There was no chain of command. Nobody in charge.' In the aftermath of the explosion and oil spill, several federal agencies are also in the hot seat because of loose oversight and confusion over responsibility that led to delays and disagreements that prolonged the suffering of local communities.[15]

TAKE A MOMENT

Go to the Ethical Dilemma at the end of the chapter that pertains to issues of authority, responsibility and delegation.

Span of management

The span of management is the number of employees reporting to a supervisor. Sometimes called the *span of control*, this characteristic of structure determines how closely a supervisor can monitor subordinates. Traditional views of organization design recommended a span of management of about seven to ten subordinates per manager. However, many lean organizations today have spans of management as high as 30 or 40, and even higher. At PepsiCo, Inc.'s Gamesa cookie operation in Mexico, for instance, employees are trained to keep production running smoothly and are rewarded for quality, teamwork and productivity. Teams are so productive and efficient that Gamesa factories operate with around 56 subordinates per manager.[16] Research over the past 40 or so years shows that span of management varies widely and that several factors influence the span.[17] Generally, when supervisors must be closely involved with subordinates, the span should be small, and when supervisors need little involvement with subordinates, it can be large. The following list describes the factors that are associated with less supervisor involvement and thus larger spans of control:

- Work performed by subordinates is stable and routine.

- Subordinates perform similar work tasks.

- Subordinates are concentrated in a single location.

- Subordinates are highly trained and need little direction in performing tasks.

- Rules and procedures defining task activities are available.

- Support systems and personnel are available for the manager.

- Little time is required in non-supervisory activities, such as coordination with other departments or planning.

- Managers' personal preferences and styles favour a large span.

The average span of control used in an organization determines whether the structure is tall or flat. A tall structure has an overall narrow span and more hierarchical levels. A flat structure has a wide span, is horizontally dispersed, and has fewer hierarchical levels.

Having too many hierarchical levels and narrow spans of control is a common structural problem for organizations. In a survey conducted for The Conference Board, 72 per cent of managers surveyed said they believed their organizations had too many levels of management.[18] The result may be that routine decisions are made too high in the organization, which pulls higher-level executives away from important, long-range strategic issues and limits the creativity, innovativeness and accountability of lower-level managers.[19] The trend in recent years has been towards wider spans of control as a way to facilitate delegation.[20] One recent study found that the span of management for CEOs has doubled over the past two decades, rising from about five to around ten managers reporting directly to the top executive, with the span of management for those managers also increasing. At the same time, the types of positions in the top team are shifting, with the position of chief operating officer (COO) declining and positions such as CIO or chief marketing officer being added to the top team.[21] Exhibit 4.2 illustrates how an international metals company was reorganized. The multilevel set of managers shown in panel *a* was replaced with ten operating managers and nine staff specialists reporting directly to the CEO, as shown in panel *b*. The CEO welcomed this wide span of 19 management subordinates because it fits his style, his management team was top quality and needed little supervision, and they were all located on the same floor of an office building.

Centralization and decentralization

Centralization and decentralization pertain to the hierarchical level at which decisions are made. Centralization means that decision authority is located near the top of the organization. With decentralization, decision authority is pushed downwards to lower organization levels. Organizations may have to experiment to find the correct hierarchical level at which to make decisions. For example, most large school systems are highly centralized. However, a study by William Ouchi found that three large urban school systems that shifted to a decentralized structure which gave school principals and teachers more control over staffing, scheduling, and teaching methods and materials, performed better and more efficiently than centralized systems of similar size.[22] Government leaders in Great Britain hope the same thing will happen for the country's National Health Service (NHS). The system has undergone the most radical restructuring since it was founded in 1948, with a key part of the plan to shift control of the multibillion annual health care budget to doctors at the local level. Leaders believe decentralization will cut costs, simplify and streamline procedures, and reduce inefficiency by 'putting power in the hands of patients and clinicians'.[23]

In the USA and Canada, the trend over the past 30 years has been towards greater decentralization of organizations. Decentralization is believed to relieve the burden on top managers, make greater use of employees' skills and abilities, ensure that decisions are made close to the action by well-informed people and permit

EXHIBIT 4.2 Reorganization to increase span of management for president of an international metals company

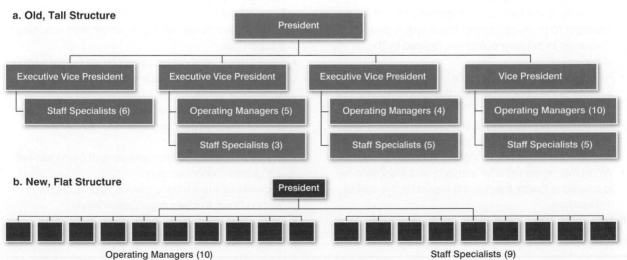

more rapid response to external changes. Stanley McChrystal, former commander of US and NATO forces in Afghanistan, once said, '*I learned … that any complex task is best approached by flattening hierarchies. It gets everybody feeling like they're in the inner circle, so that they develop a sense of ownership.*'[24] Nearly a decade of fighting a complex, decentralized enemy has pushed the US armed forces to decentralize as well. The US Army recently implemented its Starfish Programme to train leaders to think, act and operate in a decentralized fashion. The programme is based on ideas in Ori Brafman and Rod Beckstrom's book *The Starfish and the Spider*, which makes the case that decentralized 'starfish' are less vulnerable to attack than centralized 'spiders'.[25]

However, not every organization should decentralize all decisions. Within many companies, there is often a 'tug of war between centralization and decentralization' as top executives want to centralize some operations to eliminate duplication, while business division managers want to maintain decentralized control.[26] Managers should diagnose the organizational situation and select the decision-making level that will best meet the organization's needs. Factors that typically influence centralization versus decentralization are as follows:

- ■ *Greater change and uncertainty in the environment are usually associated with decentralization.* A good example of how decentralization can help cope with rapid change and uncertainty occurred following Hurricane Katrina. Mississippi Power restored power in just 12 days, thanks largely to a decentralized management system that empowered people at the electrical substations to make rapid on-the-spot decisions.[27]

- ■ *The amount of centralization or decentralization should fit the firm's strategy.* Top executives at the Walt Disney Company adopt a decentralization approach when they buy small creative companies such as Pixar Animation Studios and Marvel Entertainment. Disney CEO Bob Iger believed in allowing the managers of these companies to run the organizations as they saw fit. Decentralization fits with the strategy of allowing creative units to respond quickly and innovatively to changes in the entertainment industry.[28] Taking the opposite approach, to compete better with Kohl's and Macy's, managers at JCPenney centralized product planning and buying operations, enabling the company to get more fashionable merchandise to stores quickly and at lower prices.[29]

- ■ *In times of crisis or risk of company failure, authority may be centralized at the top.* When Honda could not get agreement among divisions about new car models, President Nobuhiko Kawamoto made the decision himself.[30]

REFLECTION

- The **chain of command** is an unbroken line of authority that links all individuals in the organization and specifies who reports to whom.
- **Authority** is the formal and legitimate right of a manager to make decisions, issue orders and allocate resources to achieve outcomes desired by the organization.
- **Responsibility** is the flip side of the authority coin; it refers to the duty to perform the task or activity that one has been assigned.
- **Accountability** means that people with authority and responsibility are subject to reporting and justifying task outcomes to those above them in the chain of command.
- When managers transfer authority and responsibility to positions below them in the hierarchy, it is called **delegation**.
- Managers may have **line authority**, which refers to the formal power to direct and control immediate

subordinates, or **staff authority**, which refers to the right to advise, counsel and recommend in the manager's area of expertise.
- **Span of management**, sometimes called *span of control*, refers to the number of employees reporting to a supervisor.
- A **tall structure** is characterized by an overall narrow span of management and a relatively large number of hierarchical levels.
- A **flat structure** is characterized by an overall broad span of management and relatively few hierarchical levels.
- The trend is towards broader spans of management and greater decentralization.
- **Decentralization** means that decision authority is pushed down to lower organization levels.
- **Centralization** means that decision authority is located near top organization levels.

Departmentalization

Another fundamental characteristic of organization structure is departmentalization, which is the basis for grouping positions into departments and departments into the total organization. Managers make choices about how to use the chain of command to group people together to perform their work. Five approaches to structural design reflect different uses of the chain of command in departmentalization, as illustrated in Exhibit 4.3. The functional, divisional and matrix are traditional approaches that rely on the chain of command to define departmental groupings and reporting relationships along the hierarchy. Two innovative approaches are the fuller use of teams and virtual networks, which have emerged to meet changing organizational needs in a turbulent global environment. Virtual networks are seen to be an essential element in facilitating Open Innovation (OI).

The basic difference among structures illustrated in Exhibit 4.3 is the way in which employees are departmentalized and to whom they report.[31] Each structural approach is described in detail in the following sections.

Vertical functional approach
What it is

In a functional structure, also called a **U-form** (unitary structure), activities are grouped together by common function from the bottom to the top of the organization.[32] The functional structure groups positions into departments based on similar skills, expertise, work activities and resource use. A functional structure can be thought of as departmentalization by organizational resources, because each type of functional activity – accounting, human resources, engineering and manufacturing – represents specific resources for performing the organization's task. People, facilities and other resources representing a common function are grouped into a single department. One example is Blue Bell Creameries, which relies on in-depth expertise in its various functional departments to produce high-quality ice cream for a limited regional market. The quality control department, for example, tests all incoming ingredients and ensures that only the best go into Blue Bell's ice cream. Quality inspectors also test outgoing products and, because of their years of experience, can detect the slightest deviation from expected quality. Blue Bell also has functional departments such as sales, production, maintenance, distribution, research and development, and finance.[33]

How it works

Refer to Exhibit 4.1 for an example of a functional structure. The major departments under the president are groupings of similar expertise and resources, such as accounting, human resources, production and marketing. Each of the functional departments is concerned with the organization as a whole. The marketing department is responsible for all sales and marketing, for example, and the accounting department handles financial issues for the entire company.

The functional structure is a strong vertical design. Information flows up and down the vertical hierarchy, and the chain of command converges at the top of the organization. In a functional structure, people within a department communicate primarily with others in the same department to coordinate work and accomplish tasks or implement decisions that are passed down the hierarchy. Managers and employees are compatible because of similar training and expertise. Typically, rules and procedures govern the duties and responsibilities of each employee, and employees at lower hierarchical levels accept the right of those higher in the hierarchy to make decisions and issue orders.

Functional advantages and disadvantages

Grouping employees by common tasks permits economies of scale and efficient resource use. For example, at American Airlines, all information technology (IT) people work in the same large department. They have the expertise and skills to handle almost any issue related to IT for the organization. Large, functionally based departments enhance the development of in-depth skills, because people work on a variety of related

EXHIBIT 4.3 Five approaches to structural design

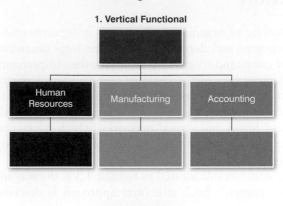

1. Vertical Functional

Human Resources | Manufacturing | Accounting

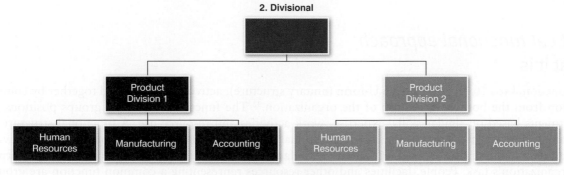

2. Divisional

Product Division 1 — Human Resources | Manufacturing | Accounting

Product Division 2 — Human Resources | Manufacturing | Accounting

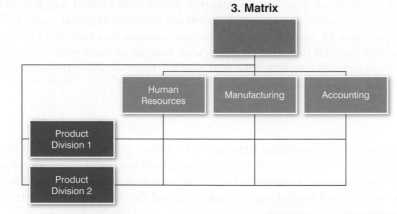

3. Matrix

Human Resources | Manufacturing | Accounting

Product Division 1

Product Division 2

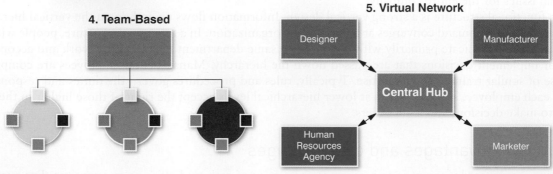

4. Team-Based

5. Virtual Network

Designer

Manufacturer

Central Hub

Human Resources Agency

Marketer

problems and are associated with other experts within their own department. Because the chain of command converges at the top, the functional structure also offers a way to centralize decision-making and provide unified direction from top managers. The primary disadvantages reflect barriers that exist across departments. Because people are separated into distinct departments, communication and coordination across functions are often poor, causing a slow response to environmental changes. Innovation and change require involvement of several departments. Another problem is that decisions involving more than one department may pile up at the top of the organization and be delayed. Effective boundary management is essential where the functions and divisions intercept.

Divisional approach

In contrast to the functional approach, in which people are grouped by common skills and resources, the divisional structure occurs when departments are grouped together based on similar organizational outputs. With a divisional structure, also called an **M-form** (multidivisional) *or a* decentralized form, separate divisions can be organized with responsibility for individual products, services, product groups, major projects or programmes, divisions, businesses or profit centres.[34] The divisional structure is also sometimes called a product structure, programme structure *or* a self-contained unit structure. Each of these terms means essentially the same thing: diverse departments are brought together to produce a single organizational output, whether it is a product, a programme or a service to a single customer.

Most large corporations have separate divisions that perform different tasks, use different technologies or serve different customers. When a MNC organization produces products for different markets, the divisional structure works well, as each division is an autonomous business. For example, Walmart uses divisions for Wal-Mart Stores, Sam's Club (US) and International Stores. Each of these large divisions is further subdivided into smaller geographical divisions to better serve customers in different regions.[35]

 CONCEPT CONNECTION

The health science company, Nordion Inc., manufacturer of products used for the prevention, diagnosis and treatment of diseases, split into two new business units: Targeted Therapies and Specialty Isotopes. Nordion's CEO Steve West explained that the new **divisional structure** is strategically designed to *'take into account the unique product life cycles and the needs of our customers in each of our businesses'*. Based in Ottawa in Canada, Nordion does business in 60 countries around the world.

How divisionalization works

Functional and divisional structures are illustrated in Exhibit 4.4. In a divisional structure, divisions are created as self-contained units, with separate functional departments for each division. For example, in Exhibit 4.4, each functional department resource needed to produce the product is assigned to each division. Whereas in a functional structure all R&D engineers are grouped together and work on all products, in a divisional structure, separate R&D departments are created within each division. Each department is smaller and focuses on a single product line or customer segment. Departments are duplicated across product lines.

The primary difference between divisional and functional structures is that in a divisional structure, the chain of command from each function converges lower in the hierarchy. In a divisional structure, differences of opinion among R&D, marketing, manufacturing and finance would be resolved at the divisional level rather than by the president. Thus, the divisional structure encourages decentralization. Decision-making is pushed down at least one level in the hierarchy, freeing the president and other top managers for strategic planning. Top-level executives should not be

EXHIBIT 4.4 Functional versus divisional structures

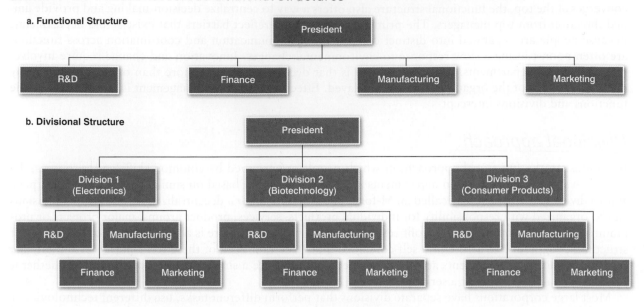

EXHIBIT 4.5 Geographic-based global organization structure

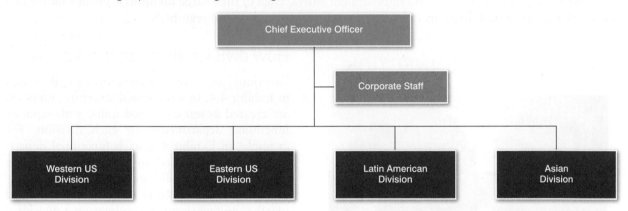

burdened by too many general management duties as their task is to heed entrepreneurial imperatives of strategic leadership. There is a definite balancing act to be fully taken into account. First, that the organization can meet current and new client needs. Second, that the organization is synchronized to respond and meet future market requirements.

Geographic or customer-based divisions

An alternative for assigning divisional responsibility is to group company activities by geographic region, or by customer group. For example, the Internal Revenue Service (IRS) shifted to a structure focused on four distinct taxpayer (customer) groups: individuals, small businesses, corporations and non-profit or government agencies.[36] A global geographic structure is illustrated in Exhibit 4.5. In a geographic-based structure, all functions in a specific country or region report to the same division manager. The structure thus focuses company activities on local market conditions. Competitive advantage may come from the production or sale of a product or service adapted to a given country or region. Walt Disney Company CEO, Bob Iger, reorganized the Disney Channel into geographic divisions, because what appeals to people in different countries varies. Studio executives in Burbank, California, were displeased at the reorganization, but it paid off. Iger learned that the number 1 programme on Italy's Disney Channel was one he had never heard of – 'Il Mondo di Patty', an inexpensive, telenovela-style show about an Argentine girl. *'It's important that Disney's products are presented in ways that are culturally relevant,'* Iger said about the geographic reorganization.[37] Large non-profit organizations such as the YMCAs and the Scouts and Lions International also frequently use a type of geographical structure, with a central headquarters and semiautonomous local units.[38]

Divisional advantages and disadvantages

By dividing employees and resources along divisional lines, the organization will be more flexible and responsive to change, because each unit is small and tuned in to its environment. By having employees working on a single product line, the concern for customers' needs is potentially very high. Coordination across functional departments is improved because employees are grouped together in a single location and committed to the one product line. Great coordination therefore exists within divisions; however, coordination *across* divisions is often poor. Problems occurred at Hewlett-Packard (HP), for example, when over-autonomous divisions went in opposite directions. The software produced in one division did not fit the hardware produced in another. Thus, the divisional structure was realigned to establish adequate coordination across divisions. Another major disadvantage is duplication of resources and the high cost of running separate divisions. Instead of a single research department in which all research people use a single facility, each division may have its own research facility. The organization loses efficiency and economies of scale. In addition, the small size of departments within each division may result in a lack of technical specialization, expertise and training.

The matrix: a plurality approach

The matrix approach combines aspects of both functional and divisional structures simultaneously in the same part of the organization. The matrix structure evolved as a way to improve horizontal coordination and information sharing.[39] One unique feature of the matrix is that it has plural lines of authority. In Exhibit 4.6, the functional hierarchy of authority runs vertically, and the divisional hierarchy of authority runs horizontally. The vertical structure provides traditional control within functional departments, and the horizontal structure provides coordination across departments. The US operation of Starbucks, for example,

EXHIBIT 4.6 Dual-authority structure in a matrix organization

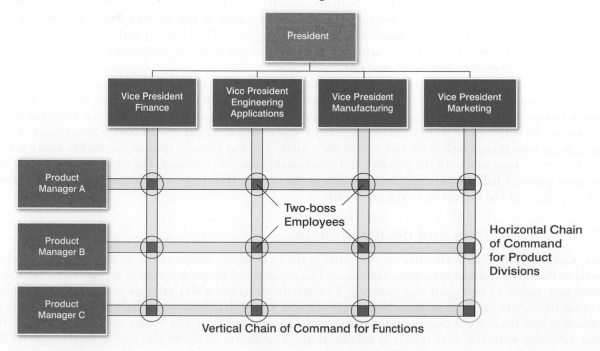

EXHIBIT 4.7 Global matrix structure

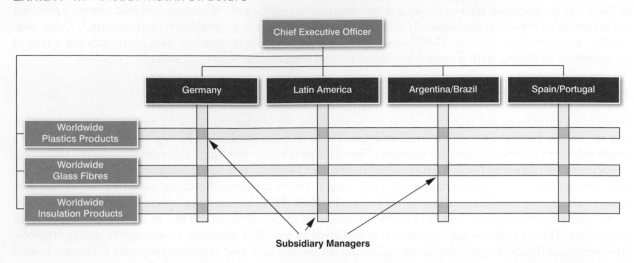

uses geographic divisions for Western/Pacific, Northwest/Mountain, Southeast/Plains and Northeast/Atlantic. Functional departments including finance, marketing and so forth are centralized and operate as their own vertical units, as well as supporting the horizontal divisions.[40] The matrix structure therefore supports a formal chain of command for both functional (vertical) and divisional (horizontal) relationships. As a result of this dual structure, some employees actually report to two supervisors/managers simultaneously. It is a common structure in management consultancies.

How the matrix works

The dual lines of authority make the matrix unique. To see how the matrix works, consider the global matrix structure illustrated in Exhibit 4.7. The two lines of authority are geographic and product. The geographic boss in Germany coordinates all subsidiaries in Germany, and the plastics products boss coordinates the manufacturing and sale of plastics products around the world. Managers of local subsidiary companies in Germany would report to two superiors, both the country boss and the product boss. The dual authority structure violates the unity-of-command concept described earlier in this chapter, but is necessary to give equal emphasis to both functional and divisional lines of authority. Dual lines of authority can be confusing, but after managers learn to use this structure the matrix provides excellent coordination simultaneously for each geographic region and each product line.

The success of the matrix structure depends on the abilities of people in key matrix roles. Two-boss employees, those who report to two supervisors simultaneously, must resolve conflicting demands from the matrix bosses. They must work with senior managers to reach joint decisions. They need excellent human relations skills with which to confront managers and resolve conflicts. The matrix boss is the product or functional boss, who is responsible for one side of the matrix. The top leader is responsible for the entire matrix. The top leader oversees both the product and functional chains of command. His or her responsibility is to maintain a power balance between the two sides of the matrix. If disputes arise between them, the problem will be passed up the hierarchy to the top leader.

Matrix advantages and disadvantages

The matrix can be highly effective in a complex, rapidly changing environment in which the organization needs to be flexible, innovative and adaptable.[41] The conflict and frequent meetings generated by the matrix allow new issues to be raised and resolved. The matrix structure makes efficient use of human resources because specialists can be transferred from one division to another. A major problem with the matrix is the confusion and frustration caused by the dual chain of command.[42] Matrix bosses and two-boss employees have difficulty with the dual reporting relationships. The matrix structure also can generate high conflict because it pits divisional against functional goals in a domestic structure, or product line versus country goals in a global structure. Rivalry between the two sides of the matrix can be exceedingly difficult for two-boss employees to manage. This problem leads to the third disadvantage: time lost to meetings and discussions devoted to resolving this type of recurring conflict. Often the matrix structure leads to more discussion than action because different goals and points of view are being addressed. Managers may spend a great deal of time coordinating meetings and assignments, which takes time resources away from core work activities.

REFLECTION

- **Departmentalization** is the basis for grouping individual positions into departments and departments into the total organization.
- Three traditional approaches to departmentalization are functional, divisional and matrix.
- A **functional structure** groups employees into departments based on similar skills, tasks and use of resources.
- The **divisional structure** groups employees and departments based on similar organizational outputs (products or services), such that each division has a mix of functional skills and tasks.
- An alternative approach to divisional structure is to group employees and departments based on geographic region or customer group.

- The Disney Channel is structured into geographic divisions to better address the interests of children and teens in different parts of the world.
- The **matrix approach** uses both functional and divisional chains of command simultaneously, in the same part of the organization.
- In a matrix structure, some employees, called **two-boss employees**, report to two supervisors simultaneously.
- A **matrix boss** is a functional or product supervisor responsible for one side of the matrix.
- In a matrix structure, the **top leader** oversees both the product and the functional chains of command and is responsible for the entire matrix.
- Each approach to departmentalization has distinct advantages and disadvantages.

Team approach
What teams achieve

Probably the most widespread trend in departmentalization in recent years has been the implementation of team concepts. The vertical chain of command is a powerful means of control, but passing all decisions up the hierarchy takes too long and keeps responsibility at the top. The team approach gives managers a way to delegate authority, push responsibility to lower levels, and be more flexible and responsive in a complex and competitive global environment. Chapter 16 will discuss teams in detail.

How it works

One approach to using teams in organizations is through cross-functional teams, which consist of employees from various functional departments who are responsible to meet as a team and resolve mutual problems. For example, at Total Attorneys, a Chicago-based company that provides software and services to small law firms, CEO Ed Scanlan realized that the functional structure, which broke projects down into sequential stages that moved from one department to another, was slowing things down so much that clients' needs had sometimes changed by the time the product was completed. He solved the problem by creating small, cross-functional teams to increase horizontal **coordination**. Now, designers, coders and quality-assurance testers work closely together on each project.[43] Cross-functional teams can provide needed horizontal coordination to complement an existing divisional or functional structure. A frequent use of cross-functional teams is for change projects, such as new product or service innovation. Team members typically still report to their functional departments, but they also report to the team, one member of whom may be the leader.

The second approach is to use permanent teams, groups of employees who are organized in a way similar to a formal department. Each team brings together employees from all functional areas focused on a specific task or project, such as parts supply and logistics for an automobile plant. Emphasis is on horizontal

🔗 CONCEPT CONNECTION

Hospitals and other health care providers face a great need for **coordination** because medical care needs to be integrated. For instance, collaborative care, like this **cross-functional team** of a nurse, doctor and dietitian, helps patients with chronic illnesses require fewer emergency department visits. Rush University Medical Center in Chicago started its Virtual Integrated Practice (VIP) project to give physicians in private practice access to teams of physicians, dieticians, pharmacists and social workers. VIP replicates the collaboration that can occur in a hospital setting by enabling members to share information via email, telephone and fax.

communication and information sharing because representatives from all functions are coordinating their work and skills to complete a specific organizational task. Authority is pushed down to lower levels, and front-line employees are often given the freedom to make decisions and take action on their own. Team members may share or rotate team leadership. With a team-based structure, the entire organization is made up of horizontal teams that coordinate their work and work directly with customers to accomplish the organization's goals.[44]

Team advantages and disadvantages

The team approach breaks down barriers across departments and improves coordination and cooperation. Team members get to know one another's problems and often compromise, rather than blindly pursue their own goals. The team concept also enables the organization to adapt more quickly to customer requests and environmental changes and speeds decision-making because less decisions need to go to the top of the hierarchy for approval. Another major advantage is the boost to employee morale. Employees are typically more enthusiastic about their involvement in bigger projects rather than narrow departmental tasks. At video games company Ubisoft, for example, each studio is set up so that teams of employees and managers work collaboratively to develop new games. Employees don't make much money, but they're motivated by the freedom they have to propose new ideas and put them into action.[45]

However, the team approach has disadvantages as well. Employees may be enthusiastic about team participation, but they may also experience conflicts and dual loyalties. A cross-functional team may make different work demands on members than do their department managers, and members who participate in more than one team must resolve these conflicts. A large amount of time is devoted to meetings, thus increasing coordination time. Unless the organization truly needs teams to coordinate complex projects and adapt to the environment, it will lose production efficiency with them. Finally, the team approach may cause too much decentralization. Senior department managers who traditionally made decisions might feel left out when a team moves ahead on its own. Team members often do not see the big picture of the corporation and may make decisions that are good for their group but bad for the organization as a whole.

Virtual network approach
What do networks achieve?

The most recent approach to departmentalization extends the idea of horizontal coordination and collaboration beyond the boundaries of the organization. In a variety of industries, vertically integrated, hierarchical organizations are giving way to loosely interconnected groups of companies with permeable boundaries.[46] *Outsourcing*, which means farming out certain activities, such as manufacturing or credit processing, has become a significant trend. British retailer J. Sainsbury, for example, lets Accenture handle its entire IT department. Ohio State University plans to outsource its parking system. And the City

CONCEPT CONNECTION

William Wang, founder of Vizio, Inc., produces competitively priced LCD and plasma televisions using the **virtual network approach**. Wang keeps costs down by running a lean operation, outsourcing manufacturing, research and development, and technical support. Vizio televisions are priced about 50 per cent lower than most brands. The network approach has paid off. After only 7 years in business, the company surpassed Sony in 2010 to become the second best-selling brand in the USA.

of Manwood, California, decided to outsource everything from street maintenance to policing and public safety. The budget for the police department used to be nearly $8 million. Now the city pays about half that to the Los Angeles County Sheriff's Department and residents say service has improved.[47] The pharmaceuticals company Pfizer is using an innovative approach that lets some employees pass off certain parts of their jobs to an outsourcing firm in India with a click of a button. Rather than shifting entire functions to contractors, this 'personal outsourcing' approach allows people to shift only certain tedious and time-consuming tasks to be handled by the outsourcing partner, while they focus on higher-value work.[48]

Some organizations take this networking approach to the extreme to create an innovative structure. The virtual network structure means that the firm subcontracts most of its major functions to separate companies and coordinates their activities from a small headquarters organization.[49] How would you feel about working as a freelance employee for a virtual company? The Shoptalk describes some pros and cons of 'never having to go to the office'.

How it works

The organization may be viewed as a central hub surrounded by a network of outside specialists, sometimes spread all over the world, as illustrated in Exhibit 4.8. Rather than being housed under one roof, services such as accounting, design, manufacturing and distribution are outsourced to separate organizations that are connected electronically to the central office.[50] Networked computer systems, collaborative software and the Internet enable organizations to exchange data and information so rapidly and smoothly that a loosely connected network of suppliers, manufacturers, assemblers and distributors can look and act like one seamless company.

The idea behind networks is that a company can concentrate on what it does best and contract out other activities to companies with distinctive competence in those specific areas, which enables a company to do more with less.[51] The 'heart-healthy' US food company Smart Balance has been able to innovate and expand rapidly by using a virtual network approach.

With a network structure such as that used at Smart Balance, it is difficult to answer the question 'Where is the organization?' in traditional terms. The different organizational parts are drawn together contractually

INNOVATIVE WAY

Smart Balance

Smart Balance has about 67 employees, but nearly 400 people are working for the company. Smart Balance started by making a buttery spread and now has a line of spreads, all-natural peanut butter, nutrient-enhanced

milk, cheese, sour cream, popcorn and other products. Managers credit the virtual network approach with helping the company innovate and expand rapidly.

Smart Balance keeps product development and marketing in-house but uses contractors to do just about everything else, including manufacturing, distribution, sales, IT services, and research and testing. The way the company got into the milk business shows how the network structure increases speed and flexibility. Peter Dray, vice president of product development, was able to get the help he needed to perfect the product from contractors. Outside scientists and research and development consultants worked on the formula. The company contracted with a dairy processor to do tests and trial production runs. An outside laboratory assessed nutritional claims and another company managed consumer taste tests.

Each morning, full-time employees and virtual workers exchange a flurry of email messages and telephone calls to update each other on what took place the day before and what needs to happen today. Executives spend much of their time managing relationships. Twice a year they hold all-company meetings that include permanent staff and contractors. Information is shared widely, and managers make a point of recognizing the contributions of contractors to the company's success, which helps create a sense of unity and commitment.[52]

EXHIBIT 4.8 Network approach to departmentalization

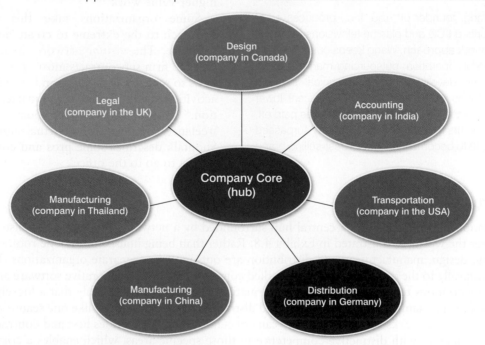

and coordinated electronically, creating a new form of organization. Much like building blocks, parts of the network can be added or taken away to meet changing needs.[53]

A similar approach to networking is called the modular approach, in which a manufacturing company uses outside suppliers to provide entire chunks of a product, which are then assembled into a final product by a handful of workers. The modular approach passes off responsibility for engineering and production of entire sections of a product, such as a Volkswagen automobile or a Boeing airplane, to outside suppliers. Suppliers design a module, making some of the parts themselves and subcontracting others. Parts for the Boeing 787 Dreamliner jet, for example, came from 135 companies in two dozen countries.[54] These modules are delivered right to the assembly line, where a handful of employees bolt and weld them together into the aeroplane.

Virtual network advantages and disadvantages

The biggest advantages to a virtual network approach are flexibility and competitiveness on a global scale. The extreme flexibility of a network approach is illustrated by recent anti-government protests and the 2011 overthrow of leaders in Tunisia and Egypt.[55] A far-flung collection of groups that share a similar mission and

🌐 MANAGER'S SHOPTALK

Would you like to work in your pyjamas?

There are about 34 million Americans who work from home at least part of the time, and millions more in other countries. Some of these people are freelancers, or 'solopreneurs', who enter into outsourcing contracts to perform services for companies around the world. Escaping the 9-to-5 office grind sounds like a dream to many people, but working solo has its down side. Most people who are accustomed to working in an office go through a bumpy transition when they switch to working virtually. Here are just a few of the good and bad things about working on your own.

Pro: You can be more productive. Many people find they can get more done working from home. For one thing, you might gain a couple of extra hours a day that you used to spend commuting. When reporters, editors, designers and the numerous other professionals who put together *Inc.* magazine experimented with putting out an issue by working entirely outside the office, most of them found that they accomplished more work in an environment where they could focus for long stretches of time without distractions. However, Ms Meyer as the incoming CEO of Yahoo, quickly changed the company ethos by insisting that employees did more work in the Yahoo office environment, as she thought that face-to-face engagement was an important aspect that was not strong enough for the corporation's competitiveness.

Con: It's all up to you to make it work. It takes discipline, self-management and organization skills to make sure you complete all the jobs you've agreed to do. Some people can't resist funny websites, the television, the kids and pets or raiding the refrigerator, long enough to actually get any work done. These types typically don't do well working from home and need the structure of an office to keep them motivated and productive. On the other hand, some people find that they work *too much* and have to learn to set boundaries.

Pro: You can set your own schedule and define your own work. If you want to sleep in and work later in the day, fine. If you want to take a 3-hour lunch break, there's no one telling you that you can't. You can choose your own projects and organize the activities and tasks the way it makes sense to you rather than having someone else dictating how to do things. You can choose the companies you want to work for – anywhere in the world.

Con: Lack of recognition and feedback can create self-doubt, stress and frustration. Lack of recognition is a common complaint among virtual workers. In addition, it's often hard to assess what your client really thinks of you and your performance. A lot of virtual solo entrepreneurs don't get regular feedback which can lead to self-doubt – and the solitary nature of the work doesn't help. 'I was spending all day in my tiny apartment, not talking to anyone,' said one virtual worker. Many people counteract the isolation of virtual work by taking their laptop to a coffee shop or spending some time at a 'co-working centre', where they can rent office space on a daily basis.

And finally … A blog on the thereitis website offered a lighthearted look at some of the pros and cons of virtual work: You never again have to worry about a bad hair day or spend an hour getting dressed for work. But you just might miss the chance to 'power dress' once in a while.

SOURCES: Max Chafkin, 'The Office Is Dead. Long Live the Office: The Case, and the Plan, for the Virtual Company', *Inc.* (April 2010): 62–73; Laurie Sheppard, 'Challenges to Working Virtually', *Creating at Will* website, 2011, www.creatingatwill.com/challenges-to-working-virtually/ (accessed August 17, 2012); Sara Fletcher, '5 Challenges of Working from Home', *RecruitingBlogs,* August 14, 2012, www.recruitingblogs.com/profiles/blogs/5-challenges-of-working-from-home (accessed August 16, 2012); and 'Perks and Challenges of Virtual Work', *thereitis.com*, www.blog.thereitis.com/post/22640167629/challenges-of-virtual-work (accessed 17 August 2012).

goals but are free to act on their own joined together to mastermind the 'Arab Spring' uprisings, much in the same way as terrorist groups have masterminded attacks against the USA and other countries. *'Attack any single part of it, and the rest carries on largely untouched,'* wrote one journalist about the terrorist network. *'It cannot be decapitated, because the insurgency, for the most part, has no head.'*[56]

Similarly, today's business organizations can benefit from a flexible network approach that lets them shift resources and respond quickly. A network organization can draw on resources and expertise worldwide to achieve the best quality and price and can sell its products and services worldwide. Flexibility comes from the ability to hire whatever services are needed and to change a few months later without constraints from owning plant, equipment and facilities. The organization can redefine itself continually to fit new product and market opportunities. This structure is perhaps the leanest of all organization forms because little supervision is required. Large teams of staff specialists and administrators are not needed. A network organization may have only two or three levels of hierarchy, compared with ten or more in traditional organizations.[57]

One of the major disadvantages is lack of hands-on control.[58] Managers do not have all operations under one roof and must rely on contracts, coordination, negotiation and electronic linkages to hold things together. Each partner in the network necessarily acts in its own self-interest. The weak and ambiguous boundaries create higher uncertainty and greater demands on managers for defining shared goals, managing relationships, keeping people focused and motivated, and coordinating activities so that everything functions as intended. Consider, for instance, that production of Boeing's 787 Dreamliner fell 2 years behind schedule because the 'modules' from various contractors that were supposed to be fitted together didn't always fit.[59] Customer service and loyalty can also suffer if outsourcing partners fail to perform as expected.[60] The reputation of United Airlines was severely damaged when the employee assigned by an outsourcing contractor to supervise an unaccompanied 10-year-old at Chicago's busy O'Hare Airport, didn't show up. The story made the national news when United's own employees failed to respond appropriately and the parents couldn't locate their missing child for nearly an hour.[61] Finally, in this type of organization, employee loyalty can weaken. Employees might feel they can be replaced by contract services. A cohesive corporate culture is less likely to develop, and employee turnover tends to be higher, because emotional commitment between organization and employee is fragile.

Exhibit 4.9 summarizes the major advantages and disadvantages of each type of structure we have discussed.

EXHIBIT 4.9 Structural advantages and disadvantages

Structural approach	Advantages	Disadvantages
Functional	Efficient use of resources; economies of scale In-depth skill specialization and development Top manager direction and control	Poor communication across functional departments Slow response to external changes; lagging innovation Decisions concentrated at top of hierarchy, creating delay
Divisional	Fast response, flexibility in unstable environment Fosters concern for customer needs Excellent coordination across functional departments	Duplication of resources across divisions Less technical depth and specialization Poor coordination across divisions
Matrix	More efficient use of resources than single hierarchy Flexibility, adaptability to changing environment Interdisciplinary cooperation, expertise available to all divisions	Frustration and confusion from dual chain of command High conflict between two sides of the matrix Many meetings, more discussion than action
Team	Reduced barriers among departments, increased compromise Shorter response time, quicker decisions Better morale, enthusiasm from employee involvement	Dual loyalties and conflict Time and resources spent on meetings Unplanned decentralization
Virtual network	Can draw on expertise worldwide Highly flexible and responsive Reduced overhead costs	Lack of control; weak boundaries Greater demands on managers Weaker employee loyalty

REFLECTION

- Popular contemporary approaches to departmentalization include team and virtual network structures.
- A **cross-functional team** is a group of employees from various functional departments that meet as a team to resolve mutual problems.
- Total Attorneys uses cross-functional teams to improve coordination on software and services projects for small law firm clients.
- A **permanent team** is a group of employees from all functional areas permanently assigned to focus on a specific task or activity.
- A **team-based structure** is one in which the entire organization is made up of horizontal teams that

coordinate their activities and work directly with customers to accomplish organizational goals.
- With a **virtual network structure**, the organization subcontracts most of its major functions to separate companies and coordinates their activities from a small headquarters organization.
- The **modular approach** is one in which a manufacturing company uses outside suppliers to provide large modular sections of a product, such as an automobile, which are then assembled into a final product by a few employees.
- Both the team and the network approach have distinct advantages and disadvantages.

Organizing for horizontal coordination

One reason for the growing use of teams and networks is that many managers recognize the limits of traditional vertical organization structures in a fast-shifting environment. In general, the trend is towards breaking down barriers between departments, and many companies are moving towards horizontal structures based on work processes rather than departmental functions.[62] However, regardless of the type of structure, every organization needs mechanisms for horizontal integration and coordination. The structure of an organization is not complete without designing the horizontal as well as the vertical dimensions of structure.[63]

The need for coordination

As organizations grow and evolve, two things happen. First, new positions and departments are added to deal with factors in the external environment or with new strategic needs, as described earlier in the chapter. As companies add positions and departments to meet changing needs, they grow more complex, with hundreds of positions and departments performing incredibly diverse activities.

Second, senior managers have to find a way to tie all these departments together. The formal chain of command and the supervision it provides is effective, but it is not enough. The organization needs systems to process information and enable communication among people in different departments and at different levels. Coordination refers to the managerial task of adjusting and synchronizing the diverse activities among different individuals and departments. Collaboration means a joint effort between people from two or more departments to produce outcomes that meet a common goal or shared purpose and that are typically greater than what any of the individuals or departments could achieve working alone.[64] To understand the value of collaboration, consider the 2011 US mission to raid Osama bin Laden's compound in Pakistan. The raid could not have succeeded without close collaboration between the Central Intelligence Agency (CIA) and the US military. There has traditionally been insufficient interaction between the nation's intelligence officers and its military officers, but the war on terrorism has changed that mindset. During planning for the bin Laden mission, military officers spent every day for months working closely with the CIA team in a remote, secure facility on the CIA campus. *'This is the kind of thing that, in the past, people who watched movies thought was possible, but no one in the government thought was possible,'* one official later said of the collaborative mission.[65]

Collaboration and coordination within business organizations is just as important. Without coordination, a company's left hand will not act in concert with the right hand, causing problems and conflicts. Coordination is required regardless of whether the organization has a functional, divisional or team structure. Employees identify with their immediate department or team, taking its interest to heart, and they may not want to

EXHIBIT 4.10 Evolution of organization structures

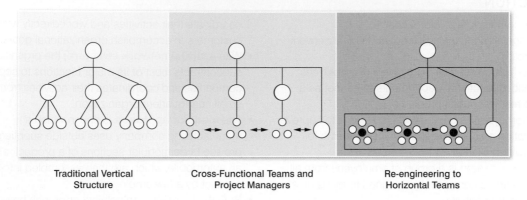

| Traditional Vertical Structure | Cross-Functional Teams and Project Managers | Re-engineering to Horizontal Teams |

compromise and collaborate with other units for the good of the organization as a whole. The dangers of poor coordination are reflected in recent quality and safety issues with Toyota vehicles and the inadequate initial response by top managers. A panel investigating the situation pinpointed lack of information sharing and poor communication and collaboration across different units as one distinct problem.[66]

The problem is amplified in the international arena because organizational units are differentiated not only by goals and work activities, but also by geographical distance, time differences, cultural values and perhaps language. Toyota, for instance, is a huge organization with divisions all over the world. How can managers ensure that needed coordination and collaboration will take place in their company, both domestically and globally? Coordination is the outcome of information and cooperation. Managers can design systems and structures to promote the fullest horizontal coordination and collaboration.

Exhibit 4.10 illustrates the evolution of organizational structures, with a growing emphasis on horizontal coordination. Although the vertical functional structure is effective in stable environments, it does not provide the horizontal coordination needed in times of rapid change. Innovations such as cross-functional teams, task forces and project managers, work within the vertical structure but provide a means to increase horizontal communication and cooperation. The next stage involves re-engineering to structure the organization into teams working on horizontal processes. Re-engineering refers to the radical redesign of business processes to achieve dramatic improvements in cost, quality, service and speed. Because the focus of re-engineering is on horizontal workflows rather than function, re-engineering generally leads to a shift away from a strong vertical structure to one emphasizing stronger horizontal coordination. The vertical hierarchy is flattened, with perhaps only a few senior executives in traditional support functions such as finance and human resources.

Task forces, teams and project management

A task force is a temporary team or committee designed to solve a problem involving several departments.[67] Task force members represent their departments and share information that enables coordination. For example, at Irving Medical Center, a unit of Kaiser Permanente in California, a task force made up of operating room nurses, surgeons, technicians, housekeeping staff and others, came together to streamline the procedure for performing total-hip and knee-joint replacements, the hospital's costliest and most time-consuming surgeries. The resulting combination of enhanced coordination and reallocated resources meant that the number of these surgeries that could be performed increased from one or two a day up to four a day. Better coordination freed up 188 hours of operating room time a year, reflecting significant cost savings.[68] In addition to creating task forces, companies also set up *cross-functional teams*, such as the ones at Total Attorneys described earlier. A cross-functional team furthers horizontal coordination because participants from several departments meet regularly to solve ongoing problems of common interest.[69] This team is similar to a task force except that it works with continuing rather than temporary problems and might exist for several years. Team members think in terms

CONCEPT CONNECTION

The SciFi Channel had outgrown its brand image. Managers assembled a **task force** to create a new image that better represented the network's fantasy programming and appealed to a broader audience, especially women. After reviewing more than 300 names, the task force settled on *Syfy* because, said President David Howe, *'it's changing your name without changing your name'*. It also chose a logo (pictured) with softer, warmer-looking letters and created a short film, chockfull of special effects, to introduce the new name, logo and slogan ('Imagine Greater') to advertisers. It worked: the number of *Syfy* female viewers has grown substantially.

of working together for the good of the whole, rather than just for their own department.

Companies also use project managers to increase coordination. A project manager is a person who is responsible for coordinating the activities of several departments for the completion of a specific project.[70] Project managers might also have titles such as product manager, integrator, programme manager or process owner. The distinctive feature of the project manager position is that the person is not a member of one of the departments being coordinated. Project managers are located outside the departments and have responsibility for coordinating several departments to achieve desired project outcomes. At General Mills, for example, a manager is assigned to each product line, such as Cheerios, Bisquick and Hamburger Helper. Product managers set budget goals, marketing targets and strategies and obtain the cooperation from advertising, production and sales personnel needed for implementing product strategy.

In some organizations, project managers are included on the organization chart, as illustrated in Exhibit 4.11. The project manager is drawn to one side of the chart to indicate authority over the project but not over the people assigned to it. The *dashed lines* to the project manager indicate responsibility for coordination and communication with assigned team members, but department managers retain line authority over functional employees.

Relational coordination

The highest level of horizontal coordination is relational coordination. Relational coordination refers to *'frequent, timely, problem-solving communication carried out through [employee] relationships of shared goals, shared knowledge and mutual respect'*.[71] Relational coordination isn't a structural device or mechanism such as a project manager, but rather is part of the very fabric and culture of the organization. In an organization with a high level of relational coordination, people share information freely across departmental boundaries, and people interact on a continuous basis to share knowledge and solve problems. Coordination is carried out through a web of ongoing positive relationships rather than because of formal coordination roles or mechanisms.[72] Employees coordinate directly with each other across units.

To build relational coordination into the fabric of the organization, managers invest in training people in the skills needed to interact with one another and resolve cross-departmental conflicts based on shared goals rather than emphasizing goals of their separate departments. People are given freedom from strict work rules so they have the flexibility to interact and contribute wherever they are needed, and rewards are based on

EXHIBIT 4.11 Example of project manager relationships to other departments

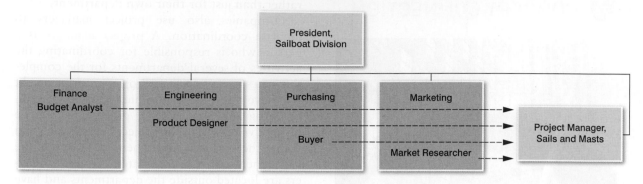

 INNOVATIVE **WAY**

Southwest Airlines

Airlines face many challenges, but one that they face hundreds of times on a daily basis is getting airplanes loaded and off the ground safely and on time. Flight departure is a highly complex process. It involves numerous employees from various departments – such as ticket agents, pilots, flight attendants, baggage handlers, gate agents, mechanics, ramp agents, fuel attendants and so forth – performing multiple tasks within a limited time period, under uncertain and ever-changing conditions. If all these groups aren't tightly coordinated, a successful on-time departure is difficult to achieve.

Southwest Airlines has the shortest turnaround time in the business, partly because managers promote relational coordination to achieve superior on-time performance and a high level of customer satisfaction. In any airline, there can be serious disagreements

among employees about who is to blame when a flight is delayed, so Southwest managers created what they call *team delay*. Rather than searching for who is to blame when something goes wrong, the team delay is used to point out problems in coordination between various groups. The emphasis on the team focuses everyone on their shared goals of on-time departure, accurate baggage handling and customer satisfaction. Because delay becomes a team problem, people are motivated to work closely together and coordinate their activities rather than looking out for themselves and trying to avoid or shift blame. Supervisors work closely with employees, but their role is less 'being the boss' as it is facilitating learning and helping people do their jobs. Southwest uses a small supervisory span of control – about one supervisor for every eight or nine front-line employees – so that supervisors have the time to coach and assist employees, who are viewed as internal customers.[73]

team efforts and accomplishments. Front-line supervisors typically have smaller spans of control so they can develop close working relationships with subordinates and coach and mentor employees. Southwest Airlines provides a good illustration.

By using practices that facilitate relational coordination, managers ensure that all the departments involved in flight departure are tightly coordinated. When relational coordination is high, people share information and coordinate their activities without having to have bosses or formal mechanisms telling them to do so. The team is thus self-functioning.

Factors shaping structure

Vertical hierarchies continue to thrive because they provide important benefits for organizations. Some degree of vertical hierarchy is often needed to organize a large number of people effectively to accomplish complex

REFLECTION

- In addition to the vertical structure, every organization needs mechanisms for horizontal integration and coordination.
- Coordination refers to the managerial task of adjusting and synchronizing the diverse activities among different individuals and departments.
- Collaboration means a joint effort between people from two or more departments to produce outcomes that meet a common goal or shared purpose.
- The successful US mission to raid Osama bin Laden's compound in Pakistan was a result of collaboration between the nation's intelligence officers and its military officers.
- As organizations grow, they add new positions, departments and hierarchical levels, which leads to greater coordination problems.
- Ways to increase horizontal coordination include task forces, teams, project managers and relational coordination.

- A task force is a temporary team or committee formed to solve a specific short-term problem involving several departments.
- A project manager is a person responsible for coordinating the activities of several departments for the completion of a specific project.
- Companies often shift to a more horizontal approach after going through re-engineering, which refers to the radical redesign of business processes to achieve dramatic improvements in cost, quality, service and speed.
- Relational coordination refers to frequent horizontal coordination and communication carried out through ongoing relationships of shared goals, shared knowledge and mutual respect.
- Southwest Airlines achieves the shortest turnaround time in the airline industry because managers foster relational coordination among the varied people and departments involved in the flight departure process.

tasks within a coherent framework. Without a vertical structure, people in a large, global firm wouldn't know what to do. However, in today's environment, an organization's vertical structure often needs to be balanced with strong horizontal mechanisms to achieve peak performance.[74]

How do managers know whether to design a structure that emphasizes the formal, vertical hierarchy or one with an emphasis on horizontal communication and collaboration? The answer lies in the organization's strategic goals and the nature of its technology. Exhibit 4.12 illustrates that forces affecting organization structure come from both outside and inside the organization. External strategic needs, such as environmental conditions, strategic direction and organizational goals, create top-down pressure for designing the organization in such a way as to fit the environment and accomplish strategic goals. Structural decisions also take into consideration pressures from the bottom up – that is, from the technology and work processes that are performed to produce the organization's products and services.

'The organizations that are most likely to survive are those that can balance themselves on the edge of chaos – and between the forces of change and the forces of stability.'
— CHRISTIAN GIBBONS, DIRECTOR, BUSINESS AND INDUSTRY
AFFAIRS, NEW ECONOMY PROJECT

Structure follows strategy

Studies demonstrate that business performance is strongly influenced by how well the company's structure is aligned with its strategic intent and the needs of the environment, so managers strive to pick strategies and structures that are congruent.[75] In Chapter 9, we discuss several strategies that business firms can adopt. Two strategies proposed by Professor Michael E. Porter are differentiation and cost leadership.[76] With a differentiation strategy, the organization attempts to develop innovative products unique to the market. With a cost leadership strategy, the organization strives for internal efficiency. The two strategies can of course work together.

Typically, strategic goals of cost efficiency occur in more stable environments, while goals of innovation and flexibility occur in more uncertain environments. The terms *mechanistic* and *organic* can be used to explain structural responses to strategy and the environment.[77] Goals of efficiency and a stable environment are associated

EXHIBIT 4.12 Factors affecting organization structure

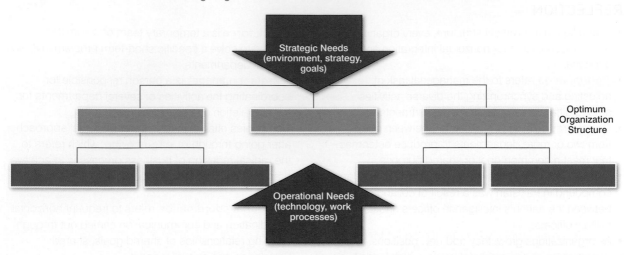

SOURCE: David A. Nadler and Michael L. Tushman with Mark B. Nadler, *Competing by Design: The Power of Organizational Architecture* (New York: Oxford University Press, 1997), p. 54.

with a mechanistic system. This type of organization typically has a rigid, vertical centralized structure, with most decisions made at the top. The organization is highly specialized and characterized by rules, procedures and a clear hierarchy of authority. With goals of innovation and a rapidly changing environment, however, the organization tends to be much looser, free-flowing and adaptive, using an organic system. The structure is more horizontal, and decision-making authority is decentralized. People at lower levels have more responsibility and authority for solving problems, enabling the organization to be more fluid and adaptable to changes.[78]

TAKE A MOMENT

Go to the Experiential Exercise online that pertains to organic versus mechanistic structure.

Exhibit 4.13 shows a simplified continuum that illustrates how different structural approaches are associated with strategy and the environment. The pure functional structure is appropriate for achieving internal efficiency goals in a stable environment. The vertical functional structure uses task specialization and a strict chain of command to gain efficient use of scarce resources, but it does not enable the organization to be flexible or innovative. In contrast, horizontal teams are appropriate when the primary goal is innovation and the organization needs flexibility to cope with an uncertain environment. Each team is small, is able to be responsive and has the people and resources necessary for performing its task. The flexible horizontal structure enables organizations to differentiate themselves and respond more quickly to the demands of a shifting environment but at the expense of efficient resource use.

Exhibit 4.13 also illustrates how other forms of structure represent intermediate steps on the organization's path to efficiency or innovation. The functional structure with cross-functional teams and project managers provides greater coordination and flexibility than the pure functional structure. The divisional structure promotes differentiation because each division can focus on specific products and customers, although divisions tend to be larger and less flexible than small teams. Exhibit 4.13 does not include all possible structures, but it illustrates how structures can be used to facilitate the organization's strategic goals.

TAKE A MOMENT

The Small Group Breakout Exercise online will give you a chance to practise organizing to meet strategic needs.

EXHIBIT 4.13 Relationship of structural approach to strategy and the environment

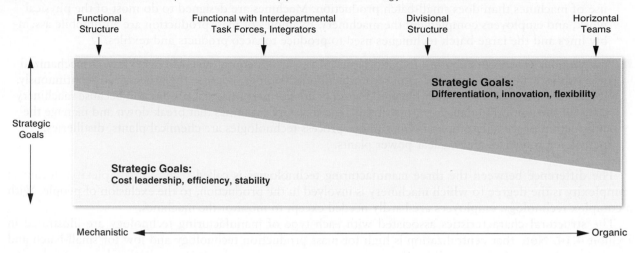

REFLECTION

- Contingency factors of strategic goals, environment and technology influence the correct structural approach.
- A mechanistic, vertical structure is appropriate for a cost leadership strategy, which typically occurs in a stable environment.

- An organic, horizontal approach is needed for a differentiation strategy and when the organization needs flexibility to cope with an uncertain environment.

Structure fits the technology

Technology includes the knowledge, tools, techniques and activities used to transform organizational inputs into outputs.[79] Technology includes machinery, employee skills and work procedures. A useful way to think about technology is as 'production activities'. The production activities may be to produce website content, steel castings, television programmes or computer software. Technologies vary between manufacturing and service organizations.

Woodward's manufacturing technology

The most influential research into the relationship between manufacturing technology and organization structure was conducted decades ago by Joan Woodward, a British industrial sociologist.[80] She gathered data from 100 British firms to determine whether basic structural characteristics, such as administrative overhead, span of control and centralization, were different across firms. She found that manufacturing firms could be categorized according to three basic types of production technology:

- *Small-batch and unit production.* Small-batch production firms produce goods in batches of one or a few products designed to customer specification. This technology also is used to make large, one-of-a-kind products, such as computer-controlled machines. Small-batch manufacturing is close to traditional skilled-craft work, because human beings are a large part of the process. Examples of items produced through small-batch manufacturing include custom clothing, special-order machine tools, space capsules, satellites and submarines.

- *Large-batch and mass production.* Mass production technology is distinguished by standardized production runs. A large volume of products is produced, and all customers receive the same product.

Standard products go into inventory for sale as customers need them. This technology makes greater use of machines than does small-batch production. Machines are designed to do most of the physical work, and employees complement the machinery. Examples of mass production are automobile assembly lines and the large-batch techniques used to produce tobacco products and textiles.

■ *Continuous process production.* In continuous process production, the entire workflow is mechanized in a sophisticated and complex form of production technology. Because the process runs continuously, it has no starting and stopping. Human operators are not part of actual production because machinery does all the work. Human operators simply read dials, fix machines that break down and manage the production process. Examples of continuous process technologies are chemical plants, distilleries, petroleum refineries and nuclear power plants.

The difference between the three manufacturing technologies is called technical complexity. Technical complexity is the degree to which machinery is involved in the production, to the exclusion of people. With a complex technology, employees are hardly needed except to monitor the machines.

The structural characteristics associated with each type of manufacturing technology are illustrated in Exhibit 4.14. Note that centralization is high for mass production technology and low for small-batch and continuous process. Unlike small-batch and continuous process production, standardized mass-production machinery requires centralized decision-making and well-defined rules and procedures. The administrative ratio and the percentage of indirect labour required also increase with technological complexity. Because the production process is non-routine, closer supervision is needed. More indirect labour in the form of maintenance people is required because of the machinery's complexity; thus, the indirect/direct labour ratio is high. Span of control for first-line supervisors is greatest for mass production. On an assembly line, jobs are so routinized that a supervisor can handle an average of 48 employees. The number of employees per supervisor in small-batch and continuous process production is lower because closer supervision is needed. Overall, small-batch and continuous process firms have somewhat loose, flexible structures (organic), and mass production firms have tight vertical structures (mechanistic).

Woodward found that the relationship between structure and technology was directly related to company performance. Low-performing firms tended to deviate from the preferred structural form, often adopting a structure appropriate for another type of technology. These findings still have relevance in today's manufacturing companies. High-performing organizations had characteristics similar to those listed below in Exhibit 4.14.

EXHIBIT 4.14   Relationship between manufacturing technology and organization structure

	Manufacturing technology		
	Small batch	Mass production	Continuous process
Technical complexity of production technology	Low	Medium	High
Structural characteristics: Centralization	Low	High	Low
Top administrator ratio	Low	Medium	High
Indirect/direct labour ratio	1/9	1/4	1/1
Supervisor span of control	23	48	15
Communication:			
Written (vertical)	Low	High	Low
Verbal (horizontal)	High	Low	High
Overall structure	Organic	Mechanistic	Organic

SOURCE: Joan Woodward, *Industrial Organizations: Theory and Practice* (London: Oxford University Press, 1965).

Service technology

Examples of service organizations include consulting companies, law firms, brokerage houses, airlines, hotels, advertising companies, amusement parks and educational organizations. In addition, service technology characterizes many departments in large corporations, even manufacturing firms. In a manufacturing company such as Ford Motor Company, the legal, human resources, finance and market research departments all provide service. Thus, the structure and design of these departments reflect their own service technology rather than the manufacturing plant's technology. Service technology can be defined as follows:

- ◼ *Intangible output.* The output of a service firm is intangible. Services are perishable and, unlike physical products, cannot be stored in inventory. The service is either consumed immediately or lost forever. Manufactured products are produced at one point in time and can be stored until sold at another time.

- ◼ *Direct contact with customers.* Employees and customers interact directly to provide and purchase the service. Production and consumption are simultaneous. Service firm employees have direct contact with customers. In a manufacturing firm, technical employees are separated from customers, and hence no direct interactions occur.[81]

One distinct feature of service technology that directly influences structure is the need for employees to be close to the customer.[82] Structural characteristics are similar to those for continuous manufacturing technology, shown in Exhibit 4.14. Service firms tend to be flexible, informal and decentralized. Horizontal communication is high because employees must share information and resources to serve customers and solve problems. Services also are dispersed, hence each unit is often small and located geographically close to customers. For example, banks, hotels, fast-food franchises and doctors' offices disperse their facilities into regional and local offices to provide faster and better service to customers.

Some services can be broken down into explicit steps, so that employees can follow set rules and procedures. An interesting example comes from India, where Dr Devi Shetty runs a hospital that performs open heart surgery for about 10 per cent of the cost charged by hospitals in the USA, without reduced quality, by applying standardized operating procedures and principles of mass production. His approach is in line with a trend towards *lean services* that looks at how to design service work to improve both quality and efficiency. '*In healthcare, you can't do one thing and reduce the price,*' Dr. Shetty says. '*We have to do 1000 small things*'.[83] When services can be standardized, a tight centralized structure can be effective, but service firms in general tend to be more organic, flexible and decentralized.

Outsourcing of services

A major trend observed in recent years has been the outsourcing of services by MNCs. Indeed, many UK-domiciled banks now have service call centres located in the Philippines and India, producing high cost savings. But the consequence of the transfer from the UK to non-nationals has been, for many customers, a reduction in the quality of their customer experience. The amount of government funds spent on outsourcing public services roughly doubled during the period 2010–2014. Gill Plimmer, writing in *the Financial Times*, (April 2015) states: '*This highlights an accelerating pace in justice, welfare and defence. Tens of thousands of staff have been transferred to private sector management, as the coalition [government] sought cost savings, according to figures from the Information Services Group (ISG) consultancy.*' [and] '*The UK outsourcing market is now the second largest in the world outside the USA.*' states the ISG report. ISG's data also discloses the top five outsourcers winning government contracts to be: Hays, Carillion, BT Group, Serco and Capita (the biggest winner of deals). The chair of the UK public accounts committee has called the privatization of public services (cited in Plimmer's article of 30 April 2015) as being: 'The most important policy issue of our time'.

REFLECTION

- Types of technologies include manufacturing and service.
- **Small-batch production** is a type of manufacturing technology that involves the production of goods in batches of one or a few products designed to customer specification.
- **Mass production** is characterized by long production runs to manufacture a large volume of products with the same specifications.
- **Continuous process production** involves mechanization of the entire workflow and non-stop production, such as in chemical plants or petroleum refineries.
- Small-batch and continuous process technologies are associated with a more flexible horizontal structure,

whereas a tighter vertical structure is appropriate for mass production.
- Manufacturing technologies differ in terms of **technical complexity**, which refers to the degree to which complex machinery is involved in the production process to the exclusion of people.
- **Service technology** is characterized by intangible outputs and direct contact between employees and customers.
- Examples of service firms include banks, hotels and fast-food restaurants.
- Service technologies tend to have more flexible horizontal structures.

DISCUSSION QUESTIONS

1   'The matrix structure should be adopted only as a last resort because the dual chains of command can create more problems than they solve'. Discuss this statement.

2   Describe the virtual network approach to organizational structure, with illustrative examples. Discuss how variations in authority and commitment differ when compared to other forms of departmentalization.

3   Describe the primary differences between manufacturing and service organizations. How do these differences influence the type of structure that will be most effective?

4   Organizations are becoming increasingly decentralized, with authority, decision-making

responsibility and accountability being pushed farther down the organization hierarchy. How will this trend affect the manager of the future?

5   An organizational consultant was heard to say, 'Some aspects of functional structure appears in every organization.' Discuss this statement providing illustrative examples.

6   Compare and contrast the organization structure of an Internet company, such as eBay, that operates almost entirely online, to one of a bricks-and-mortar company such as Vodafone that uses the Internet for some functions, such as customer service and business-to-business transactions?

What are your leadership beliefs?[84]

INSTRUCTIONS The fit between a new manager and the organization is often based on personal beliefs about the role of leaders. Things work best when organization design matches a new manager's beliefs about his or her leadership role.

Think about the extent to which each statement reflects your beliefs about a leader's role in an organization. Mark as 'Mostly true' the four statements that are *most* true for you, and mark as 'Mostly false' the four that are *least* true for you.

		Mostly true	Mostly false
1	A leader should take charge of the group or organization.	☐	☐
2	The major tasks of a leader are to make and communicate decisions.	☐	☐
3	Group and organization members should be loyal to designated leaders.	☐	☐
4	The responsibility for taking risks lies with the leaders.	☐	☐
5	Leaders should foster discussions among members about the future.	☐	☐
6	Successful leaders make everyone's learning their highest priority.	☐	☐
7	An organization needs to be always changing the way it does things to adapt to a changing world.	☐	☐
8	Everyone in an organization should be responsible for accomplishing organizational goals.	☐	☐

SCORING & INTERPRETATION Each question pertains to one of two subscales of *leadership beliefs*. Questions 1–4 reflect *position-based* leadership beliefs. This is the belief that the most competent and loyal people are placed in positions of leadership where they assume responsibility and authority for the group or organization. Questions 5–8 reflect *non-hierarchical* leadership beliefs. This belief is that the group or organization faces a complex system of adaptive challenges, and leaders see their job as facilitating the flow of information among members and their full engagement to respond to those challenges. The subscale for which you checked more items 'Mostly true' may reveal your personal beliefs about position-based versus non-hierarchical leadership.

Position-based beliefs typically work for managers in a traditional vertical hierarchy or mechanistic organization. Non-hierarchical beliefs typically work for managers engaged with horizontal organizing or organic organizations, such as managing teams, projects and networks.

APPLY YOUR SKILLS: ETHICAL DILEMMA

A matter of delegation[85]

Tom Harrington loved his job as an assistant quality control officer for Rockingham Toys. After 6 months of unemployment, he was anxious to make a good impression on his boss, Frank Golopolus. One of his responsibilities was ensuring that new product lines met federal safety guidelines. Rockingham had made several manufacturing changes over the past year. Golopolus and the rest of the quality-control team had been working 60-hour weeks to troubleshoot the new production process.

Harrington was aware of numerous changes in product safety guidelines that he knew would affect the new Rockingham toys. Golopolus was also aware of the guidelines, but he was taking no action to implement them. Harrington wasn't sure whether his boss expected him to implement the new procedures. The ultimate responsibility was his boss's, and Harrington was concerned about moving ahead on his own. To cover for his boss, he continued to avoid the questions he received from the factory floor, but he was beginning to wonder whether Rockingham would have time to make changes with the Christmas season rapidly approaching.

Harrington felt loyalty to Golopolus for giving him a job and didn't want to alienate him by interfering. However, he was beginning to worry what might happen if he didn't act. Rockingham had a fine product safety reputation and was rarely challenged on matters of quality. Should he question Golopolus about implementing the new safety guidelines?

What would you do?

1   Prepare a memo to Golopolus, summarizing the new safety guidelines that affect the Rockingham product line and requesting his authorization for implementation.

2   Mind your own business. Golopolus hasn't said anything about the new guidelines, and you don't want to overstep your authority. You've been unemployed and need this job.

3   Send copies of the reports anonymously to the operations manager, who is Golopolus's boss.

APPLY YOUR SKILLS: CASE FOR CRITICAL ANALYSIS

The Church of Scotland: A democratic or adaptive structure?

The Church of Scotland government is organized on the basis of courts, mainly along lines set between 1560 and 1690. Each of these courts has committees, which may include other members of the Church, and at national level employ full-time staff. At a local level, the parish, the court is a kirk session. Kirk sessions oversee the local congregation and its parish, and consist of elders presided over by a minister.

At district level, the court is a presbytery. Presbyteries consist of all the ministers in the district and an equal number of elders, along with members of the diaconate (a form of ordained ministry, usually working in a complementary role in a ministry team in both parish and industry sector contexts). There are 46 presbyteries across Scotland, England, Europe and Jerusalem.

At national level, the court is the highest court of the Kirk, the General Assembly. The General Assembly consists of around 400 ministers, 400 elders and members of the diaconate, all representing the presbyteries.

The Queen is not the supreme governor of the Church of Scotland, as she is in the Church of England. The sovereign has the right to attend the General Assembly, but not to take part in its deliberations.

As business organizations respond to changing circumstances they adopt a structural form that best meets their requirements at that point in time. Firms often grow by expanding the sale of their products or services to new geographic areas. In these areas, they frequently encounter differences that necessitate different approaches in producing, providing or selling their products or services. Structuring by geographic areas is usually required to accommodate these differences.

Functional structures involve specialization according to organizational activity or function. This subdivision by function remains commonplace where each key activity is carried out by a semi-autonomous group, e.g. finance, production, marketing and human resources. Functional structures predominate in firms with a single or narrow product focus. Such firms require well-defined skills and areas of specialization to build competitive advantages in providing their products or services. Dividing tasks into functional specialties enables the organizational members to concentrate on only one aspect of the necessary work. This allows use of the latest technical skills and develops a high level of efficiency.

Divisional structures are associated with market expansion and product or service diversification. The driving force for divisionalization is the need to enhance coordination and control. Each main division operates as a profit-centre with a high degree of autonomy. Divisions can be grouped around markets, products or services or combinations thereof. Within divisions there may be functional sub-divisions. A divisional/strategic business unit (SBU) structure allows corporate management to delegate authority for the strategic management of distinct business entities – the divisions or SBUs. This expedites decision-making in response to varied competitive environments and enables corporate management to concentrate on corporate-level strategic decisions.

Networking is a product of advances in communications technology that facilitates the establishment of individual and team links within and between organizations.   Franchising involves a parent company assisting in the start-up of a new business.

Product-team structure: Cross-functional collaboration has become an increasing concern for companies facing rapid change and global competitors in the twenty-first century. The product-team structure has emerged as a way many firms are restructuring to meet this challenge. Drawing on the ideas underlying the matrix structure and the divisional/SBU structure, this new approach seeks to allocate people across all functions onto teams that manage a particular product or process.

Virtual structures: New technologies and globalization have led to changing organizational forms where organizational members interact with colleagues, customers and suppliers remotely through IT and systems, negating the need for office premises and face-to-face meetings.

Critical analysis is the process of evaluating academic findings and challenging accepted views and orthodox thinking around the subject matter. It may take someone to view the issue in a different light to further understanding of the subject matter. In this case a critical approach to the existing understanding of organization design and adaptation would form the basis for developing new theories or ways of looking at the issue or subject

matter. Orthodox thinking tends to obstruct the development of alternative ways of understanding a phenomenon and should be challenged according to critical management theorists.

Reference www.churchofscotland.org.uk/

Questions

1   Critically appraise the disadvantages in the current structures of the Church of Scotland.

2   Put yourself in the role of a management consultant and make recommendations on changing the organization structure of the Church of Scotland.

3   Comment on the assertion that third sector organizations are often criticized for being managed 'like a business' instead of being managed in a 'business-like' manner.

END NOTES

1. Claire Suddath, 'Why There Are No Bosses at Valve', *Bloomberg Businessweek*, April 27, 2012, www.businessweek.com/articles/2012-04-27/why-there-are-no-bosses-at-valve (accessed August 10, 2012); Rachel Emma Silverman, 'Who's the Boss? There Isn't One', *The Wall Street Journal*, June 20, 2012, B1; and Alex Hern, 'Valve Software: Free Marketer's Dream, or Nightmare?' *New Statesman*, August 3, 2012, www.newstatesman.com/blogs/economics/2012/08/valve-software-free-marketeers-dream-or-nightmare (accessed August 10, 2012).

2. Russell Adams, 'Hachette to Break Through "Silos" As It Restructures Women's Magazines', *The Wall Street Journal*, March 2, 2009; Justin Scheck, 'Dell Reorganizes, Creating New Mobile Device Division', *The Wall Street Journal*, December 5, 2009, B6; and Sony example from John Bussey, 'Has Time Come for More CIOs to Start Reporting to the Top?' *The Wall Street Journal*, May 17, 2011, www.online.wsj.com/article/SB10001424052748704281504576327510720752684.html (accessed August 14, 2012).

3. John Child, *Organization: A Guide to Problems and Practice*, 2nd ed. (London: Harper & Row, 1984).

4. Adam Smith, *The Wealth of Nations* (New York: Modern Library, 1937).

5. Leslie Kwoh, 'Firms Hail New Chiefs (of Diversity)', *The Wall Street Journal* (January 5, 2012), www.online.wsj.com/article/SB10001424052970203899504577129261732884578.html (accessed August 13, 2012); Brian Knowlton, 'White House Names First Chief Information Officer', *The New York Times*, March 5, 2009, www.thecaucus.blogs.nytimes.com/2009/03/05/white-house-names-first-chief-information-officer/ (accessed August 13, 2012).

6. Bussey, 'Has Time Come for More CIOs to Start Reporting to the Top?'

7. This discussion is based on A. J. Grimes, 'Authority, Power, Influence and Social Control: A Theoretical Synthesis', *Academy of Management Review* 3 (1978): 724–735; and W. Graham Astley and Paramjit S. Sachdeva, 'Structural Sources of Intraorganizational Power: A Theoretical Synthesis', *Academy of Management Review* 9 (1984): 104–113.

8. C. I. Barnard, *The Functions of the Executive* (Cambridge, MA: Harvard University Press, 1938).

9. Thomas A. Stewart, 'CEOs See Clout Shifting', *Fortune* (November 6, 1989): 66.

10. Michael G. O'Loughlin, 'What Is Bureaucratic Accountability and How Can We Measure It?' *Administration & Society* 22, no. 3 (November 1990): 275–302; and Brian Dive, 'When Is an Organization Too Flat?' *Across the Board* (July–August 2003): 20–23.

11. Adam Lashinsky, 'Inside Apple', *Fortune* (May 23, 2011): 125–134.

12. Carrie R. Leana, 'Predictors and Consequences of Delegation', *Academy of Management Journal* 29 (1986): 754–774.

13. Chris Taylor, 'Democracy Works', *Fortune Small Business* (May 2009): 40; and Heather Green, 'How Meetup Tore Up the Rule Book', *BusinessWeek* (June 16, 2008): 88–89.

14. Clifford Krauss and Julia Werdigier, 'BP's New Chief, Not Formally in the Role, Is Already Realigning Senior Managers', *The New York Times*, September 30, 2010, B3; and Guy Chazan, 'BP's New Chief Puts Emphasis on Safety', *The Wall Street Journal*, September 29, 2010, www.online.wsj.com/article/SB100014240527487041160045755213 94170919842.html (accessed August 14, 2012).

15. Ian Urbina, 'In Gulf, It Was Unclear Who Was in Charge of Oil Rig', *The New York Times,* June 5, 2010; and Douglas A. Blackmon et al., 'There Was "Nobody in Charge" ', *The Wall Street Journal,* May 27, 2010.

16. George Anders, 'Overseeing More Employees – With Fewer Managers' (Theory & Practice column), *The Wall Street Journal,* March 24, 2008.

17. Barbara Davison, 'Management Span of Control: How Wide Is Too Wide?' *Journal of Business Strategy* 24, no. 4 (2003): 22–29; Paul D. Collins and Frank Hull, 'Technology and Span of Control: Woodward Revisited', *Journal of Management Studies* 23 (March 1986): 143–164; David D. Van Fleet and Arthur G. Bedeian, 'A History of the Span of Management', *Academy of Management Review* 2 (1977): 356–372; and C. W. Barkdull, 'Span of Control – A Method of Evaluation', *Michigan Business Review* 15 (May 1963): 25–32.

18. Reported in Brian Dive, 'Hierarchies for Flow and Profit', *Strategy + Business,* August 26, 2008, www.strategy-business.com/article/08315 (accessed May 25, 2010).

19. Dive, 'Hierarchies for Flow and Profit'; and Gary Neilson, Bruce A. Pasternack and Decio Mendes, 'The Four Bases of Organizational DNA', *Strategy + Business*, Issue 33 (December 10, 2003): 48–57.

20. Anders, 'Overseeing More Employees'; Barbara Davison, 'Management Span of Control'; Brian Dive, 'When Is an Organization Too Flat?'; Brian Dumaine, 'What the Leaders of Tomorrow See', *Fortune* (July 3, 1989): 48–62; and Raghuram G. Rajan and Julie Wulf, 'The Flattening Firm: Evidence from Panel Data on the Changing Nature of Corporate Hierarchies', working paper, reported in Caroline Ellis, 'The Flattening Corporation', *MIT Sloan Management Review* (Summer 2003): 5.

21. Gary L. Neilson and Julie Wulf, 'How Many Direct Reports?' *Harvard Business Review* (April 2012): 112–119; and Bussey, 'Has Time Come for More CIOs to Start Reporting to the Top?'

22. William G. Ouchi, 'Power to the Principals: Decentralization in Three Large School Districts', *Organization Science* 17, no. 2 (March–April 2006): 298–307.

23. Sarah Lyall, 'Britain Plans to Decentralize Health Care', *The New York Times*, July 24, 2010, www.nytimes.com/2010/07/25/world/europe/25britain.html?pagewanted=all (accessed August 14, 2012).

24. Quoted in Robert D. Kaplan, 'Man Versus Afghanistan', *The Atlantic* (April 2010): 60–71.

25. Gen. Martin E. Dempsey, 'The Army's Starfish Program and an Emphasis on Decentralization', Official Army website, April 26, 2010, www.army.mil/-news/2010/04/26/37979-the-armys-starfish-program-and-an-emphasis-on-decentralization/ (accessed August 30, 2010); and Bruce E. DeFeyter, 'The Lion, the Starfish and the Spider: Hitting Terrorists Where It Hurts', *Special Warfare* (March–April 2010): 26; Ori Brafman and Rod Beckstrom, *The Starfish and the Spider: The Unstoppable Power of Leaderless Organizations* (New York: Portfolio/Penguin 2006).

26. Andrew Campbell, Sven Kunisch and Günter Müller-Stewens, 'To Centralize or Not to Centralize?' *McKinsey Quarterly*, June 2011, www.mckinseyquarterly.com/To_centralize_or_not_to_centralize_2815 (accessed August 14, 2012).

27. Dennis Cauchon, 'The Little Company That Could', *USA Today*, October 9, 2005, www.usatoday.com/money/companies/

28. Jennifer Reingold, 'The Fun King', *Fortune* (May 21, 2012): 166–174.

29. Penney example reported in Ann Zimmerman, 'Home Depot Learns to Go Local', *The Wall Street Journal,* October 7, 2008.

30. Clay Chandler and Paul Ingrassia, 'Just As US Firms Try Japanese Management, Honda Is Centralizing', *The Wall Street Journal*, April 11, 1991.

31. The following discussion of structural alternatives draws from Jay R. Galbraith, *Designing Complex Organizations* (Reading, MA: Addison-Wesley, 1973); Jay R. Galbraith, *Organization Design* (Reading, MA: Addison-Wesley, 1977); Jay R. Galbraith, *Designing Dynamic Organizations* (New York: AMACOM, 2002); Robert Duncan, 'What Is the Right Organization Structure?' *Organizational Dynamics* (Winter 1979): 59–80; N. Anand and Richard L. Daft, 'What Is the Right Organization Design?' *Organizational Dynamics* 36, no. 4 (2007): 329–344; and J. McCann and Jay R. Galbraith, 'Interdepartmental Relations', in *Handbook of Organizational Design*, ed. P. Nystrom and W. Starbuck (New York: Oxford University Press, 1981), pp. 60–84.

32. Raymond E. Miles, Charles C. Snow, Øystein D. Fjeldstad, Grant Miles and Christopher Letti, 'Designing Organizations to Meet 21st-Century Opportunities and Challenges', *Organizational Dynamics* 39, no. 2 (2010): 93–103.

33. Based on the story of Blue Bell Creameries in Richard L. Daft, *Organization Theory and Design,* 9th ed. (Mason, OH: South-Western, 2007), p. 103.

34. R. E. Miles et al., 'Designing Organizations to Meet 21st Century Opportunities and Challenges'.

35. Jaimelynn Hitt, 'The Organizational Structure of Starbucks, Unilever and Wal-Mart', www.voices.yahoo.com/the-organizational-structure-starbucks-unilever-1495147.html (accessed August 15, 2012); Mae Anderson, 'Wal-Mart Reorganizes U.S. Operations to Help Spur Growth', *USA Today*, January 28, 2010, www.usatoday.com/money/industries/retail/2010-01-28-walmart-reorganization_N.htm (accessed August 15, 2012); and 'Walmart', *The OfficialBoard.com*, www.theofficialboard.com/org-chart/wal-mart-stores (accessed August 15, 2012).

36. Eliza Newlin Carney, 'Calm in the Storm', *Government Executive* (October 2003): 57–63; and the Internal Revenue Service website, www.irs.gov (accessed April 20, 2004).

37. Brooks Barnes, 'Is Disney's Chief Having a Cinderella Moment?' *The New York Times*, April 11, 2010, BU1.

38. Maisie O'Flanagan and Lynn K. Taliento, 'Nonprofits: Ensuring That Bigger Is Better', *McKinsey Quarterly,* no. 2 (2004): 112ff.

39. The discussion of matrix structure is based on S. H. Appelbaum, D. Nadeau and M. Cyr, 'Performance Evaluation in a Matrix Organization: A Case Study', *Industrial and Commercial Training* 40, no. 5 (2008): 236–241; T. Sy and S. Cote, 'Emotional Intelligence: A Key Ability to Succeed in the Matrix Organization', *Journal of Management Development* 23, no. 5 (2004): 439; L. R. Burns, 'Matrix Management in Hospitals: Testing Theories of Matrix Structure and Development', *Administrative Science Quarterly* 34 (1989): 349–368; Carol Hymowitz, 'Managers Suddenly Have to Answer to a Crowd of Bosses', *The Wall Street*

management/2005-10-09-mississippi-power-usat_x.htm.

Journal, August 12, 2003; and Stanley M. Davis and Paul R. Lawrence, *Matrix* (Reading, MA: Addison-Wesley, 1977).

40. Howard Schultz, 'Starbucks Makes Organizational Changes to Enhance Customer Experience', February 11, 2008, www.news.starbucks.com/article_display.cfm?article_id=66 (accessed August 15, 2012).

41. Robert C. Ford and W. Alan Randolph, 'Cross-Functional Structures: A Review and Integration of Matrix Organization and Project Management', *Journal of Management* 18, no. 2 (1992): 267–294; and Thomas Sy and Laura Sue D'Annunzio, 'Challenges and Strategies of Matrix Organizations: Top-Level and Mid-Level Managers' Perspectives', *Human Resources Planning* 28, no. 1 (2005): 39–48.

42. These disadvantages are based on Sy and D'Annunzio, 'Challenges and Strategies of Matrix Organizations'; and Michael Goold and Andrew Campbell, 'Making Matrix Structures Work: Creating Clarity on Unit Roles and Responsibilities', *European Management Journal* 21, no. 3 (June 2003): 351–363.

43. Darren Dahl, 'Strategy: Managing Fast, Flexible and Full of Team Spirit', *Inc.* (May 2009): 95–97.

44. Gary Hamel, 'Break Free', *Fortune* (October 1, 2007): 119–126, excerpted from Gary Hamel, *The Future of Management* (Boston: Harvard Business School Press, 2007); and Nick Paumgarten, 'Food Fighter: The Whole Foods CEO vs His Customers' (Profiles column), *The New Yorker* (January 4, 2010): 36.

45. Geoff Keighley, 'Massively Multinational Player', *Business 2.0* (September 2005): 64–66.

46. Melissa A. Schilling and H. Kevin Steensma, 'The Use of Modular Organizational Forms: An Industry-Level Analysis', *Academy of Management Journal* 44, no. 6 (December 2001): 1149–1169.

47. Bob Sechler, 'Colleges Shedding Non-Core Operations', *The Wall Street Journal*, April 2, 2012, A6; David Streitfeld, 'A City Outsources Everything. California's Sky Doesn't Fall', *The New York Times*, July 20, 2010, A1.

48. Jena McGregor, 'The Chore Goes Offshore', *BusinessWeek* (March 23 and 30, 2009): 50–51.

49. Raymond E. Miles and Charles C. Snow, 'The New Network Firm: A Spherical Structure Built on a Human Investment Philosophy', *Organizational Dynamics* (Spring 1995): 5–18; and Raymond E. Miles et al., 'Organizing in the Knowledge Age: Anticipating the Cellular Form', *Academy of Management Executive* 11, no. 4 (1997): 7–24.

50. Raymond E. Miles and Charles C. Snow, 'Organizations: New Concepts for New Forms', *California Management Review* 28 (Spring 1986): 62–73; and John W. Wilson and Judith H. Dobrzynski, 'And Now, the Post-Industrial Corporation', *BusinessWeek* (March 3, 1986): 64–74.

51. N. Anand, 'Modular, Virtual and Hollow Forms of Organization Design', working paper, London Business School (2000); Don Tapscott, 'Rethinking Strategy in a Networked World', *Strategy + Business*, Issue 24 (Third Quarter 2001): 34–41.

52. Joann S. Lublin, 'Smart Balance Keeps Tight Focus on Creativity' (Theory & Practice column), *The Wall Street Journal,* June 8, 2009; and Rebecca Reisner, 'A Smart Balance of Staff and Contractors', *BusinessWeek Online*, June 16, 2009, www.businessweek.com/managing/content/jun2009/ca20090616_217232.htm (accessed April 30, 2010).

53. Gregory G. Dess, Abdul M. A. Rasheed, Kevin J. McLaughlin, Richard L. Priem and Gail Robinson, 'The New Corporate Architecture', *Academy of Management Executive* 9, no. 3 (1995): 7–20.

54. Harry Hurt III, 'The Pain of Change at Boeing', *The New York Times*, November 20, 2011, www.nytimes.com/2010/11/21/business/21shelf.html (accessed August 15, 2012).

55. Charles Levinson and Margaret Coker, 'The Secret Rally That Sparked an Uprising; Cairo Protest Organizers Describe Ruses Used to Gain Foothold Against Police', *The Wall Street Journal Online*, February 11, 2011, www.online.wsj.com/article/SB10001424052748704132204576135882356532702.html (accessed August 16, 2012).

56. Dexter Filkins, 'Profusion of Rebel Groups Helps Them Survive in Iraq', *The New York Times*, December 2, 2005, www.nytimes.com/2005/12/02/international/middleeast/02insurgency.html (accessed August 30, 2010).

57. Raymond E. Miles, 'Adapting to Technology and Competition: A New Industrial Relations System for the Twenty-First Century', *California Management Review* (Winter 1989): 9–28; and Miles and Snow, 'The New Network Firm'.

58. These disadvantages are based on Cecily A. Raiborn, Janet B. Butler and Marc F. Massoud, 'Outsourcing Support Functions: Identifying and Managing the Good, the Bad and the Ugly', *Business Horizons* 52 (2009): 347–356; Dess et al., 'The New Corporate Architecture'; Anand and Daft, 'What Is the Right Organization Design?'; Henry W. Chesbrough and David J. Teece, 'Organizing for Innovation: When Is Virtual Virtuous?' *The Innovative Entrepreneur* (August 2002): 127–134; N. Anand, 'Modular, Virtual and Hollow Forms of Organization Design'; and M. Lynne Markus, Brook Manville and Carole E. Agres, 'What Makes a Virtual Organization Work?' *Sloan Management Review* (Fall 2000): 13–26.

59. Hurt, 'The Pain of Change at Boeing'.

60. Steven Pearlstein, 'Lifeguard's Ordeal Is Parable about Outsourcing', *The Washington Post*, July 14, 2012, www.washingtonpost.com/business/lifeguards-ordeal-is-parable-about-outsourcing/2012/07/13/gJQAN6TtkW_story.html (accessed August 16, 2012).

61. Bob Sutton, 'United Airlines Lost My Friends' 10-Year-Old Daughter and Didn't Care', *Bob Sutton Work Matters Blog*, www.bobsutton.typepad.com/my_weblog/2012/08/united-airlines-lost-my-friends-10-year-old-daughter-and-didnt-care.html (accessed August 16, 2012).

62. Laurie P. O'Leary, 'Curing the Monday Blues: A U.S. Navy Guide for Structuring Cross-Functional Teams', *National Productivity Review* (Spring 1996): 43–51; and Alan Hurwitz, 'Organizational Structures for the 'New World Order,'' *Business Horizons* (May–June 1996): 5–14.

63. Jay Galbraith, Diane Downey and Amy Kates, 'Processes and Lateral Capability', *Designing Dynamic Organizations* (New York: AMACOM, 2002) Chapter 4.

64. Thomas Kayser, 'Six Ingredients for Collaborative Partnerships', *Leader to Leader* (Summer 2011): 48–54.

65. Siobhan Gorman and Julian E. Barnes, 'Spy, Military Ties Aided bin Laden Raid', *The Wall Street Journal*, May 23, 2011, www.online.wsj.com/article/SB10001424052748704083904576334160172068344.html (accessed May 23, 2011).

66. 'Panel Says Toyota Failed to Listen to Outsiders', *USA Today*, May 23, 2011, www.content.usatoday.com/communities/driveon/post/2011/05/toyota-panel-calls-for-single-us-chief-paying-heed-to-criticism/1 (accessed August 16, 2012).

67. William J. Altier, 'Task Forces: An Effective Management Tool', *Management Review* (February 1987): 52–57.

68. Example from Paul Adler and Laurence Prusak, 'Building a Collaborative Enterprise', *Harvard Business Review* (July–August 2011): 95–101.

69. Henry Mintzberg, *The Structure of Organizations* (Englewood Cliffs, NJ: Prentice Hall, 1979).

70. Paul R. Lawrence and Jay W. Lorsch, 'New Managerial Job: The Integrator', *Harvard Business Review* (November–December 1967): 142–151; and Ronald N. Ashkenas and Suzanne C. Francis, 'Integration Managers: Special Leaders for Special Times', *Harvard Business Review* (November–December 2000): 108–116.

71. Jody Hoffer Gittell, *The Southwest Airlines Way: Using the Power of Relationships to Achieve High Performance* (New York: McGraw-Hill, 2003).

72. This discussion is based on Jody Hoffer Gittell, 'Coordinating Mechanisms in Care Provider Groups: Relational Coordination as a Mediator and Input Uncertainty as a Moderator of Performance Effects', *Management Science* 48, no 11 (November 2002), 1408–1426; J. H. Gittell, 'The Power of Relationships', *Sloan Management Review* (Winter 2004),16–17; and J. H. Gittell, *The Southwest Airlines Way*.

73. Jody Hoffer Gittell, 'Paradox of Coordination and Control', *California Management Review* 42, no 3 (Spring 2000): 101–117.

74. Claudio Feser, 'Long Live Bureaucracy', *Leader to Leader* (Summer 2012): 57–65; and Harold J. Leavitt, 'Why Hierarchies Thrive', *Harvard Business Review* (March 2003): 96–102, discuss the benefits and problems of vertical hierarchies. See Timothy Galpin, Rod Hilpirt and Bruce Evans, 'The Connected Enterprise: Beyond Division of Labor', *Journal of Business Strategy* 28, no. 2 (2007): 38–47, for a discussion of the advantages of horizontal over vertical designs.

75. Eric M. Olson, Stanley F. Slater and G. Tomas M. Hult, 'The Importance of Structure and Process to Strategy Implementation', *Business Horizons* 48 (2005): 47–54; and Dale E. Zand, 'Strategic Renewal: How an Organization Realigned Structure with Strategy', *Strategy & Leadership* 37, no. 3 (2009): 23–28.

76. Michael E. Porter, *Competitive Strategy* (New York: Free Press, 1980), pp. 36–46.

77. Tom Burns and G. M. Stalker, *The Management of Innovation* (London: Tavistock, 1961).

78. John A. Coutright, Gail T. Fairhurst and L. Edna Rogers, 'Interaction Patterns in Organic and Mechanistic Systems', *Academy of Management Journal* 32 (1989): 773–802.

79. For more on technology and structure, see Denise M. Rousseau and Robert A. Cooke, 'Technology and Structure: The Concrete, Abstract and Activity Systems of Organizations', *Journal of Management* 10 (1984): 345–361; Charles Perrow, 'A Framework for the Comparative Analysis of Organizations', *American Sociological Review* 32 (1967): 194–208; and Denise M. Rousseau, 'Assessment of Technology in Organizations: Closed versus Open Systems Approaches', *Academy of Management Review* 4 (1979): 531–542.

80. Joan Woodward, *Industrial Organizations: Theory and Practice* (London: Oxford University Press, 1965); and Joan Woodward, *Management and Technology* (London: Her Majesty's Stationery Office, 1958).

81. Peter K. Mills and Thomas Kurk, 'A Preliminary Investigation into the Influence of Customer-Firm Interface on Information Processing and Task Activity in Service Organizations', *Journal of Management* 12 (1986): 91–104; Peter K. Mills and Dennis J. Moberg, 'Perspectives on the Technology of Service Operations', *Academy of Management Review* 7 (1982): 467–478; and Roger W. Schmenner, 'How Can Service Businesses Survive and Prosper?' *Sloan Management Review* 27 (Spring 1986): 21–32.

82. Richard B. Chase and David A. Tansik, 'The Customer Contact Model for Organization Design', *Management Science* 29 (1983): 1037–1050; and Gregory B. Northcraft and Richard B. Chase, 'Managing Service Demand at the Point of Delivery', *Academy of Management Review* 10 (1985): 66–75.

83. Geeta Anand, 'The Henry Ford of Heart Surgery', *The Wall Street Journal*, November 25, 2009, A16.

84. This questionnaire is based on Richard M. Wielkiewicz, 'The Leadership Attitudes and Beliefs Scale: An Instrument for Evaluating College Students' Thinking About Leadership and Organizations', *Journal of College Student Development* 41 (May–June 2000): 335–346.

85. Based on Doug Wallace, 'The Man Who Knew Too Much', *Business Ethics* 2 (March–April 1993): 7–8.

CHAPTER 5

MANAGING IN A GLOBAL ENVIRONMENT

LEARNING OBJECTIVES

After studying this chapter, you should be able to:

1 Define globalization and explain how it is creating a borderless world for today's managers.

2 Describe a global mindset and why it has become imperative for companies operating internationally.

3 Describe the characteristics of a multinational corporation and explain the 'bottom of the pyramid' concept.

4 Define international management and explain how it differs from the management of domestic business operations.

5 Indicate how dissimilarities in the economic, sociocultural and legal-political environments throughout the world can affect business operations.

6 Discuss how the international landscape is changing, including the growing power of China and India.

7 Describe how regional trading alliances are reshaping the international business environment.

Japan's Nissan has headquarters in Yokohama, but the chief executive of its luxury Infiniti division has his office in Hong Kong. The skin, cosmetics and personal care business of Procter & Gamble (P&G) is based in Singapore. The entire senior management team for Starwood, a hotel company based in Stamford, Connecticut, relocated to Shanghai for a month, so managers could immerse themselves in the local culture, and gain a better understanding of how the Chinese market differs from that in the USA.[1] The trend towards moving executives and divisions to Asia is both practical and symbolic. Hong Kong is considered a gateway to mainland China, while Singapore is a springboard into Southeast Asia and India. In addition, locating in the region '.... *is a visible demonstration of your commitment*,' said Michael Andrew, global chairman of KPMG International, who is based in Hong Kong.[2]

Rolls Royce is now manufacturing aero engines in Singapore bringing the advantages of proximity to their major Asian markets. Furthermore, this is a clear signal of commitment to their major customers, the Asia airlines, in the region.

Managers around the world are eager to make a substantial commitment to China and India, where the potential for growth is huge. Brazil, Russia, India and China (often referred to as the BRICs), as well as other emerging economies, are growing rapidly as providers of both products and services to the USA, Canada, Europe and other developed nations. At the same time, these regions are becoming major markets for the products and services of these producing neighbours. Finding managers with the mindset needed to succeed in these countries is proving difficult for multinational firms. China, India and Brazil are expected to see the greatest shortage of executive talent for the next few years.[3]

Managers today are required to think and act globally, because the whole world is a source of business threats and opportunities. Even managers who spend their entire careers working in their hometowns have to be aware of the international environment and probably interact with people from other cultures. The international dimension is an increasingly important part of the external environment as discussed in Chapter 3. This chapter introduces basic concepts about the global environment and international management. First, we provide an overview of today's borderless world and the global mindset needed to be effective. Next, we discuss multinational corporations, consider the globalization backlash, and describe the 'bottom of the pyramid' concept. We then touch on various strategies and techniques for entering the global arena and take a look at the economic, legal-political and sociocultural challenges that companies encounter, especially within the global business environment. The chapter also describes how emerging markets and regional trade agreements are reshaping the international business landscape. Of particular interest at the time of writing, are the impacts of the trade sanctions against Russia following its annexation of the Crimea and political intervention in the Ukraine.

The exclusion of the R(ussia) letter along with the B(razil) is likely from the 'BRIC' anagram of developing markets, much applauded by many commentators in the period up to the end of 2014. China's growth also stalled during 2015. Its gross domestic product slowed to around 7 per cent p.a. in 2015 and some commentators are claiming that the intensity of the ruling party's aggressive anti-corruption programme is a significant factor in slowing down the volume of trading transactions.

CONCEPT CONNECTION

Today's companies compete in a borderless world. Procter & Gamble's sales in Southeast Asia are a rapidly growing percentage of the company's worldwide sales and account for 16 per cent of total sales.

SOURCE: Procter & Gamble 2014 Annual Report.

Are we in a borderless world?

The reality facing most managers is that isolation from international forces is no longer possible. Organizations in all fields are being reordered around the goal of addressing needs and desires that transcend national boundaries. Consider that the Federal Bureau of Investigation (FBI) now ranks international cybercrime as one of its top priorities: because electronic boundaries between countries are virtually non-existent.[4] *'The whole boundary mindset has been obliterated,'* says John Hering, the CEO of US Lookout Mobile Security. Hering's company has customers in 170 countries using 400 mobile networks around the world. *'For many people, this is the only computer they have,'* he says. *'The thought of something bad happening to your phone is untenable.'*[5]

Globalization

Business, just like crime, has become a unified, global field. Globalization refers to the extent to which trade and investments, information, social and cultural ideas, and political cooperation flow between countries. One consequence is that countries, businesses and people become increasingly interdependent. India-based Tata Consultancy Services gets more than half of its revenue from North America. Japan's Honda gets 65 per cent of its parts for the Accord from the USA or Canada and assembles the vehicle in Ohio, US-based General Motors (GM) makes the Chevrolet HHR in Mexico with parts that come from all over the world.[6]

Globalization has been on the rise since the 1970s, and most industrialized nations show a high degree of globalization today.[7] The KOF Swiss Economic Institute measures economic, political and social aspects of globalization and ranks countries on a globalization index. Not surprisingly, the pace of economic globalization slowed in the most recent survey, reflecting the impact of the global financial and economic crisis, but social and political globalization continued its upward trend. Exhibit 5.1 shows how selected countries ranked on the 2012 KOF Index of Globalization (based on the year 2009) compared to their degree of globalization in the mid-1970s. Note that the USA is the least globalized of the countries shown in the exhibit. Among the 187 countries on the KOF Index, the USA ranks number 35, down from number 27 on the 2011 index. The 10 most globalized countries, according to the KOF Index, are Belgium, Ireland, the Netherlands, Austria, Singapore, Sweden, Denmark, Hungary, Portugal and Switzerland.[8]

EXHIBIT 5.1 Ranking of six countries on the globalization index

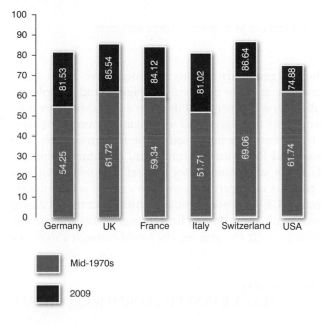

SOURCE: '2012 KOF Index of Globalization', KOF Swiss Economic Institute, www.kof.ethz.ch/static_media/filer/2012/03/15/rankings_2012. pdf (accessed June 26, 2012) and 'KOF Index of Globalization 2010', Press Release (January 22, 2010), www.globalization.kof.ethz. ch/ (accessed 22 January 2010). Note: The 2012 KOF analysis of globalization dimensions is based on the year 2009.

TAKE A MOMENT

Complete the Experiential Exercise online that pertains to your global management potential. How well do your knowledge and preferences reflect a global mindset?

Developing a global mindset

Succeeding on a global level requires more than a desire to go global and a new set of skills and techniques; it requires that managers develop a *global mindset*. As more managers find themselves working in foreign countries or working with foreign firms within their own country, they need a mindset that enables them to navigate through ambiguities and complexities that far exceed anything they encounter within their traditional management responsibilities.[9] A global mindset can be defined as the ability of managers to appreciate and influence individuals, groups, organizations and systems that represent different social, cultural, political, institutional, intellectual and psychological characteristics.[10] A manager with a global mindset can perceive and respond to many different perspectives at the same time, rather than being stuck in a domestic mindset that sees everything from one's own perspective. Reliance Industries, the largest private sector company in India, specifically lists 'global mindset' as one of the core competencies for its managers.[11]

People who have had exposure to different cultures develop a global mindset more easily. For example, the Dutch have to learn English, German and French, as well as Dutch, to interact and trade with their economically dominant neighbours. English Canadians must not only be well versed in American culture and politics, but they also have to consider the views and ideas of French Canadians, who, in turn, must learn to think like North Americans, members of a global French community, Canadians and Quebecois.[12] People in the USA who have grown up without language and cultural diversity typically have more difficulties with foreign assignments, but willing managers from any country can and should learn to open their minds and appreciate other viewpoints. Ethnocentric behaviour is often harmful to negotiations with foreign partners.

TAKE A MOMENT

Go to the Small Group Breakout Exercise online that pertains to exposure to different cultures and ideas.

Developing a global mindset requires managers who are genuinely curious and inquisitive about other people and cultures, are open-minded and non-judgemental, and can deal with ambiguity and complexity without becoming overwhelmed or frustrated. One of the best ways managers develop a global mindset is by engaging with people from different cultures. In the past, many managers who were sent on overseas assignments lived an insular lifestyle, which kept them from truly becoming immersed in the foreign culture. '*You can lead a true-blue German lifestyle in China,*' says Siegfried Russwurm, former head of human resources at Siemens. '*You can live in a gated community with German neighbours. They will tell you where you can find a German baker and butcher.*'[13] Today, though, the goal for managers who want to succeed is to globalize their thinking. John Rice, vice chairman of General Electric (GE) and president and chief executive of global growth and operations for the company, recently moved with his wife to Hong Kong. '*Being outside the United States makes you smarter about global issues,*' Rice said. '*It lets you see the world through a different lens.*'[14]

'*Global managers are made, not born. This is not a natural process.*'
— PERCY BARNEVIK, FORMER CEO OF ABB

REFLECTION

- A majority of today's companies and managers operate in a **borderless** world that provides both risks and opportunities.
- Globalization refers to the extent to which trade and investments, information, ideas and political cooperation flow between countries.
- The most globalized countries according to one ranking are Belgium, Ireland, Austria, the Netherlands and Singapore.

- To succeed on a global level requires managers at all levels to have a global mindset, which is the ability to appreciate and influence individuals, groups, organizations and systems that represent different social, cultural, political, institutional, intellectual and psychological characteristics.

Multinational corporations

The size and volume of international businesses are so large that they are hard to comprehend. For example, if revenues were valued at the equivalent of a country's gross domestic product (GDP), the revenue of ExxonMobil is comparable in size to the GDP of Egypt. The revenue of Walmart is comparable to Greece's GDP, that of Toyota to Algeria's GDP and that of General Electric to the GDP of Kazakhstan.[15]

A large volume of international business is being carried out by large international businesses that can be thought of as *global corporations, stateless corporations* or *transnational corporations*. In the business world, these large international firms typically are called *multinational corporations*, which have been the subject of enormous media attention. There has been considerable international collaboration to get US corporations such as Starbucks and Google (with EU operations based in Eire) to pay a fairer level of tax to those nations where they are trading from. To date they have legally minimized their effective tax payments through various means. MNCs can move a wealth of assets from country to country and influence national economies, politics and cultures.

Although the term has no precise definition, a multinational corporation (MNC) typically receives more than 25 per cent of its total sales revenues from operations outside the parent's home country. During the recent economic slump, the percentage of revenue from foreign operations increased for many multinationals because of stronger sales in developing markets such as China and India. In the third quarter of 2010, revenues for Yum! Brands (including restaurants such as KFC and Pizza Hut) in China surpassed those in the USA for the first time, and the company's China business may be twice as large as that in the USA by 2015.[16] MNCs also have the following distinctive managerial characteristics:

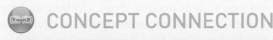

CONCEPT CONNECTION

The Maharaja Mac and Vegetable Burger served at McDonald's in New Delhi, India, represent how this very well-known MNC has changed its business model, by decentralizing its operations. When McDonald's initiated international units, it copied what it did and sold in the USA. Today, the fast-food giant seeks local managers who understand the culture and laws of each country. Country managers have a degree of freedom to use different furnishings and develop new products to suit local tastes. The expression 'Glocalization' has been used to explain this phenomenon.

1 An MNC is managed as an integrated worldwide business system, in which foreign affiliates act in close alliance and cooperation with one another. Capital, technology and people are transferred among country affiliates. The MNC can acquire materials and manufacture parts wherever in the world it is most advantageous to do so.

2 An MNC is ultimately controlled by a single management authority that makes key strategic decisions relating to the parent and all affiliates. Although some headquarters are *binational*, such as the Royal Dutch/Shell Group, some centralization of management is required to maintain worldwide integration and profit maximization for the enterprise as a whole.

3 MNC top managers are presumed to possess and exercise global perspective. They regard the entire world as one market for strategic decisions, resource acquisition and location of production, advertising and marketing efficiency.

In a few cases, the MNC management philosophy may differ from that just described. For example, some researchers have distinguished among *ethnocentric companies*, which place emphasis on their home countries; *polycentric companies*, which are oriented towards the markets of individual foreign host countries; and *geocentric companies*, which are truly world oriented and favour no specific country.[17] Truly global companies that transcend national boundaries, are growing in number. These companies no longer see themselves as American, Chinese or German; they operate globally and serve a global market. Nestlé SA provides a good example. The company gets most of its sales from outside the 'home' country of Switzerland, and its 280 000 employees are spread all over the world. CEO Paul Bulcke is Belgian, Chairman Peter Brabeck-Letmathe was born in Austria and more than half of the company's managers are non-Swiss. Nestlé has hundreds of brands and has production facilities or other operations in almost every country in the world.[18]

A globalization backlash

The size and power of multinationals, combined with the growth of free trade agreements, which we will discuss later in this chapter, has sparked a backlash over globalization. In a *Fortune* magazine poll, 68 per cent of Americans say other countries benefit the most from free trade, and a survey by *The Wall Street Journal* and NBC News found that 53 per cent of Americans surveyed said free trade had actually hurt the USA. That figure is up from 46 per cent in 2007 and 32 per cent in 1999. The sentiment is reflected in other countries such as Germany, France and even India. *'For some reason, everyone thinks they are the loser,'* said former US trade representative, Mickey Kantor.[19]

In the USA, the primary concern has been the loss of jobs as companies expanded their offshoring activities by exporting more and more work overseas. The transfer of jobs such as making shoes, clothing and toys began decades ago, and in recent years services and knowledge work have also been outsourced to developing countries. Many American shoppers say they'd be willing to pay higher prices for US-made products to keep jobs from going overseas.[20]

Business leaders, meanwhile, insist that economic benefits of globalization flow back to the US economy in the form of lower prices, expanded markets and increased profits that can fund innovation.[21] However, another troubling issue for some people in the USA is how overseas contractors and suppliers treat their employees. In the first few months of 2010, ten employees at Foxconn Technologies (a China-based contract manufacturer) that makes electronic products for Apple, Dell and other US companies, committed suicide. After a coalition of advocacy groups sent an open letter to Apple calling for an investigation to ensure safe and decent working conditions at all its suppliers, managers asked the Fair Labor Association to investigate Foxconn. The group found widespread problems, including excessively long work hours, low pay and unsafe working conditions. In a symbolic gesture to emphasize the company's commitment, in 2012 Apple's CEO, Tim Cook, visited Foxconn's manufacturing plant where the iPhone is made and met with both company and government leaders in China.[22]

With concerns over jobs and labour practices, the anti-globalization fervour is just getting hotter – and is not likely to dissipate anytime soon. In the end, it is not whether globalization is good or bad, but how business managers and government agencies can work together to ensure that the advantages of a global world are fully and fairly shared.

 CONCEPT CONNECTION

Having dominated almost every market in the world, Coca-Cola turned its sights on Africa in recent years. The beverage giant sees tremendous potential in countries across the Africa continent, many of whose inhabitants would be considered to be part of the bottom of the pyramid. The company is working closely with distributors and small business owners to promote its products by offering plenty of incentives and rewards as well as marketing support.

Serving the bottom of the pyramid

Although large multinational organizations are accused of many negative contributions to society, they also have the resources needed to do good things in the world. One approach that combines business with social responsibility is referred to as *serving the bottom of the pyramid*.

The bottom of the pyramid (BOP) concept proposes that corporations can alleviate poverty and other social ills, as well as make significant profits, by selling to the world's poorest people. The term *bottom of the pyramid* refers to the more than 4 billion people who make up the lowest level of the world's economic 'pyramid' as defined by per-capita income. These people earn less than €1300 a year, with about one-quarter of them earning less than a cent a day.[23] Traditionally, these people haven't been served by most large businesses because products and services are too expensive, inaccessible and not suited to their needs; therefore, in many countries, the poor end up paying significantly more that their wealthier counterparts for some basic needs.

 INNOVATIVE WAY

Godrej & Boyce

By one estimate, a third of India's food is lost to spoilage, but in 2007, refrigerator market penetration was just 18 per cent. Many lower-income people couldn't afford even a basic refrigerator. Another problem for poor people, particularly in rural areas, was that electric service was usually unreliable. Godrej & Boyce managers decided it was time to do something about this.

'As a company that made refrigerators for more than 50 years, we asked ourselves why it was that refrigerator penetration was just 18 per cent,' said G. Sunderraman, vice president of corporate development. The first major insight was that many people not only couldn't afford a refrigerator, but didn't *need* a large refrigerator that took up too much space in a small house and used a lot of electricity. What they needed was the ChotuKool

('The Little Cool'), an innovative appliance introduced by Godrej & Boyce in 2010. The ChotuKool, a mini-fridge designed to cool five or six bottles of water and store a few kilos of food, was portable, ran on batteries, and sold for about 3250 rupees (€44), about 35 per cent less than the cheapest refrigerator on the market. To sell the new product, Godrej & Boyce trained rural villagers as salespeople. The villagers earn a commission of about €2 for each refrigerator sold, and the system reduces Godrej's distribution costs. When asked how many ChotuKools the company expected to sell, George Menezes, COO of Godrej Appliances, said, 'In 3 years, probably millions.' Godrej & Boyce managers spend a lot of time working directly with consumers and are now testing ideas for other low-cost products aimed at rural markets. 'Currently, the rural market accounts for only 10 per cent, but it is all set to expand in a huge way,' said Menezes.[24]

A number of leading companies are changing by adopting BOP business models geared to serving the poorest of the world's consumers. Consider this example from India's Godrej & Boyce.

US companies are getting in on the BOP act too. P&G researchers are visiting homes in China, Brazil, India and other developing countries, to see how the company can come up with entirely new products and services for consumers living at the bottom of the pyramid. However, P&G is late getting into marketing to the BOP poor. Rival Unilever, for instance, introduced Lifebuoy soap to India more than a century ago, promoting it as the enemy of dirt and disease.[25] Unilever gets more than 50 per cent of its sales from developing markets. 'P&G is still very US-centric,' said Unilever's then CEO, Paul Polman. '*Emerging markets are in the DNA of our company.*' To try to catch up, P&G's previous top executive, Robert McDonald, began focusing company employees on the mission of 'touching and improving more lives, in more parts of the world, more completely.' When people feel they are changing lives, '*it's almost like you don't have to pay us to do this,*' said one R&D scientist.[26] Proponents of BOP thinking believe multinational firms can contribute to positive lasting change when the profit motive goes hand in hand with the desire to make a contribution to humankind.

REFLECTION

- A **multinational corporation (MNC)** is an organization that receives more than 25 per cent of its total sales revenues from operations outside the parent company's home country and has a number of distinctive managerial characteristics.
- Nestlé SA is a good example of a MNC.
- Some researchers distinguish among *ethnocentric companies*, which place emphasis on their home countries, *polycentric companies*, which are oriented towards the markets of individual host countries, and *geocentric companies*, which are truly world oriented.
- The increasing size and power of MNCs has sparked a globalization backlash.

- MNCs have the resources to reach and serve the world's poorest people who cannot afford the typical products and services offered by big companies. P&G has done this by supplying Asian kiosks with small size shampoos and other products, excluding the costly enzymes that products for Western markets require, often for product differentiation.
- The **bottom of the pyramid (BOP) concept** proposes that corporations can alleviate poverty and other social ills, as well as make significant profits, by selling to the world's poor. Godrej & Boyce created an innovative battery-powered refrigerator called the ChotuKool for rural markets in India. Haier of China is also a great product innovator of refrigerators and washing machines for their domestic rural markets in China.

Getting started internationally

Organizations have a number of ways of becoming involved internationally. One is to seek cheaper resources such as materials or labour offshore, which is called *offshoring* or *global outsourcing*. Another is to develop markets for intermediates, finished products or services outside their home countries, which may include exporting, licensing and direct investing. Exporting, licensing and direct investing are called market entry strategies, because they represent alternative ways to sell products and services in foreign markets. Exhibit 5.2 shows the strategies that companies can use to engage in the international arena, either to acquire resources or to enter new markets.

EXHIBIT 5.2 Strategies for entering the international arena

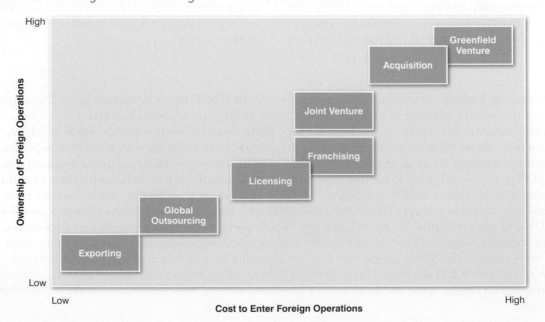

Exporting

With exporting, the company maintains its production facilities within the home nation and transfers its products for sale in foreign countries.[27] Exporting enables a company to market its products in other countries at modest resource cost and with limited risk. Exporting does entail numerous problems based on physical distances, government regulations, foreign currencies and cultural differences, but it is less expensive than committing the firm's own capital to build plants in host countries. For example, Skooba Designs, a New York, manufacturer of carrying cases for laptops, iPads and other tools, exports to more than 30 countries. Service companies can also export. Netflix is exporting its movie streaming service to customers in Latin America, the UK and Ireland, as well as exploring other countries to move into.[28] Hollywood movie studios have long exported films to foreign countries, but they're taking a different approach than in the past.

 INNOVATIVE WAY

Hollywood studios

Hollywood films have long been quintessentially American products, and years ago, audiences in Japan, Brazil or South Korea would faithfully go to watch movies that were written for and marketed primarily to American audiences. This is no longer the case as local films are giving Hollywood a 'run for its money'. At the same time, audiences are declining in the USA but growing overseas. Hollywood movies typically get about 70 per cent of their revenue from abroad. Today, a few Hollywood studios have gone as far as making movies specifically for certain foreign markets, and almost all of them are reframing their films to suit foreign tastes. Here are some examples of tactics they are using:

- **Use foreign actors.** For Paramount's *GI Joe*, Byung-hun Lee, a major Korean movie star, was placed in a title role and a South African actor played another key character.

- **Set the movie in a growing market – or in no man's land.** Several recent films, such as *Rio* and

Fast Five, have been set in Brazil, which is a rapidly growing market for Hollywood movies. Others, like *Avatar* and *The Lord of the Rings* films, are set in fantasy worlds that are home to no one specific nationality.

- **Stuff the film with foreign brands.** In the latest *Transformers* movie, DreamWorks Studios had a character observed gulping Shuhua low-lactase milk from China's Yili dairy company.

- **Shoot in foreign cities.** Pixar's *Cars* didn't do well abroad, so the studio set the sequel in Paris, London, Tokyo and on the Italian Riviera.

These and other techniques represent a whole new approach to making movies. Rather than trying to lure audiences to their films, studios are targeting their films to the audiences. In addition, managers are increasingly looking for films with global appeal. *'I can tell you that no studio is going to make a big expensive movie that costs $150 million or $200 million unless it has worldwide appeal,'* said Mark Zoradi, former president of Walt Disney Company's Motion Pictures Group.[29]

Outsourcing

Global outsourcing, also called *offshoring*, means engaging in the international division of labour so that work activities can be done in countries with the cheapest sources of labour and supplies. Millions of low-level jobs such as textile manufacturing, call centre operations and credit card processing have been outsourced to low-wage countries in recent years. The Internet and plunging telecommunications costs have enabled companies to outsource more and higher-level work as well, such as software development, accounting or medical services. A patient might have a magnetic resonance imaging (MRI) test performed in Minneapolis and have it read by doctors in India. After the US Sarbanes-Oxley Act (2002) went into effect requiring extensive new financial and management accounting reporting procedures with enhanced oversight, Unisys had a hard time finding enough additional internal auditors in the USA, so managers outsourced their core auditing practice to China. Large pharmaceutical companies farm out much of their early-stage chemistry research to cheaper labs in China and India.[30]

Licensing

With licensing, a corporation (the licensor) in one country makes certain resources available to companies in another country (the licensee). These resources include technology, managerial skills and patent or trademark rights. They enable the licensee to produce and market a product or service similar to what the licensor has been producing. Heineken, which has been called the world's first truly global brand of beer, usually begins by exporting to help boost familiarity with its products; if the market looks enticing enough, Heineken then licenses its brands to a local brewer. Licensing offers a business firm relatively easy access to international markets at low cost, but it limits the company's participation in and control over the development of those markets.

One special form of licensing is franchising, which occurs when a franchisee buys a complete package of materials and services, including equipment, products, product ingredients, trademark and trade name rights, managerial advice and a standardized operating system. Whereas with licensing, a licensee generally keeps its own company name, autonomy and operating systems, a franchise takes the name and systems of the franchisor. The fast-food chains are some of the best-known franchisors. The story is often told of the Japanese child visiting Los Angeles who excitedly pointed out to his parents, 'They have McDonald's in America.'

Direct investing

A higher level of involvement in international trade is direct investment in facilities in a foreign country. Direct investing means that the company is involved in managing the productive assets, which distinguishes it from other entry strategies that permit less managerial control.

Currently, the most popular type of direct investment is to engage in strategic alliances and partnerships. In a joint venture, a company shares costs and risks with another firm, typically in the host country, to develop new products, build a manufacturing facility or set up a sales and distribution network.[31] A partnership is often the fastest, cheapest and least risky way to get into the global game. For example, Abbott Laboratories has teamed up with an Indian drug firm, Biocon Ltd, to develop nutritional supplements and generic drugs tailored to the local market.[32] A Chinese firm has formed a joint venture with an American partner to refurbish New York City's Alexander Hamilton Bridge and work on other construction projects in the USA.[33] In addition to joint ventures, the complexity of today's global business environment is causing managers at many companies to develop alliance networks, which are collections of partnerships with various other firms, often across international boundaries.[34]

The other choice is to have a wholly owned foreign affiliate, over which the company has complete control. Direct *acquisition* of an affiliate may provide cost savings over exporting by shortening distribution channels and reducing storage and transportation costs. Local managers also have a better understanding of economic, cultural and political conditions. Kraft Foods bought Cadbury plc in large part because the firm had established local contacts and distribution networks in emerging markets. Home Depot purchased Home Mart, the number two home-improvement retailer in Mexico, Philip Morris acquired Indonesia's third-largest cigarette maker to tap into the lucrative Asian cigarette market, and Walmart bought Africa's Massmart.[35] The most costly and risky direct investment is called a greenfield venture, which means a company builds a subsidiary from scratch in a foreign country. The advantage is that the subsidiary is exactly what the company wants and has the potential to be highly profitable. For example, in 2012, Airbus announced plans to build jetliners in its first assembly plant in the USA. By building a huge plant in Alabama and employing American workers, Airbus managers expect to become part of US culture, thereby reducing political opposition to the purchase of the company's airplanes.[36] The disadvantage is that the company has to acquire all the market knowledge, materials, people and know-how needed of a different culture, and mistakes in analysis are possible. Another example of a greenfield venture is the Nissan plant in Canton, Mississippi. The plant represents the first auto factory ever built in Mississippi, where the Japanese company had to rely on an untested and largely inexperienced workforce. The logistical and cultural hurdles were so enormous and the risks so high that one Nissan executive later said, '*We did what nobody thought was possible.*'[37]

REFLECTION

- Two major alternatives for engaging in the international arena are to seek cheaper resources via outsourcing and to develop markets outside the home country.
- **Global outsourcing**, sometimes called *offshoring*, means engaging in the international division of labour so as to obtain the cheapest sources of labour and supplies, regardless of country.
- **Market entry strategies** are various tactics that managers use to enter foreign markets.
- **Exporting** is a market entry strategy in which a company maintains production facilities within its home country and transfers products for sale in foreign countries.
- With a market entry strategy of **licensing**, a company in one country makes certain resources available to companies in other countries to participate in the production and sale of its products abroad.
- **Franchising** is a form of licensing in which a company provides its foreign franchisees with a complete package of materials and services.

- McDonald's and other US fast food companies have franchises all over the world.
- **Direct investing** is a market entry strategy in which the organization is directly involved in managing its production facilities in a foreign country.
- Alternatives for direct investing include engaging in joint ventures, acquiring foreign affiliates and initiating a greenfield venture.
- With a **joint venture**, an organization shares costs and risks with another firm in a foreign country to build a facility, develop new products or set up a sales and distribution network.
- A **wholly owned foreign affiliate** is a foreign subsidiary over which an organization has complete control.
- Home Depot purchased the chain Home Mart in Mexico as a wholly owned foreign affiliate.
- The most risky type of direct investment is the **greenfield venture**, in which a company builds a subsidiary from scratch in a foreign country.

The international business environment

International management is the management of business operations conducted in more than one country. The fundamental tasks of business management – including the financing, production and distribution of products and services – do not change in any substantive way when a firm is transacting business across international borders. The basic management functions of planning, organizing, leading and controlling are the same whether a company operates domestically or internationally. However, managers will experience greater difficulties and risks when performing these management functions on an international scale. Consider the following blunders:

■ It took McDonald's more than a year to understand that Hindus in India do not eat beef because they consider the cow sacred. The company's sales took off only after McDonald's started using lamb to make burgers sold in India.[38]

■ When IKEA launched a superstore in Bangkok, managers learned that some of its Swedish product names sound like crude terms for sex when pronounced in Thai.[39]

■ In Africa, the labels on bottles show pictures of what is inside so illiterate shoppers can know what they're buying. When a baby-food company showed a picture of an infant on its label, the product didn't sell very well.[40]

■ United Airlines discovered that even colours can doom a product. The airline handed out white carnations when it started flying from Hong Kong, only to discover that, for many Asians, such flowers represent death and bad luck.[41]

Some of these examples might seem humorous, but there's nothing funny about them to managers trying to operate in a highly competitive global environment. What should managers of emerging global companies look for to avoid making obvious international mistakes? When they are comparing one country with another, the economic, legal-political and sociocultural sectors present the greatest difficulties. Key factors to understand in the international environment are summarized in Exhibit 5.3.[42]

EXHIBIT 5.3 Key factors in the international environment

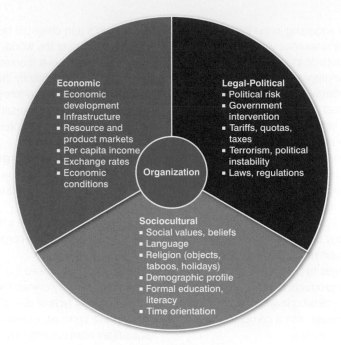

REFLECTION

- The basic management functions are the same in either a domestic or an international subsidiary, but managers will experience greater difficulties and risks when performing these functions internationally.

- **International management** means managing business operations in more than one country.
- When operating on an international basis, it is important for managers to give considerable thought to economic, legal-political and sociocultural factors.

Economic environment

The economic environment represents the economic conditions in the country where the international organization operates. This part of the environment includes factors such as economic development and resource and product markets. In addition, factors such as inflation, interest rates and economic growth are also part of the international economic environment.

TAKE A MOMENT

Read the Ethical Dilemma at the end of the chapter that pertains to conducting business in less-developed countries.

Economic development

Economic development differs widely among the countries and regions of the world. Countries can be categorized as either *developing or developed*. Developing countries are referred to as *less-developed*

CONCEPT CONNECTION

While working as a New York investment banker, Bangladeshi Iqbal Quadir realized that connectivity equals productivity. He also knew his impoverished homeland was one of the least connected places on Earth. That prompted him to collaborate with countryman Muhammad Yunus, Grameen Bank founder and 2006 Nobel Peace Prize winner, to create Village Phone. Entrepreneurs, mostly women, use Grameen Bank microloans to purchase mobile phones. 'Telephone ladies', such as Monwara Begum, then earn the money to repay the debt by providing a telephone service to fellow villagers. Village Phone has resulted in thousands of new small businesses, as well as an improved communication infrastructure that makes economic development possible.

countries (LDCs). The criterion traditionally used to classify countries as developed or developing is *per-capita income*, which is the income generated by the nation's production of goods and services divided by total population. The developing countries have low per capita incomes. LDCs generally are located in Asia, Africa and South America. Developed countries are generally located in North America, Europe and Japan. Most international business firms are headquartered in the wealthier, economically advanced countries, but smart managers are investing heavily in Asia, Eastern Europe, Latin America and Africa.[43] These companies face risks and challenges today, but they stand to reap huge benefits in the future.

Each year, the World Economic Forum analyzes data to gauge how companics are doing in the economic development race and releases its Global Competitiveness Report, which tallies numerous factors that contribute to an economy's competitiveness.[44] The report considers both hard data and perceptions of business leaders around the world and considers government policies, institutions, market size, the sophistication of financial markets and other factors that drive productivity and thus enable sustained economic growth. Exhibit 5.4 shows the top ten countries in the overall ranking for 2011–2012, along with several other countries for comparison. The USA has steadily fallen to fifth place, from first place in 2008–2009. Note that highly developed countries typically rank higher in the competitiveness index. One important factor in gauging competitiveness is the country's infrastructure, that is, the physical facilities such as highways, airports, utilities and telephone lines that support economic activities.

Economic interdependence

One thing the recent global financial crisis has made abundantly clear is how economically interconnected the world is. Although the recent crisis might seem atypical, informed international managers realize that their companies will probably be buffeted by similar crises fairly regularly. For example, most students are probably familiar with the bursting of the dot-com bubble in the early part of this century, which caused a severe drop in the stock market and affected companies around the globe. The Asian financial crisis of 1997–98 similarly affected firms in North America, Europe and other parts of the world. More recently, Greece's inability to make payments on its debt sparked a panic that devalued the euro and threatened the stability of financial markets worldwide.[45]

Recent financial woes have left a number of countries reeling, as reflected in a 'misery index' created by a Moody's economist and illustrated in Exhibit 5.5. The misery index adds together a country's

EXHIBIT 5.4 Country competitiveness comparison

Country	World Economic Forum competitiveness ranking	Gross domestic product	Number of people in labour force
Switzerland	1	$ 344 200 000 000	4 899 000
Singapore	2	$ 318 900 000 000	3 237 000
Sweden	3	$ 386 600 000 000	5 018 000
Finland	4	$ 198 200 000 000	2 682 000
USA	5	$ 15 290 000 000 000	153 600 000
Germany	6	$ 3 139 000 000 000	43 670 000
Netherlands	7	$ 713 100 000 000	7 809 000
Denmark	8	$ 209 200 000 000	2 851 000
Japan	9	$ 4 497 000 000 000	65 910 000
UK	10	$ 2 290 000 000 000	31 720 000
Canada	12	$ 1 414 000 000 000	18 700 000
Saudi Arabia	17	$ 691 500 000 000	7 630 000
China	26	$ 11 440 000 000 000	795 500 000
Kuwait	34	$ 155 500 000 000	2 227 000
South Africa	50	$ 562 200 000 000	17 660 000
Brazil	53	$ 2 324 000 000 000	104 700 000
India	56	$ 4 515 000 000 000	487 600 000

SOURCE: 'The Global Competitiveness Report 2011–2012', World Economic Forum, www3.weforum.org/docs/WEF_GCR_Report_2011-12.pdf (accessed June 27, 2012); CIA World Factbook 2011, www.cia.gov/library/publications/the-world-factbook (accessed 15 November 2012).

EXHIBIT 5.5 How countries are bearing the economic crisis: misery index, 2010 compared to 2000

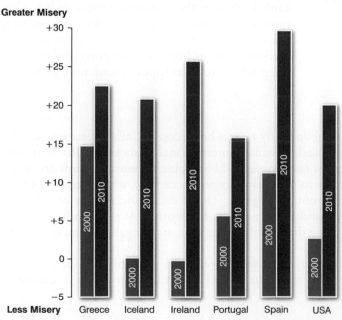

SOURCE: 'A New Definition of Misery', *The New York Times* (December 18, 2009), based on data from Moody's; www.nytimes.com/imagepages/2009/12/18/business/economy/20091219_CHARTS_GRAPHIC.html (accessed 19 December 2009).

unemployment rate and the budget deficit as a percentage of GDP. The 2010 figures suggest significantly greater misery for almost every country compared to the beginning of this century. Iceland and Ireland, two countries hit particularly hard by the recent economic crisis, had a negative misery index in 2000 but registered high scores for misery in 2010. The USA went from a misery score of less than 5 in 2000 to about 21 in 2010.[46]

Another reflection of economic interdependence is the fact that parts and supplies for many companies come from around the world, which presents managers with new complexities. For example, a challenge for Honda and Toyota automotive plants in the USA, Canada and Asia was getting the electronics and other parts they needed from suppliers in Thailand, where flooding swamped huge industrial sections of the country. At a recent shareholder meeting, a Bangladeshi labour organizer complained that many factories that produce goods for Walmart, the giant US-based chair, mistreat workers and he presented a proposal that the company require suppliers to describe working conditions in detail.[47]

REFLECTION

- Countries vary widely in terms of **economic development** and are classified as either developed countries or less-developed countries (LDCs).
- **Infrastructure** refers to a country's physical facilities, such as highways, utilities and airports, which support economic activities.
- The USA has fallen from first to third place on a 2014 ranking of global competitiveness.

- As recent financial crises in the USA and Europe show, countries are economically deeply interconnected, and financial problems in one area of the world can spread contagiously and rapidly around the globe. International business managers can expect their companies to be affected periodically by economic problems that cross geographical boundaries.

The legal-political environment

Differing laws and regulations make doing business a challenge for international firms. Host governments have myriad laws concerning libel statutes, consumer protection, information and labelling, employment and safety, and wages. International managers must learn these rules and regulations and abide by them. In addition, managers must deal with unfamiliar political systems when they go international, as well as with more government supervision and regulation. Government officials and the general public often view foreign companies as outsiders (or even intruders) and are suspicious of their impact on economic independence and political sovereignty.

Political risk is defined as the risk of loss of assets, earning power or managerial control due to politically based events or actions by host governments. Although many developing countries today welcome and support foreign firms, political risk is a major concern for international companies, which face a broader and more complex array of threats than ever.[48] For example, National Security Agency (NSA) investigators say they traced a series of online attacks on Google and dozens of other US corporations to two Chinese educational institutions with ties to the Chinese military. The attacks were aimed at stealing trade secrets and tapping into the email of suspected Chinese human rights activists.[49] Political risk also includes government takeovers of property and acts of violence directed against a firm's properties or employees. We have witnessed the disabling effects of cyber-attacks on Sony Pictures in the USA and the terrorist attacks on Charlie Hebdo in Paris, during January 2015. These events have led to a top-level summit in Washington where politicians are arguing the case for nation states to have greater snooping rights over Internet traffic – even encrypted emails between B2B communications and to journalists. These additional rights could lead to Western businessmen moving out of the USA and EU where their business intelligence could be compromised.

Another frequently cited problem for international companies is political instability, which includes riots, revolutions, civil disorders and frequent changes in government. The Arab Spring, for instance, a revolutionary wave of protests in the Arab world that began in late 2010, has created a tumultuous environment for

CONCEPT CONNECTION

Amway, the US-based network marketing company, spent many years patiently negotiating in China's legal-political environment. In 1998, the Chinese government closed down Amway operations in China, because it suspected the company was either an illegal pyramid scheme or a sinister cult. Amway survived by cultivating better relationships with government officials and by departing from its business model. For example, it opened more than 200 retail stores such as this one to demonstrate its commitment. In 2006, the Chinese government once again allowed Amway to sell directly to consumers, and the company now earns $billions in annual revenue from China. Another interesting case to follow is that of Bieresdorf AG, who bought 85 per cent of C-Bons and within a short period of time wrote off more than €200m as they had retrospectively paid far too much for the Hong Kong-listed company.

businesses operating in the region (including Tunisia, Egypt, Libya, Syria, Yemen and Bahrain). '*No president, no government, no police,*' said Jalilia Mezni, owner of Société d'Articles Hygiéniques in Tunisia. '*Only complete disorder.*'[50] Political risk and political instability remain elevated throughout the Arab world, causing problems for both local and foreign organizations. Zaid Qadoumi, the CEO of Canada's BroadGrain, which has been delivering agricultural commodities to emerging markets and political hot spots since the company was founded, offered extra pay for a crew to deliver a load of wheat to Libya, but advised workers to '*cut the ropes and leave*' if they believed the situation was too dangerous.[51]

Further radical Islamic radical terrorism and resulting turmoil is evident in the Yemen which prompted India and China to airlift its citizens out of the country in April 2015. Saudi Arabia is very active in bombing locations where radicals are operating, regrettably with collateral damage to the civilian population.

The sociocultural environment

A nation's culture includes the shared knowledge, beliefs and values, as well as the common modes of behaviour and ways of thinking amongst members of a society. Cultural factors sometimes can be more perplexing than political and economic factors when working or living in a foreign country. They are interconnected and affect the way business is done. However, the tolerance for non-ethical business practices in the EU, following various banking scandals, (post the 2008 crisis) has predictably intensified. Several post 2008 scandals have involved foreign exchange rate fixing in London and also the manipulation of the all-important LIBOR rate. The later rate is now determined in the USA having been moved from London in 2014. It was reported that a whistle-blower divulged considerable knowledge of the banks involved in the unethical fixing of these major market settlement rates.

Social values

Many managers fail to realize that the values and behaviours that typically govern how business is done in their own country don't always translate to the rest of the world. American managers in particular are regularly accused of an ethnocentric attitude that assumes their way is the best way. This chapter looks further at how American managers are often perceived by people in other countries. Ethnocentrism refers to a natural tendency of people to regard their own culture as superior and to downgrade, or dismiss, other cultural values. Ethnocentrism can be found in all countries, and strong ethnocentric attitudes within a country make it difficult for foreign firms to operate there. One way that managers can fight their own ethnocentric tendencies is to better understand and appreciate differences in social values. Ethnocentrism is largely blamed for ebay's failure to gain meaningful market share in China during the first decade of this century, and subsequently being driven out of China by Jack Ma's Alibaba. This case is a very interesting one that involved Jack Ma and his team of software engineers developing Alibaba's platform in total secrecy.

REFLECTION

- Complicated legal and political forces can create huge risks for international managers and organizations.
- Political risk refers to a company's risk of loss of assets, earning power or managerial control, due to politically based events or actions by host governments.
- Political instability includes events such as riots, revolutions or government upheavals that can affect the operations of an international company.
- A revolutionary wave of protests known as the *Arab Spring* which began in the Arab world in late 2010 has created a tumultuous environment for businesses operating in the region. But amongst chaos and confusion entrepreneurial opportunities can and do exist!

- Managers must understand and follow the differing laws and regulations in the various countries where they do business. Such an understanding of the 'rules of the game' is gained by multicultural firms through cultural diversity. Keeping abreast of regulatory changes is a major challenge for EU and US firms.
- US federal supervisors are holding regular meetings with directors of US banks. *'This change (per McGrane and Hilsenrath) has Washington overseeing the overseers, as regulators home in on whether directors are adequately challenging management and monitoring risks in the banking system.'*

Hofstede's value dimensions

In research that included 116 000 IBM employees in 40 countries, Dutch social scientist Geert Hofstede identified four dimensions of national value systems that influence organizational and employee working relationships.[52] Examples of how countries rate on the four dimensions are shown in Exhibit 5.6.

1 *Power distance.* High power distance means that people accept inequality in power among institutions, organizations and people. Low power distance means that people expect equality in power. Countries that value high power distance are Malaysia, India and the Philippines. Countries that value low power distance are Denmark, Israel and New Zealand.

2 *Uncertainty avoidance.* High uncertainty avoidance means that members of a society feel uncomfortable with uncertainty and ambiguity and thus support beliefs that promise certainty and conformity. Low uncertainty avoidance means that people have high tolerance for the unstructured, the unclear and the unpredictable. High uncertainty avoidance countries include Greece, Portugal and Uruguay. Countries with low uncertainty avoidance values are Sweden, Singapore and Jamaica.

3 *Individualism and collectivism.* Individualism reflects a value for a loosely knit social framework in which individuals are expected to take care of themselves. Collectivism means a preference for a tightly knit social framework in which individuals look after one another and organizations protect their members' interests. Countries with individualist values include the USA, Canada and Great Britain. Countries with collectivist values are China, Mexico and Brazil.

4 *Masculinity/femininity.* Masculinity stands for preference for achievement, heroism, assertiveness, work centrality (with resultant high stress) and material success. Femininity reflects the values of relationships, cooperation, group decision-making and quality of life. Societies with strong masculine values are Japan,

Germany, Italy and Mexico. Countries with feminine values are Sweden, Costa Rica, Norway and France. Both men and women subscribe to the dominant value in masculine and feminine cultures.

Hofstede and his colleagues later identified a fifth dimension, long-term orientation versus short-term orientation. The long-term orientation, found in China and other Asian countries, includes a greater concern for the future and highly values thrift and perseverance. A short-term orientation found in Russia and West Africa, is more concerned with the past and the present and places a high value on tradition and meeting social obligations.[53] Researchers continue to explore and expand on Hofstede's findings.[54] For example, in the last 30 years, more than 1400 articles and numerous books have been published on individualism and collectivism alone.[55]

 MANAGER'S SHOPTALK

How do you perceive America?

Americans have been frequently accused of a tendency to think everyone does things the way they are done in the USA and to believe 'the American way is the best way'. Those attitudes have hurt US firms, such as ebay, Facebook and Google in the global business environment – especially in China.

How people in developing countries view corporate America

PepsiCo conducted a perception study to see how corporate America is viewed in developing countries. One finding is that US companies are rarely perceived as being multinational; rather, they are perceived as US companies doing business internationally. Here are a few other perceptions:

- American managers are 'travelling salesmen' who come in fast, give a quick presentation, make promises and then disappear. Carpetbaggers!

- When things go wrong, American managers don't fix them; they dump them and move on.

- American managers take a mercenary approach and do not build or value consistency and stability.

Americans as global managers

One expert on business etiquette says inexperienced American managers commit blunders more than 70 per cent of the time, when doing business abroad.

Here are a few typical cultural mistakes American managers frequently make when working overseas or with people from foreign countries:

- American managers can often come across as cold or insensitive. In relationship-oriented societies such as Latin America, Asia and Mexico, for example, managers are expected to use a warm, personal approach and show interest and concern for the personal lives of subordinates as well as colleagues.

- American managers demonstrate a take-charge attitude that is considered impolite or offensive in some countries. Cultural values in China, for example, emphasize that the leader is much more modest, less visible and accomplishes things behind the scenes. In India, a take-charge attitude in the workplace may be considered disrespectful.

- American managers are typically informal and refer to everyone by their first names, which can be insulting to people in areas such as Mexico and some Asian and Latin American countries, where business is conducted much more formally.

SOURCES: Carlos Sanchez-Runde, Luciara Nardon and Richard M. Steers, 'Looking Beyond Western Leadership Models: Implications for Global Managers', *Organizational Dynamics* 40 (2011): 207–213; Christine Uber Grosse, 'Global Managers' Perceptions of Cultural Competence', *Business Horizons* 54 (2011): 307–314; Sarah Salas, 'Business Etiquette in Latin America', BellaOnline website, www.bellaonline.com/articles/art40307.asp (accessed June 29, 2012); 'PepsiCo's Perception Study', in *Managing Diversity for Sustained Competitiveness: A Conference Report* (New York: The Conference Board, 1997), p. 16.

EXHIBIT 5.6 Rank orderings of ten countries along four dimensions of national value systems

Country	Power distance[a]	Uncertainty avoidance[b]	Individualism[c]	Masculinity[d]
Australia	7	7	2	5
Costa Rica	8 (tie)	2 (tie)	10	9
France	3	2 (tie)	4	7
West Germany	8 (tie)	5	5	3
India	2	9	6	6
Japan	5	1	7	1
Mexico	1	4	8	2
Sweden	10	10	3	10
Thailand	4	6	9	8
USA	6	8	1	4

a. 1 = Highest power distance
   10 = Lowest power distance
c. 1 = Highest individualism
   10 = Lowest individualism

b. 1 = Highest uncertainty avoidance
   10 = Lowest uncertainty avoidance
d. 1 = Highest masculinity
   10 = Lowest masculinity

SOURCES: Dorothy Marcic, *Organizational Behavior and Cases*, 4th ed. (St. Paul, MN: West, 1995). Based on two books by Geert Hofstede: *Culture's Consequences* (London: Sage Publications, 1984) and *Cultures and Organizations: Software of the Mind* (New York: McGraw-Hill, 1991).

TAKE A MOMENT

Answer the questions in the New Manager Self-Test to see how you rate on some of the value dimensions described by Hofstede and the GLOBE project.

GLOBE Project value dimensions

Recent research by the Global Leadership and Organizational Behavior Effectiveness (GLOBE) Project extends Hofstede's assessment and offers a broader understanding for today's managers. The GLOBE Project used data collected from 18 000 managers in 62 countries to identify nine dimensions that explain cultural differences. In addition to the ones identified by Hofstede, the GLOBE Project identifies the following characteristics:[56]

1 *Assertiveness.* A high value on assertiveness means a society encourages toughness, assertiveness and competitiveness. Low assertiveness means that people value tenderness and concern for others over being competitive.

2 *Future orientation.* Similar to Hofstede's time orientation, this dimension refers to the extent to which a society encourages and rewards planning for the future over short-term results and quick gratification.

3 *Gender differentiation.* This dimension refers to the extent to which a society maximizes gender role differences. In countries with low gender differentiation, such as Denmark, women typically have a higher status and play a stronger role in decision-making. Countries with high gender differentiation accord men higher social, political and economic status.

4 *Performance orientation.* A society with a high performance orientation places high emphasis on performance and rewards people for performance improvements and excellence. A low performance orientation means people pay less attention to performance and more attention to loyalty, belonging and background.

5 *Humane orientation.* The final dimension refers to the degree to which a society encourages and rewards people for being fair, altruistic, generous and caring. A country high on humane orientation places a great value on helping others and being kind. A country low on this orientation expects people to take care of themselves. Self-enhancement and gratification are of high importance.

'Because management deals with the integration of people in a common venture, it is deeply embedded in culture. What managers do in Germany, in the UK, in the USA, in Japan or in Brazil is exactly the same. How they do it may be quite different.'

— PETER DRUCKER, MANAGEMENT GURU

Exhibit 5.7 gives examples of how some countries rank on these GLOBE dimensions. These dimensions give managers an added tool for identifying and managing cultural differences. Social values greatly influence organizational functioning and management styles. Consider the difficulty that Emerson Electric managers had when Emerson opened a new manufacturing facility in Suzhou, China. One area in which the American view and the Chinese view differed widely was in terms of time orientation. The American managers favoured a short time horizon and quick results, and they viewed their assignments as stepping stones to future career advancement. The Chinese managers, on the other hand, favoured a long-term approach, building a system and setting a proper course of action to enable long-term success.[57] Other companies have encountered similar cultural differences. Consider the American concept of self-directed teams, which emphasizes shared power and authority, with team members working on a variety of problems without formal guidelines, rules and structure. Managers trying to implement teams have had trouble in areas where cultural values support high power distance and a low tolerance for uncertainty, such as Mexico. Many workers in Mexico, as well as in France and Mediterranean countries, expect organizations to be hierarchical. In Russia, people are good at working in groups and like competing as a team, rather than on an individual basis. Organizations in Germany and other central European countries typically strive to be impersonal, well-oiled machines. Effective management styles differ in each country, depending on cultural characteristics.[58]

EXHIBIT 5.7 Examples of country rankings on selected GLOBE value dimensions

Dimension	Low	Medium	High
Assertiveness	Sweden Switzerland Japan	Egypt Iceland France	Spain USA Germany (former East)
Future orientation	Russia Italy Kuwait	Slovenia Australia India	Denmark Canada Singapore
Gender differentiation	Sweden Denmark Poland	Italy Brazil Netherlands	South Korea Egypt China
Performance orientation	Russia Greece Venezuela	Israel England Japan	USA Taiwan Hong Kong
Humane orientation	Germany France Singapore	New Zealand Sweden USA	Indonesia Egypt Iceland

SOURCE: Mansour Javidan and Robert J. House, 'Cultural Acumen for the Global Manager: Lessons from Project GLOBE', *Organizational Dynamics* 29, no. 4 (2001): 289–305, with permission from Elsevier.

NEW MANAGER SELF-TEST

What are your social values?

INSTRUCTIONS: Respond to each of the following statements based on your beliefs, indicating whether the statement is 'Mostly true' or 'Mostly false' for you.

	Mostly true	*Mostly false*
1 Achieving one's personal goals is more important than achieving team or organization goals.	☐	☐
2 Children should take great pride in the individual accomplishments of their parents and vice versa.	☐	☐
3 Pay and bonus systems should be designed to maximize individual interests over mutual interests.	☐	☐
4 I believe that orderliness and consistency should be stressed in society, even at the expense of experimentation and innovation.	☐	☐
5 Organizations work better when people do not break rules.	☐	☐
6 Organizations should spell out job requirements in detail so employees know what they are supposed to do.	☐	☐
7 I want to compete for high-level jobs and high earnings.	☐	☐
8 People should be encouraged to be assertive rather than non-assertive.	☐	☐
9 In an organization, people should be encouraged to be tough more than tender.	☐	☐
10 As a manager, I would want an egalitarian working relationship with my direct reports rather than maintaining distance from them.	☐	☐
11 Organizations should encourage subordinates to question their leaders.	☐	☐
12 Authority should be based on one's ability and contribution rather than on one's position in the hierarchy.	☐	☐
13 People in society will be happier if they accept the status quo rather than try to change things for the days ahead.	☐	☐
14 I prefer a norm of taking life events as they occur rather than constantly planning ahead.	☐	☐
15 I believe in focusing on current problems rather than trying to make things happen for the future	☐	☐

SCORING & INTERPRETATION These questions represent a measure of five cultural values as described by Geert Hofstede and the GLOBE Project mentioned earlier. Give yourself one point for each answer marked 'Mostly true'. Questions 1–3 are for *individualism-collectivism*. A higher score of 2–3 represents a belief towards individualism; a lower score of 0–1 means a belief more towards collectivism. Questions 4–6 are about *uncertainty avoidance*. A higher score of 2–3 means a value for low uncertainty in life; a lower score of 0–1 means a value for higher uncertainty. Questions 7–9 represent *assertiveness*. A higher score of 2–3 represents a value for people being assertive; a lower score of 0–1 means a value for people being non-assertive. Questions 10–12 represent *power distance*. A higher score of 2–3 means a value for low power distance; a lower score of 0–1 means a value for high power distance. Questions 13–15 represent *time orientation*. A higher score of 2–3 means an orientation towards the present; a lower score of 0–1 represents a future orientation.

Your scores have both individual and societal meaning. Compare your scores to other students to understand your perception of the different values in your colleague group. On which of the five values would you personally like to score higher? Lower? These five values also differ widely across national cultures. Go to the website www.geert-hofstede.com/hofstededimensions.php and compare your country's scores on the five values to the scores of people from other countries. At this site, the term *masculinity* is used instead of *assertiveness*. What surprises you most about the differences across countries?

SOURCES: Robert J. House, Paul J. Hanges, Mansour Javidan, Peter W. Dorfman and Vipin Gupta (eds), *Culture, Leadership, and Organizations: The GLOBE Study of 62 Societies* (Thousand Oaks, CA: Sage Publications, 2004); Geert Hofstede, *Culture's Consequences* (London: Sage Publications, 1984); and David Matsumoto, Michelle D. Weissman, Ken Preston, Bonny R. Brown and Cenita Kupperbusch, 'Context-Specific Measurement of Individualism-Collectivism on the Individual Level: The Individualism-Collectivism Interpersonal Assessment Inventory', *Journal of Cross-Cultural Psychology* 28, no. 6 (1997): 743–767.

REFLECTION

- Managers working internationally should guard against ethnocentrism, which is the natural tendency among people to regard their own culture as superior to others.
- Hofstede's sociocultural value dimensions measure power distance, uncertainty avoidance, individualism-collectivism and masculinity-femininity.
- Power distance is the degree to which people accept inequality in power among institutions, organizations and people.
- Uncertainty avoidance is characterized by people's intolerance for uncertainty and ambiguity and resulting support for beliefs that promise certainty and conformity.
- Individualism refers to a preference for a loosely knit social framework in which individuals are expected to take care of themselves.
- Collectivism refers to a preference for a tightly knit social framework in which individuals look after one another and organizations protect their members' interests.
- Masculinity is a cultural preference for achievement, heroism, assertiveness, work centrality and material success.
- Femininity is a cultural preference for relationships, cooperation, group decision-making and quality of life.
- Hofstede later identified another dimension: long-term orientation, which reflects a greater concern for the future and a high value on thrift and perseverance, versus short-term orientation, which reflects a concern with the past and present and a high value on meeting current obligations.
- Additional value dimensions recently identified by Project GLOBE are assertiveness, future orientation, gender differentiation, performance orientation and humane orientation.

Communication differences

People from some cultures tend to pay more attention to the social context (social setting, non-verbal behaviour, social status, etc.) of their verbal communication than Americans do. For example, American managers working in China have discovered that social context is considerably more important in that culture, and they need to learn to suppress their impatience and devote the time necessary to establish personal and social relationships. See Guan Xi in Chapter 3 for more detail.

Exhibit 5.8 indicates how the emphasis on social context varies among countries. In a high-context culture, people are sensitive to circumstances surrounding social exchanges. People use communication primarily to

EXHIBIT 5.8 High-context and low-context cultures

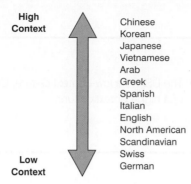

High
Context

Chinese
Korean
Japanese
Vietnamese
Arab
Greek
Spanish
Italian
English
North American
Scandinavian
Swiss
German

Low
Context

SOURCES: Edward T. Hall, *Beyond Culture*
(Garden City, NY: Anchor Press/Doubleday, 1976);
and J. Kennedy and A. Everest, 'Put Diversity in
Context', *Personnel Journal* (September 1991):
50–54.

build personal social relationships; meaning is derived from context – setting, status and non-verbal behaviour – more than from explicit words; relationships and trust are more important than business; and the welfare and harmony of the group are valued. In a low-context culture, people use communication primarily to exchange facts and information; meaning is derived primarily from words; business transactions are more important than building relationships and trust; and individual welfare and achievement are more important than the group.[59]

 CONCEPT CONNECTION

Pictured at a traditional Japanese ceremony is Hiroshi Mikitani (second from right), Rakuten, Inc.'s founder and CEO. Tokyo-based Rakuten is an Internet group that includes Rakuten Marketplace, a flourishing e-commerce site. In keeping with Rakuten's ambitious global expansion plans, Mikitari holds all board meetings, strategy discussions and weekly employee gatherings in English, the most commonly used language in international business. As Rakuten expands, managers from Japan's high-context culture, where communication is used to build relationships, must not only become proficient in a foreign language, but also learn to communicate effectively with managers from low-context cultures, where communication is used primarily to conduct business.

There is a need to understand how differences in cultural context affect communications; consider the American expression, 'The squeaky wheel gets the grease'. It means that the loudest person will get the most attention, and attention is assumed to be favourable. Equivalent sayings in China and Japan are 'Quacking ducks get shot', and 'The nail that sticks up gets hammered down', respectively. In these latter two cultures, standing out as an individual merits unfavourable attention. Consider the huge culture gap when China's Lenovo Group acquired IBM's PC business. In meetings and conference calls, Western executives were frustrated by their Chinese counterparts' reluctance to speak up, while the Chinese managers were irritated by the Americans' propensity to 'just talk and talk', as one vice president of human resources put it.[60]

High-context cultures include Asian and Arab countries. Low-context cultures tend to be American and Northern European. Even within North America, cultural subgroups vary in the extent to which context counts, explaining why differences among groups can hinder successful communication. White females, Native Americans and African-Americans all tend to prefer higher context communication than do white males. A high-context interaction requires more time because a relationship has to be developed, and trust and friendship must be established. Furthermore, most male managers and most people doing the hiring in organizations are from low-context cultures, which conflicts with people entering the organization from a background in a higher-context culture.

REFLECTION

- A **high-context culture** is one in which people use communication to build personal relationships.
- In a **low-context culture**, people use communication primarily to exchange facts and information.

- The USA is a low-context culture. China is an example of a high-context culture.

Changing international landscape

Many companies today are going straight to China or India as a first step into international business, either through outsourcing or by using various market entry strategies. China and India have been the world's fastest growing economies in recent years. In addition, Brazil is emerging as a major player on the international business landscape, although this view has been challenged by some commentators.

China, Inc.

In recent years, foreign companies have invested more in business in China than they spent anywhere else in the world. A market that was of little interest a decade ago has become the one place nearly every manager is thinking about. China is German car maker BMW's biggest market for its largest and most profitable autos.[61] The US-based company Apple has two stores in Shanghai, and they are so busy that the company is opening a third, along with dozens of other stores throughout China. Apple's stores in Beijing and Shanghai are the company's most heavily used – as well as the most profitable.[62] Apple had to jump through all sorts of legal and regulatory hurdles to sell in China, but it was worth it to get the iPhone into the largest mobile phone market in the world.[63] Although outsourcing has been the most widespread approach to involvement in China, the country is rapidly moving towards a consumer-driven economy, with the fastest-growing middle class in history. China is the largest or second-largest market for a variety of products and services, including mobile phones, automobiles, consumer electronics, luxury goods and Internet use.[64]

 **GREEN POWER**

When Bentonville met Beijing

Establishing his business in Bentonville, Arkansas, in 1962, entrepreneur Sam Walton could not have imagined eventual expansion to over 350 stores and 20 000 suppliers in China. In 2008, the Walmart CEO publicly addressed environmental concerns in China and put Walmart's vast resources behind his pledge to make sustainability a priority in the Chinese market. To address waste and pollution, Walmart trained and monitored workers across the Chinese supply chain, from factory and transport to retail stores, and then set environmental standards as a *requirement* for other companies to do business with Walmart. The company also joined forces with China's Institute of Public and Environmental Affairs, to map water pollution and wastewater management. The efforts resulted in dramatic drops in water use at many supplier factories. To address mounting food safety concerns amongst the Chinese, Walmart established the Direct Farm Program, offering local farmers higher incomes for providing safe supplies of fresh food to consumers through the giant retailer.

SOURCE: Orville Schell, 'How Walmart Is Changing China – and Vice Versa', *The Atlantic* (December 2011): 80–98.

Yet, doing business in China has never been smooth, and it appears to be getting even tougher. New regulations and government policies are making life hard for foreign companies in all industries. For Internet companies such as Facebook, Twitter, eBay and Google, China's regulated business environment has been more a source of trouble and frustration than of its new customers.[65] Google closed its Chinese site, *Google.cn*, in early 2010, because of government restrictions and censorship, although the company later had its licence renewed to provide limited services in China. Some multinational firms doing business with Chinese organizations, particularly big state-owned companies, have also had problems getting payments on their contracts. '*A contract is not an unchangeable bible for Chinese companies*,' said Beijing-based lawyer Jingzhou Tao. Chinese managers frequently withhold payments as a tactic in price negotiations. Part of the reason is that these organizations are not just companies but also political entities. But another reason is because of cultural differences. '*Chinese culture will build a relationship before the contract*,' said Arthur Bowring, managing director of the Hong Kong Shipowners Association. '*The relationship is always something that can be talked about. The contract is just a set of papers that you keep in your bottom drawer.*'[66]

Despite the problems, China is a market that foreign managers can't afford to ignore. However, competition from domestic companies in China is growing fast. In some industries, local companies have already become market leaders, such as Haier in consumer white good products and service, and 7 Days Inn for budget hotels.[67] One Chinese company that is rapidly becoming a global leader is Lenovo, which bought out the hardware side of IBM.

 ## INNOVATIVE **WAY**

Lenovo

The fastest-growing company in the PC industry is one that most people outside China hadn't even heard of a few years ago, even after it bought IBM's Think-Pad brand in 2005. Lenovo is now the No. 2 seller of computers in the world (behind Hewlett-Packard) and is innovating in new product categories such as tablets, smartphones and smart TVs. Lenovo's CEO, Yang Yuanqing, who started as a salesman and once delivered computers by bicycle, was China's highest-paid executive.

With its emphasis on quality (its machines rank tops for reliability), Lenovo is redefining the perception of the phrase 'made in China'. Moreover, it is redefining the meaning of a Chinese company, blending the best of Eastern philosophy and culture with the best of Western business and management thinking. The company has headquarters in Beijing, but Yang spends a third of his time at Lenovo's offices in Raleigh, North Carolina. Lenovo's top managers, once almost all Chinese with no international experience, now come from 14 different nations. Most members of the top leadership team speak two or more languages. They live and work in six different cities on three continents. Dan Stone, who was born in Israel, had his office in the USA, while Gerry Smith, born in the USA, worked out of Singapore.

Lenovo's top executives know that appreciating and merging Chinese and non-Chinese perspectives is crucial to success. It's an idea that US managers need to be paying attention to. '*Chinese people know Americans or the USA more than vice versa,*' says Lenovo's founder and chairman, Liu Chuanzhi. '*Much more.*'[68]

India, the service giant

India, second only to China in population, has taken a different path towards economic development. Whereas China is strong in manufacturing, India is a rising power in software design, services and precision engineering. Numerous companies see India as a major source of technological and scientific brainpower, and the country's large English-speaking population makes it a natural for US companies wanting to outsource services. One index lists more than 900 business services companies in India, which employ around 575 000 people.[69]

One of the fastest-growing industries in India is pharmaceuticals, medical devices and diagnostics. The country has a large number of highly trained scientists, doctors and researchers. US firms Abbott Laboratories and Covidien have both opened research and development centres there. India is also a growing manufacturer of pharmaceuticals and is the world's largest exporter of generic drugs. By 2020, India's pharmaceuticals

CONCEPT CONNECTION

Companies such as Bug Agentes Biologicos, located in Piracicaba, Brazil, reflect the changing international landscape. One of Forbes magazine's top 50 most innovative companies worldwide, Bug Agentes Biologicos supplies the agriculture industry with predatory insect eggs and parasitoids, which are a natural alternative to harmful agricultural pesticides. Bug sells its products throughout the three largest agricultural producers – the USA, the European Union (EU) and Brazil – and far beyond.

industry will likely be a global leader, according to a report by PricewaterhouseCoopers.[70]

Brazil's growing clout

Brazil is another country that is increasingly gaining managers' attention. Although Brazil's economic growth has slowed, it is still regarded as one of the fastest-growing emerging economies in the developing world, with large and growing agricultural, mining, manufacturing and service sectors.[71] The country's economy, already the seventh-largest in the world, is projected, by some commentators to move into fourth place by 2050. The choice of Rio de Janeiro to host the 2016 Summer Olympics is also an indication of Brazil's growing presence in the international arena.

Brazil has a young, vibrant population, the largest in Latin America, and a rapidly growing middle class, which is eager to experience the finer things in life. Consumer spending represents about 60 per cent of Brazil's economy. The Brazilian government has initiated major investments in the development of infrastructure such as highways, ports and electricity projects, which is creating jobs as well as spurring the development of other businesses. In addition, in 2010, Brazil announced a \$22 billion investment in science and technology innovation.

REFLECTION

- Many companies are going directly into China or India as a first and often major step into international business.
- Outsourcing is the most widespread involvement by foreign firms in these two countries.
- China is strong in manufacturing, whereas India is a major provider of services.
- The Chinese company Lenovo is emerging as the country's first global corporation, with managers coming from 14 different nations, living and working in six cities on three continents.

- Brazil, with its rapidly growing consumer market, is becoming a major player in the shifting international landscape.
- Managers also look to China, India and Brazil as sources of lower-cost technological and scientific brainpower.
- China has bought agricultural land in Africa and is now buying assets in the EU, with an emphasis on acquiring Intellectual Property.

International trade alliances

Another highly visible change in the international business environment in recent years has been the development of regional trading alliances and international trade agreements.

GATT and the WTO

The General Agreement on Tariffs and Trade (GATT), signed by 23 nations in 1947, started as a set of rules to ensure non-discrimination, clear procedures, the negotiation of disputes and the participation of lesser-developed countries in international trade.[72] GATT sponsored eight rounds of international trade negotiations aimed at reducing trade restrictions. The 1986 to 1994 Uruguay Round (the first to be named for a developing country) involved 125 countries and cut more tariffs than ever before. In addition to lowering tariffs 30 per cent from the previous level, it boldly moved the world closer to global free trade by calling for the establishment of the World Trade Organization (WTO) in 1995.

The WTO represents the maturation of GATT into a permanent global institution that can monitor international trade and has legal authority to arbitrate disputes on some 400 trade issues. As of July 2008, 153 countries, including China, Vietnam and Ukraine, were members of the organization. As a permanent membership organization, the WTO is bringing greater trade liberalization in goods, information, technological developments and services; stronger enforcement of rules and regulations; and greater power to resolve disputes among trading partners.

European Union

An alliance begun in 1957 to improve economic and social conditions among its members, the European Economic Community has evolved into the 28-nation European Union (EU) illustrated in Exhibit 5.9. The biggest expansion came in 2004, when the EU welcomed ten new members from central and eastern Europe.[73] Turkey and the Ukraine are potential future new members.

The declared goal of the EU is to create a powerful single-market system for Europe's millions of consumers, allowing people, goods and services to move freely. The increased competition and economies of scale within Europe enable companies to grow large and efficient, and become more competitive in the USA

EXHIBIT 5.9 The nations of the European Union

and other world markets. Another aspect of European unification has been the introduction of a common currency. The euro has replaced national currencies in Austria, Belgium, Cyprus, Finland, France, Germany, Greece, Ireland, Italy, Luxembourg, Malta, the Netherlands, Portugal, Slovakia, Slovenia, Spain, Latvia, Lithuania and Estonia.[74]

However, not all has gone smoothly for the integration, particularly since the global recession began. As economic stability varied from country to country, pitting winners against losers, the economic crisis revived national loyalties and cross-border resentments, slowing the move towards a unified and cohesive 'European identity'.[75] Spain, Ireland and particularly Greece have all had trouble paying their debts, putting the entire eurozone at risk and leading to a possible breakup of the euro system. As EU officials scrambled to dispel the fears that Greece would exit the euro, multinational firms doing business in EU countries were bracing themselves for the worst and taking steps to protect their interests. Managers at companies such as Heineken NV and GlaxoSmithKline plc, for instance, moved all cash reserves out of the eurozone and into currencies such as the US dollar or British pound. Some analysts now express the view that a broad breakup of the eurozone is most unlikely, but the uncertainty has smart managers rethinking what they would have to do in the event of a return to national currencies or a two-tier euro system.[76]

North American Free Trade Agreement (NAFTA)

The North American Free Trade Agreement (NAFTA), which came into effect on 1 January, 1994, merged the USA, Canada and Mexico into a single market. Intended to spur growth and investment, increase exports and expand jobs in all three nations, NAFTA broke down tariffs and trade restrictions over a 15-year period in a number of key areas. Thus, by 2008, virtually all US industrial exports into Canada and Mexico were duty-free.

Over the first decade of NAFTA, US trade with Mexico increased more than threefold, while trade with Canada also rose dramatically.[77] Significantly, NAFTA spurred the entry of small businesses into the global arena. However, opinions over the benefits of NAFTA appear to be as divided as they were when talks began, with some people calling it a spectacular success and others referring to it as a dismal failure.[78] In Bain & Company's 2011 survey of managers, only 53 per cent of North American managers surveyed said they thought reducing trade barriers and increasing free trade was a positive thing, down from 74 per cent in 2003.[79] Although NAFTA has not lived up to its grand expectations, experts stress that it increased trade, investment and income and continues to enable companies in all three countries to compete more effectively with rival Asian and European firms.[80]

TAKE A MOMENT

Take the questionnaire at the end of this chapter, which will give you some insight into whether you lean towards low-context or high-context communications. A higher score indicates low-context behaviour, which would clash when trying to do business in a high-context culture.

REFLECTION

- Regional trading alliances and international trade agreements are reshaping global business.
- The World Trade Organization (WTO) is a permanent membership organization that monitors trade and has authority to arbitrate disputes among 153 member countries.

- Two important, yet sometimes controversial, regional alliances are the European Union (EU) and the North American Free Trade Agreement (NAFTA).
- The euro is a single European currency that has replaced the currencies of 16 EU member nations.

DISCUSSION QUESTIONS

1 To what extent could the experience of living and working in another country contribute to the skills and effectiveness of a manager in his/her home country?

2 Somnio, a start-up running shoe company in California, decided to start selling its products around the world from its beginning. In general terms, discuss some of the significant challenges a 'born global' company might face internationally.

3 Discuss the ways and means of developing a global mindset within the management group.

4 How will trade alliances such as NAFTA, the EU and TTIP might affect you as a future international manager?

5 What steps could a company take to avoid making product design and marketing mistakes when introducing new products in to India? How would you go about hiring a plant manager for a facility you are planning to build in India?

6 Explain the difference between licensing, exporting and direct investment as market entry strategies providing examples of each.

Are you ready to work internationally?[81]

INSTRUCTIONS Are you ready to negotiate a sales contract with someone from another country? Companies large and small deal on a global basis. To what extent are you guilty of the behaviours below?

Please answer each item as 'Mostly true' or 'Mostly false' for you.

Are you typically:	Mostly true	Mostly false
1 Impatient? Do you have a short attention span? Do you want to keep moving to the next topic?	☐	☐
2 A poor listener? Are you uncomfortable with silence? Does your mind think about what you want to say next?	☐	☐
3 Argumentative? Do you enjoy arguing for its own sake?	☐	☐
4 Unfamiliar with cultural specifics in other countries? Do you have limited experience in other countries?	☐	☐
5 Short-term-oriented? Do you place more emphasis on the short term than on the long term in your thinking and planning?	☐	☐
6 'All business'? Do you think that it is a waste of time getting to know someone personally before discussing business?	☐	☐
7 Legalistic to win your point? Do you hold others to an agreement regardless of changing circumstances?	☐	☐
8 Thinking 'win/lose' when negotiating? Do you usually try to win a negotiation at the other's expense?	☐	☐

SCORING & INTERPRETATION American managers often display cross-cultural ignorance during business negotiations when compared to counterparts in other countries. American habits can be disturbing, such as emphasizing areas of disagreement over agreement, spending little time understanding the views and interests of the other side, and adopting an adversarial attitude. Americans often like to leave a negotiation thinking that they have won, which can be embarrassing to the other side. For this quiz, a low score shows better international presence. If you answered 'Mostly true' to three or fewer questions, then consider yourself ready to assist with an international negotiation. If you scored six or more 'Mostly true' responses, it is time to learn more about other national cultures before participating in international business deals. Try to develop a greater focus on other people's needs and an appreciation for different viewpoints. Be open to compromise and develop empathy for people who are different from you.

APPLY YOUR SKILLS: ETHICAL DILEMMA

AH Biotech[82]

Dr Abraham Hassan knew he couldn't put off the decision any longer. AH Biotech, the Bound Brook, New Jersey-based company started by this psychiatrist-turned-entrepreneur, had developed a novel drug that seemed to promise long-term relief from panic attacks. If it gained approval from the Food and Drug Administration (FDA), it would be the company's first product. It was now time for large-scale clinical trials. But where should AH Biotech conduct those tests?

David Berger, who headed up research and development, was certain he already knew the answer to that question: Albania. 'Look, doing these trials in Albania will be quicker, easier and a lot cheaper than doing them in the States,' he pointed out. 'What's not to like?'

Dr Hassan had to concede that Berger's arguments were sound. If they did trials in the USA, AH Biotech would spend considerable time and money advertising for patients and then finding physicians who'd be willing to serve as clinical trial investigators. Rounding up US doctors prepared to take on that job was getting increasingly difficult. They just didn't want to take time out of their busy practices to do the testing, not to mention all the recordkeeping that such a study entailed.

In Albania it was an entirely different story. It was one of the poorest Eastern European countries – if not *the* poorest – with a just barely functioning health-care system. Albanian physicians and patients would practically line up at AH Biotech's doorstep begging to take part. Physicians there could earn much better money as clinical investigators for a US company than they could actually practising medicine, and patients saw signing up as test subjects as their best chance for receiving any treatment at all, let alone cutting-edge Western medicine. All these factors meant that the company could count on realizing at least a 25 per cent saving (maybe even more) by running the tests overseas.

What's not to like? As the Egyptian-born CEO of a start-up biotech company with investors and employees hoping for its first marketable drug, there was absolutely nothing to dislike. It was when he thought like a US-trained physician that he felt qualms. If he used US test subjects, he knew they'd be likely to continue receiving the drug until it was approved. At that point nearly everyone would have insurance that covered most of the cost of their prescriptions. But he already knew it wasn't going to make any sense to market the drug in a poor country like Albania, so when the study was over, he'd have to cut off treatment. Sure, he conceded, panic attacks weren't usually fatal. But he knew how debilitating these sudden bouts of feeling completely terrified were – the pounding heart, chest pain, choking sensation and nausea. The severity and unpredictability of these attacks often made a normal life all but impossible. How could he offer people dramatic relief and then snatch it away?

What would you do?

1   Do the clinical trials in Albania. You'll be able to bring the drug to market faster and cheaper, which will be good for AH Biotech's employees and investors and good for the millions of people who suffer from anxiety attacks.

2 Do the clinical trials in the USA. Even though it will certainly be more expensive and time-consuming, you'll feel as if you're living up to the part of the Hippocratic oath that instructed you to 'prescribe regimens for the good of my patients according to my ability and my judgement and never do harm to anyone.'

3 Do the clinical trials in Albania, and if the drug is approved, use part of the profits to set up a compassionate use programme in Albania, even though setting up a distribution system and training doctors to administer the drug, monitor patients for adverse effects and track results, will entail considerable expense.

APPLY YOUR SKILLS: CASE FOR CRITICAL ANALYSIS

HSBC and global environmental sensitivity

According to their Annual Report, the purpose of HSBC Bank plc is to connect customers to opportunities, enable businesses to thrive and economies to prosper, and ultimately help people to fulfil their hopes and realize their ambitions. HSBC aims to be the world's leading and most respected international bank and plans to achieve this by focusing on the needs of its customers and the societies it serves, thereby delivering long-term sustainable value to all its stakeholders.

HSBC recently announced a set of three interconnected and equally weighted priorities to help deliver its strategy:

■ grow the business and dividends

■ implement global standards, and

■ streamline processes and procedures.

Each priority is complementary and underpinned by initiatives being undertaken within its day-to-day business. Together they create value for customers of HSBC and contribute to the long-term sustainability of the group and HSBC.

In Europe the group's aim is to be the leading and most respected international bank connecting Europe with the rest of the world. On an operational level the group has developed a strategy for each of four global businesses following HSBC's strategic priorities while also focusing on increasing capital and cost efficiency.

Progress in implementing this strategy is tracked with a range of financial and non-financial measures or key performance indicators. Targets have recently been revised to better reflect the changing regulatory and operating environment.

The HSBC group continues to follow the vision for the long-term strategic vision which was first outlined in 2011 along with a clear strategy that will help it to achieve its aspirations. The strategy guides where and how it seeks to compete in what is increasingly a global market. HSBC constantly assesses its progress against this strategy and provides regular updates to stakeholders.

Through its principal activities – making payments, holding savings, enabling trade, providing finance and managing risks – it plays a central role in society and in the economic system. The HSBC target is to build and maintain a business which is sustainable in the long term.

HSBC competitive advantages

What matters in this environment is:

■ having an international network and global product capabilities to capture international trade and movements in capital, and

■ being able to take advantage of organic investment opportunities in the most attractive growth markets and maintaining the capacity to invest.

The group's competitive advantages come from:

■ its meaningful presence in and long-term commitment to HSBC's key strategic markets

■ its business network

■ its balanced business portfolio centred on its global client franchise

■ its strong ability to add to its capital base while also providing competitive rewards to its staff and good returns to its shareholder.

Leaked HSBC files – which were published by *The Guardian* and other media outlets and cover the period from 2005/2007 – revealed that HSBC's

Swiss bankers aggressively marketed a device that would allow clients to avoid a new tax. Stephen Green, who left HSBC to join the House of Lords as a Conservative peer and trade minister in 2010 after nearly three decades at the bank, has yet to be called by any of the parliamentary committees holding inquiries into the scandal. In his lecture on banking and finance, Green acknowledged the 'widespread public perception that some multinational businesses and some wealthy individuals play fast and loose with the tax rules, so as to squirrel away income into low-tax jurisdictions and avoid making their rightful contribution to the public well-being.'

Stephen Green, who was chairman of HSBC for 5 years and is also an ordained Church of England minister, acknowledged that big business had lost respect and trust as society became 'more questioning, more suspicious, more atomized.' He said this attitude could be turned around by responsible boards promoting proactive engagement by their staff and 'responsiveness to both clients and community.'

Questions

1 Evaluate the organizational implications of Stephen Green's assertion.

2 Discuss the extent to which Hofstede's 'value dimensions' remain significant today for a company such as HSBC.

3 Design a 2-day (12 hours) training programme for HSBC managers to enhance their sensitivity to economic, legal-political and sociocultural influences.

END NOTES

1. Bettina Wassener, 'Living in Asia Appeals to More Company Leaders', *The New York Times*, June 21, 2012, B3; and Emily Glazer, 'P&G Unit Bids Goodbye to Cincinnati, Hello to Asia', *The Wall Street Journal*, May 10, 2012, B1.

2. Quoted in Wassener, 'Living in Asia Appeals to More Company Leaders'.

3. Joann S. Lublin, 'Hunt Is on for Fresh Executive Talent – Cultural Flexibility in Demand', *The Wall Street Journal*, April 11, 2011, B1.

4. Lolita C. Baldor, 'FBI Sends More Agents Abroad to Shield U.S. from Cybercrime; Foreign Hackers Stepping up Their Attacks', *South Florida Sun-Sentinel,* December 10, 2009; and Cassell Bryan-Low, 'Criminal Network: To Catch Crooks in Cyberspace, FBI Goes Global', *The Wall Street Journal*, November 21, 2006.

5. Ryan Underwood, 'Going Global', *Inc.* (March 2011): 96–98.

6. Chris Woodyard, 'The American Car', *USA Today,* February 17, 2009.

7. 'KOF Index of Globalization 2012', press release, KOF Swiss Economic Institute (March 26, 2012), www.kof.ethz.ch/static_media/filer/2012/03/16/kof_index_of_globalization_2012_1.pdf (accessed June 26, 2012).

8. '2012 KOF Index of Globalization', www.kof.ethz.ch/static_media/filer/2012/03/15/rankings_2012.pdf (accessed June 26, 2012). Note: The 2012 KOF analysis of globalization dimensions is based on the year 2009.

9. This section is based on Schon Beechler and Dennis Baltzley, 'Creating a Global Mindset', *Chief Learning Officer* (May 29, 2008), www.clomedia.com/articles/view/creating_a_global_mindset/1 (accessed June 26, 2012); Joana S. P. Story and John E. Barbuto, Jr., 'Global Mindset: A Construct Clarification and Framework', *Journal of Leadership and Organizational Studies* 18, no. 3 (2011): 377–384; and Stephen L. Cohen, 'Effective Global Leadership Requires a Global Mindset', *Industrial and Commercial Training* 42, no. 1 (2010): 3–10.

10. Definition based on Mansour Javidan and Mary B. Teagarden, 'Conceptualizing and Measuring Global Mindset', *Advances in Global Leadership* 6 (2011): 13–39; and Beechler and Baltzley, 'Creating a Global Mindset'.

11. Amol Titus, 'Competency of Intercultural Management', *The Jakarta Post*, March 11, 2009, www.thejakartapost.com/news/2009/03/11/competency-intercultural-management.html (accessed June 30, 2012).

12. Karl Moore, 'Great Global Managers', *Across the Board* (May–June 2003): 40–43.

13. Siegfried Russwurm, Luis Hernandez, Susan Chambers, Keumyong Chung, Daniel McGinn, Lothar Kuhn and Cornelia Geissler 'Developing Your Global Know-How', *Harvard Business Review* (March 2011): 70–75.

14. Quoted in Wassener, 'Living in Asia Appeals to More Company Leaders'.

15. 'Count: *Really* Big Business', *Fast Company* (December 2008–January 2009): 46.

16. David E. Bell and Mary L. Shelman, 'KFC's Radical Approach to China', *Harvard Business Review* (November 2011): 137–142.

17. Howard V. Perlmutter, 'The Tortuous Evolution of the Multinational Corporation', *Columbia Journal of World Business* (January–February 1969): 9–18; and Youram Wind, Susan P. Douglas and Howard V. Perlmutter, 'Guidelines for Developing International Marketing Strategies', *Journal of Marketing* (April 1973): 14–23.

18. Deborah Ball, 'Boss Talk: Nestlé Focuses on Long Term', *The Wall Street Journal,* November 2, 2009; Transnationale website, www.transnationale.org/companies/nestle.php (accessed March 17, 2010); Company Analytics website, www.company-analytics.org/company/nestle.php (accessed March 17, 2010); and Nestlé SA website, www.nestle.com (accessed March 17, 2010).

19. Sara Murray and Douglas Belkin, 'Americans Sour on Trade: Majority Say Free-Trade Pacts Have Hurt U.S.', *The Wall Street Journal*, October 4, 2010; and Nina Easton,

'Make the World Go Away', *Fortune* (February 4, 2008): 105–108.

20. Easton, 'Make the World Go Away'.

21. Michael Schroeder and Timothy Aeppel, 'Skilled Workers Sway Politicians with Fervor Against Free Trade', *The Wall Street Journal*, December 10, 2003.

22. Stephanie Wong, John Liu and Tim Culpan, 'Life and Death at the iPad Factory', *Bloomberg Businessweek* (June 7–June 13, 2010): 35–36; Charles Duhigg and Steven Greenhouse, 'Apple Supplier in China Pledges Big Labor Changes', *The New York Times*, March 29, 2012, www.nytimes.com/2012/03/30/business/apple-supplier-in-china-pledges-changes-in-working-conditions.html?pagewanted=all (accessed June 30, 2012); and Kevin Drew, 'Apple's Chief Visits iPhone Factory in China', *The New York Times*, March 29, 2012, www.nytimes.com/2012/03/30/technology/apples-chief-timothy-cook-visits-foxconn-factory.html (accessed June 30, 2012).

23. C. K. Prahalad, 'The Fortune at the Bottom of the Pyramid', *Fast Company* (April 13, 2011), www.fastcompany.com/1746818/fortune-at-the-bottom- of-the-pyramid ck prahalad (accessed June 30, 2012); C. K. Prahalad and S. L. Hart, 'The Fortune at the Bottom of the Pyramid', *Strategy + Business* 26 (2002): 54–67; and Scott Johnson, 'SC Johnson Builds Business at the Base of the Pyramid', *Global Business and Organizational Excellence* (September–October, 2007): 6–17.

24. Bala Chakravarthy and Sophie Coughlan, 'Emerging Market Strategy: Innovating Both Products and Delivery Systems', *Strategy & Leadership* 40, no. 1 (2012): 27–32; T. V. Mahalingam, 'Godrej's Rediscovery of India: They Say They Touch More Consumers than Any Other Indian Company', *Business Today* (July 25, 2010): 58–64; and 'Godrej Eyes Youth to Expand Portfolio', *Mail Today*, July 12, 2009.

25. Rob Walker, 'Cleaning Up', *New York Times Magazine* (June 10, 2007): 20.

26. Jennifer Reingold, 'Can P&G Make Money in Places Where People Earn $2 a Day?' *Fortune* (January 17, 2011): 86–91.

27. Jean Kerr, 'Export Strategies', *Small Business Reports* (May 1989): 20–25.

28. Mark Sweney, 'Netflix Non-US Losses Hit $100m But Subscribers Increase', *The Guardian*, April 24, 2012, www.guardian.co.uk/media/2012/apr/24/netflix-losses-100m-subscribers-increase (accessed June 27, 2012).

29. Lauren A. E. Schuker, 'Plot Change: Foreign Forces Transform Hollywood Films', *The Wall Street Journal*, July 31, 2010, A1; and Nicole Allan, 'How to Make a Hollywood Hit', *The Atlantic* (May 2012); 70–71.

30. Alison Stein Wellner, 'Turning the Tables', *Inc.* (May 2006): 55–59.

31. Kathryn Rudie Harrigan, 'Managing Joint Ventures', *Management Review* (February 1987): 24–41; and Therese R. Revesz and Mimi Cauley de Da La Sierra, 'Competitive Alliances: Forging Ties Abroad', *Management Review* (March 1987): 57–59.

32. Christopher Weaver, 'Abbott Looks to Consumer for Growth', *The Wall Street Journal*, May 2, 2012, www.online.wsj.com/article/SB10001424052702303990604577367760661436198.html (accessed June 28, 2012).

33. James T. Areddy, 'European Project Trips China Builder', *The Wall Street Journal*, June 4, 2012, A1; and Kirk Semple, 'Bridge Repairs by a Company Tied to Beijing', *The New York Times*, August 10, 2011, www.nytimes.com/2011/08/11/nyregion/china-construction-co-involved-in-new-yorks-public-works.html (accessed June 27, 2012).

34. Anthony Goerzen, 'Managing Alliance Networks: Emerging Practices of Multinational Corporations', *Academy of Management Executive* 19, no. 2 (2005): 94–107.

35. Anjali Cordeiro, 'Tang in India and Other Kraft Synergies', *The Wall Street Journal Online*, April 19, 2010, www.online.wsj.com/article/SB10001424052702303348504575184103106388686.html (accessed June 28, 2012); Lorrie Grant, 'An 'Infinite' Opportunity for Growth: CEO Bob Nardelli Sees Expansion in Home Depot's Future', *USA Today*, July 28, 2005; Donald Greenlees, 'Philip Morris to Buy Indonesian Cigarette Maker', *The New York Times*, March 14, 2005; and Tiisetso Motsoeneng and Wendell Roelf, 'Wal-Mart Wins Final Go-Ahead for Massmart Deal', Reuters.com, March 9, 2012, www.reuters.com/article/2012/03/09/us-massmart-walmart-idUSBRE8280KH20120309 (accessed June 27, 2012).

36. Daniel Michaels, Jon Ostrower and David Pearson, 'Airbus's New Push: Made in the U.S.A.', *The Wall Street Journal*, July 2, 2012.

37. G. Pascal Zachary, 'Dream Factory', *Business 2.0* (June 2005): 96–102.

38. Jim Holt, 'Gone Global?' *Management Review* (March 2000): 13.

39. James Hookway, 'IKEA's Products Make Shoppers Blush in Thailand', *The Wall Street Journal*, June 5, 2012, A1.

40. Holt, 'Gone Global?'

41. 'Slogans Often Lose Something in Translation', *The New Mexican*, July 3, 1994.

42. For a recent overview of various environmental factors influencing firms that operate internationally, see David Conklin, 'The Global Environment of Business: New Paradigms for International Management', *Ivey Business Journal* (July–August 2011), www.iveybusinessjournal.com/topics/global-business/the-global-environment-of-business-new-paradigms-for-international-management (accessed June 27, 2012).

43. Louis S. Richman, 'Global Growth Is on a Tear', in *International Business 97/98, Annual Editions*, ed. Fred Maidment (Guilford, CT: Dushkin Publishing Group, 1997), pp. 6–11.

44. 'The Global Competitiveness Report 2011–2012', World Economic Forum, www3.weforum.org/docs/WEF_GCR_Report_2011-12.pdf (accessed June 27, 2012).

45. M. Walker, C. Forelle and D. Gauthier-Villars, 'Europe Bailout Lifts Gloom', *The Wall Street Journal*, May 11, 2010; and G. Bowley and C. Hauser, 'Stocks Plunge on Fears of a Spreading European Crisis', *The New York Times*, May 21, 2010.

46. 'A New Definition of Misery', *The New York Times*, December 18, 2009 (based on data from *Moody's*), www.nytimes.com/imagepages/2009/12/18/business/economy/20091219_CHARTS_GRAPHIC.html (accessed September 27, 2012).

47. Mike Ramsey and Yoshio Takahashi, 'Car Wreck: Honda and Toyota', *The Wall Street Journal Online*, November 1, 2011, www.online.wsj.com/article/SB10001424052970204528204577009044170787650.html (accessed June 29, 2012); Stephanie Clifford, 'Rattling Wal-Mart's Supply Chain', *International Herald Tribune*, June 1, 2011, 17.

48. Ian Bremmer, 'Managing Risk in an Unstable World', *Harvard Business Review* (June 2005): 51–60; Mark Fitzpatrick,

'The Definition and Assessment of Political Risk in International Business: A Review of the Literature', *Academy of Management Review* 8 (1983): 249–254; and Jo Jakobsen, 'Old Problems Remain, New Ones Crop Up: Political Risk in the 21st Century', *Business Horizons* 53 (2010): 481–490.

49. John Markoff and David Barboza, 'Inquiry Is Said to Link Attack on Google to Chinese Schools', *The New York Times*, February 19, 2010.

50. Peter Wonacott, 'An Entrepreneur Weathers a Tumultuous Arab Spring', *The Wall Street Journal*, January 17, 2012, www.online.wsj.com/article/SB1000142405297020343690 4577150690233235850.html (accessed June 27, 2012).

51. Mary Gooderham, 'Companies That Go Where Others Fear to Tread', *The Globe and Mail*, June 21, 2012, B7.

52. Geert Hofstede, *Culture's Consequences: International Differences in Work-Related Values* (Beverly Hills, CA: Sage, 1980); G. Hofstede, 'The Interaction Between National and Organizational Value Systems', *Journal of Management Studies* 22 (1985): 347–357; and G. Hofstede, *Cultures and Organizations: Software of the Mind* (revised and expanded 2d ed.) (New York: McGraw-Hill, 2005).

53. Geert Hofstede, 'Cultural Constraints in Management Theory', *Academy of Management Executive* 7 (1993): 81–94; and G. Hofstede and M. H. Bond, 'The Confucian Connection: From Cultural Roots to Economic Growth', *Organizational Dynamics* 16 (1988): 4–21.

54. Vas Taras, Piers Steel and Bradley L. Kirkman, 'Three Decades of Research on National Culture in the Workplace: Do the Differences Still Make a Difference?' *Organizational Dynamics* 40 (2011): 189–198.

55. For an overview of the research and publications related to Hofstede's dimensions, see 'Retrospective: *Culture's Consequences*', a collection of articles focusing on Hofstede's work, in *The Academy of Management Executive* 18, no. 1 (February 2004): 72–93. See also Michele J. Gelfand et al., 'Individualism and Collectivism', in *Culture, Leadership and Organizations: The Globe Study of 62 Societies*, ed. R. J. House et al. (Thousand Oaks, CA: Sage, 2004).

56. Mansour Javidan, Peter W. Dorfman, Mary Sully de Luque and Robert J. House, 'In the Eye of the Beholder: Cross-Cultural Lessons from Project GLOBE', *Academy of Management Perspectives* (February 2006): 67–90; Robert J. House et al., eds, *Culture, Leadership, and Organizations: The GLOBE Study of 62 Societies* (Thousand Oaks, CA: Sage Publications, 2004); M. Javidan and R. J. House, 'Cultural Acumen for the Global Manager: Lessons from Project GLOBE', *Organizational Dynamics* 29, no. 4 (2001): 289–305; and R. J. House et al., 'Understanding Cultures and Implicit Leadership Theories Across the Globe: An Introduction to Project GLOBE', *Journal of World Business* 37 (2002): 3–10.

57. Carlos Sanchez-Runde, Luciara Nardon and Richard Steers, 'Looking Beyond Western Leadership Models: Implications for Global Managers', *Organizational Dynamics* 40 (2011): 207–213.

58. Chantell E. Nicholls, Henry W. Lane and Mauricio Brehm Brechu, 'Taking Self-Managed Teams to Mexico', *Academy of Management Executive* 13, no. 2 (1999): 15–27; Carl F. Fey and Daniel R. Denison, 'Organizational Culture and Effectiveness: Can American Theory Be Applied in Russia?' *Organization Science* 14, no. 6 (November–December 2003): 686–706; Ellen F. Jackofsky, John W. Slocum, Jr. and Sara J. McQuaid, 'Cultural Values and the CEO: Alluring Companions?' *Academy of Management Executive* 2 (1988): 39–49.

59. J. Kennedy and A. Everest, 'Put Diversity in Context', *Personnel Journal* (September 1991): 50–54.

60. Jane Spencer, 'Lenovo Goes Global, But Not Without Strife', *The Wall Street Journal*, November 4, 2008.

61. Bob Davis, 'As Global Economy Shifts, Companies Rethink, Retool', *The Wall Street Journal*, November 7, 2010, www.online.wsj.com/article/SB1000142405274870404990457555 4290932153112.html (accessed June 29, 2012).

62. David Barboza, 'Apple Cracks the Code for Success in China', *International Herald Tribune*, July 26, 2011, 15.

63. Loretta Chao, Lorraine Luk and Aaron Back, 'Sales of iPhone in China Set Under 3-Year Accord', *The Wall Street Journal*, August 31, 2009; and Loretta Chao, Juliet Ye and Yukari Iwatani Kane, 'Apple, Facing Competition, Readies iPhone for Launch in Giant China Market', *The Wall Street Journal*, August 28, 2009.

64. George Stalk and David Michael, 'What the West Doesn't Get About China', *Harvard Business Review* (June 2011): 25–27; Zoe McKay, 'Consumer Spending in China: To Buy or Not to Buy', *Forbes.com*, June 15, 2012, www.forbes.com/sites/insead/2012/06/15/consumer-spending-in-china-to-buy-or-not-to-buy/ (accessed June 29, 2012); and Adam Davidson, 'Come On, China, Buy Our Stuff!' *The New York Times*, January 25, 2012, www.nytimes.com/2012/01/29/magazine/come-on-china-buy-our-stuff.html?pagewanted=all (accessed June 29, 2012).

65. David Barboza and Brad Stone, 'A Nation That Trips up Many', *The New York Times*, January 16, 2010.

66. Andrew Galbraith and Jason Dean, 'In China, Some Firms Defy Business Norms', *The Wall Street Journal Online*, September 6, 2011, www.online.wsj.com/article/SB10001424 05311190389590457654638151201572z.html (accessed June 29, 2012).

67. Stalk and Michael, 'What the West Doesn't Get About China'.

68. Chuck Salter, 'Lenovo: Protect and Attack', *Fast Company* (December 2011–January 2012): 116–121, 154–155.

69. W. Michael Cox and Richard Alm, 'China and India: Two Paths to Economic Power', *Economic Letter*, Federal Reserve Bank of Dallas, August 2008, www.dallasfed.org / research/eclett/2008/el0808.html (accessed July 14, 2010).

70. 'Pharmaceuticals', India Brand Equity Foundation, IBEF .org, May 2012, www.ibef.org/industry/pharmaceuticals .aspx (accessed June 29, 2012); and Sushmi Dey, 'Indian Pharma Eyes US Generic Gold Rush', *Business Standard*, June 27, 2012, www.business-standard.com/india/news/indian-pharma-eyes-us-generic-gold-rush/478593/ (accessed June 29, 2012).

71. This section is based on 'Brazil GDP Growth Rate', Trading Economics website, www.tradingeconomics.com/brazil/gdp-growth (accessed June 29, 2012); 'Brazil', The World Factbook, Central Intelligence Agency website, www.cia.gov/library/publications/the-world-factbook/geos/br.html#top (accessed June 29, 2012); Paulo Prada, 'For Brazil, It's Finally Tomorrow', *The Wall Street Journal*, March 29, 2010; Melanie Eversley, 'Brazil's Olympian Growth', *USA Today*, October 5, 2009; and Liam Denning,

'Are Cracks Forming in the BRICs?' *The Wall Street Journal*, February 16, 2010.

72. This discussion is based on 'For Richer, for Poorer', *The Economist* (December 1993): 66; Richard Harmsen, 'The Uruguay Round: A Boon for the World Economy', *Finance & Development* (March 1995): 24–26; Salil S. Pitroda, 'From GATT to WTO: The Institutionalization of World Trade', *Harvard International Review* (Spring 1995): 46–47, 66–67; and World Trade Organization website, www.wto.org (accessed February 11, 2008).

73. EUROPA website, 'The History of the European Union', www.europa.eu/about-eu/eu-history/index_en.htm (accessed July 14, 2010).

74. European Commission Economic and Financial Affairs website, www.ec.europa.eu/economy_finance/euro/index_en.htm (accessed March 18, 2010).

75. Clive Crook, 'Opening Remarks: Who Lost the Euro?' part of a 'Special Euro Crisis' section, *Bloomberg Businessweek* (May 28–June 3, 2012): 10–12; and Howard Schneider, 'In Greece, The Money Flowed Freely, Until It Didn't', *The Washington Post*, June 14, 2012, www.washingtonpost.com/business/economy/in-greece-the-money-flowed-freely-until-it-didnt/2012/06/14/gJQA7Z4YcV_story.html (accessed June 30, 2012).

76. Vanessa Fuhrmans and Dana Cimilluca, 'Business Braces for Europe's Worst – Multinationals Scramble to Protect Cash, Revise Contracts, Tighten Payment Terms', *The Wall Street Journal*, June 1, 2012, B1.

77. Tapan Munroe, 'NAFTA Still a Work in Progress', *Knight Ridder/Tribune News Service*, January 9, 2004; and J. S. McClenahan, 'NAFTA Works', *IW* (January 10, 2000): 5–6.

78. Eric Alterman, 'A Spectacular Success?' *The Nation* (February 2, 2004): 10; Jeff Faux, 'NAFTA at 10: Where Do We Go from Here?' *The Nation* (February 2, 2004): 11; Geri Smith and Cristina Lindblad, 'Mexico: Was NAFTA Worth It? A Tale of What Free Trade Can and Cannot Do', *BusinessWeek* (December 22, 2003): 66; Jeffrey Sparshott, 'NAFTA Gets Mixed Reviews', *The Washington Times*, December 18, 2003; and Munroe, 'NAFTA Still a Work in Progress'.

79. Darrell Rigby and Barbara Bilodeau, 'Management Tools and Trends 2011', Bain & Company, Inc., www.bain.com/publications/articles/Management-tools-trends-2011.aspx (accessed June 22, 2012).

80. Munroe, 'NAFTA Still a Work in Progress'; Sparshott, 'NAFTA Gets Mixed Reviews'; and Amy Borrus, 'A Free-Trade Milestone, with Many More Miles to Go', *BusinessWeek* (August 24, 1992): 30–31.

81. Adapted from Cynthia Barnum and Natasha Wolniansky, 'Why Americans Fail at Overseas Negotiations', *Management Review* (October 1989): 54–57.

82. Based on Gina Kolata, 'Companies Facing Ethical Issue as Drugs Are Tested Overseas', *The New York Times*, March 5, 2004; and Julie Schmit, 'Costs, Regulations Move More Drug Tests Outside USA', *USA Today*, June 16, 2005.

CHAPTER 6

MANAGING ETHICS AND SOCIAL CORPORATE GOVERNANCE

LEARNING OBJECTIVES

After studying this chapter, you should be able to:

1 Define ethics and explain how ethical behaviour relates to behaviour governed by law and free choice.

2 Discuss why ethics is important for managers and identify recent events that call for a renewed commitment to ethical management.

3 Explain the utilitarian, individualism, moral rights, justice and practical approaches for making ethical decisions.

4 Describe the factors that shape a manager's ethical decision-making, including levels of moral development.

5 Identify important stakeholders for an organization and discuss how managers balance the interests of various stakeholders.

6 Explain the philosophy of sustainability and why organizations are embracing it.

7 Describe what is meant by 'the triple bottom line'.

8 Define corporate social responsibility and how to evaluate it along economic, legal, ethical and discretionary criteria.

9 Discuss how ethical organizations are created through ethical leadership and organizational structures and systems.

What does courage have to do with a chapter on ethics? If you read articles about the US Secret Service prostitution scandal, the subprime mortgage fiasco in the USA and the contagion that affected the EU and the UK banks in particular, the implosion of financial icons such as Lehman Brothers and Bear Stearns, it soon becomes apparent that this is a major issue that cannot be swept under the carpet! These organizations not only had senior managers and executives behaving unethically, but they also had many managers who thought the behaviour was wrong but lacked the courage to challenge their superiors, or call attention to the misdeeds. There is a need for defining channels of legitimate dissent to be developed and participants (including whistle-blowers) to be afforded a higher degree of legal protection and even financial rewards. The bounty system recently introduced by US legislators has moved strongly in this direction (see section 6.4 in the KPMG 2013 Survey for details) of the Dodd-Frank Wall Street Reform and Consumer Protection Law).

Unfortunately, many managers slide into unethical or even illegal behaviour simply because they don't have the courage to stand up and do the right thing. Lack of courage isn't the only problem, of course. Managers and organizations engage in unethical behaviour for any number of reasons, such as personal ego, greed or pressures to increase profits or appear successful. Mark Hurd was fired as CEO of Hewlett-Packard, after an investigation revealed that he submitted inaccurate expense reports, in an attempt to cover up an inappropriate relationship with a female contractor.[1] Interviews with people in the mortgage wholesale industry reveal that many wholesalers (who work for banks and buy loan applications from independent mortgage brokers) operated from pure commission-seeking greed. They frequently altered documents, coached brokers on how to skirt the rules, and even offered bribes and sexual favours to generate more loans – and thus more profits. And the former CEO of Yahoo!, Scott Thompson, resigned under pressure after only 4 months in the job because reports revealed he had inaccurately claimed on his resumé that he had a degree in computer science. Moreover, initially Thompson tried to blame the inaccuracy on the executive search firm that had placed him in an earlier job at PayPal. *'The cover-up became worse than the crime,'* said one anonymous person familiar with the fiasco.[2]

This chapter expands on the ideas about environment, corporate culture and the international environment discussed in Chapters 3 and 4. We first focus on the topic of ethical values, which builds deeply on the concept of corporate culture. We look at the current ethical climate in corporate America and Europe to examine fundamental approaches that can help managers think through difficult ethical issues; and consider various factors that influence how managers make ethical choices. Understanding these ideas will help you build a solid foundation on which to base future decision-making. We also examine organizational relationships to the external environment, as reflected in corporate social responsibility. The final section of this chapter describes how managers build and sustain an ethical organization using codes of ethics, organizational policies, structures and control systems. The holistic approach to all of these aspects is now firmly within the developing academic discipline of Corporate Governance.

What are managerial ethics?

Ethical behaviour is difficult to define in a precise way. In a general sense, ethics is the code of moral principles and values that governs the behaviours of a person, or group, with respect to what is right or wrong. Ethics sets standards as to what is good or bad in conduct and decision-making.[3] An ethical issue is present in a situation when the actions of a person or organization may harm and/or benefit others.[4] Yet ethical issues sometimes can be exceedingly complex. People may hold widely divergent views about the most ethically appropriate or inappropriate actions related to a situation.[5] But most transactions invariably involve winners and losers and therefore judgement calls have to be made. *'It is equally reasonable to expect different role players, such as senior executives, not to evade their moral responsibilities, hiding behind the notion of corporate moral responsibility, to execute actions in the organization's name that would be condemned by civil society, which could never be justified as moral actions if executed by them as individuals in the community'* (McEwan 2001).

Consider the issue of competitive intelligence. Companies are increasingly using social media sites to learn more about their competition, some even going so far as to befriend customers or employees of rival firms and post seemingly innocuous questions to gather information that can provide them with a competitive advantage.[6] The laws regarding information gathering are not clear-cut, and neither are opinions regarding the ethics of such tactics. Whereas some people believe any form of corporate espionage is wrong, many think it is an acceptable way of learning about the competition.[7] Managers frequently face situations in which it is difficult (at that time) to determine what is right and what is wrong. In addition, they might be torn between their misgivings and their sense of duty to their bosses and the organization. Ethics can be more clearly understood when compared with behaviours governed by law and by free choice. Exhibit 6.1 illustrates that human behaviour falls into three categories. The first is codified law, in which values and standards are written into the legal system and enforceable in the courts. In this area, lawmakers set rules that people and corporations must follow in a certain way, such as obtaining licences for cars, paying corporate taxes or following other local, state and national laws. Behaviours such as fraud and tax evasion are clearly against the law and blatantly unethical. The EU is cracking down on aggressive tax avoidance schemes and the US is currently taking a stance of 'tax-inversion' that is moving a company's tax domicile away from the USA (say from the USA to Eire) that would be very financially advantageous to the US company involved in the M&A (Mergers and Acquisitions). Other USA corporations such as Starbucks (with clever transfer pricing of coffee beans and marketing costs) have agreed to pay more $millions of corporation tax to the UK tax authorities. The domain of free choice is at the opposite end of the scale and pertains to behaviour about which the law has no guidance and for which an individual or organization enjoys complete freedom. The UK government has taken a number of regulatory steps following the near collapse of many of the UK's clearing banks. 'The Salz Review: An Independent Review of Barclay's Business Practices' (2013) made 32 recommendations to their executive board to facilitate improved corporate governance. The review noted in section 6.24, inter alia, that *'Barclays was slow to deal with emerging regulatory concerns'* and that *'the culture of the bank had developed into one which at times valued meeting financial targets more than meeting customer needs. It should be recognized that executives are not homogeneous actors so there cannot be a standardized set of behavioural controls that can be applied to their individual performance. We have an expectation that executive managers will behave in a rational way when making decisions that impact on the company's stakeholders'*

The following is an extract from the Salz Review (2013, p.58) that encapsulates the complexity of industry regulation for the banking industry:

The industry has been vocal in asserting that regulators and others involved in redress have sometimes developed and adapted their approach over time to specific conduct issues, ultimately relating to the settlement of customer claims, to the material disadvantage of the banks. We are not in a position to judge whether this is a fair viewpoint. Effective regulation at its best is based on mutual trust and respect. For this, it will be important that, wherever possible, banks fully understand how the regulators intend to approach issues and how any rules will be applied. Certainty is impossible and consistency on the part of the regulator will in turn depend upon the industry applying regulation in line with its spirit. This will, of course, be assisted by the efforts of banks to apply the highest standards of customer care.

In September 2014 the Financial Reporting Council (FRC) issued The UK Corporate Governance Code. The publication (point 4 of 6) states that: *'The code is a guide to a number of key components of effective board practice. It is based on the underlying principles of all good governance: accountability, transparency, probity and focus on the sustainable success of an entity over the long term.'*

Also, under point 5 of 6 it states: *'The Code has been enduring, but it is not immutable. Its fitness for purpose in a permanently changing economic and social business environment requires its evaluation at appropriate intervals.'*

In conclusion, it can be observed that regulators are frequently playing 'catch-up' to exercise managerial control over often devious and self-seeking opportunistic executives.

Between these domains lies the area of ethics. This domain has no specific laws, yet it does have standards of conduct based on shared principles and core values concerning moral conduct that guide an individual,

EXHIBIT 6.1 Three domains of human action

CONCEPT CONNECTION

Goldman Sachs CEO, Lloyd Blankfein, was in the hot seat as he defended the firm's role in creating Abacus, a mortgage-backed investment fund that was allegedly designed to fail. While Goldman bet against the fund as a way to hedge against a weakening housing market, its trading side facilitated sales of Abacus to institutional customers. The manoeuvre helped Goldman weather the financial crisis but raised serious questions about its **managerial ethics**. Blankfein said that the firm's trading side is simply '*A machine that lets people buy and sell what they want to buy and sell.*' Despite this defence, Goldman agreed in 2010 to pay $550 million to settle federal claims that it misled investors.

or a company. For example, it was not illegal for Harry Stonecipher, the former CEO of Boeing, to have an extramarital affair with a female executive, but his behaviour violated Boeing's code of ethical conduct, and Stonecipher was therefore replaced. However, a manager who commits sexual harassment is not just being unethical but is breaking US, EU and other national laws. Steven J. Heyer was fired as CEO of Starwood Hotels & Resorts Worldwide Inc. after the board received an anonymous letter (from a whistle-blower) that accused Heyer of inappropriately touching female employees and creating a hostile work environment.[8]

Many companies and individuals get into trouble with the simplified view that decisions are governed by either law or free choice. This view leads people to mistakenly assume that if it's not illegal, it must be ethical, as if there were no third domain.[9] A better option is to recognize the domain of ethics and accept moral values as a powerful force for good that can regulate behaviours both inside and outside organizations. Codes of ethics need to be embedded in a firm's corporate culture, understood and clearly communicated. Transgressions need to be dealt with promptly and transparently. History tells us when the truth is suppressed the outcome is far worse because of inept attempts to conceal or change the story.

REFLECTION

- Managers face many pressures that can sometimes tempt them to engage in unethical behaviour.
- **Ethics** is the code of moral principles and values that governs the behaviours of a person or group with respect to what is right or wrong.
- Just because managers aren't breaking the law doesn't necessarily mean they are being ethical.

- An ethical issue is present in any situation when the actions of an individual or organization may harm or benefit others.
- Managers sometimes need courage to stand up and do the right thing.

Ethical management today

Every decade seems to experience its share of scoundrels, but the pervasiveness of ethical lapses during the first decade or so of this century has been astounding. In Gallup's 2010 poll regarding the perception of business leaders, just 15 per cent of respondents rated leaders' honesty and ethical standards as 'high' or 'very high'.[10] Although public confidence in business managers in particular is at an all-time low, politics sports and non-profit organizations also have been affected. Cycling star Lance Armstrong was stripped of his seven Tour de France championship titles, after conclusive evidence of his drug abuse proved that he was using performance-enhancing drugs, before each of his victories.[11]

In the business world, the names of once-revered corporations have become synonymous with greed, deceit, irresponsibility and lack of moral conscience: Lehman Brothers, Enron, Bear Stearns, RBS and Barclays Bank. No wonder a poll found that 76 per cent of people surveyed say corporate America's moral compass was '*pointing in the wrong direction*'; 69 per cent said executives rarely consider the public good in making decisions; and 94 per cent said executives make decisions based primarily on advancing their own careers.[12] Extracts from the extensive 12 month KPMG survey of 2013 now follow and provide rich insights of misconduct and warnings that fraud and corporate misconduct still prevail in US corporations. They have been paraphrased for conciseness.

a) A majority of respondents (73 per cent) reported that they had observed misconduct over the 12 month period covered by the survey.

b) The prevalence of misconduct could cause a significant loss of public confidence if discovered.

c) One of the most commonly cited drivers of misconduct continues to be attributed to pressure to do 'whatever' it takes to meet business goals and [encouraged] by having systems in place that rewarded results over means, and a fear of job loss if targets were not met.

d) Employee propensity to report misconduct to an ethics hotline has increased, [whilst] their willingness to look the other way and do nothing, or to report misconduct outside the organization, has also increased.

e) Having in place formal ethics and compliance programmes continue to makes a positive difference.

f) Finally, the executive summary contains this advice to policymakers, which is provided in full below:

'Such results demonstrate a continuing need for organizations to enhance the effectiveness of their internal reporting mechanisms, especially in the light of the provision of various federal and state whistle-blowing laws – including the recently enacted Dodd-Frank Law.'

'The bottom line is that when shareholder value capitalism is paramount, the rest of us suffer. CEOs will readily dupe customers, sack employees and spoil the environment to meet expectations.'

— ROGER MARTIN, DEAN AND PROFESSOR AT THE ROTMAN SCHOOL OF MANAGEMENT, TORONTO

Managers carry a tremendous responsibility for setting the ethical climate in an organization and can act as role models for others.[13] Managers are responsible for seeing that resources are used to serve the interests of stakeholders, including shareholders, employees, customers and society. Exhibit 6.2 details various ways that organizations sometimes behave unethically towards customers, employees and other stakeholders.[14] Unfortunately, in today's environment, an overemphasis on pleasing shareholders may cause some managers to behave unethically towards customers, employees and the broader society. Managers are under enormous pressure to meet short-term earnings goals, and some even use creative accounting or other techniques to show returns that meet market expectations rather than ones that reflect true performance. Moreover, most executive compensation plans include hefty stock-based incentives, a practice that encourages managers to do whatever will increase the share price, even if it hurts the company in the long run. When managers 'fall prey to the siren call of shareholder value', all other stakeholders may suffer.[15] Executives have been found guilty (retrospectively) of having overconfidence that has seriously eroded shareholder value.

Executive compensation has become a hot-button issue.[16] In 2011, the average pay of CEOs at large US corporations was 380 times what the average employee was paid. A study by the Economic Policy Institute found that between 1978 and 2011, the average worker's annual pay grew 5.7 per cent, while average CEO pay increased a whopping 726.7 per cent.[17] The question of whether it is ethical for managers to rake in huge sums of money compared to other employees is of growing concern, and in general the widespread ethical lapses of the past decade have put managers under increasing scrutiny.

EXHIBIT 6.2 Examples of unethical and illegal organizational behaviour

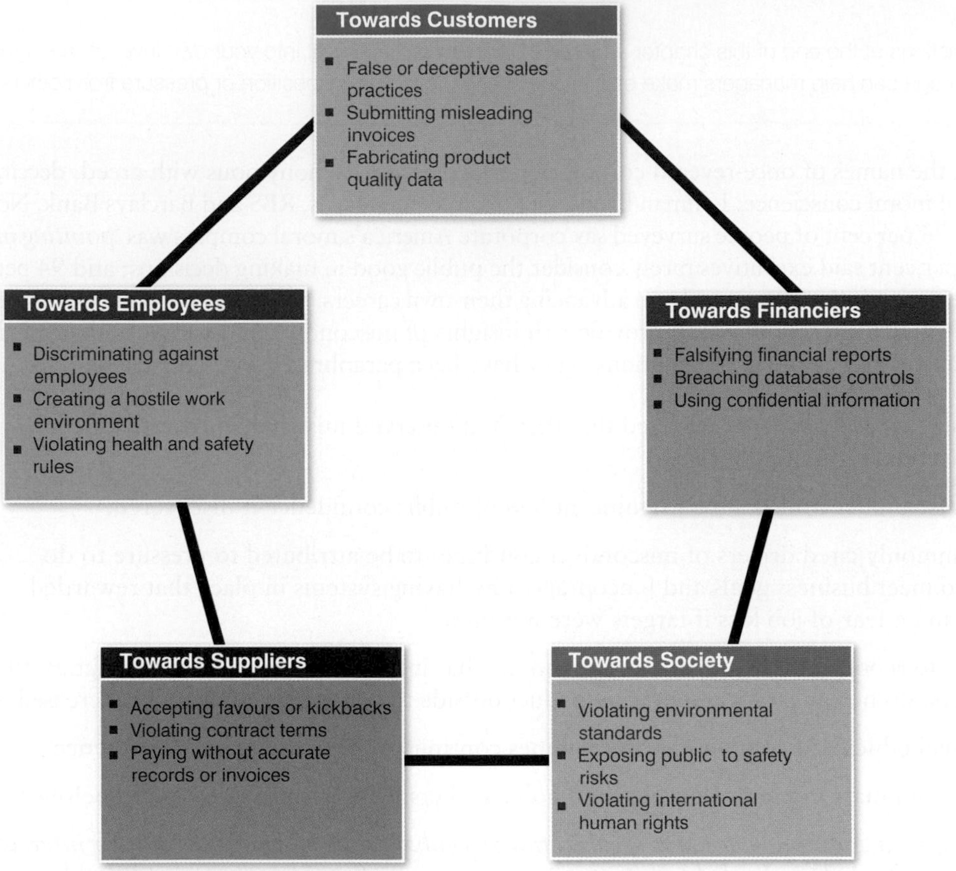

Towards Customers
- False or deceptive sales practices
- Submitting misleading invoices
- Fabricating product quality data

Towards Employees
- Discriminating against employees
- Creating a hostile work environment
- Violating health and safety rules

Towards Financiers
- Falsifying financial reports
- Breaching database controls
- Using confidential information

Towards Suppliers
- Accepting favours or kickbacks
- Violating contract terms
- Paying without accurate records or invoices

Towards Society
- Violating environmental standards
- Exposing public to safety risks
- Violating international human rights

SOURCE: Muel Kaptein, 'Developing a Measure of Unethical Behavior in the Workplace: A Stakeholder Perspective', *Journal of Management* 34, no. 5 (October 2008): 978–1008.

REFLECTION

- Managers are ethically responsible for seeing that organizational resources are used to serve the interests of stakeholders, including shareholders, employees, customers and the broader society.
- Unethical managers seek to serve their own needs and interests at the expense of stakeholders.
- Confidence in business managers and leaders in all walks of life is at an all-time low.
- One hot-button ethical issue concerns excessive executive compensation.

Ethical dilemmas: what would you do?

Being ethical is always about making decisions, and some issues are difficult to resolve. Although most companies have codes of ethics that specify expected behaviour, disagreements and dilemmas about what is appropriate often occur. An ethical dilemma arises in a situation concerning right or wrong when values are in conflict.[18] Right and wrong cannot be clearly identified.

The individual who must make an ethical choice in an organization is the *moral agent*.[19]

Below are some dilemmas that a manager in an organization might face. Determine how you would handle them:

1   Your small company has clear procedures for providing supplies to employees who choose to work from home, as well as a strict code of conduct specifying that any employee caught taking supplies without authorization will be fired. At the end of a long hard day, you notice Sarah, one of your best employees, putting printer paper, highlighters and notepads in her laptop bag. According to company policy you are required to report her immediately to your superior, who is the only one who can authorize employees taking supplies. But your boss has left for the day, and you know Sarah often works from home.[20]

2   As a sales manager for a major pharmaceuticals company, you've been asked to promote a new drug that costs €2500 per dose. You've read the reports saying the drug is only 1 per cent more effective than an alternative drug that costs less than €625 per dose. The vice president of sales wants you to promote the €2500-per-dose drug aggressively. He reminds you that if you don't, lives could be lost that might have been saved with that 1 per cent increase in the drug's effectiveness.

3   You work at a large corporation that requires a terrorist watch list screening for all new customers, which takes approximately 24 hours from the time an order is placed. You can close a lucrative deal with a potential long-term customer if you agree to ship the products overnight, even though that means the required watch list screening will have to be done after the fact.[21]

4   On the train ride from your home in Ipswich to your office in London, your peaceful morning routine is disturbed by neighbouring passengers carrying on a loud mobile business meeting. After trying to quiet them with cold stares, you eventually decide to just listen in. Within minutes, you realize they are discussing a client that your own firm has been courting. Furthermore, you soon have the time, telephone number and passcode for a conference call the consultants are having with the client later that day. It isn't your fault that they gave out that information in a public place, but you wonder what you should do with it.[22]

These kinds of dilemmas and issues fall squarely in the domain of ethics. How would you handle each of the above situations?

Now consider the following hypothetical dilemma which scientists are using to study human morality:[23]

■   A runaway trolley is heading down the tracks towards five unsuspecting people. You're standing near a switch that will divert the trolley onto a siding, but there is a single workman on the siding who cannot be warned in time to escape and almost certainly will be killed. Would you throw the switch?

■   Now, what if the workman is standing on a bridge over the tracks and you have to push him off the bridge to stop the trolley with his body in order to save the five unsuspecting people? (Assume that his body is large enough to stop the trolley, and yours is not.) Would you push the man, even though he almost certainly will be killed?

These dilemmas show how complex questions of ethics and morality can sometimes be. In *Time* magazine's readers' poll, 97 per cent of respondents said they could throw the switch (which would almost certainly lead to the death of the workman), but only 42 per cent said they could actually push the man to his death.[24]

REFLECTION

- Ethics is about making choices.
- Most managers encounter ethical dilemmas that are tough to resolve.

- An **ethical dilemma** is a situation in which all alternative choices or behaviours have potentially negative consequences. Right and wrong cannot be clearly distinguished.

Criteria for ethical decision-making

Most ethical dilemmas involve a conflict between the needs of the part and the whole – the individual versus the organization, or the organization versus society as a whole. For example, should a company scrutinize job candidates' or employees' social media postings, which might benefit the organization as a whole, but reduce the individual privacy and freedom of employees? Or should products that fail to meet Food and Drug Administration (FDA) and EU approval standards be exported to other countries? Where government standards are lower, benefiting the company but potentially harming world citizens? Sometimes ethical decisions entail a conflict of interest between two groups. For example, should the potential for local health problems resulting from a company's effluents take precedence over the jobs it creates as the town's leading employer?

Managers faced with these kinds of tough ethical choices often benefit from a normative strategy – one based on norms and values – to guide their decision-making. Normative ethics uses several approaches to describe values for guiding ethical decision-making. Five approaches that are relevant to managers are the utilitarian approach, individualism approach, moral-rights approach, justice approach and practical approach.[25] Barclays Bank was the subject of a major government review chaired by Salz – access to this report is available via the Internet. Highlights of the report are covered in Chapter 12.

Utilitarian approach

The utilitarian approach, espoused by the nineteenth-century philosophers Jeremy Bentham and John Stuart Mill, holds that moral behaviour produces the greatest good for the greatest number. Under this approach, a decision-maker is expected to consider the effect of each decision alternative on all parties and select the one that optimizes the benefits for the greatest number of people. In the trolley dilemma earlier in this chapter, for instance, the utilitarian approach would hold that it would be moral to push one person to his death in order to save five. The utilitarian ethic is cited as the basis for the recent trend among companies to monitor employee use of the Internet and police personal habits such as alcohol and tobacco consumption, because such behaviour affects the entire workplace.[26]

Individualism approach

The individualism approach contends that acts are moral when they promote the individual's best long-term interests.[27] In theory, with everyone pursuing self-direction, the greater good is arguably ultimately served, because people learn to accommodate each other in their own long-term interest. Individualism is believed to lead to honesty and integrity because that works best in the long run. Lying and cheating for immediate self-interest just causes business associates to lie and cheat in return. Thus, proponents say, individualism ultimately leads to behaviour towards others that fits standards of behaviour that people want towards themselves.[28] However, because individualism is easily misinterpreted to support immediate self-gain, it is not popular in the highly organized and group-oriented society of today.

Moral-rights approach

The moral-rights approach asserts that human beings have fundamental rights and liberties that cannot be taken away by an individual's decision. Thus, an ethically correct decision is one that best maintains the rights of those affected by it. To make ethical decisions, managers need to avoid interfering with the fundamental rights of others, such as the right to privacy, the right of free consent or the right to freedom of speech. Performing experimental treatments on unconscious trauma patients, for example, might be construed to violate the right to free consent. A decision to monitor employees' non-work activities violates the right to privacy. The right of free speech would support whistle-blowers, who call attention to illegal or inappropriate actions within a company. There is now a code for whistle-blowers provided by UK legislation.

Justice approach

The justice approach holds that moral decisions must be based on standards of equity, fairness and impartiality. Three types of justice are of concern to managers. Distributive justice requires that different treatment of people not be based on arbitrary characteristics. For example, men and women should not receive different salaries if they have the same qualifications and are performing the same job. Procedural justice requires that rules be administered fairly. Rules should be clearly stated and consistently and impartially enforced. Compensatory justice argues that individuals should be compensated for the cost of their injuries by the party responsible. The justice approach is closest to the thinking underlying the domain of law in Exhibit 6.1 because it assumes that justice is applied through rules and regulations. Managers are expected to define attributes on which different treatment of employees is acceptable.

Practical approach

The approaches discussed so far presume to determine what is 'right' or good in a moral sense. However, as has been mentioned, ethical issues are frequently not clear-cut and there are disagreements over what is the ethical choice. The practical approach sidesteps debates about what is right, good or just and bases decisions on prevailing standards of the profession and the larger society, taking the interests of all stakeholders into account.[29] The decision of Paula Reid, the manager who set the US Secret Service prostitution scandal in motion by reporting the misconduct of agents in Cartagena, Colombia, was based largely on the practical approach.

With the practical approach, a decision would be considered ethical if it is one that would be considered acceptable by the professional community, one that the manager would not hesitate to publicize on the evening news, and one that a person would typically feel comfortable explaining to family and friends. One Secret Service agency director offered this practical advice to his staff in a recent memo: 'You should

 INNOVATIVE WAY

Paula Reid, US Secret Service

Put aside the issue of whether it is morally wrong to hire a prostitute, particularly in a country where prostitution is legal in certain areas. The bottom line for Paula Reid is that visits to strip clubs, heavy drinking and payments to prostitutes are not acceptable behaviour for Secret Service agents, charged with protecting the president of the USA.

'If every boss was Paula Reid,' said a former agent, 'the Secret Service would never have a problem. It would be a lot more boring, but never a problem.' Reid, the new supervising manager for the Miami office, a prestigious division that oversees the South American region, acted swiftly when she received a report of a disturbance at the hotel where agents preparing for President Barack Obama's visit to Cartagena were staying. Based on information from the hotel manager, Reid swiftly rounded up a dozen agents, ordered them out of the country, and notified her superiors that she had found evidence of 'egregious misconduct.' She acted in spite of a potential internal backlash because she believed the actions of the agents had both hurt the agency's reputation and damaged its ability to fulfil its protective and investigative missions.

The resulting scandal threw the Secret Service into turmoil and put Director Mark Sullivan and other managers in the hot seat. Four of the agents dismissed for engaging in inappropriate conduct have since challenged their dismissals, saying they are being made scapegoats for behaviour that the agency has long tolerated as long as there is no breach of operational security. Yet, for Reid and others, the 'boys will be boys' mentality is not acceptable in today's world. According to former director, Ralph Basham, there are many former and current agents who are 'deeply ashamed of what these people did.'[30]

always assume you are being watched when on an official assignment. Do not put yourself in a situation in your personal or professional life that would cause embarrassment to you, your family or the Secret Service.'[31] Using the practical approach, managers may combine elements of the utilitarian, moral rights and justice approaches in their thinking and decision-making. For example, one expert on business ethics suggests managers can ask themselves the following five questions to help resolve ethical dilemmas.[32] NB: these questions cover a variety of the approaches, as discussed above.

1 What's in it for me?

2 What decision would lead to the greatest good for the greatest number?

3 What rules, policies or social norms apply in the given context?

4 What are my obligations to others?

5 What will be the long term impact for myself and important stakeholders?

REFLECTION

- Most ethical dilemmas involve a conflict between the interests of different groups or between the needs of the individual versus the needs of the organization.
- Managers can use various approaches based on norms and values to help them make ethical decisions.
- The **utilitarian approach** to ethical decision-making says that the ethical choice is the one that produces the greatest good for the greatest number.
- The **individualism approach** suggests that actions are ethical when they promote the individual's best long-term interests, because with everyone pursuing self-interest, the greater good is ultimately served.
- The individualism approach is not considered appropriate today because it is easily misused to support one's personal gain at the expense of others.
- Some managers rely on a **moral-rights approach**, which holds that ethical decisions are those that best maintain the fundamental rights of the people affected by them.
- The **justice approach** says that ethical decisions must be based on standards of equity, fairness and impartiality.
- **Distributive justice** requires that different treatment of individuals are not based on arbitrary characteristics.
- **Procedural justice** holds that rules should be clearly stated and consistently and impartially enforced.
- **Compensatory justice** argues that individuals should be compensated for the cost of their injuries by the party responsible, and individuals should not be held responsible for matters over which they have no control.
- Many managers also use the **practical approach**, which sidesteps debates about what is right, good or just, and bases decisions on prevailing standards of the profession and the larger society, taking the interests of all stakeholders into account.

The individual manager and ethical choices

A number of factors influence a manager's ability to make ethical decisions. Individuals bring specific personality and behavioural traits to the job. Personal needs, family influence and religious background all shape a manager's value system. In addition, the corporate culture and pressures from superiors and colleagues can also influence an individual's ethical choices. A recent study found that organizational pressures can indeed induce employees to behave unethically. Moreover, when people experience organizational pressure to go against their sense of what is right, they typically become frustrated and emotionally exhausted.[33] Clearly, unethical behaviour inhibits a person's ability to do his or her best for the company, as well as hindering the individual's personal and professional well-being. Specific personality characteristics, such as ego strength, self confidence and a strong sense of independence, may enable managers to make more ethical choices despite outside pressures and personal risks.

One important personal trait is the stage of moral development.[34] A simplified version of one model of personal moral development is shown in Exhibit 6.3.

EXHIBIT 6.3 Three levels of personal moral development

Level 1 Pre-conventional	Level 2 Conventional	Level 3 Post-conventional
Follows rules to avoid punishment. Acts in own interest. Obedience for its own sake.	Lives up to expectations of others. Fulfills duties and obligations of social system. Upholds laws.	Follows self-chosen principles of justice and right. Aware that people hold different values and seeks creative solutions to ethical dilemmas. Balances concern for individual with concern for common good.

← Self-Interest — Societal Expectations — Internal Values →

Leader Style:	Autocratic/coercive	Guiding/encouraging, team oriented	Transforming, or servant leadership
Employee Behaviour:	Task accomplishment	Work-group collaboration	Empowered employees, full participation

SOURCE: L. Kohlberg, 'Moral Stages and Moralization: The Cognitive-Developmental Approach', in *Moral Development and Behavior: Theory, Research, and Social Issues,* ed. T. Lickona (New York: Holt, Rinehart and Winston, 1976), pp. 31–53; and Jill W. Graham, 'Leadership, Moral Development and Citizenship Behavior', *Business Ethics Quarterly* 5, no. 1 (January 1995): 43–54.

🔗 CONCEPT CONNECTION

In many cases, the people of Africa have relatively few natural resources to use in creating goods to sell. Fortunately, some business leaders, functioning at the **post-conventional level of moral development**, have been inspired to help African entrepreneurs create opportunities for themselves, either through microfinancing or through non-profit organizations. The Africa InKNITiative is just one example. The organization provides Ugandan widows and refugees with raw materials for knitting scarves out of old T-shirts. The scarves are then shipped to the USA, where they're sold, and the proceeds go back to the women in Uganda.

At the *pre-conventional level*, individuals are concerned with external rewards and punishments and obey authority to avoid detrimental personal consequences. In an organizational context, this level may be associated with managers who use an autocratic or coercive leadership style, with employees oriented towards dependable accomplishment of specific tasks.

At level two, called the *conventional level*, people learn to conform to the expectations of good behaviour as defined by colleagues, family, friends and society. Meeting social and interpersonal obligations is important. Work-group collaboration is the preferred manner of accomplishing organizational goals, and managers use a leadership style that encourages interpersonal relationships and cooperation.

At the *post-conventional*, or *principled* level, individuals are guided by an internal set of values based on universal principles of justice and right and will even disobey rules or laws that violate these principles. Internal values become more important than the expectations of significant others. One recent example of the post-conventional or principled approach was the lifeguard in Hallandale Beach, Florida, who was fired for leaving his assigned zone to help a drowning man. Tomas Lopez rushed to offer assistance when he saw a man struggling, even though his supervisor ordered him not to leave his zone and to call 911 instead. 'What he did was his own decision,' said manager Susan Ellis. 'He knew the rules.' The company cited liability issues as the reason for the rules, and later offered Lopez his job back (he refused).[35] When managers operate from this highest level of development, they use transformative or servant leadership, focusing on the needs of followers and encouraging others to think for themselves and to engage in higher levels of moral reasoning. Employees are empowered and given opportunities for constructive participation in governance of the organization.

TAKE A MOMENT

Complete the New Manager Self-Test below to assess your capacity for servant leadership, which is related to a high level of moral development.

 NEW MANAGER SELF-TEST

Servant Leadership

Managers differ in how they view other people and the tactics they use to get things done. Respond to the items below based on how you view yourself and others. Please answer whether each item is 'Mostly true' or 'Mostly false' for you.

		Mostly true	Mostly false
1	My actions meet the needs of others before my own needs.	☐	☐
2	I am always offering a helping hand to those around me.	☐	☐
3	I give away credit and recognition to others.	☐	☐
4	I tend to feel competitive with my coworkers.	☐	☐
5	I often interrupt someone to make my point.	☐	☐
6	I encourage the growth of others, expecting nothing in return.	☐	☐
7	I like to be of service to others.	☐	☐
8	Giving makes me happier than receiving.	☐	☐
9	I reach out to orient new people even though it is not required.	☐	☐

SCORING & INTERPRETATION Sum questions 1–3 and 6–9 with one point for each 'Mostly true', and sum questions 4–5 with one point for each 'Mostly false'. Your score pertains to a concept that was introduced by Robert Greenleaf in his book, *Servant Leadership*. Servant leadership means that managers try to place service to others before self-interest, listen as a way to care about others, and nourish others to help them become whole. This approach to management was based on Greenleaf's Quaker beliefs. A score of 7–9 would be considered high on servant leadership, and 0–3 low, with a score of 4–6 in the middle range. How do you feel about your score? Are you attracted to the qualities of servant leadership, or would you prefer a different approach to managing others?

SOURCE: Robert Greenleaf, *Servant Leadership: A Journey into the Nature of Legitimate Power and Greatness*, 25th anniversary ed. (New York: Paulist Press, 2002).

The great majority of managers operate at level two, meaning their ethical thought and behaviour is greatly influenced by their superiors, colleagues and other significant people in the organization or industry. A few have not advanced beyond level one. Only about 20 per cent of American adults reach the level three post-conventional stage of moral development. People at level three are able to act in an independent, ethical manner regardless of expectations from others inside or outside the organization. Managers at level three of moral development will make ethical decisions whatever the organizational consequences are for them.

REFLECTION

- Organizational pressures can influence people to go against their own sense of right or wrong, and the resulting stress can lead to mental exhaustion and burnout.
- Personality characteristics, family influence, religious background and other factors influence a manager's ability to make ethical choices.
- One important factor is whether a manager is at a pre-conventional, conventional or post-conventional level of moral development.

- Most managers operate at a *conventional level*, conforming to standards of behaviour expected by society.
- Only about 20 per cent of adults reach the *post-conventional level* and are able to act in an independent, ethical manner regardless of the expectations of others.

What is corporate social responsibility?

Now let's turn to the issue of corporate social responsibility. In one sense, the concept of social responsibility, like ethics, is easy to understand: It means distinguishing right from wrong and doing right. It means being a good corporate citizen. The formal definition of corporate social responsibility (CSR) is management's obligation to make choices and take actions that will contribute to the welfare and interests of society, not just the organization.[36]

As straightforward as this definition seems, CSR can be a difficult concept to grasp because different people have different beliefs as to which actions improve society's welfare.[37] To make matters worse, social responsibility covers a range of issues, many of which are ambiguous with respect to right or wrong. If a bank deposits the money from a trust fund into a low-interest account for 90 days, from which it makes a substantial profit, is it being a responsible corporate citizen? How about two companies engaging in intense competition? Is it socially responsible for the stronger corporation to drive the weaker one out of business or into a forced merger? Or consider General Motors (GM), Kmart, Lehman Brothers and the numerous other companies that have declared bankruptcy in recent years – which is perfectly legal – and thus avoided having to meet their full financial obligations to suppliers, labour unions or competitors. These examples contain moral, legal and economic complexities that make socially responsible behaviour hard to define.

Organizational stakeholders

One reason for the difficulty of understanding and applying CSR is that managers must confront the question, 'Responsibility to whom?' Recall from Chapter 3 that the organization's environment consists of several sectors, in both the task and the general environment. From a social responsibility perspective, enlightened organizations view the internal and external environment as a variety of stakeholders.

A stakeholder is any group or person within or outside the organization that has some type of investment or interest in the organization's performance and is affected by the organization's actions (employees, customers, shareholders and so forth). Each stakeholder has a different criterion of responsiveness because it has a different interest in the organization.[38] There is growing interest in a technique called stakeholder mapping, which basically provides a systematic way to identify the expectations, needs, importance and relative power of various stakeholders, which may change over time.[39] Stakeholder mapping helps managers

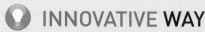

INNOVATIVE WAY

Gap Inc.

When reports surfaced in 2009 that a contractor in Lesotho, Africa, making clothing for Gap Inc. and other US companies was dumping toxic materials into local landfills and discharging chemicals into the Caledon River, Gap managers swung into action. A similar crisis related to child labour and unsafe conditions 10 years earlier had resulted in global protests that raged for months and tarnished Gap's reputation, damaged employee morale and devastated the firm's performance. In contrast, the 2009 Lesotho story died down quickly and Gap came out stronger on the other side.

What happened in those 10 years to make a difference? It's certainly not that the public was less outraged by the stories of poor children being harmed by dangerous chemicals while playing near the river or scavenging through refuse. The result was different this time because Gap managers had carefully cultivated open relationships with labour groups, human rights organizations, trade unions, non-governmental organizations and other stakeholders that enabled them to swing into action immediately and take specific steps to solve the problem. In the past, managers' approach would have been to deny responsibility and blame the subcontractor. With the Lesotho incident, though, Gap's top leaders immediately stepped forward to declare the company's commitment to fair and safe conditions and outline the steps it would take. The company later joined Levi Strauss, which also had clothing made by this contractor, to issue a statement detailing actions that had been taken or were in progress. Because of the relationships Gap had developed with numerous stakeholder groups, the company had the support of labour and human rights organizations, which praised managers' commitment and actions.

Gap embarked on the process of engaging with key stakeholders because even though the company had made a strong commitment to social and environmental responsibility since 1992, the previous approach wasn't working. Multimillion-dollar efforts at solving ethical problems in the supply chain had failed. So managers drew up a stakeholder map that listed as many stakeholders as possible, then ranked them by their importance. Starting with mapping gave managers a way to focus their efforts and join with the most influential stakeholders to improve labour practices. It was a long and difficult journey, but the results have been well worth it. The company has received awards and public recognition as a leader in ethics and social responsibility.[40]

identify or prioritize the key stakeholders related to a specific issue or project. For instance, Gap Inc., struggling to cope with the turmoil that erupted after the company was targeted by protesters for using contractors that polluted the environment and engaged in child labour practices, decided to use mapping to identify key stakeholders with which the firm could develop deeper, and more transparent relationships. Royal Mail Group did a similar exercise several years before its privatization in 2014.

The global supply chain is a source of ongoing challenges for managers today. As Dan Rees, former director of the Ethical Trading Initiative (ETI) said, '*It is not a crime to find child labour in your supply chain. What is important is what you do about it when you find out.*' By using stakeholder mapping and cultivating open, trust-based relationships with key stakeholders, Gap has ensured that managers are able to do the right thing swiftly, sometimes even turning crises into opportunities.[41]

Exhibit 6.4 illustrates important stakeholders for a large organization such as Gap. Most organizations are influenced by a similar variety of stakeholder groups. Investors and shareholders, employees, customers and suppliers are considered primary stakeholders, without whom the organization cannot survive. Investors, shareholders and suppliers' interests are served by managerial efficiency – that is, use of resources to achieve profits. Employees expect work satisfaction, pay and good supervision. Customers are concerned with decisions about the quality, safety and availability of goods and services. When any primary stakeholder group becomes seriously dissatisfied, the organization's viability is threatened.[42]

Other important stakeholders are the government and the community, which have become increasingly important in recent years. Most corporations exist only under the proper charter and licences and operate within the limits of safety laws, environmental protection requirements, antitrust regulations, anti-bribery legislation, and other laws and regulations in the government sector. Government regulations affecting

EXHIBIT 6.4 Major stakeholders relevant to Gap Inc.

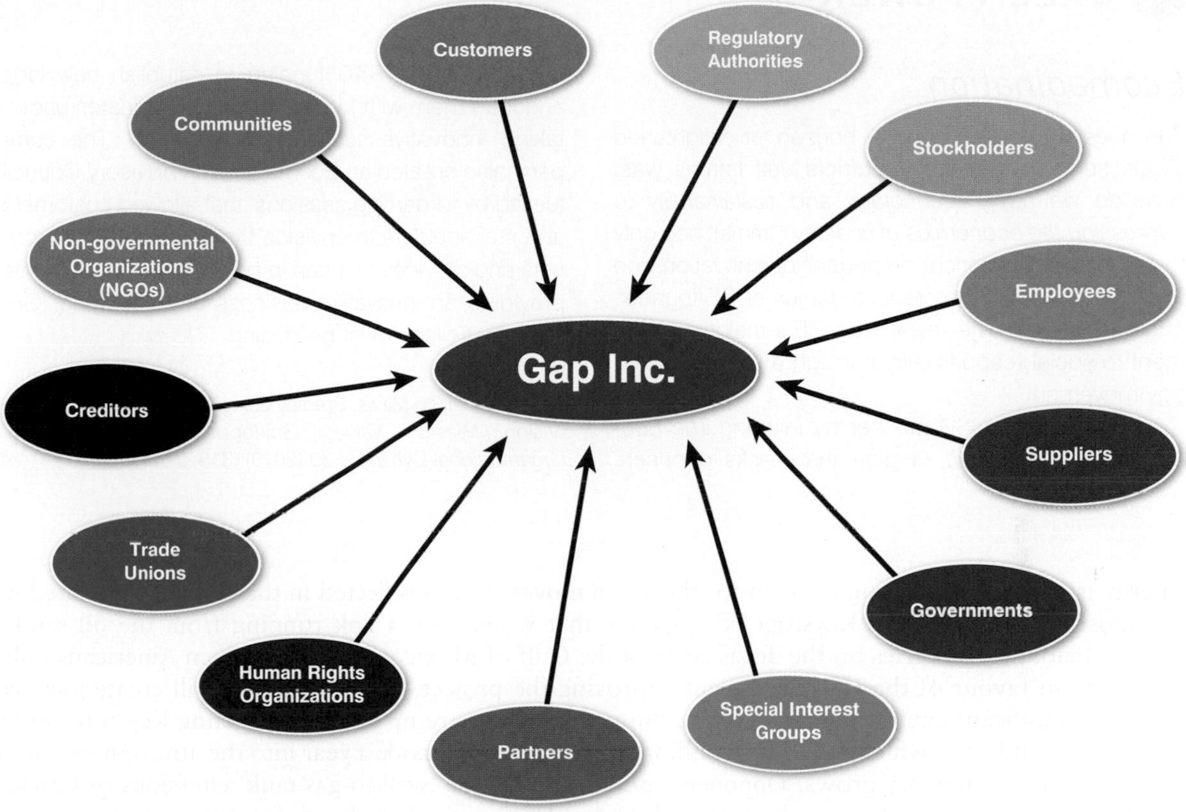

SOURCE: D. Wheeler, B. Colbert and R. E. Freeman, 'Focusing on Value: Reconciling Corporate Social Responsibility, Sustainability and a Stakeholder Approach in a Networked World', *Journal of General Management* 28, no. 3 (Spring 2003): 1–28; J. E. Post, L. E. Preston and S. Sachs, 'Managing the Extended Enterprise: The New Stakeholder View', *California Management Review* 45, no. 1 (Fall 2002): 6–28; and N. Craig Smith, Sean Ansett and Lior Erex, 'How Gap Inc. Engaged with Its Stakeholders', *MIT Sloan Management Review* 52, no. 4 (Summer 2011): 69–76.

business are increasing because of recent events. The community includes local governments, the natural environment and the quality of life provided for residents. For many companies such as Gap, trade unions and human rights organizations are highly important stakeholders. Special interest groups may include trade associations, political action committees, professional associations and consumerists. One special interest group of particular importance today is the green movement.

The green movement

The year was 2004, and Jeffrey Immelt, CEO of General Electric (GE), had just presented a plan for a 'green' business initiative to 35 top GE executives. They voted it down. But Immelt, in a rare move, overruled them, and Ecomagination was born. Today, GE's Ecomagination is one of the world's most widely recognized corporate green programmes. It has not only cut GE's greenhouse gas emissions by 30 per cent but also added innovative products that are generating billions in annual revenue.[43]

Going green has become a new business imperative, driven by shifting social attitudes, new governmental policies, climate changes and information technology (IT) that quickly spreads any news of a corporation's negative impact on the environment. A recent survey found that 90 per cent of Americans agree that there are important 'green' issues and problems, and 82 per cent think that businesses should implement environmentally friendly practices.[44] Each chapter of this text contains a Green Power example that highlights what companies are doing to improve their environmental performance.

🌱 GREEN POWER

Ecomagination

The question hovering on the horizon for enlightened CEOs such as **General Electric's** Jeff Immelt was: *How do we apply technology and sustainability to addressing the economics of scarcity?* Immelt had only to tap into the historical precedent of innovation and imagination set by the creative genius of GE founder, Thomas Edison. The result was GE's major commitment to social responsibility through a green technology movement.

GE became a CSR pioneer by initiating *The Ecomagination Campaign,* a plan that packs a punch.

Immelt doubled R&D funding to establish new labs and load them with highly educated graduates undertaking innovative sustainability research. The company also created an Ecomagination Advisory Council fuelled by 'dreaming sessions' that allowed customers and stakeholders to envision the future and the products and services that can improve those futures while providing an innovative business opportunity for GE. Founder Edison must be smiling.

SOURCE: Philip Mirvis, Bradley Googins and Sylvia Kinnicutt, 'Vision, Mission, Values: Guideposts to Sustainability', *Organizational Dynamics* 39 (2010): 316–324.

Energy is an area of ongoing concern for the green movement, as reflected in the conflict associated with the proposed building of the Keystone XL pipeline that would add a link running from the oil sands of Alberta, Canada, to refineries on the Texas coast of the Gulf of Mexico. Nearly six in ten Americans polled, in 2014, are in favour of the US government approving the project, believing that it will create jobs without causing significant environmental damage. But green groups are up in arms, targeting Keystone and the entire oil sands industry, which releases 30 million tons of carbon dioxide a year into the atmosphere and will release more as the industry grows. Opponents point out that the 'well-to-gas tank' emissions of Canadian oil sands are about twice as high as the average barrel of US imported crude oil. Supporters insist it is better to tap the oil sands of Canada than to continue helping oil-rich countries that may abuse both people and the environment.[45]

Sustainability and the triple bottom line

Some corporations are embracing an idea called *sustainability* or *sustainable development.* Sustainability refers to economic development that generates wealth and meets the needs of the current generation while preserving the environment and society so future generations can meet their needs as well.[46] With a philosophy of sustainability, managers weave environmental and social concerns into every strategic decision, so that financial goals are achieved in a way that is socially and environmentally responsible. Managers in organizations that embrace sustainability measure their success in terms of a triple bottom line. The term triple bottom line refers to Elkington's work on measuring an organization's social performance, its environmental performance and its financial performance. This is sometimes called the three Ps: People, Planet and Profit.[47]

The People part of the triple bottom line looks at how socially responsible the organization is in terms of fair labour practices, diversity, supplier relationships, treatment of employees, contributions to the community and so forth. The Planet aspect measures the organization's commitment to environmental sustainability. The third P, of course, looks at the organization's profit, the financial bottom line. Based on the principle that what you measure is what you strive for and achieve, using a triple bottom line approach to measuring performance ensures that managers take social and environmental factors into account, rather than blindly pursuing profit no matter the cost to society and the natural environment.

Evaluating corporate social responsibility

A model for evaluating corporate social performance is presented in Exhibit 6.5. The model indicates that total corporate social responsibility can be divided into four primary criteria: economic, legal, ethical and

REFLECTION

- **Corporate social responsibility** refers to the obligation of organizational managers to make choices and take actions that will enhance the welfare and interests of society, as well as the organization.
- Different stakeholders have different interests in the organization and thus different criteria for social responsiveness.
- The term **stakeholder** refers to any group or person within or outside the organization that has some type of investment or interest in the organization's performance.
- Shareholders, employees, customers and suppliers are considered primary stakeholders, without whom the organization could not survive.
- Government, the community and special interest groups are also important stakeholders.
- **Stakeholder mapping** provides a systematic way to identify the expectations, needs, importance and relative power of various stakeholders.

- The *green movement* is a special interest group of particular importance today.
- **Sustainability** refers to economic development that generates wealth and meets the needs of the current population while preserving society and the environment for the needs of future generations.
- Companies that embrace sustainability measure performance in terms of financial performance, social performance and environmental performance, referred to as the **triple bottom line**.
- A recent survey found that 90 per cent of Americans agree that there are important 'green' issues and problems, and 82 per cent think that businesses should implement environmentally friendly practices.

---

discretionary responsibilities.[48] These four criteria fit together to form the whole of a company's social responsiveness.

'For a long time, people believed that the only purpose of industry was to make a profit. They are wrong. Its purpose is to serve the general welfare.'

— HENRY FORD, SR (1863–1947), AMERICAN INDUSTRIALIST

The first criterion of social responsibility is *economic responsibility*. The business institution is, above all, the basic economic unit of society. Its responsibility is to produce the goods and services that society wants and to

EXHIBIT 6.5 Criteria of corporate social performance

SOURCE: Archie B. Carroll, 'A Three-Dimensional Conceptual Model of Corporate Performance', *Academy of Management Review* 4 (1979): 499; A. B. Carroll, 'The Pyramid of Corporate Social Responsibility: Toward the Moral Management of Corporate Stakeholders', *Business Horizons* 34 (July–August 1991): 42; and Mark S. Schwartz and Archie B. Carroll, 'Corporate Social Responsibility: A Three-Domain Approach', *Business Ethics Quarterly* 13, no. 4 (2003): 503–530.

⊶ CONCEPT CONNECTION

In the European Union, employers have a **legal responsibility** to comply with laws designed to protect workers, such as the health and safety laws recommended by the European Agency for Safety and Health at Work. For example, companies that run manufacturing plants like this one are required to provide employees with safety goggles, earplugs, hard hats and other protective gear as needed for various jobs.

maximize profits for its owners and shareholders. Economic responsibility, carried to the extreme, is called the *profit-maximizing view*, advocated by Nobel economist Milton Friedman. This view argues that the corporation should be operated on a profit-oriented basis, with its sole mission to increase its profits as long as it stays within the rules of the game.[49] The purely profit-maximizing view is no longer considered an adequate criterion of social performance in Canada, the USA and Europe. This approach means that economic gain is the only responsibility and can lead companies into trouble, as recent events in the mortgage and finance industries have clearly shown.

Legal responsibility defines what society deems as important with respect to appropriate corporate behaviour.[50] That is, businesses are expected to fulfil their economic goals within the framework of legal requirements imposed by local town councils, state legislators and federal regulatory agencies. Examples of illegal acts by corporations include corporate fraud, intentionally selling defective goods, performing unnecessary repairs or procedures, deliberately misleading consumers and billing clients for work not done. Organizations that knowingly break the law are poor performers in this category. Walmart, for example, is currently embroiled in a bribery scandal amid allegations that the company's largest foreign subsidiary, Walmart de Mexico, paid bribes to local officials and covered up the wrongdoing to corner every edge of the market in that country. Investigators found 'reasonable suspicion' that Walmart managers had violated US and Mexican laws and called for a broader inquiry into the allegations.[51]

Ethical responsibility includes behaviours that are not necessarily codified into law and may not serve the corporation's direct economic interests. As described earlier in this chapter, to be *ethical*, organization decision-makers should act with equity, fairness and impartiality, respect the rights of individuals, and provide different treatment of individuals only when relevant to the organization's goals and tasks.[52] *Unethical* behaviour occurs when decisions enable an individual or company to gain at the expense of other people or society as a whole. Managers at Merck & Company, for example, seriously damaged the company's reputation by continuing to market the arthritis medication *Vioxx* aggressively, even after they had information suggesting that there were heart attack and stroke risks associated with the drug. Merck was facing stiff competition from Pfizer's *Celebrex* and chose to pursue profits, even at the risk of harming patients.

Discretionary responsibility is purely voluntary and is guided by a company's desire to make social contributions not mandated by economics, law or ethics. Discretionary activities include generous philanthropic contributions that offer no payback to the company and are not expected. For example, Royal DSM, a Netherlands-based company that produces nutritional supplements, pharmaceutical ingredients and energy-efficient building products, partners with the World Food Programme to give vitamins, supplements and fortified food products to malnourished people in Nepal, Kenya, Bangladesh and Afghanistan. DSM also offers free medical services to poor villagers in India, and has donated building supplies to construct schools in poor countries. 'We don't really put a value on it. . . . ,' said Fokko Wientjes, DSM's director of sustainability. 'But shareholders haven't ever called me up and said, 'Please stop.''[53] Gap Inc., described earlier, donates 50 per cent of profits on a particular line of 'Red'-branded Gap products to lead U2 singer Bono's Red campaign against HIV/AIDS.[54] As another example, a week after a massive earthquake and tsunami devastated Japan, corporations had pledged about $151 million in cash and in-kind donations for disaster relief.[55] Discretionary responsibility is the highest criterion of social responsibility because it goes beyond societal expectations to contribute to the community's welfare.

TAKE A MOMENT

Read the Ethical Dilemma at the end of this chapter that pertains to legal and ethical responsibilities.

REFLECTION

- The model for evaluating a company's social performance uses four criteria: economic, legal, ethical and discretionary.
- Companies may get into trouble when they use economic criteria as their only measure of responsibility, sometimes called the *profit-maximizing* view.

- **Discretionary responsibility** is purely voluntary and is guided by the organization's desire to make social contributions not mandated by economics, laws or ethics.
- Corporations that sent generous donations to Japan following the devastating earthquake and tsunami were practising discretionary responsibility.

Managing company ethics and social responsibility

An expert on the topic of ethics said, 'Management is responsible for creating and sustaining conditions in which people are likely to behave themselves.'[56] Exhibit 6.6 illustrates ways in which managers create and support an ethical organization. One of the most important steps managers can take is to practise ethical leadership. *Ethical leadership* means that managers are honest and trustworthy, fair in their dealings with employees and customers, and behave ethically in both their personal and professional lives. In response to recent ethical violations and critics of management education saying MBA stands for 'Me Before Anyone',[57] some business schools and students are taking a fresh look at how future managers are trained.

Changing how future managers are trained could be one key to solving the ethics deficit pervading organizations. Managers and first-line supervisors are important role models for ethical behaviour, and they strongly influence the ethical climate in the organization by adhering to high ethical standards in their own

EXHIBIT 6.6 Building an ethical organization

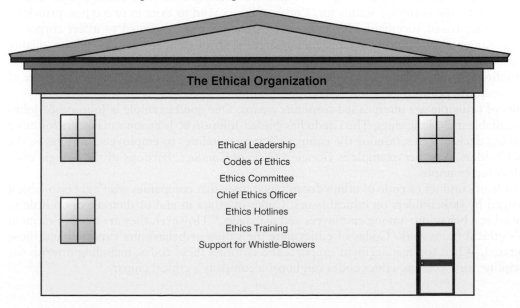

The Ethical Organization

Ethical Leadership
Codes of Ethics
Ethics Committee
Chief Ethics Officer
Ethics Hotlines
Ethics Training
Support for Whistle-Blowers

SOURCE: Linda Klebe Treviño, Laura Pincus Hartman and Michael Brown, 'Moral Person and Moral Manager', *California Management Review* 42, no. 4 (Summer 2000): 128–142.

💡 INNOVATIVE WAY

Harvard Business School, Columbia Business School, Yale School of Management

Some members of a recent graduating class of Harvard Business School did something unusual. They signed a voluntary student-led pledge saying that the goal of a business manager is to 'serve the greater good' and promising that they will act responsibly and ethically and refrain from advancing their 'own narrow ambitions' at the expense of others.

At Harvard and other business schools, there has been an explosion of interest in ethics classes and activities that focus on personal and corporate responsibility. Many students, as well as educators, are recognizing a need to give future managers a deeper understanding of how to practise ethical leadership rather than just how to make money. At Columbia Business School, which requires an ethics course, students formed a popular Leadership and Ethics Board that sponsors lectures and other activities. Yale School of Management developed sessions in its core curriculum related to the recent ethical crisis in the mortgage and finance industries and worked with the Aspen Institute to create a curriculum aimed at teaching business students how to act on their values at work. About 55 business schools are using all or part of the curriculum in pilot programmes. 'There is a feeling that we want our lives to mean something more and to run organizations for the greater good,' said Max Anderson, one of the organizers of Harvard's pledge. 'No one wants to have their future criticized as a place filled with unethical behaviours.'[58]

behaviour and decisions. Moreover, managers are proactive in influencing employees to embody and reflect ethical values.[59] This chapter's Shoptalk describes an approach that some leading companies are taking to strengthen managers' ethical and socially responsible underpinning.

Managers can also implement organizational mechanisms to help employees and the company stay on an ethical footing. Some of the primary ones are codes of ethics, ethical structures and measures to protect whistle-blowers.

Code of ethics

A code of ethics is a formal statement of the company's values concerning ethics and social issues; it communicates to employees what the company stands for. Codes of ethics tend to exist in two types: principle-based statements and policy-based statements. *Principle-based statements* are designed to affect corporate culture; they define fundamental values and contain general language about company responsibilities, quality of products and treatment of employees. *Policy-based statements* generally outline the procedures to be used in specific ethical situations. These situations include marketing practices, conflicts of interest, observance of laws, proprietary information, political gifts and equal opportunities.

General statements of principle are often called *corporate credos*. One good example is Johnson & Johnson's 'The Credo'. Available in 36 languages, The Credo has guided Johnson & Johnson's managers for more than 60 years in making decisions that honour the company's responsibilities to employees, customers, the community and stockholders. Another example is Google's *Code of Conduct*. Portions of the Google code are shown in the following example.

Having a strong code of conduct or code of ethics doesn't guarantee that companies won't get into ethical trouble or be challenged by stakeholders on ethical issues. Codes of ethics in and of themselves do little to influence and ensure ethical behaviour among employees and managers.[60] However, they are one key element of the organization's ethical framework. Codes of ethics state the values or behaviours expected and those that will not be tolerated. When top management supports and enforces these codes, including rewards for compliance and discipline for violation, ethics codes can boost a company's ethical climate.[61]

⊕ MANAGER'S SHOPTALK

Cultivating a service mindset

Some of today's best companies are taking a new approach to developing managers – global service programmes that place employees with not-for-profit organizations or small businesses, often in developing countries, to provide free or low-cost technical and managerial assistance. In line with the growing emphasis on sustainability and the triple bottom line, organizations want managers who have a service and sustainability mindset rather than an attitude of getting all they can for themselves. In one survey, 88 per cent of top executives said it was important that future managers have the mindset and skills to address sustainability issues.

1   **Global service programmes benefit everyone.** Global service programmes have been described as a 'win–win–win'. It might seem obvious that the non-profit organizations served by these programmes benefit, but the companies investing in them and the employees participating in them gain just as much. IBM credits its programme with generating about $5 billion in new business. Companies gain greater knowledge of emerging markets, develop social capital and goodwill, and get more well-rounded managers with the service and sustainability mindset needed in today's world. Participants benefit in numerous ways, including increased self-awareness, new skill and greater cross-cultural understanding.

2   **Many managers view these opportunities as plum assignments.** Laura Benetti of Dow Corning spent 4 weeks working 9 hour days with women in rural India, helping them learn how to price and market the garments they made. She and nine colleagues slept in a lodge with limited access to hot water and electricity. 'It gives more meaning to your career,' said Benetti. Participants in global service also appreciate the opportunity to expand their understanding of global issues. 'We all *know* about things like poverty in Africa and corruption and bribery . . .,' said one IBM participant who spent time in Nigeria. 'This kind of experience really brings . . . things to life, you really feel it.'

3   **How widespread is the trend?** In early 2012, at least 27 *Fortune* 500 companies, including PepsiCo, IBM, FedEx, Dow Corning and Pfizer, had some type of global service programme, up from only six in 2006. Since 2008, IBM has sent more than 1400 employees to work with projects such as reforming Kenya's postal system or developing ecotourism in Tanzania. Pfizer's programme lends employees to non-governmental organizations (NGOs) to address health care needs in Asia and Africa. The Accenture Development Partnership has been involved in more than 200 projects in 55 countries, where Accenture's professionals work at 50 per cent pay for up to 6 months with organizations such as UNICEF and Freedom from Hunger.

SOURCES: Philip Mirvis, Kevin Thompson and John Gohring, 'Toward Next-Generation Leadership: Global Service', *Leader to Leader* (Spring 2012): 20–26; Matthew Gitsham, 'Experiential Learning for Leadership and Sustainability at IBM and HSBC', *Journal of Management Development* 31, no, 3 (2012): 298–307; and Anne Tergesen, 'Doing Good to Do Well', *The Wall Street Journal*, 9 January 2012, B7.

Ethical structures

Ethical structures represent the various systems, positions and programmes that a company can undertake to encourage and support ethical behaviour.[63] An ethics committee is a group of executives (and sometimes lower-level employees as well) appointed to oversee company ethics. The committee provides rulings on questionable ethical issues and assumes responsibility for disciplining wrongdoers. Motorola's Ethics Compliance Committee, for instance, was charged with interpreting, clarifying and communicating the company's code of ethics and with adjudicating suspected code violations. Universities also have codes of practices covering cheating and plagiarism by students, as well as ethical practices concerning research activities.

Many companies set up ethics offices with full-time staff to ensure that ethical standards are an integral part of company operations. These offices are headed by a chief ethics officer, sometimes called a *chief ethics*

INNOVATIVE WAY

Google

Google is one of the best-known companies in the world, and managers take seriously its reputation for both technological superiority and a commitment to ethics and social responsibility. Google's code of conduct starts with these words: "Don't be evil". Googlers generally apply those words to how we serve our users. But "Don't be evil" is much more than that.'

Google uses a well-designed code of conduct to put the motto 'Don't be evil' into practice. The code is divided into seven sections, each further subdivided into sections that describe specific values, policies and expectations. The code also clearly states that employees will be protected if they call attention to ethical violations or misconduct. Here are some excerpts from Google's code:

Serve our users

Our users value Google not only because we deliver great products and services, but because we hold ourselves to a higher standard in how we treat users and operate more generally.

Respect each other

We are committed to a supportive work environment, where employees have the opportunity to reach their fullest potential. Each Googler is expected to do his or her utmost to create a respectful workplace culture that is free of harassment, intimidation, bias and unlawful discrimination of any kind.

Preserve confidentiality

We get a lot of press attention around our innovations and our culture, and that's usually fine. However, company information that leaks prematurely into the press or to competitors can hurt our product launches, eliminate our competitive advantage and prove costly in other ways.

Ensure financial integrity and responsibility

Financial integrity and fiscal responsibility are core aspects of corporate professionalism. . . . The money we spend on behalf of Google is not ours; it's the company's and, ultimately, our shareholders.

Obey the law

Google takes its responsibilities to comply with laws and regulations very seriously and each of us is expected to comply with applicable legal requirements and prohibitions.

Conclusion

Google aspires to be a different kind of company. It's impossible to spell out every possible ethical scenario we might face. Instead, we rely on one another's good judgement to uphold a high standard of integrity for ourselves and our company.

And remember . . . don't be evil, and if you see something that you think isn't right – speak up![62] Google, of late, has responded to requests from individuals who have asked for reports on them to be eliminated from Google's search engines. The right of privacy of individuals to have past data removed has been observed.

and compliance officer, a company executive who oversees all aspects of ethics and legal compliance, including establishing and broadly communicating standards, ethics training, dealing with exceptions or problems, and advising senior managers in the ethical and compliance aspects of decisions.[64] The title *chief ethics officer* was almost unheard of a decade ago, but highly publicized ethical and legal problems in recent years have sparked a growing demand for these ethics specialists. The Ethics and Compliance Officer Association, a trade group, reports that membership soared 70 per cent, to more than 1260 companies, in the 5 years following the collapse of Enron due to financial wrongdoing.[65] Most ethics offices also work as counselling

TAKE A MOMENT

Complete the Experiential Exercise online that pertains to ethical work environments.

centres to help employees resolve difficult ethical issues. A toll-free confidential *ethics hotline* allows employees to report questionable behaviour, as well as seek guidance concerning ethical dilemmas.

Whistle-blowing

Employee disclosure of illegal, unethical or illegitimate practices on the employer's part is called whistle-blowing.[66] No organization can rely exclusively on codes of conduct and ethical structures to prevent all unethical behaviour. Holding organizations accountable depends to some degree on individuals who are willing to speak up if they detect illegal, dangerous or unethical activities. Whistle-blowers often report wrongdoing to outsiders, such as regulatory agencies, senators or newspaper reporters. Some firms have instituted innovative programmes and confidential hotlines to encourage and support internal whistle-blowing. For this practice to be an effective ethical safeguard, however, companies must view whistle-blowing as a benefit to the company and make dedicated efforts to encourage and protect whistle-blowers.[67]

The US Office of Special Counsel recently found three Air Force officials guilty of retaliating against civilian employees who reported the mishandling of the remains of deceased soldiers at Dover Air Force Base, for example. A former executive at Countrywide Financial Corporation says he was bullied and eventually fired after he questioned the company's use of so-called 'Ninja loans' (no income, no job, no assets) at the height of the subprime mortgage craze. And Matthew Lee, a former senior vice president in Lehman Brothers' accounting division, lost his job just weeks after he raised concerns about how the firm was masking risks by temporarily 'parking' $50 billion in risky loan assets off its balance sheet.[68]

Unfortunately, many managers still look on whistle-blowers as disgruntled employees who aren't good team players. Yet to maintain high ethical standards, organizations need people who are willing to point out wrongdoing. Managers can be trained to view whistle-blowing as a benefit rather than a threat, and systems can be set up to protect employees who report illegal or unethical activities.

 CONCEPT CONNECTION

'GenYers' throughout the world expect a serious **commitment to sustainability** from their employers. In fact, one study found that more than 95 per cent of Gen-Y respondents wanted to work for an organization that goes beyond merely complying with existing environmental legislation. That's why Cleveland-based Eaton Corporation, a diversified power management company, prominently features its commitment to sustainability on its career web page and at career fairs. 'It's actually helped us in acquiring top talent at a lot of top universities,' says Joel Wolfsberger, Eaton vice president for environment, health, and safety.

The business case for ethics and social responsibility

Most managers now realize that paying attention to ethics and social responsibility is as important a business issue as paying attention to costs, profits and growth. For one thing, in today's information age, bad behaviour is increasingly hard to hide, and 'outbehaving the competition' can provide a real competitive advantage.[69]

Naturally, the relationship of a corporation's ethics and social responsibility to its financial performance concerns both managers and management scholars and has generated a lively debate.[70] One concern of managers is whether good citizenship will hurt performance – after all, ethics programmes and social responsibility cost money. A commitment to sustainability means that things often have to be done in a more costly way. Hundreds of studies have been undertaken to determine whether heightened ethical and social responsiveness increases or decreases a company's financial performance. Studies have provided varying results, but they have generally found a positive relationship between ethical and socially responsible behaviour and firm financial performance.[71] For example, a recent study of the top 100 sustainable global companies found that they had significantly higher sales growth, return on assets, profits and cash flow from operations in at least some areas of business.[72] Another review of the financial performance of large US corporations considered 'best corporate citizens' found that they enjoy both superior reputations and superior financial performance.[73] Similarly, Governance Metrics International, an independent corporate governance ratings agency in New York, reports that the stocks of companies run on more selfless principles perform better than those run in a self-serving manner.[74] Although results from these studies are not proof, they do provide an indication that using resources for ethics and social responsibility does not hurt companies.[75]

Review your responses to the questions at the end of this chapter, which will give you some insight into your own level of manager courage. A high level of courage can help managers make ethical choices in the face of opposition or pressure from others.

Companies are also making an effort to measure the non-financial factors that create value. Researchers find, for example, that people prefer to work for sustainable companies or companies that demonstrate a high level of ethics and social responsibility; thus, these organizations can attract and retain high-quality employees.[76] Customers pay attention too. A study by Walker Research indicates that, price and quality being equal, two-thirds of customers say they would switch brands to do business with a company that is ethical and socially responsible.[77] Another series of experiments by Remi Trudel and June Cotte of the University of Western Ontario's Ivey School of Business, found that consumers were willing to pay slightly more for products they were told had been made using high ethical standards.[78]

Enlightened managers realize that integrity and trust are essential elements in sustaining successful and profitable business relationships with an increasingly connected and well-informed web of employees, customers, suppliers and partners. Although doing the right thing might not always be profitable in the short run, many managers believe that it can provide a competitive advantage by developing a level of trust that money can't buy.

REFLECTION

- Managers are role models. One of the most important ways that managers create ethical and socially responsible organizations is by practising ethical leadership.
- Some students at Harvard Business School sign a pledge promising to act responsibly and ethically as managers.
- A **code of ethics** is a formal statement of the organization's values regarding ethics and social issues.
- An **ethics committee** is a group of executives (and sometimes lower-level employees as well) charged with overseeing company ethics by ruling on questionable issues and disciplining violators.

- Some organizations have ethics offices headed by a **chief ethics officer**, a manager who oversees all aspects of ethics and legal compliance.
- Managers who want ethical organizations support **whistle-blowing**, the disclosure by employees of unethical, illegitimate or illegal practices by the organization.
- Companies that are ethical and socially responsible perform as well as – often even better than – those that are not socially responsible.
- One study found that sustainable companies have significantly higher sales growth, return on assets and profits than companies that are not run on a philosophy of sustainability.

DISCUSSION QUESTIONS

1   Is it reasonable to expect that managers measure their social and environmental performance on the same level as they measure financial performance, with Elkington's triple bottom line approach? Discuss.

2 Environmentalists are trying to pass laws for oil spills that would remove all liability limits for the oil companies. This change would punish corporations financially. Is this approach the best way to influence companies to be socially responsible?

3 To what extent is it socially responsible for organizations to undertake political activity, or join with others in a trade association to influence the government? Discuss.

4 Discuss the view that it is ethical for organizational managers and human resource specialists to request access to and to scrutinize the Facebook pages of job applicants?

5 Do you think bottom-of-the-pyramid business practices can really have a positive effect on poverty and social problems in the developing world? Discuss.

6 Imagine you are a manager of a clothing company (such as Gap) and you discover that child labour is being used in your supply chain, how might you deal with this situation?

Will you be a courageous manager?

INSTRUCTIONS It probably won't happen right away, but soon enough in your duties as a new manager, you will be confronted with a situation that will test the strength of your moral beliefs or your sense of justice. Are you ready to deal with these difficult situations? To find out, think deeply regarding a recent period within your life when you were faced with a moral dilemma and how you dealt with it. Record your core values within a confidential file and reflect on whether your approach was consistent with your core values.

Are you typically:	Mostly true	Mostly false
1 I risked substantial personal loss to achieve a goal.	☐	☐
2 I took personal risks to defend my beliefs.	☐	☐
3 I would say no to inappropriate things, even if I had a lot to lose.	☐	☐
4 My significant actions were linked to higher values.	☐	☐
5 I easily acted against the opinions and approval of others.	☐	☐
6 I quickly told people the truth as I saw it, even when it was negative.	☐	☐
7 I spoke out against group or organizational injustice.	☐	☐
8 I acted according to my conscience, even if I could lose my standing in my community stature.	☐	☐

SCORING & INTERPRETATION Each of these questions pertains to some aspect of displaying courage in a group situation, which often reflects a person's level of moral development. Count the number of checks for 'Mostly true'. If you scored 5 or more, congratulations! That behaviour would enable you to become a courageous manager about moral issues. A score below 4 indicates that you may avoid difficult issues or have not been in situations that challenged your moral courage.

Study the specific questions for which you scored 'Mostly true' and 'Mostly false' to learn more about your specific strengths and weaknesses. Think about what influences your moral behaviour and decisions, such as need for success or approval. Study the behaviour of others whom you consider to be moral individuals. How might you increase your courage as a new manager?

APPLY YOUR SKILLS: ETHICAL DILEMMA

Should we go beyond the law?[79]

Nathan Rosillo stared out his office window at the lazy curves and lush, green, flower-lined banks of the Dutch Valley River. He'd grown up near here, and he envisioned the day his children would enjoy the river as he had as a child. But now his own company might make that a risky proposition.

Nathan is a key product developer at Chem-Tech Corporation, an industry leader. Despite its competitive position, Chem-Tech experienced several quarters of dismal financial performance. Nathan and his team developed a new lubricant product that the company sees as the turning point in its declining fortunes. Top executives are thrilled that they can produce the new product at a significant cost saving because of recent changes in environmental regulations. Regulatory agencies loosened requirements on reducing and recycling wastes, which means that Chem-Tech can now release waste directly into the Dutch Valley River.

Nathan is as eager as anyone to see Chem-Tech survive this economic downturn, but he doesn't think this route is the way to do it. He expressed his opposition regarding the waste dumping to both the plant manager and his direct supervisor, Martin Feldman. Martin has always supported Nathan, but this time was different. The plant manager, too, turned a deaf ear. 'We're meeting government standards,' he'd said. 'It's up to them to protect the water. It's up to us to make a profit and stay in business.'

Frustrated and confused, Nathan turned away from the window, his prime office view mocking his inability to protect the river he loved. He knew the manufacturing vice president was visiting the plant next week. Maybe if he talked with her, she would agree that the decision to dump waste materials in the river was ethically and socially irresponsible. But if she didn't, he would be skating on thin ice. His supervisor had already accused him of not being a team player. Maybe he should just be a passive bystander – after all, the company isn't breaking any laws.

What would you do?

1 Talk to the manufacturing vice president and emphasize the responsibility that Chem-Tech has as an industry leader to set an example. Present her with a recommendation that Chem-Tech participate in voluntary pollution reduction as a marketing tool, positioning itself as the environmentally friendly choice.

2 Mind your own business and just do your job. The company isn't breaking any laws, and if Chem-Tech's economic situation doesn't improve, a lot of people will be thrown out of work.

3 Call the local environmental advocacy group and get them to stage a protest of the company.

APPLY YOUR SKILLS: CASE FOR CRITICAL ANALYSIS

Barclays Bank PLC and the London Interbank Offered Rate (The LIBOR)

The LIBOR developed in response to rising demand around the mid-1980s for 'Euro' currencies – offshore, stateless and often in dollars – that swept London and allowed companies and countries to borrow, deposit and repay while dodging domestic regulation and taxes The LIBOR has become integrated into a majority of the world's financial markets and currently provides the reference point for nearly all interest rate derivatives and variable rate loans available.

It is currently calculated for 15 different loan durations, ranging from overnight to a year, and in ten currencies, including the pound, the dollar, the euro and the Swedish krona. The LIBOR rates are used as a benchmark to set payments on about $800 trillion-worth of financial instruments, ranging from complex interest-rate derivatives to simple mortgages. The number determines the global flow of billions of dollars each year. The rates signal a bank's health to financial markets, rising when banks are in trouble, and create the basis for payments on trillions of dollars in corporate debt, home mortgages and financial contracts worldwide.

The impact of even small rate shifts can be critical. A small increase in the LIBOR can make a big difference for borrowers. Because of its pervasiveness in, and significance for, the financial markets, the rate has come to be known as 'the world's most important number'.

Currently, member banks report their LIBOR rates each morning to the British Bankers' Association (BBA) and European Banking Federation (EBF), respectively. The BBA and EBF require that reporting banks use their subjective judgements in determining the submitted rates; therefore, the accuracy of the LIBOR and EURIBOR, as interest rates, relies upon the accuracy of the subjective judgement of the individual reporting banks.

Derivatives traders are strictly prohibited from considering their own financial positions in exercising their subjective judgement. Thomson Reuters, on behalf of the BBA and EBF, then collates the submissions, calculates the final benchmark rates and publishes the daily rates.

According to the US Financial Stability Oversight Council (FSOC) and the UK's Financial Services Authority (FSA), two regulatory bodies charged with investigating alleged market manipulation, as early as 2005 evidence surfaced that the major global financial and banking services company, Barclays Bank PLC (Barclays), was falsifying its reported EURIBOR rates, and, to a lesser extent, its LIBOR rates, at the request of its own derivatives traders and other banks.

On 2 July 2012, Barclays' chairman, Marcus Agius, chief executive officer, Robert Diamond, and chief operating officer, Jerry del Missier, resigned amid allegations of misconduct. By the spring of 2012, US and UK investigators had uncovered substantial evidence that Barclays and several other unnamed banks had tried to manipulate the LIBOR. In June 2012, following an extensive investigation, Barclays finally admitted to misconduct. The FSA imposed a £59.5 million ($92.8 million) penalty on Barclays. On 27 June 2012, Barclays agreed to pay a $360 million fine to settle charges brought against it by the US Department of Justice and the US Commodity Futures Trading Commission (CFTC).

Also in July 2012, the UK's Serious Fraud Office launched a criminal investigation into the LIBOR scandal, investigating a total of 18 banks including Citigroup, Inc., Royal Bank of Scotland Group plc and UBS AG.

In December 2012, UBS was fined $1.5 billion for LIBOR rigging. It was fined an additional $14.5 million by Britain's financial regulators for exposing customers to unacceptable risk when UBS sold an AIG investment fund to customers. The Royal Bank of Scotland was fined $610 million by US and UK authorities in February 2013. European Union regulators continue to investigate other banks involved in the scandal.

The Royal Bank of Scotland was fined $610 million by US and UK authorities in February 2013. EU regulators continue to investigate other banks involved in the scandal, including Citigroup, reportedly J.P. Morgan Chase, Deutsche Bank and various other European lenders.

The US Department of Justice has already brought criminal charges against several individual traders and may bring more.

Questions

1   Discuss the extent to which the outcome of the LIBOR fixing illustrates the correct application of procedural and compensatory justice.

2   According to Barclays plc chairman, Sir David Walker, 'we have made significant advances in resolving legacy issues in the course of 2014 through working more closely and constructively than ever with our regulators across the world. The Board and I consider the conduct and practices that led to these issues are entirely inconsistent with the values to which we hold ourselves today. Our proactive efforts in resolving these issues will continue throughout 2015 and stand testament to our commitment to do business in the right way, putting issues that have been so damaging to our reputation behind us and supporting greater resilience, transparency and sustainability for term.' Evaluate this response of Barclays plc to the ethical failures of the LIBOR fixing scandal.

3   Propose further measures that Barclays plc should take to promote greater ethics and enhanced corporate social responsibility.

END NOTES

1. Ben Worthen and Joann S. Lublin, 'Mark Hurd Neglected to Follow H-P Code', *The Wall Street Journal*, August 9, 2010, B1.

2. Mara Der Hovanesian, 'Sex, Lies, and Mortgage Deals', *BusinessWeek* (November 24, 2009): 71–74; Amir Efrati and Joann S. Lublin, 'Yahoo CEO's Downfall', *The Wall Street Journal Online*, May 15, 2012, www.online.wsj.com/article/SB10001424052702304192704577404530999458956.htm (accessed July 2, 2012).

3. Gordon F. Shea, *Practical Ethics* (New York: American Management Association, 1988); and Linda K. Treviño, 'Ethical Decision Making in Organizations: A Person-Situation Interactionist Model', *Academy of Management Review* 11 (1986): 601–617.

4. Thomas M. Jones, 'Ethical Decision Making by Individuals in Organizations: An Issue-Contingent Model', *Academy of Management Review* 16 (1991): 366–395.

5. Shelby D. Hunt and Jared M. Hansen, 'Understanding Ethical Diversity in Organizations', *Organizational Dynamics* 36, no 2 (2007): 202–216.

6. 'Socializing for Intelligence', *Computer News Middle East*, November 2, 2011.

7. Justin Scheck, 'Accusations of Snooping in Ink-Cartridge Dispute', *The Wall Street Journal Online*, August 11, 2009, www.online.wsj.com/article/SB124995836273921661.html?KEYWORDS=%22Accusations+of+Snooping+in+Ink-Cartridge+Dispute%22 (accessed August 14, 2009).

8. These examples are from Jones and Koppel, 'Ethical Lapses Felled Long List of Company Executives'.

9. Rushworth M. Kidder, 'The Three Great Domains of Human Action', *Christian Science Monitor*, January 30, 1990.

10. Gallup Survey results reported in Roger Martin, 'The CEO's Ethical Dilemma in the Era of Earnings Management', *Strategy & Leadership* 39, no. 6 (2011): 43–47.

11. John Revill and Vanessa O'Connell, 'Armstrong is Stripped of Titles in Cycling', *The Wall Street Journal*, October 23, 2012, A4; and Anemona Hartocollis, 'At Ailing Brooklyn Hospital, Insider Deals and Lavish Perks', *The New York Times*, March 26, 2012, A1.

12. Marist College Institute for Public Opinion and Knights of Columbus survey, results reported in Kevin Turner, 'Corporate Execs: Nobody Trusts Us; U.S. Lacks Confidence in Business Ethics, Poll Says', *Florida Times Union*, February 27, 2009.

13. Gary R. Weaver, Linda Klebe Treviño and Bradley Agle, ' 'Somebody I Look Up To:' Ethical Role Models in Organizations', *Organizational Dynamics* 34, no. 4 (2005): 313–330.

14. These measures of unethical behaviour are from Muel Kaptein, 'Developing a Measure of Unethical Behavior in the Workplace: A Stakeholder Perspective', *Journal of Management* 34, no. 5 (October 2008): 978–1008.

15. Roger Martin, 'The CEO's Ethical Dilemma in the Era of Earnings Management', *Strategy & Leadership* 39, no. 6 (2011): 43–47.

16. Nicholas D. Kristof, 'Lehman CEO Fuld Takes the Prize; Need a Job?: $17,000 an Hour; No Success Required', *The Gazette*, September 19, 2008; Paul Goodsell, 'Are CEOs Worth Their Salt?' *Omaha World-Herald*, October 5, 2008; Jackie Calmes and Louise Story, 'AIG Bonus Outcry Builds: Troubled Insurance Giant Gave out More Millions Last Week', *Pittsburgh Post Gazette*, March 18, 2009; Graham Bowley, 'Wall Street '09 Bonuses Increase 17% to $20 Billion', *The New York Times*, February 24, 2010; and Adam Shell, 'Despite Recession, Average Wall Street Bonus Leaps 25%; About $20.3 Billion Distributed in 2009', *USA Today*, February 24, 2010.

17. Jennifer Liberto, 'CEO Pay Is 380 Times Average Worker's – AFL-CIO', *CNNMoney*, April 19, 2012, www.money.cnn.com/2012/04/19/news/economy/ceo-pay/index.htm (accessed July 3, 2012); and Jena McGregor, 'Crazy Data Point of the Day: How Much CEO Pay vs. Worker Pay Has Grown', Post Leadership Blog, *WashingtonPost.com*, May 11, 2012, www.washingtonpost.com/blogs/post-leadership/post/crazy-data-point-of-the-day-how-much-ceo-vs-worker-pay-has-grown/2012/05/11/gIQArUISIU_blog.html (accessed July 3, 2012).

18. Linda K. Treviño and Katherine A. Nelson, *Managing Business Ethics: Straight Talk About How to Do It Right* (New York: John Wiley & Sons, Inc. 1995), p. 4.

19. Jones, 'Ethical Decision Making by Individuals in Organizations'.

20. This example is from Francis J. Flynn and Scott S. Wiltermuth, 'Who's with Me? False Consensus, Brokerage, and Ethical Decision Making in Organizations', *Academy of Management Journal* 53, no. 5 (2010): 1074–1089.

21. Based on a question from a General Electric (GE) employee ethics guide, reported in Kathryn Kranhold, 'U.S. Firms Raise Ethics Focus', *The Wall Street Journal*, November 28, 2005.

22. D. Wallis, 'Loose Lips Can Sink Trips', *The New York Times*, May 3, 2012, F1.

23. From Jeffrey Kluger, 'What Makes Us Moral?' *Time* (December 3, 2007): 54–60.

24. 'The Morality Quiz', *Time*, www.time.com/morality (accessed February 19, 2008).

25. This discussion is based on Gerald F. Cavanagh, Dennis J. Moberg and Manuel Velasquez, 'The Ethics of Organizational Politics', *Academy of Management Review* 6 (1981): 363–374; Justin G. Longenecker, Joseph A. McKinney and Carlos W. Moore, 'Egoism and Independence: Entrepreneurial Ethics', *Organizational Dynamics* (Winter 1988): 64–72; Carolyn Wiley, 'The ABCs of Business Ethics: Definitions, Philosophies, and Implementation', *IM* (February 1995): 22–27; and Mark Mallinger, 'Decisive Decision Making: An Exercise Using Ethical Frameworks', *Journal of Management Education* (August 1997): 411–417.

26. Michael J. McCarthy, 'Now the Boss Knows Where You're Clicking', and 'Virtual Morality: A New Workplace Quandary', *The Wall Street Journal*, October 21, 1999; and Jeffrey L. Seglin, 'Who's Snooping on You?' *Business 2.0* (August 8, 2000): 202–203.

27. John Kekes, 'Self-Direction: The Core of Ethical Individualism', in *Organizations and Ethical Individualism*, ed. Konstanian Kolenda (New York: Praeger, 1988), pp. 1–18.

28. Tad Tulega, *Beyond the Bottom Line* (New York: Penguin Books, 1987).

29. Bill Lynn, 'Ethics', Practical Ethics website, www.practicalethics.net/ethics.html (accessed March 23, 2010); Richard E. Thompson, 'So, Greed's Not Good After All', *Trustee* (January 2003): 28; and Dennis F. Thompson, *'What Is Practical Ethics?'* Harvard University Edmond J. Safra Foundation Center for Ethics website, www.ethics.harvard.edu/the-center/what-is-practical-ethics (accessed March 23, 2010).

30. Carol D. Leonnig and David Nakamura, 'Official Quickly Corralled Agents', *The Washington Post*, April 22, 2012, A1; David Nakamura, 'Out of Public Eye, a Disgusted Secret Service Director', *The Washington Post*, April 26, 2012, A1; and Carol D. Leonnig and David Nakamura, 'Four in Secret Service Fight Back', *The Washington Post*, May 23, 2012, A1.

31. Anonymous official quoted in Leonnig and Nakamura, 'Four in Secret Service Fight Back'.

32. Gerard L. Rossy, 'Five Questions for Addressing Ethical Dilemmas', *Strategy & Leadership* 39, no. 6 (2011): 35–42.

33. John D. Kammeyer-Mueller, Lauren S. Simon and Bruce L. Rich, 'The Psychic Cost of Doing Wrong: Ethical Conflict, Divestiture Socialization and Emotional Exhaustion', *Journal of Management* 38, no. 3 (May 2012): 784–808.

34. L. Kohlberg, 'Moral Stages and Moralization: The Cognitive-Developmental Approach', in *Moral Development and Behavior: Theory, Research, and Social Issues,* ed. T. Lickona (New York: Holt, Rinehart and Winston, 1976), pp. 31–83; L. Kohlberg, 'Stage and Sequence: The Cognitive-Developmental Approach to Socialization', in *Handbook of Socialization Theory and Research,* ed. D. A. Goslin (Chicago: Rand McNally, 1969); Linda K. Treviño, Gary R. Weaver and Scott J. Reynolds, 'Behavioral Ethics in Organizations: A Review', *Journal of Management* 32, no 6 (December 2006): 951–990; and Jill W. Graham, 'Leadership, Moral Development, and Citizenship Behavior', *Business Ethics Quarterly* 5, no. 1 (January 1995): 43–54.

35. Ihosvani Rodriguez, 'Hallandale Beach Lifeguard Fired After Participating in Beach Rescue', *Sun Sentinel*, July 3, 2012, www.articles.sun-sentinel.com/2012-07-03/news/fl-hallandale-beach-lifeguards-20120703_1_lifeguard-services-jeff-ellis-beach-rescue (accessed July 9, 2012); and Gilma Avalos and Ari Odzer, 'Hallandale Beach Lifeguard Fired for Leaving His Zone to Rescue Drowning Man', *NBCMiami.com*, July 5, 2012, www.nbcmiami.com/news/local/Hallandale-Beach-Lifeguard-Fired-For-Leaving-His-Zone-For-Rescue-161372785.html (accessed July 9, 2012).

36. Eugene W. Szwajkowski, 'The Myths and Realities of Research on Organizational Misconduct', in *Research in Corporate Social Performance and Policy*, ed. James E. Post (Greenwich, CT: JAI Press, 1986), 9: 103–122; and Keith Davis, William C. Frederick and Robert L. Blostrom, *Business and Society: Concepts and Policy Issues* (New York: McGraw-Hill, 1979).

37. Douglas S. Sherwin, 'The Ethical Roots of the Business System', *Harvard Business Review* 61 (November–December 1983): 183–192.

38. Nancy C. Roberts and Paula J. King, 'The Stakeholder Audit Goes Public', *Organizational Dynamics* (Winter 1989): 63–79; Thomas Donaldson and Lee E. Preston, 'The Stakeholder Theory of the Corporation: Concepts, Evidence, and Implications', *Academy of Management Review* 20, no. 1

(1995): 65–91; and Jeffrey S. Harrison and Caron H. St. John, 'Managing and Partnering with External Stakeholders', *Academy of Management Executive* 10, no. 2 (1996): 46–60.

39. R. Mitchell, B. Agle and D. J. Wood, 'Toward a Theory of Stakeholder Identification and Salience: Defining the Principle of Who or What Really Counts', *Academy of Management Review* 22 (1997): 853–886; Virginie Vial, 'Taking a Stakeholders' Approach to Corporate Social Responsibility', *Global Business and Organizational Excellence* (September–October 2011): 37–47; and Martijn Poel, Linda Kool and Annelieke van der Giessen, 'How to Decide on the Priorities and Coordination of Information Society Policy? Analytical Framework and Three Case Studies', *Info: The Journal of Policy, Regulation and Strategy for Telecommunications, Information, and Media* 12, no. 6 (2010): 21–39.

40. N. Craig Smith, Sean Ansett and Lior Erex, 'How Gap Inc. Engaged with Its Stakeholders', *MIT Sloan Management Review* 52, no. 4 (Summer 2011): 69–76.

41. *Ibid.*

42. Max B. E. Clarkson, 'A Stakeholder Framework for Analyzing and Evaluating Corporate Social Performance', *Academy of Management Review* 20, no. 1 (1995): 92–117.

43. Rich Kauffeld, Abhishek Malhotra and Susan Higgins, 'Green Is a Strategy', *Strategy + Business* (December 21, 2009).

44. Reported in Dung K. Nguyen and Stanley F. Slater, 'Hitting the Sustainability Sweet Spot: Having It All', *Journal of Business Strategy* 31, no. 3 (2010): 5–11.

45. Steven Mufson, 'Keystone XL Pipeline Expansion Driven by Oil-Rich Tar Sands in Alberta', *The Washington Post*, June 30, 2012, www.washingtonpost.com/business/economy/keystone-xl-pipeline-expansion-driven-by-oil-rich-tar-sands-in-alberta/2012/06/30/gJQAVe4ZEW_story.html?wpisrc (accessed July 4, 2012).

46. This definition is based on Marc J. Epstein and Marie-Josée Roy, 'Improving Sustainability Performance: Specifying, Implementing and Measuring Key Principles', *Journal of General Management* 29, no. 1 (Autumn 2003): 15–31; World Commission on Economic Development, *Our Common Future* (Oxford, U.K.: Oxford University Press, 1987); and A. W. Savitz and K. Weber, *The Triple Bottom Line: How Today's Best-Run Companies Are Achieving Economic, Social, and Environmental Success* (San Francisco: Jossey-Bass, 2006).

47. This discussion is based on Nguyen and Slater, 'Hitting the Sustainability Sweet Spot'; Savitz and Weber, *The Triple Bottom Line*; and 'Triple Bottom Line', an article adapted from *The Economist Guide to Management Ideas and Gurus*, by Tim Hindle (London: Profile Books, 2008), *The Economist* (November 17, 2009), www.economist.com/node/14301663 (accessed July 5, 2012). The 'people, planet, profit' phase was first coined in 1994 by John Elkington, founder of a British consulting firm called SustainAbility.

48. Mark S. Schwartz and Archie B. Carroll, 'Corporate Social Responsibility: A Three-Domain Approach', *Business Ethics Quarterly* 13, no. 4 (2003): 503–530; and Archie B. Carroll, 'A Three-Dimensional Conceptual Model of Corporate Performance', *Academy of Management Review* 4 (1979): 497–505. For a discussion of various models for evaluating corporate social performance, also see Diane L. Swanson,

'Addressing a Theoretical Problem by Reorienting the Corporate Social Performance Model', *Academy of Management Review* 20, no. 1 (1995): 43–64.

49. Milton Friedman, *Capitalism and Freedom* (Chicago: University of Chicago Press, 1962), p. 133; and Milton Friedman and Rose Friedman, *Free to Choose* (New York: Harcourt Brace Jovanovich, 1979).

50. Eugene W. Szwjakowski, 'Organizational Illegality: Theoretical Integration and Illustrative Application', *Academy of Management Review* 10 (1985): 558–567.

51. David Barstow, 'Vast Mexico Bribery Case Hushed up by Walmart After Top-Level Struggle', *The New York Times*, April 21, 2012, www.nytimes.com/2012/04/22/business/at-walmart-in-mexico-a-bribe-inquiry-silenced.html?pagewanted=all (accessed July 6, 2012).

52. David J. Fritzsche and Helmut Becker, 'Linking Management Behavior to Ethical Philosophy – An Empirical Investigation', *Academy of Management Journal* 27 (1984): 165–175.

53. 'Royal DSM', segment in Alison Beard and Richard Hornik, 'Spotlight on the Good Company: It's Hard to Be Good', *Harvard Business Review* (November 2011): 88–94.

54. Smith, Ansett and Erex, 'How Gap Inc. Engaged with Its Stakeholders'.

55. Jessica Dickler, 'Donations to Japan Lag Far Behind Haiti or Katrina', *CNNMoney.com*, March 18, 2011, www.money.cnn.com/2011/03/18/pf/japan_earthquake_aid/index.htm (accessed July 6, 2012).

56. Saul W. Gellerman, 'Managing Ethics from the Top Down', *Sloan Management Review* (Winter 1989): 73–79.

57. Attributed to Philip Delves Broughton in David A. Kaplan, 'MBAs Get Schooled in Ethics', *Fortune* (October 26, 2009): 27–28.

58. Leslie Wayne, 'A Promise to Be Ethical in an Era of Temptation', *The New York Times*, May 30, 2009; and Kelley Holland, 'Is It Time to Retrain B-Schools?' *The New York Times*, March 15, 2009.

59. Michael E. Brown and Linda K. Treviño, 'Ethical Leadership: A Review and Future Directions', *The Leadership Quarterly* 17 (2006): 595–616; Weaver, Treviño and Agle, "Somebody I Look Up To"; and L. K. Treviño et al., 'Managing Ethics and Legal Compliance: What Works and What Hurts?' *California Management Review* 41, no. 2 (Winter 1999): 131–151.

60. M. A. Cleek and S. L. Leonard, 'Can Corporate Codes of Ethics Influence Behavior?' *Journal of Business Ethics* 17, no. 6 (1998): 619–630.

61. K. Matthew Gilley, Chris Robertson and Tim Mazur, 'The Bottom-Line Benefits of Ethics Code Commitment', *Business Horizons* 53 (January–February 2010): 31–37; Joseph L. Badaracco and Allen P. Webb, 'Business Ethics: A View from the Trenches', *California Management Review* 37, no. 2 (Winter 1995): 8–28; and Ronald B. Morgan, 'Self- and Co-Worker Perceptions of Ethics and Their Relationships to Leadership and Salary', *Academy of Management Journal* 36, no. 1 (February 1993): 200–214.

62. 'Code of Conduct', Google Investor Relations, April 25, 2012, www.investor.google.com/corporate/code-of-conduct.html (accessed September 28, 2012).

63. Cheryl Rosen, 'A Measure of Success? Ethics After Enron', *Business Ethics* (Summer 2006): 22–26.

64. Alan Yuspeh, 'Do the Right Thing', *CIO* (August 1, 2000): 56–58.

65. Reported in Rosen, 'A Measure of Success? Ethics After Enron'.

66. Marcia P. Miceli and Janet P. Near, 'The Relationship Among Beliefs, Organizational Positions, and Whistle-Blowing Status: A Discriminant Analysis', *Academy of Management Journal* 27 (1984): 687–705; Michael T. Rehg, Marcia P. Miceli, Janet P. Near and James R. Van Scotter, 'Antecedents and Outcomes of Retaliation Against Whistleblowers: Gender Differences and Power Relationships', *Organization Science* 19, no. 2 (March–April 2008): 221–240.

67. Eugene Garaventa, '*An Enemy of the People* by Henrik Ibsen: The Politics of Whistle-Blowing', *Journal of Management Inquiry* 3, no. 4 (December 1994): 369–374; Marcia P. Miceli and Janet P. Near, 'Whistleblowing: Reaping the Benefits', *Academy of Management Executive* 8, no. 3 (1994): 65–74.

68. Nicole Gaudiano, 'Report: Air Force Whistle-Blowers Targeted', *USA Today*, February 1, 2012, 3A; Gretchen Morgenson, 'How a Whistle-Blower Conquered Countrywide', *The New York Times*, February 20, 2011, BU1; and Christine Seib and Alexandra Frean, 'Lehman Whistleblower Lost Job Month After Speaking Out', *The Times*, March 17, 2010, 43.

69. Richard McGill Murphy, 'Why Doing Good Is Good For Business', *Fortune* (February 8, 2010): 90–95.

70. Homer H. Johnson, 'Does It Pay to Be Good? Social Responsibility and Financial Performance', *Business Horizons* (November–December 2003): 34–40; Jennifer J. Griffin and John F. Mahon, 'The Corporate Social Performance and Corporate Financial Performance Debate: Twenty-Five Years of Incomparable Research', *Business and Society* 36, no. 1 (March 1997): 5–31; Bernadette M. Ruf, Krishnamurty Muralidhar, Robert M. Brown, Jay J. Janney and Karen Paul, 'An Empirical Investigation of the Relationship Between Change in Corporate Social Performance and Financial Performance: A Stakeholder Theory Perspective', *Journal of Business Ethics* 32, no. 2 (July 2001): 143ff; Philip L. Cochran and Robert A. Wood, 'Corporate Social Responsibility and Financial Performance', *Academy of Management Journal* 27 (1984): 42–56.

71. Heli Wang, Jaepil Choi and Jiatao Li, 'Too Little or Too Much? Untangling the Relationship Between Corporate Philanthropy and Firm Financial Performance', *Organization Science* 19, no. 1 (January–February 2008): 143–159; Philip L. Cochran, 'The Evolution of Corporate Social Responsibility', *Business Horizons* 50 (2007): 449–454; Paul C. Godfrey, 'The Relationship Between Corporate Philanthropy and Shareholder Wealth: A Risk Management Perspective', *Academy of Management Review* 30, no. 4 (2005): 777–798; Oliver Falck and Stephan Heblich, 'Corporate Social Responsibility: Doing Well by Doing Good', *Business Horizons* 50 (2007): 247–254; J. A. Pearce II and J. P. Doh, 'The High Impact of Collaborative Social Initiatives', *MIT Sloan Management Review* (Spring 2005): 31–39; Curtis C. Verschoor and Elizabeth A. Murphy, 'The Financial Performance of Large U.S. Firms and Those with Global Prominence: How Do the Best Corporate Citizens Rate?' *Business and Society Review* 107, no. 3 (Fall 2002): 371–381; Johnson, 'Does It Pay to Be Good?'; Dale Kurschner, '5

Ways Ethical Business Creates Fatter Profits', *Business Ethics* (March–April 1996): 20–23.

72. Rashid Ameer and Radiah Othman, 'Sustainability Practices and Corporate Financial Performance: A Study Based on the Top Global Corporations', *Journal of Business Ethics* 108, no. 1 (June 2012): 61–79.

73. Verschoor and Murphy, 'The Financial Performance of Large U.S. Firms'.

74. Phred Dvorak, 'Finding the Best Measure of 'Corporate Citizenship,'' *The Wall Street Journal*, July 2, 2007.

75. Jean B. McGuire, Alison Sundgren and Thomas Schneeweis, 'Corporate Social Responsibility and Firm Financial Performance', *Academy of Management Journal* 31 (1988): 854–872; and Falck and Heblich, 'Corporate Social Responsibility: Doing Well by Doing Good'.

76. Daniel W. Greening and Daniel B. Turban, 'Corporate Social Performance as a Competitive Advantage in Attracting a Quality Workforce', *Business and Society* 39, no. 3 (September 2000): 254; and Kate O'Sullivan, 'Virtue Rewarded', *CFO* (October 2006): 47–52.

77. 'The Socially Correct Corporate Business', in Leslie Holstrom and Simon Brady, 'The Changing Face of Global Business', a special advertising section, *Fortune* (July 24, 2000): S1–S38.

78. Remi Trudel and June Cotte, 'Does Being Ethical Pay?' *The Wall Street Journal,* May 12, 2008.

79. Adapted from Janet Q. Evans, 'What Do You Do: What If Polluting Is Legal?' *Business Ethics* (Fall 2002): 20.

PART 2 INTEGRATIVE CASE
PART TWO: THE ENVIRONMENT
OF MANAGEMENT

Brown goes green: UPS embraces natural gas trucking fleet

Can 3 million commercial trucks consuming nearly 4 billion gallons of diesel fuel annually in the USA really 'go green'? To find out, the White House in 2008 launched a National Clean Fleets Partnership aimed at helping businesses embrace vehicles that run on natural gas, electricity, hydrogen and other alternative fuels. Since it was first announced, the public-private partnership has sparked close collaboration between the US Department of Energy and top fleet operators like United Parcel Service (UPS) nicknamed 'Brown'.

UPS's participation in a national green highways initiative may seem counterintuitive to many – but it shouldn't. Brown's quest to attain cost savings through fuel-efficient motoring stretches back to the 1930s, when the parcel delivery service used 20-mph electric cars to deliver packages in New York City. In the 1980s, UPS introduced vehicles that ran on compressed natural gas. In 2006, the company partnered with the US Environmental Protection Agency (EPA) to design and build the world's first hydraulic delivery vehicle – a truck propelled by hydraulic pumps that store and release energy captured during braking. Today, the Georgia-based delivery giant continues to test alternative-fuel technologies, seeking to transform 95 000 delivery vehicles into fuel-efficient green machines.

Although numerous alternative-fuel technologies are competing for dominance at UPS, liquefied natural gas (LNG) has gained significant momentum in recent years, especially for Brown's largest trucks. Like most eighteen-wheelers, UPS's 17 000 tractor-trailers run on diesel fuel. This is beginning to change, however. In the years since the 2004 discovery of massive shale gas fields in the Marcellus Shale region of the USA, natural gas supplies have skyrocketed, causing methane prices to drop to about half the price of diesel. This development has had a significant influence on business. In particular, transportation managers faced with an affordable supply of domestic clean energy have begun evaluating the efficiency and environmental impact of their fleets.

In 2011, UPS embraced the new natural gas boom by ordering 48 LNG-engine tractor-trailers – an investment that boosted the company's long-haul natural gas fleet total to 59. Brown was not alone; similar moves by Ryder Systems, Waste Management Inc., and AT&T led *Wall Street Journal* energy reporter Rebecca Smith to wonder if the entire trucking industry was about to 'ditch diesel'. As Smith noted, 'Never before has the price gap between natural gas and diesel been so large, suddenly making natural-gas-powered trucks an alluring option for company fleets.'

According to Mike Britt, the director of vehicle engineering at UPS, Brown has good reason to switch from diesel to LNG. 'The added advantage of LNG,' says Britt, 'is it does not compromise the tractor's abilities, fuel economy or drivability, and it significantly reduces greenhouse gases.' The benefits of LNG are numerous indeed. While most alternative-fuel vehicles can drive only limited distances, LNG trucks have a 600-mile single-tank range, plus a reliable network of fuelling stations. In addition, LNG-fuelled trucks produce 25 per cent less carbon emissions and consume 95 per cent less diesel than conventional trucks. Most importantly, natural gas engines deliver full horsepower. Highlighting a stark contrast between LNG and electric-powered vehicles, Britt quips that 'a 450-horsepower eighteen-wheeler uses so much power that to haul two trailers through mountainous terrain, the first trailer would have to be all batteries.' The performance gap leads Britt to conclude: 'LNG is the only suitable alternative to diesel for the really heavy long-haul tractor trailers you see on the highway.'

At UPS, terms like 'fleet efficiency' and 'environmental impact' aren't mere buzzwords – they are increasingly part of Brown's corporate culture. In 2011, UPS created its first executive-level management position for green concerns: the chief sustainability officer (CSO). Scott Wicker, a longtime company veteran appointed to the new post, has been instrumental in defining what a CSO does. 'The key thing I do in my job is try to keep UPS focused on the environmental impacts that we have as an organization – and we're constantly working to reduce those environmental impacts,' Wicker states. 'But it's not just the environment: sustainability is also about what we do as a company in terms of our people, our customers and the communities in which we live and work.' Under Wicker's leadership, sustainability has garnered significant attention at UPS, appearing prominently in the company's policy book, upside blog, and corporate website. In addition, Wicker and his management teams develop and roll out sustainability initiatives to UPS's 400 000 employees.

According to the new green chief, effective sustainability reinforces a company's economic responsibility. 'Above all else, sustainability is about being able to maintain a balance between our impacts on the environment and society, but at the same time keep the company economically prosperous,' Wicker says. Kurt Kuehn, UPS's chief financial officer (CFO), underscores this point, citing two key objectives of sustainability: 'Doing what's right for the environment and society, and also being mindful of the bottom line so we're a healthy company financially.'

Minding the bottom line is especially relevant to Brown's pursuit of alternative-fuel technologies. At $195 000 each, LNG tractor-trailers cost twice as much as conventional semi-trailers – a high premium for going green. However, Mike Britt says that UPS can offset that expense through a combination of government subsidies and natural-gas-related fuel savings. For Britt, added investment in LNG reaps added reward for companies and communities: 'LNG is a cheaper, cleaner-burning fuel that is better for the environment and more sustainable than conventional diesel. It's also a fuel that's in abundant supply inside the USA – it doesn't have to be imported.'

Questions

1 Explain how UPS's alternative-fuels fleet is a response to trends taking place in the company's general environment.

2 Describe how UPS is using *boundary-spanning roles* to adapt to energy-related uncertainty in its environment.

3 How does UPS's clean fleets initiative illustrate the concepts of *sustainability and corporate social responsibility?*

SOURCES: Based on White House Fact Sheet: 'National Clean Fleets Partnership', press release, April 1, 2011, www.whitehouse.gov/the-press-office/2011/04/01/fact-sheet-national-clean-fleets-partnership (accessed June 14, 2012); Rebecca Smith, 'Will Truckers Ditch Diesel?' *The Wall Street Journal*, May 23, 2012, www.online.wsj.com/article/SB100014240 52702304707604577422192910235090.html (accessed June 14, 2012); Matthew L. Wald, 'UPS Finds a Substitute for Diesel: Natural Gas, at 260 Degrees Below Zero', *The New York Times*, February 22, 2011, www.green.blogs.nytimes.com/2011/02/22/u-p-s-finds-a-substitute-for-diesel-natural-gas-at-260-degrees-below-zero (accessed June 14, 2012); Jeffrey Ball, 'Natural-Gas Trucks Face Long Haul', *The Wall Street Journal*, May 17, 2011, www.online.wsj.com/article/SB10001424052748704740604 576301550341227910.html (accessed June 15, 2012); 'UPS Adds to Its Natural Gas Truck Fleet'. *Environmental Leader,* February 25, 2011, www.environmentalleader.com/2011/02/25/ups-adds-to-its-natural-gas-truck-fleet (accessed June 15, 2012); Scott Wicker (CSO, United Parcel Service), interview by Kevin Coffey, upside blog, April 13, 2012, www.blog.ups.com/2012/04/13/talkin-sustainable-logistics-fortune-brainstorm-green (accessed June 16, 2012); William Smith, 'New Terminology, Same Priority: Sustainability Engrained at UPS', upside blog, April 30, 2012, www.blog.ups.com/2012/04/30/new-terminology-same-priority-sustainability-engrained-at-ups (accessed June 16, 2012); Jill Swiecichowski, 'Brown's Legacy of Being Green', upside blog, July 21, 2010, www.blog.ups.com/2010/07/21/browns-legacy-of-being-green (accessed June 15, 2012); 'UPS Replaces Diesel with Cleaner LNG Tractor Trucks', Environment News Service, February 22, 2011, www.ens-newswire.com/ens/feb2011/2011-02-22-091.html (accessed 14 June 2012).

PART 3

PLANNING

CHAPTER 7

MANAGERIAL PLANNING AND GOAL SETTING

LEARNING OBJECTIVES

After studying this chapter, you should be able to:

1 Define goals and plans and explain the relationship between them.

2 Explain the concept of organizational mission and how it influences goal setting and planning.

3 Describe the types of goals an organization should have and how managers use strategy maps to align goals.

4 Define the characteristics of effective goals.

5 Describe the four essential steps in the management-by-objectives (MBO) process.

6 Explain the difference between single-use plans and standing plans.

7 Discuss the benefits and limitations of planning.

8 Describe and explain the importance of contingency planning, scenario building and crisis planning for today's managers.

9 Identify innovative planning approaches that managers use in a fast-changing environment.

Walmart's mission for its US stores is to provide everyday low prices for America's working-class consumer. Sounds familiar? It's the old formula that made Walmart the world's largest retailer, but several years ago, in the midst of a US sales slump, senior managers tried a new direction. Instead of sticking with its well established goals of strict operational efficiency and everyday low prices, they decided to court upscale customers with remodelled, less cluttered stores, organic foods and trendy merchandise. The store raised prices on many items and promoted price cuts on only selected merchandise. Walmart succeeded in meeting its goal of attracting a more upscale clientele, but many of its core customers – people making less than $70 000 a year – decided they'd start shopping at other discount and dollar store chains. Longtime suppliers were alienated as well, because of the cuts Walmart made in its selection of merchandise. Walmart's sales took a sharp downturn. 'I think we tried to stretch the brand a little too far,' said William Simon, head of the US division. Managers are now reformulating goals to try to recapture a winning formula. The company still wants to grow its customer base in the USA, but it plans to do so primarily by building smaller stores in urban areas. 'Every Day Low Prices' can happen in 15 000 square feet,' said Simon.[1]

One of the primary responsibilities of managers is to set goals for where the organization or department should go in the future and plan how to get it there. Walmart managers are facing a struggle that executives in every organization encounter as they try to decide what goals to pursue and how to achieve them. Lack of planning, or poor planning of an implementation, can seriously hurt an organization. For example, the nuclear accident at the Fukushima Daiichi nuclear power plant, after the earthquake and tsunami in Japan in 2011, has been blamed partly on poor planning. Kiyoshi Kurokawa, the chairman of the Fukushima Nuclear Accident Independent Investigation Commission, said: *'It was a profoundly manmade disaster – that could and should have been foreseen and prevented. And its effect could have been mitigated by a more effective human response.'*[2]

Managers cannot see the future, unless they have the rare gift of foresight, nor can they prevent natural disasters such as earthquakes, but proper planning can enable them to respond more swiftly and more effectively to such unexpected events. There are a number of software tools including 'Delphi' that can be used for scenario modelling. At Fukushima, chaos reigned as communications broke down, the chain of command was confused, and no one seemed to know what to do to maintain safety, or to follow up once the accident had occurred.

Of the four management functions – planning, organizing, leading and controlling – described in Chapter 1, planning is considered by many practitioners to be the most fundamental as arguably everything else stems from planning. Yet planning is also the most controversial management function. How do managers plan for the future in a constantly changing environment? The economic, political and social turmoil of recent years has sparked a renewed interest in organizational planning, particularly planning for crises and unexpected events, yet it also has some managers questioning whether planning is even worthwhile in a world that is in constant flux. Planners cannot fully determine uncertain futures. Planning cannot tame a turbulent environment. However, although history does not repeat itself, themes do and signals from the market can be interpreted by astute managers. A statement by General Colin Powell, former US secretary of state, offers a warning for managers: *'No battle plan survives contact with the enemy.'*[3]

Does that mean it is useless for managers to make plans? Of course not. No plan can be perfect, but without plans and goals, organizations and employees flounder. However, good managers understand that plans should be flexible and react to necessary change to meet shifting conditions. Admiral Lord Nelson used to discuss battle plans with his captains before his many sea battles (primarily against Bonaparte's navy) in the nineteenth century; but his captains were instructed to use their own judgement in the battle once it had got under way. Nelson had a battle plan but knew that the enemy could well vary their strategy on the day of engagement itself. Nelson also was concerned about restoring social order in the defeated country when the enemy was vanquished. Military intervention without subsequent plans to restore order, especially when dictatorships are eliminated, has too often been the case in current geo-politics.

In this chapter, we explore the process of planning and consider how managers develop effective plans. Special attention is given to goal setting, for that is where planning starts. Then we discuss the various types of plans that managers use to help the organization achieve those goals. We also take a look at planning approaches that help managers deal with uncertainty, such as contingency planning, scenario building and crisis planning. Finally, we examine new approaches to planning that emphasize[4] the involvement of employees (and sometimes other stakeholders) in strategic thinking and execution. Chapter 8 will look at strategic planning in depth and examine a number of strategic options that managers can use in a competitive environment. In Chapter 9, we look at management decision-making. Appropriate decision-making techniques are crucial to selecting the organization's goals, plans and strategic options. Perhaps in the future artificial intelligence can be deployed with complex algorithms to aid decision-makers. It is evident that Google and Facebook as well as major stockbrokers use decision-making algorithms within their business models.

Goal setting and planning overview

A goal is a desired future circumstance or condition that the organization attempts to realize. Goals are important because organizations exist for a purpose, and goals define and state that purpose. A plan is a blueprint for goal achievement and specifies the necessary resource allocations, schedules, tasks and other actions. Goals specify future ends; plans specify today's means. The concept of planning usually incorporates both ideas; it means determining the organization's goals and defining the means for achieving them.[5]

Levels of goals and plans

Exhibit 7.1 illustrates the levels of goals and plans in an organization. The planning process starts with a formal mission that defines the basic purpose of the organization, especially for external audiences. The mission is the basis for the strategic (company) level of goals and plans, which in turn shapes the tactical (divisional) level and the operational (departmental) level.[6] Top managers are typically responsible for establishing *strategic* goals and plans that reflect a commitment to both organizational efficiency and effectiveness, as described in Chapter 1. *Tactical* goals and plans are the responsibility of middle managers, such as the heads of major divisions or functional units. A division manager will formulate tactical plans that focus on the major actions the division must take to fulfil its part in the strategic plan set by top management. *Operational* plans identify the specific procedures or processes needed at lower levels of the organization, such as individual departments and employees. Frontline managers and supervisors develop operational plans that focus on specific tasks and processes and that help meet tactical and strategic goals. Planning at each level supports the other levels.

The overall planning process, illustrated in Exhibit 7.2, prevents managers from thinking merely in terms of day-to-day activities. The process begins when managers develop the overall plan for the organization by clearly defining mission and strategic (company-level) goals. Second, they translate the plan into action, which includes defining tactical objectives and plans, developing a 'strategy map' to

EXHIBIT 7.1 Levels of goals and plans

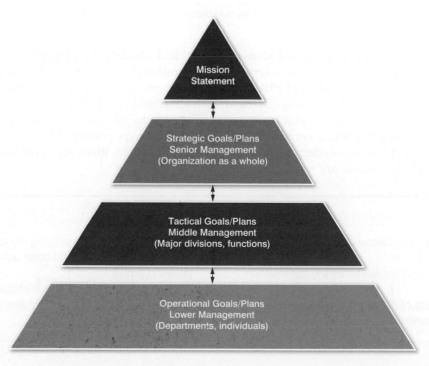

EXHIBIT 7.2 The organizational planning process

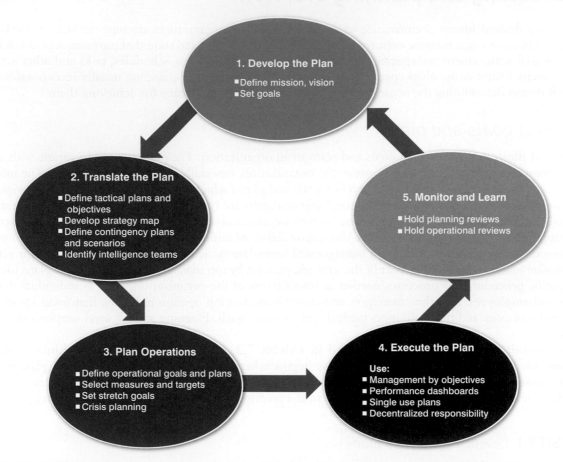

1. Develop the Plan
- Define mission, vision
- Set goals

2. Translate the Plan
- Define tactical plans and objectives
- Develop strategy map
- Define contingency plans and scenarios
- Identify intelligence teams

5. Monitor and Learn
- Hold planning reviews
- Hold operational reviews

3. Plan Operations
- Define operational goals and plans
- Select measures and targets
- Set stretch goals
- Crisis planning

4. Execute the Plan

Use:
- Management by objectives
- Performance dashboards
- Single use plans
- Decentralized responsibility

SOURCE: Robert S. Kaplan and David P. Norton, 'Mastering the Management System', *Harvard Business Review* (January 2008): 63–77.

align goals, formulating contingency and scenario plans, and identifying intelligence teams to analyze major competitive issues. Third, managers lay out the operational factors needed to achieve goals. This involves devising operational goals and plans, selecting the measures and targets that will be used to determine if things are on track, and identifying stretch goals and crisis plans that might need to be put into action. Tools for executing the plan include management by objectives, performance dashboards, single-use plans and decentralized responsibility. Finally, managers periodically review plans to learn from results and shift plans as needed, starting a new planning cycle. Planning is far from being a static activity and multiple iterations are often necessary.

REFLECTION

- Planning is the most fundamental of the four management functions.
- A **goal** is a desired future state that the organization wants to realize.
- **Planning** is the act of determining goals and defining the means of achieving them.

- A **plan** is a blueprint specifying the resource allocations, schedules and other actions necessary for attaining goals.
- Planning helps managers think about the future rather than thinking merely in terms of day-to-day activities.

Goal setting in organizations

The overall planning process begins with a mission statement and goals for the organization as a whole. Goals don't just appear on their own in organizations. Goals are *socially constructed*, which means they are defined by an individual or group. Managers typically have different ideas about what goals should be, so they discuss and negotiate which goals to pursue. Cultural diversity in a MNC complicates the process but there is a consensus in the literature that the planning process is more comprehensive as multiple viewpoints surface to be debated,

The Shoptalk section below describes the process of coalition building that often occurs during goal setting.

 MANAGER'S SHOPTALK

Who sets the goals? Individual manager versus coalition

Organizations perform many activities and pursue many goals simultaneously to accomplish an overall mission. But who decides what mission and goals to strive for? Pursuing some goals means that others have to be delayed or set aside, which means managers often disagree about priorities. After China's Zhejiang Geely Holding Group bought Volvo Car Corporation, the Chinese and European managers disagreed strongly. The European managers wanted to continue pursuing goals of providing safe, reliable, family-friendly vehicles for a stable market. The new Chinese owners and managers, on the other hand, wanted to expand aggressively into the super-luxury car market. The goals of the two sides were mutually exclusive, so managers had to negotiate and come to some agreement on which direction the company would take.

In April 2012, following a main board reorganization at Beiersdorf AG, a new CEO was appointed from outside the industry of skin care and other personal products. The incoming CEO was described in the media at the time as being more aggressive than his predecessor. Stefan F. Heidenreich was regarded as bringing to Beiersdorf AG (known worldwide for its NIVEA brand) a number of required executive qualities. These included his proven track record of corporate restructuring and dealing with powerful equity 'blockholders'. As an industry outsider he knew that he would have to work hard to gain the trust of employees who were used to a stable corporate culture based on reliability, consis-

tency and trust. One significant strategic issue he had to address early was financial failure – arising from the acquisition of C-Bons, a Chinese equity investment that the previous board had executed. The financial statements for 2011 show the multi million impairment costs that were written off.

Powerful, motivating goals that unite people are typically established not by a single manager, but by developing a coalition. *Coalitional management* involves building an alliance of people who support a manager's goals and can influence other people to accept and work towards them. Being an effective 'coalitional' manager involves three key steps:

- **Talk to customers and other managers.** Building a coalition requires talking to many people both inside and outside the organization. Coalitional managers solicit the views of employees and key customers. They talk to other managers all across the organization to get a sense of what people care about and learn what challenges and opportunities they face. A manager can learn who believes in and supports a particular direction and goals, and who is opposed to them and the reasons for the opposition. The senior management of Singapore-based fashion company, Zanora, personally telephone customers who complain – they do not leave it to customer service representatives.

- **Address conflicts.** Good managers don't let conflicts over goals simmer and detract from goal accomplishment or hurt the organization. At Toyota, for example, the recent recall crisis exposed a longstanding internal conflict between managers who wanted to pursue goals of faster growth and higher profit margins, and those who believed that rapid growth would strain the company's ability to ensure quality and reliability. Each side is blaming the other for the recent problems, but it is the failure of managers to unite towards a shared goal that is largely to blame. There is a need for cohesion in the senior management team.

- **Break down barriers and promote cross-silo cooperation.** A final step is to break down boundaries and get people to cooperate and collaborate across departments, divisions and levels. When Colin Powell was chairman of the US Joint Chiefs of Staff, he regularly brought together the heads of the Army, Air Force, Navy and Marines so they could understand one another's viewpoints and come together around key goals. Cross-enterprise understanding and cooperation is essential so that the entire organization will be aligned towards accomplishing desired goals.

As a manager, remember that you will accomplish more and be more effective as part of a coalition, rather than as an individual actor. When there are goals that are highly important to you, take steps to build a coalition to support them. Throw your support behind other managers when appropriate. Do remember that building positive relationships, discussion and especially negotiation are key skills to development and maintain for good management interaction.

SOURCES: Stephen Friedman and James K. Sebenius, 'Organization Transformation: The Quiet Role of Coalitional Leadership', *Ivey Business Journal* (January–February 2009), www.iveybusinessjournal.com/topics/leadership/organizational-transformation-the-quiet-role-of-coalitional-leadership (accessed January 27, 2012); G. R. Ferris, R. Blass, C. Douglas, R.W. Kolodinsky and D.C.Treadway,, 'Political Skill in Organizations',*Journal of Management* (June 2007): 290–320; Norihiko Shirouzu, 'Chinese Begin Volvo Overhaul', *The Wall Street Journal*, June 7, 2011, B1; and Norihiko Shirouzu, 'Inside Toyota, Executives Trade Blame Over Debacle', *The Wall Street Journal*, April 14, 2010, A1.

Organizational mission

At the top of the goal hierarchy is the mission being the organization's primary reason for existence. The mission describes the organization's values, aspirations and its reason for being. A well-defined mission is the basis for development of all subsequent goals and plans. Without a mission clarity, goals and plans may be developed haphazardly and are unlikely to take the organization in the direction it needs to go. One of the defining attributes of successful companies is that they have a clear mission that guides decisions and actions. When management actions and decisions go against the mission, organizations may get into trouble. Sam Walton, founder of Walmart, told his managers that the fledgling company was going to overtake Sears on the day he heard that Sears had reneged on its satisfaction guaranteed policy. At the time, Walmart had $20 billion less in sales than Sears, but Walton believed that stepping away from a core part of its mission would set Sears on a downhill path and indeed, the company never recovered. Some people share the view that Walmart made a similar blunder when it began trying to court upscale customers, as described in the opening example.[7]

The formal mission statement is a broadly stated definition of purpose that distinguishes the organization from others of a similar type. Too often they can be rhetoric and have low impact on employee behaviour or how the organization really behaves with its public. The difference between the espoused values and the real values if made public can be very damaging to corporate reputations.

'A real purpose can't just be words on paper. . . . If you get it right, people will feel great about what they're doing, clear about their goals and excited to get to work every morning.'
      — ROY M. SPENCE JR, AUTHOR OF IT'S NOT WHAT YOU SELL, IT'S WHAT YOU STAND FOR

Although most corporate mission statements aren't as broad or quite as inspiring as Holstee's as illustrated in Exhibit 7.3, a well-designed mission statement can enhance employee motivation and organizational performance.[8]

The content of a mission statement often describes the company's basic business activities and purpose, as well as the values that guide the company. Some mission statements also describe company characteristics such as desired markets and customers, product quality, location of facilities and attitude towards employees. An example of a short, straightforward mission statement comes from Waitrose, part of the UK-based John

EXHIBIT 7.3 An innovative mission statement: the Holstee Manifesto

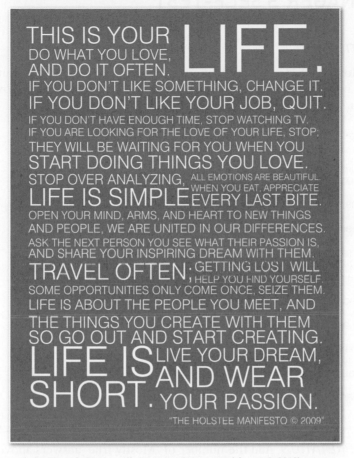

Lewis Partnership. 'Waitrose believes in championing British produce, treading lightly on the environment, supporting responsible sourcing and treating people fairly.'

The core values of Norwegian Air Shuttle ASA are concisely expressed as just three values: simplicity, directness and relevance. Fedex has several core values in its mission statement that address people, service, innovation, efficiency, integrity and loyalty.

TAKE A MOMENT

As a new manager, you will need to understand what you want for your own future. Complete the New Manager Self-Test to get some insight into whether you have a personal mission that guides your life.

Goals and plans

Strategic goals, sometimes called *official goals*, are broad statements describing where the organization wants to be in the future. These goals pertain to the organization as a whole rather than to specific divisions or departments.

Strategic plans define the action steps by which the company intends to attain strategic goals. The strategic plan is the blueprint that defines the organizational activities and resource allocations – in the form of cash, personnel, space and facilities – required for meeting these targets. Strategic planning tends to be long term and may define organizational action steps from 2 to 5 years in the future. The purpose of strategic plans is to turn organizational goals into realities within that time period.

NEW MANAGER'S SELF-TEST

My personal mission

INSTRUCTIONS: How much do you think about the positive outcomes you want in your future? Do you have a personal mission to guide your life? Indicate whether each item below is 'Mostly false' or 'Mostly true' for you.

		Mostly true	Mostly false
1	I can describe a compelling image of my future.	☐	☐
2	Life to me seems more exciting than routine.	☐	☐
3	I have created very clear life goals and aims.	☐	☐
4	I feel that my personal existence is very meaningful.	☐	☐
5	In my life, I see a reason for being here.	☐	☐
6	I have discovered a satisfying 'calling' in life.	☐	☐
7	I feel that I have a unique life purpose to fulfil.	☐	☐
8	I will know when I have achieved my purpose.	☐	☐
9	I talk to people about my personal mission in life.	☐	☐
10	I know how to harness my creativity and use my talents.	☐	☐

SCORING & INTERPRETATION Add the number of 'Mostly true' answers above for your score: ___. A score of 7 or above indicates that you are in great shape with respect to your life's personal mission. A score of 3 or below would suggest that you have not given much thought to a mission for your life. A score of 4–6 would be about average.

Creating or discovering a personal mission is difficult work for most people. It doesn't happen easily, or by accident. A personal mission is just like an organizational mission in that it requires focused thought and effort. Spend some time thinking about a mission for yourself and write it down.

SOURCES: The ideas for this questionnaire were drawn primarily from Chris Rogers, 'Are You Deciding on Purpose?' *Fast Company* (February–March 1998): 114–117; and J. Crumbaugh, 'Cross-Validation of a Purpose-in-Life Test Based on Frankl's Concepts', *Journal of Individual Psychology* 24 (1968): 74–81.

After strategic goals are formulated, the next step is to define tactical goals, which are the results that major divisions and departments within the organization intend to achieve. These goals apply to middle management and describe what major subunits must do for the organization to achieve its overall goals. Tactical plans are designed to help execute the major strategic plans and to accomplish a specific part of the company's strategy.[9]

Tactical plans typically have a shorter time horizon than strategic plans – over the next year or so. The word *tactical* originally comes from the military. In a business or non-profit organization, tactical plans define what major departments and organizational subunits will do to implement the organization's strategic plan. For example, a tactical goal for a location's scouting division might be to identify three new locations a year that fit a target market of educated, adventurous consumers and could support a given venture store. Tactical goals and plans help top managers implement their overall strategic plan. Normally, it is the middle manager's job to take the broad strategic plan and identify specific tactical plans.

TAKE A MOMENT

Go to the Experiential Exercise online that pertains to developing action plans for accomplishing strategic goals.

 CONCEPT CONNECTION

Walt Disney used to say, 'I make movies for children and the child in all of us.' DreamWorks, according to CEO Jeffrey Katzenberg, 'makes movies for adults and the adult that exists in every child.' That subtle difference in wording provides the key to the studio's sense of **mission** and the way it sets itself apart. Starting with *Shrek* in 2001, a film where the villain tortured the Gingerbread Man by dipping him into a glass of milk, DreamWorks has produced feature-length animated films aimed at appealing equally to adults and children by being irreverent and a little subversive.

The results expected from departments, work groups and individuals are the operational goals. They are precise and measurable. 'Process 150 sales applications each week', 'Achieve 90 per cent of deliveries on time', 'Reduce overtime by 10 per cent next month', and 'Develop two new online courses in accounting' are examples of operational goals. An operational goal for a product development department could be to identify ten new and intriguing items a week to phase into stores. In the human resources department, an operational goal might be to keep turnover to less than 5 per cent a year so that there are longtime employees who have close relationships with customers.

Operational plans are developed at the lower levels of the organization to specify action steps towards achieving operational goals and to support tactical plans. The operational plan is the department manager's tool for daily and weekly operations. Goals are stated in quantitative terms, and the department plan describes how goals will be achieved. Operational planning specifies plans for department managers, supervisors and individual employees. Schedules are an important component of operational planning. Schedules define precise time frames for the completion of each operational goal required for the organization's tactical and strategic goals. Operational planning also must be coordinated with the budget because resources must be allocated for desired activities.

Align goals using a strategy map

Effectively designed organizational goals are aligned; that is, they are consistent and mutually supportive so that the achievement of goals at low levels permits the attainment of high-level goals. Organizational performance is an outcome of how well these interdependent elements are aligned, so that individuals, teams and departments are working in concert to attain specific goals that ultimately help the organization achieve high performance and fulfil its mission.[10]

An increasingly popular technique for aligning goals into a hierarchy is the strategy map. A strategy map is a visual representation of the key drivers of an organization's success. Because the strategy map shows how specific goals and plans[11] in each area are linked, it provides a very useful way for managers to see the cause-and-effect relationships among goals and plans. The simplified strategy map in Exhibit 7.4 illustrates four key areas that contribute to a firm's long-term success – learning and growth, internal processes, customer service and financial performance – and how the various goals and plans in each area link to the other areas. This framework was reintroduced by Kaplan and Cooper in 2008. The idea is that learning and growth goals serve as a foundation to help achieve goals for excellent internal business processes. Meeting business process goals, in its turn, enables the organization to meet goals for customer service and satisfaction, which helps the organization achieve its financial goals and optimize its value to all stakeholders. The three other perspectives of Kaplan's balanced scorecard clearly interact and ultimately reflect on the financial perspective. Surprisingly, the customer perspective was no part of Kaplan and Coopers' original 'four perspectives' analytical framework.

In the strategy map shown in Exhibit 7.4, the organization has learning and growth goals that include developing employees, enabling continuous learning and knowledge sharing, and building a culture of innovation. Achieving these will help the organization build internal business processes that promote good relationships with suppliers and partners, improve the quality and flexibility of operations, and excel at developing innovative products and services. Accomplishing internal process goals, in turn, enables the organization to maintain strong relationships with customers, be a leader in quality and reliability, and provide innovative solutions to emerging customer needs. At the top of the strategy map, the accomplishment of these lower-level goals facilitates the organization to increase revenues in existing markets, increasing productivity and efficiency, and growing through selling new products and services and serving new market segments.

In a real-life organization, its tailored strategy map would typically be much more complex and would state concrete, specific goals relevant to the particular business. However, the generic map in Exhibit 7.4

EXHIBIT 7.4 A strategy map for aligning goals

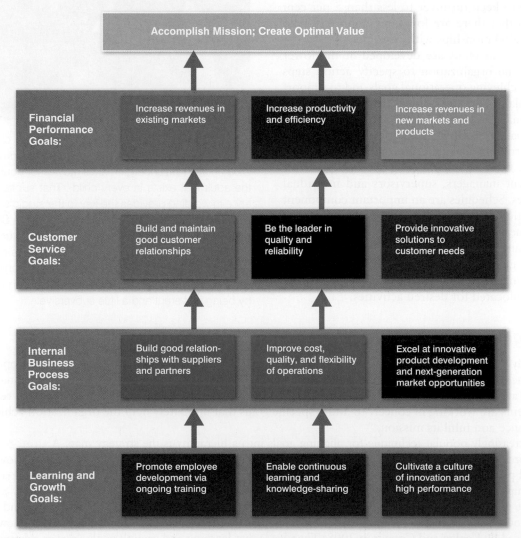

SOURCES: Robert S. Kaplan and David P. Norton, 'Mastering the Management System', *Harvard Business Review* (January 2008): 63–77; and R. S. Kaplan and D. P. Norton, 'Having Trouble with Your Strategy? Then Map It', *Harvard Business Review* (September–October 2000): 167–176.

gives an idea of how managers can map goals and plans so that they are mutually supportive. The strategy map is also a good way to communicate goals because all employees can see what part they play in helping the organization accomplish its mission.

REFLECTION

- Planning starts with the organization's purpose or reason for existence, which is called its **mission**.
- A **mission statement** is a broadly stated definition of the organization's basic business scope and operations that distinguishes it from similar types of organizations.
- Goals begin with broad strategic goals, followed by more specific tactical goals and then operational goals.
- Plans are defined similarly, with strategic, tactical and operational plans used to achieve the goals.
- **Strategic goals** are broad statements of where the organization wants to be in the future and pertain to the organization as a whole rather than to specific divisions or departments.
- **Strategic plans** are the action steps by which an organization intends to attain strategic goals.

- The outcomes that major divisions and departments must achieve for the organization to reach its overall goals are called **tactical goals**.
- **Tactical plans** are designed to help execute major strategic plans and to accomplish a specific part of the company's strategy.
- **Operational goals** are specific, measurable results that are expected from departments, work groups and individuals.
- **Operational plans** specify the action steps towards achieving operational goals and support tactical activities.
- Goals and plans need to be in alignment so that they are consistent and mutually supportive.
- A **strategy map** is a visual representation of the key drivers of an organization's success, showing the cause-and-effect relationship among goals and plans.

Operational planning

Managers use operational goals to direct employees and resources towards achieving specific outcomes that enable the organization to perform efficiently and effectively. One consideration is how to establish effective goals. Then managers use a number of planning approaches, including management by objectives (MBO), single-use plans and standing plans. Some companies use disaster planning so they are better prepared for dealing with crises that may arise in the future.

Criteria for effective goals

Research has identified certain factors, shown in Exhibit 7.5, that characterize effective goals. First and foremost, goals need to be *specific and measurable*. When possible, operational goals should be expressed in quantitative terms, such as increasing profits by 2 per cent, having zero incomplete sales order forms or increasing average teacher effectiveness ratings from 3.5 to 3.7. Not all goals can be expressed in numerical terms, but vague goals have little motivating power for employees. By necessity, goals are qualitative as well as quantitative. The important point is that the goals be precisely defined and allow for measurable progress. Effective goals also have a *defined time period* that specifies the date on which goal attainment will be measured. For instance, school administrators might set a deadline for improving teacher effectiveness ratings by the end of the 2013 school term. When a goal involves a 2- to 3-year time horizon, setting specific dates for achieving parts of it is a good way to keep people on track towards the goal.

Goals should *cover key result areas*. Goals cannot be set for every aspect of employee behaviour or organizational performance; if they were, their sheer number would render them meaningless. Instead, managers establish goals based on the idea of *choice and clarity*. A few carefully chosen, clear and direct goals can focus organizational attention, energy and resources more powerfully.[12]

Managers should set goals that are *challenging but realistic*. When goals are unrealistic, they set employees up for failure and lead to a decrease in employee morale. However, if goals are too easy, employees may not feel motivated. Goals should also be *linked to rewards*. The ultimate impact of goals depends on the extent

🌱 GREEN POWER

The Bees buzz

Moving sustainability beyond fashionable 'buzz-words' is a focus of North Carolina-based **Burt's Bees** – makers of personal care products made from natural substances (including, but not limited to, beeswax). Employees at Burt's Bees get down and dirty with the annual companywide Dumpster Dive, sorting through accumulated rubbish that reached monthly totals of up to 40 tons in one recent year. Employees recommitted to a zero-waste goal, which the company achieved in 2009. With 100 per cent employee engagement, Burt's Bees has now focused on achieving a loftier 'zero-waste, zero-carbon' goal by 2020.

Sustainability planning and goal-setting at Burt's Bees engages employees in activities such as reducing water use by 'steam-cleaning' containers (resulting in a 90 per cent water reduction) or extending the paper label on lip balm to eliminate shrink-wrapping (eliminating 900 miles of film). Managerial goals also extend to consumer education through the 'Natural Vs' campaign (aimed at clarifying industry terms, such as *natural*). Through all its efforts, Burt's Bees works towards a goal of helping take the 'sting' out of environmental problems.

SOURCE: Christopher Marquis and Bobbi Thomason, 'Leadership and the First and Last Mile of Sustainability', *Ivey Business Journal,* September–October 2010, www. iveybusinessjournal.com/topics/leadership/leadership-and-the-first-and-last-mile-of-sustainability (accessed August 2, 2012).

EXHIBIT 7.5 Characteristics of effective goals

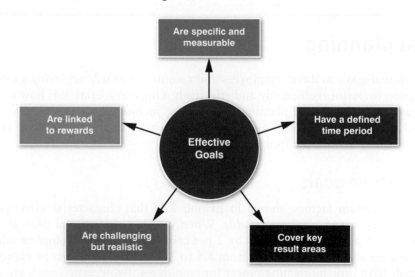

to which salary increases, promotions and awards are based on goal achievement. Employees pay attention to what gets noticed and rewarded in the organization.[13]

Management by objectives (MBO)

Described by renowned management scholar Peter Drucker in his 1954 book, *The Practice of Management*, management by objectives has remained a popular and compelling method for defining goals and monitoring progress towards achieving them. Management by objectives (MBO) is a system whereby managers and employees define goals for every department, project and person and use them to monitor subsequent performance.[14]

A model of the essential steps of the MBO system is presented in Exhibit 7.6. Four major activities make MBO successful:

1 *Set goals.* Setting goals involves employees at all levels and looks beyond day-to-day activities to answer the question, 'What are we trying to accomplish?' Managers heed the criteria of effective goals described in the previous section and make sure to assign responsibility for goal accomplishment. However, goals should be derived jointly. Mutual agreement between employee and supervisor creates the strongest commitment to achieving goals. In the case of teams, all team members may participate in setting goals.

2 *Develop action plans.* An *action plan* defines the course of action needed to achieve the stated goals. Action plans are made for both individuals and departments.

3 *Review progress.* A periodic progress review is important to ensure that action plans are working. These reviews can occur informally between managers and subordinates, where the organization may wish to conduct 3-, 6-, or 9-month reviews during the year. This periodic checkup allows managers and employees to see whether they are on target or whether corrective action is needed. Managers and employees should not be locked into predefined behaviour and must be willing to take whatever steps are necessary to produce meaningful results. The point of MBO is to achieve goals. The action plan can be changed whenever goals are not being met.

4 *Appraise overall performance.*[15] The final step in MBO is to evaluate whether annual goals have been achieved for both individuals and departments. Success or failure to achieve goals can become part of the performance appraisal system and the designation of salary increases and other rewards. The appraisal of departmental and overall corporate performance shapes goals for the next year. The MBO cycle repeats itself annually.

EXHIBIT 7.6 Model of the MBO process

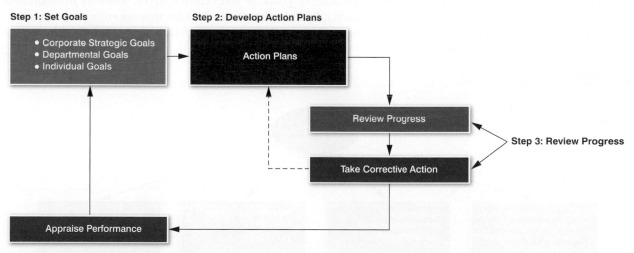

Many companies, including Intel, Tenneco, Black & Decker and DuPont, have used MBO, and most managers think that it is an effective management tool. Tim O'Shaughnessy, founder and CEO of US Living-Social, a daily deal website with more than 5000 employees and 46 million members in 25 countries, uses the principles of MBO to keep the fast-growing business on track. O'Shaughnessy meets regularly with the heads of every department to set goals for items such as sales and membership growth and develop action plans for how to achieve them. He is obsessive about tracking metrics to see whether things are on target towards meeting the numbers. Each week, O'Shaughnessy meets with department heads to talk about their key metrics and review their progress. *'The more data you gather, the more likely you'll be successful in the long term,'* he says.[16]

Most managers, like Tim O'Shaughnessy, believe they are better oriented towards goal achievement when MBO is used.

MBO can provide a number of benefits which are summarized in Exhibit 7.7. Corporate goals are more likely to be achieved when they focus manager and employee efforts. Using a performance measurement system such as MBO helps employees see how their jobs and performance contribute to the business, giving them a sense of ownership and commitment.[17]

Performance is improved when employees are committed to attaining the goal, are motivated because they help decide what is expected, and are free to be resourceful. Goals at lower levels are aligned with and enable the attainment of goals at top management levels.

TAKE A MOMENT

You can practice setting goals and developing action plans by completing the Small Group Breakout Exercise online.

However, like any system, MBO can cause problems when used improperly. For example, an overemphasis on 'meeting the goals' can obscure the means that people use to get there. People may cut corners, ignore potential problems, or behave unethically just to meet the targets. In addition, MBO cannot stand alone; it is only a part of effectively managing people to achieve goals. MBO is 'like training wheels on a bicycle'.[18]

It gets you started, but it isn't all you need. In the USA, for example, the implementation of rigorous MBO-type systems in urban police departments and school systems led to cheating on the numbers, with people lying about their work performance in order to score well on the metrics. The means for achieving goals is just as important as the outcomes. 'What gets measured gets done' is a well-known truism. A new systematic approach that has recently emerged is called management by means (MBM), which focuses attention on the methods and processes used to achieve goals. A term coined by H. Thomas Johnson and his co-authors in their book *Profit Beyond Measures*, MBM is based on the idea that when managers pursue their activities in the right way, positive outcomes will result. MBM focuses people on considering the means rather than just on reaching the goals.[19]

EXHIBIT 7.7 MBO benefits

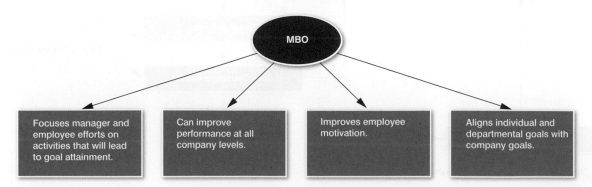

At Toyota, the 'sticky accelerator' problem has been blamed in part on a breakdown between goals[20] and the methods used to achieve them. Years of aggressive growth goals eventually strained managers' ability to control the means by which the goals were achieved. People had to be hired quickly, with little time for adequate training and development. Therefore, the limited number of highly trained managers and engineers had to do more to keep pace towards the goals. Since the crisis, Toyota has refocused on improving the abilities of managers and employees to use the right means of achieving ambitious goals. Toyota Motor Company pursues the Truth North vision of perfectionism, based on the pillars of respect for people and continuous improvement. By following the plan-do-check-adjust cycle, it constantly reinvents itself in order to reach ever-higher quality and performance standards at low costs. Their culture of contradictions has driven the success of the Toyota Production System, which has become a worldwide-recognized model for business excellence. However, the paradoxical nature of this business concept had put increasing pressure on management who were no longer able to control the means of goal achievement. People had to be hired quickly, with little time for adequate training and development, so that a limited number of highly trained managers and engineers had to do more to keep pace towards the goals. Recent recalls of cars with 'sticky accelerators' showed how fundamental principles of the Toyota Way of quality and reliability had been violated as a result. Since the crisis, Toyota has refocused on improving the abilities of managers and employees to use the right means of achieving ambitious goals.

Single-use and standing plans

Single-use plans are developed to achieve a set of goals that are not likely to be repeated in the future. Standing plans are ongoing plans that provide guidance for tasks or situations that occur repeatedly within the organization. Exhibit 7.8 outlines the major types of single-use and standing plans. Single-use plans typically include both programmes and projects. The primary standing plans are organizational policies, rules[21] and procedures. Standing plans generally pertain to matters such as employee illness, absences, smoking, discipline, hiring and dismissal. Many companies are discovering a need to develop standing plans regarding the use of social media. According to the Society for Human Resource Management, 40 per cent of organizations surveyed have a formal social media policy, and more than half of them include a statement about the company's right to monitor social media usage. Good social media policies are clear, simple and specific. They define appropriate behaviour, clearly specify what is off-limits, let employees know the company can monitor their online activities, and explain the consequences for breaking the rules.

EXHIBIT 7.8 Major types of single-use and standing plans

Single-use plans	Standing plans
Programme	**Policy**
■ Plans for attaining a one-time organizational goal	■ Broad in scope – general guide to action
■ Major undertaking that may take several years to complete	■ Based on organization's overall goals/strategic plan
■ Large in scope; may be associated with several projects	■ Defines boundaries within which to make decisions

Examples Building a new headquarters
        Converting all paper files to digital
	Examples Sexual harassment policies
	        Internet and social media policies

Project	**Rule**
■ Also a set of plans for attaining a one-time goal	■ Narrow in scope
■ Smaller in scope and complexity than a programme; shorter in horizon	■ Describes how a specific action is to be performed
■ Often one part of a larger programme	■ May apply to specific setting

Examples Renovating the office
        Setting up a company intranet
	Example No eating rule in areas of company where
	        employees are visible to the public

	Procedure
	■ Sometimes called a standard operating procedure
	■ Defines a precise series of steps to attain certain goals
	Examples Procedures for issuing refunds Procedures for handling employee grievances

REFLECTION

- Managers formulate goals that are specific and measurable, cover key result areas, are challenging but realistic, have a defined time period and are linked to rewards.
- Types of operational planning include management by objectives, single-use plans and standing plans.
- **Management by objectives (MBO)** is a method whereby managers and employees define goals for every department, project and person and use them to monitor subsequent performance.[22]
- MBO includes the steps of setting goals, developing action plans, reviewing progress and appraising performance.

- A recent approach that focuses people on the methods and processes used to attain results, rather than on the results themselves, is called **management by means (MBM)**.
- **Single-use plans** are plans that are developed to achieve a set of goals that are unlikely to be repeated in the future.
- **Standing plans** are ongoing plans that are used to provide guidance for tasks that occur repeatedly in the organization.
- One example of a standing plan is a social media policy.

Benefits and limitations of planning

Some managers believe planning ahead is necessary to accomplish anything, whereas others think planning limits personal and organizational performance. Both opinions have merit, because planning can have both advantages and disadvantages.

Research indicates that planning generally positively affects a company's performance. Some reasons for this are:[23]

- *Goals and plans provide a source of motivation and commitment.* Planning can reduce uncertainty for employees and clarify what they should accomplish. The lack of a clear goal hampers motivation because people don't understand what they're working towards.

- *Goals and plans guide resource allocation.* Planning helps managers decide where they need to allocate resources, such as employees, money and equipment. At Netflix, for example, a goal of having more video offerings online rather than in DVD format means allocating more funds for Internet movie rights and spending more of managers' time developing alliances with other companies.[24]

- *Goals and plans are a guide to action.* Planning focuses attention on specific targets and directs employee efforts towards important outcomes. Planning helps managers and other employees know what actions they need to take to achieve the goal.

- *Goals and plans set a standard of performance.* Because planning and goal setting define desired outcomes, they also establish performance criteria so managers can measure whether things are on- or off-track. Goals and plans provide a standard of assessment.

Despite these benefits, some researchers also think planning can hurt organizational performance in some ways.[25]

Thus, managers should understand the limitations to planning, particularly when the organization is operating in a turbulent environment:

- *Goals and plans can create a false sense of certainty.* Having a plan can give managers a false sense that they know what the future will be like. However, all planning is based on assumptions, and managers can't know what the future holds for their industry or for their competitors, suppliers and customers.

- *Goals and plans may cause rigidity in a turbulent environment.* A related problem is that planning can lock the organization into specific goals, plans and time frames, which may no longer be appropriate. Managing under conditions of change and uncertainty requires a degree of flexibility. Managers who believe in 'staying the course' will often stick with a faulty plan even when conditions change dramatically.

■ *Goals and plans can get in the way of intuition and creativity.* Success often comes from creativity and intuition, which can be hampered by too much routine planning. For example, during the process of setting goals in the MBO process described earlier, employees might play it safe to achieve objectives rather than offer creative ideas. Similarly, managers sometimes quash creative ideas from employees that do not fit with predetermined action plans.[26]

'In preparing for battle, I have always found that plans are useless, but planning is indispensable.'
– DWIGHT D. EISENHOWER (1890–1969), US PRESIDENT

REFLECTION

- Benefits of planning and goal setting include serving as a source of motivation, determining resource allocation, providing a guide to action and setting a standard for performance measurement.

- Limitations of planning and goal setting include the potential to create a false sense of certainty, create rigidity that hinders response to a turbulent environment, and get in the way of creativity and intuition.

Planning for a turbulent environment

Considering the limitations to planning, what are managers to do? One way managers can gain benefits from planning and control its limitations is by using innovative planning approaches that are in tune with today's turbulent environment. Three approaches that help brace the organization for unexpected – even unimaginable – events are contingency planning, building scenarios and crisis planning.

Contingency planning

When organizations are operating in a highly uncertain environment or dealing with long time horizons, sometimes planning can seem like a waste of time. Indeed, inflexible plans may hinder rather than help an organization's performance in the face of rapid technological, social, economic or other environmental change. In these cases,[27] managers can develop multiple future alternatives to help them form more adaptive plans.

Contingency plans define company responses to be taken in the case of emergencies, setbacks or unexpected conditions. To develop contingency plans, managers identify important factors in the environment, such as possible economic downturns, declining markets, increases in cost of supplies, new technological developments or safety accidents. Managers then forecast a range of alternative responses to the most likely high-impact contingencies, focusing on the worst case. For example, if sales fall 20 per cent and prices drop 8 per cent, what will the company do? Managers can develop contingency plans that might include layoffs, emergency budgets, new sales efforts or new markets. A real-life example comes from the Oscars Ceremonies. What happens if writers or actors go on strike just before the annual Academy[28] Awards show? The Academy of Motion Picture Arts and Sciences has to have contingency plans in place to put the show on using alternatives such as film clips, historical background and other out-of-the-ordinary ideas. *'We have an obligation to the art form to present the Oscars, so we have to deal with the possibility of not being able to do the show because of pickets or agreements not being concluded,'* said Sid Ganis of the academy.

TAKE A MOMENT

As a new manager, get in the mindset of scenario planning. Go to www.shell.com/home/content/future_energy/scenarios/, where Shell Oil publishes the outline of its annual scenario-planning exercise. You might also want to do an Internet search and type in 'national intelligence agency scenarios' to find links to reports of global trends and scenario planning done by various organizations.

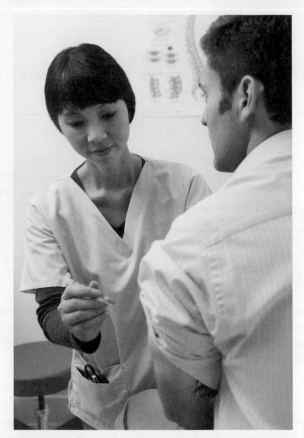

CONCEPT CONNECTION

After several outbreaks of the H1N1 flu revealed the dangers of widespread diseases, Mike Claver, State Farm Insurance Company's emergency management superintendent, oversaw the development of a thorough **contingency plan** designed to protect State Farm employees during any potential outbreaks in the future. In addition to coordinating with area agencies and encouraging employees to get vaccines, Claver tested the company's ability to function should managers have to ask employees to work at home during an outbreak. More than 1000 people, about 10 per cent of the workforce at the Bloomington, Illinois, headquarters, logged into the company computer network from their homes one August day. Managers used the results of the dry run to fine-tune contingency plans.

Building[29] scenarios

An extension of contingency planning is a forecasting technique known as *scenario building*. Scenario building involves looking at current trends and discontinuities and visualizing future possibilities. Rather than looking only at history and thinking about what has been, managers think about what *could be*. The events that cause the most damage to companies are those that no one even conceived of. In today's tumultuous world, traditional planning can't help managers cope with the many shifting and complex variables that might affect their organizations.

Managers can't predict the future, but they can rehearse a framework within which future events can be managed. Some managers use published global scenarios, such as debt problems in Europe, a slowdown in Asia or global warming, to analyze patterns and driving forces that might affect their industry as a starting point for scenario building. This *abbreviated scenario thinking* can give managers a head start on asking 'What if', leading to increased understanding even before any scenarios are written.[30]

Next, a broad base of managers mentally rehearses different scenarios based on anticipating the varied changes that could affect the organization. Scenarios are like stories that offer alternative vivid pictures of what the future will be like and how managers will respond.[31]

Typically, two to five scenarios are developed for each set of factors, ranging from the most optimistic to the most pessimistic view. For example, after the USA became involved in a military operation in Libya in early 2011, leaders created four broad scenarios of what might happen – two that were positive for the USA and two that could have highly troublesome consequences – and developed plans for how to respond. Similarly, in businesses and other organizations, scenario building forces managers to rehearse mentally what they would do if their best-laid plans collapse.

Crisis planning

Many firms also engage in *crisis planning* to enable them to cope with unexpected events that are so sudden and devastating that they have the potential to destroy the organization if managers aren't prepared with a quick and appropriate response. Because so many things can go wrong in their business, most airlines, such as JetBlue, have teams of people dedicated to crisis planning.

Airlines aren't the only organizations that have to be prepared for potentially devastating events. Crises have become integral features of the organizational environment. Past crises include Hurricane Sandy on the east coast, with massive destruction in New York and New Jersey; the earthquake, tsunami and subsequent

INNOVATIVE **WAY**

JetBlue

Penny Neferis has been the 'worrier in chief' at JetBlue Airways for more than 16 years. As director of care and emergency response, she leads a team that is always thinking about what could go wrong. Neferis's team develops JetBlue's emergency response plan and trains employees in handling a crisis, whether it be an accident, health scare, terrorist attack or natural disaster.

Many organizations weren't prepared when the swine flu outbreak hit the USA in 2009, but JetBlue had procedures in place that could be adapted to the crisis. They quickly set up training to help employees recognize symptoms, provided hand sanitizer and gloves for planes, established reporting procedures and created a plan for how to operate if staff or headquarters personnel were affected. Regardless of where a crisis occurs in the world, Neferis and her team swing into action. Following the earthquake in Haiti, for instance, Neferis immediately set up a task force that coordi-

nated with the Haitian consulate and the Red Cross. The airport in Haiti was closed, but JetBlue, which flies to the Dominican Republic, was able to get supplies and people in.

Neferis has always known that anything can happen in the airline business, but that was never clearer than on 11 September 2001. Neferis says she 'went on autopilot' during the emergency response at Kennedy Airport following the terrorist attacks. Because the airline had crisis plans in place, JetBlue was able to help passengers and ease some of the chaos. The team set up a passenger assistance centre that took passengers from any carrier, not just JetBlue. 'You've got to stay strong and grounded in a crisis,' Neferis says, 'but eventually you have to deal with what you've experienced.' She adds, '*You're also never done with planning. The minute you get comfortable, think you're ready for anything and become overconfident, it's an indication that you're not in the right field. You've got to stay humble.*'[32]

EXHIBIT 7.9 Essential stages of crisis planning

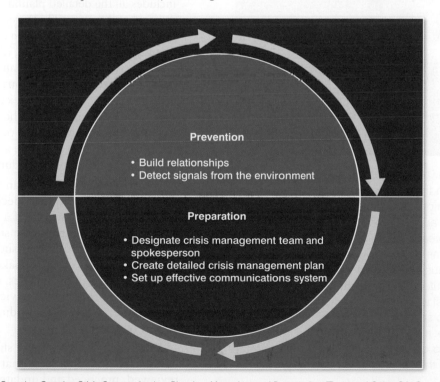

SOURCE: W. Timothy Coombs, *Ongoing Crisis Communication: Planning, Managing, and Responding* (Thousand Oaks, CA: Sage Publications, 1999).

nuclear disaster in Japan; the mass shooting in Aurora, Colorado, movie theatre during the premiere of *The Dark Knight Rises;* the massive BP oil spill in the Gulf of Mexico and the 2015 shootings in the offices of the Charlie Hebdo satirical magazine by jihadists, could be replicated throughout the EU and Africa.

Although crises may vary, a carefully thought-out and coordinated plan can be used to respond to any disaster. In addition, crisis planning reduces the incidence of trouble, just as putting a good lock on a door reduces burglaries.[33]

Exhibit 7.9 outlines two essential stages of crisis planning.[34]

- **Crisis prevention.** The *crisis prevention* stage involves activities that managers undertake to try to prevent crises from occurring and to detect warning signs of potential crises. A critical part of the prevention stage is building open, trusting relationships with key stakeholders such as employees, customers, suppliers, governments, unions and the community. By developing favourable relationships, managers can often prevent crises from happening and respond more effectively to those that cannot be avoided.[35]

  For example, organizations that have open, trusting relationships with employees and unions may avoid crippling labour strikes. At the software firm 37signals, managers prevented a crisis by responding quickly and openly when Campfire, a real-time chat tool for small businesses, kept turning off and on unexpectedly. Customers were furious because they used Campfire to run their organizations. Managers immediately began tweeting with customers and posting regular updates on the company's website to let people know what was going on and that they were working on the problem. If they didn't understand something, they admitted it. 'We responded to every complaint and took the blame every time – even when people went overboard and launched into personal attacks,' said Jason Fried of 37signals. Once the problem was fixed, they gave all customers a free month of service. Thanks to quick action, 37signals came out of the episode with stronger customer loyalty and goodwill than ever.[36]

 CONCEPT CONNECTION

After the Deepwater Horizon oil rig drilling a well for BP exploded in the Gulf of Mexico, US congressman Henry Waxman observed that '*a striking feature of the incident is the apparent lack of an adequate plan to contain the spreading environmental damage.*' BP's CEO at the time, Tony Hayward, admitted Waxman was right. Because BP saw a deep water leak as highly unlikely and touted the Deepwater Horizon as one of the world's most technologically advanced drilling platforms, it had no specific **crisis plan** for an uncontrolled blowout. Since then, BP has committed more than \$US18 billion to cleaning up both the damage to the gulf region and the damage to the BP brand.

- **Crisis preparation.** The *crisis preparation* stage includes all the detailed planning to handle a crisis when it occurs. Three steps in the preparation stage are (1) designating a crisis management team and spokesperson, (2) creating a detailed crisis management plan and (3) setting up an effective communications system. The crisis management team, for example, is a cross-functional group of people who are designated to swing into action if a crisis occurs. The organization should also designate a spokesperson to be the voice of the company during the crisis.[37]

  The crisis management plan (CMP) is a detailed, written plan that specifies the steps to be taken, and by whom, if a crisis occurs. The CMP should include the steps for dealing with various types of crises, such as natural disasters like fires or earthquakes; normal accidents like economic crises, industrial accidents or product and service failures; and abnormal events such as product tampering or acts of terrorism.[38]

  A key point is that a CMP should be a living, changing document that is regularly reviewed, practiced and updated as needed.

REFLECTION

- Managers use innovative planning approaches to cope with today's turbulent environment.
- **Contingency planning** identifies important factors in the environment and defines a range of alternative responses to be taken in the case of emergencies, setbacks or unexpected conditions.
- With **scenario building**, managers look at trends and discontinuities and imagine possible alternative futures to build a framework within which unexpected future events can be managed.

- Scenarios are alternative vivid pictures of what the future might be like.
- Many companies increased their use contingency and scenario planning because of the global financial crisis and volatile economic conditions.
- Crisis planning involves the two major stages of prevention and preparation.

Innovative approaches to planning

The process of planning changes over time, like other aspects of managing, to become more in tune with shifts in the environment and employee[39] attitudes. A fresh approach to planning is to involve everyone in the organization, and sometimes outside stakeholders as well, in the planning process. The evolution to a new approach began with a shift to decentralized planning, which means that planning experts work with managers in major divisions or departments to develop their own goals and plans. Managers throughout the company come up with their own creative solutions to problems and become more committed to following through on the plans. As the environment became even more volatile, top executives saw the benefits of pushing decentralized planning even further by having planning experts work directly with line managers and frontline employees to develop dynamic plans that meet fast-changing needs.

In a complex and competitive business environment, strategic thinking and execution become the expectation of every employee. Planning comes alive when employees are involved in setting goals and determining the means to reach them. The following sections provide some guidelines for innovative planning.

TAKE A MOMENT

Go to the Ethical Dilemma at the end of this chapter that pertains to potential problems with innovative planning approaches.

Set stretch goals for excellence

Stretch goals are reasonable yet highly ambitious goals that are so clear, compelling and imaginative that they fire up employees and engender excellence. Stretch goals are typically so far beyond the current levels that people have to be innovative to find ways to reach them. Consider the following example from Amazon.com.

Asking a group of engineers to create the first Kindle e-reader might be considered what James Collins and Jerry Porras have called a *big hairy audacious goal (BHAG)*. This phrase was first proposed by Collins and Porras in their 1996 article entitled 'Building Your Company's Vision'.[41]

Since then, it has evolved into a term used to describe any goal that is so big, inspiring and outside the prevailing paradigm that it hits people in the gut and shifts their thinking. At the same time, however, goals must be seen as achievable or employees will be discouraged and demotivated, and some might resort to extreme or unethical measures to meet the targets.[42]

Stretch goals and BHAGs have become extremely important because things move fast. A company that focuses on gradual, incremental improvements in products, processes or systems will be left behind. Managers can use these goals to compel employees to think in new ways that can lead to bold, innovative breakthroughs.[43]

INNOVATIVE WAY

Amazon

When Jeff Bezos, CEO of Amazon, first asked engineers in 2004 to create a lightweight, simple e-reader with built-in cellular access, systems engineer Jateen Parekh said, 'I thought it was insane. I really did.' At the time, nothing like that had ever been tried. But Bezos believed that configuring devices to Wi-Fi networks would be too complicated for many users, and he didn't want people to have to connect to a personal computer. Essentially, he didn't want people to even have to think about the wireless connection. The challenge eventually got Parekh and others highly motivated.

It took the development group several years, but in 2007 the Kindle was born. It proved to be such a hit that the first batch sold out in just a few hours. Amazon had to scramble to find a key part that had been discontinued by a supplier to get more on the market. 'You look at the history of the Kindle, they developed some real skills around the creation of that product. They cut their teeth, so to speak,' said Brian Blair, an analyst with Wedge Partners.

Building its own hardware – much less something that hadn't been done before – was an audacious, high-stakes bet for Amazon, but it paid off. Moreover, making four successive generations of the Kindle e-reader led down the path to the Kindle Fire, which is today the only serious competitor to Apple's iPad.[40]

 CONCEPT CONNECTION

Back in 2005, Netflix CEO Reed Hastings announced a **stretch goal** of quadrupling the company's subscriber base to 20 million by 2012. 'That's a bit aggressive,' he said at the time, 'but it's theoretically possible.' Fast forward to 2012, and Netflix had not only met this goal but surpassed it, achieving a total of 33 million US streaming subscribers! The UK penetration was a million – a very competitive market with entrenched competition from Amazon Prime and others. With success like this, it's no surprise that Hastings set a new and possibly unachievable stretch goal of 60 million to 90 million subscribers in the future.

Use performance dashboards

People need a way to see how plans are progressing and gauge their progress towards achieving goals. Companies began using *business performance dashboards* as a way for executives to keep track of key performance metrics, such as sales in relation to targets, number of products on back order, or percentage of customer service calls resolved within specified time periods. Dashboards have evolved into organization-wide systems that help align and track goals across the enterprise. Exhibit 7.10 shows an example of a business performance dashboard that can deliver real-time key performance metrics. The true power of dashboards comes from applying them throughout the company, even on the factory or sales floor, so that all employees can track progress towards goals, see when things are falling short, and find innovative ways to get back on course towards reaching the specified targets. At Emergency Medical Associates, a physician-owned medical group that manages emergency rooms for hospitals[44] in New York and New Jersey, dashboards enable the staff to see when performance thresholds related to patient wait times, for example, aren't being met at various hospitals. Some dashboard systems also incorporate software that lets users perform what-if scenarios to evaluate the impact of various alternatives for meeting goals.

Deploy intelligence teams

Anticipating and managing uncertainty and turbulence in the environment is a crucial part of planning, which means managers need good intelligence to make informed choices about goals and plans. A growing number of leading companies are using intelligence teams to manage this challenge. An intelligence team is a cross-functional group of managers and employees, usually led by a competitive intelligence professional, who work together to gain a deep understanding of a specific business issue, with the aim of presenting insights, possibilities and recommendations about goals and plans related to that issue.[45]

Intelligence teams are useful when the organization confronts a major intelligence challenge. For example, consider a large financial services firm that learns that an even-larger rival is potentially moving to compete directly with one of its major profit-generating businesses. Top managers might form an intelligence team to identify when and how this might happen and how it might affect the organization. Intelligence teams can provide insights that enable managers to make more informed decisions about goals, as well as to devise contingency plans and scenarios related to major strategic issues.

EXHIBIT 7.10 A performance dashboard for planning

SOURCE: Sample Dashboard by Conflair, 'Management Dashboards', Conflair.com, www.conflair.com/ConflairServices/41_ManagementDashboards.asp (accessed July 23, 2012).

REFLECTION

- Approaches to planning change with the times. In many companies today, planning is decentralized.
- **Decentralized planning** means that top executives or planning experts work with managers in major divisions or departments to develop their own goals and plans.
- **Stretch goals** are reasonable yet highly ambitious and compelling goals that energize people and inspire excellence.

- At Amazon, a stretch goal was to build the first Kindle e-reader with built-in cellular access so people didn't have to connect to a PC.
- Business performance dashboards can help managers oversee plans and measure progress towards goals.
- An **intelligence team** is a cross-functional group of people who work together to gain a deep understanding of a specific competitive issue and offer insight and recommendations for planning.

DISCUSSION QUESTIONS

1 Review a published mission statement for a multinational corporation (MNC) for example, Google. Evaluate the extent to which the stated values are consistent with reality.

2 One of the stated benefits of a strategy map is that goals are clarified and how they are interlinked and can be communicated clearly to everyone in the organization. To what extent is it necessary and desirable for employees at all levels to understand the strategic goals of their company?

3 A general view is that a new business venture must develop a comprehensive business plan to borrow money to get started. Companies such as FedEx and Nike claim that they did not follow their original plans closely. Critically discuss the viewpoint that developing the plan was a waste of time for these eventually successful companies.

4 There have been many changes to planning processes in today's organizations when compared to planning 25 years ago. Do you consider that planning has become more important, or less important, in a world where everything is changing so quickly and crises seem a regular part of organizational life?.

5 Some commentators have expressed the view that an organization could never be well prepared for a disaster such as Japan's nuclear disaster, or the BP oil spill in the Gulf of Mexico. Discuss the potential value of crisis planning in situations such as these.

6 Goals that are overly ambitious can discourage employees and decrease motivation, yet the idea of stretch goals is proposed as a way to get people enthusiastic and motivated. As a manager, how do you balance objectives with employee morale?

Does goal setting fit your management style?

INSTRUCTIONS Are you a good planner? Do you set goals and identify ways to accomplish them? This questionnaire will help you understand how your work habits fit with making plans and setting goals. Answer the following questions as they apply to your work or study habits. Please indicate whether each item is 'Mostly true' or 'Mostly false' for you.

	Mostly true	Mostly false
1 I have clear, specific goals in several areas of my life.	☐	☐
2 I have a definite outcome in life I want to achieve.	☐	☐
3 I prefer general to specific goals.	☐	☐
4 I work better without specific deadlines.	☐	☐
5 I set aside time each day or week to plan my work.	☐	☐
6 I am clear about the measures that indicate when I have achieved a goal.	☐	☐
7 I work better when I set more challenging goals for myself.	☐	☐
8 I help other people clarify and define their goals.	☐	☐

SCORING AND INTERPRETATION Give yourself one point for each item you marked as 'Mostly true', except items 3 and 4. For items 3 and 4, give yourself one point for each one that you marked

'Mostly false'. A score of 5 or higher suggests a positive level of goal-setting behaviour and good preparation for a new manager role in an organization. If you scored 4 or less, you might want to evaluate and begin to change your goal-setting behaviour. An important part of a new manager's job is setting goals, measuring results and reviewing progress for the department and subordinates.

These questions indicate the extent to which you have already adopted the disciplined use of goals in your life and work. But if you scored low, don't despair. Goal setting can be learned. Most organizations have goal setting and review systems that managers use. Not everyone thrives under a disciplined goal-setting system, but as a new manager, setting goals and assessing results are tools that will enhance your influence. Research indicates that setting clear, specific and challenging goals in key areas will produce better performance.

APPLY YOUR SKILLS: ETHICAL DILEMMA

Inspire Learning Corporation[46]

When the idea first occurred to her, it seemed like such a win–win situation. Now she wasn't so sure.

Marge Brygay was a hardworking sales rep for Inspire Learning Corporation, a company intent on becoming the top educational software provider in 5 years. That newly adopted strategic goal translated into an ambitious, million-dollar sales target for each of Inspire's sales reps. At the beginning of the fiscal year, her share of the sales department's operational goal seemed entirely reasonable to Marge. She believed in Inspire's products. The company had developed innovative, highly regarded math, language, science and social studies programs for the K–12 market. What set the software apart was a foundation in truly cutting-edge research. Marge had seen for herself how Inspire programs could engage whole classrooms of normally unmotivated kids; the significant rise in test scores on those increasingly important standardized tests bore out her subjective impressions.

But now, just days before the end of the year, Marge's sales were $1000 short of her million-dollar goal. The sale that would have put her comfortably over the top fell through due to last-minute cuts in one large school system's budget. At first, she was nearly overwhelmed with frustration, but then it occurred to her that if she contributed $1000 to Central High, the inner-city high school in her territory probably most in need of what she had for sale, they could purchase the software and put her over the top.

Her scheme would certainly benefit Central High students. Achieving her sales goal would make Inspire happy, and it wouldn't do her any harm, either professionally or financially. Making the goal would earn her a $10 000 bonus cheque that would come in handy when the time came to write out that first tuition cheque for her oldest child, who had just been accepted to a well-known, private university.

Initially, it seemed like the perfect solution all the way around. The more she thought about it, however, the more it didn't quite sit well with her conscience. Time was running out. She needed to decide what to do.

What would you do?

1   Donate the $1000 to Central High, and consider the $10 000 bonus a good return on your investment.

2   Accept the fact that you didn't quite make your sales goal this year. Figure out ways to work smarter next year to increase the odds of achieving your target.

3   Don't make the donation, but investigate whether any other ways are available to help Central High raise the funds that would allow them to purchase the much-needed educational software.

APPLY YOUR SKILLS: CASE FOR CRITICAL ANALYSIS

Government goals and controls

Scotland Performs

The key purpose of organizational performance management is to introduce systematic controls in the management process to guide and regulate the activities of an organization or any of its parts, by means of management judgement, decision and action for the purposes of attaining agreed objectives.

In an organization, control consists of verifying whether everything occurs in conformity with the plan adopted, instructions issued and the principles established. Controls can be either strategic or operational. All such controls check whether the organization's strategic and operational plans are being realized, and put into effect corrective measures where deviations from expected performance levels or shortfalls are occurring.

Control can take place before, during or after an event, (the earlier the better), but many controls can only realistically be introduced after organizational activity has taken place as they gauge the effect of organizational actions.

Scotland Performs measures and reports on progress of government in Scotland. Progress towards the Purpose is tracked by seven Purpose Targets and it is supported by 16 National Outcomes and 50 National Indicators, covering key areas of health, justice, environment, economy and education measure progress. Individuals can judge for themselves how Scotland is progressing through 'direction of travel' arrows on the 'Performance at a Glance' page which indicate whether performance is improving, worsening or maintaining. Assessments of progress are regularly updated from the latest evidence and each has explanatory notes attached.

There are ten guiding principles for Scotland Performs:

- Openness and transparency
- Accountability and responsibility
- Objectivity
- Independent assessment
- Dynamic site: real data, real time
- Accessibility 24/7
- Simplicity and clarity
- Credibility to parliament and the wider public
- Shared responsibility for outcomes-based performance (with our partners)
- Sharpening focus – driving improvement.

Progress against the 50 National Indicators and seven Purpose Targets set out in the National Performance Framework is tracked and reported through Scotland Performs. The website reports on how the Scottish Government and Scotland's public services are doing at a national level.

Scotland Performs does this by providing a **graph** that shows the long term trend in the figures for each indicator and purpose target (where appropriate). Additional graphs are used in some cases to help the interpretability of more complex measures. **Narratives** are added to the 'Current status' and 'How are we performing' sections on the relevant indicator or target pages which contain further analysis on the recent change in performance, the longer trend and the change since the baseline. They might also include – to some extent – assessment of delivery, where appropriate. The data also reveal a **direction of travel performance arrow**, to each National Indicator and Purpose Target, which aim to evaluate the direction of **change between the two most recent comparable data points.**

Four types of symbols are used:

↑ Performance improving

←→ Performance maintaining

↓ Performance worsening

● Data being collected (for the ones where there are no two comparable data points available).

Research shows that there are multiple tools and techniques being used globally in organizational performance management. There is clearly a tendency towards dashboards, colour charts and diagrams providing a snapshot of the current status of actual performance against planned performance using information which is as close as possible to real time. These tools have most significance where the focus of the performance relates to all organizational activity. Corrective action can be introduced relatively quickly and the expectation is that the corrective action will have a short term impact.

Organizational performance management literature identified the core elements of organizational performance management and has confirmed that it is global development. Reports by the World Bank (2007), the US Government Accountability Office (GAO) (2007) and the OECD (2008) identify the pervasive characteristics of global organizational performance management in a government context. According to these influential organizations, comprehensive systems of organizational performance management should be modelled on these pervasive characteristics.

1   High level aspirations expressed as outcomes

2   Strategic business plan

3   Performance measurement tools and techniques

4   Targets

5   Implementation

6   Monitoring

7   Measuring results

8   Verification

9   Communication

10   Review and evaluation

11   **Continuous sensitivity**

12   **Commitment**

References Organization for Economic Co-operation and Development (OECD) (2008), *Performance Budgeting in OECD Countries,* Paris: OECD.
Scottish Government: www.scotland.gov.uk
United States Government Accountability Office (2007), *Performance and Accountability Report: Fiscal Year 2007*, Washington, United States Government Accountability Office.
World Bank (2007), *How to Build M&E Systems to Support Better Government,* Washington DC, The World Bank.

Questions

1   Do you think that organizational performance management tools such as *Scotland Performs* lead to a clearer focus on organizational goals?

2   What would be your concerns as a politician or senior public servant in continuously making performance information available to the public?

3   What would be your concerns as a manager in continuously making performance information available to employees?

END NOTES

1. Miguel Bustillo, 'Corporate News – Boss Talk: Wal-Mart's US Chief Aims for Turnaround', *The Asian Wall Street Journal*, March 22, 2011, 22; and Miguel Bustillo, 'Wal-Mart Tries to Recapture Mr Sam's Winning Formula', *The Wall Street Journal Online*, February 22, 2011, www.online.wsj.com/article/SB100014240527487038039045761527531117889930.html (accessed July 17, 2012).

2. Hiroko Tabuchi, 'Inquiry Declares Fukushima Crisis a Man-Made Disaster', *The New York Times*, July 5, 2012, www.nytimes.com/2012/07/06/world/asia/fukushima-nuclear-crisis-a-man-made-disaster-report-says.html (accessed July 19, 2012).

3. Quoted in Oren Harari, 'Good/Bad News About Strategy', *Management Review* (July 1995): 29–31.

4. Amitai Etzioni, *Modern Organizations* (Englewood Cliffs, NJ: Prentice Hall, 1984), p. 6.

5. *Ibid.*

6. Max D. Richards, *Setting Strategic Goals and Objectives*, 2nd ed. (St. Paul, MN: West, 1986).

7. Reported in Matthew Budman, 'Why Are We In Business? Ad Man Roy Spence Wants to Know What Your *Purpose* Is', *The Conference Board Review* (March–April 2009): 35–41.

8. Mary Klemm, Stuart Sanderson and George Luffman, 'Mission Statements: Selling Corporate Values to Employees', *Long-Range Planning* 24, no. 3 (1991): 73–78; John A. Pearce II and Fred David, 'Corporate Mission Statements: The Bottom Line', *Academy of Management Executive* (1987): 109–116; Jerome H. Want, 'Corporate Mission: The Intangible Contributor to Performance', *Management Review* (August 1986): 46–50; and Forest R. David and Fred R. David, 'It's Time to Redraft Your Mission Statement', *Journal of Business Strategy* (January–February 2003): 11–14.

9. Paul Meising and Joseph Wolfe, 'The Art and Science of Planning at the Business Unit Level', *Management Science* 31 (1985): 773–781.

10. Geary A. Rummler and Kimberly Morrill, 'The Results Chain', *TD* (February 2005): 27–35; and John C. Crotts, Duncan R. Dickson and Robert C. Ford, 'Aligning Organizational Processes with Mission: The Case of Service Excellence', *Academy of Management Executive* 19, no. 3 (August 2005): 54–68.

11. This discussion is based on Robert S. Kaplan and David P. Norton, 'Mastering the Management System', *Harvard Business Review* (January 2008): 63–77; and Robert S. Kaplan and David P. Norton, 'Having Trouble with Your Strategy? Then Map It', *Harvard Business Review* (September–October 2000): 167–176.

12. Sayan Chatterjee, 'Core Objectives: Clarity in Designing Strategy', *California Management Review* 47, no. 2 (Winter 2005): 33–49.

13. Edwin A. Locke, Gary P. Latham and Miriam Erez, 'The Determinants of Goal Commitment', *Academy of Management Review* 13 (1988): 23–39.

14. Peter F. Drucker, *The Practice of Management* (New York: Harper & Row, 1954); George S. Odiorne, 'MBO: A Backward Glance', *Business Horizons* 21 (October 1978): 14–24; and William F. Roth, 'Is Management by Objectives Obsolete?' *Global Business and Organizational Excellence* (May–June 2009): 36–43.

15. J. Ivancevich, J. T. McMahon, J. W. Streidl and A. D.Szilagi, Jr,, 'Goal Setting: The Tenneco Approach to Personnel Development and Management Effectiveness', *Organizational Dynamics* (Winter 1978): 48–80.

16. Tim O'Shaughnessy, as told to Liz Welch, 'The Way I Work: Tim O'Shaughnessy, LivingSocial', *Inc.* (March 2012): 104–108.

17. Eileen M. Van Aken and Garry D. Coleman, 'Building Better Measurement', *Industrial Management* (July–August 2002): 28–33.

18. This analogy is from Jeffrey K. Liker and Timothy N. Ogden, 'The Toyota Recall: Missing the Forest for the Trees', *Ivey Business Journal* (November–December 2011), www.iveybusinessjournal.com/topics/marketing/the-toyota-recall-missing-the-forest-for-the-trees (accessed July 19, 2012).

19. Reylito A. H. Elbo, 'MBM: Management by Means, Not Results', *The Manila Times*, June 11, 2012, www.manila-times.net/index.php/business/business-columnist/24633-mbm-management-by-means-not-results (accessed August 8, 2012); and Liker and Ogden, 'The Toyota Recall'.

20. Liker and Ogden, 'The Toyota Recall'.

21. Sarah Fister Gale, 'Big Brother Is Watching: Why Social Media Policies Make Good Business Sense', *Workforce*, June 21, 2012, www.workforce.com/article/20120621/NEWS02/120629994/big-brother-is-watching-why-social-media-policies-make-good-business-sense# (accessed July 18, 2012); and Sarah Fister Gale, 'Five Things Every Social Media Policy Should Do', *Workforce*, June 21 2012, www.workforce.com/article/20120621/NEWS02/120629995 (accessed July 18, 2012).

22. C. Chet Miller and Laura B. Cardinal, 'Strategic Planning and Firm Performance: A Synthesis of More than Two Decades of Research', *Academy of Management Journal* 37, no. 6 (1994): 1649–1685.

23. These are based on E. A. Locke and G. P. Latham, *A Theory of Goal Setting & Task Performance* (Englewood Cliffs, N.J.: Prentice Hall, 1990); Richard L. Daft and Richard M. Steers, *Organizations: A Micro/Macro Approach* (Glenview, IL: Scott, Foresman, 1986), pp. 319–321; Herbert A. Simon, 'On the Concept of Organizational Goals', *Administrative Science Quarterly* 9 (1964): 1–22; and Charles B. Saunders and Francis D. Tuggel, 'Corporate Goals', *Journal of General Management* 5 (1980): 3–13.

24. Nick Wingfield, 'Netflix Boss Plots Life After the DVD', *The Wall Street Journal*, June 23, 2009.

25. These are based on Henry Mintzberg, *The Rise and Fall of Strategic Planning* (New York: The Free Press, 1994); H. Mintzberg, 'Rethinking Strategic Planning, Part I: Pitfalls and Fallacies', *Long Range Planning* 27 (1994): 12–21; and H. Mintzberg, 'The Pitfalls of Strategic Planning', *California Management Review* 36 (1993): 32–47.

26. Roth, 'Is Management by Objectives Obsolete?'

27. Curtis W. Roney, 'Planning for Strategic Contingencies', *Business Horizons* (March–April 2003): 35–42; and 'Corporate Planning: Drafting a Blueprint for Success', *Small Business Report* (August 1987): 40–44.

28. Sandy Cohen, 'Oscars Contingency Plan', *USAToday*, January 30, 2008, www.usatoday.com/life/music/2008-01-30-1092823826_x.htm (accessed July 20, 2012).

29. This section is based on Steven Schnaars and Paschalina Ziamou, 'The Essentials of Scenario Writing', *Business Horizons* (July–August 2001): 25–31; Peter Cornelius, Alexander Van de Putte and Mattia Romani, 'Three Decades of Scenario Planning in Shell', *California Management Review* 48, no. 1 (Fall 2005): 92–109; Audrey Schriefer and Michael Sales, 'Creating Strategic Advantage with Dynamic Scenarios', *Strategy & Leadership* 34, no. 3 (2006): 31–42; William J. Worthington, Jamie D. Collins and Michael A. Hitt, 'Beyond Risk Mitigation: Enhancing Corporate Innovation with Scenario Planning', *Business Horizons* 52 (2009): 441–450; and Gill Ringland, 'Innovation: Scenarios of Alternative Futures Can Discover New Opportunities for Creativity', *Strategy & Leadership* 36, no. 5 (2008): 22–27.

30. Kathleen Wilburn and Ralph Wilburn, 'Abbreviated Scenario Thinking', *Business Horizons* 54 (2011): 541–550.

31. Gerald F. Seib, 'Four Scenarios for Libya – Some Good and Some Bad', *The Wall Street Journal*, March 29, 2011, www.online.wsj.com/article/SB10001424052748703739204576228620384027448.html (accessed July 20, 2012).

32. Penny Neferis, as told to Patricia R. Olsen, 'Call Her the Worrier in Chief', *The New York Times*, April 30, 2011, www.nytimes.com/2011/05/01/jobs/01pre.html (accessed July 20, 2012).

33. Ian Mitroff with Gus Anagnos, *Managing Crises Before They Happen* (New York: AMACOM, 2001); Ian Mitroff and Murat C. Alpaslan, 'Preparing for Evil', *Harvard Business Review* (April 2003): 109–115.

34. The following discussion is based largely on W. Timothy Coombs, *Ongoing Crisis Communication: Planning, Managing and Responding* (Thousand Oaks, CA: Sage Publications, 1999).

35. Ian I. Mitroff, 'Crisis Leadership', *Executive Excellence* (August 2001): 19; Andy Bowen, 'Crisis Procedures that Stand the Test of Time', *Public Relations Tactics* (August 2001): 16.

36. Jason Fried, 'How to Ride a Storm', *Inc.* (February 2011): 37–39.

37. Christine Pearson, 'A Blueprint for Crisis Management', *Ivey Business Journal* (January–February 2002): 69–73.

38. See Mitroff and Alpaslan, 'Preparing for Evil', for a discussion of the 'wheel of crises' outlining the many different kinds of crises that organizations may face.

39. Harari, 'Good/Bad News About Strategy'.

40. Brad Stone, 'The Omnivore', *Bloomberg Businessweek* (October 3–October 9, 2011): 58–65.

41. James C. Collins and Jerry I. Porras, 'Building Your Company's Vision', *Harvard Business Review* (September–October 1996): 65–77.

42. Steven Kerr and Steffan Landauer, 'Using Stretch Goals to Promote Organizational Effectiveness and Personal Growth: General Electric and Goldman Sachs', *Academy of Management Executive* 18, no. 4 (November 2004): 134–138; and Lisa D. Ordóñez, Maurice E. Schweitzer, Adam D. Galinsky and Max H. Bazerman, 'Goals Gone Wild: The Systematic Side Effects of Overprescribing Goal Setting', *Academy of Management Perspectives* (February 2009): 6–16.

43. See Kenneth R. Thompson, Wayne A. Hockwarter and Nicholas J. Mathys, 'Stretch Targets: What Makes Them Effective?' *Academy of Management Executive* 11, no. 3 (August 1997): 48.

44. Doug Bartholomew, 'Gauging Success', *CFO-IT* (Summer 2005): 17–19.

45. This section is based on Liam Fahey and Jan Herring, 'Intelligence Teams', *Strategy & Leadership* 35, no. 1 (2007): 13–20.

46. Based on Shel Horowitz, 'Should Mary Buy Her Own Bonus?' *Business Ethics* (Summer 2005): 34.

CHAPTER 8

STRATEGY FORMULATION AND EXECUTION

LEARNING OBJECTIVES

After studying this chapter, you should be able to:

1 Define the components of strategic management and discuss the levels of strategy.

2 Describe the strategic management process and SWOT analysis for evaluating the company's strengths, weaknesses, opportunities and threats.

3 Define corporate-level strategies and explain the Boston Consulting Group (BCG) matrix, portfolio and diversification approaches.

4 Describe Michael Porter's competitive strategies.

5 Discuss organizational dimensions that managers use to execute strategy.

How important is strategic management? It largely determines which organizations succeed and which ones struggle. Differences in the strategies that managers choose and how effectively they *execute* them help to explain why Amazon.com and Alibaba.com are thriving and others are floundering, how Facebook diminished MySpace's presence in the sphere of social networking and why Apple is continuing to beat Microsoft and others in the world of mobile computing. Chief executive officer (CEO) and founder, Jack Ma, took Alibaba to the NASDAQ in 2014 – being the highest value IPO that the exchange handled at $B250!

Every company is concerned with strategy. In the fast food industry, managers revived Domino's by formulating and aggressively advertising a new pizza recipe that responded to changing consumer tastes. McDonald's has succeeded with a revamped strategy of adding the McCafe line of hot and iced coffee drinks, offering snacks and small dessert items throughout the day, and enhancing its line of products for health-conscious consumers. YUM Brands' KFC chain is thriving with an ambitious global strategy, rapidly expanding overseas, particularly in China.[1]

Strategic blunders can hurt a company. For instance, Kodak still hasn't recovered from its managers' failure to plan for the rapid rise of digital photography, particularly as Kodak also had the patents for digital photography. A recent article touting the success of a thriving, innovative, adaptive company referred to the firm as the 'anti-Kodak'. Liz Claiborne was once one of the most popular clothing brands around. The company that pioneered career apparel for women has been in decline for years, with managers failing to latch onto a strategy that could keep the clothing brand relevant as baby boomers retired and began spending less money on career outfits.[2]

'It's hard to outrun the future if you don't see it coming.'
— GARY HAMEL, MANAGEMENT SCHOLAR AND AUTHOR

Managers at Liz Claiborne, McDonald's, Kodak and Facebook are all involved in determining and implementing strategic management initiatives. They look for dynamic and novel ways to respond to competitors, cope with difficult environmental challenges, meet changing customer needs and effectively use available resources. Strategic management has taken on greater importance in today's environment, because managers are responsible for positioning their organizations for success in a world that is constantly changing. Top level managers must pay due regard to the imperatives of entrepreneurial strategic leadership which may well be inconsistent to the firm's future businesses. They have to be truly ambidextrous – simultaneously coping with current market needs and refining their products and services to stay abreast or ahead of the competition.

Chapter 7 provided an overview of the types of goals and plans that organizations use. In this chapter, we explore strategic management, which is one specific type of planning. First, we define the components of strategic management and discuss the purposes and levels of strategy. Next, we examine several models of strategy formulation at the corporate, business and functional levels. Finally, we discuss the tools that managers use to execute their strategic plans.

Thinking strategically

What does it mean to think strategically? Strategic thinking means to take the long-term view and to see the big picture, including the organization and the competitive environment, and consider how they fit together. Strategic thinking is important for both businesses and non-profit organizations. In for-profit firms, strategic planning typically pertains to competitive actions in the marketplace. In non-profit organizations such as the Red Cross or the Salvation Army, strategic planning pertains to events in the external environment.

Some research has shown that strategic thinking and planning positively affect a firm's performance and financial success.[3] Most managers are aware of the importance of strategic planning, as evidenced by a *McKinsey Quarterly* survey. Of responding executives whose companies had no formal strategic planning process, 51 per cent said they were dissatisfied with the company's development of strategy, compared to only 20 per cent of those at companies that had a formal planning process.[4] CEOs at successful companies make strategic thinking and planning a top management priority. For an organization to succeed, the CEO must be actively involved in making the tough choices and trade-offs that define and support strategy.[5] However, senior executives at today's leading companies want middle- and lower-level managers to think strategically as well. Understanding the strategy concept and the levels of strategy is an important start towards strategic thinking.

What is strategic management?

Strategic management refers to the set of decisions and actions used to formulate and execute strategies that will provide a competitively superior fit between the organization and its environment so as to achieve organizational goals.[6] Managers ask questions such as the following: What changes and trends are occurring in the competitive environment? Who are our competitors and what are their strengths and weaknesses? eBay had little or no knowledge of Alibaba's competitive Taobao product being developed for the Chinese market that eBay entered and subsequently exited with considerable losses. Competitor analysis with unknown competitors is obviously incomplete. Who are our customers? What products or services should we offer and how can we offer them most efficiently? What does the future hold for our industry, and how can we change the rules of the game? Answers to these questions help managers make choices about how to position their organizations in the environment with respect to rival companies.[7] Superior organizational performance is not a matter of luck. It is determined by the choices that managers make.

🌐 NEW MANAGER SELF-TEST

Systemic thinking

INSTRUCTIONS Respond to each of the following statements based on how you have *actually* approached a difficult problem. Please indicate whether each item is 'Mostly true' or 'Mostly false' for you.

		Mostly true	Mostly false
1	I tried to see the problem in its entirety and how it affected other people.	☐	☐
2	I started by acquiring and integrating information from different areas.	☐	☐
3	I enjoyed solving a complex rather than a simple problem.	☐	☐
4	I systematically talked to people who had diverse perspectives on the problem.	☐	☐
5	I attempted to link a solution to an overall strategy or plan.	☐	☐
6	I analyzed root causes of the problem to find leverage points for a solution.	☐	☐
7	My approach was to focus on one part of the problem at a time.	☐	☐
8	I took time to consider the situation from all angles.	☐	☐
9	I studied how different parts of the organization interacted to affect the problem.	☐	☐

SCORING & INTERPRETATION Systemic thinking represents a strategic approach to problem solving that seeks the big picture of how things fit together, rather than focusing on a specific part. Systemic thinking is considered strategic because it welcomes the challenge of system complexity and how all the parts interact. Analytical thinkers, for example, may break a problem down into individual parts, whereas a systemic thinker would strive to understand how the parts fit together in a larger context. Give yourself 2 points for each 'Mostly true' answer and 1 point for each 'Mostly false' answer, except for question 7, which should be reverse-scored – 2 points for 'Mostly false' and 1 point for 'Mostly true'. If your score is 14 or higher, you probably have a tendency towards systemic thinking. If your score is 6 or less, you probably approach problems by focusing on individual parts of a system, rather than on the interaction of the parts to create the whole system. A score of 7–13 implies that you use some elements of systemic thinking some of the time.

TAKE A MOMENT

Completing the New Manager Self-Test at the end of the chapter will give you an idea about your ability to see the big picture and how different aspects of the organization and its environment interact, which is an important part of strategic thinking.

- To think strategically means to take the long-term view and see the big picture.
- Managers in all types of organizations, including businesses, not-for-profit organizations and

government agencies, have to think about how the organization fits in the environment.

Purpose of strategy

The first step in strategic management is to define an explicit strategy, which is the plan of action that describes resource allocation and activities for dealing with the environment, achieving a competitive advantage and attaining the organization's goals. Competitive advantage refers to what sets the organization apart from others and provides it with a distinctive edge for meeting customer or client needs in the marketplace. The essence of formulating strategy is choosing how the organization will be different.[8] Managers make decisions about whether the company will perform different activities or will execute similar activities differently from its rivals. Strategy necessarily changes over time to fit environmental conditions, but to achieve competitive advantage companies must at least develop strategies that incorporate the elements illustrated in Exhibit 8.1: target specific customers, focus on core competencies, provide synergy and create value.

Target customers

An effective strategy defines the customers and which of their needs are to be served by the company.[9] Managers can define a target market geographically, such as serving people in a certain part of the country; demographically, such as aiming at a demographic with certain characteristics, e.g., a certain income bracket or targeting pre-teen girls; or by a variety of other means. Some firms target people who purchase primarily over the Internet, whereas others aim to serve people who like to shop in small stores with a limited selection of high-quality merchandise. When Southwest Airlines was founded, managers identified their target customer as regular bus travellers, people who wanted to get from one place to another in a convenient, low-cost way.[10] Volvo's new owners and managers are shifting the company's strategy towards a new target customer. Rather than aiming for people who appreciate the brand's reputation for safe, reliable family vehicles, Li Shufu, the company's new Chinese owner, is aiming to expand aggressively into the luxury car market. Volvo is particularly courting the emerging class of rich consumers in China and other overseas markets. Li wants Volvo to offer innovative, electrifying designs that turn heads and win new luxury-minded customers with flashy tastes.[11]

Managers develop their ability to think strategically through both work experiences and formal study. Some claim other sources of experience of 'reading competitors thinking' such as observing non-verbal communication (NVC) when playing poker. See if any of your experiences have given you a good start towards strategic thinking by completing the Experiential Exercise online.

Exploit core competence

A company's core competence is something that the organization does especially well in comparison to its competitors. A core competence represents a competitive advantage because the company acquires expertise that competitors do not have. A core competence may be in the area of superior research and development, expert technological know-how, process efficiency or exceptional customer service.[12] Managers at companies such as Southwest Airlines, for example, focus on a core competence of operational efficiency that enables them to keep costs low. Robinson Helicopter succeeds through superior technological know-how for building small, two-seater helicopters used for everything from police patrols in Los Angeles to herding cattle in

EXHIBIT 8.1 The elements of competitive advantage

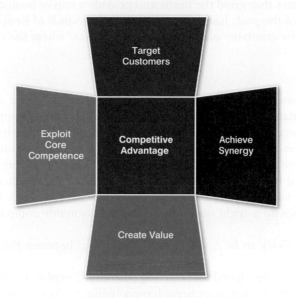

 CONCEPT CONNECTION

When the US Marines needed rugged motorcycles, they looked to manufacturers of on- and off-road bikes. But most motorcycles run on petrol, which is the wrong fuel for military purposes. Hayes Diversified Technologies had the competitive advantage. After 20 years of building adapted motorcycles for the Marines and the Army Special Forces, Hayes had developed a **core competence** in technology that addresses the fuel limitations faced by the military. Most US military machines run on JB8 fuel, a formulation of diesel and kerosene. Hayes Diversified's HDT M1030M1 motorcycle is designed for diesel service, so Hayes readily won the contract.

Australia.[13] In each case, their leaders identified what their company does especially well and built strategy around it.

Build synergy

When organizational parts interact to produce a joint effect that is greater than the sum of the parts acting alone, synergy occurs. The organization may attain a special advantage with respect to cost, market power, technology or management skill. When properly managed, synergy can create additional value with existing resources, providing a big boost to the bottom line.[14] Synergy was the motivation for Kraft to buy UK's Cadbury, for instance, and for Oracle to buy Sun Microsystems. Kraft used Cadbury's established distribution network in emerging markets to share trucks and store contacts and sell more Kraft products. Oracle's purchase of Sun gives the software company a giant hardware business, enabling Oracle to provide corporations with most of the technology they need in a single package.[15]

Synergy can also be obtained by good relationships between organizations. For example, Coinstar, the company behind Redbox movie rentals, uses partnerships to attain synergy. As rentals of physical videos decline, the Redbox division has partnered with Verizon Communications on a service that combines DVD rental and streaming video, benefiting both companies. In another partnership, Coinstar has joined with Starbucks to provide self-service coffee vending machines that grind the beans and provide a cup of fresh coffee that is miles away from the vending machine coffee of the past. Just as there are now thousands of Redbox kiosks in Walmarts, drugstores, and other locations, the company plans to put coffee kiosks 'where the consumer goes every day'.[16]

Deliver value

Delivering value to the customer is at the heart of strategy. *Value* can be defined as the combination of benefits received and costs paid. Managers help their companies create value by devising strategies that exploit core competencies and attain synergy. Starbucks introduced the Starbucks Card, which works like a typical retail gift card except that users get benefits like points for free coffee.[17] Cable companies such as Time Warner Cable and Comcast offer *value packages* that provide a combination of basic cable, digital premium channels, video-on-demand, high-speed Internet and digital telephone service for a reduced cost. Some movie theatres are trying to provide greater value by offering 'dinner and a movie'. In-theatre dining provides a more time-efficient way for people to spend a night out, and costs are reasonable compared to eating in a restaurant before or after the film.[18]

In the UK there is more likely to be a symbiotic relationship between the cinema and a neighbouring restaurant.

Amazon is thriving with a strategy based on targeting customers, exploiting its core competencies, building synergy and providing value. Such dominant firms have a 'winner takes all' mentality and acute knowledge of tax-efficient organization developed with their accounting advisors.

 INNOVATIVE WAY

Amazon

It's hard to believe Amazon was once a struggling online bookseller. Today, it is 'an existential threat' to every retailer, as observed by Fiona Dias, executive vice president of GSI Commerce. Amazon targets customers who want to find good deals and purchase products conveniently over the Internet. Those customers can find many products they want on Amazon. They will often pay less for it than they would anywhere else and if they belong to Amazon Prime, they get free one-day shipping.

Amazon wants to provide 'premium products at non-premium prices'. To do that, it has developed an extensive network of third-party merchants – partners with whom it maintains close, mutually beneficial relationships, and is constantly honing its operational efficiency. It has created one of the most finely tuned retail distribution systems. As if all that wasn't enough, along came Prime. For £79 a year, UK customers get free one-day shipping, as well as free streaming video and discounted DVDs and other short-term promotions. Prime allows Amazon to capitalize on its core competencies of wide selection, cost efficiency and slick distribution. When asked how they decided on the £79 price tag, a member of the Prime team said it *'was never about the £79. It was really about changing people's mentality so they wouldn't shop anywhere else.'*

Prime was conceived as a way to further cement the loyalty of Amazon's best customers, and it has been more successful than even CEO Jeff Bezos imagined. 'Amazon Prime,' said one recent business article 'turns casual shoppers . . . into Amazon addicts.' It provides value to customers, but it also increases sales for Amazon. According to some estimates, customers increase their purchases on the site by about 150 per cent after joining Prime. It is credited for helping Amazon's sales zoom 30 per cent during the 2008 recession while other retailers struggled to attract customers.[19]

Levels of strategy

Another aspect of strategic management concerns the organizational level to which strategic issues apply. Strategic managers normally think in terms of three levels of strategy, as illustrated in Exhibit 8.2.[20]

EXHIBIT 8.2 Three levels of strategy in organizations

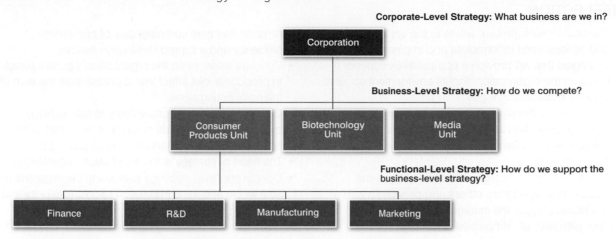

- *What business are we in?* Managers ask this question when they consider corporate-level strategy. Corporate-level strategy pertains to the organization as a whole and the combination of business units and product lines that make up the corporate entity. Strategic actions at this level usually relate to the acquisition of new businesses; additions or divestments of business units, plants, or product lines; and joint ventures with other corporations in new areas. An example of corporate-level strategy is Garmin. Founded by Gary Burrell and Min Kao, Garmin is the company that first became known for stand-alone GPS products. Garmin has evolved into an international corporation that has a consumer products division; a division making dashboard-embedded GPS for the automotive market; a division that makes guidance and avionics systems for airplanes and marine vessels; a division that provides mobile weather solutions; and a division that focuses on personal monitoring technology such as foot pods and heart rate monitors for sports and fitness products. The company's growth has been fuelled by acquisitions, including the purchase of UPS Aviation Technologies, Inc. (now Garmin AT) and Dynastream Innovations (personal monitoring products).[21]

- *How do we compete?* Business-level strategy pertains to each business unit or product line. Strategic decisions at this level concern amount of advertising, direction and extent of research and development, product changes, new-product development, equipment and facilities, and expansion or contraction of product and service lines. At Garmin, sales of GPS devices to consumers have been hurt because so many people use their smartphones to get directions or Google maps, so Garmin's consumer products division decided to create a phone of its own. The company partnered with computer maker Asus to develop a Garmin-branded smartphone with built-in GPS. In addition, Garmin's consumer division created its own app for the iPhone that lets users do everything from check for traffic jams to look up their destinations on Wikipedia.[22]

- *How do we support the business-level strategy?* Functional-level strategy pertains to the major functional departments within the business unit. Functional strategies involve all of the major functions, including finance, research and development, marketing and manufacturing. One element of functional-level strategy for Gap's marketing department is to use mobile technology to offer targeted deals to customers. Gap created a mobile app that uses GPS technology, so that when a customer opens the app near a Gap store, it provides special sales offers exclusive to that location.[23]

TAKE A MOMENT

Go to the Ethical Dilemma at the end of this chapter that pertains to business and functional level strategy.

REFLECTION

- **Strategic management** refers to the set of decisions and actions used to formulate and implement strategies that will provide a competitively superior fit between the organization and its environment so as to achieve organizational goals.
- A **strategy** is the plan of action that describes resource allocation and activities for dealing with the environment, achieving a competitive advantage and attaining goals.
- **Competitive advantage** refers to what sets the organization apart from others and provides it with a distinctive edge in the marketplace.
- Four elements of competitive advantage are the company's target customer, core competencies, synergy and value.
- A **core competence** is something that the organization does particularly well in comparison to others.
- Amazon has core competencies of operational efficiency and a superb distribution system.
- **Synergy** exists when the organization's parts interact to produce a joint effect that is greater than the sum of the parts acting alone.
- Oracle bought Sun Microsystems to gain synergy by being able to provide customers with most of the technology that they need in a single package.
- The heart of strategy is to deliver value to customers.
- **Corporate-level strategy** pertains to the organization as a whole and the combination of business units and products that make it up.
- **Business-level strategy** pertains to each business unit or product line within the organization.
- **Functional-level strategy** pertains to the major functional departments within each business unit, such as manufacturing, marketing, and research and development.

The strategic management process

The overall strategic management process is illustrated in Exhibit 8.3. It begins when executives evaluate their current position with respect to mission, goals and strategies. They then scan the organization's internal and external environments and identify strategic issues that might require change. Managers at BP didn't have to look far to see a need for change after a giant drilling rig exploded and sank in April 2010, killing 11 crew members and spilling massive amounts of oil into the Gulf of Mexico. BP's strategy had been based on being a leader in pushing the frontiers of the oil industry, such as drilling the world's deepest wells, scouting

EXHIBIT 8.3 The strategic management process

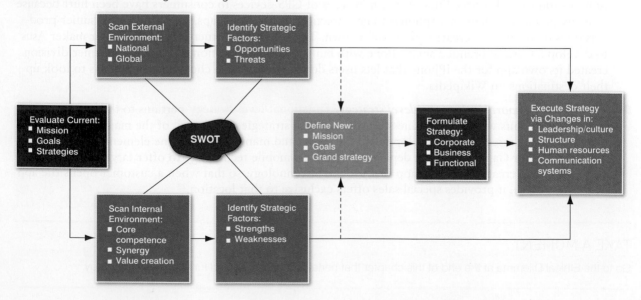

🌐 MANAGER'S SHOPTALK

Will strategy ever be the same?

'*Strategy, as we knew it, is dead,'* said Walt Shill, head of management consulting in North America for Accenture Ltd. It might be an overstatement, but during the economic turmoil of the past few years many managers have discovered they need new approaches to strategy:

- *Managers build flexibility into strategic plans.* Management scholar and strategic thinker Gary Hamel uses the term *strategic decay* to describe the fact that the value of even the most brilliant strategy declines over time. Static long-range strategic plans can be a liability in a topsy-turvy world. What was a strength yesterday, might be the beginnings of a weakness today. To overcome the natural tendency to depend on what has worked in the past, managers at organizations such as McKinsey & Company build a culture of inquiry, healthy debate and constructive conflict.

- *Strategy is built actively and interactively.* Managers don't sit at their desks and dream up strategy. They get out and talk to employees, customers, suppliers and other stakeholders. In the early days of Hewlett-Packard, for example, Dave Packard and Bill Hewlett were seldom at their desks. They were out talking to people and gaining a solid, realistic grounding for the creation of effective strategy.

- *Strategic partnerships are key components of strategy.* Collaboration with other organizations is an important part of how successful companies enter new areas of business. To find new ways to make money as e-books, which provide less revenue per unit than traditional hardcover books, become more popular, Random House is striking deals with videogame publishers to write original stories for games and offer advice to developers on their own storylines.

- *Strategy comes to life with creative execution.* Creative execution is the implementation of a strategy that is so well conceived, compelling and embraced by everyone throughout the organization that it practically guarantees a successful outcome. For example, Google's strategy of focusing on search rather than content – on organizing existing information and making it accessible and useful – was so clear and compelling that employees rallied behind it. Managers use visionary leadership, open and honest communication, and bold action to drive strategy. Ignoring the seemingly impossible nature of the task, Google managers have inspired people with a strategic goal to digitize every book in the world's libraries.

SOURCES: Gary Hamel, 'Outrunning Change – The CliffsNotes Version', Gary Hamel's Management 2.0, *WSJ Blogs*, October 21, 2009, www.blogs.wsj.com/management/2009/10/21/outrunning-change-the-cliffsnotes-version/ (accessed July 31, 2012); Eric Beaudan, 'Creative Execution', *Ivey Business Journal* (March–April 2010), www.iveybusinessjournal.com/article.asp?intArticle_ID=891 (accessed March 26, 2010); Jeffrey A. Trachtenberg, 'Random House Harnesses Skills to Venture into Videogame Action', *The Wall Street Journal*, March 1, 2010; and Don Tapscott, 'Rethinking Strategy in a Networked World', *Strategy & Business* 24 (Third Quarter 2001): 34–41.

for oil in the Arctic and other aggressive efforts. The strategy succeeded; BP steadily increased production and overtook Royal Dutch Shell plc in market capitalization in January 2010.[24] A few months later, disaster struck, presenting a crisis that required a new approach to strategy for the oil giant. BP managers evaluated whether the company's strategy fitted the environment and its own capabilities and shifted strategic goals to focus on safety and consistency.

For all organizations, internal or external events sometimes indicate a need to redefine the mission or goals or to formulate a new strategy at either the corporate, business or functional level. Factors that alter a company's ability to achieve its goals are called *strategic issues*, as described in Chapter 3. In turbulent environments and fast-changing industries, managers have to stay alert to strategic issues that require a shift in strategy to stay in line with both internal and external changes.[25] The final stage in the strategic management process outlined in Exhibit 8.3 is execution of the new strategy. This chapter's Shoptalk discusses some recent trends in strategy formulation and execution.

CONCEPT CONNECTION

Sir Stelios Haji-Ioannou started easyJet in 1995, with just two Boeing aircraft, using a £5m loan from his Cypriot father. The conditions of the loan were simply to make money for himself, his brother and his sister. The first location of the airline's operations was determined to be the then inexpensive municipally owned Luton airport, a critical aspect of establishing a low cost and no-frills airline. The chance of obtaining expensive slots from any of the major airports in the UK (such as Heathrow and Gatwick) was not feasible. If any take-off and landing slots had been available, then the cost would have been prohibitive. This entrepreneur has adopted and adapted the low-cost business model of USA's Southwestern Airlines, and the family business venture (which was written up by the founder in a University PG dissertation) has been demonstrably successful for a number of reasons. First, there was an unsatisfied market need for air travel from the UK to mainland Europe, as alternatives were often expensive and unreliable – trains and ferries. Second, bookings were made over the Internet using a web-based non-industry (expensive) booking system. Third, astute equity block control over corporate strategy decisions – even after he resigned as the CEO of easyJet. Fourth, good luck! He executed well-judged and timed excellent strategic implementations with the making of good early acquisitions. He was able to buy a failed Zurich-based airline and get additional planes and slots in Switzerland, and also made an astute decision to buy Go – an airline sold by British Airways to its management. An interesting aspect of the company is that it made its first dividend distribution after trading for 10 years and it was a considerable payout to the principal shareholders, which included major institutional investors such as insurance companies.

Strategy formulation versus execution

Strategy formulation includes the planning and decision-making that lead to the establishment of the firm's goals and the development of a specific strategic plan.[26] Strategy formulation includes assessing the external environment and internal problems to identify strategic issues, then integrating the results into goals and strategy. This process is in contrast to strategy execution, which is the use of managerial and organizational tools to direct resources towards accomplishing strategic results.[27] Strategy execution is the administration and implementation of the strategic plan. Managers may use persuasion, new technology, changes in organization structure, or a revised reward system to ensure that employees and resources are better used to making a formulated strategy a reality.

SWOT analysis

Formulating strategy begins with understanding the circumstances, forces, events and issues that shape the organization's competitive situation, which requires that managers conduct an audit of both internal and external factors that influence the company's ability to compete.[28] SWOT analysis includes a careful assessment of strengths, weaknesses, opportunities and threats that affect organizational performance. Managers obtain external information about opportunities and threats from a variety of sources, including customers, government reports, professional journals, suppliers, bankers, critical friends in other organizations, consultants or professional association meetings. Many firms contract with special environment scanning organizations to provide them with newspaper data, Internet research, and analyses of relevant domestic and global trends. Some hire competitive intelligence professionals to scope out competitors, as we discussed in Chapter 3, and use intelligence teams, as described in Chapter 7.

Executives acquire information about internal strengths and weaknesses from a variety of reports, including budgets, financial ratios, profit and loss statements, and surveys of employee attitudes and satisfaction. In addition, managers build an understanding of the company's internal strengths and weaknesses by talking with people at all levels of the hierarchy in frequent face-to-face discussions and meetings.

Internal strengths and weaknesses

Strengths are positive internal characteristics that the organization can exploit to achieve its strategic performance goals. *Weaknesses* are internal characteristics that might inhibit or restrict the organization's performance. Some examples of what managers evaluate to interpret strengths and weaknesses are shown in the audit checklist in Exhibit 8.4. Managers perform an internal audit of specific functions such as marketing, finance, production, and research and development. Internal analysis also assesses overall organization structure, management competence and quality, and human resource characteristics. Based on their understanding of these areas, managers can determine their strengths or weaknesses compared with other companies.

TAKE A MOMENT

Go to the Small Group Breakout Exercise online that pertains to SWOT analysis. Before reading further, you might also want to review your strategic strengths as determined by your responses to the questionnaire at the end of this chapter.

External opportunities and threats

Threats are characteristics of the external environment that may prevent the organization from achieving its strategic goals. One threat to Microsoft, for example, is the proliferation of cheap or free software available over the Internet.[29] *Opportunities* are characteristics of the external environment that have the potential to help the organization achieve or exceed its strategic goals. For example, US auto manufacturers had an unprecedented opportunity to steal customers from Toyota because of the quality, safety and public relations problems that Toyota recently experienced.[30] German retailer Aldi found an opportunity to further expand in the USA because of heated opposition in urban areas to Walmart. Aldi has quietly been setting up small, drugstore-sized shops in cities around the USA, including New York City. *'Walmart has sort of become the bad guy that there's a concerted effort against,'* said Craig Johnson, president of consulting firm Customer

EXHIBIT 8.4 Audit checklist for analyzing organizational strengths and weaknesses

Management and organization	Marketing	Human resources
Management quality	Distribution channels	Employee experience,
Staff quality	Market share	education
Degree of centralization	Advertising efficiency	Union status
Organization charts	Customer satisfaction	Turnover, absenteeism
Planning, information,	Product quality	Work satisfaction
control systems	Service reputation	Grievances
	Sales force turnover	
Finance	**Production**	**Research and Development**
Profit margin	Location, resources	Basic applied research
Debt-equity ratio	Machinery obsolescence	Laboratory capabilities
Inventory ratio	Purchasing system	Research programs
Return on investment	Quality control	New-product innovations
Credit rating	Productivity/efficiency	Technology innovations

Growth Partners. *'There's no reason to oppose an Aldi.'* Because Aldi is a smaller format and has opened only a limited number of stores a year, it was able to slip in under the radar, obtaining space from small landlords while people were focused on fighting Walmart.[31]

Managers evaluate the external environment based on the ten sectors described in Chapter 3. The task environment sectors are the most relevant to strategic behaviour and include the behaviour of competitors, customers, suppliers and the labour supply. The general environment contains those sectors that have an indirect influence on the organization, but nevertheless must be understood and incorporated into strategic behaviour. The general environment includes technological developments, the economy, legal-political and international events, the natural environment and sociocultural changes. Additional areas that might reveal opportunities or threats include pressure groups, such as those opposing Walmart's expansion into urban areas, interest groups, creditors and potentially competitive industries.

A good example of SWOT analysis comes from Dana Holding Corporation, a world leader in axles, drive-shafts, transmissions and other automotive products.

Formulating corporate-level strategy

Three approaches to understanding corporate-level strategy are portfolio strategy, the BCG matrix and diversification.

 INNOVATIVE WAY

Dana Holding Corporation

Dana Holding Corporation was created in 1904, when a 29-year-old engineering student at Cornell designed the first practical universal joint to power an automobile and left school to start a business. Innovation and ingenuity still drive Dana's mission: 'To anticipate and address customers' needs with innovative solutions'. Dana Corporation is never standing still, and managers are continually evaluating the company's competitive situation and making strategic decisions based on looking at the company's strengths, weaknesses, opportunities and threats.

Dana's *strengths* include technological know-how, an innovative culture and a strong research and development department. The company has won global recognition as a technological innovator due to its cellular manufacturing methods, statistical process control techniques and flexible production. It has a well-trained workforce and major manufacturing facilities in 26 countries. Diverse products enable Dana to serve customers across the light-duty, heavy-duty and off-highway vehicle markets to improve sales and profits. A final strength comes from strong partnerships through alliances and joint ventures with other automotive component suppliers.

A primary *weakness* is that Dana is still dealing with fallout from a 2006 bankruptcy filing. The company emerged from bankruptcy in 2008, but customer and investor confidence has not fully recovered. In addition, operational costs remain high, contributing to lower profit margins.

The biggest *threats* to the company are a decline in demand for sport utility vehicles and pressures from auto manufacturing customers such as General Motors (GM), Chrysler, Ford and Volkswagen for lower prices on components. *Opportunities* exist in the ongoing development of electric and hybrid systems, where Dana has strong expertise, and in growing consumer pressures for more environmentally friendly products.

What does SWOT analysis suggest for Dana Corporation? To reduce costs and improve profit margins, managers have been selling off non-core businesses and closing weak or underperforming facilities. They are investing heavily in the Power Technologies unit, which produces products that incorporate sealing and thermal management technologies that help reduce fuel and oil consumption, cut emissions and improve vehicle durability. The investment seems to be paying off: Sales in the Power Technologies division exceeded $1 billion for the first time in 2011. The company is also working to expand its international business, with particular emphasis on emerging markets including Asia and South America, where demand for construction vehicles and industrial equipment products is growing.[32]

CONCEPT CONNECTION

On 11 March 2011, the people of Japan experienced an astounding 9.0 magnitude earthquake and tsunami, which struck the east coast of the country's main island, Honshu. The devastating natural disaster took the lives of more than 15 000 people and destroyed well over 100 million homes and businesses. The recovery efforts took many months, and during that time, many Japanese businesses suffered under the **threat** of failure due to the lack of energy, resources, labour and many other factors. And yet there were **opportunities** as well, especially through the reconstruction of the country's infrastructure and real estate development. However, valuable lessons have been learned from the catastrophe – especially regarding the safety features that new build nuclear power stations will be required to have in the future. A major nuclear power station is planned to be built in Somerset, England. It involves considerable foreign direct investment from China and involves EDF of France.

Portfolio strategy

Individual investors often wish to diversify in an investment portfolio with some high-risk stocks, some low-risk stocks, some growth stocks and perhaps a few income bonds. In much the same way, corporations like to have a balanced mix of business divisions called strategic business units (SBUs). An SBU has a unique business mission, product line, competitors and markets relative to other SBUs in the corporation.[33] Executives in charge of the entire corporation generally define an overall strategy and then bring together a portfolio of SBUs to carry it out. Some executives don't like to become over-dependent on one business. Portfolio strategy pertains to the mix of business units and product lines that fit together in a logical way to provide synergy and competitive advantage for the corporation. An interesting example of using portfolio strategy to attain synergy and competitive advantage comes from the health care industry.

It is too soon to tell if insurers' new portfolio strategy will provide value to customers or simply higher profits for insurers. Some consumer advocates are worried, while others believe the trend can be positive for patients as well as the organizations.

The BCG matrix

One coherent way to think about portfolio strategy is the BCG matrix. The BCG matrix (named for the Boston Consulting Group, which developed it) is illustrated in Exhibit 8.5. The BCG matrix organizes businesses along two dimensions – business growth rate and market share.[35] *Business growth rate* pertains to how rapidly the entire industry is increasing. *Market share* defines whether a business unit has a larger or smaller share than competitors. The combinations of high and low market share and high and low business growth, provide four categories for a corporate portfolio.

REFLECTION

- **Strategy formulation** is the stage of strategic management that includes the planning and decision-making that led to the establishment of the organization's goals and a specific strategic plan.
- Managers often start with a **SWOT analysis**, an audit or careful examination of *strengths, weaknesses, opportunities* and *threats* that affect organizational performance.

- The proliferation of free software over the Internet is a *threat* to Microsoft. Opposition to the expansion of Walmart provided German retailer Aldi with an *opportunity* to gain a foothold in urban areas.
- **Strategy execution** is the stage of strategic management that involves the use of managerial and organizational tools to direct resources towards achieving strategic outcomes.

INNOVATIVE WAY

UnitedHealth Group

UnitedHealth Group used to be an insurance company. Today, it describes itself as a health care company with a mission of 'helping people live healthier lives'. That's because UnitedHealth is now a portfolio of different companies – one subsidiary provides insurance, and others provide services such as information technology and data management for hospitals, drug delivery and clinical trial management, continuing medical education, and even physicians and other medical services. The company serves 75 million people worldwide and 'touches nearly every aspect of health care', as stated on the UnitedHealth website.

UnitedHealth might be the largest insurer, but it isn't the only one that has begun buying doctor's groups or medical facilities to develop a portfolio of divisions. WellPoint, for example, bought CareMore, a group of 26 health care clinics in the Los Angeles area. Humana bought Concentra, a chain of urgent care centres. And Highmark, which runs BlueCross BlueShield plans in Pennsylvania and West Virginia, is trying to buy a Pittsburgh-based chain of six hospitals. The strategy is partly in response to increasing financial pressure on insurers brought about by the Patient Protection and Affordable Care Act in the USA, and pressure from customers tired of paying ever-higher insurance premiums. 'It's just trying many different ways to see what appeals to the American public and what adds value,' said Gail Wilensky, a United board member.[34]

GREEN POWER

Beyond the dump

Houston-based Waste Management Inc. CEO David Steiner is leading a new 'Think Green' strategy that is reaching consumers as well as employees. This new approach began with consultants hired to examine Waste Management's sustainability strengths and weaknesses and to assess future opportunities. What emerged was a strategy to move the company beyond rubbish pickup – beyond the dump. In alignment with the company's 'Think Green' moniker, managers focus on extracting 'value' from waste by allowing consumers to place all recyclables in one container, with the various items separated on-site through forced air, magnets and optical scanning. Waste Management also responded to the need for massive clean-up efforts created by frequent natural disasters. One popular new product is the Bagster Dumpster in a Bag, with the capacity to hold up to 3300 pounds of debris and rubbish.

SOURCE: Marc Gunther, 'Waste Management's New Direction', *Fortune* (December 6, 2010): 103–108.

The *star* has a large market share in a rapidly growing industry. It is important because it has additional growth potential, and profits should be ploughed into this business as investment for future growth and profits. The star is visible and attractive and will generate profits and a positive cash flow even as the industry matures and market growth slows.

The *cash cow* exists in a mature, slow-growth industry but is a dominant business in the industry, with a large market share. Because heavy investments in advertising and plant expansion are no longer required, the corporation earns a positive cash flow. It can milk the cash cow to invest in other, riskier businesses.

The *question mark* exists in a new, rapidly growing industry, but has only a small market share. The question mark business is risky: It could become a star, or it could fail. The corporation can invest the cash earned from cash cows in question marks with the goal of nurturing them into future stars.

EXHIBIT 8.5 The BCG matrix

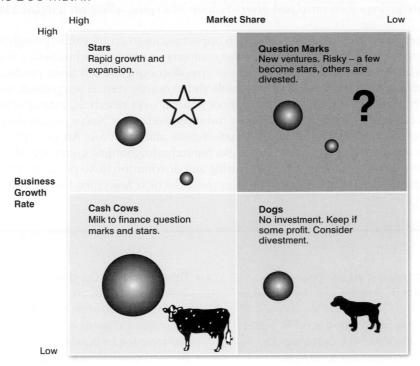

The *dog* is a poor performer. It has only a small share of a slow-growth market. The dog provides little profit for the corporation and may be targeted for divestment or liquidation if turnaround is not possible.

The circles in Exhibit 8.5 represent the business portfolio for a hypothetical corporation. Circle size represents the relative size of each business in the company's portfolio. Most large organizations, such as General Electric (GE), have businesses in more than one quadrant, thereby representing different market shares and growth rates. The most famous cash cow in GE's portfolio, for example, is the appliance division. This business holds a large share of a stable market and accounts for a big portion of GE's sales and profits. The GE Healthcare and Aviation divisions have star status, and GE is pumping money into development of new products in these fast-growing areas, such as products for wind energy. GE's consumer finance division is a question mark. The division expanded too aggressively into areas such as real estate and took a big hit during the 2008 financial crisis. The media division has probably gained dog status because it doesn't fit well in the GE portfolio. A dog for GE might be a star for someone else, so GE executives recently sold a majority stake in NBC Universal to Comcast.[36]

Diversification strategy

The strategy of moving into new lines of business, as search leader Google did by purchasing YouTube and BlackBerry, is called diversification. Other notable examples of diversification include Apple's entry into the mobile phone business with the iPhone, Amazon's move into consumer electronics with the Kindle electronic reader, and Nestlé's entry into the pet food business with the purchase of Ralston.

The purpose of diversification is to expand the firm's business operations to produce new kinds of valuable products and services. When the new business is related to the company's existing business activities, the organization is implementing a strategy of related diversification. Nestlé's move into pet foods is linked to these firms' existing health care and nutrition businesses. Unrelated diversification occurs when an organization expands into a totally new line of business, such as GE's entry into media, or food company Sara Lee's move into the intimate clothing business. With unrelated diversification, the company's lines of business aren't logically associated with one another; therefore, it can be difficult to make the strategy successful. Many companies are giving up on unrelated diversification strategies, selling off unrelated businesses to focus on core areas.

A firm's managers may also pursue diversification opportunities to create value through a strategy of vertical integration. Vertical integration means that the company expands into businesses that either produce the supplies needed to make products and services or that distribute and sell those products and services to customers. In recent years, there has been a noticeable shift towards vertical integration, with large corporations getting into businesses that will give them more control over materials, manufacturing and distribution.[37] To gain more control over raw materials, for instance, steelmaker Nucor acquired a major scrap-metal processor, and rival Arcelor bought mines in Brazil, Russia and the USA. An example of diversifying to distribute products comes from PepsiCo, which began repurchasing bottling companies that it spun off in the late 1990s. PepsiCo controls marketing, manufacturing and distribution in 80 per cent of North America and is expected to buy the remaining independent bottlers over the next few years. Service companies can pursue vertical integration too.

REFLECTION

- Frameworks for corporate-level strategy include portfolio strategy, the BCG matrix and diversification strategy.
- Portfolio strategy pertains to the mix of SBUs and product lines that fit together in a logical way to provide synergy and competitive advantage.
- A strategic business unit (SBU) is a division of the organization that has a unique business, mission, product or service line, competitors and markets relative to other units of the same organization.
- The BCG matrix is a concept developed by the Boston Consulting Group that evaluates SBUs with respect to two dimensions – business growth rate and market share – and classifies them as cash cows, stars, question marks or dogs.

- The strategy of moving into new lines of business is called diversification.
- Apple diversified when it moved into the mobile phone business, and Nestlé diversified by purchasing the Ralston pet food business.
- Related diversification means moving into a new business that is related to the corporation's existing business activities.
- Unrelated diversification refers to expanding into totally new lines of business.
- Some managers pursue diversification through a strategy of vertical integration, which means expanding into businesses that either provide the supplies needed to make products or distribute and sell the company's products.

Formulating business-level strategy

Now we turn to strategy formulation within the SBU, in which the concern is how to compete. A popular and effective model for formulating strategy is Porter's competitive strategies. Michael E. Porter studied a number of business organizations and proposed that business-level strategies are the result of understanding competitive forces in the company's environment.[38]

The competitive environment

The competitive environment is different for different kinds of businesses. Most large companies have separate business lines and do an industry analysis for each line of business or SBU. Mars, Inc., for example, operates in six business segments: chocolate (Snickers); pet care (Pedigree); gum and confections (Juicy Fruit); food (Uncle Ben's); drinks (Flavia); and symbioscience (veterinary care, plant care). The competitive environment for the chocolate division would be different from that for the symbioscience division, so managers would do a competitive analysis for each business segment, looking at factors such as competitors, customers, suppliers, the threat of substitute products or services, potential new markets and so forth.

Porter's competitive strategies

To find a competitive edge within the specific business environment, Porter suggests that a company can adopt one of three strategies: differentiation, cost leadership or focus. The organizational characteristics typically associated with each strategy are summarized in Exhibit 8.6.

EXHIBIT 8.6 Organizational characteristics of Porter's competitive strategies

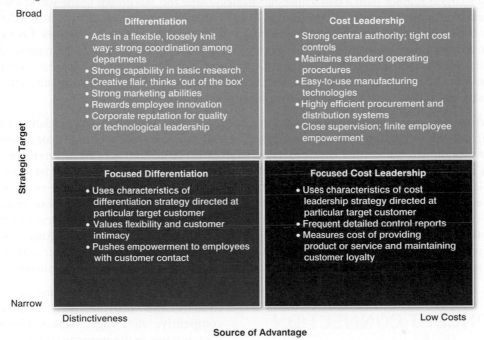

SOURCES: Michael E. Porter, *Competitive Strategy: Techniques for Analyzing Industries and Competitors* (New York: The Free Press, 1980); Michael Treacy and Fred Wiersema, 'How Market Leaders Keep Their Edge', *Fortune* (February 6, 1995): 88–98; and Michael A. Hitt, R. Duane Ireland and Robert E. Hoskisson, *Strategic Management* (St. Paul, MN: West, 1995), pp. 100–113.

- **Differentiation.** The differentiation strategy involves an attempt to distinguish the firm's products or services from others in the industry. The organization may use creative advertising, distinctive product features, exceptional service or new technology to achieve a product perceived as unique. Examples of products that have benefited from a differentiation strategy include Harley-Davidson motorcycles, Apple computers and phones, and Gore-Tex fabrics, all of which are perceived as distinctive in their markets. Apple computers, the iPhone and the iPad, for example, can command significantly higher prices because of their distinctiveness. Apple has never tried to compete on price and likes being perceived as an 'elite' brand. Service companies such as Starbucks, Whole Foods Market and IKEA also use a differentiation strategy.

  A differentiation strategy can reduce rivalry with competitors and fight off the threat of substitute products because customers are loyal to the company's brand. However, a differentiation strategy requires a number of costly activities, such as product research and design and extensive advertising. Companies need a robust marketing department and creative employees who are given the time and resources to seek innovation.

- **Cost leadership.** With a cost leadership strategy, the organization aggressively seeks efficient facilities, pursues cost reductions and uses tight cost controls to produce products more efficiently than competitors. Although cost leadership doesn't always mean low prices, most cost leadership companies keep internal costs low so that they can provide products and services to customers at lower prices and still make a profit. A cost leadership position means that the company can undercut competitors' prices and still offer comparable quality and earn a reasonable profit. For example, Spirit Airlines, which has taken cut-rate fares to new extremes, is one of the most profitable companies in the airline industry, earning 40 per cent more per plane than any other US airline.[39]

The cost leadership strategy is concerned with maintaining stability rather than pursuing innovation and growth. However, cost leadership can certainly lead to growth, as evidenced by Walmart, which became the world's largest retailer with a cost leadership strategy. Acer Inc. has grown to the world's second-largest computer maker with a cost leadership strategy. Acer has a bare-bones cost structure. Its overhead expenses are about 8 per cent of sales, compared to around 14 to 15 per cent for rival companies. Cost savings are passed on to consumers, with a high-quality ultrathin laptop selling for around £600, compared to £1700 for a similar Hewlett-Packard (HP) model and £800 for Dell's ultrathin version. Acer has now moved into the smartphone market. With its cost leadership position, Acer can give consumers quality smartphones at lower prices and still see profit margins in the range of 15 to 20 per cent.[40]

■ **Focus.** With a focus strategy the organization concentrates on a specific regional market or buyer group. The company will use either a differentiation or cost leadership approach, but only for a narrow target market. An example of a focused cost leadership strategy is Poundstretcher. Poundstretcher stores offer prices on major brands such as Tide washing powder or Colgate toothpaste that can be more than 40 per cent lower than those found in major supermarkets. The company locates its stores on inexpensive real estate and markets to mainly low income people rather than trying to court a more upscale clientele. Proamérica Bank succeeds with a focused differentiation strategy. Mexican-born Maria Contreras-Sweet founded the bank to concentrate on serving largely family-owned businesses in Los Angeles's Hispanic community. She believes the Latino-owned bank can differentiate itself from its larger commercial competitors, such as Bank of America, by establishing close personal relationships with customers.[41]

CONCEPT CONNECTION

While Americans and Europeans enjoy snapping up the latest and more expensive smartphones that feature all kinds of special features, many mobile phone users around the world look for simple, reliable mobile phones at affordable prices. China's ZTE is there to meet their needs. ZTE has employed a **cost leadership strategy**, using efficient production to keep prices low for many of its models. The approach has made the company one of the biggest mobile phone producers in the world.

Managers should think carefully about which strategy will provide their company with a competitive advantage. Gibson Guitar Corporation, famous in the music world for its innovative, high-quality products, found that switching to a cost leadership strategy to compete against Japanese rivals such as Yamaha and Ibanez actually hurt the company. When managers realized that people wanted Gibson products because of their reputation, not their price, they went back to a differentiation strategy and invested in new technology and marketing.[42]

In his studies, Porter found that some businesses did not consciously adopt one of these three strategies and were stuck with no strategic advantage. Without a strategic advantage, businesses earned below-average profits compared with those that used differentiation, cost leadership, or focus strategies. Similarly, a 5-year study of management practices in hundreds of businesses, referred to as the 'Evergreen Project', found that a clear strategic direction was a key factor that distinguished winners from losers.[43] JCPenney floundered through a transition because customers were confused by a strategy that seems to combine cost leadership and differentiation.

INNOVATIVE WAY

JCPenney

Ron Johnson, the CEO of JCPenney, is a former Apple executive largely responsible for creating Apple's innovative retail store concept. With that kind of success, can he transform the struggling JCPenney stores? Maybe, maybe not, Penney's has been under pressure for years, and at the time of his appointment, Johnson was hailed as just the right executive to get the retailer back on track at long last.

Johnson introduced a new strategy that did away with the company's hundreds of annual sales events (there were nearly 600 of them in 2011) in favour of an 'everyday fair and square' price model. Prices were cut about 40 per cent across the board. The strategy also included a new logo and a makeover of stores into distinctive vendor-branded and themed 'boutiques'. Regular customers haven't responded favourably, though. The retailer's sales have plummeted since the 'fair and square' pricing model was introduced. Johnson says

customers were initially confused by the change, and he believes the new model will pay off as they realize that store prices are low every day and they don't have to wait for sales.

The problem, though, say some analysts, is that JCPenney isn't Apple. The company doesn't have the brand recognition, distinctiveness and customer loyalty that Apple enjoys. Apple's status-symbol products keep customers coming to the stores no matter what. JCPenney, on the other hand, needed those regular sales to bring people in – and to get them to buy once they were there. Everyday low pricing takes away the fun of searching for deals and getting a bargain. 'A discount gives shoppers the incentive to buy today,' said Kit Yarrow, consumer psychologist and author of *Gen BuY: How Tweens, Teens, and Twenty-Somethings Are Revolutionizing Retail.* 'Without that, there's no sense of urgency for people to purchase things that, frankly, they probably don't need.' Johnson might agree. He recently reintroduced the word *sale* into the company's lexicon.[44]

Although he is making adjustments, Johnson is sticking with his basic strategy to revolutionize JCPenney with across-the-board low prices, a boutique approach, and eventually, a checkout-free concept that uses Wi-Fi and mobile technology to let customers pay without having to go through a checkout counter. Getting rid of cashiers, cash registers and checkout stands could save millions of dollars that can be put towards lowering prices and providing superior customer service, Johnson says.[45] Will it work? Old-time customers might be alienated, but a new generation of customers might find it just the right approach.

Formulating functional-level strategy

Functional-level strategies are the action plans used by major departments to support the execution of business-level strategy. Major organizational functions include marketing, production, finance, human resources and research and development. Managers in these and other departments adopt strategies that are coordinated with business-level strategy to achieve the organization's strategic goals.

For example, consider a company that has adopted a differentiation strategy and is introducing new products that are expected to experience rapid growth. The human resources department should adopt a strategy appropriate for growth, which would mean recruiting additional personnel and training middle- and lower-level managers for new positions. The marketing department should undertake test marketing, aggressive advertising campaigns and consumer product trials. The finance department should adopt plans to borrow money, handle large cash investments and authorize construction of new facilities.

A company with mature products or a cost leadership strategy will have different functional-level strategies. The human resources department should develop strategies for retaining and developing a stable workforce. Marketing should stress brand loyalty and the development of established, reliable distribution channels. Production should use a strategy of long production runs, standard procedures and cost reduction. Finance should focus on net cash flows and positive cash balances.

REFLECTION

- A popular framework for formulating business-level strategy is Porter's competitive strategies.
- Managers analyze the competitive environment and adopt one of three types of strategy: differentiation, cost leadership or focus.
- A differentiation strategy is a strategy with which managers seek to distinguish the organization's products and services from those of others in the industry.
- A cost leadership strategy is a strategy with which managers aggressively seek efficient facilities, cut

costs and use tight cost controls to be more efficient than others in the industry.
- With a focus strategy, managers use either a differentiation or a cost leadership approach, but they concentrate on a specific regional market or buyer group.
- Managers at Poundstretcher stores use a focus strategy by concentrating on selling to low income people.
- Once business-level strategies are formulated, managers in functional departments devise functional-level strategies to support them.

Global strategy

Many organizations operate globally and pursue a distinct strategy as the focus of global business. Senior executives try to formulate coherent strategies to provide synergy among worldwide operations for the purpose of fulfilling common goals.

One consideration for managers is the strategic dilemma between the need for global standardization and national responsiveness. The various global strategies are shown in Exhibit 8.7. The first step towards a greater international presence is when companies begin exporting domestically produced products to selected

EXHIBIT 8.7 Global corporate strategies

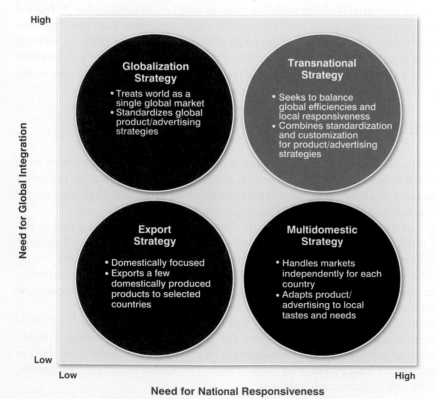

SOURCES: Michael A. Hitt, R. Duane Ireland and Robert E. Hoskisson, *Strategic Management: Competitiveness and Globalization* (St. Paul, MN; West Publishing, 1995), p. 239; and Thomas M. Begley and David P. Boyd, 'The Need for a Corporate Global Mindset', *MIT Sloan Management Review* (Winter 2003): 25–32.

countries. The *export strategy* is shown in the lower-left corner of the exhibit. Because the organization is domestically focused, with only a few exports, managers have little need to pay attention to issues of either local responsiveness or global standardization. Organizations that pursue further international expansion must decide whether they want each global affiliate to act autonomously or if activities should be standardized and centralized across countries. This choice leads managers to select a basic strategy alternative, such as globalization versus multidomestic strategy. Some corporations may seek to achieve a degree of both global standardization and national responsiveness by using a transnational strategy.

Globalization strategy

When an organization chooses a globalization strategy, it means that product design and advertising strategies are standardized throughout the world.[46] This approach is based on the assumption that a single global market exists for many consumer and industrial products. The theory is that people everywhere want to buy the same products and live the same way. The idea is that people everywhere want to eat McDonald's hamburgers and use iPhones.[47] A globalization strategy can help an organization reap efficiencies by standardizing product design and manufacturing, using common suppliers, introducing products around the world faster, coordinating prices and eliminating overlapping facilities. For example, Gillette has large production facilities that use common suppliers and processes to manufacture razors and other products with technical specifications that are standardized around the world.[48]

Globalization enables marketing departments alone to save millions of dollars. One consumer products company reports that, for every country where the same commercial runs, the company saves $1 million to $2 million in production costs. More millions have been saved by standardizing the look and packaging of brands.[49] Domino's Pizza is using a globalization strategy as it expands into emerging markets such as India, China, Russia and Brazil. Although local franchisees can modify ingredients to suit local tastes, Domino's managers say the strategy in emerging markets is '*to go in there with a tried-and-true business model of delivery and carryout pizza that we deploy around the world.*' Domino's facilities, packaging and marketing materials look essentially the same in Russia, India or the USA.[50]

CONCEPT CONNECTION

Since first going international in 1971, Dallas-based Mary Kay Inc. (cosmetics) has expanded to more than 30 markets on five continents. The company uses a **multidomestic strategy** that handles competition independently in each country. In China, for example, Mary Kay has developed products that appeal to the unique tastes and preferences of Chinese women. Under the direction of Mary Kay China president, Paul Mak (centre), the company has built a $25 million distribution centre in Hangzhou, the first such location outside the United States. Within the next several years, China is poised to become Mary Kay's biggest market, surpassing all others, including its home market.

Multidomestic strategy

When an organization chooses a multidomestic strategy, it means that competition in each country is handled independently of industry competition in other countries. Thus, a multinational company is present in many countries, but it encourages marketing, advertising and product design to be modified and adapted to the specific needs of each country.[51] Many companies reject the idea of a single global market. They have found that the French do not drink orange juice for breakfast, that laundry detergent is used to wash dishes in parts of Mexico, and that people in the Middle East prefer toothpaste that tastes spicy. Kraft Foods Inc. has introduced new products, reformulated recipes and redesigned packaging to suit local tastes in various countries. In China, for instance, Kraft cookie flavours include green tea, ice cream, and mango and mandarin orange; and Ritz crackers are offered in flavours such as 'fantastic beef stew' and 'very spicy chicken' and sold in portable cuplike packages that resemble ramen-noodle containers.[52] Service companies also have to consider their global strategy carefully. The 7-Eleven convenience store chain uses a multidomestic strategy because the product mix, advertising approach and payment methods need to be tailored to the preferences, values and government regulations in different parts of the world. For example, in Japan, customers like to use convenience stores to pay utility and other bills. 7-Eleven Japan responded by offering that as a service, as well as setting up a way for people to pick up and pay for purchases made over the Internet at their local 7-Eleven store.[53]

Transnational strategy

A transnational strategy seeks to achieve both global standardization and national responsiveness.[54] A true transnational strategy is difficult to achieve though, because one goal requires close global coordination while the other requires local flexibility. However, many industries are finding that, although increased competition means that they must achieve global efficiency, growing pressure to meet local needs demands national responsiveness.[55] One company that effectively achieves both aspects of a transnational strategy is Coca-Cola. The giant soft drink company can attain efficiencies by manufacturing, advertising and distributing well-known brands such as Coke, Fanta and Sprite on a global basis. However, CEO Muhtar Kent has pushed the company to expand beyond well-known brands and embrace local tastes. The company sells more than 400 different drinks globally.

Although most multinational companies want to achieve some degree of global standardization to hold costs down, even global products may require some customization to meet government regulations in various countries, or some tailoring to fit consumer preferences. In addition, increased competition means many organizations need to take advantage of global opportunities as well as respond to the heterogeneity of the international marketplace.

REFLECTION

- When formulating a strategy as the focus for global operations, managers face a dilemma between the need for global standardization and the need for local responsiveness.
- With a globalization strategy, product design and advertising are standardized throughout the world.
- A multidomestic strategy means that competition in each country is handled independently; product design and advertising are modified to suit the specific needs of individual countries.

- Kraft has reformulated cookie and cracker recipes and redesigned packaging to suit tastes in China.
- A transnational strategy is a strategy that combines global coordination to attain efficiency with local flexibility to meet needs in different countries.
- Most large companies use a combination of global strategies to achieve global standardization and efficiency, as well as respond to local needs and preferences in various countries.

Strategy execution

The final step in the strategic management process is strategy execution – how strategy is implemented or put into action. Many companies have file drawers full of winning strategies, but they still struggle to succeed. Why? Practising managers remind us that 'strategy is easy, but execution is hard'.[56] Indeed, many strategy experts agree that execution is the most important, yet the most difficult, part of strategic management.[57]

No matter how brilliant the formulated strategy, the organization will not benefit if it is not skilfully executed. One key to effective strategy execution is *alignment*, so that all aspects of the organization are in congruence with the strategy and every department and individual's efforts are coordinated towards accomplishing strategic goals. Alignment basically means that everyone is moving in the same direction. Grand goals have to be translated into a clear blueprint for execution, so that everyone's actions are in line with managers' strategic intentions.[58] Recall our discussion of strategy maps from the previous chapter. Just as managers make sure goals are in alignment, they check that all aspects of the organization are coordinated to be supportive of the strategies designed to achieve those goals.

Exhibit 8.8 illustrates the primary tools that managers use to implement strategy effectively: visible leadership, clear roles and accountability, candid communication and appropriate human resource practices.[59]

'If you want to build a ship, don't drum up the men to gather wood, divide the work and give orders. Instead, teach them to yearn for the vast and endless sea.'
— ANTOINE DE SAINT-EXUPÉRY (1900–1944), *CITADELLE (THE WISDOM OF THE SANDS)*

- *Visible leadership.* The primary key to successful strategy execution is good leadership. *Leadership* is the ability to influence people to adopt the new behaviours needed for putting the strategy into action. Leaders actively use persuasion, motivation techniques and cultural values that support the new strategy. They might make speeches to employees, build coalitions of people who support the new strategic direction, and persuade middle managers to go along with their vision for the company. Most important, they lead by example.[60] Pixar, the animation studio, has a rule about leadership that supports its strategy of producing highly creative animated films: no studio executives.

Pixar's leaders are the creative artists, an approach that maintains a 'film school without the teachers' culture that gives people maximum freedom to develop and pursue unique, innovative ideas. At Pixar, everyone from janitors to auditors is encouraged to submit ideas for new films.[61]

- *Clear roles and accountability.* People need to understand how their individual actions can contribute to achieving the strategy. Trying to execute a strategy that conflicts with structural design, particularly in relation to managers' roles, authority and accountability, is a top obstacle to putting strategy into

EXHIBIT 8.8 Tools for putting strategy into action

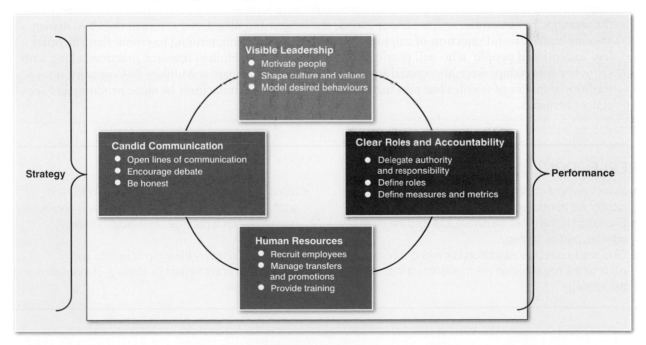

SOURCES: Jay R. Galbraith and Robert K. Kazanjian. *Strategy Implementation: Structure, Systems, and Process,* 2nd ed. (Cincinnati, OH: South-Western, Cengage Learning, 1986); Lawrence G. Hrebiniak, *Making Strategy Work: Leading Effective Execution and Change* (Upper Saddle River, NJ: Wharton School Publishing/Pearson Education Inc., 2005); and Eric Beaudan, 'Creative Execution', *Ivey Business Journal* (March–April 2010), www.iveybusinessjournal.com/article.asp?intArticle_ID=891 (accessed March 26, 2010).

action.[62] To execute strategy effectively, top executives clearly define roles and delegate authority to individuals and teams who are accountable for results. A lack of clear roles and accountability is partly to blame for the debacle at JPMorgan Chase, which announced a multibillion-dollar loss in May 2012. Why did implementation of the company's careful, low-risk trading strategy falter? Ina Drew, the senior banker who has been blamed for the problems, had won the complete trust of CEO Jamie Dimon after she steered the company through the 2008 financial crisis. However, Drew was out of the office a great deal of time due to illness beginning in 2010, and long-simmering conflicts and divisions over roles and responsibilities emerged. Drew's deputy in New York, Althea Duersten, disagreed with the risky, outsized bets being made by Achilles Macris, the deputy in London, but the London deputy used his stronger personality to shout down Duersten's objections and gain more power. *'It felt like there was a land grab where no one was pushing back because Althea and Achilles both wanted more responsibility,'* a former trader said. Another trader underscored the lack of clear roles when he said he *'didn't know who to listen to.'*[63]

■ *Candid communication.* Managers openly and avidly promote their strategic ideas, but they also listen to others and encourage disagreement and debate. They create a culture based on openness and honesty, which encourages teamwork and collaboration across hierarchical and departmental boundaries. Effective strategy execution also requires candid communication with shareholders, customers and other stakeholders. Sergey Brin and Larry Page, the founders of Google, take turns writing a direct and open letter to shareholders each year. The original letter written for the initial public offering (IPO) makes clear that Google wouldn't try to 'smooth out' its quarterly results, as some publicly traded companies do.[64] Candid communication with customers was also part of strategy implementation at JCPenney, described earlier. When Ron Johnson announced his new 'fair and square price' strategy, he told customers that the regular prices in stores have long been 'fake and inflated'. Johnson felt that the company's rejection of marketing gimmicks would win trust and support for the new strategy.[65]

■ *Appropriate human resource practices.* The organization's *human resources* are its employees. The human resource function recruits, selects, trains, compensates, transfers, promotes and lays off employees to achieve strategic goals. Managers make sure human resource practices are aligned with the strategy. For example, at Broadmoor Hotel, the longest-reigning 5-star resort in the USA, managers emphasize careful selection of employees and extensive ongoing training to ensure that the hotel has 'exceptional people' who will provide exceptional service.[66] Human resource practices, along with visionary leadership, were also crucial to execution of a new strategy at Milliken & Company, once a traditional maker of textiles but now thriving as a diversified manufacturer of niche products and specialty chemicals.

REFLECTION

- Even the most creative strategies have no value if they cannot be translated into action.
- Execution is the most important, but also the most difficult, part of strategy.
- One key to effective execution is making sure that all parts of the organization are in alignment to support the strategy.

- Managers use visible leadership, clear roles and accountability, candid communication and appropriate human resource practices to execute strategy effectively.
- Milliken & Company hires top scientists and researchers to implement its strategy of innovation and diversification.

INNOVATIVE WAY

Milliken & Company

'All of Milliken's traditional textile competitors are gone,' says John Fly, a top executive at Milliken & Company in Spartanburg, South Carolina. 'They're out of business. And Milliken is having the best economic performance it's ever had. It's clear we did something different.'

What Milliken did differently was adopt a strategy of innovation and diversification. Traditional textile manufacturing began leaving the USA long ago to take advantage of lower labour costs overseas. Milliken's managers knew they had to change – and they had to change fast. Visible and visionary leadership was crucial to implementing a new strategy. Roger Milliken, who died at the age of 95 in 2010, was constantly 'pounding the drum' for new ideas, new products and new techniques. Ever wonder who makes the fabric that reinforces duct tape? How about the additives that make children's markers washable or that make combat gear protective? Those products, and hundreds of others that touch our lives every day, are made by Milliken. Milliken still makes textiles, but it isn't a textile company. 'We're an innovation company,' says CEO Joe Salley.

Getting the right people on board was essential to executing the strategy. Around 350 of Milliken's managers and supervisors have advanced degrees, a third of them PhDs. Hiring scientists and researchers from top schools is a priority. The company is able to get them because when they come to Milliken, they know they'll have the opportunity to work seriously in the sciences. The Milliken Hall of Fame posts employee names alongside their patents (thousands of them). Researchers can use 15 per cent of their time to work on anything they like, and proven innovators get 50 per cent of their time to work on projects of their own choosing.[67]

DISCUSSION QUESTIONS

1   Based on data acquired and analyzed of the following companies, how effective has (any one) of the following four acquisitions been, in terms of creating corporate synergy:

 a) The purchase of MySpace by News Corporation (owner of Fox Broadcasting)

 b) Facebook's purchase of Instagram

 c) Coca Cola's purchase of Innocent Smoothies

 d) Kraft's acquisition of Cadbury?

2   A corporate management team is determining whether the company should diversify into new markets. Determine what factors pre-entry they should consider including competitor data they could/should analyze.

3   Assume you are a middle manager tasked with the implementation of a new corporate cost-cutting strategy and you are meeting resistance from your subordinates. Discuss how the momentum of the change management process could be regained.

4   Using Porter's competitive strategies, how would you describe the strategies of Waitrose, Tesco and Aldi?

5   What is meant by 'vertical integration'? Discuss why some business are increasingly shifting towards vertical integration.

6   Describe the differences between globalization, multidomestic and transnational strategies. As the CEO of a fast growing food and drink company, which strategy would be best for your enterprise?

What is your strategy's strength?[68]

INSTRUCTIONS As a new manager, what are your strengths concerning strategy formulation and implementation? To find out, think about *how you handle challenges and issues* in your business school or job.

Then mark (a) or (b) for each of the following items, depending on which is more descriptive of your behaviour. There is no right or wrong answer to these questions. Respond to each item as it best describes how you respond to work situations.

1 When keeping records, I tend to:

   a. Be careful about documentation.   ___ ___

   b. Be haphazard about documentation.

2 If I run a group or a project, I:

   a. Have the general idea and let others figure out how to do the tasks.   ___ ___

   b. Try to figure out specific goals, timelines and expected outcomes.

3 My thinking style could be more accurately described as:

   a. Linear thinker, going from A to B to C.   ___ ___

   b. Thinking like a grasshopper, hopping from one idea to another.

4 In my office or home, things are:

   a. Here and there, in various piles.   ___ ___

   b. Laid out neatly, or at least in reasonable order.

5 I take pride in developing:

   a. Ways to overcome a barrier to a solution.   ___ ___

   b. New hypotheses about the underlying cause of a problem.

6 I can best help strategy by encouraging:

   a. Openness to a wide range of assumptions and ideas.   ___ ___

   b. Thoroughness when implementing new ideas.

7 One of my strengths is:

   a. Commitment to making things work.   ___ ___

   b. Commitment to a dream for the future.

8 I am most effective when I emphasize:

   a. Inventing original solutions.   ___ ___

   b. Making practical improvements.

SCORING & INTERPRETATION Managers have differing strengths and capabilities when it comes to formulating and implementing strategy. Here's how to determine yours. For *Strategic Formulator* strength, score 1 point for each (a) answer marked for questions 2, 4, 6 and 8, and for each (b) answer marked for questions 1, 3, 5 and 7. For *Strategic Implementer* strength, score 1 point for each (b) answer marked for questions 2, 4, 6 and 8, and for each (a) answer marked for questions 1, 3, 5 and 7. Which of your two scores is higher, and by how much? The higher score indicates your strategy strength.

New managers bring value to strategic management as formulators, implementers or both. New managers with implementer strengths tend to work within the situation and improve it by making it more efficient and reliable. Managers with the formulator strength push towards out-of-the-box strategies and like to seek out dramatic breakthroughs. Both styles are essential to strategic management. Strategic formulators often use their skills in creating whole new strategies and strategic implementers often work with strategic improvements and implementation.

If the difference between your two scores is 2 or less, you have a balanced formulator/implementer style and work well in both arenas. If the difference is 4 or 5 points, you have a moderately strong style and probably work best in the area of your strength. If the difference is 7 or 8 points, you have a distinctive strength and almost certainly would want to work in the area of your strength rather than in the opposite domain.

APPLY YOUR SKILLS: ETHICAL DILEMMA

The Spitzer Group[69]

Irving Silberstein, marketing director for the Spitzer Group, a growing regional marketing and corporate communications firm, was hard at work on an exciting project. He was designing Spitzer's first word-of-mouth campaign for an important client, a manufacturer of beauty products.

In a matter of just a few years, word-of-mouth advertising campaigns morphed from a small fringe specialty to a mainstream marketing technique embraced by no less than consumer products giant Procter & Gamble (P&G). The basic idea was simple, really. You harnessed the power of existing social networks to sell your products and services. The place to start, Irving knew, was to take a close look at how P&G's in-house unit, Vocalpoint, conducted its highly successful campaigns, both for its own products and those of its clients.

Because women were key purchasers of P&G consumer products, Vocalpoint focused on recruiting mothers with extensive social networks, participants known internally by the somewhat awkward term *connectors*. The Vocalpoint web page took care to emphasize that participants were members of an 'exclusive' community of mums who exerted significant influence on P&G and other major companies. Vocalpoint not only sent the women new product samples and solicited their opinions, but it also carefully tailored its pitch to the group's interests and preoccupations so the women would want to tell their friends about a product. For example, it described a new dishwashing foam that was so much fun to use, kids would actually volunteer to clean up the kitchen (music to any mother's ears). P&G then furnished the mothers with coupons to hand out if

they wished. It was all voluntary, P&G pointed out. According to a company press release issued shortly before Vocalpoint went national in early 2006, members 'are never obligated to do or say anything'.

One of the things Vocalpoint members weren't obligated to say, Irving knew, was that the women were essentially unpaid participants in a P&G-sponsored marketing programme. When asked about the policy, Vocalpoint CEO Steve Reed replied, '*We have a deeply held belief you don't tell the consumer what to say.*' However, sceptical observers speculated that what the company really feared was that the women's credibility might be affected adversely if their Vocalpoint affiliation were known. Non-disclosure really amounted to lying for financial gain, Vocalpoint's critics argued, and furthermore, the whole campaign shamelessly exploited personal relationships for commercial purposes. Others thought the critics were making mountains out of molehills. P&G wasn't forbidding participants from disclosing their ties to Vocalpoint and P&G. And the fact that they weren't paid meant the women had no vested interest in endorsing the products.

So, as Irving designs the word-of-mouth campaign for his agency's client, just how far should he emulate the company that even its detractors acknowledge is a master of the technique?

What would you do?

1 Don't require Spitzer 'connectors' to reveal their affiliation with the corporate word-of-mouth marketing campaign. They don't have to recommend a product they don't believe in.

2   Require that Spitzer participants reveal their ties to the corporate marketing programme right up front before they make a recommendation.

3   Instruct Spitzer participants to reveal their participation in the corporate marketing programme only if directly asked by the person they are talking to about the client's products.

APPLY YOUR SKILLS: CASE FOR CRITICAL ANALYSIS

Comparing retailers Marks and Spencer and Tesco

Marks and Spencer

Marks and Spencer (M&S) is one of the UK's best known retailers with over 100 years of experience. Its core aspirations are to promote quality value, service, innovation and trust. It has a rich history and an extraordinary global reach with over 34 million customers. These are some of the attributes that make M&S unique. The company predominantly operates in the UK but has global outlets and employs over 65 000 people. The M&S strategy focuses on sustainable consumption and production offering customers good value, high quality products and services, sold through an efficient multichannel operation based on a transparent value chain and comprehensive reporting. The M&S strategy is to reassert M&S as a brand of style and substance and to showcase the quality, innovation and provenance of its food. In order to promote this aspiration the aim is to deliver a holistic brand experience that spans its products, its sub-brands, its marketing and, critically, its in-store environments. M&S has a broad range of customers, but within that it has clear customer groups, and works hard, strategically, to remain relevant to each one of these groups via compelling and relevant targeted marketing initiatives.

The retail industry is going through a period of profound change. Many of the actions set out as part of M&S strategy have been implemented; this puts M&S in a stronger position to compete. M&S has also delivered major infrastructure projects that have strengthened its business. Its new M&S.com website and new distribution centre are both essential in its strategy to transform M&S from a traditional British retailer into an international, multichannel retailer. It has repositioned its website as its flagship and its design has been centred on the needs of its customers.

Tesco

Tesco is the biggest private sector employer in the UK and has 360 000 employees worldwide. Tesco also operates in 12 countries outside the UK. Its new core purpose is: We make what matters better, together. Its new core value is: We use our scale for good. Tesco has set three big ambitions in areas where it believes it can make a real contribution and create value for society as a whole. This new core value is also about building on the essential work Tesco does as a responsible corporate citizen.

Tesco has three strategic priorities:

1   Continuing to invest in a strong UK business.

2   Establishing multichannel leadership in all of its markets.

3   Pursuing disciplined international growth.

As a retailer, Tesco's business model is based on core activities:

- Tesco buys products and services from suppliers.

- Tesco moves them through its distribution network

- Tesco sells them to customers.

- Tesco aims to improve these activities for customers each time they shop.

Customers purchase instore, online or through a combination of different formats and channels. Tesco aims to provide customers with the most compelling offer and the best shopping trip. It works with its suppliers to offer an excellent range of products and services. It moves the products through its modern and efficient supply chain into its well-located, multiformat store network, ready for customers to shop 24 hours a day. The core activities form a cycle. Tesco is now accelerating plans to deliver the most compelling offer for customers with sharper prices, improved quality, stronger ranges and better service, in addition to accelerating growth in new channels.

In 2015 Tesco crashed to the biggest loss ever recorded on the UK high street, slumping £6.4 billion into the red as a result of huge writedowns on the value of its property portfolio and stock.

Dave Lewis, the chief executive parachuted in to mastermind a turnaround last year, described the loss as a 'big significant number'. But the former Unilever executive insisted the supermarket was on the road to recovery after a tough 2014 in which it suffered a £263 million accounting scandal and the exit of the former chief executive, Philip Clarke, following slumping sales and profits.

'This patient is okay … Our job is to allow it to be healthier. There is nothing critical about its finances,' he said.

After years of growth in the UK, Tesco suffered five profit warnings in 2014 as analysts said it had opened too many large stores, let prices rise and shop floor standards slip. All supermarkets are under pressure as shoppers switch to the Internet, small local shops and discounters such as Aldi and Lidl, but Tesco has been hardest hit as a result of its scale. Lewis, who has never run a retailer before, was brought in to provide a fresh approach.

Two shoppers were recently overheard having the following conversation:

'Did you see on the news last night that Tesco are closing down some of their stores and delaying major investment?'

'Yes I heard that, they seem to be worried about their market share and profitability given the growth in the discount food retailers such as Aldi and Lidl. Tesco has even started trying to compete with a cheaper food range but I still like to go to Marks and Spencer once a week to buy something nice to eat for the weekend and to have a look at their latest clothes range – even if it does cost a little more the quality is excellent'.

Questions

1 How do you think shopping at Marks and Spencer compares to Tesco? What do you value most when selecting a retailer for food shopping/clothes shopping?

2 With respect to competitive strategy, identify and evaluate Marks and Spencer's and Tesco's target customers, core competencies and how they build synergy and deliver value.

3 Examine Marks and Spencer's competitive strategy commenting on the extent to which it pursues differentiation, cost-leadership and focus, or some combination.

END NOTES

1. Bruce Horovitz, 'New Pizza Recipe Did Wonders for Domino's Sales', *USA Today*, May 5, 2010, B1; Julie Jargon, 'How McDonald's Hit the Spot', *The Wall Street Journal*, December 13, 2011; Paul Lilley, 'Weight Watchers Reveals New Partner: McDonald's', *Virginian-Pilot*, March 4, 2010; David E. Bell and Mary Shelman, 'KFC's Radical Approach to China', *Harvard Business Review* (November 2011): 137–142.

2. John Bussey, 'The Anti-Kodak: How a U.S. Firm Innovates', *The Wall Street Journal*, January 13, 2012, B1; Rachel Dodes, 'Targeting Younger Buyers, Liz Claiborne Hits a Snag', *The Wall Street Journal*, August 16, 2010, A1.

3. Chet Miller and Laura B. Cardinal, 'Strategic Planning and Firm Performance: A Synthesis of More than Two Decades of Research', *Academy of Management Journal* 37, no. 6 (1994): 1649–1665.

4. Renée Dye and Olivier Sibony, 'How to Improve Strategic Planning', *McKinsey Quarterly*, no. 3 (2007).

5. Keith H. Hammonds, 'Michael Porter's Big Ideas', *Fast Company* (March 2001): 150–156.

6. John E. Prescott, 'Environments as Moderators of the Relationship Between Strategy and Performance', *Academy of*

Management Journal 29 (1986): 329–346; John A. Pearce II and Richard B. Robinson, Jr., *Strategic Management: Strategy, Formulation and Implementation*, 2d ed. (Homewood, IL: Irwin, 1985); and David J. Teece, 'Economic Analysis and Strategic Management', *California Management Review* 26 (Spring 1984): 87–110.

7. Jack Welch, 'It's All in the Sauce', excerpt from his book, *Winning*, published in *Fortune* (April 18, 2005): 138–144; and Constantinos Markides, 'Strategic Innovation', *Sloan Management Review* (Spring 1997): 9–23.

8. Michael E. Porter, 'What Is Strategy?' *Harvard Business Review* (November–December 1996): 61–78.

9. This discussion is based on Ken Favaro with Kasturi Rangan and Evan Hirsh, 'Strategy: An Executive's Definition', *Strategy + Business* (March 5, 2012), www.strategy-business.com/article/cs00002?gko=d59c2 (accessed July 24, 2012).

10. Example from Favaro et al., 'Strategy: An Executive's Definition'.

11. Norihiko Shirouzu, 'Chinese Begin Volvo Overhaul', *The Wall Street Journal*, June 7, 2011, B1.

12. Arthur A. Thompson, Jr. and A. J. Strickland III, *Strategic Management: Concepts and Cases,* 6th ed. (Homewood, IL:

Irwin, 1992); and Briance Mascarenhas, Alok Baveja and Mamnoon Jamil, 'Dynamics of Core Competencies in Leading Multinational Companies', *California Management Review* 40, no. 4 (Summer 1998): 117–132.

13. Chris Woodyard, 'Big Dreams for Small Choppers Paid Off', *USA Today*, September 11, 2005.

14. Michael Goold and Andrew Campbell, 'Desperately Seeking Synergy', *Harvard Business Review* (September–October 1998): 131–143.

15. Anjali Cordeiro 'Boss Talk: Tang in India and Other Kraft Synergies', *The Wall Street Journal Online*, April 19, 2010, www.online.wsj.com/article/SB1000142405270230334850 4575184103106388686.html (accessed October 8, 2012); and Ashlee Vance, 'Oracle Elbows Its Way into a Crowded Fight; With Close of Sun Deal, It Hopes to Beat Out Rivals Offering One-Stop Shops', *International Herald Tribune*, January 28, 2010.

16. Nick Wingfield, 'Thinking Outside the Redbox', *The New York Times*, February 18, 2012, B1.

17. John Jannarone, 'Starbucks Sees New Growth on the Card', *The Wall Street Journal*, January 17, 2012, C10.

18. Lauren A. E. Schuker, 'Double Feature: Dinner and a Movie – To Upgrade from Dirty Carpets and Tubs of Popcorn, Theater Chains Try Full Menus, Seat-Side Service', *The Wall Street Journal*, January 5, 2011, D1.

19. Brad Stone, 'What's in the Box? Instant Gratification', *Bloomberg Businessweek* (November 29–December 5, 2010): 39–40; and S. Levy, 'CEO of the Internet: Jeff Bezos Owns the Web in More Ways than You Think', *Wired* (December 2011), www.wired.com/magazine/2011/11/ff_bezos/ (accessed July 24, 2012).

20. Milton Leontiades, *Strategies for Diversification and Change* (Boston: Little, Brown, 1980), p. 63; and Dan E. Schendel and Charles W. Hofer, eds., *Strategic Management: A New View of Business Policy and Planning* (Boston: Little, Brown, 1979), pp. 11–14.

21. Erik Rhey, 'A GPS Maker Shifts Gears', *Fortune* (March 19, 2012): 62; 'Garmin International, Inc. Announces Completion of the Acquisition of UPS Aviation Technologies, Inc.', *PR Newswire*, August 22, 2003, www.prnewswire.com/news-releases/garmin-international-inc-announces-completion-of-the-acquisition-of-ups-aviation-technologies-inc-70979722.html (accessed July 25, 2012); and 'Garmin Ltd. Acquires Dynastream Innovations, Inc'. Garmin Press Release, December 1, 2006, Garmin website, www8.garmin.com/pressroom/corporate/120106.html (accessed July 25, 2012).

22. Rhey, 'A GPS Maker Shifts Gears'.

23. Example reported in Armen Ovanessoff and Mark Purdy, 'Global Competition 2021: Key Capabilities for Emerging Opportunities', *Strategy & Leadership* 39, no. 5 (2011): 46–55.

24. Guy Chazan, 'BP's Worsening Spill Crisis Undermines CEO's Reforms', *The Wall Street Journal*, May 3, 2010.

25. Bruce E. Perrott, 'Strategic Issue Management as Change Catalyst', *Strategy & Leadership* 39, no. 5 (2011): 20–29.

26. Milton Leontiades, 'The Confusing Words of Business Policy', *Academy of Management Review* 7 (1982): 45–48.

27. Lawrence G. Hrebiniak and William F. Joyce, *Implementing Strategy* (New York: Macmillan, 1984).

28. Christopher B. Bingham, Kathleen M. Eisenhardt and Nathan R. Furr, 'Which Strategy When?' *MIT Sloan Management Review* (Fall 2011): 71–78.

29. Peter Burrows, 'Microsoft Defends Its Empire', *BusinessWeek* (July 6, 2009): 28–33.

30. David Welch, Keith Naughton and Burt Helm, 'Detroit's Big Chance', *Bloomberg BusinessWeek* (February 22, 2010): 38–44.

31. Stephanie Clifford, 'Where Wal-Mart Failed, Aldi Succeeds', *The New York Times* (March 29, 2011), www.nytimes.com/2011/03/30/business/30aldi.html?pagewanted=all (accessed July 26, 2012).

32. 'Company Overview and Quick Facts', Dana Holding Corporation website, www.dana.com/wps/wcm/connect/dext/Dana/Company/ (accessed July 26, 2012); 'Dana History', www.dana.com/wps/wcm/connect/dext/Dana/Company/History/ (accessed July 26, 2012); 'Dana: 2009 Company Profile Edition 1: SWOT Analysis', *Just-Auto* (February 2009): 14–16; 'Dana: 2009 Company Profile Edition 2: Chapter 6 SWOT Analysis', *Just-Auto* (June 2009): 16–18; and Dana Holding Corporation 2012 Fact Sheet, www.dana.com/wps/wcm/connect/0642380041f3cfb59a8 0be1c9e250a89/dext-2012DanaFact.pdf?MOD=AJPERES (accessed July 26, 2012).

33. Frederick W. Gluck, 'A Fresh Look at Strategic Management', *Journal of Business Strategy* 6 (Fall 1985): 4–19.

34. Christopher Weaver, 'Managed Care Enters the Exam Room as Insurers Buy Doctors Groups', *The Washington Post*, July 1, 2011, www.washingtonpost.com/insurers-quietly-gaining-control-of-doctors-covered-by-companies-plans/2011/06/29/AG5DNftH_story.html (accessed July 27, 2012); Anna Wilde Matthews, 'Corporate News: UnitedHealth Buys California Group of 2,300 Doctors', *The Wall Street Journal*, September 1, 2011, B3; 'About Us', UnitedHealth Group website, www.unitedhealthgroup.com/main/aboutus.aspx (accessed July 27, 2012).

35. Thompson and Strickland, *Strategic Management*; and William L. Shanklin and John K. Ryans, Jr., 'Is the International Cash Cow Really a Prize Heifer?' *Business Horizons* 24 (1981): 10–16.

36. William E. Rothschild, 'GE and Its Naysayers', *Chief Executive* (November–December 2009): 46–50; Paul Glader, 'Corporate News: GE's Immelt to Cite Lessons Learned', *The Wall Street Journal*, December 15, 2009; Shital Vakhariya and Menaka Rao, 'Innovate for Growth: Immelt's Strategy for GE', *Journal of Operations Management* 8, no. 3–4 (August–November 2009): 86–92; and General Electric website, www .ge.com/products_services/index.html (accessed August 10, 2010).

37. This discussion and the following examples are from Ben Worthen, Cari Tuna and Justin Scheck, 'Companies More Prone to Go Vertical', *The Wall Street Journal*, November 30, 2009; and Jacqueline Doherty, 'At Pepsi, the Glass Is Half Full', *Barron's* (November 30, 2009): 24–25.

38. Michael E. Porter, 'The Five Competitive Forces That Shape Strategy', *Harvard Business Review* (January 2008): 79–93; Michael E. Porter, *Competitive Strategy* (New York: Free Press, 1980), pp. 36–46; Danny Miller, 'Relating Porter's Business Strategies to Environment and Structure: Analysis and Performance Implementations', *Academy of Management Journal* 31 (1988): 280–308; and Michael E. Porter, 'From Competitive Advantage to Corporate Strategy', *Harvard Business Review* (May–June 1987): 43–59.

39. Jack Nicas, 'A Stingy Spirit Lifts Airline's Profit', *The Wall Street Journal*, May 12, 2012, A1.

40. Bruce Einhorn, 'Acer's Game-Changing PC Offensive', *BusinessWeek* (April 20, 2009): 65; Charmian Kok and Ting-I Tsai, 'Acer Makes China Push from Taiwan; PC Maker's Chief Expects Best Gains in New Markets, Including Brazil, as Aims to Surpass H-P', *The Wall Street Journal*, April 1, 2010; and 'Experience Will Propel Acer to Top of Smartphone Market by 2013', *Gulf News,* January 22, 2010.

41. 'Building Wealth', Proamérica Bank website, www.proamericabank.com/en/index.asp (accessed July 31, 2012).

42. Joshua Rosenbaum, 'Guitar Maker Looks for a New Key', *The Wall Street Journal*, February 11, 1998.

43. Nitin Nohria, William Joyce and Bruce Roberson, 'What Really Works', *Harvard Business Review* (July 2003): 43–52.

44. 'Issue of the Week: J.C. Penney's No-Sales Misfire', *The Week* (July 6–13, 2012), 36; Brad Tuttle, 'The Price Is Righter', *Time* (February 13, 2012), www.time.com/time/magazine/article/0,9171,2105961,00.html#ixzz2275GLNTv (accessed July 30, 2012); Dana Mattioli, 'Penney's to Make Deeper Price Cuts', *The Wall Street Journal*, July 26, 2012, B1.

45. Brad Tuttle, 'A Store Without a Checkout Counter? JCPenney Presses on with Retail Revolution', *Time* (July 20, 2012), www.moneyland.time.com/2012/07/20/a-store-without-a-checkout-counter-jcpenney-presses-on-with-retail-revolution/ (accessed July 30, 2012).

46. Kenichi Ohmae, 'Managing in a Borderless World', *Harvard Business Review* (May–June 1990): 152–161.

47. Theodore Levitt, 'The Globalization of Markets', *Harvard Business Review* (May–June 1983): 92–102.

48. Cesare Mainardi, Martin Salva and Muir Sanderson, 'Label of Origin: Made on Earth', *strategy + business*, Issue 15, Second Quarter, 1999, www.strategy-business.com/article/16620 (accessed August 10, 2010).

49. Joanne Lipman, 'Marketers Turn Sour on Global Sales Pitch Harvard Guru Makes', *The Wall Street Journal*, May 12, 1988.

50. Annie Gasparro, 'Domino's Sticks to Its Ways Abroad', *The Wall Street Journal*, April 17, 2012, B10.

51. Michael E. Porter, 'Changing Patterns of International Competition', *California Management Review* 28 (Winter 1986): 40.

52. Laurie Burkitt, 'Kraft Craves More of China's Snacks Market', *The Wall Street Journal*, May 30, 2012, B6.

53. Mohanbir Sawhney and Sumant Mandal, 'What Kind of Global Organization Should You Build?' *Business 2.0* (May 2000): 213.

54. Based on Michael A. Hitt, R. Duane Ireland and Robert E. Hoskisson, *Strategic Management: Competitiveness and Globalization* (St. Paul, MN: West, 1995), p. 238.

55. Anil K. Gupta and Vijay Govindarajan, 'Converting Global Presence into Global Competitive Advantage', *Academy of Management Executive* 15, no. 2 (2001): 45–56.

56. Quote from Gary Getz, Chris Jones and Pierre Loewe, 'Migration Management: An Approach for Improving Strategy Implementation', *Strategy & Leadership* 37, no. 6 (2009): 18–24.

57. Lawrence G. Hrebiniak, 'Obstacles to Effective Strategy Implementation', *Organizational Dynamics* 35, no. 1 (2006): 12–31; Eric M. Olson, Stanley F. Slater and G. Tomas M. Hult, 'The Importance of Structure and Process to Strategy Implementation', *Business Horizons* 48 (2005): 47–54; L. J. Bourgeois III and David R. Brodwin, 'Strategic Implementation: Five Approaches to an Elusive Phenomenon', *Strategic Management Journal* 5 (1984): 241–264; Anil K. Gupta and V. Govindarajan, 'Business Unit Strategy, Managerial Characteristics and Business Unit Effectiveness at Strategy Implementation', *Academy of Management Journal* (1984): 25–41; and Jeffrey G. Covin, Dennis P. Slevin and Randall L. Schultz, 'Implementing Strategic Missions: Effective Strategic, Structural and Tactical Choices', *Journal of Management Studies* 31, no. 4 (1994): 481–505.

58. Riaz Khadem, 'Alignment and Follow-Up: Steps to Strategy Execution', *Journal of Business Strategy* 29, no. 6 (2008): 29–35; Stephen Bungay, 'How to Make the Most of Your Company's Strategy', *Harvard Business Review* (January–February 2011): 132–140; and Olson, Slater and Hult, 'The Importance of Structure and Process to Strategy Implementation'.

59. This discussion is based on Eric Beaudan, 'Creative Execution', *Ivey Business Journal,* March–April 2010, www.iveybusinessjournal.com/article.asp?intArticle_ID=891 (accessed March 26, 2010); Jay R. Galbraith and Robert K. Kazanjian, *Strategy Implementation: Structure, Systems and Process,* 2d ed. (St. Paul, MN: West, 1986); Victoria L. Crittenden and William F. Crittenden, 'Building a Capable Organization: The Eight Levers of Strategy Implementation', *Business Horizons* 51 (2008): 301–309; Paul C. Nutt, 'Selecting Tactics to Implement Strategic Plans', *Strategic Management Journal* 10 (1989): 145–161; and Lawrence G. Hrebiniak, *Making Strategy Work: Leading Effective Execution and Change* (Upper Saddle River, NJ: Wharton School Publishing/Pearson Education Inc., 2005).

60. Crittenden and Crittenden, 'Building a Capable Organization'.

61. This example is from Bingham, Eisenhardt and Furr, 'Which Strategy When?'

62. Based on survey results reported in Hrebiniak, 'Obstacles to Effective Strategy Implementation'.

63. Jessica Silver-Greenberg and Nelson D. Schwartz, 'Discord at Key JPMorgan Unit Is Blamed in Bank's Huge Loss', *The New York Times*, May 20, 2012, A1.

64. Beaudan, 'Creative Execution'.

65. Tuttle, 'The Price Is Righter'.

66. Example reported in Stanley F. Slater, Eric M. Olson and G. Tomas M. Hult, 'Worried About Strategy Implementation? Don't Overlook Marketing's Role', *Business Horizons* 53 (2010): 469–479.

67. John Bussey, 'The Anti-Kodak: How a U.S. Firm Innovates', *The Wall Street Journal*, January 13, 2012, B1.

68. This questionnaire is adapted from Dorothy Marcic and Joe Seltzer, *Organizational Behavior: Experiences and Cases* (Cincinnati, OH: SouthWestern, 1998), pp. 284–287, and William Miller, *Innovation Styles* (Global Creativity Corporation, 1997).

69. Based on Robert Berner, 'I Sold It Through the Grapevine', *BusinessWeek* (May 29, 2006): 32–34; 'Savvy Moms Share Maternal Instincts; Vocalpoint Offers Online Moms the Opportunity to be a Valuable Resource to Their Communities', *Business Wire* (December 6, 2005); and Steve Hall, 'Word of Mouth Marketing: To Tell or Not to Tell', *AdRants.com*, May 2006, www.adrants.com/2006/05/word-of-mouth-marketing-to-tell-or-not-to.php (accessed August 23, 2010).

CHAPTER 9

MANAGERIAL
DECISION-MAKING

LEARNING OBJECTIVES

After studying this chapter, you should be able to:

1 Explain why decision-making is an important component of good management.

2 Discuss the difference between programmed and non-programmed decisions and the decision characteristics of certainty and uncertainty.

3 Describe the ideal, rational model of decision-making and the political model of decision-making.

4 Explain the process by which managers actually make decisions in the real world.

5 Identify the six steps used in managerial decision-making.

6 Describe four personal decision styles used by managers, and explain the biases that frequently cause managers to make bad decisions.

7 Identify and explain innovative techniques for decision-making, including brainstorming, evidence-based management and after-action reviews.

New managers typically use a different decision behaviour than seasoned executives. The decision behaviour of a successful CEO may be almost the opposite of a first-level supervisor. The difference is due partly to the types of decisions and partly to learning what works at each level. New managers often start out with a more directive, decisive, command-oriented behaviour to establish their standing and decisiveness and gradually move towards more openness, diversity of viewpoints and interactions with others as they move up the hierarchy.

Solar energy is a great idea. US President Barack Obama agrees, and when visiting the Solyndra plant in 2010, he proudly proclaimed that 'companies like Solyndra are leading the way towards a brighter and more prosperous future.' The solar panel manufacturing start-up had received a $535 million federal stimulus loan guarantee to help the USA gain dominance in solar technology while generating thousands of jobs. The problem, however, was that Solyndra's managers had made decisions based on faulty assumptions, and the company was losing money fast, with no likelihood of turning things around. Barely a year after Obama's visit, Solyndra declared bankruptcy, dismissed more than 1000 employees and was raided by the Federal Bureau of Investigation (FBI) seeking evidence of possible fraud. Meanwhile, the Obama administration's flawed decision to back Solyndra could cost taxpayers a half billion dollars.[1]

Welcome to the world of managerial decision-making. Managers often are referred to as *decision-makers,* and every organization grows, prospers or fails as a result of decisions made by its managers. Yet decision-making, particularly in relation to complex problems, is not always easy. Solyndra's executives based many of their decisions on the assumption that the price of silicon, a primary component in solar panels made by competitors, would remain high. Solyndra's innovative panels didn't use silicon, but the higher manufacturing costs meant the company had to charge a premium to make a profit. When the price of silicon dropped, competitors had a huge advantage. As for the US government's decision to invest in Solyndra, there are charges that administration officials failed to evaluate the risks properly and heed the troubling signs that the company was financially unstable.[2] Managers can sometimes make the wrong decision, even when their intentions are right. Managers frequently must make decisions amid ever-changing factors, unclear information and alternative points of view.

The business world is full of evidence of both good and bad decisions. YouTube was once referred to as 'Google's Folly', but decisions made by the video platform's managers have more than justified the $1.65 billion that Google paid for it and turned YouTube into a highly admired company, that is redefining the entertainment industry.[3] On the other hand, Microsoft's decision to purchase ad giant aQuantive for $6.3 billion hasn't turned out so well. Microsoft managers believed that aQuantive, at the time a thriving 2600-employee company with rapidly growing sales and profits, would help the software giant be more competitive against Google and establish it as a leader in online advertising. But poor decision-making regarding how to integrate aQuantive into the larger software company contributed to a disaster that required Microsoft to take a $6.2 billion writedown. Today, aQuantive is a shell of its former self. '*From the initial decision to put aQuantive under the absolutely wrong Microsoft leadership – who had no knowledge or interest or skills in it . . . this acquisition had snafu written on it from day one,*' said a former aQuantive employee.[4]

Good decision-making is a vital part of good management because decisions determine how the organization solves problems, allocates resources and accomplishes its goals. This chapter describes decision-making in considerable detail. First, we examine decision characteristics. Then we look at decision-making models and the steps executives could/should take when making important decisions. The chapter also explores some biases that can cause managers to make poor decisions. Finally, we examine some specific techniques for innovative decision-making in today's fast-changing business environment.

Types of decisions and problems

A decision is a choice made from available alternatives. For example, an accounting manager's selection among Colin, Tasha and/or Chris for the position of a junior level auditor, is a decision. Many people assume that making a choice is the major part of decision-making, but it is only a part of it.

Decision-making is the process of identifying problems and opportunities and then resolving them. Decision-making involves effort both before and after the actual choice. Thus, the decision of whether to select Colin, Tasha or Chris requires the accounting manager to ascertain whether a new junior auditor is needed, then to determine the availability of potential job candidates, interview candidates to acquire necessary information, select one candidate and follow up with the induction of the new employee into the organization and its culture to ensure the decision is successful.

Programmed and non-programmed decisions

Management decisions typically fall into one of two categories: programmed and non-programmed. Programmed decisions involve situations that have occurred often enough to enable decision rules to be developed and applied in the future.[5] Programmed decisions are made in response to recurring organizational problems. The decision to reorder office supplies when inventories drop to a certain level is a programmed decision. Other programmed decisions concern the types of skills required to fill certain jobs, the reorder point for manufacturing inventory and selection of freight routes for product deliveries. Once managers formulate decision rules, subordinates and others can make the decision, freeing managers for other tasks. For example, when staffing banquets, many hotels use a rule that specifies having one server per 20 guests for a sit-down function and one server per 30 guests for a buffet.[6]

TAKE A MOMENT

Go to the Ethical Dilemma at the end of this chapter that pertains to making non-programmed decisions.

GREEN POWER

Revitalizing small farms

PepsiCo executives discovered for themselves that sustainability decisions can be observed and measured in the lives of individuals. Management's decision to launch a pilot project cutting the middleman from the supply chain for Sabritas, its Mexican line of snacks, by initiating direct purchase of corn from 300 small farmers in Mexico brought unimagined benefits.

The decision resulted in visible, measureable outcomes, including lower transportation costs and a stronger relationship with small farmers, who were able to develop pride and a businesslike approach to farming. The arrangement with PepsiCo gave farmers a financial edge in securing much-needed credit for purchasing equipment, fertilizer and other necessities, resulting in higher crop yields. New levels of financial security also reduced the once-rampant and highly dangerous treks back and forth across the US border that farmers made at great personal risk as they sought ways to support their families. Within 3 years, PepsiCo's pilot programme was expanded to 850 farmers.

SOURCE: Stephanie Strom, 'For Pepsi, a Business Decision with Social Benefits', *The New York Times*, February 21, 2011, www.nytimes.com/2011/02/22/business/global/22pepsi.html?pagewanted=all (accessed August 2, 2012).

Non-programmed decisions are made in response to situations that are unique, are weakly defined and largely unstructured, and have important consequences for the organization. Sprint Nextel's decision about carrying the iPhone is a good example of a non-programmed decision. Apple has strong power over wireless carriers and is able to require them to make long-term volume commitments. Sprint managers had to decide whether to agree to purchase at least 30.5 million iPhones over a period of 4 years at a cost of $20 billion or more – regardless of whether the company could sell them to their customers. For Sprint, the stakes were high as the company was losing customers and hadn't been profitable for years. To sell that many iPhones, Sprint managers realized they would have to double their contract customers and commit all of them to purchasing iPhones. However, not carrying the iPhone might mean Sprint wouldn't stand much chance against other carriers such as AT&T and Verizon. As one person said of Sprint's decision process, it was '*a bet-the-company kind of thing.*' Managers eventually decided to go with the Apple contract.[7]

Many non-programmed decisions, such as the ones at Sprint Nextel, are related to strategic planning because uncertainty is great and decisions are complex. Decisions to acquire a company, build a new factory, develop a new product or service, enter a new geographical market, or relocate headquarters to another city, are all non-programmed decisions.

Facing certainty and uncertainty

One primary difference between programmed and non-programmed decisions relates to the degree of certainty or uncertainty that managers deal with in making the decision. In a perfect world, managers would have all the information necessary for making decisions. In reality, however, some aspects are unknowable. Thus, some decisions will fail to solve the problem and/or attain the desired outcomes. Managers should try

CONCEPT CONNECTION

Having filled in for Steve Jobs during three medical leaves, COO Tim Cook was ready and able to take the helm of Apple when Jobs had to step down shortly before his death in 2011. The choice of Cook as the new CEO was a **non-programmed decision** that had been made well in advance, giving Cook some time to prepare for a seamless transition to his new role. Since then, investors, employees and customers alike seem impressed with his abilities and generally happy with his performance. Whether Apple's new CEO will have the depth of vision that Jobs clearly had is an opinion reserved by some commentators.

to obtain information about decision alternatives that will reduce the level of decision uncertainty. Every decision situation can be organized on a scale according to the availability of information and the possibility of failure. The four positions on the scale are certainty, risk, uncertainty and ambiguity, as illustrated in Exhibit 9.1. Whereas programmed decisions can be made in situations involving near to full certainty, many situations that managers deal with on a daily basis involve at least some degree of uncertainty and require non-programmed decision-making.

Certainty

Certainty means that all the information the decision-maker needs is fully available.[9] Managers have information on operating conditions, resource costs or constraints, and each course of action and possible outcome. For example, if a company considers a €10 000 investment in new equipment that it knows for certain will yield €4000 in cost savings per year over the next 5 years, managers can calculate a before-tax rate of return of about 40 per cent. If managers compare this investment with one that will yield only €3000 per year in cost savings, they can confidently select the better 40 per cent return. However, few decisions are certain in the real world. Most contain risk or uncertainty.

Risk

Risk means that a decision has clear-cut goals and that good information is available, but the future outcomes associated with each alternative are subject to some chance of loss or failure. However, enough information is available to estimate the probability of a successful outcome versus failure.[10] In some cases, managers use statistical software analysis to calculate the probabilities of success or failure for each alternative. At Boeing, managers had to decide whether to build a new version of the company's single-aisle 737 jet. They noted that European rival Airbus was getting high orders for the redesigned A320, which included more fuel-efficient engines, something Boeing's customers also wanted. Perhaps installing new engines on 737 jets was a better alternative than building a completely new plane, Boeing managers thought. They projected production costs for designing and building a new plane versus designing and installing new engines, calculated potential increases in fuel efficiency, considered whether new engines rather than a new plane would meet customer's needs, and looked at total operating costs. CEO James McNerney and other managers eventually decided to go with the new engines. McNerney said Boeing believed that new engines would yield 10 to 12 per cent fuel savings on 737 planes, also enabling the company to maintain a significant cost advantage over the Airbus A320. It proved to be a

💡 INNOVATIVE WAY

Bremen Castings Inc.

What do you do if you're about halfway into a $10 million expansion when the economy crashes, the stock market tumbles, and the USA is grappling with its first credit downgrade? You've already invested $5 million. If you continue with the expansion plan, it will require getting another $5 million bank loan right away.

That's the situation that J. B. Brown, president of Bremen Castings, discussed for 4 hours with his top managers in the midst of the largest expansion plan in the company's 72-year history. Should they halt the expansion and start cutting costs rather than spending more money? Would the increased capacity be worth the risk they were taking? The uncertainties were tremendous. The executive team reviewed order rates and relationships with customers and considered what-ifs: What would happen if Bremen's 15 largest

customers cut their order rates by 30 to 40 per cent, or if agricultural customers stopped picking cotton and corn, or if new Environmental Protection Agency (EPA) regulations created a decline in demand from trucking customers? 'If we go out and spend another 3 or 4 million and that work is not there,' Brown asked, 'what are we going to do to capture more market share?'

The team also looked at the positive side of the slow economy. Casting companies in the USA, like Bremen, face tough competition from lower-cost Chinese producers, but the uncertain economy means some customers have turned back to smaller domestic suppliers who will fill small orders. Eventually, the team decided to go forward with the planned expansion. 'If we don't, someone else will,' said Brown. 'Those are the chances you take in business.'[8]

EXHIBIT 9.1 Conditions that affect the possibility of decision failure

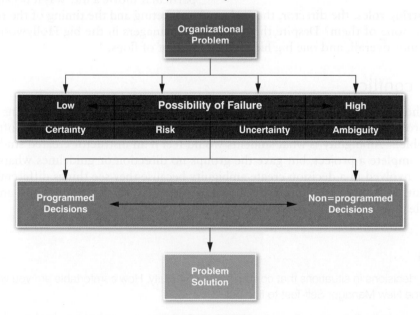

good decision. In early 2012, Boeing was already on track to retake the lead from Airbus as the world's top producer of commercial airplanes.[11]

Uncertainty

Uncertainty means that managers know which goals they wish to achieve, but information about alternatives and future events is incomplete. Factors that may affect a decision, such as price, production costs, volume or

CONCEPT CONNECTION

Uncertainty is a standard feature in the life of any farmer. Changing weather patterns and unexpected events, such as the UK floods of 2013–2014, can have devastating effects on crops that no amount of planning can prevent. Yet, despite these unforeseeable situations, farmers must make decisions and continue to operate based on assumptions and expectations.

future interest rates, are difficult to analyze and predict. Managers may have to make assumptions from which to influence the decision, even though it will be wrong if the underlying assumptions are incorrect. Former US treasury secretary, Robert Rubin, defined uncertainty as: *a situation in which even a good decision might produce a bad outcome.*[12] Managers face uncertainty every day. Many problems have no clear-cut solution, but managers rely on creativity, judgement, intuition and experience to craft an optimum response.

Consider the uncertainty faced by managers in the movie industry. The movie *Men in Black 3* cost $250 million to make and at least that much in marketing expenses. The movie managed to break even, but many films don't, which reflects the tremendous uncertainty in the film industry. What do people want to see this summer? Will comic book heroes, vampires or aliens once again be popular? Will animated films, disaster epics, classics or romantic comedies attract larger audiences? The interests and preferences of moviegoers are fickle and extremely difficult to accurately predict. Moreover, it is hard for managers to understand even after the fact what made a particular movie a hit. Was it because of the storyline, the actors in starring roles, the director, the prelaunch marketing and the timing of the release? Perhaps all of those things or none of them? Despite the uncertainty, managers in the big Hollywood studios make relatively good decisions overall, and one big hit can pay for a lot of flops.[13]

Ambiguity and conflict

Ambiguity is by far the most difficult aspect of the 'what decision' situation. Ambiguity means that the goal to be achieved or the problem to be solved is unclear, alternatives are difficult to define and information about outcomes is unavailable.[14] Ambiguity is what students would feel if an instructor created student groups and told each group to complete a project, but gave the groups no direction or guidelines whatsoever. In some situations, managers involved in a decision create ambiguity because they see things differently and disagree about what they want. Managers in different departments often have different priorities and goals for the decision, which can lead to conflicts over decision alternatives.

TAKE A MOMENT

Managers make many decisions in situations that contain some ambiguity. How comfortable are you when dealing with ambiguity? Complete the New Manager Self-Test to find out.

A highly ambiguous situation can create what is sometimes called a *wicked decision problem*. Wicked decisions are associated with conflicts over goals and decision alternatives, rapidly changing circumstances, fuzzy information, unclear links among decision elements and the inability to evaluate whether a proposed solution will work. For wicked problems, there often is no 'right' answer.[15] Managers have a difficult time coming to grips with the issues and must conjure up reasonable scenarios in the absence of clear information. Consider the differing opinions regarding whether to blast a gap in the Birds Point levee as water levels on the Ohio

NEW MANAGER SELF-TEST

Intolerance of ambiguity

INSTRUCTIONS Rate each statement below from 1–7, based on how strongly you disagree or agree with it. There are no right or wrong answers, so answer honestly to receive accurate feedback.

	Strongly disagree	Moderately disagree	Slightly disagree	Neither agree nor disagree	Slightly agree	Moderately agree	Strongly agree
	1	2	3	4	5	6	7

1 An expert who doesn't come up with a definite answer probably doesn't know too much.

2 I would like to live in a foreign country for a while.

3 There is really no such thing as a problem that can't be solved.

4 People who live their lives to a schedule probably miss most of the joy of living.

5 A good job is one where what is done and how it is to be done are always clear.

6 It is more fun to tackle a complicated problem than to solve a simple one.

7 In the long run, it is possible to get more done by tackling small, simple problems rather than large and complicated ones.

8 Often the most interesting and stimulating people are those who don't mind being different and original.

		Strongly disagree	Moderately disagree	Slightly disagree	Neither agree nor disagree	Slightly agree	Moderately agree	Strongly agree
		1	2	3	4	5	6	7
9	What we are used to is always preferable to what is unfamiliar.							
10	People who insist upon a yes or no answer just don't know how complicated things really are.							
11	A person who leads an even, regular life in which few surprises or unexpected happenings arise really has a lot to be grateful for.							
12	Many of our most important decisions are based on insufficient information.							
13	I like parties where I know most of the people more than ones where all or most of the people are complete strangers.							
14	Teachers or supervisors who hand out vague assignments give one a chance to show initiative and originality.							
15	The sooner we all acquire similar values and ideals the better.							
16	A good teacher is one who makes you wonder about your way of looking at things.							

SCORING & INTERPRETATION Sum the odd-numbered statements, giving 7 points for each 'Strongly agree', 6 points for each 'Moderately agree', 5 points for each 'Slightly agree', 4 points for 'Neither agree nor disagree', 3 points for 'Slightly disagree', 2 points for 'Moderately disagree', and 1 point for each 'Strongly disagree'. Reverse-score the even-numbered statements, giving 7 points for each 'Strongly disagree' through 1 point for each 'Strongly agree'.

These questions were originally designed to help identify students who would be comfortable with the ambiguity associated with the practice of medicine. Managers also must manage ambiguity in their decisions about the following: rapid change, strategy, people, and social and political dynamics. Intolerance of ambiguity means that an individual tends to perceive novel, complex and ambiguous situations as potentially threatening rather than as desirable. A high score means greater *intolerance* of ambiguity. A low score means that you tolerate ambiguity and likely see promise and potential in ambiguous situations. Managers make many decisions under conditions of some or much ambiguity, so learning to be comfortable with ambiguity is something to work towards as a manager.

SOURCE: S. Budner, 'Intolerance of Ambiguity as a Personality Variable', *The Journal of Personality* (30), pp. 29–59. Copyright (1962) John Wiley & Sons. Reproduced with permission of John Wiley & Sons Inc.

River near the confluence with the Mississippi reached 18 metres. Some people believed strongly that the breach was necessary to prevent the town of Cairo, Illinois, from flooding and to relieve pressure on the over-burdened system of levees protecting the entire region. Others questioned whether breaking the levee would have the intended result and said the one sure thing it would do would be to destroy about 90 homes and flood 130 000 acres of farmland in Missouri. Major-General Michael J. Walsh, head of the Mississippi Valley Division of the Army Corps of Engineers, had to consult with experts and consider varied opinions, as well as weigh the interests of people whose homes and farms in Missouri would be flooded, against the safety of Cairo, a poverty-ridden town with a population of around 3000. 'These are people's homes, their livelihoods,' said the chief of the corps' operations division. 'We really don't want to do this.' The situation was changing from minute to minute as flood waters continued to rise. Missouri's state attorney general even asked the US Supreme Court to overturn a decision that would allow the Corps to blast the levee. *'There are still a lot of decision points as we move forward,'* Major-General Walsh said. *'He'll still have to make the decision,'* said one person involved with the situation. Another said: *'I don't figure it's going to do what they think it's going to do.'*[16] There were similar issues to address in Somerset county in England in 2014 with many farms and houses flooding, with accusations that government agencies had seriously neglected flood defences.

REFLECTION

- Good decision-making is a vital part of good management, but decision-making is far from easy.
- **Decision-making** is the process of identifying problems and opportunities and then resolving them.
- A **decision** is a choice made from available alternatives.
- A **programmed decision** is one made in response to a situation that has occurred often enough to enable managers to develop decision rules that can be consistently applied in the future.
- A **non-programmed decision** is one made in response to a situation that is unique, is poorly defined and largely unstructured, and has important consequences for the organization.
- Decisions differ according to the amount of certainty, risk, uncertainty or ambiguity in the situation.

- **Certainty** is a situation in which all the information the decision-maker needs is fully available.
- **Risk** means that a decision has clear-cut goals and good information is available, but the future outcomes associated with each alternative are subject to chance.
- **Uncertainty** occurs when managers know which goals they want to achieve, but information about alternatives and future events is incomplete.
- **Ambiguity** is a condition in which the goals to be achieved or the problem to be solved is unclear, alternatives are difficult to define and information about outcomes is unavailable.
- Highly ambiguous circumstances can create a wicked decision problem, the most difficult decision situation that managers face.

Decision-making models

The approach that managers use to make decisions usually falls into one of three types – the classical model, the administrative model or the political model. The choice of model depends on the manager's personal preference, whether the decision is programmed or non-programmed and the degree of uncertainty associated with the decision.

The ideal, rational model

The classical model of decision-making is based on rational economic assumptions and managerial beliefs about what ideal decision-making should be. This model has arisen within the management literature because managers are expected to make decisions that are economically sensible and in the organization's best economic interests. The four assumptions underlying this model are as follows:

■ The decision-maker operates to accomplish goals that are known of and agreed on. Problems are required to be precisely formulated and defined.

■ The decision-maker strives for conditions of high certainty, gathering complete information. All alternatives and the potential results of each are calculated.

■ Criteria for evaluating alternatives are known. The decision-maker selects the alternative that will maximize the economic return to the organization.

■ The decision-maker is rational and uses logic to assign values, order preferences, evaluate alternatives and make the decision that will maximize the attainment of organizational goals.

The classical model of decision-making is considered to be normative, which means it defines how a decision-maker *should* make decisions. It does not so much describe how managers actually make decisions as it provides guidelines on how to reach an ideal outcome for the organization. The ideal, rational approach of the classical model is often unattainable by real people in real organizations. However, the model has value because it helps decision-makers be more rational and not to rely entirely on personal preference in making decisions. Indeed, a global survey by McKinsey & Company found that when managers incorporate thoughtful analysis into decision-making, they get better results. Studying the responses of more than 2000 executives regarding how their companies made a specific decision, McKinsey concluded that techniques such as detailed analysis, risk assessment, financial models and considering comparable situations typically contribute to better financial and operational outcomes.[17]

The classical model is most useful when applied to programmed decisions and to decisions characterized by certainty or risk, because relevant information is available and probabilities can be calculated. For example, new analytical software programs automate many programmed decisions, such as freezing the account of a customer who has failed to make payments, determining the mobile phone service plan that is most appropriate for a particular customer, or sorting insurance claims so that cases are handled most efficiently.[18]

The growth of quantitative decision techniques that use computers has expanded the use of the classical approach. The New York City Police Department uses computerized mapping and analysis of arrest patterns, paydays, sporting events, concerts, rainfall, holidays and other variables to predict likely 'hot spots' and decide where to assign officers. Major US retailers such as Target and Walmart, make decisions about what to stock and how to price it based on analysis of sales, economic and demographic data and so forth.[19] Airlines use automated systems to optimize seat pricing, flight scheduling and crew assignment decisions.

How managers actually make decisions

Another approach to decision-making, called the administrative model, is considered to be descriptive in nature, meaning that it describes how managers actually make decisions in complex situations, rather than dictating how they *should* make decisions according to a theoretical ideal. The administrative model recognizes the human and environmental limitations that affect the degree to which managers can pursue a rational decision-making process. In difficult situations, such as those characterized by non-programmed decisions, uncertainty and ambiguity, managers are typically unable to make economically rational decisions, even if they want to.[20]

Bounded rationality and satisficing

The administrative model of decision-making is based on the published work of Herbert A. Simon. Simon proposed two concepts that were instrumental in shaping the administrative model: bounded rationality and satisficing. Bounded rationality means that people have limits, or boundaries, on how rational they can be. Organizations are incredibly complex, and managers often have the time and ability to process only a limited amount of information with which to make decisions.[21] Because managers do not have the time or sufficiency of cognitive ability to process complete information about complex decisions, they must satisfice. Satisficing means that decision-makers choose the first solution alternative that satisfies minimal decision criteria. Rather than pursuing all alternatives to identify the single solution that will maximize economic returns, managers will opt for the first solution that appears to solve the problem, even if better solutions are presumed to exist. The decision-maker cannot justify the time and expense of obtaining complete information.[22]

Managers sometimes generate alternatives for complex problems only until they find one that they believe will work. For example, Liz Claiborne managers hired designer Isaac Mizrahi and targeted younger consumers in an effort to revive the flagging Liz Claiborne brand, but sales and profits continued to decline. Faced with the failure of the new youth-oriented line, a 90 per cent reduction in orders from Macy's, high unemployment, a weak economy, and other complex and multifaceted problems, managers weren't sure how to stem the years-long tide of losses and get the company back in the black. They satisficed with a quick decision to form a licencing agreement to have Liz Claiborne clothing sold exclusively at JCPenney, which will handle all manufacturing and marketing for the brand.[23]

The administrative model relies on assumptions different from those of the classical model and focuses on organizational factors that influence individual decisions. According to the administrative model:

- Decision goals often are vague, conflicting and lack consensus among managers. Managers often are unaware of problems or opportunities that exist in the organization.

- Rational procedures are not always used, and, when they are, they are confined to a simplistic view of the problem that does not capture the complexity of real organizational events.

- Managers' searches for alternatives are limited because of human, information and resource constraints.

- Most managers settle for a satisficing rather than a maximizing solution, partly because they have limited information and partly because they have only vague criteria for what constitutes a maximizing solution.

Intuition

Another aspect of administrative decision-making is intuition. Intuition represents a quick apprehension of a decision situation based on past experience but without conscious thought.[24] Intuitive decision-making is not arbitrary or irrational because it is based on years of practice and hands-on experience. Movie mogul Harvey Weinstein, co-chairman of independent film production and distribution studio The Weinstein Company (TWC), has been in the movie business since he and his brother Bob founded Miramax in 1979. Many people told Weinstein he was crazy to even think about making a black-and-white silent film called *The Artist*, but Weinstein thought it would work and it did. The film earned TWC a Best Picture Oscar (among other awards) at the 2012 Academy Awards.[25] In today's fast-paced business environment, intuition plays an increasingly important role in decision-making. Numerous studies have found that effective managers use a combination of rational analysis and intuition in making complex decisions under time pressure.[26]

Psychologists and neuroscientists have studied how people make good decisions using their intuition under extreme time pressure and uncertainty.[27] Good intuitive decision-making is based on an ability to recognize

CONCEPT CONNECTION

'Lots of people hear what I'm doing and think, "That's a crazy idea!,"' says Russell Simmons. The successful entrepreneur, who heads the New York–based media firm Rush Communications, has relied on his **intuition** to build a half-billion-dollar empire on one profitable 'crazy idea' after another. It all began with his belief that he could go mainstream with the vibrant rap music he heard in African-American neighbourhoods. In 1983, he started the pioneering hip-hop Def Jam record label, launching the careers of Beastie Boys, LL Cool J and Run-DMC, among others. He has since moved on to successful ventures in fashion, media, consumer products and finance.

patterns at lightning speed. When people have a depth of experience and knowledge in a particular area, the right decision often comes quickly and effortlessly as recognition of information that has been largely forgotten by the conscious mind. For example, firefighters make decisions by recognizing what is typical or abnormal about a fire, based on their past experience. This ability can also be seen among soldiers in Iraq, who have been responsible for stopping many roadside bomb attacks based on 'gut feelings'. High-tech gear designed to detect improvised explosive devices (IEDs), is merely a supplement rather than a replacement for the ability of the human brain to sense danger and act on it. Soldiers with experience in the Iraq war subconsciously knew when something doesn't look or feel right. It might be a rock that wasn't there yesterday, a piece of concrete that looks too symmetrical, odd patterns of behaviour or just a different feeling of tension in the air.[28] Similarly, in the business world, managers continuously perceive and process information that they may not consciously be aware of, and their base of knowledge and experience helps them make decisions that may be characterized by uncertainty and ambiguity.

However, intuitive decisions don't always work out, and managers should take care to apply intuition under the right circumstances and in the right way, rather than considering it a magical technique for making all important decisions.[29] Managers may walk a fine line between two extremes: on the one hand, making arbitrary decisions without careful study, and on the other, relying obsessively on rational analysis. One is not better than the other, managers need to take a balanced approach by considering both rationality and intuition as important components of effective decision-making.[30]

The political model

The third model of decision-making is useful for making non-programmed decisions when conditions are uncertain, information is limited, and there are manager conflicts about what goals to pursue or what course of action to take. Most organizational decisions involve many managers who are pursuing different goals, and they have to talk with one another to share information and reach an agreement. Managers often engage in coalition building for making complex organizational decisions.[31] A coalition is an informal alliance among managers who support a specific goal. *Coalition building* is the process of forming alliances among managers. In other words, a manager who supports a specific alternative, such as increasing the corporation's growth by acquiring another company, talks informally to other executives and tries to persuade them to support the decision. Without a coalition, a powerful individual or group could derail the decision-making process. Coalition building provides managers with the opportunity to contribute to decision-making, enhancing their commitment to the alternative that is ultimately adopted. Results from the global survey by McKinsey & Company mentioned earlier suggest that informal coalition building is associated with faster implementation of decisions, because managers have developed consensus about which action to pursue.[32]

Failing to build a coalition can allow conflict and disagreements to derail a decision, particularly if the opposition builds a powerful coalition of its own.

Managers always have to anticipate resistance, talk with people all across the organization and make sure that their decisions will benefit the overall organization. The political model closely resembles the real environment in which most managers and decision-makers operate. For example, interviews with CEOs in high-tech industries found that they strived to use some type of rational process in making decisions, but the way they actually decided things was through a complex interaction with other managers, subordinates, environmental factors and organizational events.[33] Decisions are complex and involve many people, information is often ambiguous, and disagreement and conflict over problems and solutions are normal. The political model begins with four basic assumptions:

■ Organizations are made up of groups with diverse interests, goals and values. Managers disagree about problem priorities and may not understand, or share, the goals and interests of other managers.

■ Information is ambiguous and incomplete. The attempt to be rational is limited by the complexity of many problems, as well as personal and organizational constraints.

■ Managers do not have the time, resources or mental capacity to comprehensively identify all the dimensions of the problem and process all relevant information. Managers interact with each other exchanging viewpoints to gather information and reduce ambiguity.

■ Managers engage in the push and pull of debate to decide goals and discuss alternatives. Decisions are the result of bargaining and discussion among coalition members.

The key dimensions of the classical, administrative and political models are listed in Exhibit 9.2. Research into decision-making procedures found rational, classical procedures to be associated with high performance for organizations in stable environments. However, administrative and political decision-making procedures and intuition have been associated with high performance in unstable environments, in which decisions must be made rapidly and under more difficult conditions.[34]

Decision-making steps

Whether a decision is programmed or non-programmed and regardless of managers' choice of the classical, administrative or political models of decision-making, six steps are typically associated with effective decision processes. These steps are summarized in Exhibit 9.3.

Recognition of decision requirement

Managers confront a decision requirement in the form of either a problem or an opportunity. A problem occurs when organizational accomplishment is less than established goals. Some aspect of performance is unsatisfactory. An opportunity exists when managers see a potential accomplishment that significantly exceeds specified current goals. Managers see the possibility of enhancing performance beyond current levels.

Awareness of a problem or opportunity is the first step in the decision-making sequence and requires surveillance of the internal and external environment for issues that merit executive attention.[35] This process

EXHIBIT 9.2 Characteristics of classical, administrative and political decision-making models

Classical model	Administrative model	Political model
Clear-cut problem and goals	Vague problem and goals	Pluralistic; conflicting goals
Condition of certainty	Condition of uncertainty	Condition of uncertainty or ambiguity
Full information about alternatives and their outcomes	Limited information about alternatives and their outcomes	Inconsistent viewpoints; ambiguous information
Rational choice by individual for maximizing outcomes	Satisficing choice for resolving problem using intuition	Bargaining and discussion among coalition members

REFLECTION

- The ideal, rational approach to decision-making, called the **classical model**, is based on the assumption that managers should make logical decisions that are economically sensible and in the organization's best economic interest.
- The classical model is **normative**, meaning that it defines how a manager *should* make logical decisions and provides guidelines for reaching an ideal outcome.
- Software programs based on the classical model are being applied to programmed decisions, such as how to schedule airline crews or how to process insurance claims most efficiently.
- The **administrative model** includes the concepts of *bounded rationality* and *satisficing* and describes how managers make decisions in situations that are characterized by uncertainty and ambiguity.
- The administrative model is **descriptive**, an approach that describes how managers actually make decisions,

rather than how they should make decisions according to a theoretical model.
- **Bounded rationality** means that people have restricted time and cognitive ability to process only a limited amount of information, on which to base decisions.
- **Satisficing** means choosing the first alternative that satisfies minimal decision criteria, regardless of whether better solutions are presumed to exist.
- **Intuition** is an aspect of administrative decision-making that refers to a quick comprehension of a decision situation based on past experience, but without conscious thought.
- Soldiers in the Iraq war were known to detect roadside bombs using their intuition.
- The political model takes into consideration that many decisions require debate, discussion and coalition building.
- A **coalition** is an informal alliance among managers who support a specific goal or solution.

EXHIBIT 9.3 Six steps in the managerial decision-making process

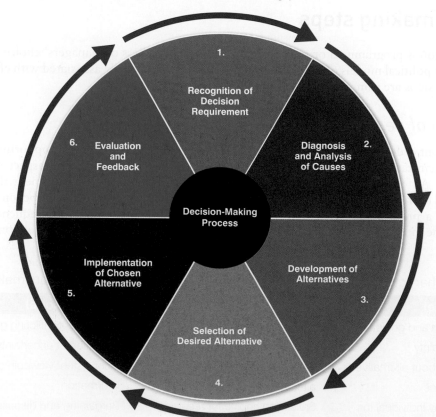

resembles the military concept of gathering intelligence. Managers scan the world around them to determine whether the organization is satisfactorily progressing towards its goals.

Some information comes from periodic financial reports, performance reports and other sources that are designed to discover problems before they become too serious. Managers also take advantage of informal sources. They talk to other managers, gather opinions on how things are going and seek advice on which problems should be tackled or which opportunities embraced.[36] For example, the board of Hewlett-Packard fired Leo Apotheker after only 11 months as CEO because they heard from other managers that Apotheker did not seem to keep his team informed of plans, failed to rally the troops behind his efforts and was unclear on strategic direction for the company.[37] Recognizing decision requirements is difficult because it often means integrating disparate bits and pieces of information in novel ways.

Diagnosis and analysis of causes

Once a problem or opportunity comes to a manager's attention, the understanding of the situation should be refined. Diagnosis is the first stage in the decision-making process in which managers analyze underlying causal factors associated with the decision situation.

Many times, the real problem lies hidden behind the problem that managers *think* exists. By looking at a situation from different angles, managers can identify the true problem. In addition, they often discover opportunities they didn't realize were there.[38] Kepner and Tregoe (1965), who conducted extensive studies of managerial decision-making, recommend that managers ask a series of questions to specify underlying causes, including the following eight questions:

1 What is the state of disequilibrium affecting us?

2 When did it occur?

3 Where did it occur?

4 How did it occur?

5 To whom did it occur?

6 What is the urgency of the problem?

7 What is the interconnectedness of events?

8 What result came from which activity?[39]

'It isn't that they can't see the solution. It's that they can't see the problem.'
— G. K. CHESTERTON, ENGLISH NOVELIST

Such structured questions help to specify what actually happened and why. Diagnosing a problem can be thought of as peeling an onion, layer by layer. Management Consultant Daniel Burrus tells of meeting with the CEO of a large accounting and professional services firm who said the company's biggest problem was the inability to hire enough qualified people to serve their global clients. As the two peeled the onion further, they got down to the real problem, which was not the lack of staff – but inefficiency in internal collaboration and communication. The CEO discovered that he might actually be able to *reduce* staff with more effective and efficient systems.[40] Managers cannot solve problems if they don't know enough about them, or if they are addressing the wrong issues.

TAKE A MOMENT

The Small Group Breakout Exercise online will give you a chance to practise a new approach to decision-making that focuses on desired outcomes rather than looking at the cause of problems.

CONCEPT CONNECTION

Reid Carr, founder and CEO of San Diego-based Red Door Interactive, Inc., a firm that manages clients' online presence, involves his staff throughout the decision-making process. Carr believes that when **developing, selecting and implementing alternatives**, managers should 'decide slowly and collaboratively so that you have the best plan produced by those who are tasked with execution. Then, let them execute.' Red Door's annual 'Start, Stop and Keep' survey is one way Carr gathers feedback. It asks employees to suggest which internal processes and practices should be introduced, continued or discontinued.

Development of alternatives

The next stage is to generate possible alternative solutions that will respond to the needs of the situation and correct the underlying causes.

For a programmed decision, feasible alternatives are easy to identify and in larger organizations they are usually available within the organization's rules and procedures. Non-programmed decisions, however, require developing new courses of action that will meet the company's needs. For decisions made under conditions of high uncertainty, managers may develop only one or two custom solutions that will satisfice for handling the problem. However, studies find that limiting the search for alternatives is a primary cause of decision failure in organizations.[41]

Decision alternatives can be thought of as tools for reducing the difference between the organization's current and desired performance. Smart managers tap into the knowledge of people throughout the organization for decision alternatives.

Selection of the desired alternative

Once feasible alternatives are developed, one must be selected. In this stage, managers try to select the most promising of several alternative courses of action. The best alternative solution is one which best fits the overall goals and values of the organization and achieves the desired results using the fewest resources.[42] Managers want to select the choice with the least amount of risk and uncertainty. Because some risk is inherent for most non-programmed decisions, managers try to gauge prospects for success. They might rely on their intuition and experience to estimate whether a given course of action is likely to succeed. Basing choices on overall goals and values can also guide the selection of best alternatives.

Choosing among alternatives also depends on managers' personality factors and willingness to accept risk and uncertainty. Risk propensity is the willingness to undertake risk with the opportunity of gaining an increased payoff. At drug maker Novartis, for example, researchers wanted CEO Vasella to give the go-ahead for an experimental vaccine for Alzheimer's disease. The potential payoff is huge, but Vasella thought at the time that the risks were far too high. He prefers to focus research on smaller, narrowly defined groups of patients, often suffering from rare diseases that are well understood scientifically but that desperately need new drugs. For Vasella, investing in a drug for Alzheimer's before the disease is better understood is wasting time and money.[43] The level of risk that a manager is willing to accept will influence the analysis of costs and benefits to be derived from any decision. Consider the situations in Exhibit 9.4. In each situation, which alternative would you choose? A person with a low risk propensity would tend to take ensured moderate returns by going for a tie score, building a domestic plant or pursuing a career as a physician. A risk taker would go for the victory, build a plant in a foreign country or embark on an acting career.

Implementation of the chosen alternative

The implementation stage involves the use of managerial, administrative and persuasive abilities to ensure that the chosen alternative is carried out. This step is similar to the idea of strategy execution described

EXHIBIT 9.4 Decision alternatives with different levels of risk

In each of the following situations, which alternative would you choose?	
You're the coach of a university football team and in the final seconds of a game with the team's archrival, you face a choice:	Choose a play that has a 95 per cent chance of producing a tie score OR Go for a play that has a 30 per cent chance of victory but will lead to certain defeat if it fails.
As president of a German manufacturing company, you face a decision about building a new factory. You can:	Build a plant in Germany that has a 90 per cent chance of producing a modest return on investment OR Build a plant in a foreign country that has an unstable political history. This alternative has a 40 per cent chance of failing, but the returns will be enormous if it succeeds.
It's your final year, and it is time to decide your next move. Here are the alternatives you're considering:	Go to medical school and become a physician, a career in which you are 80 per cent likely to succeed OR Follow your dreams and be an actor, even though the opportunity for success is only around 20 per cent.

in Chapter 8. The ultimate success of the chosen alternative depends on whether it can be translated into action.[44] Sometimes an alternative never becomes reality because managers lack the resources or energy needed to make things happen. Implementation may require discussion with many people affected by the decision. Communication, motivation and leadership skills must be used to see that the decision is carried out. When employees see that managers follow up on their decisions by tracking implementation success, they are more committed to positive action.[45]

 ## INNOVATIVE WAY

The New York Times

In March 2011, *The New York Times* took a giant strategic leap – it asked readers to begin paying for access to its journalism online. The decision wasn't made lightly. In reality, executives and senior editors had spent years studying the problem, analyzing various alternatives and reaching an agreement to implement the new subscription plan.

Managers agreed on the major issue that had to be addressed: declining revenues. Analyzing the causes of this problem, they recognized that the economic recession had hit the newspaper's revenue hard, and that both print and online advertising had gone down steeply since the recession began. However, another major cause was the continuing decline in print subscriptions. Why should people pay for a subscription when they could simply go to the *Times*' website and access the paper's high-quality journalism free of charge? Managers believed that some type of online subscription business model was needed. Debate and discussion of various alternatives went on for months, both formally and informally. Eventually, a coalition of managers came together around the idea of a tiered subscription service that would allow website visitors to read 20 articles a month at no charge, before being asked to select one of three subscription models at various price levels.

Evaluation and feedback began immediately and continues to this day. On the day the paper launched the subscription model, executives gathered with Web developers around two long tables, 'their heads buried in their laptops monitoring the launch,' as one writer put it. The first subscriber signed up at practically the same moment the announcement was made. One year later, managers were surprised by the success of this decision. They had set a measure of 300 000 subscribers during the first year as a benchmark for success, and the total was actually around 390 000. Interestingly, at the same time, home delivery subscriptions of the print edition increased for the first time in 5 years, perhaps because some readers feared losing the paper edition altogether if they didn't support it. In addition, advertising revenues began to grow again as advertisers saw that the new digital subscription model was working.[46]

Evaluation and feedback

In the evaluation stage of the decision process, decision-makers gather information that informs them how well the decision was implemented and whether it was effective in achieving its goals. Feedback is important because decision-making is an ongoing process. Decision-making is not completed when a manager or board of directors votes yes or no. Feedback provides decision-makers with information that can precipitate a new iterative decision cycle. The decision taken may fail, thus generating a new analysis of the problem, evaluation of alternatives and selection of a new alternative. Many big problems are solved by trying several alternatives in sequence, each providing modest improvement. Feedback is the part of monitoring that assesses whether a new decision needs to be made.

To illustrate the overall decision-making process, including evaluation and feedback, consider the decision at *The New York Times* to begin a paid subscription plan for the newspaper's website.

The decision at *The New York Times* to implement a digital subscription strategic plan illustrates all the decision steps, and the launch process ultimately ended in great success.[47] Strategic decisions always contain some risk, but feedback and follow-up can help keep companies on track. When decisions don't work out so well, managers can learn from their mistakes – and sometimes turn problems into opportunities.

Personal decision framework

Imagine you were a manager at Google, *The New York Times*, a VUE cinema or the local public library. How would you go about making important decisions that might shape the future of your department or company? So far in this chapter, we have discussed a number of factors that affect how managers make decisions. For example, decisions may be programmed or non-programmed, situations are characterized by various levels of uncertainty, and managers may use the classical, administrative or political model of decision-making. In addition, the decision-making process typically follows six recognized steps.

However, not all managers go about making decisions in the same way. In fact, significant differences distinguish the ways in which individual managers may approach problems and make decisions concerning them. These differences can be explained by the concept of personal decision styles. Exhibit 9.5 illustrates the role of personal style in the decision-making process. Personal decision style refers to distinctions amongst

REFLECTION

- Managers face the need to make a decision when they either confront a problem or see an opportunity.
- A **problem** is a situation in which organizational accomplishments have failed to meet established goals.
- An **opportunity** is a situation in which managers see potential organizational accomplishments that exceed current goals.
- The decision-making process typically involves six steps: recognition of the need for a decision; diagnosing causes; developing alternatives; selecting

an alternative; implementing the alternative; and evaluating decision effectiveness.
- **Diagnosis** is the step in which managers analyze underlying causal factors associated with the decision situation.
- Selection of an alternative depends partly on managers' **risk propensity**, or their willingness to undertake risk with the opportunity of gaining an increased payoff.
- The **implementation** step involves using managerial, administrative and persuasive abilities to translate the chosen alternative into action.

people with respect to how they evaluate problems, generate alternatives and make choices. Research has identified four major decision styles: directive, analytical, conceptual and behavioural.[48]

1   The *directive style* is used by people who prefer simple, clear-cut solutions to problems. Managers who use this style often make decisions quickly because they do not like to deal with a lot of information and may consider only one or two alternatives. People who prefer the directive style generally are efficient and rational and prefer to rely on existing rules or procedures for making decisions.

2   Managers with an *analytical style* like to consider complex solutions based on as much data as they can gather. These individuals carefully consider alternatives and often base their decisions on objective, rational data from management control systems and other sources. They search for the best possible decision based on the information available.

3   People who tend towards a *conceptual style* also like to consider a broad amount of information. However, they are more socially oriented than those with an analytical style and have dialogue with others about the problem(s) and possible alternatives for solving them. Managers using a conceptual style consider many broad alternatives, rely on information from both people and systems, and like to creatively solve problems.

4   The *behavioural style* is often the style adopted by managers having a deep concern for others as individuals. Managers using this style like to engage with people on a one-on-one basis, understand their feelings about the problem, and consider the effect of a given decision on them. People with a behavioural style usually are much concerned with the personal development of others and may make decisions that help others achieve their goals.

Many managers have a dominant decision style. For example, US President Barack Obama's decision to increase troop strength in Afghanistan reflected his primarily conceptual style of decision-making. The president held ten meetings with key military decision-makers in a decision process that was called 'intense, methodical, earnest and at times deeply frustrating'. Obama requested detailed reports, asked numerous questions and showed an almost insatiable need for information. One participant described him as '*a cross between a college professor and a gentle cross-examiner.*'[49]

EXHIBIT 9.5 Personal decision framework

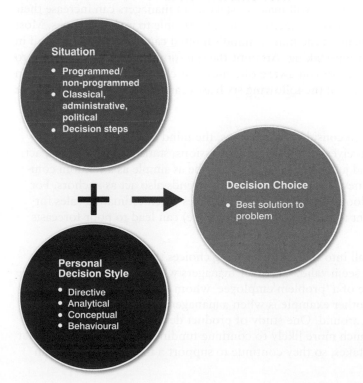

SOURCES: A. J. Rowe, J. D. Boulgaides and M. R. McGrath, *Managerial Decision Making* (Chicago: Science Research Associates, 1984); and Alan J. Rowe and Richard O. Mason, *Managing with Style: A Guide to Understanding, Assessing, and Improving Your Decision Making* (San Francisco: Jossey-Bass, 1987).

However, managers frequently use several different styles or a combination of styles in making the varied decisions that they confront daily. A manager might use a directive style for determining which company to use for standard office supplies, yet would shift to a more conceptual style when handling an interdepartmental conflict. The most effective managers are able to shift among styles, as needed, to meet the situation. Being strongly aware of one's dominant decision style can help a manager avoid making critical mistakes when his/her usual style may be inappropriate to the problem at hand.

TAKE A MOMENT

To learn more about how you make decisions, go to the Experiential Exercise online that evaluates your personal decision style.

REFLECTION

- A manager's personal decision style influences how he or she makes decisions.
- Decision styles are differences among people with respect to how they perceive problems and make choices.
- Four major decision styles are directive, analytical, conceptual and behavioural.

- President Barack Obama mostly uses a primarily conceptual style of decision-making.
- Most experienced managers use a variety of styles depending on the decision's contextual situation.

Why do managers make poor decisions?

Managers are faced with a relentless flow of demand for decisions, from solving minor problems to implementing major strategic changes. Even the best manager will make mistakes, but managers can increase their percentage of good decisions by understanding some of the factors that cause people to make bad ones. Most bad decisions are errors in judgement that originate in the human mind's limited capacity, or fatigue, and in the natural biases managers display during decision-making. Attempt the questions in the Shoptalk box to learn how biases can affect decisions and choices. Are you aware of biases that cloud your judgement when you make decisions and solve problems? Awareness of the following six biases can help managers make more enlightened choices.[50]

1   *Being influenced by initial impressions.* When considering decisions, the mind often gives disproportionate weight to the early information it receives. These initial impressions, statistics or estimates, act as an anchor to our subsequent thoughts and judgements. Anchors can be as simple as a random comment by a colleague, or a statistic read in a newspaper. Past events and trends also act as anchors. For example, in business, managers frequently look at the previous year's sales when estimating sales for the coming year. Giving far too much weight to the past (rarely replicable) can lead to poor forecasts and misguided decisions.

2   *Justifying past decisions.* Many managers fall into the trap of making choices that justify their past decisions, even if those decisions no longer seem valid. Consider managers who invest tremendous time and energy into improving the performance of a 'problem employee' whom they now realize should never have been hired in the first place. Another example is when a manager continues to pour money into a failing project, hoping to turn things around. One study of product development found that managers who initiate a new product are much more likely to continue funding it despite evidence that it is failing.[51] People don't like to make mistakes, so they continue to support a flawed decision in an effort to justify or correct the past.

CONCEPT CONNECTION

By most accounts, Facebook's initial public offering (IPO) in 2012 was considered something of a flop, as it was shrouded in controversy and allegations of misconduct and wrongdoing. The IPO was just one in a series of missteps and mistakes by Facebook's leaders, including founder Mark Zuckerberg. Many critics attribute Zuckerberg's lapses in good judgement to his **overconfidence** and the fact that he surrounded himself with board members who didn't question his decisions perhaps as thoroughly as they should have. It is argued that overconfidence is a prerequisite of visionary leadership and there is support in the finance literature for this viewpoint.

3   ***Seeing what you want to see.*** People frequently look for information that supports their existing instinct or point of view and avoid information that contradicts it.

This bias affects where managers look for information, as well as how they interpret the information they find. People tend to give too much weight to supporting information and too little to information that conflicts with their established viewpoints. For example, managers at Tokyo Electric Power Company (Tepco) have been accused of delaying far too long the decision to use seawater to cool nuclear reactors at Fukushima Daiichi following the 2011 Japan earthquake and tsunami. Tepco managers knew that seawater would destroy the reactors, so they gave greater weight to information that supported their decision to delay its use, emphasizing that they were *'taking the safety of the whole plant into consideration'* in judging the appropriate timing to use seawater in the cooldown efforts. Unfortunately, it took an explosion at the plant to convince managers that using seawater was essential to control the overheating of the reactors.[52]

4   ***Perpetuating the status quo.*** Managers may base decisions on what has worked in the past and fail to explore new options, dig for additional information or investigate new technologies. For example, General Motors (GM) was stuck with its strategic decision to offer a multitude of brands long after there was clear evidence that trying to cover the whole range of the auto market was paving the way to disaster. The strategy started to fray in the 1970s with increased competition from Japanese automakers and spikes in oil prices. Yet, in February 2008, managers were saying that talk about killing brands was 'not a thoughtful discussion.' Only bankruptcy and a forced restructuring finally pushed managers to cut GM's brands from eight down to four.[53]

5   ***Being influenced by emotions.*** If you've ever made a decision when you were angry, upset or even ecstatically happy, you might already know the danger of being over-influenced by emotions. A study of traders in London investment banks found that effective regulation of emotions was a characteristic of higher-performing traders. Lower-performing traders were less effective in managing and modulating their emotional responses.[54] Another finding is that doctors make less effective decisions when they feel emotions of like or dislike for a patient. If they like a patient, they are less likely to prescribe a painful procedure. If they feel dislike, they may blame the patient for the condition and provide less treatment.[55] Unfortunately, some managers let their emotions influence their decisions on a regular basis. There is some evidence that when people make poor decisions under the influence of strong emotions (such as firing off an angry email message), they tend to continue to make poor decisions because it becomes part of the mind's blueprint for how to behave.[56] Managers make better decisions when – to the extent possible – they take emotions out of the decision-making process.

6   ***Overconfidence.*** Most people overestimate their ability to predict uncertain outcomes. For example, when people are asked to define quantities about which they have little direct knowledge ('What was the market value of Facebook as of 14 August 2012?'), they overestimate their memory recall accuracy.

MANAGER'S SHOPTALK

Do biases influence your decision-making?

All of us have biases, but most of us have a hard time seeing our own. What biases influence your decisions and solutions to problems? Answer the following questions to get an idea of the difficulties and mistakes that you can expect as a new manager.

1   A piece of paper is folded in half, in half again, etc. After 100 folds, how thick will it be? Take your best guess: _____. I am 90 per cent sure that the correct answer lies between _____ and _____.

2   Which figure below is most different from the others?

3   As owner and CEO of your company, you decided to invest $100 million to build pilotless drones that cannot be detected by enemy radar. When the project is 90 per cent complete, a competing firm begins marketing a completed drone that cannot be detected by radar. In addition, their drone is much faster, smaller, cheaper and more sophisticated than the drone that your company is developing. The question is: Should you invest the last 10 per cent of the research funds to finish your drone? Check one of the following answers.

_____ No _____ There is no reason to continue spending money on the project.

_____ Yes _____ After investing $90 million, we might as well finish the project.

4   Give a quick (5-second) estimate of the following product without actually calculating:

$8 \times 7 \times 6 \times 5 \times 4 \times 3 \times 2 \times 1 =$ _____

5   Robert is envious, stubborn, critical, impulsive, industrious and intelligent. In general, how emotional do you think Robert is? (Circle one number.)

Not emotional   Extremely
at all

1 2 3 4 5 6 7 8 9   emotional

6   Which would you choose between the two alternatives below?

_____ Alternative A: A 50 per cent chance of gaining $1000.00

_____ Alternative B: A sure gain of $500.00

Which would you choose between the two alternatives below?

_____ Alternative C: A 50 per cent chance of losing $1000.00

_____ Alternative D: A sure loss of $500.00

After you have specified an answer to each problem, you will find the answers and a description of the potential related bias on page 300.

SOURCES: Questions 1 and 3–6 are from research studies reviewed in Scott Plous, *The Psychology of Judgment and Decision Making* (Philadelphia: Temple University Press, 1993); question 2 is based on an item in the *Creativity in Action Newsletter,* as reported in Arthur B. VanGundy, *Idea Power: Techniques & Resources to Unleash the Creativity in Your Organization* (New York: Amacom, 1992).

Similarly, many managers have unrealistic expectations of their ability to understand the risks and make the right choice. Consider how overconfidence contributed to decisions at JPMorgan Chase's chief investment office, made by the so-called 'London Whale', that led to a multibillion-dollar loss. All banks take risks, but JPMorgan was praised for not taking the kind of outsized risks that many banks took during the mortgage boom – and that contributed to the collapse of the US economy. After the Wall Street crisis, JPMorgan's CEO, Jamie Dimon, was called 'the world's most important banker', and his top executives were hailed as a management team that could seemingly do no wrong. The company's chief investment office in London, which was created to protect the bank from volatility caused by complex global financial transactions, gained a reputation for its trading prowess. The unit was a star performer and became a profit centre for JPMorgan at a time when industry earnings were under pressure. But managers got excessively overconfident of their ability to spot and manage risks. They began taking larger and larger bets and gambles, including involvement in a highly complicated trading strategy involving derivatives – similar in some ways to the risks that led to the Wall Street crisis. The strategy backfired, eventually causing a loss of almost $6 billion, leading to the firing of several key executives, and damaging the reputation of both the bank and its CEO. Moreover, federal investigators were known to be looking into potential fraud, suspecting that some traders improperly marked their trades to obscure the magnitude of the losses.[57]

REFLECTION

- Being aware of biases that cloud good judgement helps managers avoid decision traps and make better decisions.
- Biases to watch out for include: being influenced by initial impressions, trying to correct or justify past flawed decisions, seeing only what you want to see, perpetuating the status quo, being influenced by emotions and being overconfident.

Innovative decision-making

The ability to make fast, widely supported, high-quality decisions on a frequent basis is a critical skill in today's fast-moving organizations.[58] Considering that managers are under pressure to decide quickly and that biases creep in and cloud judgement, how do managers ever make good decisions? Some innovative techniques can help managers watch out for and avoid mistakes caused by cognitive biases. It is difficult for most managers to see their own biases, but they can build in mechanisms that neutralize or reduce bias-related decision errors at the organizational level.[59]

Start with brainstorming

Brainstorming uses a face-to-face interactive group to spontaneously suggest a wide range of alternatives for decision-making. The accepted rules for effective brainstorming are as follows: that people can build on one another's ideas; all ideas are acceptable, no matter how crazy they seem; and criticism and premature evaluation are not allowed. The goal is to generate as many ideas (variety) as possible. Brainstorming has been found to be highly effective for quickly generating a wide range of alternate solutions to a problem, but it does have some drawbacks.[60] For one aspect, people in a group often want to conform to what others are saying. Others may be concerned about pleasing the boss or impressing colleagues. In addition, many creative people simply have social inhibitions that limit their participation in a group session, or make it difficult to come up with ideas in a group setting. One study found that when four people are asked to 'brainstorm' individually, they typically come up with twice as many ideas as a group of four brainstorming together.

One recent approach, electronic brainstorming, takes advantage of the group approach while overcoming some disadvantages. Electronic brainstorming, sometimes called *brainwriting*, brings people together in an interactive group over a computer network.[61] One member writes an idea, another reads it and adds other ideas, and so on. Studies show that electronic brainstorming generates about 40 per cent more ideas than individuals brainstorming alone, and 25 to 200 per cent more ideas than regular brainstorming groups, depending on group size.[62] Why should this be the case? Because the process is anonymous, the sky's the limit in terms of what people feel free to say. People can write down their ideas immediately, avoiding the possibility that a good idea might slip away while the person is waiting for a chance to speak in a face-to-face group. Social inhibitions and concerns are avoided, which typically allows for a broader range of participation. Another advantage is that electronic brainstorming can potentially be done with groups made up of employees from around the world, further increasing the diversity of alternatives.

CONCEPT CONNECTION

Brainstorming has its share of critics. Some say that it prevents the quiet people from participating, and that a group can be too easily influenced by the emotions of some of the dominant players. In response, a number of brainstorming alternatives have been developed. In fact, some companies bring in certified trainers to teach employees how to use methods, such as the Six Thinking Hats, Lateral Thinking, Nominal Group Technique, Ideation, and more.

Use hard evidence

Using hard evidence can help take emotion out of the decision-making process, keep people from relying on faulty assumptions and prevent managers from 'seeing what they want to see', as described earlier. Evidence-based decision-making means a commitment to make more informed and intelligent decisions based on the best available facts and evidence. It means being alert to potential biases and seeking and examining the evidence with rigour. Managers practise evidence-based decision-making by being careful and thoughtful – rather than carelessly relying on assumptions, past experience, rules of thumb or intuition.[63] For example, the Educational Testing Service (ETS), which develops and administers tests such as the Scholastic Aptitude Test (SAT) and the Graduate Record Examination (GRE), created a task force to examine the company's decision-making processes for new products and services. The team found that many product decisions were made without clear information about intellectual property, cycle times or even the expected market opportunities. The team then worked with managers to create a more systematic, evidence-based decision-making process, including the use of forms that required specific metrics and information about each proposal and defined standards for what constituted strong evidence that the product or service would fit with ETS strategy and likely market demand.[64]

A recent study by Brynjolfsson, an economist at the Sloan School of Management at Massachusetts Institute of Technology (MIT), provided some evidence that organizational decisions can be improved with the use of evidence-based decision-making. Brynjolfsson and his colleagues studied 179 large companies and found that the ones that have adopted data-driven decision-making achieved productivity that was 5 to 6 per cent higher than could be explained by any other factors.[65]

Engage in rigorous debate

An important key to better decision-making is to encourage a rigorous debate of the issue at hand. Good managers recognize that constructive conflict based on divergent points of view can bring a problem into focus, clarify people's ideas, stimulate creative thinking, limit the role of bias, create a broader understanding of issues and alternatives and improve decision quality.[66] Reed Hastings, CEO of Netflix, built more rigorous debate into the decision-making process to avoid another calamity, such as the one the company experienced following two successive unpopular decisions: a) to increase the price of the service, and b) to split Netflix into two separate businesses – one for Internet streaming and one for DVD rentals. Customers were furious, and they showed it by cancelling their Netflix memberships in droves. When Hastings had told a friend before the decision that he was thinking of splitting the business, the friend said, *'That is awful. I don't want to deal with two accounts.'* But Hastings didn't listen. He admits now that he was guilty of overconfidence and being out of touch with customers' thinking. By using rigorous debate about major decisions, Hastings hopes to get Netflix back on the right track – gaining rather than losing customers.[67]

Stimulating rigorous debate can be done in several ways. One way is by ensuring that the group is diverse in terms of age and gender, functional area of expertise, hierarchical level and experience with the business. Some groups assign a devil's advocate, who has the role of challenging the assumptions and assertions made by the group.[68] The devil's advocate may force the group to rethink its approach to the problem and avoid reaching premature conclusions. Jeffrey McKeever, a CEO of MicroAge, often played the devil's advocate, changing his position in the middle of a debate to ensure that other executives don't just go along with his opinions.[69]

Another approach is to have group members develop as many alternatives as they can as quickly as they can.[70] It allows the team to work with multiple alternatives and encourages people to advocate ideas they might not prefer, simply to encourage debate. Still another way to encourage constructive conflict is to use a technique called point-counterpoint, which breaks a decision-making group into two subgroups and assigns them different, often competing, responsibilities.[71] The groups then develop and exchange proposals and discuss and debate the various options until they arrive at a common set of understandings and recommendations.

Avoid groupthink

It is important for managers to remember that some disagreement and conflict is much healthier than blind agreement. Pressures for conformity exist in almost any group, and particularly when people in a group like one another, they tend to avoid anything that might create disharmony. Groupthink refers to the tendency of people in groups to suppress contrary opinions.[72] When people slip into groupthink, the desire for harmony outweighs concerns over decision quality. Group members emphasize maintaining unity rather than realistically challenging problems and alternatives. People censor their personal opinions and are reluctant to criticize the opinions of others.

Author and scholar Jerry Harvey coined the related term *Abilene paradox* to illustrate the hidden pressures for conformity that can exist in groups.[73] Harvey tells the story of how members of his extended family sat sweltering on the porch in 104-degree heat in a small town about 50 miles from Abilene, Texas. When someone suggested driving to a café in Abilene, everyone went along with the idea, even though the car was not air conditioned. Everyone was miserable and returned home exhausted and irritable. Later, each person admitted that they hadn't wanted to make the trip and thought it was a ridiculous idea. They only went because they thought the others wanted to go.

Know when to bail out

In a fast-paced environment, good managers encourage risk taking and learning from mistakes, but they also aren't hesitant to pull the plug on something that isn't working. Walt Disney Company managers wanted to shut down production of the remake of *The Lone Ranger* with Johnny Depp, because they considered the budget far too high. Although production had begun and set construction was underway, the budget had increased out of line with what managers considered reasonable. CEO Bob Iger said: '*the company would rather skip a project entirely than commit too many resources to a risky bet.*'[74] Unlike the Disney managers involved with *The Lone Ranger* movie, however, research has found that managers and organizations often continue to invest time and money in a solution, even when there is strong evidence that it is not appropriate. This tendency is referred to as escalating commitment. Managers might block or distort negative information because they don't want to be responsible for a bad decision, or they might simply refuse to accept that their solution is wrong.[75] A study in Europe verified that even highly successful managers often miss or ignore warning signals because they become committed to a decision and believe that if they persevere, it will pay off.[76] As companies face increasing competition, complexity and change, it is important that managers don't get so attached to their own ideas that they're unwilling to recognize when to move on. According to Stanford University professor, Robert Sutton, the key to successful creative decision-making is to '*fail early, fail often and pull the plug early.*'[77]

'*The most dangerous thing is to be successful. You then think every decision is the right one.*'
— WONG WAI MING, CFO OF LENOVO

Do a postmortem

To improve decision-making, managers need to reflect and learn from every decision they make. When people review the results of their decisions, they learn valuable lessons for how to do things better in the future. A technique many companies have adopted from the US Army to encourage examination of the evidence and continuous learning is the after-action review, a disciplined procedure whereby managers invest time to review the results of decisions on a regular basis and learn from them.[78] After implementation of any significant decision, managers meet to evaluate what worked, what didn't and how to do things better. Many problems are solved by trial and error. For example, postmortem reviews of decisions regarding attacks from roadside bombs in Iraq led soldiers to suggest implementation of an overall counter-insurgency strategy rather than relying so much on technology.[79] Numerous business organizations have adopted some form of after-action review. A similar technique emphasized by Lenovo founder Liu Chuanzhi is called *fu pan*, which means 'replaying the chess board'. The idea is to review every move to improve the next one. Lenovo managers are trained to apply *fu pan* in everything from a small quick review of a workday incident to a full, in-depth review of a major decision.[80] When managers get prompt feedback on decisions through after-action reviews, it gives them the chance to incorporate new information and greater understanding into their thinking and decision-making.

REFLECTION

- Most decisions within organizations are made as part of a group, and whereas managers can't always see their own biases, they can build in mechanisms to prevent bias from influencing major decisions at the organizational level.
- Brainstorming is a technique that uses a face-to-face group to spontaneously suggest a broad range of alternatives for making a decision.
- Electronic brainstorming brings people together in an interactive group over a computer network, rather than meeting face to face.
- Evidence-based decision-making is founded on a commitment to examining potential biases, seeking and examining evidence with rigour and making informed and intelligent decisions based on the best available facts and evidence.
- A devil's advocate is a person who is assigned the role of challenging the assumptions and assertions made by the group to prevent premature consensus.

- A group decision-making technique that breaks people into subgroups and assigns them to express competing points of view regarding the decision is called point-counterpoint.
- Groupthink refers to the tendency of people in groups to suppress contrary opinions in a desire for harmony.
- Escalating commitment refers to continuing to invest time and money in a decision despite evidence that it is failing.
- A technique adopted from the US Army, the after-action review is a disciplined procedure whereby managers review the results of decisions to evaluate what worked, what didn't and how to do things better.
- Managers at Lenovo apply a technique called *fu pan*, which means 'replaying the chess board', reviewing every move to improve the next one.

DISCUSSION QUESTIONS

1 *'Chamelion Clothing'* is a UK-based clothing retailer that has made a series of decisions that have damaged the company's half year profits and their reputation for stylish fashion. They expanded in 2015 far too quickly and as a consequence they lost touch with their mainstream customers' needs and wants. Their business model was to copy the successful approach of rivals, rather than pursuing their own course. This involved reducing product quality to reduce costs and rapidly shifting from one fashion approach to another as each failed, leaving slow moving inventory. Suggest improvements they could make to their decision-making that would help them implement a more effective business model.

2 Explain the difference between risk and uncertainty. How might you approach a risky

situation differently to an uncertain situation?

3 Using the six steps of decision making as demonstrated in Exhibit 9.3, describe how you might apply these to deciding which higher education university to apply for.

4 What do you see as the possible advantages and disadvantages of face-to-face brainstorming versus electronic brainstorming? Provide examples of when one might be preferred over the other.

5 Can the classical model and the administrative model of decision making exist side by side? If so, how might managers combine the two?

How do you make decisions?

INSTRUCTIONS Most of us make decisions automatically, without realizing that people have diverse decision-making behaviours which they bring to management positions.[81] Think back to how you make decisions in your personal, student or work life, especially where other people are involved. Please answer whether each of the following items is 'Mostly true' or 'Mostly false' for you.

		Mostly true	Mostly false
1	I like to decide quickly and move on to the next thing.	☐	☐
2	Most decisions within organizations are made as I would use my authority to make a decision if certain I am right.	☐	☐
3	I appreciate decisiveness.	☐	☐
4	Most decisions within organizations are made as there is usually one correct solution to a problem.	☐	☐
5	I identify everyone who needs to be involved in the decision.	☐	☐
6	Most decisions within organizations are made as I explicitly seek conflicting perspectives.	☐	☐
7	I use discussion strategies to reach a solution.	☐	☐
8	Most decisions within organizations are made as I look for different meanings when faced with a great deal of data.	☐	☐
9	I take time to reason things through and use systematic logic.	☐	☐

SCORING & INTERPRETATION All nine items in the list reflect appropriate decision-making behaviour, but items 1–4 are more typical of new managers. Items 5–8 are typical of successful senior manager decision-making. Item 9 is considered part of good decision-making at all levels. If you checked 'Mostly true' for three or four of items 1–4 and 9, consider yourself typical of a new manager. If you checked 'Mostly true' for three or four of items 5–8 and 9, you are using behaviour consistent with top managers. If you checked a similar number of both sets of items, your behaviour is probably flexible and balanced.

APPLY YOUR SKILLS: ETHICAL DILEMMA

The no-show consultant[82]

Jeffrey Moses was facing one of the toughest decisions of his short career as a manager with International Consulting. Andrew Carpenter, one of his best consultants, was clearly in trouble, and his problems were affecting his work. International Consulting designs, installs and implements complex back-office software systems for companies all over the world. About half the consultants work out of the main office, while the rest, including Carpenter, work primarily from home.

This Monday morning, Moses received an irate call from a major New York client saying Carpenter hadn't showed up at the company's headquarters, where the client had been expecting his new computer system to go live for the first time. In calling around to other customers on the East Coast trying to locate the missing consultant, Moses heard other stories. Carpenter had also missed a few other appointments – all on Monday mornings – but no one had felt the need to report it because he had called to reschedule. In addition, he practically came to blows with an employee who challenged him about the capabilities of the new system, and he inexplicably walked out of one customer's office in the middle of the day, without a word to anyone. Another client reported that the last time he saw Carpenter, he appeared to have a serious hangover. Most of the clients liked Carpenter, but they were concerned that his behaviour was increasingly erratic. One client suggested that she would prefer to work with someone else. As for the major New York customer, he preferred that Carpenter rather than a new consultant finish the project, but he also demanded that International reduce by half the $250 000 consultant's fee.

After Moses finally located Carpenter by calling his next-door neighbour, Carpenter confessed that he'd had a 'lost weekend' and been too drunk to get on the plane. He then told Moses that his wife had left and taken their 2-year-old son with her. He admitted that he had been drinking a little more than usual lately, but insisted that he was getting himself under control and promised no more problems. 'I'm really not an alcoholic or anything,' he said. 'I've just been upset about Brenda leaving, and I let it get out of hand this weekend.' Moses told Carpenter that if he would go to New York and complete the project, all would be forgiven.

Now, however, he wondered whether he should really just let things slide. Moses talked to Carpenter's team leader about the situation and was told that the leader was aware of his recent problems but thought everything would smooth itself over. 'Consultants with his knowledge, level of skill and willingness to travel are hard to find. He's well liked among all the customers; he'll get his act together.' However, when Moses discussed the problem with Carolyn Walter, vice president of operations, she argued that Carpenter should be dismissed. 'You're under no obligation to keep him just because you said you would,' she pointed out. 'This was a major screw-up, and it's perfectly legal to fire someone for absenteeism. Your calls to customers should make it clear to you that this situation was not a onetime thing. Get rid of him now before things get worse. If you think that reducing the $250 000 fee by half hurts now, just think what could happen if this behaviour continues.'

What would you do?

1 Give Carpenter a month's notice and terminate. He's known as a good consultant, so he probably won't have any trouble finding a new job, and you'll avoid any further problems associated with his emotional difficulties and his possible alcohol problem.

2 Overlook the misconduct. Missing the New York appointment is Carpenter's first big mistake. He says he is getting things under control, and you believe that he should be given a chance to get himself back on track.

3 Let Carpenter know that you care about what he's going through, but insist that he take a short paid leave and get counselling to deal with his emotional difficulties and evaluate the seriousness of his problems with alcohol. If the alcohol abuse continues, require him to attend a treatment programme or find another job.

APPLY YOUR SKILLS: CASE FOR CRITICAL ANALYSIS

Career planning: Rational or incremental decision-making

There are several key theoretical developments in managerial decision-making research, with researchers devoting increased attention to bounded rationality. There are a number of potential concerns associated with the assumptions of dominant rational decision-making models and with models that omit decision-makers. These concerns support the need for a greater understanding of the benefits of, and opportunities for, models that incorporate bounded rationality, decision-making biases, judgements by managers and scenario planning.

Two models commonly used to illustrate different approaches to decision-making are the rationalist model and the incrementalist model.

Simon's rationality model (1947)

The main activities involved in rational decision-making are set out below:

(a) Intelligence gathering: Intelligence is here used as in the sense of 'military intelligence', namely the gathering of information prior to taking action. In a completely rational world, decision-makers would continually and systematically scan the horizon, seeking to identify all present and potential problems and opportunities relevant to its strategic and operational issues.

(b) Identifying all options: Several responses (or 'behaviour alternatives') are usually possible when a problem or opportunity is perceived. The completely rational decision-maker would identify all such options and consider them in detail.

(c) Assessing consequences of options: In considering each option, it would be necessary to know what would happen if it were to be adopted. Thus the fully rational decision-maker would identify all the costs and benefits ('consequences') of all identified options.

(d) Relating consequences to values: From the preceding gathering of data about problems,

options and consequences, the rational decision-maker would now have comprehensive data. But the data need to be related to a set of criteria or some sort of preference-ordering procedure. Thus for Simon, 'rationality is concerned with the selection of preferred behaviour alternatives in terms of some system of values, whereby the consequences of behaviour can be evaluated.'

(e) Choosing preferred option: Given full understanding of, and information about, all problems and opportunities, all the possible decision responses, all the consequences of each and every option, and the criteria to be employed in valuing these consequences and thus assessing decision options then, and only then, would the decision-maker be able to arrive at a fully rational decision.

Simon indicates the extent to which decision-makers fall short of rationality but, nevertheless, (he believes) there is a need for decision-makers to become more rational.

Lindblom's incrementalist model (1959)

Charles Lindblom recognizes limits to rationality in real-life decision-making. He emphasizes the 'costliness of analysis', and is particularly strong on the political environment of decision-making and the constraints of the given situation in which decisions are made. Lindblom's model has the following characteristics.

(a) Attempts at understanding are limited to decisions that differ only incrementally from existing decisions.

(b) Instead of simply adjusting means to ends, ends are chosen that are appropriate to available means.

(c) A relatively small number of means (alternative possible decisions) are considered, as follows from (a).

(d) Instead of comparing alternative means in the light of postulated ends or objectives, alternative ends or objectives are also compared in the light of postulated means and their consequences.

(e) While these actors are self-interested they are not blindly partisan, and are capable of adjusting to one another, through bargaining, negotiating and compromise ('partisan mutual adjustment').

(f) A value is placed upon 'consensus seeking', so that what emerges is not necessarily the one best decision but rather that compromise decision upon which most groups can agree.

Decisions by consent, however, will ultimately reflect the interests of the most powerful. Incrementalism also neglects innovation and change as it focuses on the short run and tries to achieve no more than limited variations from past policies. The result can be action without direction.

References: Lindblom, C.E. (1959), 'The science of muddling through', *Public Administration Review*, 19, 78–88. Simon H.A. (1947), *Administrative Behaviour*, London, Macmillan.

Questions

1 Propose a rational decision-making approach to career planning.

2 Propose an incremental decision-making approach to career planning.

3 Analyze the following approach and explain which model it most closely resembles:

First, consider all the career options available. Then consider the pros and cons of each career possibility in great detail, including such considerations as job security, career earnings, social status, opportunities for travel, length of holidays and other benefits (monetary and non-monetary). These data would be useless if you did not know how to value job security against high earnings and both against, say, social status and opportunities for travel. Thus you would have to think through the value system very comprehensively. Given both comprehensive information and a fully worked-out preference-ordering set of criteria or values, a career choice decision would be possible.

Answers to questions in manager's *shoptalk*

1 The answer is unbelievably huge: roughly 800 000 000 000 000 times the distance between the Earth and the Sun. Your mind was likely anchored in the thinness of a sheet of paper, thereby leading you to dramatically underestimate the effect of doubling the thickness 100 times. Initial mental anchoring to a low or high point leads to frequent incorrect solutions. How certain did you feel about your answer? This is an example of *overconfidence*, a major cause of manager mistakes.

2 Every figure is different in some way. Figure (a) has the greatest area, (b) has the least area, (c) is the only square, (d) is the only three-sided figure, (e) is most narrow and lopsided, and (f) is least symmetrical and five-sided. Did you stop after finding one correct answer? *Failure to go beyond initial impressions and dig below the surface* often prevents managers from understanding what the real problem is or identifying the correct or best solution.

3 If you checked 'yes', you felt the desire to continue investing in a previous decision even when it was failing, which is called *escalating commitment*. This is a mistake many managers make because they are *emotionally attached* to the previous decision, even one as hopeless as this inadequate drone.

4 The median estimate from students is 2250. When the numbers are given in reverse order starting with 1×2, etc., the median estimate is 512. The correct answer is 40 320. The *order in which information is presented* makes a difference to a person's solution, and acting quickly produces an answer that is far from correct.

5 When judging people, early information has more impact than later information, called the *primacy effect*. Reversing the word sequence so that *intelligent* and *industrious* come first creates a more favorable impression. Respondents rate Robert more or less emotional depending on the order of the descriptive words. Were you guilty of rating Robert as more emotional because of being *influenced by initial impressions*?

6 Although the options are numerically equivalent, most people choose alternatives B and C. People hate losing more than they enjoy winning, and hence about 80 per cent choose a sure small gain (B), and 70 per cent will take more risk in the hope of avoiding a loss (C). *Taking emotions out of the process* typically leads to better decisions.

END NOTES

1. Eric Lipton and John M. Broder, 'In Rush to Assist a Solar Company, U.S. Missed Warning Signs', *The New York Times*, September 23, 2011, A1.

2. *Ibid.*

3. Danielle Sacks, 'Blown Away', *Fast Company* (February 2011): 58–65, 104.

4. John Cook, 'After the Writedown: How Microsoft Squandered Its $6.3B Buy of Ad Giant aQuantive', *Geek Wire*, July 12, 2012, www.geekwire.com/2012/writedown-microsoft-squandered-62b-purchase-ad-giant-aquantive/ (accessed August 2, 2012).

5. Herbert A. Simon, *The New Science of Management Decision* (Englewood Cliffs, NJ: Prentice Hall, 1977), p. 47.

6. Paul J. H. Schoemaker and J. Edward Russo, 'A Pyramid of Decision Approaches', *California Management Review* (Fall, 1993): 9–31.

7. Joann S. Lublin and Spencer E. Ante, 'Inside Sprint's Bet on iPhone', *The Wall Street Journal*, October 4, 2011, A1.

8. Kris Maher, 'At Indiana Machine Shop, Tough Calls Amid Turmoil', *The Wall Street Journal*, August 10, 2011, B1.

9. Samuel Eilon, 'Structuring Unstructured Decisions', *Omega* 13 (1985): 369–377; and Max H. Bazerman, *Judgment in Managerial Decision Making* (New York: Wiley, 1986).

10. James G. March and Zur Shapira, 'Managerial Perspectives on Risk and Risk Taking', *Management Science* 33 (1987): 1404–1418; and Inga Skromme Baird and Howard Thomas, 'Toward a Contingency Model of Strategic Risk Taking', *Academy of Management Review* 10 (1985): 230–243.

11. Christopher Drew, 'Improved Sales Help Boeing Beat Forecasts', *The New York Times*, July 28, 2011, B7, and Christopher Drew, 'Deliveries Up, Boeing Beats Forecasts of Analysts', *The New York Times*, July 26, 2012, B3.

12. Reported in David Leonhardt, 'This Fed Chief May Yet Get a Honeymoon', *The New York Times*, August 23, 2006.

13. Adam Davidson, 'When You Wish Upon 'Ishtar': How Does the Film Industry Actually Make Money?' *The New York Times Magazine* (July 1, 2012): 16–17.

14. Michael Masuch and Perry LaPotin, 'Beyond Garbage Cans: An AI Model of Organizational Choice', *Administrative Science Quarterly* 34 (1989): 38–67; and Richard L. Daft and Robert H. Lengel, 'Organizational Information Requirements, Media Richness and Structural Design', *Management Science* 32 (1986): 554–571.

15. Peter C. Cairo, David L. Dotlich and Stephen H. Rhinesmith, 'Embracing Ambiguity', *The Conference Board Review* (Summer 2009): 56–61; John C. Camillus, 'Strategy as a Wicked Problem', *Harvard Business Review* (May 2008): 98–106; and Richard O. Mason and Ian I. Mitroff, *Challenging Strategic Planning Assumptions* (New York: Wiley Interscience, 1981).

16. Malcolm Gay, 'Preparations Advance in Plan to Breach a Levee in Missouri as a Storm Brews', *The New York Times*, May 2, 2011, A19; and Malcolm Gay, 'Levee Breach Moves One Step Closer', *The New York Times*, May 1, 2011, A31.

17. 'How Companies Make Good Decisions: McKinsey Global Survey Results', *The McKinsey Quarterly*, January 2009, www.mckinseyquarterly.com (accessed February 3, 2009).

18. Thomas H. Davenport and Jeanne G. Harris, 'Automated Decision Making Comes of Age', *MIT Sloan Management Review* (Summer 2005): 83–89; and Stacie McCullough, 'On the Front Lines', *CIO* (October 15, 1999): 78–81.

19. These examples are from Steve Lohr, 'The Age of Big Data', *The New York Times*, February 12, 2012, SR1.

20. Herbert A. Simon, *The New Science of Management Decision* (New York: Harper & Row, 1960), pp. 5–6; and Amitai Etzioni, 'Humble Decision Making', *Harvard Business Review* (July–August 1989): 122–126.

21. James G. March and Herbert A. Simon, *Organizations* (New York: Wiley, 1958).

22. Herbert A. Simon, *Models of Man* (New York: Wiley, 1957), pp. 196–205; and Herbert A. Simon, *Administrative Behavior*, 2d ed. (New York: Free Press, 1957).

23. Rachel Dodes, 'Targeting Younger Buyers, Liz Claiborne Hits a Snag', *The Wall Street Journal*, August 16, 2010, A1.

24. Weston H. Agor, 'The Logic of Intuition: How Top Executives Make Important Decisions', *Organizational Dynamics* 14 (Winter 1986): 5–18; and Herbert A. Simon, 'Making Management Decisions: The Role of Intuition and Emotion', *Academy of Management Executive* 1 (1987): 57–64. For a recent review of research, see Erik Dane and Michael G. Pratt, 'Exploring Intuition and Its Role in Managerial Decision Making', *Academy of Management Review* 32, no. 1 (2007): 33–54.

25. Harvey Weinstein, as told to Diane Brady, 'Etc.: Hard Choices', *Bloomberg Businessweek* (January 30–February 5, 2012): 84.

26. Jaana Woiceshyn, 'Lessons from "Good Minds": How CEOs Use Intuition, Analysis, and Guiding Principles to Make Strategic Decisions', *Long-Range Planning* 42 (2009): 298–319; Ann Hensman and Eugene Sadler-Smith, 'Intuitive Decision Making in Banking and Finance', *European Management Journal* 29 (2011): 51–66; Eugene Sadler-Smith and Erella Shefy, 'The Intuitive Executive: Understanding and Applying "Gut Feel" in Decision-Making', *The Academy of Management Executive* 18, no. 4 (November 2004): 76–91.

27. See Gary Klein, *Intuition at Work: Why Developing Your Gut Instincts Will Make You Better at What You Do* (New York: Doubleday, 2002); Kurt Matzler, Franz Bailom and Todd A. Mooradian, 'Intuitive Decision Making', *MIT Sloan Management Review* 49, no. 1 (Fall 2007): 13–15; Malcolm Gladwell, *Blink: The Power of Thinking Without Thinking* (New York: Little Brown, 2005); and Sharon Begley, 'Follow Your Intuition: The Unconscious You May Be the Wiser Half', *The Wall Street Journal*, August 30, 2002.

28. Benedict Carey, 'Hunches Prove to Be Valuable Assets in Battle', *The New York Times*, July 28, 2009.

29. C. Chet Miller and R. Duane Ireland, 'Intuition in Strategic Decision Making: Friend or Foe in the Fast-Paced 21st Century?' *Academy of Management Executive* 19, no. 1 (2005): 19–30; and Eric Bonabeau, 'Don't Trust Your Gut', *Harvard Business Review* (May 2003): 116ff.

30. Sadler-Smith and Shefy, 'The Intuitive Executive'; Simon, 'Making Management Decisions'; and Ann Langley, 'Between "Paralysis by Analysis" and "Extinction by Instinct", *Sloan Management Review* (Spring 1995): 63–76.

31. This discussion is based on Stephen Friedman and James K. Sebenius, 'Organizational Transformation: The Quiet Role of Coalitional Leadership', *Ivey Business Journal* (January–February 2009): 1ff; Gerald R. Ferris, Darren C. Treadway, Pamela L. Perrewé, Robyn L. Brouer, Ceasar Douglas and Sean Lux, 'Political Skill in Organizations', *Journal of Management* (June 2007): 290–320; and William B. Stevenson, Jon L. Pierce and Lyman W. Porter, 'The Concept of "Coalition" in Organization Theory and Research', *Academy of Management Review* 10 (1985): 256–268.

32. 'How Companies Make Good Decisions'.

33. George T. Doran and Jack Gunn, 'Decision Making in High-Tech Firms: Perspectives of Three Executives', *Business Horizons* (November–December 2002): 7–16.

34. James W. Fredrickson, 'Effects of Decision Motive and Organizational Performance Level on Strategic Decision Processes', *Academy of Management Journal* 28 (1985): 821–843; James W. Fredrickson, 'The Comprehensiveness of Strategic Decision Processes: Extension, Observations, Future Directions', *Academy of Management Journal* 27 (1984): 445–466; James W. Dean, Jr. and Mark P. Sharfman, 'Procedural Rationality in the Strategic Decision-Making Process', *Journal of Management Studies* 30, no. 4 (July 1993): 587–610; Nandini Rajagopalan, Abdul M. A. Rasheed and Deepak K. Datta, 'Strategic Decision Processes: Critical Review and Future Directions', *Journal of Management* 19, no. 2 (1993): 349–384; and Paul J. H. Schoemaker, 'Strategic Decisions in Organizations: Rational and Behavioral Views', *Journal of Management Studies* 30, no. 1 (January 1993): 107–129.

35. Marjorie A. Lyles and Howard Thomas, 'Strategic Problem Formulation: Biases and Assumptions Embedded in Alternative Decision-Making Models', *Journal of Management Studies* 25 (1988): 131–145; and Susan E. Jackson and Jane E. Dutton, 'Discerning Threats and Opportunities', *Administrative Science Quarterly* 33 (1988): 370–387.

36. Richard L. Daft, Juhani Sormumen and Don Parks, 'Chief Executive Scanning, Environmental Characteristics, and Company Performance: An Empirical Study' (unpublished manuscript, Texas A&M University, 1988).

37. Ben Worthen, Justin Scheck and Joann S. Lublin, 'H-P Defends Hasty Whitman Hire', *The Wall Street Journal*, September 23, 2011, www.online.wsj.com/article/SB1000142405311190370360457658675382739051 0.html (accessed August 6, 2012).

38. Daniel Burrus and John David Mann, 'Whatever Your Problem . . . That's Not Likely to Be Your Real Problem', *Leadership Excellence* (February 2011): 7–8.

39. C. Kepner and B. Tregoe, *The Rational Manager* (New York: McGraw-Hill, 1965).

40. This image and example is from Burrus and Mann, 'Whatever Your Problem'.

41. Paul C. Nutt, 'Expanding the Search for Alternatives During Strategic Decision Making', *Academy of Management Executive* 18, no. 4 (2004): 13–28; and P. C. Nutt, 'Surprising But True: Half the Decisions in Organizations Fail', *Academy of Management Executive* 13, no. 4 (1999): 75–90.

42. Peter Mayer, 'A Surprisingly Simple Way to Make Better Decisions', *Executive Female* (March–April 1995): 13–14; and Ralph L. Keeney, 'Creativity in Decision Making with Value-Focused Thinking', *Sloan Management Review* (Summer 1994): 33–41.

43. Kerry Capell, 'Novartis: Radically Remaking Its Drug Business', *BusinessWeek* (June 22, 2009): 30–35.

44. Mark McNeilly, 'Gathering Information for Strategic Decisions, Routinely', *Strategy & Leadership* 30, no. 5 (2002): 29–34.

45. *Ibid.*

46. Joe Pompeo, 'A Year into the *Times*' Digital Subscription Program, Analysts and Insiders See Surprising Success, and More Challenges to Come', *Capital New York Website*, March 19, 2012, www.capitalnewyork.com/article/media/2012/03/5509293/year-times-digital-subscription-program-analysts-and-insiders-see-surp (accessed August 3, 2012); Jeremy W. Peters, 'The Times's Online Pay Model Was Years in the Making', *The New York Times* (March 20, 2011), www.nytimes.com/2011/03/21/business/media/21times.html?pagewanted=all (accessed September 27, 2011); and J. W. Peters, 'New York Times is Set to Begin Charging for Web Access; Chairman Concedes Plan is Risky But Says It's an "Investment in Our Future"', *International Herald Tribune* (March 18, 2011), 15.

47. Pompeo, 'A Year into the *Times*' Digital Subscription Program'.

48. Based on A. J. Rowe, J. D. Boulgaides and M. R. McGrath, *Managerial Decision Making* (Chicago: Science Research Associates, 1984); and Alan J. Rowe and Richard O. Mason, *Managing with Style: A Guide to Understanding, Assessing, and Improving Your Decision Making* (San Francisco: Jossey-Bass, 1987).

49. Peter Baker, 'How Obama's Afghanistan War Plan Came to Be', *International Herald Tribune*, December 7, 2009; and Ron Walters, 'Afghanistan: The Big Decision', *The Washington Informer*, December 10–16, 2009.

50. This section is based on John S. Hammond, Ralph L. Keeney and Howard Raiffa, *Smart Choices: A Practical Guide to Making Better Decisions* (Boston: Harvard Business School Press, 1999); Max H. Bazerman and Dolly Chugh, 'Decisions Without Blinders', *Harvard Business Review* (January 2006): 88–97; J. S. Hammond, R. L. Keeney and H. Raiffa, 'The Hidden Traps in Decision Making', *Harvard Business Review* (September–October 1998): 47–58; Oren Harari, 'The Thomas Lawson Syndrome', *Management Review* (February 1994): 58–61; Dan Ariely, 'Q&A: Why Good CIOs Make Bad Decisions', *CIO* (May 1, 2003): 83–87; Leigh Buchanan, 'How to Take Risks in a Time of Anxiety', *Inc.* (May 2003): 76–81; and Max H. Bazerman, *Judgment in Managerial Decision Making*, 5th ed. (New York: John Wiley & Sons, 2002).

51. J. B. Schmidt and R. J. Calantone, 'Escalation of Commitment During New Product Development', *Journal of the Academy of Marketing Science* 30, no. 2 (2002): 103–118.

52. Norihiko Shirouzu, Phred Dvorak, Yuka Hayashi and Andrew Morse, 'Bid to "Protect   Assets" Slowed Reactor

Fight', *The Wall Street Journal*, March 19, 2011, www.on-line.wsj.com/article/SB100014240527487046085045762079126426299904.html (accessed August 6, 2012).

53. John D. Stoll, Kevin Helliker and Neil E. Boudette, 'A Saga of Decline and Denial', *The Wall Street Journal,* June 2, 2009.

54. Mark Fenton-O'Creevy, Emma Soane, Nigel Nicholson and Paul Willman, 'Thinking, Feeling, and Deciding: The Influence of Emotions on the Decision Making and Performance of Traders', *Journal of Organizational Behavior* 32 (2011): 1044–1061.

55. Example from Jerome Groopman, *How Doctors Think* (New York: Houghton Mifflin, 2007).

56. Dan Ariely, 'The Long-Term Effects of Short-Term Emotions', *Harvard Business Review* (January–February 2010): 38.

57. Jessica Silver-Greenberg, 'New Fraud Inquiry as JPMorgan's Loss Mounts', *The New York Times*, July 13, 2012, www.dealbook.nytimes.com/2012/07/13/jpmorgan-says-traders-obscured-losses-in-first-quarter/ (accessed August 7, 2012); Ben Protess, Andrew Ross Sorkin, Mark Scott and Nathaniel Popper, 'In JPMorgan Chase Trading Bet, Its Confidence Yields to Loss', *The New York Times*, May 11, 2012, www.dealbook.nytimes.com/2012/05/11/in-jpmorgan-chase-trading-bet-its-confidence-yields-to-loss/ (accessed May 15, 2012); Peter Eavis and Susanne Craig, 'The Bet That Blew Up for JPMorgan Chase', *The New York Times*, May 11, 2012, www.dealbook.nytimes.com/2012/05/11/the-bet-that-blew-up-for-jpmorgan-chase/ (accessed May 15, 2012); and Jessica Silver-Greenberg and Nelson D. Schwartz, 'Red Flags Said to Go Unheeded by Bosses at JPMorgan', *The New York Times*, May 14, 2012, www.dealbook.nytimes.com/2012/05/14/warnings-said-to-go-unheeded-by-chase-bosses/ (accessed May 15, 2012).

58. Kathleen M. Eisenhardt, 'Strategy as Strategic Decision Making', *Sloan Management Review* (Spring 1999): 65–72.

59. Daniel Kahneman, Dan Lovallo and Olivier Sibony, 'Before You Make That Big Decision', *Harvard Business Review* (June 2011): 50–60.

60. Josh Hyatt, 'Where the Best – and Worst – Ideas Come From' (a brief synopsis of 'Idea Generation and the Quality of the Best Idea', by Karen Girotra, Christian Terwiesch and Karl T. Ulrich), *MIT Sloan Management Review* (Summer 2008): 11–12; and Robert C. Litchfield, 'Brainstorming Reconsidered: A Goal-Based View', *Academy of Management Review* 33, no. 3 (2008): 649–668.

61. R. B. Gallupe, L. Bastianutti and W. H. Cooper, 'Blocking Electronic Brainstorms', *Journal of Applied Psychology* 79 (1994): 77–86; R. B. Gallupe and W. H. Cooper, 'Brainstorming Electronically', *Sloan Management Review* (Fall 1993): 27–36; and Alison Stein Wellner, 'A Perfect Brainstorm', *Inc.* (October 2003): 31–35.

62. Wellner, 'A Perfect Brainstorm'; Gallupe and Cooper, 'Brainstorming Electronically'.

63. This section is based on Jeffrey Pfeffer and Robert I. Sutton, 'Evidence-Based Management', *Harvard Business Review* (January 2006), 62–74; Rosemary Stewart, *Evidence-based Decision Making* (Radcliffe Publishing, 2002); and Joshua Klayman, Richard P. Larrick and Chip Heath, 'Organizational Repairs', *Across the Board* (February 2000), 26–31.

64. Thomas H. Davenport, 'Make Better Decisions', *Harvard Business Review* (November 2009), 117–123.

65. Study by Erik Brynjolfsson, Lorin Hitt and Heekyung Kim; results reported in Steve Lohr, 'The Age of Big Data', *The New York Times*, February 12, 2012, SR1.

66. Sydney Finkelstein, 'Think Again: Good Leaders, Bad Decisions', *Leadership Excellence* (June 2009): 7; 'Flaws in Strategic Decision Making: McKinsey Global Survey Results', *The McKinsey Quarterly*, January 2009, www .mckinsey.com; Michael A. Roberto, 'Making Difficult Decisions in Turbulent Times', *Ivey Business Journal* (May–June 2003): 1–7; Eisenhardt, 'Strategy As Strategic Decision Making'; and David A. Garvin and Michael A. Roberto, 'What You Don't Know About Making Decisions', *Harvard Business Review* (September 2001): 108–116.

67. Nick Wingfield and Brian Stelter, 'A Juggernaut Stumbles', *The New York Times*, October 25, 2011, B1.

68. David M. Schweiger and William R. Sandberg, 'The Utilization of Individual Capabilities in Group Approaches to Strategic Decision Making', *Strategic Management Journal* 10 (1989): 31–43; 'Avoiding Disasters', sidebar in Paul B. Carroll and Chunka Mui, '7 Ways to Fail Big', *Harvard Business Review* (September 2008): 82–91; and 'The Devil's Advocate', *Small Business Report* (December 1987): 38–41.

69. Doran and Gunn, 'Decision Making in High-Tech Firms'.

70. Eisenhardt, 'Strategy As Strategic Decision Making'.

71. Garvin and Roberto, 'What You Don't Know About Making Decisions'.

72. Irving L. Janis, *Groupthink: Psychological Studies of Policy Decisions and Fiascoes,* 2d ed. (Boston: Houghton Mifflin, 1982).

73. Jerry B. Harvey, 'The Abilene Paradox: The Management of Agreement', *Organizational Dynamics* (Summer 1988): 17–43.

74. Ethan Smith, 'Disney Hobbles "Lone Ranger,"', *The Wall Street Journal*, August 15, 2011, B1.

75. S. Trevis Certo, Brian L. Connelly and Laszlo Tihanyi, 'Managers and Their Not-So-Rational Decisions', *Business Horizons* 51 (2008): 113–119.

76. Hans Wissema, 'Driving Through Red Lights; How Warning Signals Are Missed or Ignored', *Long Range Planning* 35 (2002): 521–539.

77. *Ibid.*

78. Thomas E. Ricks, 'Army Devises System to Decide What Does, Does Not, Work', *The Wall Street Journal*, May 23, 1997, A1; David W. Cannon and Jeffrey McCollum, 'Army Medical Department Lessons Learned Program Marks 25th Anniversary', *Military Medicine* (November 2011): 1212–1214.

79. Peter Eisler, Blake Morrison and Tom Vanden Brook, 'Strategy That's Making Iraq Safer Was Snubbed for Years', *USA Today*, December 19, 2007.

80. Chuck Salter, 'Lenovo: Protect and Attack', *Fast Company* (December 2011–January 2012): 116–121, 154–155.

81. See Stephen J. Sauer, 'Why Bossy Is Better for Rookie Managers', *Harvard Business Review* (May 2012): 30; and Kenneth R. Brousseau, Michael J. Driver, Gary Hourihan and Rikard Larsson, 'The Seasoned Executive's Decision Making Style', *Harvard Business Review* (February 2006): 110–121, for a discussion of how decision-making behaviour evolves as managers progress in their careers.

82. Based on information in Jeffrey L. Seglin, 'The Savior Complex', *Inc.* (February 1999): 67–69; and Nora Johnson, "He's Been Beating Me,' She Confided', *Business Ethics* (Summer 2001): 21.

PART 3 INTEGRATIVE CASE
PART THREE: PLANNING

Companies form strategic partnership to build America's Natural Gas Highway

Consumers face a series of important questions when shopping for a new vehicle: Electric or hybrid? Petrol or diesel? Powerful or fuel-efficient? Sporty or economical? Yet for eco-minded consumers who seek the ultimate in green motoring, the decision to purchase a vehicle often comes down to one simple question: Where do I fill it up?

Where to refuel is a perplexing issue for buyers of alternative-fuel vehicles. This is because cutting-edge green vehicles lack a nationwide fuelling infrastructure. The USA has more than 100 000 standard petrol stations, yet few are equipped to fuel vehicles that run on electricity, natural gas or biofuel. For most consumers, that's a deal breaker.

Despite the push for cleaner autos, today's car buyers find themselves in a Catch-22: an ecologically responsible vehicle might fit in with their needs and desires, but if there is no place to fill up, they can't drive it, so why consider buying one? A similar dilemma exists for fleet purchasers, automakers and gas station chains: why purchase or even manufacture alternative-fuel vehicles if there aren't any filling stations? On the other hand, why build filling stations if no one is purchasing or making alternative-fuel vehicles?

Fortunately for consumers and the environment, Clean Energy Fuels Corp. and Navistar International have a plan to solve this chicken-and-egg dilemma. In 2012, the California alternative fuels provider and the Illinois semi-trailer truck giant announced a strategic partnership to build America's Natural Gas Highway, a first-of-its-kind network of natural gas fuelling stations across the USA. Slated for completion by the end of 2013 and still under construction, America's Natural Gas Highway will feature 150 liquefied natural gas (LNG) filling stations in major

metropolitan areas across the country – San Diego, Los Angeles and Las Vegas out west; Houston, San Antonio and Dallas in the Texas Triangle; New York in the east; and major cities in the Midwest and South. Well-placed stations on in-between routes will tie the whole network together, resulting in a coast-to-coast refuelling infrastructure for natural gas vehicles.

Top-level planners behind America's Natural Gas Highway say their goal is to offer transport companies a package deal made up of eco-friendly fleets, inexpensive fuel and reliable fuelling stations. 'Navistar and Clean Energy have come up with a breakthrough programme that offers customers a quicker payback on their investment, plus added fuel cost savings from day one of operation,' says Navistar CEO Dan Ustian. 'Together our companies will demonstrate how a natural-gas-integrated vehicle offering the right distribution and fuelling solution can be integrated into a fleet's operations to reduce costs and drive efficiencies.'

For a natural gas highway to work, effective collaboration must occur between a truck maker, a fuel supplier, a truck stop chain and a natural gas driller. Navistar and Clean Energy have the first two bases covered: Navistar will sell its best-in-class LNG truck fleets to shippers, along with a mandatory 5-year fuel-purchase contract through Clean Energy. News releases indicate that two other companies are included in the plan. Pilot Flying J Travel Centers, the largest network of truck and travel stops, is providing service locations where trucks can refuel. Likewise, Chesapeake Energy, the No. 2 natural gas driller in the USA, is investing $150 million towards the initial rollout. So Navistar sells natural gas trucks to shippers, Clean Energy supplies the fuel, Pilot Flying J provides the fueling stations and Chesapeake drills natural gas and provides investment capital.

The plan sounds good on paper, but can it work? Clean Energy CEO Andrew Littlefair says America's Natural Gas Highway is already well underway. 'Clean Energy has already engaged over 100 shippers, private fleets and for-hire carriers that have shared their operations to qualify for the economic opportunity of operating natural gas trucks. This has helped us in turn plan the first phase of the natural gas fuelling highway,' Littlefair says. Clean Energy's chief marketing guru, Jim Harger, adds that the financial advantages of the plan are such that transport businesses simply can't refuse. 'You get the same lease cost of a diesel truck and get fuel savings too,' Harger says.

There are many good reasons to think that America's Natural Gas Highway will succeed. However, executives at Navistar and Clean Energy say their plan will work because natural gas is the energy of the future and requires no government subsidies. 'We remain committed to provide natural gas fuel for transportation because it has genuinely proven to be the cleaner, cheaper, domestic alternative fuel choice,' says Andrew Littlefair. Navistar's chief agrees, adding that natural gas is both economically sustainable and good for the environment. 'The programme will allow the industry to transition to natural gas-powered vehicles without relying on government handouts,' Ustian says. 'This is going to work far differently than any other programme in this field for alternative fuels. It can stand on its own and stand very tall, and that's why it's going to be successful.'

Integrative case questions

1 Why do businesses form strategic partnerships? Does the creation of America's Natural Gas Highway require such a partnership? Why or why not?

2 What opportunities in the external environment may have led Navistar and Clean Energy to formulate their plan for America's Natural Gas Highway?

3 What threats in the external environment could cause this comprehensive natural gas strategy to fail? What can managers do to help ensure that the plan is executed successfully?

SOURCES: Based on Clean Energy Fuels Corp., *America's Natural Gas Highway: The Clean Energy Solution* (Seal Beach, CA: Clean Energy, 2012), www.cleanenergyfuels.com/pdf/CE-OS.ANGH.011212.ff.pdf (accessed July 10, 2012); John Stodder, 'Natural Gas Vehicles Face Chicken-and-Egg Syndrome,' *The Daily Reporter,* May 9, 2012, www.dailyreporter.com/2012/05/09/natural-gas-vehicles-face-chicken-and-egg-syndrome/ (accessed July 10, 2012); 'Navistar International and Clean Energy Fuels Team on Natural Gas Trucks,' *Fleets & Fuels,* February 2, 2012, www.fleetsandfuels.com/fuels/ngvs/2012/02/ navistar-clean-energy-team-on-natural-gas-trucks-2012/ (accessed July 10, 2012); James Menzies, 'Navistar Partnership with Clean Energy Takes Sting out of Cost of NG-Powered Trucks,' *Truck News,* February 3, 2012, www.trucknews.com/news/navistar-partnership-with-clean-energy-takes-sting-out-of-cost-of-ng-powered-trucks/1000876051/ (accessed July 12, 2012); Dave Hurst, 'Clean Energy Fuels and Navistar Agreement: More than Marketing Hype?' Pike Research, May 30, 2012, www.pikeresearch.com/blog/clean-energy-fuels-and-navistar-agreement-more-than-marketing-hype (accessed July 12, 2012); Clean Energy Fuels, 'Clean Energy Unveils Backbone Network for America's Natural Gas Highway,' press release, January 12, 2012, www.businesswire.com/news/home/20120112005432/en/Clean-Energy-Unveils-Backbone-Network-America's-Natural (accessed July 10, 2012); 'Clean Energy Unveils Network Plan for Natural Gas Highway,' Trucker News Service, January 16, 2012, www.thetrucker.com/News/Stories/2012/1/16/CleanEnergyunveilsnetworkplanfornaturalgashighway.aspx (accessed July 12, 2012).

PART 4

ORGANIZING

CHAPTER 10

MANAGING SMALL BUSINESS START-UPS

LEARNING OBJECTIVES

After studying this chapter, you should be able to:

1 Define entrepreneurship and the four classifications of entrepreneurs.

2 Describe the importance of entrepreneurship to global economies.

3 Appreciate the impact of minority- and women-owned businesses.

4 Define the personality characteristics of a typical entrepreneur.

5 Explain social entrepreneurship as a vital part of today's small business environment.

6 Outline the planning necessary to launch an entrepreneurial start-up.

7 Describe the five stages of growth for an entrepreneurial company.

8 Explain how the management activities of planning, organizing, decision-making and controlling apply to a growing entrepreneurial company.

Scott Adams, the writer of the satirical *Dilbert* comic strip, was a budding entrepreneur during his college years at Hartwick College in New York. An economics major who aspired to be a banker, Adams grew to see the world through an entrepreneur's eyes during a variety of small-business ventures. First, he convinced his accounting professor to hire him as 'Minister of Finance' at the campus coffeehouse, where he created and oversaw an accounting system. The system replaced a previous one that Adams described as *'seven students trying to remember where all the money went.'* Adams's next venture was a plan to become student manager of his dormitory and get paid to do it. *'For the next 2 years, my friends and I each had a private room at no cost, a base salary and the experience of managing the dorm. On some nights, I also got paid to do overnight security, while also getting paid to clean the laundry room,'* Adams said.

After college, Adams started his career in banking, but it didn't work out as he'd hoped, so he left to pursue a career in writing. He is convinced that his experiences during his entrepreneurial stints in college paid off. '*Every good thing that has happened to me as an adult can be traced back to that training*,' he says. What is Scott Adams's advice to up-and-coming entrepreneurs? First, he says, take risks and try to get paid while you're doing the failing and learn new skills that will be useful later. Second, replace fear and shyness with enthusiasm and learn to enjoy speaking to a crowd. Third, learn how to persuade. '*Students of entrepreneurship should learn the art of persuasion in all its forms, including psychology, sales, marketing, negotiating, statistics and even design*,' says Adams.[1]

Starting and growing your own business requires a combination of many skills to be successful. Adams, a highly successful entrepreneur, with experience gained from business start-ups, combined this with creativity and passion when he left the corporate world for a writing career. His passion is shared by many other courageous self-starters, who take the leap and start a sole proprietorship, one of the fastest-growing segments of small and medium sized (SMEs) businesses in both the USA and Canada. Approximately 600 000 new businesses are launched in the USA each year by self-starting entrepreneurs.[2]

What is entrepreneurship?

Entrepreneurship can be defined in several ways including: *The process of initiating a business venture, organizing the necessary resources and assuming the associated risks and rewards*.[3] An entrepreneur is someone who engages in entrepreneurial activity. An entrepreneur recognizes a viable idea for a business product or service and carries it out by finding and accessing the necessary resources – money, people, machinery, location – to undertake the business venture. Entrepreneurs also assume the risks and take rewards from the business. They assume the financial and legal risks of ownership and are due the business's profits.

Successful entrepreneurs have many different motivations and they measure rewards in different ways. One study, published in the year 2000, classified small business owners into five different categories, as illustrated in Exhibit 10.1. Some people are *idealists*, who like the idea of working on something that is new, creative or personally meaningful. *Optimizers* are rewarded by the personal satisfaction of being business owners. Entrepreneurs in the *sustainer* category like the chance to balance work and personal life and often don't want the business to grow too large, while *hard workers* enjoy putting in the long hours and dedication to build a larger, more profitable business. The *juggler* category includes entrepreneurs who like the chance that a small business gives them to handle everything themselves. These high-energy people thrive on the pressure of paying bills, meeting deadlines and making money.[4]

Compare the motivation of Susan Polis Schutz, the owner of Blue Mountain Arts, to that of Jeff Bezos, founder of Amazon. Schutz has always written poetry about love and nature. On a whim, her husband illustrated one of her poems and created 12 posters to sell at a local bookstore. The posters sold quickly, and the bookstore placed another order. That was the start of Blue Mountain Arts. With her husband working as illustrator and her mother working as sales manager, Schutz was content with a life that blended work and family. When the company exploded to more than 300 employees, this perfect balance was jeopardized.

EXHIBIT 10.1 Five types of small business owners

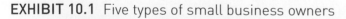

Rewarded by chance to work on something new and creative		Thrive on the challenge of building a larger, more profitable business		Enjoy chance to balance work and personal life

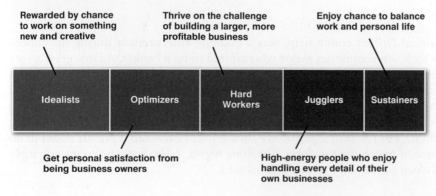

| Idealists | Optimizers | Hard Workers | Jugglers | Sustainers |

Get personal satisfaction from being business owners

High-energy people who enjoy handling every detail of their own businesses

SOURCE: Based on a study conducted by Yankelovich Partners for Pitney Bowes in Mark Henricks, 'Type-Cast', *Entrepreneur* (March 2000): 14–16.

To give herself more family time, Schutz hired a business manager to take over daily operations. '*I still love connecting to people's emotions on love, nature, friendship and family in my work, but my favourite thing these days is doting on my grandson, who is 5 years old,*' said Schutz.[5] In contrast, Jeff Bezos launched Amazon in 1994 with a vision to build 'an important and lasting company'. Bezos was in no hurry, then or now, to boost profits. Instead, he focused on revenue growth and customer service. Leading this closely watched, high-growth business is demanding and requires that Bezos continuously seeks out new ideas and products. Jeff Bezos reflects the motivation of a *hard worker*, whereas Susan Polis Schutz's motivation is more that of a *sustainer*.

REFLECTION

- **Entrepreneurship** is the process of initiating a business, organizing the necessary resources and assuming the associated risks and rewards.
- One of the fastest-growing segments of small business is in one-owner operations, called *sole proprietorships*.
- An **entrepreneur** recognizes a viable idea for a business product or service and carries it out by finding and allocating the necessary resources to start the business.
- Scott Adams, creator of *Dilbert*, started his first entrepreneurial ventures while still in college. This 'moonlighting' approach is often used to test a business model whilst having a paid occupation.
- Entrepreneurs may be classified as *idealists, optimizers, sustainers, hard workers* or *jugglers*.

Impact of entrepreneurial companies

Small businesses were hit particularly hard by the 2008 global economic crisis and weakened consumer demand. But rejuvenation in the economy is underway, and small businesses and entrepreneurs are the engine behind the rebound that has occurred in many US and UK markets.

Entrepreneurship internationally

Globally, entrepreneurship has experienced a tremendous boost due to huge advances in technology and the rapid expansion of the volume of middle class consumers in countries such as China and India. Consider one of India's most successful entrepreneurs, Narayana Murthy. He and several co-founders launched Infosys and sparked an outsourcing revolution that has brought billions of dollars into the Indian economy. Infosys offers business consulting, technology, engineering and outsourcing services, and has been ranked Number 1 on the list of India's most admired companies in the *Wall Street Journal Asia 200* survey in most years since 2000. Murthy started the organization from scratch and typical of most start-ups, endured years of hardship. '*It is all about sacrifice, hard work, lots of frustration, being away from your family, in the hope that someday you will get adequate returns from that,*' explains Murthy.[6]

Entrepreneurship in other countries is also booming. The list of entrepreneurial countries around the world, shown in Exhibit 10.2, is intriguing. A 2011 project monitoring entrepreneurial activity, reported that an estimated 24 per cent of adults aged 18 to 64 in China are either starting or managing new enterprises. The percentage in Chile is 24 per cent; in Peru, 23 per cent. Argentina, Brazil and Jamaica also show higher rates of entrepreneurial activity than the US rate of 12 per cent.[7]

Entrepreneurship in the United States

The impact of entrepreneurial companies on the US economy is astonishing. In the USA, small businesses – including outsourcing firms in Chicago and high-tech start-ups in California – create two out of every three new jobs. There are 28 million small firms in the USA that employ 60 million Americans, about half of the private sector workforce.[8] According to the Small Business Administration (SBA), small businesses represent 98 per cent of all businesses in the USA.[9] In addition, small businesses represent 97 per cent of America's exporters and produce 30.2 per cent of all export value.[10]

EXHIBIT 10.2 Entrepreneurial activity around the world

Country	Percentage of individuals age 18 to 64 active in starting or managing a new business, 2011
China	24
Chile	24
Peru	23
Argentina	22
Brazil	15
Jamaica	13
Turkey	12
USA	12
Mexico	9
Poland	8
Greece	8
Portugal	8
UK	7
Germany	6
Belgium	6
Japan	5

SOURCE: From Donna J. Kelley, Slavica Singer and Mike Herrington, *Global Entrepreneurship Monitor 2011 Executive Report*. Permission to reproduce a figure from the GEM 2011 Global Report, which appears here, has been kindly granted by the copyright holders. The Global Entrepreneurship Monitor (GEM) is an international consortium, and this report was produced from data collected in, and received from, 54 countries in 2011. Our thanks go to the authors, national teams, researchers, funding bodies and other contributors who have made this possible.

NOTE: Total early-stage Entrepreneurial Activity (TEA): Percentage of 18–64 population who are either a 'nascent entrepreneur' or owner-manager of a 'new business'. A 'nascent entrepreneur' is defined as someone actively involved in setting up a business they will own or co-own; and he or she has no prior experience of running a business. A 'new business' is defined in the USA as a running business that has paid salaries, wages or any other payments to the owners for more than 3 months, but not more than 42 months.

Not surprisingly, online businesses are forming at record rates. Powerful technology, such as Google's application engine, Amazon's Web services and Facebook's authentication technology, is readily available and inexpensive. These building blocks make it easier for tech start-ups to create products and services within a year of being founded. A decade ago, it was pricey to start a company. But in the past few years, with each new breakthrough in Internet and mobile technology, entrepreneurs '*can start a company for little money and run it almost anywhere*,' says Joe Beninato, CEO of Tello, a free customer-service rating application on the iPhone and iPad. '*It used to take the first $5 million to set up the infrastructure*,' he says. '*Now you can pull out your credit card and spend $5000 on Amazon Web services.*'[11]

In the USA, entrepreneurship and small business are the engines behind job creation and innovation:

- **Job creation.** Researchers disagree over what percentage of new jobs are created by small businesses. Research indicates that the *age* of a company, more than its size, determines the number of jobs it creates. That is, virtually *all* new jobs in recent years have come from new companies, which include not only small companies, but also new branches of huge, multinational organizations.[12] However, small companies still are thought to create a large percentage of new jobs in the USA. Jobs created by small businesses give the USA an economic vitality that not many other countries can claim.

- **Innovation.** Small business owners typically gain an intimate understanding of their customers, which places them in an ideal position to innovate. Research by entrepreneurship commentator, David Birch, traced the employment and sales records of some 9 million companies with the findings that new smaller firms have been responsible for 55 per cent of the innovations in 362 different industries, and 95 per cent of all radical innovations. In addition, fast-growing businesses, which Birch calls *gazelles*, produce twice as many product innovations per employee as do larger firms. Small firms that file for patents typically produce 13 times more patents per employee than large patenting firms.[13]

Who are entrepreneurs?

The heroes of American business – Henry Ford, Mary Kay Ash, Sam Walton, Oprah Winfrey, Steve Jobs – are almost always true entrepreneurs. Entrepreneurs start with a vision. Often they are unhappy with their current jobs and see an opportunity to bring together the resources needed for a new venture. However, the image of entrepreneurs as bold pioneers probably is overly romantic. A survey of the CEOs of the nation's fastest-growing small firms found that these entrepreneurs could be best characterized as hard-working and practical, with great familiarity with their market and industry.[14]

Minority-owned businesses

As the minority population of European countries has grown, so has the number of minority-owned businesses. *'The rise in minorities is a reflection of demographic changes,'* said Matthew Haller of the International Franchising Association. *'As more minorities establish themselves in the USA, they are looking to control their destiny through business ownership.'*[15] Consider former veterinarian Salvador Guzman, who moved from Mexico to become a waiter in a friend's Mexican restaurant in Nashville, Tennessee. Energized by the opportunities to succeed in the USA as an entrepreneur, Guzman started his own restaurant with three partners and savings of $18 000, joining more than 2.4 million self-employed immigrants in the USA. Now he owns 14 restaurants and two Spanish-language radio stations in Tennessee.[16]

The number of minority-owned businesses increased by 45.6 per cent between 2002 and 2007, to 5.8 million firms, according to the recent data available. That's more than twice the national rate of all US businesses. These new firms generated $1.0 trillion in revenues and employed 5.9 million people. Increases in the number of minority-owned businesses range from 60.5 per cent for black-owned businesses to 17.9 per cent for Native American- and Alaska Native-owned businesses. Hispanic-owned businesses increased by 43.6 per cent.[17] Exhibit 10.3 summarizes the racial and ethnic composition of business owners in the USA.

The types of businesses launched by minority entrepreneurs are also increasingly sophisticated. The traditional minority-owned family retail store or restaurant is being replaced by firms in industries such as financial services, insurance and online businesses. Several successful Silicon Valley companies have been

EXHIBIT 10.3 Racial and ethnic composition of small business owners

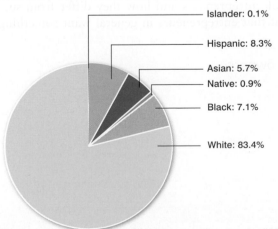

Islander: 0.1%
Hispanic: 8.3%
Asian: 5.7%
Native: 0.9%
Black: 7.1%
White: 83.4%

SOURCE: Summary of Findings, 'Preliminary Estimates of Business Ownership by Gender, Ethnicity, Race and Veteran Status: 2007', Survey of Business Owners (SBO), US Census Bureau, www.census.gov/econ/sbo/#nhpi (accessed August 23, 2010).

NOTE: The survey permitted multiple counts (for example, an owner might be counted as both Hispanic and Black) so figures add up to more than 100 per cent.

CONCEPT CONNECTION

Many people are motivated to start their own businesses by a desire for **autonomy** – meaning the freedom to work the way they want to work under the conditions they choose for themselves – or by a desire for **power** or **influence**. But for an entrepreneur to be successful, he or she needs to have a number of other important personal traits, such as unflagging enthusiasm, perseverance and self-efficacy. Entrepreneurs are also typically comfortable with calculated risk uncertainty and ambiguity.

founded or co-founded by minority entrepreneurs, including textbook-rental start-up Chegg, online dating service Zoosk and online craft marketplace Etsy.

Women-owned businesses

Women are also embracing entrepreneurial opportunities in greater numbers. Women own nearly 8 million firms, or 28 per cent of all businesses, according to the Center for Women's Business Research. Sales of these businesses generated $1.9 million as of 2008 and provided 16 per cent of all jobs in a range of industries like business services, personal services, retail, health care and communication. While these numbers are impressive, the results could be much better. Only 20 per cent of women-owned businesses have employees, an area of great growth and opportunity. '*The reason most businesses don't grow is [women] try to do everything themselves,*' claims Nell Merlino, who created the Take Our Daughters to Work campaign. '*The most important thing to do is hire people. With 10 million out of work,*' she added, '*there is an extraordinary labour pool.*'[18] Another challenge faced by women is the stark imbalance of the sexes in high-tech fields. Statistics show that women created only 8 per cent of the venture-backed technology start-ups.[19] Exhibit 10.4 displays the gender composition of business owners in the USA.

As the cost of launching an online business falls, more women are taking a gamble in this competitive market. When Apple introduced the iPhone in 2007, the market for smartphone applications skyrocketed. Today, over 350 000 apps are available, and the market is crowded with developers trying to create apps that mobile consumers will use loyally.

Traits of entrepreneurs

A number of studies have investigated the characteristics of entrepreneurs and how they differ from successful managers in established organizations. Some suggest that entrepreneurs in general want something

EXHIBIT 10.4 Gender composition of small business owners

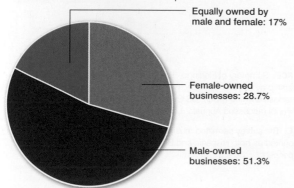

Equally owned by male and female: 17%

Female-owned businesses: 28.7%

Male-owned businesses: 51.3%

SOURCE: 'Summary Statistics for All U.S. Firms by Gender: 2007', *Survey of Business Owners – Women-Owned Firms*, U.S. Census Bureau, www.census.gov/econ/sbo/get07sof.html?12# (accessed August 9, 2012).

different from life than do traditional managers. Entrepreneurs seem to place high importance on being free to achieve and maximize their potential. Some 40 traits are identified as being associated with entrepreneurship, but seven have special importance.[20] These characteristics are illustrated in Exhibit 10.5.

EXHIBIT 10.5 Characteristics of entrepreneurs

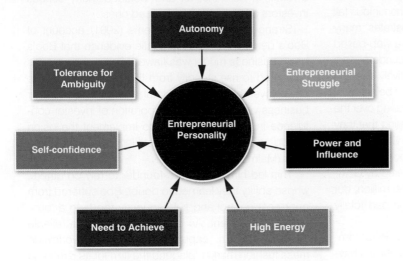

SOURCE: Leigh Buchanan, 'The Motivation Matrix', *Inc.*, March 2012, www.inc.com/magazine/201203/motivation-matrix.html (accessed August 20, 2012); and Charles R. Kuehl and Peggy A. Lambing, *Small Business: Planning and Management* (Ft. Worth, TX: The Dryden Press, 1994), p. 45.

'When you reach an obstacle, turn it into an opportunity. You have the choice. You can overcome and be a winner, or you can allow it to overcome you and be a loser. The choice is yours and yours alone.'
— MARY KAY ASH, AMERICAN BUSINESSWOMAN AND FOUNDER OF MARY KAY COSMETICS

Autonomy

In a 2012 survey of 2000 entrepreneurs, the desire for autonomy was the primary motivator for pursuing an entrepreneurial life. Entrepreneurs are driven by the desire for autonomy and cherish the freedom of making their own decisions about their business. Because of this desire for independent planning and decision-making, these entrepreneurs may consider operating solo, without partners or significant investors. But going solo has drawbacks. It may limit a firm's growth and result in a smaller-scale business.[21] For start-ups to succeed in the long run, a founder may have to forego autonomy and allow someone else with a different set of managerial skills to lead the company into the next phase of growth. *'When you're facing that tradeoff, you have to strike a stark balance. You're going to have to give up something dear to you in order to get something that is even more dear to you,'* said Noam Wasserman, author of *The Founder's Dilemmas: Anticipating and Avoiding the Pitfalls That Can Sink a Startup*.[22] Sometimes, this means giving up the autonomy that motivated an entrepreneur to start a business in the first place.

Entrepreneurial struggle

Another common trait among entrepreneurs is the ability to persevere and stay positive after long periods of struggle. Consider Justin Carden, a 29-year-old software engineer, who shared cramped communal housing with other aspiring tech entrepreneurs near Silicon Valley. He and other hopeful entrepreneurs toiled for long hours in tiny living spaces, working to develop ideas for new apps and websites. These 'hacker hostels' often house ten or more people, crammed into two bedrooms. People try out their sales talks on one another before pitching them to investors. *'We work so hard and we don't care about where we're staying,'* said Ethan Mollick, a former graduate student at the Massachusetts Institute of Technology (MIT) and assistant professor at the Wharton School of the University of Pennsylvania. *'People always complain that academic study of computer science doesn't do a lot for you as a programmer. What does [work] are these sorts of environments,'* he said.[23] In another example of entrepreneurial struggle, two surfing buddies endured years of financial struggle as they built a new microbrewery, described in the following example.

INNOVATIVE WAY

Leander and Malmsten (Boo.com)

A case study charting the rapid rise and ignominious fall in 2001 of web-based Boo.com, demonstrates many of the challenges and risks of starting up a web-based venture during dotcom1. The company's founders, Kaja Leander and Ernst Malmsten, were respectively a model and an arts impresario. Both had a history of being serial entrepreneurs. An earlier foray into book retailing over the Web in Sweden, gave them a taste for e-tailing that they were to rapidly develop on a gigantic scale via Boo.com. They had ridden the Internet bubble to the point where, in late 1999, they were being seriously considered by Goldman Sachs for an IPO at a valuation of $390 million, but the company's credibility and market value had totally collapsed by April 2000.

The dot.com period's boom saw many IPOs coming to the market, with some young entrepreneurs having 'self-efficacy' in that they could start and grow an international business. There was at this time a glut of willing investors' money that had flowed into the stock markets. The flow of investment funding was partly a result of herd instinct and included many serious investors as well as inexperienced ones.

Strangely, in Ernst Malmsten's (2001) account of Boo's demise there appears little evidence that Boo's basic business model was flawed. Sales and margins continued to rise steadily from the site going fully live on 3 November 1999. The fatal blow perhaps to their business venture was the evaporation of investor confidence in Malmsten's ability to implement the vision of Boo as the premier online retailer of sports/fashionwear (Malmsten, 2001, p. 342).

This led him and his co-founder to rely on others, whose ability they learned to doubt. Boo suffered from poor cost control and subsequently too high a 'burn rate' of investment. An inability to produce a reliable Internet platform, capable of serving a worldwide mass fashion market, plagued the firm for its 5 months of online trading. This reflected the technical weakness of the founders, who had previously only tested their entrepreneurial drive in the Arts and Literature.

Power and influence

Some entrepreneurs are driven by the desire for power and influence. Sam Walton, founder of Walmart, was the most successful retailer in US history, partly because he was way ahead of his competitors in bringing efficiency to the supply chain and selling goods at the lowest possible prices. Walton was able to exert significant pressure on manufacturers to improve their efficiency and bring down costs. As Walmart's influence grew, so did Walton's power to dictate price, volume, delivery, packaging and quality of many of its suppliers' products. Walton was a man who was driven by power and influence and will long be recognized as the entrepreneur who flipped the supplier-retailer relationship upside down.[24]

High energy

A business start-up requires great effort. A survey of small business owners by Staples found that 43 per cent of small business owners work more than a regular 40-hour week, 31 per cent report working during holidays, and 13 per cent say they regularly work more than 80 hours a week.[25] High levels of passion also help entrepreneurs overcome inevitable obstacles and traumas.[26] You can recognize entrepreneurial passion in people by their unwavering belief in a dream, intense focus and unconventional risk taking. *'To succeed, you have to believe in something with such a passion that it becomes a reality,'* said Anita Roddick of the Body Shop.[27] Long before 'going green' was popular, Roddick created a business that was socially and environmentally responsible. By 2007, she had a chain of more than 2000 Body Shop stores in 50 countries.[28]

TAKE A MOMENT

Are you an entrepreneur in the making? Do you have the persistence to endure setbacks and disappointments? Take the questionnaire at the end of the chapter to assess your potential to start and manage your own business.

Need to achieve

Another characteristic closely linked to entrepreneurship is the need to achieve, which means that people are motivated to excel and pick situations in which success is likely.[29] People who have high achievement needs like to set their own goals, which are moderately difficult. Easy goals present no challenge; unrealistically difficult goals cannot be achieved. Intermediate goals are challenging and provide great satisfaction when achieved. High achievers also like to pursue goals for which they can obtain feedback about their success. '*I was very low and I had to achieve something,*' recalls *Harry Potter* creator and billionaire author J. K. Rowling. '*Without the challenge, I would have gone stark raving mad.*'[30]

Self-efficacy

People who start and run a business must act decisively. They need confidence about their ability to master the day-to-day tasks of the business. They need to feel sure about their ability to win customers, handle the technical details and keep the business moving. Entrepreneurs also have a general feeling of confidence that they can deal with anything in the future; complex, unanticipated problems can be handled as they arise.

Tolerance for ambiguity

Many people need work situations characterized by clear structure, specific instructions and complete information. Tolerance for ambiguity is the psychological characteristic that allows a person to be untroubled by disorder and uncertainty. This trait is important for entrepreneurs because few situations present more uncertainty than starting a new business. Decisions are often made without clear understanding of options or certainty about which option will succeed.

These traits and the demographic characteristics discussed earlier offer an insightful but imprecise picture of the entrepreneur. Successful entrepreneurs come in all ages, from all backgrounds, and may have a combination of personality traits and other characteristics. No one should be discouraged from starting a business because he or she doesn't fit a specific profile. One review of small business suggests that the three most important traits of successful entrepreneurs, particularly in a turbulent environment, are realism, flexibility and passion. Even the most realistic entrepreneurs tend to underestimate the difficulties of building a business, so they need flexibility and a passion for their idea to survive the hurdles.[31]

REFLECTION

- Entrepreneurs often have backgrounds, demographic characteristics and personalities that distinguish them from successful managers in established organizations.
- One survey suggests that the desire for autonomy is the primary motivator for people to pursue entrepreneurship.
- Characteristics common to entrepreneurs include the ability to persevere, a desire for power and influence, self-confidence, a high energy level, a need to achieve and a tolerance of ambiguity.
- The need to achieve means that entrepreneurs are motivated to excel and pick situations in which success is likely.
- Tolerance for ambiguity is the psychological characteristic that allows a person to be untroubled by disorder and uncertainty.

Social entrepreneurship

Today's consumers have a growing expectation that organizations will operate in socially responsible ways. In response, a new breed of business is emerging that is motivated to help society solve all types of social problems, including environmental pollution, global hunger and deaths from treatable diseases. In many ways, these businesses function like traditional businesses, but their primary focus is on providing social benefits, not maximizing financial returns. Social entrepreneurship focuses primarily on creating social value by providing solutions to social problems, with a secondary purpose of generating profit

CONCEPT CONNECTION

Social entrepreneurs Eric Schwartz and Ned Rimer created Citizen Schools to reach out to middle school students with after-school programmes that include hands-on apprenticeships taught by volunteer professionals. The apprentices create actual products, ranging from solar cars to well-managed stock portfolios. The goal is to give students the skills and motivation to do well in their academic and personal lives. One reason the organization is so successful is that it is run on solid business principles, with a well-honed strategy and growth plan that includes concrete objectives and specific performance measures.

and returns.[32] A well-known social entrepreneur is Muhammad Yunus, who founded Grameen Bank. Yunus pioneered the concept of lending small amounts of money, called *microcredit*, to small businesses in poverty-stricken villages in India. By 2006, when Yunus won the Nobel Peace Prize, the Grameen Bank had outstanding loans to nearly 7 million poor people in 73 000 villages in Bangladesh. The Grameen model expanded into more than 100 countries and helped millions of people rise out of poverty.[33] As another example, Kathy Giusti unexpectedly became a social entrepreneur after a devastating medical diagnosis.

Launching an entrepreneurial start-up

Whether one starts a non-profit organization, a socially oriented business or a traditional for-profit small company, the first step in pursuing an entrepreneurial dream is to come up with a viable idea and then plan like crazy. Once someone has a new idea in mind, a business plan must be drawn up and decisions must be made about legal structure, financing and basic tactics, such as whether to start the business from scratch and whether to pursue international opportunities from the start.

GREEN POWER

Star power

Jessica Alba is not the first movie beauty lured by a desire to find solutions to social problems, but she may be the first to start a company focused on a problem that many new mothers are concerned with: *How to have healthy baby products that also assure a healthy environment.*

While researching healthy-baby issues during her own pregnancy, Alba read Christopher Gavigan's book *Healthy Child, Healthy World.* Concerned by Gavigan's reports on toxin levels in baby products, Alba (in her own words) *hounded* the author, urging him to join forces with her in the creation of eco-friendly baby care products. The duo launched **The Honest Company**

with a flagship product necessary to every new mum – the disposable nappy. Independent testing demonstrated a 33 per cent increase in nappy absorbency through a natural combination of wheat, corn and wood fluff from sustainable forests, appealing to eco-conscious consumers. The new nappies are also 85 per cent biodegradable, right down to the addition of 'green tab' fasteners. Today, The Honest Company offers a variety of products aimed at helping children grow up in a world free of toxins and carcinogens.

SOURCES: 'The 100 Most Creative People in Business 2012: #17 Jessica Alba', *Fast Company* (June 2012): 96–97; and 'About Us: Health and Sustainability Standards', The Honest Company website, https://www.honest.com/about-us/health-and-sustainability (accessed October 2, 2012).

INNOVATIVE **WAY**

The reluctant social entrepreneur

Kathy Giusti never dreamed she would leave the corporate world to become an entrepreneur. She was on the fast track at the pharmaceutical company G. D. Searle and aspired to be one of the first women on the executive committee. At Searle, she was quickly identified as a 'high-potential' employee. Alan Heller, who was Searle's co-president, described Giusti as 'highly intelligent, highly analytical and very driven'. At Searle, she played an instrumental role in launching two successful drugs: Ambien and Daypro. An introvert by nature, she loved working for a big corporation and didn't consider herself a risk taker.

Then, Giusti received news that would change her life. She was diagnosed with multiple myeloma, a deadly blood cancer, and told that myeloma patients were living, on average, 3 or 4 years. She extensively researched treatments and was devastated by what she learned. The drugs used to fight the disease were from the 1960s, and no one was devoting research and development resources to it. Her next move was surprising. She resigned from Searle and started a non-profit business. She channelled her business acumen,

passion for a cure and high energy level to start two organizations for helping accelerate the development of treatments for the disease: the Multiple Myeloma Research Foundation and the Multiple Myeloma Research Consortium.

As a self-described 'big-company person', Giusti had little respect for non-profits because she thought most were not professionally managed. 'I wanted people to see that I wasn't going to run some schlocky non-profit. I was going to try to do this right,' she says. Giusti requires the foundation and the consortium to use metrics, benchmarking and scorecards so that all parties know their individual and collective performance and are consistently striving to do better. The leaders of a 24-person staff hold a strategy meeting every Monday and an operations meeting every Tuesday. To date, Giusti has raised more than $165 million for myeloma research, an extraordinary achievement given that the vast majority of US non-profits never surpass $1 million. 'What Kathy brought to the table was an unwillingness to accept the norm,' says Keith Stewart, dean for research at the Mayo Clinic in Arizona. 'She's a demanding person. She knows what she wants, and she doesn't rest until she's found a solution to thorny problems.'[34]

REFLECTION

- A **social entrepreneur** is an entrepreneurial leader who is committed to both good business and changing the world for the better.
- Social entrepreneurs are creating new business models that meet critical human needs and resolve important problems unsolved by current economic and social institutions.
- Social entrepreneurship combines the creativity, business acumen, passion and work of the traditional entrepreneur with a social mission.

Starting with an idea

To some people, the idea for a new business is the easy part. They do not even consider entrepreneurship until they are inspired by an exciting idea. Other people decide they want to run their own business and set about looking for an idea or opportunity. Exhibit 10.6 shows the most important reasons that people start a new business and the source of new business ideas. Note that 37 per cent of business founders got their idea from an in-depth understanding of the industry, primarily because of past job experience. Interestingly, almost as many – 36 per cent – spotted a market niche that wasn't being filled.[35] An example is Spanx founder Sara Blakely, who was eagerly looking for a new business idea while working full-time selling office equipment. 'I had been thinking about a product I could come up with on my own,' says Blakely. 'I liked to sell and I was good at it. But I [wanted] to sell something that I was really passionate about.' While trying to find

EXHIBIT 10.6 Sources of entrepreneurial motivation and new business ideas

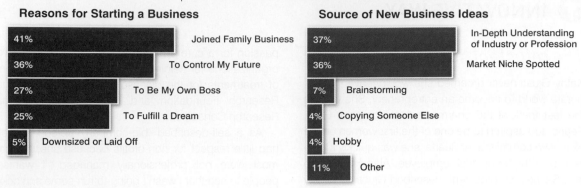

SOURCE: John Case, 'The Rewards', *Inc.* (May 15, 2001): 50–51; and Leslie Brokaw, 'How to Start an Inc. 500 Company', *Inc.* (October 15, 1994): 51–65. Copyright 1994 and 2001 by Mansueto Ventures LLC. Reproduced with permission of Mansueto Ventures LLC.

some figure-flattering hosiery to wear under white trousers, she came up with the idea for a new business. She created Spanx, a footless, body-shaping pantyhose that skyrocketed to success after Oprah Winfrey selected Spanx to be featured on the popular 'favourite things' episode of her TV show. Today, Spanx has more than 100 employees and products that include swimwear, trousers, skirts and underwear.[36]

The trick for entrepreneurs is to blend their own skills and experience with a need in the marketplace. Acting strictly on one's own skills may produce something no one wants to buy. On the other hand, finding a market niche that one does not have the ability to fill doesn't work either. Both personal skill and market need typically must be present.

Writing the business plan

Once an entrepreneur is inspired by a new business idea, careful planning is crucial. A business plan is a document specifying the business details prepared by an entrepreneur prior to opening a new business. Planning forces the entrepreneur to think carefully through the issues and problems associated with starting and developing the business. Most entrepreneurs have to borrow money, and a business plan is absolutely critical for persuading lenders and investors to participate in the business. Studies show that small businesses with a carefully thought-out, written business plan are much more likely to succeed than those without one.[37] To attract the interest of venture capitalists or other potential investors, the entrepreneur should keep the plan crisp and compelling.

The details of a business plan may vary, but successful business plans generally share several characteristics:[38]

- Demonstrate a clear, compelling vision that creates an air of excitement.
- Provide clear and realistic financial projections.
- Profile potential customers and the target market.
- Include detailed information about the industry and competitors.
- Provide evidence of an effective entrepreneurial management team.
- Pay attention to good formatting and clear writing.
- Keep the plan short – no more than 50 pages.
- Highlight critical risks that may threaten business success.
- Spell out the sources and uses of start-up funds and operating funds.
- Capture the reader's interest with a killer summary.

Starting a business is a rewarding and complex process that starts with good planning, preparation and insight. A well-crafted business plan summarizes the road map for success. As the business begins to grow, however, the entrepreneur should be prepared to handle common pitfalls, as described in this chapter's Manager's Shoptalk.

'The first purpose of the business plan is to convince yourself that it's an idea you really want to do. If you're not convinced, you'll never be able to convince anyone else.'
— MAXINE CLARK, CHIEF EXECUTIVE, BUILD-A-BEAR WORKSHOP

Choosing a legal structure

Before entrepreneurs begin a business, and perhaps again as it expands, they must choose an appropriate legal structure for the company. The three basic choices are proprietorship, partnership or corporation.

Sole proprietorship

A sole proprietorship is defined as an unincorporated business owned by an individual for profit. Proprietorships make up the majority of businesses in the USA. This form is popular because it is easy to start and has few legal requirements. A proprietor has total ownership and control of the company and can make all decisions without consulting anyone. However, this type of organization also has drawbacks. The owner has unlimited liability for the business, meaning that if someone sues, the owner's personal as well as business assets are at risk. Also, financing can be harder to obtain because business success rests on one person's shoulders.

Partnership

A partnership is an unincorporated business owned by two or more people. Partnerships, like proprietorships, are relatively easy to start. Two friends may reach an agreement to start a graphic arts company. To avoid misunderstandings and to make sure the business is well planned, it is wise to draw up and sign a formal partnership agreement with the help of an attorney lawyer. The agreement specifies how partners are to share responsibility and resources and how they will contribute their expertise. The disadvantages of partnerships are the unlimited liability of the partners and the disagreements that almost always occur among strong-minded people. A poll by *Inc.* magazine illustrated the volatility of partnerships. According to the poll, 59 per cent of respondents considered partnerships a bad business move, citing reasons such as partner problems and conflicts. Partnerships often dissolve within 5 years. Respondents who liked partnerships pointed to the equality of partners (sharing of workload and emotional and financial burdens) as the key to a successful partnership.[39]

Corporation

A corporation is an artificial entity created by the state and existing apart from its owners. As a separate legal entity, the corporation is liable for its actions and must pay taxes on its income. Unlike other forms of ownership, the corporation has a legal life of its own; it continues to exist regardless of whether the owners live or die. And the corporation, not the owners, is liable in case the company gets sued. Thus, continuity and limits on owners' liability are two principal advantages of forming a corporation. For example, a physician can form a corporation so that liability for malpractice will not affect his or her personal assets. The major disadvantage of the corporation is that it is expensive and complex to do the paperwork required to incorporate the business and to keep the records required by law. When proprietorships and partnerships are successful and grow large, they often incorporate to limit liability and to raise funds through the sale of stock to investors.

Arranging financing

Most entrepreneurs are particularly concerned with financing the business. A few types of businesses can still be started with a few thousand dollars, but starting a business usually requires coming up with a significant amount of initial funding. An investment is required to acquire labour and raw materials, and perhaps a building and equipment as well. High-tech businesses, for example, typically need from $50 000 to $500 000 just to get through the first 6 months, even with the founder drawing no salary.[40]

 MANAGER'S SHOPTALK

Why start-ups fail

Small businesses face many challenges as they navigate through today's economy and confront issues that jeopardize their success: slow job growth, weak consumer confidence and a slow housing recovery. It's no wonder that small business failure rates increased by 40 per cent from 2007 to 2010. To keep a small business running successfully, an entrepreneur should know how to avoid potential land mines that can knock a business off course. While it is impossible to avoid all risks, a savvy entrepreneur will be alert to the most frequent reasons small business ventures fail.

- **Poor management.** Many small business owners lack the necessary business skills to manage all areas of their business, such as finance, purchasing, inventory, sales, production and hiring. When Jay Bean founded sunglassesonly.com, he had no experience of managing inventory. 'Having inventory requires you to deal with a different set of complex issues, including theft control,' he said. Bean's sales plummeted during the economic recession, and he closed the business in November 2010, selling the assets at a loss.

- **Overexpansion.** Some overzealous business owners confuse success with the need to expand. This may include moving into markets that are not as profitable, or borrowing too much money in an attempt to keep growth at a particular rate. When the cofounders of Large Format Digital spent $1 million to build their own installation facility, they believed it would save them money in the long term. The business had been growing at about 60 per cent each year since 2006. Within a month of building the facility in 2008, sales dropped 50 per cent, and the company closed in March 2011.

- **Sloppy accounting.** Financial statements are the backbone of a small business, and owners need to understand the numbers to control the business. The income statement and balance sheet help diagnose potential problems before they become fatal. It's also important to understand the ratio of sales to expenses that will result in profitability. Managing cash flow is another important role of the small business owner. Businesses go through cycles and smart managers have a cash cushion that helps them recover from the inevitable bumps.

- **No website.** As the number of online customers increases, it's important for every business to have a professional, well-designed website. According to the US Department of Commerce, e-commerce sales totalled $165.4 billion in 2010. The key to a successful website is to make it easy for users to navigate. Wesabe, a personal finance website, helped consumers budget their money and make smart buying decisions. With 150 000 members in the first year, the co-founders were ecstatic. A new competitor, Mint.com, launched a website with a better design and a more memorable name. Within 3 months, Mint had 300 000 users and $17 million in venture financing. Wesabe was unable to compete and closed its site soon after. Co-founder Marc Hedlund says the managers at Wesabe should have made the site easier to use. 'We wanted to help people,' he said, 'but it was too much work to get that help.'

- **Operational mediocrity.** An important role of the entrepreneur is to set high standards in essential areas such as quality control, customer service and the company's public image. Most businesses depend on repeat and referral business, so it's important to create a positive first impression with customers. Franchisors often assist in providing high-quality products and services, reducing some of the stress entrepreneurs can face. Immigrant Lyudmila Khonomov pursued her American dream by opening a Subway restaurant in Brooklyn. *'You don't have to prepare the foods from scratch,'* she said. *'Subway takes the guesswork out of preparing high-quality sandwiches in a consistent way.'*

- **Fear of firing.** Firing an employee is uncomfortable and difficult, but if business owners plan to outperform competitors, it's important to build and maintain an excellent staff. Unfortunately, it's very easy to keep mediocre employees around, especially those who are nice and loyal. However, it will hurt the business in the long run. Ask yourself, 'Would I be relieved if anyone on my team quit tomorrow?' If the answer is yes, you may have a problem.

SOURCES: Patricia Schaefer, 'The Seven Pitfalls of Business Failures and How to Avoid Them', *BusinessKnow-How.com*, April, 2011, www.businessknowhow.com/startup/business-failure.htm (accessed August 14, 2012); Jay Goltz, 'You're the Boss: The Art of Running a Small Business', *The New York Times*, January 5, 2011, www.boss.blogs.nytimes.com/2011/01/05/top-10-reasons-small-businesses-fail/ (accessed August 14, 2012); Eilene Zimmerman, 'How Six Companies Failed to Survive 2010', *The New York Times*, January 5, 2011, www.nytimes.com/2011/01/06/business/smallbusiness/06sbiz.html (accessed August 14, 2012); 'The State of Small Businesses Post Great Recession: An Analysis of Small Businesses Between 2007 and 2011', Dun & Bradstreet, May 2011, www.dnbgov.com/pdf/DNB_SMB_Report_May2011.pdf (accessed August 14, 2012); Adriana Gardella, 'Advice From a Sticky Web Site on How to Make Yours the Same', *The New York Times*, April 13, 2011, www.nytimes.com/2011/04/14/business/smallbusiness/14sbiz.html (accessed August 14, 2012).

Many entrepreneurs rely on their own resources for initial funding, but they often have to mortgage their homes, depend on credit cards, borrow money from a bank or give part of the business to a venture capitalist.[41] Exhibit 10.7 summarizes the most common sources of start-up capital for entrepreneurs. The financing decision initially involves two options – whether to obtain loans that must be repaid (debt financing) or whether to share ownership (equity financing).

EXHIBIT 10.7 Sources of start-up capital for entrepreneurs

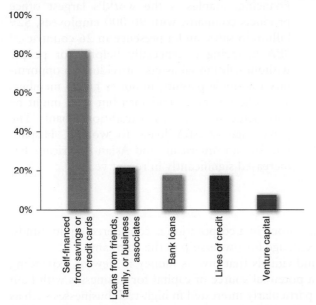

SOURCE: Jim Melloan, 'The Inc. 5000', *Inc.* (September 1, 2006): 187. Copyright © 2006 by Mansueto Ventures LLC. Reproduced with permission of Mansueto Ventures LLC.

TAKE A MOMENT

How effective would you be at pitching a new business idea to potential investors? You can get an idea by completing the New Manager Self-Test.

Debt financing

Borrowing money that has to be repaid at a later date to start a business is referred to as debt financing. One common source of debt financing for a start-up is to borrow from family and friends. Increasingly, entre-

CONCEPT CONNECTION

Chipotle Mexican Grill founder, chairman and CEO, Steve Ells, used both **debt** and **equity financing** when he launched his 'quick gourmet' restaurant chain. An $85 000 loan from his father made the first Denver restaurant possible. Later, Ells borrowed more from his father, took out an SBA (Small Business Administration) loan, and raised $1.8 million from friends and private investors. Eventually, the chain received equity financing: first from McDonald's, and later from the stock that Chipotle issued when it went public. Ironically, Ells's main reason for starting Chipotle was to generate cash to finance an upscale restaurant. With Chipotle's success, he no longer has any plans to open that fancy restaurant.

preneurs are using their personal credit cards as a form of debt financing. Another common source is a bank loan. Banks provide some 25 per cent of all financing for small business. Sometimes entrepreneurs can obtain money from a finance company, wealthy individuals or potential customers. A typical source of funds for businesses with high potential is through angel financing. Angels are wealthy individuals, typically with business experience and contacts, who believe in the idea for the start-up and are willing to invest their personal funds to help the business get started. Significantly, angels also provide advice and assistance as the entrepreneur is developing the company. The entrepreneur wants angels who can make business contacts, help find talented employees and serve as all-around advisors.

Another form of loan financing is provided by the Small Business Administration (SBA). Staples, which started with one office supply store in Brighton, Massachusetts, in 1986, got its start towards rapid growth with the assistance of SBA financing. Staples is the world's largest office products company, with 90 000 employees, $29 billion in sales, and a presence in 26 countries.[42] SBA financing is especially helpful for people without substantial assets, providing an opportunity for single parents, minority group members and others with a good idea but who might be considered high-risk by a traditional bank. The percentage of SBA loans to women, Hispanics, African-Americans and Asian-Americans has increased significantly in recent years.[43]

Equity financing

Any money invested by owners or by those who purchase stock in a corporation is considered equity funds. Equity financing consists of funds that are invested in exchange for ownership in the company.

A venture capital firm is a group of companies or individuals that invests money in new or expanding businesses for ownership and potential profits. This is a potential source of capital for businesses with high earning and growth possibilities. Venture capitalists are particularly interested in high-tech businesses such as biotechnology, innovative online ventures or telecommunications, because they have the potential for high rates of return on investment.[44] Venture capitalist Andreessen Horowitz, a Facebook investor, contributed part of the $1 million seed money for an e-commerce start-up called the Dollar Shave Club, which hopes to claim a part of the razor market with home delivery and low prices. At the Dollar Shave Club, customers sign up for one of three plans that give them a razor and a supply of blades for $3 to $9 per month. Venture capitalists are hoping that the Dollar Shave Club totally upends the market for men's razors and blades, where competitor Gillette controls 66 per cent of the market.[45]

A new option available to entrepreneurs is called crowdfunding, which is a way of raising capital by receiving small amounts of money from a large number of investors, usually through social media and the Internet. The Jumpstart Our Business Startups (JOBS) Act, signed into law by President Barack Obama in April 2012, opened the door for this type of fundraising from a wide pool of small investors who are not burdened with

NEW MANAGER SELF-TEST

Perceived passion

INSTRUCTIONS An entrepreneur starting a business often has to make presentations to investors in order to raise money. Respond to the following statements about how you would normally make a persuasive presentation to investors for a business you are starting. Answer whether each statement is 'Mostly true' or 'Mostly false' for you.

When making a formal presentation, I would:

		Mostly true	Mostly false
1	Use energetic body movements to act out the idea.	☐	☐
2	Show animated facial expressions.	☐	☐
3	Use a lot of gestures.	☐	☐
4	Talk with varied tone and pitch.	☐	☐
5	Dramatize my excitement.	☐	☐
6	Point out explicitly the relationship between the topic and its broader context.	☐	☐
7	Make sure my content has real substance.	☐	☐
8	Confirm that the presentation is coherent and logical.	☐	☐
9	Make certain the presentation is thoughtful and in-depth.	☐	☐
10	Cite facts and examples to support my points and arguments.	☐	☐

SCORING & INTERPRETATION This questionnaire was developed to measure the persuasiveness of presentations to venture capitalists by entrepreneurs in an effort to obtain investment money. Two aspects of presentation are measured above   passion and preparedness. Give yourself one point for each 'Mostly true' answer.

Passion: Items 1–5 score ____.
Preparedness: Items 6–10 score ___.

The research showed consistently that preparedness, not passion, had the most positive impact on decisions to invest money with entrepreneurs. Thus, a higher score on preparedness is more important for an effective presentation to investors than is a high score on presentation passion. Compare your scores to other students. Why do you think preparedness has more impact than passion on potential investors?

SOURCE: Xiao-Ping Chen, Xin Yao and Suresh Kotha, 'Entrepreneur Passion and Preparedness in Business Plan Presentations: A Persuasion Analysis of Venture Capitalists' Funding Decisions', *Academy of Management Journal* 52, no. 1 (2009): 199–214.

restrictions. The law allows businesses to raise money from investors in exchange for equity in the company and allows non-accredited investors (like relatives) to sink their own cash into start-ups.[46] Currently, the most successful crowdfunding website is Kickstarter, which began as a way for people to raise money for quirky projects like offbeat documentaries and pop-up wedding chapels. Kickstarter has expanded to include video game production and innovative new gadgets. It enables budding entrepreneurs to test new ideas and see if there's a market for them before they trade ownership of their company for money from venture capitalists. To date, Kickstarter has raised more than \$200 million for 290 000 projects, or about 44 per cent of those that sought financing on the site.[47]

REFLECTION

- The two most common sources of new business ideas come from a thorough understanding of an industry, often derived from past job experience, and identifying a market niche.
- Prior to opening a business, an entrepreneur should prepare a **business plan**, a document specifying the details of the business.
- Businesses with carefully written business plans are more likely to succeed than those without business plans.
- An unincorporated for-profit business owned by an individual is called a **sole proprietorship**.
- A **partnership** is formed when two or more people choose to own an unincorporated business.
- A **corporation** is an artificial entity created by the state and existing apart from its owners.

- **Debt financing** involves borrowing money from friends, family or a bank, that has to be repaid at a later date in order to start a business.
- **Angel financing** occurs when a wealthy individual who believes in the idea for a start-up provides personal funds and advice to help the business get started.
- **Equity financing** consists of funds that are invested in exchange for ownership in the company.
- A **venture capital firm** is a group of companies or individuals that invests money in new or expanding businesses for ownership and potential profits.
- **Crowdfunding** is a way of raising capital that involves getting small amounts of money from a large number of investors, typically using social media or the Internet.

Tactics for becoming a business owner

Aspiring entrepreneurs can become business owners in several different ways. They can start a new business from scratch, buy an existing business or start a franchise. Another popular entrepreneurial tactic is to participate in a business incubator.

Start a new business

One of the most common ways to become an entrepreneur is to start a new business from scratch. This approach is exciting because the entrepreneur sees a need for a product or service that has not been filled before and then sees the idea or dream become a reality. Sara and Warren Wilson, co-founders of the Snack Factory, built a \$42 million business by coming up with new snack-sized versions of traditional foods. Together, they dreamed up the concept of bagel chips, which are flat, crunchy chips made from bagels. '*We didn't just daydream ideas; we figured out a way to make them happen,*' said Warren Wilson. After selling Bagel Chips to Nabisco in 1992, the dream continued, and they went on to create pitta chips and pretzel chips. '*As with our two previous businesses, we built Pretzel Chips little by little and with great attention to detail and care,*' he said.[48]

The advantage of starting a business is the ability to develop and design the business in the entrepreneur's own way. The entrepreneur is solely responsible for its success. A potential disadvantage is the long time it can take to get the business off the ground and make it profitable. The uphill battle is caused by the lack of established clientele and the many mistakes made by someone new to the business. Moreover, no matter how much planning is done, a start-up is risky, with no guarantee that the new idea will work. Some entrepreneurs, especially in high-risk industries, develop partnerships with established companies that can help the new company get established and grow. Others use the technique of outsourcing – having some activities handled by outside contractors – to minimize the costs and risks of doing everything in-house.[49]

Buy an existing business

Because of the long start-up time and the inevitable mistakes, some entrepreneurs prefer to reduce risk by purchasing an existing business. This direction offers the advantage of a shorter time to get started and an existing track record. The entrepreneur may get a bargain price if the owner wishes to retire or has other family considerations. Moreover, a new business may overwhelm an entrepreneur with the amount of work to be done and procedures to be determined. An established business already has filing systems, a payroll tax system, and other operating procedures. Potential disadvantages are the need to pay for goodwill that the owner believes exists and the possible existence of ill will towards the business. In addition, the company may have bad habits and procedures or outdated technology, which may be why the business is for sale.

Buy a franchise

Franchising is a business arrangement where a firm (franchisor) collects upfront and ongoing fees in exchange for other firms (franchisees) to offer products and services under its brand name and using its processes.[50] The franchisee invests his or her money and owns the business but does not have to develop a new product, create a new company or test the market. According to the International Franchising Association, the 735 571 franchise outlets in the USA employed nearly 8 million people in 2011, a decline since 2007. Franchise growth stalled by weak consumer spending and tighter credit standards, which limit small business owners from borrowing sufficient money. But after 3 years of decline, the number of franchises was around 2 per cent in 2012.[51] Exhibit 10.8 lists some of the fastest-growing franchises, including the type of business, the number of outlets worldwide and the initial franchise fee. Initial franchise fees don't include the other start-up costs that the entrepreneur will have to cover.

TAKE A MOMENT

How motivated are you to keep working towards a goal despite setbacks? The answer may reveal your entrepreneurial potential. For a better assessment, complete the Experiential Exercise online.

EXHIBIT 10.8 Some of today's fastest-growing franchises (in US$)

Franchise	Type of business	Number of outlets*	Franchise Fee
Subway	Submarine sandwiches	37 003	$15 000
Pizza Hut	Pizza, pasta, wings	13 432	$25 000
Dunkin' Donuts	Doughnuts, coffee, baked goods	8 924	$40 000–$80 000
McDonald's	Hamburgers, chicken, salads	33 427	$45 000
Hampton Hotels	Mid-priced hotel	1 868	$65 000

*Does not include company-owned outlets.

SOURCE: '2011 Fastest-Growing Franchise Rankings', *Entrepreneur*, www.entrepreneur.com/franchises/rankings/fastestgrowing-115162/2011,-1.html (accessed August 14, 2012).

The powerful advantage of a franchise is that management help is provided by the owner. Franchisors provide an established name and national advertising to stimulate local demand for the product or service. For example, Dunkin' Donuts supports its franchisees with recipes, employee training and ongoing marketing support in exchange for a franchising fee of between $40 000 to $80 000 and an ongoing royalty fee of 5.9 per cent.[52] Potential disadvantages are the lack of control that occurs when franchisors want every business managed in exactly the same way. In some cases, franchisors dictate the prices of products or require franchisees to purchase expensive equipment to support new product offerings. Vince Eupierre, a 70 plus-year-old immigrant from Cuba, owns 34 Burger King franchises in Southern California and employs 2500 workers. His sales are down 25 per cent from 3 years previously due to the economic recession. As part of his franchising agreement with Burger King, he was required to purchase $1.3 million in smoothie stations and new freezers when Burger King added smoothies and frappés to its menu. Facing declining sales, Eupierre is concerned about the future. *'If you ask me, "Will you buy another store today?" I'd say, Let's wait a little bit and see what happens in the next 60 to 90 days,'* he said.[53] In addition, franchises can be expensive, and the high start-up costs are followed with monthly payments to the franchisor that can run from 2 per cent to 15 per cent of gross sales.[54]

Entrepreneurs who are considering buying a franchise should investigate the company thoroughly. The prospective franchisee is legally entitled to a copy of franchisor disclosure statements, which include information on 20 topics, including litigation and bankruptcy history, identities of the directors and executive officers, financial information, identification of any products that the franchisee is required to buy, and from whom those purchases must be made. The entrepreneur also should talk with as many franchise owners as possible because they are among the best sources of information about how the company really operates.[55] Exhibit 10.9 lists some specific questions entrepreneurs should ask when considering buying a franchise. Answering such questions can reduce the risks and improve the chances of success.

EXHIBIT 10.9 Sample questions for choosing a franchise

Questions about the franchisor	Questions about financing
1 Does the franchisor provide support such as marketing and training?	**1** Do I understand the risks associated with this business, and am I willing to assume them?
2 How long does it take the typical franchise owner to start making a profit?	**2** Have I had a lawyer review the disclosure documents and franchise agreement?
3 How many franchisees are there and what is the failure rate?	**3** What is the initial investment?
4 How do the products or services of the franchise differ from those of competitors?	**4** How much working capital is required?
5 Does the company have a history of litigation?	**5** Is an existing franchise a better purchase than opening a new one?
6 What is the background of top management?	**6** Is the franchisor willing to negotiate the franchise agreement?

SOURCE: Kermit Pattison, 'A Guide to Assessing Franchising Opportunities', *The New York Times,* (September 17, 2009); Thomas Love, 'The Perfect Franchisee', *Nation's Business* (April 1998): 59–65; and Roberta Maynard, 'Choosing a Franchise', *Nation's Business* (October 1996): 56–63.

Participate in a business incubator

An attractive option for entrepreneurs who want to start a business from scratch is to join a business incubator. A business incubator typically provides shared office space, management support services and management and legal advice to entrepreneurs. Incubators also give entrepreneurs a chance to share information with one another about local business, financial aid and market opportunities. A recent innovation is the *virtual incubator*, which does not require that people set up on-site. These virtual organizations connect entrepreneurs with a wide range of experts and mentors and offer lower overhead and cost savings for cash-strapped small business owners. Christie Stone, co-founder of Ticobeans, a coffee distributor in New Orleans, likes the virtual approach because it gives her access to top-notch advice while allowing her to keep her office near her inventory.[56]

Business incubators have become a significant segment of the small business economy, with approximately 1400 in operation in North America and an estimated 7000 worldwide.[57] The incubators that are thriving are primarily non-profits and those that cater to niches or focus on helping women or minority entrepreneurs. These incubators include those run by government agencies and universities to boost the viability of small business and spur job creation. The great value of an incubator is the expertise of a mentor, who serves as advisor, role model and cheerleader, and ready access to a team of lawyers, accountants and other advisors. Incubators also give budding entrepreneurs a chance to network and learn from one another.[58] *'The really cool thing about a business incubator is that when you get entrepreneurial people in one place, there's a*

CONCEPT CONNECTION

Etsy.com is a textbook example of how to start an online company. Co-founder and CEO Rob Kalin identified a clear **market niche**: providing an online store where crafters and artisans can sell handmade items like these. He built an engaging, user-friendly **professional website** that includes a community section that nurtures **online relationships**. Finally, Etsy's **domain name** is intriguing. Kalin once said he came up with it after noticing that characters in Fellini movies kept saying *et si*, but others insist Etsy stands for 'easy to sell yourself'.

synergistic effect,' said Tracy Kitts, vice president and chief operating officer of the National Business Incubation Association. '*Not only do they learn from staff, they learn tons from each other, and this really contributes to their successes.*'[59]

Starting an online business

Many entrepreneurs are turning to the Internet to expand their small businesses or launch a new venture. Anyone with an idea, a computer, access to the Internet and the tools to create a website can start an online business. These factors certainly fuelled Ashley Qualls's motivation to create a website that has become a destination for millions of teenage girls. Starting at age 15, Ashley launched Whateverlife.com with a clever website, an $8 domain name, and a vision to provide free designs (hearts, flowers, celebrities) for social networking pages. Her hobby has exploded into a thriving business, with advertising revenue of more than $1 million so far.[60]

As Whateverlife.com illustrates, one incentive for starting an online business is that an entrepreneur can take a simple idea and turn it into a lucrative business. Another example comes from entrepreneurs Andrew Miller and Michael Zapolin. When they bought the generic domain name *chocolate.com*, Miller and Zapolin aspired to turn a simple domain name into an online emporium. '*We knew nobody was doing a good job with chocolate in the online space,*' says Miller. In 2 years, the partners have built a business that is on track to clear $2 million in annual revenue. Always in pursuit of the next big online success story, Miller and Zapolin now own 17 domain names, including *software.com* and *relationship.com*.[61]

Entrepreneurs who aspire to start online businesses follow the usual steps required to start a traditional business: identify a profitable market niche, develop an inspiring business plan, choose a legal structure and determine financial backing. Beyond that, they need to be unusually nimble, persistent in marketing, savvy with technology and skilful at building online relationships. Several steps required to start an online business are highlighted here.

- **Find a market niche.** To succeed in the competitive online market, the entrepreneur needs to identify a market niche that isn't being served by other companies. Online businesses succeed when they sell unique, customized or narrowly focused products or services to a well-defined target audience.

- **Create a professional website.** Online shoppers have short attention spans, so a website should entice them to linger. In addition, websites should be easy to navigate and intuitive, and also offer menus that are easy to read and understand. Even 'small-time' sites need 'big-time' designs and should avoid common mistakes such as typos, excessively large files that are slow to load, too much information and sensory overload. FragranceNet.com competes with big-time competitors with a website that clearly communicates its value proposition (designer brands at discount prices), easy navigation and superior customer service.[62]

- **Choose a domain name.** A domain name gives a company an address on the Web and a unique identity. Domain names should be chosen carefully and be easy to remember, pronounce and spell. How is a domain name selected? The crux of Miller and Zapolin's business, described above, is the simplicity of their domain names. Chocolate.com, for example, gets thousands of visitors a day from anyone keying 'chocolate' into the address line of their Web browser. There are many options for creating a domain name, including (1) using the company name (Dell.com); (2) creating a domain name that describes your product or service (seranataflowers.com); or (3) choosing a domain name that doesn't have a specific meaning and provides options for expanding (Google.com).[63]

■ **Use social media.** Social media sites, such as Facebook, Twitter and YouTube, have the potential to be powerful tools for small business owners. The benefits of using social media include gaining valuable feedback on products and services, building communities of loyal followers and promoting special events and pricing. Under the best of circumstances, loyal customers view the business as a social activity itself, making recommendations that will stream on the Facebook newsfeeds of all their friends. Facebook won't reveal how many businesses combine its core features with commerce, but more than 7 million apps and websites are integrated with the popular social network.[64] For some start-ups, social media will help them grow. For others, such as Instagram, recently purchased by Facebook, it is the basis of the business.

 ## INNOVATIVE WAY

Instagram

Crammed into a small ground-floor office in the South Park neighbourhood of San Francisco, Kevin Systrom and Mike Krieger worked tirelessly to develop a mobile app that would let people share pictures with friends. Recognizing that consumers are increasingly mobile, the two Stanford graduates wanted to design a social network built around photography. Initially, they launched Burbn, which let people post photos and other updates. Burbn only attracted a few hundred users, but they uploaded thousands of photos. So Systrom and Krieger went back to work and released a sleeker version for the iPhone, calling it Instagram.

Instagram lets people add quirky effects to their smartphone snapshots and share them with friends on Facebook and Twitter. Instagram became an immediate, out-of-nowhere Internet success. Early users posted their pictures to Twitter, which then sparked greater interest when people saw links to the photos in their feeds.

Today, Instagram has nearly a billion users. *'It's the Web fairy tale that all start-ups dream of,'* said Melissa Parrish, an analyst with Forrester Research, who added: *'They took a simple behaviour – sharing pictures with friends – and made it a utility that people want.'* In September 2012, Facebook bought Instagram for around $750 million in cash and stock. Buying Instagram helps Facebook with one of its most urgent needs – making its service more appealing on smartphones. *'It's easier to update Facebook when you're on the go with a snapshot rather than with text,'* says Rebecca Lieb of the Altimeter Group.[65]

REFLECTION

- The most common way to become an entrepreneur is to create a new business based on a marketable idea.
- The advantage of building a business from scratch is that the entrepreneur is solely responsible for its success; a potential drawback is the time required to make the business profitable.
- An entrepreneur may also choose to buy an existing business, shortening the time required to get started.
- **Franchising** is an arrangement by which the owner of a product or service allows others to purchase the right to distribute the product or service with help from the owner.
- **Business incubators** help start-up companies by connecting them with a range of experts and mentors who nurture them, thus increasing their likelihood of success.
- The steps in starting an online business include finding a market niche, creating a professional website, choosing a domain name and using social media.

Managing a growing business

Once an entrepreneurial business is up and running, how does the owner manage it? Often the traits of self-confidence, creativity and internal locus of control lead to financial and personal grief as the enterprise grows. A hands-on entrepreneur who gave birth to the organization loves perfecting every detail. But after the start-up, continued growth requires a shift in management style. Those who fail to adjust to a growing business can be the cause of the problems rather than the solution.[66] In this section, we look at the stages through which entrepreneurial companies move and then consider how managers should carry out their planning, organizing, decision-making and controlling.

Stages of growth

Entrepreneurial businesses go through distinct stages of growth, with each stage requiring different management skills. The five stages are illustrated in Exhibit 10.10.

1 *Start-up*. In this stage, the main challenges include funding the business and adjusting the product or service in response to market demands. For example, technology entrepreneurs may cycle through several ideas for a new business idea before ultimately landing on the one that takes off. Because it's relatively cheap and easy to tinker with software and create new products, Internet businesses frequently pivot, which means to change the strategic direction of the business. '*Pivot to me is not a four-letter word*,' says Tony Conrad, a partner in the early-stage venture capital firm True Ventures. '*It represents some of the best methodology that the Valley has invented. Starting something, determining it's not working, and then leveraging aspects of that technology is extremely powerful.*'[67]

2 *Survival*. At this stage, the business demonstrates that it is a workable business entity. It produces a product or service and has sufficient customers. Concerns here involve finances – generating sufficient cash flow to run the business and making sure that revenues exceed expenses. The organization will grow in size and profitability during this period. At this critical stage, businesses must sustain their early momentum and chart a course for long-term success. Foursquare, a mobile app that lets people share their locations with friends, has nearly 1 million new users each month, yet has failed to generate income. To reach the next stage, Foursquare needs to continuously innovate, appeal to the ever-changing demands of the mobile consumer and find ways to bring in revenues.[68]

EXHIBIT 10.10 Five stages of growth for an entrepreneurial company

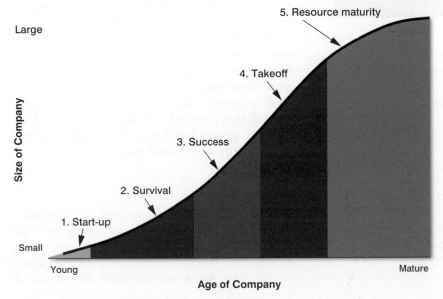

SOURCE: Neil C. Churchill and Virginia L. Lewis, 'The Five Stages of Small Business Growth', *Harvard Business Review* (May–June 1993): 30–50.

3   *Success.* At this point, the company is solidly based and profitable. Systems and procedures are in place to allow the founder to slow down if desired. Another choice the founder needs to make is whether to stay involved or turn the business over to professional managers. In making this decision, the founder who led the charge during the early years of development may confront 'the paradox of entrepreneurial success'. Although entrepreneurs possess the passion needed to build the business, they may have the wrong set of skills for the next stage of development. Research shows that for founders who hang onto the CEO position, their own personal equity stake is worth half as much as if they give up control to a new CEO with the skill set to grow the value of the business.[69]

4   *Takeoff.* Here the key problem is how to grow rapidly and finance that growth. The owner must learn to delegate, and the company must find sufficient capital to invest in major growth. This period is crucial in an entrepreneurial company's life. Properly managed, the company can become a big business.

5   *Resource maturity.* At this stage, the company's substantial financial gains may come at the cost of losing its advantages of small size, including flexibility and the entrepreneurial spirit. To keep that entrepreneurial spirit alive during the maturity stage, many companies fuel innovation through investments in research and development. Google, for example, spent $11.8 billion on research and development in the 3 years up to 2012. Managing a massive organization while stimulating continuous innovation is often the most challenging stage for any company.[70]

 CONCEPT CONNECTION

In 1999, Luis Brandwayn, Jochen Fischer and Troy McConnell co-founded Batanga.com, a Hispanic online media company. McConnell is shown here in Batanga's original offices in the Nussbaum Center for Entrepreneurship **business incubator** in Greensboro, North Carolina. Initially, Batanga streamed audio and video online aimed at a Spanish-speaking audience. Its 2005 merger with Planeta Networks of Miami, a broadband platform supplier, propelled it into the **take-off stage of growth**. Now based in Coral Gables, Florida, it has continued its rapid growth by partnering with iTunes, raising $30 million in equity funding, and acquiring both LatCom Communications, a publishing and events company, and advertising network HispanoClick.

Planning

In the early start-up stage, formal planning tends to be non-existent except for the business plan described earlier in this chapter. The primary goal is simply to remain alive. As the organization grows, formal planning usually is not instituted until the success stage. Recall from Chapter 1 that planning means defining goals and deciding on the tasks and use of resources needed to attain them. Chapters 7, 8 and 9 describe how entrepreneurs can define goals and implement strategies and plans to meet them. It is important that entrepreneurs view their original business plan as a living document that evolves as the company grows, the market changes, or both.

One planning concern for today's small businesses is the need to plan and allocate resources for Internet operations from the beginning and grow those plans as the company grows. Of the small companies that have websites, more than half say that the site has broken even or paid for itself in greater efficiency, improved customer relationships or increased business.[71]

Organizing

In the first two stages of growth, the organization's structure is typically informal, with all employees reporting to the owner. At about stage 3 – success – functional managers often are hired to take over duties performed by the owner. A functional organization structure will begin to evolve with managers in charge of finance, manufacturing and marketing. Another organizational approach is to use outsourcing, as described earlier. Method, a company launched by two 20-something entrepreneurs to develop a line of non-toxic cleaning products in fresh scents and stylish packaging, contracted with an industrial designer for its unique dish soap bottle and uses contract manufacturers in every region of the country to rapidly make products and get them to stores.[72]

During the latter stages of entrepreneurial growth, managers must learn to delegate and decentralize authority. If the business has multiple product lines, the owner may consider creating teams or divisions responsible for each line. The organization must hire competent managers and have sufficient management talent to handle fast growth and eliminate problems caused by increasing size. As an organization grows, it might also be characterized by greater use of rules, procedures and written job descriptions.

Decision-making

When managing a growing business, owners face a multitude of decisions that affect the organization's performance. These decisions may include determining inventory levels, hiring new employees, choosing a domain name for a website or expanding into a new market. Every decision has the potential to alter the direction and success of the business. Paul Downs, who founded Paul Downs Cabinetmakers in 1986, confronts difficult decisions on a daily basis. With each decision, he considers alternatives, makes choices and then follows up with necessary actions. Sometimes the decisions are easy to make. Others require careful consideration on how to best allocate limited resources. Consider the following examples of decisions that Downs has had to make:

- Should I buy a sander that will decrease production time, or use that money to give my staff a 5 per cent bonus?

- Do I purchase and move into a new building or renew my current lease that comes up next year?

- What are the risks of outsourcing work to Dubai, where I can hire ten workers for the price of one US employee?

- How can I create a learning organization where workers are improving work processes constantly?

- Should I upgrade our database and customer files from an ageing server and move everything to cloud computing?[73]

Several models that can help managers make better decisions were discussed in Chapter 9.

Controlling

Financial control is important in each stage of the entrepreneurial firm's growth. In the initial stages, control is exercised by simple accounting records and by personal supervision. By stage 3 – success – operational budgets are in place, and the owner should start implementing more structured control systems. During the takeoff stage, the company will need to make greater use of budgets and standard cost systems and use computer systems to provide statistical reports. These control techniques will become more sophisticated during the resource maturity stage.

REFLECTION

- Small businesses generally proceed through five stages of growth: start-up, survival, success, takeoff and resource maturity.
- In the start-up stage, Internet businesses frequently **pivot**, which means to change the strategic direction of the business.

- The management activities of planning, organizing, decision-making and controlling should be tailored to each stage of growth.

As Amazon grew and expanded internationally, for example, entrepreneur and CEO Jeff Bezos needed increasingly sophisticated control mechanisms. Bezos hired a computer systems expert to develop a system to track and control all the company's operations.[74] Control is more fully discussed online in Chapter 16 and the Appendix.

DISCUSSION QUESTIONS

1 Identify and discuss the four major risks for an undergraduate to evaluate *before* entering a new start-up upon his/her graduation.

2 What is the importance of writing a clear business plan at the start of a new venture? Give examples of what might be needed in a business plan for a new technology company.

3 Identify and discuss the major barriers preventing the launch of a new business venture.

4 How might you approach buying a franchise differently to starting your own business from scratch? What are the different considerations you would need to bear in mind?

5 'The most successful entrepreneurs *tend* to have special personality characteristics.' Provide a set of desirable entrepreneurial characteristics that facilitate business success, for class discussion.

6 Do you think entrepreneurs who launched a new business after deciding to leave a job on their own versus those who have been forced to leave a job as a result of downsizing are likely to have different traits? Which group is likely to succeed in your opinion?

Do you think like an entrepreneur?[75]

INSTRUCTIONS An entrepreneur faces many demands. Do you have the proclivity to start and build your own business? To find out, consider the extent to which each of the following statements characterizes your behaviour. Please answer each of the following items as 'Mostly true' or 'Mostly false' for you.

		Mostly true	Mostly false
1	Give me a little information and I can come up with a lot of ideas.	☐	☐
2	I like pressure in order to focus.	☐	☐
3	I don't get easily frustrated when things don't go my way.	☐	☐
4	I identify how resources can be recombined to produce novel outcomes.	☐	☐
5	I enjoy competing against the clock to meet deadlines.	☐	☐
6	People in my life have to accept that nothing is more important than the achievement of my school, my sport or my career goals.	☐	☐
7	I serve as a role model for creativity.	☐	☐
8	I think 'on my feet' when carrying out tasks.	☐	☐
9	I am determined and action-oriented.	☐	☐

SCORING & INTERPRETATION Each question pertains to some aspect of improvisation, which is a correlate of entrepreneurial intentions. Entrepreneurial improvisation consists of three elements. Questions 1, 4 and 7 pertain to creativity and ingenuity, the ability to produce novel solutions under constrained conditions. Questions 2, 5 and 8 pertain to working under pressure and stress, the ability to excel in pressure-filled circumstances. Questions 3, 6 and 9 pertain to action and persistence, the determination to achieve goals and solve problems in the moment. If you answered 'Mostly true' to at least two of three questions for each subscale, or six of all the nine questions, then consider yourself an entrepreneur in the making, with the potential to manage your own business. If you scored one or fewer 'Mostly true' on each subscale or three or fewer for all nine questions, you might want to consider becoming a manager by working for someone else.

APPLY YOUR SKILLS: ETHICAL DILEMMA

Closing the deal[76]

As the new, heavily recruited CEO of a high-technology start-up, backed by several of Silicon Valley's leading venture capitalists, Chuck Campbell is flying high – great job, good salary, stock options and a chance to be in on the ground floor and build one of the truly great twenty-first-century organizations. Just a few days into the job, Chuck participated in a presentation to a new group of potential investors for funding that could help the company expand marketing, improve its services and invest in growth. By the end of the meeting, the investors had verbally committed $16 million in funding.

But things turned sour pretty fast. As Chuck was leaving about 9 pm, the corporate controller, Betty Mars, who had just returned from an extended leave, cornered him. He was surprised to find her working so late, but before he could even open his mouth, Betty blurted out her problem: The numbers that Chuck had presented to the venture capitalists were flawed. 'The assumptions behind the revenue growth plan are absolutely untenable,' she said. 'Not a chance of ever happening.' Chuck was stunned. He told Betty to go home and he'd stay and take a look at the figures.

At 11 pm, Chuck was still sitting in his office wondering what to do. His research showed that the numbers were indeed grossly exaggerated, but most of them were at least statistically possible (however remote that possibility was!). However, what really troubled him was that the renewal income figure was just flat-out false – and it was clear that one member of the management team who participated in the presentation knew that it was incorrect all along. To make matters worse, it was the renewal income figure that ultimately had made the investment so attractive to the venture capital firm. Chuck knew what was at stake – no less than the life or death of the company itself. If he told the truth about the deceptive numbers, the company's valuation would almost certainly be slashed and the $16 million possibly cancelled. On the other hand, if he didn't come clean now, the numbers didn't pan out, and the investors found out later that he knew about the flawed numbers, the company could be ruined.

What would you do?

1   Say nothing about the false numbers. Of course, the company will miss the projections and have to come up with a good explanation, but, after all, isn't that par for the course among fledgling high-tech companies? Chances are, the whole thing will blow over without a problem.

2   Go ahead and close the deal, but come clean later. Explain that the controller had been on an extended leave of absence, and because you had been on the job only a few days, you had not had time to do an analysis of the numbers yourself.

3   Take swift action to notify the venture capitalists of the truth of the situation – and start cleaning house to get rid of people who would knowingly lie to close a deal.

APPLY YOUR SKILLS: CASE FOR CRITICAL ANALYSIS

Business start ups: The role of governments and managers

Comprehensive approaches by government bodies often provide core services of business information, and advice on start-ups and business growth. This is backed up with targeted support including e-business, technology and innovation, skills and finance. And there is built-in flexibility for discretionary services at a local level. The aim is to provide high quality, easily accessible services – and an end to the duplication between different public agencies.

■ **Entrepreneurship** is a mind set seeking new opportunities which can be turned into sustained business growth. Entrepreneurs are those who seek to generate value through the creation or expansion of economic activity by identifying and exploiting new products, processes or markets.

■ **Innovation** is the process by which ideas can be turned into new or significantly improved products, services or business processes. While products and services vary widely, the innovation process requires creativity and connectivity between customers, suppliers, financiers and other partners.

To succeed, businesses need both these elements: entrepreneurs who can identify real market opportunities and the innovative skills to translate a good idea into a marketable product. Government's role is often to provide the supportive environment in which such businesses can succeed and accelerate economic growth.

The ability of businesses to grow and be successful will depend upon:

1 A diverse, robust and adaptive business base, where all businesses are important and some are truly world class.

2 A skilled, educated and adaptable workforce.

3 An ability to secure a competitive advantage from utilizing natural and energy resources more efficiently.

4 A research and business base that supports commercialization and innovation.

5 A culture of entrepreneurship, leadership, creativity and international ambition.

6 Attractive well-connected places to live and work that build on a country's natural assets in terms of cities, towns and rural areas.

7 A robust and reliable physical and digital infrastructure that helps businesses grow and compete internationally.

8 A competitive tax regime.

9 Effective and efficient public services that promote competition and help businesses thrive.

10 An effective justice system which supports the rule of law, protects communities and individuals, reduces the cost of crime, safeguards economic activity, and promotes equality and fairness

Any increase in the business stock is a good indicator of an active entrepreneurship climate in the economy. Also, competition drives innovation, efficiency and quality improvements thereby improving productivity. The number of businesses in (stock) reflects a combination of both the numbers of new businesses created (start-ups) and the survival of existing businesses. A strong private sector is essential for economic growth and wealth creation, and small businesses – which account for 98 per cent of all enterprises – create vital jobs and are often the lifeblood of local communities. That's why a fundamental aim of government is to improve the business creation, sustainability and growth of small businesses.

The provision of good quality support and assistance will remain crucial. The exposure of students in further and higher education to entrepreneurship and the enterprise experience will increase the prospect of graduates forming new businesses and introducing new products and ideas to the marketplace. All business development and business start-up is important to an economy. The focus of a government's entrepreneurship and innovation framework, however, is often on those businesses and business ideas which have the greatest potential for growth, internationalization and economic benefit.

The Business Growth fund (BGF) provides long-term capital for fast growing British companies. Since its launch in May 2011 it has made over 60 investments, providing more than £300m of new capital to UK enterprises. The BGF provides growth capital to take successful small- and medium-sized businesses to the next level, helping to boost the rate of their growth without asking the owners to give away large parts of the company they have worked hard to build. BGF provides business owners in the scheme with support to grow their company and a highly experienced business person to sit on the board.

Reference: www.businessgrowthfund.co.uk

Questions

1 Explain why governments should support business creation, sustainability and growth of small businesses.

2 Of the ten suggestions which impact on the ability of businesses to grow and be successful, which are more important?

3 Discuss the distinctive features of managing a small business start-up.

END NOTES

1. Scott Adams, 'How to Get a Real Education', *The Wall Street Journal*, April 9–10, 2011, C1.
2. US Small Business Administration, www.sba.gov/content/entrepreneurship-you-0 (accessed August 6, 2012).
3. Donald F. Kuratko and Richard M. Hodgetts, *Entrepreneurship: A Contemporary Approach,* 4th ed. (Fort Worth, TX: The Dryden Press, 1998), p. 30.
4. Study conducted by Yankelovich Partners, reported in Mark Henricks, 'Type-Cast', *Entrepreneur* (March 2000): 14–16.
5. Susan Polis Schutz, 'Poetry and a Pickup Truck', *The New York Times*, March 3, 2012, www.nytimes.com/2012/03/04/jobs/blue-mountain-arts-chief-on-how-the-business-began.html?_r=1&pagewanted=print (accessed August 6, 2012).
6. John A. Byrne, 'The 12 Greatest Entrepreneurs of Our Time', *Fortune* (April 9, 2012): 67–86; 'Asia 200: Infosys Tops India's Most Admired Companies', *The Wall Street Journal Asia Online,* November 2, 2010, www.online.wsj.com/article/SB100014240527023041737045755776836132563 68.html (accessed October 2, 2012); and 'Asia 200 Interactive', *The Wall Street Journal Online,* www.online.wsj.com/article/SB10001424052702304410504575559363431123480.html (accessed October 2, 2012).
7. Donna J. Kelley, Slavica Singer and Mike Herrington, *Global Entrepreneurship Monitor 2011 Executive Report,* July 26, 2012, www.gemconsortium.org/docs/2409/gem-2011-global-report (accessed October 9, 2012).
8. 'Moving America's Small Businesses & Entrepreneurs Forward: Creating an Economy Built to Last', *National Economic Council* (May 2012), www.whitehouse.gov/sites/default/files/docs/small_business_report_05_16_12.pdf (accessed August 7, 2012).
9. Major L. Clark, III and Radwan N. Saade, Office of Advocacy US Small Business Administration, September 2010, www.archive.sba.gov/advo/research/rs372tot.pdf (accessed August 6, 2012).
10. U.S. Small Business Administration, www.sba.gov/advo/stats/sbfaq.pdf (accessed August 7, 2012).
11. Jon Swartz, 'Google, Amazon, Facebook Put Start-ups on Fast Track', *USA Today,* February 22, 2011, www.google.com/search?sourceid=navclient&aq=4&oq=google+amazon&ie=UTF-8&rlz=1T4ADRA_enUS426US427&q=google+amazon+facebook+put+startups+on+fast+track&gs_upl=0l0l0l5065lllllllllll0&aqi=g4s1&pbx=1 (accessed August 7, 2012).
12. Research and statistics reported in 'The Job Factory', *Inc.* (May 29, 2001): 40–43.
13. Ian Mount, 'The Return of the Lone Inventor', *Fortune Small Business* (March 2005): 18; Magnus Aronsson, 'Education Matters – But Does Entrepreneurship Education? An Interview with David Birch', *Academy of Management Learning and Education* 3, no. 3 (2004): 289–292; Office of Advocacy, U.S. Small Business Administration, www.sba.gov/advo/stats/sbfaq.pdf (accessed August 19, 2010).
14. John Case, 'The Origins of Entrepreneurship', *Inc.* (June 1989): 51–53.
15. Dinah Wisenberg Brin, 'Franchises a Draw for Minority Entrepreneurs', *Entrepreneur*, December 22, 2011, www.entrepreneur.com/blog/222525 (accessed August 8, 2012).
16. 'Small Business Ambassador', *Fortune Small Business* (February 2007): 28; and 'Salvador Guzman Buys Second AM Radio Station', July 8, 2009, www.hispanicnashville.com/2009/07/salvador-guzman-buys-second-am-radio.html (accessed October 9, 2012).
17. U.S. Census Bureau, www.factfinder2.census.gov/faces/tableservices/jsf/pages/productview.xhtml?pid=SBO_2007_00CSA01&prodType=table (accessed August 8, 2012).
18. Mickey Meece, 'One in Four Businesses Calls the Owner "Ma"am,"' *The New York Times* (November 5, 2009), www.nytimes.com/2009/11/05/business/smallbusiness/05sbiz.html?scp=1&sq=one%20in%20four%20businesses%20calls%20the%20owner%20maam&st=Search (accessed November 4, 2009).
19. Claire Cain Miller, 'Out of the Loop in the Silicon Valley', *The New York Times,* April 16, 2010, www.dealbook.blogs.nytimes.com/2010/04/19/out-of-the-loop-in-silicon-valley/?scp=1&sq=OUT%20OF%20THE%20LOOP%20IN%20SILICON%20VALLEY&st=Search (accessed June 1, 2010).
20. This discussion is based in part on Charles R. Kuehl and Peggy A. Lambing, *Small Business: Planning and Management,* 3d ed. (Ft. Worth, TX: The Dryden Press, 1994).
21. Leigh Buchanan, 'The Motivation Matrix', *Inc.*, March 2012, www.inc.com/magazine/201203/motivation-matrix.html (accessed August 20, 2012).
22. Quoted in Jessica Bruder, 'A Harvard Professor Analyzes Why Start-Ups Fail', *The New York Times*, May 25, 2012, www.boss.blogs.nytimes.com/2012/05/25/a-harvard-professor-analyzes-why-start-ups-fail/ (accessed August 9, 2012).

23. Brian X. Chen, 'Crammed Into Cheap Bunks, Dreaming of Future Digital Glory', *The New York Times*, July 5, 2012, www.nytimes.com/2012/07/06/technology/at-hacker-hostels-living-on-the-cheap-and-dreaming-of-digital-glory.html?pagewanted=all (accessed August 9, 2012).

24. Byrne, 'The 12 Greatest Entrepreneurs of Our Time'.

25. Reported in 'Crunching the Numbers: Work-Life Balance', *Inc.* (July–August, 2011): 30.

26. Melissa S. Cardon, Joakim Wincent, Jagdip Singh and Mateja Drnsovek, 'The Nature and Experience of Entrepreneurial Passion', *Academy of Management Review* 34, no. 3 (2009): 511–532.

27. Quote from www.evancarmichael.com.

28. Byrne, 'The 12 Greatest Entrepreneurs of Our Time'.

29. David C. McClelland, *The Achieving Society* (New York: Van Nostrand, 1961).

30. Quote from www.evancarmichael.com.

31. Paulette Thomas, 'Entrepreneurs' Biggest Problems – and How They Solve Them', *The Wall Street Journal*, March 17, 2003.

32. M. Tina Dacin, Peter A. Dacin and Paul Tracey, 'Social Entrepreneurship: A Critique and Future Directions', *Organization Science* 22, no. 5 (September–October 2011): 1203–1213.

33. Byrne, 'The 12 Greatest Entrepreneurs of Our Time'.

34. Steven Prokesch, 'The Reluctant Social Entrepreneur', *Harvard Business Review* (June 2011): 124 – 126.

35. Leslie Brokaw, 'How to Start an *Inc.* 500 Company', *Inc.* 500 (1994): 51–65.

36. Lottie L. Joiner, 'How to Work Full-time While Launching a Business, Spanx', *USA Today*, June 25, 2011, www.usatoday.com/money/smallbusiness/2011-07-22-work-full-time-and-launch-small-business_n.htm (accessed August 13, 2012).

37. Paul Reynolds, 'The Truth About Start-ups', *Inc.* (February 1995): 23; Brian O'Reilly, 'The New Face of Small Businesses', *Fortune* (May 2, 1994): 82–88.

38. Based on Ellyn E. Spragins, 'Venture Capital Express: How to Write a Business Plan That Will Get You in the Door', *Small Business Success,* November 1,1990, www.inc.com/magazine/19901101/5472.html (accessed August 18, 2010); Linda Elkins, 'Tips for Preparing a Business Plan', *Nation's Business* (June 1996): 60R–61R; Carolyn M. Brown, 'The Do's and Don'ts of Writing a Winning Business Plan', *Black Enterprise* (April 1996): 114–116; and Kuratko and Hodgetts, *Entrepreneurship,* pp. 295–397. For a clear, thorough, step-by-step guide to writing an effective business plan, see Linda Pinson and Jerry Jinnett, *Anatomy of a Business Plan,* 5th ed. (Virginia Beach, VA: Dearborn, 2001).

39. The INC. FAXPOLL, *Inc.* (February 1992): 24.

40. Duncan MacVicar, 'Ten Steps to a High-Tech Start-up', *The Industrial Physicist* (October 1999): 27–31.

41. 'Venture Capitalists' Criteria', *Management Review* (November 1985): 7–8.

42. 'Staples Makes Big Business from Helping Small Businesses', *SBA Success Stories,* www.sba.gov/ successstories.html (accessed March 12, 2004); and Staples website, www.staples.com/sbd/cre/marketing/about_us/index.html (accessed August 24, 2012).

43. Elizabeth Olson, 'From One Business to 23 Million', *The New York Times*, March 7, 2004, www.query.nytimes.com/gst/fullpage.html?res=9C03E6D6113FF934A35750C0A9629C8B63 (accessed July 16, 2008).

44. 'Where the Venture Money Is Going', *Business 2.0* (January–February 2004): 98.

45. Emily Glazer, 'A David and Gillette Story', *The Wall Street Journal*, April 12, 2012, www.online.wsj.com/article/SB10001424052702303624004577338103789934144.html (accessed August 14, 2012).

46. Catherine Clifford, 'Want to Raise Money With Crowdfunding? Consider These Tips', *Entrepreneur*, April 4, 2012, www.entrepreneur.com/article/223270 (accessed August 14, 2012).

47. Jenna Wortham, 'Start-ups Look to the Crowd', *The New York Times*, April 29, 2012, www.nytimes.com/2012/04/30/technology/kickstarter-sets-off-financing-rush-for-a-watch-not-yet-made.html?pagewanted=all (accessed August 14, 2012).

48. Aviva Yael, 'How We Did It', *Inc.* (September 2008): 143.

49. Wendy Lea, 'Dancing with a Partner', *Fast Company* (March 2000): 159–161.

50. James G. Combs, David J. Ketchen Jr, Christopher L. Shook and Jeremy C. Short, 'Antecedents and Consequences of Franchising: Past Accomplishments and Future Challenges', *Journal of Management* 37, no. 1 (January 2011): 99–126.

51. Data from 'The Franchise Business Economic Outlook: 2012', Prepared by IHS Global Insight for the International Franchising Association, www.emarket.franchise.org/2012FranchiseBusinessOutlook.pdf (accessed August 15, 2012).

52. www.entrepreneur.com/franchises/dunkindonuts/282304-0.html.

53. Sarah E. Needleman and Angus Loten, 'Fast-Food Franchises Bulking Up', *The Wall Street Journal*, April 12, 2012, www.online.wsj.com/article/SB10001424052702304587704577333443052487330.html (accessed August 15, 2012).

54. For a discussion of the risks and disadvantages of owning a franchise, see Anne Fisher, 'Risk Reward', *Fortune Small Business* (December 2005–January 2006): 44.

55. Anne Field, 'Your Ticket to a New Career? Franchising Can Put Your Skills to Work in Your Own Business', in *Business Week Investor: Small Business* section, *BusinessWeek* (May 12, 2003): 100; and Roberta Maynard, 'Choosing a Franchise', *Nation's Business* (October 1996): 56–63.

56. Darren Dahl, 'Getting Started: Percolating Profits', *Inc.* (February 2005): 38.

57. Statistics from the National Business Incubation Association, www.nbia.org/resource_library/faq/index.php#3 (accessed July 31, 2010).

58. Amy Oringel, 'Sowing Success', *Working Woman* (May 2001): 72.

59. Laura Novak, 'For Women, a Recipe to Create a Successful Business', *The New York Times*, June 23, 2007, www.nytimes.com/2007/06/23/business/smallbusiness/23cocina.html?_r=1&sq=Laura%20Novak,%20â œFor%20Women,%20a%20Recipe%20to%20Create%20a%20Successful%20Business&st=cse&adxnnl=1&oref=slogin&scp=1&adxnnlx=1225894278-APkyZ4   kswGDrm3QtejIg6A (accessed June 23, 2007).

60. Chuck Salter, 'Girl Power', *Fast Company* (September 2007): 104.

61. Aaron Pressman, 'The Domains of the Day', *BusinessWeek* (June 25, 2007): 74.

62. Ellen Reid Smith, *e-loyalty: How to Keep Customers Coming Back to Your Website* (New York: HarperBusiness, 2000), p. 19.

63. *Ibid.*, p. 127.

64. Dennis Nishi, 'Click "Like" if This Tactic Makes Sense at Start-Ups', *The Wall Street Journal,* November 14, 2011, R6.

65. Jenna Wortham, 'Facebook to Buy Photo-Sharing Service Instagram for $1 Billion', *The New York Times,* April 9, 2012, www.bits.blogs.nytimes.com/2012/04/09/facebook-acquires-photo-sharing-service-instagram/?pagewanted=print (accessed August 17, 2012); and Benny Evangelista, 'Facebook's Instagram Purchase Final', *The San Francisco Chronicle*, September 6, 2012, www.sfgate.com/technology/article/Facebook-s-Instagram-purchase-final-3845127.php (accessed September 8, 2012).

66. Carrie Dolan, 'Entrepreneurs Often Fail as Managers', *The Wall Street Journal*, May 15, 1989.

67. Lizette Chapman, "Pivoting" Pays Off for Tech Entrepreneurs, *The Wall Street Journal*, April 26, 2012, www.online.wsj.com/article/SB10001424052702303592404577364171598999252.html (accessed August 17, 2012).

68. Jenna Wortham, 'Rather Than Share Your Location, Foursquare Wants to Suggest One', *The New York Times,* June 7, 2012, www.nytimes.com/2012/06/07/technology/in-app-overhaul-foursquare-shifts-focus-to-recommendations.html (accessed August 17, 2012).

69. Jessica Bruder, 'A Harvard Professor Analyzes Why Start-Ups Fail', *The New York Times*, May 25, 2012, www.boss. blogs.nytimes.com/2012/05/25/a-harvard-professor-analyzes-why-start-ups-fail/ (accessed August 17, 2012).

70. Byrne, 'The 12 Greatest Entrepreneurs of Our Time'.

71. George Mannes, 'Don't Give Up on the Web', *Fortune* (March 5, 2001): 184[B]–184[L].

72. Bridgett Finn, 'Selling Cool in a Bottle', *Business 2.0,* December 1, 2003, www.money.cnn.com/magazines/business2/business2_archive/2003/12/01/354202/index.htm (accessed November 5, 2008).

73. Paul Downs, 'My Business Problems This Week', *The New York Times*, March 11, 2011, www.boss.blogs.nytimes.com/2011/03/11/my-business-problems-this-week/ (accessed August 20, 2012).

74. Saul Hansell, 'Listen Up! It's Time for a Profit: A Front-Row Seat as Amazon Gets Serious', *The New York Times,* May 20, 2001.

75. Based on Keith M. Hmieleski and Andrew C. Corbett, 'Proclivity for Improvisation as a Predictor of Entrepreneurial Intentions', *Journal of Small Business Management* 44, no. 1 (January 2006): 45–63; and 'Do You Have an Entrepreneurial Mind?' *Inc.com,* October 19, 2005, www.inc.com (accessed October 19, 2005).

76. Adapted from Kent Weber, 'The Truth Could Cost You $16 Million', *Business Ethics* (March–April 2001): 18.

CHAPTER 11

MANAGING CHANGE AND INNOVATION

LEARNING OBJECTIVES

After studying this chapter, you should be able to:

1 Define organizational change and explain the forces driving innovation and change in today's organizations.

2 Identify the three innovation strategies that managers implement for changing products and technologies.

3 Explain the value of creativity, a bottom-up approach, internal contests, idea incubators, idea champions and new-venture teams for innovation.

4 Describe the horizontal linkage model and how it contributes to successful product and service innovations.

5 Explain open innovation and how it is being used by today's organizations.

6 Discuss why changes in people and culture are critical to any change process.

7 Define organization development (OD) and large group interventions.

8 Explain the OD stages of unfreezing, changing and refreezing.

9 Identify sources of resistance to change and describe the implementation tactics that managers can use to overcome resistance.

Have you ever dreamed of designing vehicles, weapons or other equipment for the military? You might get a chance. The Defense Advanced Research Projects Agency (DARPA) believes that by opening up innovation to a range of participants – including small businesses, academic research labs, corporations and individual engineers – it can tap more brainpower than with the traditional defence contractor approach, while also saving time and money. The first step in this new model is a competition to see if volunteers can come up with a design for a new amphibious vehicle to replace the 1970s-era one the Marines are now using. Military leaders – and taxpayers – can hope that the competition produces a design that can be manufactured in a timely and cost-efficient way. In 2011, the military cancelled its contract on a project for a new amphibious vehicle led by General Dynamics Corporation because it concluded it would be too expensive – after spending more than $3 billion on development.[1]

The military is similar to organizations in all industries in searching for any innovation edge they can find. Companies might still be struggling through a tough economy, but smart managers know they can't let innovation take a back seat. Winning companies are continually innovating in both large and small ways. Apple once again produced a groundbreaking innovation with the launch of communications technology Siri, prompting Amazon and Google to buy technologies to provide their own similar services.[2]

If organizations don't change and innovate successfully, they die. Consider that only a small number of large companies reach the age of 40, according to a 2010 published study of more than 6 million firms. The ones that survive are ruthless about innovation and change.[3] Every organization sometimes faces the need to change swiftly and dramatically to cope with a changing environment. Consider General Motors (GM). After sinking into bankruptcy and being bailed out by the US government just a few years ago, GM amazingly regained its position as the world's largest automaker by implementing a combination of management, structure, strategy, culture and product changes.[4]

In this chapter, we look at how organizations can be designed to respond to the environment through internal change and development. First, we look at two key aspects of change in organizations: introducing new products and technologies, and changing people and culture. Then we examine how managers implement change, including overcoming resistance.

Innovation and the changing workplace

Organizational change can be defined as the adoption of a new idea or behaviour by an organization.[5] Sometimes change and innovation are spurred by forces outside the organization, such as when a powerful customer demands annual price cuts, when a key supplier goes out of business or when new government regulations go into effect. In China, for example, organizations are under pressure from the government to increase wages to help workers cope with rising food costs.[6] Managers in all types of organizations in the USA are facing a need for change to be in line with provisions of the new Patient Protection and Affordable Care Act (a health care law passed in March 2010), which was upheld by the Supreme Court as constitutional in 2012. Insurance companies will no longer be able to deny coverage based on pre-existing conditions. Small businesses will be required to provide health insurance for employees or pay penalties. State governments are evaluating options for expanding Medicaid coverage or creating new insurance exchanges where people can purchase affordable coverage. Health care providers are entering into partnerships with each other and with insurance providers to stave off financial pressures that may result from mandates and price controls.[7]

These types of outside forces compel managers to look for greater efficiencies in operations and other changes to keep their organizations profitable. Other times, managers within the company want to initiate major changes, such as forming employee-participation teams, introducing new products or instituting new training systems, but they don't know how to make the changes successful. Or do they lack the courage to implement changes?

Embracing disruptive innovation is becoming a prerequisite for companies that want to remain competitive on a global basis. Disruptive innovation refers to innovations in products, services or processes that radically change an industry's rules of the game for producers and consumers. DVDs all but wiped out the videotape industry, and now streaming video is threatening the same fate for DVDs. Digital cameras are eliminating the demand for general photographic film industry. Square, an American company based in California, has developed a credit card reader that plugs into a smartphone. This is a disruptive innovation in the trillion-dollar financial services system for credit card payments. Square has enabled millions of small businesses that couldn't afford the transaction fees charged by financial companies to begin accepting credit cards.[8] Many disruptive innovations come from small entrepreneurial firms like Square, created by Twitter's founder Jack Dorsey. Some observers believe that companies in emerging markets such as China and India will produce a great percentage of such innovations in the coming years.[9]

🔗 CONCEPT CONNECTION

Technological advances in smartphones have paved the way for mobile credit card readers from providers such as Square, Intuit GoPayment and Merchant Anywhere. This **disruptive innovation** has been a major step forwards for small business owners, allowing them to accept credit card payments on the move and with minimal transaction fees. The mobile readers are especially useful for merchants who sell their wares in outdoor environments, such as flea markets, arts and crafts fairs, and farmer's markets.

In addition, Western firms are increasingly using an approach referred to as *trickle-up innovation* or *reverse innovation*. Rather than innovating in affluent countries and transferring products to emerging markets, companies such as General Electric (GE), John Deere, Nestlé, Procter & Gamble (P&G) and Xerox are creating innovative low-cost products for emerging markets and then quickly and inexpensively repackaging them for sale in developed countries. GE Healthcare's team in China created a portable ultrasound machine that sold for less than 15 per cent of the cost of the company's high-end machines. GE now sells the product around the world, and it grew to a \$278 million global product line within 6 years. John Deere developed a high-quality, low-cost tractor for farmers in India that is increasingly in demand in the USA among farmers reeling from the recession.[10]

However, change – especially major change – is not easy, and many organizations struggle with changing successfully. In some cases, employees don't have the desire or motivation to come up with new ideas, or their ideas never get heard by managers who could put them into practice. In other cases, managers learn about good ideas but have trouble getting cooperation from employees for implementation. Successful change requires that organizations are capable of both creating and implementing ideas, which means the organization must learn to be *ambidextrous*.

An ambidextrous approach means incorporating structures and processes that are appropriate for both the creative impulse and for the systematic implementation of innovations. For example, a loose, flexible structure and greater employee freedom are excellent for the creation and initiation of ideas; however, these same conditions often make it difficult to implement a change because employees are less likely to comply. With an ambidextrous approach, managers encourage flexibility and freedom to innovate and propose new ideas with creative departments and other mechanisms we will discuss in this chapter, but they use a more rigid, centralized and standardized approach for implementing innovations.[11] For example, Mike Lawrie, CEO of the London-based software company Misys, created a separate unit for Misys Open Source Solutions, a venture aimed at creating a potentially disruptive technology in the health care industry. Lawrie wanted creative people to have the time and resources they needed to work on new software that holds the promise of seamless data exchange among hospitals, physicians, insurers and others involved in the health care system. Implementation of new ideas, where routine and precision is important, occurs within the regular organization.[12]

REFLECTION

- Every organization must change and innovate to survive.
- Organizational change is defined as the adoption of a new idea or behaviour by an organization.
- Disruptive innovation refers to innovations in products, services or processes that radically change

competition in an industry, such as the advent of streaming video or e-books.
- An ambidextrous approach means incorporating structures and processes that are appropriate for both the creative impulse and the systematic implementation of innovations.

Changing things: new products and technologies

Organizations must embrace many types of change. One vital area of innovation is the introduction of new products and technologies. A product change is a change in the organization's product or service outputs. Product and service innovation is the primary way in which organizations adapt to changes in markets, technology and competition.[13] Examples of new products include the Amazon Kindle Fire; Frigidaire's Double Oven Range, which fits two ovens in the space of a standard 76 cm appliance; and the Yonanas countertop blender, which transforms frozen bananas into an ice-cream-like treat.[14] HBO Go, the first comprehensive mobile television service, is an example of a service innovation, as is the launch of online programmes for undergraduate and graduate education. Southern New Hampshire University (SNHU) zoomed to number 12 on *Fast Company's* list of the world's 50 most innovative companies due to managers' creative reinvention of online education. SNHU president Paul LeBlanc hired the former CEO of an online customer relationship company to retool the college's operations in the style of Zappos.com, to provide exceptional customer service. And he didn't stop there. '*We want to create the business model that blows up our current business model, because if we don't, someone else will,*' LeBlanc said.[15]

Product and service changes are related to changes in the technology of the organization. A technology change is a change in the organization's production process – how the organization does its work. Technology changes are designed to make the production of a product or service more efficient. Examples of technology change include the introduction of efficiency-boosting winglets on aircraft at Southwest Airlines, the adoption of automatic mail-sorting machines by the US Postal Service, and the use of biosimulation software to run virtual tests on new drugs at Johnson & Johnson pharmaceutical research and development. British Airways and Virgin Atlantic are developing biofuels as substitutes for kerosene for their jets to use in the future.

Three critical innovation strategies for changing products and technologies are illustrated in Exhibit 11.1.[16] The first strategy, *exploration*, involves designing the organization to encourage creativity and the initiation of new ideas. The strategy of *cooperation* refers to creating conditions and systems to facilitate internal and external coordination and knowledge sharing. Finally, *innovation roles* means that managers put in place processes and structures to ensure that new ideas are carried forward for acceptance and implementation.

GREEN POWER

Building a better mouse . . .

We all have them: old laptops stuffed into closets, BlackBerry's, computer monitors, hard drives and printers crammed into the corners of the garage. And who can forget the mouse (five of them, actually, still attached to cords) jammed into a drawer? In a world focused on sustainability, the challenge for managers in the electronics industry is how to change and innovate when the large outer casings for our products *won't* go away. **Fujitsu** broke this barrier by developing a keyboard made from renewable materials. A year

later, using organic materials as a substitute for plastic, the company unveiled a mouse casing that was 100 per cent biodegradable. Now, the race is on. Fujitsu's innovations offer a visionary promise that one day, all our electronic devices will be part of the sustainability revolution. Increasingly, governments in the developed world are legislating for recyclability of electrical components to be a requirement of the product design.

SOURCE: Staff writers, 'Fujitsu Unveils "World's First" Biodegradable Mouse', *Business Green*, January 25, 2011, www.businessgreen.com/bg/news/1939343/fujitsu-unveils-worlds-biodegradable-mouse (accessed January 25, 2011).

TAKE A MOMENT

Assess your creativity by completing the New Manager Self-Test.

EXHIBIT 11.1 Three innovation strategies for new products and technologies

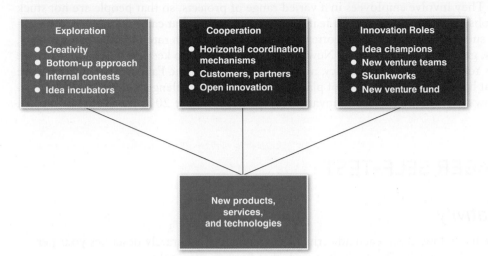

Exploration	Cooperation	Innovation Roles
● Creativity ● Bottom-up approach ● Internal contests ● Idea incubators	● Horizontal coordination mechanisms ● Customers, partners ● Open innovation	● Idea champions ● New venture teams ● Skunkworks ● New venture fund

New products, services, and technologies

SOURCE: Patrick Reinmoeller and Nicole van Baardwijk, 'The Link Between Diversity and Resilience', *MIT Sloan Management Review* (Summer 2005): 61–65.

CONCEPT CONNECTION

Innovative companies such as Intuit want everyone to be continually coming up with new ideas. Managers encourage **creativity** during the **exploration phase** by embracing failure as readily as they do success. *'I've had my share of really bad ideas,'* founder Scott Cook, pictured here with former CEO Steve Bennett, admits. Yet failure can have hidden possibilities. Sticky notes, such as those shown here on Intuit's board, were invented at 3M Corporation based on a failed product – a not-very-sticky adhesive that resulted from a chemist's attempts to create a superglue. Post-it Notes subsequently became one of the best-selling office products ever.

Exploration

Exploration is the stage where ideas for new products and technologies are born. Managers design the organization for exploration by establishing conditions that encourage creativity and allow new ideas to spring forth. Creativity is the generation of novel ideas that might meet perceived needs or respond to opportunities for the organization. People noted for their creativity include Thomas Edison who invented the electric light bulb and Swiss engineer George de Mestral, who created Velcro after noticing the tiny hooks on some burrs caught on his wool socks. These people saw unique and creative opportunities in familiar situations. They are sometimes described as a Eureka moment, but they can be the result of sustained experimentation.

Characteristics of highly creative people are illustrated in the left column of Exhibit 11.2. Creative people often are known for originality, open-mindedness, curiosity, a focused approach to problem solving, persistence, a relaxed and playful attitude, and receptiveness to new ideas.[17] Creativity can also be designed into organizations. Most companies want more creative employees and often seek to hire creative individuals. However, the individual is only part of the story, and each of us has some potential for creativity. Managers are responsible for creating a work environment that allows creativity to flourish.[18]

The characteristics of creative organizations correspond to those of individuals, as illustrated in the right column of Exhibit 11.2. Creative organizations are loosely structured. People find themselves in a situation of ambiguity, assignments are vague, territories overlap, tasks are loosely defined and much work is done by teams. Managers in creative companies embrace risk and experimentation. They involve employees in a varied range of projects, so that people are not stuck in the rhythm of routine jobs, and they drive out the fear of making mistakes that can inhibit creative thinking.[19] Research shows that successful innovations are often accompanied by a high rate of failure. SurePayroll, a payroll-services company, gives out an annual 'Best New Mistake' cash award to keep people taking creative risks. Similarly, Grey New York, an advertising agency, awards an annual 'Heroic Failure' trophy.[20] Creative organizations are those that have an internal culture of playfulness, freedom, challenge and grass-roots participation.[21] Exhibit 11.3 shows the world's top ten innovative companies from the 2012 list in Fast Company.

 NEW MANAGER SELF-TEST

Assess your creativity

INSTRUCTIONS In the list below, check each adjective that you believe accurately describes your personality. Be very honest with yourself. Check all the words that fit your personality.

1 affected___	11 honest___	21 original___
2 capable___	12 humorous___	22 reflective___
3 cautious___	13 individualistic___	23 resourceful___
4 clever___	14 informal___	24 self-confident___
5 commonplace___	15 insightful___	25 sexy___
6 confident___	16 intelligent___	26 snobbish___
7 conservative___	17 interests narrow___	27 sincere___
8 conventional___	18 interests wide___	28 submissive___
9 egotistical___	19 inventive___	29 suspicious___
10 dissatisfied___	20 mannerly___	30 unconventional___

SCORING & INTERPRETATION Add one point for checking each of the following words: 2, 4, 6, 9, 12, 13, 14, 15, 16, 18, 19, 21, 22, 23, 24, 25, 26 and 30. Subtract one point for checking each of the following words: 1, 3, 5, 7, 8, 10, 11, 17, 20, 27, 28 and 29. Score = ___. The highest possible score is +18; the lowest possible score is –12.

Innovation starts with creativity. Your score on this questionnaire reflects your creativity for solving problems and finding novel solutions. The average score for a set of 256 males on this creativity scale was 3.57, and for 126 females was 4.4. A group of 45 male research scientists and a group of 530 male psychology graduate students both had average scores of 6.0, and 124 male architects received an average score of 5.3. A group of 335 female psychology students had an average score of 3.34. If you have a score above 5.0, your personality would be considered above average in creativity. To what extent do you think your score reflects your true creativity? Compare your score to others in your class. Which adjectives were more important for your score compared to other students?

SOURCE: Harrison G. Clough, 'A Creative Personality Scale for the Adjective Check List', *Journal of Personality and Social Psychology* 37, no. 8 (1979): 1398–1405.

EXHIBIT 11.2 Characteristics of creative people and organizations

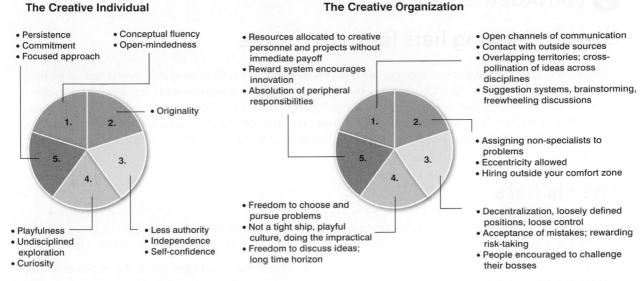

The Creative Individual

- Persistence
- Commitment
- Focused approach

- Conceptual fluency
- Open-mindedness

- Originality

- Playfulness
- Undisciplined exploration
- Curiosity

- Less authority
- Independence
- Self-confidence

The Creative Organization

- Resources allocated to creative personnel and projects without immediate payoff
- Reward system encourages innovation
- Absolution of peripheral responsibilities

- Open channels of communication
- Contact with outside sources
- Overlapping territories; cross-pollination of ideas across disciplines
- Suggestion systems, brainstorming, freewheeling discussions

- Assigning non-specialists to problems
- Eccentricity allowed
- Hiring outside your comfort zone

- Freedom to choose and pursue problems
- Not a tight ship, playful culture, doing the impractical
- Freedom to discuss ideas; long time horizon

- Decentralization, loosely defined positions, loose control
- Acceptance of mistakes; rewarding risk-taking
- People encouraged to challenge their bosses

SOURCES: Gary A. Steiner, ed., *The Creative Organization* (Chicago: University of Chicago Press, 1965): 16–18; Rosabeth Moss Kanter, 'The Middle Manager as Innovator', *Harvard Business Review* (July–August 1982): 104–105; James Brian Quinn, 'Managing Innovation: Controlled Chaos', *Harvard Business Review* (May–June 1985): 73–84; Robert I. Sutton, 'The Weird Rules of Creativity', *Harvard Business Review* (September 2001): 94–103; and Bridget Finn, 'Playbook: Brainstorming for Better Brainstorming', *Business* 2.0 (April 2005), 109–114.

Innovative companies can use a bottom-up approach, which means *encouraging the flow of ideas from lower levels and making sure they get heard and acted upon by top executives.*[22] At Intuit, managers sponsor Design for Delight (D4D) forums, typically attended by more than 1000 employees. Two employees who had been at Intuit for only a few months came up with the idea of an online social network for the D4D initiative. In the first year, the network generated 32 ideas that made it to market.[23] Japanese pharmaceutical firm Eisai Company encourages a bottom-up flow of ideas with innovation community forums that focus on specific health-care-related issues. One idea now on the market in Japan is technology for dispensing medications in a jellylike substance that Alzheimer's patients can swallow easily.[24] This chapter's Shoptalk describes a fun technique some companies use to get people to come up with creative ideas for solving specific problems.

EXHIBIT 11.3 The world's most innovative companies 2012

Rank	Company	Reason
1	Apple	Creating markets others have to compete in
2	Facebook	Ever-widening platform for people to share information
3	Google	Transforming from search to a diversified Web power
4	Amazon	Constantly transforming itself
5	Square	Reinventing the process of making and taking credit payments
6	Twitter	Strengthening global dialogue
7	The Occupy Movement	Challenging the political, financial and social establishment
8	Tencent	Advancing China's Internet boom
9	Life Technologies	Products that speed up genetic sequencing
10	SolarCity	Being a full-service provider of new solar technology

SOURCE: 'The World's 50 Most Innovative Companies', *Fast Company* (March 2012): 70–149.

MANAGER'S SHOPTALK

Use six thinking hats for better ideas

A lateral thinking technique that can promote broader thinking is called the *six thinking hats,* which was developed by Edward de Bono. The model encourages people in a group to combine negative and critical thinking with positive and creative thinking. Participants either literally or figuratively wear a hat to represent a distinct perspective. The wearing of the hats helps individuals step out of their comfort zone and generate creative ideas in a risk-free way. The six hats technique can transform a typical non-productive meeting into a highly creative problem-solving endeavour.

The six hats

- *White hat:* This hat is neutral and concerned with just the objective facts, figures and information pertaining to a problem.

- *Red hat:* This hat allows an emotional response to the subject. It is a perspective based on feelings, intuitions, instincts and hunches.

- *Green hat:* The green hat is the one that generates new ideas, possibilities, alternatives and unique solutions for better problem solving.

- *Black hat:* This is the negative, pessimistic and critical hat that focuses on why a suggestion will

not work. When people wear this hat, they point out the flaws and false assumptions in an idea.

- *Yellow hat:* The yellow hat is the opposite of the black hat. It is optimistic and focuses on the values and benefits of an idea. Its focus is on what *will* work.

- *Blue hat:* This hat is concerned with group facilitation. The group leader typically assumes the blue hat role, although any member can wear the blue hat from time to time.

Using the technique

To apply the six hats technique, schedule a specific time during a creative problem-solving meeting when every person in the group wears the same colour of hat – that is, takes the same perspective. A time is set aside when everyone uses rational, fact-based thinking (white hat), emotional thinking (red hat), creative thinking (green hat), and so forth. The result is that each

perspective (hat) is heard in sequence, and negative views or arguments do not overwhelm creativity. Everyone together has a time to think of good ideas, as well as a time for finding weak points.

SOURCE: Edward de Bono, *Serious Creativity: Using the Power of Lateral Thinking to Create New Ideas* (New York: HarperBusiness, 1992).

Some companies also use internal *innovation contests*. Managers at the accounting and consulting firm PricewaterhouseCoopers challenged the stereotype that accountants are boring and unimaginative by sponsoring an *American Idol*-style contest to spur employees to come up with creative ideas.

Just as important as creating ideas is turning them into action. Sadly, some past research indicates that, on average, a US employee's ideas are implemented only once every 6 years.[26] '*There's nothing worse for morale than when employees feel like their ideas go nowhere,*' says Larry Bennett, a professor of entrepreneurship.[27] At PricewaterhouseCoopers, all of the final ideas were assigned to a senior 'champion', who will help the teams further develop and implement their proposals. Other ideas from the top 20 semi-finalists were assigned to an idea incubator group. An idea incubator is a mechanism that provides a safe harbour where ideas from employees throughout the company can be developed without interference from company bureaucracy or politics.[28]

💡 INNOVATIVE WAY

PricewaterhouseCoopers

'We have an average age of 27, but we have roots in tax and assurance,' said PricewaterhouseCoopers (PwC) US chairman Bob Moritz. 'So how do you make this place feel like a Google or a Facebook? A place that feels leading edge?'

Like other companies, PwC has felt the sting of increased competition and a shaky global economy. Harnessing the creativity of all employees in the search for profitable ideas seemed not only like a good thing to do, but like a business imperative. Mitra Best, PwC's 'innovation leader' and a fan of *American Idol*, took ideas from that show, plus ideas from the videogame world of live chats and online discussions, to create PowerPitch, a fun, collaborative competition that would connect and inspire 30 000 PwC employees. The competition, structured in three stages over a 9 month period, was open to any US employee below the partner level. Each contestant had to recruit a team and pitch either a new service or a radical rethinking of an existing service that could be worth $100 million in revenue. The winning team would get a $100 000 prize, plus the chance to help implement the new idea.

Employees loved it and nearly 800 proposals were pitched at round one, and by the time of the grand finale, nearly 60 per cent of people in the firm had participated in one way or another – direct participation, voting, comments and suggestions, and so forth. The five finalist teams were flown to PwC headquarters in New York to present their proposals and answer questions from judges in a packed corporate auditorium. Offices around the country held viewing parties, watching the competition via live Webcast. The winning team, led by 25-year-old financial services associate Zachary Capozzi, proposed creating a sophisticated data-mining practice within PwC that uses the sort of analytics that Netflix uses to predict which movies customers are interested in. For clients who don't have that capability in-house, the service can be invaluable – and it can be a source of new clients and a big new revenue stream for PwC.[25]

TAKE A MOMENT

Go to the Experiential Exercise online that pertains to creativity in organizations.

REFLECTION

- A **product change** is a change in the organization's products or services, such as the Frigidaire double-oven range or the Amazon Kindle Fire.
- **Technology change** refers to a change in production processes – how the organization does its work.
- **Exploration** involves designing the organization to encourage creativity and the initiation of new ideas.
- **Creativity** is the generation of novel ideas that may meet perceived needs or respond to opportunities for the organization.

- PricewaterhouseCoopers applied a **bottom-up approach**, using an *American Idol-style* contest to encourage employee ideas for new services at the giant accounting and consulting firm.
- An **idea incubator** is an organizational programme that provides a safe harbour where employees can generate and develop ideas without interference from company bureaucracy or politics.

Cooperation

Another important aspect of innovation is providing mechanisms for both internal and external cooperation. Ideas for product and technology innovations typically originate at lower levels of the organization and need to flow horizontally across departments. In addition, people and organizations outside the firm can be rich sources of innovative ideas. Lack of innovation is widely recognized as one of the biggest problems facing today's businesses. Consider that 72 per cent of top executives surveyed by *BusinessWeek* and the *Boston Consulting Group* reported that innovation is a top priority, yet almost half said they are dissatisfied with their results in that area.[29] Thus, many companies are undergoing a transformation in the way they find and use new ideas, focusing on improving both internal and external coordination and cooperation.

Internal coordination

Successful innovation requires expertise from several departments simultaneously, and failed innovation is often the result of failed cooperation.[30] Sony, once the epitome of Japanese business and innovation success, is literally fighting to stay alive because the company had not had a hit product in years and hasn't turned a profit since 2008. To be sure, Sony was battered by one after another disruptive new technology or unexpected competitor, but the biggest problem was that managers were unable to fight back because of poor cooperation within the organization. The company had the technology to create a music player like the iPod long before Apple came out with it (co-founder Akio Morita actually envisioned such a device in the 1980s), but divisions couldn't cooperate to bring the idea to fruition. Today, some top executives complain about managers who refuse to share information or work with other divisions. Consequently, the company makes a lot of different gadgets that overlap and cannibalize one another and offers disjointed services for different products rather than an integrated common platform to deliver music, movies and games.[31] '*Innovation is a team sport,*' says Drew Boyd, a businessman who speaks about innovation to other companies.[32]

Companies that successfully innovate usually have the following characteristics:

- People in research and marketing actively work with customers to understand their needs and develop solutions.

- Technical specialists are aware of recent developments and make effective use of new technology.

- A shared new product development process that is advocated and supported by top management cuts across organizational functions and units.

- Members from key departments – research, manufacturing, marketing – cooperate in the development of the new product or service.

- Each project is guided by a core cross-functional team from beginning to end.[33]

One approach to successful innovation is called the horizontal linkage model, which is illustrated in the centre circle of Exhibit 11.4.[34] The model shows that the research, manufacturing, and sales and marketing departments within an organization simultaneously contribute to new products and technologies. People from these departments meet frequently in teams and task forces to share ideas and solve problems. Research people inform marketing of new technical developments to learn whether they will be useful to customers. Marketing people pass customer complaints to research to use in the design of new products and to manufacturing people to develop new ideas for improving production speed and quality. Manufacturing informs other departments whether a product idea can be manufactured within cost limits. Throughout the process, development teams keep in close touch with customers. A study by McKinsey found that 80 per cent of successful innovators periodically test and validate customer preferences during development of new products and services.[35] Unfortunately, '*new products can take on a life of their own within an organization, becoming so hyped that there's no turning back,*' wrote Joan Schneider and Julie Hall, coauthors of *The New Launch Plan: 152 Tips, Tactics, and Trends from the Most Memorable New Products*. This is probably what happened with Coca-Cola's failed introduction of 'New Coke' in the mid-1980s and its more recent launch of Coke C2, a failed product aimed at 20- to 40-year old men that promised half the calories and carbs but all the taste of original Coke. The product development team became so committed to the new product that it failed to look objectively at marketing data.[36]

The horizontal linkage model is increasingly important in a high-pressure business environment that requires rapidly developing and commercializing products and services. Speed is a pivotal strategic weapon in today's global marketplace.[37] This kind of teamwork is similar to a rugby match, wherein players run together, passing the ball back and forth as they move downfield.[38] Corning used a horizontal linkage model to create a new product for the mobile phone industry.

EXHIBIT 11.4 Coordination model for innovation

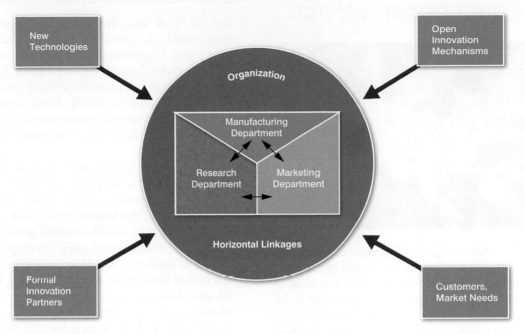

INNOVATIVE WAY

Corning Inc.

Plastic screens on mobile phones are easily scratched and broken, which gave a small team in Corning's speciality materials division an idea: What if they could find a way to make mobile screens out of a super-strong but flexible glass that the company had originally attempted (unsuccessfully) to sell for automobile windshields in the 1960s? Just producing an experimental batch to gauge customer interest would cost as much as $300 000, but managers took the risk because the project had a strong idea champion.

Once the test run was completed and potential customers expressed excitement, managers had to move quickly. Corning took the project from concept to commercial success in an amazingly short period of time. One reason is that the company had both the right culture and the right systems. Corning

divisions and departments know that top managers expect, support and reward collaboration on promising new product launches. Innovation at Corning is managed not by lone inventors or small teams in groups, but rather by multidisciplinary groups all across the organization. The company has two units – the Corporate Technology Council and the Growth and Strategy Council – that are charged with overseeing the innovation process and making sure departments effectively cooperate in new product development efforts that are sanctioned by management. Thus, employees from R&D, manufacturing and sales quickly agreed to serve on the team developing the new glass product.

By 2010, Corning's mobile phone glass, called Gorilla Glass, was used on more than three dozen mobile phones as well as some laptops and other devices. Gorilla Glass was projected to be a $500 million business by 2015.[39]

By using a horizontal linkage model for new product development, Corning has been highly effective in rapidly taking products from idea to success in the marketplace. Famous innovation failures – such as Microsoft's Zune music player and the US Mint's Susan B. Anthony dollar, perhaps the most unpopular coin in American history – usually violate the horizontal linkage model.

CONCEPT CONNECTION

Innovation often requires **internal coordination** because it takes the combined expertise of a number of different team players, each with their own areas of specialization, to come up with a single creative, yet realistic, solution. In architecture, for example, projects are often designed by teams of people. One may be a specialist in structural engineering, another may focus on the plumbing and electrical systems, while yet others are concerned about the look of the interior and exterior of the structure. Working together, they ensure that all aspects of an innovative design will work together to meet the needs of the customer.

External coordination

Exhibit 11.4 also illustrates that organizations look outside their boundaries to find and develop new ideas. Engineers and researchers stay aware of new technological developments. Marketing personnel pay attention to shifting market conditions and customer needs. Some organizations build formal strategic partnerships such as alliances and joint ventures to improve innovation success.

Successful companies often include customers, strategic partners, suppliers and other outsiders directly in the product and service development process. One of the hottest trends is *open innovation*.[40] In the past, most businesses generated their own ideas in-house and then developed, manufactured, marketed and distributed them, which is a closed innovation approach. Today, however, forward-looking companies such as P&G are trying a different method. Open innovation means extending the search for and commercialization of new ideas beyond the boundaries of the organization and even beyond the boundaries of the industry, sharing knowledge and resources with other organizations and individuals outside the firm.

For example, game maker Rovio extended the commercialization of the Angry Birds brand into books, movies and toys by letting outsiders licence the popular gaming app.[41] Some of the best-selling products from consumer products company P&G, including the Swiffer SweeperVac, Olay Regenerist and Mr Clean Magic Eraser, were developed in whole or in part by someone outside the firm.[42] Even Apple, which has always been famously 'closed' in many ways, has found a way to tap into the power of open innovation. For example, although the company sets guidelines and technological constraints, it allows anyone to create and market mobile applications for the iPhone in exchange for a small share of the revenue generated by the apps. Apple generates around $75 million in revenue a month through its App Store.[43]

'Successful innovation requires rich cross-pollination both inside and outside the organization.'
– BRUCE BROWN AND SCOTT D. ANTHONY, IN 'HOW P&G TRIPLED ITS INNOVATION SUCCESS RATE'

The Internet has made it possible for companies to tap into ideas from around the world and let hundreds of thousands of people contribute to the innovation process, which is why some approaches to open innovation are referred to as *crowdsourcing*. Fiat introduced the first crowdsourced car, the Mio, in 2010. The automaker launched a website asking people to think about what the car of the future should be like, and more than 17 000 people around the world submitted ideas.[44] Oscar de la Renta has a 'digital inspiration board' on the Internet, where anyone can upload images for new designs to inspire the next fashion collection. Goldcorp, a Canadian gold mining firm, asked people to examine its geologic data over the Web and submit proposals for locations to find more gold. With a prize to the top 25 finalists of $500 000, the company received more than 475 000 tips and solutions, which confirmed many suspected deposits and identified some new ones.[45]

Crowdsourcing is also being used to gather creative ideas for solving social problems. After the 2010 devastating earthquake in Haiti, for example, relief workers trying to dispatch health care workers and supplies had 400 street addresses that might be clinics. They asked for help over the Internet in 'geotagging' the addresses (putting coordinates on a map), and nearly all 400 were mapped within 24 hours. Having people physically check addresses might have taken weeks. Similarly, following the 2011 earthquake and tsunami in Japan, crowdsourced maps gave local relief workers a better picture of the situation and helped them set priorities for distribution of food, shelter and sanitation services.[46]

REFLECTION

- Successful product and service innovation depends on cooperation, both within the organization and with customers and others outside the organization.
- Using a horizontal linkage model means that several departments, such as marketing, research and manufacturing, work closely together to develop new products.
- Some companies, such as P&G and Rovio, creator of the Angry Birds game, extend the search for and

commercialization of innovative ideas beyond the boundaries of the organization – a process called open innovation.
- *Crowdsourcing,* an open innovation approach used by Fiat, Oscar de la Renta and many other companies, taps into ideas from around the world and lets thousands or hundreds of thousands of people participate in the innovation process, usually via the Internet.

Innovation roles

The third aspect of product and technology innovation is creating structural mechanisms to make sure new ideas are carried forward, accepted and implemented. Managers can directly influence whether entrepreneurship flourishes in the organization by expressing support of entrepreneurial activities, giving employees a degree of autonomy, and rewarding learning and risk-taking.[47] One important factor is fostering idea champions. The formal definition of an idea champion is a person who sees the need for and champions productive change within the organization.

Remember: Change does not occur by itself. Personal energy and effort are required to promote a new idea successfully. When Texas Instruments studied 50 of its new-product introductions, a surprising fact emerged: Without exception, every new product that failed lacked a zealous champion. In contrast, most of the new products that succeeded had a champion. Managers made an immediate decision: No new product would be approved unless someone championed it. Similarly, at SRI International, a contract research and development firm, managers use the saying 'No champion, no product, no exception'.[48] Research confirms that successful new ideas are generally those that are backed by someone who believes in the idea wholeheartedly and is determined to convince others of its value.[49] Recall how the winning proposals at PricewaterhouseCoopers innovation contest were all assigned to a senior champion so they didn't get lost in the everyday shuffle.

Sometimes a new idea is rejected by top managers, but champions are passionately committed to a new idea or product despite rejection by others. For example, Robert Vincent was fired twice by two different division managers at a semiconductor company. Both times, he convinced the president and chairman of the board to reinstate him to continue working on his idea for an airbag sensor that measures acceleration and deceleration. He couldn't get approval for research funding, so Vincent pushed to finish another project in half the time and used the savings to support the new product development.[50]

Championing an idea successfully requires roles in organizations, as illustrated in Exhibit 11.5. Sometimes a single person may play two or more of these roles, but successful innovation in most companies involves the interplay of different people, each adopting one role. The *inventor* comes up with a new idea and understands its technical value but has neither the ability nor the interest to promote it for acceptance within the organization. The *champion* believes in the idea, confronts the organizational realities of costs and benefits, and gains the political and financial support needed to bring it to reality. The *sponsor* is a high-level manager who approves the idea, protects the idea and removes major organizational barriers to acceptance. The *critic* counterbalances the zeal of the champion by challenging the concept and providing a reality test against hardnosed criteria. The critic prevents people in the other roles from adopting a bad idea.[51]

EXHIBIT 11.5 Four roles in organizational change

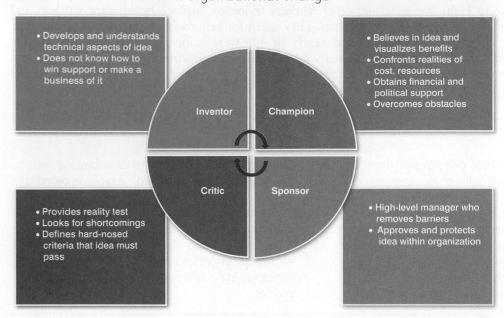

- Develops and understands technical aspects of idea
- Does not know how to win support or make a business of it

Inventor

Champion

- Believes in idea and visualizes benefits
- Confronts realities of cost, resources
- Obtains financial and political support
- Overcomes obstacles

Critic

Sponsor

- Provides reality test
- Looks for shortcomings
- Defines hard-nosed criteria that idea must pass

- High-level manager who removes barriers
- Approves and protects idea within organization

SOURCES: Harold L. Angle and Andrew H. Van de Ven, 'Suggestions for Managing the Innovation Journey', in *Research in the Management of Innovation: The Minnesota Studies*, ed. A. H. Van de Ven, H. L. Angle, and Marshall Scott Poole (Cambridge, MA: Ballinger/Harper & Row, 1989); and Jay R. Galbraith, 'Designing the Innovating Organization', *Organizational Dynamics* (Winter 1982): 5–25.

Another way to facilitate entrepreneurship is through a new-venture team. A new-venture team is a unit separate from the rest of the organization that is responsible for developing and initiating a major innovation.[52] New-venture teams give free rein to members' creativity because their separate facilities and location unleash people from the restrictions imposed by organizational rules and procedures. These teams typically are small, loosely structured and flexible, reflecting the characteristics of creative organizations described in Exhibit 11.2. One good example is Nestlé's Nespresso venture, which developed a line of high-quality coffees packaged in individual capsules for use in specially designed coffee machines. The team found itself hampered by the large company's rules, structures and regulations. In addition, the project faced resistance from managers who feared the new premium line would hurt the existing Nescafé brand. Top managers moved the Nespresso business outside the existing structure so it could thrive with an entrepreneurial culture and promote innovative ideas.[53] P&G has established several new-business-creation groups that search for and develop breakthrough ideas that cross multiple businesses and divisions. These teams are partly responsible for a dramatic increase in P&G's innovation success rate.[54]

One variation of a new-venture team is called a skunkworks.[55] A skunkworks is a separate small, informal, highly autonomous and often secretive group that focuses on breakthrough ideas for a business. The original skunkworks, which still exists, was created by Lockheed Martin more than 50 years ago. The essence of a skunkworks is that highly talented people are given the time and freedom to let creativity reign.[56] Consider the clandestine Google X lab, which was so hush-hush until *The New York Times* wrote about it that even many of Google's employees didn't know it existed. Google X is a top-secret lab in an undisclosed location where engineers are working on shoot-for-the-moon ideas like driverless cars, space elevators that can collect information from or haul things into space, and robots that can attend a conference for you while you stay at the office.[57] Similarly, at GM, the location of the skunkworks facility known as Studio X is kept secret even from the automaker's top executives.[58]

TAKE A MOMENT

Go to the Ethical Dilemma at the end of the chapter that pertains to structural change.

A related idea is the new-venture fund, which provides resources from which individuals and groups can draw to develop new ideas products or businesses. At Pitney Bowes, for example, the New Business Opportunity (NBO) programme provides funding for teams to explore potentially lucrative but unproven ideas. The NBO programme is intended to generate a pipeline of new businesses for the mail and document management services company. Similarly, Royal Dutch Shell puts 10 per cent of its R&D budget into the GameChanger programme, which provides seed money for innovation projects that are highly ambitious, radical or long-term and would get lost in the larger product development system.[59] With these programmes, the support and assistance of senior managers are often just as important as the funding.[60]

REFLECTION

- To increase innovation, managers develop an internal culture, philosophy and structure that encourage entrepreneurial activity.
- An **idea champion** is a person who sees the need for change and is passionately committed to making it happen.
- One structural mechanism that promotes entrepreneurship is the **new-venture team**, which is a unit separate from the mainstream organization that is responsible for initiating and developing innovations.

- A variation of the new-venture team is a **skunkworks**, a separate informal, highly autonomous and often secretive group that focuses on breakthrough ideas.
- The top-secret Google X lab is an example of a skunkworks.
- A **new-venture fund** provides financial resources from which individuals or teams can draw to develop new ideas, products or businesses.

Changing people and culture

All successful changes involve changes in people as well as culture. Changes in people and culture pertain to how employees think – changes in mind set. People change concerns just a few employees, such as sending a handful of middle managers to a training course to improve their leadership skills. Culture change pertains to the organization as a whole, such as when the US Internal Revenue Service (IRS) shifted its basic mind set from an organization focused on collection and compliance to one dedicated to informing, educating and serving customers (taxpayers).[61] Large-scale culture change is not easy. Indeed, managers routinely report that changing people and culture is their most difficult job.[62] New top managers at GM, for instance, have received praise for pulling the company back from bankruptcy (liquidation in the UK) and achieving impressive financial results, but even CEO Dan Akerson admits that in terms of changing the bureaucratic, tradition-bound culture, they are at only about 25 per cent of where they want to be. One of Akerson's goals has been to get more women into top jobs, partly because he believes they can lead the radical culture change GM needs. Today, four of the company's 12 directors are female, a woman heads global product development, and some of the company's biggest plants are run by women.[63] Two specific tools that can smooth the culture change process are training and development programmes and organization development (OD).

Training and development

Training is one of the most frequently used approaches to changing people's mind sets. A company might offer training programmes to large blocks of employees on subjects such as teamwork, diversity, emotional intelligence, quality circles, communication skills or participative management.

Successful companies want to provide training and development opportunities for everyone, but they might particularly emphasize training and development for managers, with the idea that the behaviour and attitudes of managers will influence people throughout the organization and lead to culture change. A number of Silicon Valley companies, including Intel and Advanced Micro Devices (AMD), regularly send managers to the Growth and Leadership Center (GLC), where they learn to use emotional intelligence to build better relationships. Nick Kepler, director of technology development at AMD, was surprised to learn how his emotionless approach to work was intimidating people and destroying the rapport needed to shift to a culture based on collaborative teamwork.[64]

Organization development

Organization development (OD) is a planned, systematic process of change that uses behavioural science knowledge and techniques to improve an organization's health and effectiveness through its ability to adapt to the environment, improve internal relationships and increase learning and problem-solving capabilities.[65] OD focuses on the human and social aspects of the organization and works to change attitudes and relationships among employees, helping to strengthen the organization's capacity for adaptation and renewal.[66]

OD can help managers address at least three types of current problems:[67]

- *Mergers/acquisitions.* The disappointing financial results of many mergers and acquisitions are caused by the failure of executives to determine whether the administrative style and corporate culture of the two companies fit. Executives may concentrate on potential synergies in technology, products, marketing and control systems but fail to recognize that two firms may have widely different values, beliefs and practices. These differences create stress and anxiety for employees, and these negative emotions affect future performance. Cultural differences should be evaluated during the acquisition process, and OD experts can be used to smooth the integration of two firms.

- *Organizational decline/revitalization.* Organizations undergoing a period of decline and revitalization experience a variety of problems, including a low level of trust, lack of innovation, high turnover and high levels of conflict and stress. The period of transition requires opposite behaviours, including confronting stress, creating open communication and fostering creative innovation to emerge with high levels of productivity. OD techniques can contribute greatly to cultural revitalization by managing conflicts, fostering commitment and facilitating communication.

 CONCEPT CONNECTION

Google managers rely on **survey feedback** to make sure they're providing the environment and benefits employees value. But Google doesn't stop there. In addition to the annual survey, managers solicit feedback on an ongoing basis through various innovative **organization development** tools. One example is the TGIF (Thank Goodness It's Friday) meeting held each week. Managers share the latest news, and employees ask questions and offer opinions about matters ranging from product decisions to human resource policies. Those unable to attend in person can participate online.

- *Conflict management.* Conflict can occur at any time and place within a healthy organization. For example, a product team for the introduction of a new software package was formed at a computer company. Made up of strong-willed individuals, the team made little progress because members could not agree on project goals. At a manufacturing firm, salespeople promised delivery dates to customers that were in conflict with shop supervisor priorities for assembling customer orders. In a publishing company, two managers disliked each other intensely. They argued at meetings, lobbied politically against each other and hurt the achievement of both departments. Organization development efforts can help resolve these kinds of conflicts, as well as conflicts that are related to growing diversity and the global nature of today's organizations.

Organization development can be used to solve the types of problems just described and many others. However, to be truly valuable to companies and employees, organization development practitioners go beyond looking at ways to settle specific problems. Instead, they become involved in broader issues that contribute to improving organizational life, such as encouraging a sense of community, pushing for an organizational climate of openness and trust, and making sure the company provides employees with opportunities for personal growth and development.[68] One fairly recent study looked at the results of an OD project in a large US metropolitan sheriff's department that was plagued by extremely high turnover, low morale, ineffective leadership and internal conflicts. OD consultants used a variety of activities over a period of 4 years to solve the crisis threatening the department. It was a long, and sometimes difficult, process, but the study not only found that the OD interventions had highly beneficial results but the positive impact lasted over a period of 30 years to the present day.[69]

OD activities

OD consultants use a variety of specialized techniques to help meet OD goals. Three of the most popular and effective are the following:

- *Team-building activities.* Team building enhances the cohesiveness and success of organizational groups and teams. For example, a series of OD exercises can be used with members of cross-departmental teams to help them learn to act and function as a team. An OD expert can work with team members to increase their communication skills, facilitate their ability to confront one another and help them accept common goals.

- *Survey-feedback activities.* Survey feedback begins with a questionnaire distributed to employees on values, climate, participation, leadership and group cohesion within their organization. After the survey is completed, an OD consultant meets with groups of employees to provide feedback about their responses and the problems identified. Employees are engaged in problem solving based on the data.

- *Large-group interventions.* In recent years, the need for bringing about fundamental organizational change in today's complex, fast-changing world prompted a growing interest in applications of OD techniques to large group settings.[70] The large-group intervention approach brings together participants from all parts of the organization – often including key stakeholders from outside the organization as well – to discuss problems or opportunities and plan for change. A large-group intervention might involve 50 to 500 people and last several days. The idea is to include everyone who has a stake in the change, gather perspectives from all parts of the system and enable people to create a collective future through sustained, guided dialogue.

Large-group interventions are one of the most popular and fastest-growing OD activities and reflect a significant shift in the approach to organizational change from earlier OD concepts and approaches.[71] Exhibit 11.6 lists the primary differences between the traditional OD model and the large-scale intervention model of organizational change.[72]

EXHIBIT 11.6 OD approaches to culture change

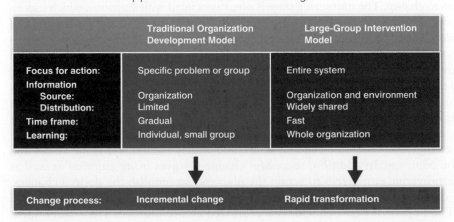

	Traditional Organization Development Model	Large-Group Intervention Model
Focus for action:	Specific problem or group	Entire system
Information Source:	Organization	Organization and environment
Distribution:	Limited	Widely shared
Time frame:	Gradual	Fast
Learning:	Individual, small group	Whole organization
Change process:	Incremental change	Rapid transformation

SOURCE: Barbara Benedict Bunker and Billie T. Alban, 'Conclusion: What Makes Large Group Interventions Effective?' *Journal of Applied Behavioral Science* 28, no. 4 (December 1992): 579–591.

In the newer approach, the focus is on the entire system, which takes into account the organization's interaction with its environment. The sources of information for discussion are expanded to include customers, suppliers, community members and even competitors, and this information is shared widely so that everyone has the same picture of the organization and its environment. The acceleration of change when the entire system is involved can be remarkable. In addition, learning occurs across all parts of the organization simultaneously, rather than in individuals, small groups or business units. The result is that the large-group approach offers greater possibilities for fundamental, radical transformation of the entire culture, whereas the traditional approach creates incremental change in a few individuals or small groups at a time.

REFLECTION

- Often, a manager's toughest job is changing people and an embedded corporate culture.
- **People change** refers to a change in the attitudes and behaviours of a few employees.
- **Culture change** is a major shift in the norms, values and mindset of the entire organization.
- **Organization development (OD)** is a planned, systematic process of change that uses behavioural science techniques to improve an organization's health and effectiveness through its ability to cope with environmental changes, improve internal relationships and increase learning and problem-solving capabilities.
- OD can help managers with the task of blending corporate cultures following mergers and acquisitions, as well as with many other people-related problems.

- **Team building** is an OD intervention that enhances cohesiveness by helping groups of people learn to work together as a team.
- With **survey feedback**, OD change agents survey employees to gather their opinions regarding corporate values, leadership, participation, cohesiveness and other aspects of the organization, then meet with small groups to share the results and brainstorm solutions to problems identified by the results.
- **Large-group intervention** is an OD approach that brings together people from different parts of the organization (and often including outside stakeholders) to discuss problems or opportunities and plan for change.

OD steps

OD experts acknowledge that changes in corporate culture and human behaviour are tough to accomplish and require major effort. The theory underlying OD process proposed by Kotter has three distinct stages for achieving behavioural and attitudinal change: (1) unfreezing, (2) changing and (3) refreezing.[73]

The first stage, unfreezing, makes people throughout the organization aware of problems and the need for change. This stage creates the motivation for people to change their attitudes and behaviours. Unfreezing may begin when managers present information that shows discrepancies between desired behaviours or performance and the current state of affairs. In addition, managers need to establish a sense of urgency to unfreeze people and create an openness and willingness to change. The unfreezing stage is often associated with *diagnosis*, which uses an outside expert called a *change agent*. The change agent is an OD specialist who performs a systematic diagnosis of the organization and identifies work-related problems. He or she gathers and analyzes data through personal interviews, questionnaires and observations of meetings. The diagnosis helps determine the extent of organizational problems and helps unfreeze managers by making them aware of problems in their behaviour.

The second stage, changing, occurs when individuals experiment with new behaviour and learn new skills to be used in the workplace. This process is sometimes known as *intervention*, during which the change agent implements a specific plan for training managers and employees. The changing stage might involve a number of specific steps.[74] For example, managers put together a coalition of people with the will and power to guide the change, create a vision for change that everyone can believe in, and widely communicate the vision and plans for change throughout the company. In addition, successful change involves using emotion as well as logic to persuade people and empowering employees to act on the plan and accomplish the desired changes.

The third stage, refreezing, occurs when individuals acquire new attitudes or values and are rewarded for them by the organization. The impact of new behaviours is evaluated and reinforced. The change agent supplies new data that show positive changes in performance. Managers may provide updated data to employees that demonstrate positive changes in individual and organizational performance. Top executives celebrate successes and reward positive behavioural changes. At this stage, changes are institutionalized in the organizational culture, so that employees begin to view the changes as a normal, integral part of how the organization operates. Employees may also participate in refresher courses to maintain and reinforce the new behaviours.

The process of unfreezing-changing-refreezing can be illustrated by efforts of managers at ENSR to create a high-performance, employee-focused culture.

 INNOVATIVE WAY

ENSR

When top executives at ENSR began hearing that high employee turnover was hurting the company's relationships with clients, they knew something had to be done. ENSR is a full-service environmental services firm with around 3000 employees in 90 locations around the world. Long-term relationships with clients are the key to ENSR's success.

To attack the turnover problem, managers embarked on a process of changing the culture. To make people aware of the need for change (unfreezing), ENSR's president and CEO travelled with the senior vice president of human resources to the largest 50 or so of ENSR's global locations. They held town-hall-style meetings with employees and leadership workshops with ENSR managers. The *changing* stage included training. Surveys were conducted to find out what employees considered their primary needs. For example, supervisors were trained in how to help lower-performing employees improve their performance and how to provide greater challenge and rewards to employees who showed high potential for leadership.

Within a few years, new behaviours became the norm. Turnover dropped from 22 per cent to only 9 per cent, one of the lowest rates in the industry, and employees were recognized and rewarded for meeting high individual and collective goals (refreezing). ENSR continues to attract high-quality employees to fill job openings, which helps to keep the high-performance culture alive.[75]

REFLECTION

- OD practitioners recommend a three stage approach for changing people's attitudes and behaviour.
- **Unfreezing** is the stage in which people are made aware of problems and the need for change.
- Unfreezing requires diagnosing problems, which uses a **change agent** – an OD specialist who contracts with an organization to help managers facilitate change.

- **Changing** is the 'intervention' stage of OD, when change agents teach people new behaviours and skills and guide them in using them in the workplace.
- At the **refreezing** stage, people have incorporated new values, attitudes and behaviours into their everyday work and the changes [optimistically] become institutionalized in the culture.

Implementing change

The final step to be managed in the change process is *implementation*. A new, creative idea will not benefit the organization until it is in place and being used fully. One frustration for managers is that employees often seem to resist change for no apparent reason. To manage the implementation process effectively, managers should be aware of the reasons people resist change and use techniques to enlist employee cooperation.

Need for change

Many people are not willing to change unless they perceive a problem or a crisis. A crisis or strong need for change lowers resistance. The shifting relationship between GM and the United Auto Workers (UAW) provides a good example. GM managers' efforts to build a more collaborative relationship typically met with resistance from UAW leaders until bankruptcy proved the urgent need for working more closely together.[76] Sometimes, though, there is no obvious crisis. Many organizational problems are subtle, so managers have to recognize and then make others aware of the need for change.[77] A need for change is a disparity between existing and desired performance levels.

Resistance to change

Getting others to understand the need for change is the first step in implementation. Yet most changes will encounter some degree of resistance. Idea champions often discover that other employees are unenthusiastic about their new ideas. Members of a new-venture group may be surprised when managers in the regular organization do not support or approve their innovations. Managers and employees not involved in an innovation often seem to prefer the status quo. People resist change for several reasons, and understanding them can help managers implement change more effectively.

Self-interest

People typically resist a change they believe conflicts with their self-interests. A proposed change in job design, structure or technology may increase employees' workload, for example, or cause a real or perceived loss of power, prestige, pay or benefits. The fear of personal loss is perhaps the biggest obstacle to organizational change.[78] Consider what is happening at Anheuser-Busch, which was acquired by the Belgian company InBev. The lavish executive suites at Anheuser-Busch headquarters have been demolished in favour of an open floor plan that has staff members and executives working side by side. Managers accustomed to flying first class or on company planes are now required to fly economy class. It has become a competition to get a company-provided smartphone, as InBev has dramatically cut the number it will provide for employees. Free beer is a thing of the past, and complimentary tickets to sporting events are few and far between. Once the envy of others in the industry because of their lavish perks, Anheuser-Busch employees are resisting the new managers' wide-ranging changes because they feel they are losing both financially and in terms of status.[79]

Lack of understanding and trust

Employees often distrust the intentions behind a change or do not understand the intended purpose of a change. If previous working relationships with an idea champion have been negative, resistance may occur. When CareFusion Corporation was spun off as a subsidiary of Cardinal Health, CEO David L. Schlotterbeck and other top executives wanted to implement new values of collaboration and teamwork, but lower-level managers were initially suspicious of their intentions. Only when they saw that top leaders were fully committed to the values and honoured them in their own behaviour did others begin to support the changes.[80]

'Change hurts. It makes people insecure, confused and angry. People want things to be the same as they've always been, because that makes life easier. But, if you're a leader, you can't let your people hang on to the past.'
  – RICHARD MARCINKO, FORMER US NAVY SEAL, AUTHOR, AND CHAIRMAN OF RED CELL INTERNATIONAL CORPORATION

Uncertainty

Uncertainty is the lack of information about future events. It represents a fear of the unknown. Uncertainty is especially threatening for employees who have a low tolerance for change and fear anything out of the ordinary. They do not know how a change will affect them and worry about whether they will be able to meet the demands of a new procedure or technology.[81] For example, employees at one mail-order company resisted the introduction of teams because they were comfortable with their working environment and uncertain about how the implementation of teams would alter it. People had developed good collaborative working relationships informally and they didn't see the need for being forced to work in teams.

Different assessments and goals

Another reason for resistance to change is that people who will be affected by a change or innovation may assess the situation differently from an idea champion or new-venture group. Critics frequently voice legitimate disagreements over the proposed benefits of a change. Managers in each department pursue different goals, and an innovation may detract from performance and goal achievement for some departments. For example, if marketing gets the new product it wants for customers, the cost of manufacturing may increase, and the manufacturing superintendent thus will resist. Apple executives are currently encountering this type of resistance. In August 2010, Apple became the largest US corporation in terms of market valuation. But executives are currently under pressure for change because of poor working conditions in overseas supplier factories, including ones in China. More than half of the suppliers audited were found to have violated aspects of Apple's code of conduct and some have broken laws. However, there is conflict within the company because although top executives want to improve conditions, some managers argue that a radical overhaul will derail crucial supplier relationships and slow innovation and the delivery of new products.[82]

TAKE A MOMENT

The Small Group Breakout Exercise online will give you an idea of how difficult it can sometimes be for people to change.

These reasons for resistance are legitimate in the eyes of employees affected by the change. Managers should not ignore resistance but instead diagnose the reasons and design strategies to gain acceptance by users.[83] Strategies for overcoming resistance to change typically involve two approaches: the analysis of resistance through the force-field technique and the use of selective implementation tactics to overcome resistance.

Force-field analysis

Force-field analysis grew from the work of Kurt Lewin, who proposed that change was a result of the competition between *driving* and *restraining forces*.[84] Driving forces can be thought of as problems or opportunities that provide motivation for change within the organization. Restraining forces are the various barriers to change, such as a lack of resources, resistance from middle managers or inadequate employee skills. When a change is introduced, managers should analyze both the forces that drive change (problems and opportunities) and the forces that resist it (barriers to change). By selectively removing forces that restrain change, the driving forces will be strong enough to enable implementation, as illustrated by the move from A to B in Exhibit 11.7. As barriers are reduced or removed, behaviour will shift to incorporate the desired changes.

EXHIBIT 11.7 Using force-field analysis to change from traditional to just-in-time inventory system

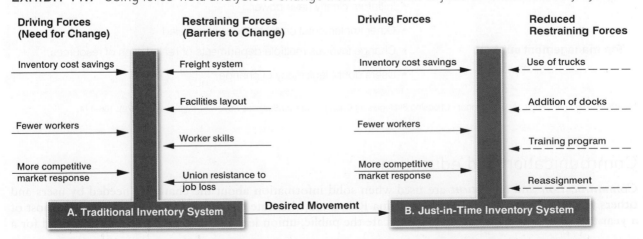

Just-in-time (JIT) inventory control systems schedule materials to arrive at a company just as they are needed on the production line. In an Ohio manufacturing company, management's analysis showed that the driving forces (opportunities) associated with the implementation of JIT were (1) the large cost savings from reduced inventories; (2) savings from needing fewer workers to handle the inventory and (3) a quicker, more competitive market response for the company. Restraining forces (barriers) that managers discovered were (1) a freight system that was too slow to deliver inventory on time; (2) a facility layout that emphasized inventory maintenance over new deliveries; (3) worker skills that were inappropriate for handling rapid inventory deployment and (4) union resistance to loss of jobs. The driving forces were not sufficient to overcome the restraining forces.

To shift the behaviour to JIT, managers attacked the barriers. An analysis of the freight system showed that delivery by truck provided the flexibility and quickness needed to schedule inventory arrival at a specific time each day. The problem with facility layout was met by adding four new loading docks. Inappropriate worker skills were attacked with a training programme to instruct workers in JIT methods and in assembling products with uninspected parts. Union resistance was overcome by agreeing to reassign workers no longer needed for maintaining inventory to jobs in another plant. With the restraining forces reduced, the driving forces were sufficient to allow the JIT system to be implemented.

Implementation tactics

The other approach to managing implementation is to adopt specific tactics to overcome resistance. Researchers have studied various methods for dealing with resistance to change. The following five tactics, summarized in Exhibit 11.8, have proven successful.[85]

EXHIBIT 11.8 Tactics for overcoming resistance to change

Approach	When to use
Communication, education	• Change is technical.
	• Users need accurate information and analysis to understand change.
Participation	• Users need to feel involved.
	• Design requires information from others.
	• Users have power to resist.
Negotiation	• Group has power over implementation.
	• Group will lose out in the change.
Coercion	• A crisis exists.
	• Initiators clearly have power.
	• Other implementation techniques have failed.
Top management support	• Change involves multiple departments or reallocation of resources.
	• Users doubt legitimacy of change.

SOURCE: J. P. Kotter and L. A. Schlesinger, 'Choosing Strategies for Change', *Harvard Business Review* 57 (March–April 1979): 106–114.

Communication and education

Communication and *education* are used when solid information about the change is needed by users and others who may resist implementation. Gina Raimondo, the state treasurer of Rhode Island, spent most of a year travelling all across the state to educate the public, union leaders and legislators about the need for a radical overhaul of the state's pension system. I would talk to social workers or social-service agencies who . . . would ask, 'Why should I care about pensions?' And I said, 'Because if you don't, your whatever it is, homeless shelter, is going to lose X thousand dollars of funding,' she said. Raimondo 'conducted a long, relentless, public-education campaign' because she believed reform was essential to keep the state from going broke.[86] Within organizations, education can be especially important when the change involves new technical knowledge or users are unfamiliar with the idea. Managers should also remember that implementing change requires speaking to people's hearts (touching their feelings) as well as to their minds (communicating facts). Emotion is a key component in persuading and influencing others. People are much more likely to change their behaviour when they both understand the rational reasons for doing so and see a picture of change that influences their feelings.[87]

 CONCEPT CONNECTION

In the wake of the 2008 global economic crisis, many people felt that Wall Street and other financial institutions around the world were primarily responsible for the poor state of the world's economy. Motivated by a desire to change the way global financial systems operate, people took to the streets in protests like Occupy Wall Street, Occupy London, and many more. Their goal was to **educate** the public through **communication**, and to encourage **participation** in the change process.

Participation

Participation involves users and potential resisters in designing the change. This approach is time-consuming, but it pays off because users understand and become committed to the change. At Learning Point Associates, which needed to change dramatically to meet new challenges, the change team drew up a comprehensive road map for transformation but had trouble getting the support of most managers. The managers argued that they hadn't been consulted about the plans and didn't feel compelled to participate in implementing them.[88] Research studies have shown that proactively engaging frontline employees in upfront planning and decision-making about changes that affect their work results in much smoother implementation.[89] Participation also helps managers determine potential problems and understand the differences in perceptions of change among employees.

Negotiation

Negotiation is a more formal means of achieving cooperation. *Negotiation* uses formal bargaining to win acceptance and approval of a desired change. For example, if the marketing department fears losing power if a new management structure is implemented, top managers may negotiate with marketing to reach a resolution. Companies that have strong unions frequently must formally negotiate change with the unions. The change may become part of the union contract reflecting the agreement of both parties.

Coercion

Coercion means that managers use formal power to force employees to change. Resisters are told to accept the change or lose rewards (or even their jobs). In most cases, this approach should not be used because employees feel like victims, are angry at change managers and may even sabotage the changes. However, coercion may be necessary in crisis situations when a rapid response is urgent. For example, at the struggling Chrysler Group, some insiders say new CEO Sergio Marchionne 'injected an element of fear into [Chrysler's] ranks' to get people to change. Several top managers were reassigned or terminated because they wouldn't go along with Marchionne's changes for returning Chrysler to profitability after it emerged from bankruptcy protection.[90]

Top management support

One survey found that 80 per cent of companies that are successful innovators have top executives who frequently reinforce the importance of innovation both verbally and symbolically.[91] The visible support of top management helps overcome resistance. For instance, one of the primary correlates of the success of new business ventures is the strong support of top managers, which gives the project legitimacy.[92] *Top management support* symbolizes to all employees that the change is important for the organization. Top management support is especially important when a change involves multiple departments or when resources are being reallocated among departments. Without top management support, changes can get bogged down in squabbling among departments or contradictory orders from lower-level managers.

Managers can soften resistance and facilitate change and innovation by using smart techniques. By communicating with employees, providing training and closely involving employees in the change process, managers can smooth implementation. In addition, change agents should never underestimate the importance of top management support for any change effort to succeed.

REFLECTION

- A **need for change** is a disparity between actual and desired performance.
- When managers see a need, they want to make changes to fill it, but they may be frustrated because employees seem to resist change for no apparent reason.
- Many people aren't willing to change unless they perceive a crisis.
- There are many legitimate reasons why people resist change, such as self-interest, uncertainty or lack of trust.

- **Force-field analysis** is a technique for determining which forces drive a proposed change and which forces restrain it.
- Driving forces are problems or opportunities that provide motivation to change. Restraining forces are barriers such as a lack of resources or inadequate employee skills.
- The support of top executives is crucial to the successful implementation of a change. In addition, managers use a variety of techniques to smooth the implementation process.

DISCUSSION QUESTIONS

1   As a manager, how would you deal with resistance to change when you know employees' fears of significant job losses are well founded? What factors might a human resource management director need to consider?

2   Explain the meaning of coercion and why it might occasionally be used to implement change under particular situations. Give at least one example.

3   Analyze the driving and restraining forces of a change initiative which you consider is required in an organization familiar to you.

4   Summarize these various roles in the innovation process: inventor, champion, sponsor and critic. Which roles do you think are most important for the initiation of change, and which for the implementation of change? Discuss.

5 'Core values relating to organizational development can be drivers of organization adaptability'. Critically discuss this statement.

6 Evaluate the major advantages and disadvantages of a company moving to open innovation, using 'models', as suggested by Tidd and Bessant (2009) and other academics.

Are you innovative?[93]

INSTRUCTIONS Think about your current life. Indicate whether each item below is 'Mostly true' or 'Mostly false' for you.

		Mostly true	Mostly false
1	I am always seeking new ways to do things.	☐	☐
2	I consider myself creative and original in my thinking and behaviour.	☐	☐
3	I rarely trust new gadgets until I see whether they work for people around me.	☐	☐
4	In a group or at work, I am often sceptical of new ideas.	☐	☐
5	I typically buy new foods, gear and other innovations before other people.	☐	☐
6	I like to spend time trying new things.	☐	☐
7	My behaviour influences others to try new things.	☐	☐
8	Among my co-workers, I will be among the first to try out a new idea or method.	☐	☐

SCORING & INTERPRETATION *Personal innovativeness* reflects the awareness of the need to innovate and a readiness to try new things. Innovativeness is also thought of as the degree to which a person adopts innovations earlier than other people in the peer group. Innovativeness is considered a positive characteristic for people in many companies where individuals and organizations are faced with a constant need to change.

To compute your score on the Personal Innovativeness scale, add the number of 'Mostly true' answers to items 1, 2, 5, 6, 7 and 8 above and the 'Mostly false' answers to items 3 and 4 to get your score. A score of 6–8 indicates that you are very innovative and likely are one of the first people to adopt changes. A score of 4–5 would suggest that you are average or slightly above average in innovativeness compared to others. A score of 0–3 means that you might prefer the tried and true and hence are not excited about new ideas or innovations. As a new manager, a high score suggests you will emphasize innovation and change. A low score suggests you may prefer stability and established methods.

APPLY YOUR SKILLS: ETHICAL DILEMMA

Crowdsourcing[94]

Last year, when Ai-Lan Nguyen told her friend Greg Barnwell that Off the Hook Tees, based in Asheville, North Carolina, was going to experiment with crowdsourcing, he warned her she wouldn't like the results. Now, as she was about to walk into a meeting to decide whether to adopt this new business model, she was afraid her friend had been right.

Crowdsourcing uses the Internet to invite anyone, professionals and amateurs alike, to perform tasks such as product design that employees usually perform. In exchange, contributors receive recognition – but little or no pay. Ai-Lan, as vice president of operations for Off the Hook, a company specializing in witty T-shirts aimed at young adults, upheld the values of founder Chris Woodhouse, who, like Ai-Lan, was a graphic artist. Before he sold the company, the founder always insisted that T-shirts be well designed by top-notch graphic artists to make sure each screen print was a work of art. Those graphic artists reported to Ai-Lan.

During the past 18 months, Off the Hook's sales stagnated for the first time in its history. The crowdsourcing experiment was the latest in a series of attempts to jump-start sales growth. Last spring, Off the Hook issued its first open call for T-shirt designs and then posted the entries on the Web so people could vote for their favorites. The top five vote-getters were handed over to the in-house designers, who tweaked the submissions until they met the company's usual quality standards.

When CEO Rob Taylor first announced the company's foray into crowdsourcing, Ai-Lan found herself reassuring the designers that their positions were not in jeopardy. Now Ai-Lan was all but certain she would have to go back on her word. Not only had the crowdsourced tees sold well, but Rob had put a handful of winning designs directly into production, bypassing the design department altogether. Customers didn't notice the difference.

Ai-Lan concluded that Rob was ready to adopt some form of the Web-based crowdsourcing because it made T-shirt design more responsive to consumer desires. Practically speaking, it reduced the uncertainty that surrounded new designs, and it dramatically lowered costs. The people who won the competitions were delighted with the exposure it gave them.

However, when Ai-Lan looked at the crowdsourced shirts with her graphic artist's eye, she felt that the designs were competent, but none achieved the aesthetic standards attained by her in-house designers. Crowdsourcing essentially replaced training and expertise with public opinion. That made the artist in her uncomfortable.

More distressing, it was beginning to look as if Greg had been right when he'd told her that his working definition of crowdsourcing was 'a billion amateurs want your job'. It was easy to see that if Off the Hook adopted crowdsourcing, she would be handing out pink slips to most of her design people, longtime employees whose work she admired. 'Sure, crowdsourcing costs the company less, but what about the human cost?' Greg asked.

What future course should Ai-Lan argue for at the meeting? And what personal decisions will she face if Off the Hook decide to put the crowd completely in charge when it came to T-shirt design?

What would you do?

1   Go to the meeting and argue for abandoning crowdsourcing for now in favour of maintaining the artistic integrity and values that Off the Hook has always stood for.

2   Accept the reality that because Off the Hook's CEO Rob Taylor strongly favours crowdsourcing, it's a fait accompli. Be a team player and help work out the details of the new design approach. Prepare to lay off graphic designers as needed.

3   Accept the fact that converting Off the Hook to a crowdsourcing business model is inevitable, but because it violates your own personal values, start looking for a new job elsewhere.

APPLY YOUR SKILLS: CASE FOR CRITICAL ANALYSIS

Change and Innovation at Thomas Cook

Thomas Cook is fundamentally a sound travel business with revenues in excess of £9.5 billion and with a strong market position in each of its source travel related markets. It already features as number one or two in its core markets of the UK, Continental Europe and Northern Europe. Its business mode has consistently delivered strong gross margins in excess of 20 per cent, demonstrating the trust and the value that its 23 million customers place upon its products.

A focus area for our senior team has been the breaking down of the departments that existed within the Group to enable the sharing of best practice. This change has enabled the Business Transformation progress to happen quickly whilst delivering greater synergies and efficiencies. New and objective performance based measurement criteria have been applied across the board as part of a new, relentless focus on performance as the Group looks to create a new culture, that is more agile, responsive and decisive. New values, ways of working and a comprehensive Code of Conduct have been introduced and the leadership team has been strengthened through a mix of internal promotions and external appointments, with approximately one-third of the original management team remaining. Embedding a strong focus on enterprise risk assessment and working effectively together to reshape the organization is instrumental in creating the right culture for the future.

Thomas Cook's new strategy is to drive profitable growth by delighting customers with trusted, personal holiday experiences delivered through a high-tech, high-touch approach. To do this it has identified four strategic initiatives based on facts generated from a thorough review of the industry and Thomas Cook's performance within it. The review includes one of the most comprehensive surveys of travellers ever conducted, and in-depth analysis of the attitudes of almost 18 000 people across all our key source markets.

In response the Group's strategy involves four major pillars:

- Expand and leverage: Thomas Cook's proven successful, exclusive and international hotel concepts.

  The Group already has successful concepts in Northern Europe and Continental Europe which on average earn twice the margin of our other hotels which already have a reputation for delighting customers, and this powerful customer concept will be at the heart of the Group's competitive advantage.

- Product and service innovation: This is the creation of a new portfolio of flexible trusted products and services based on feedback and trends demonstrated through the survey. Today Thomas Cook is announcing the first five innovations in this area with more innovation to come. These are: an increased emphasis on winter sun; a portfolio of dynamic packaged city break holidays; budget quality hotels with great design for the smart traveller; expanding room and flight only booking capability whilst providing an assurance of quality and a deeper engagement with customers through a suite of 'high tech services'; and through community engagement which complements the holiday

product portfolio leading to higher conversion rates, improved share of wallet and improved likelihood of repeat purchase.

- Single customer gateway: this will enable a consistent, personalized customer experience with access to a full range of products, services and personal recommendations across all channels allowing deeper, more insightful customer relationships which go beyond the booking transaction.

A key priority of the Group is to become the leading online tour operator with a digital platform that will host a full portfolio of digital products and services. Thomas Cook will reduce the number of its product brands and for its customer-facing websites there will become four in the EU (three in the UK and one in Germany), implement functionality enhancements and extend its product offering, increase its investment in offline advertising and search engine usage optimization and invest in customer engagement tools. Thomas Cook aspires to have the highest share of bookings online for a major tour operator.

- Execution supported by brand and technology: The Thomas Cook brand and other leading brands within the Group engender trust and a commitment to quality. Sixty per cent of those surveyed said it was a brand they grew up with and trust in the brand was 9 per cent higher than the market average. Drawing together the IT capabilities across the Group into a consistent platform that will enable the extension of the Group's dynamic packaging capability to customers in all markets, assist with yield management across the portfolio as well as create a seamless, unified, multi-channel customer interaction experience across mobile, web and in-store adding considerable value. Thomas Cook is building the capability to support personalized customer interaction through micro-segmentation, social media integration and powerful recommendation analytics. The IT investment plan is based on using verified, proven capabilities and systems that already exist within the Group and rolling them out to other parts of the Group. The annual investment required for this IT programme over 3 years is approximate with significant benefits as it underpins the delivery of other key parts of the strategy.

Thomas Cook CEO Harriet Green has unexpectedly stepped down and is being replaced by chief operating officer Peter Fankhauser. The change at the top of the company came as Cook released annual financial results. Green, who joined the company in 2012 and rescued it from possible collapse, said: *'The transformation of Thomas Cook into a company with a market capitalization of just under £2 billion and a share price of over 130 pence is one I have been proud to lead. I always said that I would move on to another company with fresh challenges once my work was complete. That time is now. I wish all of the team at this re-energized company continued success, as they move to the next phase of the company's development.'*

References www.thomascookgroup.com/group-strategy/

Questions

1   Discuss the extent to which Thomas Cook is following the 'Coordination Model of Innovation'.

2   Identify and comment on the reasons Thomas Cook employees might have for resisting current changes.

3   Propose managerial strategies for overcoming resistance to change at Thomas Cook.

END NOTES

1. James R. Hagerty, 'Tapping Crowds for Military Design', *The Wall Street Journal*, August 16, 2012, A3.
2. '01: Apple, For Walking the Talk', in 'The World's 50 Most Innovative Companies', *Fast Company* (March 2012): p. 81.
3. Study by Charles I. Stubbart and Michael B. Knight, reported in Spencer E. Ante, 'Avoiding Innovation's Terrible Toll', *The Wall Street Journal*, January 7, 2012, www.online.wsj.com/article/SB10001424052970204331304577144980247499346.html (accessed August 21, 2012).
4. Alex Taylor III, 'The New GM: A Report Card', *Fortune* (September 5, 2011): 38–46.
5. Richard L. Daft, 'Bureaucratic vs Nonbureaucratic Structure in the Process of Innovation and Change', in *Perspectives in Organizational Sociology: Theory and Research*, ed. Samuel B. Bacharach (Greenwich, CT: JAI Press, 1982), pp. 129–166.
6. Keith Bracsher, 'Newest Export out of China: Inflation Fears', *The New York Times*, April 16, 2004, www.nytimes.com/2004/04/16/business/newest-export-out-of-china-inflation-fears.html?scp=1&sq=Newest+Export+Out+of+China%3A+Inflation+Fears&st=nyt (accessed August 30, 2010).
7. Richard Wolf, Brad Heath and Chuck Raasch, 'How Health Care Law Survived, And What's Next', *USA Today*, June 29, 2012, www.usatoday.com/NEWS/usaedition/2012-06-29-still2_CV_U.htm (accessed August 21, 2012).
8. '05: Square, For Making Magic Out of the Mercantile', in 'The World's 50 Most Innovative Companies', *Fast Company* (March 2012): pp. 83–85, 146.
9. David W. Norton and B. Joseph Pine II, 'Unique Experiences: Disruptive Innovations Offer Customers More "Time Well Spent",' *Strategy & Leadership* 37, no. 6 (2009): 4; and 'The Power to Disrupt', *The Economist* (April 17, 2010): 16.
10. Jeffrey R. Immelt, Vijay Govindarajan and Chris Trimble, 'How GE Is Disrupting Itself', *Harvard Business Review* (October 2009): 3–11; and Navi Radjou, 'Polycentric Innovation: A New Mandate for Multinationals', *The Wall Street Journal Online*, November 9, 2009, www.online.wsj.com/article/SB125774328035737917.html (accessed November 13, 2009).
11. For more information on the ambidextrous approach, see R. Duncan, 'The Ambidextrous Organization: Designing Dual Structures for Innovation', in R. H. Killman, L. R. Pondy and D. Sleven, eds., *The Management of Organization* (New York: North Holland), pp. 167–188; S. Raisch, J. Birkinshaw, G. Probst and M. L. Tushman, 'Organizational Ambidexterity: Balancing Exploitation and Exploration for Sustained Performance', *Organization Science* 20, no. 4 (July–August 2009): 685–695; C. Brooke Dobni, 'The Innovation Blueprint', *Business Horizons* (2006): 329–339; Sebastian Raisch and Julian Birkinshaw, 'Organizational Ambidexterity: Antecedents, Outcomes, and Moderators', *Journal of Management* 34, no 3 (June 2008): 375–409; Charles A. O'Reilly III and Michael L. Tushman, 'The Ambidextrous Organization', *Harvard Business Review* (April 2004): 74–81; Duane Ireland and Justin W. Webb, 'Crossing the Great Divide of Strategic Entrepreneurship: Transitioning Between Exploration and Exploitation', *Business Horizons* 52 (2009): 469–479; and Sebastian Raisch, 'Balanced Structures: Designing Organizations for Profitable Growth', *Long Range Planning* 41 (2008): 483–508.
12. Michael L. Tushman, Wendy K. Smith and Andy Binns, 'The Ambidextrous CEO', *Harvard Business Review* (June 2011): 74–80.
13. Glenn Rifkin, 'Competing Through Innovation: The Case of Broderbund', *Strategy + Business* 11 (Second Quarter 1998): 48–58; and Deborah Dougherty and Cynthia Hardy, 'Sustained Product Innovation in Large, Mature Organizations: Overcoming Innovation-to-Organization Problems', *Academy of Management Journal* 39, no. 5 (1996): 1120–1153.
14. '2012 Good Housekeeping VIP (Very Innovative Products) Awards', www.goodhousekeeping.com/product-reviews/innovative-products-awards-2012#slide-1 (accessed August 21, 2012).
15. Anya Kamenetz, '12: Southern New Hampshire University, for Relentlessly Reinventing Higher Ed, Online and Off', in 'The World's Most Innovative Companies', pp. 94–96.

16. Adapted from Patrick Reinmoeller and Nicole van Baardwijk, 'The Link Between Diversity and Resilience', *MIT Sloan Management Review* (Summer 2005): 61–65.

17. Gordon Vessels, 'The Creative Process: An Open-Systems Conceptualization', *Journal of Creative Behavior* 16 (1982): 185–196.

18. Robert J. Sternberg, Linda A. O'Hara and Todd I. Lubart, 'Creativity as Investment', *California Management Review* 40, no. 1 (Fall 1997): 8–21; Amabile, 'Motivating Creativity in Organizations'; Leavy, 'Creativity: The New Imperative'; and Ken Lizotte, 'A Creative State of Mind', *Management Review* (May 1998): 15–17.

19. James Brian Quinn, 'Managing Innovation: Controlled Chaos', *Harvard Business Review* 63 (May–June 1985): 73–84; Howard H. Stevenson and David E. Gumpert, 'The Heart of Entrepreneurship', *Harvard Business Review* 63 (March–April 1985): 85–94; Marsha Sinetar, 'Entrepreneurs, Chaos, and Creativity – Can Creative People Really Survive Large Company Structure?' *Sloan Management Review* 6 (Winter 1985): 57–62; Constantine Andriopoulos, 'Six Paradoxes in Managing Creativity: An Embracing Act', *Long Range Planning* 36 (2003): 375–388; and Michael Laff, 'Roots of Innovation', *T&D* (July 2009): 35–39.

20. The research studies and examples are reported in Sue Shellenbarger, 'Better Ideas Through Failure', *The Wall Street Journal*, September 27, 2011, D1.

21. Cynthia Browne, 'Jest for Success', *Moonbeams* (August 1989): 3–5; and Rosabeth Moss Kanter, *The Change Masters* (New York: Simon and Schuster, 1983).

22. J. C. Spender and Bruce Strong, 'Who Has Innovative Ideas? Employees', *The Wall Street Journal* (August 23, 2010), R5; and Rachel Emma Silverman, 'How to Be Like Apple', *The Wall Street Journal* (August 29, 2011), www.online.wsj.com/article/SB10001424053111904000930457653284266785 4706.html (accessed September 16, 2011).

23. Roger L. Martin, 'The Innovation Catalysts', *Harvard Business Review* (June 2011): 82–87.

24. Spender and Strong, 'Who Has Innovative Ideas?'

25. Alison Overholt, 'American Idol: Accounting Edition', *Fortune* (October 17, 2011): 100–106.

26. Reported in Rachel Emma Silverman, 'For Bright Ideas, Ask the Staff', *The Wall Street Journal*, October 17, 2011, B7.

27. Dahl, 'Technology: Pipe Up, People!'

28. Sherry Eng, 'Hatching Schemes', *The Industry Standard* (November 27–December 4, 2000): 174–175.

29. Jena McGregor, Michael Arndt and Robert Berner, 'The World's Most Innovative Companies', *BusinessWeek* (April 24, 2006): 62ff.

30. James I. Cash, Jr, Michael J. Earl and Robert Morison, 'Teaming up to Crack Innovation and Enterprise Integration', *Harvard Business Review* (November 2008): 90–100; Barry Jaruzelski, Kevin Dehoff and Rakesh Bordia, 'Money Isn't Everything', *Strategy + Business*, no. 41 (December 5, 2005): 54–67; William L. Shanklin and John K. Ryans, Jr, 'Organizing for High-Tech Marketing', *Harvard Business Review* 62 (November–December 1984): 164–171; Arnold O. Putnam, 'A Redesign for Engineering', *Harvard Business Review* 63 (May–June 1985): 139–144; and Joan Schneider and Julie Hall, 'Why Most Product Launches Fail', *Harvard Business Review* (April 2011): 21–23.

31. Hiroko Tabuchi, 'How the Parade Passed Sony By', *The New York Times*, April 15, 2012, BU1.

32. Quoted in Janet Rae-DuPree, 'Teamwork, the True Mother of Invention', *The New York Times,* December 7, 2008.

33. Based on Gloria Barczak and Kenneth B. Kahn, 'Identifying New Product Development Best Practice', *Business Horizons* 55 (2012): 293–305; Andrew H. Van de Ven, 'Central Problems in the Management of Innovation', *Management Science* 32 (1986): 590–607; Richard L. Daft, *Organization Theory and Design* (Mason, OH: SouthWestern 2010), pp. 424–425; and Science Policy Research Unit, University of Sussex, *Success and Failure in Industrial Innovation* (London: Centre for the Study of Industrial Innovation, 1972).

34. Based on Daft, *Organization Theory and Design*; and Lee Norris Miller, 'Debugging Dysfunctional Development', *Industrial Management* (November–December 2011): 10–15.

35. Mike Gordon, Chris Musso, Eric Rebentisch and Nisheeth Gupta, 'The Path to Successful New Products', *McKinsey Quarterly* (January 2010) www.mckinseyquarterly.com/The_path_to_successful_new_products_2489 (accessed February 10, 2012).

36. Reported in Schneide and Hall, 'Why Most Product Launches Fail'.

37. Erik Brynjolfsson and Michael Schrage, 'The New, Faster Face of Innovation', *The Wall Street Journal Online*, August 17, 2009, www.online.wsj.com/article/SB1000142405297 020483030457413082018426034 0.html (accessed August 21, 2009).

38. Brian Dumaine, 'How Managers Can Succeed Through Speed', *Fortune* (February 13, 1989): 54–59; and George Stalk, Jr, 'Time – The Next Source of Competitive Advantage', *Harvard Business Review* (July–August 1988): 41–51.

39. William J. Holstein, 'Five Gates to Innovation', *Strategy + Business* (March 1, 2010), www.strategy-business.com/article/00021?gko=0bd39 (accessed September 16, 2011).

40. This discussion of open innovation is based on Henry Chesbrough, 'The Era of Open Innovation', *MIT Sloan Management Review* (Spring 2003): 35–41; Ulrich Lichtenthaler, 'Open Innovation: Past Research, Current Debates, and Future Directions', *Academy of Management Perspectives* (February 2011): 75–92; Julian Birkinshaw and Susan A. Hill, 'Corporate Venturing Units: Vehicles for Strategic Success in the New Europe', *Organizational Dynamics* 34, no. 3 (2005): 247–257; Amy Muller and Liisa Välikangas, 'Extending the Boundary of Corporate Innovation', *Strategy & Leadership* 30, no. 3 (2002): 4–9; Navi Radjou, 'Networked Innovation Drives Profits', *Industrial Management* (January–February 2005): 14–21; and Henry Chesbrough, 'The Logic of Open Innovation: Managing Intellectual Property', *California Management Review* 45, no. 3 (Spring 2003): 33–58.

41. Amy Muller, Nate Hutchins and Miguel Cardoso Pinto, 'Applying Open Innovation Where Your Company Needs It Most', *Strategy & Leadership* 40, no. 2 (2012): 35–42.

42. A. G. Lafley and Ram Charan, *The Game Changer: How You Can Drive Revenue and Profit Growth with Innovation* (New York: Crown Business, 2008); Larry Huston and Nabil Sakkab, 'Connect and Develop; Inside Procter & Gamble's New Model for Innovation', *Harvard Business Review* (March 2006): 58–66; and G. Gil Cloyd, 'P&G's Secret: Innovating Innovation', *Industry Week* (December 2004): 26–34.

43. Farhad Manjoo, 'Apple Nation', *Fortune* (July–August 2010): 68–112; and Jorge Rufat-Latre, Amy Muller and

Dave Jones, 'Delivering on the Promise of Open Innovation', *Strategy & Leadership* 38, no. 6 (2010): 23–28.

44. Reported in Muller, Hutchins and Cardoso Pinto., 'Applying Open Innovation'.

45. Elizabeth Holmes, 'Before the Dresses, the Ideas; Oscar de la Renta Invites Fans to Submit Visual Inspiration for Next Collection', *The Wall Street Journal*, February 14, 2012, www.online.wsj.com/article/SB10001424052970204883 304577221461560720548.html (accessed February 17, 2012); and Sang M. Lee, David L. Olson and Silvana Trimi, 'Innovative Collaboration for Value Creation', *Organizational Dynamics* 41 (2012): 7–12.

46. Steve Lohr, 'Online Mapping Shows Potential to Transform Relief Efforts', *The New York Times*, March 28, 2011, www.nytimes.com/2011/03/28/business/28map.html?_r=1 (accessed August 22, 2012); and Tina Rosenberg, 'Crowdsourcing a Better World', *The New York Times*, March 28, 2011, www.opinionator.blogs.nytimes.com/2011/03/28/crowdsourcing-a-better-world/ (accessed March 29, 2011).

47. Daniel T. Holt, Matthew W. Rutherford and Gretchen R. Clohessy, 'Corporate Entrepreneurship: An Empirical Look at Individual Characteristics, Context, and Process', *Journal of Leadership and Organizational Studies* 13, no. 4 (2007): 40–54.

48. Curtis R. Carlson and William W. Wilmot, *Innovation: The Five Disciplines for Creating What Customers Want* (New York: Crown Business, 2006).

49. Robert I. Sutton, 'The Weird Rules of Creativity', *Harvard Business Review* (September 2001): 94–103; and Julian Birkinshaw and Michael Mol, 'How Management Innovation Happens', *MIT Sloan Management Review* (Summer 2006): 81–88.

50. Jane M. Howell, 'The Right Stuff: Identifying and Developing Effective Champions of Innovation', *Academy of Management Executive* 19, no. 2 (2005): 108–119.

51. Harold L. Angle and Andrew H. Van de Ven, 'Suggestions for Managing the Innovation Journey', in *Research in the Management of Innovation: The Minnesota Studies*, ed. A. H. Van de Ven, H. L. Angle and Marshall Scott Poole (Cambridge, MA: Ballinger/Harper & Row, 1989).

52. C. K. Bart, 'New Venture Units: Use Them Wisely to Manage Innovation', *Sloan Management Review* (Summer 1988): 35–43; Michael Tushman and David Nadler, 'Organizing for Innovation', *California Management Review* 28 (Spring 1986): 74–92; Peter F. Drucker, *Innovation and Entrepreneurship* (New York: Harper & Row, 1985); and Henry W. Chesbrough, 'Making Sense of Corporate Venture Capital', *Harvard Business Review* 80, no. 3 (March 2002): 90–99.

53. Raisch, 'Balanced Structures'.

54. Bruce B. Brown and Scott D. Anthony, 'How P&G Tripled Its Innovation Success Rate', *Harvard Business Review* (June 2011): 64–72.

55. Christopher Hoenig, 'Skunk Works Secrets', *CIO* (July 1, 2000): 74–76; and Tom Peters and Nancy Austin, *A Passion for Excellence: The Leadership Difference* (New York: Random House, 1985).

56. Hoenig, 'Skunk Works Secrets'.

57. Claire Cain Miller and Nick Bilton, 'Google's Lab of Wildest Dreams', *The New York Times*, November 13, 2011, www.nytimes.com/2011/11/14/technology/at-google-x-a-top-secret-lab-dreaming-up-the-future.html?pagewanted=all (accessed November 14, 2011).

58. Taylor, 'The New GM'.

59. David Dobson, 'Integrated Innovation at Pitney Bowes', *Strategy + Business Online*, October 26, 2009, www.strategy-business.com/article/09404b?gko=f9661 (accessed December 30, 2009); and James Cash, Michael Earl and Robert Morison, 'Teaming up to Crack Innovation and Enterprise Integration', *Harvard Business Review* (November 2008): 90–100.

60. Robert C. Wolcott and Michael J. Lippitz, 'The Four Models of Corporate Entrepreneurship', *MIT Sloan Management Review* (Fall 2007): 75–82.

61. E. H. Schein, 'Organizational Culture', *American Psychologist* 45 (February 1990): 109–119; Eliza Newlin Carney, 'Calm in the Storm', *Government Executive* (October 2003): 57–63.

62. Rosabeth Moss Kanter, 'Execution: The Un-Idea', sidebar in Art Kleiner, 'Our 10 Most Enduring Ideas', *Strategy + Business*, no. 41 (December 12, 2005): 36–41.

63. Alan Murray, 'Women in a Man's World: Dan Akerson of General Motors on Changing a Male-Dominated Culture', *The Wall Street Journal*, May 7, 2012, B11; and Alex Taylor III, 'The New GM: A Report Card', *Fortune* (September 5, 2011): 38–46.

64. Michelle Conlin, 'Tough Love for Techie Souls', *BusinessWeek* (November 29, 1999): 164–170.

65. M. Sashkin and W. W. Burke, 'Organization Development in the 1980s', *General Management* 13 (1987): 393–417; and Richard Beckhard, 'What Is Organization Development?' in *Organization Development and Transformation: Managing Effective Change*, ed. Wendell L. French, Cecil H. Bell, Jr and Robert A. Zawacki (Burr Ridge, IL: Irwin McGraw-Hill, 2000), pp. 16–19.

66. Wendell L. French and Cecil H. Bell, Jr, 'A History of Organization Development', in French, Bell and Zawacki, *Organization Development and Transformation*, pp. 20–42; and Christopher G. Worley and Ann E. Feyerherm, 'Reflections on the Future of Organization Development', *The Journal of Applied Behavioral Science* 39, no. 1 (March 2003): 97–115.

67. Paul F. Buller, 'For Successful Strategic Change: Blend OD Practices with Strategic Management', *Organizational Dynamics* (Winter 1988): 42–55; Robert M. Fulmer and Roderick Gilkey, 'Blending Corporate Families: Management and Organization Development in a Postmerger Environment', *The Academy of Management Executive* 2 (1988): 275–283; and Worley and Feyerherm, 'Reflections on the Future of Organization Development'.

68. W. Warner Burke, 'The New Agenda for Organization Development', *Organizational Dynamics* (Summer 1997): 7–19.

69. R. Wayne Bass et al., 'Sustainable Change in the Public Sector: The Longitudinal Benefits of Organization Development', *The Journal of Applied Behavioral Science* 46, no. 4 (2010): 436–472.

70. This discussion is based on Kathleen D. Dannemiller and Robert W. Jacobs, 'Changing the Way Organizations Change: A Revolution of Common Sense', *The Journal of Applied Behavioral Science* 28, no. 4 (December 1992): 480–498; and Barbara Benedict Bunker and Billie T. Alban, 'Conclusion: What Makes Large Group Interventions Effective?' *The Journal of Applied Behavioral Science* 28, no. 4 (December 1992): 570–591.

71. For a recent review of the literature related to large group interventions, see Christopher G. Worley, Susan A. Mohrman and Jennifer A. Nevitt, 'Large Group Interventions: An Empirical Study of Their Composition, Process, and Outcomes', *The Journal of Applied Behavioral Science* 47, no. 4 (2011): 404–431.

72. Bunker and Alban, 'Conclusion: What Makes Large Group Interventions Effective?'

73. Kurt Lewin, 'Frontiers in Group Dynamics: Concepts, Method, and Reality in Social Science', *Human Relations* 1 (1947): 5–41; and E. F. Huse and T. G. Cummings, *Organization Development and Change*, 3d ed. (St. Paul, MN: West, 1985).

74. Based on John Kotter's eight-step model of planned change, which is described in John P. Kotter, *Leading Change* (Boston: Harvard Business School Press, 1996), pp. 20–25, and John Kotter, 'Leading Change: Why Transformation Efforts Fail', *Harvard Business Review* (March–April, 1995): 59–67.

75. Based on Bob Kelleher, 'Employee Engagement Carries ENSR Through Organizational Challenges and Economic Turmoil', *Global Business and Organizational Excellence* 28, no. 3 (March–April 2009): 6–19.

76. Paul Ingrassia, 'GM Gets a Second Chance', *The Wall Street Journal Europe,* July 10, 2009; and 'Ford to Seek Same No-Strike Vow from UAW as GM and Chrysler Obtained', *National Post*, June 18, 2009.

77. Kotter, *Leading Change*, pp. 20–25; and 'Leading Change: Why Transformation Efforts Fail'.

78. J. P. Kotter and L. A. Schlesinger, 'Choosing Strategies for Change', *Harvard Business Review* 57 (March–April 1979): 106–114.

79. David Kesmodel and Suzanne Vranica, 'Unease Brewing at Anheuser as New Owners Slash Costs', *The Wall Street Journal*, April 29, 2009.

80. Joann S. Lublin, 'Theory & Practice: Firm Offers Blueprint for Makeover in a Spinoff', *The Wall Street Journal,* June 29, 2009.

81. G. Zaltman and Robert B. Duncan, *Strategies for Planned Change* (New York: Wiley Interscience, 1977).

82. E. S. Browning, Steven Russolillo and Jessica Vascellaro, 'Apple Now Biggest-Ever U.S. Company', *The Wall Street Journal Europe*, August 22, 2012, 24; and Charles Duhigg and David Barboza, 'In China, Human Costs Are Built Into an iPad', *The New York Times*, January 25, 2012, www.nytimes.com/2012/01/26/business/ieconomy-apples-ipad-and-the-human-costs-for-workers-in-china.html?pagewanted=all (accessed January 26, 2012).

83. Dorothy Leonard-Barton and Isabelle Deschamps, 'Managerial Influence in the Implementation of New Technology', *Management Science* 34 (1988): 1252–1265.

84. Kurt Lewin, *Field Theory in Social Science: Selected Theoretical Papers* (New York: Harper & Brothers, 1951).

85. Paul C. Nutt, 'Tactics of Implementation', *Academy of Management Journal* 29 (1986): 230–261; Kotter and Schlesinger, 'Choosing Strategies for Change'; R. L. Daft and S. Becker, *Innovation in Organizations: Innovation Adoption in School Organizations* (New York: Elsevier, 1978); and R. Beckhard, *Organization Development: Strategies and Models* (Reading, MA: Addison-Wesley, 1969).

86. Allysia Finley, 'The Democrat Who Took On the Unions', *The Wall Street Journal*, March 24, 2012, A13.

87. Gerard H. Seijts and Grace O'Farrell, 'Engage the Heart: Appealing to the Emotions Facilitates Change', *Ivey Business Journal* (January–February 2003): 1–5; John P. Kotter and Dan S. Cohen, *The Heart of Change: Real-Life Stories of How People Change Their Organizations* (Boston: Harvard Business School Press, 2002); and Shaul Fox and Yair Amichai Hamburger, 'The Power of Emotional Appeals in Promoting Organizational Change Programs', *Academy of Management Executive* 15, no. 4 (2001): 84–95.

88. Gina Burkhardt and Diane Gerard, 'People: The Lever for Changing the Business Model at Learning Point Associates', *Journal of Organizational Excellence* (Autumn 2006): 31–43.

89. Henry Hornstein, 'Using a Change Management Approach to Implement IT Programs', *Ivey Business Journal* (January–February 2008); Philip H. Mirvis, Amy L. Sales and Edward J. Hackett, 'The Implementation and Adoption of New Technology in Organizations: The Impact on Work, People, and Culture', *Human Resource Management* 30 (Spring 1991): 113–139; Arthur E. Wallach, 'System Changes Begin in the Training Department', *Personnel Journal* 58 (1979): 846–848, 872; and Paul R. Lawrence, 'How to Deal with Resistance to Change', *Harvard Business Review* 47 (January–February 1969): 4–12, 166–176.

90. Kate Linebaugh and Jeff Bennett, 'Marchionne Upends Chrysler's Ways: CEO Decries Detroit's 'Fanatical' Focus on Market Share', *The Wall Street Journal,* January 12, 2010.

91. Strategos survey results, reported in Pierre Loewe and Jennifer Dominiquini, 'Overcoming the Barriers to Effective Innovation', *Strategy & Leadership* 34, no. 1 (2006): 24–31.

92. Donald F. Kuratko, Jeffrey G. Covin and Robert P. Garrett, 'Corporate Venturing: Insights from Actual Performance', *Business Horizons* 52 (2009): 459–467.

93. Based on H. Thomas Hurt, Katherine Joseph and Chester D. Cook, 'Scales for the Measurement of Innovativeness', *Human Communication Research* 4, no. 1 (1977): 58–65; and John E. Ettlie and Robert D. O'Keefe, 'Innovative Attitudes, Values, and Intentions in Organizations', *Journal of Management Studies* 19, no. 2 (1982): 163–182.

94. Based on Paul Boutin, 'Crowdsourcing: Consumers As Creators', *BusinessWeek Online,* July 13, 2006, www.businessweek.com/innovate/content/jul2006/id20060713_755844.htm (accessed August 30, 2010); Jeff Howe, 'The Rise of Crowdsourcing', *Wired,* June 2006, www.wired.com/wired/archive/14.06/crowds.html (accessed August 30, 2010); and Jeff Howe, Crowdsourcing blog, www.crowdsourcing.com (accessed August 30, 2010).

CHAPTER 12

MANAGING CORPORATE DIVERSITY

LEARNING OBJECTIVES

After studying this chapter, you should be able to:

1 Appreciate the pervasive demographic changes occurring in the domestic and global workforces and how corporations are responding.

2 Understand how the definition of diversity has grown to recognize a broad spectrum of differences among employees, the importance of fostering a sense of inclusion, and the dividends of a diverse workforce.

3 Recognize the complex attitudes, opinions and issues that people bring to the workplace, including prejudice, discrimination, stereotypes and ethnocentrism.

4 Recognize the factors that affect women's opportunities, including the glass ceiling, the opt-out trend and the female advantage.

5 Explain the five steps in developing cultural competence in the workplace.

6 Describe how diversity initiatives and training programmes help create a climate that values diversity.

7 Understand how multicultural teams and employee affinity groups help organizations respond to the rapidly changing and complex workplace.

Texas Instruments does a good job recruiting women engineers out of college – 20 to 24 per cent of the electrical engineers it hires are female. But there are few women in executive management positions. To help fill the pipeline to the corner office with women, Texas Instruments grooms them for positions of higher responsibility through initiatives like the Women's P&L Initiative, which puts women in positions where they will get 'profit-and-loss' experience. Managers identify star women performers and prepare them for line-management roles with training in leadership traits and skills. In addition, aspiring managers are assigned to high-ranking mentors to develop skills needed for promotion. '*We have to attract more of them into the jobs that lead to the highest levels,*' says CEO Richard K. Templeton.

Jennifer W. Christensen, a Chicago executive recruiter, knows why the Women's P&L Initiative is so important. Higher-level positions require profit-and-loss experience. *'Men dominate profit-and-loss posts, in part because they ask for them, while women often wait for them to be offered,'* says Christensen. The company's initiative is paying off, leading to a 60 per cent increase in 2012 over 2009 in the number of women in profit-and-loss positions.[1]

Managers are discovering that it makes good business sense to support diversity programmes like the Women's P&L Initiative. Not only are diversity programmes the right thing to do ethically and culturally, but these initiatives can also create new business opportunities. To capitalize on those opportunities, organizations recognize that workplaces need to reflect the diversity in the marketplace. *'Our country's consumer base is so varied,'* says Shelley Willingham-Hinton, 2007 president of the National Organization for Diversity in Sales and Marketing. *'I can't think of how a company can succeed without having that kind of diversity with their employees.'*[2] Forward-thinking managers agree and take steps to attract and retain a workforce that reflects the cultural diversity of the population. They take seriously that there is a link between the diversity of the workforce and corporate financial success in the marketplace. Exhibit 12.1 lists a few corporations that are considered leaders in diversity. They make diversity a top priority and actively pursue a corporate culture that values equality and reflects today's multicultural consumer base.

'If we don't reflect the global nature of our business in our employees, how can we possibly hope to understand our customers? In the same way, we have to have a good balance of men and women. If we only have men building our products and services, how are we going to appeal to half the world's population?'
— MARK PALMER-EDGECUMBE, GOOGLE'S HEAD OF DIVERSITY AND INCLUSION

This chapter describes how the domestic and global workforce is becoming increasingly multicultural and how corporations are responding to the challenges and opportunities this presents. We look at the myriad complex issues that face managers and employees in a diverse workplace, including prejudice, stereotypes, discrimination and ethnocentrism. Factors that specifically affect women – the glass ceiling, the opt-out trend and feminine advantages – are also considered. After a review of the steps towards fuller cultural competence, the chapter concludes by presenting an overview of initiatives taken by corporations to create an environment that welcomes and values a broad spectrum of diversity among its employees. The significant impacts of globalization and foreign direct investment (FDI) flows from China, the world's second largest economy, are also included in this chapter. There is a great deal of hype and rhetoric about the impetus of diversity-reduction in the 'new new world' – but there are underlying strands of continuity in many of the diverse national cultures on our planet. We aspire to provide a balanced view of cultural diversity that some modern scholars (e.g. Dicken, P., 2011, p.8) are expressing as a dynamic variable influencing the complexity of corporate identity. We would further argue that the world is contoured and not flat, challenging Friedman's bold statement.

EXHIBIT 12.1 Examples of leaders in corporate diversity

Company	US employees	% Minority employees
Four Seasons Hotels	11 729	67
Marriott International	106 280	61
Qualcomm	12 520	55
Genentech	11 464	45
Cisco	36 612	45
Nordstrom	49 447	41
Intel	42 694	40

SOURCE: '100 Best Companies to Work For, 2009; Top Companies: Most Diverse', www.money.cnn.com/magazines/fortune/bestcompanies/2011/minorities/ (accessed June 28, 2012).

Diversity in the workplace

When Brenda Thomson, former director of diversity and leadership education at the Las Vegas MGM Mirage, stepped into one of the company's hotel lobbies, she closes her eyes and listens. *'It's amazing all the different languages I can hear just standing in the lobbies of any of our hotels,'* she says. *'Our guests come from all over the world, and it really makes us realize the importance of reflecting that diversity in our workplace.'*[3] The diversity Thomson sees in the lobbies of the MGM Mirage hotels is a small reflection of the cultural diversity in larger domestic and globalized workplaces.

Diversity in corporate America

Faced with fewer resources, a spluttering economy, and increased domestic and global competition, US managers are searching for ways to set their organizations apart from the competition and create break-through innovations. One highly important tool for succeeding in a competitive environment is a diversi-fied workforce. Managers who cultivate a diversified workforce have demonstrated improvements of their organization's chances of success. Diverse teams that perform efficiently add value by combining individuals' strengths, making the whole greater than the sum of its parts.[4]

In the past, when managers thought of diversity, they focused on the 'problems' associated with diversity, such as discrimination, bias, affirmative action and tokenism.[5] Now managers recognize that the differences people bring to the workplace are valuable.[6] Rather than expecting all employees to adopt similar attitudes and values, managers are learning that these differences enable their companies to better compete globally and to tap into rich sources of new talent. Although diversity in North America has been a reality for some time, genuine efforts to accept and *manage* diverse people began only in recent years. Exhibit 12.2 lists some interesting milestones in the history of corporate diversity.

Diversity in corporate America has become an important issue for policymakers partly because of the vast changes occurring in today's workplace. The following data illustrate how the workplace is changing and challenging frontline managers who are trying to build cohesive teams:

■ *Unprecedented generational diversity.* Today's workforce is in a state of flux as a blend of multiple generations presents new challenges for management, *'with people staying healthy and working longer not only in the USA, but in China, Brazil, Russia and elsewhere'.*[7] Although most people from the post 1945 generation have retired, there are still some members in their late 60s, 70s and even 80s active in the workplace. In 2010, for example, this generation represented about 5 per cent of the labour force in the USA, and nearly 7 per cent in Canada. These employees, and the rapidly ageing baby boom-ers, share a 'corporate memory' that is invaluable to organizations, but as they stay in the workforce longer, there is less room for Generation X managers wanting to move quickly up the hierarchy. As Gen-X workers move into middle age, they are struggling with reduced guarantees about their financial futures and questionable longer term job security. Meanwhile, Gen-Yers, sometimes called Millennials, are characterized as ambitious, lacking loyalty to one organization, and eager for quick success. Unlike different generations working together in the past, there are strong value differences among employees from different eras today.[8]

■ *Ageing workers.* Baby boomers continue to affect the workplace as this massive group of workers pro-gresses through its life stages. A baby boomer turns 60 every 7 seconds, continuously bumping up the average age of the workforce. While the number of workers between 25 and 45-years-old is expected to decline from 66.9 per cent to 63.7 per cent by 2020, the number of boomers age 55 years and older will leap from 19.5 per cent to 25.2 in the same period.[9]

■ *Increased diversity.* Today's workplace is becoming more diverse as the number of foreign-born work-ers increases. Foreign-born workers make up one in six of the US workforce and are most likely em-ployed in service industries, such as food preparation, cleaning and maintenance. Of the total number of foreign-born workers, nearly 50 per cent are Hispanic and 23 per cent are Asian.[10] Looking ahead, the number of Hispanic employees will grow the most, expected to increase to 18.6 per cent by 2020.[11]

EXHIBIT 12.2 Milestones in the history of corporate diversity

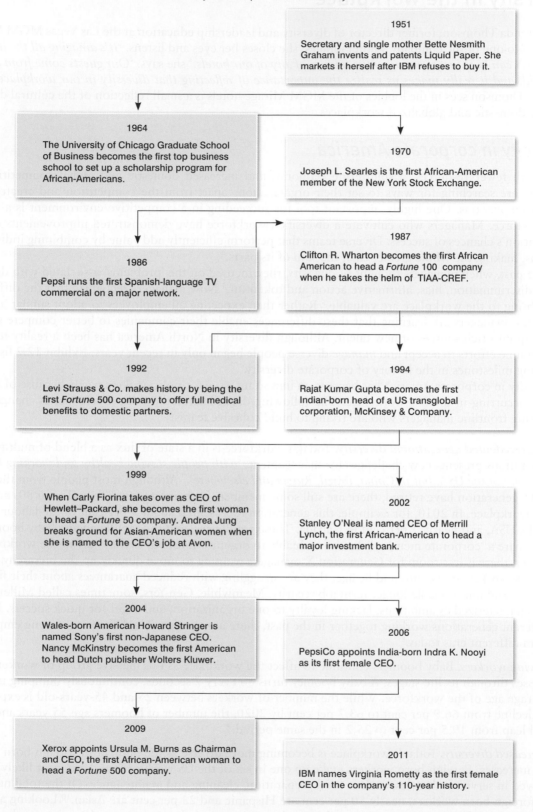

1951

Secretary and single mother Bette Nesmith Graham invents and patents Liquid Paper. She markets it herself after IBM refuses to buy it.

1964

The University of Chicago Graduate School of Business becomes the first top business school to set up a scholarship program for African-Americans.

1970

Joseph L. Searles is the first African-American member of the New York Stock Exchange.

1987

Clifton R. Wharton becomes the first African American to head a *Fortune* 100 company when he takes the helm of TIAA-CREF.

1986

Pepsi runs the first Spanish-language TV commercial on a major network.

1992

Levi Strauss & Co. makes history by being the first *Fortune* 500 company to offer full medical benefits to domestic partners.

1994

Rajat Kumar Gupta becomes the first Indian-born head of a US transglobal corporation, McKinsey & Company.

1999

When Carly Fiorina takes over as CEO of Hewlett–Packard, she becomes the first woman to head a *Fortune* 50 company. Andrea Jung breaks ground for Asian-American women when she is named to the CEO's job at Avon.

2002

Stanley O'Neal is named CEO of Merrill Lynch, the first African-American to head a major investment bank.

2004

Wales-born American Howard Stringer is named Sony's first non-Japanese CEO. Nancy McKinstry becomes the first American to head Dutch publisher Wolters Kluwer.

2006

PepsiCo appoints India-born Indra K. Nooyi as its first female CEO.

2009

Xerox appoints Ursula M. Burns as Chairman and CEO, the first African-American woman to head a *Fortune* 500 company.

2011

IBM names Virginia Rometty as the first female CEO in the company's 110-year history.

SOURCES: 'Spotlight on Diversity', special advertising section, *MBA Jungle* (March–April 2003): 58–61; and Xerox corporate website, www.news.xerox.com.

EXHIBIT 12.3 Projected changes in US labour force, 2010 to 2020

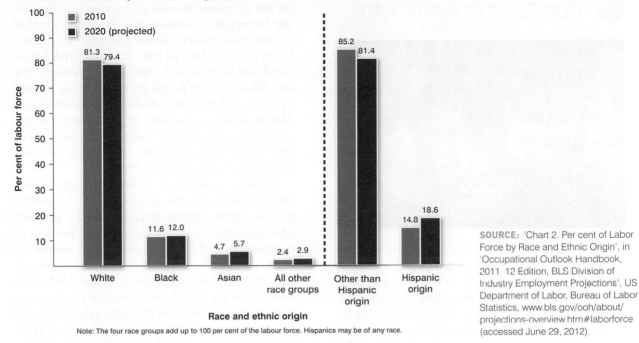

Note: The four race groups add up to 100 per cent of the labour force. Hispanics may be of any race.

SOURCE: 'Chart 2. Per cent of Labor Force by Race and Ethnic Origin', in 'Occupational Outlook Handbook, 2011 12 Edition, BLS Division of Industry Employment Projections', US Department of Labor, Bureau of Labor Statistics, www.bls.gov/ooh/about/projections-overview.htm#laborforce (accessed June 29, 2012).

Exhibit 12.3 shows the projected changes in employment among different racial and ethnic groups in the USA.

- **Growth in women workers.** Today, women outnumber men in the workplace, and their numbers are projected to grow slightly faster, at 7.4 per cent compared to 6.3 per cent for men. The good news is that nearly 73 per cent of *Fortune 500* companies have at least one female executive officer, but women comprise just 14 per cent of executive officers, according to Catalyst, a leading advocacy group for women.[12] To accelerate their progress, many corporations have initiated coaching and training programmes that prepare women for senior-level positions.

TAKE A MOMENT

As a manager, will you value the differences people bring to the workplace? Take the questionnaire at the end of this chapter to see if your biases are creating a stumbling block in your ability to embrace diversity.

These trends underscore the complex nature of today's workforce and the potential pitfalls managers face as they lead diverse teams towards common goals. While many managers recognize the value of multicultural diversity, some simply haven't kept pace with these demographic trends. In fact, as diversity has increased, so have the number of discrimination complaints with the US Equal Employment Opportunity Commission (EEOC), which investigates employee claims and sometimes brings lawsuits on behalf of workers. Claims rose nearly 100 000 in 2010, up 7 per cent from the year before.

Diversity on a global scale

Managers across the globe wrestle with many of the same diversity challenges as US managers, especially concerning the progression of women into upper management positions. Consider, for example, that in Italy, only 6 per cent of the total number of corporate board members are women, 14 per cent in Britain, and 2 per cent in Germany and India. As mentioned earlier, 14 per cent of all board members in the USA

CONCEPT CONNECTION

Successful organizations seek a **diverse and inclusive workforce**. Indra Nooyi was named CEO of PepsiCo in 2006 after 12 years with the food and beverage giant, spending most of those years leading its global strategy. Both *Fortune* and *Forbes* magazines named the Indian-born executive one of the most powerful women in America. *'I am not your normal, non-diverse CEO. I am everything that this company took forth in diversity and inclusion, and it has all come together with me,'* says Nooyi.

are women.[13] To boost the percentage of women on the corporate boards of European countries, the European Commission is studying whether to introduce quotas across the continent, similar to a recent law in Italy that required Italian listed and state-owned companies to ensure that one-third of their board members were women by 2015. *'We needed a shock to the system,'* said Alessia Mosca, a member of Parliament for the centre-left Democratic Party, who coauthored Italy's new 'pink quota' law. *'The hope is that this will set off cultural change.'*[14]

Japanese companies have an even greater struggle to bridge the gender gap on corporate boards, where women make up just 1.2 per cent of senior executives.[15] In fact, only 65 per cent of college-educated Japanese women are employed, many of them in low-paid temp jobs, compared with 80 per cent of women in the USA. The reasons for the dearth of women in the Japanese workforce are complex. Part of it relates to tepid economic growth. But over two-thirds of Japanese women leave work after their first child is born, compared to just one-third of US women, often because of insufficient childcare and societal expectations.[16]

Cultural norms, such as those that restrict the progression of women in Japan, are intangible, pervasive and difficult to comprehend. However, it is imperative that managers learn to understand local cultures and deal with them effectively.[17]

REFLECTION

- A workforce that displays characteristics of today's diversified marketplace is an important tool for managers who are striving for success in a highly competitive business environment.
- The US workforce is being transformed by a four-generation workforce: ageing baby boomers, an increase in Hispanic and Asian workers and an increasing number of women employees.

- The progression of women into executive positions continues to be slow in both US and global corporations, but innovative companies are initiating programmes to boost women's advancement into higher levels of responsibility.
- To succeed in the global marketplace managers need to fully understand other cultures and how business is to be conducted with sensitively.

Managing diversity

Managers who want to boost performance and jumpstart innovation express a consensus view that culturally diverse teams produce the best results. In one survey of 32 department heads and executives, 84 per cent stated that they prefer heterogeneous teams because they lead to multiple viewpoints and more prolific ideas.[18] The following sections describe the characteristics of a diverse workforce and the dividends of cultivating one.

🌱 GREEN POWER

Diversity and biodiversity

The preservation of diverse plant and animal life forms echoes UK academics Solomon and Solomon's words. To promote biodiversity preservation, managers at beverage maker **Bean and Body** use proceeds from the sale of its healthy coffees to sponsor *The Bean and Body Protected Grounds Initiative*, which works in collaboration with The World Land Trust to buy, protect and preserve the most threatened areas of the world's rain forests, wetlands and coastlines. The award-winning effort recognizes corporate goals to promote a healthy lifestyle, whilst taking intentional steps to promote ecological, economic and social preservation. The Bean and Body initiative works to solve biodiversity issues by helping the farmers whose cultivation of coffee beans affects the environment through ground water runoff and deep incursions into rain forests.

SOURCES: Andrew J. Hoffman, 'Climate Change as a Cultural and Behavioral Issue: Addressing Barriers and Implementing Solutions', *Organizational Dynamics* 39 (2010): 295–305; and Erin Legg, 'Coffee Re-imagined: Bean and Body Emerge as Global Leaders', *Healthy New Age* website, July 2010, www.healthynewage.com/blog/bean-and-body-wins-award/ (accessed August 1, 2012).

Diversity and inclusion

Diversity can be briefly defined as all the ways in which people differ.[19] Diversity wasn't always defined this broadly. Decades ago, many companies defined diversity in terms of race, gender, age, lifestyle and disability. That focus helped create awareness, change mindsets and create new opportunities for many. Today, companies are embracing a more inclusive definition of diversity, one that recognizes a spectrum of differences that influence how employees approach work, interact with each other, derive satisfaction from their work and define who they are as people in the workplace.[20]

Exhibit 12.4 illustrates the difference between the traditional model and the inclusive model of diversity. The dimensions of diversity shown in the traditional model include inborn differences that are immediately observable and include race, gender, age and physical ability. However, the inclusive model of diversity includes *all* of the ways in which employees differ, including aspects of diversity that can be acquired or changed throughout one's lifetime. These dimensions may have less impact than those included only in the traditional model, but they nevertheless affect a person's self-definition and worldview and the way the person is viewed by others. Many organizational leaders embrace this more inclusive definition of diversity. *'Diversity has to be looked at in its broadest sense,'* said Wally Parker, former CEO of KeySpan Energy (now National Grid). *'To me, it's all about recognizing, respecting and supporting individuals regardless of what makes up that individuality. So, yes, that's race, gender and sexual orientation. But it's also introverted and extroverted, ethnic backgrounds, cultural upbringing, all those things.'*[21]

EXHIBIT 12.4 Traditional vs inclusive models of diversity

SOURCE: Anthony Oshiotse and Richard O'Leary, 'Corning Creates an Inclusive Culture to Drive Technology Innovation and Performance', *Global Business and Organizational Excellence* 26, no. 3 (March/April 2007): 7–21.

One of the challenges of managing a diverse workforce is creating an environment where all employees feel accepted as members of the team and where their unique talents are appreciated.[22] When managers create a feeling of inclusiveness, employees display more loyalty, cooperation and trustworthiness. Inclusion is the degree to which an employee feels like an esteemed member of a group in which his or her uniqueness is highly appreciated. Inclusion creates a strong sense of belonging where all can have their voices heard and appreciated. Consider how a manager of a retail store embraced an employee's unique perspective with positive results. Hal, the manager, supervised an employee, Olivia, who was quiet and seemed to have few innovative ideas. But as Hal discussed marketing strategies for the store with Olivia, he was surprised to learn that she was a highly creative thinker, consistently interjecting novel ideas into the discussion. Over time, Hal realized that this seemingly quiet employee was one of the most creative marketing thinkers he had ever met, and together they created a very successful line of children's outerwear. Hal has become a strong supporter of inclusion and a champion for individuals who operate differently from the norm.[23]

In creating a culture of inclusion, managers may experience times of tension and discord as people with different backgrounds bring different opinions and ideas. Conflict, anxiety and misunderstandings may increase. Embracing these differences and using them to improve company performance can be challenging. Managing diversity, a key management skill in today's global economy, means creating a climate in which the potential advantages of diversity for organizational or group performance are maximized, while the potential disadvantages are minimized.[24]

It could be argued that cross-cultural management has morphed into a form of knowledge management, being synchronized, by the best firms, to the new economic world. The task of international managers is, as described by Holden (2002) '... *to facilitate and direct synergistic interaction and learning at interfaces where knowledge, values and experience are transferred into multicultural domains of implementation. Cross-cultural management is also the study of the creation, evolution and management of fusions of diversity, in relation to organizations' policies, goals, strategies and achievements.*'

Holden states that the 'know-how' and thus its benefits should be shared between individuals and transmitted across internal organizational boundaries, becoming a facet of a firm's [unique] core competence. Cultural knowledge-sharing aligned with continuous collaborative organizational learning contributes to gaining and maintaining international competitive advantage. Conceptually, a firm with rich cultural diversity could conceivably pursue two strategic objectives simultaneously, that seem to be contradictory being the exploitation of existing and the exploration of new markets. This polemic approach is one of 'Strategic Ambidexterity' described by Alukah and Sarkar cited in Judge and Blocker (2008) as: '*A firm's ability to combine exploration and exploitation strategies across product, market and resource domains.*'

The Manager's Shoptalk section describes how managers can leverage gender and ethnic differences to improve performance and strengthen corporate culture.

TAKE A MOMENT

In what ways do you feel unique from others you work or attend class with? Do these perceived differences affect your interpersonal relationships? Complete the Small Group Breakout Exercise online to assess your personal diversity and gain insights about the factors that you believe set you apart from others.

Diversity of perspective

You may have heard the expression that 'great minds think alike'. But when it comes to achieving breakthrough levels of innovation, the best minds are those that *don't* think alike. Successful managers understand the basic elements of successful teams, including competence, clear performance goals, shared vision and a supportive work environment. You will learn more about managing successful teams in Chapter 16. But managers who cultivate a team with a 'diversity of perspective' significantly increase the chance of creating hard-to-replicate competitive advantage. Diversity of perspective is achieved when a manager creates a heterogeneous team made up of individuals with diverse backgrounds and skill sets. By tapping into the strengths of diversity, teams are more likely to experience the following: higher efficiency, better quality, less duplication of effort among team members and increased innovation and creativity.[25]

🌐 MANAGER'S SHOPTALK

Change your frame

Managers who successfully manage diversity are well equipped to navigate the challenges of today's global economy. But some managers are sceptical of a 'managing diversity' philosophy that imposes a requirement to recruit and blend together people of different ethnicities, cultures and genders. (To assess your attitude towards diversity, complete the New Manager Self-Test) Instead of 'managing diversity', leaders can embrace a new frame of reference that focuses on 'leveraging differences' to build a stronger corporate culture and improve performance. The traditional frame of reference about imposing diversity '… *originated from the Civil Rights era,*' said Dr Rohini Anand, chief diversity officer at Sodexo. '*This will never go away completely. However, diversity must go beyond this mentality.*'

The real value of diversity can only be achieved when managers focus on inviting and embracing the contributions from fusing together people of different ethnic and gender backgrounds. Below are some reasons for adopting a 'leveraging differences' mindset:

- **Greater collective intelligence.** A group of employees with a high collective intelligence learns quickly and thinks creatively. Its collective intelligence has little relationship to the average IQ of its members. Instead, collective intelligence is highest in groups whose members demonstrate social sensitivity, which refers to sensitivity to others' emotions. Groups with social sensitivity communicate effectively and encourage all members to express their ideas. Groups with the highest social sensitivity include both men and women. But data show that the more women there are in a group, the better.

- **Greater creativity.** Instead of a narrow mindset that is blind to differences in a group, managers

can embrace the idea that people hold divergent perspectives and that there is something to be learned from each individual. Creativity is cultivated in environments where managers face the discomfort with the friction that can surface when group members disagree.

- **Broader perspectives.** Ideas that arise from less familiar places increase the breadth of information and knowledge to which people are normally exposed. Studies show that senior executives need a variety of perspectives, and they're much more likely to gain that if their organizations and management teams include people of different social and cultural backgrounds.

- **Preventing groupthink.** Many teams unconsciously seek to avoid conflict and place a priority on creating harmony. The term *groupthink* describes a faulty decision-making process by team members who are overly eager to agree with one another. Conforming to the consensus of the group restricts innovative thinking. A leveraging differences frame cultivates a decision-making environment that values divergent opinions and encourages healthy disagreements.

SOURCES: Glenn Llopis, 'Diversity Management Is the Key to Growth: Make It Authentic', *Forbes*, June 13, 2011, www.forbes.com/sites/glennllopis/2011/06/13/diversity (accessed July 20, 2011); Martin Davidson, 'The End of Diversity: How Leaders Make Differences Really Matter', *Executive Forum* (Spring 2012): 51–56; Peter Gwynne, 'Group Intelligence, Teamwork, and Productivity', *Perspectives* (March–April, 2012): 7–8; Anita Woolley and Thomas Malone, 'What Makes a Team Smarter? More Women', *Harvard Business Review* (June 2011): 32–33; and Natalie D. Brecher, 'Diversity Delivers: Four Tips for Embracing Differences', *Journal of Property Management* (May–June 2012): 24.

What happens when employees are homogeneous and lack a diversity of perspective? A study conducted by Jonathan Haidt, a social psychologist at the University of Virginia, suggests that when a group is homogeneous, it can develop a tribal mentality, embracing only ideas that support its own values and ditching ideas that distort or threaten the group's norms. Haidt observed that nearly 80 per cent of 1000 psychologists attending a professional meeting identified themselves as 'liberal'. Haidt claims this dominate ideology creates a bias in thinking that leads to a hostile environment for non-liberals in the profession. He also observed that the small minority of psychologists who consider themselves 'conservative' frequently hid their feelings from colleagues to avoid being shunned or ridiculed.[26] Haidt's study underscores how homogeneous groups may hinder innovative thinking and reject ideas from outsiders.

Dividends of workplace diversity

Managers who build strong, diverse organizations reap numerous dividends as described here and shown in Exhibit 12.5.[27] The dividends of diversity include the following:

- **Better use of employee talent.** Companies with the best talent are the ones with the best competitive advantage. Attracting a diverse workforce is not enough; companies must also provide career opportunities and advancement for minorities and women to retain them. The organizational talent pool must also have an absorptive capacity.

- **Increased understanding of the marketplace.** A diverse workforce is better able to anticipate and respond to changing consumer needs. US Ford Motor Company realized it could only reach its business objectives if it created a workforce that reflected the multicultural face of the host country. So it assembled a workforce made up of 25 per cent minorities (18.4 per cent are African-American) to foster a culture of inclusion, winning it a spot on *Black Enterprise's* '40 Best Companies for Diversity'.[28]

- **Enhanced breadth of understanding in leadership positions.** Homogeneous top management teams tend to be myopic in their perspectives. According to Niall FitzGerald, Chairman and CEO of Unilever until 2004, *'It is important for any business operating in an increasingly complex and rapidly changing environment to deploy a broad range of talents. That provides a breadth of understanding of the world and environment and a fusion of the very best values and different perspectives which make up that world.'*[29]

- **Increased quality of team problem solving.** Teams with diverse backgrounds bring different perspectives to a discussion that result in more creative ideas and solutions.[30] Although a large percentage of Ernst & Young's senior leadership is male, the company is taking steps to create a more diverse leadership team, because it's better for business. *'We know you get better solutions when you put a diverse team at the table. People come from different backgrounds and they have different frames of reference. When you put these people together, you get the best solution for our clients,'* says Billie Williamson, director of flexibility and gender equity strategy at Ernst & Young.[31]

- **Reduced costs associated with high turnover, absenteeism and lawsuits.** Companies that foster a diverse workforce reduce turnover, absenteeism and the risk of lawsuits. Because family responsibilities contribute to turnover and absenteeism, many companies now offer child care and elder-care benefits, flexible work arrangements, telecommuting and part-time employment to accommodate employee responsibilities at home. Discrimination lawsuits are also a costly side-effect of a discriminatory work environment. A racial harassment suit against Lockheed Martin Corporation cost the company $2.5 million, the largest individual racial-discrimination payment obtained by the EEOC.[32]

The most successful organizations appreciate the importance of diversity and recognize that their biggest asset is their people. Organizations with diverse workforces are better prepared to anticipate strategic surprises, as the Central Intelligence Agency (CIA) discovered.

CONCEPT CONNECTION

As part of its award-winning supplier diversity programme, San Francisco-based Pacific Gas & Electric (PG&E) spent $1.6 billion in 2011, or 36 per cent of its total procurement funds, on products and services from businesses owned by minorities, women and service-disabled veterans. Because many of these suppliers are also PG&E customers, the utility's managers don't have to look far to find the **diversity dividend** PG&E reaps from this programme.

EXHIBIT 12.5 Dividends of workplace diversity

- Better use of employee talent.
- Increased understanding of the marketplace.
- Enhanced breadth of understanding in leadership positions.
- Increased quality of team problem solving.
- Reduced costs associated with high turnover, absenteeism and lawsuits.

SOURCE: Gail Robinson and Kathleen Dechant, 'Building a Business Case for Diversity', *Academy of Management Executive* 11, no. 3 (1997): 21–31.

 INNOVATIVE WAY

Central Intelligence Agency (CIA)

Surprises always catch us off guard. When they happen, we ask ourselves, 'Who would have seen that coming?' The surprise attacks in the USA by Islamic terrorists on 11 September 2001, left the nation stunned, especially the CIA officers who were responsible for gathering intelligence about terrorist activities and warning of possible threats. Why didn't the CIA, one of the most influential institutions of the last 60 years, predict these attacks? Why did they have such a hard time getting inside the heads of the Islamic terrorists who crafted a devastating attack on US soil?

When an organization such as the CIA experiences a 'strategic surprise' – an unexpected, game-changing event that throws it off course – the results can be devastating. To better anticipate strategic surprises, organizations need a diverse workforce, one that reflects the diversity in the communities they serve. The CIA's workforce has long been largely homogeneous in terms of race, gender, ethnicity, class and culture. The majority of its agents and analysts have been a tight group of Caucasian, Protestant, liberal-arts-educated American males. Few travelled abroad or learned to speak a foreign language. The results of this homogeneity are intelligence failures. Consider the Cuban missile crisis of the early 1960s, where CIA analysts dismissed key intelligence about the Cuban missile buildup because of racist attitudes about Cuban informants. Even up through 11 September 2001, Robert Gates, former CIA director and secretary of defence, claimed that the CIA was less and less willing to employ *'people that are a little different, people who are eccentric, people who don't look good in a suit and tie, people who don't play well in the sandbox with others.'*[33]

Today's CIA, however, seems to be recognizing the value of a heterogeneous workforce. According to retired general David H. Petraeus, who resigned as CIA director in 2012, *'Our key challenge now is to ensure that the CIA's extraordinarily gifted and dedicated workforce is contributing to its full potential. That means we must, at every level, be as inclusive as possible in our composition and in how we make decisions. Intelligence work is teamwork, and we have a duty, in our own teams, to reinforce each day the values of diversity, fairness, respect and inclusion.'*[34]

REFLECTION

- **Diversity** is defined as all the ways in which employees differ.
- **Inclusion** is the degree to which an employee feels like an esteemed member of a group in which his or her uniqueness is highly appreciated.
- **Diversity of perspective** is achieved when a manager creates a heterogeneous team made up of individuals with diverse backgrounds and skill sets.
- **Managing diversity** is a key management skill today which means creating a climate in which the potential

advantages of diversity for enhanced organizational performance are maximized, while the potential disadvantages are minimized.
- Corporations that recruit and retain a diverse workforce reap numerous benefits, including improved team problem solving and increased understanding of the global marketplace.
- The Central Intelligence Agency (CIA) is trying to recruit a more diverse workforce to improve intelligence gathering and team problem solving.

Factors shaping personal bias

To reap the benefits of diversity described previously, organizations are seeking managers who will serve as catalysts in the workplace, to reduce barriers and eliminate obstacles for women and minorities. To successfully manage a diverse workgroup and create a positive, productive environment for all employees, managers need to start with an understanding of the complex attitudes, opinions and issues that already exist in the workplace or that employees bring into the workplace. These include several factors that shape personal bias: prejudice, discrimination, stereotypes and ethnocentrism.

TAKE A MOMENT

What judgemental beliefs or attitudes do you have that influence your feelings about diversity in the workplace? Complete the New Manager Self-Test to see how prepared you are to put stereotypes aside so you can manage effectively.

Workplace prejudice, discrimination and stereotypes

Prejudice is the tendency to view people who are different as being deficient. If someone acts out their prejudicial attitudes towards people who are the targets of their prejudice, discrimination has occurred. Paying a woman less than a man for the same grade of work is gender discrimination. Mistreating people because they have a different ethnicity is ethnic discrimination. Although blatant discrimination is not as widespread as in the past, bias in the workplace often shows up in subtle ways: a lack of choice assignments, the disregard by a subordinate of a minority manager's directions or the ignoring of comments made by women and minorities at meetings. A survey by Korn Ferry International found that 59 per cent of minority managers surveyed had observed a racially motivated double standard in the delegation of assignments.[35]

A major component of prejudice is stereotyping: rigid, exaggerated, irrational beliefs associated with a particular group of people.[36] To be successful managing diversity, managers need to eliminate harmful stereotypes from their thinking, shedding any biases that negatively affect the workplace. For example, old stereotypes often bubble up and block women's rise to higher-level positions. These silent but potent beliefs include the perception that women pose a greater risk in senior positions, or that working mothers are unable to hold positions requiring extensive travel and stress. Stereotypes also may block the honest feedback women need for improving their performance. If a man makes a bad presentation, his male superiors might slap him on the back and say, 'Buddy, what happened? You screwed up, man!' If a woman gives a bad presentation, she may never hear candid feedback. Instead, it may be spoken behind her back: 'Wow! She really screwed up.'[37]

 CONCEPT CONNECTION

Age discrimination has made a difficult situation even more trying for older workers looking for jobs in this economy. In March 2012, for instance, the average duration of unemployment for job seekers over age 55 hovered around 55 weeks, over one full year. That's 16 weeks longer than the then national average. **Stereotypes** that plague older job seekers include the beliefs that they are more expensive, harder to train, more likely to leave, and less productive, adaptable and technologically adept.

⊕ NEW MANAGER SELF-TEST

Valuing workplace diversity

INSTRUCTIONS Circle all the words below that you associate with your personal response to the idea of workplace diversity:

Abnormal	Dispute	Oppose
Accommodate	Dissatisfaction	Optimistic
Aggravation	Dread	Partake
Appreciative	Eager	Perplexed
Assist	Gratified	Please
Baseless	Hostile	Reasonable
Belittle	Impractical	Retreat
Beneficial	Irritation	Right
Biased	Join	Suitable
Committed	Just	Sympathetic
Comprehend	Listen	Uneasy
Corrupt	Necessary	Unfounded
Criticize	Noble	Valueless
Dislike	Obstinate	Welcoming

Total Score A _____. Add 1 point for each of the following words circled: Beneficial, Just, Necessary, Noble, Reasonable, Right, Suitable. Subtract 1 point for each of the following words circled: Abnormal, Baseless, Biased, Corrupt, Impractical, Unfounded, Valueless.

Total Score B _____. Add 1 point for each of the following words circled: Appreciative, Committed, Eager, Gratified, Optimistic, Pleased, Sympathetic. Subtract 1 point for each of the following words circled: Aggravation, Dislike, Dissatisfaction, Dread, Irritation, Perplexed, Uneasy.

Total Score C _____. Add 1 point for each of the following words circled: Accommodate, Assist, Comprehend, Join, Listen, Partake, Welcoming. Subtract 1 point for each of the following words circled: Belittle, Criticize, Dispute, Hostile, Obstinate, Oppose, Retreat.

SCORING & INTERPRETATION Your scores on this questionnaire pertain to your attitudes towards workplace diversity, which are reflected in your personal diversity values. Your score for Part A pertains to your intellectual judgements towards workplace diversity, Part B pertains to your affective (emotional) reaction and Part C to your behavioural response to diversity. If your scores are near zero, then your attitudes and values towards workplace diversity are neutral. Higher positive scores mean that you hold positive values towards diversity and will likely deal sympathetically with bias in the workplace. Higher negative scores mean you hold negative values towards diversity and may be ill prepared to deal with diversity issues that arise in your role as manager. What experiences have led to your diversity values? How do you think your values will contribute to a career in management for you?

SOURCES: Kenneth P. De Meuse and Todd J. Hostager, 'Developing an Instrument for Measuring Attitudes Toward and Perceptions of Workplace Diversity: An Initial Report', *Human Resource Development Quarterly* (Spring 2001): 33–51; and Alfred B. Heilbrun, 'Measurement of Masculine and Feminine Sex Role Identities as Independent Dimensions', *Journal of Consulting and Clinical Psychology* 44 (1976): 183–190.

Managers can learn to *value differences* meaning that they should recognize cultural differences and see these differences with an appreciative attitude. To facilitate this attitude, managers can learn about cultural patterns and typical beliefs of groups to help understand why people act the way they do. It helps to understand the difference between these two ways of thinking, most notably that stereotyping is a barrier to diversity, but valuing cultural differences facilitates diversity. These two different ways of thinking are listed in Exhibit 12.6 and described below.[38]

■ *Stereotypes are often based on folklore, media portrayals and other unreliable sources of information.* In contrast, legitimate cultural differences are backed up by systematic research of real differences.

■ *Stereotypes contain negative connotations.* On the other hand, managers who value diversity view differences as potentially positive or neutral. For example, the observation that Asian males are typically less aggressive does not imply they are inferior or superior to white males – it simply means that there is a difference.

■ *Stereotypes assume that all members of a group have the same characteristics.* Managers who value diversity recognize that individuals within a group of people may or may not share the same characteristics.[39]

EXHIBIT 12.6 Difference between stereotyping and valuing cultural differences

Stereotyping	Valuing cultural differences
Is based on false assumptions, anecdotal evidence, or impressions without any direct experience with a group.	Is based on cultural differences verified by scientific research methods.
Assigns negative traits to members of a group.	Views cultural differences as positive or neutral.
Assumes that all members of a group have the same characteristics.	Does not assume that all individuals within a group have the same characteristics.
Example: Suzuko Akoi is Asian, and is therefore not aggressive by white, male standards.	Example: As a group, Asians tend to be less aggressive than white, male Americans.

SOURCE: Taylor Cox, Jr, and Ruby L. Beale, *Developing Competency to Manage Diversity: Readings Cases and Activities* (San Francisco: Berrett-Koehler Publishers, Inc., 1997).

Not only should managers eliminate stereotypical thinking, they should also recognize the stereotype threat that may jeopardize the performance of at-risk employees. Stereotype threat describes the psychological experience of a person who, when engaged in a task, is aware of a stereotype about his or her identity group that suggests he or she will not perform well on that task.[40] Suppose that you are a member of a minority group presenting complicated market research results to your management team and are anxious about making a good impression. Assume that some members of your audience have a negative stereotype about your identity group. As you ponder this, your anxiety skyrockets and self-confidence is shaken. Understandably, your presentation suffers because you are distracted by worries and self-doubt as you invest energy in overcoming the stereotype. The feelings you are experiencing are called *stereotype threat*.

People most affected by stereotype threat are those we consider as disadvantaged in the workplace due to negative stereotypes – racial and ethnic minorities, members of lower socioeconomic classes, women, older people, gay and lesbian individuals and people with disabilities. Although anxiety about performing a task may be normal, people with stereotype threat feel an extra scrutiny and worry that their failure will reflect not only on themselves as individuals but on the larger group to which they belong. As Beyoncé Knowles said, '*It's like you have something to prove, and you don't want to mess it up and be a negative reflection on black women.*'[41]

Ethnocentrism

Ethnocentrism is one roadblock for managers trying to recognize, welcome and encourage differences among people so they can develop their unique talents and be effective organizational members. Ethnocentrism is the belief that one's own group and culture are inherently superior to other groups and cultures. Ethnocentrism makes it difficult to value diversity. Viewing one's own culture as the best culture is a natural tendency among most people. Moreover, the business world still tends to reflect the values, behaviours and assumptions based on the experiences of a rather homogeneous, white, middle-class, male workforce. Indeed, most theories of management presume that workers share similar values, beliefs, motivations and attitudes about work and life in general. These theories presume that one set of behaviours best helps an organization to be productive and effective and therefore should be adopted by all employees.[42]

Ethnocentric viewpoints and a standard set of cultural practices produce a monoculture, a culture that accepts only one way of doing things and one set of values and beliefs, which can cause problems for minority employees. People of colour, women, gay people, the disabled, the elderly and other diverse employees may feel undue pressure to conform, may be victims of stereotyping attitudes, and may be presumed deficient because they are different. White, heterosexual men, many of whom do not fit the notion of the 'ideal' employee, may also feel uncomfortable with the monoculture and resent stereotypes that label white males as racists and sexists. Valuing diversity means ensuring that *all* people are given equal opportunities in the workplace.[43]

The goal for organizations seeking cultural diversity is pluralism rather than a monoculture, and ethnorelativism rather than ethnocentrism. Ethnorelativism is the belief that groups and subcultures are inherently equal. Pluralism means that an organization accommodates several subcultures. Movement towards pluralism seeks to integrate fully into the organization the employees who otherwise would feel isolated and ignored. To promote pluralism in its Mountain View corporate headquarters, chefs at Google's corporate cafeteria ensure that its menu accommodates the different tastes of its ethnically diverse workforce.

TAKE A MOMENT

How tolerant are you of people who are different from you? Complete the Experiential Exercise online to assess your tolerance for diversity.

 INNOVATIVE WAY

Google

Employees in Google's corporate headquarters come from all corners of the world, but they feel a little closer to home when they see familiar foods from their homeland on the cafeteria menu. With a goal of satisfying a diverse, ethnically varied palate, Google's first food guru and chef, Charlie Ayers, designed menus that reflected his eclectic tastes yet also met the needs of an increasingly diverse workforce. He created his own dishes, searched all types of restaurants for new recipes, and often got some of his best ideas from foreign-born employees. For example, a Filipino accountant offered a recipe for chicken *adobo,* a popular dish from her native country. Scattered around the Google-plex are cafés specializing in Southwestern, Italian, California-Mediterranean and vegetarian cuisines. And because more and more Googlers originally hail from Asia, employees can find sushi at the Japanese-themed Pacific Café or Thai red curry beef at the East Meets West Café.

Google believes food can be a tool for supporting an inclusive workplace. The array of menu options gives people a chance to try new things and learn more about their co-workers. And Google knows that when people need a little comfort and familiarity, nothing takes the edge off working in a foreign country like eating food that reminds you of home.[44]

REFLECTION

- The tendency to view people who are different as being deficient is called **prejudice**.
- **Discrimination** occurs when someone acts out their negative attitudes towards people who are the targets of their prejudice.
- A rigid, exaggerated, irrational belief associated with a particular group of people is called a **stereotype**.
- **Stereotype threat** occurs when a person engaged in a task is aware of a stereotype about his or her identity group suggesting that he or she will not perform well on that task.

- **Ethnocentrism** is the belief that one's own group is inherently superior to other groups.
- A culture that accepts only one way of doing things and one set of values and beliefs is called a **monoculture**.
- **Ethnorelativism** is the belief that groups and subcultures are inherently equal.
- **Pluralism** describes an environment in which the organization accommodates several subcultures, including employees who would otherwise feel isolated and ignored.

 CONCEPT CONNECTION

A number of studies conducted around the world in recent years confirm that weight discrimination adds to the **glass ceiling** effect for women. While overweight males are disproportionately represented among CEOs, overweight and obese women are underrepresented. Several years ago, ABC News sent a woman out on job interviews twice – once appearing to be an individual of normal weight and the second time in padded clothing to appear overweight. She received more job offers as a thin person despite the fact that she handed prospective employers a stronger résumé in her overweight incarnation.

Factors affecting women's careers

Progressive organizations realize the business advantage of hiring, retaining and promoting women in the workplace. Some research indicates that companies with several senior-level women outperform those without senior-level women both financially and organizationally. One major survey of 58 000 employees in over 100 global companies revealed that companies with three or more women in top management are perceived to be more capable, have stronger leadership and inspire higher employee motivation, among other important organizational characteristics.[45] However, there is historical evidence from 2011 that women are stalling at the middle-management level. Women hold 53 per cent of entry-level professional positions, but they hold only 37 per cent of middle-management positions, 28 per cent of vice president and senior managerial roles and 14 per cent of executive positions.[46]

In addition, men as a group still have the benefit of higher wages and faster promotions. In the USA in 2009, for example, women employed full-time earned 80 cents for every dollar that men earned, compared to 79 cents in 2000.[47] Walmart, the world's largest retailer, struggled to rebound after seven women filed a class-action suit on behalf of all women working for the company in 2001. They complained of a general pattern of discrimination in pay and promotions. Six years before the lawsuit, a law firm found widespread gender disparities in pay and promotion at Walmart and Sam's Club stores and urged the company to make improvements. In response to the report and the lawsuit, Walmart took steps to reduce the disparity occurring in the promotion and pay of women and men. Walmart has told its 50 000 managers to promote more women and minorities, with 15 per cent of managers' bonuses tied to achieving diversity goals. Women now hold 46 per cent of assistant store manager positions, up from 40 per cent 5 years ago.[48]

Both the glass ceiling and the decision to 'opt out' of a high-pressure career have an impact on women's advancement opportunities and pay. Yet women are sometimes favoured in leadership roles for demonstrating behaviours and attitudes that help them succeed in the workplace, a factor called 'the female advantage'.

The glass ceiling

In 2010 for the first time in US history, women held a majority of the nation's jobs.[49] As they move up the career ladder, the numbers of men and women are comparable, with women holding 51 per cent of all lower- and mid-level managerial and professional jobs.[50] But very few women break through the glass ceiling to reach senior management positions. Only 3.6 per cent of *Fortune* 500 companies have a woman CEO.[51] The glass ceiling is an invisible barrier that exists for women and minorities that limits their upward mobility in organizations. They can look up through the ceiling and see top management, but prevailing attitudes and stereotypes are invisible obstacles to their own advancement. This barrier also impedes the career progress of minorities. In particular, Asian managers bump up against the *bamboo ceiling*, a combination of cultural and organizational barriers that impede Asians' career progress. Today, while Asians are the most educated and make up a good share of the entry-level workforce in certain industries, they make up only 1.5 per cent of corporate board members in the USA.[52]

To break through the glass ceiling into senior management roles, top executives suggest female and minority managers follow this advice:

- ▪ *Gain profit-and-loss experience.* Women and minorities are often sidetracked into staff functions, such as human resources and administrative services, rather than line positions where they can gain profit-and-loss experience. For managers who want to be considered for top-level jobs, it is important to have experience in a line position with profit-and-loss responsibilities.[53]

- ▪ *Be assertive and ask for what you want.* Many Asian managers have found themselves stereotyped as 'not top manager material' because they are too quiet and unassertive. Women, in general, are also uncomfortable asking for what they want, for fear of being perceived as too aggressive or too selfish. Sheryl Sandberg, Facebook's chief operating officer, argues that women *'need to sit at the table'*. She said *that 57 per cent of men entering the workforce negotiate their salaries, but only 7 per cent of women do likewise.*[54] In addition, women and minorities need to build their case around things that matter most to their employer – principally, the impact on the bottom line.[55]

- ▪ *Be willing to take risks.* Jump in as a problem solver when an organization is in crisis, an opportunity known as the *glass cliff.* Jack Welch, former CEO of General Electric (GE), underscored this advice when he told a group of women executives, *'To get ahead, raise your hand for line jobs and tough, risky assignments.'* When asked about her experience with the glass cliff, KeyCorp's CEO Beth Mooney said, *'I have stepped up to many 'ugly' assignments that others didn't want.'*[56]

- ▪ *Highlight your achievements.* Women tend to downplay their accomplishments to avoid being judged as unfeminine. In addition, modest women and minorities from group-oriented cultures often will not ask for rewards for themselves, but they may ask for rewards for others. White males, on the other hand, typically self-promote their successes. To achieve recognition and credit for their successes, female and minority managers should highlight their achievements and promote their own accomplishments.[57]

- ▪ *Display confidence and credibility in your body language.* Women are champions in communicating warmth and empathy but often fall short in communicating authority and power. Consultant Carol Kinsey Goman suggests that women who strive for leadership positions need to be aware of non-verbal messages that reduce their authority. Her advice includes avoiding the following actions: (1) head tilts when listening; (2) girlish behaviours such as biting a finger or twirling hair; (3) excessive smiling; (4) nodding too much; (5) delicate handshakes and (6) flirting.[58]

'The most important factor in determining whether you will succeed isn't your gender, it's you. Be open to opportunity and take risks. In fact, take the worst, the messiest, the most challenging assignment you can find, and then take control.'

— ANGELA BRALY, WELLPOINT CEO

Opt-out trend

Some women never hit the glass ceiling because they choose to get off the fast track long before it comes into view. In recent years, an ongoing discussion concerns something referred to as the *opt-out trend*. In a major survey of nearly 2500 women and 653 men, 37 per cent of highly qualified women reported that they voluntarily left the workforce at some point in their careers, compared to only 24 per cent of similarly qualified men.[59]

Quite a debate rages over the reasons for the larger number of women who drop out of mainstream careers. Opt-out proponents say women are deciding that corporate success isn't worth the price in terms of reduced family and personal time, greater stress and negative health effects.[60] Anne-Marie Slaughter, a Princeton professor and then a top aide to Hillary Clinton, left her prestigious position to spend more time at home with a rebellious teenager. Unable to balance work and family with success, Slaughter challenged the concept that women can 'have it all' in a controversial 2012 article in *The Atlantic*. In the article, Slaughter said today's workplace needs to adapt, and women who opt out have no need to apologize. *'Women of my generation have clung to the feminist credo we were raised with . . . because we are determined not to drop the flag for the next generation,'* Ms. Slaughter wrote. *'But when many members of the younger generation have stopped listening, on the grounds that glibly repeating "you can have it all" is simply airbrushing reality, it is time to talk.'*[61]

One school of thought says that women don't want corporate power and status in the same way that men do, and clawing one's way up the corporate ladder has become less appealing. Yet critics argue that this view is just another way to blame women themselves for the dearth of female managers at higher levels.[62] Vanessa Castagna, for example, says she left JCPenney after decades with the company, not because she wanted more family or personal time, but because she kept getting passed over for top jobs.[63] Although some women are voluntarily leaving the fast track, many more genuinely want to move up the corporate ladder but find their paths blocked. In a survey by Catalyst of executive women, 55 per cent said they aspire to senior leadership levels.[64] In addition, a survey of 103 women voluntarily leaving executive jobs in *Fortune* 1000 companies found that corporate culture was cited as the number one reason for leaving.[65] The greatest disadvantages of women leaders stem largely from prejudicial attitudes and a heavily male-oriented corporate culture.[66] Some years ago, when Procter & Gamble (P&G) asked the female executives whom it considered 'regretted losses' (that is, high performers that the company wanted to retain) why they left their jobs, the most common answer was that they didn't feel valued by the company.[67]

The female advantage

Some people hold the opinion that women might actually be better managers, partly because of a more collaborative, less hierarchical, relationship-oriented approach that is in tune with today's global and multicultural environment.[68] As attitudes and values change with changing generations, the qualities that women seem to possess naturally may lead to a gradual role reversal in organizations. For example, a stunning gender reversal is taking place in US education, with girls taking over almost every leadership role from kindergarten to graduate school. In addition, women of all races and ethnic groups are outpacing men in earning bachelor's and master's degrees. In most higher-education institutions, women make up 58 per cent of enrolled students.[69] Among 25- to 29-year-olds, 32 per cent of women have college degrees, compared to 27 per cent of men. Women are rapidly closing the MD and PhD gap, and they make up about half of all US law students, half of all undergraduate business majors and about 30 per cent of MBA candidates. Overall, women's participation in both the labour force and civic affairs has steadily increased since the mid-1950s, while men's participation has slowly but steadily declined.[70]

According to James Gabarino, an author and professor of human development at Cornell University, women are *'better able to deliver in terms of what modern society requires of people – paying attention, abiding by rules, being verbally competent and dealing with interpersonal relationships in offices.'*[71] His observation is supported by data that female managers are typically rated higher by subordinates on interpersonal skills, as well as on factors such as task behaviour, communication, ability to motivate others and goal accomplishment.[72] Recent research found a correlation between balanced gender composition in companies (that is, roughly equal male and female representation) and higher organizational performance. Moreover, a study by Catalyst indicates that organizations with the highest percentage of women in top management financially outperform, by about 35 per cent, those with the lowest percentage of women in higher-level jobs.[73]

REFLECTION

- Companies that promote women to senior-level positions outperform those without women in these positions, both financially and organizationally.
- The **glass ceiling** is an invisible barrier that separates women and minorities from senior management positions.
- Proponents of the opt-out trend say some women choose to leave the workforce because they decide success isn't worth it in terms of reduced family and personal time, greater stress and negative health effects.
- Critics say that opinion is just a way to blame women themselves for the scarcity of female top managers and argue that organizations must change.
- Women are likely to be more collaborative, less hierarchical and more relationship-oriented than men, qualities that prepare them to succeed in today's multicultural work environment.

Achieving cultural competence

A corporate culture, as discussed in Chapter 3, is defined by the values, beliefs, understandings and norms shared by members of the organization. Although some corporate cultures foster diversity, many managers struggle to create a culture that values and nurtures the organization's diverse employees. Managers who have made strategic decisions to foster diversity need a plan that moves the corporate culture towards one that reduces obstacles for disadvantaged types of employees. A successful diversity plan leads to a workforce that demonstrates *cultural competence* in the long run. Cultural competence is the ability to interact effectively with people of different cultures.[74]

Exhibit 12.7 illustrates the five-step process for implementing a diversity plan.[75] These steps create cultural competence among employees by helping them better understand, communicate with, and successfully interact with diverse co-workers.

Step 1: Uncover diversity problems in the organization. Most doctors can't make a medical diagnosis without first examining the patient. Similarly, organizations cannot assess their progress towards cultural competence without first investigating where the culture is right now. A *cultural audit* is a tool that identifies problems or areas needing improvement in a corporation's culture. The cultural audit is completed by employees who answer the following types of questions: How do promotion rates compare? Is there pay disparity between managers in the same pay grade? Does a glass ceiling limit the advancement of women and minorities? Answers to these questions help managers assess the cultural competence of the organization and focus their diversity efforts on specific problems.

Step 2: Strengthen top management commitment. The most important component of a successful diversity strategy is management commitment, leadership and support.[76] Some of the ways that top managers demonstrate their support of diversity efforts are by allocating time and money to diversity activities, supporting the recommendations of problem-solving task forces and communicating the commitment to diversity through speeches and vision and mission statements. Committed top managers also make diversity a priority by setting an example for others to follow.

Step 3: Choose solutions to fit a balanced strategy. The best solutions to diversity problems are those that address the organization's most pressing problems uncovered during Step 1. To be most effective, solutions should be presented in a balanced strategy and address three factors: education, enforcement and exposure. *Education* may include new training programmes that improve awareness and diversity skills. *Enforcement* means providing incentives for employees who demonstrate new behaviours and disciplinary action for those who violate diversity standards. A good example is Denny's restaurants. After facing discrimination lawsuits in the early 1990s, Denny's rebounded with a multifaceted diversity programme that included 25 per cent discretionary bonuses to all senior managers who significantly improved their record of hiring and promoting minority workers.[77] *Exposure* involves exposing traditional managers to non-traditional peers to help break down stereotypical beliefs. For example, a company might team up a white male manager with a female African-American manager.

Step 4: Demand results and revisit the goals. The truism 'What doesn't get measured doesn't get done' equally applies to diversity efforts. Diversity performance should be measured by numerical goals to ensure solutions are being implemented successfully. Numerical goals demonstrate that diversity is tied to business objectives. Examples of numerical goals might include tracking the salaries, rates of promotion and managerial positions for women and minorities. But these personnel statistics don't completely measure an organization's progress towards cultural competence. Other measures might include productivity and profitability tied to diversity efforts, employee opinions about their co-workers and an assessment of the corporation's ability to provide a satisfying work environment for all employees.[78]

Step 5: Maintain momentum to change the culture. Success with any of the previous four steps is a powerful motivator for continuing diversity efforts. Corporations should use these successes as an impetus to move forward and to provide leverage for more progress.

EXHIBIT 12.7 Five steps to cultural competence

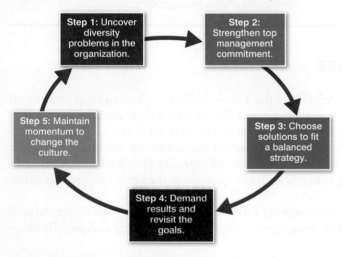

SOURCE: Ann M. Morrison, *The New Leaders: Guidelines on Leadership Diversity in America* (San Francisco: Jossey-Bass Publishers, 1992), p. 160.

REFLECTION

- **Cultural competence** is the ability to interact effectively with people of different cultures.
- When a corporate culture embraces diversity and fosters an environment where all people thrive, the organization has achieved full cultural competence.

- The five steps towards cultural competence include identifying diversity problems, strengthening top management commitment, choosing solutions, demanding results and maintaining momentum.

Diversity initiatives and programmes

In responding to a survey by the US Society for Human Resource Management, 91 per cent of companies said they believe that diversity initiatives and programmes help maintain a competitive advantage. Some specific benefits they cited include improving employee morale, decreasing interpersonal conflict, facilitating progress in new markets and increasing the organization's creativity.[79] As described in Step 3 of Exhibit 12.7, organizations can develop initiatives and programmes that address their unique diversity problems.

TAKE A MOMENT

Read the Ethical Dilemma at the end of the chapter that pertains to accommodating the religious practices of employees. Think about how you would handle this challenging management situation.

Enhancing structures and policies

Many policies within organizations originally were designed to fit the stereotypical male employee. Now leading companies are changing structures and policies to facilitate and support diversity. Most large organizations have formal policies against racial and gender discrimination, as well as structured grievance procedures and complaint review processes. Companies are also developing policies to support the recruitment and career advancement of diverse employees. Many have added a new senior management position called *chief diversity officer,* whose role is to create working environments where women and minorities can flourish. About 60 per cent of *Fortune* 500 companies have chief diversity officers. Among them, 65 per cent are women and 37 per cent are African-American.[80] Increasingly, organizations such as P&G, Ernst & Young and Allstate Insurance are tying elements of managers' bonuses and promotions to how well they DO diversify the workforce. Exhibit 12.8 illustrates some of the most common diversity initiatives.

EXHIBIT 12.8 The most common diversity initiatives: percentage of Fortune 1000 respondents

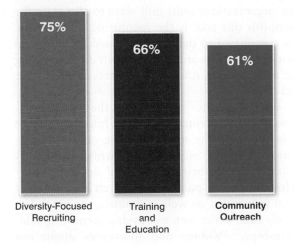

- Diversity-Focused Recruiting: 75%
- Training and Education: 66%
- Community Outreach: 61%

SOURCE: 'Impact of Diversity Initiatives on the Bottom Line: A SHRM Survey of the *Fortune* 1000', pp. S12–S14, in *Fortune*, special advertising section, 'Keeping Your Edge: Managing a Diverse Corporate Culture', produced in association with the Society for Human Resource Management, www.fortune.com/sections.

 INNOVATIVE WAY

IBM

For years, many corporate leaders paid lip service to diversity, as reflected in the comments of one consumer goods executive: *'Diversity is another way of saying affirmative action, and we are forced to support it in order to protect our brand in the trade and with consumers.'* Unfortunately, many executives still share this opinion.

IBM, however, considers diversity a time-sensitive business imperative. IBM's chief diversity officer Ron Glover believes that diversity must be an embedded mindset with common threads that touch all functional areas because diversity fuels innovation and business growth. *'Innovation is about looking at complex problems and bringing new views to the table'* Glover says. *'Diversity has allowed IBM to be innovative and successful for 100 years and to work across lines of differences in 172 countries, amongst 427 000 employees.'*

IBM has a long history of pioneering diversity efforts. The organization hired its first professional women, 25 college seniors working in systems services, in 1935. In 1943, it named its first female vice president. It instituted a 3-month family leave policy in 1956, 37 years before it became required by law. In 2011, IBM hired its first female CEO, Virginia M. Rometty.[81]

IBM has a long history of notable and innovative policies for developing a richly diverse workforce. IBM currently has one of the most diverse workforces in corporate America, and managers strongly encourage and support an inclusive culture. *'IBM sees their ability to compete in today's marketplace, to approach new markets and to make money as being tied to diversity,'* said Caroline Simard, vice president of research at the Anita Borg Institute for Women and Technology. *'It really is a business imperative and not just a responsibility of HR.'*[82]

Expanding recruitment efforts

For many organizations, a new approach to recruitment means making better use of formal recruiting strategies, offering internship programmes to give people opportunities, and developing creative ways to draw on previously unused labour markets. US-based Nationwide's Scholars Program brings in Hispanic and African-American college students for a 3-year programme that includes summer internships and year long mentoring.[83] Marathon Petroleum created a six-point recruiting strategy to increase diversity, including (1) recruiting corporate-wide and cross-functionally; (2) building relationships with first and second-tiered schools to recruit minority students; (3) offering internships for racial and ethnic minorities; (4) offering minority scholarships; (5) establishing informal mentoring programmes and (6) forming affiliations with minority organizations.[84]

Establishing mentor relationships

The successful advancement of diverse employees means that organizations must find ways to eliminate the glass ceiling. One of the most successful structures to accomplish this goal is the mentoring relationship. A mentor is a higher-ranking organizational member who is committed to providing upward mobility and support to a protégé's professional career.[85] Mentoring provides minorities and women with direct training and inside information on the norms and expectations of the organization. A mentor also acts as a friend or counsellor, enabling the employee to feel more confident and capable.

 CONCEPT CONNECTION

A counsellor for CAMBA, a social services group in New York City, directs a role-playing session during a course to help immigrants apply for jobs at Whole Foods Market. The grocer helped CAMBA develop the course to support its **diversity recruiting goals**. The classes include instruction on organic foods, customer service and tours of Whole Foods Markets.

One researcher who studied the career progress of high-potential minorities found that those who advance the most all share one characteristic – a strong mentor or network of mentors who nurtured their professional development.[86] However, some published research also indicates that minorities, as well as women, are much less likely than white men to develop mentoring relationships.[87] Women and minorities might not seek mentors because they feel that job competency should be enough to succeed, or they might feel uncomfortable seeking out a mentor when most of their senior executives are white males. Women might fear that initiating a mentoring relationship could be misunderstood as a romantic overture, whereas male mentors may think of women as mothers, wives, or sisters rather than as potential executives. Cross-race mentoring relationships sometimes leave both parties uncomfortable, but the mentoring of minority employees must often be across race, because of the low number of minorities in upper-level positions. The few minorities and women who have reached the upper ranks often are overwhelmed with mentoring requests from people like themselves, and they may feel uncomfortable in highly visible minority–minority or female–female mentoring relationships, which isolate them from the white male status quo.

The solution for many organizations is to overcome some of the barriers to mentor relationships between white males and minorities. When organizations can institutionalize the value of white males actively seeking women and minority protégés, the benefits will mean that women and minorities will be steered into pivotal jobs and positions critical to advancement. Mentoring programmes also are consistent with the US Civil Rights Act of 1991, which requires the diversification of middle and upper management.

Increasing awareness of sexual harassment

Although psychological closeness between men and women in the workplace may be a positive experience, sexual harassment is not as it is illegal. As a form of sexual discrimination, sexual harassment in the workplace is a violation of Title VII of the US 1964 Civil Rights Act. Sexual harassment in the classroom is a violation of Title VIII of the US Education Amendment of 1972. Many companies offer sexual harassment awareness programmes that create awareness of what defines sexual harassment and the legal ramifications of violations. The following list categorizes various forms of sexual harassment as defined by one university:

- *Generalized.* This form involves sexual remarks and actions that are not intended to lead to sexual activity but that are directed towards a co-worker based solely on gender and reflect on the entire group.

- *Inappropriate/offensive.* Though not sexually threatening, the behaviour causes discomfort in a co-worker, whose reaction in avoiding the harasser may limit his or her freedom and ability to function in the workplace.

- *Solicitation with promise of reward.* This action treads a fine line as an attempt to 'purchase' sex, with the potential for criminal prosecution.

- *Coercion with threat of punishment.* The harasser coerces a co-worker into sexual activity by using the threat of power (through recommendations, grades, promotions and so on) to jeopardize the victim's career.

- *Sexual crimes and misdemeanors.* The highest level of sexual harassment, these acts would, if reported to the police, be considered felonies or misdemeanours.[88]

Using multicultural teams

Companies have long known that putting together teams made up of members from different functional areas results in better problem solving and decision-making. Now, they are recognizing that multicultural teams – teams made up of members from diverse national, racial, ethnic and cultural backgrounds – provide even greater potential for enhanced creativity, innovation and value in today's global marketplace.[89] Research indicates that diverse teams generate more and better alternatives to problems and produce more creative solutions than homogeneous teams.[90] A team made up of people with different perspectives, backgrounds and cultural values creates a healthy mix of ideas and leads to greater creativity and better decisions.

Despite their many advantages,[91] multicultural teams are more difficult to manage because of the increased potential for miscommunication and misunderstanding. Multicultural teams typically have more difficulty learning to communicate and work together smoothly, but with effective cross-cultural training and good management, teams can learn to work well together.[92] One management team videotaped its meetings so members could see how their body language reflects cultural differences. An American manager remarked, '*I couldn't believe how even my physical movements dominated the table, while Ron [a Filipino American] . . . actually worked his way off-camera within the first 5 minutes.*'[93]

Encouraging employee affinity groups

Employee affinity groups are based on social identity, such as gender or race, and are organized by employees to focus on concerns of employees from that group.[94] Affinity groups pursue a variety of activities, such

CONCEPT CONNECTION

Caterpillar's commitment to diversity and to the development of leaders from diverse backgrounds is supported by the number of affinity groups within the company. Employees are invited to participate in **support networks and affinity groups** for African-Americans, Chinese, Asian Indians, Koreans and Latinos, as well as young professionals, women, armed forces veterans, experienced professionals and gay, lesbian, bisexual and transgendered employees.

as meetings to educate top managers, mentoring programmes, networking events, training sessions and skills seminars, minority intern programmes and community volunteer activities. These activities give people a chance to meet, interact with and develop social and professional ties to others throughout the organization, which may include key decision-makers. Affinity groups are a powerful way to reduce social isolation for women and minorities, help these employees be more effective and enable members to achieve greater career advancement. A recent study confirms that affinity groups can be important tools for helping organizations retain managerial-level minority employees.[95] For example, when she was a senior vice president at Best Buy, Julie Gilbert launched a women's leadership forum, known as WOLF, to get more women involved in solving core business problems and to pull frontline employees into the top ranks. As a result of these 'WOLF packs', recruitment of female regional sales managers increased 100 per cent over the previous year, and turnover among women managers dropped almost 10 percentage points.[96]

An important characteristic of affinity groups is that they are created informally by employees, not the organization, and membership is voluntary. Affinity groups for minorities who have faced barriers to advancement in organizations, including African-Americans, Hispanics, American Indians, Asian-Americans, women, gays and lesbians and disabled employees, show tremendous growth. Even managers who once thought of these as 'gripe groups' are now seeing them as essential to organizational success because they help to retain minority employees, enhance diversity efforts and spark new ideas that can benefit the organization.[97]

REFLECTION

- Many organizations have added a new senior management position called *chief diversity officer,* whose role is to spearhead diversity efforts and cultivate working environments that help women and minorities flourish.
- A **mentor** is a higher-ranking senior member of the organization who is committed to providing upward mobility and support to a protégé's professional career.
- To eliminate sexual harassment, companies may offer sexual harassment awareness programmes

that define harassment and the legal ramifications of harassment.
- **Multicultural teams** are made up of members from diverse national, racial, ethnic and cultural backgrounds.
- **Employee affinity groups** are based on social identity, such as gender or race, and are organized by employees to focus on concerns of employees from that group.

At Kraft Foods, affinity groups are considered critical to the success of multicultural teams because they build awareness and acceptance of cultural differences and help people feel more comfortable working together.[98] In general, female and minority employees who participate in an affinity group feel more pride about their work and are more optimistic about their careers than those who do not have the support of a group.[99]

DISCUSSION QUESTIONS

1 Determine and discuss several effective strategies that a manager could beneficially employ to create a work environment that fosters high cultural inclusion.

2 Evaluate your own personal experiences with people from other cultural backgrounds. To what extent have 'critical incidents' prepared you to better understand the unique needs and dilemmas within a diverse workforce?

3 Describe some of the challenges which organizations face when managing multicultural teams. Discuss ways in which these can be overcome.

4 Explain the meaning of the 'glass ceiling'. What support can employers offer to help women overcome this challenge?

5 Describe how diversity of perspective boosts creativity and innovation in the workplace. To what extent can a diversity of perspective deliver a sustainable competitive advantage?

6 'Organizations must strike a balance between respecting and meeting the needs of a diverse workforce and shaping a high-performance corporate culture where shared values contribute to the accomplishment of strategic goals.' Critically evaluate this statement.

Do you know your biases?[100]

INSTRUCTIONS As a new manager, your day-to-day behaviour will send signals about your biases and values. Some personal biases are active and well known to yourself and others. Other biases are more subtle, and the following questions may provide some hints about where you are biased and don't know it. Please answer whether each item is 'Mostly true' or 'Mostly false' for you.

	Mostly true	*Mostly false*
1 I prefer to be in work teams with people who think like me.	☐	☐
2 I have avoided talking about culture differences with people I met from different cultures because I didn't want to say the wrong thing.	☐	☐
3 I have jumped to a conclusion without first hearing all sides of a story.	☐	☐
4 The first thing I notice about people is the physical characteristics that make them different from the norm.	☐	☐
5 Before I hire someone, I have a picture in mind of what they should look like.	☐	☐
6 I typically ignore movies, magazines and TV programmes that are targeted towards groups and values that are different from mine.	☐	☐
7 When someone makes a bigoted remark or joke, I don't confront him or her about it.	☐	☐

	Mostly true	Mostly false
8 I prefer to not discuss sensitive topics such as race, age, gender, sexuality or religion at work.	☐	☐
9 There are people I like but would feel uncomfortable inviting to be with my family or close friends.	☐	☐

SCORING & INTERPRETATION Give yourself one point for each item you marked as 'Mostly true'. The ideal score is zero, but few people reach the ideal. Each question reflects an element of 'passive bias', which can cause people different from you to feel ignored or disrespected by you. Passive bias may be more insidious than active discrimination because it excludes people from opportunities for expression and interaction. If you scored 5 or more, you should take a careful look at how you think and act towards people different from yourself. The sooner you learn to actively include diverse views and people, the better a new manager you will be.

APPLY YOUR SKILLS: ETHICAL DILEMMA

Sunset prayers[101]

Frank Piechowski, plant manager for a Minnesota North Woods Appliance Corporation refrigerator plant, just received his instructions from the vice president for manufacturing. He was to hire 40 more temporary workers through Twin Cities Staffing, the local labour agency that North Woods used. Frank already knew from past experience that most, if not all, of the new hires available to work the assembly line would be Muslim Somali refugees, people who had immigrated to Minnesota from their war-torn native country en masse over the past 15 years.

North Woods, like all appliance manufacturers, was trying to survive in a highly competitive, mature industry. Appliance companies were competing mainly on price. The entrance of large chains such as Best Buy and Home Depot only intensified the price wars, not to mention that consumers could easily do comparison shopping before leaving home by logging on to the Internet. The pressure to keep production costs low was considerable.

That's where the Somali workers came in. In an effort to keep labour costs low, North Woods was relying more and more on temporary workers rather than increasing the ranks of permanent employees. Frank was quite pleased with the Somalis already at work on the assembly line. Although few in number, they were responsible, hard-working and willing to work for the wages that he could afford to pay.

It was the first time this son of Polish immigrants had ever come into contact with Muslims, but so far, it had gone well. Frank had established a good working relationship with the Somalis' spokesperson, Halima Adan, who explained that unlike most Western faiths, Islamic religious practices were inextricably woven into everyday life. So together, they worked out ways to accommodate Muslim customs. Frank authorized changes in the plant's cafeteria menu so the Somali workers had more options that conformed to their dietary restrictions, and he allowed women to wear traditional clothing, so long as they weren't violating safety standards.

After learning that the Somalis would need to perform at least some of the ceremonial washing and prayers they were required to do five times a day during work hours, the plant manager set aside a quiet, clean room where they could observe their 15-minute rituals during their breaks and at sunset. The Maghrib sunset prayers that second shift workers had to perform were disruptive to a smooth workflow. Compared to their midday and afternoon rituals, the Muslim faithful had considerably less leeway as to when they said the sunset prayers, and of course, the sun set at a slightly different time each day. But so far, they'd all coped.

But what was he going to do about the sunset prayers with an influx of 40 Somali workers that would dramatically increase the number of people who would need to leave the line to pray? Was it time to modify his policy? He knew that Title VII of the Civil Right Act required that he make 'reasonable' accommodations to his employees' religious practices unless doing so would impose an 'undue hardship' on the employer. Had he reached the point where the accommodations that Halima Adan would probably request crossed the line from reasonable to unreasonable? But if he changed his policy, did he risk alienating his workforce?

What would you do?

1 Continue the current policy that leaves it up to the Muslim workers as to when they leave the assembly line to perform their sunset rituals.

2 Try to hire the fewest possible Muslim workers so the work line will be efficient on second shift.

3 Ask the Muslim workers to delay their sunset prayers until a regularly scheduled break occurs, pointing out that North Woods is primarily a place of business, not a house of worship.

APPLY YOUR SKILLS: CASE FOR CRITICAL ANALYSIS

Managing diversity in global organizations: The ASEAN Retail Corporation (ARC)

The ASEAN Retail Corporation (ARC) has been expanding its operations in Asia since establishing ARC Stores in Malaysia in 1977 and currently has approximately 1000 overseas outlets, including general merchandise stores (GMS), supermarkets and convenience stores. In addition, ARC's group companies including financial service operators, speciality store companies, service operators and others are accelerating overseas expansion.

ARC's fundamental management principles are the pursuit of peace, respect for humanity and contributions to local communities, with the customer's point of view as the core. On the basis of this unchanging philosophy, the ARC Group focuses first and foremost on its customers and ensuring customer satisfaction, constantly innovating to promptly and precisely respond to changes in the external environment and customer needs.

ARC aims to be a 'glocal' company, meaning that management must both meet global quality standards and at the same time remain rooted in local communities. ARC recently launched the 'ARC Group 5-Year Plan (FY2015–2020)'. Under the new plan, it will accelerate the shift to Asian markets, urban markets, senior markets and digital markets; a strategy implemented under the previous ARC Management Plan (FY2010–2015).

In fast-growing Asia, ARC has established various national headquarters to lead the strengthening of existing businesses. It is also pursuing new growth through the opening of shopping centres in Vietnam, Cambodia and China. Aeon also has plans to open shopping centres in Hubei Province, China and Indonesia which will further solidify its shift to Asian markets. In urban markets, it is enhancing its business foundation through the expansion of its chain of small-scale urban-type supermarkets. In senior markets, it has announced a business and capital alliance agreement to respond to the rising health-consciousness of Japan's growing number of senior citizens by offering a broad spectrum of high-quality services. In digital markets, it is promoting an omni-channel strategy which combines experience, product and Internet. ARC continues to develop digital business models that match changes in the management environment and leverages the comprehensive capabilities of the Group.

The driving force behind ARC's future growth is the diversification of human resources, which is stated as their greatest management resource. ARC believe it is important to raise the profile of women, who represent their main customer, as well as to promote the active involvement of local employees in all regions as it shifts towards Asian markets and localize its management there. ARC has set a target of raising the ratio of female at management level in group companies to 40 per cent by 2016 and to 50 per cent by 2020. At the same time, it will promote the hiring and nurturing of human resources reflecting a diversity of languages, cultures and values in order to support the sustainable group growth.

ARC aims to be an enterprise that continually innovates by promoting world-class management quality and ensuring its management is deeply rooted in local communities. The kinds of people

ARC is seeking to hire are those with a strong desire to improve the quality of life of customers through commercial activities across various countries. They should also have a strong sense of commitment and a broadminded outlook with the ability to adapt to different local cultures, customs and languages and work in a globalized business environment. ARC plans to hire those who have studied abroad or have a strong interest in the culture and customs of other countries, those with an excellent command of one or more foreign languages, and those with an ambition to improve their language ability and work overseas in the future. In so doing ARC hopes to create a 'talent pool' of global managers.

Since its establishment, ARC has held fast to the principles of fair treatment and equal opportunity, eliminating discrimination on the basis of national origin, gender, age or any other factor. It has always evaluated its employees solely on the basis of their ability and performance. After joining ARC, employees of all group companies are given fair opportunities for promotion and ARC places a special focus on employee training and talent management to help employees, wherever they are and whatever their position, to always be the best they can be.

Reference: www.cipd.co.uk/hr-resources/factsheets/international-culture.aspx

Questions

1. How would a 'cultural audit' help ARC assess its diversity issues?

2. Comment on the focus on gender diversity in ARC's management plans.

3. Evaluate the equality implications of ARC's recruitment and talent development plans.

END NOTES

1. Joann S. Lublin, 'TI Battles a Gender Gap in Job Experience', *The Wall Street Journal*, June 13, 2012, B10.
2. Quoted in Susan Caminiti, 'The Diversity Factor', *Fortune* (October 19, 2007): 95–105.
3. Caminiti, 'The Diversity Factor'.
4. Yair Holtzman and Johan Anderberg, 'Diversify Your Teams and Collaborate: Because Great Minds Don't Think Alike', *Journal of Management Development* 30, no. 1 (2011): 75–92.
5. Lynn M. Shore, Amy E. Randel, Beth G. Chung, Michelle A. Dean, Karen Holcombe Ehrhart and Gangaram Singh, 'Inclusion and Diversity in Work Groups: A Review and Model for Future Research', *Journal of Management* 37, no. 4 (July 2011): 1262–1289.
6. Taylor H. Cox, 'Managing Cultural Diversity: Implications for Organizational Competitiveness', *Academy of Management Executive* 5, no. 3 (1991): 45–56; and Faye Rice, 'How to Make Diversity Pay', *Fortune* (August 8, 1994): 78–86.
7. Rawn Shah, 'Working with Five Generations in the Workplace', *Forbes.com*, April 20, 2011, www.forbes.com/sites/rawnshah/2011/04/20/working-with-five-generations-in-the-workplace/ (accessed August 9, 2012); and Jeanne Meister and Karie Willyerd, *The 2020 Workplace* (New York: HarperCollins 2010).
8. 'Generations in the Workplace in the United States and Canada', Catalyst.org, May 2012, www.catalyst.org/publication/434/generations-in-the-workplace-in-the-united-states-canada (accessed August 9, 2012); Lisa Beyer, Samuel Greengard, Susan G. Hauser and Todd Henneman, 'Workforce 90th Anniversary: Workforce Management Looks Back at Workplace History', *Workforce.com*, July 2, 2012, www.workforce.com/article/20120702/WORKFORCE90/120629967/1066/newsletter01 (accessed August 9, 2012); and Shah, 'Working with Five Generations in the Workplace'.
9. Occupational Outlook Handbook, *Bureau of Labor Statistics*, www.bls.gov/ooh/about/projections-overview.htm#laborforce (accessed June 29, 2012).
10. 'Foreign-Born Workers and Labor Force Characteristics: 2011', *United States Labor Department Bureau of Labor Statistics*, www.bls.gov/news.release/pdf/forbrn.pdf (accessed June 29, 2012).
11. Occupational Outlook Handbook, *Bureau of Labor Statistics*, www.bls.gov/ooh/about/projections-overview.htm#labor force (accessed June 29, 2012).
12. Joann S. Lublin and Kelly Eggers, 'More Women Are Primed to Land CEO Roles', *The Wall Street Journal Online*, April 30, 2012, www.online.wsj.com/article/SB10001424052702303990604577368344256435440.html (accessed June 29, 2012).
13. Giada Zampano, 'Italy to Push Pink Quotas', *The Wall Street Journal Online*, June 5, 2012, www.google.com/search?sourceid=navclient&aq=0&oq=italy+to+push&ie=UTF-8&rlz=1T4ADRA_enUS426US427&q=italy+to+push+'pink+quotes'&gs_upl=0l0l0l4406llllllllll0&aqi=g4&pbx=1 (accessed July 2, 2012); Katrin Bennhold, 'Women Nudged out of German Workforce', *The New York Times Online*, June 28, 2011, www.nytimes.com/2011/06/29/world/europe/29iht-FFgermany29.html?pagewanted=all.
14. Zampano, 'Italy to Push Pink Quotas'.
15. Mariko Sanchanta, 'Japan's Women Reach Job Milestones', *The Wall Street Journal*, July 14, 2010, A15.
16. Hiroka Tabuchi, 'Leading in 3-D TV, Breaking Japan's Glass Ceiling', *The New York Times Online*, January 17, 2011, www.nytimes.com/2011/01/18/business/global/18screen.html?pagewanted=all (accessed July 3, 2012).
17. Richard L. Daft, *The Leadership Experience* (Cincinnati, OH: Cengage Learning, 2008), p. 340.
18. Holtzman and Anderberg, 'Diversify Your Teams and Collaborate'.'

19. Michael L. Wheeler, 'Diversity: Business Rationale and Strategies', *The Conference Board*, Report No. 1130-95-RR, 1995, p. 25.

20. Anthony Oshiotse and Richard O'Leary, 'Corning Creates an Inclusive Culture to Drive Technology Innovation and Performance', Wiley InterScience, *Global Business and Organizational Excellence* 26, no. 3 (March/April 2007): 7–21.

21. 'When CEOs Drive Diversity, Everybody Wins', *Chief Executive*, July 2005, www.chiefexecutive.net/ME2/dirmod.asp?sid=&nm=&type=Publishing&mod= Publications%3A%3AArticle&mid=8F3A7027421841978F18BE895F87F791&tier=4&id=201D3B11B9D4419893E78DDA4B7ACDC8 (accessed September 21, 2010).

22. Shore et al., 'Inclusion and Diversity in Work Groups'.

23. Martin N. Davidson, 'The End of Diversity: How Leaders Make Differences Really Matter', *Leader to Leader* (Spring 2012): 51–55.

24. Taylor Cox, Jr., and Ruby L. Beale, *Developing Competency to Manage Diversity* (San Francisco: Berrett-Koehler Publishers, Inc., 1997), p. 2.

25. Holtzman and Anderberg, 'Diversify Your Teams and Collaborate.''

26. Reported in John Tierney, 'Social Scientist Sees Bias Within', *The New York Times Online*, www.nytimes.com/2011/02/08/science/08tier.html (accessed July 5, 2012).

27. Gail Robinson and Kathleen Dechant, 'Building a Business Case for Diversity', *Academy of Management Executive* 11, no. 3 (1997): 21–31.

28. Sonie Alleyne and Nicole Marie Richardson, 'The 40 Best Companies for Diversity', *Black Enterprise* 36, no. 12 (July 2006): 15.

29. Robinson and Dechant, 'Building a Business Case for Diversity'.

30. *Ibid.*

31. Quoted in Carol Hymowitz, 'Coaching Men on Mentoring Women Is Ernst & Young Partner's Mission', *The Wall Street Journal Online*, June 14, 2007, www.online.wsj.com/article/SB118167178575132768search.html (accessed July 9, 2007).

32. Kris Maher, 'Lockheed Settles Racial-Discrimination Suit', *The Wall Street Journal*, January 3, 2008.

33. Frederick E. Allen, 'Lack of Diversity Paralyzed the CIA. It Can Cripple Your Organization Too', *Forbes*, April 26, 2012, www.forbes.com/sites/frederickallen/2012/04/26/lack-of-diversity-paralyzed-the-cia-it-can-cripple-your-organization-too/ (accessed July 19, 2012).

34. CIA website, https://www.cia.gov/careers/diversity/directors-diversity-commitment.html (accessed July 19, 2012).

35. Reported in Roy Harris, 'The Illusion of Inclusion', *CFO* (May 2001): 42–50.

36. Carr-Ruffino, *Managing Diversity*, pp. 98–99.

37. Based on an interview with PepsiCo chairman and CEO Indra Nooyi, in Rebecca Blumenstein, 'View from the Top', *The Wall Street Journal*, April 11, 2011, R9.

38. Cox and Beale, 'Developing Competency to Manage Diversity', p. 79.

39. *Ibid.*, pp. 80–81.

40. Loriann Roberson and Carol T. Kulik, 'Stereotype Threat at Work', *Academy of Management Perspectives* 21, no. 2 (May 2007): 25–27.

41. *Ibid.*, 26.

42. Robert Doktor, Rosalie Tung and Mary Ann von Glinow, 'Future Directions for Management Theory Development', *Academy of Management Review* 16 (1991): 362–365; and Mary Munter, 'Cross-Cultural Communication for Managers', *Business Horizons* (May–June 1993): 69–78.

43. Renee Blank and Sandra Slipp, 'The White Male: An Endangered Species?' *Management Review* (September 1994): 27–32; Michael S. Kimmel, 'What Do Men Want?' *Harvard Business Review* (November–December 1993): 50–63; and Sharon Nelton, 'Nurturing Diversity', *Nation's Business* (June 1995): 25–27.

44. Jim Carlton, 'Dig In', *The Wall Street Journal*, November 14, 2005; Tony DiRomualdo, 'Is Google's Cafeteria a Competitive Weapon?' *Wisconsin Technology Network*, August 30, 2005, www.wistechnology.com/article.php?id=2190 (accessed August 31, 2005); and Marc Ramirez, 'Tray Chic: At Work, Cool Cafeterias, Imaginative Menus', *The Seattle Times*, November 21, 2005, www.seattletimes.nwsource.com/html/living/2002634266_cafés21.html?pageid=display-in-thenews.module&pageregion=itnbody (accessed November 22, 2005).

45. Georges Desvaux, Sandrine Devillard-Hoellinger, and Mary C. Meaney, 'A Business Case for Women', *The McKinsey Quarterly: The Online Journal of McKinsey & Co.*, September 2008, www.mckinseyquarterly.com/A_business_case_for_women_2192 (accessed June 17, 2010).

46. Joanna Barsh and Lareina Yee, 'Changing Companies' Minds About Women', *McKinsey Quarterly Online*, September, 2011, www.mckinsey.com/careers/women/~/media/Reports/Women/Changing_companies_minds_about_women.ashx (accessed June 29, 2012).

47. Jena McGregor, 'Why the Pay Gap Persists', *The Washington Post*, September 28, 2010, www.washingtonpost.com/wp-dyn/content/article/2010/09/28/AR2010092806188.html (accessed July 9, 2012).

48. Steven Greenhouse, 'Report Warned Wal-Mart of Risks Before Bias Suit', *The New York Times*, June 3, 2010, www.nytimes.com/2010/06/04/business/04lawsuit.html (accessed June 4, 2010).

49. Hanna Rosin, 'The End of Men', *The Atlantic*, July/ August 2010, www.theatlantic.com/magazine/print/2010/07/the-end-of-men/8135/ (accessed July 9, 2012).

50. Jenny M. Hoobler, Grace Lemmon and Sandy J. Wayne, 'Women's Underrepresentation in Upper Management: New Insights on a Persistent Problem', *Organizational Dynamics* 40 (2011): 151–156.

51. John Bussey, 'How Women Can Get Ahead: Advice from Female CEOs', *The Wall Street Journal Online*, May 18, 2012, www.online.wsj.com/article/SB10001424052702303879604577410520511235252.html (accessed July 8, 2012).

52. Jane Hyun, 'Leadership Principles for Capitalizing on Culturally Diverse Teams: The Bamboo Ceiling Revisited', *Leader to Leader* (Spring 2012): 14–19.

53. Hoobler, Lemmon and Wayne, 'Women's Underrepresentation in Upper Management',

54. Ken Auletta, 'A Woman's Place', *The New Yorker*, (July 11 and 18, 2011): 55–63.

55. Peggy Klaus, 'Don't Fret. Just Ask for What You Need', *The New York Times*, July 9, 2011, www.nytimes.com/2011/07/10/jobs/10pre.html (accessed July 8, 2012).

56. Bussey, 'How Women Can Get Ahead: Advice from Female CEOs'.

57. Marie-Helene Budworth and Sara L. Mann, 'Becoming a Leader: The Challenge of Modesty for Women', *Journal of Management Development* 29, no. 2 (2010): 177–186.

58. Carol Kinsey Goman, 'Body Language', *Leadership Excellence* (August, 2010): 9.

59. Sylvia Ann Hewlett and Carolyn Buck Luce, 'Off-Ramps and On-Ramps: Keeping Talented Women on the Road to Success', *Harvard Business Review* (March 2005): 43–54.

60. Lisa Belkin, 'The Opt-Out Revolution', *The New York Times Magazine* (October 26, 2002): 43–47, 58.

61. Jodi Kantor, 'Elite Women Put a New Spin on an Old Debate', *The New York Times*, June 21, 2012, www.nytimes.com/2012/06/22/us/elite-women-put-a-new-spin-on-work-life-debate.html (accessed July 9, 2012); Anne-Marie Slaughter, 'Why Women Still Can't Have It All', *The Atlantic*, July–August 2012, www.theatlantic.com/magazine/archive/2012/07/why-women-still-cant-have-it-all/309020/ (accessed October 15, 2012).

62. C. J. Prince, 'Media Myths: The Truth About the Opt-Out Hype', *NAFE Magazine* (Second Quarter 2004): 14–18; Patricia Sellers, 'Power: Do Women Really Want It?' *Fortune* (October 13, 2003): 80–100.

63. Jia Lynn Yang, 'Goodbye to All That', *Fortune* (November 14, 2005): 169–170.

64. Sheila Wellington, Marcia Brumit Kropf and Paulette R. Gerkovich, 'What's Holding Women Back?' *Harvard Business Review* (June 2003): 18–19.

65. The Leader's Edge/Executive Women Research 2002 survey, reported in 'Why Women Leave', *Executive Female* (Summer 2003): 4.

66. Barbara Reinhold, 'Smashing Glass Ceilings: Why Women Still Find It Tough to Advance to the Executive Suite', *Journal of Organizational Excellence* (Summer 2005): 43–55; Jory Des Jardins, 'I Am Woman (I Think)', *Fast Company* (May 2005): 25–26; and Alice H. Eagly and Linda L. Carli, 'The Female Leadership Advantage: An Evaluation of the Evidence', *The Leadership Quarterly* 14 (2003): 807–834.

67. Claudia H. Deutsch, 'Behind the Exodus of Executive Women: Boredom', *USA Today,* May 2, 2005.

68. Eagly and Carli, 'The Female Leadership Advantage'; Reinhold, 'Smashing Glass Ceilings'; Sally Helgesen, *The Female Advantage: Women's Ways of Leadership* (New York: Doubleday Currency, 1990); Rochelle Sharpe, 'As Leaders, Women Rule: New Studies Find that Female Managers Outshine Their Male Counterparts in Almost Every Measure', *BusinessWeek* (November 20, 2000): 5ff; and Del Jones, '2003: Year of the Woman Among the *Fortune* 500?' *USAToday*, December 30, 2003.

69. Tamar Lewin, 'At Colleges, Women Are Leaving Men in the Dust', *The New York Times Online,* July 9, 2006, www.nytimes.com/2006/07/09/education/09college.html?_r=1&scp=1&sq=at%20colleges,%20women%20are%20leaving%20men%20in%20the%20dust&st=cse&oref=slogin (accessed March 13, 2008).

70. Michelle Conlin, 'The New Gender Gap', *BusinessWeek* (May 26, 2003): 74–82.

71. Quoted in Conlin, 'The New Gender Gap'.

72. Kathryn M. Bartol, David C. Martin and Julie A. Kromkowski, 'Leadership and the Glass Ceiling: Gender and Ethnic Group Influences on Leader Behaviors at Middle and Executive Managerial Levels', *The Journal of Leadership and Organizational Studies* 9, no. 3 (2003): 8–19; Bernard M. Bass and Bruce J. Avolio, 'Shatter the Glass Ceiling: Women May Make Better Managers', *Human Resource Management* 33, no. 4 (Winter 1994): 549–560; and Sharpe, 'As Leaders, Women Rule'.

73. Dwight D. Frink, Robert K. Robinson, Brian Reithel, Michelle M. Arthur, Anthony P. Ammeter, Gerald R. Ferris, David M. Kaplan and Hubert S. Morrisette, 'Gender Demography and Organization Performance: A Two-Study Investigation with Convergence', *Group & Organization Management* 28, no. 1 (March 2003): 127–147; Catalyst research project cited in Reinhold, 'Smashing Glass Ceilings'.

74. Mercedes Martin and Billy Vaughn, 'Cultural Competence: The Nuts & Bolts of Diversity & Inclusion', *Diversity Officer Magazine*, October 25, 2010, www.diversityofficermagazine.com/uncategorized/cultural-competence-the-nuts-bolts-of-diversity-inclusion/ (accessed October 15, 2012).

75. Ann M. Morrison, *The New Leaders: Guidelines on Leadership Diversity in America* (San Francisco: Jossey-Bass Publishers, 1992), p. 235.

76. Wheeler, 'Diversity: Business Rationale and Strategies'.

77. Alleyne and Richardson, 'The 40 Best Companies for Diversity', 100.

78. Morrison, *The New Leaders*.

79. 'Impact of Diversity Initiatives on the Bottom Line: A SHRM Survey of the *Fortune* 1000', in 'Keeping Your Edge: Managing a Diverse Corporate Culture', special advertising section produced in association with the Society for Human Resource Management, *Fortune* (June 3, 2001): S12–S14.

80. Leslie Kwoh, 'Firms Hail New Chiefs (of Diversity)', *The Wall Street Journal Online*, January 5, 2012, www.online.wsj.com/article/SB10001424052970203899504577129261732884578.html (accessed July 9, 2012).

81. Glenn Llopis, 'Diversity Management Is the Key to Growth: Make It Authentic', *Forbes*, June 13, 2011, www.forbes.com/sites/glennllopis/2011/06/13/diversity (accessed July 20, 2011); and Claire Cain Miller, 'For Incoming I.B.M. Chief, Self-Confidence Is Rewarded', *The New York Times*, October 27, 2011, www.nytimes.com/2011/10/28/business/for-incoming-ibm-chief-self-confidence-rewarded.html (accessed July 20, 2012).

82. Miller, 'For Incoming I.B.M. Chief, Self-Confidence Is Rewarded'.

83. Annie Finnigan, 'Different Strokes', *Working Woman* (April 2001): 42–48.

84. 'Diversity in an Affiliated Company', cited in Vanessa J. Weaver, 'Winning with Diversity', *BusinessWeek* (September 10, 2001).

85. Melanie Trottman, 'A Helping Hand', *The Wall Street Journal,* November 14, 2005; B. Ragins, 'Barriers to Mentoring: The Female Manager's Dilemma', *Human Relations* 42, no. 1 (1989): 1–22; and Belle Rose Ragins, Bickley Townsend and Mary Mattis, 'Gender Gap in the Executive Suite: CEOs and Female Executives Report on Breaking the Glass Ceiling', *Academy of Management Executive* 12, no. 1 (1998): 28–42.

86. David A. Thomas, 'The Truth About Mentoring Minorities – Race Matters', *Harvard Business Review* (April 2001): 99–107.

87. Mary Zey, 'A Mentor for All', *Personnel Journal* (January 1988): 46–51.

88. 'Sexual Harassment: Vanderbilt University Policy' (Nashville, TN: Vanderbilt University, 1993).

89. Joseph J. Distefano and Martha L. Maznevski, 'Creating Value with Diverse Teams in Global Management', *Organizational Dynamics* 29, no. 1 (Summer 2000): 45–63; and Finnigan, 'Different Strokes'.

90. W. E. Watson, K. Kumar and L. K. Michaelsen, 'Cultural Diversity's Impact on Interaction Process and Performance: Comparing Homogeneous and Diverse Task Groups', *Academy of Management Journal* 36 (1993): 590–602; Robinson and Dechant, 'Building a Business Case for Diversity'; and D. A. Thomas and R. J. Ely, 'Making Differences Matter: A New Paradigm for Managing Diversity', *Harvard Business Review* (September–October 1996): 79–90.

91. See Distefano and Maznevski, 'Creating Value with Diverse Teams' for a discussion of the advantages of multicultural teams.

92. Watson, Kumar and Michaelsen, 'Cultural Diversity's Impact on Interaction Process and Performance'.

93. Distefano and Maznevski, 'Creating Value with Diverse Teams'.

94. This definition and discussion is based on Raymond A. Friedman, 'Employee Network Groups: Self-Help Strategy for Women and Minorities', *Performance Improvement Quarterly* 12, no. 1 (1999): 148–163.

95. Raymond A. Friedman and Brooks Holtom, 'The Effects of Network Groups on Minority Employee Turnover

Intentions', *Human Resource Management* 41, no. 4 (Winter 2002): 405–421.

96. Diane Brady and Jena McGregor, 'What Works in Women's Networks', *BusinessWeek* (June 18, 2007): 58.

97. Elizabeth Wasserman, 'A Race for Profits', *MBA Jungle* (March–April 2003): 40–41.

98. Finnigan, 'Different Strokes'.

99. Raymond A. Friedman, Melinda Kane and Daniel B. Cornfield, 'Social Support and Career Optimism: Examining the Effectiveness of Network Groups among Black Managers', *Human Relations* 51, no. 9 (1998): 1155–1177.

100. Based on Lawrence Otis Graham, *Proversity: Getting Past Face Values and Finding the Soul of People* (New York: John Wiley & Sons, 1997).

101. Based on Rob Johnson, '30 Muslim Workers Fired for Praying on Job at Dell', *The Tennessean*, March 10, 2005; Anayat Durrani, 'Religious Accommodation for Muslim Employees', *Workforce.com*, www.workforce.com/archive/feature/religious-accommodation-muslim-employees/index.php (accessed September 21, 2010); 'Questions and Answers About Employer Responsibilities Concerning the Employment of Muslims, Arabs, South Asians, and Sikhs', The U.S. Equal Employment Opportunity Commission, www.eeoc.gov/facts/backlash-employer.html (accessed September 20, 2010); and '2006 Household Appliance Industry Outlook', U.S. Department of Commerce, International Trade Administration, www.ita.doc.gov/td/ocg/outlook06_appliances.pdf (accessed September 21, 2010).

PART 4 INTEGRATIVE CASE
PART FOUR: ORGANIZING

Westport Innovations: A look under the hood of the clean auto revolution

Despite transportation's many benefits, the idea of a clean-burning automobile has been largely unimaginable due to the car engine's link to petroleum-based gas. But with the recent introduction of natural-gas engines, the car has begun one of the biggest evolutions in its history. Not since Ford introduced the Model T has an innovation promised to transform so thoroughly the automotive industry and the carbon footprint it leaves behind.

The greening of modern transportation can be traced in part to Dr Philip Hill, a mechanical engineering professor at the University of British Columbia (UBC). In the 1980s, Hill became interested in clean energy and began a quest to improve the internal combustion engine. With an eye towards clean technology, Hill and a group of graduate students conducted experiments to see if diesel engines could run on natural gas, a clean-burning fuel that produces fewer emissions than petroleum-based gas. Hill wanted to preserve the diesel engine's astounding torque, but he envisioned a future where high-powered engines didn't leave behind smog or dirty exhaust. 'Though the diesel engine was a wonderful machine, it really needed cleaning up as far as emissions goes,' Hill says, thinking back on his early research. Hill's breakthrough came in the form of High-Pressure Direct Injection (HPDI), a new fuel injector system in which a tiny amount of diesel fuel sprays through one injector needle to ignite natural gas in another, which leads to combustion. Hill's patented duel-injector system was so ingenious that now virtually any diesel engine can be converted to run on natural gas – with no loss of horsepower.

Hill's invention might have stalled there if it hadn't found a use in the marketplace. But in 1995, UBC tapped businessman David R. Demers to commercialize Hill's HPDI system, and Westport Innovations Inc. was born. Since that time, HPDI technology has found its way under the hoods of trucking fleets, heavy machinery and consumer vehicles around the world. From Kenworth and Peterbilt to Volvo and Ford, top automotive brands are adopting Westport natural-gas engines for cars, trucks and industrial vehicles. According to founder and CEO Demers, Westport's emergence as the global leader in natural gas engines is owed to Hill's system. 'The initial research conducted by Hill and his team at UBC was the genesis of our company's leadership in developing and commercializing low-emissions, environmentally friendly engine systems,' Demers says. 'Westporters continue to draw inspiration from Dr Hill's design and technical brilliance.'

How did Westport Innovations grow from a start-up to a global leader of the green automotive revolution? With Hill's HPDI technology as a principal strategic asset, Demers resolved to bring natural-gas engines to various gasoline-based automotive sectors. In 2001, Westport and diesel engine giant Cummins Inc. formed a joint venture to introduce HPDI technology to the trucking market. With Hill's injector system and Cummins's heavy-duty engine blocks, Cummins Westport Inc. has succeeded in manufacturing over 34 000 natural gas engines for high-powered buses and semi-trailer trucks. The success of the venture led Demers to establish Westport's first business unit, Westport HD, which specializes in liquefied natural gas (LNG) systems for heavy-duty Class 8 trucks – eighteen-wheel road warriors manufactured by companies like Kenworth and Peterbilt. In 2007, Demers launched a joint venture with Italy's OMVL SpA and began producing light-duty engines for consumer vehicles, including the Volvo V70 station wagon and Ford F-250 pickup. Westport acquired OMVL in 2010, and a new light-duty division was established – Westport LD. The creation of Westport LD opened the door for Westport to build natural-gas engines for General Motors (GM). Most recently, in 2012, Westport and equipment manufacturer Caterpillar formed a partnership to make natural gas engines for mining vehicles, locomotives and off-road machines. These changes to Westport's structure have positioned the company to dominate multiple markets for years to come.

Why are automakers and equipment manufacturers suddenly snatching up natural-gas engines? According to Hill, market forces are at work. 'For a decade, emissions was a primary driving motive for alternative fuels for diesels,' says Hill. 'But economic factors are a huge driving force right now, particularly with the abundance of shale gas reserves being discovered, and the economic advantages of domestically produced fuels.' As Hill notes, shale gas discoveries in the USA have boosted domestic supply, driving down methane prices to approximately half the cost of diesel. The change is leading businesses and industries to switch to natural gas. If the trend continues, the Westport brand could become as recognizable as Navistar, Ford or Mopar.

As for Hill, the UBC professor and 2011 Manning Innovation Award recipient says helping transportation go green has been humbling. 'I feel grateful for being able to play a small part in the beginning of what's turned out to be a fascinating venture,' he says. 'It has been an eye-opener to me how people of wonderful talents can come together, trust each other and work cooperatively, not worrying about who gets the credit, but just being focused on the job and getting it done.'

Integrative case questions

1 What type of change and innovation is taking place at Westport Innovations Inc.? Which innovation strategies helped turn Hill's research ideas into successful new products?

2 Which structural design approach are managers using to organize and grow Westport Innovations Inc.?

3 In what way has Westport's organization structure followed its business strategy?

SOURCES: University-Industry Liaison Office, 'Dr. Phil Hill Wins Manning Award for Innovation', the University of British Columbia, November 2, 2011, www.uilo.ubc.ca/uilo/dr-phil-hill-wins-manning-award-innovation (accessed July 2, 2012); '2011 Encana Principal Award Winner Dr. Philip G. Hill: High-Pressure Direct Injection (HPDI) of Natural Gas into Diesel Engines', Ernest C. Manning Awards Foundation, Online Video, www.manningawards.ca/awards/winners/2011-principal-award-hill.shtml (accessed July 2, 2012); Daniel Ferry, 'Westport & Caterpillar: Natural Gas is Taking Over the World', Motley Fool, June 5, 2012, www.beta.fool.com/catominor/2012/06/05/westport-caterpillar-natural-gas-taking-over-world/5399/ (accessed July 1, 2012); Westport Corporate website, 'Westport History', www.westport.com/corporate/history (accessed July 1, 2012); 'Could British Columbia Become the Next Cleantech Mecca?' Cantech Letter, August 2, 2011, www.cantechletter.com/2011/08/tech-sparks-could-bc-become-the-next-cleantech-mecca (accessed July 1, 2012); and Glenn Rogers, 'Boone Pickens Is Right: Natural Gas Is the Future', Seeking Alpha, June 21, 2012, www.seekingalpha.com/article/675311-boone-pickens-is-right-natural-gas-is-the-future-at-least-for-now-buy-westport-innovations (accessed July 1, 2012).

PART 5

LEADING

LEADING

CHAPTER 13

LEADERSHIP

LEARNING OBJECTIVES

After studying this chapter, you should be able to:

1 Define leadership and explain its importance for organizations.

2 Describe how leadership is changing in today's organizations, including Level 5 leadership, servant leadership and authentic leadership.

3 Discuss how women's style of leading is typically different from men's.

4 Identify personal characteristics associated with effective leaders.

5 Define task-oriented behaviour and people-oriented behaviour and explain how these categories are used to evaluate and adapt leadership style.

6 Describe the situational model of leadership and its application to subordinate participation.

7 Discuss how leadership fits the organizational situation and how organizational characteristics can substitute for leadership behaviours.

8 Describe transformational leadership and when it should be used.

9 Explain how followership is related to effective leadership.

10 Identify sources of leader power and the tactics that leaders use to influence others.

Being selfless and having a 'servant's mentality' are not phrases often thought about in terms of powerful leaders, but respected leaders generally have the virtue of humility in many corporations and do not have a strong public profile – indeed many shun publicity and keep their privates lives very private. Such a new kind of leadership style is arguably one for today's collaborative world – a leader who quietly builds strong teams and organizations, rather than touting his or her own abilities and accomplishments. This is contrary to the Premier League in England where the media focus strongly on the highly paid egotistical team's

CONCEPT CONNECTION

Steven Gerrard has been a loyal servant of Liverpool Football Club for the whole of his football playing career in the English Premier League, as well as being an excellent captain of the English national team, until 2014. During his final season at Liverpool FC it became clear to a number of commentators that he had lost some of his drive and lost his way during a league match in March 2015. He was given a 'red card' meaning he was sent off the field of play. Clearly there is a time for top sportsmen to retire from a competitive environment and this also applies to top businessmen.

Oliver Kay of *The Times* reported that: *'Gerrard, though, is a super hero no more. After spending much of last season defying predictions of his decline, he has been confronted, more and more regularly, with his footballing mortality. Perhaps, in some strange way, it was logic – and the knowledge that he could no longer defeat it – that was behind his moment of madness on Sunday. Allowing his heart to rule his head has been his undoing at times, but has also been the secret of his success.'*

coaches. Humility is not a quality that several demonstrate – especially on the touchline when they disagree with the referee's decisions. In the previous chapter, we explored differences in attitudes and personality that affect behaviour. Some of the most important attitudes for the organization's success are those of its leaders because leader attitudes and behaviours play a critical role in shaping employee attitudes and performance. In this chapter we define leadership and explore how managers develop leadership qualities. We look at some important leadership approaches for contemporary organizations, as well as examine trait, behavioural and contingency theories of leadership effectiveness; discuss charismatic and transformational leadership; explore the role of followership; and consider how leaders use power and influence to get things done. We will explore the views of contemporary writers on the abuses of leadership as well as those who have taken novel approaches to leadership and team development. Chapters 14 through 16 will look in detail at many of the functions of leadership, including employee motivation, communication and facilitating effective teamwork.

The nature of leadership

In most situations, a team, military unit, department or volunteer group is only as good as its leadership. Yet there are as many variations among leaders as there are among other individuals, and many different styles of leadership can be effective.

An extreme view, expressed by some authors, (Boddy (2005) and Kets de Vries (2010) is that managers can exert manipulation and coercion on others, without any conscience, for their personal career advancement. The descriptive term these two writers have adopted is that of 'Corporate Psychopaths' being described by Boddy as: '... *self-serving, opportunistic, egocentric, ruthless and shameless but who can be charming, manipulative and ambitious.'* This area is one that is of considerable interest to academics as these individuals, as CEOs, wield considerable power and influence at the top level and, at worst, they can damage corporate reputations and misdirect corporate resources to value destroying business ventures. We argue that a certain level of overconfidence is a requirement of a leader along with a strong degree of self-efficacy – but checks and balances must be in place. Ruthless ambition has jeopardized many UK banks with Fred Goodwin, CEO of RBS, being cited by the media as a CEO who wanted the acquisition of the Dutch bank ABN Amro at all costs and retrospectively grossly overpaid for the bank. Hubristic behaviour such as Goodwin's can be both value-adding and value destroying to corporations, and detection systems are very difficult to design and implement.

So, what does it mean to be a leader? Among all the ideas and writings about leadership, three aspects stand out – people, influence and goals. Leadership occurs among people, involves the use of influence and is used to attain goals.[1] *Influence* means that the relationship amongst people is not a passive one. Moreover, influence should be designed to achieve some meaningful result and/or goal. Thus, leadership, as defined here, is the ability to influence people towards the attainment of negotiated goals. This definition captures the idea that leaders are engaged with other people in the achievement of organizational goals. Leadership is reciprocal, occurring *among* people.[2] Leadership is a 'people' activity, distinct from excessive administrative activities.

REFLECTION

- The attitudes and behaviours of leaders shape the conditions that facilitate how well employees can do their jobs; thus, leaders play a tremendous role in the organization's success.

- Leadership is the ability to influence people towards the attainment of organizational goals.
- Many different styles of leadership can be effective.

Contemporary leadership

The concept of what is appropriate leadership should evolve as the needs of organizations change. That is, the environmental context in which leadership is practised, influences which approach might be most effective, as well as what types of leaders are most admired by society. Technology, economic conditions, labour conditions, social and cultural norms of the times, all play a major role. A significant influence on leadership styles, in recent and future years, has been and will continue to be the turbulence and uncertainty of the environment. Ethical and economic difficulties, corporate governance concerns, globalization, changes in technology, new ways of working, shifting employee expectations, and significant social transitions, have all contributed to a radical shift in how we reflect on and practice pragmatic and excellent leadership. It is interesting that industry regulators for banking have moved dramatically from light touch oversight to much tighter regulation. This has serious impacts on the international banking community that has been exposed as having weak internal supervision of its commercial activities. Barclays Bank was subject to a major UK Government review in 2013 following its near collapse in 2008. HSBC is currently replacing all its Independent Directors, and extracts that follow from the *Wall Street Journal* of 1 April 2015 are revealing. For an in-depth review of integrity within several industries the KPMG review of 2013 is highly informative of the level of concern for honesty and integrity in the business world. Corporate governance should be high on the agenda for executive boards.

'The Federal Reserve and other bank regulators are holding frequent, in some cases monthly, meetings with individual directors at the nation's biggest banks, demanding detailed minutes and other documentation of board meetings and singling out boards in internal regulatory critiques of bank operations and oversight. This change has Washington overseeing the overseers, as regulators home in on whether directors are adequately challenging and monitoring risks in the bankng system.'

– WSJ REPORTERS MCGANE AND HILSENRATH

Four approaches that are arguably still in synchronization with leadership for today's turbulent times are: Collins' Level 5 leadership theories, servant leadership, authentic leadership and interactive leadership – which has been most associated with different aspects of women's style of leading.

Level 5 leadership

A study conducted by Jim Collins and his research associates identified the critical importance of what Collins calls *Level 5 leadership* in transforming companies from merely good to truly great organizations.[3] As described in his book *Good to Great: Why Some Companies Make the Leap . . . and Others Don't*, Level 5 leadership refers to the highest level in a hierarchy of manager capabilities, as illustrated in Exhibit 13.1.

As reflected in the exhibit, a key characteristic of Level 5 leaders is an almost complete lack of ego (humility) coupled with a fierce resolve to do what is best for the organization (will). Humility means being

EXHIBIT 13.1 Level 5 hierarchy

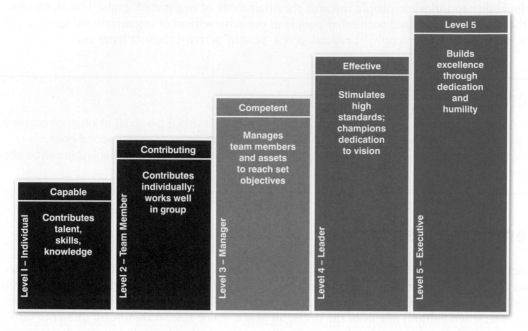

SOURCE: Jim Collins, *Good to Great: Why Some Companies Make the Leap ... and Others Don't* (New York: HarperCollins, 2001), p. 20.

unpretentious and modest rather than arrogant and prideful. In contrast to the view of great leaders as larger-than-life personalities with strong egos and big ambitions, Level 5 leaders often seem reserved and self-effacing. Although they accept full responsibility for mistakes, poor results or failures, Level 5 leaders give and share credit for business and social successes with others. Level 5 leaders build organizations based on solid values that go far beyond just making money, with an unwavering resolve to do whatever is needed to make the company successful over the long term.[4]

One leader who demonstrates such Level 5 leadership qualities is Qi Lu with Microsoft.

 INNOVATIVE WAY

Qi Lu, Microsoft

Qi Lu grew up in a rural village in China with no electricity or running water. He became the president of Microsoft's Online Services division. How did he get there? Not from personal ambition, say former colleagues at Yahoo!. '*He shunned the limelight,*' said Tim Cadogan, now CEO of OpenX, '*but he was considered one of the stars.*'

Lu rose through the ranks at Yahoo!, and he got the senior level job at Microsoft not on aggressiveness and pursuit of personal advancement, but based on his intellectual abilities and his commitment to go above and beyond the call of duty, to accomplish organizational goals. Lu transmitted a strong sense of duty and loyalty to his employers, pouring his heart and soul into the mission rather than spending his energies promoting himself. On his last day of work at Yahoo!, a problem came up with a database. Rather than leaving the problem for others, Lu worked side by side with his soon-to-be former employees to try to fix it. He finally left at midnight, when his network access was automatically cut off.[5]

Level 5 leaders like Qi Lu are extremely ambitious for their companies rather than for themselves. As another example, consider Darwin Smith, CEO of Kimberly-Clark from 1971–1991. Over those 20 years, Smith transformed Kimberly-Clark from a stodgy paper product maker with falling stock prices, into the leading consumer paper products company in the world. The company generated cumulative stock returns that were 4.1 times greater than those of the general market. Yet few people had heard of this Mr Smith.

He shunned the spotlight and was never featured in high profile articles in *Fortune* magazine or *The Wall Street Journal*. He was ambitious for the company, not for himself.[6]

This attitude of humility becomes more highly evident in the area of succession planning. Level 5 leaders develop a solid talent pool of future leaders throughout the organization, so that when they leave, the company can continue to thrive and grow even stronger. Egocentric leaders, by contrast, often set their successors up for failure, because it will become a testament to their own greatness if the company doesn't perform as well without them. Rather than building an organization around 'a corporate hero', Level 5 leaders want the maximum of subordinates to develop to their fullest potential.

Servant leadership

When Jack Welch, longtime CEO of General Electric (GE), and now a high level consultant, addresses an audience of MBA students, he reminds them that '*any time you are managing people, your job is not about you, it's about them. It starts out about you as . . . an individual in a company,*' Welch says. '*But once you get a leadership job, it moves very quickly to being about them.*'[7] Some leaders operate from the assumption that work exists for the development of the worker as much as the worker exists to do the work.[8] The concept of servant leadership, first described by Robert Greenleaf in 1970, has gained renewed interest in recent years, as companies recover from ethical scandals and compete to attract and retain the best human talent.[9]

A servant leader transcends self-interest to serve others, the organization and society.[10] Marilyn Nelson, CEO of the Carlson Companies (Radisson Hotels, TGI Fridays, Regent Seven Seas Cruises), says being a true leader means you 'have to subordinate your own emotions, your own desires, even make decisions on behalf of the whole that might conflict with what you would do on an individual basis.'[11] A stunning example of this occurred in the spring of 2009 when a US-flagged cargo ship, the *Maersk Alabama*, was seized and raided by Somali pirates. Captain Richard Phillips ordered crew members of the unarmed ship not to fight and gave himself up as a hostage to free the ship and crew. Contrast his behaviour with that of Captain Francesco Schettino, who allegedly abandoned his ship, the *Costa Concordia*, while passengers were still aboard after the luxury cruise liner hit a rock and sank off the coast of Italy, killing at least 30 people. Schettino was subsequently found guilty of manslaughter, shipwreck and abandoning ship.[12] In organizations, true servant leaders operate on two levels: for the fulfilment of their subordinates' goals and needs and for the realization of the larger purpose or mission of their organization. Servant leaders are altruistic, sharing power, ideas, information, recognition, credit for accomplishments, even money. Servant leaders often work in the non-government organization world because it offers a natural way to apply their leadership drive and skills to serve others. But servant leaders also succeed in business. Fred Keller has built a $250 million plastics manufacturing company, Cascade Engineering, by continuously asking one question: *What good can we do?* Keller started the business over 40 years ago with six employees. Today, it has 1000 employees in 15 business divisions. Keller has made social responsibility a cornerstone of the business. The company offers jobs to welfare recipients. Keller has also donated large amounts to various philanthropic causes, both as an individual and through Cascade.[13]

TAKE A MOMENT

Answer the 'What's Your Personal Style?' questions at the end of this chapter. What does your score say about your humility? Read the Ethical Dilemma at the end of this chapter that pertains to leadership for turbulent times.

Authentic leadership

Another popular concept in leadership today is the idea of authentic leadership, which refers to individuals who know and understand themselves, who espouse and act consistent with higher-order ethical values, and who empower and inspire others with their openness and authenticity.[14] To be authentic means being *real*, staying true to one's values and beliefs, and acting based on one's true self rather than emulating what others do. Authentic leaders inspire trust and commitment because they respect diverse viewpoints, encourage collaboration, and help others learn, grow and develop as leaders.

Exhibit 13.2 outlines the key characteristics of authentic leaders, and each is discussed below.[15]

■ *Authentic leaders pursue their purpose with passion*. Leaders who lead without a purpose can fall prey to greed and the desires of the ego. When leaders demonstrate a high level of passion and commitment to a purpose, they inspire commitment from followers.

■ *Authentic leaders practise solid values*. Authentic leaders have values that are shaped by their personal beliefs, and they stay true to them even under pressure. People come to know what the leader stands for, which inspires trust.

■ *Authentic leaders lead with their hearts as well as their heads*. All leaders sometimes have to make tough choices, but authentic leaders maintain a compassion for others as well as the courage to make difficult decisions.

■ *Authentic leaders establish connected relationships*. Authentic leaders build positive and enduring relationships, which makes followers want to do their best. In addition, authentic leaders surround themselves with good people and work to help others grow and develop.

■ *Authentic leaders demonstrate self-discipline*. A high degree of self-control and self-discipline keeps leaders from taking excessive or unethical risks that could harm others and the organization. When authentic leaders make mistakes, they openly admit them.

'True leadership is a fire in the mind. . . . It is a strength of purpose and belief in a cause that reaches out to others, touches their hearts, and makes them eager to follow.'
– ROBERT M.GATES, FORMER US SECRETARY OF DEFENSE

EXHIBIT 13.2 Components of authentic leadership

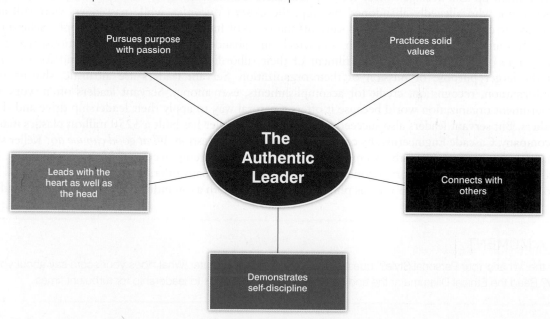

SOURCE: Bill George, *Authentic Leadership: Rediscovering the Secrets to Lasting Value* (San Francisco: Jossey-Bass, 2003).

Gender differences

Some of the general characteristics associated with Level 5 leaders and authentic leaders are also hallmarks of interactive leadership, which has been found to be associated with female leaders. Interactive leadership means that the leader favours a consensual and collaborative process, and influence derives from relationships rather than position power and formal authority.[16]

CONCEPT CONNECTION

The 2008 financial collapse put Debra Cafaro's leadership skills to the test. The CEO of Ventas Inc. saw the housing crisis approaching and insisted the Louisville-based health care real estate investment trust build cash reserves. Although she wanted to project calmness and certainty when the economic downturn hit, Cafaro says that 'in order to be authentic, I also had to acknowledge, I'm scared, too.' Throughout the crisis, Cafaro operated as an **interactive leader**, one who, in her words, makes sure 'we're working together, collaborating – marching in the same direction.' Ventas survived the recession. In a recent *Harvard Business Review* article, 29 CEOs were interviewed and expressed worry and anxiety of being CEOs and not making mistakes.

Although both men and women can practice interactive leadership, research indicates that women's style of leadership is typically different from that of most men and is particularly suited to today's organizations.[17] Using data from actual performance evaluations, one study [2000] found that when rated by peers, subordinates and bosses, female managers scored significantly higher than men on abilities such as motivating others, fostering communication and listening.[18] Another 2005 study of leaders and their followers in businesses, universities and government agencies found that women were rated higher on social and emotional skills, which are crucial for interactive leadership.[19] Indeed, a past review of more than 7000 360-degree performance evaluations discovered that women outshone men in almost every leadership dimension measured, even some considered typically masculine qualities, such as driving for results. The exception was that women were typically rated lower on developing a strategic perspective, which some researchers believe hinders female managers' career advancement despite their exceptional ratings on other leadership dimensions.[20] Exhibit 13.3 shows results for five of the 16 dimensions measured by the study.

One good example of an interactive leader is Cindy Szadokierski, who started as a reservations agent for United Airlines and became the vice president in charge of operations for United's largest hub, at O'Hare International Airport. As she oversees 4000 employees and 600 flights a day, her favourite times are the weekly afternoon walkabouts on the O'Hare ramp, and the weekly morning strolls through the terminal, where she can connect with employees and customers. Pete McDonald, then chief operating officer of United's parent, UAL Corporation, says there were serious operations problems at O'Hare, so they put 'the most communicative person' in the job. Szadokierski's approach to leadership is demonstrably more collaborative than command and control.[21]

Men can also be interactive leaders as well, as illustrated by the example of Pat McGovern, founder and chairman of IDG, a technology publishing and research firm owning magazines such as *CIO, PC World* and *Computerworld*. McGovern believes that having personal contact with employees and letting them know they're appreciated is a primary responsibility of leaders.[22] The characteristics associated with interactive leadership are emerging as valuable qualities for both male and female leaders in today's workplace. Values associated with interactive leadership include personal humility, inclusion, relationship building and caring for people.

EXHIBIT 13.3 Gender differences in leadership behaviours

Leadership ability	Who does it best?
Develops others	(Women rated higher)
Drives for results	(Women rated higher)
Inspires and motivates others	(Women rated higher)
Innovates	(Women and men rated about equally)
Builds relationships	(Women rated higher)
Technical or professional expertise	(Women and men rated about equally)

SOURCE: Data from Zenger Folkman, Inc., reported in Jack Zenger and Joseph Folkman, 'Are Women Better Leaders than Men?' HBR Blog Network, *Harvard Business Review,* March 15, 2012, www.blogs.hbr.org/cs/2012/03/a_study_in_leadership_women_do.html (accessed September 12, 2012).

REFLECTION

- A significant influence on leadership styles in recent years is the turbulence and uncertainty of the environment.
- One effective approach in today's environment is Level 5 leadership, which is characterized by an almost complete lack of ego (humility), coupled with a fierce resolve to do what is best for the organization (will).
- **Humility** means being unpretentious and modest rather than arrogant and prideful.
- A **servant leader** is a leader who serves others by working to fulfil followers' needs and goals, as well as to achieve the organization's larger mission.
- **Authentic leadership** refers to leadership by individuals who know and understand themselves,

who espouse and act consistent with higher-order ethical values, and who empower and inspire others with their openness and authenticity.
- Women leaders typically score significantly higher than men on abilities such as motivating others, building relationships and developing others – skills that are based on humility and authenticity and are particularly suited to today's organizations.
- **Interactive leadership** is a leadership style characterized by values such as inclusion, collaboration, relationship building and caring.
- Although interactive leadership is associated with women's style of leading, both men and women can be effective interactive leaders.

From management to leadership

Hundreds of books and articles have been written in recent years about the differences between management and leadership. Good management is essential in organizations, yet managers have to be leaders too, because distinctive qualities are associated with management and leadership that provide different strengths for the organization. A good way to think of the distinction between management and leadership is that:

'Management organizes the production and supply of fish to people, whereas leadership teaches and motivates people to fish. Organizations need both types of skills.'[23]

As shown in Exhibit 13.4, management and leadership reflect two different sets of qualities and skills that frequently overlap within a single individual. A person might have more of one set of qualities than the other,

EXHIBIT 13.4 Leader and manager qualities

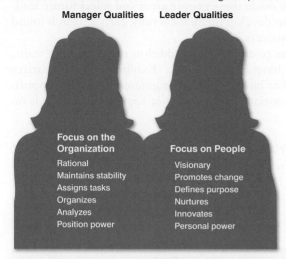

Manager Qualities | Leader Qualities

Focus on the Organization
Rational
Maintains stability
Assigns tasks
Organizes
Analyzes
Position power

Focus on People
Visionary
Promotes change
Defines purpose
Nurtures
Innovates
Personal power

SOURCE: 'What Is the Difference Between Management and Leadership?' *The Wall Street Journal Online,* www.guides.wsj.com/management/developing-a-leadership-style/what-is-the-difference-between-management-and-leadership (accessed June 28, 2009); and Genevieve Capowski, 'Anatomy of a Leader: Where Are the Leaders of Tomorrow?' *Management Review* (March 1994): 12.

but ideally, a manager develops a balance of both manager and leader qualities.[24] A primary distinction between management and leadership is that management promotes stability and order within the existing organizational structure and systems. This ensures that suppliers are paid, customers invoiced, products and services produced on time, and so forth. Leadership, on the other hand, promotes vision and change. Leadership means questioning the status quo and being willing to take reasonable risks so that outdated, unproductive or socially irresponsible norms can be replaced to meet new challenges. This was a view strongly expressed as denouement by Professor R. F. Flood (1996) in his textbook *Diversity Management: Triple Loop Learning* (Wiley).

Consider how Alan Mulally applied both management and leadership to revive Ford Motor Company. Ford was losing $83 million a day in 2008. Three years later, in 2011, the company had a net profit of $20 billion. Ford was the only one of the Big Three automakers that didn't accept a bailout from the US government. Mulally needed excellent management skills to expose operating inefficiencies, cut costs, streamline the structure and improve quality. Yet the turnaround of Ford also depended on consummate leadership. Mulally inspired people with a vision of saving a storied American company and transforming it to meet the challenges of the twenty-first century. He shifted the culture from one of ego-driven infighting to one of cooperation, accountability and commitment. He motivated thousands of employees to embrace change and execute the vision and strategy. Mulally ate in the company cafeteria rather than the executive dining room so that he could talk with people at all levels of the company, occasionally popped into meetings to offer encouragement and support, and personally answered emails from employees.[25]

Leadership cannot replace management; it should be in addition to management. Good management is needed to help the organization meet current commitments, while good leadership is needed to move the organization into the future. Leadership's power comes from being built on the foundation of a well-managed organization.

REFLECTION

- Leadership and management reflect two different sets of qualities and skills that provide different benefits for the organization.
- Management promotes stability and efficient organizing to meet current commitments, whereas leadership often inspires engagement and organizational change to meet new conditions.

- Both leadership and management are important to organizations, and people can learn to be good leaders as well as good managers.
- Alan Mulally applied both skilled management and good leadership in his turnaround of Ford Motor Company.

Leadership traits

Early efforts to understand leadership success focused on the leader's traits. Traits are the distinguishing personal characteristics of a leader, such as intelligence, honesty, self-confidence and even appearance. The early research looked at leaders who had achieved a level of greatness, and hence was referred to as the 'Great Man' approach. The idea was relatively simple: Find out what made these people great and select future leaders who already exhibited the same traits or could be trained to develop them. Generally, early research found only a weak relationship between personal traits and leader success.[26]

In recent years, interest in examining leadership traits has re-emerged. In addition to personality traits, physical, social and work-related characteristics of leaders have been studied.[27] Exhibit 13.5 summarizes the physical, social and personal leadership characteristics that have received the greatest research support. However, these characteristics do not stand alone. The appropriateness of a trait or set of traits depends on the contextual leadership situation.

'The good news: these [leadership] traits are not genetic. It's not as if you have to be tall or left-handed. These qualities are developed through attitude, habit and discipline – factors that are within your control.'
– ADAM BRYANT, SENIOR EDITOR FOR FEATURES AT *THE NEW YORK TIMES*, IN THE 'CORNER OFFICE' COLUMN

EXHIBIT 13.5 Personal characteristics of leaders

Physical characteristics	Personality	Work-related characteristics
Energy	Self-confidence	Achievement drive, desire to excel
Physical stamina	Honesty and integrity	Conscientiousness in pursuit of goals
	Optimism	Persistence against obstacles, tenacity
	Desire to lead	
	Independence	
Intelligence and ability	**Social characteristics**	**Social background**
Intelligence, cognitive ability	Sociability, interpersonal skills	Education
Knowledge	Cooperativeness	Mobility
Judgement, decisiveness	Ability to enlist cooperation	
	Tact, diplomacy	

SOURCE: Bernard M. Bass, *Bass & Stogdill's Handbook of Leadership: Theory, Research, and Managerial Applications,* 3rd ed. (New York: The Free Press, 1990), pp. 80–81; and S. A. Kirkpatrick and E. A. Locke, 'Leadership: Do Traits Matter?' *Academy of Management Executive* 5, no. 2 (1991): 48–60.

Effective leaders typically possess varied traits, and no single leader can have a complete set of characteristics that is appropriate for handling any problem, challenge or opportunity that comes along. In addition, traits that are typically considered positive can sometimes have negative consequences, and traits sometimes considered negative can have positive consequences. For example, optimism is a highly desirable trait for a leader. As described in the previous chapter, studies have shown that optimism is the single characteristic most common to top executives.[28] Leaders need to be able to see possibilities where others see problems and instill in others a sense of hope for a better future. However, optimism can also lull leaders into laziness and overconfidence, causing them to miss danger signals and underestimate risks. The 2007–2008 crisis in the financial services industry can be blamed partly on leaders who grew overconfident and led their organizations astray. Optimism has to be paired with 'reality testing' and conscientiousness, another trait common to successful leaders, as shown in the exhibit.[29]

Therefore, rather than just understanding their *traits*, the best leaders recognize and hone their *strengths*.[30] Strengths are natural talents and abilities that have been supported and reinforced with learned knowledge and skills and provide each individual with his or her best tools for accomplishment and satisfaction.[31] Every manager has a limited capacity; those who become good leaders are the ones who maximize their key inner strengths that can make a difference. Effective leadership is not about having the 'right' traits, but rather about finding the strengths that one can best exemplify and apply as a leader.

REFLECTION

- **Traits** are distinguishing personal characteristics, such as intelligence, self-confidence, energy and independence.

- **Strengths** are natural talents and abilities that have been supported and reinforced with learned knowledge and skills.

Behavioural approaches

The inability to define effective leadership based solely on traits led to an interest in looking at the behaviour of leaders and how it might contribute to leadership success or failure. Two basic leadership behaviours identified as important for leadership are attention to tasks and attention to people. Land Rover Jaguar of the UK assess their managers in a four quadrant box – the best performers have both high performance teams and they must manage them with high empathy.

Task versus people bias

Two types of behaviour that have been identified as applicable to effective leadership in a variety of situations and time periods are *task-oriented behaviour* and *people-oriented behaviour*.[32] Although they are not the only important leadership behaviours, concern for tasks and concern for people must be shown at some reasonable level. Thus, many approaches to understanding leadership use these *metacategories*, or broadly defined behaviour categories, as a basis for study and comparison.

Important early research programmes on leadership were conducted at The Ohio State University and the University of Michigan.[33] Ohio State researchers identified two major behaviours they called consideration and initiating structure. Consideration falls in the category of people-oriented behaviour and is the extent to which the leader is mindful of subordinates, respects their ideas and feelings and establishes mutual trust. Initiating structure is the degree of task behaviour; that is, the extent to which the leader is task oriented and directs subordinate work activities towards goal attainment. Studies suggest that effective leaders may be high on consideration and low on initiating structure or low on consideration and high on initiating structure, depending on the situation.[34]

TAKE A MOMENT

As a new manager, realize that both task-oriented behaviour and people-oriented behaviour are important, although some situations call for a greater degree of one over the other. Go to the Experiential Exercise online to measure your degree of task orientation and people orientation.

Research at the University of Michigan also considered task and people-oriented behaviours by comparing the behaviour of effective and ineffective supervisors.[35] The most effective supervisors were those who established high performance goals and displayed supportive behaviour towards subordinates. These were referred to as *employee-centred leaders*. The less-effective leaders were called *job-centred leaders*; these leaders tended to be less concerned with goal achievement and human needs in favour of meeting schedules, keeping costs low and achieving production efficiency.

The leadership grid

Building on the work of the Ohio State and Michigan studies, Blake and Mouton of the University of Texas proposed a two-dimensional theory called the Managerial Grid®, which was later restated by Blake and

McCanse as the Leadership Grid®.[36] The model and five of its major management styles are depicted in Exhibit 13.6. Each axis on the grid is a nine-point scale, with 1 meaning low concern and 9 meaning high concern.

Team management (9, 9) often is considered the most effective style and is recommended for leaders because organization members work together to accomplish tasks. *Country club management* (1, 9) occurs when primary emphasis is given to people rather than to work outputs. *Authority-compliance management* (9, 1) occurs when efficiency in operations is the dominant orientation. *Middle-of-the-road management* (5, 5) reflects a moderate amount of concern for both people and production. *Impoverished management* (1, 1) means the absence of a management philosophy; managers exert little effort towards interpersonal relationships or work accomplishment.

EXHIBIT 13.6 The leadership grid figure

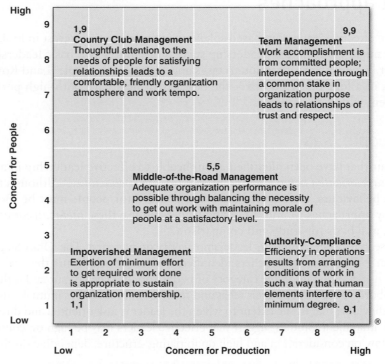

REFLECTION

- Two basic leadership behaviours identified as important for leadership are attention to tasks and attention to people.
- Consideration is the term used by researchers at The Ohio State University to describe the extent to which a leader is sensitive to subordinates, respects their ideas and feelings and establishes mutual trust.
- Initiating structure is the term that describes the extent to which a leader is task oriented and directs subordinates' work activities towards goal accomplishment.

- Researchers at the University of Michigan used the terms *employee-centred leaders* and *job-centred leaders* to describe the same two basic leadership behaviours.
- The Leadership Grid® is a two-dimensional leadership model that measures the leader's concern for people and concern for production to categorize the leader in one of five different leadership styles.

Contingency approaches

Steven Sinofsky led a team of Microsoft software engineers working on the next generation of Windows operating system software. At Apple, Bertrand Serlet was leading a team to ensure the new Macintosh operating system is better. Although they hold the same type of job, Sinofsky and Serlet are widely different in their approaches to leadership. Sinofsky is a meticulous planner and likes to run a tight ship. *'Under Sinofsky,'* one engineer said, *'you plan and you stick to the plan.' Serlet, on the other hand, prefers things to be a little chaotic. He isn't a stickler for rules and procedures, emphasizing a more flexible, laid-back style.* A programmer who has worked under both leaders compared Sinofsky's style to that of a martial marching band, while Serlet's was compared to an improvisational jazz group.[37]

How can two people with widely different styles both be effective leaders? The answer lies in understanding contingency approaches to leadership, which explore how the organizational situation influences leader effectiveness. Contingency approaches include the situational model based on the work of Hersey and Blanchard, the leadership model developed by Fiedler and his associates and the substitutes-for-leadership concept.

TAKE A MOMENT

As a new manager, will you emphasize a task-oriented or a people-oriented leadership style? To find out, complete the New Manager Self-Test.

The situational model of leadership

The situational model of leadership, which originated with Hersey and Blanchard, is an interesting extension of the behavioural theories summarized in the leadership grid (see Exhibit 13.6). This approach focuses a great deal of attention on the characteristics of followers, in determining appropriate leadership behaviour. The point of the situational model is that subordinates vary in readiness, which is determined by the degree of willingness and ability a subordinate demonstrates while performing a specific task. *Willingness* refers to a combination of confidence, commitment and motivation, and a follower may be high or low on any of the three variables. *Ability* refers to the amount of knowledge, experience and demonstrated skill a subordinate brings to the task. Effective leaders adapt their style according to the readiness level of the people they are managing. People low in readiness – because of little ability or training or insecurity – need a different leadership style than those who are high in readiness and have good ability, skills, confidence and willingness to work.[38]

According to the situational model, a leader can adopt one of four leadership styles, as shown in Exhibit 13.7. The *directing style* is a highly directed dictating style and involves giving explicit directions about how tasks should be accomplished. The *coaching style* is one where the leader explains decisions and gives subordinates a chance to ask questions and gain clarity and understanding about work tasks. The *supporting style* is one where the leader shares ideas with subordinates, gives them a chance to participate and facilitates decision-making. The fourth style, the *entrusting style*, provides little direction and little support because the leader turns over responsibility for decisions and their implementation to subordinates.

Exhibit 13.7 summarizes the situational relationship between leader style and follower readiness. The directing style has the highest probability of successfully influencing low readiness followers who are unable or unwilling – because of poor ability and skills, little experience or insecurity – to take responsibility for their own task behaviour. The leader is specific, directing people exactly what to do, how to do it and when. The coaching and supporting styles work for followers at moderate readiness levels. For example, followers might lack some education and experience for the job but have high confidence, interest and willingness to learn. As shown in the exhibit, the coaching style is effective in this situation because it involves giving direction but also includes seeking input from others and clarifying tasks rather than simply instructing that they be performed. When followers have the necessary skills and experience but are somewhat insecure in their abilities or lack high willingness, the supporting style enables the leader to guide followers' development

NEW MANAGER SELF-TEST

Task versus people orientation

INSTRUCTIONS Responding to the statements below can help you diagnose your approach to dealing with others when you are in a leadership role. If you have been a leader at work with people reporting to you, think back to that experience. Or you can think about how you usually behave as a formal or informal leader in a group to get an assignment completed. Please answer honestly about how frequently you display each behaviour.

		Mostly true	Mostly false
1	I intentionally try to make people's work on the job more pleasant.	☐	☐
2	I focus more on execution than on being pleasant with people.	☐	☐
3	I go out of my way to help others.	☐	☐
4	I personally hold people accountable for their performance.	☐	☐
5	I work hard to maintain a friendly atmosphere on the team.	☐	☐
6	I clearly tell people what I expect of them.	☐	☐
7	I think a lot about people's personal welfare.	☐	☐
8	I check up on people to know how they are doing.	☐	☐
9	I am concerned more with relationships than with results.	☐	☐
10	I assign people to specific roles and tasks.	☐	☐
11	I focus more on being pleasant with people than on execution of tasks.	☐	☐
12	I am concerned more with results than with peoples' feelings.	☐	☐

SCORING & INTERPRETATION Give yourself 2 points for each 'Mostly true' and 1 point for each 'Mostly false'.

People orientation: Sum your points for the odd-numbered questions: ___.

Task orientation: Sum your points for the even-numbered questions: ___.

Your *People orientation* score reveals your orientation towards people and relationships as described in the chapter. A score of 10 or higher suggests that you may be 'high' on people behaviour. A score of 9 or below suggests that you may be 'low' on people orientation. Your *Task orientation* score reveals your orientation towards tasks and outcomes. A score of 10 or higher suggests that you may be 'high' on task-oriented behaviour. A score of 9 or below suggests that you may be 'low' on task orientation.

What is your primary leadership orientation? Which of the following best represents your leadership style? (Check one) Look at Exhibit 13.7 to see the quadrant in which you fit.

___Low task, Low people = Entrusting style

___Low task, High people = Supporting style

___High task, Low people = Directing style

___High task, High people = Coaching style

Does your quadrant seem correct based on your experience? Compare your scores with other students.

EXHIBIT 13.7 The situational model of leadership

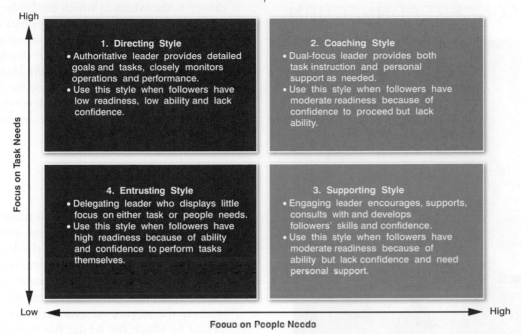

SOURCE: Gary Yukl, Angela Gordon and Tom Taber, 'A Hierarchical Taxonomy of Leadership Behaviour: Integrating a Half Century of Behaviour Research', *Journal of Leadership and Organization Studies* 9, no. 1 (2002): 15–32, and Paul Hersey, Kenneth Blanchard and Dewey Johnson, *Management of Organizational Behaviour: Utilizing Human Resources,* 7th ed. (Upper Saddle River, NJ: Prentice Hall, 1996).

and act as a resource for advice and assistance. When followers demonstrate high readiness, that is, they have high levels of education, experience and readiness to accept responsibility for their own task behaviour, the entrusting style can effectively be used. Because of the high readiness level of followers, the leader can delegate responsibility for decisions and their implementation to subordinates who have the skills, abilities and positive attitudes to follow through. The leader provides a general goal and sufficient authority to do the task as followers see fit.

To apply the situational model, the leader diagnoses the readiness level of followers and adopts the appropriate style – directing, coaching, supporting or entrusting. For example, Jo Newton, an impulse import category leadership manager at Mars' Slough office near London, uses primarily a supporting style. Most members of Newton's team are at moderate to high readiness levels, so Newton advises them of the results the company wants and then steps back, providing guidance and support as needed. *'I like people to come up with their own way of doing things...,'* she says. *'I like to support people as opposed to directing them to do things.'*[39] A leader taking over a new team of inexperienced or uncertain members would likely have to provide more direction with either a directing or coaching style. On the other hand, Warren Buffett uses a primarily entrusting style. The octogenarian CEO of Berkshire Hathaway is considered one of the world's best managers, but he isn't closely involved in the day-to-day management of all the businesses that Berkshire owns. He trusts the managers of the various units, who are highly skilled professionals able and willing to take responsibility for their own task behaviour.[40] An entrusting leader style is not always appropriate, but all managers need to be able to delegate some tasks and decisions for the organization to work smoothly. The Shoptalk discusses techniques for effective delegation.

Fiedler's contingency theory

Whereas the situational model focused on the characteristics of followers, Fiedler and his associates looked at some other elements of the organizational situation to assess when one leadership style is more effective

CONCEPT CONNECTION

'Let's get going. Let's do something, let's move, and let's not be constrained by something that has happened in the past.' That's how Edward Whitacre, Jr, transitional CEO and chairman of General Motors (GM), described his leadership style. In the wake of the 2008 economic crisis and federal bailout, he faced a tough situation trying to restore the newly reorganized company's profitability so it could end government ownership. Whitacre used a **task-oriented style**, demanding quality and efficiency improvements and setting high standards. By the end of his brief tenure in 2010, GM had returned to profitability, paid back loans to US and Canadian governments ahead of schedule, and begun the process of returning to private ownership.

than another.[41] The starting point for Fiedler's theory is the extent to which the leader's style is task oriented or relationship (people) oriented. Fiedler considered a person's leadership style to be relatively fixed and difficult to change; therefore, the basic idea is to match the leader's style with the situation most favourable for his or her effectiveness. By diagnosing leadership style and the organizational situation, the correct fit can be arranged.

Situation: favourable or unfavourable?

The suitability of a person's leadership style is determined by whether the situation is favourable or unfavourable to the leader. The favourability of a leadership situation can be analyzed in terms of three elements: the quality of relationships between leader and followers, the degree of task structure and the extent to which the leader has formal authority over followers.[42]

A situation would be considered *highly favourable* to the leader when leader-member relationships are positive, tasks are highly structured and the leader has formal authority over followers. In this situation, followers trust, respect and have confidence in the leader. The group's tasks are clearly defined, involve specific procedures and have clear, explicit goals. In addition, the leader has formal authority to direct and evaluate followers, along with the power to reward or punish. A situation would be considered *highly unfavourable* to the leader when leader-member relationships are poor, tasks are highly unstructured and the leader has little formal authority. In a highly unfavourable situation, followers have little respect for or confidence and trust in the leader. Tasks are vague and ill-defined and lack clear-cut procedures and guidelines. The leader has little formal authority to direct subordinates and does not have the power to issue rewards or punishments.

Matching leader style to the situation

When Fiedler examined the relationships among leadership style and situational favourability, he found the pattern shown in Exhibit 13.8. Task-oriented leaders are more effective when the situation is either highly favourable or highly unfavourable. Relationship-oriented leaders are more effective in situations of moderate favourability.

🌐 MANAGER'S SHOPTALK

How to delegate

Sometimes, managers cling too tightly to their decision-making and task responsibilities. Failure to delegate occurs for a number of reasons: Managers are most comfortable making familiar decisions; they feel they will lose personal status by delegating tasks; they believe they can do a better job themselves; or they have an aversion to risk – they will not take a chance on delegating because performance responsibility ultimately rests with them.

Yet delegating tasks and decision-making offers an organization many advantages. Decisions are made at the right level, lower-level employees are motivated and employees have the opportunity to develop decision-making skills. The following approach can help you delegate more effectively as a manager:

- **Delegate the whole task.** A manager should delegate an entire task to one person rather than dividing it among several people. This type of delegation gives the individual complete responsibility and increases his or her initiative while giving the manager some control over the results.

- **Select the right person.** Not all employees have the same capabilities and degree of motivation. Managers must match talent to task if delegation is to be effective. They should identify subordinates who made good independent decisions in the past and show a desire for more responsibility. Track record of past success is a strong indicator.

- **Ensure that authority equals responsibility.** Merely assigning a task is not effective delegation. Managers often load subordinates with increased responsibility but do not extend their decision-making range. In addition to having responsibility for completing a task, the worker must be given the authority to make decisions about how best to do the job.

- **Give thorough instruction.** Successful delegation includes information on what, when, why, where, who and how. The subordinate must clearly understand the task and the expected results. It is a good idea to write down all the requirements discussed, including required resources and when and how the results will be reported. Project milestones are normally established for review points.

- **Maintain feedback.** Feedback means keeping open lines of communication with the subordinate to answer questions and provide advice, but without exerting too much control. Open lines of communication make it easier to trust subordinates. Feedback keeps the subordinate on the right track.

- **Evaluate and reward performance.** Once the task is completed, the manager should evaluate results, not methods. When results do not meet expectations, the manager must assess the consequences. When they do meet expectations, the manager should reward employees for a job well done with praise, financial rewards when appropriate, and delegation of future assignments. Haier America changed the Chinese company's ethos of chastising under-performers publically, to one of praising high performers publically and the corporate culture was improved with this 'about face' change of substituting praise for good behaviours versus the opposite – punishment of bad behaviours.

Are you a positive delegator?

Do you help or hinder the decentralization process? If you answer yes to more than three of the following questions, you may have a problem delegating:

- I tend to be a perfectionist.
- My boss expects me to know all the details of my job.
- I don't have the time to explain clearly and concisely how a task should be accomplished.

- I often end up doing tasks myself.
- My subordinates typically are not as committed as I am.
- I get upset when other people don't do the task right.
- I really enjoy doing the details of my job to the best of my ability.
- I like to be in control of task outcomes.

SOURCES: Thomas R. Horton, 'Delegation and Team Building: No Solo Acts Please', *Management Review* (September 1992): 58–61; Andrew E. Schwartz, 'The Why, What, and to Whom of Delegation', *Management Solutions* (June 1987): 31–38; 'Delegation', *Small Business Report* (June 1986): 38–43; and Russell Wild, 'Clone Yourself', *Working Woman* (May 2000): 79–80.

EXHIBIT 13.8 How leader style fits the situation

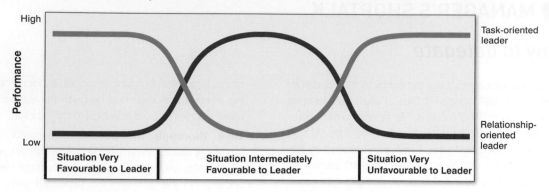

SOURCE: Fred E. Fiedler, 'The Effects of Leadership Training and Experience: A Contingency Model Interpretation', *Administrative Science Quarterly* 17 (1972): 455.

The task-oriented leader excels in the favourable situation because everyone gets along, the task is clear and the leader has power; all that is needed is for someone to lead the charge and provide direction. Similarly, if the situation is highly unfavourable to the leader, a great deal of structure and task direction is needed. A strong leader will define task structure and establish strong authority. Because leader-member relations are typically poor, a strong task orientation will make no difference in the leader's popularity. Sergio Marchionne used strong task-oriented leadership in an unfavourable situation at Chrysler.

Sergio Marchionne's tough, task-oriented approach is suitable for the difficult situation at Chrysler. Researchers at the University of Chicago who looked at CEOs in turnaround situations – where companies typically have high debt loads and a need to improve results in a hurry – found that tough-minded, task-focused characteristics such as analytical skills, a focus on efficiency and setting high standards were more valuable leader qualities than were relationship skills such as good communication, listening and teamwork.[43]

The relationship-oriented leader performs better in situations of intermediate favourability because human relations skills are important in achieving high group performance. In these situations, the leader may be moderately well liked, have some power and supervise jobs that contain some ambiguity. A leader with good interpersonal skills can create a positive group atmosphere that will improve relationships, clarify task structure and establish position power.

A leader, then, needs to know two things when using Fiedler's contingency theory. First, the leader should know whether he or she has a relationship or task-oriented style. Second, the leader should diagnose the situation and determine whether leader-member relations, task structure and position power are favourable or unfavourable.

Fiedler believed fitting leader style to the situation can yield big dividends in profits and efficiency.[44] On the other hand, the model has also been criticized.[45] For one thing, some researchers have challenged the idea that leaders cannot adjust their styles as situational characteristics change. Despite criticisms, Fiedler's model has continued to influence leadership studies. Fiedler's research called attention to the importance of finding the correct fit between leadership style and situation.

Situational substitutes for leadership

The contingency leadership approaches considered so far focus on the leader's style, the subordinates' nature and the situation's characteristics. The final contingency approach suggests that situational variables can be so powerful that they actually substitute for or neutralize the need for leadership.[46] This approach outlines those organizational settings in which a leadership style is unimportant or unnecessary.

Exhibit 13.9 shows the situational variables that tend to substitute for or neutralize leadership characteristics. A substitute for leadership makes the solo leadership style unnecessary or redundant. For example, highly professional subordinates who know how to do their tasks do not need a leader who initiates structure for them and tells them what to do. A neutralizer counteracts the leadership style and prevents the leader

INNOVATIVE WAY

Steve Case (America Online)

Steve Case at AOL represents a successful entrepreneurial leader in the sense that he took AOL from its inception to maturity in the worldwide media conglomerate AOL Time Warner. Steve Case finally departed from AOL Time Warner in May 2003, following investor discontent about the 70 per cent decline in share price, in the wake of AOL's merger with Time Warner in 2001. He did not immediately impress everyone, one journalist after taking an early lacklustre interview with Case, was quoted by Klein (2003, p. 28) as observing *'If you told me Steve Case was Chairman of AOL/Time Warner you would have to hospitalize me for internal haemorrhaging.'*

Case seemed to keep his job at Control Video (the chrysalis from which AOL would grow) by being the hardest working and the lowest paid of those in the marketing section (Swisher and Dickey, 2003, p. 27). Case's background in marketing at Procter & Gamble was ideal to help him bring Von Meister's strange creations to market as attractive products. While Case played a central role from day one, he largely supported Kimsey (a lead investor), who acted as CEO. But as an early colleague Randy Dean saw it *'At the end of the day Steve was the company and Jim knew that'* (Kein, p. 44). This tendency to take a back seat role remained after Case had both founded America Online and acted as Chief Executive of the newly formed enterprise. Jim Kerr, his then Chairman, claimed Case was 'in need of adult supervision' (Swisher, 1998, p. 142) a role initially provided by William Razzbouk and later Bob Pittman of MTV.

While Case was a visionary and a business-builder he lacked the requisite attention to detail necessary to run a large, rapidly growing corporation. He had the creative flair, but neither the gravitas, nor administrative experience, to implement his vision. What Case did not lack was tenacity – his tenacity was so legendary that AOL became dubbed 'the cockroach of the Net' and Case personally 'The Wall'. But with this tenacity and self-confidence could come certain remoteness, as one key investor in AOL noted: *'He's got a Tourette's syndrome of arrogance. He acts humble but then he bursts out with these arrogant comments'* (Swisher and Dickens, 2003, p.21). This combination of personality traits would prove costly for Case as the enterprise grew and sharing control became important.

While Case continued to promulgate the big picture of a new-economy media empire, his new-found colleagues conspired his demise, by reference to very old economy benchmarks. Klein's history of the construction of the AOL Time Warner's empire begins with 'Home Box Office' Chairman and Chief Executive Jeff Bewkes declaring, to the AOL Time Warner Board, *'I'm tired of this bullshit. The only division that's not performing is yours. Every one of us is growing, making numbers. The only problem in this construct is AOL.'* (Klein, 2003, p.2).

A victor of the new economy was impaled on an old economy rhetoric, one he had perhaps hoped to expunge forever. The final indignity for Case occurred when AOL Time Warner reverted back to Time Warner; signalling the extent of an extreme reversal of fortunes involved.

SOURCE: 'The Boys in the Bubble: Searching for intangible value in Internet Stocks' by William Forbes and published by The Institute of Chartered Accountants of Scotland (ICAS) © 2007. This case has been reproduced by kind permission of William Forbes and ICAS.

from displaying certain behaviours. For example, if a leader has absolutely no position power or is physically removed from subordinates, the leader's ability to give directions to subordinates is greatly reduced.

Situational variables in Exhibit 13.9 include characteristics of the group, the task and the organization itself. When followers are highly professional and experienced, both leadership styles are less important. People do not need much direction or consideration. With respect to task characteristics, highly structured tasks substitute for a task-oriented style, and a satisfying task substitutes for a people-oriented style. With respect to the organization itself, group cohesiveness substitutes for both leader styles. Formalized rules and procedures substitute for leader task orientation. Physical separation of leader and subordinate neutralizes both leadership styles.

EXHIBIT 13.9 Substitutes and neutralizers for leadership

Variable		Task-oriented leadership	People-oriented leadership
Organizational variables	Group cohesiveness	Substitutes for	Substitutes for
	Formalization	Substitutes for	No effect on
	Inflexibility	Neutralizes	No effect on
	Low position power	Neutralizes	Neutralizes
	Physical separation	Neutralizes	Neutralizes
Task characteristics	Highly structured task	Substitutes for	No effect on
	Automatic feedback	Substitutes for	No effect on
	Intrinsic satisfaction	No effect on	Substitutes for
Group characteristics	Professionalism	Substitutes for	Substitutes for
	Training/experience	Substitutes for	No effect on

The value of the situations described in Exhibit 13.9 is that they help leaders avoid leadership overkill. Leaders should adopt a style with which to complement the organizational situation. Consider the work situation for bank cashiers. A bank cashier performs highly structured tasks, follows clearly written rules and procedures, and has little flexibility in terms of how to do the work. The head cashier should not adopt a task-oriented style because the organization already provides structure and direction. The head cashier should concentrate on a people-oriented style to provide a more pleasant work environment. In other organizations, if group cohesiveness or intrinsic satisfaction meets employees' social needs, the leader is free to concentrate on task-oriented behaviours. The leader can adopt a style complementary to the organizational situation to ensure that both task needs and people needs of the work group will be met.

REFLECTION

- A **contingency approach** is a model of leadership that describes the relationship between leadership styles and specific situations.
- One contingency approach is the **situational model**, which links the leader's behavioural style with the readiness level of followers.
- In general, a task-oriented leader style fits a low-readiness follower, and a relationship leader style fits a higher-readiness follower.
- In Fiedler's contingency theory, the suitability of a leader's style is determined by whether the situation is considered favourable or unfavourable to the leader.

- Task-oriented leaders are considered to perform better in either highly favourable or highly unfavourable situations.
- Relationship-oriented leaders are considered to perform better in situations of intermediate favourability.
- A **substitute for leadership** is a situational variable that makes a leadership style redundant or unnecessary.
- A **neutralizer** is a situational variable that counteracts a leadership style and prevents the leader from displaying certain behaviours.

Charismatic and transformational leadership

Research has also looked at how leadership can inspire and motivate people beyond their normal levels of performance. Some leadership approaches are more effective than others for bringing about high levels of commitment and enthusiasm. Two types with a substantial impact are charismatic and transformational.

Charismatic leadership

Charisma has been referred to as 'a fire that ignites followers' energy and commitment, producing results above and beyond the call of duty.'[47] The charismatic leader has the ability to inspire and motivate people to do more than they would normally do, despite obstacles and personal sacrifice. Followers are willing to put aside their own interests for the sake of the team, department or organization. The impact of charismatic leaders normally comes from (1) stating a lofty vision of an imagined future that employees identify with, (2) displaying an ability to understand and empathize with followers and (3) empowering and trusting subordinates to accomplish results.[48] Charismatic leaders tend to be less predictable because they create an atmosphere of change, and they may be obsessed by visionary ideas that excite, stimulate and drive other people to work hard. One of the best known charismatic leaders in the business world in recent years was Apple co-founder and CEO Steve Jobs.

 INNOVATIVE **WAY**

Steve Jobs, Apple

Steve Jobs was a legend long before he died in October 2011. His creativity and obsession with innovative product design, combined with the force of his personality, made Apple what it is today. Since his death, managers have been reading books and articles that describe his leadership style to try to tap into some of the Steve Jobs magic. Part of that magic relied on Jobs's charisma.

Jobs commanded a rock-star-like following. The tale of how he dropped out of college, co-founded Apple, got fired from his own company, returned years later to save it, and then transformed it by creating a whole new business with the iPod and iPhone, is the stuff of legend. Jobs provided the *pizzazz* for Apple employees, business partners and the public. His charismatic personality played an important role in persuading media companies to make their content available on Apple products. '*When Steve talks, people listen,*' a Harvard Business School professor said a few months before Jobs's death. His passion and commitment inspired and motivated millions of employees and customers. However, his quick, unpredictable temper, driven, wilful personality, impatience and relentless demands, and hypercritical attitude sometimes undermined individual and team performance.

Jobs challenged and inspired teams to reach beyond the possible, yet he could easily dismiss a promising idea or effort as 'a piece of crap', contributing to disillusionment and the loss of potential. Despite this, many people – even some he mistreated – admired and respected (some have even said *worshipped*) Steve Jobs. They tell their 'Steve-Jobs-yelled-in-my-face' stories with pride. His energizing personality and his refusal to 'sell out' made people want to be around him and want to be *like* him. Indeed, one magazine article commented that the amazing staff loyalty he inspired turned Apple into 'Steve Jobs with a thousand lives'.[49]

As the example of Steve Jobs illustrates, there can be both positive and negative aspects of charisma. Other charismatic leaders include Mother Teresa, David Koresh, Sam Walton, Oprah Winfrey, Martin Luther King, Jr, and for Islamic radicals Osama bin Laden. Charisma can be used for positive outcomes that benefit the group, but it can also be used for self-serving purposes that lead to the deception, manipulation and exploitation of others. When charismatic leaders respond to organizational problems in terms of the needs of the entire group rather than their own emotional needs, they can have a powerful, positive influence on organizational performance.[50] At Apple, Steve Jobs's personal identity was so closely aligned with his company that serving Apple and serving his own emotional needs were likely one and the same! As with the Level 5 and authentic leadership approaches that we discussed earlier in the chapter, *humility* typically plays an important part in distinguishing whether a charismatic leader will work to benefit primarily the larger organization or use his or her gifts for ego-building and personal gain.[51]

Charismatic leaders are skilled in the art of *visionary leadership*. A vision is an attractive, ideal future that is credible yet not readily attainable. Vision is an important component of both charismatic and transformational leadership. Visionary leaders speak to the hearts of employees, letting them be part of something bigger than themselves. Where others see obstacles or failures, they see possibility and hope.

Charismatic leaders typically have a strong vision for the future, almost an obsession, and they can motivate others to help realize it.[52] These leaders have an emotional impact on subordinates because they strongly believe in the vision and can communicate it to others in a way that makes the vision real, personal and meaningful. Brin and Page the founders of Google are exemplars of these qualities.

 GREEN POWER

In the hands of a matador

It was, by any standard, a bold move. Taking the leadership reins in 2004 as CEO and president of Spain-based **Acciona**, one of Europe's most profitable real estate and construction businesses, José Manuel Entrecanales envisioned a future in which businesses would balance economic gain with environmental standards. Entrecanales convinced his board to address climate change and promote renewable energy development. The company wasted no time making a public announcement of its long-term sustainability plans and undertaking new strategies led by a Sustainability Committee. Over the next 6 years, Acciona managers made investments in sustainability including wind generators. By 2009, Acciona had risen to third in the world in wind energy production. In less than a decade, Acciona has established a green reputation, and it was the leadership of Entrecanales, with the precise timing and calculated moves of a great matador, that envisioned the new spheres of action.

SOURCES: Daniel Arenas, Jeremie Fosse and Matthew Murphy, 'Acciona: a Process of Transformation Towards Sustainability', in *The Journal of Management Development* 30, no. 10 (2011): 1027–1048; and Patricia McCormick, 'A Brave Matador Explains the Bullfight', *Sports Illustrated*, March 11, 1963, www.sportsillustrated.cnn.com/vault/article/magazine/MAG1074594/2/index.htm (accessed August 4, 2012).

Transformational versus transactional leadership

Transformational leaders are similar to charismatic leaders, but they are distinguished by their special ability to bring about innovation and change by recognizing followers' needs and concerns, providing meaning, challenging people to look at old problems in new ways, and acting as role models for the new values and behaviours. Transformational leaders inspire followers not just to believe in the leader personally, but to believe in their own potential to imagine and create a better future for the organization. Transformational leaders create significant change in both followers and the organization.[53]

Transformational leadership can be better understood in comparison to *transactional leadership*.[54] Transactional leaders clarify the role and task requirements of subordinates, initiate structure, provide appropriate rewards and try to be considerate and meet the social needs of subordinates. The transactional leader's ability to satisfy subordinates may improve productivity. Transactional leaders excel at management functions. They are hardworking, tolerant and fair minded. They take pride in keeping things running smoothly and efficiently. Transactional leaders often stress the impersonal aspects of performance, such as plans, schedules and budgets. They have a sense of commitment to the organization and conform to organizational norms and values. Transactional leadership is important to all organizations, but leading change requires a different approach.

Transformational leaders have the ability to lead changes in the organization's mission, strategy, structure and culture, as well as to promote innovation in products and technologies. Transformational leaders do not rely solely on tangible rules and incentives to control specific transactions with followers. They focus on intangible qualities such as vision, shared values and ideas to build relationships, give larger meaning to diverse activities and find common ground to enlist followers in the change process.[55] Studies show that transformational leadership has a positive impact on follower development and follower performance.[56] Moreover, transformational leadership skills can be learned and they are not totally ingrained personality characteristics. However, some personality traits may make it easier for a leader to display transformational leadership behaviours. For example, studies of transformational leadership have found that the trait of agreeableness, as discussed in the previous chapter, is often associated with transformational leaders.[57] In addition, transformational leaders are typically emotionally stable and positively engaged with the world around them, and they have a strong ability to recognize and understand others' emotions.[58] These characteristics are not surprising, considering that these leaders accomplish change by building networks of positive relationships.

REFLECTION

- A **charismatic leader** is a leader who has the ability to inspire and motivate people to transcend their expected performance, even to the point of personal sacrifice. Both Wellington and Napoleon Bonaparte had these qualities as great generals and a common characteristic – ruthlessness.
- Both charismatic and transformational leaders provide followers with an inspiring **vision**, an attractive, ideal future that is credible yet not readily attainable.

- A **transformational leader** is distinguished by a special ability to bring about innovation and change by creating an inspiring vision, shaping values, building relationships and providing meaning for followers.
- A **transactional leader** clarifies subordinates' roles and task requirements, initiates structure, provides rewards and displays consideration for followers.

Followership

No discussion of leadership is complete without a consideration of followership. Leadership matters, but without effective followers no organization can survive. People have different expectations of what constitutes a good follower versus a good leader, as illustrated by the results of studies asking people to rank the desired characteristics of leaders and followers. The top five qualities desired in each are as follows:[59]

Leader	Follower
Honest	Honest
Competent	Competent
Forward-looking	Dependable
Inspiring	Cooperative
Intelligent	Loyal

There may be some differences, but overall, many of the qualities that define a good follower are the same qualities as those possessed by a good leader. Leaders can develop an understanding of their followers and create the conditions that help them be most effective.[60]

One model of followership is illustrated in Exhibit 13.10. Robert E. Kelley conducted extensive interviews with managers and their subordinates and came up with five *follower styles*, which are categorized according to two dimensions, as shown in the exhibit.[61]

The first dimension is the quality of independent, critical thinking versus dependent, uncritical thinking. Independent critical thinkers are mindful of the effects of their own and others' behaviour on achieving organizational goals. They can weigh the impact of their boss's and their own decisions and offer constructive criticism, creativity and innovation. Conversely, a dependent, uncritical thinker does not consider possibilities beyond what he or she is told, does not contribute to the cultivation of the organization and accepts the supervisor's ideas without thinking.

The second dimension of follower style is active versus passive behaviour. An active follower participates fully in the organization, engages in behaviour that is beyond the limits of the job, demonstrates a sense of ownership and initiates problem solving and decision-making. A passive follower, by contrast, is characterized by a need for constant supervision and prodding by superiors. Passivity is often regarded as laziness; a passive person only does what is required and avoids added responsibility.

EXHIBIT 13.10 Styles of followership

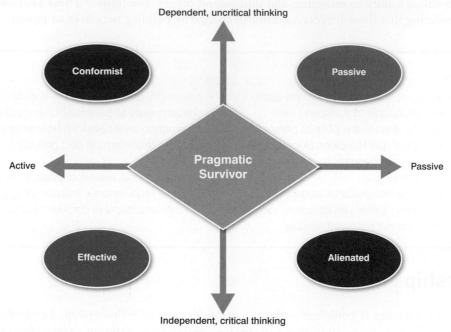

SOURCE: Robert E. Kelley, *The Power of Followership* (New York: Doubleday, 1992).

The extent to which an individual is active or passive and is an independent, critical thinker or a dependent, uncritical thinker determines whether the person will be an alienated follower, a passive follower, a conformist, a pragmatic survivor or an effective follower, as illustrated in Exhibit 13.10:

■ The alienated follower is a passive, yet independent, critical thinker. Alienated employees are often effective followers who have experienced setbacks and obstacles, perhaps promises broken by their superiors. Thus, they are capable, but they focus exclusively on the shortcomings of their boss. Often cynical, alienated followers are able to think independently, but they do not participate in developing solutions to the problems or deficiencies that they see. These people waste valuable time complaining about their boss without offering constructive feedback.

■ The conformist participates actively in a relationship with the boss but doesn't use critical thinking skills. In other words, a conformist typically carries out any and all orders, regardless of the nature of the request. The conformist participates willingly, but without considering the consequences of what he or she is being asked to do – even at the risk of contributing to a harmful endeavour. A conformist is concerned only with avoiding conflict. This follower style might reflect an individual's overdependent attitude towards authority, yet it can also result from rigid rules and authoritarian environments that create a culture of conformity.

■ The pragmatic survivor has qualities of all four extremes – depending on which style fits with the prevalent situation. This type of person uses whatever style best benefits his or her own position and minimizes risk. Pragmatic survivors often emerge when an organization is going through desperate times, and individuals find themselves doing whatever is needed to get through the difficulty. Within any given company, some 25 to 35 per cent of people tend to be pragmatic survivors, avoiding risks and fostering the status quo.[62]

■ The passive follower exhibits neither critical, independent thinking nor active participation. Being passive and uncritical, these people show neither initiative nor a sense of responsibility. Their activity is limited to what they are told to do, and they accomplish things only with a great deal of supervision. Passive followers leave the thinking to the boss. Often, this style is the result of a micromanaging boss who encourages passive behaviour. People learn that to show initiative, accept responsibility or think creatively is not rewarded, and may even be punished by the boss, so they grow increasingly passive.

■ The effective follower is both a critical, independent thinker and active in the organization. Effective followers behave the same towards everyone, regardless of their position in the organization. They develop an equitable relationship with their leaders and do not try to avoid risk or conflict. These people are capable of self-management, they discern strengths and weaknesses in themselves and their bosses, they are committed to something bigger than themselves, and they work towards competency, solutions and positive impact.

Consider the effective followership of the night janitor at FAVI, a French copper-alloy foundry. While the janitor was cleaning one night, the telephone rang, and she answered it to discover that an important visitor to the company had been delayed and was now waiting at the airport without the promised ride to his hotel. (FAVI's CEO had left the airport when the visitor didn't arrive as expected.) What did the janitor do? She simply took the keys to one of the company cars, drove 90 minutes to pick up the visitor and deliver him to his hotel, then went back to finish the cleaning that she had stopped 3 hours earlier.[63]

Effective followers recognize that they have power in their relationships with superiors; thus, they have the courage to manage upwards, to initiate change, and to put themselves at risk or in conflict with the boss if they believe that it serves the best interest of the team or organization. Cognitive and affective conflict situations are often seen to arise, often in the public eye, between Premier League coaches and their star players. Forde and Kuper, writing *in The Financial Times* (15 May 2015) provide copious examples of how top coaches have handled difficult situations with their club players, many possessing huge egos and potentially unique match-winning talents. Forde was Chelsea FC director of football operations from 2007–2013 and he has identified 11 sporting lessons for male talent management, as follows:

1 Big talent usually comes with a big ego – accept it.

2 Look for big egos that have 'got over' themselves.

3 Single out and praise those who make sacrifices for the organization.

4 The manager should not aspire to dominate the talent.

5 Ask the talent for advice – but only for advice.

6 The manager's job is not to motivate.

7 The talent needs to trust each other more than it needs to trust the manager.

8 Improve the talent.

9 Ninety-nine per cent of recruitment is about who you do not sign.

10 Accept that the talent will eventually leave.

11 Gauge the moment when a talent reaches his peak.

The full FT article *'Game of talents: management lessons from top football coaches'* can be accessed from ft.com, where details and examples against each of the 11 sporting lessons are explained in detail.

REFLECTION

- Leaders can accomplish little without effective followers.
- Critical thinking means thinking independently and being mindful of the effect of one's behaviour on achieving goals.
- Uncritical thinking means failing to consider the possibilities beyond what one is told, accepting others' ideas without thinking.
- An effective follower is a critical, independent thinker who actively participates in the organization.

- An alienated follower is a person who is an independent, critical thinker but is passive in the organization.
- A conformist is a follower who participates actively in the organization but does not use critical thinking skills.
- A passive follower is one who exhibits neither critical independent thinking nor active participation.
- A follower who has qualities of all four follower styles, depending on which fits the prevalent situation, is called a pragmatic survivor.

Power and influence

Both followers and leaders use power and influence to get things done in organizations. Sometimes the terms *power* and *influence* are used synonymously, but there are distinctions between the two. Power is the potential ability to influence the behaviour of others.[64] Influence is the effect that a person's actions have on the attitudes, values, beliefs or behaviour of others. Whereas power is the capacity to cause a change in a person, influence may be thought of as the degree of actual change.

Most discussions of power include five types that are available to leaders,[65] and these can be categorized as either *hard power* or *soft power*. Hard power is power that stems largely from a person's position of authority and includes legitimate, reward and coercive power. Soft power includes expert power and referent power, which are based on personal characteristics and interpersonal relationships more than on a position of authority.

Position power

The traditional manager's power comes from the organization (hard power). The manager's position gives him or her the power to reward or punish subordinates to influence their behaviour. Legitimate power, reward power and coercive power are all forms of position power used by managers to change employee behaviour.

Legitimate power

Power coming from a formal management position in an organization and the authority granted to it is called legitimate power. Once a person has been selected as a supervisor, most employees understand that they are obligated to follow his or her direction with respect to work activities. Subordinates accept this source of power as legitimate, which is why they comply.

Reward power

Another kind of power, reward power, stems from the authority to bestow rewards on other people. Managers may have access to formal rewards, such as pay increases or promotions. They also have at their disposal rewards such as praise, attention, and recognition. Managers can use rewards to influence subordinates' behaviour.

Coercive power

The opposite of reward power is coercive power. It refers to the authority to punish or recommend punishment. Managers have coercive power when they have the right to fire or demote employees, criticize them or withhold pay increases. If an employee does not perform as expected, the manager has the coercive power to reprimand him, put a negative letter in his file, deny him a raise and hurt his chances for a promotion.

Personal power

Effective leaders don't rely solely on the hard power of their formal position to influence others. Jeff Immelt, CEO of GE, considers himself a failure if he exercises his formal authority more than seven or eight times a year. The rest of the time he is using softer means to persuade and influence others and to resolve conflicting ideas and opinions.[66] In contrast to the external sources of position power, personal power most often comes from internal sources, such as an individual's special knowledge or personal characteristics. Personal power is the primary tool of the leader, and it is becoming increasingly important as more businesses are run by teams of workers who are less tolerant of authoritarian management.[67] Two types of personal power are expert power and referent power.

CONCEPT CONNECTION

'*In business*,' says Daniel Amos, Aflac chairman and CEO, '*you should treat your employees like they can vote.*' The insurance company that Amos heads has been named to *Fortune's* '100 Best Companies to Work For in America' for 10 consecutive years. Amos (pictured here with the Aflac duck) influences employees using a combination of **reward power** and **referent power**. '*You kind of try to kiss the babies and shake the hands and tell 'em you appreciate 'em and would like them to support you. You can do it like a dictator, but I'm not sure very many of them in the long run are successful.*'

Expert power

Power resulting from a person's special knowledge or skill regarding the tasks being performed is referred to as expert power. When someone is a true expert, others go along with recommendations because of his or her superior knowledge. Followers as well as leaders can possess expert power. For example, some managers lead teams in which members have expertise that the leader lacks. Some leaders at top management levels may lack expert power because subordinates know more about technical details than they do.

Referent power

Referent power comes from an individual's personal characteristics that command others' identification, respect and admiration so they wish to emulate that individual. Referent power does not depend on a formal title or position. When employees admire a supervisor because of the way that she deals with them, the influence is based on referent power. Referent power is most visible in the area of charismatic leadership. In social and religious movements, we often see charismatic leaders who emerge and gain a tremendous following based solely on their personal power. They communicate with missionary zeal and theatrical style.

Other sources of power

There are additional sources of power that are not linked to a particular person or position, but rather to the role an individual plays in the overall functioning of the organization. These important sources include personal effort, relationships with others and information.

Personal effort

People who show initiative, work beyond what is expected of them, take on undesirable but important projects and show interest in learning about the organization and industry often gain power as a result. Stephen Holmes says he got his start towards the CEO's office at Wyndham Worldwide because of personal effort. As a young internal auditor at a private-equity firm in the early 1980s, Holmes was spending his evenings trying to learn a new spreadsheet program. Noted investor Henry Silverman noticed him night after night and, intrigued by the young auditor's efforts, stopped by to see what he was doing. Silverman asked Holmes to move with him to future companies, including Blackstone, HMS and eventually Wyndham. '*I was a kid*,' Holmes says, '*[but he] put me into positions that no one else my age was getting to do.*'[68]

Network of relationships

People who are enmeshed in a network of relationships have greater power. A leader or employee with many relationships knows what's going on in the organization and industry, whereas one who has few interpersonal connections is often in the dark about important activities or changes. Developing positive associations with superiors or other powerful people is a good way to gain power, but people with the greatest power are those who cultivate relationships with individuals at all levels, both inside and outside the organization.

Information gatekeepers

Information is a primary business resource, and people who have access to information and control over how and to whom it is distributed are typically powerful. To some extent, access to information is determined by a person's position in the organization. Top managers typically have access to more information than middle managers, who in turn have access to more information than lower-level supervisors or front-line employees.

Both leaders and followers can tap into these additional sources of power. Leaders succeed when they take the time to build relationships both inside and outside the organization and to talk informally about important projects and priorities. Jack Griffin was forced out as CEO of Time Inc., after less than 6 months in the job, largely because he failed to develop positive relationships. Griffin tried to use the hard power of his position to make needed changes at Time without building the soft power connections needed to implement the changes. Board members began to realize that Griffin had become so unpopular that the company was likely to lose valuable employees if he stayed on as CEO.[69] There are similar high level CEO dismissals to refer to such as McDonald and Durk Jager both at Procter & Gamble.

Interpersonal influence tactics

Leaders often use a combination of influence strategies, and people who are perceived as having greater power and influence typically are those who use a wider variety of tactics. One survey of a few hundred leaders identified more than 4000 different techniques that these people used to influence others.[70]

However, these tactics fall into basic categories that rely on understanding the principles that cause people to change their behaviour and attitudes. Exhibit 13.11 lists six principles for asserting influence. Notice that most of these involve the use of personal power rather than relying solely on position power or the use of rewards and punishments.[71]

1 *Use rational persuasion.* The most frequently used influence strategy is to use facts, data and logical argument to persuade others that a proposed idea, request or decision is appropriate. Using rational persuasion can often be highly effective because most people have faith in facts and analysis.[72] Rational persuasion is most successful when a leader has technical knowledge and expertise related to the issue at hand (expert power), although referent power is also used. That is, in addition to facts and figures, people have to believe in the leader's credibility.

2 *Help people to like you.* People would rather say yes to someone they like than to someone they don't. Effective leaders strive to create goodwill and favourable impressions. When a leader shows consideration and respect, treats people fairly and demonstrates trust in others, people are more likely to want to help and support the leader by doing what he or she asks. In addition, most people like a leader who makes them feel good about themselves, so leaders should never underestimate the power of praise.

3 *Rely on the rule of reciprocity.* Leaders can influence others through the exchange of benefits and favours. Leaders share what they have – whether it is time, resources, services or emotional support. The feeling among people is nearly universal that others should be paid back for what they do, in one form or another. This unwritten 'rule of reciprocity' means that leaders who do favours for others, can expect that others will do favours for them in return.[73] Quid pro quo.

4 *Develop allies.* Effective leaders develop networks of allies – people who can help the leader accomplish his or her goals. Leaders talk with followers and others outside of formal meetings to understand their needs and concerns as well as to explain problems and describe the leader's point of view. They strive to reach a meeting of minds with others about the best approach to a problem or decision.[74]

5 *Ask for what you want.* Another way to influence others is to make a direct and personal request. Leaders have to be explicit about what they want, or they aren't likely to get it. An explicit proposal is sometimes accepted simply because others have no better alternative. Also, a clear proposal or alternative will often receive support if other options are less well defined.

6   *Make use of higher authority.* Sometimes to get things done leaders have to use their formal authority, as well as gain the support of people at higher levels to back them up. However, research has found that the key to successful use of formal authority is to be knowledgeable, credible and trustworthy – that is, to demonstrate expert and referent power as well as legitimate power. Managers who become known for their expertise, who are honest and straightforward with others, and who inspire trust can exert greater influence than those who simply issue orders.[75]

Research indicates that people rate leaders as 'more effective' when they are perceived to use a variety of influence tactics. But not all managers use influence in the same way. Studies have found that leaders in human resources, for example, tend to use softer, more subtle approaches such as building goodwill, using favours and developing allies, whereas those in finance are inclined to use harder, more direct tactics such as formal authority and assertiveness.[76]

EXHIBIT 13.11 Six interpersonal influence tactics for leaders

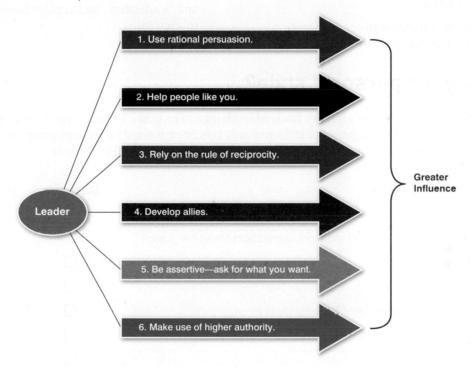

1. Use rational persuasion.

2. Help people like you.

3. Rely on the rule of reciprocity.

Leader

4. Develop allies.

5. Be assertive—ask for what you want.

6. Make use of higher authority.

Greater Influence

REFLECTION

- **Power** is the potential ability to influence the behaviour of others.
- All leaders use power to influence people and accomplish organizational goals.
- **Influence** is the effect a person's actions have on the attitudes, values, beliefs or behaviour of others.
- **Legitimate power** is power that stems from a manager's formal position in an organization and the authority granted by that position.
- **Reward power** results from the authority to bestow rewards.
- **Coercive power** stems from the authority to punish or recommend punishment.

- **Expert power** is power that results from a leader's special knowledge or skill in the tasks performed by subordinates.
- **Referent power** results from characteristics that command subordinates' identification with, respect and admiration for, and desire to emulate the leader.
- Both leaders and followers can tap into other sources of power, including personal effort, networks of relationships, and access to or control over information.
- Leaders use a wide range of interpersonal influence tactics, and people who use a wider variety of tactics are typically perceived as having greater power.

DISCUSSION QUESTIONS

1 Explain the differences between trait theories and behavioural theories of leadership.

2 Describe the key components of 'authentic leadership'. Explain why authentic leaders inspire trust and commitment.

3 Discuss the importance for a manager of demonstrating executive self-efficacy (ESE) recommending how dysfunctional levels of ESE might be negated.

4 Determine the various sources of power available to a manager, evaluating their

effectiveness in the influencing of followers and peers.

5 Provide some examples of organizational situations that would call for either one of the following leadership styles: a) transformational, b) transactional, or c) charismatic leadership.

6 Discuss the differences between 'followership' and 'leadership', and explain how they relate to each other.

What's your personal style?

INSTRUCTIONS Ideas about effective leadership change over time. To understand your approach to leadership, think about your personal style towards others or towards a student group to which you belong, and then answer each item below as 'Mostly true' or 'Mostly false' for you.

		Mostly true	*Mostly false*
1	I am a modest, unassuming person.	☐	☐
2	When a part of a group, I am more concerned about how the group does than how I do.	☐	☐
3	I prefer to lead with quiet modesty rather than personal assertiveness.	☐	☐
4	I feel personally responsible if the team does poorly.	☐	☐
5	I act with quiet determination.	☐	☐
6	I resolve to do whatever needs doing to produce the best result for the group.	☐	☐
7	I am proactive to help the group succeed.	☐	☐
8	I facilitate high standards for my group's performance.	☐	☐

SCORING & INTERPRETATION A recent view of leadership called Level 5 leadership says that the most successful leaders have two prominent qualities: humility and will. Give 1 point for each item marked 'Mostly true'.

Humility: Items 1, 2, 3, 4
Will: Items 5, 6, 7, 8

'Humility' means a quiet, modest, self-effacing manner. A humble person puts group or organizational success ahead of personal success. 'Will' means a quiet but fierce resolve to stay the course to achieve the group's desired outcome and to help the group succeed. The traits of humility and will are opposite the traditional idea of leadership as loud and self-centred. If you scored 3 or 4 on either humility or will, you are on track to Level 5 leadership, which says that ordinary people often make excellent leaders. Exemplars follow in a later section of such leaders with high levels of humility.

APPLY YOUR SKILLS: ETHICAL DILEMMA

Too much of a good thing?

Not long ago, Jessica Armstrong, vice president of administration for Delaware Valley Chemical Inc., a New Jersey-based multinational company, made a point of stopping by department head Darius Harris's office and lavishly praising him for his volunteer work with an after-school programme for disadvantaged children in a nearby urban neighbourhood. Now she was about to summon him to her office so she could take him to task for his dedication to the same volunteer work.

It was Carolyn Clark, Harris's secretary, who'd alerted her to the problem. 'Darius told the community centre he'd take responsibility for a fund-raising mass mailing. And then he asked me to edit the letter he'd drafted, make all the copies, stuff the envelopes and get it into the mail – most of this on my own time,' she reported, still obviously indignant. 'When I told him, "I'm sorry, but that's not my job," he looked me straight in the eye and asked when I'd like to schedule my upcoming performance appraisal.'

Several of Harris's subordinates also volunteered with the programme. After chatting with them, Armstrong concluded most were volunteering out of a desire to stay on the boss's good side. It was time to talk to Harris.

'Oh, come on,' responded Harris impatiently when Armstrong confronted him. 'Yes, I asked for her help as a personal favour to me. But I only brought up the appraisal because I was going out of town, and we needed to set some time aside to do the evaluation.' Harris went on to talk about how important working for the after-school programme was to him personally. 'I grew up in that neighbourhood, and if it hadn't been for the people at the centre, I wouldn't be here today,' he said. Besides, even if he had pressured employees to help out – and he wasn't saying he had – didn't all the emphasis the company was putting on employee volunteerism make it okay to use employees' time and company resources?

After Harris left, Armstrong thought about the conversation. There was no question that Delaware Valley actively encouraged employee volunteerism – and not just because it was the right thing to do. The chemical company had suffered a couple of unfortunate accidental spills in its recent past that caused environmental damage and sparked community anger.

Volunteering had the potential to help employees acquire new skills, create a sense of camaraderie and play a role in recruiting and retaining talented people. But most of all, it gave a badly needed boost to the company's public image. Recently, Delaware Valley took every opportunity to publicize its employees' extracurricular community work on its website and in company publications. And the company created the annual Delaware Prize, which granted cash awards ranging from $1000 to $5000 to outstanding volunteers.

So now that Armstrong had talked with everyone concerned, just what was she going to do about the dispute between Darius Harris and Carolyn Clark?

What would you do?

1 Tell Carolyn Clark that employee volunteerism is important to the company and that while her performance evaluation will not be affected by her decision, she should consider helping Harris because it is an opportunity to help a worthy community project.

2 Tell Darius Harris that the employee volunteer programme is just that: a volunteer programme. Even though the company sees volunteerism as an important piece of its campaign to repair its tarnished image, employees must be free to choose whether to volunteer. He should not ask for the help of his direct employees with the after-school programme.

3 Discipline Darius Harris for coercing his subordinates to spend their own time on his volunteer work at the community after-school programme. This action will send a signal that coercing employees is a clear violation of leadership authority.

APPLY YOUR SKILLS: CASE FOR CRITICAL ANALYSIS

Fred Goodwin and the Royal Bank of Scotland

When case studies are used in management education they can serve three distinct purposes:

- Description (what actually happened).

- Prescription (what should be done in the future).

- Proscription (what should not be done in the future).

Often in leadership cases information is presented in a descriptive manner highlighting particularly successful leaders and seeking to identify what has led to their success (traits-style-contingency).

Royal Bank of Scotland was very much at the forefront of banking in the eighteenth century, pioneering innovations like overdrafts and joint stock banking and spreading a model of Scots banking around the world. In the 1980s the Royal Bank of Scotland (RBS) began to slip back, realizing that it had perhaps been resting on its banking traditions for too long. George Mathewson was appointed as its new Chief Executive – an engineer, not a banker – who promptly launched 'Project Columbus' to allow it to reclaim its place on the world stage.

Mathewson's hand-picked successor, first as his deputy in 1998 and then as CEO, was Fred Goodwin – again, an accountant rather than a banker, with a reputation for detailed project management and 'manufacturing fear' to improve performance. Mathewson became Goodwin's chairman. They were the heroes of RBS's rise to success (it became RBS, rather than Royal Bank of Scotland, only in 2003 in order to foster its global ambitions). In 2007, those early ambitions were finally fulfilled. RBS – at precisely the worst possible moment – became the biggest bank in the world. Its £1.9 trillion balance sheet was bigger than UK GDP. But in order to maintain this position it needed to borrow tens of billions daily… just as credit was drying up. The rest is history.

The leadership characteristics of Fred Goodwin ('manufacturing fear') are often talked up in management and organizational culture but such a culture inhibits constructive criticism and legitimate rational challenges to leadership decision-making.

That took his attention away from things that were much more important. Goodwin's focus on detail and getting things just right might have been a useful trait when he was working at a lower level but as individuals progress to higher managerial levels they require a different skills set. Goodwin did not adjust his leadership style.

The RBS Head of Strategy raised doubts about CDOs (collateralized debt obligations) and the ABN-AMRO merger. But he was frozen out, went on sick leave and eventually left. There were others. But for the most part misgivings were voiced in private, outside the senior management meetings. Goodwin himself was still insisting to colleagues, even as they prepared their *mea culpas*, that 'you've got to remember we didn't make any mistakes.' Financial journalists and commentators were also guilty of failing to critique the leadership of Fred Goodwin. What is more, RBS was aggressively attentive to any hint of criticism in the press and more than willing to take legal action.

Goodwin's appointment was substantially influenced by the CEO George Mathewson. Goodwin had strategic vision but was reluctant to listen to alternative perspectives and to take on board new information not available at the time of the formulation of the strategy. This approach failed to inspire the organizational members. Organizational members need to believe in the personal integrity of their leadership with tangible evidence of good practice, consideration, listening to the voice of others, empathizing with employees regardless of organizational position, sound ethics and a track record of delivering on promises.

A good leader is someone that employees want to follow, not somebody they have no choice but to follow. Employees that feel threatened if they speak out against management tend to be resentful and this leads to under-performance (individual and organizational). Employees that are inspired by respect give their best.

The most obvious remedy in the case of RBS is to look at corporate governance, recruitment and succession planning.

Reference Fraser, I. (2014) *Shredded: Inside RBE: The Bank that Broke Britain*, Berlinn.

Questions

1 Evaluate Fred Goodwin's leadership style. What were its strengths and weaknesses? What were the sources of his influence?

2 Analyze Fred Goodwin as a 'transformational leader'.

3 Discuss the extent to which leaders are identified and developed at an early point in their careers and their talents nurtured by their employing organization.

END NOTES

1. Gary Yukl, 'Managerial Leadership: A Review of Theory and Research', *Journal of Management* 15 (1989): 251–289.
2. James M. Kouzes and Barry Z. Posner, 'The Credibility Factor: What Followers Expect from Their Leaders', *Management Review* (January 1990): 29–33.
3. Jim Collins, 'Level 5 Leadership: The Triumph of Humility and Fierce Resolve', *Harvard Business Review* (January 2001): 67–76; Jim Collins, 'Good to Great', *Fast Company* (October 2001): 90–104; A. J. Vogl, 'Onward and Upward' (an interview with Jim Collins), *Across the Board* (September–October 2001): 29–34; and Jerry Useem, 'Conquering Vertical Limits', *Fortune* (February 19, 2001): 84–96.
4. Jim Collins, 'Enduring Greatness', *Leadership Excellence* (January 2011): 8.
5. Miguel Helft, 'A Hired Gun for Microsoft, in Dogged Pursuit of Google', *The New York Times,* August 31, 2009, www.nytimes.com/2009/08/31/technology/internet/31search.html (accessed August 31, 2009).
6. Collins, 'Level 5 Leadership'.
7. Quoted in William J. Holstein, 'The View's Still Great from the Corner Office', *The New York Times,* May 8, 2005.
8. Richard L. Daft and Robert H. Lengel, *Fusion Leadership: Unlocking the Subtle Forces That Change People and Organizations* (San Francisco: Berrett-Koehler, 1998).
9. Leigh Buchanan, 'In Praise of Selflessness: Why the Best Leaders Are Servants', *Inc.* (May 2007): 33–35.
10. Robert K. Greenleaf, *Servant Leadership: A Journey into the Nature of Legitimate Power and Greatness* (Mahwah, NJ: Paulist Press, 1977).
11. 'Not Her Father's Chief Executive' (an interview with Marilyn Carlson Nelson), *U.S. News & World Report* (October 30, 2006): 64–65.
12. 'Maersk Alabama Crew Recalls Pirate Attack', *USA Today* (April 16, 2009), www.usatoday.com/news/nation/2009-04-16-pirates_N.htm (accessed April 30, 2009); Stacy Meichtry, Arian Campo-Flores and Leslie Scism, 'Cruise Company Blames Captain', *The Wall Street Journal,* January 17, 2012, www.online.wsj.com/article/SB10001424052970203735304577165290656739300.html (accessed January 20, 2012); and 'Death Toll of Italy's Costa Concordia Wreck Rises to 30', *Philippine Star,* March 23, 2012, www.philstar.com/article.aspx?articleid=790169&publicationsubcategoryid=200 (accessed September 14, 2012).
13. Adam Bluestein, 'Start a Company. Change the World'. *Inc.* (May 2011): 71–80.
14. Bill George, Peter Sims, Andrew N. McLean and Diana Mayer, 'Discovering Your Authentic Leadership', *Harvard Business Review* (February 2007): 129–138; and Bill George, *Authentic Leadership: Rediscovering the Secrets to Lasting Value* (San Francisco: Jossey-Bass, 2003). For a recent review of the literature on authentic leadership, see William L. Gardner, C. C. Cogliser, K. M. Davis and M.P. Dickens, 'Authentic Leadership: A Review of the Literature and Research Agenda', *The Leadership Quarterly* 22 (2011): 1120–1145.
15. George, *Authentic Leadership*; and Bill George, 'Truly Authentic Leadership', Special Report: America's Best Leaders, *U.S. News & World Report,* October 22, 2006, www.usnews.com/usnews/news/articles/061022/30authentic.htm (accessed October 5, 2010).
16. Judy B. Rosener, *America's Competitive Secret: Utilizing Women as a Management Strategy* (New York: Oxford University Press, 1995), pp. 129–135.
17. Alice H. Eagly and Linda L. Carli, 'The Female Leadership Advantage: An Evaluation of the Evidence', *The Leadership Quarterly* 14 (2003): 807–834; Rosener, *America's Competitive Secret*; Judy B. Rosener, 'Ways Women Lead', *Harvard Business Review* (November–December 1990): 119–125; Sally Helgesen, *The Female Advantage: Women's Ways of Leadership* (New York: Currency/Doubleday, 1990); Bernard M. Bass and Bruce J. Avolio, 'Shatter the Glass Ceiling: Women May Make Better Managers', *Human Resource Management* 33, no. 4 (Winter 1994): 549–560; and Carol Kinsey Goman, 'What Men Can Learn from Women about Leadership in the 21st Century', *The Washington Post,* August 10, 2011, www.washingtonpost.com/national/on-leadership/what-men-can-learn-from-women-about-leadership/2011/08/10/gIQA4J9n6I_story.html (accessed September 12, 2012).
18. Rochelle Sharpe, 'As Leaders, Women Rule', *BusinessWeek* (November 20, 2000): 75–84.
19. Kevin S. Groves, 'Gender Differences in Social and Emotional Skills and Charismatic Leadership', *Journal of Leadership and Organizational Studies* 11, no. 3 (2005): 30ff.
20. Jack Zenger and Joseph Folkman, 'Are Women Better Leaders Than Men?' HBR Blog Network, *Harvard Business Review,* March 15, 2012, www.blogs.hbr.org/cs/2012/03/a_study_in_leadership_women_do.html (accessed September 12, 2012); and Herminia Ibarra and Otilia Obodaru, 'Women and the Vision Thing', *Harvard Business Review* (January 2009): 62–70.
21. Susan Carey, 'More Women Take Flight in Airline Operations', *The Wall Street Journal,* August 14, 2007, B1; and Ann Therese Palmer, 'Teacher Learns All About Airline;

United VP Began as Reservations Clerk, Rose Through Ranks', *Chicago Tribune*, December 24, 2006, 3.

22. Leigh Buchanan, 'Pat McGovern . . . For Knowing the Power of Respect', segment in '25 Entrepreneurs We Love', *Inc.* (April 2004): 110–147.

23. This analogy is from Gordon P. Rabey, 'Leadership Is Response: A Paper for Discussion', *Industrial and Commercial Training* 42, no. 2 (2010): 87–92.

24. This discussion is based on Philip A. Dover and Udo Dierk, 'The Ambidextrous Organization: Integrating Managers, Entrepreneurs, and Leaders', *Journal of Business Strategy* 31, no. 5 (2010): 49–58; Gary Yukl and Richard Lepsinger, 'Why Integrating the Leading and Managing Roles Is Essential for Organizational Effectiveness', *Organizational Dynamics* 34, no. 4 (2005): 361–375; and Henry Mintzberg, *Managing* (San Francisco: Berrett-Kohler Publishers, 2009).

25. Nancy F. Koehn, 'The Driver in Ford's Amazing Race', *The New York Times*, April 1, 2012, BU.1.

26. G. A. Yukl, *Leadership in Organizations* (Englewood Cliffs, NJ: Prentice Hall, 1981); and S. C. Kohs and K. W. Irle, 'Prophesying Army Promotion', *Journal of Applied Psychology* 4 (1920): 73–87.

27. R. Albanese and D. D. Van Fleet, *Organizational Behaviour: A Managerial Viewpoint* (Hinsdale, IL: The Dryden Press, 1983); and S. A. Kirkpatrick and E. A. Locke, 'Leadership: Do Traits Matter?' *Academy of Management Executive* 5, no. 2 (1991): 48–60.

28. A summary of various studies and surveys is reported in Del Jones, 'Optimism Puts Rose-Colored Tint in Glasses of Top Execs', *USA Today*, December 15, 2005.

29. Annie Murphy Paul, 'The Uses and Abuses of Optimism (and Pessimism)', *Psychology Today* (November–December 2011): 56–63.

30. Tom Rath and Barry Conchie, *Strengths Based Leadership* (Gallup Press, 2009); Marcus Buckingham and Donald O. Clifton, *Now, Discover Your Strengths* (New York: The Free Press, 2001), p. 12.

31. Buckingham and Clifton, *Now, Discover Your Strengths*.

32. Gary Yukl, Angela Gordon and Tom Taber, 'A Hierarchical Taxonomy of Leadership Behaviour: Integrating a Half Century of Behaviour Research', *Journal of Leadership and Organizational Studies* 9, no. 1 (2002): 13–32.

33. C. A. Schriesheim and B. J. Bird, 'Contributions of the Ohio State Studies to the Field of Leadership', *Journal of Management* 5 (1979): 135–145; C. L. Shartle, 'Early Years of the Ohio State University Leadership Studies', *Journal of Management* 5 (1979): 126–134; and R. Likert, 'From Production- and Employee-Centeredness to Systems 1–4', *Journal of Management* 5 (1979): 147–156.

34. P. C. Nystrom, 'Managers and the High-High Leader Myth', *Academy of Management Journal* 21 (1978): 325–331; and L. L. Larson, J. G. Hunt and Richard N. Osborn, 'The Great High-High Leader Behavior Myth: A Lesson from Occam's Razor', *Academy of Management Journal* 19 (1976): 628–641.

35. R. Likert, 'From Production- and Employee-Centeredness to Systems 1–4'.

36. Robert R. Blake and Jane S. Mouton, *The Managerial Grid III* (Houston, TX: Gulf, 1985).

37. John Markoff, 'Competing as Software Goes to Web', *The New York Times*, June 5, 2007, C1, C5.

38. This discussion is based on Paul Hersey and Ken Blanchard, 'Revisiting the Life-Cycle Theory of Leadership', in 'Great Ideas Revisited', *Training & Development* (January 1996): 42–47; Kenneth H. Blanchard and Paul Hersey, 'Life-Cycle Theory of Leadership', in 'Great Ideas Revisited', *Training & Development* (January 1996): 42–47; Paul Hersey, 'Situational Leaders: Use the Model in Your Work', *Leadership Excellence* (February 2009): 12; and Paul Hersey and Kenneth H. Blanchard, *Management of Organizational Behaviour: Utilizing Human Resources*, 4th ed. (Englewood Cliffs, NJ: Prentice Hall, 1982). The concept of *readiness* comes from Hersey, 'Situational Leaders'.

39. Jennifer Robison, 'Many Paths to Engagement: How Very Different Management Styles Get the Same Great Results at Mars Incorporated', *Gallup Management Journal*, January 10, 2008, www.gmj.gallup.com/content/103513/Many-Paths-Engagement.aspx (accessed July 31, 2010).

40. Andrew Ross Sorkin, 'Warren Buffett, Delegator in Chief', *The New York Times*, www.nytimes.com/2011/04/24/weekinreview/24buffett.html (accessed September 14, 2012).

41. Fred E. Fiedler, 'Assumed Similarity Measures as Predictors of Team Effectiveness', *Journal of Abnormal and Social Psychology* 49 (1954): 381–388; F. E. Fiedler, *Leader Attitudes and Group Effectiveness* (Urbana, IL: University of Illinois Press, 1958); and F. E. Fiedler, *A Theory of Leadership Effectiveness* (New York: McGraw-Hill, 1967).

42. Fred E. Fiedler and M. M. Chemers, *Leadership and Effective Management* (Glenview, IL: Scott, Foresman, 1974).

43. Reported in George Anders, 'Theory & Practice: Tough CEOs Often Most Successful, a Study Finds', *The Wall Street Journal*, November 19, 2007.

44. Fred E. Fiedler, 'Engineer the Job to Fit the Manager', *Harvard Business Review* 43 (1965): 115–122; and F. E. Fiedler, M. M. Chemers and L. Mahar, *Improving Leadership Effectiveness: The Leader Match Concept* (New York: Wiley, 1976).

45. R. Singh, 'Leadership Style and Reward Allocation: Does Least Preferred Coworker Scale Measure Tasks and Relation Orientation?' *Organizational Behaviour and Human Performance* 27 (1983): 178–197; and D. Hosking, 'A Critical Evaluation of Fiedler's Contingency Hypotheses', *Progress in Applied Psychology* 1 (1981): 103–154.

46. S. Kerr and J. M. Jermier, 'Substitutes for Leadership: Their Meaning and Measurement', *Organizational Behaviour and Human Performance* 22 (1978): 375–403; and Jon P. Howell and Peter W. Dorfman, 'Leadership and Substitutes for Leadership among Professional and Nonprofessional Workers', *Journal of Applied Behavioural Science* 22 (1986): 29–46.

47. Katherine J. Klein and Robert J. House, 'On Fire: Charismatic Leadership and Levels of Analysis', *Leadership Quarterly* 6, no. 2 (1995): 183–198.

48. Jay A. Conger and Rabindra N. Kanungo, 'Toward a Behavioural Theory of Charismatic Leadership in Organizational Settings', *Academy of Management Review* 12 (1987): 637–647; Jaepil Choi, 'A Motivational Theory of Charismatic Leadership: Envisioning, Empathy, and Empowerment', *Journal of Leadership and Organizational Studies* 13, no. 1 (2006): 24ff; and William L. Gardner and Bruce J. Avolio, 'The Charismatic Relationship: A Dramaturgical Perspec-

tive', *Academy of Management Review* 23, no. 1 (1998): 32–58.

49. Jon Katzenbach, 'The Steve Jobs Way', *Strategy + Business* (Summer 2012), www.strategy-business.com/article/00109?gko=d331b (accessed June 11, 2012); Steve Moore, 'Not Bad for a Hippie Dropout', *Management Today* (March 2009): 27; Connie Guglielmo, 'What Makes Steve Jobs Run?' *National Post* (May 17, 2008), FW–8; 'Editorial: Apple – and U.S. – Need Steve Jobs', *McClatchy-Tribune Business News* (January 18, 2009); Leslie Kwoh and Emma Silverman, 'Bio as Bible: Managers Imitate Steve Jobs', *The Wall Street Journal* (March 31, 2012), B1; and Miguel Helft and Claire Cain Miller, 'A Deep Bench of Leadership at Apple', *The New York Times*, January 17, 2011, www.nytimes.com/2011/01/18/technology/18cook.html?_r=0 (accessed January 18, 2011).

50. Robert J. House and Jane M. Howell, 'Personality and Charismatic Leadership', *Leadership Quarterly* 3, no. 2 (1992): 81–108; and Jennifer O'Connor, M. D. Mumford, T. C. Clifton, T. L. Gessner and M. S. Connelly, 'Charismatic Leaders and Destructiveness: A Historiometric Study', *Leadership Quarterly* 6, no. 4 (1995): 529–555.

51. Rob Nielsen, Jennifer A. Marrone and Holly S. Slay, 'A New Look at Humility: Exploring the Humility Concept and Its Role in Socialized Charismatic Leadership', *Journal of Leadership and Organizational Studies* 17, no. 1 (February 2010): 33–44.

52. Robert J. House, 'Research Contrasting the Behaviour and Effects of Reputed Charismatic vs Reputed Non-Charismatic Leaders', paper presented as part of a symposium, 'Charismatic Leadership: Theory and Evidence', Academy of Management, San Diego, 1985.

53. Bernard M. Bass, 'Theory of Transformational Leadership Redux', *Leadership Quarterly* 6, no. 4 (1995): 463–478; Noel M. Tichy and Mary Anne Devanna, *The Transformational Leader* (New York: John Wiley & Sons, 1986); James C. Sarros, Brian K. Cooper and Joseph C. Santora, 'Building a Climate for Innovation Through Transformational Leadership and Organizational Culture', *Journal of Leadership and Organizational Studies* 15, no. 2 (November 2008): 145–158; and P. D. Harms and Marcus Crede, 'Emotional Intelligence and Transformational and Transactional Leadership: A Meta-Analysis', *Journal of Leadership and Organizational Studies* 17, no. 1 (February 2010): 5–17.

54. The terms *transactional* and *transformational* come from James M. Burns, *Leadership* (New York: Harper & Row, 1978); and Bernard M. Bass, 'Leadership: Good, Better, Best', *Organizational Dynamics* 13 (Winter 1985): 26–40.

55. Daft and Lengel, *Fusion Leadership*.

56. Gang Wang, In-Sue Oh, Stephen Courtright and Amy Colbert, 'Transformational Leadership and Performance Across Criteria and Levels: A Meta-Analytic Review of 25 Years of Research', *Group & Organization Management* 36, no. 2 (2011): 223–270; Taly Dvir et al., 'Impact of Transformational Leadership on Follower Development and Performance: A Field Experiment', *Academy of Management Journal* 45, no. 4 (2002): 735–744.

57. Robert S. Rubin, David C. Munz and William H. Bommer, 'Leading from Within: The Effects of Emotion Recognition and Personality on Transformational Leadership Behaviour', *Academy of Management Journal* 48, no. 5 (2005): 845–858; and Timothy A. Judge and Joyce E. Bono, 'Five-Factor Model of Personality and Transformational Leadership', *Journal of Applied Psychology* 85, no. 5 (October 2000): 751ff.

58. Rubin, Munz and Bommer, 'Leading from Within'.

59. Augustine O. Agho, 'Perspectives of Senior-Level Executives on Effective Followership and Leadership', *Journal of Leadership and Organizational Studies* 16, no. 2 (November 2009): 159–166; and James M. Kouzes and Barry Z. Posner, *The Leadership Challenge: How to Get Extraordinary Things Done in Organizations* (San Francisco: Jossey-Bass, 1990).

60. Barbara Kellerman, 'What Every Leader Needs to Know About Followers', *Harvard Business Review* (December 2007): 84–91.

61. Robert E. Kelley, *The Power of Followership* (New York: Doubleday, 1992).

62. *Ibid.*, 117–118.

63. Vignette recounted in Isaac Getz, 'Liberating Leadership: How the Initiative-Freeing Radical Organizational Form Has Been Successfully Adopted', *California Management Review* (Summer 2009): 32–58.

64. Henry Mintzberg, *Power In and Around Organizations* (Englewood Cliffs, NJ: Prentice Hall, 1983); and Jeffrey Pfeffer, *Power in Organizations* (Marshfield, MA: Pitman, 1981).

65. John R. P. French, Jr and Bertram Raven, 'The Bases of Social Power', in D. Cartwright and A. F. Zander, eds, *Group Dynamics* (Evanston, IL: Row Peterson, 1960), pp. 607–623.

66. Reported in Vadim Liberman, 'Mario Moussa Wants You to Win Your Next Argument' (Questioning Authority column), *Conference Board Review* (November–December 2007): 25–26.

67. Jay A. Conger, 'The Necessary Art of Persuasion', *Harvard Business Review* (May–June 1998): 84–95.

68. Roger Yu, 'Co-Workers Praise Wyndham CEO's Welcoming Demeanor', *USA Today*, November 22, 2010, www.usatoday.com/money/companies/management/profile/2010-11-22-wyndhamceo22_ST_N.htm (accessed September 14, 2012).

69. Jeremy W. Peters, 'Time Inc. Chief Executive Jack Griffin Out', *The New York Times*, February 17, 2011, www.mediadecoder.blogs.nytimes.com/2011/02/17/time-inc-chief-executive-jack-griffin-out/ (accessed February 18, 2011).

70. David Kipnis, Stuart Schmidt, Chris Swaffin-Smith and Ian Wilkinson, 'Patterns of Managerial Influence: Shotgun Managers, Tacticians, and Politicians', *Organizational Dynamics* (Winter 1984): 58–67.

71. These tactics are based on Kipnis et al., 'Patterns of Managerial Influence'; and Robert B. Cialdini, 'Harnessing the Science of Persuasion', *Harvard Business Review* (October 2001): 72–79.

72. Kipnis et al., 'Patterns of Managerial Influence'; and Jeffrey Pfeffer, *Managing with Power: Politics and Influence in Organizations* (Boston: Harvard Business School Press, 1992), Chapter 13.

73. *Ibid.*

74. V. Dallas Merrell, *Huddling: The Informal Way to Management Success* (New York: AMACOM, 1979).

75. Robert B. Cialdini, *Influence: Science and Practice*, 4th ed. (Boston: Pearson Allyn & Bacon, 2000).

76. Harvey G. Enns and Dean B. McFarlin, 'When Executives Influence Peers, Does Function Matter?' *Human Resource Management* 4, no. 2 (Summer 2003): 125–142.

CHAPTER 14

MANAGING HUMAN RESOURCES

By Anne Cox, University of Wollongong, Australia

LEARNING OBJECTIVES

After studying this chapter, you should be able to:

1   Explain the strategic role of human resource management.

2   Show how organizations determine their future staffing needs through human resource planning.

3   Describe the tools that managers use to recruit and select employees.

4   Describe how organizations develop an effective workforce through training and performance appraisal.

5   Explain how organizations maintain a workforce through the administration of wages and salaries, benefits, and terminations.

6   Define *motivation* and explain the difference between intrinsic and extrinsic rewards.

7   Identify and describe theories of motivation based on employee needs.

8   Discuss major approaches to job design and how job design influences motivation.

Every hour or so throughout the night, big brown trucks back into the bays at UPS's distribution centre in Lagos, Nigeria, where part-time workers load, unload and sort packages at a rate of 1200 boxes an hour. A typical employee handles a box every 3 seconds. The packages don't stop until the shift is over, which allows little time for friendly banter and chitchat, even if you could hear over the din of the belts and ramps that carry packages through the cavernous 270 000-square-foot warehouse. It's not the easiest job in the world, and many people don't stick around for long. When Okogbua Okechukwu started work in Lagos as the new district manager, the attrition rate of part-time workers, who account for half of Lagos's workforce, was 50 per cent a year. With people deserting at that rate, hiring and training costs were through the roof, not to mention the slowdown in operations caused by continually training new workers. Something had to be done to bring in the right employees and make them want to stay longer than a few weeks.

TAKE A MOMENT

How would you address this enormous human resources challenge? What changes in recruiting, hiring, training and other human resource practices can help to solve Okogbua Okechukwu's problem in Lagos?

The situation at UPS's Lagos distribution centre provides a dramatic example of the challenges managers face every day. Hiring and retaining quality employees is one of the most urgent concerns of today's managers.[1] The people who make up an organization give the company its primary source of competitive advantage and human resource management plays a key role in finding and developing the organization's people as it is human resources that contribute to and directly affect company success. The term human resource management (HRM) refers to the design and application of formal systems in an organization to ensure the effective and efficient use of human talent to accomplish organizational goals.[2] This system includes activities undertaken to attract, develop and maintain an effective workforce.

Managers at Electronic Arts, the world's largest maker of computer games, include a commitment to human resources as one of the company's four worldwide goals. They have to, in a company where the creativity and mind power of artists, designers, model makers, mathematicians and filmmakers determines strategic success, and the competition for talent is intense.[3] HRM is equally important for government and non-profit organizations. For example, non-fee-paying or state funded schools all over the world are facing a severe teacher shortage with an increasing number of teacher vacancies to be filled over the next decade. Many schools are trying innovative programmes such as recruiting in foreign countries, establishing relationships with leaders at top universities, and having their most motivated and enthusiastic teachers work with university students who are considering teaching careers.[4]

As in many other countries, convincing the best and brightest students to consider a teaching career over the lure of other prestigious professions, such as medicine, finance, law, etc. is not an easy task in Singapore. The Singapore's Ministry of Education (MOE) has created an aggressive recruitment strategy to attract a strong candidate pool. They have worked out an attractive incentive structure, offering teachers opportunities to earn additional pay and benefits. Singapore's MOE overhauled its existing teacher evaluation system and replaced it with a more comprehensive approach, which it called the Enhanced Performance Management System. The new system represents a major shift from the traditional model of performance appraisal which focused on observable characteristics, such as subject matter expertise, classroom management and instructional skills, to emphasizing the underlying characteristics, or 'competencies', that lead to exceptional teacher's performance and distinguish top performers from the rest. The development and measurement of individual competencies are used in conjunction with other human resource functions such as professional training and development, managing career track, promotion and payment. As a result, Singapore is well known for the achievements of their education system, including extraordinary student learning results and teaching excellence.[5]

Over the past decade, HRM has shed its old 'personnel' image and gained recognition as a vital player in corporate strategy.[6] Increasingly, large corporations are outsourcing routine human resource administrative activities, freeing HRM staff from time-consuming paperwork and enabling them to take on more strategic responsibilities. In 2003, human resources topped Gartner Inc.'s list of most commonly outsourced business activities.[7] Today's best human resources departments not only support the organization's strategic objective but actively pursue an ongoing, integrated plan for furthering the organization's performance.[8] Human resource managers are key players on the executive team. Research has found that effective HRM has a positive impact on strategic performance, including higher employee productivity and stronger financial results.[9]

CONCEPT CONNECTION

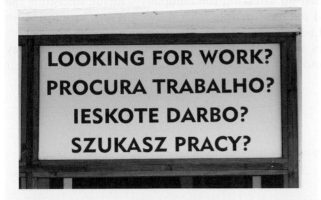

With a booming economy, the Republic of Ireland had employers looking for workers. Poland, on the other hand, had plenty of workers looking for jobs. The result was the Warsaw job fair, an example of how globalization affects HRM. Because both countries are European Union members, Irish construction companies were free to come to the Polish capital in search of the engineers, project managers and skilled carpenters they needed. Polish applicants flocked to the job fair from all over the country, seeking to escape high unemployment and a job market where the take-home pay for even an experienced engineer is roughly $800 a month.

Today, all managers need to be skilled in the basics of HRM. Flatter organizations often require that managers throughout the organization play an active role in recruiting and selecting the right personnel, developing an effective training programme or creating appropriate performance appraisal systems. HRM professionals act to guide and assist line managers in managing their human resources to achieve the organization's strategic goals.

The strategic role of human resource management

HRM strategies outline the organization's people objectives and must be an integrated part of its overall business strategy. The strategic approach to HRM recognizes three key elements. First, all managers are human resource managers. For example, at IBM every manager is expected to pay attention to the development and satisfaction of subordinates. Line managers use surveys, career planning, performance appraisal and compensation to encourage commitment to IBM.[10] Second, employees are viewed as assets. Employees, not buildings and machinery, give a company its competitive advantage. How a company manages its workforce may be the single most important factor in sustained competitive success.[11] Third, HRM is a matching process, integrating the organization's strategy and goals with the correct approach to managing the firm's human capital.[12] Current strategic issues of particular concern to managers include hiring and retaining the right people with the following competencies:

- Becoming more competitive on a global basis.

- Improving quality, innovation and customer service.

- Applying new information technologies for e-business.

All of these strategic decisions determine a company's need for skills and employees.

Just as strategic HRM must support the organization's overall aims and objectives, it must maintain and reinforce the organization's culture and core values. The culture represents the values, beliefs, assumptions and symbols that define how the organization conducts its business. Organizational culture tells employees how things are done, what is important and what kind of behaviour is rewarded.[13] Zappos, for example, realized the importance of explicitly defining the core values from which they develop their culture, brand and business strategies. The ten core values that they live by are: 1) Deliver WOW through service; 2) Embrace and drive change; 3) Create fun and a little weirdness; 4) Be adventurous, creative and open-minded; 5) Pursue growth and learning; 6) Build open and honest relationships with communication; 7) Build a positive team and family spirit; 8) Do more with less; 9) Be passionate and determined and 10) Be humble. Zappos is willing to make short-term sacrifices (including lost revenue or profits) to protect the company's culture and core values, which are considered as a long-term benefit. Their HR department developed interview questions for each of the core values and used them in the selection process. Tony Hsieh, CEO of Zappos, revealed that 'Be Humble' was probably the core value that ended up affecting the company's hiring decisions the most. They have rejected a lot of experienced and talented people who showed traces of egotism in the selection process, although these people could have made an immediate impact on the company's top or bottom line. When selected, new employees are required to sign a document stating that they have read the core values document and understand that living up to the core values is part of their job expectation.[14]

TAKE A MOMENT

Go to the Experiential Exercise online that pertains to assessing your potential for strategic HRM.

This chapter examines the three primary goals of HRM as illustrated in Exhibit 14.1. The broad HRM activities are determining and attracting an effective workforce, rewarding and developing the workforce to its potential and maintaining the workforce over the long term.[15] Achieving these goals requires skills in job analysis, planning, recruiting, selecting, training, performance appraisal, wage and salary administration, benefit programmes, motivating and even terminating. Each of the activities in Exhibit 14.1 will be discussed in this chapter.

EXHIBIT 14.1 Strategic human resource management

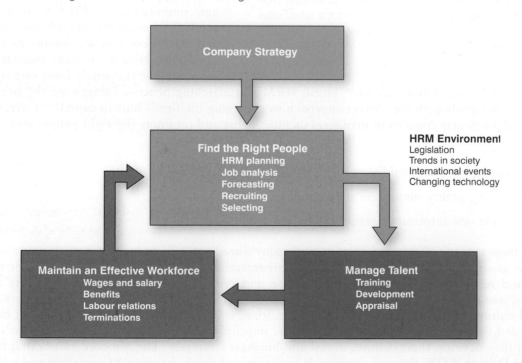

🌱 GREEN POWER

The 'you' in sustainability

'*You* are our sustainability edge!' is the new slogan to bring employees on board for sustainability. **HSBC** carried employee involvement to a new level by promoting individual projects and action plans through its Climate Champions Programme. HSBC paved the way by partnering with powerful environmental organizations, including the Smithsonian Institution, Earthwatch and the Climate Group. Participants must go through an application process for a 12-month residential programme.

Working alongside Earthwatch scientists, HSBC employees complete climate-related business projects, gaining skills and developing methods that can be transferred to the workplace. HSBC's Climate Champions programme has ignited employee curiosity and excitement. The programme tells participants, 'You have a voice in sustainability. You *own* this project. *You* are our sustainability edge.'

SOURCE: Matthew Gitsham, 'Experiential Learning for Leadership and Sustainability at IBM and HSBC,' *The Journal of Management Development* 31, no. 3 (2012): 298–307.

The influence of globalization on HRM

The recent trends of regional integration, removal of trade barriers, the deregulation and opening of closed national markets to international competition, the rise of Asian countries and the integration of Central and Eastern Europe and China into the world economy, etc. have inevitably led to a more globalized world, in which an increasing number of companies widen their horizon of activities outside their countries' borders. An issue of significant concern for today's organizations is competing on a global basis, which brings tremendous new challenges for HRM. Most companies are still in the early stages of developing effective HRM policies, structures and services that respond to the current reality of globalization.[16] In a study of more than 200 global companies, including Eli Lilly, PPG Industries and UPS, managers reported that the biggest challenge for HRM is leadership development and training for the international arena. In addition, HRM is responsible for recruitment, training and performance management of employees who might have to work across geographical, technical and cultural boundaries to help the organization achieve its goals. The success of global business strategies is closely tied to the effectiveness of the organization's global HR strategies.[17]

A subfield known as international human resource management (IHRM) specifically addresses the added complexity that results from coordinating and managing diverse people on a global scale.[18] Research in IHRM has revealed that, as the world becomes increasingly interconnected, some human resource practices and trends are converging. However, IHRM managers need a high degree of cultural sensitivity and the ability to tailor and communicate policies and practices to different cultures.[19] What works in one country may not translate well to another.

There is strong evidence that the multinational companies are distinctive in the way they manage their workforce. The parent company is embedded in an institutional environment located in the home country.[20] To varying degrees, the particular features of the home country become an ingrained part of each multinational corporation (MNC) corporate identity and shape its international orientation as the general philosophy or approach taken by the parent company in the design of the HRM systems to be used in its overseas subsidiaries. The difference in American and Japanese MNCs' attitudes regarding union recognition in their subsidiaries abroad is a good example. American MNCs are said to avoid union recognition,[21] while Japanese MNCs are also more likely to have single enterprise unions, non-strike clauses and collective bargaining.[22]

On the other hand, national differences, including cultural and institutional differences, are the most important constraints on 'context generalizability' of HRM practices. Each subsidiary of the MNC is faced with the task of establishing and maintaining both external legitimacy in its host environment and internal legitimacy within the MNC.[23] MNCs do not necessarily adapt to the local environments, but, rather, manage their legitimacy through negotiation processes with their multiple environments.[24] Adaptation and hybridization are the result of these processes. Almost all empirical studies that look at the cross-border transfer of HRM come to the conclusion that a certain amount of change is always necessary to successfully implement a HRM system developed in the home business system. For example, Honda has transferred their seniority-based wage system to their Vietnamese subsidiaries with some adaptations. There are three determinants in the basic salary in Honda. The first determinant, the job salary, is determined by job grade (based on job complexity and position responsibilities). The second determinant, the personal salary, is determined by each employee's qualifications, experience and skills and the result of their performance appraisal. The third determinant is the age-linked salary. The Vietnamese life module is the result of the research conducted in Vietnam by salary specialists from the Japanese headquarters with the support of the Vietnamese staff at the subsidiaries. The life module estimates the cost of living of an average employee from the age of 18 to 60. The salary of the employee is supposed to increase in pace with his/her promotion in the firms (from team member to team leader to supervisor, etc.) and his/her personal needs (from being single to being married, having children, paying for children's tuition fees, buying a house in the early or mid-40s, etc.). The age-linked salary rises more sharply in the younger ages and then is held constant after the age of 50 till retirement. In the Vietnamese subsidiary, Honda gives greater weight to individual merit in determining wages and promotions, due to the much greater influence of the external labour market compared with Japan. Furthermore, due to the limited number of qualified professionals and upper levels in the Vietnamese labour market, in order to attract candidates for their vacancies, the starting salary paid is relatively higher than what would be expected in Japan.[25]

Exhibit 14.2 lists some interesting trends related to selection, compensation, performance appraisal and training in different countries.

EXHIBIT 14.2 Some trends in international human resource management

Selection	• In Japan, HR managers focus on a job applicant's potential and his or her ability to get along with others. Less emphasis is placed on job-related skills and experience. • Employment tests are considered a crucial part of the selection process in Korea, whereas in Taiwan, the job interview is considered the most important criterion for selection.
Compensation	• Seniority-based pay is used to a greater extent in Asian and Latin countries. • China has surprisingly high use of pay incentives, and are moving towards more incentives based on individual rather than group performance.
Performance appraisal	• Across ten countries surveyed, managers consider recognizing subordinates' accomplishments, evaluating their goal achievement, planning their development and improving their performance to be the most important reasons for performance appraisals.
Training	• In Mexico, managers consider training and development a reward to employees for good performance. • HR managers in Korea incorporate team-building into nearly all training and development practices.

SOURCE: Mary Ann Von Glinow, Ellen A. Drost and Mary B. Teagarden, 'Converging on IHRM Best Practices: Lessons Learned from a Globally Distributed Consortium on Theory and Practice', *Human Resource Management* 41, no. 1 (Spring 2002): 123–140.

Determining and attracting an effective workforce

The first goal of HRM emphasizes the importance of meeting the organization's human resource requirements through job analysis, human resource planning, employee recruitment and selection. The first step involves job analysis, which identifies what employees are expected to do and the knowledge, skills, abilities and other characteristics that the employees need to perform their jobs. The second step involves human resource planning, in which managers or HRM professionals predict the need for new employees based on the types of vacancies that will exist. The third step is to use recruiting procedures to communicate with potential applicants. The fourth step is to select from the applicants those persons believed to be the best potential contributors to the future organization. Finally, the new employee is welcomed into the organization, normally through an induction programme.

Job analysis

Job analysis is the foundation of HR activities. 'It is in fact difficult to imagine how an organization could effectively hire, train, appraise, compensate or use its human resources without the kinds of information derived from job analysis'.[26] It is a systematic process of gathering and interpreting information about the essential duties, tasks and responsibilities of a job, as well as about the context within which the job is performed.[27] To perform job analysis, managers or specialists ask about work activities and workflow, the degree of supervision given and received in the job, knowledge and skills needed, performance standards, working conditions, and so forth. The manager then prepares a written job description, which is a clear and concise summary of the specific tasks, duties and responsibilities, and a job specification, which outlines the knowledge, skills, education, physical abilities and other characteristics needed to adequately perform the job.

Job analysis helps organizations recruit the right kind of people and match them to appropriate jobs. For example, to enhance internal recruiting, Sara Lee Corporation identified six functional areas and 24 significant skills that it wants its finance executives to develop, as illustrated in Exhibit 14.3. Managers are tracked on their development and moved into other positions to help them acquire the needed skills.[28] New software programs and web-based, on-demand subscription services are aiding today's companies in more efficiently and effectively recruiting and matching the right candidates with the right jobs.

EXHIBIT 14.3　Sara Lee's required skills for finance executives

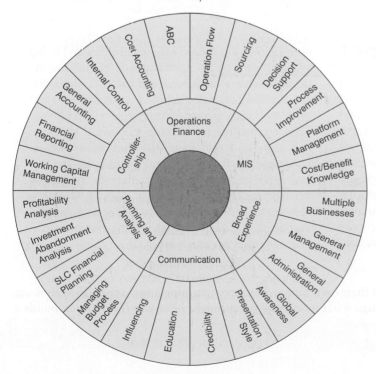

SOURCE: Victoria Griffith, 'When Only Internal Expertise Will Do', *CFO* (October 1998): 95–96, 102.

Human resource planning

Human resource planning is the forecasting of human resource needs and the projected matching of individuals with expected vacancies. Human resource planning begins with several questions:

- What new technologies are emerging, and how will these affect the work system?
- What is the volume of the business likely to be in the next 5–10 years?
- What is the turnover rate, and how much, if any, is avoidable?

The responses to these questions are used to formulate specific questions pertaining to HR activities, such as the following:

- How many senior managers will we need during this time period?
- What types of engineers will we need, and how many?
- Are persons with adequate computer skills available for meeting our projected needs?
- How many administrative personnel – technicians, IT specialists – will we need to support the additional managers and engineers?
- Can we use temporary, contingent or virtual workers to handle some tasks?[29]

Answers to these questions help define the direction for the organization's HRM strategy. For example, if forecasting suggests a strong upcoming need for more technically trained individuals, the organization can (1) define the jobs and skills needed in some detail, (2) hire and train recruiters to look for the specified skills and (3) provide new training for existing employees. By anticipating future human resource needs, the organization can prepare itself to meet competitive challenges more effectively than organizations that react to problems only as they arise.

 INNOVATIVE WAY

Tennessee Valley Authority (TVA)

TVA created an eight-step plan that assesses future human resource needs and formulates actions to meet those needs. The first step is laying the groundwork for later implementation of the programme by creating planning and oversight teams within each business unit. Step two involves assessing processes and functions that can be benchmarked. Step three involves projecting the skills and employee numbers (demand data) that will be necessary to reach goals within each business unit. Once these numbers are in place, step four involves projecting the current employee numbers (supply data) over the planning horizon without new hires and taking into consideration the normal attrition of staff through death, retirement, resignation, and so forth. Comparison of the difference between supply and demand (step five) gives the future gap, or surplus situation. This knowledge enables human resource to develop strategies and operational plans (step six). Step seven involves communicating the action plan to employees. The final step is periodically to evaluate and update the plan as the organization's needs change. When TVA faces a demand for additional employees, this process enables the company to recruit workers with the skills needed to help meet organizational goals.[30]

A number of organizations have developed their own human resource planning approaches. IBM looks at trends in information technology to try to gauge what its clients' needs might be in the future, then builds a plan for finding people with the right skills to meet those needs. Recently, for example, the company has built up its roster of people with skills in areas such as open software standards, grid computing and autonomic computing.[31]

Recruiting

Recruiting is defined as 'activities or practices that define the characteristics of applicants to whom selection procedures are ultimately applied'.[32] Today, recruiting is sometimes referred to as *talent acquisition* to reflect the importance of the human factor in the organization's success.[33] Although we frequently think of campus recruiting as a typical recruiting activity, many organizations use *internal recruiting,* or *promote-from-within* policies, to fill their high-level positions.[34] At oil field services company Schlumberger, Ltd, for example, current employees are given preference when a position opens. With 84 000 people of more than 140 nationalities working in approximately 80 countries, the company can identify potential career opportunities in North American, European, CIS, African, Middle Eastern or Asian branches. Some 80 per cent of top managers have been moved up the ranks based on the promote-from-within philosophy; many of them started fresh out of school as field engineers.[35] Internal recruiting has several advantages: it is less costly than an external search, and it generates higher employee commitment, development and satisfaction because it offers opportunities for career advancement to employees rather than outsiders.

Frequently, however, *external recruiting* – recruiting newcomers from outside the organization – is needed. Applicants are provided by a variety of outside sources including advertising, state employment services, online recruiting services, professional organizations, private employment agencies (*headhunters*), job fairs, educational institutions, employee referrals and unsolicited applications ('write ins' and 'walk ins'). Advantages of external recruiting include new insights, skills and know-how that can be introduced into the organization, the pool of talent is bigger, and outside employees not being members of existing cliques.

A research conducted by Swaroff, Barclay and Bass (1985) found no relationship between recruitment method and job tenure or employee productivity.[36] Each organization should conduct its own recruitment evaluation in terms of cost, candidate quality, turnover and job performance to identify the most effective recruitment methods for the organization.

Realistic job previews

Job analysis also helps enhance recruiting effectiveness by enabling the creation of realistic job previews. A realistic job preview (RJP) gives applicants all pertinent and realistic information – positive and negative – about the job and the organization.[37] RJPs enhance employee satisfaction and reduce turnover, because they facilitate matching individuals, jobs and organizations. Individuals have a better basis on which to determine their suitability to the organization and 'self-select' into or out of positions based on full information.

Legal considerations

Organizations must ensure that their recruiting practices conform to the law. As discussed earlier in this chapter, equal employment opportunity (EEO) laws stipulate that recruiting and hiring decisions cannot discriminate on the basis of race, national origin, religion or gender. The Disability Discrimination Act 1995, an Act of the Parliament of the UK which has now been repealed and replaced by the Equality Act 2010 (except in Northern Ireland where the Act still applies), underscored the need for well-written job descriptions and specifications that accurately reflect the mental and physical dimensions of jobs, so that people with disabilities will not be discriminated against. Affirmative action refers to the use of goals, timetables or other methods in recruiting to promote the hiring, development and retention of protected groups – persons historically under-represented in the workplace. For example, a city might establish a goal of recruiting one black firefighter for every white firefighter until the proportion of black firefighters is commensurate with the black population in the community.

Most large companies try to comply with affirmative action and EEO guidelines. Prudential Insurance Company's policy is presented in Exhibit 14.4. Prudential actively recruits employees and takes affirmative action steps to recruit individuals from all walks of life.

EXHIBIT 14.4 Prudential's corporate recruiting policy

An equal opportunity employer

Prudential recruits, hires, trains, promotes and compensates individuals without regard to race, colour, religion or creed, age, sex, marital status, national origin, ancestry, liability for service in the armed forces of the USA, status as a special disabled veteran or veteran of the Vietnam era, or physical or mental handicap.

This is official company policy because:

- we believe it is right.
- it makes good business sense.
- it is the law.

We are also committed to an ongoing programme of affirmative action in which members of under-represented groups are actively sought out and employed for opportunities in all parts and at all levels of the company. In employing people from all walks of life, Prudential gains access to the full experience of our diverse society.

 CONCEPT CONNECTION

e-Recruiting has grown exponentially in recent years with a 2008 CIPD survey revealing 75 per cent of British organizations using their own website for recruiting. Originating in 1994, Monster has been at the forefront of this online growth with 4200 employees operating in 36 countries in 2010. Earning commission from employers is now only part of Monster's strategy, with a massive job contacts database providing rich opportunities for everything from online jobs fairs to data mining analyses of specific roles and industries.

e-Recruiting

One of the fastest-growing approaches to recruiting is use of the Internet for recruiting, or *e-cruiting*.[38] Recruiting job applicants online dramatically extends the organization's recruiting reach, offering access to a wider pool of applicants and saving time and money. Besides posting job openings on company websites, many organizations use commercial recruiting sites such as Monster.com, where job seekers can post their CVs and companies can search for qualified applicants. In addition, as competition for high-quality employees heats up, new online companies, such as TopJob, Monster, Jobster and JobThread, emerge to help companies search for 'passive candidates', people who aren't looking for jobs but might be the best fit for a company's opening. Expedia calls it 'anti-in-box recruiting'. Instead of waiting until it has job openings, it uses online recruitment agencies to build up a ready supply of passive prospects who have the skills and experience the company might need.[39]

LinkedIn is a business-oriented social networking service. As of June 2013, LinkedIn reported more than 259 million acquired users in more than 200 countries and territories. It connects professionals, allows them to market their skills, to share knowledge and experiences, and to plan future career steps.[40] It presents a major change to the way in which companies recruit personnel. Potential candidates can increase their visibility through the website, and can get their friends and colleagues to write them referrals online. Companies can accomplish research, networking and referrals much faster and without engaging costly employment agencies or head-hunters. However, the use of LinkedIn may affect decision-making in the selection phase as it hands organizations the opportunity to screen their applicants on the Internet, searching for personal information that could be added to the information available in a paper curriculum vitae. This allows selection bias to occur even before the first interview has taken place. LinkedIn also heightens the risk of guilt-by-association errors to occur, as applicants' networks are explicitly visualized.[41]

Companies as diverse as Deloitte Touche Tohmatsu, Cisco Systems, John Lewis, L'Oréal and Tesco use the Web for recruiting. Organizations have not given up their traditional recruiting strategies, but the Internet gives HR managers new tools for searching the world to find the best available talent.

Other recent approaches to recruiting

Organizations are finding other ways to enhance their recruiting success. One highly effective approach is getting referrals from current employees. A company's employees often know of someone who would be qualified for a position and fit in with the organization's culture. Many organizations offer cash rewards to employees who submit names of people who subsequently accept employment, because referral by current employees is one of the cheapest and most reliable methods of external recruiting.[42] At many of today's top companies, managers emphasize that recruiting is part of everyone's job.

Having employees assist with recruiting has the added bonus of providing potential candidates with a realistic job preview. At the Container Store, employees share with customers what it's like to work for the company. They want people to know the positive and potentially negative aspects of the job, because it's important to get people who will fit in.

Some companies turn to non-traditional sources to find dedicated employees, particularly in a tight labour market. For example, when Walker Harris couldn't find workers for his ice company on the west side of Chicago, Harris Ice, he began hiring former prison inmates, many of whom have turned out to be reliable, loyal employees.[43] Manufacturer Dee Zee, which makes aluminium truck accessories in a factory in Des Moines, Iowa, found a source of hard-working employees among refugees from Bosnia, Vietnam and Kosovo.[44] Since 1998, Bank of America has hired and trained more than 3000 former welfare recipients in positions that offer the potential for promotions and long-term careers. Numerous companies recruit older workers, who typically have lower turnover rates, especially for part-time jobs. The Home Depot offers 'snowbird specials' – winter work in Florida and summers in Maine.[45] Recruiting on a global basis is on the rise as well. Non-fee-paying schools are recruiting teachers from overseas. High-tech companies are looking for qualified workers in foreign countries because they cannot find people with the right skills in the USA.[46]

Selecting

The next step for managers is to select desired employees from the pool of recruited applicants. In the selection process, employers assess applicants' characteristics in an attempt to determine the 'fit' between the job and applicant characteristics. Given the wide variation among personalities and among jobs, an important responsibility of managers is to try to match employee and job characteristics so that work is done by people who are well suited to do it. This goal requires that managers be clear about what they expect employees to do and have a sense of the kinds of people who would succeed at various types of assignments. The extent to which a person's ability and personality match the requirements of a job is called *person–job fit*. When managers achieve person–job fit, employees are more likely to contribute and have higher levels of job satisfaction and commitment.[47] The importance of person–job fit became especially apparent during the dot-com heyday of the late 1990s. People who rushed to Internet companies in hopes of finding a new challenge – or making a quick buck – found themselves floundering in jobs for which they were unsuited. One manager recruited by a leading executive search firm lasted less than 2 hours at his new job. The search firm, a division of Russell Reynolds Associates, later developed a 'Web Factor' diagnostic to help determine whether people have the right personality for the Internet, including such things as a tolerance for risk and uncertainty, an obsession with learning and a willingness to do whatever needs doing, regardless of job title.[48]

🔗 CONCEPT CONNECTION

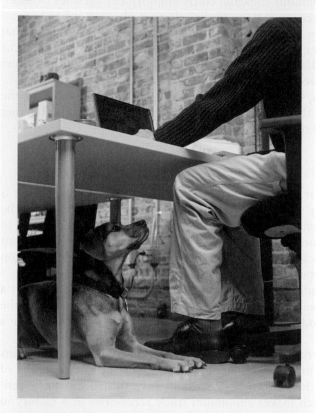

Dogs are such a huge part of our lives that many of us dream of having them come to work with us. Well, more and more companies are allowing dogs in the office and yours may be next. At Google Headquarters (Googleplex) Googlers are permitted to bring their dogs to the workplace. Research has shown that having pets in the workplace reduces stress and increases the feeling of well-being. And that's precisely why Relay Recruitment, a company in West Yorkshire, UK brought in Rupert, a Cocker Spaniel. What management experienced was beyond their expectations. Rupert indeed helped with the post-holiday blues, but also encouraged four people to quit smoking and others to lose weight by going on walks during breaks. For a lot of companies with rules such as owner accountability, a dog review board and a dog-approval process, employees find that the dogs are a great release for stress. This dog policy helps managers make good recruitment decisions; candidates who respond favourably to the canine rule are likely to fit in with the existing office culture. It worked out so well that 'Bosses now plan to provide dogs for their staff in Leeds, Halifax and York.'[50]

A related concern is *person–environment fit*, which looks not only at whether the person and job are suited to one another but also at how well the individual will fit in the overall organizational environment. An employee who is by nature strongly authoritarian, for example, would have a hard time in an organization such as W. L. Gore and Associates, which has few rules, no hierarchy, no fixed or assigned authority and no bosses. Many of today's organizations pay attention to person–environment fit from the beginning of the recruitment process. Texas Instruments' webpage includes an area called Fit Check that evaluates personality types anonymously and gives prospective job candidates a chance to evaluate for themselves whether they would be a good match with the company.[49]

Several selection devices are used for assessing applicant qualifications. The most frequently used are the application form, interview, employment test, assessment centre and to a lesser extent personality test. Studies indicate that the greater the skill requirements and work demands of an open position, the greater the number and variety of selection tools the organization will use.[51] Human resource professionals may use a combination of devices to obtain a valid prediction of employee job performance. Validity refers to the relationship between one's score on a selection device and one's future job performance. A valid selection procedure will provide high scores that correspond to subsequent high job performance.

Application form

The application form is used to collect information about the applicant's education, previous job experience and other background characteristics. Research in the life insurance industry shows that biographical information inventories can validly predict future job success.[52]

One pitfall to be avoided is the inclusion of questions that are irrelevant to job success. In line with affirmative action, the application form should not ask questions that will create an adverse impact on protected groups unless the questions are clearly related to the job.[53] For example, employers should not ask whether the applicant rents or owns his or her own home because (1) an applicant's response might adversely affect his or her chances of getting the job, (2) minorities and women may be less likely

💡 INNOVATIVE WAY

Africon

Africon is ranked the Number 1 consulting engineering firm in South Africa, as well as one of the Top 200 International Design Firms worldwide. Established more than half a century ago, the firm has grown into a multinational player in the arena of infrastructure design and management, with an enviable track record spanning a wide range of engineering disciplines, from asset and facility management, civil engineering, construction supervision and electrical and power system engineering to mining engineering, project management, structural engineering, traffic engineering and water engineering.

The firm has an extensive office network encompassing 17 offices throughout South Africa, 11 offices in Portuguese- and English-speaking African countries, and a further two offices in the Middle East. Its staff complement comprises more than 1500 dedicated and competent individuals, including more than 1000 engineers and other professionals.

Part of that success is due to the popular track record Africon has on project completion, e.g. the R-1000 traffic study for the Dubai Municipality;

the construction of a new Central Terminal Building at OR Tambo International Airport in Johannesburg; the Nova Vida Housing Development in Luanda, Angola; the Rabat Corniche mixed-use property development in Rabat, Morocco; the 45 000-seat Peter Mokaba sports stadium, which was constructed in the Limpopo Province as part of the preparations for the 2010 Soccer World Cup; and the Moatize Coal project in Mozambique. But another, perhaps even greater, element is Africon's approach to recruiting, which turns the company's best stakeholders into loyal, top-performing employees.

The in-company head-hunting approach has been so successful that approximately a third of the company's workers come from employee referrals. In an industry where most companies are running classified ads or recruiting through recruitment consultants every week or two for new staff, Africon often goes 6 to 8 months without placing a single help-wanted ad. However, this does not mean that they do not use partners for recruitment. Every year they participate in recruitment events like 'Careers in Africa', which bring a healthy flow of applicants.

---

to own a home and (3) home ownership is probably unrelated to job performance. By contrast, the US Certified Public Accountant (CPA) exam is relevant to job performance in a CPA firm; thus, it is appropriate to ask whether an applicant for employment has passed the CPA exam, even if only one-half of all female or minority applicants have done so versus nine-tenths of male applicants.

Interview

The *interview* serves as a two-way communication channel that allows both the organization and the applicant to collect information that would otherwise be difficult to obtain. This selection technique is used in almost every job category in nearly every organization. It is another area where the organization can get into legal trouble if the interviewer asks questions that violate EEO guidelines. Exhibit 14.5 lists some examples of appropriate and inappropriate interview questions.

Although widely used, the interview is not generally a valid predictor of job performance. Studies of interviewing suggest that people tend to make snap judgements of others within the first few seconds of meeting them and only rarely change their opinions based on anything that occurs in the interview.[54] However, the interview as a selection tool has high *face validity*. That is, it seems valid to employers, and managers prefer to hire someone only after they have been through some form of interview, preferably face-to-face. Exhibit 14.5 offers some tips for effective interviewing.

🌐 NEW MANAGER SELF-TEST

What is your HR work orientation?

INSTRUCTIONS As a new manager, what is your orientation concerning day-to-day work issues? To find out, think about your preferences for the questions below. Circle *a* or *b* for each item depending on which one is accurate for you. There are no right or wrong answers.

1 The work elements I prefer are

    a. Administrative

    b. Conceptualizing

2 The work elements I prefer are

    a. Creative

    b. Organizing

3 My mode of living is

    a. Conventional

    b. Original

4 Which is more important to you?

    a. How something looks (form)

    b. How well it works (function)

5 I like to work with

    a. A practical person

    b. An idea person

6 I am more

    a. Idealistic

    b. Realistic

7 For weekend activities, I prefer to

    a. Plan in advance

    b. Be free to do what I want

8 A daily work routine for me is

    a. Painful

    b. Comfortable

SCORING & INTERPRETATION The human resources department typically is responsible for monitoring compliance with federal laws, and it provides detailed and specific employee procedures and records for an organization. Every new manager is involved in human resource activities for his or her direct reports, which involves systematic record keeping, awareness of applicable laws, and follow-through. For your human resource work orientation, score one point for each 'a' answer circled for questions 1, 3, 5, 7 and one point for each 'b' answer circled for questions 2, 4, 6, 8.

New managers with a high score (7 or 8) for human resource work orientation tend to be practical, organized, good at record keeping and meet commitments on time. New managers with a low score (1 or 2) on human resource work orientation tend to be more free-spirited, creative and conceptual. These managers tend to think out-of-the-box and may dislike the organization, routine and legal record keeping required for efficient HRM. If your score is midrange (3 to 6), you may do well with human resource work if you put your mind to it, but human resources may not be your area of greatest strength.

EXHIBIT 14.5 Employment applications and interviews: what can you ask?

Category	Okay to ask	Inappropriate or illegal to ask
National origin	• The applicant's name • If applicant has ever worked under a different name	• The origin of applicant's name • Applicant's ancestry/ethnicity
Race	• Nothing	• Race or colour of skin
Disabilities	• Whether applicant has any disabilities that might inhibit performance of job	• If applicant has any physical or mental defects • If applicant has ever filed workers' compensation claim
Age	• If applicant is over 18	• Applicant's age • When applicant left full-time education
Religion	• Nothing	• Applicant's religious affiliation • What religious holidays applicant observes
Criminal record	• If applicant has ever been convicted of a crime	• If applicant has ever been arrested
Marital/family status Education and experience	• Nothing • Where applicant went to school • Prior work experience	• Marital status, number of children or planned children • Childcare arrangements • When applicant graduated • Hobbies
Citizenship	• If applicant has a legal right to work in the country	• If applicant is a citizen of another country

SOURCES: 'Appropriate and Inappropriate Interview Questions', in George Bohlander, Scott Snell and Arthur Sherman, *Managing Human Resources*, 12th ed. (Cincinnati, OH: South-Western, 2001): 207; and 'Guidelines to Lawful and Unlawful Preemployment Inquiries', Appendix E, in Robert L. Mathis and John H. Jackson, *Human Resource Management*, 2nd ed. (Cincinnati, OH: South-Western, 2002), 189–190.

Today's organizations are trying different approaches to overcome the limitations of the interview. Some put candidates through a series of interviews, each one conducted by a different person and each one probing a different aspect of the candidate. At Microsoft, for example, interviewers include HRM professionals, managers of the appropriate functional department, peers and people outside the department who are well grounded in the corporate culture.[55] Other companies, including universities in Europe and Asia use *panel interviews,* in which the candidate meets with several interviewers who take turns asking questions, to increase interview validity.[56] For the graduate management positions, companies tend to use group interviews, in which as many as ten candidates are asked to make a pitch for a product that solves a particular organization challenge. This approach gives managers a chance to see how people function as part of a team.[57]

Some organizations also supplement traditional interviewing information with *computer-based interviews*. This type of interview typically requires a candidate to answer a series of multiple-choice questions tailored to the specific job. The answers are compared to an ideal profile or to a profile developed on the basis of other candidates. Companies such as Pinkerton Security, Coopers & Lybrand and Pic n' Pay Shoe Stores found computer-based interviews to be valuable for searching out information regarding the applicant's honesty, work attitude, drug history, candour, dependability and self-motivation.[58]

TAKE A MOMENT

As a new manager, get the right people in the right jobs by assessing your team's or department's needs, offering realistic job previews, using a variety of recruiting methods, and striving to match the needs and interests of the individual to those of the organization. It is typically wise to use a variety of selection tools. For lower-skilled jobs, an application and brief interview might be enough, but higher-skilled jobs call for a combination of interviews, aptitude and skills tests, and assessment exercises.

Employment test

The majority of multinational companies use *psychometric tests* that measure attributes like intelligence, aptitude and personality. They provide a potential employer with an insight into how well an applicant works with other people, how well an applicant handles stress and whether an applicant is able to cope with the intellectual demands of the job. Most of the established psychometric tests used in recruitment and selection make no attempt to analyze emotional or psychological stability. However, in recent years there has been rapid growth (particularly in the USA) of tests that claim to measure your integrity or honesty and your predisposition to anger. These tests have attracted a lot of controversy, because of questions about their validity, but their popularity with employers has continued to increase. Psychometric testing is now used by over 80 per cent of the Fortune 500 companies in the USA and by over 75 per cent of the *Times* Top 100 companies in the UK. Information technology companies, financial institutions, management consultancies, local authorities, the civil service, police forces, fire services and the armed forces all make extensive use of psychometric testing, as shown in Exhibit 14.6.[59]

Assessment centres

The quest for a more reliable method of identifying people with high potential is not new. Assessment Centres were originally developed for the military, first by the German military and later by the US Office of Strategic Services in World War II. The first business application of the Assessment Centre in the USA was conducted by AT&T in 1956. Assessment centres are now a popular method to select individuals with high potential for managerial careers by such organizations as IBM, General Electric and others.[60] Assessment centres

EXHIBIT 14.6 Percentage of companies using psychometric testing

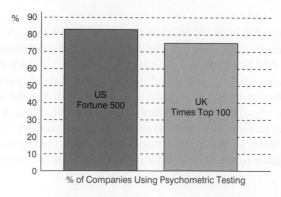

present a series of managerial situations to groups of applicants over a 2- or 3-day period. One technique is the in-basket simulation, which requires the applicant to play the role of a manager who must decide how to respond to ten memos in his or her in-basket within a 2-hour period. Panels of two or three trained judges observe the applicant's decisions and assess the extent to which they reflect interpersonal, communication and problem-solving skills.

Assessment centres have proven to be valid predictors of managerial success, and some organizations now use them for hiring frontline workers as well. Mercury Communications in England uses an assessment centre to select customer assistants. Applicants participate in simulated exercises with customers and in various other exercises designed to assess their listening skills, customer sensitivity and ability to cope under pressure.[61]

In recent years, many employers showed heightened interest in matching people's personalities to the needs of the job and the organization. An individual's personality is the set of characteristics that underlie a relatively stable pattern of behaviour in response to ideas, objects or people in the environment. Understanding personality can help managers predict how a person might act in a particular situation.

Personality traits

In common usage, people think of personality in terms of traits, the fairly consistent characteristics a person exhibits. Researchers investigated whether any traits stand up to scientific scrutiny. Although investigators examined thousands of traits over the years, their findings fit into five general dimensions that describe personality. These dimensions, often called the 'Big Five' personality factors, are illustrated in Exhibit 14.7.[62] Each factor may contain a wide range of specific traits. The Big Five personality factors describe an individual's extroversion, agreeableness, conscientiousness, emotional stability and openness to experience:

1 *Extroversion.* The degree to which a person is outgoing, sociable, assertive and comfortable with interpersonal relationships.

2 *Agreeableness.* The degree to which a person is able to get along with others by being good-natured, likeable, cooperative, forgiving, understanding and trusting.

3 *Conscientiousness.* The degree to which a person is focused on a few goals, thus behaving in ways that are responsible, dependable, persistent and achievement oriented.

4 *Emotional stability.* The degree to which a person is calm, enthusiastic and self-confident, rather than tense, depressed, moody or insecure.

5 *Openness to experience.* The degree to which a person has a broad range of interests and is imaginative, creative, artistically sensitive and willing to consider new ideas.

As illustrated in the exhibit, these factors represent a continuum. That is, a person may have a low, moderate or high degree of each quality. Answer the questions in Exhibit 14.7 to see where you fall on the Big Five scale for each of the factors. Having a moderate-to-high degree of each of the Big Five personality factors is considered desirable for a wide range of employees, but this isn't always a key to success. For example, having an outgoing, sociable personality (extroversion) is considered desirable for managers, but many successful top leaders, including Richard Branson, Herbert Heiner, Phillip Rose, Bill Gates, Charles Schwab and Steven Spielberg are introverts, people who become drained by social encounters and need time alone to reflect and recharge their batteries. One study found that four in ten top executives test out to be introverts.[63] Thus, the quality of extroversion is not as significant as is often presumed. Traits of agreeableness, on the other hand, seem to be particularly important in today's collaborative organizations. The days are over when a hard-driving manager can run roughshod over others to earn a promotion. Companies want managers who work smoothly with others and get help from lots of people inside and outside the organization. Today's successful CEOs are not the tough guys of the past but those men and women who know how to get people to like and trust them. Philip Purcell was forced out as CEO of Morgan Stanley largely because he was a remote, autocratic leader who treated many employees with contempt and failed to build positive relationships with clients. Purcell had little goodwill to back him up when things started going against him. Many people just didn't like him. In contrast, Sainsbury's CEO Justin King stresses good relationships with employees, suppliers, partners and customers as a key to effective management.[64]

EXHIBIT 14.7 The Big Five personality traits

Each individual's collection of personality traits is different; it is what makes us unique. But, although each *collection* of traits varies, we all share many common traits. The following phrases describe various traits and behaviours. Rate how accurately each statement describes you, based on a scale of 1 to 5, with 1 being very inaccurate and 5 very accurate. Describe yourself as you are now, not as you wish to be. There are no right or wrong answers.

	1	2	3	4	5	
Very inaccurate						Very accurate

Extroversion

I am usually the life of the party.	1	2	3	4	5
I feel comfortable around people.	1	2	3	4	5
I am talkative.	1	2	3	4	5

Agreeableness

I am kind and sympathetic.	1	2	3	4	5
I have a good word for everyone.	1	2	3	4	5
I never insult people.	1	2	3	4	5

Conscientiousness

I am systematic and efficient.	1	2	3	4	5
I pay attention to details.	1	2	3	4	5
I am always prepared for class.	1	2	3	4	5

Neuroticism (Low emotional stability)

I often feel critical of myself.	1	2	3	4	5
I often envy others.	1	2	3	4	5
I am temperamental.	1	2	3	4	5

Openness to new experiences

I am imaginative.	1	2	3	4	5
I prefer to vote for liberal political candidates.	1	2	3	4	5
I really like art.	1	2	3	4	5

Which are your most prominent traits? For fun and discussion, compare your responses with those of peers.

One recent book argues that the secret to success in work and in life is *likeability*. We all know we're more willing to do something for someone we like than for someone we don't, whether it be a team-mate, a neighbour, a professor or a supervisor. Managers can increase their likeability by developing traits of agreeableness, including being friendly and cooperative, understanding other people in a genuine way and striving to make people feel positive about themselves.[65]

Many companies, including HSBC, the UK's National Health Service, Toys'R'Us, Next, Lancôme and others, use personality testing to hire, evaluate or promote employees. Surveys show that at least 30 per cent of organizations use some kind of personality testing for hiring.[66] In the USA, MultiCinema (AMC), one of the largest theatre chains in the USA, looks for frontline workers with high conscientiousness and high emotional stability.[67] Marriott Hotels look for people who score high on conscientiousness and agreeableness because they believe these individuals will provide better service to guests.[68] Companies also use personality testing for managers. Hewlett-Packard, Apple, Google, Dell Computer and General Electric all put candidates for top positions through testing, interviews with psychologists, or both, to see whether they have the 'right stuff' for the job.[69] Executives at franchises such as Little Gym International and Yum Brands, which owns Pizza Hut and KFC are using personality testing to make sure potential franchisees can fit into their system and be successful.[70] It is noted that despite growing use of personality tests, little hard evidence shows them to be valid predictors of job performance. In addition, the applicants can easily fabricate the answers.[71] Finally, in the USA, questions about religion affiliations and sexual orientation, for example, have been construed as both invasive and discriminatory and have resulted in heavy financial penalties.[72]

Rewarding and developing an effective workforce

Following selection, the next goal of HRM is to reward and develop employees into an effective workforce, which includes performance appraisal, compensation and benefits, and training and development as illustrated in Exhibit 14.8.

Training and development

Training and development represent a planned effort by an organization to facilitate employees' learning of job-related skills and behaviours.[73] The training budget of IBM alone in 2005 was $750 million.[74] The most common method of training is on-the-job training. In on-the-job training (OJT), an experienced employee is asked to take a new employee 'under his or her wing' and show the newcomer how to perform job duties. OJT has many advantages, such as minimal out-of-pocket costs for training facilities, materials or instructor fees and easy transfer of learning back to the job. When implemented well, OJT is considered the fastest and most effective means of facilitating learning in the workplace.[75] One type of on-the-job training involves moving people to various types of jobs within the organization, where they work with experienced employees to learn different tasks. This *cross-training* may place an employee in a new position for as short a time as a few hours or for as long as a year, enabling the employee to develop new skills and giving the organization greater flexibility.

Another type of on-the-job training is *mentoring,* which means a more experienced employee is paired with a newcomer or a less-experienced worker to provide guidance, support and learning opportunities. Other frequently used training methods include the following:

- *Orientation training*, in which newcomers are introduced to the organization's culture, standards and goals.

- *Classroom training,* including lectures, films, audiovisual techniques and simulations, makes up approximately 70 per cent of all formal corporate training.[76]

- *Self-directed learning*, also called programmed instruction, which involves the use of books, manuals or computers to provide subject matter in highly organized and logical sequences that require employees to answer a series of questions about the material.

- *Computer-based training,* sometimes called *e-training,* including computer-assisted instruction, Web-based training, and teletraining. As with self-directed learning, the employee works at his or her own pace and instruction is individualized, but as the training programme is interactive and more complex, non-structured information can be communicated. e-Training has soared in recent years because it offers cost savings to organizations and allows people to learn at their own pace.[77]

Corporate universities

A recent popular approach to training and development is the corporate university. A corporate university is an in-house training and education facility that offers broad-based learning opportunities for employees – and frequently for customers, suppliers and strategic partners as well – throughout their careers.[78] One well-known corporate university is Hamburger University, McDonald's worldwide training centre, which has been

EXHIBIT 14.8 Types and methods of training

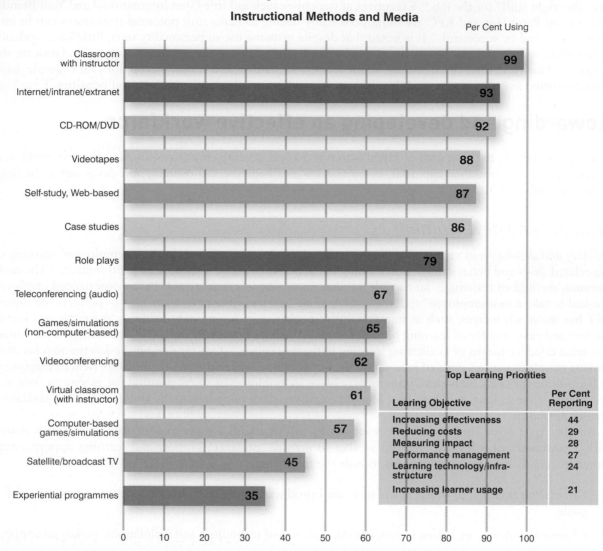

Instructional Methods and Media

Per Cent Using

Method	Per Cent Using
Classroom with instructor	99
Internet/intranet/extranet	93
CD-ROM/DVD	92
Videotapes	88
Self-study, Web-based	87
Case studies	86
Role plays	79
Teleconferencing (audio)	67
Games/simulations (non-computer-based)	65
Videoconferencing	62
Virtual classroom (with instructor)	61
Computer-based games/simulations	57
Satellite/broadcast TV	45
Experiential programmes	35

Top Learning Priorities	
Learing Objective	Per Cent Reporting
Increasing effectiveness	44
Reducing costs	29
Measuring impact	28
Performance management	27
Learning technology/infra-structure	24
Increasing learner usage	21

SOURCES: Methods data from Tammy Galvin, '2003 Industry Report', *Training* (October 2003): 21+. Reprinted with permission from the October 2003 issue of *Training* magazine, Copyright 2003, Bill Communications, Minneapolis, Minn. All rights reserved. Not for resale. Types data from Holly Dolezalek, '2005 Industry Report', *Training* (December 2005): 14–28.

in existence for more than 40 years. Numerous other companies, including IBM, FedEx, General Electric, Intel, Harley-Davidson and Capital One, pump millions of dollars into corporate universities to continually build human capital.[79] Employees at Caterpillar attend courses at Caterpillar University, which combines e-training, classroom session and hands-on training activities. Although corporate universities have extended their reach with new technology that enables distance learning via videoconferencing and online education, most emphasize the importance of classroom interaction.[80]

Promotion from within

Another way to further employee development is through promotion from within, which helps companies retain valuable people. This provides challenging assignments, prescribes new responsibilities and helps

CONCEPT CONNECTION

'We don't do training,' says Equifax senior vice president and chief learning officer, Lynn Slavenski. 'We do change.' Slavenski oversaw the establishment of Equifax University for the consumer credit reporting company. What distinguishes corporate universities from most old-style training programmes is that the courses – from classes teaching a specific technical skill to corporate-run MBA programmes – are intentionally designed to foster the changes needed to achieve the organization's strategy. It's clearly an idea whose time has come. In 1993, there were just 400 in-house corporate universities. By 2005, that number increased five-fold, and observers predict it will reach 3700 by 2010.

employees grow by expanding and developing their abilities.

In the old social contract between organization and employee, the employee could contribute ability, education, loyalty and commitment and expect in return that the company would provide wages and benefits, work, advancement and training throughout the employee's working life. But volatile changes in the environment have disrupted this contract. As many organizations downsized, significant numbers of employees were eliminated. Employees who are left may feel little stability. In a fast-moving company, a person is hired and assigned to a project. The project changes over time, as do the person's tasks. Then the person is assigned to another project and then to still another. These new projects require working with different groups and leaders and schedules, and people may be working in a virtual environment, where they rarely see their colleagues face-to-face.[81] Careers no longer progress up a vertical hierarchy but move across jobs horizontally. In many of today's companies, everyone is expected to be a self-motivated worker, with excellent interpersonal relationships, who is continuously acquiring new skills.

Workforce optimization

A related approach is workforce optimization, which can be defined as putting the right person in the right place at the right time.[82] With today's emphasis on managing and building human capital, human resource professionals are pursuing a range of strategies that help organizations make the best use of the talent they have and effectively develop that talent for the future. New software programs and information technology can help identify people with the right mix of skills to tackle a new project, for example, as well as pinpoint where to move staff internally to ensure they have opportunities for growth and development. IBM is a leader in workforce optimization with a technology-based staff-deployment tool it calls the Workforce Management Initiative. One use of the system is a sort of in-house recruiting tool that lets managers search for employees with the precise skills needed for particular projects. However, the system's greatest impact is that it helps human resource professionals and managers analyze what skills employees have, see how those talents match up with current and anticipated needs in the business and technology environment, and devise job transfers and other training to help close skills-gaps.[83]

Performance appraisal

Performance appraisal comprises the steps of observing and assessing employee performance, recording the assessment and providing feedback to the employee. During performance appraisal, skilful managers give feedback and praise concerning the acceptable elements of the employee's performance. They also describe performance areas that need improvement. Employees can use this information to change their job performance.

Performance appraisal can also reward high performers with merit pay, recognition and other rewards. However, the most recent thinking is that linking performance appraisal to rewards has unintended consequences. The idea is that performance appraisal should be ongoing, not something that is done once a year as part of a consideration of salary increases.

Managers are responsible for evaluating the performance of their employees and for accurately communicating that assessment. Communicating clear, specific expectations and giving both negative and positive feedback are essential parts of the performance appraisal process. Unfortunately, discussing such matters can be stressful to both the manager and the subordinate. A common method to overcome this problem is the 'sandwich approach', in which the negative feedback is sandwiched between two pieces of positive feedback. The method is believed to provide balanced feedback and reduce discomfort and anxiety. However, it is claimed that the 'sandwich approach' may undermine feedback, with subordinates discounting positive feedback, believing it is not genuine.[84]

Generally, HRM professionals concentrate on two things to make performance appraisal a positive force in their organizations: (1) the accurate assessment of performance through the development and application of assessment systems such as rating scales and (2) training managers effectively to use the performance appraisal interview, so they can provide feedback that will reinforce good performance and motivate employee development.

Assessing performance accurately

To obtain an accurate performance rating, managers acknowledge that jobs are multidimensional and performance thus may be multidimensional as well. For example, a sports broadcaster might perform well on the job-knowledge dimension; that is, he or she might be able to report facts and figures about the players and describe which rule applies when there is a questionable play on the field. But the same broadcaster might not perform as well on another dimension, such as effective communication. The person might be unable to express the information in a stimulating way that interests the audience or might interrupt the other broadcasters.

For performance to be rated accurately, the appraisal system should require the rater to assess each relevant performance dimension. A multidimensional form increases the usefulness of the performance appraisal and facilitates employee growth and development.

A recent trend in performance appraisal is called 360-degree feedback, a process that uses multiple raters, including self-rating, as a way to increase awareness of strengths and weaknesses and guide employee development. Members of the appraisal group may include supervisors, co-workers and customers, as well as the individual, thus providing appraisal of the employee from a variety of perspectives. One study found that 26 per cent of companies used some type of multirater performance appraisal.[85]

Another alternative performance-evaluation method is the *performance review ranking system*.[86] This method has become quite popular over the past several years, with as many as one-third of US corporations using some type of forced ranking system.[87] However, because these systems essentially evaluate employees by pitting them against one another, the method is increasingly coming under fire. As most commonly used, a manager evaluates his or her direct reports relative to one another and categorizes each on a scale, such as A = outstanding performance, B = high-middle performance or C = in need of improvement. Most companies routinely fire those managers falling in the bottom 10 per cent of the ranking. Proponents say the technique provides an effective way to assess performance and offer guidance for employee development. But critics of these systems, sometimes called *rank and yank,* argue that they are based on subjective judgements, produce skewed results and discriminate against employees who are 'different' from the mainstream. A class-action lawsuit charges that Ford's ranking system discriminates against older managers. Use of the system has also triggered employee lawsuits at Conoco and Microsoft, and employment lawyers warn that other law suits will follow.[88]

In addition, critics warn that ranking systems significantly hinder collaboration and risk taking, which are increasingly important for today's companies striving for innovation. One recent study found that forced rankings that include firing the bottom 5 or 10 per cent can lead to a dramatic improvement in organizational performance in the short term, but the benefits dissipate over several years as people become focused on competing with one another rather than improving the business.[89] Many companies, including General Electric, the most famous advocate of forced rankings in recent years, are building more flexibility into the performance review ranking system, and some are abandoning it altogether.[90] Despite these concerns, the appropriate use of performance ranking has been useful for many companies, especially as a short-term way to improve performance. A variation of the system is helping UK supermarket chain Sainsbury's retain quality workers in fairly turbulent market conditions.

Performance evaluation errors

Although we would like to believe that every manager assesses employees' performance in a careful and bias-free manner, researchers have identified several rating problems.[91]

One of the most dangerous is stereotyping, which occurs when a rater places an employee into a class or category based on one or a few traits or characteristics – for example, stereotyping an older worker as slower and more difficult to train. Another rating error is the halo effect or horn effect, in which a manager's rating of a subordinate on one positive factor (the halo effect) or negative factor (the horn effect) biases the rating of that person on other factors. **Central tendency** error occurs when every employee is incorrectly rated near the average or middle of the scale. A **leniency** or **strictness bias** occurs when managers rate their employees either consistently high or low. The **recency effect** occurs when managers overemphasize the employee's most recent behaviour. Finally, **relationship effect** occurs when the nature of the supervisor/subordinate relationship influences a performance rating.

One approach to overcome performance evaluation errors is to use a behaviour-based rating technique, such as the behaviourally anchored rating scale. The behaviourally anchored rating scale (BARS) is developed from critical incidents pertaining to job performance. Each job performance scale is anchored with specific behavioural statements that describe varying degrees of performance. By relating employee performance to specific incidents, raters can more accurately evaluate an employee's performance.[92]

Exhibit 14.9 illustrates the BARS method for evaluating a production line supervisor. The production supervisor's job can be broken down into several dimensions, such as equipment maintenance, employee training or work scheduling. A behaviourally anchored rating scale should be developed for each dimension. The dimension in Exhibit 14.9 is work scheduling. Good performance is represented by a 4 or 5 on the scale and unacceptable performance as a 1 or 2. If a production supervisor's job has eight dimensions, the total performance evaluation will be the sum of the scores for each of eight scales.

EXHIBIT 14.9 Example of a behaviourally anchored rating scale

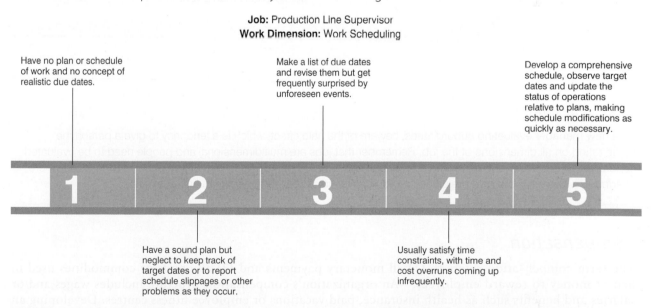

Job: Production Line Supervisor
Work Dimension: Work Scheduling

Have no plan or schedule of work and no concept of realistic due dates.

Make a list of due dates and revise them but get frequently surprised by unforeseen events.

Develop a comprehensive schedule, observe target dates and update the status of operations relative to plans, making schedule modifications as quickly as necessary.

Have a sound plan but neglect to keep track of target dates or to report schedule slippages or other problems as they occur.

Usually satisfy time constraints, with time and cost overruns coming up infrequently.

SOURCES: J. P. Campbell, M. D. Dunnette, R. D. Arvey and L. V. Hellervik, 'The Development and Evaluation of Behaviourally Based Rating Scales', *Journal of Applied Psychology* 57 (1973), 15–22; and Francine Alexander, 'Performance Appraisals', *Small Business Reports* (March 1989), 20–29.

◉ INNOVATIVE WAY

Sainsbury's[93]

Sainsbury's Supermarkets is the UK's longest standing major food retailing chain, having opened its first store in 1869. The Sainsbury's brand is built upon a heritage of providing customers with healthy, safe, fresh and tasty food. Today it differentiates itself by offering a broad range of quality products at fair prices with particular emphasis on fresh food, a strong ethical approach to business and continuous leadership and innovation.

Products are improved and developed to ensure the company leads in terms of the ingredients used and integrity of sourcing. A large Sainsbury's store offers around 30 000 products and an increasing number of stores also offer complementary non-food products and services. Sainsbury's has 147 stores which also operate an Internet-based home delivery shopping service.

The HRM policies, covering areas such as health and safety, employee relations, fair treatment, and learning and development, help make working life better for every employee. Staff are invited to share their thoughts with the Chief Executive, to make sure they are listened to from the highest level. And the company ensures there is a strong focus on diversity in the workplace by actively recruiting people from a wide range of ages and backgrounds.

A key aspect of the new retention strategy is the Sainsbury's Performance Management system, which took performance appraisal to the Web, making it easier for managers to complete the evaluations and – more importantly – put the results to good use. Twice a year each hourly paid employee conducts a self-evaluation that covers nine areas: appearance, reliability, fun (including the ability to tolerate frustration), ability, customer service, willingness to be a team player, initiative, stamina and cooperation. The store manager does the same for each employee; then they meet, compare results and discuss areas for improvement. But the feedback loop doesn't end there. With a few mouse clicks the manager looks at how each employee ranks with respect to all others in the store, separating employees into the top 20 per cent, the middle 60 per cent and the bottom 20 per cent.

The system is not the basis for firing low-ranking employees, but they usually leave soon enough anyway. Its value lies in helping managers focus their retention efforts on the top 20 per cent, who have management potential, and provide training and development opportunities to the middle 60 per cent, who have the potential to move up the ranking. Concentrating on certain employees is paying off for Sainsbury's. The staff turnover rate dropped almost 50 percentage points in less than 2 years.

TAKE A MOMENT

As a new manager evaluating subordinates, beware of the halo effect, which is a tendency to give a person the same rating on all dimensions of the job. Remember that jobs are multidimensional and people need to be evaluated separately on each relevant dimension so they can be rewarded appropriately and improve their performance where needed. Be aware of your own prejudices so you can avoid stereotyping people during evaluations.

Compensation

The term compensation refers to (1) all monetary payments and (2) all goods or commodities used in lieu of money to reward employees.[94] An organization's compensation structure includes wages and/or salaries and benefits such as health insurance, paid vacations or employee fitness centres. Developing an effective compensation system is an important part of HRM because it helps to attract and retain talented workers. In addition, a company's compensation system has an impact on strategic performance.[95] Human resource managers design the pay and benefits systems to fit company strategy and to provide compensation equity.

Wage and salary systems

Ideally, management's strategy for the organization should be a critical determinant of the features and operations of the pay system.[96] For example, managers may have the goal of maintaining or improving profitability or market share by stimulating employee performance. Thus, they should design and use a merit pay system rather than a system based on other criteria such as seniority.

The most common approach to employee compensation is *job-based pay,* which means linking compensation to the specific tasks an employee performs. However, these systems present several problems. For one thing, job-based pay may fail to reward the type of learning behaviour needed for the organization to adapt and survive in today's environment. In addition, these systems reinforce an emphasis on organizational hierarchy and centralized decision-making and control, which are inconsistent with the growing emphasis on employee participation and increased responsibility.[97]

Skill-based pay systems are becoming increasingly popular in both large and small companies, including Welland Valley Feeds in Market Harborough, UK and Orijen, part of Champion Pet Foods in Canada. Employees with higher skill levels receive higher pay than those with lower skill levels. Located in the heart of Alberta's prairie farmlands, Orijen is a reputable producer of high quality dog and cat foods that have been exported worldwide since 1975. At Orijen pet food plant, for example, employees might start at something like $8.75 per hour but reach a top hourly rate of $14.50 when they master a series of skills.[98] Also called *competency-based pay,* skill-based pay systems encourage employees to develop their skills and competencies, thus making them more valuable to the organization as well as more employable if they leave their current jobs.

Compensation equity

Whether the organization uses job-based pay or skill-based pay, good managers strive to maintain a sense of fairness and equity within the pay structure and thereby fortify employee morale. Job evaluation refers to the process of determining the value or worth of jobs within an organization through an examination of job content. Job evaluation techniques enable managers to compare similar and dissimilar jobs and to determine internally equitable pay rates – that is, pay rates that employees believe are fair compared with those for other jobs in the organization.

Organizations also want to make sure their pay rates are fair compared to other companies. HRM managers may obtain wage and salary surveys that show what other organizations pay incumbents in jobs that match a sample of 'key' jobs selected by the organization.

Pay-for-performance

Many of today's organizations develop compensation plans based on a *pay-for-performance standard* to raise productivity and cut labour costs in a competitive global environment. Pay-for-performance, also called *incentive pay,* means tying at least part of compensation to employee effort and performance, whether it be through merit-based pay, bonuses, team incentives or various gain-sharing or profit-sharing plans. Data show that, while growth in base wages is slowing in many industries, the use of pay-for-performance has steadily increased since the early 1990s, with approximately 70 per cent of companies now offering some form of incentive pay.[99] US President, George W. Bush, called for implementing performance-based pay in agencies of the federal government. The seniority-based pay system used by most federal agencies has come under intense scrutiny in recent years, with critics arguing that it creates an environment where poor performers tend to stay and the best and brightest leave out of frustration. A survey conducted in 2003 by the Office of Personnel Management found that only one in four federal employees believe adequate steps are taken to deal with poor performers, and only two in five think strong performers are appropriately recognized and rewarded.[100]

With pay-for-performance, incentives are aligned with the behaviours needed to help the organization achieve its strategic goals. Employees have an incentive to make the company more efficient and profitable because if goals are not met, no bonuses are paid.

Benefits

The best human resource managers know that a compensation package requires more than money. Although wage/salary is an important component, it is only a part. Equally important are the benefits offered by the organization. Benefits make up 40 per cent of labour costs.[101]

In the USA, some benefits are required by law, such as Social Security, unemployment compensation and workers' compensation. In addition, companies with 50 or more employees are required by the Family and Medical Leave Act to give up to 12 weeks of unpaid leave for such things as the birth or adoption of a child, the serious illness of a spouse or family member, or an employee's serious illness. Other types of benefits, such as health insurance, vacations and such things as on-site day-care or fitness centres are not required by law but are provided by organizations to maintain an effective workforce.

One reason benefits make up such a large portion of the US compensation package is that health care costs continue to increase. Many organizations are requiring that employees absorb a greater share of the cost of medical benefits, such as through higher co-payments and deductibles. Microsoft, for example, recently sliced health care benefits by requiring a higher co-pay on prescription drugs.[102]

Computerization cuts the time and expense of administering benefits programmes tremendously. At many companies, such as Wells Fargo and LG&E Energy, employees access their benefits package through an intranet, creating a 'self-service' benefits administration.[103] This access also enables employees to change their benefits selections easily. Today's organizations realize that the 'one-size-fits-all' benefits package is no longer appropriate, so they frequently offer *cafeteria-plan benefits packages* that allow employees to select the benefits of greatest value to them.[104] Other companies use surveys to determine which combination of fixed benefits is most desirable. The benefits packages provided by large companies attempt to meet the needs of all employees.

Maintaining an effective workforce

Now we turn to the topic of how managers and HRM professionals maintain a workforce that has been recruited and rewarded and developed. Maintenance of the current workforce involves motivation, job design and occasional terminations.

 ## CONCEPT CONNECTION

Managers at Swedish retailer ICA in Sweden believe that creating a work environment that is rich in opportunity, challenge and reward and motivates employees is key to the company's success. By providing clear goals and objectives, performance reviews, formal and informal education programmes, functional training, lateral promotions and individual mentoring, managers help employees such as Lars Bengtsson, find both intrinsic and extrinsic rewards in their work. Bengtsson has been assisting shoppers and winning hearts at ICA supermarket in Almhult since the store opened in 1976. 'He's the Mayor of ICA,' says Store Director Madelene Gummesson.

Motivation

Most people begin a new job with energy and enthusiasm, but employees can lose their drive if managers fail in their role as motivators. It can be a problem for even the most successful of organizations and the most admired of managers, when experienced, valuable employees lose the motivation and commitment they once felt, causing a decline in their performance. Motivation refers to the forces either within or external to a person that arouse enthusiasm and persistence to pursue a certain course of action. Employee motivation affects productivity, and part of a manager's job is to channel motivation towards the accomplishment of organizational goals.[105] The study of motivation helps managers understand what prompts people to initiate action, what influences their choice of action and why they persist in that action over time.

The contemporary approach to employee motivation is dominated by three types of theories, each of which will be discussed in the following sections. The first are *content theories*, which stress the analysis of underlying human needs. Content theories provide insight into the needs of people in organizations and help managers understand how needs can be satisfied in the workplace. *Process theories* concern the thought processes that influence behaviour. They focus on how people seek rewards in work circumstances. *Reinforcement theories* focus on employee learning of desired work behaviours.

Content perspectives on motivation

Content theories emphasize the needs that motivate people. At any point in time, people have basic needs such as those for monetary reward, achievement or recognition. These needs translate into an internal drive that motivates specific behaviours in an attempt to fulfil the needs. In other words, our needs are like a hidden catalogue of the things we want and will work to get. To the extent that managers understand employees' needs, they can design reward systems to meet them and direct employees' energies and priorities towards attaining organizational goals.

Hierarchy of needs theory

Hierarchy of needs theory is one of the early management theories proposed by Abraham Maslow in 1943 and is probably the most famous content theory.[106] It proposes that people are motivated by multiple needs and that these needs exist in a hierarchical order, as illustrated in Exhibit 14.10. Maslow identified five general types of motivating needs in order of ascendance:

1 *Physiological needs.* These most basic human physical needs include food, water and oxygen. In the organizational setting, they are reflected in the needs for adequate heat, air and basic salary to ensure survival.

2 *Safety needs.* These needs include a safe and secure physical and emotional environment and freedom from threats – that is, for freedom from violence and for an orderly society. In an organizational workplace, safety needs reflect the needs for safe jobs, fringe benefits and job security.

3 *Belongingness needs.* These needs reflect the desire to be accepted by one's peers, have friendships, be part of a group and be loved. In the organization, these needs influence the desire for good relationships with co-workers, participation in a work group and a positive relationship with supervisors.

4 *Esteem needs.* These needs relate to the desire for a positive self-image and to receive attention, recognition and appreciation from others. Within organizations, esteem needs reflect a motivation for recognition, an increase in responsibility, high status and credit for contributions to the organization.

5 *Self-actualization needs.* These needs include the need for self-fulfilment, which is the highest need category. They concern developing one's full potential, increasing one's competence and becoming a better person. Self-actualization needs can be met in the organization by providing people with opportunities to grow, be creative and acquire training for challenging assignments and advancement.

EXHIBIT 14.10 Maslow's hierarchy of needs

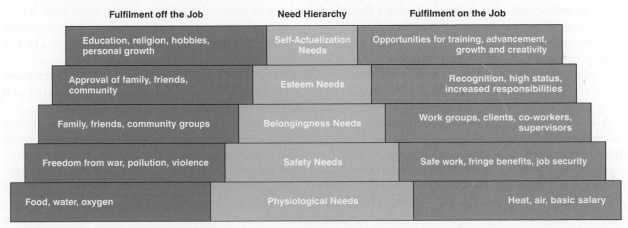

According to Maslow's theory, low-order needs take priority – they must be satisfied before higher-order needs are activated. The needs are satisfied in sequence: physiological needs come before safety needs, safety needs before social needs, and so on. A person desiring physical safety will devote his or her efforts to securing a safer environment and will not be concerned with esteem needs or self-actualization needs. Once a need is satisfied, it declines in importance and the next higher need is activated.

A study of employees in the manufacturing department of a major health care company in the UK provides some support for Maslow's theory. Most line workers emphasized that they worked at the company primarily because of the good pay, benefits and job security. Thus, employees' lower level physiological and safety needs were being met. When questioned about their motivation, employees indicated the importance of positive social relationships with both peers and supervisors (belongingness needs) and a desire for greater respect and recognition from management (esteem needs).[107]

TAKE A MOMENT

As a new manager, recognize that some people are motivated primarily to satisfy lower-level physiological and safety needs, while others want to satisfy higher-level needs. Learn which lower- and higher-level needs motivate you by completing the Experiential Exercise online.

ERG theory

Clayton Alderfer proposed a modification of Maslow's theory in an effort to simplify it and respond to criticisms of its lack of empirical verification.[108] His ERG theory identified three categories of needs:

1 *Existence needs.* The needs for physical well-being.

2 *Relatedness needs.* The needs for satisfactory relationships with others.

3 *Growth needs.* The needs that focus on the development of human potential and the desire for personal growth and increased competence.

The ERG model and Maslow's need hierarchy are similar because both are in hierarchical form and presume that individuals move up the hierarchy one step at a time. However, Alderfer reduced the number of need categories to three and proposed that movement up the hierarchy is more complex, reflecting a frustration–regression principle, namely, that failure to meet a high-order need may trigger a regression to an already fulfilled lower-order need. Thus, a worker who cannot fulfil a need for personal growth may revert to a lower-order need and redirect his or her efforts towards making a lot of money. The ERG model therefore is less rigid than Maslow's need hierarchy, suggesting that individuals may move down as well as up the hierarchy, depending on their ability to satisfy needs.

Need hierarchy theory helps explain why organizations find ways to recognize employees, encourage their participation in decision-making, and give them opportunities to make significant contributions to the organization and society. For example, Cahoot Bank, a subsidiary of Santander UK plc, is not using bank tellers or cashiers. These positions are now frontline managers who are expected to make decisions and contribute ideas for improving the business.[109] USAA, which offers insurance, mutual funds and banking services to five million members of the military and their families in the USA, provides another example.

A recent survey found that employees who contribute ideas at work, such as those at USAA, are more likely to feel valued, committed and motivated. In addition, when employees' ideas are implemented and recognized, a motivational effect often ripples throughout the workforce.[111]

Many companies are finding that creating a humane work environment that allows people to achieve a balance between work and personal life is also a great high-level motivator. Flexibility in the workplace, including options such as telecommuting, flexible hours and job sharing, is highly valued by today's employees because it enables them to manage their work and personal responsibilities. Flexibility is good for organizations too. Employees who have control over their work schedules are significantly less likely to suffer job burnout and are more highly committed to their employers, as shown in Exhibit 14.11. This idea was supported by a survey conducted at Deloitte, which found that client service professionals cited workplace

INNOVATIVE WAY

USAA

USAA's customer service agents are on the frontline in helping families challenged by war and overseas deployment manage their financial responsibilities. Managers recognize that the most important factor in the company's success is the relationship between USAA members and these frontline employees.

To make sure that relationship is a good one, USAA treats customer service reps, who are often considered the lowest rung on the corporate ladder, like professionals. People have a real sense that they're making life just a little easier for military members and their families, which instils them with a feeling of pride and accomplishment. Employees are organized into small,

tightly knit 'expert teams' and are encouraged to suggest changes that will benefit customers. One service rep suggested that the company offer insurance premium billing timed to coincide with the military's bi-weekly pay cheques. Service reps don't have scripts to follow, and calls aren't timed. Employees know they can take whatever time they need to give the customer the best possible service.

Giving people the opportunity to make real contributions has paid off. In a study by Forrester Research, 81 per cent of USAA customers said they believe the company does what's best for them, rather than what's best for the bottom line. Compare that to about 20 per cent of customers for financial services firms such as JP Morgan Chase and Citibank.[110]

---

flexibility as a strong reason for wanting to stay with the firm. Another study at Prudential Insurance found that work–life satisfaction and work flexibility directly correlated to job satisfaction, organizational commitment and employee retention.[112]

Making work fun can play a role in creating this balance. One psychologist recently updated Maslow's hierarchy of needs for a new generation and included the need to have fun as a substantial motivator for today's employees.[113] Having fun at work relieves stress and enables people to feel more 'whole', rather than feeling that their personal lives are totally separate from their work lives. Something as simple as a manager's choice of language can create a lighter, more fun environment. Research suggests the use of phrases such as 'Play around with this … Explore the possibility of … Have fun with … Don't worry about little mistakes … View this as a game …' and so forth can effectively build elements of fun and playfulness into a workplace.[114]

EXHIBIT 14.11 The motivational benefits of job flexibility

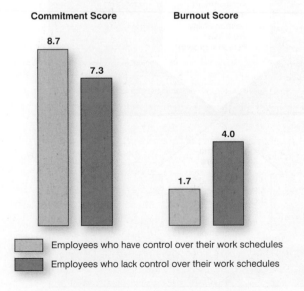

SOURCE: WFD Consulting data, as reported in Karol Rose, 'Work–Life Effectiveness', *Fortune* (September 29, 2003): S1–S17.

Two-factor theory

Frederick Herzberg developed another popular theory of motivation called the *two-factor theory*.[115] Herzberg interviewed hundreds of workers about times when they were highly motivated to work and other times when they were dissatisfied and unmotivated at work. His findings suggested that the work characteristics associated with dissatisfaction were quite different from those pertaining to satisfaction, which prompted the notion that two factors influence work motivation.

The two-factor theory is illustrated in Exhibit 14.12. The centre of the scale is neutral, meaning that workers are neither satisfied nor dissatisfied. Herzberg believed that two entirely separate dimensions contribute to an employee's behaviour at work. The first, called hygiene factors, involves the presence or absence of job dissatisfiers, such as working conditions, pay, company policies and interpersonal relationships. When hygiene factors are poor, work is dissatisfying. However, good hygiene factors simply remove the dissatisfaction; they do not in themselves cause people to become highly satisfied and motivated in their work.

The second set of factors does influence job satisfaction. Motivators focus on high-level needs and include achievement, recognition, responsibility and opportunity for growth. Herzberg believed that when motivators are absent, workers are neutral towards work, but when motivators are present, workers are highly motivated and satisfied. Thus, hygiene factors and motivators represent two distinct factors that influence motivation. Hygiene factors work only in the area of dissatisfaction. Unsafe working conditions or a noisy work environment will cause people to be dissatisfied, but their correction will not lead to a high level of motivation and satisfaction. Motivators such as challenge, responsibility and recognition must be in place before employees will be highly motivated to excel at their work.

The implication of the two-factor theory for managers is clear. On the one hand, providing hygiene factors will eliminate employee dissatisfaction but will not motivate workers to high achievement levels. On the other, recognition, challenge and opportunities for personal growth are powerful motivators and will promote high satisfaction and performance. The manager's role is to remove dissatisfiers – that is, to provide hygiene factors sufficient to meet basic needs – and then to use motivators to meet higher-level needs and propel employees towards greater achievement and satisfaction. Consider how Vision Express, one of the UK and Europe's largest providers of eye care benefits, uses both hygiene factors and motivators.

EXHIBIT 14.12 Herzberg's two-factor theory

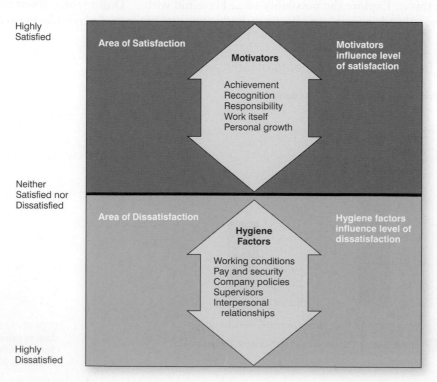

⦿ INNOVATIVE **WAY**

Vision Express[116]

Based in Nottingham, UK, Vision Express has seen its workforce nearly triple over the past few decades. Despite the challenges of rapid growth, employee satisfaction levels have climbed to an astonishing high of 98 per cent. Vision Express is a subsidiary of Grand Vision, which employs 3600 people and operates 873 stores throughout Europe, including the GrandOptical, Generale D'Optique and Solaris multiple chains.

Vision Express doesn't offer outrageous salaries and stock options; it does make sure people are paid fairly and provided with solid benefits. The real key to high motivation and satisfaction at Vision Express, though, is that people feel valued and respected. The process starts the minute someone is hired. Managers use a checklist of items that should be waiting for the new employee upon arrival. Having such basics as a computer, voicemail and email accounts, a nameplate and business cards, helps the newcomer feel like a member of the team. Supervisors give each new employee a picture frame with a note from the CEO encouraging

them to use it to display the important people in their lives. A career development programme gives employees opportunities to examine their personal priorities, develop their skills and discuss their career objectives. If someone wants a new job in the company that he or she is not qualified for, Vision Express sets up an individualized training programme to help bridge the gap.

Open communication is another high-level motivator. Issues are raised, debated and dealt with openly, and people have all the information they need to do their best work. CEO Bryan Magraph personally answers emails from any employee, randomly sits with employees in the company cafeteria, and holds biannual employee meetings where he shares all company information and answers any employee question on the spot. This openness is motivating to employees, who appreciate the higher responsibility and the respect and trust that it implies.

By incorporating both hygiene factors and motivators, managers at Vision Express have created an environment where people are highly motivated and want to stay.

Acquired needs theory

The final content theory was developed by David McClelland. The *acquired needs theory* proposes that certain types of needs are acquired during the individual's lifetime. In other words, people are not born with these needs but may learn them through their life experiences.[117] The three needs most frequently studied are these:

1 *Need for achievement.* The desire to accomplish something difficult, attain a high standard of success, master complex tasks and surpass others.

2 *Need for affiliation.* The desire to form close personal relationships, avoid conflict and establish warm friendships.

3 *Need for power.* The desire to influence or control others, be responsible for others and have authority over others.

Early life experiences determine whether people acquire these needs. If children are encouraged to do things for themselves and receive reinforcement, they will acquire a need to achieve. If they are reinforced for forming warm human relationships, they will develop a need for affiliation. If they get satisfaction from controlling others, they will acquire a need for power.

For more than 20 years, McClelland studied human needs and their implications for management. People with a high need for achievement are frequently entrepreneurs. The parents of social entrepreneur Bill Strickland, the charismatic leader who established Manchester Bidwell, always encouraged him to follow his dreams. When he wanted to go south to work with the Freedom Riders in the 1960s, they supported him. His plans for tearing up the family basement and making a photography studio were met with equal enthusiasm.

CONCEPT CONNECTION

According to General Electric CEO, Jeffrey Immelt, people who succeed at GE are usually those who have a strong need for achievement or need for affiliation. 'We lose people who just want to make a lot of money, or just want to be powerful. But if you like building stuff, and you like who you work with, this is a pretty energizing place to work.' Immelt is counting on those highly motivated employees as he tries to steer the multi-national conglomerate towards unprecedented growth by transforming it into a customer-driven company that thrives on innovation as well as superior productivity.

Strickland thus developed a need for *achievement* that enabled him to accomplish amazing results later in life.[118] People who have a high need for *affiliation* are successful integrators, whose job is to coordinate the work of several departments in an organization.[119] Integrators include brand managers and project managers who must have excellent people skills. People high in need for affiliation are able to establish positive working relationships with others.

A high need for *power* often is associated with successful attainment of top levels in the organizational hierarchy. For example, McClelland studied managers at AT&T for 16 years and found that those with a high need for power were more likely to follow a path of continued promotion over time. More than half of the employees at the top levels had a high need for power. In contrast, managers with a high need for achievement but a low need for power tended to peak earlier in their careers and at a lower level. The reason is that achievement needs can be met through the task itself, but power needs can be met only by ascending to a level at which a person has power over others.

In summary, content theories focus on people's underlying needs and label those particular needs that motivate behaviour. The hierarchy of needs theory, the ERG theory, the two-factor theory and the acquired needs theory all help managers understand what motivates people. In this way, managers can design work to meet needs and hence elicit appropriate and successful work behaviours.

Process perspectives on motivation

Process theories explain how people select behavioural actions to meet their needs and determine whether their choices were successful. The most popular process theory is probably equity theory.

Equity theory

Equity theory focuses on individuals' perceptions of how fairly they are treated compared with others. Developed by J. Stacy Adams, equity theory proposes that people are motivated to seek social equity in the rewards they expect for performance.[120]

According to equity theory, if people perceive their compensation as equal to what others receive for similar contributions, they will believe that their treatment is fair and equitable. People evaluate equity by a ratio of inputs to outcomes. Inputs to a job include education, experience, effort and ability. Outcomes from a job include pay, recognition, benefits and promotions. The input-to-outcome ratio may be compared to another person in the work group or to a perceived group average. A state of equity exists whenever the ratio of one person's outcomes to inputs equals the ratio of another's outcomes to inputs.

Inequity occurs when the input-to-outcome ratios are out of balance, such as when a person with a high level of education or experience receives the same salary as a new, less-educated employee. Interestingly, perceived inequity also occurs in the other direction. Thus, if an employee discovers she is making more money than other people who contribute the same inputs to the company, she may feel the need to correct the inequity by working harder, getting more education or considering lower pay. Studies of the brain have shown that people get less satisfaction from money they receive without having to earn it than they do from money they work to receive.[121] Perceived inequity creates tensions within individuals that motivate them to bring equity into balance.[122]

The most common methods for reducing a perceived inequity are these:

- *Change inputs.* A person may choose to increase or decrease his or her inputs to the organization. For example, underpaid individuals may reduce their level of effort or increase their absenteeism. Overpaid people may increase effort on the job.

- *Change outcomes.* A person may change his or her outcomes. An underpaid person may request a salary increase or a bigger office. A union may try to improve wages and working conditions in order to be consistent with a comparable union whose members make more money.

- *Distort perceptions.* Research suggests that people may distort perceptions of equity if they are unable to change inputs or outcomes. They may artificially increase the status attached to their jobs or distort others' perceived rewards to bring equity into balance.

- *Leave the job.* People who feel inequitably treated may decide to leave their jobs rather than suffer the inequity of being under- or overpaid. In their new jobs, they expect to find a more favourable balance of rewards.

The implication of equity theory for managers is that employees indeed evaluate the perceived equity of their rewards compared to others. An increase in salary or a promotion will have no motivational effect if it is perceived as inequitable relative to that of other employees.

Inequitable pay puts pressure on employees that is sometimes almost too great to bear. They attempt to change their work habits, try to change the system or leave the job.[123] Consider Deb Allen, who went into the office on a weekend to catch up on work and found a document accidentally left on the copy machine. When she saw that some new employees were earning €200 000 more than her counterparts with more experience, and that 'a noted screw-up' was making more than highly competent people, Allen began questioning why she was working on weekends for less pay than many others were receiving. Allen became so demoralized by the inequity that she left her job 3 months later.[124]

TAKE A MOMENT

As a new manager, be aware of equity feeling on your team. Don't play favourites, such as regularly praising some while overlooking others making similar contributions. Keep equity in mind when you make decisions about compensation and other rewards.

Goal-setting theory

Recall from Chapter 7 our discussion of the importance and purposes of goals. Numerous studies have shown that people are more motivated when they have specific targets or objectives to work towards.[125] You have probably noticed in your own life that you are more motivated when you have a specific goal, such as making an A on a final exam, losing 5 kilograms over the next 3 months or earning enough money during the summer to buy a used car.

Goal-setting theory, described by Edwin Locke and Gary Latham, proposes that managers can increase motivation by setting specific, challenging goals that are accepted as valid by subordinates, then helping people track their progress towards goal achievement by providing timely feedback. The four key components of goal-setting theory include the following:[126]

■ *Goal specificity* refers to the degree to which goals are concrete and unambiguous. Specific goals such as 'Visit one new customer each day', or 'Sell €1000 worth of merchandise a week' are more motivating than vague goals such as 'Keep in touch with new customers' or 'Increase merchandise sales'. The first, critical step in any pay-for-performance system is to clearly define exactly what managers want people to accomplish. Lack of clear, specific goals is a major cause of the failure of incentive plans in many organizations.[127]

■ In terms of *goal difficulty*, hard goals are more motivating than easy ones. Easy goals provide little challenge for employees and don't require them to increase their output. Highly ambitious but achievable goals ask people to stretch their abilities.

■ *Goal acceptance* means that employees have to 'buy into' the goals and be committed to them. Managers often find that having people participate in setting goals is a good way to increase acceptance and commitment. At Aluminio del Caroni, a state-owned aluminium company in south-eastern Venezuela, plant workers felt a renewed sense of commitment when top leaders implemented a *co-management* initiative that has managers and lower-level employees working together to set budgets, determine goals and make decisions. 'The managers and the workers are running this business together,' said one employee who spends his days shovelling molten aluminium down a channel from an industrial oven to a cast. 'It gives us the motivation to work hard.'[128]

■ Finally, the component of *feedback* means that people get information about how well they are doing in progressing towards goal achievement. It is important for managers to provide performance feedback on a regular, ongoing basis. However, self-feedback, where people are able to monitor their own progress towards a goal, has been found to be an even stronger motivator than external feedback.[129] Managers at Sanmina France S.A.S., which makes custom-printed circuit boards, steer employee performance towards goals by giving everyone ongoing numerical feedback about every aspect of the business. Employees are so fired up that they check the data on the intranet throughout the day as if they were checking the latest sports scores. The system enables people to track their progress towards achieving goals, such as reaching sales targets or solving customer problems within specified time limits.

Why does goal-setting increase motivation? For one thing, it enables people to focus their energies in the right direction. People know what to work towards, so they can direct their efforts towards the most important activities to accomplish the goals. Goals also energize behaviour because people feel compelled to develop plans and strategies that keep them focused on achieving the target. Specific, difficult goals provide a challenge and encourage people to put forth high levels of effort. In addition, when goals are achieved, pride and satisfaction increase, contributing to higher motivation and morale.[130]

TAKE A MOMENT

As a new manager, use specific, challenging goals to keep people focused and motivated. Have team members participate in setting goals and determining how to achieve them. Give regular feedback on how people are doing.

Reinforcement perspective on motivation

The reinforcement approach to employee motivation sidesteps the issues of employee needs and thinking processes described in the content and process theories. Reinforcement theory simply looks at the relationship between behaviour and its consequences. It focuses on changing or modifying employees' on-the-job behaviour through the appropriate use of immediate rewards and punishments.

Reinforcement tools

Behaviour modification is the name given to the set of techniques by which reinforcement theory is used to modify human behaviour.[131] The basic assumption underlying behaviour modification is the **law of effect**, which states that behaviour that is positively reinforced tends to be repeated, and behaviour that is not reinforced tends not to be repeated. **Reinforcement** is defined as anything that causes a certain behaviour to be repeated or inhibited. The four reinforcement tools are positive reinforcement, avoidance learning, punishment and extinction. Each type of reinforcement is a consequence of either a pleasant or unpleasant event being applied or withdrawn following a person's behaviour. The four types of reinforcement are summarized in Exhibit 14.13.

Positive reinforcement

Positive reinforcement is the administration of a pleasant and rewarding consequence following a desired behaviour. A good example of positive reinforcement is immediate praise for an employee who arrives on time or does a little extra work. The pleasant consequence will increase the likelihood of the excellent work behaviour occurring again. Studies have shown that positive reinforcement does help to improve performance. In addition, non-financial reinforcements such as positive feedback, social recognition and attention are just as effective as financial incentives.[132] Indeed, many people consider factors other than money to be more important. Nelson Motivation Inc. conducted a survey of 750 employees across various industries to assess the value they placed on various rewards. Cash and other monetary awards came in last. The most valued rewards involved praise and manager support and involvement.[133]

Avoidance learning

Avoidance learning is the removal of an unpleasant consequence following a desired behaviour. Avoidance learning is sometimes called *negative reinforcement*. Employees learn to do the right thing by avoiding unpleasant situations. Avoidance learning occurs when a supervisor stops criticizing or reprimanding an employee once the incorrect behaviour has stopped.

Punishment

Punishment is the imposition of unpleasant outcomes on an employee. Punishment typically occurs following undesirable behaviour. For example, a supervisor may berate an employee for performing a task incorrectly. The supervisor expects that the negative outcome will serve as a punishment and reduce the likelihood of the behaviour recurring. The use of punishment in organizations is controversial and often criticized because it fails to indicate the correct behaviour. However, almost all managers report that they find it necessary to occasionally impose forms of punishment ranging from verbal reprimands to employee suspensions or firings.[134]

 CONCEPT CONNECTION

Faranagers often use a fixed-rate reinforcement schedule by basing a fruit or vegetable picker's pay on the amount he or she harvests. A variation on this individual piece-rate system is a relative incentive plan that bases each worker's pay on the ratio of the individual's productivity to average productivity among all co-workers. A study of Eastern and Central European pickers in the UK found that workers' productivity declined under the relative plan. Researchers theorized that fast workers didn't want to hurt their slower colleagues, so they reduced their efforts. The study authors suggested a team-based scheme – where everyone's pay increased if the team did well – would be more effective.

EXHIBIT 14.13 Changing behaviour with reinforcement

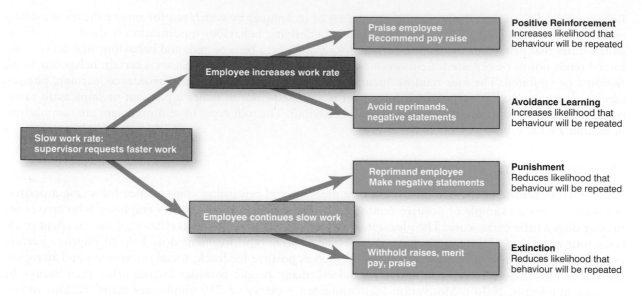

SOURCE: Richard L. Daft and Richard M. Steers, *Organizations: A Micro/Macro Approach* (Scott, Foresman Glenview, IL, 1986): 109.

Extinction

Extinction is the withdrawal of a positive reward. Whereas with punishment, the supervisor imposes an unpleasant outcome such as a reprimand, extinction involves withholding pay raises, bonuses, praise or other positive outcomes. The idea is that behaviour that is not positively reinforced will be less likely to occur in the future. For example, if a perpetually tardy employee fails to receive praise and pay raises, he or she will begin to realize that the behaviour is not producing desired outcomes. The behaviour will gradually disappear if it is continually not reinforced.

Executives can use aspects of reinforcement theory to shape employees' behaviour. Garry Ridge, CEO of WD-40 Company, which makes the popular lubricant used for everything from loosening bolts to removing scuff marks from floors, wanted to encourage people to talk about their failures so the company could learn from them. He offered prizes to anyone who would email and share their 'learning moments', and each respondent would have the chance to win an all-expenses-paid vacation. The positive reinforcement, combined with the company's 'blame-free' policy, motivated people to share ideas that have helped WD-40 keep learning and growing.[135]

Schedules of reinforcement

A great deal of research into reinforcement theory suggests that the timing of reinforcement has an impact on how quickly employees learn and respond with the desired behaviour. Schedules of reinforcement pertain to the frequency with which, and intervals over which, reinforcement occurs. A reinforcement schedule can be selected to have maximum impact on employees' job behaviour. Five basic types of reinforcement schedules include continuous and four types of partial reinforcement.

Continuous reinforcement

With a continuous reinforcement schedule, every occurrence of the desired behaviour is reinforced. This schedule can be especially effective in the early stages of learning new types of behaviour, because every attempt has a pleasant consequence. Some companies use a continuous reinforcement schedule by offering people cash, game tokens, or points that can be redeemed for prizes each time they perform the desired behaviour. Many companies are developing continuous reinforcement programmes so that employees make a clear connection between their behaviour and the desired reward.

Partial reinforcement

However, in the real world of organizations, it is often impossible to reinforce every correct behaviour. With a partial reinforcement schedule, the reinforcement is administered only after some occurrences of the correct behaviour. The four types of partial reinforcement schedules are fixed interval, fixed ratio, variable interval and variable ratio.

1 *Fixed-interval schedule.* The fixed-interval schedule rewards employees at specified time intervals. If an employee displays the correct behaviour each day, reinforcement may occur every week, for example. Regular pay cheques or quarterly bonuses are examples of fixed-interval reinforcement. At Mikael Grahn's Mini Maid franchise in Terjärv, Finland, workers are rewarded with an attendance bonus each pay period if they have gone to work every day on time and in uniform.[136]

2 *Fixed-ratio schedule.* With a fixed-ratio schedule, reinforcement occurs after a specified number of desired responses, say, after every fifth. For example, paying a field hand €2 for picking 10 pounds of peppers is a fixed-ratio schedule. Most piece-rate pay systems are considered fixed-ratio schedules.

3 *Variable-interval schedule.* With a variable-interval schedule, reinforcement is administered at random times that cannot be predicted by the employee. An example would be a random inspection by the manufacturing superintendent of the production floor, at which time he or she commends employees on their good behaviour.

4 *Variable-ratio schedule.* The variable-ratio schedule is based on a random number of desired behaviours rather than on variable time periods. Reinforcement may occur sometimes after 5, 10, 15 or 20 displays of behaviour. One example is random monitoring of telemarketers, who may be rewarded after a certain number of calls in which they perform the appropriate behaviours and meet call performance specifications. Employees know they may be monitored but are never sure when checks will occur and when rewards may be given.

The schedules of reinforcement are illustrated in Exhibit 14.14. Continuous reinforcement is most effective for establishing new learning, but behaviour is vulnerable to extinction. Partial reinforcement schedules are more effective for maintaining behaviour over extended time periods. The most powerful is the variable-ratio schedule, because employee behaviour will persist for a long time due to the random administration of reinforcement only after a long interval.[137]

EXHIBIT 14.14 Schedules of reinforcement

Schedule of reinforcement	Nature of reinforcement	Effect on behaviour when applied	Effect on behaviour when withdrawn	Example
Continuous	Reward given after each desired behaviour	Leads to fast learning of new behaviour	Rapid extinction	Praise
Fixed-interval	Reward given at fixed time intervals	Leads to average and irregular performance	Rapid extinction	Weekly pay cheque
Fixed-ratio	Reward given at fixed amounts of output	Quickly leads to very high and stable performance	Rapid extinction	Piece-rate pay system
Variable-interval	Reward given at variable times	Leads to moderately high and stable performance	Slow extinction	Performance appraisal and awards given at random times each month
Variable-ratio	Reward given at variable amounts of output	Leads to very high performance	Slow extinction	Sales bonus tied to number of sales calls, with random cheques

💡 INNOVATIVE WAY

PinnacleHealth System

Federal health regulations in the USA are carefully designed to prevent hospitals from paying doctors to economize on care. But one hospital system in Pennsylvania obtained special approval for an innovative programme.

Administrators at PinnacleHealth System wanted to make doctors cost-sensitive and reward them for saving money. So they developed an incentive plan that allows doctors to share in any money they save the hospital, which is positive reinforcement to doctors for using cost-efficient procedures or less-expensive medical devices. For example, in the past, many cardiologists at PinnacleHealth hospitals would inflate a new artery-opening balloon each time they inserted a stent into a patient's clogged arteries. Now, when possible, they use a single balloon throughout the procedure. The doctors say this poses no risk to the patient, and the simple step cuts a couple of hundred dollars per procedure, amounting to big savings over time. When they can, PinnacleHealth doctors also use stents, pacemakers and other medical devices that the hospital buys at a negotiated volume discount, rather than using more costly products. Doctors can use any device they feel is in the best interest of the patient, but incentives focus doctors on manufacturers with whom the company has low-cost supplier contracts.

It's working. Annual savings in 2004 amounted to about $1 million, with participating physicians each earning an estimated $10 000 to $15 000 from the payouts that year.[138]

PinnacleHealth System provides an excellent, though somewhat controversial, example of the successful use of reinforcement theory.

Reinforcement also works at such organizations as Campbell Soup Co., Emery Air Freight, Hallmark Consumer Services, Michigan Bell, Barrie Stephen Hair and PC World, because managers reward the desired behaviours. They tell employees what they can do to receive rewards, tell them what they are doing wrong, distribute rewards equitably, tailor rewards to behaviours and keep in mind that failure to reward deserving behaviour has an equally powerful impact on employees.

Reward and punishment motivational practices dominate organizations. According to the Society for Human Resource Management, 84 per cent of all companies in the USA offer some type of monetary or non-monetary reward system and 69 per cent offer incentive pay, such as bonuses, based on an employee's performance.[139] However, in other studies, more than 80 per cent of employers with incentive programmes have reported that their programmes are only somewhat successful or not working at all.[140] Despite the testimonies of organizations that enjoy successful incentive programmes, criticism of these 'carrot-and-stick' methods is growing.

Innovative ideas for motivating

Organizations are increasingly using various types of incentive compensation as a way to motivate employees to higher levels of performance. Exhibit 14.15 summarizes several popular methods of incentive pay.

Variable compensation and forms of 'at risk' pay are key motivational tools and are becoming more common than fixed salaries at many companies. These programmes can be effective if they are used appropriately and combined with motivational ideas that also provide employees with intrinsic rewards and meet higher-level needs. Effective managers don't use incentive plans as the sole basis of motivation. At steelmaker Nucor, for example, the amount of money employees and managers take home depends on company profits and how effective the plants are at producing defect-free steel.

Some organizations give employees a voice in how pay and incentive systems are designed, which boosts motivation by increasing people's sense of involvement and control.[141] Managers at Premium Standard Farms' pork-processing plant hired a consultant to help slaughterhouse workers design and implement an incentive programme. Annual payouts to employees in one recent year were around $1000 per employee. More important, though, is that workers feel a greater sense of dignity and purpose in their jobs, which has helped to reduce turnover significantly. As one employee put it, 'Now I have the feeling that this is my company, too.'[142] The most effective motivational programmes typically involve much more than money or other external rewards. Two recent motivational trends are empowering employees and framing work to have greater meaning.

EXHIBIT 14.15 New motivational compensation programmes

Program	Purpose
Pay for performance	Rewards individual employees in proportion to their performance contributions. Also called *merit pay*.
Gain sharing	Rewards all employees and managers within a business unit when predetermined performance targets are met. Encourages teamwork.
Employee stock ownership plan (ESOP)	Gives employees part ownership of the organization, enabling them to share in improved profit performance.
Lump-sum bonuses	Rewards employees with a one-time cash payment based on performance.
Pay for knowledge	Links employee salary with the number of task skills acquired. Workers are motivated to learn the skills for many jobs, thus increasing company flexibility and efficiency.
Flexible work schedule	*Flextime* allows workers to set their own hours. *Job sharing* allows two or more part-time workers to jointly cover one job. *Telecommuting,* sometimes called *flex-place,* allows employees to work from home or an alternative workplace.
Team-based compensation	Rewards employees for behaviour and activities that benefit the team, such as cooperation, listening and empowering others.
Lifestyle awards	Rewards employees for meeting ambitious goals with luxury items, such as high-definition televisions, tickets to big-name sporting events and exotic travel.

Empowering people to meet higher needs

One significant way managers can meet higher motivational needs is to shift power down from the top of the organization and share it with employees to enable them to achieve goals. Empowerment is power sharing, the delegation of power or authority to subordinates in an organization.[143] Increasing employee power heightens motivation for task accomplishment because people improve their own effectiveness, choosing how to do a task and using their creativity.[144] Most people come into an organization with the desire to do a good job, and empowerment releases the motivation that is already there. Research indicates that most people have a need for *self-efficacy*, which is the capacity to produce results or outcomes, to feel that they are effective.[145] By meeting this higher-level need, empowerment can provide powerful motivation.

Empowering employees involves giving them four elements that enable them to act more freely to accomplish their jobs: information, knowledge, power and rewards.[146]

1 *Employees receive information about company performance.* In companies where employees are fully empowered, all employees have access to all financial and operational information. At Reflexite Corporation, for example, which is largely owned by employees, managers sit down each month to analyze data related to operational and financial performance and then share the results with employees throughout the company. In addition to these monthly updates, employees have access to any information about the company at any time they want or need it.[147]

2 *Employees have knowledge and skills to contribute to company goals.* Companies use training programmes to help employees acquire the knowledge and skills they need to contribute to organizational performance. For example, when DMC, which makes pet supplies, gave employee teams the authority and responsibility for assembly-line shutdowns, it provided extensive training on how to diagnose and interpret line malfunctions, as well as data related to the costs of shutdown and start-up. People worked through several case studies to practice decision-making related to line shutdowns.[148]

3 *Employees have the power to make substantive decisions.* Empowered employees have the authority to directly influence work procedures and organizational performance, such as through quality circles

or self-directed work teams. At Venezuela's Aluminio del Caroní, employees participate in round table discussions and make recommendations to management regarding new equipment purchases or other operational matters. In addition, workers vote to elect managers and board members.[149] The Brazilian manufacturer Semco pushes empowerment to the limits by allowing its employees to choose what they do, how they do it, and even how they get compensated for it. Many employees set their own pay by choosing from a list of 11 different pay options, such as set salary or a combination of salary and incentives.[150]

4 *Employees are rewarded based on company performance.* Organizations that empower workers often reward them based on the results shown in the company's bottom line. For example, at Semco, in addition to employee-determined compensation, a company profit-sharing plan gives each employee an even share of 23 per cent of his or her department's profits each quarter.[151] Organizations may also use other motivational compensation programmes described in Exhibit 14.16 to tie employee efforts to company performance.

Many of today's organizations are implementing empowerment programmes, but they are empowering workers to varying degrees. At some companies, empowerment means encouraging workers' ideas while managers retain final authority for decisions; at others it means giving employees almost complete freedom and power to make decisions and exercise initiative and imagination.[152] Current methods of empowerment fall along a continuum, as illustrated in Exhibit 14.16. The continuum runs from a situation in which frontline

EXHIBIT 14.16 A continuum of empowerment

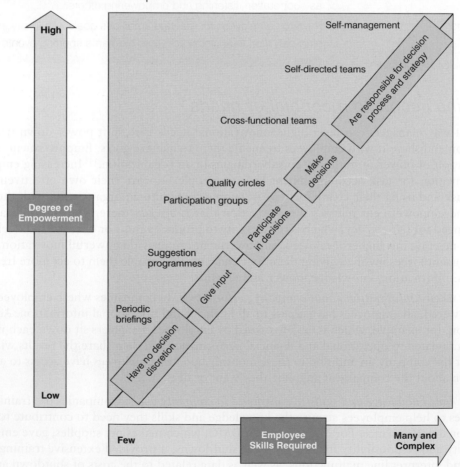

SOURCE: Robert C. Ford and Myron D. Fottler, 'Empowerment: A Matter of Degree', *Academy of Management Executive* 9, no. 3 (1995), 21–31; Lawrence Holpp, 'Applied Empowerment', *Training* (February 1994), 39–44; and David P. McCaffrey, Sue R. Faerman and David W. Hart, 'The Appeal and Difficulties of Participative Systems', *Organization Science* 6, no. 6 (November–December 1995), 603–627.

workers have almost no discretion, such as on a traditional assembly line, to full empowerment, where workers even participate in formulating organizational strategy. Studies indicate that higher-level empowerment programmes, where employees have input and decision-making power related to both everyday operational issues and higher-level strategic decisions, are still relatively rare.[153]

Giving meaning to work

Another way to meet higher-level motivational needs and help people get intrinsic rewards from their work is to instil a sense of importance and meaningfulness. *Fortune* magazine finds that one of the primary characteristics shared by companies on its annual list of 'The 100 Best Companies to Work For' is that they are *purpose-driven*, that is, people have a sense that what they are doing matters and makes a positive difference in the world.[154] Consider the motivation of employees at Swarovski.

It is easy to understand why employees at Swarovski feel they are serving an important cause. But managers in any organization can tap into people's desire to contribute and make a difference. Former Coca-Cola CEO Roberto Goizueta spent a lot of time talking to employees about the company's charitable work and emphasized that millions of small merchants could make a living because they sold Coca-Cola. Employees at FedEx take pride in getting people the items they need on time, whether it be a work report that is due, a passport for a holiday trip to Jamaica or an emergency order of medical supplies.[155]

INNOVATIVE WAY

Swarovski[156]

Since 1895, Swarovski has held true to its vision of maintaining a balance between economic success, social responsibility and stewardship of the environment. Throughout the Swarovski group, there is a strong emphasis on respect for all cultures, ethical business practice and generosity towards others. From the upper management to production, Swarovski employees take pride in living up to the axiom of the founder – 'continually improve on what is good.' This axiom, in fact, is regarded as a driving force behind the company's innovativeness, entrepreneurship and success.

In daily working lives, Swarovski stays faithful to the founder's vision by cultivating ways to improve on successes and by looking towards the future at all times. As a family-run company, Swarovski feels that sustainable growth is as important as generating profits. The latter is reinvested in the company in order to keep the future secure. All employees benefit from this sustainability.

There is another way personal growth and economic success is kept in balance at Swarovski: development. By offering employees ongoing opportunities to fine-tune and enhance existing skills and also acquire new ones, the company ensures that at the end of the day everyone has the opportunity to contribute to the company's success according to their strengths and abilities.

These opportunities are available through line managers. In addition, it is up to every employee to seek out and take advantage of the growth opportunities appropriate to them. This can take numerous forms, for instance through Swarovski Academy, where leadership and management skills are developed for all. By acting as a company-wide competence centre, Swarovski Academy builds a 'leadership culture' of shared values that employees embody in their behaviour – improving on-the-job performance. The Academy offers customized, multicultural programmes supported by preparation and a follow-up process, helps leaders develop 'their' style in accordance with company principles and core competencies, improves speakers' effectiveness and fosters a dialogue across businesses, regions and functions. There is also an opportunity for employees to sign up for in-house training, which is tailored to the needs of each region, culture and location. On top of this there are numerous external training opportunities and executive development at well-known business schools. There is a possibility for employees to be sent on international assignments that expose them to other cultures within the global Swarovski environment. The learning of the way things are done at Swarovski can also be cultivated through project assignments and general on-the-job training. Naturally, all training courses stand in relation to the personal strengths and needs that arise in a changing market environment. All these programmes have one aim at their heart – to appropriately prepare staff for this constant change.

Another example is Les Schwab Tire Centers, where employees feel like partners united towards a goal of making people's lives easier. Stores fix flat tyres for free, and some have been known to install tyres hours before opening time for an emergency trip. Employees frequently stop to help stranded motorists. Schwab rewards people with a generous profit-sharing plan for everyone and promotes store managers solely from within. However, these external rewards only supplement, not create, the high motivation employees feel.[157]

In recent years, managers have focused on employee *engagement*, which has less to do with extrinsic rewards such as pay and much more to do with fostering an environment in which people can flourish. Engaged employees are more satisfied and motivated because they feel appreciated by their supervisors and the organization, and they thrive on work challenges rather than feeling frustrated by them.[158] Engaged employees are motivated, enthusiastic and committed employees. In addition, there is a growing recognition that it is the behaviour of managers that makes the biggest difference in whether people feel engaged at work. When David A. Brandon took over as CEO of Domino's Pizza, he commissioned research to identify the factors that contributed to a store's success. What he learned was that the quality of the manager and how he or she treats employees has a much greater impact than neighbourhood demographics, packaging, marketing or other factors.[159] Indeed, a Gallup Organization study conducted over 25 years found that the single most important variable in whether employees feel good about their work is the relationship between employees and their direct supervisors.[160]

The role of today's manager is not to control others but to organize the workplace in such a way that each person can learn, contribute and grow. Good managers channel employee motivation towards the accomplishment of organizational goals by tapping into each individual's unique set of talents, skills, interests, attitudes and needs. By treating each employee as an individual, managers can put people in the right jobs and provide intrinsic rewards to every employee every day. Then, managers make sure people have what they need to perform, clearly define the desired outcomes and get out of the way.

One way to evaluate how a manager or a company is doing in engaging employees by meeting higher-level needs is a metric developed by the Gallup researchers called the Q12. When a majority of employees can answer these 12 questions positively, the organization enjoys a highly motivated and productive workforce:

1 Do I know what is expected of me at work?

2 Do I have the materials and equipment that I need in order to do my work right?

3 At work, do I have the opportunity to do what I do best every day?

4 In the past 7 days, have I received recognition or praise for doing good work?

5 Does my supervisor, or someone at work, seem to care about me as a person?

6 Is there someone at work who encourages my development?

7 At work, do my opinions seem to count?

8 Does the mission or purpose of my company make me feel that my job is important?

9 Are my co-workers committed to doing quality work?

10 Do I have a best friend at work?

11 In the past 6 months, has someone at work talked to me about my progress?

12 This past year, have I had opportunities to learn and grow?[161]

Results of the Gallup study show that organizations where employees give high marks on the Q12 have less turnover, are more productive and profitable and enjoy greater employee and customer loyalty.[162] Many companies have used the Q12 to pinpoint problems with motivation in the organization. Best Buy, for example, uses the survey and includes employee engagement as a key item on each manager's scorecard. Eric Taverna, the general manager of a Best Buy store in Manchester, Connecticut, took to heart the finding that his employees didn't think their opinions mattered. Taverna responded by implementing significant changes based on employee ideas and suggestions. The Manchester store's engagement levels improved significantly, as did the store's financial performance, while turnover has been substantially reduced.[163] When employees are more engaged and motivated, they – and their organizations – thrive.

Job design

Job design is an important consideration for motivation because productivity, job stress and quality of work life are tied to job design. Managers need to know what aspects of a job provide motivation as well as how to compensate for routine tasks that have little inherent satisfaction. Job design is the application of motivational theories to the structure of work for improving productivity and satisfaction. Approaches to job design are generally classified as job simplification, job rotation, job enlargement and job enrichment.

Job simplification

Job simplification pursues task efficiency by reducing the number of tasks one person must do. Job simplification is based on principles drawn from scientific management and industrial engineering. Tasks are designed to be simple, repetitive and standardized. As complexity is stripped from a job, the worker has more time to concentrate on doing more of the same routine task. Workers with low skill levels can perform the job, and the organization achieves a high level of efficiency. Indeed, workers are interchangeable, because they need little training or skill and exercise little judgement. As a motivational technique, however, job simplification has failed. People dislike routine and boring jobs and react in a number of negative ways, including sabotage, absenteeism and unionization. Job simplification is compared with job rotation and job enlargement in Exhibit 14.17.

Job rotation

Job rotation systematically moves employees from one job to another, thereby increasing the number of different tasks an employee performs without increasing the complexity of any one job. For example, an auto-worker might install windscreens one week and front bumpers the next. Job rotation still takes advantage of engineering efficiencies, but it provides variety and stimulation for employees.

Although employees might find the new job interesting at first, the novelty soon wears off as the repetitive work is mastered.

Companies such as B&Q, Motorola, McDonald's and KLM Royal Dutch Airline have built on the notion of job rotation to train a flexible workforce. As companies break away from ossified job categories, workers can perform several jobs, thereby reducing labour costs and giving people opportunities to develop new skills. At B&Q, for example, workers scattered throughout the company's vast chain of stores can get a taste of the corporate climate by working at in-store support centres, while associate managers can dirty their hands on the sales floor.[164] Job rotation also gives companies greater flexibility. One production worker might shift among the jobs of drill operator, punch operator and assembler, depending on the company's need at the moment. Some unions have resisted the idea, but many now go along with it, realizing that it helps the company be more competitive.[165]

EXHIBIT 14.17 Types of job design

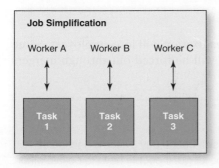
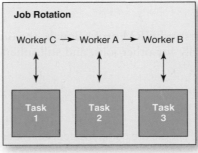
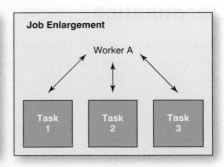

CONCEPT CONNECTION

At the Walkers Crisps plant in Leicester, UK, Julia Gardner used to just pack bags of crisps into cardboard cartons. Today, she's interviewing new employees, refusing products that don't meet quality standards and sending home excess workers if machines shut down. Hourly workers have been enjoying the benefits of job enlargement and job enrichment since Walkers Crisps introduced work teams 6 years ago. Gardner's potato chip team is responsible for everything from potato processing to equipment maintenance.

Job enlargement

Job enlargement combines a series of tasks into one new, broader job. This type of design is a response to the dissatisfaction of employees with oversimplified jobs. Instead of only one job, an employee may be responsible for three or four and will have more time to do them. Job enlargement provides job variety and a greater challenge for employees. At Tupolev PSC in Russia, jobs were enlarged when work was redesigned so that workers assembled an entire part of the plane rather than doing each part as it reached them on the assembly line. Similarly, rather than just changing the oil at a Kwik Fit location in the UK, a mechanic changes the oil, greases the car, inflates the tyres, checks fluid levels, battery, air filter, and so forth. Then the same employee is responsible for consulting with the customer about routine maintenance or any problems he or she sees with the vehicle.

Job enrichment

Recall the discussion of Maslow's need hierarchy and Herzberg's two-factor theory. Rather than just changing the number and frequency of tasks a worker performs, job enrichment incorporates high-level motivators into the work, including job responsibility, recognition and opportunities for growth, learning and achievement. In an enriched job, employees have control over the resources necessary for performing it, make decisions on how to do the work, experience personal growth and set their own work pace. Research shows that when jobs are designed to be controlled more by employees than by managers, people typically feel a greater sense of involvement, commitment and motivation, which in turn contributes to higher morale, lower turnover and stronger organizational performance.[166]

Many companies have undertaken job enrichment programmes to increase employees' involvement, motivation and job satisfaction. At La Jaboneria, a Spanish cosmetics manufacturer, for example, managers enriched jobs by combining several packing positions into a single job and cross-training employees to operate all of the packing line's equipment. In addition, assembly-line employees screen, interview and train all new employees. They are responsible for managing the production flow to and from their upstream and downstream partners, making daily decisions that affect their work, managing quality and contributing to continuous improvement. Enriched jobs have improved employee motivation and satisfaction, and the company has benefited from higher long-term productivity, reduced costs and happier, more motivated employees.[167]

Termination

Despite the best efforts of line managers and HRM professionals, the organization will lose employees. Some will retire, others will depart voluntarily for other jobs, and still others will be forced out through mergers and cutbacks or for poor performance.

TAKE A MOMENT

Even as a new manager, play a role in how people are compensated. Consider skill-based pay systems and incentive pay to encourage high performers. Don't be dismayed if some people have to be let go. If people have to be laid off or fired, do it humanely.

The value of termination for maintaining an effective workforce is two-fold. First, employees who are poor performers can be dismissed. Productive employees often resent disruptive, low-performing employees who are allowed to stay with the company and receive pay and benefits comparable to theirs. Second, employers can use exit interviews as a valuable human resource tool, regardless of whether the employee leaves voluntarily or is forced out. An exit interview is an interview conducted with departing employees to determine why they are leaving. The value of the exit interview is to provide an inexpensive way to learn about pockets of dissatisfaction within the organization and hence reduce future turnover. The oil services giant Schlumberger includes an exit interview as part of a full-scale investigation of every departure, with the results posted online so managers all around the company can get insight into problems.[168] However, in many cases, employees who leave voluntarily are reluctant to air uncomfortable complaints or discuss their real reasons for leaving. Companies such as T-Mobile, Campbell Soup and Conair found that having people complete an online exit questionnaire yields more open and honest information. When people have negative things to say about managers or the company, the online format is a chance to speak their mind without having to do it in a face-to-face meeting.[169]

For companies experiencing downsizing through mergers or because of global competition or a shifting economy, often a large number of managers and workers are terminated at the same time. In these cases, enlightened companies try to find a smooth transition for departing employees. For example, General Electric laid off employees in three gradual steps. It also set up a re-employment centre to assist employees in finding new jobs or in learning new skills. It provided counselling in how to write a résumé and conduct a job search. Additionally, GE placed an advertisement in local newspapers saying that these employees were available.[170] By showing genuine concern in helping laid-off employees, a company communicates the value of human resources and helps maintain a positive corporate culture.

DISCUSSION QUESTIONS

1   It is the year 2018. In your company, central planning has given way to frontline decision-making, and bureaucracy has given way to teamwork. Shop floor workers use handheld computers and robots extensively. A labour shortage currently affects many job openings, and the few applicants you do attract lack the required skills to work in teams, make their own production decisions or use sophisticated technology. As vice president of HRM since 2015, what should you have done to prepare for this dynamic situation? Discuss.

2   'The human resource activities of recruiting, performance appraisal and compensation should be related to corporate strategy.' Discuss this statement including viewpoints from relevant literature.

3   Discuss the 'validity' of the information obtained from a personal interview versus employment tests, and versus an assessment centre, what would be the best for predicting effective job performance for a graduate level entry manager.

4   As a human resources specialist in charge of training and development, which training option or options – such as on-the-job training, cross-training, classroom, self-directed or computer-based – would you be likely to choose for your company's production line manager? A customer service representative? An entry-level accountant?

5   Determine how you would decide whether to use a job-based, skills-based or pay-for-performance compensation plan for employees in: a textile manufacturing plant? Waiting staff in a restaurant? Salespeople in an insurance company?

6   Discuss the value that exit interviews serve for HRM.

Getting the right people on the bus[171]

INSTRUCTIONS As a new manager, how much emphasis will you give to getting the right people on your team? Find out by answering the following questions based on your expectations and beliefs for handling the people part of your management job. Please answer whether each item is 'Mostly True' or 'Mostly False' for you.

		Mostly true	Mostly false
1	I will readily fire someone who isn't working out for the interests of the organization.	☐	☐
2	Selecting the right people for a winning business team is as important to me as it is to a winning sports team.	☐	☐
3	I expect to spend 40 to 60 per cent of my management time on issues such as recruiting, developing and placing people.	☐	☐
4	I will paint a realistic picture of negative job aspects that will help scare off the wrong people for the job.	☐	☐
5	My priority as a manager is first to hire the right people, second to put people in the right positions and third to decide strategy and vision.	☐	☐
6	With the right people on my team, problems of motivation and supervision will largely go away.	☐	☐
7	I expect that hiring the right people is a lengthy and arduous process.	☐	☐
8	I view firing people as helping them find the place where they belong to find fulfilment.	☐	☐

SCORING & INTERPRETATION Most new managers are shocked at the large amount of time, effort and skill required to recruit, place and retain the right people. In recent years, the importance of 'getting the right people on the bus' has been described in popular business books such as *Good to Great (Jim Collins, Random House Business, 2001)* and *Execution (Charles Burck, Larry Bossidy and Ram Charan, Random House Business, 2011)*. The right people can make an organization great; the wrong people can be catastrophic.

Give yourself 1 point for each item you marked as 'Mostly true'. If you scored 4 or less, you may be in for a shock as a new manager. People issues will take up most of your time, and if you don't handle people correctly, your effectiveness will suffer. You should learn how to get the right people on the bus and how to get the wrong people off the bus. The faster you learn these lessons, the better a new manager you will be. A score of 5 or more suggests that you have the right understanding and expectations for becoming a manager and dealing with people on the bus.

APPLY YOUR SKILLS: ETHICAL DILEMMA

A conflict of responsibilities

As a director of human resources, Brian Schipper was asked to negotiate a severance deal with Terry Winston, the European sales manager for Network Management Systems at Cisco Systems. Winston's problems with alcohol had become severe enough to precipitate his dismissal. His customers were devoted to him, but top management was reluctant to continue gambling on his reliability. Lives depended on his work as the salesperson and installer of Network Management software. Winston had been warned twice to clean up his act, but had never succeeded. Only his unique blend of technical knowledge and high-powered sales ability had saved him before.

Now the vice president of sales asked Schipper to offer Winston the option of resigning rather than being fired if he would sign a non-compete agreement and agree to go into rehabilitation. Cisco Systems would also extend a guarantee of confidentiality on the abuse issue and a good work reference as thanks for the millions of dollars of business that Winston had brought to the company. Winston agreed to take the deal. After his departure, a series of near disasters was uncovered as a result of Winston's mismanagement. Some of his manoeuvres to cover up his mistakes bordered on fraud.

Today, Schipper received a message to call the human resource director at a distant rival company to give a personal reference on Terry Winston. From the area code, Schipper could see that he was not in violation of the non-compete agreement. He had also heard that Winston had completed a 30-day treatment programme as promised. Brian knew he was expected to honour the confidentiality agree-

ment, but he also knew that if his shady dealings had been discovered before his departure, he would have been fired without any agreement. Now he was being asked to give Winston a reference for another sales management position.

What would you do?

1 Honour the agreement, trusting Winston's rehabilitation is complete on all levels and that he is now ready for a responsible position. Give a good recommendation.

2 Contact the vice president of sales and ask him to release you from the agreement or to give the reference himself. After all, he made the agreement. You don't want to lie.

3 Without mentioning specifics, give Winston such an unenthusiastic reference that you hope the other human resources director can read between the lines and believe that Winston will be a poor choice.

APPLY YOUR SKILLS: CASE FOR CRITICAL ANALYSIS

Red Sea Waterworld

Lee Carter and her husband, Jack Schiffer, became two of Red Sea Waterworld Sports most valuable Dive Centre managers almost by accident. But now, if the snatch of conversation CEO Cyrus Maher just overheard on his way to get coffee meant what he thought it did, he was in danger of losing the very people who'd contributed most to RSWW's recent growth surge.

Cyrus had met Lee and Jack, both diving enthusiasts, when he was a PADI Instructor to Red Sea Waterworld in Taba, Egypt. Lee and Jack were doing their Dive Master course. Cyrus got on really well with them, and when they started talking it appeared that Lee had a degree in marketing, and Jack was from an engineering background. He took a liking to the young couple and offered them a nice relaxing job for 3 months in the first instance; the couple decided to stay on full-time and take a breather before launching their demanding professional careers. That was 10 years ago.

When Lee and Jack joined RSWW, they found a laid-back atmosphere. Even as the diving centre had grown steadily over the years, it continued to attract employees from all over the world who loved water sports and enjoyed the customer interaction. Employees spent time good-naturedly horsing around with each other, but they got their work done on time. In fact, on nice days, they often completed their tasks on time and then stayed at the centre to socialize with their colleagues.

In late 2003, Lee took a hard look at the slow demand for diving and the rapidly growing extreme sports market, which included wakeboarding, water-skiing and parasailing. 'Cyrus,' she asked, 'have you ever thought about extreme sports?' Intrigued, Cyrus gave Lee and Jack the go-ahead to see what they could do. Jack responded by sourcing the equipment: Malibu I-Ride wakeboard boat and a Malibu Response water-ski boat both with Indmar Monsoon 350 hp engines. The I-Ride included a Waketower, Wakewedge, Malibu Launch System (Mid-ship Ballast system) to increase the air time for the customer, These immediately found favour among the tourists looking for a way to have some fun. Lee established a formal marketing department to drive sales. That's when things really took off. Many RSWW customers placed sizable orders on extreme water sports.

Energized by their success, Cyrus, Lee, Jack (who'd recently been named Sales and Marketing department head) and other RSWW managers developed a long-range strategic plan that called for aggressive growth, a portfolio of new services and international marketing by 2010. These ambitious plans resulted in an increased workload and a faster-paced work environment. RSWW managers provided employees with across-the-board pay raises.

In Cyrus's opinion, the pay increases were more than reasonable, but lately he has heard complaints, both from the shop floor and from managers. He is dealing with compensation issues the way he always has – on a case-by-case basis. When a Dive Centre manager suggested top performers receive additional wage increases, Cyrus turned it down, contending that RSWW's wages were in line with other dive centres in Egypt. Shortly afterwards, a new Diving centre offering a slightly higher wage lured away three of RSWW's best diving instructors.

When the company's finance director threatened to leave unless his compensation package included share options, Cyrus appeased him with a pay increase and extra vacation. But Lee and Jack have been more insistent. What they feel they deserve, in view of their contribution to the company's growth, is a share in the profits too. He turned them down, and now, if he heard correctly, they are considering a lucrative job offer from a competing company.

What should Cyrus do? He sees Lee and Jack's point of view, but would the other managers understand if he granted the couple the part ownership in the company he'd denied the others? And how would the hourly workers react?

Questions

1   Does RSWW's current compensation system seem to fit the dive centre's strategy of aggressive growth and innovation? How might it be changed to achieve a better fit?

2   Specifically, how would you gather the data and design a competitive compensation system for RSWW? Would your approach be different for hourly workers versus managers? Would you treat all managers equally?

3   How might non-financial incentives play a role in helping RSWW retain their best talent? How can they help keep aggressive and ambitious professionals such as Lee and Jack?

SOURCE Robert D. Nicoson, 'Growing Pains', *Harvard Business Review* (July–August 1996): 20–36.

END NOTES

1. Results of a McKinsey Consulting survey, reported in Branham, 'Planning to Become an Employer of Choice'.
2. Robert L. Mathis and John H. Jackson, *Human Resource Management: Essential Perspectives*, 2nd ed. (Cincinnati, OH: South-Western Publishing, 2002): 1.
3. Joy Persaud, 'Game On', *People Management* (September 25, 2003): 40–41.
4. Jonathan Poet, *Schools Looking Overseas for Teachers*, (Johnson City Press, 2001): 6; and Jill Rosenfeld, 'How's This for a Tough Assignment?' *Fast Company* (November 1999): 104–106.
5. Lucy Steiner, 'Using Competency-Based Evaluation to Drive Teacher Excellence, Lessons from Singapore', Public Impact (2010).
6. See James C. Wimbush, 'Spotlight on Human Resource Management', *Business Horizons* 48 (2005): 463–467; Jonathan Tompkins, 'Strategic Human Resources Management in Government: Unresolved Issues', *Public Personnel Management* (Spring 2002): 95–110; Noel M. Tichy, Charles J. Fombrun and Mary Anne Devanna, 'Strategic Human Resource Management', *Sloan Management Review* 23 (Winter 1982): 47–61; Cynthia A. Lengnick-Hall and Mark L. Lengnick-Hall, 'Strategic Human Resources Management: A Review of the Literature and a Proposed Typology', *Academy of Management Review* 13 (July 1988): 454–470; Eugene B. McGregor, *Strategic Management of Human Knowledge, Skills, and Abilities* (San Francisco: Jossey-Bass, 1991).
7. Edward E. Lawler III, 'HR on Top', *Strategy + Business*, no. 35 (Second Quarter 2004): 21–25.
8. Tompkins, 'Strategic Human Resource Management in Government: Unresolved Issues'; and Wimbush, 'Spotlight on Human Resource Management'.
9. Mark A. Huselid, Susan E. Jackson and Randall S. Schuler, 'Technical and Strategic Human Resource Management Effectiveness as Determinants of Firm Performance', *Academy of Management Journal* 40, no. 1 (1997): 171–188; and John T. Delaney and Mark A. Huselid, 'The Impact of Human Resource Management Practices on Perceptions of Organizational Performance', *Academy of Management Journal* 39, no. 4 (1996): 949–969.
10. D. Kneale, 'Working at IBM: Intense Loyalty in a Rigid Culture', *The Wall Street Journal* (April 7, 1986): 17.
11. Jeffrey Pfeffer, 'Producing Sustainable Competitive Advantage Through the Effective Management of People', *Academy of Management Executive* 9, no. 1 (1995): 55–72; and Harry Scarbrough, 'Recipe for Success', *People Management* (January 23, 2003): 32–25.
12. James N. Baron and David M. Kreps, 'Consistent Human Resource Practices', *California Management Review* 41, no. 3 (Spring 1999): 29–53.

13. Stone, R., *Managing Human Resources* ,4th ed. (John Wiley & Sons, Milton, 2013): p.30.

14. Tony Hsieh, 'How Zappos Infuses Culture Using Core Values', *Harvard Business Review* (2010). https://hbr.org/2010/05/how-zappos-infuses-culture-using-core-values.

15. Cynthia D. Fisher, 'Current and Recurrent Challenges in HRM', *Journal of Management* 15 (1989): 157–180.

16. Rich Wellins and Sheila Rioux, 'The Growing Pains of Globalizing HR', *Training and Development* (May 2000): 79–85.

17. Ibid.

18. Helen DeCieri, Julie Wolfram Cox and Marilyn S. Fenwick, 'Think Global, Act Local: From Naive Comparison to Critical Participation in the Teaching of Strategic International Human Resource Management', *Tamara: Journal of Critical Postmodern Organization Science* 1, no. 1 (2001): 68; S. Taylor, S. Beecher and N. Napier, 'Towards an Integrative Model of Strategic Human Resource Management', *Academy of Management Review* 21 (1996): 959–985; Mary Ann Von Glinow, Ellen A. Drost and Mary B. Teagarden, 'Converging on IHRM Best Practices: Lessons Learned from a Globally Distributed Consortium on Theory and Practice', *Human Resource Management* 41, no. 1 (Spring 2002): 123–140.

19. M. Von Glinow, E. Drost and M. Teagarden, 'Converging on IHRM Best Practices'; and Jennifer J. Laabs, 'Must-Have Global HR Competencies', *Workforce* 4, no. 2 (1999): 30–32.

20. Ferner, A. 'Country of origin effects and HRM in multinational companies', *Human Resource Management Journal*, 7, no.1 (1997): 19–37.

21. DeVos, T., *US Multinationals and Worker Participation in Management. The American Experience in the European Community*, London: Aldwych (1981).

22. Innes, E. and Morris, J. 'Multinational corporations and employee relations: Continuity and change in a mature industrial region', *Employee Relations,* 17, no.6 (1995): 25–42.

23. Kostova, T. and Roth, K. 'Adoption of an organisational practice by subsidiaries of multinational corporations: institutional and relational effects', *Academy of Management Journal*, 45, no.1 (2002): 215–233.

24. Kostova, T. and Zaheer, S. 'Organisational legitimacy under conditions of complexity: the case of the multinational enterprise', *Academy of Management Review*, 24, no.1 (1999): 64–81.

25. Vo, N. T. 'Localization or globalization? The case of Japanese multinational companies in Vietnam'. In APROS 12 Colloquium; Asia-Pacific Researchers in Organization Studies (APROS): Gurgaon, India (2007): 15.

26. Ivancevich, J. M., *Human Resource Management: Foundations of Personnel*, 8th edn, Homewood: Irwin, p. 156.

27. Nanette Byrnes, 'Star Search', *BusinessWeek* (October 10, 2005): 68–78.

28. This discussion is based on Mathis and Jackson, *Human Resource Management*, Chapter 4, 49–60.

29. Dennis J. Kravetz, *The Human Resources Revolution* (San Francisco: Jossey-Bass, 1989).

30. David E. Ripley, 'How to Determine Future Workforce Needs', *Personnel Journal* (January 1995): 83–89.

31. Ted Hoff, interviewed by Ryan Underwood, in 'Fast Talk: Now Hiring', *Fast Company* (May 2004): 57–64.

32. Ibid.

33. J. W. Boudreau and S. L. Rynes, 'Role of Recruitment in Staffing Utility Analysis', *Journal of Applied Psychology* 70 (1985): 354–366.

34. Megan Santosus, 'The Human Capital Factor', *CFO-IT* (Fall 2005): 26–27.

35. Brian Dumaine, 'The New Art of Hiring Smart', *Fortune* (August 17, 1987): 78–81.

36. Swaroff, P.G., Barclay, L.A. and Bass, A.R. 'Recruiting sources: another look', *Journal of Applied Psychology*, 70(4): 720–8.

37. Victoria Griffith, 'When Only Internal Expertise Will Do', *CFO* (October 1998): 95–96, 102.

38. Samuel Greengard, 'Technology Finally Advances HR', *Workforce* (January 2000): 38–41; and Scott Hays, 'Hiring on the Web', *Workforce* (August 1999): 77–84.

39. Jessica Mintz, 'Online Tools Aid Job Recruiters in Search of "Passise" Prospects', *The Wall Street Journal* (July 12, 2005): B6.

40. Trusov, M., Bucklin, R. E. and Pauwels, K. 'Effects of word-of-mouth versus traditional marketing: Findings from an internet social networking site', *Journal of Marketing* (September 2009):73, 90–102.

41. Ralf Caers and Vanessa Castelyns 'LinkedIn and Facebook in Belgium: The Influences and Biases of Social Network Sites in Recruitment and Selection Procedures', *Social Science Computer Review* (November 2011), 29 no. 4: 437–448.

42. Kathryn Tyler, 'Employees Can Help Recruit New Talent', *HR Magazine* (September 1996): 57–60.

43. Ron Stodghill, 'Soul on Ice', *FSB* (October 2005):129–134.

44. Ann Harrington, 'Anybody Here Want a Job'? *Fortune* (May 15, 2000): 489–498.

45. Milt Freudenheim, 'More Help Wanted: Older Workers Please Apply', *The New York Times* (March 23, 2005), http://www.nytimes.com.

46. 'Bank of America to Hire 850 Ex-Welfare Recipients', *Johnson City Press* (January 14, 2001): 29; E. Blacharczyk, 'Recruiters Challenged by Economy, Shortages, Unskilled', *HR News* (February 1990): B1; Victoria Rivkin, 'Visa Relief', *Working Woman* (January 2001): 15.

47. Charles A. O'Reilly III, Jennifer Chatman and David F. Caldwell, 'People and Organizational Culture: A Profile Comparison Approach to Assessing Person-Organization Fit', *Academy of Management Journal* 34, no. 3 (1991): 487–516.

48. Anna Muoio, 'Should I Go.Com?' *Fast Company* (July 2000): 164–172.

49. Leder, 'Is That Your Final Answer'?

50. Dogs at the Office – Good for Dogs, People and Business (online) available from http://www.bigpawsonly.com/dogblog/dogs-at-the-office-good-for-dogs-people-and-business (accessed November 15, 2008).

51. Wimbush, 'Spotlight on Human Resource Management'.

52. P. W. Thayer, 'Somethings Old, Somethings New', *Personnel Psychology* 30 (1977): 513–524.

53. J. Ledvinka, *Federal Regulation of Personnel and Human Resource Management* (Boston: Kent, 1982); and Civil Rights Act, Title VII, 42 U.S.C. Section 2000e *et seq.* (1964).

54. Studies reported in William Poundstone, 'Impossible Questions', *Across the Board* (September–October 2003): 44–48.

55. Anne S. Tsui and Joshua B. Wu, 'The New Employment Relationship Versus the Mutual Investment Approach: Im-

plications for Human Resource Management', *Human Resource Management* 44, no. 2 (Summer 2005): 115– 121.

56. Bohlander, Snell and Sherman, *Managing Human Resources*, 202.

57. Powers, 'Finding Workers Who Fit'.

58. Bohlander, Snell and Sherman, *Managing Human Resources*.

59. Psychometric Success online available from http:// www. psychometric-success.com/index.htm, (accessed on November 29, 2008).

60. 'Assessment Centers: Identifying Leadership through Testing', *Small Business Report* (June 1987): 22–24; and W. C. Byham, 'Assessment Centers for Spotting Future Managers', *Harvard Business Review* (July–August 1970): 150–167.

61. Mike Thatcher, '"Front-line" Staff Selected by Assessment Center', *Personnel Management* (November 1993): 83.

62. See J. M. Digman, 'Personality Structure: Emergence of the Five-Factor Model', *Annual Review of Psychology* 41 (1990): 417–440; M. R. Barrick and M. K. Mount, 'Autonomy as a Moderator of the Relationships Between the Big Five Personality Dimensions and Job Performance', *Journal of Applied Psychology* (February 1993): 111–118; and J. S. Wiggins and A. L. Pincus, 'Personality: Structure and Assessment', *Annual Review of Psychology* 43 (1992): 473–504.

63. Del Jones, 'Not All Successful CEOs Are Extroverts', *USA Today* (June 6, 2006), http://www.usatoday.com.

64. Joseph Nocera, 'In Business, Tough Guys Finish Last', *The New York Times* (June 18, 2005): C1; Carol Hymowitz, 'Rewarding Competitors Over Collaborators No Longer Makes Sense', *The Wall Street Journal* (February 13, 2006): B1.

65. Tim Sanders, *The Likeability Factor: How to Boost Your L-Factor and Achieve the Life of Your Dreams* (New York: Crown, 2005).

66. Lisa Takeuchi Cullen, 'SATs for J-O-B-S', *Time* (April 3, 2006): 89.

67. Michelle Leder, 'Is That Your Final Answer?', *Working Woman* (December–January 2001): 18; 'Can You Pass the Job Test'? *Newsweek* (May 5, 1986): 46–51.

68. Alan Farnham, 'Are You Smart Enough to Keep Your Job?', *Fortune* (January 15, 1996): 34–47.

69. Cora Daniels, 'Does This Man Need a Shrink?', *Fortune* (February 5, 2001): 205–208.

70. Julie Bennett, 'Franchising: Do You Have What It Takes?', *The Wall Street Journal* (September 19, 2005): R11.

71. Spillane, R. and Martin, J. *Personality and Performance* (Sydney: UNSW Press) (2005) p. 254.

72. Mello, J.A. (1996) Personality tests and privacy rights, *HR Focus* (March): 22–3.

73. Bernard Keys and Joseph Wolfe, 'Management Education and Development: Current Issues and Emerging Trends', *Journal of Management* 14 (1988): 205–229.

74. '2005 Industry Report', *Training* (December 2005): 14– 28; 'Pinpointing Inside Up-and-Comers', sidebar in Nanette Byrnes, 'Star Search', *BusinessWeek* (October 10, 2005): 68–78.

75. William J. Rothwell and H. C. Kazanas, Improving On-the-Job Training: How to Establish and Operate a Comprehensive OJT Program (San Francisco: Jossey-Bass, 1994).

76. '2005 Industry Report'.

77. Doug Bartholomew, 'Taking the E-Train', *Industry Week* (June 2005): 34–37.

78. Jeanne C. Meister, 'The Brave New World of Corporate Education'. *The Chronicle of Higher Education* (February

79. 9, 2001): B10; and Meryl Davids Landau, 'Corporate Universities Crack Open Their Doors', *The Journal of Business Strategy* (May–June 2000): 18–23.

79. Meister, 'The Brave New World of Corporate Education'; Edward E. Gordon, 'Bridging the Gap', *Training* (September 2003): 30; and John Byrne, 'The Search for the Young and Gifted', *BusinessWeek* (October 4, 1999): 108–116.

80. Bartholomew, 'Taking the E-Train'; Joel Schettler, 'Defense Acquisition University: Weapons of Mass Instruction', *Training* (February 2003): 20–27.

81. Charles F. Falk and Kathleen A. Carlson, 'Newer Patterns in Management for the Post=Social Contract Era', *Midwest Management Society Proceedings* (1995): 45–52.

82. Scott Leibs, 'Building a Better Workforce', *CFO-IT* (Fall 2005): 20–27; and Charles Forelle, 'IBM Tool Dispatches Employees Efficiently', *The Wall Street Journal* (July 14, 2005).

83. 'Pinpointing Inside Up-and-Comers'; and Forelle, 'IBM Tool Dispatches Employees Efficiently'.

84. Roger Schwarz, 'The "Sandwich Approach" Undermines Your Feedback', *Harvard Business Review*, (April 19, 2013). https://hbr.org/2013/04/the-sandwich-approach-undermin/

85. Walter W. Tornow, 'Editor's Note: Introduction to Special Issue on 360-Degree Feedback', *Human Resource Management* 32, no. 2–3 (Summer–Fall 1993): 211–219; and Brian O'Reilly, '360 Feedback Can Change Your Life', *Fortune* (October 17, 1994): 93–100.

86. This discussion is based on Dick Grote, 'Forced Ranking: Behind the Scenes', *Across the Board* (November–December 2002): 40–45; Matthew Boyle, 'Performance Reviews: Perilous Curves Ahead', *Fortune* (May 28, 2001): 187– 188; Carol Hymowitz, 'Ranking Systems Gain Popularity But Have Many Staffers Riled', *The Wall Street Journal* (May 15, 2001): B1; and Frieswick, 'Truth & Consequences'.

87. Dick Grote, *Forced Ranking: Making Performance Management Work* (Boston: Harvard Business School Press, 2005); Jena McGregor, 'The Struggle to Measure Performance', *BusinessWeek* (January 9, 2006): 26–28.

88. Hymowitz, 'Ranking Systems Gain Popularity'; and Boyle, 'Performance Reviews'.

89. Reported in McGregor, 'The Struggle to Measure Performance'.

90. Ibid.

91. V. R. Buzzotta, 'Improve Your Performance Appraisals', *Management Review* (August 1988): 40–43; and H. J. Bernardin and R. W. Beatty, *Performance Appraisal: Assessing Human Behaviour at Work* (Boston: Kent, 1984).

92. Ibid.

93. Sainsbury's online available from www.sainsburys.co.uk (accessed on November 25, 2008)

94. Richard I. Henderson, *Compensation Management: Rewarding Performance*, 4th ed. (Reston, VA: Reston, 1985).

95. L. R. Gomez-Mejia, 'Structure and Process Diversification, Compensation Strategy, and Firm Performance', *Strategic Management Journal* 13 (1992): 381–397; and E. Monte-Mayor, 'Congruence Between Pay Policy and Competitive Strategy in High-Performing Firms', *Journal of Management* 22, no. 6 (1996): 889–908.

96. Renée F. Broderick and George T. Milkovich, 'Pay Planning, Organization Strategy, Structure and "Fit": A Prescriptive Model of Pay', paper presented at the 45th Annual Meeting of the Academy of Management, San Diego (August 1985).

97. E. F. Lawler, III, *Strategic Pay: Aligning Organizational Strategies and Pay Systems* (San Francisco: Jossey-Bass, 1990); and R. J. Greene, 'Person-Focused Pay: Should It Replace Job-Based Pay'? *Compensation and Benefits Management* 9, no. 4 (1993): 46–55.

98. L. Wiener, 'No New Skills? No Raise', *US News and World Report* (October 26, 1992): 78.

99. Data from Hewitt Associates, Bureau of Labor Statistics, reported in Michelle Conlin and Peter Coy, with Ann Therese Palmer and Gabrielle Saveri, 'The Wild New Workforce', *BusinessWeek* (December 6, 1999): 39–44.

100. Brian Friel, 'The Rating Game', *Government Executive* (August 2003): 46–52.

101. *Employee Benefits*, (Washington, DC: US Chamber of Commerce, 1997): 7.

102. Jay Greene, 'Troubling Exits at Microsoft', *BusinessWeek* (September 26, 2005): 98–108.

103. Frank E. Kuzmits, 'Communicating Benefits: A Double-Click Away', *Compensation and Benefits Review* 30, no. 5 (September–October 1998): 60–64; and Lynn Asinof, 'Click and Shift: Workers Control Their Benefits Online', *The Wall Street Journal* (November 27, 1997): C1.

104. Robert S. Catapano-Friedman, 'Cafeteria Plans: New Menu for the '90s', *Management Review* (November 1991): 25–29.

105. Richard M. Steers and Lyman W. Porter, eds, *Motivation and Work Behavior,* 3rd ed. (New York: McGraw-Hill, 1983); Don Hellriegel, John W. Slocum, Jr. and Richard W. Woodman, *Organizational Behavior,* 7th ed. (St. Paul, MN: West, 1995): 170; and Jerry L. Gray and Frederick A. Starke, *Organizational Behavior: Concepts and Applications,* 4th ed. (New York: Macmillan, 1988): 104–105.

106. Abraham F. Maslow, 'A Theory of Human Motivation', *Psychological Review* 50 (1943): 370–396.

107. Sarah Pass, 'On the Line', *People Management* (September 15, 2005).

108. Clayton Alderfer, *Existence, Relatedness, and Growth* (New York: Free Press, 1972).

109. Robert Levering and Milton Moskowitz, '2004 Special Report: The 100 Best Companies To Work For', *Fortune* (January 12, 2004): 56–78.

110. Jena McGregor, 'Employee Innovator; Winner: USAA', *Fast Company* (October 2005): 57.

111. Jeff Barbian, 'C'mon, Get Happy', *Training* (January 2001): 92–96.

112. Karol Rose, 'Work-Life Effectiveness', *Fortune* (September 29, 2003): S1–S17.

113. W. Glaser, *The Control Theory Manager* (New York: Harper-Business, 1994); and John W. Newstrom, 'Making Work Fun: An Important Role for Managers', *SAM Advanced Management Journal* (Winter 2002): 4–8, 21.

114. Newstrom, 'Making Work Fun'.

115. Frederick Herzberg, 'One More Time: How Do You Motivate Employees?', *Harvard Business Review* (January 2003): 87–96.

116. 'Vision Express appoints CEO', online available from http://www.opticianonline.net/Articles/2007/11/16/19855/Vision+Express+appoints+CEO.html (accessed November 2008); 'Vision Express sets sights on franchising', *Small Business,* online available from http://www.smallbusiness.co.uk/channels/start-a-business/news/22294/vision-express-sets-sights-on-franchising.thtml (accessed November 2008).

117. David C. McClelland, *Human Motivation* (Glenview, IL: Scott, Foresman, 1985).

118. John Brant, 'What One Man Can Do', *Inc.* (September 2005): 145–153.

119. David C. McClelland, 'The Two Faces of Power', in *Organizational Psychology,* ed. D. A. Colb, I. M. Rubin and J. M. McIntyre (Englewood Cliffs, NJ: Prentice Hall, 1971): 73–86.

120. J. Stacy Adams, 'Injustice in Social Exchange', in *Advances in Experimental Social Psychology,* 2d ed., ed. L. Berkowitz (New York: Academic Press, 1965); and J. Stacy Adams, 'Toward an Understanding of Inequity', *Journal of Abnormal and Social Psychology* (November 1963): 422–436.

121. 'Study: The Brain Prefers Working Over Getting Money for Nothing', *TheJournalNews.com* (May 14, 2004), www.thejournalnews.com/apps/pbcs.dll/frontpage.

122. Ray V. Montagno, 'The Effects of Comparison to Others and Primary Experience on Responses to Task Design', *Academy of Management Journal* 28 (1985): 491–498; and Robert P. Vecchio, 'Predicting Worker Performance in Inequitable Settings', *Academy of Management Review* 7 (1982): 103–110.

123. James E. Martin and Melanie M. Peterson, 'Two-Tier Wage Structures: Implications for Equity Theory', *Academy of Management Journal* 30 (1987): 297–315.

124. Jared Sandberg, 'Why You May Regret Looking at Papers Left on the Office Copier', *The Wall Street Journal* (June 20, 2006): B1.

125. See Edwin A. Locke and Gary P. Latham, 'Building a Practically Useful Theory of Goal Setting and Task Motivation: A 35-Year Odyssey', *The American Psychologist* 57, no. 9 (September 2002): 705+; Gary P. Latham and Edwin A. Locke, 'Self-Regulation through Goal Setting', *Organizational Behavior and Human Decision Processes* 50, no. 2 (1991): 212+; G. P. Latham and G. H. Seijts, 'The Effects of Proximal and Distal Goals on Performance of a Moderately Complex Task', *Journal of Organizational Behavior* 20, no. 4 (1999): 421+; P. C. Early, T. Connolly and G. Ekegren, 'Goals, Strategy Development, and Task Performance: Some Limits on the Efficacy of Goal Setting', *Journal of Applied Psychology* 74 (1989): 24–33; E. A. Locke, 'Toward a Theory of Task Motivation and Incentives', *Organizational Behavior and Human Performance* 3 (1968): 157–189; Gerard H. Seijts, Ree M. Meertens and Gerjo Kok, 'The Effects of Task Importance and Publicness on the Relation Between Goal Difficulty and Performance', *Canadian Journal of Behavioural Science* 29, no. 1 (1997): 54+.

126. Locke and Latham, 'Building a Practically Useful Theory of Goal Setting and Task Motivation'.

127. Edwin A. Locke, 'Linking Goals to Monetary Incentives', *Academy of Management Executive* 18, no. 4 (2005): 130–133.

128. Brian Ellsworth, 'Making a Place for Blue Collars in the Boardroom', *The New York Times* (August 3, 2005), www.nytimes.com.

129. J. M. Ivancevich and J. T. McMahon, 'The Effects of Goal Setting, External Feedback, and Self-Generated Feedback on Outcome Variables: A Field Experiment', *Academy of Management Journal* (June 1982): 359+; G. P. Latham and E. A. Locke, 'Self-Regulation Through Goal Setting', *Organizational Behavior and Human Decision Processes* 50, no. 2 (1991): 212+.

130. Gary P. Latham, 'The Motivational Benefits of Goal-Setting', *Academy of Management Executive* 18, no. 4 (2004): 126–129.

131. Alexander D. Stajkovic and Fred Luthans, 'A Meta-Analysis of the Effects of Organizational Behavior Modification on Task Performance, 1975–95', *Academy of Management Journal* (October 1997): 1122–1149; H. Richlin, *Modern Behaviorism* (San

Francisco: Freeman, 1970); and B. F. Skinner, *Science and Human Behavior* (New York: Macmillan, 1953).

132. Stajkovic and Luthans, 'A Meta-Analysis of the Effects of Organizational Behavior Modification on Task Performance, 1975–95', and Fred Luthans and Alexander D. Stajkovic, 'Reinforce for Performance: The Need to Go Beyond Pay and Even Rewards', *Academy of Management Executive* 13, no. 2 (1999): 49–57.

133. Reported in Charlotte Garvey, 'Meaningful Tokens of Appreciation', *HR Magazine* (August 2004): 101–105.

134. Kenneth D. Butterfield and Linda Klebe Treviño, 'Punishment from the Manager's Perspective: A Grounded Investigation and Inductive Model', *Academy of Management Journal* 39, no. 6 (December 1996): 1479–1512; and Andrea Casey, 'Voices from the Firing Line: Managers Discuss Punishment in the Workplace', *Academy of Management Executive* 11, no. 3 (1997): 93–94.

135. Gwendolyn Bounds, 'Boss Talk: No More Squeaking By – WD-40 CEO Garry Ridge Repackages a Core Product', *The Wall Street Journal* (May 23, 2006): B1.

136. Roberta Maynard, 'How to Motivate Low-Wage Workers', *Nation's Business* (May 1997): 35–39.

137. L. M. Sarri and G. P. Latham, 'Employee Reaction to Continuous and Variable Ratio Reinforcement Schedules Involving a Monetary Incentive', *Journal of Applied Psychology* 67 (1982): 506–508; and R. D. Pritchard, J. Hollenback and P. J. DeLeo, 'The Effects of Continuous and Partial Schedules of Reinforcement on Effort, Performance, and Satisfaction', *Organizational Behavior and Human Performance* 25 (1980): 336–353.

138. Reed Abelson, 'To Fight Rising Costs, Hospitals Seek Allies in the Operating Room', *The New York Times* (November 18, 2005), www.nytimes.com.

139. Amy Joyce, 'The Bonus Question; Some Managers Still Strive to Reward Merit', *The Washington Post* (November 13, 2005): F6.

140. Survey results from World at Work and Hewitt Associates, reported in Karen Kroll, 'Benefits: Paying for Performance', *Inc.* (November 2004): 46; and Kathy Chu, 'Firms Report Lackluster Results from Pay-for-Performance Plans', *The Wall Street Journal* (June 15, 2004): D2.

141. Ann Podolske, 'Giving Employees a Voice in Pay Structures', *Business Ethics* (March–April 1998): 12.

142. Rekha Balu, 'Bonuses Aren't Just for the Bosses', *Fast Company* (December 2000): 74–76.

143. Edwin P. Hollander and Lynn R. Offermann, 'Power and Leadership in Organizations', *American Psychologist* 45 (February 1990): 179–189.

144. Jay A. Conger and Rabindra N. Kanungo, 'The Empowerment Process: Integrating Theory and Practice', *Academy of Management Review* 13 (1988): 471–482.

145. *Ibid.*

146. David E. Bowen and Edward E. Lawler III, 'The Empowerment of Service Workers: What, Why, How, and When', *Sloan Management Review* (Spring 1992): 31–39; and Ray W. Coye and James A. Belohav, 'An Exploratory Analysis of Employee Participation', *Group and Organization Management* 20, no. 1, (March 1995): 4–17

147. William C. Taylor, 'Under New Management; These Workers Act Like Owners (Because They Are)', *The New York Times* (May 21, 2006), www.nytimes.com.

148. Russ Forrester, 'Empowerment: Rejuvenating a Potent Idea', *Academy of Management Executive* 14, no. 3 (2000): 67–80.

149. Ellsworth, 'Making a Place for Blue Collars in the Boardroom'.

150. Ricardo Semler, 'How We Went Digital Without a Strategy', *Harvard Business Review* (September–October 2000): 51–58.

151. Podolske, 'Giving Employees a Voice in Pay Structures'.

152. This discussion is based on Robert C. Ford and Myron D. Fottler, 'Empowerment: A Matter of Degree', *Academy of Management Executive* 9, no. 3 (1995): 21–31.

153. Bruce E. Kaufman, 'High-Level Employee Involvement at Delta Air Lines', *Human Resource Management* 42, no. 2 (Summer 2003): 175–190.

154. Geoff Colvin, 'The 100 Best Companies to Work For'.

155. Colvin, 'The 100 Best Companies to Work For'; Levering and Moskowitz, 'And the Winners Are …'; and Daniel Roth, 'Trading Places', *Fortune* (January 23, 2006): 120–128.

156. Adapted from Swarovski Sparkles online available from http:// www.swarovskisparkles.com/fashion/armani/n-189. html#docs acceded on November 2008; Svarovski Cristall – The Story online available from http://www.swarovski. com/is-bin/INTERSHOP.enfinity/WFS/SCO-Web_GB-Site/ en_US/-/GBP/SPAG_TheStory-ViewPage?origin=landing (accessed on November 2008).

157. Cheryl Dahle, 'Four Tires, Free Beef', *Fast Company* (September 2003): 36.

158. Jerry Krueger and Emily Killham, 'At Work, Feeling Good Matters', *Gallup Management Journal* (December 8, 2005).

159. Erin White, 'New Recipe; To Keep Employees, Domino's Decides It's Not All About Pay', *The Wall Street Journal* (February 17, 2005): A1, A9.

160. This discussion is based on Tony Schwartz, 'The Greatest Sources of Satisfaction in the Workplace are Internal and Emotional', *Fast Company* (November 2000): 398–402; Marcus Buckingham and Curt Coffman, *First, Break All the Rules: What the World's Greatest Managers Do Differently* (New York: Simon and Schuster, 1999); and Krueger and Killham, 'At Work, Feeling Good Matters'.

161. This discussion is based on Tony Schwartz, 'The Greatest Sources of Satisfaction in the Workplace are Internal and Emotional', *Fast Company* (November 2000): 398–402; Marcus Buckingham and Curt Coffman, *First, Break All the Rules: What the World's Greatest Managers Do Differently* (New York: Simon and Schuster, 1999); and Krueger and Killham, 'At Work, Feeling Good Matters'.

162. Curt Coffman and Gabriel Gonzalez-Molina, *Follow This Path: How the World's Greatest Organizations Drive Growth by Unleashing Human Potential* (New York: Warner Books, 2002), as reported in Anne Fisher, 'Why Passion Pays', *FSB* (September 2002): 58.

163. Rodd Wagner, "One Store, One Team' at Best Buy', *Gallup Management Journal* (August 12, 2004).

164. Barbian, 'C'mon, Get Happy'.

165. Norm Alster, 'What Flexible Workers Can Do', *Fortune* (February 13, 1989): 62–66.

166. Christine M. Riordan, Robert J. Vandenberg and Hettie A. Richardson, 'Employee Involvement Climate and Organizational Effectiveness', *Human Resource Management* 44, no. 4 (Winter 2005): 471–488.

167. Glenn L. Dalton, 'The Collective Stretch', *Management Review* (December 1998): 54–59.

168. Byrnes, 'Star Search'.

169. Mike Brewster, 'No Exit', *Fast Company* (April 2005): 93.

170. Yvette Debow, 'GE: Easing the Pain of Layoffs', *Management Review* (September 1997): 15–18.

171. Based on ideas presented in Jim Collins, *Good to Great: Why Some Companies Make the Leap … and Others Don't* (New York: Harper Business, 2001).

CHAPTER 15

MANAGING COMMUNICATION

LEARNING OBJECTIVES

After studying this chapter, you should be able to:

1 Explain why communication is essential for effective management, and appreciate the scope for misunderstanding.

2 Describe how an open communication climate and the choice of a communication channel influence the quality of communication.

3 Understand how communicating with candour, asking questions, listening and non-verbal communication affect communication between a manager and employee.

4 Explain the difference between formal and informal organizational communications.

5 Appreciate the role of personal communication channels, including the grapevine, in enhancing organizational communication.

6 Recognize the manager's role in using social media to improve organizational communication.

7 Explain strategies for managing communication during a crisis.

Nick Chen loved his job as a software engineer designing programs for mobile phones. The work was rewarding, the pay was good and the working conditions were excellent. 'The best part of being a software engineer,' said Nick, 'is working with a team of professionals who are excited about finding the next breakthrough in mobile technology.' Nick's team had recently designed a chipset that would revolutionize the way people communicate with their mobile phones. Nick's managers recognized his contributions with a year-end bonus, so he was feeling confident about his future with the company. However, Nick had become eager for more responsibility, so he began looking for a management position. During his 1-hour commute to work every morning, he used LinkedIn to strengthen his professional network and explore job openings in the mobile technology industry. As one morning while updating his profile, Nick got a message from a former colleague who had recently taken a position at Qualcomm in San Diego. She recommended that Nick apply for a new position as product manager for the Android smartphone. Eager to learn more, Nick started following Qualcomm as one of the company's 54 000 LinkedIn followers in 2012. He learned Qualcomm had earned a strong reputation as a great place to work and had been named in *Fortune* magazine's list of '100 Best Companies to Work For' 14 years in a row. Nick quickly updated his resume and applied for the position.[1]

Personal networking, enhanced through social and professional networking sites such as LinkedIn, is an important skill for managers because it enables them to interact with professionals more effectively and make better progress than they could do in isolation. Networking builds social, work and career relationships that can facilitate mutual and reciprocal benefits. How do managers build a personal network that includes a broad range of professional and social relationships? One important skill is to know how to communicate most effectively. In fact, communication is a vital factor in every aspect of the manager's job. This includes for some top executives public speaking and dealing with media attention, such as the Lufthansa executives in March 2015 when one of their pilots deliberately crashed a Germanwings flight in the French Alps on its way to Dusseldorf from Barcelona. This is an example of crisis management which we will deal with in a later section of this chapter.

The most successful organizations are the ones whose managers keep the lines of communication fully open. They must have the courage to talk to employees about what they want to hear and to explain difficult decisions, especially during tough economic times. In fact, one longitudinal study shows that companies with highly effective communication had 47 per cent higher total returns to shareholders between 2004 and 2009, compared to companies with less effective communication practices.[2]

Not only does effective communication lead to better bottom-line results, but also much of a manager's time is spent communicating.

This chapter explains why managers should make effective communication a high priority. First, we examine communication as a crucial part of the manager's job and describe a model of the communication process. Second, we consider how the interpersonal aspects of communication, including open communication climates, communication channels, persuasion, communicating with candour, asking questions and listening, affect managers' ability to communicate. Third, we look at the organization holistically and consider formal upwards, downwards and horizontal communications and filtering noise. Fourth, we address maintaining personal networks and utilizing informal communication channels. Finally, we describe the manager's role in using social media to enhance internal and external organizational communication and developing strategies to manage crisis management communication.

CONCEPT CONNECTION

Michael Newcombe climbed the corporate ladder of the prestigious Four Seasons Hotel chain successfully, due to his exceptional management capabilities, including his **communication skills**. Newcombe firmly believes in routinely talking with all his workers at all levels in order to understand their changing needs and to prevent problems before they occur. His personal interest shown in every employee also makes them feel invested as individuals valued in the organization.

Communication is the manager's overarching role

Exhibit 15.1 illustrates the crucial role of managers as critical agents of communication. Managers

EXHIBIT 15.1 The manager as a champion of communication

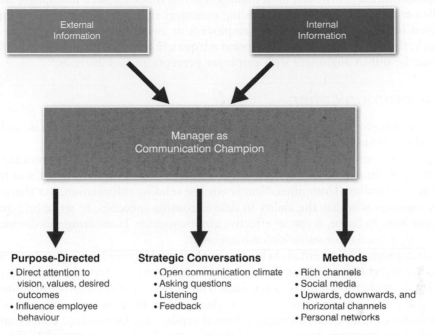

SOURCES: Henry Mintzberg, *The Nature of Managerial Work* (New York: Harper and Row, 1973); and Richard L. Daft, *The Leadership Experience,* 3rd ed. (Cincinnati, OH: South-Western, 2005), p. 346.

gather important information from both inside and outside the organization and then distribute appropriate information to others who need it for optimum decision-making. Managers' communication should be *purpose-directed* in that it directs attention *inter alia* towards the vision, values and desired goals of the team or organization influencing people to act in the best way to achieve the desired goals. Managers facilitate *strategic conversations* by using open communication, actively listening to others, asking probing questions and using purposeful and timely feedback for learning and change. Strategic conversation refers to people talking across boundaries and hierarchical levels about the team or organization's vision, critical strategic themes and the values that help achieve important goals.[3]

Managers should use different *methods* and media to communicate, depending on the purpose of the communication and the audience. Social media is one medium that is growing exponentially in its popularity. In a survey taken in 2014, *65 per cent of managers surveyed said that they expected to use social media more next year to communicate with employees.*[4]

What is communication?

Most of us think of spoken or written language when we think about communication, but words are only a small part of human communication. Managers are carefully observed by employees, so it's important to remember that everything a manager does and says will communicate something. In addition, real communication is a two-way process that involves asking questions, seeking and receiving feedback, paying attention to non-verbal communication of others and listening actively. Communication is the process by which information is exchanged and hopefully understood by two or more people, usually with an intention to influence, or motivate, appropriate responses. Of course it could be used to clarify the context and meaning of earlier communications, for better understanding of why a decision was made – or even reversed.

Many surveys of managers have shown that they consider communication their most critical skill and one of their top responsibilities.[5] However, most managers reveal that they need to improve their communication effectiveness. Fewer than half of these responding managers tailor their messages to employees, customers or suppliers. Even fewer seek feedback from employees or customers because they fear hearing bad news. Without feedback, though, managers can't respond adequately to problems or opportunities, and their plans and decisions may be out of alignment with employee perceptions and interests.[6]

A model of communication

Being a good communicator starts with appreciating how complex communication is, and understanding the key elements of the communication process, as illustrated in Exhibit 15.2.

Many people think communication is simple and natural. After all, we communicate every day without even thinking about it. In reality, though, human communication is quite complex and fraught with opportunities for misunderstanding. Communication is not just sending information, but sharing information in a planned way. A manager who has the ability to deliver rousing speeches, or write brilliant commentary, but who doesn't know how to listen, is not an effective communicator. Honouring this distinction between *sharing* and *proclaiming* is crucial for successful management.

Knowing what communication entails helps you appreciate the complexity of it. As shown in Exhibit 15.2, a manager who wants to communicate with an employee encodes a thought or idea by selecting symbols (such as words) with which to compose a message. The message is the tangible formulation of the thought or idea sent to the employee, and the channel is the medium by which the message is sent. The channel might be a telephone call, an email message, a formal report or a face-to-face conversation. The employee decodes the symbols to interpret the meaning of the message. Feedback occurs when the employee responds to a manager's communication with a return message. As illustrated in the exhibit, the nature of effective communication is cyclical, in that a sender and receiver may exchange messages several times to achieve a mutual understanding.

Encoding and decoding sometimes can cause communication errors. Have you heard someone say, 'But that's not what I meant!' or wasted time and energy on misunderstood instructions? Individual differences, knowledge, values, attitudes and backgrounds act as filters and may create 'noise' when translating from symbols to meanings. We've all experienced communication breakdowns – because people can easily misinterpret messages. Feedback enables a manager to determine whether the employee correctly interpreted the

EXHIBIT 15.2 A schematic of communication

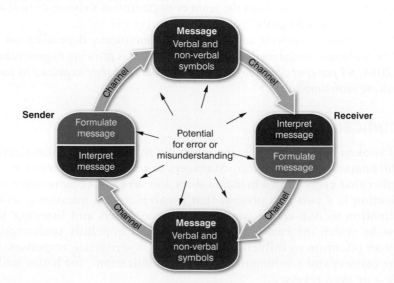

message. The strong potential for communication errors is why feedback is so important. Without feedback, the communication cycle is incomplete. Effective communication involves both the transference and the mutual understanding of information.[7]

REFLECTION

- Effective managers build broad personal communication networks through which they accomplish their jobs.
- The manager's role as communication champion means to engage in purpose-driven strategic conversations via multiple channels.
- Social media is a method of communication that is growing in popularity as an effective way to communicate information within an organization.
- Strategic conversation refers to dialogue across boundaries and hierarchical levels about the team or organization's vision, critical strategic themes and the values that help achieve important goals.

- Communication is the process by which information is exchanged and understood by two or more people.
- The sender encodes the idea by selecting symbols with which to compose a message and selecting a communication channel; the receiver decodes the symbols to interpret the meaning of the message.
- The message is the tangible formulation of an idea to be sent to the employee.
- The term channel refers to the medium by which a message is sent, such as a telephone call, blog or text message.
- Feedback occurs when the receiver responds to the sender's communication with a return message.

Communicating amongst people

Many top managers admit their performance as communication champions probably fell short during the worst of the recent economic crisis as they spent more time trying to make sure the financial status of their companies remained sound.

To achieve the best possible outcome, managers must understand how factors such as open communication climates, communication channels, the ability to persuade, communicating with candour, asking questions, listening and non-verbal behaviour all work to enhance or detract from communication. Managers should also consider how gender affects communication. The Shoptalk explores how gender differences influence the effectiveness of communication between men and women.

Open communication climate

A survey of US employees reveals that people genuinely want open and honest communication from their managers, including the bad news as well as the good.[8] This created a dilemma for Tom Szaky, CEO of TerraCycle, a waste-recycling business, because he was hesitant to share bad news with his employees. He didn't want them worrying about something that didn't affect their jobs and becoming distracted and unproductive. '*The problem with hiding information*,' Szaky said, '*was that when challenges came up, I felt pretty much alone on them, and the staff was left guessing what was happening. Predictably, the lack of information fuelled rumours and damaged morale.*' Today, Szaky encourages transparency and promotes open, honest communication. Employees see everything in great detail, even the bad news. This new climate has fostered a feeling of ownership and trust. It also brings issues to the forefront faster than ever before.[9]

Open communication means sharing all types of information throughout the organization, across functional and hierarchical boundaries. People throughout the organization need to see the bigger picture, understand the decisions that managers make and know how their work activities contribute to the success of the company. Particularly in times of change, if people don't hear what's happening from managers, they rely on rumours and will often assume the worst.[10] In an open communication environment, people know where they stand and what rules they need to play by. Open communication helps people accept, understand and commit to goals. People can see how their actions interact with and affect others in the organization. When people have access to more complete information, they are more likely to come up with creative solutions to problems and make decisions that are good for the company.

🌐 MANAGER'S SHOPTALK

Gender differences in communication

To improve the effectiveness of workplace communication, managers should be aware of various factors that influence how people communicate. One important consideration is gender roles, the learned behaviours associated with being male or female. Deborah Tannen, author of *You Just Don't Understand: Women and Men in Conversation,* has spent three decades studying gender differences in communication. Grasping the following different communication styles of men and women can help managers maximize every employee's talents and encourage both men and women to contribute more fully to the organization.

- **Purposes of conversations.** Men's conversations tend to focus on hierarchy – competition for relative power. To many men, talk is primarily a means to preserve independence and to negotiate and maintain status in a hierarchy. Men tend to use verbal language to exhibit knowledge and skill, such as by telling stories, joking or passing on information. For most women, although certainly not all, conversation is primarily a language of rapport, a way to establish connections and negotiate relationships. Women use their unique conversational style to show involvement, connection and participation, such as by seeking similarities and matching experiences with others. They seemingly have bonding sessions that are gender specific such as watching Rom-Coms and sad dramas.

- **Decision-making styles.** When women make decisions, they tend to process and think of options out loud. Men process internally until they come up with a solution. Men can sometimes misunderstand women's verbal brainstorming and assume a woman is seeking approval rather than just thinking aloud.

- **Success in collaborative environments.** A report from McKinsey & Company, 'Leadership Through the Crisis and After', notes that the types of behaviours that executives say will help their companies through an economic crisis, are most often practised by female managers. Women typically score higher than men on abilities such as motivating others, fostering communication and listening; abilities that are more important than ever when organizations are going through tough times.

- **Interpretation of non-verbal messages.** About 70 per cent of communication occurs non-verbally, but men and women generally interpret non-verbal communication differently. Women believe that good listening skills involve making eye contact and demonstrating understanding by nodding. To men, listening can take place with minimum eye contact and little supportive non-verbal feedback. Further, when a man nods, it means he agrees. When a woman nods, it communicates that she is listening. Women tend to be better at interpreting non-verbal communication. They are able to assess coalitions and alliances just by noting who is making eye contact during critical points in a meeting.

Interestingly, some male managers may be shifting to a more female-oriented communication style in today's challenging economic environment because women's approach to leadership and communication may be more suited to inspiring employees and helping people pull together towards goals during difficult economic cycles.

SOURCES: Deborah Tannen, 'He Said, She Said', *Scientific American Mind* (May–June 2010): 55–59; and Carol Kinsey Goman, 'Men and Women and Workplace Communication', *Business Analyst Times,* May 26, 2009, www.batimes.com/articles/men-and-women-and-workplace-communication.html (accessed September 20, 2012).

When the employees in the survey mentioned above were asked to evaluate how well their managers were doing in providing open and honest communication, the average score on a scale of zero to 100 was 69.[11] Managers can build an open communication climate by breaking down conventional hierarchical and department boundaries that may be barriers to communication. They can take care to communicate honestly with subordinates, keep people posted when things change in either a positive or negative direction and help people see the financial impact of their decisions and actions.[12]

CONCEPT CONNECTION

Research has shown that a culture of **open communication** offers many benefits to an organization and its employees, including higher productivity, better decision-making and lower turnover rates. Expert opinion is that, even in the largest organizations, face-to-face communication is still the best means of being really open and honest. Staff meetings or larger 'town hall' meetings like this one emphasize the importance of the information being shared, more so than any form of written communication, such as email. In developing a new flagship MBA, a major UK Business School held 'Big Tent' meetings in 2011 to brainstorm the syllabus in an inclusive academic forum. They were very successful and the unique MBA programme, based on sustainability, launched a year later.

To achieve the advantages of open communication, managers should use the type of communication network that maximizes employee performance and job satisfaction. Research into employee communication has focused on two characteristics of effective communication: the extent to which team communications are centralized and the nature of the team's task.[13] The relationship between these characteristics is illustrated in Exhibit 15.3. In a centralized network, team members must communicate through one individual to solve problems or make decisions. Centralized communication can be effective for large teams because it limits the number of people involved in decision-making. The result is a faster decision that involves fewer people.[14] In a decentralized network, individuals can communicate freely with other team members. Members process information equally among themselves until all agree on a decision.[15] Decentralized communication is best for complex, difficult work environments where teams need a free flow of communication in all directions.[16]

Communication channels

Managers have a choice of many channels through which to communicate. A manager may discuss a problem face-to-face, make a telephone call, use text messaging, send an email, write a memo or letter or post an entry to a company blog, depending on the nature of the message. Research attempted to explain how managers select communication channels to enhance communication effectiveness.[17] One approach to selecting an effective communication channel is to interpret the emotions of the person who will be receiving the message and then select the channel that will

EXHIBIT 15.3 Communication networks

Centralized Network

Decentralized Network

result in the best outcome. Scientists have shown that managers can understand how a person is feeling by studying important clues: facial expressions, gestures, body posture and tone of voice. A smirk, a furrowed brow or sagging body posture are strong indicators of a person's emotions.[18]

Another factor that shapes a manager's selection of a communication channel is the type and amount of information to be communicated. Research has shown that channels differ in their capacity to convey data. Just as a pipeline's physical characteristics limit the type and amount of liquid that can be pumped through it, a communication channel's physical characteristics limit the type and amount of information that can be conveyed through it. The channels available to managers can be classified into a hierarchy based on information richness.

The hierarchy of channel richness

Channel richness is the amount of information that can be transmitted during a communication episode. The hierarchy of channel richness is illustrated in Exhibit 15.4. The capacity of an information channel is influenced by three characteristics: (1) the ability to handle multiple cues simultaneously; (2) the ability to facilitate rapid, two-way feedback and (3) the ability to establish a personal focus for the communication. Face-to-face discussion is the richest medium because it permits direct experience, multiple information cues, immediate feedback and personal focus. Because of its richness, it is the best channel when communicating to people who are exhibiting strong emotions, such as anxiety, fear or defensiveness. Face-to-face discussions facilitate the assimilation of broad cues and deep emotional understanding of the situation. Telephone conversations are next in the richness hierarchy. Although eye contact, posture and other body language cues are missing, the human voice still can carry a tremendous amount of emotional information.

Electronic communication, such as email, instant messaging, Skype and text messaging, is increasingly being used for messages that were once handled face-to-face or by telephone. However, in a survey by researchers at The Ohio State University, most respondents said they preferred the telephone or face-to-face conversation for communicating difficult news, giving advice or expressing affection.[19] Because email messages lack both visual and verbal cues and don't allow for interaction and feedback, messages can sometimes be misunderstood. Using email to discuss disputes, for example, can lead to an escalation rather than a resolution of conflict.[20] Too often, managers use email or text messaging to avoid the emotional discomfort of a real-time conversation, hiding behind their computers to send rebukes or criticisms that they would never deliver in person. '*Because we can't see their hurt, it doesn't matter as much,*' says business consultant Margie Warrell. She advises managers to never use email in the following circumstances:

- **When you are angry.** As our anger increases, so does our inability to communicate effectively. Wait at least 2 hours to cool off before sending an email message. Then you will be more able to choose the most constructive way to convey that you are upset.

- **When your message may be misunderstood.** Meet in person with someone who may be defensive about certain issues. A face-to-face conversation ensures that the other person hears your message in the most positive way.

- **When you are cancelling or apologizing.** To cancel an engagement, pick up the telephone and call instead of emailing to demonstrate that you care about the relationship. When an apology is called for, meet in person so you can ask and receive forgiveness, which goes a long way towards restoring a damaged relationship.

- **When you are rebuking or criticizing.** While it is never easy to deliver negative feedback, it is better to communicate rebukes or criticisms in person so you can read visual cues and address any issues the other person might raise.[21]

Still lower on the hierarchy of channel richness are written letters and memos. Written communication can be personally focused, but it conveys only the cues written on paper and is slower to provide feedback. Impersonal written media, including flyers, bulletins and standard computer reports, are the lowest in richness. These channels are not focused on a single receiver, use limited information cues and do not permit feedback.

EXHIBIT 15.4 A continuum of channel richness

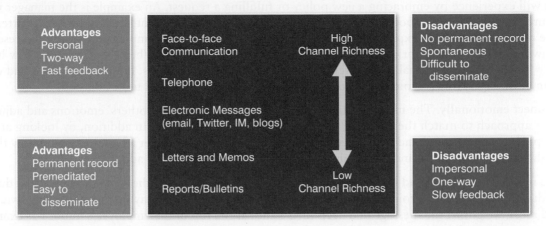

> 'Electric communication will never be a substitute for the face of someone who with their soul encourages another person to be brave and true.'
>
> – CHARLES DICKENS (1812–1870), ENGLISH NOVELIST

Selecting the appropriate channel

It is important for managers to understand that each communication channel has advantages and disadvantages and that each can be an effective means of communication in the appropriate circumstances.[22] Channel selection depends on whether the message is routine or non-routine. *Non-routine messages* typically are ambiguous, concern novel events and involve great potential for misunderstanding. They often are characterized by time pressure and surprise. Managers can communicate non-routine messages effectively by selecting rich channels. *Routine* messages are simple and straightforward. They convey data or statistics or simply put into words what managers already agree on and understand. Routine messages can be efficiently communicated through a channel lower in richness, such as a memo, email, text message or Twitter. Written communications should be used when the communication is official and a permanent record is required.[23]

The prerequisite is to select a channel to fit the message. During a major acquisition, a firm decided to send top executives to all major work sites of the acquired company, where most of the workers met the managers in person, heard about their plans for the company and had a chance to ask questions. The results were well worth the time and expense of the personal face-to-face meetings because the acquired workforce saw their new managers as understanding, open and willing to listen.[24] Communicating their non-routine message about the acquisition in person prevented damaging rumours and misunderstandings. The choice of a communication channel can also convey a symbolic meaning to the receiver; in a sense, the medium becomes part of the message. The firm's decision to communicate face-to-face with the acquired workforce signalled to employees that managers cared about them as individuals.

Communicating to persuade and influence others

Communication is not just for conveying information, but also to persuade and influence people. Although communication skills have always been important to managers, the ability to persuade and influence others is even more critical today. The command-and-control mindset of managers telling workers what to do and how to do it is gone. Key points for practising the art of persuasion include the following:[25]

■ **Establish credibility.** A manager's credibility is based on knowledge, expertise and interpersonal skills. By demonstrating a consistent ability to make well-informed, sound decisions, managers inspire employees to have stronger confidence in the manager's leadership abilities.

- **Build goals on common ground.** To be persuasive, managers should describe the benefits that employees will experience by embracing a new policy or fulfilling a request. An example is the manager who wanted to persuade fast food franchisees to support new pricing discounts desired by headquarters. The manager didn't just explain that headquarters wanted the policies implemented; he cited research showing that the revised pricing would increase franchisees' profits.[26] When the franchisees saw how they would benefit personally, they were eager to adopt the new policies. If a manager can't find common advantages, this is typically a good signal that goals and plans need to be adjusted.

- **Connect emotionally.** The most effective managers learn to understand others' emotions and adjust their approach to match the audience's ability to receive their message. In addition, by looking at how people have interpreted and responded to past events, a manager can get a better grasp on how they might react to new ideas and proposals that the manager wants them to adopt.

- **Use multiple media to send important messages.** When managers send the same message using different media, they move their projects forward faster and more smoothly. By saying the same thing twice, they add more weight to the message and keep their issues at the top of the employee's mind. For example, one manager explained a request to an employee in person. He immediately composed a follow-up email to the same employee that summarized the request in writing.[27]

To persuade and influence, managers have to communicate frequently and easily with others. Yet some people find interpersonal communication experiences unrewarding or difficult and thus tend to avoid situations where communication is required. The term communication apprehension describes this avoidance behaviour and is defined as '*an individual's level of fear or anxiety associated with either real or anticipated communication.*' With training and practice, managers can overcome their communication apprehension and become more effective communicators.

TAKE A MOMENT

Becoming an effective communicator may require you to overcome your fears and anxiety when communicating. Go to the Experiential Exercise online to assess your communication apprehension in a variety of communication settings.

Communicating with candour

To influence and persuade, managers also have to be honest and straightforward about what they want and need from others. Communicating with candour means being direct, honest and clear about what employees need to do for meeting objectives, while also expressing respect for others and not making people feel slighted, controlled or exploited. Unfortunately, communicating with candour is a problem for many managers. Jack Welch, speaker, author and former CEO of General Electric (GE), says that when he asks groups of managers how many of them have received candid performance appraisals, only about 10 per cent of people raise their hands. When he asks how many have given candid appraisals to their employees, the results aren't much better.[28]

Communicating with candour is a confident, positive approach that lets others know exactly where you stand and what you're asking of them. The appropriate use of candid communication acknowledges the other person's perspective and opinion, yet is very specific about what the manager wants and why. Some valuable techniques for communicating with candour include:[29]

- **Use 'I statements'.** To communicate with candour, you should keep the focus on the specific perception you have, how it makes you feel and the effect it is having on you, rather than accusing or blaming the other person. Suppose that you share office space with a sloppy colleague. Rather than saying, 'You drive me crazy by leaving food wrappers scattered all over the place,' you might say, 'I'm finding it really hard to get our work done with all this clutter on the work table.'

- **Stick to facts rather than judgements.** Don't tell your colleague that she's grossly untidy; just let her know that the clutter she's leaving on the table is interfering with your ability to do your work.

■ **Be clear, specific and direct in your requests.** Say 'I'd like you to keep the work table clear and clean because we both have to use it to get our jobs done,' rather than 'Why don't you clean up the mess you leave around here?'

Communicating with candour is an important part of creating an open communication climate. When managers communicate with candour, they encourage others to do the same. In an organization where candid communication is the norm, everything works faster and better.[30] When everyone feels free to open up and speak frankly, more people get involved in organizational conversations, which leads to more ideas and faster learning. In addition, candour means that ideas get debated, adapted and acted upon more quickly. Candid communication leads to genuine ongoing conversations and limits common problems such as meaningless meetings, workplace incivility or rancorous silence.

Carol Bartz, former CEO of Yahoo! and Autodesk, has always been a straight talker. She believes that if a person has an opinion, they should state it, which allows others to either try to change the opinion, to agree with it or to agree to disagree. '*Agreeing is easy*' she said. '*Disagreeing takes more guts.*' At Autodesk, Bartz noticed that a successful senior-level woman was wearing inappropriate clothing at work. Her attire was

 NEW MANAGER SELF-TEST

Candour

INSTRUCTIONS Respond to the statements below based on how you speak to others during personal or work conversations. Answer whether each statement is 'Mostly true' or 'Mostly false' for you. There are no right or wrong answers, so answer honestly.

		Mostly true	Mostly false
1	I try to be courteous and respectful of people's feelings.	☐	☐
2	I say exactly what I think to people.	☐	☐
3	I never hesitate to upset someone by telling the truth.	☐	☐
4	I like to be strictly candid about what I say.	☐	☐
5	I am very straightforward when giving feedback.	☐	☐
6	I present evidence for my opinions.	☐	☐
7	I am an extremely frank communicator.	☐	☐
8	I would not deliberately say something that would hurt someone's feelings.	☐	☐

SCORING & INTERPRETATION Give yourself one point for each 'Mostly true' answer to items 2–7, plus one point for each 'Mostly false' answer to items 1 and 8. Total score: ___.

Your score reflects the level of candour with which you communicate. Many people have a hard time giving straightforward opinions and feedback because they don't want to hurt a person's feelings, nor do they want people to dislike them. Hence, the sharing of honest observations is limited. A score of 6–8 on this scale suggests that you may have a habit of candour, which will add to your managerial effectiveness. A score of 1–3 may mean that you have a hard time speaking your mind and you may want to practise to improve your candour.

distracting, and she was not being taken seriously. Bartz called her in and frankly stated, '*You're not getting the respect you deserve. Go to Nordstrom and get a personal shopper. Just say, "I'm a senior businessperson and need help dressing like one".' The employee returned with a professional wardrobe, and her credibility within the workplace improved considerably.[31]

TAKE A MOMENT

Take the New Manager Self-Test on the previous page to see if you typically communicate with candour.

Asking questions

The traditional top-down, command-and-control approach to organizational communication is no longer viable in today's global, technologically sophisticated workplace. This traditional model is giving way to a more dynamic form of communication that is characterized by *organizational conversations*, which involve a give-and-take exchange of information.[32] To have successful organizational conversations, managers need to learn to ask questions. Most managers do 80 per cent telling and 20 per cent asking, while it should be the other way around. Asking questions can benefit both managers and employees in numerous ways.[33]

- **Asking questions builds trust and openness between managers and employees.** Managers who ask questions encourage their employees to share ideas and offer feedback. Duke Energy's president and CEO, James E. Rogers, holds listening sessions with groups of 90–100 employees, where he asks questions and offers responses. By engaging with employees in a format that resembles ordinary person-to-person conversation, Rogers is developing a culture built on trust and authenticity.[34]

- **Asking questions builds critical thinking skills.** In one survey, 99 per cent of top managers said critical thinking skills at all levels are crucial to the success of their organizations.[35] Asking questions stimulates critical, independent thinking, encourages people to use their creativity and leads to deeper, more lasting learning.

- **Questions stimulate the mind and give people a chance to make a difference.** When a manager asks a question of someone, it puts the individual on alert in a way that making a statement does not. People have to think in order to respond to a question. If a plant foreman says, 'We have to increase production to fill this order,' workers can listen to him or not and try to speed things up or continue working as they have been. If, instead, the foreman asks employees, 'What can we do to make sure we fill this order on time?' people can't ignore him; they have to start looking for solutions. Thus, asking questions gets people to accept responsibility for solving their own problems.

Asking questions is an important dimension of the organizational conversation. Consider how Cisco Systems uses powerful technology and instant connectivity to facilitate fluid and open conversations among managers and employees.

 INNOVATIVE WAY

How not to write ...

It is a truism that executive communication from a MNC is scrutinized very carefully by the media and a consistent target for many has been Mr Elop, the former CEO of Nokia, which was substantially absorbed into

Microsoft's empire, post-acquisition. Lucy Kellway, writing in the UK's *Financial Times* (27 July 2014), critically described CEO Stephen Elop's Microsoft major job loss announcement as: '... *being a case study in how not to write, think, or lead a business.*' The ultimate acknowledgement of his jargon-riddled provocative communication style was his short-listing by Kellaway of the *Financial Times*; for the 'Golden Flannel Award' in 2015. One would have expected a sensitive well-crafted communication from an executive whose task 3 years earlier was to revitalize Nokia's outdated handsets against intensive competition from smartphone providers such as Apple and Samsung. Below is a summary of his gross miscommunication style which has been dubbed as his 'hello there' address to his division's workforce.

Stephen Elop, Nokia' former chief executive, announced that Microsoft was shedding 12 500 jobs in 2014. Many losses fell upon former Nokians who remembered Mr Elop's infamous 2011 'burning platform' memo, extracts from which are reproduced below. His intention, expressed in a somewhat poetical way, was to inspire Nokia employees (Nokians) to help him turn the ailing MNC around: *'Nokia, our platform is burning. We are working on a path forward – a path to rebuild our market leadership. When we share the new strategy… it will be a huge effort to transform our company. But, I believe that together we can face the challenges ahead of us. Together, we can choose to define our future. The burning platform, upon which the man found himself, caused the man to shift his behaviour, and take a bold and brave step into an uncertain future. He was able to tell his story. Now, we have a great opportunity to do the same.'*

Three years later, Elop turned from trying to be pseudo-inspirational to a more pseudo-informational mode, laced with business school metaphors. The whole formal statement was steeped in jargon as Elop described how Microsoft planned to deeply reduce Nokia's mobile phone workforce in its native Finland and other countries.

Below is a representative passage *(in italics)* from his 1110 word memo sent to Microsoft's Mobile Phone division employees, in July 2014, for which Kellaway in her article stated: 'This is a classic example of how not to fire people.'

'It is particularly important to recognize that the role of phones within Microsoft is different than it was within Nokia. Whereas the hardware business of phones within Nokia was an end unto itself, within Microsoft all our devices are intended to embody the finest of Microsoft's digital work and digital life experiences, while accruing value to Microsoft's overall strategy. Our device strategy must reflect Microsoft's strategy and must be accomplished within an appropriate financial envelope. Therefore, we plan to make some changes.'

Kellaway, as many observers, found the text was extremely hard to interpret and provided her readers with eight golden rules that clearly Elop had breached. Here we provide our interpretation of Kellaway's eight guidance rules for CEO communication:

Rule 1: Do not use inappropriate quips such as *'Hello there'* in a serious situation such as announcing mass redundancies.

Rule 2: When you use simple expressions such as 'we must do more' provide concrete examples.

Rule 3: There are obnoxious words not to overuse when you are vaguely discussing future strategy such as: focus, major, milestones, breakthrough and delivering.

Rule 4: Do not alienate listeners with jargon – just say it how it is.

Rule 5: Avoid saying 'experience' this is a greatly overused buzzword in both industry, politics and education.

Rule 6: As in rule 5, the word strategy can be overused, as overusage can imply that a real strategy does not exist.

Rule 7: Abstract nouns should never be overused.

Rule 8: Do not end a memo such as the Elop one with insincere words such as 'regards.'

Mr Elop received a very generous severance package from Microsoft in 2015.

Listening

Of all the competencies critical to successful managerial communication, listening is at the top of the list. Yet listening seems to be a rare skill among managers, and the inability to listen is one of the key reasons that managers fail. In fact, a startling 67 per cent of new managers fail within 18 months because they don't listen.[36]

Listening involves the skill of grasping both facts and feelings to interpret a message's genuine meaning. Only then can the manager provide the appropriate response. Listening requires attention, energy and skill. Although about 75 per cent of effective communication is listening, most people spend only 30 to 40 per cent of their time listening, which leads to many communication errors.[37] One of the

CONCEPT CONNECTION

Messages are conveyed not only by what is said, but by how it is said and the facial expressions and body language of the people involved. Face-to-face communication is the richest **communication channel** because it facilitates these **non-verbal cues** and allows for immediate feedback. Important issues should be discussed face-to-face.

secrets of highly successful salespeople is that they spend 60 to 70 per cent of a sales call letting the customer talk.[38] However, listening involves much more than just not talking. Many people do not know how to listen effectively. They concentrate on formulating what they are going to say next rather than on what is being said to them. Our listening efficiency, as measured by the amount of material understood and remembered by subjects 48 hours after listening to a 10-minute message, is, on average, no better than 25 per cent.[39]

Most managers now recognize that important information flows from the bottom up, not the top down, and managers had better be tuned in.[40] Some organizations use innovative techniques for finding out what's really on employees' and customers' minds. Intuit, for example, instituted an annual employee survey that gives managers an opportunity to listen to employees' feelings on a range of company practices. Then, during the year, managers are encouraged to meet with subordinates to gather more feedback. Since instituting these listening strategies, turnover at Intuit has dropped from 24 per cent to 12 per cent. *'Employees know that we are serious about asking for their feedback, and we listen and do something about it,'* said former CEO Stephen Bennett.[41]

Managers are also tapping into the interactive nature of blogs to stay in touch with employees and customers. *Blogs*, running Web logs that allow people to post opinions, ideas and information, provide a low-cost, fresh, real-time link between organizations and customers, employees, the media and investors.[42] One past estimate is that 16 per cent of *Fortune* 500 companies use blogs to keep in touch with stakeholders.[43] Blogs give managers another way to get valuable feedback. If done correctly, listening is a vital link in the communication process, shown in the model of communication in Exhibit 15.2.

What constitutes good listening? Exhibit 15.5 gives ten keys to effective listening and illustrates a number of ways to distinguish a bad listener from a good listener. A good listener finds areas of interest, is flexible, works hard at listening and uses thought speed to mentally summarize, weigh and anticipate what the speaker says. Good listening means shifting from thinking about self to empathizing with the other person, which requires a high degree of emotional intelligence.

Non-verbal communication

Managers should be aware that their body language – facial expressions, gestures, touch and use of space – can communicate a range of messages, from enthusiasm, warmth and confidence to arrogance, indifference and displeasure.[44] Non-verbal communication refers to messages sent through human actions and behaviour rather than through words.[45] Managers are watched, and their behaviour, appearance, actions and attitudes are symbolic of what they value and expect of others.

Most of us have heard the saying 'Actions speak louder than words'. Indeed, we communicate without words all the time, whether we realize it or not. Most managers are astonished to learn that words can, of themselves, carry little meaning. A significant portion of the shared understanding from communication comes from the non-verbal messages of facial expression, voice, mannerisms, posture and dress. Consider

EXHIBIT 15.5 Ten keys to effective listening

Keys to effective listening	Poor listener	Good listener
1. Listen actively	Is passive, laid back	Asks questions, paraphrases what is said
2. Find areas of interest	Tunes out dry subjects	Looks for new learning
3. Resist distractions	Is easily distracted; answers telephone or sends text messages	Gives full attention, fights distractions, maintains concentration
4. Capitalize on the fact that thought is faster	Tends to daydream	Mentally summarizes; weighs the evidence
5. Be responsive	Avoids eye contact; is minimally involved	Nods and shows interest
6. Judge content, not delivery	Tunes out if delivery is poor	Judges content; skips over delivery errors
7. Avoid premature judgement	Has preconceptions	Does not judge until comprehension is complete
8. Listen for ideas	Listens for facts	Listens to central themes
9. Work at listening	Shows no energy; forgets what the speaker says	Works hard; exhibits active body state and eye contact
10. Exercise one's mind	Resists difficult material in favour of light, recreational material	Uses heavier material as exercise for the mind

SOURCE: Diann Daniel, 'Seven Deadly Sins of (Not) Listening', *CIO*, September 7, 2004, www.cio.com/article/134801/Seven_Deadly_Sins_of_Not_Listening_ (accessed December 7, 2012; Sherman K. Okum, 'How to Be a Better Listener', *Nation's Business* (August 1975): 62; and Philip Morgan and Kent Baker, 'Building a Professional Image: Improving Listening Behavior', *Supervisory Management* (November 1985): 34–38.

the following example. During an interview about Facebook's latest privacy policy with reporters from *The Wall Street Journal*, Mark Zuckerberg, then Facebook's 26-year old chief executive, sweated profusely and appeared shaken. As he defended the company's policy, so much sweat was dripping from his forehead that the interviewer suggested he take off his hoodie. While his verbal responses provided plausible explanations for the new privacy policy, Zuckerberg's non-verbal cues suggested that he was unprepared and lacked confidence in the new direction.[46]

Non-verbal communication occurs mostly face-to-face. One researcher found three sources of communication cues during face-to-face communication: the *verbal*, which are the actual spoken words; the *vocal*, which include the pitch, tone and timbre of a person's voice; and *facial expressions*. According to this study, the relative weights of these three factors in message interpretation are as follows: verbal impact, 7 per cent; vocal impact, 38 per cent; and facial impact, 55 per cent.[47] To some extent, we are all natural *face readers*, but at the same time, facial expressions can be misinterpreted, suggesting that managers need to ask questions to make sure they're getting the right message. Managers can hone their skills at reading facial expressions and improve their ability to connect with and influence followers. Studies indicate that managers who seem responsive to the unspoken emotions of employees are more effective and successful in the workplace.[48]

Managers should take care to align their facial expressions and body language to support an intended message. When non-verbal signals contradict a manager's words, people become confused and may discount what is being said and believe the body language instead.[49] One manager who was a master at using body language to convey credibility and confidence was Steve Jobs of Apple. When he unveiled Apple's new cloud service, iCloud, in June 2011, Jobs fully faced the audience, made eye contact, kept his movements relaxed and natural and stood tall. Through his body language, he communicated credibility, commitment and honesty.[50]

REFLECTION

- **Open communication** means sharing all types of information throughout the organization and across functional and hierarchical boundaries.
- A **centralized network** is a communication structure in which team members communicate through a single individual to solve problems or make decisions.
- A **decentralized network** is a communication structure in which team members freely communicate with one another and arrive at decisions together.
- **Channel richness** is the amount of information that can be transmitted during a communication episode.
- Although communication skills have always been important to managers, the ability to persuade and influence others is even more critical today.
- **Communication apprehension** is an individual's level of fear or anxiety associated with interpersonal communication.

- Communicating with candour means being direct, honest and clear about what employees need to do to meet objectives, while also expressing respect for others and not making people feel slighted, controlled or exploited.
- To encourage a give-and-take exchange of information between managers and employees, managers need to learn to ask questions.
- **Listening** involves the skill of grasping both facts and feelings to interpret a message's genuine meaning.
- **Non-verbal communication** means communicating through actions, gestures, facial expressions and behaviour rather than through words.

Organizational communication

Another aspect of management communication concerns the organization as a whole. Organization-wide communications typically flow in three directions – downwards, upwards and horizontally. Managers are responsible for establishing and maintaining formal channels of communication in these three directions. Managers also use informal channels, meaning that they get out of their offices and mingle with employees. This has been referred to as 'MBWA': managing by walking about.

Formal communication channels

Formal communication channels are those that flow within the chain of command or task responsibility defined by the organization. The three formal channels and the types of information conveyed in each are illustrated in Exhibit 15.6.[51] Downwards and upwards communications are the primary forms of

EXHIBIT 15.6 Downwards, upwards and horizontal communication in organizations

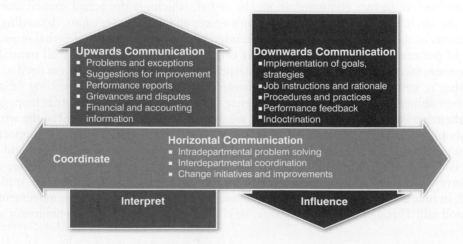

CONCEPT CONNECTION

When the US Mayo Clinic formulated a strategic plan for its world-famous medical centre in 2007, the communications department experimented with a new way to facilitate **upwards and downwards communications**. They created 'Let's Talk', an internal blog that allowed managers to use videos and blog posts to explain the plan. The clinic's employees found the blog to be so useful that it continues to be used years later as an ongoing, open communication channel. The Mayo Clinic has since added numerous external blogs to facilitate greater **horizontal communication** with customers and other stakeholders as well.

communication used in most traditional, vertically organized companies. However, many of today's organizations emphasize horizontal communication, with people continuously sharing information across departments and levels.

Electronic communication methods such as email and instant messaging have made it easier than ever for information to flow in all directions. For example, the US Army has used technology to rapidly transmit communications about weather conditions and the latest intelligence on the insurgency to lieutenants in the field in Afghanistan and Iraq. Similarly, the US Navy uses instant messaging to communicate within ships, across Navy divisions and even back to the Pentagon in Washington. '*Instant messaging has allowed us to keep our crew members on the same page at the same time*,' says Lt Cmdr Mike Houston, who oversees the navy's communications programme. '*Lives are at stake in real time, and we're seeing a new level of communication and readiness.*'[52]

Downwards communication

The most familiar and obvious flow of formal communication, downwards communication, refers to the messages and information sent from top management to subordinates in a downwards direction. Managers can communicate downwards to employees in many ways. Some of the most common are through speeches, videos, blogs, podcasts and company intranets.

It is impossible for managers to communicate with employees about everything that goes on in the organization, so they have to make choices about the important information to communicate.[53] Unfortunately, many US managers could do a better job of effective downwards communication. The results of one survey showed that employees wanted open and honest communication about both the good and the bad aspects of the organization's performance. But when asked to rate their company's communication effectiveness on a scale of 0 to 100, the survey respondents' score averaged 69. In addition, a study of 1500 managers, mostly at first and second management levels, found that 84 per cent of these leaders perceive communication as one of their most important tasks, yet only 38 per cent believe they have adequate communication skills.[54]

Managers can do a better job of downwards communication by focusing on specific areas that require regular communication. Downwards communication usually encompasses these five forthcoming topics:

- *Goals and strategies.* Communicating new strategies and goals provides information about specific targets and expected behaviours. It gives direction for lower levels of the organization. *Example:* 'The new quality campaign is for real. We must improve product quality if we are to survive.'

- *Job instructions and rationale.* These directives indicate how to do a specific task and how the job relates to other organizational activities. For high-priority or time-sensitive issues, some managers use Twitter as a preferred channel of downwards communication. With a limit of 140 characters, reading and replying to a 'tweet' is a lot faster than other forms of communication.[55] *Example of a Twitter message:* 'Brand managers from Adele will attend our presentation at the trade show on October 24. We'll meet Friday at 9 a.m. to outline the presentation.'

■ **Procedures and practices.** These messages define the organization's policies, rules, regulations, benefits and structural arrangements. *Example:* 'After your first 90 days of employment, you are eligible to enroll in our company-sponsored savings plan.'

■ **Performance feedback.** These messages appraise how well individuals and departments are doing their jobs. *Example:* 'Joe, your work on the computer network has greatly improved the efficiency of our ordering process.'

■ **Indoctrination.** These messages are designed to motivate employees to adopt the company's mission and cultural values and to participate in special ceremonies, such as picnics and United Way campaigns. *Example:* 'The company thinks of its employees as family and would like to invite everyone to attend the annual picnic and fair on 3 March.'

A major problem with downwards communication is *drop-off*, the distortion or loss of message content. Although formal communications are a powerful way to reach all employees, much information gets lost – 25 per cent or so each time a message is passed from one person to the next. In addition, the message can be distorted if it travels a great distance from its originating source to the ultimate receiver. A tragic example is the following historical case.

A reporter was present at a hamlet (village) burned down by the US Army 1st Air Cavalry Division in 1967. Investigations showed that the order from the division headquarters to the brigade was: 'On no occasion must hamlets be burned down.'

The brigade radioed the battalion: 'Do not burn down any hamlets unless you are absolutely convinced that the Viet Cong are in them.'

The battalion radioed the infantry company at the scene: 'If you think there are any Viet Cong in the hamlet, burn it down.'

The company commander ordered his troops: 'Burn down that hamlet.'[56]

Information drop-off cannot be avoided completely, but the techniques described in the previous sections can reduce it substantially. Using the right communication channel, consistency between verbal and non-verbal messages, and active listening can maintain communication accuracy as it moves down the organization.

Upwards communication

Formal upwards communication includes messages that flow from the lower to the higher levels of the organization's hierarchy. Most organizations take pains to build in healthy channels for upwards communication. Employees need to air grievances, report progress and provide feedback on management initiatives. Coupling a healthy flow of upwards and downwards communication ensures that the communication circuit between managers and employees is complete.[57] Five types of information communicated upwards are the following:

■ **Problems and exceptions.** These messages describe serious problems with and exceptions to routine performance to make senior managers aware of difficulties. *Example:* 'The website went down at 2:00 a.m., and our engineers are currently working to resolve the problem.'

■ **Suggestions for improvement.** These messages are ideas for improving task-related procedures to increase quality or efficiency. *Example:* 'I think we should eliminate step 2 in the audit procedure because it takes a lot of time and produces no results.'

■ **Performance reports.** These messages include periodic reports that inform management how individuals and departments are performing. *Example:* 'We completed the audit report for Smith & Smith on schedule, but are 1 week behind on the Jackson report.'

■ *Grievances and disputes.* These messages are employee complaints and conflicts that travel up the hierarchy for a hearing and possible resolution. *Example:* 'After the reorganization of my district, I am working excessively long hours. I have lost any semblance of a work/life balance.'

■ *Financial and accounting information.* These messages pertain to costs, accounts receivable, sales volume, anticipated profits, return on investment and other matters of interest to senior managers. *Example:* 'Costs are 2 per cent over budget, but sales are 10 per cent ahead of target, so the profit picture for the third quarter is excellent.'

Smart managers make a serious effort to facilitate upwards communication. For example, Mike Hall, CEO of Borrego Solar Systems, found an effective way to encourage his introverted engineers to speak up and submit ideas for improving the business. To get his staff to offer feedback and suggestions, Hall organized an internal contest he called the Innovation Challenge. All employees were encouraged to submit ideas about improving the business using the company intranet. Once all of the ideas were submitted, employees voted for their favourite idea, and the winner won $500 in cash. Nearly all of Borrego's employees participated in the contest. '*We've been able to generate a lot of great ideas by tapping everyone's brains,*' Hall said.[58]

TAKE A MOMENT

You can polish your professional listening skills by completing the Small Group Breakout Exercise online.

Horizontal communication

Horizontal communication is the lateral or diagonal exchange of messages among peers or co-workers. It may occur within or across departments. The purpose of horizontal communication is not only to inform, but also to request support and coordinate activities. Horizontal communication falls into one of three categories:

■ *Intradepartmental problem solving.* These messages take place among members of the same department and concern task accomplishment. *Example:* 'Kelly, can you help us figure out how to complete this medical expense report form?'

■ *Interdepartmental coordination.* Interdepartmental messages facilitate the accomplishment of joint projects or tasks. *Example:* 'Michael, please ask your team to edit the report by using Google Docs by Monday morning.'

■ *Change initiatives and improvements.* These messages are designed to share information among teams and departments that can help the organization change, grow and improve. *Example:* 'We are streamlining the company travel procedures and would like to discuss them with your department.'

Recall from Chapter 4 that many organizations build in horizontal communications in the form of task forces, committees or even a matrix or horizontal structure to encourage coordination. At Chicago's Northwestern Memorial Hospital, two doctors created a horizontal task force to reduce the incidence of hospital-borne infections. The infection epidemic that kills nearly 100 000 people a year was growing worse worldwide, but Northwestern reversed the trend by breaking down communication barriers. Infectious-disease specialists Peterson and Noskin launched a regular Monday morning meeting involving doctors and nurses, lab technicians, pharmacists, computer technicians, admissions representatives and even the maintenance staff. The enhanced communication paid off. Over a 3-year period, Northwestern's rate of hospital-borne infections plunged 22 per cent and was roughly half the national average.[59]

Personal communication channels

Personal communication channels exist outside the formally authorized channels. These informal communications coexist with formal channels but may avoid hierarchical levels, cutting across vertical chains of command to connect virtually anyone in the organization. In most organizations, these informal channels are the primary way that information spreads and work gets accomplished. Three important types of personal communication channels are *personal networks*, the *grapevine and written communication*. In all organizations there are information gatekeepers who are worth cultivating, as they know or can get to know the answers through their personal networks.

Developing personal communication networks

Personal networking refers to the acquisition and cultivation of personal relationships that cross departmental, hierarchical and even organizational boundaries.[60] Successful managers consciously develop personal communication networks and encourage others to do so. In a communication network, people share information across boundaries and reach out to anyone who can further the goals of the team and organization. Exhibit 15.7 illustrates a communication network. Some people are central to the network while others play only a peripheral role. The key is that relationships are built across functional and hierarchical boundaries.

The value of personal networks for managers is that people who have more contacts have greater influence in the organization and can get more accomplished. For example, in Exhibit 15.7, Sharon has a well-developed personal communication network, sharing information and assistance with many people across the marketing, manufacturing and engineering departments. Contrast Sharon's contacts with those of Mike or Jasmine, who are on the periphery of the network. Who do you think is likely to have greater access to resources and more influence in the organization? Here are a few tips from one expert networker for building a personal communication network:[61]

■ **Build it before you need it.** Smart managers don't wait until they need something to start building a network of personal relationships – by then, it's too late. Instead, they show genuine interest in others and develop honest connections.

■ **Never eat lunch alone.** People who excel at networking make an effort to be visible and connect with as many people as possible. Masterful networkers keep their social as well as business conference and event calendars full.

■ **Make it win–win.** Successful networking isn't just about getting what *you* want; it's also about making sure that other people in the network get what *they* want.

EXHIBIT 15.7 An organizational communication network

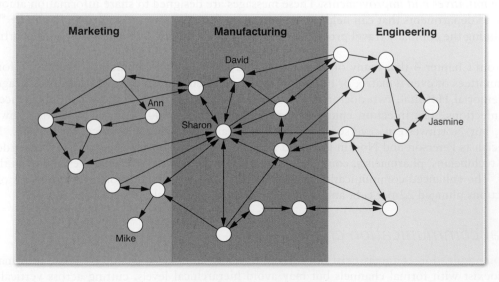

■ *Focus on diversity.* The broader your base of contacts, the broader your range of influence. Build connections with people from as many different areas of interest as possible (both within and outside the organization).

Most of us know from personal experience that 'who you know' sometimes counts for more than what you know. By cultivating a broad network of contacts, managers can extend their influence significantly and accomplish greater results.

The grapevine

Because 90 per cent of employees engage in gossip, every manager eventually will have to contend with its effects in the workplace.[62] Although the word *gossip* has a negative connotation, it may actually be good for a company, especially during times of significant organizational change, such as layoffs or downsizing. In fact, gossip can be an invaluable tool for managers. Gossip provides an efficient channel to communicate information, because it will move more rapidly than through a formal channel. Another advantage of gossip is that managers who tap into the gossip network may find it a useful 'early warning system' that helps them learn about internal situations or events that might need their attention. Plus, gossip is one way employees relieve feelings of tension and anxiety, especially during periods of change. Another benefit is that gossip may give marginalized employees an opportunity to have a voice within the organization.[63]

Gossip typically travels along the grapevine, an informal, person-to-person communication network that is not officially sanctioned by the organization.[64] The grapevine links employees in all directions, ranging from the CEO through middle management, support staff and line employees. The grapevine will always exist in an organization, but it can become a dominant force when formal channels are closed. In such cases, the grapevine is actually a service because the information that it provides helps make sense of an unclear or uncertain situation. Employees use grapevine rumours to fill in information gaps and clarify management decisions. One estimate is that as much as 70 per cent of all communication in a firm is carried through its grapevine.[65] The grapevine tends to be more active during periods of change, excitement, anxiety and sagging economic conditions. For example, a survey by professional employment services firm Randstad found that about half of all employees reported first hearing of major company changes through the grapevine.[66]

Surprising aspects of the grapevine are its accuracy and its relevance to the organization. About 80 per cent of grapevine communications pertain to business-related topics rather than personal gossip. Moreover, 70 to 90 per cent of the details passed through a grapevine are accurate.[67] Many managers would like the grapevine to be destroyed because they consider its rumours to be untrue, malicious and harmful, which typically is not the case. Managers should be aware that roughly five of every six important messages are carried to some extent by the grapevine rather than through official channels. In a survey of 22 000 shift workers in varied industries, 55 per cent said they get most of their information via the grapevine.[68] Smart managers understand the company's grapevine. *'If a leader has his ear to the ground, gossip can be a way for him to get a sense of what his employees are thinking or feeling,'* says Mitch Kusy, an organizational consultant, psychologist and professor at Antioch University.[69] In all cases, but particularly in times of crisis, executives need to manage communications effectively so that the grapevine is not the only source of information.[70]

TAKE A MOMENT

As a new manager, it is essential to build and nurture a personal communication network. Refer to the questionnaire at the end of the chapter to determine the effectiveness of your networking skills.

Written communication

Written communication skills are becoming increasingly important in today's collaborative workplace. *'With the fast pace of today's electronic communications, one might think that the value of fundamental writing skills has diminished in the workplace,'* said Joseph M. Tucci, president and CEO of EMC Corporation.

'*Actually, the need to write clearly and quickly has never been more important than in today's highly competitive, technology-driven global economy.*'[71]

Managers who are unable to communicate in writing will limit their opportunities for advancement. '*Writing is both a "marker" of high-skill, high-wage professional work and a "gatekeeper" with clear equity implications,*' says Bob Kerrey, as president of New School University in New York and chair of the National Commission on Writing. Managers can improve their writing skills by following these guidelines:[72]

■ **Respect the reader.** The reader's time is valuable; don't waste it with a rambling, confusing memo or email that has to be read several times to try to make sense of it. Pay attention to your grammar and spelling. Sloppy writing indicates that you think your time is more important than that of your readers. You'll lose their interest – and their respect.

■ **Know your point and get to it.** What is the key piece of information that you want the reader to remember? Many people just sit and write, without clarifying in their own mind what it is they're trying to say. To write effectively, know what your central point is and write to support it.

■ **Write clearly rather than impressively.** Don't use pretentious or inflated language, and avoid jargon. The goal of good writing for business is to be understood the first time. State your message as simply and as clearly as possible.

■ **Get a second opinion.** When the communication is highly important, such as a formal memo to the department or organization, ask someone you consider to be a good writer to read it – before you send it. Don't be too proud to take their advice. In all cases, read and revise the memo or email a second and third time before you hit the send button.

A former manager of communication services at consulting firm Arthur D. Little Inc. has estimated that around 30 per cent of all business memos and emails are written simply to get clarification about an earlier written communication, that didn't make sense to the reader.[73] By following the guidelines above, you can get your message across the first time.

REFLECTION

- A communication channel that flows within the chain of command is called a formal communication channel.
- Downwards communication refers to messages sent from top management down to subordinates; upwards communication includes messages that flow from the lower to the higher levels in the organization's hierarchy.
- Horizontal communication is the lateral or diagonal exchange of messages among peers or co-workers and includes team communication.

- Personal communication channels exist outside formally authorized channels and include personal networks, the grapevine and written communication.
- Personal networking refers to the acquisition and cultivation of personal relationships that cross departmental, hierarchical and even organizational boundaries.
- The grapevine carries workplace gossip, a dominant force in organization communication when formal channels are not functioning effectively.

Workplace communication

Two additional aspects of effective manager communication are using social media to improve internal and external communication and developing strategies for managing crisis communication.

Social media

Social media is a cluster of Internet-based applications that allow the creation and exchange of user-generated content. Social media covers a broad number of applications including wikis, blogs, micro-blogs (e.g., Twitter and China's Weibo), content communities (e.g., YouTube), social networking sites (e.g., Facebook) and virtual social networks (e.g., Social Life).[74] Social media is redefining how organizations communicate. Dr Pepper, for example, uses social media to listen to its customers by building an 8.5 million-strong fan base on Facebook. These loyal followers who 'like' the soft drink help the brand hone its marketing messages. The company sends out two messages daily on its Facebook fan page and then monitors the fans' reactions. Using tools from Facebook, Dr Pepper measures how many times a message is viewed, how many times it is shared with other Facebook users and what responses it gets. These data help managers adjust their brand messaging. '*We mine data to understand what is appreciated, and what is not,*' says Robert Stone, director of interactive media services for Dr Pepper Snapple Group Inc. '*It helps us shape what we are.*'[75]

Companies also use social media to build teams that solve problems faster, share information better among their employees and partners and respond to customer ideas for new product designs. In fact, big business is embracing social media in a big way. Forrester Research says that sales of software to run corporate social networks will grow 61 per cent a year and be a $6.4 billion business by 2016.[76] So far, social media hasn't boosted US productivity significantly, but economists such as MIT's Erik Brynjolfsson say that it takes about 5 years for a new technology to show its full impact on companies that use it. Social media has been used for only 2 or 3 years in most companies, largely for communicating with customers and enhancing employee collaboration.[77]

Listening to customers

Managers in many organizations, from small entrepreneurial firms and non-profit agencies to huge corporations, are experimenting with using social media to listen to customers. One organization that has implemented a clearly thought-out social media strategy is Dell's computer division. Through its IdeaStorm site, Dell received 17 000 ideas for new or improved products and adopted nearly 500, including backlit keyboards that are much better for working on airplanes. Dell also promotes its own new product ideas on IdeaStorm and requests customer feedback – before moving forwards with product development. After posting an idea related to a specialty laptop, customers posted 83 ideas for refinements to the machine, more feedback than Dell would receive from traditional focus groups.[78]

Communicating to customers

Managers also use social media to communicate corporate news quickly to customers. Domino's relied on the popularity of online communities to calm jittery customers after an image-damaging prank video, showing two employees defacing pizzas and sandwiches, was uploaded to YouTube. Domino's managers chose to respond with a viral video of their own. The company president apologized and thanked the online community for bringing the issue to his attention. He announced that the wrongdoers would be prosecuted and outlined the steps that Domino's was taking to ensure that the episode would never happen again. By engaging in an online conversation about the crisis, Domino's demonstrated concern for its customers and quashed further rumours and fears.[79]

'Don't think of social media as just another checkbox on your list of things to do. . . . It's not just about putting information out there, but listening and engaging in conversation.'
– LASANDRA BRILL, SENIOR MANAGER OF GLOBAL SOCIAL MEDIA, CISCO

Connecting employees

Using social media can enable people to connect with one another easily across organizational and geographical boundaries based on professional relationships, shared interests, problems or other criteria. Social networking, both through public sites and corporate networks, offers peer-to-peer communication channels where employees interact in an online community, sharing personal and professional information and photos, producing and sharing all sorts of ideas and opinions. Social networks designed for business use, such as Yammer and Chatter, increase productivity by making it easier for employees to share their knowledge. 7-Eleven, a Dallas-based convenience store, has 2000 employees who use Yammer to help the company's field consultants and franchisees share their knowledge and learn best practices from one another. A local franchisee might post a picture of a display that worked particularly well in one location, for instance, so that others can see it and try the same approach in their own stores.[80]

 INNOVATIVE **WAY**

Steve Jobs – Apple's CEO

Steve Jobs had a reputation in his industry of seeking perfection, with an obsession for control that shaped his approach to his full on style of running Apple. From his authorized biography written by Isaacson, Chapter 29 demonstrates his attention to detail and influencing skills with the opening of an early 'Apple Store' in Stanford, USA.

The following is an *extract* from Chapter 29 of his authorized biography (Isaacson 2011).

Jobs hated to cede control of anything, especially when it might affect the customer experience. But he faced a problem [as] there was one part of the process that he did not control: the experience of buying an Apple computer in a store. Other companies were pretty generic, but Apple's had innovative features and a higher price tag. Steve did not want an iMac to sit on a shelf between a Dell and a Compaq, while an uninformed clerk recited the specs of each. '*Unless we could find ways to get our message to customers at the store, we were screwed.*' In great secrecy Jobs began to interview executives who might be able to develop a string of Apple retail stores. One of the candidates was Ron Johnson the vice president for merchandising, at Target. '*Steve is very easy to talk to,*' said Johnson in recalling their first meeting. '*All of a sudden there's a torn pair of jeans and turtleneck and he's off and running about why he needed great stores.*' [Johnson recalled Jobs' mantra] '*If Apple is to succeed we're going to win on innovation and you cannot win on innovation unless you have a way to communicate to customers.*'

Crisis communication

A manager's skill at communicating becomes even more crucial during times of rapid change, uncertainty or crisis. Over the past few years, the sheer number and scope of crises have made communication a more demanding job for managers. Consider the importance of communication in the success of Robert Dudley, appointed as CEO for BP in the midst of the 2010 oil spill crisis in the Gulf of Mexico. Dudley faced the massive task of helping BP survive the greatest environmental disaster in history, caused when a rig drilling a well for BP exploded, killing 11 workers and making hundreds of millions of gallons of oil spew into the Gulf. Dudley entered his new role facing a myriad of challenges, all requiring superior communication skills: restoring trust among communities and the public, dealing with the costs and legal consequences of the oil spill, repairing damaged relationships with federal and state authorities, bolstering morale among BP employees and winning back investors. His ability to communicate confidence, concern and stability were critically important. '*I can't think of any new chief executive of an oil company stepping into a more complicated situation,*' said Daniel Yergin, chairman of IHS Cambridge Energy Research Associates. '*BP is going to be in a rebuilding mode, and the aftermath of the spill will go on for a long time.*'[81]

As a manager, your ability to communicate effectively during a crisis will determine how effectively the organization survives the upheaval. Consider the mistakes made by the luxury cruise ship captain who ran his ship aground in January 2012, causing a disaster that claimed 32 lives. The *Costa Concordia* ran aground and capsized off the coast of the Tuscan island of Giglio after Captain Francesco Schettino took it off course as part of a stunt. Schettino was accused of manslaughter and abandoning the ship before all passengers had been evacuated. Schettino is said to have contributed to the crisis by failing to respond for 45 minutes after the crew told him that the ship was flooding and its motors were dead. He issued the 'abandon ship order' nearly an hour after the ship had run aground – too late to save many lives. Schettino also failed to step forward, accept responsibility and explain what happened during the days following the disaster.[82]

Four primary skills for managers to follow when communicating in a crisis are outlined next. As you read them, consider how (in)effective Captain Schettino was in communicating during and after the cruise ship crisis.[83]

■ *Stay calm, listen hard.* Good crisis communicators don't allow themselves to be overwhelmed by the situation. Calmness and listening become more important than ever. Managers also learn to tailor their communications to reflect hope and optimism as they acknowledge current difficulties.

■ *Be visible.* Many managers underestimate just how important their presence is during a crisis.[84] A manager's job is to step out immediately, both to reassure employees and respond to public concerns. Face-to-face communication with employees is crucial for letting people know that managers care about them and what they're going through.

■ *Get the awful truth out.*[85] Effective managers gather as much information as they can, do their best to determine the facts and tell the truth to employees and the public as soon as possible. Getting the truth out quickly prevents harmful rumours and misunderstandings.

■ *Communicate a vision for the future.* People need to feel that they have something to work for and look forward to. Moments of crisis present opportunities for managers to communicate a vision of a better future and unite people towards common goals.

REFLECTION

- **Social media** is a group of Internet-based applications that allow the creation and exchange of user-generated content.
- **Social networking** sites offer peer-to-peer communication channels where employees interact in an online community, sharing personal and professional information, ideas and opinions.

- During a communication crisis, a manager should stay calm and listen carefully, reassure employees and the public, tell the truth and communicate a vision for the future.

DISCUSSION QUESTIONS

1 Identify and discuss the various personality, group and other situational factors etc. that affect the way information is transmitted and received by others.

2 Identify and evaluate five specific functions of non-verbal communication, discussing their importance for the senders of data.

3 In the event of a corporate crisis what particular skills should the company's spokesperson have to deal with the media?

4 Discuss the importance of listening for actors in a negotiation situation. Provide several guidelines for a manager to pay attention to.

5 Describe the types of noise that can exist in a corporate situation and provide advice on how the negative impacts of these aspects can be minimized.

Are you building a personal network?

INSTRUCTIONS How much effort do you put into developing connections with other people? Personal networks may help a new manager in the workplace. To learn something about your networking skills, answer the questions below. Please indicate whether each item is 'Mostly true' or 'Mostly false' for you in school or at work.

		Mostly true	Mostly false
1	I learn early on about changes in the organization and how they might affect me or my position.	☐	☐
2	I network as much to help other people solve problems as to help myself.	☐	☐
3	I am fascinated by other people and what they do.	☐	☐
4	I frequently use lunches to meet and network with new people.	☐	☐
5	I regularly participate in charitable causes.	☐	☐
6	I maintain a list of friends and colleagues to whom I send holiday greeting cards.	☐	☐
7	I maintain contact with people from previous organizations and school groups.	☐	☐
8	I actively give information to subordinates, peers and my boss.	☐	☐

SCORING & INTERPRETATION Give yourself one point for each item marked as 'Mostly true'. A score of 6 or higher suggests active networking and a solid foundation on which to begin your career as a new manager. When you create a personal network, you become well connected to get things done through a variety of relationships. Having sources of information and support helps a new manager gain career traction. If you scored 3 or less, you may want to focus more on building relationships if you are serious about a career as a manager. People with active networks tend to be more effective managers and have broader impact on the organization.

APPLY YOUR SKILLS: ETHICAL DILEMMA

On trial[86]

When Werner and Thompson, a Los Angeles business and financial management firm, offered Iranian-born Firoz Bahmania a position as an accountant assistant one Spring day in 2007, Bahmani felt a sense of genuine relief, but his relief was short-lived.

With his degree in accounting from a top-notch American university, he knew he was more than a little overqualified for the job. But time after time, he'd been rejected for suitable positions. His language difficulties were the reason most often

given for his unsuccessful candidacy. Although the young man had grown up speaking both Farsi and French in his native land, he'd begun to pick up English only shortly before his arrival in the USA a few years ago. Impressed by his educational credentials and his quiet, courtly manner, managing partner Beatrice Werner overlooked his heavy accent and actively recruited him for the position, the only one available at the time. During his interview, she assured him that he would advance in time.

It was clear to Beatrice that Firoz was committed to succeeding at all costs. But it soon also became apparent that Firoz and his immediate supervisor, Cathy Putnam, were at odds. Cathy was a seasoned account manager who had just transferred to Los Angeles from the New York office. Saddled with an enormous workload, she let Firoz know right from the start, speaking in her rapid-fire Brooklyn accent, that he'd need to get up to speed as quickly as possible.

Shortly before Cathy was to give Firoz his 3-month probationary review, she came to Beatrice, expressed her frustration with Firoz's performance and suggested that he be let go. 'His bank reconciliations and financial report preparations are first-rate,' Cathy admitted, 'but his communication skills leave a lot to be desired. In the first place, I simply don't have the time to keep repeating the same directions over and over again when I'm trying to teach him his responsibilities. Then there's the fact that public contact is part of his written job description. Typically, he puts off making phone calls to dispute credit card charges or ask a client's staff for the information he needs. When he does finally pick up the phone . . . well, let's just say I've had more than one client mention how hard it is to understand what he's trying to say. Some of them are getting pretty exasperated.'

'You know, some firms feel it's their corporate responsibility to help foreign-born employees learn English,' Beatrice began. 'Maybe we should help him find an English-as-a-second-language course and pay for it.'

'With all due respect, I don't think that's our job,' Cathy replied, with barely concealed irritation. 'If you come to the USA, you should learn our language. That's what my mom's parents did when they came over from Italy. They certainly didn't expect anyone to hold their hands. Besides,' she added, almost inaudibly, 'Firoz's lucky we let him into this country.'

Beatrice had mixed feelings. On the one hand, she recognized that Werner and Thompson had every right to expect someone in Firoz's position to be capable of carrying out his public contact duties. Perhaps she had made a mistake in hiring him. But as the daughter of German immigrants herself, she knew firsthand both how daunting language and cultural barriers could be and that they could be overcome in time. Perhaps in part because of her family background, she had a passionate commitment to the firm's stated goals of creating a diverse workforce and a caring, supportive culture. Besides, she felt a personal sense of obligation to help a hard-working, promising employee realize his potential. What will she advise Cathy to do now that Firoz's probationary period is drawing to a close?

What would you do?

1 Agree with Cathy Putnam. Despite your personal feelings, accept that Firoz Bahmani is not capable of carrying out the accountant assistant's responsibilities. Make the break now, and give him his notice on the grounds that he cannot carry out one of the key stated job requirements. Advise him that a position that primarily involves paperwork would be a better fit for him.

2 Place Firoz with a more sympathetic account manager who is open to finding ways to help him improve his English and has the time to help him develop his assertiveness and telephone skills. Send Cathy Putnam to diversity awareness training.

3 Create a new position at the firm that will allow Firoz to do the reports and reconciliations for several account managers, freeing the account assistants to concentrate on public contact work. Make it clear that he will have little chance of future promotion unless his English improves markedly.

APPLY YOUR SKILLS: CASE FOR CRITICAL ANALYSIS

Global Sparks: Formal and informal communication channels

Global Sparks is a global organization which positions itself along the electrification value chain. It has the know-how that extends from power generation to power transmission, power distribution and smart grid to the efficient application of electrical energy. Its strategy entitled 'Global Sparks Vision 2025' defines an entrepreneurial concept that will enable Global Sparks to consistently occupy attractive growth fields, sustainably strengthen its core business and outpace its competitors in efficiency and performance.

Excellent employees are one of Global Sparks' greatest strengths. According to Global Sparks chief executive, Gerhardt Neef, 'Our people have made Global Sparks what it is today – and their expertise, capabilities and outstanding commitment are the foundation for our ongoing success.' Neef added, 'Our people make us and therefore we are the people.' To remain competitive, Global Sparks has to continuously recruit and retain the best and brightest people worldwide. As an employer of choice, Global Sparks fosters the diversity and commitment of its workforce in a high-performance culture; encourages life long learning and development; offers an attractive working environment; operates a health management system; promotes talent management and career planning; and guarantees occupational safety. Global Sparks operates an inclusive approach to its 'Talent Management Strategy' encouraging applications for managerial roles from its diverse employees wherever they are located and from all levels of organizational employees.

It is against this background that Global Sparks recently undertook a selection process for Global Internal Management Consultants (Human Resources). These are highly sought positions and ten candidates (seven European-based and three International) were interviewed at the Munich head office for four new posts. Two of the candidates for the Global Internal Consultant (Human Resources) were employed at the Munich head office (Hans and Lotte). The interviews were conducted over 2 days by a committee of five senior executives, chaired by Dr Hans Dalmac, with each interview lasting about 60 minutes. The two Munich employees were interviewed last.

At the conclusion of the interview Dr Dalmac asked each of the members of the committee to nominate one of the ten candidates for the four new posts. These decisions were made very quickly and the committee dispersed. Catering staff (Franz and Fritz) entered the office where the interviews were being held to clear up, and asked one of the senior executives how the interviews had gone as they recognized two of the candidates, Hans and Lotte.

The senior executive stated that Lotte, who was last to be interviewed, had not been successful.

Frans and Fritz completed the clearing up and took the lift to the basement. In the basement they met one of the secretarial staff (Greta) from Lotte's department and they told her that Lotte had been unsuccessful. Greta returned to her office and as she entered the office, Lotte passed her in the corridor. Greta said to Lotte 'Sorry to hear that you were unsuccessful in your interview today.'

Lotte was furious and asked Greta 'Where and when did you hear that I was unsuccessful and who told you?' Greta replied that she had no idea where the information came from and apologised to her for passing on what was no more than gossip. Lotte contacted Dr Dalmac, asking if the rumour was true. He apologized but confirmed that she had been unsuccessful and he immediately requested information from the other members of the selection committee on how this communication leak had happened and how it had happened so quickly.

Lotte has raised a formal grievance against Dr Hans Dalmac claiming he was responsible for the breakdown in the system of formal communications and that she has suffered personal distress as a consequence of this communications failure.

References Ruck, K. and Welch, M. (2012) Valuing internal communication; management and employee perspectives, *Public Relations Review*, Volume 38, Issue 2, June 2012, Pages 294–302.

Questions

1 Critically evaluate what has happened in this case.

2 Discuss the ways in which corrective action could be taken to address this breakdown in the formal communications system.

3 Propose a course of action to avoid a further repetition of this nature.

END NOTES

1. Careercast.com website, www.careercast.com/jobs-rated/10-best-jobs-2012 (accessed September 21, 2012); George Anders, 'LinkedIn's Edge: The 7 Habits of a Well-Run Social Network', *Forbes*, August 3, 2012, www.forbes.com/sites/georgeanders/2012/08/03/linkedins-edge-the-7-habits-of-a-well-run-social-network/ (accessed September 3, 2012);

CNNmoney .com website, http://money.cnn.com/magazines/fortune/best-companies/2012/full_list/.

2. 'Capitalizing on Effective Communication: How Courage, Innovation, and Discipline Drive Business Results in Challenging Times', Communication ROI Study Report by Watson, Wyatt, Worldwide, 2009/2010, www.towerswatson.

com/assets/pdf/670/Capitalizing%20on%20Effective%20 Communication.pdf (accessed September 5, 2012).

3. Phillip G. Clampitt, Laurey Berk and M. Lee Williams, 'Leaders as Strategic Communicators', *Ivey Business Journal* (May–June 2002): 51–55.

4. Communication ROI Study Report.

5. Eric Berkman, 'Skills', *CIO* (March 1, 2002): 78-82; Louise van der Does and Stephen J. Caldeira, 'Effective Leaders Champion Communication Skills', *Nation's Restaurant News* (March 27, 2006): 20; and Byron Reimus, 'Ready, Aim, Communicate', *Management Review* (July 1996).

6. Reimus, 'Ready, Aim, Communicate'; and Dennis Tourish, 'Critical Upward Communication: Ten Commandments for Improving Strategy and Decision Making', *Long Range Planning* 38 (2005): 485–503.

7. Bernard M. Bass, *Bass & Stogdill's Handbook of Leadership*, 3rd ed. (New York: The Free Press, 1990).

8. Reported in van der Does and Caldeira, 'Effective Leaders Champion Communication Skills'.

9. Tom Szaky, 'How Much Information Do You Share With Employees?' *The New York Times*, September 8, 2011, http://boss.blogs.nytimes.com/author/tom-szaky/page/2/ (accessed September 5, 2012).

10. Quint Studer, 'Case for Transparency', *Leadership Excellence* (April 2010): 19.

11. Van der Does and Caldeira, 'Effective Leaders Champion Communication Skills'.

12. Studer, 'Case for Transparency'.

13. E. M. Rogers and R. A. Rogers, *Communication in Organizations* (New York: Free Press, 1976); and A. Bavelas and D. Barrett, 'An Experimental Approach to Organization Communication', *Personnel* 27 (1951): 366–371.

14. Joel Spolsky, 'A Little Less Conversation', *Inc.* (February, 2010): 28–29.

15. This discussion is based on Richard L. Daft and Richard M. Steers, *Organizations: A Micro/Macro Approach* (New York: HarperCollins, 1986).

16. Richard L. Daft and Norman B. Macintosh, 'A Tentative Exploration into the Amount and Equivocality of Information Processing in Organizational Work Units', *Administrative Science Quarterly* 26 (1981): 207–224.

17. Robert H. Lengel and Richard L. Daft, 'The Selection of Communication Media as an Executive Skill', *Academy of Management Executive* 2 (August 1988): 225–232; Richard L. Daft and Robert H. Lengel, 'Organizational Information Requirements, Media Richness, and Structural Design', *Managerial Science* 32 (May 1986): 554–572; and Jane Webster and Linda Klebe Treviño, 'Rational and Social Theories as Complementary Explanations of Communication Media Choices: Two Policy-Capturing Studies', *Academy of Management Journal* 38, no. 6 (1995): 1544–1572.

18. Janina Seubert and Christina Regenbogen, 'I Know How You Feel', *Scientific American Mind* (March/April 2012): 54–58.

19. Research reported in 'E-mail Can't Mimic Phone Calls', *Johnson City Press*, September 17, 2000.

20. Raymond E. Friedman and Steven C. Currall, 'E-Mail Escalation: Dispute Exacerbating Elements of Electronic Communication', http://papers.ssrn.com/sol3/papers.cfm?abstract_id=459429 (accessed September 21, 2010); Lauren Keller Johnson, 'Does E-Mail Escalate Conflict?' *MIT Sloan Management Review* (Fall 2002): 14–15; and

Alison Stein Wellner, 'Lost in Translation', *Inc. Magazine* (September 2005): 37–38.

21. Margie Warrell, 'Hiding Behind E-mail? Four Times You Should Never Use E-mail', *Forbes*, www.forbes.com/sites/margiewarrell/2012/08/27/do-you-hide-behind-email/ (accessed September 10, 2012).

22. Ronald E. Rice, 'Task Analyzability, Use of New Media, and Effectiveness: A Multi-Site Exploration of Media Richness', *Organizational Science* 3, no. 4 (November 1992): 475–500; and M. Lynne Markus, 'Electronic Mail as the Medium of Managerial Choice', *Organizational Science* 5, no. 4 (November 1994): 502–527.

23. Richard L. Daft, Robert H. Lengel and Linda Klebe Treviño, 'Message Equivocality, Media Selection and Manager Performance: Implication for Information Systems', *MIS Quarterly* 11 (1987): 355–368.

24. Mary Young and James E. Post, 'Managing to Communicate, Communicating to Manage: How Leading Companies Communicate with Employees', *Organizational Dynamics* (Summer 1993): 31–43.

25. This section is based heavily on Jay A. Conger, 'The Necessary Art of Persuasion', *Harvard Business Review* (May–June 1998): 84–95.

26. Conger, 'The Necessary Art of Persuasion'.

27. Tsedal Neeley and Paul Leonardi, 'Effective Managers Say the Same Thing Twice (and More)', *Harvard Business Review* (May 2011): 38–39.

28. This discussion is based in part on Jack Welch with Suzy Welch, *Winning* (New York: HarperBusiness, 2005), Chapter 2.

29. These are based on E. Raudsepp, 'Are You Properly Assertive?' *Supervision* (June 1992); and M. J. Smith, *When I Say No, I Feel Guilty* (New York: Bantam Books, 1975).

30. Based on Welch, *Winning*, Chapter 2.

31. Carol Bartz, 'Speak Your Mind', *BusinessWeek*, www.businessweek.com/articles/2012-04-12/how-to-speak-your-mind-carol-bartz#r=auth-s (accessed September 12, 2012).

32. Boris Groysberg and Michael Slind, 'Leadership Is a Conversation', *Harvard Business Review* (June 2012): 75–84.

33. Many of these benefits are based on 'The Power of Questions', *Leader to Leader* (Spring 2005): 59–60; Quinn Spitzer and Ron Evans, 'The New Business Leader: Socrates with a Baton', *Strategy & Leadership* (September–October 1997): 32–38; and Gary B. Cohen, 'Just Ask Leadership: Why Great Managers Always Ask the Right Questions', *Ivey Business Journal*, July–August 2010, www.iveybusinessjournal.com/topics/leadership/just-ask-leadership-why-great-managers-always-ask-the-right-questions (accessed March 7, 2011).

34. Groysberg and Slind, 'Leadership Is a Conversation'.

35. Reported in Spitzer and Evans, 'The New Business Leader: Socrates with a Baton'.

36. Kevin Cashman, 'Powerful Pause: Listening Is Leadership', *Leadership Excellence* (January 2012): 5.

37. M. P. Nichols, *The Lost Art of Listening* (New York: Guilford Publishing, 1995).

38. 'Benchmarking the Sales Function', a report based on a study of 100 salespeople from small, medium, and large businesses, conducted by the Ron Volper Group, White Plains, New York, as reported in 'Nine Habits of Highly Effective Salespeople', *Inc.com*, June 1, 1997, www.inc.com/articles/1997/06/12054.html (accessed September 23, 2010).

39. Gerald M. Goldhaber, *Organizational Communication*, 4th ed. (Dubuque, IA: Brown, 1980), p. 189.

40. C. Glenn Pearce, 'Doing Something About Your Listening Ability', *Supervisory Management* (March 1989): 29–34; and Tom Peters, 'Learning to Listen', *Hyatt Magazine* (Spring 1988): 16–21.

41. Kelley Holland, 'Under New Management; The Silent May Have Something to Say', *The New York Times*, November 5, 2006.

42. Debbie Weil, *The Corporate Blogging Book* (New York: Penguin Group, 2006), p. 3.

43. *Fortune* 500 Business Blogging Wiki, www.socialtext.net/bizblogs/index.cgi (accessed July 26, 2010).

44. Carol Kinsey Goman, 'Body Language: Mastering the Silent Language of Leadership' (The Leadership Playlist column), *The Washington Post Online,* July 17, 2009, http://views.washingtonpost.com/leadership/leadership_playlist/2009/07/body-language-mastering-the-silent-language-of-leadership.html (accessed July 17, 2009).

45. Thomas Sheppard, 'Silent Signals', *Supervisory Management* (March 1986): 31–33.

46. Carmine Gallo, 'How to Stay Cool in the Hot Seat', *BusinessWeek,* June 22, 2010, www.businessweek.com/print/smallbiz/content/jun2010/sb20100622_820980.htm (accessed July 28, 2010).

47. Albert Mehrabian, *Silent Messages* (Belmont, CA: Wadsworth, 1971); and Albert Mehrabian, 'Communicating Without Words', *Psychology Today* (September 1968): 53–55.

48. Meridith Levinson, 'How to Be a Mind Reader', *CIO* (December 1, 2004): 72–76; Mac Fulfer, 'Non-verbal Communication: How to Read What's Plain as the Nose . . . ', *Journal of Organizational Excellence* (Spring 2001): 19–27; and Paul Ekman, *Emotions Revealed: Recognizing Faces and Feelings to Improve Communication and Emotional Life* (New York: Time Books, 2003).

49. Goman, 'Body Language: Mastering the Silent Language of Leadership'.

50. *Ibid.*

51. Daft and Steers, *Organizations*; and Daniel Katz and Robert Kahn, *The Social Psychology of Organizations*, 2nd ed. (New York: Wiley, 1978).

52. Greg Jaffe, 'Tug of War: In the New Military, Technology May Alter Chain of Command', *The Wall Street Journal*, March 30, 2001; and Aaron Pressman, 'Business Gets the Message', *The Industry Standard* (February 26, 2001): 58–59.

53. Phillip G. Clampitt, Robert J. DeKoch and Thomas Cashman, 'A Strategy for Communicating about Uncertainty', *Academy of Management Executive* 14, no. 4 (2000): 41–57.

54. Reported in van der Does and Caldeira, 'Effective Leaders Champion Communication Skills'.

55. Alexandra Samuel, 'Better Leadership Through Social Media', *The Wall Street Journal*, http://online.wsj.com/article/SB10001424052970203753704577255531558650636.html (accessed September 12, 2012).

56. Story recounted in J. G. Miller, 'Living Systems: The Organization', *Behavioural Science* 17 (1972): 69.

57. Michael J. Glauser, 'Upward Information Flow in Organizations: Review and Conceptual Analysis', *Human Relations* 37 (1984): 613–643; and 'Upward/Downward Communi-

cation: Critical Information Channels', *Small Business Report* (October 1985): 85–88.

58. Darren Dahl, 'Pipe Up People! Rounding Up Staff', *Inc.* (February 2010): 80–81.

59. Thomas Petzinger, 'A Hospital Applies Teamwork to Thwart an Insidious Enemy', *The Wall Street Journal*, May 8, 1998.

60. This discussion of informal networks is based on Rob Cross, Nitin Nohria and Andrew Parker, 'Six Myths About Informal Networks', *MIT Sloan Management Review* (Spring 2002): 67–75; and Rob Cross and Laurence Prusak, 'The People Who Make Organizations Go – or Stop', *Harvard Business Review* (June 2002): 105–112.

61. Tahl Raz, 'The 10 Secrets of a Master Networker', *Inc.* (January 2003).

62. Travis J. Grosser, Virginie Lopez-Kidwell, Giuseppe Labianca and Lea Ellwardt 'Hearing It Through the Grapevine: Positive and Negative Workplace Gossip', *Organizational Dynamics* 41 (2012): 52–61.

63. Grant Michelson, Ad van Iterson and Kathryn Waddington, 'Gossip in Organizations: Contexts, Consequences, and Controversies', *Group & Organizational Management* 35, no. 4 (2010): 371–390.

64. Keith Davis and John W. Newstrom, *Human Behavior at Work: Organizational Behavior*, 7th ed. (New York: McGraw-Hill, 1985).

65. Suzanne M. Crampton, John W. Hodge and Jitendra M. Mishra, 'The Informal Communication Network: Factors Influencing Grapevine Activity', *Public Personnel Management* 27, no. 4 (Winter 1998): 569–584.

66. Survey results reported in Jared Sandberg, 'Ruthless Rumors and the Managers Who Enable Them', *The Wall Street Journal*, October 29, 2003.

67. Donald B. Simmons, 'The Nature of the Organizational Grapevine', *Supervisory Management* (November 1985): 39–42; and Davis and Newstrom, *Human Behavior at Work*.

68. Barbara Ettorre, 'Hellooo. Anybody Listening?' *Management Review* (November 1997): 9.

69. Eilene Zimmerman, 'Gossip Is Information by Another Name', *The New York Times*, February 3, 2008, www.nytimes.com/2008/02/03/jobs/03career.html?scp=1&sq=Gossip%20Is%20Information%20by%20Another%20Name&st=cse (accessed February 3, 2008).

70. Lisa A. Burke and Jessica Morris Wise, 'The Effective Care, Handling, and Pruning of the Office Grapevine', *Business Horizons* (May–June 2003): 71–74; 'They Hear It Through the Grapevine', cited in Michael Warshaw, 'The Good Guy's Guide to Office Politics', *Fast Company* (April–May 1998): 157–178; and Carol Hildebrand, 'Mapping the Invisible Workplace', *CIO Enterprise*, section 2 (July 15, 1998): 18–20.

71. The National Commission on Writing, 'Writing Skills Necessary for Employment, Says Big Business', September 14, 2004, www.writingcommission.org/pr/writing_for_employ.html (accessed April 8, 2008).

72. Based on Michael Fitzgerald, 'How to Write a Memorable Memo', *CIO* (October 15, 2005): 85–87; and Jonathan Hershberg, 'It's Not Just What You Say', *Training* (May 2005): 50.

73. Mary Anne Donovan, 'E-Mail Exposes the Literacy Gap', *Workforce* (November 2002): 15.

74. Andreas M. Kaplan and Michael Haenlein, 'Social Media: Back to the Roots and Back to the Future', *Journal*

of Systems and Information Technology 14, no. 2 (2012): 101–104.

75. Geoffrey A. Fowler, 'Are You Talking to Me?' *The Wall Street Journal*, April 25, 2011, http://online.wsj.com/article/SB1000142405274870411640457626083970961862.html (accessed September 18, 2012).

76. Mullaney, 'Social Media Is Reinventing How Business Is Done'.

77. *Ibid*.

78. *Ibid*.

79. Richard S. Levick, 'Domino's Discovers Social Media', *BusinessWeek*, April 21, 2009, www.businessweek.com/print/managing/content/apr2009/ca20090421_555468.htm (accessed April 21, 2009).

80. Shayndi Raice, 'Social Networking Heads to the Office', *The Wall Street Journal*, http://online.wsj.com/article/SB10001424052702304459804577285354046601614.html (accessed September 18, 2012).

81. Julia Werdigier and Jad Mouawad, 'Road to New Confidence at BP Runs Through US.', *The New York Times*, July 26, 2010, www.nytimes.com/2010/07/27/business/27dudley.html?_r=1&sq=BP%20Hayward&st=cse&adxnnl=1&scp=7&adxnnlx=1280315332-P6V5i9wUaL40EYFeOSH52w (accessed July 27, 2010).

82. Stacy Meichtry, Arian Camp-Flores and Leslie Scism, 'Cruise Company Blames Captain', *The Wall Street Journal*, January 17, 2012, http://online.wsj.com/article/SB10001424052970203735304577165290656739300.html (accessed September 19, 2012).

83. This section is based on Leslie Wayne and Leslie Kaufman, 'Leadership, Put to a New Test', *The New York Times*, September 16, 2001; Ian I. Mitroff, 'Crisis Leadership', *Executive Excellence* (August 2001): 19; Jerry Useem, 'What It Takes', *Fortune* (November 12, 2001): 126–132; Andy Bowen, 'Crisis Procedures That Stand the Test of Time', *Public Relations Tactics* (August 2001): 16; and Matthew Boyle, 'Nothing Really Matters', *Fortune* (October 15, 2001): 261–264.

84. Stephen Bernhut, 'Leadership, with Michael Useem' (interview), *Ivey Business Journal* (January–February 2002): 42–43.

85. Mitroff, 'Crisis Leadership'.

86. Mary Gillis, 'Iranian Americans', *Multicultural America*, www.everyculture.com/multi/Ha-La/Iranian-Americans.html (accessed September 19, 2006); and Charlene Marmer Solomon, 'Managing Today's Immigrants', *Personnel Journal* 72, no. 3 (February 1993): 56–65.

CHAPTER 16

LEADING TEAMS

LEARNING OBJECTIVES

After studying this chapter, you should be able to:

1   Identify the types of teams in organizations.

2   Explain contributions that teams make and how managers can make teams more effective.

3   Discuss some of the problems and challenges of teamwork.

4   Identify roles within teams and the type of role that you could play to help a team be effective.

5   Explain the general stages of team development.

6   Identify ways in which team size and diversity of membership affect team performance.

7   Explain the concepts of team cohesiveness and team norms and their relationship to team performance.

8   Understand the causes of conflict within and among teams, and how to reduce conflict.

9   Describe the different characteristics and consequences of task conflict versus relationship conflict.

Managers at Boeing knew it was a good problem to have – demand for the company's 737 jetliner was soaring. But they had to find a way to keep pace with the demand without jeopardizing Boeing's future with a rapid expansion of factories and operating costs. How to produce more aircraft without expanding became the driving question at Boeing – and cross-functional teams provided the innovative answers. One team made up of engineers, mechanics and other employees came up with a new process for assembling the hydraulic tubes that go into the landing gear wheel-well of the 737. The new process saves about 30 hours of mechanics' time (and a lot of money) on each system. Another team redesigned the workspace so that four engines rather than three could be produced at a time. Boeing has about 1300 of these 'innovation teams' across its commercial jet programmes. Each team of seven to ten workers typically focuses on a specific part of a jet; teams meet each week to work on problems or come up with new processes. Overall, Boeing's teams have come up with ideas that have boosted 737 output to 35 jets a month, up from 31, and the goal is to be producing 42 a month.[1]

Many people get their first management experience in a team setting, and you will sometimes have to work in a team as a new manager. Many companies, like Boeing, have discovered that teams have real advantages, but it can be tough to work in a team. You may have already experienced the challenges of teamwork as a student, where you've had to give up some of your independence and rely on the team to perform well in order to earn a good grade.

Good teams can produce amazing results, but teams aren't always successful. In a survey of manufacturing organizations, about 80 per cent of respondents reported using some kind of team, but only 14 per cent of those companies rated their teaming efforts as highly effective. Just over half of the respondents said their efforts were only 'somewhat effective', and 15 per cent considered their efforts not effective at all.[2]

This chapter focuses on teams and their applications within organizations. We define what a team is, look at the contributions that teams can make and define various types of teams. Then we discuss the dilemma of teamwork and present a model of work team effectiveness, explore the stages of team development and examine how characteristics such as size, cohesiveness, diversity and norms influence team effectiveness. The chapter also looks at the roles that individuals play in teams, discusses techniques for managing team conflict and describes how negotiation can facilitate cooperation and teamwork. Teams are a central aspect of organizational life, and the ability to manage them is a vital component of manager and organization success.

The value of teams

Why aren't organizations just collections of individuals going their own way and doing their own thing? Clearly, teamwork provides benefits or companies wouldn't continue to use this structural mechanism. One illustration of the value of teamwork comes from the military, where forward surgical teams made up of US Navy surgeons, nurses, anesthesiologists and technicians operated for the first time ever in combat during Operation Iraqi Freedom. These teams were scattered over Iraq and were able to move to new locations and be set up within an hour. With a goal of saving the lives of the 15 to 20 per cent of wounded soldiers and civilians who die unless they receive critical care within 24 hours, members of these teams smoothly coordinated their activities to accomplish a critical shared mission.[3]

Although their missions might not involve life or death, all organizations are made up of various individuals and groups that have to work together and coordinate their activities to accomplish objectives. Much work in organizations is *interdependent*, which means that individuals and departments rely on other individuals and departments for information or resources to accomplish their work. When tasks are highly interdependent, a team can be the best approach to ensuring the level of coordination, information sharing and exchange of materials necessary for successful task accomplishment.

 GREEN **POWER**

The Team's the Thing

Managers at **Subaru Indiana Automotive** (SIA) put the company's desire to reduce, reuse and recycle waste squarely on the line with television ads boasting 'zero-landfill'. SIA was not hedging, maintaining that 'zero means zero', and managers placed confidence in every member of every team in every manufacturing process to hit the target. And the teams proved to be up to the challenge. For example, shop floor initiatives within the stamping unit led to partnering agreements with suppliers for more precise steel sheeting that reduced 100 pounds of steel per vehicle. Teams initiated efforts to use plant water flow to drive mini-hydraulic electric generators, and the company's Green Payback Curve recycled a variety of waste products. Assembly-line lights were turned down during breaks and shift changes to decrease the company's carbon footprint. Respect for and confidence in its teams has made SIA a recognized leader of sustainability in manufacturing.

SOURCES: Brad Kenney, 'The Zero Effect: How to Green Your Facility', *Industry Week* (July 2008): 36–41; and Dean M. Schroeder and Alan G. Robinson, 'Green Is Free: Creating Sustainable Competitive Advantage Through Green Excellence', *Organizational Dynamics* 39, no. 4 (2010): 345–352.

What is a team?

A team is a unit of two or more people who interact and coordinate their work to accomplish a common goal to which they are committed and hold themselves mutually accountable.[4] The definition of a team has four components. First, two or more people are required. Second, people in a team have regular interaction. Third, people in a team share a performance goal, whether it is to design a new smartphone, build an engine or complete a class project. Fourth, people in a team are committed to the goal and hold themselves mutually accountable for performance. Although a *team* is a *group* of people, these two terms are not interchangeable. An employer, a teacher or a coach can put together a group of people and never build a team. The team concept implies a sense of shared mission and collective responsibility. Exhibit 16.1 lists the primary differences between groups and teams.

EXHIBIT 16.1 Differences between groups and teams

Group	Team
• Has a designated strong leader	• Shares or rotates leadership roles
• Holds individuals accountable	• Holds team members accountable to each other
• Sets identical purpose for group and organization	• Sets specific team vision or purpose
• Has individual work products	• Has collective work products
• Runs efficient meetings	• Runs meetings that encourage open-ended discussion and problem solving
• Measures effectiveness indirectly by influence on business (such as financial performance)	• Measures effectiveness directly by assessing collective work
• Discusses, decides and delegates work to individuals	• Discusses, decides and shares work

SOURCE: Jon R. Katzenbach and Douglas K. Smith, 'The Discipline of Teams', *Harvard Business Review* (March–April 1995): 111–120.

'Individual commitment to a group effort – that is what makes a team work, a company work, a society work, a civilization work.'

— VINCE LOMBARDI (1913–1970), NFL FOOTBALL COACH

Contributions of teams

Effective teams can provide many advantages in organizations, as illustrated in Exhibit 16.2. These contributions of teams lead to stronger competitive advantage and higher overall organizational performance.

■ **Creativity and innovation:** Because teams include people with diverse skills, strengths, experiences and perspectives, they contribute to a higher level of creativity and innovation in the organization.[5] One factor overlooked by some commentators in the success of Apple, for instance, is that Steve Jobs built a top management team of superb technologists, marketers, designers and others who kept the company's innovative juices flowing. Most of Jobs' top management team had worked with him for a decade or more.[6]

■ **Improved quality:** One criterion for organizational effectiveness is whether products and services meet customer requirements for quality. Perhaps nowhere is this more essential than in health care. The days when a lone physician could master all the skills, keep all the information in his or her head, and manage everything required to treat a patient, are long gone. Organizations that provide the highest quality of patient care are those in which teams of closely coordinated professionals provide an integrated system of care.[7]

EXHIBIT 16.2 Five contributions teams make

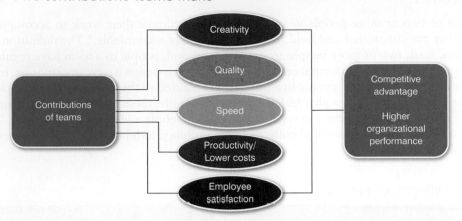

CONCEPT CONNECTION

In recent years, hundreds of hospitals have been forming palliative care **teams** to address the unique needs of patients with terminal illnesses. These teams consist of doctors, nurses, social workers and various types of spiritual advisors, who work together to treat each patient holistically – physically, mentally, emotionally and spiritually. Dr Diane Meier, a leader in the palliative care trend, notes, '*Patients [typically] see a different person for every single part of their body or every problem. The patient as a whole person gets lost.*' Hospitals are adopting these teams because they **improve the quality** of care provided to patients just when they need it most.

■ **Speed of response:** Tightly integrated teams can manoeuvre incredibly fast. Apple again provides an example. Apple's close-knit team has changed pricing as late as 48 hours before the launch of a new product, which would be inconceivable at most companies.[8] In addition, teams can speed product development (as we discussed in Chapter 4), respond more quickly to changing customer needs and solve cross-departmental problems more quickly.

■ **Higher productivity and lower costs:** Effective teams can unleash enormous energy from employees. Social facilitation refers to the tendency for the presence of others to enhance one's performance. Simply being around others has an energizing effect.[9] In addition, the blend of perspectives enables creative ideas to percolate. As described in the opening example, teams at Boeing have come up with numerous ideas that help them build planes faster and at lower cost.

■ **Enhanced motivation and satisfaction:** As described in Chapter 14, people have needs for belongingness and affiliation. Working in teams can meet these needs and create greater camaraderie across the organization. Teams also reduce boredom, increase people's feelings of dignity and self-worth and give people a chance to develop new skills. Individuals who work in an effective team cope better with stress, enjoy their jobs more and have a higher level of motivation and commitment to the organization.

Types of teams

Organizations use many types of teams to achieve the advantages discussed in the previous section. Two common types of teams in organizations are functional and cross-functional, as illustrated in Exhibit 16.3. Organizations also use self-managed teams to increase employee participation.

EXHIBIT 16.3 Functional and cross-functional teams in an organization

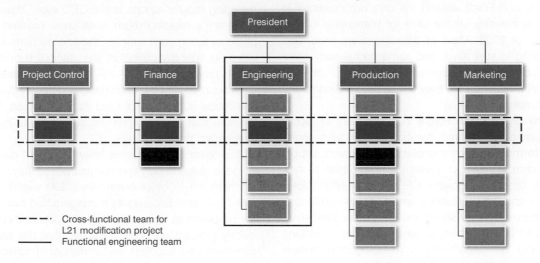

Functional teams

A functional team is composed of a manager and his or her subordinates in the formal chain of command. Sometimes called a *command team*, the functional team in some cases may include three or four levels of hierarchy within a functional department. Typically, the team includes a single department in an organization. A financial analysis department, a quality control department, an engineering department and a human resource department are all functional teams. Each is created by the organization to attain specific goals through members' joint activities and interactions.

Cross-functional teams

A cross-functional team is composed of employees from about the same hierarchical level, but from different areas of expertise. One type of cross-functional team is a *task force*, which is a group of employees from different departments formed to deal with a specific activity and existing only until the task is completed.

Another type of cross-functional team, the special-purpose team, is created outside the formal organization structure to undertake a project of special importance or creativity.[10] Sometimes called a *project team*, a special-purpose team still is part of the formal organization structure, but members perceive themselves as a separate entity. Special-purpose teams are often created for developing a new product or service. In 2008, Ford Motor Company created a special-purpose team to solve a problem that could determine whether the organization survived the turmoil in the automotive industry.

This special-purpose team played a critical role in helping Ford prevent a supply breakdown – and ultimately in helping Alan Mulally and other managers revive the company. The Project Quark team illustrates many of the advantages of teams discussed earlier, particularly creativity and speed.

Self-managed teams

The third common type of team used in organizations is designed to increase the participation of workers in decision-making and the conduct of their jobs, with the goal of improving performance. Self-managed teams typically consist of 5 to 20 multi-skilled workers who rotate jobs to produce an entire product or

💡 INNOVATIVE **WAY**

Ford Motor Company

The Big Three US automakers [General Motors (GM), Chrysler and Ford] weren't the only organizations in the auto industry on the brink of bankruptcy by the autumn of 2008. Most of their suppliers were also struggling to stay alive, and some had already gone out of business. Managers at Ford knew that without parts, nothing else they did to save the company would matter.

Tony Brown, then Ford's vice president of global purchasing, suggested creating a special-purpose team to monitor parts manufacturers, prevent supply chain disruptions and speed up Ford's plan to narrow its base of suppliers. CEO Alan Mulally quickly agreed, and Project Quark (named after the family dog in the movie *Honey, I Shrunk the Kids*) came into being. The team included people from all of Ford's divisions and functional departments – manufacturing, human resources, engineering, finance, information technology, legal, and others.

Time was of the essence, so the team started out in high gear – meeting every day, sometimes gathering before 7:00 am and working late into the night, and providing regular reports to the CEO every Thursday. The team's meeting room walls were covered with printouts listing each supplier, the specific parts it provided, its financial condition, the plants it supported, and its other customers. A risk profile was created for each supplier, and the team narrowed the list down to 850 critical suppliers that Ford wanted to keep. Making sure that these companies survived was Project Quark's top priority.

The team and managers knew that Ford couldn't save the global supply base on its own, so they began reaching out to other automakers. GM wasn't interested (perhaps because its managers had even bigger problems to worry about), but Toyota and Honda quickly jumped on board, realizing that the web of interconnected suppliers was in danger of collapsing. In some cases, the three companies agreed to share the costs of keeping a particular supplier in business.[11]

REFLECTION

- A **team** is a unit of two or more people who interact and coordinate their work to accomplish a goal to which they are committed and hold themselves mutually accountable.
- Organizations as diverse as Ford Motor Company, Apple and the US Navy use teams to perform tasks that are highly interdependent and require a high level of coordination.
- Teams provide distinct advantages in the areas of innovation, quality, speed, productivity and employee satisfaction.
- **Social facilitation** is the tendency for the presence of other people to influence an individual's motivation and performance.
- A **functional team** is composed of a manager and his or her subordinates in the formal chain of command.
- A **cross-functional team** is made up of employees from about the same hierarchical level but from different areas of expertise.

- Cross-functional teams include task forces and special purpose teams.
- A task force is a group of employees from different departments who deal with a specific activity and exist as a team only until the task is completed.
- A **special-purpose team** is a team created outside the formal structure to undertake a project of special importance, such as developing a new product.
- A **self-managed team** consists of multi-skilled employees who rotate jobs to produce an entire product or service, often led by an elected team member.
- Self-managed teams take responsibility for their work, make decisions, monitor their own performance and alter their work behaviour as needed to solve problems and meet goals.

service or at least one complete aspect or portion of a product or service (e.g., engine assembly or insurance claim processing). The central idea is that the teams themselves, rather than managers or supervisors, take responsibility for their work, make decisions, monitor their own performance and alter their

CONCEPT CONNECTION

At Lucasfilm Ltd, teams form around projects. To facilitate these **self-managed teams**, the company responsible for the *Star Wars* and *Indiana Jones* franchises moved its formerly separate divisions to a campus in the Presidio of San Francisco. An easily reconfigurable work environment encourages the sharing of ideas and technology between the visual effects division Industrial Light & Magic and LucasArts, the video game company. Project teams also work on visual effects for other films, such as the visual effects for the *Transformers* and the *Pirates of the Caribbean* franchises. In this photo, Chairman of the Board of LucasFilm Ltd and filmmaker George Lucas attends a panel discussion to review future work.

work behaviour as needed to solve problems, meet goals and adapt to changing conditions.[12] At the Chicago-based software firm 37signals, for example, customer service is run by a self-managed team that handles everything associated with providing service and support. The role of team leader rotates each week. Customer service, support and satisfaction have improved since the company started using a self-managed team. '*We've measured the difference, and we know it works*,' says co-founder Jason Fried. Today, 37signals is run almost entirely by self-managed teams.[13]

Self-managed teams are permanent teams that typically include the following elements:

■ The team includes employees with several skills and functions, and the combined skills are sufficient to perform a major organizational task. For example, in a manufacturing plant, a team may include members from the foundry, machining, grinding, fabrication and sales departments, with members cross-trained to perform one another's jobs. The team eliminates barriers among departments, enabling excellent coordination to produce a product or service.

■ The team is given access to resources; such as information, equipment, machinery and supplies needed to perform the complete task.

■ The team is empowered with decision-making authority, which means that members have the freedom to select new members, solve problems, spend money, monitor results and plan for the future. Self-managed teams can enable employees to feel challenged, find their work meaningful and develop a stronger sense of identity with the organization.

The dilemma of teams

When David Ferrucci was trying to recruit scientists to participate on a team at IBM to build a computer smart enough to beat grand champions at the game of *Jeopardy*, he learned first-hand that teamwork presents a dilemma for many people. To be sure, building 'Watson' was an unusual project, and its results would be put to the test in a televised 'human versus machine' competition. If it failed, it would be a public fiasco that would hurt the credibility of everyone involved. And if it succeeded, the hero would be the team, not any individual team member. Many of the scientists that Ferrucci approached preferred to work on their individual projects, where the success would be theirs alone. Eventually, he pulled together a core team of people willing to take the risk. '*It was a proud moment, frankly, just to have the courage as a team to move forward*,' Ferrucci says.[14] In organizations all over the world, some people love the idea of teamwork, others hate it and many people have both positive and negative emotions about being part of a team. There are three primary reasons teams present a dilemma for many people:

■ *We have to give up our independence.* When people become part of a team, their success depends on the team's success; therefore, they must depend on how well other people perform, not just on their own individual initiative and actions. Most people are comfortable with the idea of making sacrifices to achieve their own individual success, yet teamwork demands that they make sacrifices for *group* success.[15] The idea is that each person should put the team first, even if it hurts the individual at times. Many employees, particularly in individualistic cultures such as the USA, have a hard time appreciating and accepting that concept. A recent study suggests that Americans have become increasingly focused on the individual over the group since 1960, reflecting 'a sea change in American culture towards more individualism'.[16] Some cultures, such as Japan, have had greater success with teams because traditional Japanese culture values the group over the individual.

■ *We have to put up with free riders.* Teams are sometimes made up of people who have different work ethics. The term free rider refers to a team member who attains benefits from team membership but does not actively participate in and contribute to the team's work. You might have experienced this frustration in a student project team, where one member put little effort into the group project, but benefited from the hard work of others when grades were handed out. Free riding is sometimes called *social loafing* because some members do not exert equal effort.[17]

■ *Teams are sometimes dysfunctional.* Some companies have had great success with teams, but there are also numerous examples of how teams in organizations fail spectacularly.[18] '*The best groups will be better than their individual members, and the worst groups will be worse than the worst individual,*' says organizational psychologist Robert Sutton.[19] A great deal of research and team experience over the past few decades has produced significant insights into what causes teams to succeed or fail. Handling talented individuals is and always will be a challenge for managers. The evidence shows that the way teams are managed plays the most critical role in determining how well they function.[20] Exhibit 16.4 lists five dysfunctions that are common in teams and describes the contrasting desirable characteristics that effective team leaders develop.

TAKE A MOMENT

The Small Group Breakout Exercise online gives you a chance to evaluate and discuss various team member behaviours.

EXHIBIT 16.4 Five common dysfunctions of teams

Dysfunction	Effective team characteristics
Lack of trust – People don't feel safe to reveal mistakes, share concerns or express ideas.	*Trust* – Members trust one another on a deep emotional level; feel comfortable being vulnerable with one another.
Fear of conflict – People go along with others for the sake of harmony; don't express conflicting opinions.	*Healthy conflict* – Members feel comfortable disagreeing and challenging one another in the interest of finding the best solution.
Lack of commitment – If people are afraid to express their true opinions, it's difficult to gain their true commitment to decisions.	*Commitment* – Because all ideas are put on the table, people can achieve genuine buy-in around important goals and decisions.
Avoidance of accountability – People don't accept responsibility for outcomes; engage in finger-pointing when things go wrong.	*Accountability* – Members hold one another accountable rather than relying on managers as the source of accountability.
Inattention to results – Members put personal ambition or the needs of their individual departments ahead of collective results.	*Results orientation* – Individual members set aside personal agendas; focus on what's best for the team. Collective results define success.

SOURCES: Patrick Lencioni, *The Five Dysfunctions of a Team* (New York: John Wiley & Sons, 2002); and P. Lencioni, 'Dissolve Dysfunction: Begin Building Your Dream Team', *Leadership Excellence* (October 2009): 20.

REFLECTION

- Teams present a dilemma for most people because individual success depends on how well others perform, there are common dysfunctions that afflict teams and there is a potential for free riders.
- A **free rider** is a person who benefits from team membership but does not make a proportionate contribution to the team's work.

- Five common dysfunctions of teams are lack of trust, fear of conflict, lack of commitment, avoidance of accountability and inattention to results.

Model of team effectiveness

Smoothly functioning teams don't just happen. Stanford sociologist Elizabeth Cohen studied group work among young schoolchildren and found that only when teachers took the time to define roles, establish norms and set goals, did the groups function effectively as a team.[21] In organizations, effective teams are built by managers who take specific actions to help people come together and perform well as a team. The Shop-talk examines the role of the team leader in creating an effective team.

Some of the factors associated with team effectiveness are illustrated in Exhibit 16.5. Work team effectiveness is based on three outcomes – productive output, personal satisfaction and the capacity to adapt and learn.[22] *Satisfaction* pertains to the team's ability to meet the personal needs of its members and hence maintain their membership and commitment. *Productive output* pertains to performance and the quality and quantity of task outputs as defined by team goals. *Capacity to adapt and learn* refers to the ability of teams to bring greater knowledge and skills to job tasks and enhance the potential of the organization to respond to new threats or opportunities in the environment.

The model of team effectiveness in Exhibit 16.5 provides a structure for this chapter. The factors that influence team effectiveness begin with the organizational context.[23] The organizational context in which the team operates is described in other chapters and includes such matters as overall leadership, strategy, environment, culture and systems for controlling and rewarding employees. Within that context, managers define teams. Important team characteristics are the type of team, the team structure and team composition. Managers must decide when to create permanent self-managed teams and when to use a temporary task force or special-purpose team. The diversity of the team in terms of task-related knowledge and skills can have a tremendous impact on team processes and effectiveness. In addition, diversity in terms of gender and race affect a team's performance.[24] Team size and roles also are important.

EXHIBIT 16.5 Work team effectiveness model

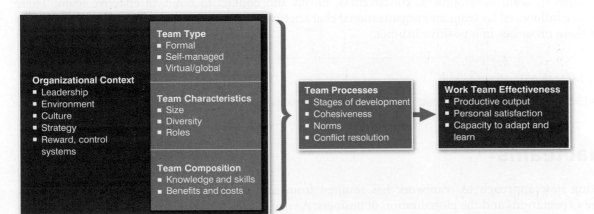

MANAGER'S SHOPTALK

How to be a great team leader

Perhaps no single factor plays a greater role in determining team effectiveness than the team leader. Teams fail when leaders try to manage them in traditional command-and-control fashion. There are four specific ways in which leaders contribute to team success:

- **Rally people around a compelling purpose.** It is the leader's responsibility to articulate a clear, compelling purpose, one of the key elements of effective teams. This ensures that everyone is moving in the same direction rather than floundering, wondering why the team was created and where it's supposed to be going. Effective leaders also establish clear goals and timelines.

- **Share control to spur commitment and motivation.** Overly controlling leaders sabotage team effectiveness. Good team leaders share power, information, control and genuine responsibility. Sharing power and control requires that the leaders have faith that team members will make good decisions, even if those decisions might not be the ones that the leader would make.

- **Clarify norms and expectations.** Leaders should define roles and expectations clearly from the start so that everyone knows what they should be doing and what they can expect from their team-mates. Team members who are confused about their roles will be unproductive, which will spark resentment

from other members. Sometimes a leader might need to meet with each team member individually to make sure that each person understands and accepts his or her obligations.

- **Admit ignorance.** Often, people appointed to lead teams find that they don't know nearly as much as their team-mates know. Good team leaders aren't afraid to admit their ignorance and ask for help. This serves as a *fallibility model* that lets people know that lack of knowledge, problems, concerns and mistakes can be discussed openly without fear of appearing incompetent. Although it's hard for many managers to believe, admitting ignorance and being willing to learn from others can earn the respect of team members faster than almost any other behaviour.

SOURCES: J. Richard Hackman, *Leading Teams: Setting the Stage for Great Performances* (Boston, MA: Harvard Business School Press, 2002); Lee G. Bolman and Terrence E. Deal, 'What Makes a Team Work?' *Organizational Dynamics* (August 1992): 34–44; Amy Edmondson, Richard Bohmer and Gary Pisano, 'Speeding up Team Learning', *Harvard Business Review* (October 2001): 125–132; Jeanne M. Wilson, Jill George and Richard S. Wellings, with William C. Byham, *Leadership Trapeze: Strategies for Leadership in Team-Based Organizations* (San Francisco: Jossey-Bass, 1994); Sarah Fister Gale, 'The Turn Around Artist', *PM Network* (October 2007): 28–35; and Eric Matson, 'Congratulations, You're Promoted (Now What?)', *Fast Company* (June-July 1997): 116–130.

These team characteristics influence processes that are internal to the team, which, in turn, affect output, satisfaction and the team's contribution to organizational adaptability. Good team leaders understand and manage stages of team development, cohesiveness, norms and conflict to build an effective team. These processes are influenced by team and organizational characteristics and by the ability of members and leaders to direct these processes in a positive manner.

TAKE A MOMENT

Go to the Experiential Exercise online that pertains to effective versus ineffective teams.

Virtual teams

An exciting new approach to teamwork has resulted from advances in information technology, shifting employee expectations and the globalization of business. A virtual team is a group made up of geographically

CONCEPT CONNECTION

To update Lotus Symphony, a package of PC software applications, IBM assigned the project to teams in Beijing, China; Austin, Texas; Raleigh, North Carolina; and Böblingen, Germany. Leading the project, the Beijing group – shown here with Michael Karasick (centre), who runs the Beijing lab, and lead developer Yue Ma (right) – navigated the **global team** through the programming challenges. To help bridge the distance gap, IBM used Beehive, a corporate social network similar to Facebook, where employees create profiles, list their interests and post photos.

or organizationally dispersed members who are linked primarily through advanced information and telecommunications technologies.[25]

A 2010 survey of employees at multinational corporations found that 80 per cent of respondents belong to virtual teams.[26] In a virtual team, members use groupware, email, instant messaging, telephone and text messaging, wikis and blogs, videoconferencing and other technology tools to collaborate and perform their work, although they also might meet face-to-face at times. Although some virtual teams are made up of only organizational members, virtual teams often include contingent workers, members of partner organizations, customers, suppliers, consultants or other outsiders. Many virtual teams are also global teams. A global team is a cross-border team made up of members of different nationalities whose activities span multiple countries.[27]

One of the primary advantages of virtual teams is the ability to assemble the most talented group of people to complete a complex project, solve a particular problem or exploit a specific strategic opportunity. The diverse mix of people can fuel creativity and innovation. On a practical level, organizations can save employees time and cut travel expenses when people meet in virtual rather than physical space. IBM reported that it saved more than $50 million in travel-related expenses in 2007 by using virtual teams.[28]

However, virtual teams also present unique challenges. Exhibit 16.6 lists some critical areas that managers should address when leading virtual teams. Each of these areas is discussed in more detail in the following list:[29]

EXHIBIT 16.6 What effective virtual team leaders do

Practice	How it's done
Use technology to build relationships	• Bring attention to and appreciate diverse skills and opinions • Use technology to enhance communication and trust • Ensure timely responses online • Manage online socialization
Shape culture through technology	• Create a psychologically safe virtual culture • Share members' special experience/strengths • Engage members from cultures where they may be hesitant to share ideas
Monitor progress and rewards	• Scrutinize electronic communication patterns • Post targets and scorecards in virtual work space • Reward people through online ceremonies, recognition

SOURCES: Table 1, 'Practices of Effective Virtual Team Leaders', in Arvind Malhotra, Ann Majchrzak and Benson Rosen, 'Leading Virtual Teams', *Academy of Management Perspectives* 21, no. 1 (February 2007): 60–69; and Table 2, ' 'Best Practices' Solutions for Overcoming Barriers to Knowledge Sharing in Virtual Teams', in Benson Rosen, Stacie Furst and Richard Blackburn, 'Overcoming Barriers to Knowledge Sharing in Virtual Teams', *Organizational Dynamics* 36, no. 3 (2007): 259–273.

- *Using technology to build trust and relationships is crucial for effective virtual teamwork.* Leaders first select people who have the right mix of technical, interpersonal and communication skills to work in a virtual environment, and then make sure that they have opportunities to get to know one another and establish trusting relationships. Encouraging online social networking, where people can share photos and personal biographies, is one key to virtual team success. One study suggests that higher levels of online communication increase team cohesiveness and trust.[30] Leaders also build trust by making everyone's roles, responsibilities and authority clear from the beginning, by shaping norms of full disclosure and respectful interaction and by providing a way for everyone to stay up to date. In a study of which technologies make virtual teams successful, researchers found that round-the-clock virtual work spaces, where team members can access the latest versions of files, keep track of deadlines and timelines, monitor one another's progress and carry on discussions between formal meetings, got top marks.[31]

- *Shaping culture through technology reinforces productive norms.* This involves creating a virtual environment in which people feel safe to express concerns, admit mistakes, share ideas, acknowledge fears or ask for help. Leaders reinforce a norm of sharing all forms of knowledge, and they encourage people to express 'off-the-wall' ideas and ask for help when it's needed. Team leaders set the example by their own behaviour. Leaders also make sure that they bring diversity issues into the open and educate members early on regarding possible cultural differences that could cause communication problems or misunderstandings in a virtual environment.

- *Monitoring progress and rewarding members keep the team progressing towards goals.* Leaders stay on top of the project's development and make sure that everyone knows how the team is progressing towards meeting its goals. Posting targets, measurements and milestones in the virtual work space can make progress explicit. Leaders also provide regular feedback, and they reward both individual and team accomplishments through avenues such as virtual award ceremonies and recognition at virtual meetings. They are liberal with praise and congratulations, but criticism or reprimands are handled individually, rather than in the virtual presence of the team.

As the use of virtual teams grows, there is growing understanding of what makes them successful. Some experts suggest that managers solicit volunteers as much as possible for virtual teams, and interviews with virtual team members and leaders support the idea that members who truly want to work as a virtual team are more effective.[32]

 INNOVATIVE WAY

Nokia

In a 2007 study of 52 virtual teams in 15 leading multinational companies, London Business School researchers found that Nokia's teams were among the most effective, even though they were made up of people working in several different countries, across time zones and cultures.

Nokia managers were careful then to select people who have a collaborative mind set, and they form many teams with volunteers who are highly committed to the task or project. The company also tries to make sure that some members of a team have worked together before, providing a base for trusting relationships. Making the best use of technology is critical. In addition to a virtual work space that team members can access 24 hours a day, Nokia provides an online resource where virtual workers are encouraged to post photos and share personal information. With the inability of members to get to know each another being one of the biggest barriers to effective virtual teamwork, encouraging and supporting social networking has paid off for Nokia.[33]

Global teams such as the ones at Nokia present even greater challenges for team leaders, who have to bridge gaps of time, distance and culture. Different cultural attitudes can affect work pacing, team communications, decision-making, the perception of deadlines and other issues and provide rich soil for misunderstandings and conflict. No wonder when the executive council of *CIO* magazine asked global chief information officers (CIOs) to rank their greatest challenges, managing virtual global teams ranked as the most pressing issue.[34]

REFLECTION

- A **virtual team** is a team made up of members who are geographically or organizationally dispersed, rarely meet face-to-face, and interact to accomplish their work primarily using advanced information and telecommunications technologies.

- A **global team** is a group made up of employees who come from different countries and whose collective activities span multiple countries.
- Virtual teams provide many advantages, but they also present new challenges for leaders, who must learn to build trusting relationships in a virtual environment.

Team characteristics

After deciding the type of team to use, the next issue of concern to managers is designing the team for greatest effectiveness. Team characteristics of particular concern are size, diversity and member roles.

Size

More than 30 years ago, psychologist Ivan Steiner examined what happened each time the size of a team increased, and he proposed that a team's performance and productivity peaked when it had about five members – a quite small number. He found that adding members beyond five caused a decrease in motivation, an increase in coordination problems and a general decline in performance.[35] Since then, numerous studies have found that smaller teams perform better, although most researchers say that it's impossible to specify an optimal team size. One investigation of team size based on data from 58 software development teams found that the best-performing teams ranged in size from three to six members.[36]

Teams need to be large enough to incorporate the diverse skills needed to complete a task, enable members to express good and bad feelings and aggressively solve problems. However, they also should be small enough to permit members to feel an intimate part of the team and to communicate effectively and efficiently. The ability of people to identify with the team is an important determinant of high performance.[37] At Amazon.com, CEO Jeff Bezos established a simple 'two-pizza rule'. If a team gets so large that members can't be fed with two pizzas, it should be split into smaller teams.[38] In general, as a team increases in size, it becomes harder for each member to interact with and influence the others. Subgroups often form in larger teams, and conflicts among them can occur. Turnover and absenteeism are higher because members feel less like an important part of the team.[39]

Although the Internet and advanced technologies are enabling larger groups of people to work more effectively in virtual teams, studies show that members of smaller virtual teams participate more actively, are more committed to the team, are more focused on team goals and have higher levels of rapport than larger virtual teams.[40]

Diversity

Because teams require a variety of skills, knowledge and experience, it seems likely that heterogeneous teams would be more effective than homogeneous ones. In general, research supports this idea, showing that diverse teams produce more innovative solutions to problems.[41] Diversity in terms of functional area and skills, thinking styles and personal characteristics is often a source of creativity. In addition, diversity may contribute to a healthy level of disagreement that leads to better decision-making.

Research studies have confirmed that both functional diversity and demographic diversity can have a positive impact on work team performance.[42] For example, recent research suggests that gender diversity, particularly with more women on a team, leads to better performance[43] Ethnic, national and racial diversity sometimes can hinder team interaction and performance in the short term, but with effective leadership, the problems fade over time.[44]

CONCEPT CONNECTION

The US women's gymnastics team excelled in the 2012 London Olympics, and team captain Aly Raisman pictured succeeded in her role as their **socioemotional** leader. In the initial round of competition, team-mate Jordyn Wieber did not perform as well as expected and failed to qualify for the all-around final, which left the entire team stunned and anxious. Raisman needed to draw upon all her leadership skills to **encourage, harmonize** and **reduce tension** among the group. The team emerged victorious, winning the team gold medal.

Member roles

For a team to be successful over the long run, it must be structured so as to both maintain its members' social well-being and accomplish its task. To understand the importance of members fulfilling various roles on a team, consider the 33 miners who were trapped underground after a copper mine collapsed in San José, Chile, in August 2010. With little food, scant water, dusty conditions and frayed nerves, the situation could have led to chaos. However, the miners organized into several teams in charge of critical activities such as communication with rescue workers, the transport of supplies from above ground, rationing and distribution of food, managing health concerns and securing the mine to prevent further collapses. Some team members were clearly focused on helping the trapped miners meet their needs for physical survival; some focused on helping people coordinate their activities; and still others focused on the group's psychological and social needs, helping people maintain hope and a sense of solidarity as the ordeal stretched to a harrowing 69 days. Experts agree that teamwork and leadership were key to the miners' survival.[45]

In successful teams, the requirements for task performance and social satisfaction are met by the emergence of two types of roles: task specialist and socioemotional.[46]

People who play a task specialist role spend time and energy helping the team reach its goal. They often display the following behaviours:

- **Initiate ideas.** Propose new solutions to team problems.
- **Give opinions.** Offer judgements on task solutions; give candid feedback on others' suggestions.
- **Seek information.** Ask for task-relevant facts.
- **Summarize.** Relate various ideas to the problem at hand; pull ideas together into a brief overview.
- **Energize.** Stimulate the team into action when interest drops.[47]

People who adopt a socioemotional role support team members' emotional needs and help strengthen the social entity. They display the following behaviours:

- **Encourage.** Are warm and receptive to others' ideas; praise and encourage others to draw forth their contributions.
- **Harmonize.** Reconcile group conflicts; help disagreeing parties reach agreement.
- **Reduce tension.** Tell jokes or diffuse emotions in other ways when the group atmosphere is tense.
- **Follow.** Go along with the team; agree to other team members' ideas.
- **Compromise.** Will shift own opinions to maintain team harmony.[48]

TAKE A MOMENT

Complete the New Manager Self-Test to see how you contribute as a team member.

🌐 NEW MANAGER SELF-TEST

Are you a contributing team member?

INSTRUCTIONS Think about how you have behaved as a member of a specific student or work team. Respond to the statements below based on how you typically behaved on that team.

	Mostly true	Mostly false
1 I engaged the team in clarifying plans and deadlines.	☐	☐
2 I suggested corrective actions to improve performance.	☐	☐
3 I kept the discussion focused on relevant items.	☐	☐
4 I came to meetings well prepared.	☐	☐
5 I was consistently on time to meetings.	☐	☐
6 I followed through on promises and commitments.	☐	☐
7 I was a focused, active listener.	☐	☐
8 I verbalized my insights and recommendations.	☐	☐
9 I provided constructive feedback to others.	☐	☐
10 I did not shy away from disputes.	☐	☐
11 I knew when to stop pushing for my own position.	☐	☐
12 I intervened constructively when conflicts arose.	☐	☐
13 I showed team members appreciation and support.	☐	☐
14 I celebrated the accomplishments of others.	☐	☐
15 I praised people for a job well done.	☐	☐

SCORING & INTERPRETATION These questions pertain to your contributions as a team member, which are important to the success of any type of formal team and especially to self-managed teams.

Give yourself one point for each 'Mostly true' answer.

Total score: ___.

Generally, if you score 11 or higher, you are considered a contributing team member. A score of 5 or lower suggests that you should be contributing more to the team.

You also can assess the specific ways in which you contributed most or least to the team.

1   Meeting the team's performance needs; one point for each 'Mostly true' answer to questions 1–3: ___.

2   Taking personal responsibility for own participation; one point for each 'Mostly true' answer to questions 4–6: ___.

3   Facilitating team communication; one point for each 'Mostly true' answer to questions 7–9: ___.

4   Managing healthy conflict among members; one point for each 'Mostly true' answer to questions 10–12: ___.

5   Meeting socioemotional needs of team members; one point for each 'Mostly true' answer to questions 13–15: ___.

A score of 3 in any of the above categories suggests a high contribution on that dimension. A score of 0 or 1 suggests a low contribution. An effective team must have someone performing each of the five parts, but no single member is expected to perform all parts. Indeed, if you scored well on most questions, you were likely playing a leadership role on the team.

There are five types of contributions that someone on a team must make, including performance management or focus on accomplishing the team's tasks (1–3), displaying personal responsibility (4–6), facilitating quality team communication (7–9), managing conflict among team members (10–12) and meeting the social needs of members (13–15). How do you feel about your contributions to the team? In what ways do you take the initiative to be an effective member? What might you do to be more effective?

Teams with mostly socioemotional roles can be satisfying, but they also can be unproductive. At the other extreme, a team made up primarily of task specialists will tend to have a singular concern for task accomplishment. This team will be effective for a short period of time but will not be satisfying for members over the long run. Effective teams have people in both task specialist and socioemotional roles. A well-balanced team will do best over the long term because it will be personally satisfying for team members, as well as permit the accomplishment of team tasks.

REFLECTION

- Issues of particular concern to managers for team effectiveness are selecting the right type of team for the task, balancing the team's size and diversity and ensuring that both task and social needs are met.
- Small teams are typically more productive and more satisfying to their members than are large teams.
- Jeff Bezos established a 'two-pizza rule' at Amazon.com: If a team gets so large that members can't be fed with two pizzas, it is split into smaller teams.
- The **task specialist role** is a team role in which an individual devotes personal time and energy to helping the team accomplish its activities and reach its goal.
- The **socioemotional role** is a team role in which an individual provides support for team members' emotional needs and helps strengthen social unity.

Team processes

Now we turn our attention to internal team processes. Team processes pertain to those dynamics that change over time and can be influenced by team leaders. In this section we discuss stages of development, cohesiveness and norms. The fourth type of team process, conflict, will be covered in the next section.

Stages of team development

After a team has been created, it develops by passing through distinct stages. New teams are different from mature teams. Recall a time when you were a member of a committee or a small team formed to do a class assignment. Over time, the team changed. In the beginning, team members had to get to know one another, establish roles and norms, divide the labour and clarify the team's task. In this way, each member became part of a smoothly operating team. The challenge for leaders is to understand the stages of development and take action that will lead to smooth functioning.

Research findings suggest that team development is not random, but evolves over definitive stages. One useful model for describing these stages is shown in Exhibit 16.7. Each stage confronts team leaders and members with unique problems and challenges.[49]

EXHIBIT 16.7 Five stages of team development

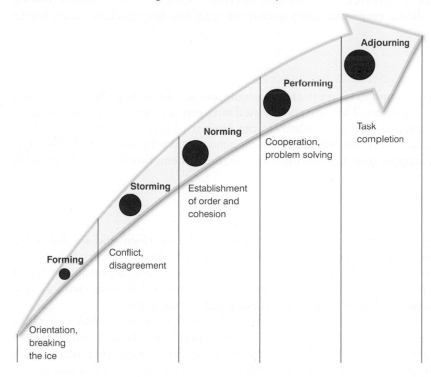

SOURCES: Based on the stages of small group development in Bruce W. Tuckman, 'Developmental Sequence in Small Groups', *Psychological Bulletin* 63 (1965): 384–399; and B. W. Tuckman and M. A. Jensen, 'Stages of Small Group Development Revisited', *Group and Organizational Studies* 2 (1977): 419–427

Forming

The **forming** stage of development is a period of orientation and getting acquainted. Members break the ice and test one another for friendship possibilities and task orientation. Uncertainty is high during this stage, and members usually accept whatever power or authority is offered by either formal or informal leaders. During this initial stage, members are concerned about things such as 'What is expected of me?', 'What behaviour is acceptable?' and 'Will I fit in?' During the forming stage, the team leader should provide time for members to get acquainted with one another and encourage them to engage in informal social discussions.

Storming

During the **storming** stage, individual personalities emerge. People become more assertive in clarifying their roles and what is expected of them. This stage is marked by conflict and disagreement. People may disagree over their perceptions of the team's goals or how to achieve them. Members may jockey for position, and coalitions or subgroups based on common interests may form. Unless teams can successfully move beyond this stage, they may get bogged down and never achieve high performance. Think of the Miami Heat basketball team, which had trouble getting a team loaded with superstar players with disparate personalities to 'gel and excel'. The team started coming together and show signs of solidarity only when it became clear that they couldn't win unless they did. 'When it's raw, when you don't get along, that's when there's the most opportunity for growth,' said head coach, Erik Spoelstra.[50] During the storming stage, the team leader should encourage participation by each team member. Members should propose ideas, disagree with one another and work through the uncertainties and conflicting perceptions about team tasks and goals.

Norming

During the norming stage, conflict is resolved, and team harmony and unity emerge. Consensus develops on who has the power, who the leaders are and what members' roles are. Members come to accept and understand one another. Differences are resolved, and members develop a sense of team cohesion. During the norming stage, the team leader should emphasize unity within the team and help to clarify team norms and values.

Performing

During the performing stage, the major emphasis is on problem solving and accomplishing the assigned task. Members are committed to the team's mission. They are coordinated with one another and handle disagreements in a mature way. They confront and resolve problems in the interest of task accomplishment. They interact frequently and direct their discussions and influence towards achieving team goals. During this stage, the leader should concentrate on managing high task performance. Both socioemotional and task specialist roles contribute to the team's functioning.

Adjourning

The adjourning stage occurs in committees and teams that have a limited task to perform and are disbanded afterwards. During this stage, the emphasis is on wrapping up and gearing down. Task performance is no longer a top priority. Members may feel heightened emotionality, strong cohesiveness and depression or regret over the team's disbanding. At this point, the leader may wish to signify the team's disbanding with a ritual or ceremony, perhaps giving out plaques and awards to signify closure and completeness.

These five stages typically occur in sequence, but in teams that are under time pressure, they may occur quite rapidly. The stages may also be accelerated for virtual teams. For example, at a large consumer goods company with a virtual team of engineers working in the USA and India, leaders started the project with a couple of days of team building to help the team move rapidly through the forming and storming stages.

Team cohesiveness

Another important aspect of the team process is cohesiveness. Team cohesiveness is defined as the extent to which members are attracted to the team and motivated to remain in it.[51] Members of highly cohesive teams are committed to team activities, attend meetings and are happy when the team succeeds. Members of less cohesive teams are less concerned about the team's welfare. High cohesiveness is normally considered an attractive feature of teams.

Determinants of team cohesiveness

Several characteristics of team structure and context influence cohesiveness. First is *team interaction*. When team members have frequent contact, they get to know one another, consider themselves a unit and become more committed to the team.[52] Second is the concept of *shared goals*. If team members agree on purpose and direction, they will be more cohesive. Third is *personal attraction to the team*, meaning that members have similar attitudes and values and enjoy being together.

💡 INNOVATIVE **WAY**

Pierre Omidyar (eBay)

Pierre Omidyar gave birth to perhaps the holy grail of the new economy, an Internet start-up that consistently made profits from the first day of operation. In June of 1995 monthly revenues hit $10 000 (Cohen, 2002, p. 29). Omidyar stated: 'I had a hobby that was making more money than my day job. So I decided it was time to quit my day job.' Omidyar was an e-entre-preneur, largely coming from a computing/technical background.

Omidyar was a venture capitalist's fantasy – an entrepreneur who actually wanted to quit once the business was financially stable. He enjoyed life outside work, went home at 5 o'clock and took regular vacations. He neither had obsessive drive nor tried to feign it. From the very start Omidyar augmented his limited business acumen with team-building with a succession of trusted lieutenants, most with a greater appetite for profits. Jeff Skoll, a Stanford MBA who had worked on Knight-Rider's attempt to move classified advertisements to the Web, was such an early appointment that he was regarded as a co-founder of eBay with Omidyar (Cohen, 2002, p. 30). Skoll focussed upon writing the business plan that would form the basis of the planned IPO. Later Meg Whitman would be brought in from Playskool, a subdivision of Hambro Toys, as CEO for her expertise in brand building and building a management team. Throughout the transition of eBay from back bedroom hobby to multi-billion pound corporation a distinct change in the prevailing e-culture took place. The old community-based, technologically driven, culture was championed by Omidyar and Mike Wilson, the chief technology officer, who was initially appointed to stabilize a fileserver, creaking under the growing load. The newly ascendant, profit driven, instrumental culture was championed by Steve Wesley, vice-president of marketing and business development (especially business alliances) and Meg Whitman herself. In recalling Wesley's group on arrival an insider said 'They wanted to know why this whole community thing was important. They just did not buy into it at all.' (Cohen, 2002, p.80). The transformation of culture took place against the background of an IPO process that made millionaires of the majority of eBay's employees. A 22 hour power-outage in May 1999, provided a convenient excuse to remove Mike Wilson and replace him with a more commercially driven alternative. By early 2000 Omidyar was largely disengaged from day-to-day management, preferring to absent himself to work with European versions of the eBay site. Omidyar is now a philanthropic multi-millionaire, having fully recognized his leadership ability limitations for eBay's long-term benefit. 'We were entrepreneurs and that was good up to a certain stage. But we didn't have the experience to take it to the next level' (Cohen, 2002, p. 110).

SOURCE: 'The Boys in the Bubble: Searching for intangible value in Internet Stocks' by William Forbes and published by The Institute of Chartered Accountants of Scotland (ICAS) © 2007. This case has been reproduced by kind permission of William Forbes and ICAS.

Two factors in the team's context also influence cohesiveness. The first is the *presence of competition*. When a team is in moderate competition with other teams, its cohesiveness increases as it strives to win. Second is *team success* and the favourable evaluation of the team by outsiders adds to cohesiveness. When a team succeeds in its task and others in the organization recognize the success, members feel good and their commitment to the team will be high.

Consequences of team cohesiveness

The outcome of team cohesiveness can fall into two categories – morale and productivity. As a general rule, morale is higher in cohesive teams because of increased communication among members, a friendly team climate, maintenance of membership because of commitment to the team, loyalty and member participation in team decisions and activities. High cohesiveness has almost uniformly good effects on the satisfaction and morale of team members.[53]

With respect to the productivity of the team as a whole, research findings suggest that teams in which members share strong feelings of connectedness and generally positive interactions tend to perform better.[54]

Thus, a friendly, positive team environment contributes to productivity, as well as member satisfaction. Other research, however, indicates that the degree of productivity in cohesive teams may depend on the relationship between management and the work team. One study surveyed more than 200 work teams and correlated job performance with their cohesiveness.[55] Highly cohesive teams were more productive when team members felt management support and less productive when they sensed management hostility and negativism.

Team norms

A team norm is an informal standard of conduct that is shared by team members and guides their behaviour.[56] Norms are valuable because they provide a frame of reference for what is expected and acceptable.

Norms begin to develop in the first interactions among members of a new team. Exhibit 16.8 illustrates four common ways in which norms develop.[57] Sometimes the first behaviours that occur in a team set a precedent. For example, at one company, a team leader began his first meeting by raising an issue and then 'leading' team members until he got the solution he wanted. The pattern became ingrained so quickly into an unproductive team norm that members dubbed meetings the 'Guess What I Think' game.[58] Other influences on team norms include critical events in the team's history, as well as behaviours, attitudes and norms that members bring with them from outside the team.

EXHIBIT 16.8 Four ways team norms develop

REFLECTION

- The **forming** stage of team development is a period of orientation and getting acquainted.
- **Storming** is the stage of team development in which individual personalities and roles emerge, along with resulting conflicts.
- **Norming** refers to the stage of development in which conflicts are resolved and team harmony and unity emerge.
- The **performing** stage is the stage in which members focus on problem solving and accomplishing the team's assigned task.

- **Adjourning** is the stage during which members of temporary teams prepare for the team's disbanding.
- **Team cohesiveness** refers to the extent to which team members are attracted to the team and motivated to remain a part of it.
- Morale is almost always higher in cohesive teams, and cohesiveness can also contribute to higher productivity.
- A **team norm** is an informal standard of conduct that is shared by team members and guides their behaviour.

Team leaders play an important role in shaping norms that will help the team be effective. For example, research shows that when leaders have high expectations for collaborative problem solving, teams develop strong collaborative norms.[59] Making explicit statements about desired team behaviours is a powerful way that leaders influence norms. When he was CEO of Ameritech, Bill Weiss established a norm of cooperation and mutual support among his top leadership team by telling them bluntly that if he caught anyone trying to undermine the others, the guilty party would be fired.[60]

Managing team conflict

The final characteristic of team process is conflict. Conflict can arise among members within a team or between one team and another. Conflict refers to antagonistic interaction in which one party attempts to block the intentions or goals of another.[61] Whenever people work together in teams, some conflict is inevitable. Bringing conflicts into the open and effectively resolving them is one of the team leader's most challenging, yet most important, jobs. Effective conflict management has a positive impact on team cohesiveness and performance.[62]

'In great teams, conflict becomes productive. The free flow of ideas and feelings is critical for creative thinking, for discovering new solutions no one individual would have come to on his own.'
— PETER SENGE, AUTHOR OF *THE FIFTH DISCIPLINE: THE ART AND PRACTICE OF THE LEARNING ORGANIZATION*

Types of conflict

Two basic types of conflict that occur in teams are task conflict and relationship conflict.[63] Task conflict refers to disagreements among people about the goals to be achieved or the content of the tasks to be performed. Two shop foremen might disagree over whether to replace a valve, or let it run despite the unusual noise that it is making. Or two members of a top management team might disagree about whether to acquire a company or enter into a joint venture as a way to expand globally. Relationship conflict refers to interpersonal incompatibility that creates tension and personal animosity among people. For example, in one team at a company that manufactures and sells upscale children's furniture, team members found their differing perspectives and working styles to be a significant source of conflict during crunch times. Members who needed peace and quiet were irked at those who wanted music playing in the background. Compulsively neat members found it almost impossible to work with those who liked working among stacks of clutter.[64]

In general, research suggests that task conflict can be beneficial because it leads to better decision-making and problem solving. On the other hand, relationship conflict is typically associated with negative consequences for team effectiveness.[65] One study of top management teams, for example, found that task conflict was associated with higher decision quality, greater commitment and more decision acceptance, while the presence of relationship conflict significantly reduced those same outcomes.[66]

Balancing conflict and cooperation

There is evidence that mild conflict can be beneficial to teams.[67] A healthy level of conflict helps to prevent *groupthink*, as discussed in Chapter 9, in which people are so committed to a cohesive team that they are reluctant to express contrary opinions. When people in work teams go along simply for the sake of harmony, problems typically result. Thus, a degree of conflict leads to better decision-making because multiple viewpoints are expressed.

However, conflict that is too strong, that is focused on personal rather than work issues or that is not managed appropriately can be damaging to the team's morale and productivity. Too much conflict can be destructive, tear relationships apart and interfere with the healthy exchange of ideas and information.[68] Team leaders have to find the right balance between conflict and cooperation, as illustrated in Exhibit 16.9. Too little conflict can decrease team performance because the team doesn't benefit from a mix of opinions and ideas – even disagreements – that might lead to better solutions or prevent the team from making mistakes. At the other end of the spectrum, too much conflict outweighs the team's cooperative efforts and leads to

EXHIBIT 16.9 Balancing conflict and cooperation

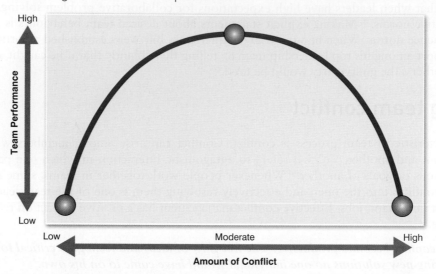

a decrease in employee satisfaction and commitment, hurting team performance. A moderate amount of conflict that is managed appropriately typically results in the highest levels of team performance. In summary, the cohesion of the team is facilitated by ensuring that there are mechanisms for legitimate dissent to be surfaced and burning issues to be resolved.

TAKE A MOMENT

Go to the Ethical Dilemma at the end of this chapter that pertains to team cohesiveness and conflict.

Causes of conflict

Several factors can lead to conflict.[69] One of the primary causes of conflict is competition over resources, such as money, information or supplies. When individuals or teams must compete for scarce or declining resources, conflict is almost inevitable. In addition, conflict often occurs simply because people are pursuing differing goals. Goal differences are natural in organizations. Individual salespeople's targets may put them in conflict with one another or with their sales manager. Moreover, the sales department's goals might conflict with those of manufacturing, and so forth.

Conflict may also arise from communication breakdowns. Poor communication can occur in any team, but virtual and global teams are particularly prone to communication breakdowns. In one virtual team developing a custom polymer for a Japanese manufacturer, the marketing team member in the USA was frustrated by a Japanese team member's failure to provide her with the manufacturer's marketing strategy. The Japanese team member, in turn, thought that her team-mate was overbearing and unsupportive. She knew that the manufacturer hadn't yet developed a clear marketing strategy, and that pushing for more information could damage the relationship by causing the customer to 'lose face'.[70] Trust issues can be a major source of conflict in virtual teams if members feel that they are being left out of important communication interactions.[71] In addition, the lack of non-verbal cues in virtual interactions leads to more misunderstandings.

Styles to handle conflict

Teams as well as individuals develop specific styles for dealing with conflict, based on the desire to satisfy their own concern versus the other party's concern. A model that describes five styles of handling conflict is in Exhibit 16.10. The two major dimensions are the extent to which an individual is assertive versus cooperative in his or her approach to conflict.[72]

EXHIBIT 16.10 A model of styles to handle conflict

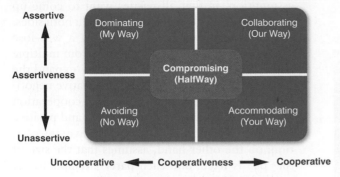

SOURCES: Kenneth Thomas, 'Conflict and Conflict Management', in *Handbook of Industrial and Organizational Behavior,* ed. M. D. Dunnette (New York: John Wiley, 1976), p. 900; and Nan Peck, 'Conflict 101: Styles of Fighting', North Virginia Community College website, September 20, 2005, www.nvcc.edu/home/npeck/conflicthome/conflict/Conflict101/conflictstyles.htm (accessed April 13, 2011).

- The *dominating style* (my way) reflects assertiveness to get one's own way and should be used when quick, decisive action is vital on important issues or unpopular actions, such as during emergencies or urgent cost cutting exercises.

- The *avoiding style* (no way) reflects neither assertiveness nor cooperativeness. It is appropriate when an issue is trivial, when there is no chance of winning, when a delay to gather more information is needed or when a disruption would be costly.

- The *compromising style* (halfway) reflects a moderate amount of both assertiveness and cooperativeness. It is appropriate when the goals on both sides are equally important, when opponents have equal power and both sides want to split the difference or when people need to arrive at temporary or expedient solutions under time pressure.

- The *accommodating style* (your way) reflects a high degree of cooperativeness, which works best when people realize that they are wrong, when an issue is more important to others than to oneself, when building social credits for use in later discussions and when maintaining harmony is especially important.

- The *collaborating style* (our way) reflects a high degree of both assertiveness and cooperativeness. The collaborating style enables both parties to win, although it may require substantial bargaining and negotiation. The collaborating style is important when both sets of concerns are too important to be compromised, when insights from different people need to be merged into an overall solution and when the commitment of both sides is needed for a consensus.

There is a pragmatic instrument for measuring one's own style: the Thomas-Kilman Instrument.

An example of the collaborating style comes from the 2008 Summer Olympics in Beijing. When building the Beijing National Aquatics Centre (typically called the 'Water Cube'), two architectural firms – one Chinese and the other Australian – developed designs that were totally different. Although this created some tension, instead of fighting for their own ideas, the two sides came up with a totally new concept that excited everyone. The resulting award-winning building is spectacular.[73] Each of the five styles is appropriate in certain cases, and effective team members and leaders vary their style to fit the specific situation.

Negotiation

One distinctive type of conflict management is negotiation, whereby people engage in give-and-take discussions and consider various alternatives to reach a joint decision that is acceptable to both parties. Negotiation is used when a conflict is formalized, such as between a union and management.

Types of negotiation

Conflicting parties may embark on negotiation from different perspectives and with different intentions, reflecting either an *integrative* approach or a *distributive* approach.

CONCEPT CONNECTION

Just who's running the Large Hadron Collider (LHC) project, an international $6 billion particle accelerator designed to simulate the universe's birth by producing high-energy proton collisions? The answer is everyone. Built at the European Organization for Nuclear Research (CERN), the European particle laboratory near Geneva, LHC involves 10 000 scientists and engineers working in hundreds of institutions. Because participants recognize that they need everyone's cooperation to succeed, they've adopted a **collaborative style of handling conflicts**. Each research group is a democratic collective; those collectives appoint members to negotiate with other groups. *'The top guy,'* notes CERN's 'top guy', Director-General Rolf-Dieter Heuer, *'can only convince the other guys to do what he wants them to do.'*

Integrative negotiation is based on a win–win assumption, in that all parties want to come up with a creative solution that can benefit both sides. Rather than viewing the conflict as a win–lose situation, people look at the issues from multiple angles, consider trade-offs and try to 'expand the pie' rather than divide it. With integrative negotiation, conflicts are managed through cooperation and compromise, which fosters trust and positive long-term relationships.[74] Distributive negotiation, on the other hand, assumes that the size of the 'pie' is fixed, and each party attempts to get as much of it as they can. One side wants to win, which means the other side must lose. With this win–lose approach, distributive negotiation is competitive and adversarial, rather than collaborative, and does not typically lead to positive long-term relationships.

Most experts emphasize the value of integrative negotiation for today's collaborative business environment. That is, the key to effectiveness is to see negotiation not as a zero-sum game, but as a process for reaching a creative solution that benefits everyone.[75]

Rules for reaching a win–win solution

Achieving a win–win solution through integrative negotiation is based on four key strategies:[76]

■ ***Separate the people from the problem.***
For successful integrative negotiation, people stay focused on the problem and the source of conflict, rather than attacking or attempting to discredit each other.

■ ***Focus on interests, not current demands.***
Demands are what each person wants from the negotiation, whereas interests represent the 'why' behind the demands. Consider two sisters arguing over the last orange in the fruit bowl. Each insisted she should get the orange and refused to give up (demands). If one sister had asked the other *why* she wanted the orange (interests), the sisters would have discovered that one wanted to eat it, and the other wanted the peel to use for a project. By focusing on interests, the sisters would be able to arrive at a solution that gave each what she wanted.[77] *Demands* create yes-or-no obstacles to effective negotiation, whereas *interests* present problems that can be solved creatively.

■ ***Listen and ask questions.*** A good strategy for most negotiations is to listen and ask questions. You can learn more about your opponent's position, their constraints and their needs, by being quiet or asking questions. Smart negotiators want to learn the other side's constraints so that they can help overcome them. Don't dismiss the opposing party's limitation as unreasonable or think 'That's their problem'. You can take it on as your own problem and try to come up with a solution for your opponent so that you can get closer to an agreement.

■ ***Insist that results be based on objective standards.*** Each party in a negotiation has its own interests and naturally would like to maximize its outcomes. Successful negotiation requires focusing on objective criteria and maintaining standards of fairness rather than using subjective judgements about the best solution.

REFLECTION

- Conflict refers to antagonistic interaction in which one party attempts to block the intentions or goals of another.
- Some conflict, particularly task conflict, can be beneficial to teams.
- Task conflict is conflict that results from disagreements about the goals to be achieved or the content of the tasks to be performed.
- Relationship conflict results from interpersonal incompatibility that creates tension and personal animosity among people.
- Causes of conflict include competition over resources, goal differences and communication breakdowns.
- Teams and individuals use a variety of styles for dealing with conflict, including the dominating style,

the avoiding style, the compromising style, the accommodating style and the collaborating style, and each can be effective under certain circumstances.

- Negotiation is a conflict management strategy whereby people engage in give-and-take discussions and consider various alternatives to reach a joint decision that is acceptable to both parties.
- Integrative negotiation is a collaborative approach that is based on a win–win assumption, whereby the parties want to come up with a creative solution that benefits both sides of the conflict.
- Distributive negotiation is a competitive and adversarial approach in which each party strives to get as much as it can, usually at the expense of the other party.

DISCUSSION QUESTIONS

1 How can organizations best use technology to help build trust and relationships between their employees?

2 Describe the five stages of team development. How do mature teams differ from new teams?

3 Explain what is meant by a cross-functional team? Discuss some of the factors which can inhibit cross-functional team effectiveness.

4 Team diversity can bring both functional and dysfunctional conflict that interferes with the

cohesion of the team. Investigate the reasons for both types of conflict arising, suggesting how a team leader can deal with the causes and the consequences of such conflict.

5 Discuss how the size of a team can directly impact its performance, and in what ways.

6 Discuss the view that the matrix structure is the optimal one to facilitate coordination of teams, when an organization has a number of complex and interdependent activities to coordinate.

How do you like to work?[78]

INSTRUCTIONS Your approach to your job or schoolwork may indicate whether you thrive on a team. Answer the questions below about your work preferences. Please answer whether each item below is 'Mostly true' or 'Mostly false' for you.

		Mostly true	Mostly false
1	Prefer to work on a team rather than do individual tasks.	☐	☐
2	Given a choice, I try to work by myself rather than face the hassles of group work.	☐	☐
3	I enjoy the personal interaction when working with others.	☐	☐
4	I prefer to do my own work and let others do theirs.	☐	☐
5	I get more satisfaction from a group victory than an individual victory.	☐	☐
6	Teamwork is not worthwhile when people do not do their share.	☐	☐
7	I feel good when I work with others, even when we disagree.	☐	☐
8	I prefer to rely on myself rather than others to do an assignment.	☐	☐

SCORING & INTERPRETATION Give yourself one point for each odd-numbered item you marked 'Mostly true' and one point for each even-numbered item you marked 'Mostly false'. As a new manager, you will both be part of a team and work alone. These items measure your preference for group work. Teamwork can be both frustrating and motivating. If you scored 2 or fewer, you definitely prefer individual work. A score of 7 or above suggests that you prefer working in teams. A score of 3 to 6 indicates comfort working alone and in a team. A new manager needs to do both.

APPLY YOUR SKILLS: ETHICAL DILEMMA

One for all and all for one?[79]

Melinda Asbel watched as three of her classmates filed out of the conference room. Then she turned back to the large wooden table and faced her fellow members (a student and three faculty members) of the university's judiciary committee.

The three students – Joe Eastridge, Brad Hamil and Lisa Baghetti – had just concluded their appeal against a plagiarism conviction stemming from a group project for an international marketing course. Melinda, who happened to be in the class with the students on trial, remembered the day that the professor, Hank Zierden, had asked Joe, Brad and Lisa, along with the group's leader, Paul Colgan, to stay after class. She happened to walk by the classroom a half hour later to see four glum students emerge. Even though Paul had a chagrined

expression on his face, Joe was the one who looked completely shattered. It didn't take long for word to spread along the ever-active grapevine that Paul had admitted to plagiarizing his part of the group paper.

At the hearing, the students recounted how they'd quickly and unanimously settled on Paul to lead the group. He was by far the most able student among them, someone who managed to maintain a stellar grade point average (GPA) even while handling a full course load and holding down a part-time job. After the group worked together for weeks analyzing the problem and devising a marketing plan, Paul assigned a section of the final paper to each member. With the pressure of all those end-of-the-semester deadlines bearing down on them, everyone was delighted when Paul volunteered to write the company and industry background, the section that typically took the most time to produce. Paul gathered in everyone's contributions, assembled them into a paper and handed the final draft to the other members. They each gave it a quick read. They liked what they saw and thought they had a good chance for an A.

Unfortunately, as Paul readily admitted when Professor Zierden confronted them, he had pulled the section that he'd contributed directly off the Internet. Pointing out the written policy that he had distributed at the beginning of the semester, which stated that each group member was equally responsible for the final product, the professor gave all four students a zero for the project. The group project and presentation counted for 30 per cent of the course grade.

Joe, Brad and Lisa maintained that they were completely unaware that Paul had cheated. 'It just never occurred to us Paul would ever need to cheat,' Brad said. They were innocent bystanders, the students argued. Why should they be penalized? Besides, the consequences weren't going to fall on each of them equally. Although Paul was suffering the embarrassment of public exposure, the failing group project grade would only put a dent in his solid GPA. Joe, on the other hand, was already on academic probation. A zero probably meant he wouldn't make the 2.5 GPA that he needed to stay in the business programme.

At least one of the faculty members of the judiciary committee supported Professor Zierden's actions. 'We're assigning more and more group projects because increasingly that's the way these students are going to find themselves working when they get real jobs in the real world,' he said. 'And the fact of the matter is that if someone obtains information illegally while on the job, it's going to put the whole corporation at risk for being sued, or worse.'

Even though she could see merit to both sides, Melinda was going to have to choose. If you were Melinda, how would you vote?

What would you do?

1   Vote to exonerate the three group project members who didn't cheat. You're convinced that they had no reason to suspect Paul Colgan of dishonesty. Exonerating them is the right thing to do.

2   Vote in support of Hank Zierden's decision to hold each individual member accountable for the entire project. The professor clearly stated his policy at the beginning of the semester, and the students should have been more vigilant. The committee should not undercut a professor's explicit policy.

3   Vote to reduce each of the three students' penalties. Instead of a zero, each student will receive only half of the possible total points for the project, which would be an F. You're still holding students responsible for the group project, but not imposing catastrophic punishment. This compromise both undercuts the professor's policy and punishes 'innocent' team members to some extent, but not as severely.

APPLY YOUR SKILLS: CASE FOR CRITICAL ANALYSIS

Manchester United: Building and rebuilding teams

Manchester United is one of the most popular and successful sports teams in the world, playing one of the most popular spectator sports on Earth. Through its 136-year heritage Manchester United has won 62 trophies, including a record 20 English league titles, enabling it to develop what it believes is one of the world's leading sports brands and a global community of 659 million followers. Its large, passionate community provides Manchester United with a worldwide platform to generate significant revenue from multiple sources, including sponsorship, merchandising, product licensing, media and content, broadcasting and match-day revenue.

Manchester United attracts leading global companies such as adidas, Aon, General Motors (Chevrolet) and Nike that want access and exposure to its community of followers and association with its global brand

At the end of the 2012–20 season, Sir Alex Ferguson retired as team manager. Sir Alex remains a key member of the club as he is a director of Manchester United FC. David Moyes was the manager during the 2013–14 season and departed the club in April 2014. David Moyes was unable to build on the success of Sir Alex Ferguson's teams. Following this departure, Ryan Giggs assumed responsibility for the first team as interim manager.

In season 2014–15 despite improved performances Manchester United did not win any trophies and the process of team rebuilding is continuing. Graeme Souness says Man United need two seasons of rebuilding to become title contenders again. However, Souness believes the club must learn from the mistakes of last summer when they failed to sign their top targets. He says supporters may need to accept that it could take four transfer windows before they have brought in enough quality players to challenge for the championship again.

'Building a team is not a quick fix.' 'From where Man United were to where they are now, the strength is nowhere near where they would want it to be.'

'You put Man United in that elite group of Barcelona, Real Madrid and Bayern Munich, but how many Man United players in the current squad would be wanted by any of those teams? I can think of two – and beyond that you're struggling.'

'The biggest problem they will have is will the quality be available? Then you're faced with the dilemma as a manager and a football club as to whether to sit and do nothing because you can't get the one you want, or go for the third or fourth or fifth choice. What do you do? That's a difficult call.'

'The supporters will want signings, that's where the pressure comes from. That's why they ended up taking players who are not their first choice. The supporters are impatient.'

Former Manchester United captain Gary Neville agrees that the new manager must be patient when he enters the transfer market this summer. He admits the season has been disappointing following the departure of Sir Alex Ferguson, but would prefer to see quality additions rather than wholesale changes.

Neville said: 'I do think Manchester United has a really good chance of getting back in the Champions League next season, I really do believe that. I think not having European football will help them.'

'If the new manager feels they need eight players, that doesn't mean they should go and sign eight players. Quality is the right thing, not the quantity.'

'We've seen many clubs sign lots of players and bedding in is always a difficulty, so sign three or four real top-quality players and improve next season and then maybe go again with two or three the year after. That's the more organic approach that I would expect Manchester United to have.'

'However, I wouldn't have expected Manchester United to sack their manager after 10 months, so what's going to happen in the next few years depends on the quality of the next manager.'

In May 2014, it was announced that Louis van Gaal would be the new team manager of Manchester United under a 3-year contract. Louis van Gaal has managed at the top level of European football for over 20 years, and, in that time, he has won domestic titles and domestic cups in three countries, as well as the UEFA Champions League, the UEFA Cup, an Intercontinental Cup, two UEFA Super Cups and domestic Super Cups in Holland and Germany. Louis van Gaal took his new post in July 2014 after the FIFA World Cup, where he managed the Dutch national team into third place position.

Reference: Beauchamp, M.R. and Eys, M.A. (2014) *Group Dynamics in Exercise and Sport Psychology*, Routledge

Questions

1 Why does team building take time?

2 Discuss the extent to which high performance teams such as professional sports teams are different from work teams?

3 Summarize what sports managers/coaches can learn from management theorists in relation to leading teams?

END NOTES

1. David Kesmodel, 'Boeing Teams Speed Up 737 Output', *The Wall Street Journal Online*, February 7, 2012, http://online.wsj.com/article/SB100014240529702034369045771552040349077744.html (accessed September 25, 2012).

2. Industry Week/Manufacturing Performance Institute's Census of Manufacturers for 2004, reported in Traci Purdum, 'Teaming, Take 2', *Industry Week* (May 2005): 41–43.

3. '"Golden Hour" Crucial Time for Surgeons on Front Line', *Johnson City Press*, April 1, 2003.

4. Carl E. Larson and Frank M. J. LaFasto, *TeamWork* (Newbury Park, CA: Sage, 1989); J. R. Katzenbach and D. K. Smith, *The Wisdom of Teams* (Boston, MA: Harvard Business School Press, 1993); and Dawn R. Utley and Stephanie E. Brown, 'Establishing Characteristic Differences Between Team and Working Group Behaviors', *Institute of Industrial Engineers Annual Conference Proceedings* (2010): 1–6.

5. Some of the advantages in this section are discussed in 'The Rewards of Teaming' sidebar in Amy C. Edmondson, 'Teamwork on the Fly', *Harvard Business Review* (April 2012): 72–80.

6. Geoff Colvin, 'First: Team Players Trump All-Stars', *Fortune* (May 21, 2012): 46–47.

7. See the excellent discussion in Atul Gawande, 'Cowboys and Pit Crews', 2011 Harvard Medical School commencement address, *The New Yorker* (May 26, 2011), www.newyorker.com/online/blogs/newsdesk/2011/05/atul-gawande-harvard-medical-school-commencement-address.html (accessed September 26, 2012).

8. Colvin, 'First: Team Players Trump All-Stars'.

9. R. B. Zajonc, 'Social Facilitation', *Science* 145 (1969): 269–274.

10. Susanne G. Scott and Walter O. Einstein, 'Strategic Performance Appraisal in Team-Based Organizations: One Size Does Not Fit All', *Academy of Management Executive* 15, no. 2 (2001): 107–116.

11. Bryce G. Hoffman, 'Inside Ford's Fight to Avoid Disaster', *The Wall Street Journal*, March 9, 2012, B1.

12. The discussion of self-managed teams is based on Ruth Wageman, 'Critical Success Factors for Creating Superb Self-Managing Teams', *Organizational Dynamics* (Summer 1997): 49–61; James H. Shonk, *Team-Based Organizations* (Homewood, IL: Business One Irwin, 1992); and Thomas Owens, 'The Self-Managing Work Team', *Small Business Report* (February 1991): 53–65.

13. Jason Fried, 'Get Real: When the Only Way Up is Out', *Inc.* (April 2011): 35–36.

14. David A. Ferrucci, 'Building the Team That Built Watson', *The New York Times*, January 7, 2012, www.nytimes.com/2012/01/08/jobs/building-the-watson-team-of-scientists.html?_r=0 (accessed October 1, 2012).

15. Study by G. Clotaire Rapaille, reported in Karen Bernowski, 'What Makes American Teams Tick?' *Quality Progress* 28, no. 1 (January 1995): 39–42.

16. Study by Jean Twenge and colleagues, reported in Sharon Jayson, 'What's on Americans' Minds? Increasingly, 'Me,'' *USA Today*, July 10, 2012, http://usatoday30.usatoday.com/LIFE/usaedition/2012-07-11-Individualism--Twenge----_ST_U.htm (accessed October 2, 2012).

17. Avan Jassawalla, Hemant Sashittal and Avinash Malshe, 'Students' Perceptions of Social Loafing: Its Antecedents and Consequences in Undergraduate Business Classroom Teams', *Academy of Management Learning and Education* 8, no. 1 (2009): 42–54; and Robert Albanese and David D. Van Fleet, 'Rational Behavior in Groups: The Free-Riding Tendency', *Academy of Management Review* 10 (1985): 244–255.

18. See David H. Freedman, 'The Idiocy of Crowds' ('What's Next' column), *Inc.* (September 2006): 61–62.

19. Quoted in Jason Zweig, 'The Intelligent Investor: How Group Decisions End Up Wrong-Footed', *The Wall Street Journal*, April 25, 2009.

20. 'Why Some Teams Succeed (and So Many Don't)', *Harvard Management Update* (October 2006): 3–4; Frederick P. Morgeson, D. Scott DeRue and Elizabeth P. Karam, 'Leadership in Teams: A Functional Approach to Understanding Leadership Structure and Processes', *Journal of Management* 36, no. 1 (January 2010): 5–39; and Patrick Lencioni, 'Dissolve Dysfunction: Begin Building Your Dream Team', *Leadership Excellence* (October 2009): 20.

21. Reported in Jerry Useem, 'What's That Spell? Teamwork!' *Fortune* (June 12, 2006): 65–66.

22. Eric Sundstrom, Kenneth P. DeMeuse and David Futtrell, 'Work Teams', *American Psychologist* 45 (February 1990): 120–133; María Isabel Delgado Piña, Ana María Romero Martínez and Luis Gómez Martínez, 'Teams in Organizations: A Review on Team Effectiveness', *Team Performance Management* 14, no. 1–2 (2008): 7–21; and Morgeson, DeRue and Karam, 'Leadership in Teams'.

23. Deborah L. Gladstein, 'Groups in Context: A Model of Task Group Effectiveness', *Administrative Science Quarterly* 29 (1984): 499–517. For an overview of research on team effectiveness, see John Mathieu, M. Travis Maynard, Tammy Rapp and Lucy Gilson, 'Team Effectiveness 1997–2007: A Review of Recent Advancements and a Glimpse into the Future', *Journal of Management* 34, no. 3 (June 2008): 410–476.

24. Sujin K. Horwitz and Irwin B. Horwitz, 'The Effects of Team Diversity on Team Outcomes: A Meta-Analytic Review of Team Demography', *Journal of Management* 33, no. 6 (December 2007): 987–1015; and Dora C. Lau and J. Keith Murnighan, 'Demographic Diversity and Faultlines: The Compositional Dynamics of Organizational Groups', *Academy of Management Review* 23, no. 2 (1998): 325–340.

25. The discussion of virtual teams is based on Phillip L. Hunsaker and Johanna S. Hunsaker, 'Virtual Teams: A Leader's Guide', *Team Performance Management* 14, no. 1–2 (2008): 86ff; Chris Kimble, 'Building Effective Virtual Teams: How to Overcome the Problems of Trust and Identity in Virtual Teams', *Global Business and Organizational Excellence* (January–February 2011): 6–15; Wayne F. Cascio and Stan Shurygailo, 'E-Leadership and Virtual Teams', *Organizational Dynamics* 31, no. 4 (2002): 362–376; Anthony M. Townsend, Samuel M. DeMarie and Anthony R. Hendrickson, 'Virtual Teams: Technology and the Workplace of the Future', *Academy of Management Executive* 12, no. 3 (August 1998): 17–29; and Deborah L. Duarte and Nancy Tennant Snyder, *Mastering Virtual Teams* (San Francisco: Jossey-Bass, 1999).

26. Survey by RW3CultureWizard, reported in Golnaz Sadri and John Condia, 'Managing the Virtual World', *Industrial Management* (January–February 2012): 21–25.

27. Vijay Govindarajan and Anil K. Gupta, 'Building an Effective Global Business Team', *MIT Sloan Management Review* 42, no. 4 (Summer 2001): 63–71.

28. Jessica Lipnack and Jeffrey Stamps, 'Virtual Teams: The New Way to Work', *Strategy & Leadership* (January–February 1999): 14–19; *and* Sadri and Condia, 'Managing the Virtual World'.

29. This discussion is based on Arvind Malhotra, Ann Majchrzak and Benson Rosen, 'Leading Virtual Teams', *Academy of Management Perspectives* 21, no. 1 (February 2007): 60–69; Benson Rosen, Stacie Furst and Richard Blackburn, 'Overcoming Barriers to Knowledge Sharing in Virtual Teams', *Organizational Dynamics* 36, no. 3 (2007): 259–273; Marshall Goldsmith, 'Crossing the Cultural Chasm; Keeping Communication Clear and Consistent with Team Members from Other Countries Isn't Easy, Says Author Maya Hu-Chan', *BusinessWeek Online,* May 31, 2007, www.businessweek.com/careers/content/may2007/ca20070530_521679.htm (accessed August 24, 2007); and Bradley L. Kirkman, Benson Rosen, Cristina B. Gibson, Paul E. Tesluk and Simon O. McPherson, 'Five Challenges to Virtual Team Success: Lessons from Sabre, Inc.', *Academy of Management Executive* 16, no. 3 (2002): 67–79.

30. Darl G. Kolb, Greg Prussia and Joline Francoeur, 'Connectivity and Leadership: The Influence of Online Activity

on Closeness and Effectiveness', *Journal of Leadership and Organizational Studies* 15, no. 4 (May 2009): 342–352.

31. Ann Majchrzak, A. Malhotra, J. Stamps and J. Lipnack, 'Can Absence Make a Team Grow Stronger?' *Harvard Business Review* 82, no. 5 (May 2004): 131.

32. Lynda Gratton, 'Working Together . . . When Apart', *The Wall Street Journal*, June 18, 2007; and Kirkman et al., 'Five Challenges to Virtual Team Success'.

33. Pete Engardio, 'A Guide for Multinationals: One of the Greatest Challenges for a Multinational Is Learning How to Build a Productive Global Team', *BusinessWeek* (August 20, 2007): 48–51; and Gratton, 'Working Together . . . When Apart'.

34. Reported in Richard Pastore, 'Global Team Management: It's a Small World After All', *CIO,* January 23, 2008, www.cio.com/article/174750/Global_Team_Management_It_s_a_Small_World_After_All (accessed May 20, 2008).

35. Reported in Jia Lynn Yang, 'The Power of Number 4.6', part of a special series, 'Secrets of Greatness: Teamwork', *Fortune* (June 12, 2006): 122.

36. Martin Hoegl, 'Smaller Teams–Better Teamwork: How to Keep Project Teams Small', *Business Horizons* 48 (2005): 209–214.

37. Stephanie T. Solansky, 'Team Identification: A Determining Factor of Performance', *Journal of Managerial Psychology* 26, no. 3 (2011): 247–258.

38. Reported in Yang, 'The Power of Number 4.6'.

39. For research findings on group size, see Erin Bradner, Gloria Mark and Tammie D. Hertel, 'Team Size and Technology Fit: Participation, Awareness, and Rapport in Distributed Teams', *IEEE Transactions on Professional Communication* 48, no. 1 (March 2005): 68–77; M. E. Shaw, *Group Dynamics*, 3d ed. (New York: McGraw-Hill, 1981); G. Manners, 'Another Look at Group Size, Group Problem-Solving, and Member Consensus', *Academy of Management Journal* 18 (1975): 715–724; and Martin Hoegl, 'Smaller Teams – Better Teamwork'.

40. Bradner, Mark and Hertel, 'Team Size and Technology Fit: Participation, Awareness, and Rapport in Distributed Teams'; Sadri and Condia, 'Managing the Virtual World'.

41. Warren E. Watson, Kamalesh Kumar and Larry K. Michaelsen, 'Cultural Diversity's Impact on Interaction Process and Performance: Comparing Homogeneous and Diverse Task Groups', *Academy of Management Journal* 36 (1993): 590–602; Gail Robinson and Kathleen Dechant, 'Building a Business Case for Diversity', *Academy of Management Executive* 11, no. 3 (1997): 21–31; and David A. Thomas and Robin J. Ely, 'Making Differences Matter: A New Paradigm for Managing Diversity', *Harvard Business Review* (September–October 1996): 79–90.

42. D. van Knippenberg and M. C. Schippers, 'Work Group Diversity', *Annual Review of Psychology* 58 (2007): 515–541; J. N. Cummings, 'Work Groups: Structural Diversity and Knowledge Sharing in a Global Organization', *Management Science* 50, no, 3 (2004): 352–364; J. Stuart Bunderson and Kathleen M. Sutcliffe, 'Comparing Alternative Conceptualizations of Functional Diversity in Management Teams: Process and Performance Effects', *Academy of Management Journal* 45, no. 5 (2002): 875–893; and Marc Orlitzky and John D. Benjamin, 'The Effects of Sex Composition on Small Group Performance in a Business School Case Competition', *Academy of Management Learning and Education* 2, no. 2 (2003): 128–138.

43. Anita Woolley and Thomas Malone, 'Defend Your Research: What Makes a Team Smarter? More Women', *Harvard Business Review* (June 2011), http://hbr.org/2011/06/defend-your-research-what-makes-a-team-smarter-more-women/ar/1 (accessed October 1, 2012).

44. Watson et al. 'Cultural Diversity's Impact on Interaction Process and Performance'; and D. C. Hambrick, S.C. Davidson, S. A. Snell and C. C. Snow, 'When Groups Consist of Multiple Nationalities: Towards a New Understanding of the Implications', *Organization Studies* 19, no. 2 (1998): 181–205.

45. Matt Moffett, 'Trapped Miners Kept Focus, Shared Tuna – Foiled Escape, Bid to Organize Marked First Two Weeks Underground in Chile', *The Wall Street Journal*, August 25, 2010; and 'Lessons on Leadership and Teamwork – From 700 Meters Below the Earth's Surface', Universia Knowledge@Wharton, September 22, 2010, www.wharton.universia.net/index.cfm?fa=viewArticle&id=1943&language=english (accessed September 29, 2010).

46. R. M. Belbin, *Team Roles at Work* (Oxford, UK: Butterworth Heinemann, 1983); Tony Manning, R. Parker and G. Pogson, 'A Revised Model of Team Roles and Some Research Findings', *Industrial and Commercial Training* 38, no. 6 (2006): 287–296; George Prince, 'Recognizing Genuine Teamwork', *Supervisory Management* (April 1989): 25–36; K. D. Benne and P. Sheats, 'Functional Roles of Group Members', *Journal of Social Issues* 4 (1948): 41–49; and R. F. Bales, *SYMLOG Case Study Kit* (New York: Free Press, 1980).

47. Robert A. Baron, *Behavior in Organizations*, 2d ed. (Boston: Allyn & Bacon, 1986).

48. *Ibid.*

49. Bruce W. Tuckman and Mary Ann C. Jensen, 'Stages of Small-Group Development Revisited', *Group and Organizational Studies* 2 (1977): 419–427; and Bruce W. Tuckman, 'Developmental Sequences in Small Groups', *Psychological Bulletin* 63 (1965): 384–399. See also Linda N. Jewell and H. Joseph Reitz, *Group Effectiveness in Organizations* (Glenview, IL: Scott Foresman, 1981).

50. Chuck Salter, 'The World's Greatest Chemistry Experiment', *Fast Company* (May 2011): 81–85, 128–130.

51. Shaw, *Group Dynamics*.

52. Daniel C. Feldman and Hugh J. Arnold, *Managing Individual and Group Behavior in Organizations* (New York: McGraw-Hill, 1983).

53. Amanuel G. Tekleab, Narda R. Quigley and Paul E. Tesluk, 'A Longitudinal Study of Team Conflict, Conflict Management, Cohesion, and Team Effectiveness', *Group & Organization Management* 34, no. 2 (April 2009): 170–205; Dorwin Cartwright and Alvin Zander, *Group Dynamics: Research and Theory*, 3d ed. (New York: Harper & Row, 1968); and Elliot Aronson, *The Social Animal* (San Francisco: W. H. Freeman, 1976).

54. Vishal K. Gupta, Rui Huang and Suman Niranjan, 'A Longitudinal Examination of the Relationship Between Team Leadership and Performance', *Journal of Leadership and Organizational Studies* 17, no. 4 (2010): 335–350; and Marcial Losada and Emily Heaphy, 'The Role of Positivity and Connectivity in the Performance of Business Teams',

American Behavioral Scientist 47, no. 6 (February 2004): 740–765.

55. Stanley E. Seashore, *Group Cohesiveness in the Industrial Work Group* (Ann Arbor, MI: Institute for Social Research, 1954).

56. J. Richard Hackman, 'Group Influences on Individuals', in *Handbook of Industrial and Organizational Psychology*, ed. M. Dunnette (Chicago: Rand McNally, 1976).

57. These are based on Daniel C. Feldman, 'The Development and Enforcement of Group Norms', *Academy of Management Review* 9 (1984): 47–53.

58. Jeanne M. Wilson, Jill George and Richard S. Wellings with William C. Byham, *Leadership Trapeze: Strategies for Leadership in Team-Based Organizations* (San Francisco: Jossey-Bass, 1994), p. 12.

59. Simon Taggar and Robert Ellis, 'The Role of Leaders in Shaping Formal Team Norms', *The Leadership Quarterly* 18 (2007): 105–120.

60. Geoffrey Colvin, 'Why Dream Teams Fail', *Fortune* (June 12, 2006): 87–92.

61. Stephen P. Robbins, *Managing Organizational Conflict: A Nontraditional Approach* (Englewood Cliffs, NJ: Prentice Hall, 1974).

62. Tekleab, Quigley and Tesluk, 'A Longitudinal Study of Team Conflict, Conflict Management, Cohesion, and Team Effectiveness'.

63. Based on K. A. Jehn, 'A Multimethod Examination of the Benefits and Determinants of Intragroup Conflict', *Administrative Science Quarterly* 40 (1995): 256–282; and K. A. Jehn, 'A Qualitative Analysis of Conflict Types and Dimensions in Organizational Groups', *Administrative Science Quarterly* 42 (1997): 530–557.

64. Linda A. Hill, 'A Note for Analyzing Work Groups', *Harvard Business School Cases,* August 28, 1995; revised April 3, 1998, Product # 9-496-026, ordered at http://hbr.org/search/linda+a+hill/4294934969/.

65. A. Amason, 'Distinguishing the Effects of Functional and Dysfunctional Conflict on Strategic Decision Making: Resolving a Paradox for Top Management Teams', *Academy of Management Journal* 39, no. 1 (1996): 123–148; Jehn, 'A Multimethod Examination of the Benefits and Determinants of Intragroup Conflict'; and K. A. Jehn and E. A. Mannix, 'The Dynamic Nature of Conflict: A Longitudinal Study of Intragroup Conflict and Group Performance', *Academy of Management Journal* 44 (2001): 238–251.

66. Amason, 'Distinguishing the Effects of Functional and Dysfunctional Conflict on Strategic Decision Making'.

67. Dean Tjosvold, Chen Hui and Daniel Z. Ding, 'Conflict Values and Team Relationships: Conflict's Contribution to Team Effectiveness and Citizenship in China', *Journal of Organizational Behavior* 24 (2003): 69–88; C. De Dreu and E. Van de Vliert, *Using Conflict in Organizations* (Beverly Hills, CA: Sage, 1997); and Kathleen M. Eisenhardt, Jean L. Kahwajy and L. J. Bourgeois III, 'Conflict and Strategic Choice: How Top Management Teams Disagree', *California Management Review* 39, no. 2 (Winter 1997): 42–62.

68. Kenneth G. Koehler, 'Effective Team Management', *Small Business Report* (July 19, 1989): 14–16; and Dean Tjosvold, 'Making Conflict Productive', *Personnel Administrator* 29 (June 1984): 121.

69. This discussion is based in part on Richard L. Daft, *Organization Theory and Design* (St. Paul, MN: West, 1992), Chapter 13; and Paul M. Terry, 'Conflict Management', *Journal of Leadership Studies* 3, no. 2 (1996): 3–21.

70. Edmondson, 'Teamwork on the Fly'.

71. Yuhyung Shin, 'Conflict Resolution in Virtual Teams', *Organizational Dynamics* 34, no. 4 (2005): 331–345.

72. This discussion is based on K. W. Thomas, 'Towards Multidimensional Values in Teaching: The Example of Conflict Behaviors', *Academy of Management Review* 2 (1977): 487.

73. Edmondson, 'Teamwork on the Fly'.

74. 'Negotiation Types', The Negotiation Experts, June 9, 2010, www.negotiations.com/articles/negotiation-types/ (accessed September 28, 2010).

75. Rob Walker, 'Take It or Leave It: The Only Guide to Negotiating You Will Ever Need', *Inc.* (August 2003): 75–82.

76. Based on Roger Fisher and William Ury, *Getting to Yes: Negotiating Agreement Without Giving In* (New York: Penguin, 1983); Walker, 'Take It or Leave It'; Robb Mandelbaum, 'How to Negotiate Effectively', *Inc.*, November 1, 2010, www.inc.com/magazine/20101101/how-to-negotiate-effectively.html (accessed April 12, 2011); and Deepak Malhotra and Max H. Bazerman, 'Investigative Negotiation', *Harvard Business Review* (September 2007): 72–78.

77. This familiar story has been reported in many publications, including 'The Six Best Questions to Ask Your Customers', Marketing and Distribution Company Limited, www.madisco.bz/articles/The%20Six%20Best%20Questions%20to%20Ask%20Your%20Customers.pdf (accessed September 28, 2010).

78. Based on Eric M. Stark, Jason D. Shaw and Michelle K. Duffy, 'Preference for Group Work, Winning Orientation, and Social Loafing Behavior in Groups', *Group & Organization Management* 32, no. 6 (December 2007): 699–723.

79. Based on Ellen R. Stapleton, 'College to Expand Policy on Plagiarism', *The Ithacan Online*, April 12, 2001, www.ithaca.edu/ithacan/articles/0104/12/news/0college_to_e.htm (accessed April 12, 2001).

PART 5 INTEGRATIVE CASE
PART FIVE: LEADING

Range Resources: Leading ethically, communicating openly

'Natural gas has been a godsend to this area. It has helped farmers see a return on all the hard work they have put into their land just to keep it,' says Bev Romanetti, a Pennsylvania cattle farmer. 'I have found that Range Resources wants to be responsible; they want to do the right things, they want to protect our environment and they want to do right by us,' remarks Albie Rinehart, a retired schoolteacher from Greene County, Pennsylvania. 'I personally know a lot of the people who work for Range Resources – it's like dealing with your neighbours,' states Buzz Meddings, a firefighter from Washington County, Pennsylvania.

Citizens of rural Pennsylvania are the people most affected by natural gas exploration in the eastern region of the USA. They are farmers, firefighters, teachers, single mums, restaurant owners and volunteers. They are hardy. They are the salt of the earth. More important, they are the face of natural gas development in the Keystone State and they provide the voices through which Texas-based energy company Range Resources communicates its message of good corporate citizenship to the public. At the company's public outreach site, MyRangeResource. com, everyday people offer video testimonials about the economic and social benefits that Range brings to local communities, whether in terms of jobs, new development or concern for the natural environment. The site, which functions as part of Range's communications strategy, is an information clearinghouse for all things related to natural gas exploration.

Since discovering the second-largest natural gas field in the world in 2004, Range has used open communication to build trust among the stakeholders most affected by the development of natural gas resources. While natural gas is recognized as a clean energy solution to America's energy needs, citizens still want to know that natural gas exploration is safe for communities and good for the environment.

As explained at MyRangeResources.com, Range makes safety a central component of its natural gas production. To extract methane from rock formations deep down in the Earth, engineers guide a 5-inch-diameter drill straight down more than a mile and then turn it horizontally to penetrate shale rock thousands of feet in all directions. This horizontal drilling method is a groundbreaking advancement that allows drillers to capture far more methane than the old vertical-only method, which requires many more wells to get a fraction of the output. Once Range's drill arrives at its destination 6500 feet below the Earth's surface, electric charges produce cracks in the rock from which methane gas escapes. To enlarge these fractures for maximum gas recovery, millions of gallons of water and sand are pumped to the area under extreme pressure, expanding the cracks and freeing even more gas to flow back up to the well head at the surface. For environmental safety, Range houses its drill in a 24-inch-diameter casing comprising five layers of steel and concrete, isolating the entire production process from contact with surrounding land and water.

In its desire to leave as small an environmental footprint as possible, Range has pioneered a way to recycle the millions of gallons of water used in the drilling process. 'One thing we've done from an environmental point of view is we now recycle 100 per cent of our water in our development areas in Pennsylvania. In fact, we're recycling nearly all of our fluid, which is a real breakthrough for the industry,' says Jeffrey Ventura, president and CEO of Range Resources. 'Back when we began that process, a lot of people felt that it couldn't be done, that it was physically impossible. Lo and behold, not only did we do it successfully, but now we're doing it large-scale.' Ventura, the leader credited with Range's decision to explore the Marcellus Shale gas formation in Pennsylvania, says water recycling is a major innovation in natural gas production. 'Just like the Marcellus Shale was a breakthrough,' Ventura says, 'on the environmental side, water recycling was a real breakthrough.'

To keep stakeholders informed about safety, Range has also led the industry in the disclosure of core production processes, especially the use of liquids for drilling and fracturing. 'In the middle of 2010, there was a lot of concern nationwide about what's in frack fluid, and Range was the first company in the industry to say exactly what's in our frack fluid,' Ventura says. 'We post it on our website and we supply it to the state for every Marcellus Shale well that we're drilling. It's 99.9 per cent water, and the 0.1 per cent is common everyday household chemicals.' Range's open communication with the public has earned the respect of environmental groups and also the US Environmental Protection Agency (EPA), which in 2012 announced that natural gas production was safe for drinking water at its test site in Dimock Township, Pennsylvania.

Safety, open communication and leadership – these are the qualities that have made Range Resources a vanguard of America's natural gas boom and a pioneer of sustainable energy development. 'I'm proud of what our technical team has done on the environmental side and the communications side,' says Ventura of his company's contribution to America's clean energy future.

Integrative case questions

1   Range Resources CEO Jeffrey Ventura emphasizes public safety, environmental concern and open communication with stakeholders. Which of the four contemporary leadership approaches do you think best describes Ventura? Explain.

2   Managers at Range Resources use communication to develop a climate of trust and openness. Why is this especially important for energy companies, and what specific actions can managers take to enhance this communication approach?

3   How might Range's leadership, communication and values affect employees' organizational commitment? Explain.

SOURCES: My Range Resources Video Interview Series, Range Resources, www.myrangeresources.com (accessed July 20, 2012); Jeffrey Ventura (President and Chief Executive Officer of Range Resources), interview by Rodney Waller, 'Range Up Close: Range's Technical Team,' Range Resources corporate site, 2010, online video, www.rangeresources.com/Media-Center/Featured-Stories.aspx (accessed July 20, 2012); Jack Z. Smith, 'New CEO Taking Helm as Range Continues Push into Marcellus,' Star-Telegram, December 17, 2011, www.star-telegram.com/2011/12/17/3601200/new-ceo-taking-helm-as-range-continues.html (accessed July 19, 2012); Rick Stouffer, 'Range Resources Recycles All Waste Water from Washington Drilling,' Pittsburgh Tribune-Review, October 19, 2009, http://triblive.com/x/pittsburghtrib/business/s_648781.html (accessed July 20, 2012); Natural Gas Company Reveals Fracking Chemical Composition,' NewsWorks, July 16, 2012, www.newsworks.org/index.php/local/healthscience/5361-natural-gas-company-reveals-fracking-chemical-composition (accessed July 19, 2012); Range Resources, 'Hydraulic Fracturing: Marcellus,' Range Resources corporate site, www.rangeresources.com/rangeresources/files/6f/6ff33c64-5acf-4270-95c7-9e991b963771.pdf (accessed July 19, 2012); Laura Legere, 'EPA to Stop Dimock Water Deliveries,' Scranton Times-Tribune, July 26, 2012, http://thetimes-tribune.com/news/gas-drilling/epa-to-stop-dimock-water-deliveries-1.1348393 (accessed July 26, 2012); Timothy Gardner, 'Dimock, PA Water Deemed Safe By EPA,' Reuters, May 11, 2012, www.huffingtonpost.com/2012/05/11/dimock-pa-water-safe-epa_n_1510035.html (accessed July 19, 2012).

GLOSSARY

360-degree feedback   Uses multiple raters, including self-rating, to appraise employee performance and guide development.

Accountability   Means that people with authority and responsibility are subject to reporting and justifying task outcomes to those above them in the chain of command.

Achievement culture   A results-oriented culture that values competitiveness, personal initiative and achievement.

Activity ratio   Measures the organization's internal performance with respect to key activities defined by management.

Adaptability culture   Characterized by values that support the company's ability to interpret and translate signals from the environment into new behaviour responses.

Adjourning   The stage during which members of temporary teams prepare for the team's disbanding.

Administrative model   A decision-making model that includes the concepts of *bounded rationality* and *satisficing* and describes how managers make decisions in situations that are characterized by uncertainty and ambiguity.

Administrative principles approach   A subfield of the classical perspective that focuses on the total organization rather than the individual worker and delineates the management functions of planning, organizing, commanding, coordinating and controlling.

After-action review   A disciplined procedure whereby managers review the results of decisions to evaluate what worked, what didn't and how to do things better.

Alienated follower   A person who is an independent, critical thinker but is passive in the organization.

Ambidextrous approach   Incorporating structures and processes that are appropriate for both the creative impulse and the systematic implementation of innovations.

Ambiguity   A condition in which the goals to be achieved or the problem to be solved is unclear, alternatives are difficult to define and information about outcomes is unavailable.

Angel financing   Occurs when a wealthy individual who believes in the idea for a start-up provides personal funds and advice to help the business get started.

Application form   A selection device that collects information about the applicant's education, previous work experience and other background characteristics.

Assessment centre   Used to select individuals with high managerial potential based on their performance on a series of simulated managerial tasks.

Authentic leadership   Leadership by individuals who know and understand themselves, who espouse and act consistent with higher-order ethical values, and who empower and inspire others with their openness and authenticity.

Authority   The formal and legitimate right of a manager to make decisions, issue orders and allocate resources to achieve outcomes desired by the organization.

BCG matrix   A concept developed by the Boston Consulting Group (BCG) that evaluates strategic business units with respect to two dimensions – business growth rate and market share – and classifies them as cash cows, stars, question marks or dogs.

Behavioural sciences approach   Draws from psychology, sociology, and other social sciences to develop theories about human behaviour and interaction in an organizational setting.

Behaviourally anchored rating scale (BARS)   A performance evaluation technique that relates an employee's performance to specific job-related incidents.

Behaviour modification   The set of techniques by which reinforcement theory is used to modify human behaviour.

Benchmarking   The continuous process of measuring products, services and practices against major competitors or industry leaders.

Big Five personality factors   Dimensions that describe an individual's extroversion, agreeableness, conscientiousness, emotional stability and openness to experience.

Bottom of the pyramid (BOP) concept   Proposes that corporations can alleviate poverty and other social ills, as well as make significant profits, by selling to the world's poor.

Bottom-up approach   Encourage the flow of ideas from lower levels and make sure they get heard and acted upon by top executives.

Bottom-up budgeting   Involves lower-level managers anticipating their department's budget needs and passing them up to top management for approval.

Boundary-spanning roles   Link to and coordinate the organization with key elements in the external environment.

Bounded rationality   Means that people have the time and cognitive ability to process only a limited amount of information on which to base decisions.

Brainstorming   A technique that uses a face-to-face group to spontaneously suggest a broad range of alternatives for making a decision.

Bureaucratic organizations approach   Emphasizes management on an impersonal, rational basis through elements such as clearly defined authority and responsibility, formal recordkeeping, and separation of management and ownership.

Business incubator   Helps start-up companies by connecting them with a range of experts and mentors who nurture them, thus increasing their likelihood of success.

Business-level strategy   Pertains to each business unit or product line within the organization.

Business plan   A document specifying the details of the business.

Capital budget   A budget that plans and reports investments in major assets to be depreciated over several years.

Cash budget   A budget that estimates receipts and expenditures of money on a daily or weekly basis to ensure that an organization has sufficient cash to meet its obligations.

Centralization   Means that decision authority is located near top organization levels.

Centralized network   A team communication structure in which team members communicate through a single individual to solve problems or make decisions.

Ceremony   A planned activity at a special event.

Certainty   A situation in which all the information the decision-maker needs is fully available.

Chain of command   An unbroken line of authority that links all individuals in the organization and specifies who reports to whom.

Change agent   An organization development (OD) specialist who contracts with an organization to help managers facilitate change.

Changing   The 'intervention' stage of organization development (OD), when change agents teach people new behaviours and skills and guide them in using them in the workplace.

Channel   The medium by which a message is sent, such as a telephone call, blog or text message.

Channel richness   The amount of information that can be transmitted during a communication episode.

Charismatic leader   A leader who has the ability to inspire and motivate people to transcend their expected performance, even to the point of personal sacrifice.

Chief ethics officer   A manager who oversees all aspects of ethics and legal compliance.

Classical model   A decision-making model based on the assumption that managers should make logical decisions that are economically sensible and in the organization's best economic interest.

Classical perspective   Takes a rational, scientific approach to management and seeks to turn organizations into efficient operating machines.

Coalition   An informal alliance among managers who support a specific goal or solution.

Code of ethics   A formal statement of the organization's values regarding ethics and social responsibility.

Coercive power   Power that stems from the authority to punish or recommend punishment.

Collaboration   A joint effort between people from two or more departments to produce outcomes that meet a common goal or shared purpose.

Collectivism   A preference for a tightly knit social framework in which individuals look after one another and organizations protect their members' interests.

Communication   The process by which information is exchanged and understood by two or more people.

Communication apprehension   An individual's level of fear or anxiety associated with interpersonal communications.

Compensation   All monetary payments and all non-monetary goods or benefits used to reward employees.

Compensatory justice   Argues that individuals should be compensated for the cost of their injuries by the party responsible, and individuals should not be held responsible for matters over which they have no control.

Competitive advantage   Refers to what sets the organization apart from others and provides it with a distinctive edge in the marketplace.

Competitors   Organizations within the same industry or type of business that vie for the same set of customers.

Conceptual skill   The cognitive ability to see the organization as a whole and the relationships among its parts.

Conflict   Antagonistic interaction in which one party attempts to block the intentions or goals of another.

Conformist   A follower who participates actively in the organization but does not use critical thinking skills.

Consideration   Describes the extent to which a leader is sensitive to subordinates, respects their ideas and feelings and establishes mutual trust.

Consistency culture   Values and rewards a methodical, rational, orderly way of doing things.

Content theories   Theories that emphasize the needs that motivate people.

Contingency approach   A model of leadership that describes the relationship between leadership styles and specific situations.

Contingency planning   Identifies important factors in the environment and defines a range of alternative responses to be taken in the case of emergencies, setbacks or unexpected conditions.

Contingency view   Tells managers that what works in one organizational situation might not work in others.

Continuous improvement   The implementation of a large number of small, incremental improvements in all areas of the organization on an ongoing basis. Also called *kaizen*.

Continuous process production   Involves mechanization of the entire workflow and non-stop production, such as in chemical plants or petroleum refineries.

Continuous reinforcement schedule   A schedule in which every occurrence of the desired behaviour is reinforced.

Controlling   Is concerned with monitoring employees' activities, keeping the organization on track towards meeting its goals and making corrections as necessary.

Coordination   The managerial task of adjusting and synchronizing the diverse activities among different individuals and departments.

Core competence   Something that the organization does particularly well in comparison to others.

Corporate governance   Refers to the framework of systems, rules and practices by which an organization ensures accountability, fairness and transparency in the firm's relationships with stakeholders.

Corporate-level strategy   Pertains to the organization as a whole and the combination of business units and products that make it up.

Corporate social responsibility (CSR)   The obligation of organizational managers to make choices and take actions that will enhance the welfare and interests of society as well as the organization.

Corporate university An in-house training and development facility that offers broad-based learning opportunities for employees.

Corporation An artificial entity created by the state and existing apart from its owners.

Cost leadership strategy A strategy with which managers aggressively seek efficient facilities, cut costs and use tight cost controls to be more efficient than others in the industry.

Creativity The generation of novel ideas that may meet perceived needs or respond to opportunities for the organization.

Critical thinking Thinking independently and being mindful of the effect of one's behaviour on achieving goals.

Cross-functional team A group of employees from various functional departments that meet as a team to resolve mutual problems.

Crowdfunding A way of raising capital that involves getting small amounts of money from a large number of investors, usually using social media or the Internet.

Cultural competence The ability to interact effectively with people of different cultures.

Cultural leader Defines and articulates important values that are tied to a clear and compelling mission.

Culture The set of key values, beliefs, understandings and norms shared by members of an organization.

Culture change A major shift in the norms, values and mindset of an entire organization.

Customers Include people and organizations that acquire goods or services from the organization.

Customer relationship management (CRM) Systems that use information technology to keep in close touch with customers, collect and manage large amounts of customer data and provide superior customer value.

Debt financing Involves borrowing money, such as from friends, family or a bank, that has to be repaid at a later date in order to start a business.

Decentralization Means that decision authority is pushed down to lower organization levels.

Decentralized control A situation where the organization fosters compliance with organizational goals through the use of organizational culture, group norms and a focus on goals rather than rules and procedures.

Decentralized network A team communication structure in which team members freely communicate with one another and arrive at decisions together.

Decentralized planning An approach where top executives or planning experts work with managers in major divisions or departments to develop their own goals and plans.

Decision A choice made from available alternatives.

Decision-making The process of identifying problems and opportunities and then resolving them.

Decision styles Differences among people with respect to how they perceive problems and make choices.

Decode To read symbols to interpret the meaning of a message.

Delegation When managers transfer authority and responsibility to positions below them in the hierarchy.

Departmentalization The basis for grouping individual positions into departments and departments into the total organization.

Descriptive in nature An approach that describes how managers actually make decisions, rather than how they should make decisions according to a theoretical model.

Devil's advocate A person who is assigned the role of challenging the assumptions and assertions made by the group to prevent premature consensus.

Diagnosis The step in which managers analyze underlying causal factors associated with the decision situation.

Differentiation strategy A strategy with which managers seek to distinguish the organization's products and services from those of others in the industry.

Direct investing A market entry strategy in which the organization is directly involved in managing its production facilities in a foreign country.

Discretionary responsibility A voluntary measure guided by the organization's desire to make social contributions not mandated by economics, laws or ethics.

Discrimination (1) Making hiring and promotion decisions based on criteria that are not job-relevant. (2) When someone acts out their negative attitudes towards people who are the targets of their prejudice.

Disruptive innovation Innovations in products, services or processes that radically change competition in an industry, such as the advent of streaming video or e-books.

Distributive justice Requires that different treatment of individuals not be based on arbitrary characteristics.

Distributive negotiation A competitive and adversarial approach in which each party strives to get as much as it can, usually at the expense of the other party.

Diversification The strategy of moving into new lines of business.

Diversity All the ways in which employees differ.

Diversity of perspective Achieved when a manager creates a heterogeneous team made up of individuals with diverse backgrounds and skill sets.

Divisional structure An organizational structure that groups employees and departments based on similar organizational outputs (products or services), such that each division has a mix of functional skills and tasks.

Downward communication Messages sent from top management down to subordinates.

Economic dimension Represents the general economic health of the country or region in which the organization operates.

Economic force Affects the availability, production and distribution of a society's resources.

Effective follower A critical, independent thinker who actively participates in the organization.

Effectiveness The degree to which the organization achieves a stated goal.

Electronic brainstorming Brainstorming that takes place in an interactive group over a computer network, rather than meeting face-to-face.

Employee affinity group A group based on social identity, such as gender or race, and organized by employees to focus on concerns of employees from that group.

Employment test A written or computer-based test designed to measure a particular attribute such as intelligence or aptitude.

Empowerment The delegation of power and authority to subordinates in an organization.

Encode To select symbols with which to compose a message.

Entrepreneur A person who recognizes a viable idea for a business product or service and carries it out by finding and assembling the necessary resources.

Entrepreneurship The process of initiating a business, organizing the necessary resources and assuming the associated risks and rewards.

Equity When the ratio of one person's outcomes to inputs equals that of another's.

Equity financing Funds that are invested in exchange for ownership in the company.

Equity theory A theory that focuses on individuals' perceptions of how fairly they are treated relative to others.

ERG theory A modification of the needs hierarchy that proposes three categories of needs: existence, relatedness and growth.

Escalating commitment Refers to continuing to invest time and money in a decision despite evidence that it is failing.

Ethical dilemma A situation in which all alternative choices or behaviours have potentially negative consequences.

Ethics The code of moral principles and values that governs the behaviours of a person or group with respect to what is right or wrong.

Ethics committee A group of executives (and sometimes lower-level employees as well) charged with overseeing company ethics by ruling on questionable issues and disciplining violators.

Ethnocentrism The natural tendency among people to regard their own culture as superior to others.

Ethnorelativism The belief that groups and cultures are inherently equal.

Euro A single European currency that has replaced the currencies of 19 member nations of the European Union (EU).

Evidence-based decision-making A process founded on a commitment to examining potential biases, seeking and examining evidence with rigour, and making informed and intelligent decisions based on the best available facts and evidence.

Exit interview An interview conducted with departing employees to determine reasons for their departure and learn about potential problems in the organization.

Expense budget A budget that outlines the anticipated and actual expenses for a responsibility centre.

Expert power Power that results from a leader's special knowledge or skill in the tasks performed by subordinates.

Exporting A market entry strategy in which a company maintains production facilities within its home country and transfers products for sale in foreign countries.

Feedback Occurs when the receiver responds to the sender's communication with a return message.

Femininity A cultural preference for relationships, cooperation, group decision-making and quality of life.

First-line manager A manager who is at the first or second level of the hierarchy and is directly responsible for overseeing a group of production employees.

Flat structure An organizational structure characterized by an overall broad span of management and relatively few hierarchical levels.

Focus strategy A strategy where managers use either a differentiation or a cost leadership approach, but they concentrate on a specific regional market or buyer group.

Force-field analysis A technique for determining which forces drive a proposed change and which forces restrain it.

Formal communication channel A communication channel that flows within the chain of command or task responsibility defined by the organization.

Forming The stage of team development involving a period of orientation and getting acquainted.

Franchising (1) A form of licensing in which a company provides its foreign franchisees with a complete package of materials and services. (2) An arrangement by which the owner of a product or service allows others to purchase the right to distribute a product or service with help from the owner.

Free rider A person who benefits from team membership but does not make a proportionate contribution to the team's work.

Frustration–regression principle Suggests that failure to meet a higher-order need may cause a regression to an already satisfied lower-order need; thus, people may move down as well as up the needs hierarchy.

Functional-level strategy Pertains to the major functional departments within each business unit, such as manufacturing, marketing, and research and development.

Functional manager A manager responsible for a department that performs a single functional task, such as finance or marketing.

Functional structure An organizational structure in which activities are grouped together by common function from the bottom to the top of the organization.

Functional team A team composed of a manager and his or her subordinates in the formal chain of command.

General environment Indirectly influences all organizations within an industry and includes five dimensions.

General manager A manager responsible for several departments that perform different functions.

Glass ceiling An invisible barrier that separates women and minorities from senior management positions.

Globalization The extent to which trade and investments, information, ideas and political cooperation flow between countries.

Globalization strategy A strategy where product design and advertising are standardized throughout the world.

Global mindset The ability to appreciate and influence individuals, groups, organizations and systems that represent different social, cultural, political, institutional, intellectual and psychological characteristics.

Global outsourcing Engaging in the international division of labour so as to obtain the cheapest sources of labour and supplies, regardless of country. Sometimes called *offshoring*.

Global team A group made up of employees who come from different countries and whose activities span multiple countries.

Goal A desired future state that the organization wants to realize.

Goal-setting theory A theory that proposes that specific, challenging goals increase motivation and performance when the goals are accepted by subordinates and these subordinates receive feedback to indicate their progress towards goal achievement.

Grapevine A system that carries workplace gossip, a dominant force in organization communication when formal channels are not functioning effectively.

Greenfield venture An investment in which a company builds a subsidiary from scratch in a foreign country.

Groupthink The tendency of people in groups to suppress contrary opinions in a desire for harmony.

Halo effect Occurs when a manager gives an employee the same rating on all dimensions of the job, even though performance may be good on some dimensions and poor on others.

Hawthorne studies A series of research efforts that was important in shaping ideas concerning how managers should treat workers.

Hero A figure who exemplifies the deeds, character and attributes of a strong culture.

Hierarchical control Involves monitoring and influencing employee behaviour through the use of rules, policies, hierarchy of authority, written documentation, reward systems and other formal mechanisms.

Hierarchy of needs theory A theory proposed by Abraham Maslow saying that people are motivated by five categories of needs – physiological, safety, belongingness, esteem and self-actualization – that exist in a hierarchical order.

High-context culture A culture in which people use communication to build personal relationships.

High-performance culture Emphasizes both cultural values and business results.

Horizontal communication The lateral or diagonal exchange of messages among peers or co-workers and includes team communication.

Horizontal linkage model Means that several departments, such as marketing, research and manufacturing, work closely together to develop new products.

Humanistic perspective Emphasizes understanding human behaviour, needs and attitudes in the workplace.

Human relations movement Stresses the satisfaction of employees' basic needs as the key to increased productivity.

Human resource management (HRM) The design and application of formal systems to ensure the effective and efficient use of human talent to accomplish organizational goals.

Human resource planning The forecasting of human resource needs and the projected matching of individuals with anticipated job vacancies.

Human resources perspective Suggests that jobs should be designed to meet people's higher-level needs by allowing employees to use their full potential.

Human skill A manager's ability to work with and through other people and to work effectively as part of a group.

Humility Being unpretentious and modest rather than arrogant and prideful.

Hygiene factors Factors that focus on lower-level needs and consider the presence or absence of job dissatisfiers, including working conditions, pay and company policies.

Idea champion A person who sees the need for change and is passionately committed to making it happen.

Idea incubator An organizational programme that provides a safe harbour where employees can generate and develop ideas without interference from company bureaucracy or politics.

Implementation Involves using managerial, administrative and persuasive abilities to translate a chosen decision alternative into action.

Inclusion The degree to which an employee feels like an esteemed member of a group in which his or her uniqueness is highly appreciated.

Income statement Summarizes the firm's financial performance for a given time interval.

Individualism A preference for a loosely knit social framework in which individuals are expected to take care of themselves.

Individualism approach A decision-making approach suggesting that actions are ethical when they promote the individual's best long-term interests, because with everyone pursuing self-interest, the greater good is ultimately served.

Influence The effect a person's actions have on the attitudes, values, beliefs or behaviour of others.

Infrastructure A country's physical facilities, such as highways, utilities and airports, that support economic activities.

Initiating structure Describes the extent to which a leader is task oriented and directs subordinates' work activities towards goal accomplishment.

Integrative negotiation A collaborative approach that is based on a win–win assumption, whereby the parties want to come up with a creative solution that benefits both sides of the conflict.

Intelligence team A cross-functional group of people who work together to gain a deep understanding of a specific competitive issue and offer insight and recommendations for planning.

Interactive leadership A leadership style characterized by values such as inclusion, collaboration, relationship building and caring.

International dimension In the external environment, represents events originating in foreign countries, as well as opportunities for companies in other countries.

International human resource management (IHRM) A subfield of human resource management that addresses the complexity that results from recruiting, selecting, developing and maintaining a diverse workforce on a global scale.

International management Managing business operations in more than one country.

Interorganizational partnership Reduces boundaries and increases collaboration with other organizations.

Intuition   An aspect of administrative decision-making that refers to a quick comprehension of a decision situation based on past experience but without conscious thought.

Involvement culture   A culture that places high value on meeting the needs of employees and values cooperation and equality.

ISO 9000 standards   Represent an international consensus of what constitutes effective quality management as outlined by the International Organization for Standardization (ISO).

Job analysis   The systematic process of gathering and interpreting information about the essential duties, tasks and responsibilities of a job.

Job description   A concise summary of the specific tasks and responsibilities of a position.

Job design   Refers to applying motivational theories to the structure of work to improve motivation, productivity and satisfaction.

Job enlargement   A job design that combines a series of tasks into one new, broader job to give employees variety and challenge.

Job enrichment   Incorporating high-level motivators, such as achievement, recognition and opportunities for growth, into the work.

Job evaluation   The process of determining the value of jobs within an organization through an examination of job content.

Job rotation   A job design that systematically moves employees from one job to another to provide them with variety and stimulation.

Job simplification   A job design whose purpose is to improve task efficiency by reducing the number of tasks a single person must do.

Job specification   Outlines the knowledge, skills, education, physical abilities and other characteristics needed to perform a specific job adequately.

Joint venture   A strategic alliance or programme by two or more organizations.

Justice approach   Says that ethical decisions must be based on standards of equity, fairness and impartiality.

Labour market   The people available for hire by the organization.

Large-group intervention   An organization development (OD) approach that brings together people from different parts of the organization (and often including outside stakeholders) to discuss problems or opportunities and plan for change.

Law of effect   Asserts that positively reinforced behaviour tends to be repeated, and unreinforced or negatively reinforced behaviour tends to be inhibited.

Leadership grid   A two-dimensional leadership model that measures the leader's concern for people and concern for production to categorize the leader in one of five different leadership styles.

Leading   Using influence to motivate employees to achieve the organization's goals.

Legal-political dimension   Includes government regulations at the local, state and federal levels, as well as political activities designed to influence company behaviour.

Legitimate power   Power that stems from a manager's formal position in an organization and the authority granted by that position.

Licensing   A strategy where a company in one country makes certain resources available to companies in other countries to participate in the production and sale of its products abroad.

Line authority   The formal power to direct and control immediate subordinates.

Liquidity ratio   Indicates the organization's ability to meet its current debt obligations.

Listening   The skill of grasping both facts and feelings to interpret a message's genuine meaning.

Long-term orientation   Reflects a greater concern for the future and a high value on thrift and perseverance.

Low-context culture   A culture where people use communication primarily to exchange facts and information.

Management   The attainment of organizational goals in an effective and efficient manner through planning, organizing, leading and controlling organizational resources.

Management by means (MBM)   An approach that focuses people on the methods and processes used to attain results, rather than on the results themselves.

Management by objectives (MBO)   A method whereby managers and employees define goals for every department, project and person and use them to monitor subsequent performance.

Management science   Uses mathematics, statistical techniques and computer technology to facilitate management decision-making, particularly for complex problems. Also called the *quantitative perspective.*

Managing diversity   Creating a climate in which the potential advantages of diversity for organizational performance are maximized while the potential disadvantages are minimized.

Market entry strategy   A tactic that managers use to enter foreign markets.

Masculinity   A cultural preference for achievement, heroism, assertiveness, work centrality and material success.

Mass production   Characterized by long production runs to manufacture a large volume of products with the same specifications.

Matrix approach   A structural approach that uses both functional and divisional chains of command simultaneously, in the same part of the organization.

Matrix boss   A functional or product supervisor responsible for one side of the matrix.

Mentor   A higher-ranking senior member of the organization who is committed to providing upward mobility and support to a protégé's professional career.

Merger   When two or more organizations combine to become one.

Message   The tangible formulation of an idea to be sent to the employee.

Middle manager   A manager who works at the middle level of the organization and is responsible for a major division or department.

Mission   An organization's purpose or reason for existence.

Mission statement   A broadly stated definition of the organization's basic business scope and operations that distinguishes it from similar types of organizations.

Modular approach An approach in which a manufacturing company uses outside suppliers to provide large chunks of a product such as an automobile, which are then assembled into a final product by a few employees.

Monoculture A culture that accepts only one way of doing things and one set of values and beliefs.

Moral-rights approach Holds that ethical decisions are those that best maintain the fundamental rights of the people affected by them.

Motivation The arousal of enthusiasm and persistence to pursue a certain course of action.

Motivators Influence job satisfaction based on fulfilling higher-level needs such as achievement, recognition, responsibility and opportunities for personal growth.

Multicultural team A team that is made up of members from diverse national, racial, ethnic and cultural backgrounds.

Multidomestic strategy Means that competition in each country is handled independently, and product design and advertising are modified to suit the specific needs of individual countries.

Multinational corporation (MNC) An organization that receives more than 25 per cent of its total sales revenues from operations outside the parent company's home country and has a number of distinctive managerial characteristics.

Natural dimension Includes all elements that occur naturally on Earth, including plants, animals, rocks and natural resources such as air, water and climate.

Need for change A disparity between actual and desired performance.

Need to achieve An individual characteristic meaning that a person is motivated to excel and will pick situations in which success is likely.

Negotiation A conflict management strategy whereby people engage in give-and-take discussions and consider various alternatives to reach a joint decision that is acceptable to both parties.

Neutralizer A situational variable that counteracts a leadership style and prevents the leader from displaying certain behaviours.

New-venture fund A fund providing resources from which individuals and groups can draw to develop new ideas, products or businesses.

New-venture team A unit separate from the mainstream organization that is responsible for initiating and developing innovations.

Non-programmed decision A decision made in response to a situation that is unique, is poorly defined and largely unstructured, and has important consequences for the organization.

Non-verbal communication Communicating through actions, gestures, facial expressions and behaviour, rather than through words.

Normative Means that it defines how a manager *should* make logical decisions and provides guidelines for reaching an ideal outcome.

Norming The stage of development in which conflicts are resolved and team harmony and unity emerge.

On-the-job-training (OJT) A process in which an experienced employee is asked to teach a new employee how to perform job duties.

Open-book management Allows employees to see for themselves the financial condition of the organization and encourages them to think and act like business owners.

Open communication Sharing all types of information throughout the organization and across functional and hierarchical boundaries.

Open innovation A process where people search for and commercialize innovative ideas beyond the boundaries of the organization.

Operational goal A specific, measurable result that is expected from departments, work groups and individuals.

Operational plan Specifies the action steps towards achieving operational goals and supports tactical activities.

Opportunity A situation in which managers see potential organizational accomplishments that exceed current goals.

Organization A social entity that is goal directed and deliberately structured.

Organizational change The adoption of a new idea or behaviour by an organization.

Organizational ecosystem Includes organizations in all the sectors of the task and general environments that provide the resource and information transactions, flows and linkages necessary for an organization to thrive.

Organizational environment Includes all elements existing outside the boundary of the organization that have the potential to affect the organization.

Organization chart A visual representation of an organization's structure.

Organization development (OD) A planned, systematic process of change that uses behavioural science techniques to improve an organization's health and effectiveness through its ability to cope with environmental changes, improve internal relationships and increase learning and problem-solving capabilities.

Organization structure The framework in which an organization defines how tasks are divided, resources are deployed and departments are coordinated.

Organizing The deployment of organizational resources to achieve strategic goals; involves assigning tasks, grouping tasks into departments and allocating resources.

Partial reinforcement schedule A schedule in which only some occurrences of the desired behaviour are reinforced.

Partnership An unincorporated business owned by two or more people.

Passive follower A person who exhibits neither critical independent thinking nor active participation.

Pay-for-performance Tying at least a portion of compensation to employee effort and performance. Also called *incentive pay*.

People change A change in the attitudes and behaviours of a few employees.

Performance The organization's ability to attain its goals by using resources in an efficient and effective manner.

Performance appraisal   The process of observing and evaluating an employee's performance, recording the assessment and providing feedback.

Performing   The stage of development in which team members focus on problem solving and accomplishing the team's assigned task.

Permanent team   A group of employees from all functional areas permanently assigned to focus on a specific task or activity.

Personal communication channels   Channels that exist outside formally authorized channels and connect people across boundaries for sharing information and accomplishing tasks.

Personality   The set of characteristics that underlie a relatively stable pattern of behaviour in response to ideas, objects or people in the environment.

Personal networking   The acquisition and cultivation of personal relationships that cross departmental, hierarchical and even organizational boundaries.

Pivot   To change the strategic direction of a business.

Plan   A blueprint specifying the resource allocations, schedules and other actions necessary for attaining goals.

Planning   The management function concerned with defining goals for future performance and how to attain them.

Pluralism   An environment in which the organization accommodates several subcultures, including employees who would otherwise feel isolated and ignored.

Point-counterpoint   A decision-making technique in which people are assigned to express competing points of view.

Political force   Relates to the influence of political and legal institutions on people and organizations.

Political instability   Events such as riots, revolutions or government upheavals that can affect the operations of an international company.

Political risk   A company's risk of loss of assets, earning power or managerial control due to politically based events or actions by host governments.

Portfolio strategy   Pertains to the mix of strategic business units and product lines that fit together in a logical way to provide synergy and competitive advantage.

Power   The potential ability to influence the behaviour of others.

Power distance   The degree to which people accept inequality in power among institutions, organizations and people.

Practical approach   A decision-making approach that sidesteps debates about what is right, good or just, and bases decisions on the prevailing standards of the profession and the larger society.

Pragmatic survivor   A follower who has qualities of all four follower styles, depending on which fits the prevalent situation.

Prejudice   The tendency to view people who are different as being deficient.

Problem   A situation in which organizational accomplishments have failed to meet established goals.

Procedural justice   Holds that rules should be clearly stated and consistently and impartially enforced.

Process theories   A set of theories, including goal-setting theory, equity theory and expectancy theory, which explains how people select behaviours with which to meet their needs and determine whether their choices were successful.

Product change   A change in an organization's products or services, such as the Whirlpool two-oven range or the Amazon Kindle Fire.

Profitability ratio   Describes the firm's profits relative to a source of profits, such as sales or assets.

Programmed decision   A decision made in response to a situation that has occurred often enough to enable managers to develop decision rules that can be applied in the future.

Project manager   A manager who is responsible for a specific work project that involves people from various functions and levels of the organization.

Quality circle   A total quality management (TQM) technique that involves a group of 6 to 12 volunteer employees who meet regularly to discuss and solve problems affecting the quality of their work.

Quality partnering   Involves assigning dedicated personnel within a particular functional area of the business to identify opportunities for quality improvements throughout the work process.

Quants   Refers to financial managers and others who make decisions based primarily on complex quantitative analysis.

Realistic job preview   Gives applicants all pertinent and realistic information, both positive and negative, about a job and the organization.

Recruiting   Activities or practices that define the desired characteristics of applicants for specific jobs. Sometimes called *talent acquisition*.

Re-engineering   The radical redesign of business processes to achieve dramatic improvements in cost, quality, service and speed.

Referent power   Power that results from characteristics that command subordinates' identification with, respect and admiration for, and desire to emulate the leader.

Refreezing   The stage of organization development (OD) where people have incorporated new values, attitudes and behaviours into their everyday work and the changes become institutionalized in the culture.

Reinforcement   Anything that causes a certain behaviour to be repeated or inhibited.

Reinforcement theory   A theory based on the relationship between a given behaviour and its consequences.

Related diversification   Moving into a new business that is related to the corporation's existing business activities.

Relational coordination   Frequent horizontal coordination and communication carried out through ongoing relationships of shared goals, shared knowledge and mutual respect.

Relationship conflict   Conflict that results from interpersonal incompatibility that creates tension and personal animosity among people.

Responsibility   The duty to perform the task or activity that one has been assigned.

Reward power   Power that results from the authority to bestow rewards.

Revenue budget A budget that lists forecasted and actual revenues of the organization.

Risk Means that a decision has clear-cut goals and good information is available, but the future outcomes associated with each alternative are subject to chance.

Risk propensity The willingness to undertake risk with the opportunity of gaining an increased payoff.

Role A set of expectations for one's behaviour.

Satisficing Refers to choosing the first alternative that satisfies minimal decision criteria, regardless of whether better solutions are presumed to exist.

Scenario building An approach where managers look at trends and discontinuities and imagine possible alternative futures to build a framework within which unexpected future events can be managed.

Schedule of reinforcement The frequency with which and intervals over which reinforcement occurs.

Scientific management A subfield of the classical perspective that emphasizes scientifically determined changes in management practices as the solution to improving labour productivity.

Selection The process of assessing the skills, abilities and other attributes of applicants in an attempt to determine the fit between the job and each applicant's characteristics.

Self-managed team A team that consists of multiskilled employees who rotate jobs to produce an entire product or service, often led by an elected team member.

Servant leader A leader who serves others by working to fulfil followers' needs and goals, as well as to achieve the organization's larger mission.

Service technology Characterized by intangible outputs and direct contact between employees and customers.

Short-term orientation Reflects a concern with the past and present and a high value on meeting current obligations.

Single-use plan A plan that is developed to achieve a set of goals that is unlikely to be repeated in the future.

Situational model A leadership model that links the leader's behavioural style with the readiness level of followers.

Six Sigma A quality control approach that emphasizes a relentless pursuit of higher quality and lower costs.

Skunkworks A separate informal, highly autonomous and often secretive group that focuses on breakthrough ideas.

Slogan A phrase.

Small-batch production A type of manufacturing technology that involves the production of goods in batches of one or a few products designed to customer specification.

Social entrepreneur An entrepreneurial leader who is committed to both good business and changing the world for the better.

Social facilitation The tendency for the presence of others to influence an individual's motivation and performance.

Social forces Aspects of a society that guide and influence relationships among people, such as their values, needs and standards of behaviour.

Social media A group of Internet-based applications that allow the creation and exchange of user-generated content.

Social media programs Include online community pages, social media sites, microblogging platforms and company online forums that enable managers to interact electronically with employees, customers, partners and other stakeholders.

Social networking Using peer-to-peer communication channels to interact in an online community, sharing personal and professional information, ideas and opinions.

Sociocultural dimension Includes demographic characteristics, norms, customs and values of a population within which the organization operates.

Socioemotional role A team role in which an individual provides support for team members' emotional needs and helps strengthen social unity.

Sole proprietorship An unincorporated for-profit business owned by an individual.

Span of management The number of employees reporting to a supervisor. Sometimes called *span of control.*

Special-purpose team A team created outside the formal structure to undertake a project of special importance, such as developing a new product.

Staff authority The right to advise, counsel and recommend in the manager's area of expertise.

Stakeholder Any group or person within or outside the organization that has some type of investment or interest in the organization's performance.

Stakeholder mapping A systematic way to identify the expectations, needs, importance and relative power of various stakeholders.

Standing plan An ongoing plan used to provide guidance for tasks that occur repeatedly in the organization.

Stereotype A rigid, exaggerated, irrational belief associated with a particular group of people.

Stereotype threat Occurs when a person who, when engaged in a task, is aware of a stereotype about his or her identity group suggesting that he or she will not perform well on that task.

Stereotyping A performance evaluation error that occurs when a manager places an employee into a class or category based on one or a few traits or characteristics.

Storming The stage of team development in which individual personalities and roles, and resulting conflicts, emerge.

Story A narrative based on true events that is repeated frequently and shared among organizational employees.

Strategic business unit (SBU) A division of the organization that has a unique business, mission, product or service line, competitors and markets relative to other units of the same organization.

Strategic conversation Dialogue across boundaries and hierarchical levels about the team or organization's vision, critical strategic themes and the values that help achieve important goals.

Strategic goal A broad statement of where an organization wants to be in the future. Pertains to the organization as a whole rather than to specific divisions or departments.

Strategic issue An event or force that alters an organization's ability to achieve its goals.

Strategic management Refers to the set of decisions and actions used to formulate and implement strategies that will provide a competitively superior fit between an organization and its environment so as to achieve organizational goals.

Strategic plan   Action steps by which an organization intends to attain strategic goals.

Strategy   A plan of action that describes resource allocation and activities for dealing with the environment, achieving a competitive advantage and attaining goals.

Strategy execution   The stage of strategic management that involves the use of managerial and organizational tools to direct resources towards achieving strategic outcomes.

Strategy formulation   The stage of strategic management that includes the planning and decision-making that lead to the establishment of the organization's goals and a specific strategic plan.

Strategy map   A visual representation of the key drivers of an organization's success, showing the cause-and-effect relationship among goals and plans.

Strengths   Natural talents and abilities that have been supported and reinforced with learned knowledge and skills.

Stretch goal   A reasonable yet highly ambitious and compelling goal that energizes people and inspires excellence.

Substitute for leadership   A situational variable that makes a leadership style redundant or unnecessary.

Subsystems   Parts of a system that depend on one another for their functioning.

Suppliers   Provide the raw materials the organization uses to produce its output.

Supply chain management   Managing the sequence of suppliers and purchasers, covering all stages of processing from obtaining raw materials to distributing finished goods to consumers.

Survey feedback   Where organization development (OD) change agents survey employees to gather their opinions regarding corporate values, leadership, participation, cohesiveness and other aspects of the organization, then meet with small groups to share the results and brainstorm solutions to problems identified by the results.

Sustainability   Economic development that generates wealth and meets the needs of the current population while preserving society and the environment for the needs of future generations.

SWOT analysis   An audit or careful examination of *strengths*, *weaknesses*, *opportunities* and *threats* that affect organizational performance.

Symbol   An object, act or event that conveys meaning to others.

Synergy   A concept that says that the whole is greater than the sum of its parts.

System   A set of interrelated parts that function as a whole to achieve a common purpose.

Systems thinking   Looking not just at discrete parts of an organizational situation, but also at the continually changing interactions among the parts.

Tactical goal   The outcome that major divisions and departments must achieve for an organization to reach its overall goals.

Tactical plan   Designed to help execute major strategic plans and to accomplish a specific part of a company's strategy.

Tall structure   An organizational structure characterized by an overall narrow span of management and a relatively large number of hierarchical levels.

Task conflict   Conflict that results from disagreements about the goals to be achieved or the content of the tasks to be performed.

Task environment   Includes the sectors that conduct day-to-day transactions with the organization and directly influence its basic operations and performance.

Task force   A temporary team or committee formed to solve a specific short-term problem involving several departments.

Task specialist role   A team role in which an individual devotes personal time and energy to helping the team accomplish its activities and reach its goal.

Team   A unit of two or more people who interact and coordinate their work to accomplish a goal to which they are committed and hold themselves mutually accountable.

Team-based structure   A structure in which an entire organization is made up of horizontal teams that coordinate their activities and work directly with customers to accomplish organizational goals.

Team building   An organization development (OD) intervention that enhances cohesiveness by helping groups of people learn to work together as a team.

Team cohesiveness   The extent to which team members are attracted to the team and motivated to remain a part of it.

Team norm   An informal standard of conduct that is shared by team members and guides their behaviour.

Technical complexity   The degree to which complex machinery is involved in the production process to the exclusion of people.

Technical skill   The understanding of and proficiency in the performance of specific tasks.

Technological dimension   In the general environment, includes scientific and technological advances in society.

Technology change   A change in production processes – how an organization does its work.

Time management   Time is a perishable resource and most important managerial decisions have to be made to strict and timed deadlines. Poor management of time is also a major factor that increases the level and intensity of stressors that could affect the quality of decision-making and corporate performance.

Tolerance for ambiguity   The psychological characteristic that allows a person to be untroubled by disorder and uncertainty.

Top-down budgeting   Means that the budgeted amounts for the coming year are literally imposed on middle- and lower-level managers.

Top leader   In a matrix structure, the person who oversees both the product and the functional chains of command and is responsible for the entire matrix.

Top manager   A manager who is at the top of the organizational hierarchy and is responsible for the entire organization.

Total quality management (TQM)   Focuses on managing the total organization to deliver quality to customers.

Transactional leader   A leader who clarifies subordinates' roles and task requirements, initiates structure, provides rewards and displays consideration for followers.

Transformational leader   A leader distinguished by a special ability to bring about innovation and change by creating an inspiring vision, shaping values, building relationships and providing meaning for followers.

Transnational strategy   A strategy that combines global coordination to attain efficiency with local flexibility to meet needs in different countries.

Triple bottom line   Refers to measuring the organization's financial performance, social performance and environmental performance.

Two-boss employee   In a matrix structure, a person who reports to two supervisors simultaneously.

Uncertainty   Occurs when managers know which goals they want to achieve, but information about alternatives and future events is incomplete.

Uncertainty avoidance   Characterized by people's intolerance for uncertainty and ambiguity and resulting support for beliefs that promise certainty and conformity.

Uncritical thinking   Failing to consider the possibilities beyond what one is told, accepting others' ideas without thinking.

Unfreezing   The stage of organization development (OD) in which people are made aware of problems and the need for change.

Unrelated diversification   Refers to expanding into totally new lines of business.

Upwards communication   Messages that flow from the lower to the higher levels in the organization's hierarchy.

Utilitarian approach   A method of ethical decision-making saying that the ethical choice is the one that produces the greatest good for the greatest number.

Validity   The relationship between an applicant's score on a selection device and his or her future job performance.

Venture capital firm   A group of companies or individuals that invests money in new or expanding businesses for ownership and potential profits.

Vertical integration   A strategy of expanding into businesses that either provide the supplies needed to make products, or distribute and sell the company's products.

Virtual network structure   An organizational structure in which the organization subcontracts most of its major functions to separate companies and coordinates their activities from a small headquarters organization.

Virtual team   A team made up of members who are geographically or organizationally dispersed, rarely meet face-to-face, and interact to accomplish their work primarily using advanced information and telecommunications technologies.

Vision   An attractive, ideal future that is credible yet not readily attainable.

Wage and salary survey   A survey that shows what other organizations pay incumbents in jobs that match a sample of key jobs selected by the organization.

Whistle-blowing   The disclosure by employees of unethical, illegitimate or illegal practices by an organization.

Wholly owned foreign affiliate   A foreign subsidiary over which an organization has complete control.

Workforce optimization   Implementing strategies to put the right people in the right jobs, make the best use of employee talent and skills and develop human capital for the future.

Work specialization   The degree to which organizational tasks are subdivided into individual jobs. Sometimes called *division of labour*.

Zero-based budgeting   An approach to planning and decision-making that requires a complete justification for every line item in a budget, instead of carrying forward a prior budget and applying a percentage change.

PHOTO CREDITS

p. 3 © Thinkstock/phloxii
p. 5 © Shutterstock/Photo Africa
p. 12 Courtesy of Tesla Motors
p. 24 Courtesy of SBTV.com
p. 35 © Thinkstock/agsandrew
p. 38 © Thinkstock/agsandrew
p. 39 Rue des Archives / The Granger Collection, New York
p. 44 Mary Parker Follette Foundation and Reading University, UK
p. 45 National Archives
p. 46 Western Electric Photographic Services
p. 53 Hyundai
p. 55 © Thinkstock/KatarzynaBialasiewicz
p. 67 © Thinkstock/Andres Garcia Martin
p. 70 © Thinkstock/marinhristov
p. 75 © Thinkstock/serezniy
p. 81 © Thinkstock/4774344sean
p. 85 © Aflo Co. Ltd. / Alamy
p. 91 © AP Photo/Bebeto Matthews
p. 99 © Thinkstock/Rawpixel Ltd
p. 103 © AP Photo/ M.Lakshman
p. 111 © Blair Gable/Reuters
p. 116 © Thinkstock/Hongqi Zhang
p. 117 © Ana Venegas/The Orange County Register/Corbis
p. 123 Alli Harvey/WireImage/Getty Images
p. 137 © Thinkstock/L_Shtandel
p. 138 © Thinkstock/Songquan Deng
p. 141 © Pradeep Paliwal / Demotix/Demotix/Corbis
p. 142 © M.Sobreira / Alamy
p. 149 © M.Sobreira / Alamy
p. 152 © GOH CHAI HIN/AFP/Getty Images
p. 159 © Kiyoshi Ota/Getty Images
p. 162 © Thinkstock/i-Stockr
p. 173 © Thinkstock/typhoonski
p. 176 © ArtPix / Alamy
p. 183 © Thinkstock/deiata
p. 190 © Thinkstock/zorandimzr
p. 195 © Thinkstock/Jacob Ammentorp Lund
p. 209 © Thinkstock/bkilzer
p. 217 © Chris Willson / Alamy
p. 226 © Thinkstock/IPGGutenbergUKLtd
p. 228 © Thinkstock/flyingrussian
p. 230 © Shutterstock/Concept Photo
p. 239 © Thinkstock/Rawpixel Ltd
p. 243 © Thinkstock/KovacsAlex
p. 248 © dpa picture alliance / Alamy
p. 251 © Thinkstock/Stocktrek Images
p. 256 © shzq/Imaginechina/AP Images
p. 259 © AP Photo/Ron Heflin
p. 271 © Thinkstock/Witez

p. 274 © Aflo Co. Ltd. / Alamy
p. 276 © Thinkstock/esentunar
p. 282 © James Leynse/Corbis
p. 286 Courtesy of Red Door Interactive
p. 291 © Kristoffer Tripplaar / Alamy
p. 294 © Thinkstock/StockRocket
p. 309 © Thinkstock/HaraldBiebel
p. 314 © Thinkstock/FogStock/Vico Images/Erik Palmer
p. 318 © Thinkstock/monkeybusinessimages
p. 324 © Thinkstock/gkrphoto
p. 329 © Thinkstock/Tuned_In
p. 332 © AP Photo/Lynn Hey
p. 341 © Thinkstock/David & Micha Sheldon
p. 343 © Thinkstock/LDProd
p. 345 © Robyn Twomey/Corbis Outline
p. 352 © Thinkstock/Rawpixel Ltd
p. 356 © Chris Gascoigne/VIEW/Corbis
p. 363 © Christina Simons/Corbis
p. 373 © Thinkstock/scanrail
p. 378 © Neville Elder/Corbis
p. 382 © Christopher J. Morris/Corbis News/Corbis
p. 384 Justin Sullivan/Getty Images News/Getty Images
p. 388 © Richard Levine/Demotix/Corbis
p. 394 © Ruby Washington/The New York Times/Redux
p. 396 © Imaginechina/Corbis
p. 409 © Thinkstock/Mike_Kiev
p. 410 © Ben Radford/Corbis
p. 415 © Jin Lee/Bloomberg /Getty Images
p. 424 © Patsy Lynch /Retna Ltd./Corbis
p. 435 © Michael A. Schwarz
p. 445 © Thinkstock/gyn9038
p. 447 © UrbanImages / Alamy
p. 454 © Shutterstock/Rawpixel
p. 456 © Thinkstock/Ryan McVay
p. 465 © Thinkstock/kasto80
p. 470 © Thinkstock/Minerva Studio
p. 476 © Philip Scalia / Alamy
p. 479 © Thinkstock/mythja
p. 488 © Alex Ramsay / Alamy
p. 497 © Thinkstock/Ingram Publishing
p. 498 © Blaine Harrington III/Corbis
p. 503 © Thinkstock/kasto80
p. 510 © Thinkstock/Milenko Bokan
p. 513 © Dan Browning/ZUMA Press/Corbis
p. 529 © Thinkstock/sculpies
p. 532 © Thinkstock/Stockbyte
p. 535 © Javier Rojas/ZUMA Press/Corbis
p. 539 © Mark Leong/Redux
p.542 © ZUMA Press,Inc./Alamy Limited
p. 552 © VIEW Pictures Ltd / Alamy

COMPANY INDEX

SUBJECT INDEX